Ugo Montanari Francesca Rossi (Eds.)

Principles and Practice
of Constraint Programming
— CP '95

First International Conference, CP '95
Cassis, France, September 19-22, 1995
Proceedings

Springer

Series Editors

Gerhard Goos, Karlsruhe University, Germany

Juris Hartmanis, Cornell University, NY, USA

Jan van Leeuwen, Utrecht University, The Netherlands

Volume Editors

Ugo Montanari
Francesca Rossi
Dipartimento di Informatica, Università di Pisa
Corso Italia, 40, I-56100 Pisa, Italy

Cataloging-in-Publication data applied for

Die Deutsche Bibliothek - CIP-Einheitsaufnahme

Principles and practice of constraint Programming : first
international conference ; proceedings / CP '95, Cassis, France,
September 19 - 22, 1995 / Ugo Montanari ; Francesca Rossi
(ed.). - Berlin ; Heidelberg ; New York : Springer, 1995
  (Lecture notes in computer science ; Vol. 976)
  ISBN 3-540-60299-2
NE: Montanari, Ugo [Hrsg.]; CP <1, 1995, Cassis>; GT

CR Subject Classification (1991): D.1, D.3.2-3, I.2.3-4, F.3.2, F.4.1, I.2.8,
H.3.3

ISBN 3-540-60299-2 Springer-Verlag Berlin Heidelberg New York

© Springer-Verlag Berlin Heidelberg 1995
Printed in Germany

Typesetting: Camera-ready by author
SPIN 10485545   06/3142 – 5 4 3 2 1 0   Printed on acid-free paper

Preface

CP'95 is the First International Conference on Principles and Practice of Constraint Programming. It is to take place at Cassis near Marseille, France, September 19-22, 1995. Conference Chair is Alain Colmerauer (LIM, Marseille) and Program Chair is Ugo Montanari (Università di Pisa).

The conference has been preceded by two workshops on the principles and practice of constraint programming organized at Orcas Island in May 1994 and at Newport in April 1993, and also by a Workshop on Constraint Logic Programming organized at Alton Jones in the Spring of 1988. Also the Workshops on Constraint Logic Programming at Marseille in 1991, 1992 and 1993, and the International Conference on Constraints in Computational Logics at Munich in September 1994, are significant antecedents.

The conference addresses the interdisciplinary area of constraint programming and constraint-based systems. This new area has recently developed an appreciable identity, which is promising in terms both of simple and general foundations and of significant practical applications. It needs an international forum to compare the results and discuss the new lines of development. The conference is hopefully a step in this direction.

Out of 108 submitted papers, the program committee selected 33 for presentation at the conference. These are grouped into sessions on efficient constraint handling, constraint satisfaction problems, constraints in databases, constraint logic programming, concurrent constraint programming, constraints in computational logic, applications of constraint programming, constraints in operation research. The program includes also: invited talks by Bruno Buchberger (RISC, Linz) and Zohar Manna (Stanford University); tutorials by Vijay Saraswat (Xerox PARC) and Pascal van Hentenryck (Brown University); and a session dedicated to industry.

The following four satellite meetings are to take place in conjunction with CP'95: "Over-constrained systems" and "Constraints for graphics and visualization" on Monday, September 18; "Set constraints and constrained logic programming" and "Studying and solving really hard problems" on Saturday, September 23.

The conference is in cooperation with AAAI and EATCS, is sponsored by ACM SIGART and SIGPLAN, and has received support from ACCLAIM, ALP, CCL, CNRS, Compulog Net, ONR, Université de la Méditerranée and Università di Pisa.

Pisa, July 1995

Ugo Montanari
Program Committee Chair

Organizing Committee:

Alan Borning (University of Washington)
Jacques Cohen (Brandeis University)
Alain Colmerauer (University of Marseille)
Eugene Freuder (University of New Hampshire)
Herve Gallaire (Xerox Corporation, Grenoble)
Jean-Pierre Jouannaud (University of Paris Sud)
Paris Kanellakis (Brown University)
Jean-Louis Lassez, chair (IBM Watson)
Ugo Montanari (University of Pisa)
Anil Nerode (Cornell University)
Vijay Saraswat (Xerox Corporation, PARC)
Ralph Wachter (Office of Naval Research)

Program Committee:

Hassan Aït-Kaci (Simon Fraser University)
Marianne Baudinet (Free University of Brussels)
Frédéric Benhamou (University of Orleans)
Rina Dechter (University of California at Irvine)
Mehmet Dincbas (COSYTEC, Orsay)
Manuel Hermenegildo (Technical University of Madrid)
Alexander Herold (ECRC, Munich)
Hoon Hong (RISC, Linz)
John Hooker (Carnegie Mellon University)
Claude Kirchner (INRIA Nancy)
Alan Mackworth (University of British Columbia)
Michael Maher (IBM Watson)
Ken McAloon (Brooklyn College)
Fumio Mizoguchi (University of Tokyo)
Ugo Montanari, chair (University of Pisa)
Luis Monteiro (New University of Lisbon)
Catuscia Palamidessi (University of Genoa)
Gert Smolka (DFKI, Saarbruecken)
Peter van Beek (University of Alberta)
Pascal Van Hentenryck (Brown University)

Referees

Contents

Constraint Logic Programming

Constraint Satisfaction Problems 2

Concurrent Constraint Programming

Computational Logic

Applications

Complete Solving of Linear Diophantine Equations and Inequations without Adding Variables*

Farid AJILI
INRIA Lorraine & CRIN
615 rue du jardin botanique BP 101 &
54602 Villers-lès-Nancy Cedex,
France
email: Farid.Ajili@loria.fr

Evelyne CONTEJEAN
LRI, CNRS URA 410
Bât 490, Université Paris-Sud,
Centre d'Orsay
91405 Orsay Cedex, France
email: Evelyne.Contejean@lri.lri.fr

Abstract. In this paper, we present an algorithm for solving *directly* linear Diophantine systems of both equations and inequations. Here directly means without adding slack variables for encoding inequalities as equalities. This algorithm is an extension of the algorithm due to Contejean and Devie [9] for solving linear Diophantine systems of equations, which is itself a generalization of the algorithm of Fortenbacher [6] for solving a single linear Diophantine equation. All the nice properties of the algorithm of Contejean and Devie are still satisfied by the new algorithm: it is complete, *i.e.* provides a (finite) description of the set of solutions, it can be implemented with a *bounded* stack, and it admits an incremental version. All of these characteristics enable its easy integration in the CLP paradigm.

1 Introduction

Research on algorithms for solving linear inequational and equational constraints, or systems of them, has been widely investigated starting from the ancient Greeks. Such constraints arise in various areas of computer science and efficient algorithms are well-known for solving systems of linear constraints over reals, rational numbers [18, 17] and integers [5, 25]. Unfortunately, restricting the domain to the natural numbers makes the problem much more difficult and the algorithms in the previous class are no longer suitable.

In the recent past, several works, related to the automatic deduction framework, have shown the key role of solving *systems of linear Diophantine [2] equations* for many important unification problems: unification modulo associativity [21], modulo associativity and commutativity [26, 14, 19, 4], modulo distributivity [8]. Hence solving such systems has been widely investigated, and a large number of algorithms (see [2] for a survey) have been proposed by numerous authors: G. Huet [15], J. L. Lambert [20], M. Clausen & A. Fortenbacher [6], E. Contejean & H. Devie [9], J. F. Romeuf [23], A. P. Tomás & M. Filgueiras [12], L. Pottier [22] and E. Domenjoud [10, 11]. All these algorithms compute a basis, *i.e* a finite subset of solutions

---

* This work was partly supported by the European Contract SOL HCM No CHRX CT92 0053

[2] *i.e.* over natural numbers

which provides a finite and complete representation of the set all solutions: any non-negative solution is an N-linear combination of the solutions of the basis. It should be noticed that in the case of systems of equations, the basis of solutions is the set of *minimal* solutions.

As for inequations, they are ubiquitous in several domains such as constraint logic programming (CLP), integer linear programming, and operational research. In the above literature, the algorithms for solving linear inequations over natural numbers are not complete but over finite domains [16] and they usually proceed by turning inequations into equations by introducing new variables generally called *slack* [24]. Such methods yield voluminous problems, which is an handicap since the solving complexity is an exponential in the number of variables.

It is therefore quite natural to investigate an appropriate solver for systems of linear constraints $AX = 0 \wedge BX \leq 0$ over natural numbers, which outputs a complete and a finite representation of the set of all non-negative solutions and avoids adding new variables. One year ago, Ajili has proposed such a solver for the case of a single inequation [3].

The set of all solutions of the system of linear Diophantine constraints $AX = 0 \wedge BX \leq 0$ where $X \in \mathbb{N}^q$ is an additive submonoïd of $\mathbb{N}^q$ finitely generated by the subset of *non-decomposable* solutions. An algorithm which computes such a subset is an adequate and complete one. Since deciding the decomposability of a solution is not as easy as deciding the minimality (*cf.* the case of equations), we avoid the decomposability tests by using the following remark: a solution X_0 of $AX = 0 \wedge BX \leq 0$ is *non-decomposable* if and only if $(X_0, -BX_0)$ is a *minimal* solution of the system of equations $AX = 0 \wedge BX + Z = 0$. Considering the tuple of new additional variables Z as a function of X (*i.e.* $Z = -BX$) and not as a tuple of plain variables enables us to avoid having to introduce and manipulate them explicitly. The same idea can be applied to improve the solving of equational system of the form $BX + Z = 0$, by removing the variables Z and solving $BX \leq 0$.

Inspired by the above ideas, in this paper (see also the full version [1] for complete proofs), we give a complete solver for homogeneous linear Diophantine systems of both equations and inequations. This solver can be extended for solving heterogeneous systems in the same way as the complete solvers for systems of equations [6, 8]. Thanks to its flexibility (solving inequations together with equations, extension to the heterogeneous case, incrementality), this new solver has a wide range of potential applications: it can be integrated in the CLP paradigm thanks to its ability to test the satisfiability and to check constraint entailment.

2 Basic Notions

2.1 Notations

As usually N denotes the set of non-negative numbers and e_j denotes the jth canonical tuple of $\mathbb{N}^q$, that is

$$e_j = (\underbrace{0,\ldots,0}_{(j-1)times} ,1, \underbrace{0,\ldots,0}_{(q-j)times}).$$

· denotes the scalar product of two tuples of N^q, but it will sometimes be omitted for short.

Definition 1 Length and Euclidean Norm. Let $X = (x_1, \ldots, x_q)$ be a tuple in N^q. Its length $\sum_{i=1}^{q} x_i$ is denoted by $|X|$ and its Euclidean norm $\sqrt{\sum_{i=1}^{q} x_i^2}$ is denoted by $\|X\|$.

Definition 2 Orderings on N^q. $\leq_q$ is the component-wise extension to N^q of the usual ordering $\leq$ defined on N. $<_q$ is the strict ordering associated with $\leq_q$.

Notice that $\leq_q$ is a partial ordering on N^q. In the following, we shall freely use $\leq$ and $<$ instead of $\leq_q$ and $<_q$ if there is no ambiguity.

Definition 3 Linear Diophantine Systems. A linear Diophantine system of m constraints in q unknowns can be written thanks to an $m \times q$ matrix $C = (c_{ij})_{1 \leq i \leq m, 1 \leq j \leq q}$ and an m-tuple $d = (d_i)_{1 \leq i \leq m}$ $(c_{ij}, d_i \in \mathbb{Z})$ as follows:

$$CX \prec d,$$

where $\prec$ belongs to $\{=, \leq\}^q$, and X is the q-tuple of unknowns.

By reindexing the lines of C, the system $CX \prec d$ can be decomposed into two parts, the equational one and the inequational one as follows $AX = a \wedge BX \leq b$. m_A and m_B are respectively the number of lines of A and B.

A non-negative solution of $CX \prec d$ is said to be *non-decomposable* if it is non-null and it cannot be written as the sum of two non-null solutions.

A linear Diophantine system $CX \prec d$ is *homogeneous* when d is null.

$Sol(CX \prec 0)$ denotes the set of all non-negative solutions of $CX \prec 0$, and $Bas(CX \prec 0)$ denotes the set of all non-negative solutions of $CX \prec 0$ which are non-decomposable.

C_i and C^j denote respectively the ith row and the jth column of C.

In the following, we shall focus on homogeneous linear Diophantine systems.

2.2 Finite representation of the solutions

In general, the set $Sol(CX \prec 0)$ is infinite, however one can represent it in a finite way. Indeed in the homogeneous case, $Sol(CX \prec 0)$ is closed under addition and contains 0, hence it is an additive sub-monoïd of N^q. By the Hilbert basis theorem [7], $Sol(CX \prec 0)$ is generated by a finite basis which is exactly $Bas(CX \prec 0)$, the set of non-decomposable solutions of $CX \prec 0$. This basis provides a finite and a complete representation of $Sol(CX \prec 0)$, in the sense that $Sol(CX \prec 0)$ is the set of all N-linear combinations of elements in $Bas(CX \prec 0)$.

When a linear Diophantine system contains only equations, the non-decomposability of a solution coincides with its minimality *w.r.t.* $\leq_q$, but this is no longer true when the system contains also some inequations. However, one can still check the non-decomposability of a solution thanks to the following remark: the solutions of

$$AX = 0 \wedge BX \leq 0$$

are the projections over the first q components of the solutions of the system of *equations*

$$AX = 0 \land BX + Z = 0,$$

where Z is a m_B-tuple whose i^{th} component is the slack variable z_i. This projection is actually a one-to-one mapping from $Sol(AX = 0 \land BX + Z = 0)$ onto $Sol(AX = 0 \land BX \leq 0)$, and its inverse maps a solution $s \in \mathbb{N}^q$ to $(s, -Bs) \in \mathbb{N}^{q+m_B}$. A solution s of $AX = 0 \land BX \leq 0$ is non-decomposable if and only if its associated solution of $AX = 0 \land BX + Z = 0$ is non-decomposable, hence if and only if $(s, -Bs)$ is minimal.

3 Solving homogeneous linear Diophantine systems of equations

In '89 Contejean and Devie [9] proposed an algorithm for solving a system of several linear Diophantine equations $AX = 0$ as a whole, by computing its set of minimal solutions. It is an extension of the algorithm of Fortenbacher [6] which solves a single linear Diophantine equation. The basis ideas of both algorithms are the following:

- Search $\mathbb{N}^q \setminus \{0\}$ for the minimal solutions starting from the canonical tuples e_js.
- Suppose that the current tuple is not yet a solution. It can be non deterministically increased component by component until it becomes a solution or greater than a solution.
- In order to insure the termination of the search, one adds a pruning criterion which does not remove any minimal solution.

The new algorithms presented below (Subsections 4.1, 4.2) are also based on the same principles.

The pruning criterion of Fortenbacher allows a non-solution y to be incremented on its jth component only if the two integers[3] Ay and Ae_j do not have the same sign.

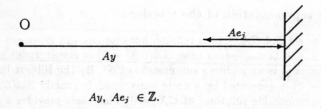

$$Ay, Ae_j \in \mathbb{Z}.$$

Fig. 1. Geometric interpretation of Fortenbacher's restriction.

Contejean and Devie have generalized this criterion for an arbitrary number of equations thanks to a geometrical interpretation: Ay should not become too large,

---

[3] Remember that there is only one equation.

hence adding Ae_j to Ay should yield a new $A(y + e_j)$ "returning to the origin", that is lying in the half-space delimited by the hyper-plan orthogonal to Ay and containing the origin. This condition can be written $Ay \cdot Ae_j < 0$.

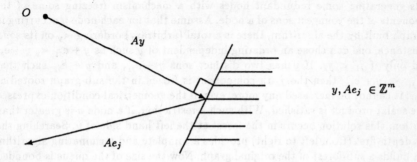

Fig. 2. Geometric interpretation of Contejean and Devie's generalized restriction.

The pruning criterion ensures the termination when $\mathbf{N}^q$ is searched breadth-first, and yields the following algorithm working on two lists, the first one being the solutions already found and the second one being the nodes already built, but not yet developed:

Initialization	$[]$; $[e_1; \ldots; e_q]$			
Solution	$\mathcal{M}$;	$[y \lvert \mathcal{P}]$	$\longrightarrow [y \lvert \mathcal{M}]$; $\mathcal{P}$	if $Ay = 0$
Leaf	$\mathcal{M}$;	$[y \lvert \mathcal{P}]$	$\longrightarrow \mathcal{M}$; $\mathcal{P}$	if $\exists s \in \mathcal{M} \ s \leq_q y$
Develop	$\mathcal{M}$;	$[y \lvert \mathcal{P}]$	$\longrightarrow \mathcal{M}$; $\mathcal{P}@[y + e_{j_1}, \ldots, y + e_{j_l}]$	

$$\text{if } Ay \neq 0, \forall s \in \mathcal{M} \ s \not\leq_q y$$
$$\text{and } \{e_{j_1}, \ldots, e_{j_l}\} = \{e_j \mid Ay \cdot Ae_j < 0\}$$

The breadth-first version of the algorithm of Contejean and Devie
for solving $AX = 0$.

Theorem 4 Contejean and Devie. *Given a system of m_A homogeneous linear Diophantine equations $AX = 0$, the above procedure reaches in a finite time a normal form $(\mathcal{M}; [])$, and $\mathcal{M}$ is exactly the set of minimal solutions of $AX = 0$.*

The termination proof is quite delicate and based on compactness properties and topology arguments. The soundness and completeness proofs are adapted from Fortenbacher's ones.

The breadth-first version of the algorithm is quite easy to explain and to understand, but one cannot guarantee that the size of the queue (that is the set of tuples waiting for development) is bounded. This problem is overcome by a depth-first version of the algorithm which can be implemented with a *bounded* stack.

One develops a forest (each tuple, but the roots, has exactly one father) and avoids generating some redundant nodes with a mechanism freezing some of the components of the youngest sons of a node. Assume that for each node y occurring in the graph built by the algorithm, there is a total (arbitrary) ordering $\prec_y$ on its sons. For instance, one can chose an ordering independent of y such as $y + e_{j_1} \prec_y y + e_{j_2}$ if and only if $j_1 < j_2$. If y has two distinct sons $y + e_{j_1}$, and $y + e_{j_2}$ such that $y + e_{j_1} \prec_y y + e_{j_2}$, then the j_2-th component is frozen in the sub-graph rooted at $y + e_{j_1}$: it cannot be increased any more, even if the geometrical condition expressed by the scalar product is satisfied. With such a restriction, if a node u is greater than a solution, this solution occurs in the forest at the left hand side of u. Searching the forest depth-first (from left to right) provides a complete and terminating algorithm which builds a sub-forest of the original graph. Now the size of the queue is bounded by the number of variables since a tuple at position l in the queue has exactly $q - l$ frozen components.

Here is a formal description of the depth-first version of the algorithm working on two lists, the first one being the solutions already found and the second one being the nodes already built, but not yet developed, equipped with their list of frozen components (written as an exponent):

Initialization	$[]$;	$[e_{j_1}^{\{j_2,\ldots,j_q\}}; \ldots ; e_{j_{q-1}}^{\{j_q\}}; e_{j_q}^{\{\}}]$		if $e_{j_1} \prec_0 \ldots \prec_0 e_{j_{q-1}} \prec_0 e_{j_q}$
Solution	$\mathcal{M}$;	$[y^{\mathcal{F}}|\mathcal{P}]$	$\longrightarrow$	$[y|\mathcal{M}]$; $\mathcal{P}$ if $Ay = 0$
Leaf	$\mathcal{M}$;	$[y^{\mathcal{F}}|\mathcal{P}]$	$\longrightarrow$	$\mathcal{M}$; $\mathcal{P}$ if $\exists s \in \mathcal{M} \; s \leq_q y$
Develop	$\mathcal{M}$;	$[y^{\mathcal{F}}|\mathcal{P}]$	$\longrightarrow$	$\mathcal{M}$; $[y + e_{j_1}^{\mathcal{F} \cup \{j_2,\ldots,j_l\}}, \ldots, y + e_{j_l}^{\mathcal{F}}]@\mathcal{P}$

$$\text{if } Ay \neq 0, \forall s \in \mathcal{M} \; s \not\leq_q y,$$
$$\{j_1, \ldots, j_l\} = \{j \mid Ay \cdot Ae_j < 0 \text{ and } j \notin \mathcal{F}\}$$
$$\text{and } y + e_{j_1} \prec_y \ldots \prec_y y + e_{j_l}$$

The depth-first version of the algorithm of Contejean and Devie

4 Solving linear Diophantine systems of constraints

It is well-known that solving the system of both equations and inequations

$$AX = 0 \wedge BX \leq 0$$

is equivalent to solve the system of *equations*

$$AX = 0 \wedge BX + Z = 0,$$

and then forget the variables Z by a projection. The key idea of the algorithms described below is that this will be done in a single step, without introducing explicitly the additional variables Z. The standard algorithm of Contejean and Devie will be applied, with the main difference that a q-tuple y does not only represent itself but also a set of $(q + m_B)$-tuples of the form

$$(y, u_1, \ldots, u_{m_B}) \text{ such that } \forall 1 \leq i \leq m_B \quad u_i \in \{0, \ldots, max(0, -B_i y)\}.$$

Hence, the algorithm for solving systems of both equations and inequations can be roughly described as follows:

- Search $N^q \setminus \{0\}$ for the non-decomposable solutions starting from the canonical tuples e_js.
- Suppose that the current tuple can still provide some non-decomposable solutions. It can be non deterministically increased component by component until it cannot provide any non-decomposable solution.
- In order to speed up the search, the new pruning criterion allows y to be incremented on its jth component ($1 \leq j \leq q$) only if there is a $(q + m_B)$-tuple represented by y which can be incremented on its jth component according to the former criterion.

Concerning the second point, the fundamental difference between solving a system of equations and a system of both equations and inequations is that in the first case, a node y greater than a solution cannot have some non-decomposable (*i.e.* *minimal*) solutions as descendants, whereas it can in the second case. Of course, this is because non-decomposability is not equivalent to minimality in this latter case as can be seen on the following example.

Example 1. Consider the inequation $x - y \leq 0$. Its set of solutions is equal to $\{(n, n + n') \mid n, n' \in N\}$.x This set is completely described as the N-linear combinations of the non-decomposable solutions $(1, 1)$ and $(0, 1)$. However these solutions are comparable with $<_2$: $(0, 1) <_2 (1, 1)$. If we take into account the hidden component corresponding to the additional variable z usually introduced for turning the inequation $x - y \leq 0$ into the equation $x - y + z = 0$, $(1, 1)$ and $(0, 1)$ respectively correspond to $(1, 1, 0)$ and $(0, 1, 1)$ which are no longer comparable.

However, we want to cut a DAG rooted at a node y as soon as possible if it does not contain any non-decomposable solution. In the case of a system of both equations and inequations $AX = 0 \wedge BX \leq 0$, a sufficient criterion is that there exists a solution s of $AX = 0 \wedge BX = 0$ such that $(s, 0) <_{q+m_B} (y, -By)$.

Every descendant $y + y'$ of y which is a solution of $AX = 0 \wedge BX \leq 0$ is decomposable into s and $y + y' - s$: by hypothesis, s is a solution, and since s is smaller than y, $y + y' - s$ is in N^q and moreover

$$A(y + y' - s) = A(y + y') - As = 0 - 0 = 0,$$
$$B(y + y' - s) = B(y + y') - Bs = B(y + y') - 0 \leq 0.$$

Hence $y + y' - s$ is a solution of $AX = 0 \wedge BX \leq 0$. This remark leads to split the set of $Sol(AX = 0 \wedge BX \leq 0)$ into two disjoint subsets, $Sol(AX = 0 \wedge BX = 0)$

and $Sol(AX = 0 \wedge BX < 0)$, and only the first one will be used for stopping the development of useless nodes.

Concerning the third point, that is the new pruning criterion, it is possible to express it in a more formal way. It is possible to increment y on its jth component $(1 \leq j \leq q)$ only if there is a $(q + m_B)$-tuple (y, z) represented by y which can be incremented on its jth component according to the former criterion, that is

$$\exists z \in \mathbf{N}^{m_B} \quad z_i \in \{0, \ldots, \max(0, -B_i y)\} \wedge (Ay \cdot Ae_j) + ((By + z) \cdot Be_j) < 0.$$

This is equivalent to the fact that the minimal value of $(Ay \cdot Ae_j) + ((By + z) \cdot Be_j)$ w.r.t z on the domain $\mathcal{D} = \{0, \ldots, \max(0, -B_1 y)\} \times \ldots \times \{0, \ldots, \max(0, -B_{m_B} y)\}$ is negative. This value can be computed as follows:

$$\min_{z \in \mathcal{D}} (Ay \cdot Ae_j) + ((By + z) \cdot Be_j)$$
$$=$$
$$\min_{z \in \mathcal{D}} (\sum_{i=1}^{m_A} (A_i y A_i e_j) + (\sum_{i=1}^{m_B} ((B_i y + z_i) B_i e_j))$$
$$=$$
$$(\sum_{i=1}^{m_A} (A_i y A_i e_j) + (\sum_{i=1}^{m_B} \min_{z_i \in \{0, \ldots, \max(0, -B_i y)\}} ((B_i y + z_i) B_i e_j))$$
$$=$$
$$(\sum_{i=1}^{m_A} (A_i y A_i e_j) + (\sum_{i=1}^{m_B} \min(B_i y B_i e_j, \max(0, B_i y) B_i e_j)).$$

Hence, the new pruning criterion $(\mathcal{C}1)$ can be expressed by: *It is possible to increment y on its jth component $(1 \leq j \leq q)$ only if*

$$\sum_{i=1}^{m_A} (A_i y A_i e_j) + (\sum_{i=1}^{m_B} min(B_i y B_i e_j, max(0, B_i y) B_i e_j)) < 0.$$

Unfortunately, in the general case we do not succeed in proving the termination with this criterion alone. We need to add another one, compatible with $(\mathcal{C}1)$, and which ensures the termination. However, we can prove the termination with $(\mathcal{C}1)$ in the case of a single inequation. The next subsection is devoted to this particular case, which is much simpler than the general case treated in the subsection 4.2.

4.1 Solving a single linear Diophantine inequation

In the case of a single inequation $B_1 X \leq 0$, the inequality used by the criterion $(\mathcal{C}1)$:

$$\sum_{i=1}^{m_A} (A_i y A_i e_j) + (\sum_{i=1}^{m_B} min(B_i y B_i e_j, max(0, B_i y) B_i e_j)) < 0,$$

can be rewritten in a simpler way: indeed $min(B_1 y B_1 e_j, max(0, B_1 y) B_1 e_j) < 0$ is equivalent to:

$$B_1 y B_1 e_j < 0.$$

This can be seen by an elementary case reasoning on the sign of $B_1 y$.

Hence, the algorithm can be formally described thanks to three lists[4], the first contains the solutions of $B_1X = 0$, the second one the solutions of $B_1X < 0$, and the last one the nodes to develop:

Initialization   [];   []; $[e_1; \ldots; e_q]$

Solution$_=$ $\mathcal{M}_=; \mathcal{M}_<; [y|\mathcal{P}] \longrightarrow [y|\mathcal{M}_=]$; $\mathcal{M}_<$; $\mathcal{P}$ if $B_1y = 0$

Leaf $\mathcal{M}_=; \mathcal{M}_<; [y|\mathcal{P}] \longrightarrow \mathcal{M}_=$; $\mathcal{M}_<$; $\mathcal{P}$ if $\exists s \in \mathcal{M}_= \; s \leq_q y$

Solution$_<$ $\mathcal{M}_=; \mathcal{M}_<; [y|\mathcal{P}] \longrightarrow \mathcal{M}_=$; $[y|\mathcal{M}_<]$; $\mathcal{P}@[y + e_{j_1}, \ldots, y + e_{j_l}]$

     if $\forall s \in \mathcal{M}_= \; s \not\leq_q y$,

     $B_1y < 0, \forall s \in \mathcal{M}_< \; (s, -B_1s) \not\leq_{q+1} (y, -B_1y)$

     and $\{e_{j_1}, \ldots, e_{j_l}\} = \{e_j \mid B_1yB_1e_j < 0\}$

Develop $\mathcal{M}_=; \mathcal{M}_<; [y|\mathcal{P}] \longrightarrow \mathcal{M}_=$; $\mathcal{M}_<$; $\mathcal{P}@[y + e_{j_1}, \ldots, y + e_{j_l}]$

     if $\forall s \in \mathcal{M}_= \; s \not\leq_q y$,

     $(B_1y \not\leq 0$ or $\exists s \in \mathcal{M}_< \; (s, -Bs) \leq_{q+1} (y, -B_1y))$

     and $\{e_{j_1}, \ldots, e_{j_l}\} = \{e_j \mid B_1yB_1e_j < 0\}$

The breadth-first version of the algorithm for solving a single inequation
$$B_1X \leq 0.$$

Theorem 5 Soundness and completeness. *Given an inequation $B_1X \leq 0$ the above procedure reaches in a finite time a normal form $(\mathcal{M}_=; \mathcal{M}_<; [])$, and $\mathcal{M}_= \cup \mathcal{M}_<$ is exactly the set of non-decomposable solutions of $B_1X \leq 0$.*

It should be noticed that running this algorithm for solving $B_1X \leq 0$ yields exactly the same DAG as the algorithm of Fortenbacher for solving $B_1X = 0$, the only difference being the way of checking the solutions: in both cases, the solutions of $B_1X = 0$ are retained, and in the case of an inequation, the solutions of $B_1X < 0$ are also retained but stored in a second set *not used for cutting the search-space by the rule* **Leaf.** Hence the termination of the algorithm is a corollary of the termination of the algorithm of Fortenbacher. The fact that $\mathcal{M}_= \cup \mathcal{M}_<$ contains only some solutions of $B_1X \leq 0$ is obvious, and the proof of completeness of the criterion $(\mathcal{C}1)$ (*i.e.* every non-decomposable solution is in $\mathcal{M}_= \cup \mathcal{M}_<$) will be sketched in the section devoted to the general case.

Example 2. Consider the inequation

$$3x_1 + 2x_2 - x_3 - 2x_4 \leq 0.$$

---

[4] In the case of systems of *equations*, two lists are enough: the list of the solutions and the list of the nodes to develop, but in the case of *inequations*, we have to split the list of solutions *cf.* the remark concerning the second point of the rough description of the general algorithm.

Running the algorithm yields the following DAG:

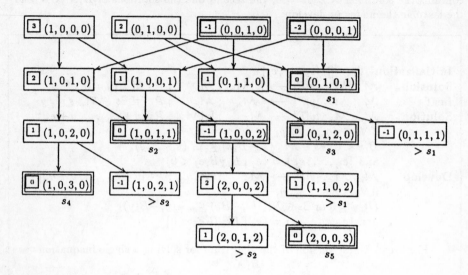

In the small box at the left hand side of each node $y = (y_1, y_2, y_3, y_4)$, there is the value $3y_1 + 2y_2 - y_3 - 2y_4$. The non-decomposable solutions have a double frame. The set $\mathcal{M}_=$ of the minimal solutions of the associated equation $3x_1 + 2x_2 - x_3 - 2x_4 = 0$ is equal to

$$\mathcal{M}_= = \{(0,1,0,1); (1,0,1,1); (0,1,2,0); (1,0,3,0); (2,0,0,3)\},$$

and the set $\mathcal{M}_<$ of the other non-decomposable solutions of the inequation $3x_1 + 2x_2 - x_3 - 2x_4 \leq 0$ is equal to

$$\mathcal{M}_< = \{(0,0,1,0); (0,0,0,1); (1,0,0,2)\}.$$

4.2 General case

In the case of a system containing a linear inequation together with at least another linear constraint, the pruning criterion $(\mathcal{C}1)$ is complete. This means that

Proposition 6 Completeness of $(\mathcal{C}1)$. *Running the procedure $\mathcal{P}roc(\mathcal{C}1)$ on a system $AX = 0 \wedge BX \leq 0$ yields in a finite number of steps a triple $(\mathcal{M}_=, \mathcal{M}_<, \mathcal{P})$ such that the set of non-decomposable solutions is exactly $\mathcal{M}_= \cup \mathcal{M}_<$.*

Initialization $[]$; $[]$; $[e_1; \ldots; e_q]$
Solution$_=$ $\mathcal{M}_=$; $\mathcal{M}_<$; $[y|\mathcal{P}] \longrightarrow [y|\mathcal{M}_=]$; $\mathcal{M}_<$; $\mathcal{P}$ if $Ay = 0 \wedge By = 0$
Leaf $\mathcal{M}_=$; $\mathcal{M}_<$; $[y|\mathcal{P}] \longrightarrow \mathcal{M}_=$; $\mathcal{M}_<$; $\mathcal{P}$ if $\exists s \in \mathcal{M}_=\ s \leq_q y$
Solution$_<$ $\mathcal{M}_=$; $\mathcal{M}_<$; $[y|\mathcal{P}] \longrightarrow \mathcal{M}_=$; $[y|\mathcal{M}_<]$; $\mathcal{P}@[y + e_{j_1}, \ldots, y + e_{j_i}]$
       if $\forall s \in \mathcal{M}_=\ s \not\leq_q y$
       $Ay = 0 \wedge By < 0, \forall s \in \mathcal{M}_<\ (s, -Bs) \not\leq_{q+m_B} (y, -By)$
       and $\{e_{j_1}, \ldots, e_{j_i}\} = \{e_j \mid (\mathcal{C})\}$
Develop $\mathcal{M}_=$; $\mathcal{M}_<$; $[y|\mathcal{P}] \longrightarrow \mathcal{M}_=$; $\mathcal{M}_<$; $\mathcal{P}@[y + e_{j_1}, \ldots, y + e_{j_i}]$
       if $\forall s \in \mathcal{M}_=\ s \not\leq_q y$,
       $(\neg(Ay = 0 \wedge By < 0)$ or $\exists s \in \mathcal{M}_<\ (s, -Bs) \leq_{q+m_B} (y, -By))$
       and $\{e_{j_1}, \ldots, e_{j_i}\} = \{e_j \mid (\mathcal{C})\}$

The procedure $\mathcal{P}roc(\mathcal{C})$ for solving a system $AX = 0 \wedge BX \leq 0$ parameterized by a pruning criterion $(\mathcal{C})$.

Sketch of the proof. The proof of the completeness of $(\mathcal{C}1)$ is by a finite induction on the length $|s|$ of a given non-decomposable solution of $AX = 0 \wedge BX \leq 0$. We can build a sequence of tuples

$$e_{j_0} = v_1 < v_2 = v_1 + e_{j_1} < v_3 \ldots < v_k < v_{k+1} = v_k + e_{j_k} < \ldots v_{|s|-1} < v_{|s|} = s,$$

such that at each step the pruning criterion allows to add e_{j_k} to v_k. This is sufficient since s is non-decomposable: there is no solution of $AX = 0 \wedge BX = 0$ which is strictly smaller that s. Hence none of the v_ks will be removed from $\mathcal{P}$ without being developed. □

Unfortunately, $(\mathcal{C}1)$ does not ensure the termination, there are some systems such that at any step $\mathcal{P}$,the last component of the triple handled by the procedure, is not empty. This is the case for the

Example 3. Let us consider the system of inequations:

$$x_1 - 3x_2 + 4x_3 \leq 0,$$
$$2x_1 + x_2 - x_3 \leq 0.$$

The system of associated equations has no solutions, hence **Solution$_=$** and **Leaf** will never apply, and it can be seen by induction on n that the procedure builds an infinite sequence of tuples

$(0, 1, 0); (0, 1, 1); (0, 2, 1); (0, 2, 2); (0, 2, 3); (0, 3, 3); (0, 4, 3); (0, 4, 4); (0, 5, 4)$
$(0, 5, 5); \ldots; (0, n, n); (0, n+1, n); (0, n+1, n+1); \ldots$

As we want to obtain a terminating algorithm for solving $AX = 0 \wedge BX \leq 0$, we add a second pruning criterion $(\mathcal{C}2)$ which ensures the termination. This is done in two steps. First, we consider $(\mathcal{C}2)$ alone. Then, we consider $(\mathcal{C}2)$ together with $(\mathcal{C}1)$, and we shall prove that they are *compatible*.

The criterion $(C2)$ is based on a the fact that the hidden part corresponding to the additional variables is bounded for the non-decomposable solutions of $AX = 0 \land BX \leq 0$. There are some uniform bounds on the minimal solutions of a system of equations $CX = 0$, in particular the following one proposed by Pottier [22]:

Lemma 7 Pottier. *Let C be an $n \times q$ matrix of rank r. Every minimal solution $m = (m_1, \ldots, m_q)$ of $CX = 0$ satisfies:*

$$max_{1 \leq j \leq q} |m_j| \leq (n - r) \left(\frac{\sum_{i,j} |c_{ij}|}{r} \right)^r.$$

Corollary 8. *Let $AX = 0 \land BX \leq 0$ be a system of linear Diophantine constraints, and r be the rank of the matrix $\begin{pmatrix} A & 0 \\ B & I \end{pmatrix}$. Let s be a non-decomposable solution of $AX = 0 \land BX \leq 0$. Then the following inequalities hold:*

$$max_{1 \leq i \leq m_B} |B_i s| \leq \mathcal{B}_2 \equiv (q + m_B - r) \left(\frac{\sum_{i,j} |a_{ij}| + \sum_{i,j} |b_{ij}| + m_B}{r} \right)^r,$$

$$\|Bs\|^2 \leq \mathcal{B}'_2 \equiv m_B \mathcal{B}_2{}^2.$$

The criterion $(C2)$ is expressed by: *It is possible to increment y on its jth component $(1 \leq j \leq q)$ only if*

$$Ay \cdot Ae_j + By \cdot Be_j \leq \mathcal{B}'_2.$$

Proposition 9 Completeness of $(C2)$. *Running the procedure $\mathcal{P}roc(C2)$ on a system $AX = 0 \land BX \leq 0$ yields in a finite number of steps a triple $(\mathcal{M}_=, \mathcal{M}_<, \mathcal{P})$ such that the set of non-decomposable solutions is exactly $\mathcal{M}_= \cup \mathcal{M}_<$.*

Proof. The completeness proof of $(C2)$ is similar to the one of $(C1)$: let us suppose that s is a non-decomposable solution of $AX = 0 \land BX \leq 0$, and that we have a sequence of tuples

$$e_{j_0} = v_1 < v_2 = v_1 + e_{j_1} < v_3 \ldots < v_k \leq s,$$

such that at each step the pruning criterion $(C2)$ is satisfied. If v_k is not yet equal to s, we shall build v_{k+1} from v_k by adding an e_{j_k} such that $e_{j_k} \leq s - v_k$. s is a solution, hence

$Av_k \cdot A(s - v_k) = -\|Av_k\|^2$ since $As = 0$,
$Av_k \cdot A(s - v_k) \leq 0$.

$B(s - v_k) + Bv_k + (-Bs) = 0$,
$\|B(s - v_k) + Bv_k + (-Bs)\|^2 = 0$,
$\underbrace{\|B(s - v_k)\|^2 + \|Bv_k\|^2 + \|-Bs\|^2}_{\geq 0} + 2(B(s - v_k) \cdot Bv_k + B(s - v_k) \cdot (-Bs) + Bv_k \cdot (-Bs)) = 0$,
$B(s - v_k) \cdot Bv_k + B(s - v_k) \cdot (-Bs) + Bv_k \cdot (-Bs)) \leq 0$,
$B(s - v_k) \cdot Bv_k + Bs \cdot (-Bs) \leq 0$,
$B(s - v_k) \cdot Bv_k \leq \|Bs\|^2$,
$B(s - v_k) \cdot Bv_k \leq \mathcal{B}'_2$.

$Av_k \cdot A(s - v_k) + Bv_k \cdot B(s - v_k) \leq \mathcal{B}'_2$.

There is necessarily a tuple $e_{j_k} \leq s - v_k$ such that $Av_k \cdot Ae_{j_k} + Bv_k \cdot Be_{j_k} \leq \mathcal{B}'_2$, otherwise the equality $Av_k \cdot A(s - v_k) + Bv_k \cdot B(s - v_k) \leq \mathcal{B}'_2$ cannot be satisfied. $(C2)$ allows to add such an e_{j_k} to v_k in order to build v_{k+1}. $\square$

Proposition 10 Termination of $(C2)$. *Running the procedure $Proc(C2)$ on a system $AX = 0 \wedge BX \leq 0$ terminates, i.e. yields in a finite number of steps a triple $(\mathcal{M}_=, \mathcal{M}_<, \emptyset)$.*

Sketch of the proof. Let Sup be the maximum of $\mathcal{B}'_2$, the $\|Ae_j\|^2$s and the $\|Be_j\|^2$s. Let $v_1, v_2 = v_1 + e_{j_1}, \ldots, v_k, v_{k+1} = v_k + e_{j_k}, \ldots$ be a sequence of tuples built according the criterion $(C2)$. It is easy to show by induction on k that $\|Av_k\|^2 + \|Bv_k\|^2 \leq 4kSup$. Hence one can deduce that $\begin{bmatrix} A \\ B \end{bmatrix} \frac{v_k}{k} \longrightarrow_{k \to \infty} 0$. Using the same arguments as in [9], it is possible to show that there exists a minimal solution s of $AX = 0 \wedge BX = 0$ and an integer k_0 such that

$$\forall k > k_0 \quad s \leq v_k.$$

Hence, such an infinite sequence will never be produced by $Proc(C2)$, since it will be cut with **Leaf**. $\square$

Proposition 11 Completeness of $(C1) \wedge (C2)$. *Running the procedure $Proc(C1 \wedge C2)$ on a system $AX = 0 \wedge BX \leq 0$ yields in a finite number of steps a triple $(\mathcal{M}_=, \mathcal{M}_<, \mathcal{P})$ such that the set of non-decomposable solutions is exactly $\mathcal{M}_= \cup \mathcal{M}_<$.*

Proof. let us suppose that s is a non-decomposable solution of $AX = 0 \wedge BX \leq 0$, and that we have a sequence of tuples

$$e_{j_0} = v_1 < v_2 = v_1 + e_{j_1} < v_3 \ldots < v_k \leq s,$$

such that at each step $(C1) \wedge (C2)$ is satisfied. If v_k is not yet equal to s, we shall build v_{k+1} from v_k by adding an e_{j_k} such that $e_{j_k} \leq s - v_k$. $(C1)$ is complete, hence there exists an $e_j \leq s - v_k$ such that

$$\sum_{i=1}^{m_A}(A_i v_k A_i e_j) + (\sum_{i=1}^{m_B} \min(B_i v_k B_i e_j, \max(0, B_i v_k)B_i e_j)) < 0.$$

If $Av_k \cdot Ae_j + Bv_k \cdot Be_j \leq \mathcal{B}'_2$, then we can chose e_j as e_{j_k}, otherwise, since

$$Av_k \cdot A(s - v_k) + Bv_k \cdot B(s - v_k) \leq \mathcal{B}'_2,$$

there is necessarily another $e_{j'} \leq s - v_k$ such that $Av_k \cdot Ae_{j'} + Bv_k \cdot Be_{j'} < 0$. Then we can chose $e_{j'}$ as e_{j_k}, since

$$\sum_{i=1}^{m_A}(A_i v_k A_i e_{j'}) + (\sum_{i=1}^{m_B} \min(B_i v_k B_i e_{j'}, \max(0, B_i v_k)B_i e_{j'})) \leq Av_k \cdot Ae_{j'} + Bv_k \cdot Be_{j'}.$$

In both cases, $(C1) \wedge (C2)$ allows to add e_{j_k} to v_k for building $v_{j_{k+1}}$. $\square$

Hence, we have designed a conjunction of criteria $(C1) \wedge (C2)$ which is complete and makes the parameterized procedure terminating.

Theorem 12. *Running the procedure $Proc(C1 \wedge C2)$ on a system $AX = 0 \wedge BX \leq 0$ yields in a finite number of steps a triple $(\mathcal{M}_=, \mathcal{M}_<, \emptyset)$ such that the set of non-decomposable solutions is exactly $\mathcal{M}_= \cup \mathcal{M}_<$.*

Example 4.

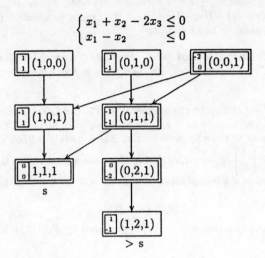

$$\begin{cases} x_1 + x_2 - 2x_3 \leq 0 \\ x_1 - x_2 \qquad \leq 0 \end{cases}$$

In this example, the criterion $(C2)$ (*i.e.* the bound) is not needed to ensure termination, it's satisfied in all the nodes. It should be noticed that solving the inequational system given above with the algorithm of E. Contejean & H. Devie (with the stack version and by adding slack variables) generates 18 nodes.

Example 5.

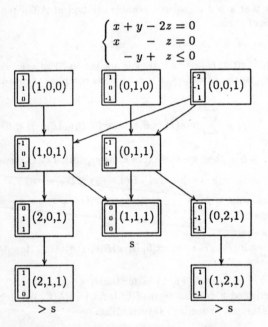

$$\begin{cases} x + y - 2z = 0 \\ x \qquad - z = 0 \\ - y + z \leq 0 \end{cases}$$

The unique non-decomposable solution of the system is $(1, 1, 1)$. Again, the criterion $(C2)$ does not cut any sub-DAG. The algorithm of E. Contejean & H. Devie builds a DAG of 12 nodes for the same constraint system.

5 Some extensions

A depth-first version of the algorithm

As in the case of systems of equations, the algorithm admits a depth-first version based on a freezing mechanism together with a total ordering for the set of sons of each node. The key point here is that we only use the solutions of associated equational system for stopping the development of useless nodes, and that if a node is greater than an "equational" solution, this solution is at its left hand side in the DAG.

Solving non-homogeneous linear Diophantine constraints

The representation of the solutions of $AX = a \wedge BX \leq b$ is a bit more complicated than in the homogeneous case since its set of solutions is no longer a monoïd. Let S_0 be the set of the non-decomposable solutions of the homogeneous system $AX = 0 \wedge BX \leq 0$ and S_1 be the set $\{s \mid (s, 1) \in \mathcal{B}as(AX - az = 0 \wedge BX - bz \leq 0)\}$. Any solution of $AX = a \wedge BX \leq b$ is a sum of a solution in S_1 and an N-linear combination of solutions in S_0. Hence the "homogeneous" solver may be extended to the heterogeneous case according to the lines of T. Guckenbiehl & A. Herold [13] and E. Contejean [9]. The sets S_0 and S_1 can be obtained by solving the homogeneous system $AX - az = 0 \wedge BX - bz \leq 0$ by the latter algorithm and freeze the new variable for each node as soon as it's equal to 1. For any (s, z) in the set $\mathcal{M}_= \cup \mathcal{M}_<$ returned by the algorithm, we test its last component: if $z = 0$ (resp $z = 1$) then s belongs to S_0 (resp S_1).

6 Some potential applications

The solver in a CLP setting

In the constraint logic programming framework, the ability of testing the constraints' entailment and the satisfiability/unsatisfiability of a set of constraints (and eventually exhibiting a solution) is a crucial issue. Propagation based solvers, as for instance in the finite domains' case, are generally not highly efficient for testing constraint entailment and unsatisfiability because propagation only reasons with local consistency [27]. The solver presented in this paper provides some effective means to decide unsatisfiability since it is complete and terminates. Moreover, it also provides an algorithm for deciding entailment.

A constraint c is *entailed* by a system of constraints C if any solution of C also satisfies c. Entailment is used in the cc(FD) frame [28] for reducing an implication constraint $c \rightarrow C$ to C if c is entailed by the constraints' store. If $\neg c$ is entailed, then $c \rightarrow C$ is reduced to *True*. Given a constraint system $AX = 0 \wedge BX \leq 0$, the proposed solver returns the basis of solutions $\{m_1, .., m_u\}$. Any inequational constraint (or system of them) $\underline{\alpha} \cdot X \leq 0$, where $\underline{\alpha}, X \in \mathbb{Z}^q$, is entailed by $AX = 0 \wedge BX \leq 0$ if and only if for all $i \in [1..u] : \underline{\alpha} \cdot m_i \leq 0$ holds. Indeed, any non-negative solution of $AX = 0 \wedge BX \leq 0$ is a N-linear combination of $\{m_1, .., m_u\}$. The strength of this procedure lies in the fact that it provides entailment in the presence of infinite solution sets.

Solving some linear programs

Let's take the integer linear program:

$$\mathcal{LP} = \begin{cases} BX \leq 0 \\ X > 0 \\ Minimize(\underline{c}X) \\ \underline{c} = (c_i)_{1 \leq i \leq q} \mid \forall i\; c_i \in \mathbf{N}^* \end{cases}$$

In order to solve $\mathcal{LP}$, some linear programming methods are characterized by constructing a sequence of trial solutions that go through the interior of the solution space until reaching an optimal one. Hence, the disadvantage of such methods is the need for a feasible solution to start. If we note that the optimal solution of $\mathcal{LP}$ must be a minimal one of $BX \leq 0$, then the solver, presented here, can be applied to compute all the minimal solutions of $BX \leq 0$ and then, the one which minimizes the objective function $\underline{c}X$ can be chosen.

7 Conclusion

We gave the *first* algorithm which computes the basis of a linear Diophantine system of both equations and *inequations* without explicitly adding some extra variables. This algorithm is actually an extension of the algorithm of E. Contejean & H. Devie, the main difference between them being the pruning criterion. Hence the new algorithm inherits all the nice characteristics of the former one: its depth-first version can be implemented with a *bounded* stack, it is incremental and compatible with the propagation traditionally used by FD solvers.

In the future, we are willing to investigate the potential applications of the new solver. This seems to be promising since many combinatorial and optimization problems (scheduling, planning, data dependence analysis...) can be formulated as: $AX = 0 \land BX \leq 0$.

References

1. F. Ajili and E. Contejean. Complete solving of linear and diophantine equational and inequational systems without adding variables. Technical Report 0175, INRIA, June 1995.
2. F. Ajili, E. Contejean, E. Domenjoud, M. Filgueiras, C. Kirchner, and A.-P. Tomás. Solving Linear Diophantine Equations: The State of the Art. in preparation, 1995.
3. Farid Ajili. Etude de la résolution de contraintes diophantiennes linéaires sur les entiers naturels. Rapport de dea, Université Henri Poincaré - Nancy 1, September 1994.
4. Alexandre Boudet, Evelyne Contejean, and Hervé Devie. A new AC-unification algorithm with a new algorithm for solving diophantine equations. In *Proc. 5th IEEE Symp. Logic in Computer Science, Philadelphia*, pages 289–299. IEEE Computer Society Press, June 1990.
5. T. J. Chou and G. E. Collins. Algorithms for the solution of systems of linear diophantine equations. *SIAM Journal on computing*, 11:687–708, 1982.
6. M. Clausen and A. Fortenbacher. Efficient solution of linear diophantine equations. *Journal of Symbolic Computation*, 8(1&2):201–216, 1989.

7. A. H. Clifford and G. B. Preston. *The algebraic theory of semigroups.* Number 7 in Mathematical surveys. American Mathematical Society, 1961. There's two volumes. The second was published in 1967.

8. Evelyne Contejean. Solving *-problems modulo distributivity by a reduction to *AC1*-unification. *Journal of Symbolic Computation*, 16:493–521, 1993.

9. Evelyne Contejean and Hervé Devie. An efficient algorithm for solving systems of diophantine equations. *Information and Computation*, 113(1):143–172, August 1994.

10. Eric Domenjoud. Outils pour la déduction automatique dans les théories associatives-commutatives. Thèse de doctorat de l'université de Nancy I, 1991.

11. Eric Domenjoud. Solving systems of linear diophantine equations: An algebraic approach. In *Proc. 16th Mathematical Foundations of Computer Science, Warsaw, LNCS 520.* Springer-Verlag, 1991.

12. M. Filgueiras and A. P. Tomás. Fast methods for solving linear diophantine equations. In M. Filgueiras and Damas L., editors, *Proceedings of the 6th Portuguese Conference on Artificial Intelligence*, 727, pages 297–306. Lecture Notes in Artificial Intelligence, Springer-Verlag, 1993.

13. T. Guckenbiehl and A. Herold. Solving linear diophantine equations. Technical Report SEKI-85-IV-KL, 1985.

14. Alexander Herold and Jorg H. Siekmann. Unification in abelian semi-groups. *Journal of Automated Reasoning*, 3(3):247–283, 1987.

15. Gérard Huet. An algorithm to generate the basis of solutions to homogeneous linear diophantine equations. *Information Processing Letters*, 7(3), April 1978.

16. E. Joxan, M. J. Maher, P. J. Stuckey, and R. H. C. Yap. Beyond finite domains. In A. Borning, editor, *Proceedings of the Second International Workshop on Principles and Practice of Constraint Programming*, volume 874 of *Lecture Notes in Computer Science*, pages 86–94. Springer-Verlag, may 1994.

17. N. Karmarkar. A new polynomial algorithm for linear programming. In *Proceedings of the 16th Annual ACM Symposium on Theory of Computing*, pages 302–311, New York, 1984. Revised version: Combinatorica 4 (1984),373-395.

18. L. G. Khachiyan. Polynomial algorithms in linear programming. *Zhurnal Vychisditel'noi Matematiki i Matematicheskoi Fiziki*, pages 51–68, 1980.

19. Claude Kirchner. From unification in combination of equational theories to a new AC unification algorithm. In H. Ait-Kaci and M. Nivat, editors, *Proc. Colloquium on Resolution of Equations in Algebraic Structures*, pages 171–210. Academic Press, 1987.

20. J. L. Lambert. Une borne pour les générateurs des solutions entières positives d'une équation diophantienne linéaire. *Comptes Rendus de l'Académie des Sciences de Paris*, 305:39,40, 1987. Série I.

21. G. S. Makanin. Algorithmic decidability of the rank of constant free equations in a free semigroup. *Dokl. Akad. Nauk. SSSR 243*, 243, 1978.

22. L. Pottier. Minimal solutions of linear diophantine systems : bounds and algorithms. In *Proceedings of the Fourth International Conference on Rewriting Techniques and Applications*, pages 162–173, Como, Italy, April 1991.

23. J. F. Romeuf. A polynomial algorithm for solving systems of two linear diophantine equations. Technical report, Laboratoire d'Informatique de Rouen et LITP, France, 1989.

24. A. Schrijver. *Theory of Linear and Integer Programming.* Wiley, 1986.

25. J. C. Sogno. Analysis of standard and new algorithms for the integer and linear constraint satisfaction problem. Technical report, INRIA, 1992.

26. M. Stickel. A unification algorithm for associative-commutative functions. *Journal of the ACM*, 28(3):423–434, 1981.

27. P Van Hentenryck. *Constraint Satisfaction in Logic Programming.* MIT Press, 1989.

28. P. Van Hentenryck, H. Simonis, and M. Dincbas. Constraint satisfaction using constraint logic programming. *Artificial Intelligence*, 58(1-3):113–159, December 1992.

From Elliott-MacMahon to an Algorithm for General Linear Constraints on Naturals*

Eric Domenjoud[1] and Ana Paula Tomás[2]

[1] CRIN/CNRS & INRIA-Lorraine
Eric.Domenjoud@loria.fr
[2] LIACC/University of Porto
apt@ncc.up.pt

Abstract. We describe a new algorithm for solving a conjunction of linear diophantine equations, inequations and disequations in natural numbers. We derive our algorithm from one proposed by Elliott in 1903 for solving a single homogeneous equation. This algorithm was then extended to solve homogeneous systems of equations by MacMahon. We show how it further extends to an algorithm which solves general linear constraints in nonnegative integers and allows a parallel implementation. This algorithm provides a parametric representation of the solutions from which minimal solutions may be extracted immediately. Moreover, it may be easily implemented in parallel. It has however one drawback: it is redundant which means that the same minimal solution is usually generated many times. We show how this redundancy may be eliminated at the cost of an increase in the space complexity.

Introduction

The problem of solving linear equations with integer coefficients over the natural numbers plays an important role in computer science. In automated deduction, this problem is at the heart of the associative commutative unification algorithm. It appears also in many other fields like data flow analysis, Petri nets or even abstract interpretation in logic programming.

Since 1978 when Huet [9] proposed his algorithm for solving a single homogeneous equation, much effort has been spent on trying to solve efficiently this problem [3, 4, 5, 8, 11]. In the last few years, several efficient algorithms have been proposed which solve systems of such equations. However, it seems that very few people have been aware of an old algorithm proposed in 1903 by Elliott [6] and later extended by MacMahon [10]. This algorithm has nice features which allowed us to extend it to solve more elaborate problems involving inequations ($\geq, \leq, <, >$) and also disequations ($\neq$). This problem was addressed very recently in two different works. One of them [2] extends the algorithm of A. Fortenbacher to solve systems of equations and inequations while the other one [1] proposes a new method for solving an arbitrary conjunction of equations,

* This work was partly supported by the SOL project, HCM *#CHRX CT92 0053*

inequations and disequations. This second algorithm is however a bit different since it does not compute a basis of the set of solutions, but rather a parametric representation of this set. This parametric representation consists in a finite set of parametric expressions which together generate all nonnegative solutions when the parameters range over the natural numbers. In addition, this parametric representation is unambiguous in the sense that each solution is generated exactly once. For instance, such a parametric representation of the solutions of $2x = y + z$ may be

$$\begin{cases} x = u_1 + u_2 \\ y = 2u_1 \\ z = 2u_2 \end{cases} \qquad \begin{cases} x = u_1 + u_2 + 1 \\ y = 2u_1 + 1 \\ z = 2u_2 + 1 \end{cases}$$

while the basis of the set of solutions is $\{(1, 2, 0), (1, 1, 1), (1, 0, 2)\}$. Note that if we are not interested in unambiguity, the basis of the set of solutions always provides a parametric representation. Unfortunately, when disequations are involved, such a basis does not exist in general. Thus a parametric representation seems to be the best one may hope. However, depending on the application we have in mind, some parametric representations may be more useful.

In this paper, we derive from the algorithm of Elliott-MacMahon a new algorithm which, given a problem $\mathcal{P}$ containing d disequations, computes at once a parametric representation of the solutions of each of the 2^d problems obtained by replacing each disequation $\alpha X + \beta \neq 0$ in $\mathcal{P}$, alternatively with $\alpha X + \beta > 0$ and $\alpha X + \beta < 0$. The advantage of this representation is that each of the solution sets of these 2^d problems may now be represented through a finite basis. Moreover, this basis may be extracted immediately from the parametric representation we obtain. Note that this last property does not hold in general for any parametric representation, even if only equations are considered. For instance,

$$\begin{cases} x = 2u + 1 \\ y = 2u \end{cases} \qquad \begin{cases} x = 2u + 2 \\ y = 2u + 1 \end{cases}$$

is a parametric representation of the solutions of $x - y - 1 = 0$. If we want to describe these solutions through minimal ones, we need both the minimal solutions of this equation and the minimal nonzero solutions of its homogeneous part $x - y = 0$. But the parametric representation does not $contain$ the solution $(x, y) = (1, 1)$ which is the only minimal nonzero solution of $x - y = 0$. The method we present does not have this problem.

The paper is organised as follows. In section 1, we introduce the main notions about linear diophantine problems. In section 2 we describe the original algorithm of Elliott-MacMahon for homogeneous equations and reformulate it as a transformation process on constrained parametric expressions. In sections 3 and 4, we extend the algorithm to solve first non-homogeneous equations and then arbitrary diophantine constraints involving equations, inequations and disequations. Finally, in section 5, we show how we can eliminate the redundancy from this algorithm. Due to lack of space, all proofs are omitted.

1 Preliminaries

We introduce here basic notions about linear diophantine constraints and their solutions. In the sequel, $\mathbb{N}$ is the set of natural numbers and $\mathbb{Z}$ is the set of integers.

A linear diophantine constraint has the form $\alpha_1 x_1 + \cdots + \alpha_n x_n + \beta \ \# \ 0$ where $\#$ is any predicate in $\{=, \geq, \leq, >, <, \neq\}$ and $\alpha_1, \ldots, \alpha_n, \beta \in \mathbb{Z}$. It is homogeneous if $\beta = 0$. We also write such a constraint as $\alpha X + \beta \ \# \ 0$ where α and X are tuples. The constraint is an *equation* if $\#$ is $=$, an *inequation* if $\# \in \{\geq, \leq, >, <\}$, and a *disequation* if $\#$ is $\neq$. For the sake of simplicity, we restrict our attention to the case where $\# \in \{=, \geq, \neq\}$. This is not really a restriction since in integers, any inequation may be reduced to $\alpha X + \beta \geq 0$.

A system of linear diophantine constraints is a finite conjunction of constraints. We also write it as $AX + B \ \# \ 0$ where A is a matrix of which the entry $\alpha_{i,j}$ is the coefficient of x_j in the ith constraint, B is a tuple of integers, and $\#$ is a tuple of predicates. We also use the notation $A^1 x_1 + \cdots + A^n x_n + B \ \# \ 0$ where A^i denotes the ith column of A. A system $AX + B \ \# \ 0$ of equations and inequations is homogeneous if $B = 0$. The *homogeneous part* of $AX + B \ \# \ 0$ is the homogeneous system $AX \ \# \ 0$.

We are only interested in nonnegative solutions of the constraints. Let $\mathcal{P} \equiv AX + B = 0 \wedge A'X + B' \geq 0$ be a system of equations and inequations and $\mathcal{P}^H$ its homogeneous part. A nonzero solution S of $\mathcal{P}^H$ is minimal if it is not the sum of two nonzero solutions of $\mathcal{P}^H$. A solution S of $\mathcal{P}$ is minimal if it is not the sum of a solution of $\mathcal{P}$ and a nonzero solution of $\mathcal{P}^H$. If Y is a tuple of n new variables where n is the number of inequations in $\mathcal{P}$ then a nonzero solution S of $\mathcal{P}^H$ is minimal if and only if $(S, A'S)$ is minimal in the componentwise ordering in the set of nonzero solutions of $AX = 0 \wedge A'X - Y = 0$. A solution S of $\mathcal{P}$ is minimal if and only if it is minimal in the componentwise ordering in the set of solutions of $AX + B = 0 \wedge A'X - Y + B' = 0$. If $\mathcal{N} = \{N_1, \ldots, N_p\}$ is the set of minimal solutions of $\mathcal{P}$ and $\mathcal{H} = \{H_1, \ldots, H_q\}$ is the set of minimal nonzero solutions of $\mathcal{P}^H$, the set of all solutions of $\mathcal{P}$ is $\{N_i + H_1 \lambda_1 + \cdots + H_q \lambda_q \mid i = 1, \ldots, p, \lambda_1, \ldots, \lambda_q \in \mathbb{N}\}$. We write this set as $\mathcal{N} + \mathcal{H}^*$ (by convention, $\varnothing^* = \{0\}$).

We shall also be interested in another description of the solutions. A parametric representation of the solutions of $AX + B \ \# \ 0$ is a finite set of expressions of the form $X = S_1 u_1 + \cdots + S_k u_k + D$ such that (i) for any natural numbers $\lambda_1, \ldots, \lambda_k$, $S_1 \lambda_1 + \cdots + S_k \lambda_k + D$ is a solution of $AX + B \ \# \ 0$; (ii) for each solution S of $AX + B \ \# \ 0$, there exists at least one expression $X = S_1 u_1 + \cdots + S_k u_k + D$ in the set and natural numbers $\lambda_1, \ldots, \lambda_k$, such that $S = S_1 \lambda_1 + \cdots + S_k \lambda_k + D$. For instance, with the previous notations, the set $\{X = N_i + H_1 u_1 + \cdots + H_q u_q \mid i = 1, \ldots, p\}$ is a parametric representation of the solutions of $\mathcal{P}$.

2 Elliott-MacMahon's method (1903/1916)

We describe here the method of Elliott for solving a single homogeneous linear diophantine equations. We give no correctness proof. The interested reader may refer to [6] for more details.

2.1 The original method

Given an homogeneous diophantine equation

$$a_1 x_1 + \cdots + a_n x_n = 0 \tag{1}$$

where $a_1, \ldots, a_n \in \mathbb{Z}$, Elliott considers the generating function

$$\prod_{i=1}^{n} (1 + Y_i \lambda^{a_i} + Y_i^2 \lambda^{2a_i} + \cdots) = \prod_{i=1}^{n} \frac{1}{1 - Y_i \lambda^{a_i}}$$

where Y_i's and λ are formal indeterminates. The expansion of this function is the sum of all terms of the form $Y^\gamma \lambda^\alpha$ where $\gamma \in \mathbb{N}^n$ and $a_1 \gamma_1 + \cdots + a_n \gamma_n = \alpha$. Thus a tuple $\gamma \in \mathbb{N}^n$ is a solution of (1) if and only if the expansion contains the term Y^γ. The idea of Elliott is to transform this generating function until factors not containing λ appear. For this, he uses the identity

$$\frac{1}{1-R} \frac{1}{1-S} = \frac{1}{1-RS} \left(\frac{1}{1-R} + \frac{1}{1-S} - 1 \right) \tag{2}$$

At each transformation step, the generating function is a sum of terms of the form $\pm \prod (1 - Y^\gamma \lambda^\alpha)^{-1}$. He selects one of these terms and two of its factors to which he applies the transformation above and distributes. This yields three new terms. When there is no *good choice* left, the process stops. He then collects in all terms the factors which do not contain λ. The set of corresponding exponents of Y contains all minimal nonzero solutions of (1).

The main question here is what a *good choice* is. The criterion for choosing the factors must fulfill two requirements: it must ensure both termination and completeness of the algorithm. By completeness, we mean that when the algorithm stops, all minimal nonzero solutions have been found. Elliott chooses two factors with respectively the smallest negative and the largest positive exponent for λ. With this criterion, termination is easily proved. At each step, either the largest difference between two exponents of λ decreases, or this difference does not change and the number of exponents that are equal to the largest one or to the smallest one decreases. A complete proof may be found in [6].

Example 1. *Let us consider the equation* $2x_1 + x_2 - 3x_3 = 0$. *The generating function is*

$$\frac{1}{1 - Y_1 \lambda^2} \frac{1}{1 - Y_2 \lambda} \frac{1}{1 - Y_3 \lambda^{-3}}$$

Applying the transformation to the first and third factors, we get

$$\frac{1}{1 - Y_2 \lambda} \frac{1}{1 - Y_1 Y_3 \lambda^{-1}} \left(\frac{1}{1 - Y_1 \lambda^2} + \frac{1}{1 - Y_3 \lambda^{-3}} - 1 \right)$$

$$= \frac{1}{1 - Y_2 \lambda} \frac{1}{1 - Y_1 Y_3 \lambda^{-1}} \frac{1}{1 - Y_1 \lambda^2} + \frac{1}{1 - Y_2 \lambda} \frac{1}{1 - Y_1 Y_3 \lambda^{-1}} \frac{1}{1 - Y_3 \lambda^{-3}}$$

$$- \frac{1}{1 - Y_2 \lambda} \frac{1}{1 - Y_1 Y_3 \lambda^{-1}}$$

which may be further transformed by selecting for instance the second and third factors in the first term. In the end, we get a sum of 19 terms among which for instance

$$\frac{1}{1 - Y_1^3 Y_3^2} \frac{1}{1 - Y_1 Y_2 Y_3} \frac{1}{1 - Y_1 Y_3 \lambda^{-1}}$$

Since the first and second factors do not contain λ, $(3,0,2)$ and $(1,1,1)$ are solutions of the equation. The set of all such tuples is $\{(3,0,2),(1,1,1),(0,3,1)\}$ which contains all minimal nonzero solutions.

Extending this algorithm to solve systems of homogeneous equations is quite straightforward and such an extension was described by MacMahon [10]. The coefficients a_i of the equation (1) are now tuples in $\mathbb{Z}^m$ where m is the number of equations in the system, and instead of a single indeterminate, λ is a tuple $(\lambda_1, \ldots, \lambda_m)$. Again, the criterion for choosing two factors to be combined must ensure both termination and completeness. The method proposed by MacMahon consists actually in handling the equations one by one. First eliminate λ_1 and then λ_2, considering only factors not containing λ_1 and so on until λ_m.

2.2 Reformulation as constraint transformations

Let us show how this algorithm may be reformulated in a way which allows for simplifications and extensions. Each term generated during the transformation process has the form

$$\pm \frac{1}{1 - Y^{M^1} \lambda^{A^1}} \cdots \frac{1}{1 - Y^{M^k} \lambda^{A^k}} \qquad (3)$$

The solutions of (1) found by transforming further this term have the form $X = M^1 u_1 + \cdots + M^k u_k$ where $u_1, \ldots, u_k$ are natural parameters satisfying $A^1 u_1 + \cdots + A^k u_k = 0$. If we interpret each term in this way, we may see the whole process as transforming constrained parametric expressions of the form

$$X = M^1 u_1 + \cdots + M^k u_k \parallel A^1 u_1 + \cdots + A^k u_k = 0 \qquad (4)$$

with $\forall i, M^i \in \mathbb{N}^n$. This may also be written in matrix form as $X = MU \parallel AU = 0$ where M and A are matrices the columns of which are respectively the M^i's and A^i's. The process is initialised with $X = U \parallel \mathcal{A}U = 0$ where $\mathcal{A}$ is the matrix of the problem we started from. The algorithm transforms this expression until a disjunction of solved forms is found. A solved form is a constrained parametric expression with an empty constraint. We write it simply as $X = MU$. We shall describe the algorithm through transformation rules operating on finite disjunctions of constrained parametric expressions. For each rule, we just describe the way it transforms one term of the disjunction.

One may check that the interpretations of the three terms resulting from the application of (2) to (3) are actually obtained by choosing $u_i \leq u_j$, $u_i \geq u_j$ or $u_i = u_j$ and performing the corresponding replacements in (4). This means replacing u_j with $u_i + u_j'$ or u_i with $u_j + u_i'$ or u_j with u_i where u_i' and u_j' are new parameters. The choice $u_i = u_j$ is obviously useless since it is contained in both other choices. After the replacement of u_i with $u_j + u_i'$, u_i completely disappears so that we may rename u_i' to u_i. The same holds for u_j'. In the end, we get a transformation rule which transforms a constrained parametric expression into a disjunction.

$$P \parallel C \quad \vdash \quad (P \parallel C)[u_i \leftarrow u_i + u_j] \vee (P \parallel C)[u_j \leftarrow u_j + u_i]$$

$(P \parallel C)[u_i \leftarrow u_i + u_j]$ denotes the replacement of u_i with $u_i + u_j$ everywhere in $P \parallel C$. Since $u_i \geq u_j \vee u_i \leq u_j$ always holds, this transformation always preserves the set of solutions regardless of how we choose u_i and u_j. We have nevertheless to choose them so as to ensure termination. We take here the same criterion as Elliott-MacMahon for choosing the two parameters u_i and u_j. Their coefficients are respectively the least negative and the greatest positive one in the first constraint. If this first constraint is $\alpha_1 u_1 + \cdots + \alpha_k u_k = 0$ where $[\alpha_1 \cdots \alpha_n]$ is the first row of A, the condition may be reformulated as $\alpha_i \alpha_j = \min\{\alpha_p \alpha_q\} < 0$. The corresponding transformation rule for constrained parametric expressions is given below. C' denotes the conjunction of remaining constraints.

$(R_1) \quad P \parallel C \quad \vdash \quad (P \parallel C)[u_i \leftarrow u_i + u_j] \vee (P \parallel C)[u_j \leftarrow u_j + u_i]$
$\qquad$ if $C \equiv \alpha_1 u_1 + \cdots + \alpha_n u_n = 0 \wedge C'$ and $\min\{\alpha_p \alpha_q\} = \alpha_i \alpha_j < 0$

This rule is however not sufficient to get solved forms. For instance, it does not apply to $X = u_1 \parallel 2u_1 = 0$ although it is unsolved. This happens when the coefficients of the first constraint are either all nonnegative or all nonpositive. In this case, all parameters with nonzero coefficients may be set to 0. We are then left with a constraint $0 = 0$ which is trivially satisfied and may be removed. This is the purpose of the two rules below.

$(R_2) \quad P \parallel C \qquad\qquad \vdash \quad (P \parallel C)[u_i \leftarrow 0]$
$\qquad$ if $C \equiv \alpha_1 u_1 + \cdots + \alpha_n u_n = 0 \wedge C'$, $\alpha_i \neq 0$ and either $\alpha \geq 0$ or $\alpha \leq 0$

$(R_3) \quad P \parallel 0 = 0 \wedge C' \quad \vdash \quad P \parallel C'$

where $\alpha \geq 0$ (resp. ≤ 0) means $\forall i$, $\alpha_i \geq 0$ (resp. ≤ 0).

Theorem 1. *Repeated application of rules R_1, R_2 and R_3 to $X = U \parallel AU = 0$ terminates and returns solved forms.*

Since each transformation rule preserves the set of solutions of $AX = 0$, when the algorithm stops, we are left with solved forms the disjunction of which is equivalent to the initial problem $AX = 0$. We want now to extract minimal solutions from this parametric representation.

Theorem 2. *Let $X = S_{i,1} u_1 + \cdots + S_{i,n_i} u_{n_i}$, $i = 1, \ldots, r$ be the solved forms obtained from $X = U \parallel AU = 0$. The set $\cup_{i=1,\ldots,r} \{S_{i,1}, \ldots, S_{i,n_i}\}$ contains all minimal nonzero solutions of $AX = 0$.*

It is also possible to see the algorithm as operating on matrices. Given a constrained parametric expression $X = MU \parallel AU = 0$, let $X' = M'U' \parallel A'U = 0$ be obtained by applying to it one of the rules R_1, R_2, R_3. If R_1 is applied, then M' and A' are obtained by adding either the ith column to the jth one in both A and M, or the jth column to the ith one. If R_2 is applied, M' and A' are obtained by removing the ith column from both M and A. Finally, if R_3 is applied, $M' = M$ and A' is obtained by removing the first row of A. In this setting, the algorithm is initialised with $M = I$ and $A = \mathcal{A}$ where I denotes the identity matrix. It stops when A has no row left.

Example 2. *We consider again the equation $2x_1 + x_2 - 3x_3 = 0$. Figure 1 shows in a tree form all applications of R_1. At each node $X = MU \parallel AU = 0$, we only represent the matrices A and M. The line delimits the matrices. The arrows above A indicate the selected parameters. Instead of showing the application of R_2 and R_3, we frame the solutions found in the end. Other columns correspond to parameters set to 0 by R_2 leaving constraints of the form $0 = 0$ which are deleted by R_3. By collecting the solutions found in the leaves, we get as before the set $\{(3, 0, 2), (1, 1, 1), (0, 3, 1)\}$.*

On this example, one may notice the main drawback of the method: its redundancy. Indeed, the same solution is in general found several times. This redundancy is due to the way we branch in the rule R_1. The two branches correspond respectively to the choices $u_i \geq u_j$ and $u_i \leq u_j$. We then find the solutions corresponding to $u_i = u_j$ in both branches. We discuss in section 5 a method which avoids this behaviour.

3   Extension to non-homogeneous equations

Up to now, we only dealt with solving homogeneous equations. Since our final aim is to solve general constraints, we first have to be able to handle the constant term $\mathcal{B}$ in $\mathcal{A}X + \mathcal{B} \ \# \ 0$. We start by showing how the previous algorithm may be extended to solve non-homogeneous equations of the form $\mathcal{A}X + \mathcal{B} = 0$. We show in the next section that the algorithm we get solves also the general case. The set of solutions of $\mathcal{A}X + \mathcal{B} = 0$ is $\mathcal{N} + \mathcal{H}^*$ where $\mathcal{N}$ is the set of minimal solutions and $\mathcal{H}$ is the set of minimal nonzero solutions of the homogeneous part $\mathcal{A}X = 0$. We show how the previous algorithm may be extended to get a parametric representation of the solutions of $\mathcal{A}X + \mathcal{B} = 0$ and how from this representation, we get immediately $\mathcal{N}$ and $\mathcal{H}$.

The constrained expressions we consider have the form $X = MU + D \parallel AU + B = 0$ and the process is initialised with $X = U \parallel \mathcal{A}U + \mathcal{B} = 0$. Provided we change slightly the condition of R_1, the transformations we gave in section 2 are still valid but do not suffice anymore. Indeed, we could not get solved forms of $2x_1 + x_2 - 3 = 0$ for instance. Therefore, we introduce a new transformation, corresponding to the choice $u_i = 0$ or $u_i \geq 1$ for some parameter u_i. The solutions are obviously preserved because $u_i = 0 \lor u_i \geq 1$ always holds in natural numbers. The meaning of $u_i \geq 1$ is $u_i = u_i' + 1$ for some new parameter u_i'. Again, replacing

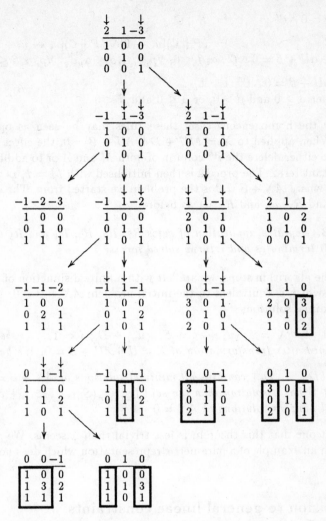

Fig. 1. solving $2x_1 + x_2 - 3x_3 = 0$

u_i with $u'_i + 1$ makes u_i disappear so that we may rename u'_i to u_i. We must also take into account the fact that a constraint may now have no solution. For instance, $u + 1 = 0$ has no solution in natural numbers. Thus, we add a deletion rule which removes expressions with an unsatisfiable constraint. The modified set of rules is given below.

(R_1) $P \parallel C$ $\vdash$ $(P \parallel C)[u_i \leftarrow u_i + u_j] \vee (P \parallel C)[u_j \leftarrow u_j + u_i]$
      if $C \equiv \alpha U + \beta = 0 \wedge C'$, $\alpha_i \alpha_j < 0$, $\forall p, q$, $\alpha_i \alpha_j \leq \alpha_p \alpha_q$, $\forall p$, $\alpha_i \alpha_j \leq \alpha_p \beta$

(R_2) $P \parallel C$ $\vdash$ $(P \parallel C)[u_i \leftarrow 0]$
      if $C \equiv \alpha U + \beta = 0 \wedge C'$, $\beta = 0$, $\alpha_i \neq 0$ and either $\alpha \geq 0$ or $\alpha \leq 0$

(R_3) $P \parallel 0 = 0 \wedge C'$ $\qquad\qquad$ $\vdash$ $\quad P \parallel C'$

(R_4) $P \parallel C$ $\qquad\qquad\qquad$ $\vdash$ $\quad (P \parallel C)[u_i \leftarrow 0] \vee (P \parallel C)[u_i \leftarrow u_i + 1]$
$\qquad$ if $C \equiv \alpha U + \beta = 0 \wedge C'$, $\alpha_i \beta < 0$, $\forall p, q$, $\alpha_i \beta \leq \alpha_p \alpha_q$, $\forall p$, $\alpha_i \beta \leq \alpha_p \beta$

(R_5) $P \parallel \alpha U + \beta = 0 \wedge C'$ $\vdash$ $\perp$
$\qquad$ if either $\alpha \geq 0$ and $\beta > 0$, or $\alpha \leq 0$ and $\beta < 0$

Like for the homogeneous case, these rules may be seen as operating on matrices. When applied to $X = MU + D \parallel AU + B = 0$, the effect of the new rule R_4 is to either delete the ith column of both M and A or to add this column to the constant term. The process is then initialised with $M = I$, $D = 0$, $A = \mathcal{A}$ and $B = \mathcal{B}$ where $\mathcal{A}X + \mathcal{B} = 0$ is the problem we started from. The effect of R_5 is obvious and R_1, R_2 and R_3 act as before.

Theorem 3. *Repeated application of rules R_1, R_2, R_3, R_4 and R_5 to $X = U \parallel \mathcal{A}U + \mathcal{B} = 0$ terminates and returns solved forms.*

When the algorithm stops, we are left with a finite disjunction of parametric expressions which is equivalent to the initial problem $\mathcal{A}X + \mathcal{B} = 0$. We want to find the minimal solutions.

Theorem 4. *Let $X = S_{i,1}u_1 + \cdots + S_{i,n_i}u_{n_i} + D_i$, $i = 1, \ldots, r$ be the solved forms obtained after transformation of $X = U \parallel \mathcal{A}U + \mathcal{B} = 0$. We have*

1. *the set $\{D_1, \ldots, D_r\}$ contains all minimal solutions of $\mathcal{A}X + \mathcal{B} = 0$.*
2. *if $\mathcal{A}X + \mathcal{B}$ has a solution then the set $\bigcup_{i=1,\ldots,r}\{S_{i,1}, \ldots, S_{i,n_i}\}$ contains all minimal nonzero solutions of $\mathcal{A}X = 0$*

Let us point out that this theorem is less trivial than it seems. We gave in the introduction an example of a parametric representation which does not have this property.

4 Extension to general linear constraints

We now extend the previous algorithm to solve a finite conjunction of linear constraints of the form $\alpha_1 x_1 + \cdots + \alpha_n x_n + \beta \ \# \ 0$ where $\#$ is any predicate in $\{=, \geq, \leq, <, >, \neq\}$. We want to solve such a problem directly, without introducing disjunctions or slack variables which would increase the complexity. As we shall see, the transformation rules described so far suffice to solve the problem. We just have to change their conditions to take the new predicates into account. For the sake of simplicity, we restrict our attention to predicates in $\{=, \geq, \neq\}$. This weakens in no way the method since $L \leq 0$, $L < 0$ and $L > 0$ are respectively equivalent to $-L \geq 0$, $-L - 1 \geq 0$ and $L - 1 \geq 0$.

Due to the presence of disequations, it is not possible anymore to represent the set of solutions as $\mathcal{N} + \mathcal{H}^*$ where $\mathcal{N}$ and $\mathcal{H}$ are finite sets. For instance, the solutions of $x - y \neq 0$ do not have such a representation. However, it is always possible to represent in this way the solutions of a problem containing only equations and inequations. Now a disequation $\alpha X + \beta \neq 0$ is clearly equivalent to the disjunction $\alpha X + \beta > 0 \vee \alpha X + \beta < 0$ so that a problem containing d disequations is equivalent to a disjunction of 2^d problems with pairwise disjoint sets of solutions which may be represented by means of two sets of minimal solutions. We do not want to introduce explicitly these disjunctions since it would lead to do most of the work several times. However, what our algorithm computes is a representation of each of these 2^d sets. Only, we handle directly the disequations and *dispatch* the solutions afterwards.

4.1 Parametric representation of the solutions

We first give the new set of transformation rules and then prove that we indeed get the representation we seek. We have to be careful about disequations when we adapt the condition of R_3. This rule is intended to remove a satisfied constraint. As already said, the disequation $L \neq 0$ is actually meant as the disjunction $L > 0 \vee L < 0$. We want to remove it only when either $L > 0$ or $L < 0$ is satisfied for all values of the parameters. For instance, the trivially satisfied disequation $2u - 1 \neq 0$ must not be removed since neither $2u - 1 < 0$ nor $2u - 1 > 0$ is satisfied.

We also have to modify slightly R_4 in order to be able to solve disequations of the form $\alpha U \neq 0$ where $\alpha \neq 0$ and either $\alpha \geq 0$ or $\alpha \leq 0$. The criterion we used until now, consisted in always choosing coefficients with opposite signs. In this case, this is not possible anymore although the disequation is neither satisfied nor unsatisfiable. We apply then R_4 by choosing any parameter u_i with a nonzero coefficient. This makes the disequation satisfied. This case is handled by the rule R_4' in the table below which gives the modified set of rules.

(R_1) $\quad P \parallel C \qquad \vdash \quad (P \parallel C)[u_i \leftarrow u_i + u_j] \vee (P \parallel C)[u_j \leftarrow u_j + u_i]$
$\qquad$ if $C \equiv \alpha U + \beta \# 0 \wedge C'$, $\alpha_i \alpha_j < 0$, $\forall p, q,\ \alpha_i \alpha_j \leq \alpha_p \alpha_q$, $\forall p,\ \alpha_i \alpha_j \leq \alpha_p \beta$

(R_2) $\quad P \parallel C \qquad \vdash \quad (P \parallel C)[u_i \leftarrow 0]$
$\qquad$ if $C \equiv \alpha U = 0 \wedge C'$, $\alpha_i \neq 0$ and either $\alpha \geq 0$ or $\alpha \leq 0$
$\qquad$ or $C \equiv \alpha U \geq 0 \wedge C'$, $\alpha_i < 0$ and $\alpha \leq 0$

(R_3) $\quad P \parallel c \wedge C' \quad \vdash \quad P \parallel C'$
$\qquad$ if $c \equiv 0 = 0$
$\qquad$ or $c \equiv \alpha U + \beta \geq 0$ and $\alpha \geq 0$ and $\beta \geq 0$
$\qquad$ or $c \equiv \alpha U + \beta \neq 0$ and either $\alpha \geq 0$ and $\beta > 0$ or $\alpha \leq 0$ and $\beta < 0$

(R_4) $\quad P \parallel C \qquad \vdash \quad (P \parallel C)[u_i \leftarrow 0] \vee (P \parallel C)[u_i \leftarrow u_i + 1]$
$\qquad$ if $C \equiv \alpha U + \beta \# 0 \wedge C'$, $\alpha_i \beta < 0$, $\forall p, q,\ \alpha_i \beta \leq \alpha_p \alpha_q$, $\forall p,\ \alpha_i \beta \leq \alpha_p \beta$

(R_4') $\quad P \parallel C \qquad \vdash \quad (P \parallel C)[u_i \leftarrow 0] \vee (P \parallel C)[u_i \leftarrow u_i + 1]$
$\qquad$ if $C \equiv \alpha U \neq 0 \wedge C'$, $\alpha_i \neq 0$ and either $\alpha \geq 0$ or $\alpha \leq 0$

(R_5) $\quad P \parallel C \qquad \vdash \quad \bot$
$\qquad$ if $C \equiv \alpha U + \beta = 0 \wedge C'$ and either $\alpha \geq 0$ and $\beta > 0$ or $\alpha \leq 0$ and $\beta < 0$
$\qquad$ or $C \equiv \alpha U + \beta \geq 0 \wedge C'$, $\alpha \leq 0$ and $\beta < 0$,
$\qquad$ or $C \equiv 0 \neq 0 \wedge C'$

Theorem 5. *The application of the transformation rules R_1, R_2, R_3, R_4, R'_4 and R_5 to $X = U \parallel AU + B \,\#\, 0$ terminates and returns solved forms.*

Example 3. *Let us consider the problem*

$$\mathcal{P} \equiv \begin{cases} 2x_1 + x_2 - 3 \geq 0 \\ x_1 - 2x_2 + 1 \neq 0 \end{cases}$$

Figure 2 shows all applications of the transformation rules in a tree form. Each node $X = MU + D \parallel AU + B \,\#\, 0$ is represented in matrix form as $\dfrac{A \,\big|\, B}{M \,\big|\, D} \#$. Struck out constraints are the ones removed by R_3, crossed leaves are the ones that are deleted by R_5 and framed leaves are solved forms.

4.2 Partition of the set of solutions

In the remaining of this section, $\mathcal{P} \equiv AX + B \,\#\, 0$ is a problem containing d disequations. When the transformation process stops, we are left with a finite disjunction of solved forms $\mathcal{F}_1, \ldots, \mathcal{F}_N$ which is equivalent to $\mathcal{P}$. Each $\mathcal{F}_i$ has the form $X = S_{i,1}u_1 + \cdots + S_{i,n_i}u_{n_i} + D_i$. As already said, $\mathcal{P}$ is equivalent to a disjunction of 2^d problems obtained by replacing each disequation in $\mathcal{P}$ with either $>$ or $<$. Given a tuple of predicates $\Delta = [\delta_1, \ldots, \delta_d] \in \{>, <\}^d$, $\mathcal{P}_\Delta$ denotes the problem obtained by replacing $\neq$ with δ_i in the ith disequation of $\mathcal{P}$. Let $\mathcal{S}_\Delta$ denote the set of solutions of $\mathcal{P}_\Delta$. We show that from $\mathcal{F}_1, \ldots, \mathcal{F}_N$, we get a representation of each $\mathcal{S}_\Delta$. For this, we first need a lemma.

Lemma 6. *Let $\alpha X + \beta \neq 0$ be a disequation in $\mathcal{P}$. For each $i = 1, \ldots, N$, either $\alpha D_i + \beta > 0$ and $\forall k = 1, \ldots, n_i$, $\alpha S_{i,k} \geq 0$ or $\alpha D_i + \beta < 0$ and $\forall k = 1, \ldots, n_i$, $\alpha S_{i,k} \leq 0$.*

This lemma implies that for each $\mathcal{F}_i$, if D_i is a solution of $\mathcal{P}_\Delta$, then any solution of $\mathcal{F}_i$ is a solution of $\mathcal{P}_\Delta$. Note that testing whether D_i is a solution of $\mathcal{P}_\Delta$ is straightforward. Since we already know that D_i is a solution of $\mathcal{P}$, we just have to look at the sign of $\alpha D_i + \beta$ for each disequation $\alpha D_i + \beta \neq 0$ in $\mathcal{P}$. We get then the following theorem.

Theorem 7. *For each $\Delta \in \{>, <\}^d$,*

1. *$\mathcal{P}_\Delta \iff \bigvee_{D_i \in \mathcal{S}_\Delta} \mathcal{F}_i$.*
2. *The set $\mathcal{N}_\Delta = \{D_i \mid D_i \in \mathcal{S}_\Delta\}$ contains all minimal solutions of $\mathcal{P}_\Delta$.*
3. *If $\mathcal{P}_\Delta$ has a solution, the set $\mathcal{H}_\Delta = \bigcup_{D_i \in \mathcal{S}_\Delta}\{S_{i,1}, \ldots, S_{i,n_i}\}$ contains all minimal nonzero solutions of its homogeneous part.*

Example 4 (example 3 continued). *Since we have one disequation, we have two sets of solutions, $S_>$ and $S_<$. Collecting the solutions in the solved forms, we get*

$$\begin{aligned} \mathcal{N}_> &= \{(2,0),(2,1),(4,2)\} & \mathcal{H}_> &= \{(1,0),(2,1)\} \\ \mathcal{N}_< &= \{(2,2),(1,2),(0,3)\} & \mathcal{H}_< &= \{(2,1),(1,1),(0,1)\} \end{aligned}$$

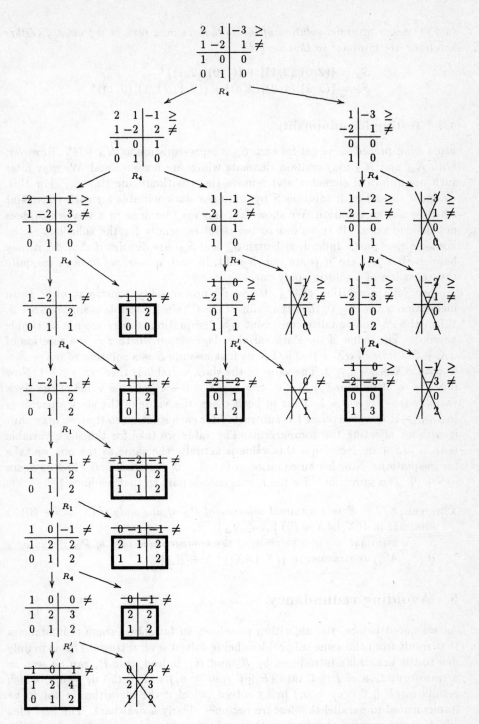

Fig. 2. solving $2x_1 + x_2 - 3 \geq 0 \wedge x_1 - 2x_2 + 1 \neq 0$

$(4, 2)$ *is a non-minimal solution of* $\mathcal{P}_>$ *so that we may remove it from* $\mathcal{N}_>$. *Other solutions are minimal so that we get*

$$S_> = \{(2, 0), (2, 1)\} + \{(1, 0), (2, 1)\}^*$$
$$S_< = \{(2, 2), (1, 2), (0, 3)\} + \{(2, 1), (1, 1), (0, 1)\}^*$$

4.3 Testing for minimality

From what precedes, we get for each $\mathcal{S}_\Delta$ a representation as $\mathcal{N}_\Delta + \mathcal{H}_\Delta^*$. However, both $\mathcal{N}_\Delta$ and $\mathcal{H}_\Delta$ may contain elements which are not minimal. We may filter such non-minimal elements and remove them without affecting $\mathcal{S}_\Delta$. For this, we must extend each solution S by adding a slack variable for each constraint which is not an equation. We show that this may be done in a way which does not depend on Δ. It turns out to be useful especially for the solutions of the homogeneous parts. Indeed, although $\mathcal{S}_\Delta$ and $\mathcal{S}_{\Delta'}$ are disjoint if $\Delta \neq \Delta'$, it may happen that $\mathcal{H}_\Delta$ are $\mathcal{H}_{\Delta'}$ are not disjoint. In such a case, we have to compute the extension of a solution only once.

Let S be a solution of $\mathcal{P}_\Delta$. If the ith non-equality constraint of $\mathcal{P}$ is an inequation $\alpha X + \beta \geq 0$, then the value of the ith slack variable is simply $\alpha S + \beta$. When the ith non-equality constraint is a disequation, things are not so simple anymore. The value of the slack variable depends on whether S is a solution of $\alpha X + \beta > 0$ or of $\alpha X + \beta < 0$. Let us first assume S is a solution of $\alpha X + \beta > 0 \iff \alpha X + \beta - 1 \geq 0$. The value of the slack variable is then $\alpha S + \beta - 1$. Now if S is a solution of $\alpha X + \beta < 0 \iff -\alpha X - \beta - 1 \geq 0$, the value of the slack variable is $-\alpha S - \beta - 1$. Thus in both cases, the value of the slack variable is $|\alpha S + \beta| - 1$. Now the offset 1 is subtracted for each solution so that we may omit it without affecting the comparisons. The value we take for the slack variable is then $|\alpha S + \beta|$. Note that this value is actually the same as the one we take for inequations. Now for an equation $\alpha X + \beta = 0$, the slack is 0 which is again $|\alpha S + \beta|$. The same holds for the homogeneous part so that we have:

Theorem 8. – S is a minimal solution of $\mathcal{P}_\Delta$ if and only if $(S, |AS + \mathcal{B}|)$ is minimal in $\{(X, |AX + \mathcal{B}|) \mid X \in \mathcal{N}_\Delta\}$.
  – S is a minimal nonzero solution of the homogeneous part of $\mathcal{P}_\Delta$ if and only if $(S, |AS|)$ is minimal in $\{(X, |AX|) \mid X \in \mathcal{H}_\Delta\}$.

5 Avoiding redundancy

As we noted before, the algorithm presented so far shows some redundancies that result from the same subproblem being solved several times. This is mainly due to the branching introduced by R_1 and R_4. Indeed, rule R_1 can be seen as a transformation of $P \parallel C$ into $(P \parallel C \wedge u_i \geq u_j) \vee (P \parallel C \wedge u_i \leq u_j)$, which results in $(P \parallel C \wedge u_j = u_i)$ being solved twice. If the algorithm is not to be implemented in parallel this feature becomes clearly a drawback. The first idea which comes in mind to overcome this problem is to replace this branching with $(P \parallel C \wedge u_i \geq u_j) \vee (P \parallel C \wedge u_i < u_j)$. But as long as we explicitly branch, we do not avoid performing twice a combination which may be needed in both branches. The changes we propose to avoid explicit branching are based on the equivalence between $X = MU \parallel AU = 0$ and

$$X = (M^i + M^j)u + MU \parallel (A^i + A^j)u + AU = 0 \wedge (u_i = 0 \vee u_j = 0)$$

If this equivalence is used as a transformation rule, the constraint $u_i = 0 \vee u_j = 0$ implies that (u_i, u_j) should not be selected afterwards. If it was, the parameter associated to the new $(A^i + A^j)$, say v, would be constrained by $v = 0$ and hence of no use to the solution. Moreover, the algorithm would not terminate.

These constraints, that *forbid some combinations*, propagate in a quite easy way. If u_i is rewritten as $u_i = u_i' + u'$ then $u_i = 0 \vee u_j = 0$ propagates as $(u_i' = 0 \vee u_j = 0) \wedge (u' = 0 \vee u_j = 0)$ since all the parameters are nonnegative integers. In general, if u_p and u_q are selected and $(u_p = 0 \vee K_p) \wedge (u_q = 0 \vee K_q)$ must hold, then for the new parameterisation, say $u_p = u_p' + u$ and $u_q = u_q' + u$, it must be $(u_p' = 0 \vee K_p) \wedge (u_q' = 0 \vee K_q) \wedge (u = 0 \vee (K_p \wedge K_q))$, and additionally $u_q' = 0 \vee u_p' = 0$. We consider expressions of the form $P \parallel C \parallel K$ where K denotes the additional constraints.

The criterion for selecting the two parameters to be replaced is slightly modified so that (u_i, u_j) is not chosen if $u_i = 0 \vee u_j = 0$ is asserted. $X = MU \parallel AU = 0 \parallel K$ rewrites as

$$X = (M^i + M^j)u + MU \parallel (A^i + A^j)u + AU = 0 \parallel K' \wedge (u_i = 0 \vee u_j = 0)$$

if $u_i \neq 0 \wedge u_j \neq 0$ is satisfiable under K, and $0 > \alpha_i \alpha_j = \min\{\alpha_p \alpha_q \mid u_p \neq 0 \wedge u_q \neq 0$ satisfiable under $K\}$. Here, K' denotes the propagation of the forbidden combinations K, that is $K[u_i \leftarrow u_i + u, u_j \leftarrow u_j + u]$. It is not difficult to conclude that at each step, either

$$\min\{\alpha_p \alpha_q \mid u_p \neq 0 \wedge u_q \neq 0 \text{ satisfiable under } K\}$$

increases, or the number of (u_p, u_q) such that $u_p \neq 0 \wedge u_q \neq 0$ is satisfiable under K and $\alpha_p \alpha_q$ is minimum decreases. This implies termination.

Now we are going to explain how this basic idea is adapted to the general case. When solving non-homogeneous problems, say $AU + B \# 0$, redundancy is also due to R_4. Since R_4 involves B which had no associated parameter, we could not express the subsequent forbidden combinations as before. The trick is to associate a parameter to B, say t, representing the initial problem by

$$X = U + 0t \parallel AU + \mathcal{B}t \# 0 \parallel t = 1$$

Then, the effect of R_4 can be seen as rewriting $X = MU + NT \parallel AU + BT \# 0 \parallel K' \wedge \sum t_i = 1$ into

$$X = MU + NT + (M^i + N^j)t \parallel AU + BT + (A^i + B^j)t \# 0 \parallel K'' \wedge \sum t_i + t = 1$$

where $K'' = K'[u_i \leftarrow u_i + t, t_j \leftarrow t_j + t] \wedge (u_i = 0 \vee t_j = 0)$. From $\sum t_i = 1$ it follows that $t_j = 0 \vee t_k = 0$, for all j and k, and thus a selection of two t's must not be eligible. If $K' \wedge \sum t_i = 1$ is denoted just as K it becomes apparent that

R_1 and R_4 may now be merged in a single rule. Also, R'_4 could be merged in the same scheme.

Let us give an example to illustrate what we have been describing. The following tables show schematically how the rules would operate on $3x - 2y - 1 = 0$. The double vertical lines make the separation between A and B, and between M and N. Below the last horizontal line we have represented the products between pairs of coefficients, and between each coefficient and b.

When u_i and u_j are selected, $\alpha_i \alpha_j$ is negative and minimum. A new column is introduced which is the sum of the columns associated to u_i and u_j. A new row is also introduced for we are not taking symmetry into account. The two entries $\alpha_i \alpha_j$ are crossed, indicating that the pair is no longer eligible. So, the table on the right results from the selection of u_1 and u_2. The one on the left was the starting table.

Coefs	3	-2	-1		Coefs	3	-2	1	-1
Tuples	1	0	0		Tuples	1	0	1	0
	0	1	0			0	1	1	0
Prods	9	-6	-3		Prods	9	×	3	-3
	-6	4	2			×	4	-2	2
						3	-2	1	-1

Crosses propagate: the result of adding something to a cross is a cross. When the selection is u_i and t_k, the sum of the columns is placed on the right-hand side and we do not introduce a new row. Just one entry has to be crossed. Since -3 is the least product, the next selection is u_1 and t_1, resulting the table below on the left. When no negative product occurs, the rules described so far do not apply, and the table is as shown on the right.

3	-2	1	-1	2		3	-2	1	-1	0	-1	2	0
1	0	1	0	1		1	0	1	1	2	0	1	1
0	1	1	0	0		0	1	1	2	3	0	0	1
9	×	3	×	6		9	×	3	×	×	×	6	×
×	4	-2	2	×		×	4	×	2	×	2	×	×
3	-2	1	-1	2		3	×	1	×	0	×	2	0
						×	2	×	1	0	1	×	×
						×	×	0	0	0	0	×	0

The equivalent problem the last table encodes can be denoted as before

$$X = \begin{bmatrix} 1 & 0 & 1 & 1 & 2 \\ 0 & 1 & 1 & 2 & 3 \end{bmatrix} U + \begin{bmatrix} 0 & 1 & 1 \\ 0 & 0 & 1 \end{bmatrix} T$$

$$\| \begin{bmatrix} 3 & -2 & 1 & -1 & 0 \end{bmatrix} U + \begin{bmatrix} -1 & 2 & 0 \end{bmatrix} T = 0$$

$$\| \sum t_i = 1 \wedge \begin{cases} u_1 = 0 \vee u_2 = u_4 = u_5 = t_1 = t_3 = 0 \\ u_2 = 0 \vee u_1 = u_3 = u_5 = t_2 = t_3 = 0 \\ u_3 = 0 \vee u_2 = u_4 = t_1 = 0 \\ u_4 = 0 \vee u_1 = u_3 = t_2 = t_3 = 0 \\ u_5 = 0 \vee u_1 = u_2 = t_2 = 0 \end{cases}$$

and the constraint part may be viewed as the disjunction

$$(3u_1 + u_3 + 2 = 0 \parallel t_2 = 1 \land u_2 = u_4 = u_5 = t_1 = t_3 = 0)$$
$$\lor (-2u_2 - u_4 - 1 = 0 \parallel t_1 = 1 \land u_1 = u_3 = u_5 = t_2 = t_3 = 0)$$
$$\lor (u_3 = 0 \parallel t_3 = 1 \land u_1 = u_2 = u_4 = t_1 = t_2 = 0)$$
$$\lor (-u_4 - 1 = 0 \parallel t_1 = 1 \land u_1 = u_2 = u_3 = t_2 = t_3 = 0)$$

It can be noted that only the third equation is satisfiable. Hence, the solution to the original problem is

$$X = \begin{bmatrix} 2 \\ 3 \end{bmatrix} u_5 + \begin{bmatrix} 1 \\ 1 \end{bmatrix}$$

The transformation rules that are then applied to get solved forms translate somehow the former R_2, R_3 and R_5. In order to describe them more easily, let L_α^i, L_β^i and R_α^i denote the sets

$$L_\alpha^i = \{u_q \mid u_q \neq 0 \land u_i \neq 0 \text{ satisfiable under } K\}$$
$$L_\beta^i = \{t_r \mid t_r \neq 0 \land u_i \neq 0 \text{ satisfiable under } K\}$$
$$R_\alpha^i = \{u_q \mid u_q \neq 0 \land t_i \neq 0 \text{ satisfiable under } K\}$$

Given a constraint $c \land C' \parallel K$ where $c \equiv \alpha U + \beta T \neq 0$,

- $u_i \leftarrow 0$ applies if either $L_\beta^i = \varnothing$ or $\alpha_i \neq 0$, $\neg(\alpha_i \# 0)$, $\forall u_q \in L_\alpha^i$, $\alpha_i \alpha_q \geq 0$ and $\forall t_r \in L_\beta^i$, $\alpha_i \beta_r \geq 0$,
- $t_i \leftarrow 0$ applies if $\neg(\beta_i \# 0)$ and either
  - $\# \in \{=, \geq\}$ and $\forall u_q \in R_\alpha^i$, $\alpha_q \beta_i \geq 0$
  - or $\# \equiv \neq$ and $\forall u_q \in R_\alpha^i$, $\alpha_q = 0$,
- $c \land C' \parallel K$ is reduced to $C' \parallel K$ if $\forall i$, $\beta_i \# 0 \land \forall u_q \in R_\alpha^i$, $\alpha_q \beta_i \geq 0$.

Finally, $P \parallel C \parallel K \vdash \perp$ if K is unsatisfiable, which happens when all t_i's have been set to 0.

Let us see how these rules apply to the example used in the previous section:

$$\begin{cases} 2x + y - 3 \geq 0 \\ x - 2y + 1 \neq 0 \end{cases}$$

If just the first constraint is represented, at the starting point we have the table on the left. After the second transformation the one in the middle, and then $t_1 \leftarrow 0$ applies.

2	1	-3	$\geq$
1	0	0	
0	1	0	
4	2	-6	
2	1	-3	

2	1	-3	-1	-2	$\geq$
1	0	0	1	0	
0	1	0	0	1	
4	2	×	-2	×	
2	1	×	-1	-2	

2	1	-1	-2	$\geq$
1	0	1	0	
0	1	0	1	
4	2	-2	×	
2	1	-1	-2	

The following tables are respectively the last for $\geq$ and the starting one for $\neq$. Because K is kept when $c \wedge C' \parallel K$ is rewritten as $C' \parallel K$, the crosses are kept.

2	1	1	0	0	$\geq$
1	0	2	1	0	
0	1	0	1	3	
4	2	2	×	×	
2	1	1	0	0	

1	−2	3	0	−5	$\neq$
1	0	2	1	0	
0	1	0	1	3	
1	−2	3	×	×	
−2	4	−6	0	10	

After some steps we get the table displayed below on the left, which has no negative products. However, since a disequation is being solved, R_4' applies twice, and then the substitutions $t_2 \leftarrow 0$ and $t_6 \leftarrow 0$, yielding the table on the right.

u_1	u_2	u_3	u_4	t_1	t_2	t_3	t_4	t_5	t_6	
1	−2	−1	0	3	0	−5	1	−1	0	$\neq$
1	0	1	2	2	1	1	2	2	3	
0	1	1	1	0	1	3	1	2	2	
1	×	×	0	3	×	×	1	×	×	
×	4	2	×	×	0	10	×	2	×	
×	2	1	0	×	×	×	×	1	0	
0	×	0	0	×	×	×	0	×	0	

u_1	u_2	u_3	u_4	t_1	t_3	t_4	t_5	t_7	t_8	
1	−2	−1	0	3	−5	1	−1	−2	−1	$\neq$
1	0	1	2	2	1	2	2	2	4	
0	1	1	1	0	3	1	2	1	3	
1	×	×	0	3	×	1	×	×	×	
×	4	2	×	×	10	×	2	4	×	
×	2	1	0	×	×	×	1	×	1	
0	×	0	0	×	×	0	×	×	0	

The constraint may be removed. In order to get the minimal solutions we proceed as in the previous section.

An aspect is worth mentioning here. The method we have proposed avoids redundancy at the cost of increasing the space complexity of the algorithm. This may become quite critical since the number of minimal solutions may be quite large, and the method solves one constraint at a time. This implies that when the ith constraint is removed there are at least as many parameters as minimal solutions of the subsystem solved so far. We say *at least* because actually there may be several non-minimal solutions which may remain until the whole system is solved. Partial solutions that are not minimal when compared with other partial solutions cannot be simply removed due to the way forbidden combinations are propagated to the next constraints.

On the other hand, although the use of pruning by solutions is an obvious improvement, it is not enough to make the Elliott-MacMahon algorithm competitive with other algorithms [7]. The major cause of lack of efficiency is inherent to constraints being solved one by one.

Conclusions

We have presented algorithms that solve systems of linear diophantine equations, inequations and disequations, yielding a parametric representation of the solution set from which it is possible to get immediately the minimal solutions. The main algorithm, which is inspired by the Elliott-MacMahon algorithm, is actually a schema parametrized by a choice criterion.

The efficiency of the instances is highly determined by the choice criterion involved. In particular, the ones described herein require solving the constraints one at a time, which is known not to be efficient. It is worth studying criteria that consider several constraints at a time. The algorithm could then be competitive.

It can be remarked that the algorithms allow the set of constraints to be changed incrementally. Moreover, they can be easily put together with other to perform satisfiability tests or efficient solvers for some kind of subproblems.

References

1. H. Abdulrab and M. Maksimenko. General solution of systems of linear diophantine equations and inequations. In J. Hsiang, editor, *Proc. 6th Conf. on Rewriting Techniques and Applications, Kaiserslautern (Germany)*, volume 914 of *Lecture Notes in Computer Science*, pages 339–351. Springer-Verlag, April 1995.

2. F. Ajili and Contejean E. Complete solving of linear diophantine equations and inequations without adding variables. In this volume.

3. A. Boudet, E. Contejean, and H. Devie. A new AC unification algorithm with a new algorithm for solving diophantine equations. In *Proc. 5th IEEE Symp. on Logic in Computer Science, Philadelphia (Pa., USA)*, pages 289–299, June 1990.

4. M. Clausen and A. Fortenbacher. Efficient solution of linear diophantine equations. *J. of Symbolic Computation*, 8(1 & 2):201–216, 1989. Special issue on unification. Part two.

5. E. Domenjoud. Solving systems of linear diophantine equations: An algebraic approach. In A. Tarlecki, editor, *Proc. 16th Int. Symp. on Mathematical Foundations of Computer Science, Kazimierz Dolny (Poland)*, volume 520 of *Lecture Notes in Computer Science*, pages 141–150. Springer-Verlag, September 1991.

6. E. B. Elliott. On linear homogeneous diophantine equations. *Quartely J. of Pure and Applied Maths*, 136, 1903.

7. M. Filgueiras and A. P. Tomás. A note on the implementation of the MacMahon-Elliott algorithm. Technical report, Centro de Informática da Universidade do Porto, 1992.

8. M. Filgueiras and A. P. Tomás. Fast methods for solving linear diophantine equations. In M. Filgueiras and L. Damas, editors, *Proc. of the 6th Portuguese Conf. on AI, Porto (Portugal)*, volume 727 of *Lecture Notes in Artificial Intelligence*, pages 297–306. Springer-Verlag, 1993.

9. G. Huet. An algorithm to generate the basis of solutions to homogenous linear diophantine equations. *Information Processing Letters*, 7(3):144–147, 1978.

10. P. A. MacMahon. *Combinatory Analysis*, volume 2, chapter II: A Syzygetic Theory, pages 111–114. Cambridge University Press, 1916. Reprinted by Chelsea, New York, 1960.

11. L. Pottier. Minimal solutions of linear diophantine systems: Bounds and algorithms. In R. V. Book, editor, *Proc. 4th Conf. on Rewriting Techniques and Applications, Como (Italy)*, volume 488 of *Lecture Notes in Computer Science*, pages 162–173. Springer-Verlag, April 1991.

The Progressive Party Problem: Integer Linear Programming and Constraint Programming Compared

Barbara M. Smith[1], Sally C. Brailsford[2], Peter M. Hubbard[2] and H. Paul Williams[2]

[1] Division of Artificial Intelligence, School of Computer Studies, University of Leeds, Leeds LS2 9JT
[2] Faculty of Mathematical Studies, University of Southampton, Southampton SO9 5NH

Abstract. Many discrete optimization problems can be formulated as either integer linear programming problems or constraint satisfaction problems. Although ILP methods appear to be more powerful, sometimes constraint programming can solve these problems more quickly. This paper describes a problem in which the difference in performance between the two approaches was particularly marked, since a solution could not be found using ILP.

The problem arose in the context of organising a "progressive party" at a yachting rally. Some yachts were to be designated hosts; the crews of the remaining yachts would then visit the hosts for six successive half-hour periods. A guest crew could not revisit the same host, and two guest crews could not meet more than once. Additional constraints were imposed by the capacities of the host yachts and the crew sizes of the guests.

Integer linear programming formulations which included all the constraints resulted in very large models, and despite trying several different strategies, all attempts to find a solution failed. Constraint programming was tried instead and solved the problem very quickly, with a little manual assistance. Reasons for the success of constraint programming in this problem are identified and discussed.

1 Introduction

Discrete optimization problems of the kind that arise in many areas of operational research can be formulated as constraint satisfaction problems (CSPs). A CSP consists of a set of variables, each with a finite set of possible values (its domain), and a set of constraints which the values assigned to the variables must satisfy. In a CSP which is also an optimization problem, there is an additional variable representing the objective; each time a solution to the CSP is found, a new constraint is added to ensure that any future solution must have an improved value of the objective, and this continues until the problem becomes infeasible, when the last solution found is known to be optimal.

Many discrete optimization problems can be modeled using linear constraints and integer variables and thus formulated as integer linear programming problems. Operational Research has developed a battery of powerful techniques for solving such problems, but although the search algorithms available for solving CSPs are at first sight less powerful than ILP methods, sometimes constraint programming is a more successful approach (see [2, 6, 7]). It would be very useful to know which of these competing techniques to choose for a given problem, but the boundary between their areas of expertise has not yet been fully mapped. This paper describes a further example of a problem where constraint programming did much better than ILP; in fact, it proved impossible to solve the problem at all using ILP. The success of constraint programming in this case appears to be due to a number of factors in combination; these are discussed in section 8.

The problem is a seemingly frivolous one arising in the context of organising the social programme for a yachting rally. The 39 yachts at the rally were all moored in a marina on the Isle of Wight[3]; their crew sizes ranged from 1 to 7. To allow people to meet as many of the other attendees as possible, an evening party was planned at which some of these boats were to be designated hosts. The crews of the remaining boats would visit the host boats in turn for six successive half-hour periods during the evening. The crew of a host boat would remain on board to act as hosts; the crew of a guest boat would stay together as a unit for the whole evening. A guest crew could not revisit a host boat, and guest crews could not meet more than once. Additional capacity constraints were imposed by the sizes of the boats. The problem facing the rally organiser was that of minimising the number of host boats, since each host had to be supplied with food and other party prerequisites.

There were a number of complicating factors in the real-life problem. For example, the rally organiser's boat was constrained to be a host boat, although it had a relatively small capacity, because he had to be readily available to deal with emergencies. Two other boats had crews consisting of parents with teenage children, and these boats were also constrained to be host boats; the crews split up so that the parents remained on board the host boat and the children became a "virtual boat" with capacity of zero. The rally organiser's children formed a third virtual boat, giving 42 boats altogether. The data for this problem is given in Table 1.

2 The Uncapacitated Problem

If we ignore the capacity constraints, just one host boat can accommodate any number of guest boats for one time period. For more than one time period, we can easily find a lower bound on the number of hosts required from the following argument. If g guest crews visit host i at time 1, then there must be at least g other hosts to accommodate them in the following time period. (The guests

---

[3] off the south coast of England.

Boat	Capacity	Crew	Boat	Capacity	Crew	Boat	Capacity	Crew
1	6	2	15	8	3	29	6	2
2	8	2	16	12	6	30	6	4
3	12	2	17	8	2	31	6	2
4	12	2	18	8	2	32	6	2
5	12	4	19	8	4	33	6	2
6	12	4	20	8	2	34	6	2
7	12	4	21	8	4	35	6	2
8	10	1	22	8	5	36	6	2
9	10	2	23	7	4	37	6	4
10	10	2	24	7	4	38	6	5
11	10	2	25	7	2	39	9	7
12	10	3	26	7	2	40	0	2
13	8	4	27	7	4	41	0	3
14	8	2	28	7	5	42	0	4

Table 1. The data

cannot visit host i again, and must visit g different hosts so as not to meet another crew again.) In fact, the required $g + 1$ hosts could each accommodate up to g visiting guest crews at time 1, without the guest crews meeting again at time 2, giving $g(g+1)$ guest crews in total. For more than 2 time periods, $g(g+1)$ is clearly an upper bound on the number of guest crews that $g + 1$ hosts can accommodate. For instance, 6 hosts can accommodate at most 30 guest boats; 7 hosts can accommodate at most 42. In fact, these limits can be attained (still assuming no constraints on the hosts' capacities, and provided that the number of time periods is not greater than the number of hosts, in which case it becomes impossible for guest crews not to visit the same host more than once), so that with 42 boats in all, we need 7 to be hosts (and therefore 35 to be guests).

However, for the real-life problem, the capacity constraints are binding and the number of host boats required is at least 13, as shown in Section 3.

3 A Lower Bound

A lower bound on the number of hosts required, taking into account the capacity constraints, was found by using linear programming to solve a considerable relaxation of the original problem. This simply required that the guest crews, as a whole, should fit into the total spare capacity of the host boats[4] for one time period.

The same lower bound can alternatively be found from a simple argument: a necessary condition for feasibility is that the total capacity of the host boats is not less than the total crew size of all the boats. The smallest number of hosts that meet this condition is therefore found by ordering the boats in descending

---

[4] i.e. the remaining capacity after accommodating the host crews themselves.

order of total capacity. With this ordering, the first 13 boats can accommodate all the crews; the first 12 boats cannot.

This suggests that in general the host boats should be chosen in descending order of total capacity. However, this heuristic was not arrived at until after the linear programming work on the problem had been completed, partly because it seemed counter-intuitive that the crew sizes should be ignored when selecting the hosts. Moreover, maximising the number of spare places is not the only consideration when selecting the host boats, since each crew has to stay together. Provided that the total capacity of the hosts is large enough, the choice of hosts may need to consider the spare capacity of each boat and how well different crew sizes fit into it.

Hence the model described below includes the selection of the host boats, even though in practice the choice of hosts was in large part guided by heuristics.

4 Integer Programming Approach

4.1 First Formulation

The first attempt at finding an optimal solution was made at the University of Southampton, where the problem was formulated as a zero-one integer programme. The variables are: $\delta_i = 1$ iff boat i is used as a host boat, and $\gamma_{ikt} = 1$ iff boat k is a guest of boat i in period t. (The rally organiser's boat was constrained to be a host in all models.)

As mentioned in Section 1, the objective was to minimise the number of hosts:

$$\text{minimise} \sum_i \delta_i \qquad \text{subject to:}$$

Constraints CD. A boat can only be visited if it is a host boat.

$$\gamma_{ikt} - \delta_i \leq 0 \qquad \text{for all } i, k, t; i \neq k$$

Constraints CCAP. The capacity of a host boat cannot be exceeded.

$$\sum_{k, k \neq i} c_k \gamma_{ikt} \leq K_i - c_i \qquad \text{for all } i, t$$

where c_i is the crew size of boat i and K_i is its total capacity.
Constraints GA. Each guest crew must always have a host.

$$\sum_{i, i \neq k} \gamma_{ikt} + \delta_k = 1 \qquad \text{for all } k, t$$

Constraints GB. A guest crew cannot visit a host boat more than once.

$$\sum_t \gamma_{ikt} \leq 1 \qquad \text{for all } i, k; i \neq k$$

Constraints W. Any pair of guests can meet at most once.

$$\gamma_{ikt} + \gamma_{ilt} + \gamma_{jks} + \gamma_{jls} \leq 3 \qquad \text{for all } i, j, k, l, t, s;$$
$$i \neq j; i \neq k; k < l; i \neq l;$$
$$k \neq j; j \neq l; s \neq t$$

The constraints W, which have six indices, clearly lead to a huge number of rows when the problem is modelled. The number of rows is $O(B^4 T^2)$, where B is the number of boats and T is the number of time periods. However, this model has a moderate number of variables, namely $O(B^2 T)$.

The size of the problem was reduced by taking account of the fact that in any optimal solution there are some boats which will always be chosen to be hosts because of their large capacity and small crew size. By the same token, some boats would clearly never be chosen to be hosts: for example, the three virtual boats with zero capacity. The data was ordered by decreasing (total capacity – crew size) and parameters *hostmin* and *hostmax* were introduced, such that the range of indices for potential hosts was restricted to 1, .. , *hostmax* and the range of indices for potential guests was restricted to *hostmin*+1, .. , 42.

The formulation was tested on a reduced problem with 15 boats and 4 time periods, and with *hostmin* = 4 and *hostmax* = 8. This resulted in a model with 379 variables and 18,212 rows. The LP relaxation solved in 259 seconds using the XPRESSMP optimiser[5] on an IBM 486 DX PC, in 816 simplex iterations.

4.2 Second Formulation

To reduce the number of constraints in the previous formulation, a further set of zero-one variables was introduced:

$$x_{iklt} = 1 \text{ iff crews } k \text{ and } l \text{ meet on boat } i \text{ in time period } t$$

and the constraints W were replaced by the three following sets S, V and Y. S and V together define the x variables in terms of the γ variables:
Constraints S.

$$2x_{iklt} - \gamma_{ikt} - \gamma_{ilt} \leq 0 \qquad \text{for all } i, k, l, t; k < l; i \neq k; i \neq l$$

Constraints V.

$$\gamma_{ikt} + \gamma_{ilt} - x_{iklt} \leq 1 \qquad \text{for all } i, k, l, t; k < l; i \neq k; i \neq l$$

and constraints Y then replace constraints W in the first formulation:
Constraints Y. Any pair of guest crews can meet at most once.

$$\sum_t \sum_{l, l > k} x_{iklt} \leq 1 \qquad \text{for all } i, k$$

The number of variables is now increased to $O(B^3 T)$, but the number of rows is reduced, also to $O(B^3 T)$.

---

[5] XPRESS MP (Version 7). Dash Associates, Blisworth House, Blisworth, Northants NN7 3BX, U.K.

5   Experiments on A Reduced Problem

The second formulation was used in a variety of computational experiments with the reduced 15-boat problem. As before, $hostmin = 4$ and $hostmax = 8$. Firstly, the problem was solved directly (model PS1). This gave an optimal solution with 5 hosts in a total time of 2214 secs. This was used as a basis for comparison in several experiments.

First, a facility of the XPRESSMP package was used which enables certain constraints to be introduced only if a particular solution violates them. This greatly reduces the initial size of a model. This facility is called MVUB (Make Variable Upper Bounds) and applies only to constraints of the form $x - My \leq 0$. The CD constraints were in this form already and the S constraints could be disaggregated to get them into the proper form, giving:

$$x_{iklt} - \gamma_{ikt} \leq 0 \text{ and } x_{iklt} - \gamma_{ilt} \leq 0$$

Normally disaggregation would result in a tighter LP relaxation, but since in this case all the coefficients of x_{iklt} in the other constraints of the model are unity, it can be shown by Fourier-Motzkin elimination that this will not be the case [8]. In the second version of the model (PS11) both the CD and the S constraints were modelled using MVUB; in the third (PS12) the S constraints were modelled explicitly and the CD constraints were modelled using MVUB. The results are shown in Table 2; the total solution time for PS1 was less than for either of the new versions. Thus the MVUB feature was not helpful in this case.

Model	PS1	PS11	PS12
Rows	4386	2130	4022
Columns	2271	2271	2271
LP solution time (secs)	101	16	19
Number of iterations	1474	696	497
LP objective value	3.42	3.42	3.42
MVUB time (secs)	n.a.	561	697
Branch-&-Bound time (secs)	2113	1852	3789
Number of nodes	287	279	311
IP objective value	5.00	5.00	5.00

Table 2. Results with MVUB

Next, special ordered sets of type I were tried. A set of variables form a special ordered set of type I if at most one of them can be nonzero. For example, the γ variables could be treated as special ordered sets: for each value of i and k, at most one of the set $\{\gamma_{ikt}, t = 1, .., 6\}$ can be nonzero. This device is useful if there is some natural ordering on the variables, when it can reduce the time spent doing branch-and-bound. However, in this case there is no natural ordering, since the time periods are interchangeable: in any solution, periods 1 and 6, say, can be swapped and the solution will still be valid. This meant that the approach was not helpful and in fact made branch-and-bound slower.

It would also be possible to tighten the LP relaxation by adding extra "covering" constraints generated from the CCAP constraints. For example, from the capacity constraint

$$\gamma_{121} + 2\gamma_{131} + 4\gamma_{141} + 3\gamma_{151} \leq 7$$

the following covering constraints could be derived:

$$\gamma_{121} + \gamma_{141} \leq 1$$

$$\gamma_{121} + \gamma_{131} + \gamma_{151} \leq 2$$

$$\gamma_{121} + \gamma_{141} + \gamma_{151} \leq 2$$

However, there would be a vast number of such constraints and so this did not seem a particularly fruitful approach.

Another approach was to omit the S, V and Y constraints, solve the LP relaxation of the resulting problem and then add in cuts of the form

$$\sum_{i \in Q} \gamma_{kit} - \sum_{i,j \in Q} x_{kijt} \leq \left\lfloor \frac{|Q|}{2} \right\rfloor$$

for index sets Q, where $|Q|$ is odd. By inspection, many of these were violated by the fractional solution. However, automating the process of inspecting the solution, identifying the appropriate index sets and then generating the corresponding cuts would have been computationally prohibitive. Equally, there would be no advantage in generating all possible cuts (even for sets of cardinality 3 only), as this would simply have resulted in another enormous model.

To summarise, the experiments with the reduced problem did not indicate a successful solution strategy for the full problem.

6 Experiments on The Full Problem

The size of the full model defeated all the available modellers, even using indices restricted by *hostmin* and *hostmax*. Therefore, a heuristic approach was adopted, based on the recognition that the total capacity of the first 13 boats (arranged, as described earlier, in decreasing order of spare capacity) was sufficient to accommodate all the crews (there would be 4 spare places), and that the largest guest crew could be accommodated on all but three of the hosts. Hence if a solution with 13 hosts was possible, these 13 hosts seemed a reasonable choice[6].

---

[6] As described in Section 3, it was later realised that the first 13 boats in order of total capacity, K_i, would give a larger number of spare places after all the guests had been accommodated. Nevertheless, the problem was in theory feasible, in terms of total capacity, with the 13 selected hosts.

A solution with 14 hosts was found, by relaxing the meeting constraints and specifying that at least the first 14 boats, and at most the first 15, had to be hosts. An integer solution was found in 598 secs. There were only a few violations of the meeting constraints and, by manually adding in the violated constraints, a feasible solution to the original problem was found.

It began to seem that this might be an optimal solution. Therefore the first 13 boats were fixed as hosts and an attempt was made to prove that this was infeasible. The indices of the guest boats in the meeting constraints were restricted to 21 to 42 (simply because this gave the largest model that XPRESSMP could handle). The model was still large by most standards: 19,470 constraints and 11,664 variables. It was run using a parallel implementation of OSL[7] on seven RS/6000 computers at IBM UK Scientific Centre, Hursley. The run was aborted after 189 hours, having failed to prove infeasibility. OSL had processed about 2,500 nodes, of which around 50% were still active: 239 were infeasible. Some nodes were taking over two hours to evaluate.

7 Constraint Programming Approach

This alternative approach was suggested by the desire to prove infeasibility for the 13-host model, in the light of the failure of OSL. However, it turned out that constraint programming was able to find a feasible solution very rapidly, albeit with a little manual intervention. The work was carried out at the University of Leeds.

The progressive party problem, with the 13 specified host boats, was formulated as a constraint satisfaction problem (CSP) and implemented in ILOG Solver [5], a constraint programming tool in the form of a C++ library. Solver has a large number of pre-defined constraint classes and provides a default backtracking search method, for solving CSPs. If necessary, new constraint classes and search algorithms can be defined, but these facilities were not required in this case. The default search algorithm is an implementation of full lookahead, as described by Haralick and Elliott [3]. The algorithm repeatedly chooses an unassigned variable, chooses a value for that variable from its current domain and makes a tentative assignment. The constraints are then used to identify the effects of the assignment on future (still unassigned) variables, and any value in the domain of a future variable which conflicts with the current assignment (and the rest of the current partial solution) is temporarily deleted. Furthermore, the subproblem consisting of the future variables and their remaining domains is made arc consistent, which may result in further values being deleted. If at any stage the domain of a future variable becomes empty, the algorithm backtracks and retracts the last assignment. The algorithm can therefore be viewed as the forward checking algorithm, a commonly-used algorithm for solving CSPs (also described in [3]), with additional constraint propagation to re-establish arc consistency after each assignment.

---

[7] Optimization Subroutine Library (OSL), IBM Corporation.

7.1 CSP Formulation

The first advantage of the constraint programming approach was that the formulation as a CSP was much more compact than had been previously possible. Since the task in this case was to show (if possible) that the problem with 13 specific host boats was infeasible, host and guest boats were treated separately in the formulation. Suppose that there are G guest boats, H host boats and T time periods.

The principal variables, h_{it}, represent the host boat that guest boat i visits at time t; the domain of each h_{it} is the set $\{1,.., H\}$, and there are GT such variables. The constraints that every guest boat must always have a host and that in any time period a guest boat can only be assigned to one host are automatically satisfied by any solution to the CSP, which must have exactly one value assigned to each h_{it}, i.e. exactly one host assigned to each guest boat in each time period.

The constraints that no guest boat can visit a host boat more than once are expressed in the CSP by:

$$h_{i1}, h_{i2}, h_{i3}, .., h_{iT} \text{ are all different} \qquad \text{for all } i$$

For each i, this gives a single Solver constraint, equivalent to $T(T-1)/2$ binary not-equals constraints, i.e. $h_{i1} \neq h_{i2}$, etc.

The capacity constraints are dealt with, as in the LP, by introducing new constrained 0-1 variables, corresponding to the γ variables of the LP formulation: $v_{ijt} = 1$ iff guest boat i visits host j at time t. The relationships between these variables and the h_{it} variables are specified by GHT Boolean constraints:

$$v_{ijt} = 1 \text{ iff } h_{it} = j \qquad \text{for all } i, j, t$$

and as in the LP, the capacity constraints are then:

$$\sum_i c_i v_{ijt} \leq C_j \qquad \text{for all } j, t$$

where c_i is the crew size of guest boat i and C_j is the spare capacity of host boat j, after accommodating its own crew.

The constraints that no pair of crews can meet twice also require the introduction of a new set of 0-1 variables: $m_{klt} = 1$ iff crews k and l meet at time t. The constraints linking the new variables to the original h variables are:

$$\text{if } h_{kt} = h_{lt} \text{ then } m_{klt} = 1 \qquad \text{for all } k, l, t; k < l$$

and the meeting constraints are expressed by:

$$\sum_t m_{klt} \leq 1 \text{ for all } k, l; k < l$$

Because the m variables have only three subscripts, rather than four as in the equivalent (x) variables in the LP, the CSP has only $O(B^2T)$ variables and $O(B^2T)$ constraints.

7.2 Symmetry Constraints

The constraints just described are sufficient to define the problem: a number of additional constraints were introduced to reduce the symmetries in the problem, as much as possible. For any solution, there are many equivalent solutions, which have, for instance, two guest boats with the same size crew interchanged throughout. Such symmetries in the problem can vastly increase the size of the search space and so the amount of work that has to be done. If there are no solutions, searching through many equivalent partial solutions can be extremely time-consuming. Symmetry can be avoided, or at least reduced, by adding constraints to eliminate equivalent solutions. (Puget [4] discusses this approach to avoiding symmetry.)

First, an ordering was imposed on the time-periods, which are otherwise interchangeable: the first guest boat must visit the host boats in order. (As described in the next section, the first guest boat was the one with the largest crew.)

The second set of constraints distinguishes between guest boats with the same size crew: if i, j are such a pair, with $i < j$, then for the first time period, we impose the constraint:

$$h_{i1} \leq h_{j1}$$

To allow for the fact that both boats may visit the same host at time 1 (i.e. $h_{i1} = h_{j1}$), but if so, they must visit different boats at time 2:

$$\text{either } h_{i1} < h_{j1} \text{ or } h_{i2} < h_{j2}$$

Finally, constraints were added to distinguish (to an extent) between host boats with the same spare capacity: if j and k are two such host boats, with $j < k$, the first guest boat cannot visit host k unless it also visits host j.

7.3 Solving the Problem

It is next necessary to choose variable and value ordering heuristics, i.e. rules for deciding which variable to consider next and which value to assign to it. Although the formulation just described has a great many variables, assigning values to the h_{it} variables is sufficient to arrive at a solution, and in devising variable and value ordering heuristics only these principal variables need be considered. Good variable ordering heuristics, in particular, are often crucial to the success of constraint programming methods. A heuristic which is commonly used is based on the "fail-first" principle, that is, choose the variable which is likely to be hardest to assign. In the forward checking algorithm, this means choosing the variable with the smallest remaining domain; ties may be broken by choosing the variable involved in most constraints. Finally, variables are considered in the order in which they are defined; to give priority to the largest crews, the guest crews, and so the corresponding h_{it} variables, were arranged in descending order of size.

In ordering the values, a general principle is to choose first those values which seem most likely to succeed, and the host boats accordingly were considered in descending order of spare capacity.

The problem formulation was first tested on smaller problems than the full 13 hosts, 29 guests, 6 time periods problem. Several smaller problems were solved very quickly (in 1 or 2 seconds on a SPARCstation IPX), with little backtracking, and the program was shown to be producing correct solutions. However, the full size problem ran for hours without producing any result.

It was then decided to assign all the variables relating to one time period before going on to the next. Hence, each time period was solved separately, but the solutions for each time period constrained future solutions. In effect, this was another variable ordering heuristic, taking priority over the others; however, the program was not able to backtrack to earlier time periods. The plan was to find a solution for as many time periods as could be solved within a short time, and then to print out the domains of the remaining variables. It was hoped that this would give some clue as to why the program could not proceed. With this modification, the program found a solution for five time periods very quickly (which it had not previously been able to do). At this point, the domain of any variable corresponding to the 6th time period contains those hosts that the corresponding boat can visit and has not already visited. An attempt was made to fit the guest crews into those host boats which they could still visit, by hand, in order to see why it could not be done. However, a solution was found which appeared to be feasible; adding some of the assignments to the program as extra constraints confirmed that a solution based on these assignments did obey all the constraints.

Hence, the 13 hosts, 29 guests, 6 time periods problem, which had been thought to be insoluble, had been solved, though with some manual assistance. An optimal solution to the original problem had therefore been found.

Subsequently, the extra constraints on the 6th time period were removed, and the program allowed to search for a solution without this intervention; it found a solution in 27 minutes, and went on to find a solution for the 7th time period in another minute, so that the party could have lasted for longer without requiring more hosts!

8 Discussion

For this particular problem, constraint programming, using constraint propagation and full-lookahead, succeeded spectacularly in finding a solution very quickly where linear programming had failed to find a solution at all. Moreover, on those problems which linear programming succeeded in solving, constraint programming found solutions much more quickly. A number of reasons to account for its success in this case can be identified.

8.1 Compactness of representation

The fundamental difficulty with linear programming appears to lie in finding a compact representation of the problem. The formulations described earlier show that the CSP representation requires far fewer constraints and variables than the ILP. This is possible because of the greater expressive power of the constraints allowed in constraint satisfaction problems, which are not restricted to linear inequalities as in linear programming. In turn, the greater expressiveness is allowed by the fact that constraint satisfaction algorithms make relatively unsophisticated (although very effective) use of the constraints, compared with the simplex algorithm, for instance; it is only necessary to be able to detect whether a particular set of assignments satisfies a given constraint or not.

Furthermore, although the total number of variables and constraints is important in constraint programming, it commonly happens, as here, that in modelling a complex combinatorial problem as a CSP, there is a set of principal variables together with subsidiary variables which are introduced for the purpose of modelling the constraints. Typically, the forward checking algorithm is applied only to the principal variables of the problem. As already mentioned, in this case the solution is found by assigning values to the h_{it} variables in turn, i.e. by assigning a host to each guest boat i for each time t. The subsidiary variables are automatically instantiated in this process, because of the constraints linking them to the principal variables, and they are used in effect as vehicles for propagating the problem constraints to the domains of other principal variables. Hence, the effective complexity of the problem is less than the total number of constraints and variables suggests. It is still, however, a large problem, having 29 × 6 variables, each with 13 possible values, giving $13^{29 \times 6}$ possible assignments.

8.2 Constraint propagation

The constraints in the progressive party problem are such that, using a CSP formulation and a lookahead algorithm, the effect of any assignment of a value to a variable can usually be propagated immediately to the domains of related variables. For instance, as soon as an assignment is made to an h_{it} variable, i.e. a host is assigned to guest crew i at time t, the same value can be removed from the domain of any variable corresponding to a crew that has already met crew i. The capacity constraints are the only ones that may not immediately prune the domains of other principal variables. However, given the capacities and crew sizes, the maximum number of guest crews that can visit a host simultaneously is 5, and in practice the number is almost always 3 or less. An assignment to an h_{it} variable will, therefore, very often result in the capacity constraints being used to prune other domains. Since the capacity constraints are binding, it is important that infeasible assignments should be detected as early as possible in this way. In other problems, by contrast, constraints on resources may only have any pruning effect once most of the variables involved in the constraint have been instantiated; this can lead to a large amount of searching before a set of assignments satisfying the constraint is found.

8.3 Solution Strategy

The attempts detailed in section 5 to find a good solution strategy using ILP are based on the mathematical properties of the model and not on the original problem. When it succeeds, this is, of course, one of the strengths of linear programming: the methods that have been developed are independent of the specific problem being addressed. However, in this case, where the attempts failed, it seems a disadvantage that the important features of the original problem cannot be used to direct the search for a solution. Indeed, the ILP model makes it difficult to see that the problem is essentially one of assigning a host boat to each guest boat in each time period: the majority of the variables are x variables, introduced solely to model the meeting constraints, and the fact that each guest boat must be assigned to exactly one host boat at any time is expressed only implicitly in the constraints.

In the CSP formulation, on the other hand, it is easy to see the essentials of the problem, because the principal variables represent precisely the assignment of a host boat to each guest boat in each time period. This allows a solution strategy to be devised around reasoning about these assignments. Although this approach may seem very problem specific, it requires only that variable and value ordering strategies be defined, and often, as here, general principles apply; choose next the variable which is likely to be hardest to assign, and choose a value for it which is likely to succeed. Solving the problem separately for each time period is admittedly a more problem-specific heuristic, but it is an example of an approach worth trying when a problem can be naturally divided into subproblems, and very quick and easy to implement.

8.4 Proof of optimality

Finally, it is easy to show that a solution with 12 hosts is impossible, from the fact that the capacity constraints cannot be met even for a single time period; hence, when a solution with 13 hosts was found, it was known to be optimal. In other situations, proving optimality can be much more difficult.

8.5 The Role of Heuristics

All these factors, together with a degree of good luck in the choice of heuristics, combined to make what was a very difficult problem for linear programming, a tractable one for constraint programming. Even so, the size of the problem meant that it was still potentially too difficult for constraint programming to solve if a great deal of search was required.

The role of heuristics in finding a solution is clearly crucial; for instance, the program was unable to find a solution with 13 hosts when all the time periods were considered together. Considering each time period in turn, as it was implemented in this case, has obvious limitations; because backtracking to earlier time periods is not allowed, this strategy is not guaranteed to find a solution if there is one, and it cannot show that a problem is infeasible. In general, it may be necessary to experiment with different combinations of heuristics on a given problem instance in order to get a good solution. Even then, it may be difficult to find a solution: a modification of the original problem, to make the individual crew sizes much more equal while keeping the total size the same, has proved much more difficult (even for one time period, where a solution can easily be found manually).

Ironically, it seems very probable that if the 13-host problem had indeed been infeasible, as originally supposed, the constraint programming approach would not have been able to prove infeasibility: although it is easy to show that a solution with 12 hosts is impossible, because the capacity constraints cannot be met even for a single time period, a problem which is 'only just' infeasible, because the meeting and capacity constraints cannot be simultaneously satisfied for the required number of time periods, would require a complete search of a very large search space, and would be extremely difficult to prove infeasible.

9 Related Work

Papers which also compare integer linear programming and constraint programming applied to particular problems are [2, 7]. Van Hentenryck and Carillon [7] describe a warehouse location problem, and suggest that the ILP model, because it has a great many variables relating to the allocation of customers to warehouses, disguises the fact that the essence of the problem is to decide which of the possible warehouse locations should be chosen. The constraint programming approach, on the other hand, is based on reasoning about the warehouses. This is similar in some respects to the progressive party problem, which also has a large number of additional ILP variables to model the meeting constraints, as described in section 8.3. However, in the warehouse location problem, the ILP and CSP models have an identical set of 0-1 variables representing whether each warehouse is to be used or not, so that the difficulty in the ILP is that the main variables are swamped by other variables. In the progressive party problem, an additional difficulty is that the ILP, unlike the CSP, has no variables representing directly the allocation of a host boat to each guest boat in each time period.

The paper by Dincbas, Simonis and van Hentenryck [2] discusses a case in which the expressive power of the constraints in constraint programming allows a radical reformulation of the obvious ILP model, giving a much smaller problem. A formulation with n variables, each with m values, and constraints which are linear inequalities, is expressed instead in terms of m variables each with n values, and more complex constraints. This changes the number of possible assignments of values to variables from m^n to n^m. Since the number of possible assignments indicates the total size of the search space, this is an advantage if m is much smaller than n. For instance, in [2], a CSP with complexity 4^{72} is reformulated to give a problem with complexity 72^4.

However, this is not the reason for the success of constraint programming in the progressive party problem: in that case, the CP formulation still has a relatively small number of values compared with the number of variables, and the number of possible assignments is $13^{29 \times 6}$. In theory, therefore, we should consider reversing the formulation in some way, making the host boats the variables. However, in this case reformulation is not a sensible option. One complication is the time dimension: the variables would have to correspond to each host boat in each time period, giving 13×6 variables in all. The values would then be the possible combinations of guest boats which could be assigned to each variable, and there are a great many such combinations; the constraints would also be very difficult to express. So although reversing the formulation can be extremely valuable in some cases, reducing a large problem to a smaller problem which can be solved much more quickly, it is not possible in this case.

A recent paper by Puget and De Backer [6] compares integer linear programming and constraint programming in general. They conclude that a crucial factor is the degree of propagation that the constraints of a problem allow: if each assignment of a value to a variable can be expected to trigger the pruning of many values from the domains of other variables, so that large parts of the search space do not have to be explored, constraint programming can be expected to be successful. As discussed in section 8.2, the constraints in the progressive party problem are very effective in propagating the effects of assignments to other variables. In other cases, for instance, where the constraints involve large numbers of variables, constraint propagation may be much less useful, and if the problem can be naturally represented by linear constraints, integer linear programming may be more efficient. Beringer and De Backer [1] discuss the combination of the two approaches for optimisation problems, where the bounds given by applying the simplex method to a linear relaxation of the problem can provide useful information which would not otherwise be available. On suitable problems, for instance multi-knapsack problems, allowing the two approaches to co-operate gives much faster solution times than could otherwise be achieved.

10 Conclusions

Although the progressive party problem may not be a practical problem, except for members of yacht clubs, it has many of the classical features of combinatorial optimization problems, and was expected to be amenable to linear programming techniques. However, as we have shown, the resulting models were too large to be solved, whereas constraint programming found an optimal solution very quickly.

The success of constraint programming in solving this problem is due to a combination of factors, discussed in section 8. Some of these reasons have been identified in other studies of problems where constraint programming outperformed ILP, as discussed in section 9. However, unlike the previous studies, in this problem both models turned out to be extremely large; ILP failed because the model was too large to be solved, but also, it would not have been possible to explore the complete search space arising from the constraint programming formulation. In practice, many real problems are too large to be able to guarantee to find a solution; this paper shows that even so, constraint programming can succeed through careful choice of heuristics to direct its search.

Our experience with this problem suggests that constraint programming may do better than integer linear programming when the following factors are present:

- The problem cannot easily be expressed in terms of linear constraints: constraint programming will then give a more compact representation.

- The constraints allow the early propagation of the effects of assignments to the domains of other variables. This happens if each constraint involves only a small number of variables, but also sometimes with global constraints, as in this case: the capacity constraints are triggered after only a small number of guest boats have been assigned to the same host at the same time.

- It is easy to devise good solution strategies for the problem and hence take advantage of the fact that the constraint programming formulation represents the problem much more directly that the ILP formulation typically does.

- A tight bound on the value of the objective in an optimal solution is available, so that if an optimal solution is found, it can be recognised as such (unless, of course, the problem is sufficiently small to be able to prove optimality by doing a complete search).

Further comparisons between the two approaches are still needed to quantify some of these factors and to give a clearer idea of when constraint programming should be chosen in preference to integer linear programming.

Acknowledgement We are very grateful to William Ricketts of IBM UK Scientific Centre, Hursley Park, Winchester, for his enthusiastic help with the computational experiments on the large LP model.

References

1. H. Beringer and B. De Backer. Combinatorial Problem Solving in Constraint Logic Programming with Cooperating Solvers. In C. Beierle and L. Plumer, editors, *Logic Programming: Formal Methods and Practical Applications*, chapter 8, pages 245–272. Elsevier Science B.V., 1995.
2. M. Dincbas, H. Simonis, and P. van Hentenryck. Solving a Cutting-Stock problem in constraint logic programming. In R. Kowalski and K. Brown, editors, *Logic Programming*, pages 42–58. 1988.
3. R. Haralick and G. Elliott. Increasing tree search efficiency for constraint satisfaction problems. *Artificial Intelligence*, 14:263–313, 1980.
4. J.-F. Puget. On the Satisfiability of Symmetrical Constrained Satisfaction Problems. In *Proceedings of ISMIS'93*, 1993.
5. J.-F. Puget. A C++ Implementation of CLP. In *Proceedings of SPICIS94 (Singapore International Conference on Intelligent Systems)*, 1994.
6. J.-F. Puget and B. De Backer. Comparing Constraint Programming and MILP. In *APMOD'95*, 1995.

7. P. van Hentenryck and J.-P. Carillon. Generality versus Specificity: an Experience with AI and OR techniques. In *Proceedings of AAAI-88*, volume 2, pages 660–664, 1988.

8. H. P. Williams. The elimination of integer variables. *JORS*, 43:387–393, 1992.

From Local to Global Consistency in Temporal Constraint Networks

Manolis Koubarakis*

Dept. of Computation
UMIST
P.O. Box 88
Manchester M60 1QD
U.K.
manolis@sna.co.umist.ac.uk

Abstract. We study the problem of global consistency for several classes of quantitative temporal constraints which include inequalities, inequations and disjunctions of inequations. In all cases that we consider we identify the level of local consistency that is necessary and sufficient for achieving global consistency and present an algorithm which achieves this level. As a byproduct of our analysis, we also develop an interesting minimal network algorithm.

1 Introduction

One of the most important notions found in the constraint satisfaction literature is global consistency [Fre78]. In a *globally consistent* constraint set all interesting constraints are explicitly represented and the projection of the solution set on any subset of the variables can be computed by simply collecting the constraints involving these variables. An important consequence of this property is that a solution can be found by *backtrack-free* search [Fre82]. Enforcing global consistency can take an exponential amount of time in the worst case [Fre78, Coo90]. As a result it is very important to identify cases in which *local consistency*, which presumably can be enforced in polynomial time, implies global consistency [Dec92].

In this paper we study the problem of enforcing global consistency for sets of quantitative temporal constraints over the rational (or real) numbers. The class of constraints that we consider includes equalities (e.g., $x_i - x_j = 5$), inequalities (e.g., $x_i - x_j \leq 5$), inequations (e.g, $x_i - x_j \neq 5$) and disjunctions of inequations ($x_i - x_j \neq 5 \ \lor \ x_k - x_l \neq 8$). For the representation of equalities, inequalities and inequations, we utilize *binary temporal constraint networks*. Disjunctions of inequations are represented separately.

Disjunctions of inequations have been introduced in [Kou92] following the observation that in the process of eliminating variables from a set of temporal

---

* Most of this work was performed while the author was at the National Technical University of Athens and at Imperial College, London. At Imperial College financial support was received from project CHRONOS funded by EPSRC and DTI.

constraints, an inequation can give rise to a disjunction of inequations.[2] In related temporal reasoning research [VK86, vB90, GS93, GSS93] have considered inequations of the form $t_1 \neq t_2$ in the context of PA networks. Also, [Mei91a] has studied inequations of the form $t \neq r$ (r a real constant) in the context of point networks with *almost-single-interval domains*. In a more general context, researchers in constraint logic programming (originally [LM89] and later [IvH93, Imb93, Imb94]) have studied disjunctions of arbitrary linear inequations (e.g., $2x_1 + 3x_2 - 4x_3 \neq 4 \ \vee \ x_2 + x_3 + x_5 \neq 7$). [LM89, IvH93] concentrate on deciding consistency and computing canonical forms while [Imb93, Imb94] deal mostly with variable elimination. It is interesting to notice that the basic algorithm for variable elimination in this case has been discovered independently in [Kou92] and [Imb93] although [Kou92] has used the result only in the context of temporal constraints.

The contributions of this paper can be summarized as follows.

1. We show that strong 5-consistency is necessary and sufficient for achieving global consistency in temporal constraint networks for inequalities and inequations (Corollary 4).[3] This result (and all subsequent ones) rely heavily on an observation of [LM89, Kou92, Imb93]: *(disjunctions of) inequations can be treated independently of one another for the purposes of deciding consistency or performing variable elimination.*

   We give an algorithm which achieves global consistency in $O(Hn^4)$ where n is the number of nodes in the network and H is the number of inequations (Theorems 3 and 5). The analysis of this algorithm demonstrates that there are situations where it is *impossible* to enforce global consistency without introducing disjunctions of inequations.

   A detailed analysis of the global consistency algorithm also gives us an algorithm for computing the minimal temporal constraint network in this case. The complexity of this algorithm is $O(\max(Hn^2, n^3))$ (Theorem 7).

2. We also consider global consistency of point algebra networks [VK86]. In this case strong 5-consistency is also necessary and sufficient for achieving global consistency (Theorem 9). This result, which answers an open problem of [vB90], also follows from [Kou92] but the bounds of the algorithms given there were not the tightest possible.

3. Finally we consider global consistency when disjunctions of inequations are also allowed in the given constraint set. This case is mostly of theoretical interest and is presented here for completeness. In this case, strong $(2V + 1)$-consistency is necessary and sufficient for achieving global consistency (Corollary 11). The parameter V is the maximum number of variables in any disjunction of inequations.

Most of the above results come from the author's Ph.D. thesis [Kou94a] or are refinements of ideas presented there.

---

[2] Elimination of variables is a very important operation in temporal constraint databases [Kou94a, Kou94b, Kou94c].

[3] As shown in [DMP91] if only inequalities are considered path consistency is necessary and sufficient for achieving global consistency.

The paper is organized as follows. The next section presents definitions and preliminaries. Section 3 discusses global consistency of temporal constraint networks while Section 4 presents an algorithm for computing the minimal network. Section 5 considers the case of point algebra networks. Section 6 considers the case of arbitrary temporal constraints. Finally Section 7 summarizes our results. Most proofs are omitted and can be found in the longer version of this paper.

2 Definition and Preliminaries

We consider time to be linear, dense and unbounded. *Points* will be our only time entities. Points are identified with the rational numbers but our results still hold if points are identified with the reals. The set of rational numbers will be denoted by Q.

A *temporal constraint* is a formula $t - t' \leq r$, $t - t' < r$, $t - t' = r$ or

$$t_1 - t'_1 \neq r_1 \lor \cdots \lor t_n - t'_n \neq r_n$$

where $t, t', t_1, \cdots, t_n, t'_1, \cdots, t'_n$ are variables and $r, r_1, \cdots, r_n$ are constants. The rationale for introducing disjunctions of inequations into the picture has been given in [Kou92]. We assume that the reader is familiar with the notions of solution and consistency for a set of temporal constraints [Kou92]. If C is a set of temporal constraints then $Sol(C)$ will denote its set of solutions.

If c is a disjunction of inequations then $\bar{c}$ denotes the *complement* of c i.e., the conjunction of equations obtained by negating c. If C is a set of equalities in n variables, the solution set of C is an affine subset of Q^n. If C is a set of inequalities in n variables, the solution set of C is a convex polyhedron in Q^n. If C is a set of disjunctions of inequations, the solution set of C is $Q^n \setminus Sol(\{\bar{c} : c \in C\})$.

Let C be a set of temporal constraints in variables $x_1, \ldots, x_n$ which contains only equations, inequalities and inequations (but not disjunctions of inequations). The *temporal constraint network* (TCN) associated with C is a labeled directed graph $G = (V, E)$ where $V = \{1, \ldots, n\}$. Node i represents variable x_i and edge (i, j) represents the binary constraints involving x_i and x_j. The set of constraints associated with a TCN N will be denoted by $Constraints(N)$.

Let us assume that the set of constraints c_{ij} on $x_j - x_i$ is

$$\{x_j - x_i \leq d_{ij}, \ x_j - x_i \geq -d_{ji}, \ x_j - x_i \neq r_{ji}^1, \ldots, x_j - x_i \neq r_{ji}^{h_{ji}}\}$$

where $-d_{ji} < r_{ji}^1 < \cdots < r_{ji}^{h_{ji}} < d_{ij}$. Then the corresponding TCN N will have an edge $i \to j$ labeled by the *almost-convex interval*

$$N_{ij} = [-d_{ji}, r_{ji}^1) \cup (r_{ji}^1, r_{ji}^2) \cup \cdots \cup (r_{ji}^{h_{ji}-1}, r_{ji}^{h_{ji}}) \cup (r_{ji}^{h_{ji}}, d_{ij}].$$

Interval N_{ij} can also be open from the right or left depending on the form of the inequalities in c_{ij}. The h_{ij} values $r_{ji}^1, \ldots, r_{ji}^{h_{ji}}$ will be called the *"holes"* of interval N_{ij}. We define a function *holes* such that, for each interval N_{ij},

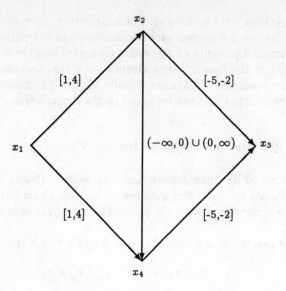

Fig. 1. A temporal constraint network

$holes(N_{ij}) = \{r_{ji}^1, \ldots, r_{ji}^{h_{ji}}\}$. As usual unary constraints will be represented as binary constraints with the introduction of a special variable $x_0 = 0$.

The TCN of Figure 1 represents the constraints

$$1 \leq x_2 - x_1 \leq 4,\ 2 \leq x_2 - x_3 \leq 5,\ 1 \leq x_4 - x_1 \leq 4,\ 2 \leq x_4 - x_3 \leq 5,\ x_4 - x_2 \neq 0.$$

Given an interval I, $conv(I)$ will denote the *convex hull* of I i.e., the minimal (in the set-theoretic sense) convex interval which includes I. Formally,

$$conv([a, r_1) \cup (r_1, r_2) \cup \cdots \cup (r_{k-1}, r_k) \cup (r_k, b]) = [a, b]$$

and $conv(I) = I$ if I is convex. If N is a TCN then $conv(N)$ denotes the TCN which is obtained from N by substituting each interval N_{ij} by $conv(N_{ij})$.

For the case of TCN, the operations of composition and intersection of almost-convex intervals are defined as usual [Mei91b]. The following proposition is straightforward.

Proposition 1. The class of *almost-convex intervals* over Q is closed under composition and intersection.

The notions of solution, consistency, equivalence and minimality for TCN are defined as usual [Mei91b].

3 Global Consistency of a TCN

We will first consider enforcing global consistency in a TCN.

Notation 3.1 Let C be a set of constraints in variables $x_1, \ldots, x_n$. For any i such that $1 \leq i \leq n$, $C(x_1, \ldots, x_i)$ will denote the set of constraints in C involving only variables $x_1, \ldots, x_i$.

The following definition is from [Dec92].

Definition 2. Let C be a set of constraints in variables $x_1, \ldots, x_n$ and $1 \leq i \leq n$. C is called *i-consistent* iff for every $i - 1$ distinct variables $x_1, \ldots, x_{i-1}$, every valuation $u = \{x_1 \leftarrow x_1^0, \ldots, x_{i-1} \leftarrow x_{i-1}^0\}$ such that u satisfies the constraints $C(x_1, \ldots, x_{i-1})$ and every variable x_i different from $x_1, \ldots, x_{i-1}$, there exists a rational number x_i^0 such that u can be extended to a valuation $u' = u \cup \{x_i \leftarrow x_i^0\}$ which satisfies the constraints $C(x_1, \ldots, x_{i-1}, x_i)$. C is called *strong i-consistent* if it is j-consistent for every j, $1 \leq j \leq i$. C is called *globally consistent* iff it is i-consistent for every i, $1 \leq i \leq n$.

Let us present some examples illustrating the above definitions.

Example 1. The constraint set $C = \{x_2 - x_1 \leq 5,\ x_1 - x_3 \leq 2,\ x_5 - x_4 \leq 1,\ x_4 - x_6 \leq 3\}$ is 1- and 2-consistent but not 3-consistent. For example, the valuation $v = \{x_2 \leftarrow 10,\ x_3 \leftarrow 2\}$ satisfies $C(x_2, x_3) = \emptyset$ but it cannot be extended to a valuation which satisfies C.

We can enforce 3-consistency by adding the constraints $x_2 - x_3 \leq 7$ and $x_5 - x_6 \leq 4$ to C. The resulting set is 3-consistent and also globally consistent.

Example 2. The constraint set $C = \{x_2 - x_1 = 5,\ x_1 - x_4 \neq 1\}$ is 1- and 2-consistent but not 3-consistent. For example, the valuation $v = \{x_2 \leftarrow 6,\ x_4 \leftarrow 0\}$ satisfies $C(x_2, x_4) = \emptyset$ but it cannot be extended to a valuation which satisfies C.

We can enforce 3-consistency by adding the constraint $x_2 - x_4 \neq 6$ to C. The resulting set is 3-consistent and also globally consistent.

Example 3. The constraint set $C = \{x_2 - x_1 \leq 5,\ x_1 - x_3 \leq 2,\ x_2 - x_3 \leq 7,\ x_1 - x_4 \neq 1\}$ is strong 3-consistent but not 4-consistent. For example, the valuation $v = \{x_2 \leftarrow 7,\ x_3 \leftarrow 0,\ x_4 \leftarrow 1\}$ satisfies $C(x_2, x_3, x_4) = \{x_2 - x_3 \leq 7\}$ but it cannot be extended to a valuation which satisfies C.

Enforcing 4-consistency amounts to adding the *disjunction*

$$x_2 - x_4 \neq 6 \ \lor \ x_3 - x_4 \neq -1.$$

The resulting set is 4-consistent and also globally consistent.

Example 4. The constraint set $C = \{x_2 - x_1 \leq 5,\ x_1 - x_3 \leq 2,\ x_2 - x_3 \leq 7,\ x_5 - x_4 \leq 1,\ x_4 - x_6 \leq 3,\ x_5 - x_6 \leq 4,\ x_1 - x_4 \neq 1\}$ is strong 3-consistent but not 4-consistent. Adding the constraint $x_2 - x_4 \neq 6 \ \lor \ x_3 - x_4 \neq -1$ (as in the previous example) is not enough. For example, the valuation $v = \{x_5 \leftarrow 2,\ x_6 \leftarrow -2,\ x_1 \leftarrow 2\}$ satisfies $C(x_5, x_6, x_1) = \{x_5 - x_6 \leq 4\}$ but it cannot be extended to a valuation which satisfies $C(x_5, x_6, x_1, x_4)$.

We can enforce 4-consistency by also adding the constraint $x_5 - x_1 \neq 0 \lor x_6 - x_1 \neq -4$ to C. Let the resulting set be C'. C' is strong 4-consistent but not 5-consistent. For example, the valuation $v = \{x_2 \leftarrow 7, \, x_3 \leftarrow 0, \, x_5 \leftarrow 2, \, x_6 \leftarrow -2\}$ satisfies $C(x_2, x_3, x_5, x_6) = \{x_2 - x_3 \leq 7, \, x_5 - x_6 \leq 4\}$ but it cannot be extended to a valuation which satisfies $C(x_2, x_3, x_5, x_6, x_1)$ (or $C(x_2, x_3, x_5, x_6, x_4)$).

We can enforce 5-consistency by adding the constraint

$$x_2 - x_3 \neq 7 \lor x_5 - x_6 \neq 4 \lor x_2 - x_5 \neq 5$$

to C'. The resulting constraint set is strong 5-consistent and also globally consistent.

Figure 2 presents algorithm TCN-GCONSISTENCY which enforces global consistency on its input TCN. TCN-GCONSISTENCY takes as input a TCN and returns an equivalent set of temporal constraints which is globally consistent. TCN-GCONSISTENCY's output is not a TCN because, as the above examples indicate, enforcing global consistency might result in the introduction of disjunctions of inequations which cannot be represented by a TCN. TCN-GCONSISTENCY takes advantage of an observation of [Kou92, Imb93]: inequations can be treated *independently* of one another for performing variable elimination.

The algorithm TCN-GCONSISTENCY essentially enforces strong 5-consistency on its input network N. As we will show shortly, this level of local consistency is enough for achieving global consistency. In step 1, TCN-GCONSISTENCY enforces strong 3-consistency on $conv(N)$. This is achieved by running the modified Floyd-Warshall algorithm of [DMP91, KL91] on $conv(N)$. Let N' denote the resulting TCN and $A' = Constraints(N')$. Then $conv(N')$ is minimal and globally consistent [DMP91, KL91].

In step 2, TCN-GCONSISTENCY completes its job. For each $r_{ik}^g \in holes(N_{ki})$ or equivalently for each inequation $x_i - x_k \neq r_{ik}^g$ of $A = Constraints(N)$, TCN-GCONSISTENCY explores the inequalities of A involving x_i and x_k in the following systematic way. Figure 3 illustrates the structure of the subnetworks of N explored in this step. Edges labeled with $\neq$ denote non-convex intervals.

1. If there are inequalities $x_m - x_i \leq d_{im}$ and $x_i - x_l \leq d_{li}$ then step 2.1 ensures that any valuation $v = \{x_l \leftarrow x_l^0, x_m \leftarrow x_m^0, x_k \leftarrow x_k^0\}$, which satisfies $A(x_l, x_m, x_k)$, can be extended to a valuation $v' = v \cup \{x_i \leftarrow x_i^0\}$ which satisfies $A(x_l, x_m, x_k, x_i)$. This is achieved with the introduction of the inequation constraint

$$x_m - x_k \neq d_{im} + r_{ik}^g \lor x_l - x_k \neq -d_{li} + r_{ik}^g.$$

If there are inequalities $x_s - x_k \leq d_{ks}$ and $x_k - x_t \leq d_{tk}$ then step 2.1 also ensures that any valuation $v = \{x_s \leftarrow x_s^0, x_t \leftarrow x_t^0, x_i \leftarrow x_i^0\}$, which satisfies $A(x_s, x_t, x_i)$, can be extended to a valuation $v' = v \cup \{x_k \leftarrow x_k^0\}$ which satisfies $A(x_s, x_t, x_i, x_k)$. This is achieved with the introduction of the inequation constraint

$$x_s - x_i \neq d_{ks} - r_{ik}^g \lor x_t - x_i \neq -d_{tk} - r_{ik}^g.$$

Algorithm TCN-GCONSISTENCY
Input: A consistent TCN N.
Output: A globally consistent set of constraints equivalent to N.

Method:
1. Step 1: Enforce path consistency on conv(N).
2. For $k, i, j = 1$ to n do
3. $N_{ij} := N_{ij} \oplus (conv(N_{ik}) \otimes conv(N_{kj}))$
4. EndFor

5. Step 2: Enforce global consistency.
6. $C := \emptyset$
7. For $i, k = 1$ to n do
8.   For $g = 1$ to h_{ik} do

9.   Step 2.1
10.   For $m, l = 1$ to n do
11.   If N_{im}, N_{li} are closed from the right then
12. $C := C \cup \{x_m - x_k \neq d_{im} + r_{ik}^g \ \vee \ x_l - x_k \neq -d_{li} + r_{ik}^g\}$
13.   EndIf
14.   EndFor

15.   Step 2.2
16.   For $m, l, s, t = 1$ to n do
17.   If $N_{im}, N_{li}, N_{ks}, N_{tk}$ are closed from the right then
18. $C := C \cup \{x_m - x_l \neq d_{im} + d_{li} \ \vee \ x_s - x_t \neq d_{ks} + d_{tk} \ \vee$
                    $x_m - x_s \neq r_{ik}^g + d_{im} - d_{ks}\}$
19.   Endif
20.   EndFor

21.   EndFor
22. EndFor

23. Return $Constraints(N) \cup C$

Fig. 2. Enforcing global consistency

2. If there are inequalities $x_m - x_i \leq d_{im}$, $x_i - x_l \leq d_{li}$, $x_s - x_k \leq d_{ks}$ and $x_k - x_t \leq d_{tk}$ then step 2.2 ensures that any valuation $v = \{x_l \leftarrow x_l^0, x_m \leftarrow x_m^0, x_s \leftarrow x_s^0, x_t \leftarrow x_t^0\}$, which satisfies $A(x_l, x_m, x_s, x_t)$, can be extended to a valuation $v' = v \cup \{x_i \leftarrow x_i^0, x_k \leftarrow x_k^0\}$ which satisfies $A(x_l, x_m, x_s, x_t, x_i, x_k)$. This is achieved with the introduction of the inequation constraint

$$x_m - x_l \neq d_{im} + d_{li} \ \vee \ x_s - x_t \neq d_{ks} + d_{tk} \ \vee \ x_m - x_s \neq r_{ik}^g + d_{im} - d_{ks}.$$

Discussion. It is possible that step 2 of algorithm TCN-GCONSISTENCY introduces constraints that are not strictly necessary for enforcing global consistency. This happens when a generated constraint is equivalent to *true* or

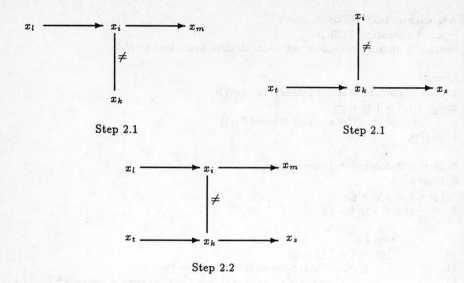

Step 2.1   Step 2.1

Step 2.2

Fig. 3. The subnetworks examined by step 2 of TCN-GCONSISTENCY

when it is implied by another constraint. TCN-GCONSISTENCY can also introduce disjunctions of inequations that are equivalent to inequations (e.g., $x_1 - x_5 \neq 2 \lor x_1 - x_5 \neq 2$). We tolerate this inefficiency because it allow us to present our ideas clearly and minimizes the case analysis in the forthcoming proofs. The reader can consult [Kou94a] for an improved but complicated version of TCN-GCONSISTENCY.

The following theorem demonstrates the correctness of algorithm TCN-GCONSISTENCY.

Theorem 3. *The algorithm* TCN-GCONSISTENCY *is correct i.e., it returns a globally consistent set of constraints equivalent to the input network.*

Corollary 4. *Strong 5-consistency is necessary and sufficient for achieving global consistency of a TCN.*

Proof. Example 4 shows the necessity of achieving strong 5-consistency. The sufficiency follows from the previous theorem; the algorithm TCN-GCONSISTENCY essentially achieves strong 5-consistency.

The following theorem gives the complexity of TCN-GCONSISTENCY.

Theorem 5. *The running time of* TCN-GCONSISTENCY *is* $O(Hn^4)$ *where* H *is the number of inequations and* n *is the number of variables in the input TCN.*

Proof. Step 1 takes $O(n^3)$ time, step 2.1 takes $O(Hn^2)$ time and step 2.2 takes $O(Hn^4)$ time.

4 Computing Minimal TCN

In this section we present an algorithm for computing the minimal network equivalent to a given TCN. The algorithm TCN-MINIMAL shown in Figure 4 is essentially a by-product of algorithm TCN-GCONSISTENCY. Notice that the constraints in the minimal TCN will be only inequalities and inequations. Therefore an algorithm for computing the minimal TCN can be constructed if we start with TCN-GCONSISTENCY and omit any part that generates a disjunction of inequations. This can be achieved by a detailed analysis of Step 2 of TCN-GCONSISTENCY.

Before proceeding with the algorithm let us clarify our notion of minimality. We will use the traditional definition of a minimal network which is as follows [DMP91, Mei91b]. A binary constraint network N is called *minimal* if there is no tighter network equivalent to it.[4] However this definition is not the only one available in the literature. [Dec92] defines a binary constraint network to be minimal if every subnetwork of size two is consistent relative to the full network (i.e, if any instantiation of two variables which is locally consistent can be extended to a solution of the full network). In our case these two definitions are not equivalent. Consider the constraint set $C = \{x_1 \leq x_2, \ x_2 \leq 5, \ x_2 \neq x_3\}$. If we adopt the first definition the minimal TCN N for C has $N_{13} = (-\infty, +\infty)$. But the valuation $v = \{x_1 \leftarrow 5, \ x_3 \leftarrow 5\}$ which satisfies the constraint express by N_{13} cannot be extended to a solution of C (C implies $x_3 \neq x_1 \vee x_3 \neq 5$ but this cannot be represented by N).

TCN-MINIMAL computes the minimal TCN in four steps. In the first step, we enforce path-consistency on the convex part $conv(N)$ of the input network N. In Step 2, TCN-MINIMAL performs constraint propagation involving equalities from $conv(N)$ and inequations from L. More precisely, for every inequation $x_i - x_j \neq r \in L$ and every equality $x_k - x_i = d_{ki} \in conv(N)$ Step 2.1 adds inequation $x_k - x_j \neq r + d_{ki}$ to N. Similarly, for every inequation $x_i - x_j \neq r \in L$ and every equality $x_j - x_k = d_{jk} \in conv(N)$ Step 2.2 adds inequation $x_i - x_k \neq r + d_{jk}$ to N.

In Step 3, TCN-MINIMAL considers subnetworks of N like the ones considered by Step 2.2 of TCN-GCONSISTENCY (see Figure 3) when $l = t$ and $m = s$.[5] In this case the constraint generated by TCN-GCONSISTENCY is equivalent to a binary inequation thus it should be reflected in the minimal TCN. This can be shown as follows. If $l = t$ and $m = s$ then Step 2.2 of TCN-GCONSISTENCY examines the constraint set

$$\{x_m - x_i \leq d_{im}, \ x_i - x_l \leq d_{li}, \ x_m - x_k \leq d_{km}, \ x_k - x_l \leq d_{lk}, \ x_i - x_k \neq r\}$$

and generates the constraint

$$x_m - x_l \neq d_{im} + d_{li} \ \vee \ x_m - x_l \neq d_{km} + d_{lk} \ \vee \ 0 \neq r + d_{im} - d_{km}.$$

---

[4] A binary constraint network M is *tighter* than N if for every i, j, $M_{ij} \subseteq N_{ij}$.

[5] The case where $l = s$ and $m = t$ does not need to be considered because it leads to disjunctions of inequations that are equivalent to *true*.

Algorithm TCN-Minimal
Input: A consistent TCN N.
Output: A minimal TCN equivalent to N.

Method:
Step 1: Enforce path consistency on $conv(N)$ (as in Step 1 of
TCN-GConsistency).

Step 2:
Let L be the list of inequations in N.
For every (i, j, r) in L do
    For $k = 1$ to n do
        If $-d_{ik} = d_{ki}$ then
            $N_{kj} := N_{kj} \oplus ((-\infty, r + d_{ki}) \cup (r + d_{ki}, \infty))$
        EndIf
    EndFor

    For $k = 1$ to n do
        If $-d_{kj} = d_{jk}$ then
            $N_{ik} := N_{ik} \oplus ((-\infty, r + d_{jk}) \cup (r + d_{jk}, \infty))$
        EndIf
    EndFor
EndFor

Step 3:
For every (i, k, r) in L do
    For $m, l = 1$ to n do
        If $N_{im}, N_{li}, N_{km}, N_{lk}$ are closed from the right and $m \neq l$ and
            $r + d_{im} - d_{km} = 0$ and $d_{li} + d_{im} = d_{lk} + d_{km}$ then
            $N_{lm} := N_{lm} \oplus ((-\infty, d_{li} + d_{im}) \cup (d_{li} + d_{im}, \infty))$
        EndIf
    EndFor
EndFor

Step 4:
For every (i, k, r) in L do
    For $m, t = 1$ to n do
        If $-d_{mi} = d_{im}$ and $-d_{kt} = d_{tk}$ then
            $N_{tm} := N_{tm} \oplus ((-\infty, d_{im} + d_{tk} + r) \cup (d_{im} + d_{tk} + r, \infty))$
        EndIf
    EndFor
EndFor

Return N

Fig. 4. A minimal TCN algorithm

If $r + d_{im} - d_{km} = 0$ and $d_{im} + d_{li} = d_{km} + d_{lk}$ then the above constraint becomes $x_m - x_l \neq d_{im} + d_{li}$ otherwise it evaluates to *true*.

Finally, in Step 4 TCN-MINIMAL considers subnetworks of N like the ones considered by Step 2.2 of TCN-GCONSISTENCY when $l = m$ and $t = s$. In this case the constraint generated by TCN-GCONSISTENCY is also equivalent to a binary inequation. This can be shown as follows. If $l = m$ and $t = s$ then Step 2.2 of TCN-GCONSISTENCY considers the constraint set

$$\{x_m - x_i \leq d_{im}, \; x_i - x_m \leq d_{mi}, \; x_t - x_k \leq d_{kt}, \; x_k - x_t \leq d_{kt}, \; x_i - x_k \neq r\}$$

and generates the constraint

$$-d_{im} \neq d_{mi} \; \vee \; -d_{kt} \neq d_{tk} \; \vee \; x_m - x_t \neq d_{im} + d_{tk} + r.$$

If $-d_{im} = d_{mi}$ and $-d_{kt} = d_{tk}$ then this constraint becomes $x_m - x_t \neq d_{im} + d_{tk} + r$ otherwise it evaluates to *true*.

The following lemma summarizes the most important property of algorithm TCN-MINIMAL.

Lemma 6. *If* TCN-GCONSISTENCY *computes a binary inequation* c *and* N *is the output of* TCN-MINIMAL *then* $c \in Constraints(N)$.

Proof. By case analysis of Step 2 of algorithm TCN-GCONSISTENCY.

The following theorem shows that the algorithm TCN-MINIMAL is correct and gives its complexity.

Theorem 7. *The algorithm* TCN-MINIMAL *computes the minimal TCN equivalent to its input in* $O(\max(Hn^2, n^3))$ *time where* H *is the number of inequations and* n *is the number of variables.*

Proof. The correctness part follows from the previous lemma. The complexity bound is achieved by either maintaining L explicitly or by having an adjacency list recording the inequations for every node of N.

An algorithm with the same complexity has also been discovered independently by Gerevini and Cristani [GC95]. without prior analysis of the global consistency problem. A careful comparison of the two algorithms shows that Step 2 of TCN-MINIMAL computes *3-path implicit inequations*, Step 3 deals with *forbidden subgraphs* and Step 4 deals with *4-path implicit inequations* (this new terminology comes from [GC95] and the reader is referred there for more details).

Independently, Isli has studied a subclass of the class of temporal constraints that we consider in this section [Isl94]. Isli does not consider inequations of the form $x - y \neq r$ where $r \neq 0$, and achieves the same complexity bound for computing the minimal network.

5 Global Consistency of Point Algebra Networks

We will now turn our attention to an important subset of TCN: the point algebra (PA) networks introduced in [VKvB89]. A *point algebra network (PAN)* is a labeled directed graph where nodes represent variables and edges represent PA constraints. The labels of the edges are chosen from the set of relations $\{<, \leq, >, \geq, =, \neq, ?\}$. The symbol ? is used to label an edge $i \to j$ whenever there is no constraint between variables x_i and x_j.

Van Beek and Cohen have studied PAN in detail [vBC90, vB92]. Theorem 7 and the following results of [vB92] show that the complexity of computing the minimal network does not change when we go from PAN to TCN.

Theorem 8. *The minimal network equivalent to a PAN can be computed in $O(\max(Hn^2, n^3))$ time where H is the number of edges labeled with $\neq$ and n is the number of nodes.*

In [vBC90] the minimal network is computed by algorithm AAC. However, in the proof of correctness of AAC (Theorem 4 of [vBC90]), Van Beek and Cohen suggest that the algorithm for computing the minimal network of a given PAN also achieves global consistency. This is not true and has been corrected in [vB90]. As the following example demonstrates, the introduction of disjunctions of inequations is necessary for achieving global consistency in this case. But algorithm AAC of [vBC90] does not introduce such disjunctions so it cannot achieve global consistency.

Example 5. For the PAN with constraints

$$x_1 \leq x_2, \ x_2 \leq x_3, \ x_4 \leq x_5, \ x_5 \leq x_6, x_2 \neq x_5$$

AAC will also introduce constraints $x_1 \leq x_3$, $x_4 \leq x_6$. The resulting PAN is strong 3-consistent but *not* globally consistent. This can be demonstrated via an argument similar to the one for Example 4. If we enforce strong 5-consistency with the addition of constraints $x_1 \neq x_5 \ \lor \ x_3 \neq x_5$, $x_4 \neq x_2 \ \lor \ x_6 \neq x_2$ and $x_1 \neq x_3 \ \lor \ x_1 \neq x_4 \ \lor \ x_1 \neq x_6$, then the resulting set is globally consistent.

Global consistency of PAN can be enforced by TCN-GCONSISTENCY if PAN are represented by their equivalent TCN. Global consistency of PAN has also been discussed (under the name decomposability) in Section 5 of [Kou92] and algorithm DECOMPOSE has been proposed for achieving this task. The algorithm is correct but it adopts a representation which is rather inappropriate for the task at hand and leads to a complexity bound which is not the tightest. The following theorem summarizes the result of Section 3 as it applies to PAN.

Theorem 9. *Strong 5-consistency is necessary and sufficient for achieving global consistency in PAN. Strong 5-consistency can be enforced in $O(Hn^4)$ time where H is the number of edges labeled with $\neq$ and n is the number of nodes.*

Let us now comment on some observations of Dechter [Dec92] on the problem of enforcing global consistency in PAN. [Dec92] discusses global consistency in general constraint networks with finite variable domains. The most important result of [Dec92] is the following. If N is a constraint network with constraints of arity r or less and domains of size k or less which is strongly $(k(r-1)+1)$-consistent, then N is globally consistent.

The above result can be applied to PAN if PAN are redefined as "traditional" constraint networks where variables represent relations between two points and constraints are defined by the transitivity table of [VKvB89]. This representation yields a constraint network with $k = 3$ and $r = 3$. Dechter's result now gives us the following. If strong 7-consistency in PAN can be enforced with ternary constraints then strong 7-consistency implies global consistency. Dechter uses the aforementioned incorrect assertion of [vBC90] to conclude that strong 7-consistency in the traditional formulation of PAN can be enforced with ternary constraints. Thus she also concludes that in the traditional formulation strong 7-consistency implies global consistency [Dec92, page 100]. In the light of Theorem 9, Dechter's conclusion remains unjustified.

6 The General Case

Let us now consider enforcing global consistency when disjunctions of inequations are allowed in the given constraint set.

Example 6. The constraint set

$$C = \{x_5 \leq x_1, \ x_1 \leq x_6, \ x_5 \leq x_6, \ x_7 \leq x_3, \ x_3 \leq x_8, \ x_7 \leq x_8, \ x_9 \leq x_2,$$
$$x_2 \leq x_{10}, \ x_9 \leq x_{10}, \ x_1 \neq y \ \vee \ x_2 \neq z \ \vee \ x_3 \neq w\}$$

is strong 7-consistent but not 8-consistent. For example, the valuation

$$v = \{y \leftarrow 0, \ z \leftarrow 0, \ w \leftarrow 0, \ x_2 \leftarrow 0, \ x_3 \leftarrow 0, \ x_5 \leftarrow 0, \ x_6 \leftarrow 0\}$$

satisfies $C(y, z, w, x_2, x_3, x_5, x_6) = \{x_5 \leq x_6\}$ but it cannot be extended to a valuation which satisfies $C(y, z, w, x_2, x_3, x_5, x_6, x_1)$. We can enforce 8-consistency by adding the constraints

$$x_5 \neq y \ \vee \ x_6 \neq y \ \vee \ x_2 \neq z \ \vee \ x_3 \neq w$$
$$x_1 \neq y \ \vee \ x_9 \neq z \ \vee \ x_{10} \neq z \ \vee \ x_3 \neq w$$
$$x_1 \neq y \ \vee \ x_2 \neq z \ \vee \ x_7 \neq w \ \vee \ x_8 \neq w.$$

The resulting set is strong 8-consistent but not 9-consistent. We can enforce 9-consistency by adding the constraints

$$x_5 \neq y \ \vee \ x_6 \neq y \ \vee \ x_9 \neq z \ \vee \ x_{10} \neq z \ \vee \ x_3 \neq w$$
$$x_1 \neq y \ \vee \ x_9 \neq z \ \vee \ x_{10} \neq z \ \vee \ x_7 \neq w \ \vee \ x_8 \neq w$$
$$x_5 \neq y \ \vee \ x_6 \neq y \ \vee \ x_2 \neq z \ \vee \ x_7 \neq w \ \vee \ x_8 \neq w.$$

Algorithm GCONSISTENCY

Input: A set of temporal constraints $C = C_i \cup C_d$ where C_i is a set of inequalities and C_d is a set of disjunctions of inequations.

Output: A globally consistent set of constraints equivalent to C.

Method:

Step 1: Enforce strong 3-consistency on C_i.

Let N be the TCN corresponding to C_i.

For $k, i, j = 1$ to n do
    $N_{ij} := N_{ij} \oplus (N_{ik} \otimes N_{kj})$
EndFor

Step 2: Enforce global consistency

$C_d' := \emptyset$

For each $c \in C_d$ do
    For all subsets $\{k_1, \ldots, k_i\}$ of the set of variables of c do
        For $m_1, \ldots, m_i, l_1, \ldots, l_i = 1$ to n do
            If $N_{k_1 m_1}, \ldots, N_{k_i m_i}, N_{l_1 k_1}, \ldots, N_{l_i k_i}$ are closed from the right then
                Eliminate variables $x_{k_1}, \ldots, x_{k_i}$ from
                $\overline{c}, \ x_{m_1} - x_{k_1} = d_{k_1 m_1}, \ x_{k_1} - x_{l_1} = d_{l_1 k_1}, \ldots, x_{m_i} - x_{k_i} = d_{i m_i},$
                $x_{k_i} - x_{l_i} = d_{l_i k_i}$
                to obtain c'
                $C_d' := C_d' \cup \{\overline{c'}\}$
        Endif
        EndFor
    EndFor
EndFor

Return $Constraints(N) \cup C_d \cup C_d'$

Fig. 5. Enforcing global consistency

The resulting set is strong 9-consistent but not 10-consistent. We can enforce 10-consistency by adding the constraint

$$x_5 \neq y \ \vee \ x_6 \neq y \ \vee \ x_9 \neq z \ \vee \ x_{10} \neq z \ \vee \ x_7 \neq w \ \vee \ x_8 \neq w.$$

The resulting set is strong 10-consistent and also globally consistent.

Figure 5 presents algorithm GCONSISTENCY which enforces global consistency on its input constraint set. The reader should have no problem understanding the details of GCONSISTENCY since it is a straightforward generalization of algorithm TCN-GCONSISTENCY.

The following theorem demonstrates the correctness of GCONSISTENCY.

Theorem 10. *The algorithm GCONSISTENCY is correct i.e., it returns a globally consistent set of constraints equivalent to the input one.*

In essence, algorithm GCONSISTENCY achieves strong $2V + 1$-consistency where V is the maximum number of variables in any disjunction of inequations. Thus we have the following corollary.

Corollary 11. *Let C be a set of temporal constraints. If C is $2V + 1$-consistent, where V is the maximum number of variables in any disjunction of inequations, then C is globally consistent.*

The time complexity of GCONSISTENCY is exponential in V. However, if V is *fixed* then the time complexity of GCONSISTENCY is polynomial in the number of variables and the number of constraints in C. This has an interesting consequence for variable elimination due to its relation to global consistency.

Corollary 12. *Let C be a set of temporal constraints such that the number of variables in every disjunction of inequations is fixed. Eliminating any number of variables from C can be done in time polynomial in the number of variables and the number of constraints. In addition, the resulting constraint set has size polynomial in the same parameters.*

Proof. Let $x_1, \ldots, x_n$ be all the variables of C. When V is fixed, the size of the constraint set generated by algorithm GCONSISTENCY is polynomial in the number of variables and the number of constraints. If C is globally consistent then for any i such that $1 \leq i \leq n$, $C(x_1, \ldots, x_i)$ is the projection of $Sol(C)$ on $\{x_1, \ldots, x_i\}$. Thus we can eliminate variables $x_1, \ldots, x_i$ from C by running GCONSISTENCY on C and returning $C(x_{i+1}, \ldots, x_n)$. This algorithm takes time polynomial in the number of variables and the number of constraints.

The above corollary complements Theorem 4.4 of [Kou92] which states that variable elimination can result in constraint sets with an exponential number of disjunctions of inequations.

7 Conclusions

We discussed the problem of enforcing global consistency in sets of quantitative temporal constraints which include inequalities, inequations and disjunctions of inequations. It would be interesting to combine our results with the results of [Mei91b] in order to identify classes of qualitative and quantitative point/interval constraints where global consistency is tractable.

8 Acknowledgements

I would like to thank Peter van Beek, Amar Isli, Alfonso Gerevini and the reviewers of CP95 for interesting discussions concerning the topics of this paper. Gerevini pointed out to us that an earlier version of Lemma 6 had been stated inaccurately.

References

[Coo90]   M.C. Cooper. An optimal k-consistency algorithm. *Artificial Intelligence*, 41(1):89–95, 1990.

[Dec92]   Rina Dechter. From local to global consistency. *Artificial Intelligence*, 55:87–107, 1992.

[DMP91]   Rina Dechter, Itay Meiri, and Judea Pearl. Temporal Constraint Networks. *Artificial Intelligence*, 49(1-3):61–95, 1991. Special Volume on Knowledge Representation.

[Fre78]   E. Freuder. Synthesizing Constraint Expressions. *Communications of ACM*, 21(11):958–966, November 1978.

[Fre82]   E. Freuder. A Sufficient Condition For Backtrack-Free Search. *Journal of ACM*, 29(1):24–32, 1982.

[GC95]   A. Gerevini and M. Cristani. Reasoning with Inequations in Temporal Constraint Networks. Technical report, IRST - Instituto per la Ricerca Scientifica e Tecnologica, Povo TN, Italy, 1995. A shorter version will be presented at the IJCAI-95 Workshop on Spatial and Temporal Reasoning, August 1995, Montreal, Canada.

[GS93]   A. Gerevini and L. Schubert. Efficient Temporal Reasoning Through Timegraphs. In *Proceedings of IJCAI-93*, pages 648–654, 1993.

[GSS93]   A. Gerevini, L. Schubert, and S. Schaeffer. Temporal Reasoning in Timegraph I-II. *SIGART Bulletin*, 4(3):21–25, 1993.

[Imb93]   J.-L. Imbert. Variable Elimination for Generalized Linear Constraints. In *Proceedings of the 10th International Conference on Logic Programming*, 1993.

[Imb94]   J.-L. Imbert. Redundancy, Variable Elimination and Linear Disequations. In *Proceedings of the International Symposium on Logic Programming*, pages 139–153, 1994.

[Isl94]   A. Isli. Constraint-Based Temporal Reasoning: a Tractable Point Algebra Combining Qualitative, Metric and Holed Constraints. Technical Report 94-06, LIPN-CNRS URA 1507, Inst. Galilée, Université Paris-Nord, 1994.

[IvH93]   J.-L. Imbert and P. van Hentenryck. On the Handling of Disequations in CLP over Linear Rational Arithmetic. In F. Benhamou and A. Colmerauer, editors, *Constraint Logic Programming: Selected Research*, Logic Programming Series, pages 49–71. MIT Press, 1993.

[KL91]   H. Kautz and P. Ladkin. Integrating Metric and Qualitative Temporal Reasoning. In *Proceedings of AAAI-91*, pages 241–246, 1991.

[Kou92]   Manolis Koubarakis. Dense Time and Temporal Constraints with $\neq$. In *Principles of Knowledge Representation and Reasoning: Proceedings of the Third International Conference (KR'92)*, pages 24–35. Morgan Kaufmann, San Mateo, CA, October 1992.

[Kou94a]   M. Koubarakis. *Foundations of Temporal Constraint Databases*. PhD thesis, Computer Science Division, Dept. of Electrical and Computer Engineering, National Technical University of Athens, February 1994. Available by anonymous ftp from host passion.doc.ic.ac.uk, file IC-Parc/Papers/M.Koubarakis/phd-thesis.ps.Z.

[Kou94b]   Manolis Koubarakis. Complexity Results for First-Order Theories of Temporal Constraints. In *Principles of Knowledge Representation and Reasoning: Proceedings of the Fourth International Conference (KR'94)*, pages 379–390. Morgan Kaufmann, San Francisco, CA, May 1994.

[Kou94c]   Manolis Koubarakis. Foundations of Indefinite Constraint Databases. In A. Borning, editor, *Proceedings of the 2nd International Workshop on the Principles and Practice of Constraint Programming (PPCP'94)*, volume 874 of *Lecture Notes in Computer Science*, pages 266–280. Springer Verlag, 1994.

[LM89]   Jean-Louis Lassez and Ken McAloon. A Canonical Form for Generalized
            Linear Costraints. Technical Report RC15004 (#67009), IBM Research Di-
            vision, T.J. Watson Research Center, 1989.

[Mei91a]   I. Meiri. Combining Qualitative and Quantitative Constraints in Temporal
            Reasoning. Technical Report R-160, Cognitive Systems Laboratory, Univer-
            sity of California, Los Angeles, 1991.

[Mei91b]   I. Meiri. Combining Qualitative and Quantitative Constraints in Temporal
            Reasoning. In *Proceedings of AAAI-91*, pages 260–267, 1991.

[vB90]   Peter van Beek. Exact and Approximate Reasoning About Qualitative Tem-
            poral Relations. Technical Report TR 90-29, Department of Computing
            Science, University of Alberta, August 1990.

[vB92]   Peter van Beek. Reasoning About Qualitative Temporal Information. *Arti-
            ficial Intelligence*, 58:297–326, 1992.

[vBC90]   Peter van Beek and Robin Cohen. Exact and Approximate Reasoning about
            Temporal Relations. *Computational Intelligence*, 6:132–144, 1990.

[VK86]   Marc Vilain and Henry Kautz. Constraint Propagation Algorithms for Tem-
            poral Reasoning. In *Proceedings of AAAI-86*, pages 377–382, 1986.

[VKvB89]   Marc Vilain, Henry Kautz, and Peter van Beek. Constraint Propagation
            Algorithms for Temporal Reasoning: a Revised Report. In D.S. Weld and
            J. de Kleer, editors, *Readings in Qualitative Reasoning about Physical Sys-
            tems*, pages 373–381. Morgan Kaufmann, 1989.

Scaling Effects in the CSP Phase Transition*

Ian P. Gent[1], Ewan MacIntyre[1], Patrick Prosser[1] and Toby Walsh[2]

[1] Department of Computer Science University of Strathclyde, Glasgow G1 1XH,
United Kingdom.
[2] Mechanized Reasoning Group, IRST, Trento, and DIST, University of Genoa, Italy.

Abstract. Phase transitions in constraint satisfaction problems (CSP's)
are the subject of intense study. We identify a control parameter for random binary CSP's. There is a rapid transition in the probability of a CSP
having a solution at a critical value of this parameter. This parameter
allows different phase transition behaviour to be compared in an uniform
manner, for example CSP's generated under different regimes. We then
show that within classes, the scaling of behaviour can be modelled by a
technique called "finite size scaling". This applies not only to probability
of solubility, as has been observed before in other NP-problems, but also
to search cost. Furthermore, the technique applies with equal validity to
several different methods of varying problem size. As well as contribut-
ing to the understanding of phase transitions, we contribute by allowing
much finer grained comparison of algorithms, and for accurate empirical
extrapolations of behaviour.

1   Introduction

A phase transition in random CSP problems has recently been the subject of in-
tensive theoretical and empirical study [30, 13, 26, 27, 21, 22, 5]. Theory predicts
approximately where the phase transition can be expected, but otherwise very
little information is available as to what behaviour can be expected at different
problem sizes and at different points with respect to the phase transition.

Compared to SAT, the model for generation of random CSP problems is
complicated, and no control parameter is used in presenting data. Yet the identification of a control parameter for random SAT problems [2, 19] is fundamental
to current research on phase transitions in SAT. In this paper we introduce a
control parameter for CSP. The phase transition is always expected at the same
value of this parameter. Using extant data, we show that it can be much more
easily understood by plotting with respect to this parameter than by raw plots
as previously presented.

In the rest of the paper, we show that the control parameter can be used to
direct detailed and meaningful comparisons of significantly different methods of

---

* The fourth author is supported by an HCM Postdoctoral Fellowship. We thank
the Department of Computer Science at the University of Strathclyde for
CPU cycles, and Judith Underwood for her help. Authors' email addresses are
ipg@cs.strath.ac.uk, ewan@hazel.demon.co.uk, pat@cs.strath.ac.uk, toby@irst.it.

generating random binary CSP's. We show that our proposed parameter gives meaningful results as we change the number of variables in our problems, change the number of values in the domain of variables, or vary both simultaneously. In each case the phase transition in probability seems to occur at similar values of the parameter with changing problem size. Furthermore, median search cost seems to peak over the same range of the parameter.

Using our results on these problems, we are able to show that the technique of "finite size scaling" can be applied to problems in CSP phase transitions. The result is an empirical prediction of how probability of solubility varies with problem size, and this prediction might be used to help derive experimental parameters for future experiments. We show this for each different method of varying problem size that we investigate. This is the first time finite size scaling has been applied to a computational phase transition on changing domain size.

The interest in how the probability of solubility varies with problem size is largely due to the correlation with peak in search cost at that phase transition. We show how remarkable a correlation this is by demonstrating that finite size scaling, applied with parameters derived only from examination of probability data, seems to apply to search cost also. The implications for the experimental analysis of algorithms are very significant.

2 Binary Constraint Satisfaction Problems

In the binary constraint satisfaction problem (CSP) we have a set of variables, where each variable has a domain of values, and a set of constraints acting between pairs of variables. The problem is then to assign values to variables, from their respective domains, such that the constraints are satisfied [3, 17, 28]. One way of addressing this problem is via systematic search using backtracking, the objectives being to find a solution, or determine that none exists, with minimal search effort, where effort is measured as the number of compatibility checks performed between pairs of variables. Given a CSP with n variables with uniform domain size of m, there will be m^n possible assignments of variables to values. The best known complete algorithms for CSP'sare exponential in the worst case.

Numerous studies have been performed on random CSP's, in order to measure the performance of algorithms [4, 24, 29] and to investigate the nature of problems [21, 26]. Random CSP'sare typically categorised using four parameters, namely $\langle n, m, p_1, p_2 \rangle$, where n is the number of variables, m is the uniform domain size, p_1 is the proportion of edges in the constraint graph (ie. the density of the constraint graph), and p_2 is the proportion of pairs of instantiations over a constraint that are disallowed (ie. the tightness of the constraints) [21, 26, 5][3] It has been observed that if n, m, and p_1 are held constant, there is a small

---

[3] That is, in a random CSP $\langle n, m, p_1, p_2 \rangle$ as defined in [21, 26] there will be exactly $p_1.n.(n - 1)/2$ constraints, and each constraint will have exactly $p_2.m^2$ conflicts. Lisp and Scheme versions of such a problem generator, and supporting search algorithms etc., are available via anonymous FTP at site ftp.cs.strath.ac.uk in directories local/pat/csp-lab/ for Lisp and local/pat/csp-lab.scm/ for Scheme.

range of values of p_2 where average search effort rapidly increases to a peak and then falls away, while at the same time the proportion of soluble problems drops to zero. That is, there is a phase transition [26, 21, 5].

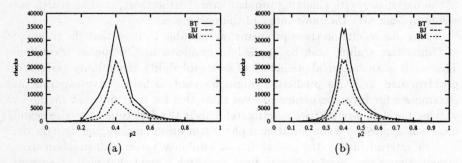

Fig. 1. Gaschnig's experiments on random 10-queens, and ours on $\langle 10, 10, 1.0 \rangle$

Probably the earliest report of the complexity peak in CSP'sis by Gaschnig [7]. One of the studies in his thesis was on random 10-queens. In the n-queens problem n non-attacking queens have to be placed on an $n \times n$ chess board, and in the random 10-queens problem a solution (or proof that none exists) has to be found for $\langle 10, 10, 1.0, p_2 \rangle$. Figure 1(a) shows a plot of the results from Gaschnig's experiments for random 10-queens. Constraint tightness p_2 is varied in steps of 0.1 (with the exception of the point $p_2 = 0.35$) and 150 problems are generated at each point. Three curves are plotted, one for chronological backtracking (BT), one for backjumping (BJ), and one for backmarking (BM) [11, 7, 6].[4] The y-axis is the average number of consistency checks and the x-axis is p_2. Figure 1(a) clearly shows a peak in average search effort at $p_2 = 0.4$ for the three algorithms.[5] In Figure 1(b) the experiments are repeated, but p_2 is varied in steps of 0.01, and this confirms that the peak in average search effort does indeed occur at $p_2 = 0.4$. Furthermore, 52% of the $\langle 10, 10, 1.0, 0.4 \rangle$ problems are soluble. It appears that Gaschnig failed to notice this phenomenon.

3 A Control Parameter for Binary CSP's

Given the random CSP $\langle n, m, p_1, p_2 \rangle$ the expected number of solutions is given by (1)

$$E(N) = m^n (1 - p_2)^{\frac{p_1 n(n-1)}{2}} \tag{1}$$

In [26] it is conjectured that average search effort will be greatest when an ensemble of problems have on average one solution, ie. $E(N) = 1$, and this

---

[4] Note that no variable or value ordering heuristics were used.

[5] Gaschnig referred to the CSP as a SAP (satisficing assignment problem) and L as the degree of a constraint (the fraction of distinct pair tests that have the value true, ie. $L = 1 - p_2$). The plot of 1(a) uses the data in Figure 4.4.3-1, page 301 of [7]. Gaschnig noted the existence of a sharp peak at $L \approx 0.6$, pages 179 and 180.

will correspond to the crossover point where half the problems are soluble. An equivalent theory was independently developed by Williams and Hogg [30]. For given values of n, m, and p_1 the critical value of constraint tightness p_{2crit}, where average search effort will be a maximum, may be predicted via (2)

$$p_{2crit} = 1 - m^{-2/((n-1)p_1)} \tag{2}$$

For example, using (2) we can predict the critical value of constraint tightness for $\langle 10, 10, 1.0 \rangle$, ie. Gaschnig's random 10-queens experiments, and that is $p_{2crit} = 0.400$, in full agreement with his observations.

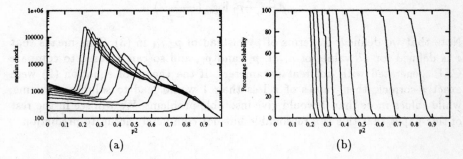

(a)   (b)

Fig. 2. $\langle 20, 10, p_1 \rangle$ (a) Median search effort against p_2, and (b) Percentage solubility against p_2

Figure 2 shows the median search effort for the CSP's $\langle 20, 10, p_1, p_2 \rangle$ (ie. 20 variables, uniform domain size of 10, p_1 varying from 0.1 to 1.0 in steps of 0.1, p_2 varying from 0.01 to 0.99 in steps of 0.01). In Figure 2(a) 10 contours are given, the leftmost is for $p_1 = 1.0$ and the rightmost for $p_1 = 0.1$. The x-axis is constraint tightness, p_2, varying in steps of 0.01, and the y-axis is the *log* of the median search effort. At each value of p_1 and p_2 one hundred problems were sampled using the algorithm forward checking with conflict-directed backjumping (FC-CBJ) [20] allied to the fail first heuristic (FF) [23, 12]. What we see is that as the density of the constraint graph increases (ie. p_1 increases) the critical value of constraint tightness falls (ie. p_2 falls). Figure 2(b) shows how the solubility of problems varies with p_1 and p_2. Again 10 contours are given, the leftmost for $p_1 = 1.0$ and the rightmost for $p_1 = 0.1$.

In some respects Figure 2 suggests that it might be difficult to compare CSP'sof different size (ie. varying n and m) or structure (ie. varying p_1 and p_2) because their graphs translate along the x-axis, changing shape as they go.[6] What we would like to find is some parameter that characterises CSP regardless of size or structure, ie. a *control parameter*. Control parameters have been identified for 3-SAT, namely $\frac{clauses}{variables}$, and in 3-COL the average degree γ [2]. We

---

[6] Although all the curves in Figure 2(a) have the same *signature*, at high values of p_1 they are more defined.

74

can derive a control parameter τ for CSP'sas follows. First, we rearrange (2) to get

$$\frac{n-1}{2}p_1 \log_m\left(\frac{1}{1-p_{2crit}}\right) = 1 \qquad (3)$$

This gives us a prediction for the location of the crossover point expressed by a function of the random generation parameters taking a certain *constant* value, and that function no longer has a first order dependency on n, ie. it does not have the exponential behaviour of (1). This immediately suggests that the LHS of (3), may be a suitable control parameter for CSP's. Accordingly, we *define* the parameter, which we call τ, by

$$\tau =_{def} \frac{n-1}{2}p_1 \log_m\left(\frac{1}{1-p_2}\right)$$

Note that we define τ in terms of p_2 instead of p_{2crit} in (3). This means that τ is defined for *all* values of n, m, p_1, and p_2, and so can be used to compare CSP'sgenerated with different parameters. If the theory of equation (2) were exactly correct, then values of τ less than 1 would lead to soluble problems, while values more than 1 would give insoluble problems. We will see in the rest of this paper that this is a reasonable but not completely accurate prediction.

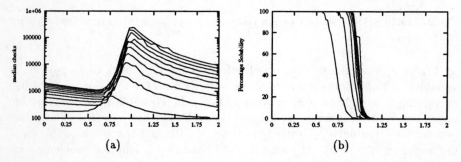

Fig. 3. $\langle 20, 10, p_1 \rangle$ (a) Median search effort against the control parameter τ, and (b) Percentage solubility against τ.

Figure 3 shows the same data as in Figure 2 but with τ on the x-axis. In Figure 3(a) the contours of median search effort peak when $0.75 \leq \tau \leq 1.0$, close to the expected value of the control parameter. However, for increasing p_1 the phase transition occurs more sharply and at values of τ nearer 1. That is, for denser constraint graphs, the prediction of Smith, Williams and Hogg for the location of the phase transition becomes more accurate.[7] Finally, it is clear that as p_1 increases towards 1, so the peak mean search effort increases considerably. Only the last of these points could have been seen clearly from the graphs as presented in Figure 2, even though in this case we have presented *less* data – we

---

[7] This change appears to be related to a decreasing variance in the number of solutions at the phase transition [27].

cut off values of p_2 where $\tau > 2.0$. These points were made in [21], but this had to be done by further analysis, and could not be read off directly from a simple plot as we did by looking at Figure 3.

We hope that our graphs argue for us the case that data should be presented with respect to the proposed parameter, τ. We show in the rest of the paper that there are further advantages in studying this parameter. Indeed we will be able to make detailed numerical predictions based on it.

4 Changing Number of Variables

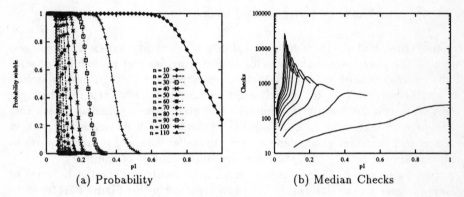

(a) Probability   (b) Median Checks

Fig. 4. $\langle n, 3, p_1, \frac{2}{9} \rangle$ plotted using p_1

A set of experiments was carried out to investigate the effect of increasing the number of variables, ie. n, on the parameter τ. In these experiments we vary the number of variables and the density of the constraint graph, while holding the domain size and tightness of constraints constant. We chose a domain size $m = 3$ and tightness of constraint $p_2 = \frac{2}{9}$, corresponding to the set of experiments reported in [5], and we will refer to them as $\langle n, 3, p_1, \frac{2}{9} \rangle$.[8] The search algorithm used for this set of experiments, and all subsequent experiments reported here, was FC-CBJ-FF, ie. forward checking with conflict-directed backjumping using the fail-first heuristic. A report on the implementation of this procedure is given in [18]. For each n from 10 to 110 in steps of 10 we tested problems from $p_1 = \frac{1}{n-1}$ to $p_1 = \frac{10}{n-1}$ in steps of $\frac{1}{5(n-1)}$. (An exception is $n = 10$ where the maximum value of p_1 is $\frac{9}{n-1}$.) These parameters are equivalent to varying the average degree of nodes in the constraint graph from 1 to 10 in steps of 0.2. For each n from 10 to 70 inclusive we tested 10,000 randomly generated problems at each value of p_1, while for n from 80 to 110 we tested 1,000 problems for each p_1.

---

[8] This corresponds to the experiments by Frost and Dechter with N and C varying, $K = 3$, and $T = \frac{2}{9}$. See Figure 1. in [5]. A problem with N variables and C constraints is exactly equivalent to a problem generated using our model and parameters $\langle N, 3, 2C/N(N-1), \frac{2}{9} \rangle$.

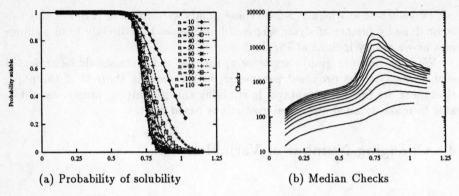

(a) Probability of solubility   (b) Median Checks

Fig. 5. $\langle n, 3, p_1, \frac{2}{9} \rangle$ plotted using control parameter τ

In Figure 4(a) we show how probability of solubility varies as n changes. Because the parameter that varies for each n is p_1, we plot probability of solubility (y-axis) against p_1 (x-axis). With increasing n, the phase transition occurs at smaller values of p_1, ie. the left most contour is for $n = 110$ and the right most contour is for $n = 10$. In Figure 4(b) we show how the median search cost changes with increasing n, on a logarithmic scale. As n increases the peak in median cost increases greatly and occurs at smaller values of p_1 and appears to coincide approximately with the transition in probability of solubility.

Just as we saw in §3, our data is much more easily understood in terms of the parameter τ than in terms of the raw parameter p_1. In Figure 5(a) we show the probability of solubility for each problem size tested, plotted against τ (x-axis). Our data covers the range of τ from 0.115 to 1.15. The phase transition in probability always starts at a value of τ slightly larger than 0.5. Comparison with equation (3) shows that this is considerably smaller than the value of 1 predicted by the theory of Smith, Williams and Hogg. Nevertheless, using their theory we have derived a parameter at a fixed value of which the phase transition seems to cluster. It is also clear that the sharpness of the phase transition tends to increase with increasing n. We show in §5 that this increasing sharpness can be characterised *precisely*.

Figure 5(b) plots median search cost against τ for each value of n tested. The peak in cost covers a similar range to the phase transition in solubility. However, as n increases, the peaks in median search cost become more sharply defined and appear at smaller values of τ.

5 Scaling of Probability

In this section we show that the probability of solubility for a given problem class scales in an astonishingly simple way. The same technique that we use has been used in other NP complete problem classes and so seems to be of very general validity. However, since the technique is borrowed from statistical physics we briefly review some analogies between phase transitions in physical and computational problems.

Similar phase transition phenomena occur in many physical systems [31]. For example, in a ferromagnet (a permanent magnet) a phase transition occurs at a critical temperature, the Curie temperature. Above this temperature, and in the absence of an external magnetic field, the ferromagnet has no magnetization. If, however, the ferromagnet is cooled then it becomes abruptly magnetized at the Curie temperature. Several other macroscopic properties like the magnetic susceptibility (the change in magnetization induced by an external field) also undergo a phase transition at the Curie temperature.

A simple model of a ferromagnet is the Ising model. This has N atoms arranged on a regular lattice. Each atom has a magnetic spin which can be either "up" or "down". The ferromagnet can therefore be in one of 2^N possible states. Magnetism is a short-range force promoting neighbouring spins to line up together. Correlations can, however, occur between more distant spins. At a high temperature, thermal fluctuations are large and spins are independent of each other. The ferromagnet therefore has no net magnetization. As the temperature is lowered towards the Curie temperature, spins become correlated over increasingly large distances. At the Curie temperature, spins are totally correlated – changing the spin of a single atom changes all other spins.

Several analogies can be made with binary CSP's. A CSP has n variables taking one of m values, so there are m^n possible variable-value pairs. Although interactions between variables are restricted to binary constraints, correlations can occur between the values of variables not directly connected via a binary constraint. Our control parameter, which is related to the expected number of solutions to the CSP, serves as a proxy for the temperature. If this parameter is small then, as there are many models, variables can take values largely independently of each other. As this parameter is increased, the values of variables become increasingly correlated. If there is only one expected model at the phase transition, the values of variables are totally correlated with each other.

Statistical mechanics describes the behaviour of a ferromagnet in the thermodynamic limit when the volume and number of atoms goes to infinity. For finite systems, a heuristical technique called "finite-size" scaling have been developed to model phase transition phenomena [1]. Finite-size scaling also appears to be useful for modelling the behaviour of the phase transition in a variety of combinatorial problems including propositional satisfiability [15, 16, 8, 9], and the traveling salesman problem [10]. Around the phase transition, finite-size scaling predicts that problems of all sizes are indistinguishable except for a change of scale. This would suggest that,

$$Prob(solution) = f(\frac{\tau - \tau_c}{\tau_c} \cdot N^{1/\nu}) \qquad (4)$$

where f is some fundamental function, τ is the control parameter, τ_c is the critical value of this parameter at the phase transition, and $N^{1/\nu}$ provides the change of scale. $\frac{\tau - \tau_c}{\tau_c}$ plays an analogous rôle to the reduced temperature, $\frac{T - T_c}{T_c}$ in physical systems.

If the prediction of (4) holds then there must be a "fixed point", a single value, τ_c of the control parameter at which all different problem sizes give the same percentage solubility, $f(0)$. This may appear not to be the case in Figure 5, except of course at 0 and 100% solubility. However, examining our data more closely in the region of high percentage solubility and interpolating between points on the plot where necessary, we did observe a fixed point.[9] We found very similar behaviour at $\tau = 0.625$, where all n gave probabilities in the range (0.974,0.982) except for $n = 10$ which gave 0.991. Taking sample sizes into account, all probabilities were within two standard deviations of an estimate for probability of solublility of 0.976 except for $n = 10$ and $n = 20$. We take 0.625 for the fixed point and thus for the critical value τ_c. It is interesting to note that this is considerably smaller than the value 1 predicted by (3). This is however consistent with observations in [21, 22, 27] that the prediction of theory seems to be less accurate in the case of sparse constraint graphs, such as these graphs are for $n > 20$ at the critical value.

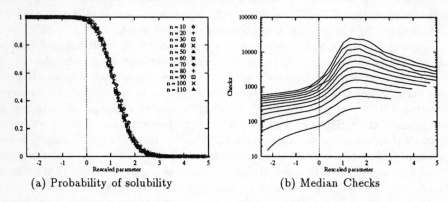

(a) Probability of solubility   (b) Median Checks

Fig. 6. $\langle n, 3, p_1, \frac{2}{9} \rangle$ Plotted with rescaled parameter τ_N

Having chosen τ_c, if (4) holds then there will be a single value ν to provide a fit to (4). Another way of seeing this is to rescale our data so that instead of plotting the control parameter τ, we define a rescaled parameter which depends on the control parameter and the problem size, N. We call this τ_N and in line with (4), using n for the problem size, define it by

$$\tau_N =_{def} \frac{\tau - \tau_c}{\tau_c} \cdot n^{1/\nu} \tag{5}$$

If the conjecture of (4) holds for the correct value of the exponent ν, we expect to see the probability curves for each n very closely aligned if we plot them against τ_N. If so, then the resulting curve gives us an empirical prediction of the function f. Having chosen τ_c, one can estimate ν empirically by assuming that

---

[9] Although the probability plots are clearly curved, locally straight line interpolation seems to be acceptable.

(5) holds. Then for a given probability of solubility, we can observe the values of τ that give that probability for different values of n. Say that for n_1 and n_2 we observe the same probability at τ_1 and τ_2. Then from (5) we expect that

$$\frac{\tau_1 - \tau_c}{\tau_c} \cdot n_1{}^{1/\nu} = \frac{\tau_2 - \tau_c}{\tau_c} \cdot n_2{}^{1/\nu}$$

Rearrangement gives us

$$\nu = \frac{\log(n_2/n_1)}{\log((\tau_1 - \tau_c)/(\tau_2 - \tau_c))} \tag{6}$$

We first estimated ν using this formula and the 50% solubility points, again using linear interpolation where necessary. The choice of 50% is because it is significantly different from the probability of 0.976 at the fixed point, giving sufficient range for the scaling to take effect. Using (6) for each of the 55 pairs of $10 \leq n_1 < n_2 \leq 110$, gave a median estimate for ν of 2.32 with a lower quartile estimate of 2.16 and an upper quartile of 2.51. Rescaling based on 25% solubility gives a very similar result, with a median estimate of 2.33. We thus choose $\nu = 2.3$. The fact that this choice gives a good fit to (4) is confirmed dramatically in Figure 6(a). (The vertical line represents $\tau_N = 0$.) Under this scaling all probability curves are almost identical, except the curve for $n = 10$ which rests slightly above the rest. This suggests that probability of solubility in this model can be described by finite size scaling with parameters $\tau_c = 0.625$, $\nu = 2.3$, and f as seen in Figure 6(a).

The implications of this result are significant. First, in this particular model it should help design future experiments. For example, should we wish a probability of solubility of 0.5, then we can interpolate the empirically predicted value of the rescaled parameter, which in this case occurs at $\tau_N \approx 1.45$, this being the median value interpolated from the 11 values of n. We can rearrange (5) to find what value of τ gives a given value of the τ_N parameter for a given n. This is given by

$$\tau = \tau_c \cdot (1 + \frac{\tau_N}{n^{1/\nu}})$$

This suggests that in an $\langle n, 3, p_1, \frac{2}{9} \rangle$ problem, 50% solubility occurs when $\tau \approx 0.625 \cdot (1 + 1.45/n^{\frac{1}{2.3}})$. We can unpack the definition of the control parameter to give the raw parameter p_1. In this problem class $p_1 = 2\tau/(n-1)\log_3(\frac{9}{7})$. We thus expect to see 50% solubility at

$$p_1 \approx (5.46 + 7.92/n^{\frac{1}{2.3}})/(n - 1)$$

Fortunately we are able to test this prediction with published data, as Frost and Dechter [5] report the number of constraints observed at 50% solubility for this model. The number of constraints C is $p_1 n(n-1)/2$, so we predict that for 50% solubility,

$$C \approx \frac{n}{2}(5.46 + 7.92/n^{\frac{1}{2.3}}) \tag{7}$$

At $n = 275$, the largest value of n reported in [5], 50% solubility occurs at 845 constraints. Equation (7) predicts 846 constraints. The largest n used to make the extrapolation was 110 variables. For smaller n, our prediction is not quite as accurate, but it is never more than 9 constraints out, which occurs at $n = 150$ with a prediction of 477 constraints compared to an observation of 468. Unlike data reported by [5], our data can also be used to interpolate for any other value of percentage solubility, and to extrapolate to any problem size.

More significant still is the likelihood that we will see similar kinds of finite scaling in other randomly generated CSP's. This is likely because once similar kinds of scaling were observed in SAT problems [15] they were observed in many different classes of SAT problems [16, 8]. We expect that similar kinds of predictions made from examining only small problems should be available for large problems in many different classes of CSP's.

6 Finite Size Scaling of Search Cost

The main feature of CSP problems that interests us is how hard it is to solve these problems. It is natural therefore to ask if changes in behaviour of search cost can be similarly corrected using finite size scaling? The remarkable answer is that this seems to be achievable using the *identical* rescaled parameter τ_N.

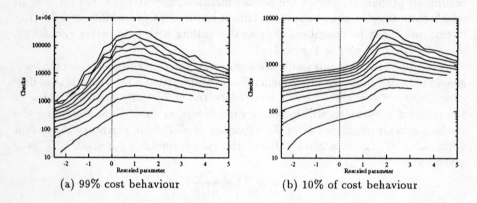

(a) 99% cost behaviour   (b) 10% of cost behaviour

Fig. 7. $\langle n, 3, p_1, \frac{2}{9} \rangle$ plotted using rescaled parameter τ_N

In Figure 6(b) we show what happens if we plot the same data previously plotted in Figure 5(b) against τ_N. Instead of the peaks in search cost occurring at different values of the parameter as seen previously, the peak appears to be at very similar values for each different n. This strongly suggests that the same finite size scaling that is effective for probability of solubility also models accurately the behaviour of search cost. Selman and Kirkpatrick have also shown that finite size scaling can be applied to search cost, in satisfiability problems [25]. It seems likely that it can be applied more generally.

It seems that not only median, but other measures of search cost scale in exactly the same way. Figure 7(a) shows how the 99 percentile behaves against

τ_N. That is, the graph plots at each point the cost that was exceeded by only 1% of problems. Just as with median behaviour, these contours line up very closely. Of course the 99 percentile is considerably worse than median behaviour, but we also note that the peaks in these curves occur at smaller values, peaking at $\tau_N \approx 0.8$ compared with $\tau_N \approx 1.6$ for median. Figure 7(b) shows behaviour of the 10 percentile, i.e. the cost exceeded by all but 10% of problems. Yet again the contours line up closely. This time the peaks are at a larger value, $\tau_N \approx 2$.

It is particularly significant that we were able to use exactly the rescaled parameter τ_N with the *same* parameters τ_c and ν as used in §5. The values $\tau_c = 0.625$ and $\nu = 2.3$ were chosen to model scaling of probability of solubility, and this is an entirely algorithm independent feature of a problem. Yet the same parameters also accurately describe the scaling of search cost in a particular algorithm, FC-CBJ-FF. This would suggest that the finite size scaling of search cost behaviour that we have observed may be algorithm independent. While the details of contours seen with different algorithms will vary, the scaling parameters may be identical in each case. Of course at this stage this is only speculation since we have only observed scaling with a single algorithm, but the implications for understanding the scaling of search cost are enormous.

7   Changing Domain Size

To test our conjecture that very similar kinds of scaling would be seen with different random CSP classes, we tested a completely different model by generating problems with parameters $\langle 10, m, 1.0, p_2 \rangle$. Notice that in §4 we fixed m and p_2 while varying n and p_1: we now fix n and p_1 while varying m and p_2. Since we have fixed $n = 10$ and $p_1 = 1$, all constraint graphs we consider are simply 10-cliques, while before we typically looked at sparse constraint graphs.

From this problem class, we tested problems for $m = 5$, 10, 15, 20, 30, 40, and 50. Except for $m = 5$, where p_2 can only vary in steps of $1/m^2 = 0.04$ we varied p_2 in steps of at most 0.01, covering at least a region of τ from 0.5 to 2. We tested 1000 problems at each value of p_2. Figure 8 shows how probability of solubility and median search effort varies with m. We give one contour in each figure for each m, plotted against p_2. As m increases, the phase transition occurs at larger values of p_2, and the peak in problem difficulty grows.

In §3 we proposed a control parameter τ for binary CSP's. If it is to be useful, it should aid comparison of our data for this problem class both with changing m and with our earlier data for $\langle n, 3, p_1, \frac{2}{9} \rangle$. This is confirmed by Figure 9 which shows our data replotted against the parameter τ. It can be seen that the probability phase transition and worst case median behaviour always occurs at similar values of τ. We observed a fixed point in probability of solubility at $\tau_c = 1.02$ where solubility was always 0.30 ± 0.01. This is much closer to the expected critical value of $\tau = 1$ than we saw in the previous problem class. Both the location of the fixed point τ_c and the probability of solubility at that point are significantly different from the values $\tau_c \approx 0.625$ and 0.976 solubility that we saw in $\langle n, 3, p_1, \frac{2}{9} \rangle$. However, just as in that class, both the probability transition and the peaks in median behaviour become sharper with increasing m.

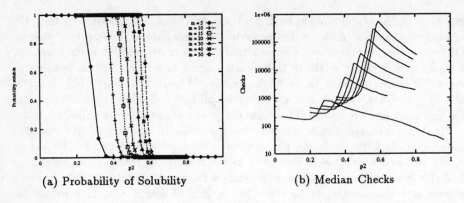

(a) Probability of Solubility

(b) Median Checks

Fig. 8. $\langle 10, m, 1.0, p_2 \rangle$ plotted using p_2

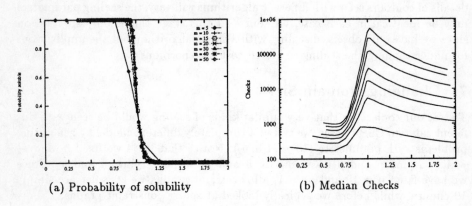

(a) Probability of solubility

(b) Median Checks

Fig. 9. $\langle 10, m, 1.0, p_2 \rangle$ plotted using control parameter τ

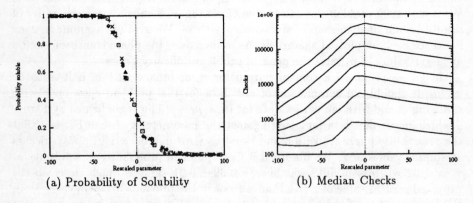

(a) Probability of Solubility

(b) Median Checks

Fig. 10. $\langle 10, m, 1.0, p_2 \rangle$ plotted using rescaled parameter τ_N

Finite size scaling may seem to be an inappropriate techique, because we are no longer changing the number of variables, n. However, we are certainly varying the problem size N by changing the number of values each variable takes, m. It is important to take account of m when considering the problem size. For example, to specify a *solution* to a binary CSP requires $n \log_2(m)$ bits, as the value each variable takes can be specified in $\log_2(m)$ bits. So, properly, this is the measure we should have used in §5 when considering finite size scaling. However, m was constant at 3 and so does not affect the parameter ν that we derived there. Here, we are varying m, so we redefine the rescaled control parameter as

$$\tau_N =_{def} \frac{\tau - \tau_c}{\tau_c} \cdot (n \log_2(m))^{1/\nu} \tag{8}$$

Having done this we can proceed as before, equation (6) becoming

$$\nu = \frac{\log(n_2 \log_2(m_2)/n_1 \log_2(m_1))}{\log((\tau_1 - \tau_c)/(\tau_2 - \tau_c))} \tag{9}$$

We estimated ν from equation (9) using the 50% probability point. We simply chose this as it is significantly different from the probability of 0.3 at the fixed point. The median estimate for ν was 0.63 with lower and upper quartiles of 0.55 and 0.68 respectively. These estimates of $\tau_c \approx 1.02$, $\nu \approx 0.63$ give an very good fit to a prediction of finite size scaling. This is seen in Figure 10 (a) which shows our data for probability of solubility plotted against the rescaled parameter τ_N.

Exactly as we saw in §6, we can use the identical parameters τ_c and ν to rescale contours of median cost. This is seen in Figure 10(b). As before the contours line up very closely, suggesting that finite size scaling can be applied to search cost in this problem class.

8 Changing Number of Variables and Domain Size

We have established that $n \log_2(m)$ provides a good measure of problem size when varying m. Finally, we ask if it also provides a good measure of problem size when varying n and m together? To test this, we return to our starting point in this paper, namely Gaschnig's random n-queens model. In the terms of §2 these are $\langle n, n, 1.0, p_2 \rangle$. Thus we vary both the number of variables and domain size, in this case keeping them identical. In our experiments we tested $n = 6, 8, 10, 12, 14,$ and 15. We varied p_2 in steps depending on n, and tested 1000 problems at each value of p_2. Figure 11 shows probability of solubility and median search cost against p_2, one contour being given for each n. As n increases the phase transition occurs at smaller values of p_2, and search cost increases.

Once again, the use of our control parameter enables us to compare our data as n increases, and to contrast our data for this problem class with data from previous problem classes. Figure 12 shows the same data replotted against the parameter τ. As in previous cases, we see the probability phase transition occurring over a similar range of τ, as do the peaks in median search cost. The curves become sharper with increasing n.

84

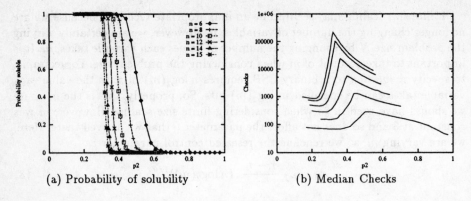

Fig. 11. $\langle n, n, 1.0, p_2 \rangle$ plotted using p_2

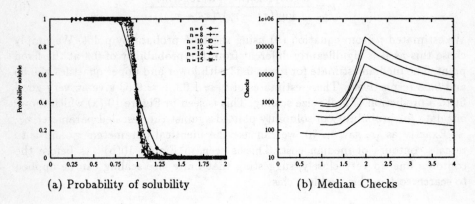

Fig. 12. $\langle n, n, 1.0, p_2 \rangle$ plotted using control parameter τ

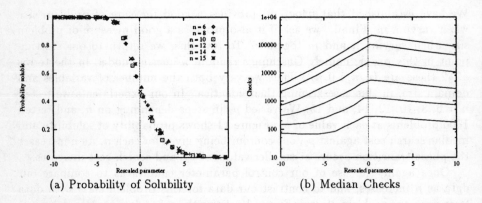

Fig. 13. $\langle n, n, 1.0, p_2 \rangle$ plotted using rescaled parameter τ_N

The fixed point in probability can be seen particularly clearly in Figure 12(a) at $\tau \approx 1$. Examining this data more closely we observed a fixed point in probability of solubility at $\tau_c = 0.99$ where it was always 0.51 ± 0.03. Note that the standard deviation at probability 0.5 in a sample of 1000 is 0.015, so all results were within 2 standard deviations of 0.51. As in §7, this is very close to the predicted critical value of $\tau = 1$, and again we note that we are looking at constraint graphs which are cliques. The critical value τ_c and the fixed point in probability of solubility are different to the previous two cases.

As in §7 we define the rescaled parameter τ_N by equation (8), using (9) to estimate ν. In this case we could not estimate ν using the 50% solubility point as it is too close to the fixed point probability of 0.51. Using 90% probability for estimation we obtained a median estimate of 1.02 with upper and lower quartiles of 0.78 and 1.09, while using 10% probability for estimation these values were 1.09, 1.03 and 1.45 respectively. Estimates of $\tau_c \approx 0.99$, $\nu \approx 1.0$ give an extremely good fit to a prediction of finite size scaling. This is seen in Figure 13 which shows our data for probability of solubility and median search cost plotted against the rescaled parameter τ_N. Again we point out the remarkable fact that finite size scaling can be applied to search cost using parameters derived solely from examination of probability data.

One of the standard becnchmark for CSP algorithms has been the n-queens, classified by Smith and Dyer as the problem class $\langle n, n, 1.0, (7n-2)/3n^2 \rangle$. Using the rescaled control parameter above τ_N for the n-queens problem, we see that as n increases τ_N decreases; for 10-queens $\tau = 0.5$ and $\tau_N = -32.3$, for 100-queens $\tau = 0.25$ and $\tau_N = -989$, and for 1000-queens $\tau = 0.17$ and $\tau_N = -16,500$. Therefore, as n increases the n-queens problem should become an easier instance of the class of problems $\langle n, n, 1.0 \rangle$. This is in full agreement with [27].

It is quite remarkable that the same kind of finite size scaling should be so accurate for three entirely different methods of varying problem size considered in this paper. We have varied n only in $\langle n, 3, p_1, \frac{2}{9} \rangle$, we have varied m only $\langle 10, m, 1.0, p_2 \rangle$, and we have varied n and m together in $\langle n, n, 1.0, p_2 \rangle$. In each case, the same equation (4) has been shown to be directly applicable, with only the parameters τ_c and ν and the function f varying between problem classes.

9 Conclusions

When presenting the results of experiments on random CSP'sgenerated from the model $\langle n, m, p_1, p_2 \rangle$ graphs have typically been plotted with either p_1 or p_2 on one axis. This tends to give a distorted view of the data, as contours rarely line up. We have proposed a control parameter τ for randomly generated CSP's, where τ characterises CSP'sregardless of size. The parameter τ is derived from a theory that predicts that on average the hardest problems will occur when the expected number of solutions $E(N) = 1$.

Analysing the empirical data for experiments with number of variables n varying, we observed a single value of τ where problems of different sizes have the same percentage solubility, ie. a fixed point τ_c. Finite-sized scaling was then applied to give a rescaled parameter τ_N. Replotting the data with respect to τ_N brought the picture into sharp focus; the solubility contours lie one on top of the other, and the peaks in median search effort coincide. Furthermore, we were able to use the rescaled parameter to estimate the critical number of constraints at the crossover point, ie. 50% solubility, for larger values of n, and these were in close agreements with results reported elsewhere; ie. we have given some evidence of the predictive power of τ_N. The same rescaling technique was then applied to data from experiments with domain size m varying, and experiments with domain size m and number of variables n varying together. In both cases problem size was taken as $N = n \log_2(m)$, and in both cases the data was again brought into sharp focus. This suggests that the technique may be quite general.

One of the surprises of this investigation is that a finite scaling of the control parameter based on the solubility of problems has carried over to a scaling of search cost. The rescaled parameter τ_N models the solubility of the problem (a problem-dependent property) *and* the behaviour of search cost (something that we might expect to be an algorithm-dependent property). The other surprise has been that finite size scaling has been so accurate for three very different classes of problems (ie. n varying, m varying, n and m varying together).

Obviously this work represents a starting point. In the future, we would like to know the detailed scaling parameters as problems are varied in more ways than we could consider in this paper. It would be very valuable if we could *size* problems with respect to graph density p_1 in order to rescale the data in §3. Finally, we note that the techniques applied in this paper effectively repair a theory which we showed to be inaccurate to a slight degree. However this repair is empirical. If our results could be used to help develop a more refined and accurate theory, it would be a pleasing validation of the empirical science of algorithms, as called for by Hooker [14].

References

1. M.N. Barber. Finite-size scaling. In *Phase Transitions and Critical Phenomena, Volume 8*, pages 145–266. Academic Press, 1983.
2. P. Cheeseman, B. Kanefsky, and W.M. Taylor. Where the really hard problems are. In *Proceedings of the 12th IJCAI*, pages 331–337. International Joint Conference on Artificial Intelligence, 1991.
3. R. Dechter, Constraint Networks, in *Encyclopedia of Artificial Intelligence*, Wiley, New York, 2nd ed., 276-286, 1992.
4. R. Dechter and I. Meiri, Experimental evaluation of preprocessing algorithms for constraint satisfaction problems, *Artif. Intell.* 68(2) (1994) 211-242.
5. D. Frost and R. Dechter, In search of the best search: an empirical evaluation, *Proceedings AAAI-94*, Seattle, WA (1994) 301-306.
6. J. Gaschnig, A general backtracking algorithm that eliminates most redundant tests, *Proceedings IJCAI-77*, Cambridge, MA (1977) 457.
7. J. Gaschnig, Performance measurement and analysis of certain search algorithms, Tech. Rept. CMU-CS-79-124, Carnegie-Mellon University, Pittsburgh, PA (1979).
8. I. P. Gent and T. Walsh. The SAT phase transition. In *Proceedings of ECAI-94*, pages 105–109, 1994.

9. I.P. Gent and T. Walsh. The satisfiability constraint gap. To appear in *Artificial Intelligence*.

10. I.P. Gent and T. Walsh. The TSP phase transition. Research report 95-178, Department of Computer Science, University of Strathclyde, 1995. Presented at First Workshop on AI and OR, Timberline, Oregon.

11. S.W. Golomb and L.D. Baumert, Backtrack programming. *JACM* **12** (1965) 516-524.

12. R.M. Haralick and G.L. Elliott, Increasing Tree Search Efficiency for Constraint Satisfaction Problems, *Artif. Intell.* **14** (1980) 263-313.

13. T. Hogg and C. Williams. The hardest constraint problems: A double phase transition. *Artificial Intelligence*, 69:359-377, 1994.

14. J.N. Hooker, Needed: An empirical science of algorithms, *Operations Research* **42** (2) (1994) 201-212.

15. S. Kirkpatrick, G. Györgyi, N. Tishby, and L. Troyansky. The statistical mechanics of k-satisfaction. In *Advances in Neural Information Processing Systems 6*, pages 439-446. Morgan Kaufmann, 1994.

16. S. Kirkpatrick and B. Selman. Critical behavior in the satisfiability of random boolean expressions. *Science*, 264:1297-1301, May 27 1994.

17. V. Kumar, Algorithms for constraint satisfaction problems: a survey, *AI magazine* 13(1) (1992) 32-44.

18. E. MacIntyre, Really hard problems, *Final Year Report for the B.Sc. degree* , Department of Computer Science, University of Strathclyde, Scotland, 1994.

19. D. Mitchell, B. Selman, and Hector Levesque. Hard and easy distributions of SAT problems. In *Proceedings, 10th National Conference on Artificial Intelligence*. AAAI Press/The MIT Press, pages 459-465, 1992.

20. P. Prosser. Hybrid algorithms for the constraint satisfaction problem. *Computational Intelligence*, 9:268-299, 1993.

21. P. Prosser. Binary constraint satisfaction problems: Some are harder than others. In *Proceedings of ECAI-94*, pages 95-99, 1994.

22. P. Prosser. An empirical study of phase transitions in binary constraint satisfaction problems. To appear in *Artificial Intelligence*.

23. P.W. Purdom, Search rearrangement backtracking and polynomial average time, *Artif. Intell.* **21** (1983) 117-133.

24. D. Sabin and E.C. Freuder, Contradicting conventional wisdom in constraint satisfaction, *Proceedings ECAI-94*, Amsterdam, The Netherlands (1994) 125-129.

25. B. Selman and S. Kirkpatrick. Critical behaviour in the computational cost of satisfiability testing. To appear in *Artificial Intelligence*.

26. B.M Smith. Phase transition and the mushy region in constraint satisfaction problems. In *Proceedings of ECAI-94*, pages 100-104, 1994.

27. B. M. Smith and M.E. Dyer. Locating the phase transition in binary constraint satisfaction problems. To appear in *Artificial Intelligence*.

28. E.P.K. Tsang, *Foundations of Constraint Satisfaction*, Academic Press, 1993.

29. E.P.K. Tsang, J. Borrett, and A.C.M. Kwan, An attempt to map the performance of a range of algorithm and heuristic combinations, In *Proceedings AISB-95*, pages 203-216, Ed. J. Hallam, IOS Press, Amsterdam, 1995.

30. C.P. Williams and T. Hogg. Exploiting the deep structure of constraint problems. *Artificial Intelligence*, 70:73-117, 1994.

31. K.G. Wilson. Problems in physics with many scales of length. *Scientific American*, 241:140-157, 1979.

Asynchronous Weak-commitment Search for Solving Distributed Constraint Satisfaction Problems

Makoto Yokoo

NTT Communication Science Laboratories
2-2 Hikaridai, Seika-cho, Soraku-gun, Kyoto 619-02, Japan
e-mail: yokoo@cslab.kecl.ntt.jp

Abstract. A distributed constraint satisfaction problem (Distributed CSP) is a CSP in which variables and constraints are distributed among multiple automated agents, and various application problems in Distributed Artificial Intelligence can be formalized as Distributed CSPs. We develop a new algorithm for solving Distributed CSPs called *asynchronous weak-commitment search*, which is inspired by the weak-commitment search algorithm for solving CSPs. This algorithm can revise a bad decision without an exhaustive search by changing the priority order of agents dynamically. Furthermore, agents can act asynchronously and concurrently based on their local knowledge without any global control, while guaranteeing the completeness of the algorithm.

The experimental results on various example problems show that this algorithm is by far more efficient than the asynchronous backtracking algorithm for solving Distributed CSPs, in which the priority order is static. The priority order represents a hierarchy of agent authority, i.e., the priority of decision making. Therefore, these results imply that a flexible agent organization, in which the hierarchical order is changed dynamically, actually performs better than an organization in which the hierarchical order is static and rigid.

1   Introduction

Distributed Artificial Intelligence (DAI) is a subfield of AI that is concerned with the interaction, especially the coordination among artificial automated agents. Since distributed computing environments are spreading very rapidly due to the advances in hardware and networking technologies, there are pressing needs for DAI techniques, thus DAI is becoming a very vital area in AI.

In [13], a distributed constraint satisfaction problem (Distributed CSP) is formalized as a CSP in which variables and constraints are distributed among multiple automated agents. It is well known that surprisingly a wide variety of AI problems can be formalized as CSPs. Similarly, various application problems in DAI which are concerned with finding a consistent combination of agent actions (e.g., distributed resource allocation problems [3], distributed scheduling problems [9], and multi-agent truth maintenance tasks [5]) can be formalized as Distributed CSPs. Therefore, we can consider a Distributed CSP as a general framework for DAI, and distributed algorithms for solving Distributed CSPs as an important infrastructure in DAI.

It must be noted that although algorithms for solving Distributed CSPs seem to be similar to parallel/distributed processing methods for solving CSPs [2, 14], research motivations are fundamentally different. The primary concern in parallel/distributed processing is the efficiency, and we can choose any type of parallel/distributed computer architecture for solving the given problem efficiently. In contrast, in a Distributed CSP, there already exists a situation where knowledge about the problem (i.e., variables and constraints) is distributed among automated agents. Therefore, the main research issue is how to reach a solution from this given situation. If all knowledge about the problem can be gathered into one agent, this agent can solve the problem alone using normal centralized constraint satisfaction algorithms. However, collecting all information about a problem requires certain communication costs, which could be prohibitively high. Furthermore, in some application problems, gathering all information to one agent is not desirable or impossible for security/privacy reasons. In such cases, multiple agents have to solve the problem without centralizing all information. The author has developed a basic algorithm for solving Distributed CSPs called *asynchronous backtracking* [13]. In this algorithm, agents act asynchronously and concurrently based on their local knowledge without any global control.

In this paper, we develop a new algorithm called *asynchronous weak-commitment search*, which is inspired by the weak-commitment search algorithm for solving CSPs [12]. The main characteristic of this algorithm is as follows.

- Agents can revise a bad decision without an exhaustive search by changing the priority order of agents dynamically.

In the asynchronous backtracking algorithm, the priority order of agents is determined, and an agent tries to find a value satisfying the constraints with the variables of higher priority agents. When an agent sets a variable value, the agent commits to the selected value strongly, i.e., the selected value will not be changed unless an exhaustive search is performed by lower priority agents. Therefore, in large-scale problems, a single mistake of value selection becomes fatal since doing such an exhaustive search is virtually impossible. This drawback is common to all backtracking algorithms. On the other hand, in the asynchronous weak-commitment search, when an agent can not find a value consistent with the higher priority agents, the priority order is changed so that the agent has the highest priority. As a result, when an agent makes a mistake in value selection, the priority of another agent becomes higher; thus the agent that made the mistake will not commit to the bad decision, and the selected value will be changed.

We will show that the asynchronous weak-commitment search algorithm can solve problems such as the distributed 1000-queens problem, the distributed graph-coloring problem, and the network resource allocation problem [8] that the asynchronous backtracking algorithm fails to solve within a reasonable amount of time. We can assume that the priority order represents a hierarchy of agent authority, i.e., the priority order of decision making. Therefore, these results imply that a flexible agent organization, in which the hierarchical order is changed dynamically, actually performs better than an organization in which the hierarchical order is static and rigid.

In the following, we briefly describe the definition of a Distributed CSP and the asynchronous backtracking algorithm (Section 2). Then, we show the basic ideas and details of the asynchronous weak-commitment search algorithm (Section 3), and empirical results which show the efficiency of the algorithm (Section 4). Finally, we examine the complexity of the algorithm (Section 5).

2 Distributed Constraint Satisfaction Problem and Asynchronous Backtracking

2.1 Formalization

A CSP consists of n variables $x_1, x_2, ..., x_n$, whose values are taken from finite, discrete domains $D_1, D_2, ..., D_n$ respectively, and a set of constraints on their values. A constraint is defined by a predicate. That is, the constraint $p_k(x_{k1}, ..., x_{kj})$ is a predicate which is defined on the Cartesian product $D_{k1} \times ... \times D_{kj}$. This predicate is true iff the value assignment of these variables satisfies this constraint. Solving a CSP is equivalent to finding an assignment of values to all variables such that all constraints are satisfied.

A Distributed CSP is a CSP in which variables and constraints are distributed among automated agents. We assume the following communication model.

- Agents communicate by sending messages. An agent can send messages to other agents iff the agent knows the addresses of the agents[1].
- The delay in delivering a message is finite, though random. For the transmission between any pair of agents, messages are received in the order in which they were sent.

Each agent has some variables and tries to determine their values. However, there exist inter-agent constraints, and the value assignment must satisfy these inter-agent constraints. Formally, there exist m agents $1, 2, ..., m$. Each variable x_j belongs to one agent i (this relation is represented as $belongs(x_j, i)$). Constraints are also distributed among agents. The fact that an agent k knows a constraint predicate p_l is represented as $known(p_l, k)$.

We say that a Distributed CSP is solved iff the following conditions are satisfied.

---

[1] This model does not necessarily mean that the physical communication network must be fully connected (i.e., a complete graph). Unlike most parallel/distributed algorithm studies, in which the topology of the physical communication network plays an important role, we assume the existence of a reliable underlying communication structure among agents and do not care about the implementation of the physical communication network. This is because our primary concern is the cooperation of intelligent agents, rather than solving CSPs by certain multi-processor architectures.

- $\forall\, i$, $\forall x_j$ where belongs(x_j, i), the value of x_j is assigned to d_j,
  and $\forall\, k$, $\forall p_l$ where known(p_l, k), p_l is true under the assignment $x_j = d_j$.

2.2 Asynchronous Backtracking

A basic algorithm for solving Distributed CSPs called *asynchronous backtrack-ing* is developed in [13]. In this algorithm, agents act asynchronously and concurrently, in contrast to traditional sequential backtracking techniques, while guaranteeing the completeness of the algorithm.

Without loss of generality, we make the following assumptions while describing our algorithms for simplicity. Relaxing these assumptions to general cases is relatively straightforward[2].

- Each agent has exactly one variable.
- All constraints are binary.
- There exists a constraint between any pair of agents.
- Each agent knows all constraint predicates relevant to its variable.

In the following, we use the same identifier x_i to represent an agent and its variable. We assume that each agent (and its variable) has a unique identifier.

In the asynchronous backtracking algorithm, each agent concurrently assigns a value to its variable, and sends the value to other agents. After that, agents wait for and respond to incoming messages. There are two kinds of messages: *ok?* messages to communicate the current value, and *nogood* messages to communicate information about constraint violations. The procedures executed at agent x_i by receiving an *ok?* message and a *nogood* message are described in Fig. 1. An overview of these procedures is given as follows.

- After receiving an *ok?* message, an agent records the values of other agents in its *agent_view*. The *agent_view* represents the state of the world recognized by this agent (Fig. 1 (i)).
- The priority order of variables/agents is determined by the alphabetical order of the identifiers, i.e., preceding variables/agents in the alphabetical order have higher priority. If the current value satisfies the constraints with higher priority agents in the *agent_view*, we say that the current value is consistent with the *agent_view*[3]. If the current value is not consistent with the *agent_view*, the agent selects a new value which is consistent with the *agent_view* (Fig. 1 (ii)).

---

[2] In [11], an algorithm in which each agent has multiple variables is described. If there exists no explicit constraint between two agents, there is a chance that an implicit constraint exists between them. In such a case, a new relation between these agents must be generated dynamically. The procedure for adding a new relation is described in [13]. The idea of making originally implicit constraints explicit can be found in the consistency algorithms for CSPs. For example, the adaptive consistency procedure [4] adds links to a constraint network while transforming the constraint network to a backtrack-free constraint network.

[3] More precisely, the agent must satisfy not only initially given constraint predicates, but also the new constraints communicated by *nogood* messages.

– If the agent can not find a value consistent with the *agent_view*, the agent sends *nogood* messages to higher priority agents (Fig. 1 (iii)). A *nogood* message contains a set of variable values that can not be a part of any final solution.

By using this algorithm, if a solution exists, agents will reach a stable state where all constraints are satisfied. If there exists no solution, an empty nogood will be found and the algorithm will terminate[4].

when received (ok?, (x_j, d_j)) **do** — (i)
   add (x_j, d_j) to *agent_view*;
   check_agent_view;
end do;

when received (nogood, x_j, *nogood*) **do**
   add *nogood* to *nogood_list*;
   check_agent_view;
end do;

procedure check_agent_view
   when *agent_view* and *current_value* are not consistent **do** — (ii)
     if no value in D_i is consistent with *agent_view* **then backtrack**; — (iii)
     else select $d \in D_i$ where *agent_view* and d are consistent;
       current_value $\leftarrow d$;
       send (ok?, (x_i, d)) to other agents; **end if**; **end do**;

procedure backtrack
   nogoods $\leftarrow \{V \mid V=$ inconsistent subset of *agent_view*$\}$;
   when an empty set is an element of *nogoods* **do**
     broadcast to other agents that there is no solution,
       terminate this algorithm; **end do**;
   for each $V \in$ *nogoods* **do**;
     select (x_j, d_j) where x_j has the lowest priority in V;
     send (nogood, x_i, V) to x_j;
   end do;

Fig. 1. Procedures for receiving messages (asynchronous backtracking)

---

[4] A set of variable values that is a *superset* of a nogood can not be a final solution. If an empty set becomes a nogood, it means that there is no solution, since any set is a superset of an empty set.

3 Asynchronous Weak-commitment Search

In this section, we briefly describe the weak-commitment search algorithm for solving CSPs [12], and describe how the asynchronous backtracking algorithm can be modified into the asynchronous weak-commitment search algorithm.

3.1 Weak-commitment Search Algorithm

In the weak-commitment search algorithm (Fig. 2), all variables have tentative initial values. We can execute this algorithm by calling **weak-commitment** $(\{(x_1, d_1), (x_2, d_2), \ldots, (x_n, d_n)\}, \{\})$, where d_i is the tentative initial value of x_i. In this algorithm, a consistent partial solution is constructed for a subset of variables, and this partial solution is extended by adding variables one by one until a complete solution is found. When a variable is added to the partial solution, its tentative initial value is revised so that the new value satisfies all constraints between the partial solution, and satisfies as many constraints between variables that are not included in the partial solution as possible. This value ordering heuristic is called the *min-conflict* heuristic [6]. The essential difference between this algorithm and the min-conflict backtracking [6] is the underlined part in Fig. 2. When there exists no value for one variable that satisfies all constraints between the partial solution, this algorithm abandons the whole partial solution, and starts constructing a new partial solution from scratch, using the current value assignment as new tentative initial values.

This algorithm records the abandoned partial solutions as new constraints, and avoids creating the same partial solution that has been created and abandoned before. Therefore, the completeness of the algorithm (always finds a solution if one exists, and terminates if no solution exists) is guaranteed. The experimental results on various example problems in [12] show that this algorithm is 3 to 10 times more efficient than the min-conflict backtracking [6] or the breakout algorithm [7].

3.2 Basic Ideas

The main characteristics of the weak-commitment search algorithm are as follows.

1. The algorithm uses the min-conflict heuristic as a value ordering heuristic.
2. It abandons the partial solution and restarts the search process if there exists no consistent value with the partial solution.

Introducing the first characteristic into the asynchronous backtracking algorithm is relatively straightforward. When selecting a variable value, if there exist multiple values consistent with the *agent_view* (those that satisfy all constraints with variables of higher priority agents), the agent prefers the value that minimizes the number of constraint violations with variables of lower priority agents.

In contrast, introducing the second characteristic into the asynchronous backtracking is not straightforward, since agents act concurrently and asynchronously,

```
procedure weak-commitment(left, partial-solution)
    when all variables in left satisfy all constraints do
        terminate the algorithm, current value assignment is a solution; end do
    (x_i, d) ← a variable and value pair in left that does not satisfy some constraint;
    values ← the list of x_i's values that are consistent with partial-solution;
    if values is an empty list;
        if partial-solution is an empty list
            then terminate the algorithm since there exists no solution;
            else record partial-solution as a new constraint (nogood);
                remove each element of partial-solution and add to left;
                call weak-commitment(left, partial-solution); end if;
        else value ← the value within values that minimizes
            the number of constraint violations with left;
        remove (x_i, d) from left;
        add (x_i, value) to partial-solution;
        call weak-commitment(left, partial-solution); end if;
```

Fig. 2. Weak-commitment search algorithm

and no agent has exact information about the partial solution. Furthermore, multiple agents may try to restart the search process simultaneously.

In the following, we show that the agents can commit to their decisions weakly by changing the priority order dynamically. We define the way of establishing the priority order by introducing *priority values*, and change the priority values by the following rules.

- For each variable/agent, a non-negative integer value representing the priority order of the variable/agent is defined. We call this value the *priority value*.
- The order is defined such that any variable/agent with a larger priority value has higher priority.
- If the priority values of multiple agents are the same, the order is determined by the alphabetical order of the identifiers.
- For each variable/agent, the initial priority value is 0.
- If there exists no consistent value for x_l, the priority value of x_l is changed to $k + 1$, where k is the largest priority value of other agents.

Furthermore, in the asynchronous backtracking algorithm, agents try to avoid situations previously found to be nogoods. However, due to the delay of messages, an *agent_view* of an agent can occasionally be a superset of a previously found nogood. In order to avoid reacting to unstable situations, and performing unnecessary changes of priority values, each agent performs the following procedure.

- Each agent records the nogoods that it has sent. When the *agent_view* is a superset of a nogood that it has already sent, the agent will not change the priority value and waits for the next message.

3.3 Details of Algorithm

In the asynchronous weak-commitment search, each agent concurrently assigns a value to its variable, and sends the value to other agents. After that, agents wait for and respond to incoming messages[5]. In Fig. 3, the procedures executed at agent x_i by receiving an *ok?* message and a *nogood* message are described[6]. The differences between these procedures and the procedures for the asynchronous backtracking algorithm are as follows.

- The priority value, as well as the current value, is communicated through the *ok?* message (Fig. 3 (i)).
- The priority order is determined by the communicated priority values. If the current value is not consistent with the *agent_view*, i.e., some constraint with variables of higher priority agents is not satisfied, the agent changes its value so that the value is consistent with the *agent_view*, and also the value minimizes the number of constraint violations with variables of lower priority agents (Fig. 3 (ii)).
- When x_i can not find a consistent value with its *agent_view*, x_i sends *nogood* messages to other agents, and increments its priority value. If x_i has already sent an identical nogood, x_i will not change the priority value and will wait for the next message (Fig. 3 (iii)).

3.4 Example of Algorithm Execution

We illustrate the execution of the algorithm using a distributed version of the well-known n-queens problem (where n=4). There exist four agents, each of which corresponds to a queen of each row. The goal of the agents is to find positions on a 4×4 chess board so that they do not threaten one another.

The initial values are shown in Fig. 4 (a). Agents communicate these values to one another. The values within parentheses represent the priority values. The initial priority values are 0. Since the priority values are equal, the priority order is determined by the alphabetical order of identifiers. Therefore, only the value of x_4 is not consistent with its *agent_view*, i.e., only x_4 is violating constraints with higher priority agents. Since there is no consistent value, agent x_4 sends *nogood* messages and increments its priority value. In this case, the value minimizing the number of constraint violations is 3, since it conflicts only with x_3. Therefore, x_4 selects 3 and sends *ok?* messages to other agents (Fig. 4 (b)). Then, x_3 tries to change its value. Since there is no consistent value, agent x_3 sends *nogood* messages, and increments its priority value. In this case, the value that minimizes

---

[5] Although the following algorithm is described in a way that an agent reacts to messages sequentially, an agent can handle multiple messages concurrently, i.e., the agent first revises *agent_view* and *nogood_list* according to the messages, and performs check_agent_view only once.

[6] It must be mentioned that the way to determine that agents as a whole have reached a stable state is not contained in this algorithm. To detect the stable state, agents must use distributed termination detection algorithms such as [1].

when received (ok?, $(x_j, d_j, priority)$) do — (i)
  add $(x_j, d_j, priority)$ to *agent_view*;
  check_agent_view;
end do;

when received (nogood, x_j, *nogood*) do
  add *nogood* to *nogood_list*;
  check_agent_view;
end do;

procedure check_agent_view
  when *agent_view* and *current_value* are not consistent do
    if no value in D_i is consistent with *agent_view* then backtrack;
    else select $d \in D_i$ where *agent_view* and d are consistent
      and d minimizes the number of constraint violations; — (ii)
      current_value $\leftarrow d$;
      send (ok?, $(x_i, d, current\_priority)$) to other agents; end if; end do;

procedure backtrack — (iii)
  nogoods $\leftarrow \{V \mid V =$ inconsistent subset of *agent_view*$\}$;
  when an empty set is an element of *nogoods* do
    broadcast to other agents that there is no solution,
      terminate this algorithm; end do;
  when no element of *nogoods* is included in *nogood_sent* do
    for each $V \in$ *nogoods* do;
      add V to *nogood_sent*
      for each (x_j, d_j) in V do;
        send (nogood, x_i, V) to x_j; end do; end do;
    $p_{max} \leftarrow max_{(x_j, d_j, p_j) \in agent\_view}(p_j)$;
    current_priority $\leftarrow 1 + p_{max}$;
    select $d \in D_i$ where d minimizes the number of constraint violations;
    current_value $\leftarrow d$;
    send (ok?, $(x_i, d, current\_priority)$) to other agents; end do;

Fig. 3. Procedures for receiving messages (asynchronous weak-commitment search)

the number of constraint violations is 1 or 2. In this example, x_3 selects 1 and sends *ok?* messages to other agents (Fig. 4 (c)). After that, x_1 changes its value to 2, and a solution is obtained (Fig. 4 (d)).

In the distributed 4-queens problem, there exists no solution when x_1's value is 1. We can see that a bad decision can be revised without an exhaustive search in the asynchronous weak-commitment search.

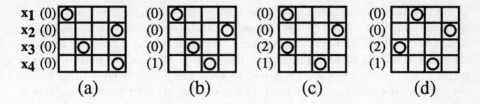

x_1 (0)
x_2 (0)
x_3 (0)
x_4 (0)

(0)
(0)
(0)
(1)

(0)
(0)
(2)
(1)

(0)
(0)
(2)
(1)

(a)   (b)   (c)   (d)

Fig. 4. Example of algorithm execution

3.5 Algorithm Completeness

The priority values are changed if and only if a new nogood is found[7]. Since the number of possible nogoods is finite, the priority values can not be changed infinitely. Therefore, after a certain time point, the priority values will be stable. Then, we show that the situations described below will not occur when the priority values are stable.

(i) There exist agents that do not satisfy some constraints, and all agents are waiting for incoming messages.

(ii) Messages are repeatedly sent/received, and the algorithm will not reach a stable state (infinite processing loop).

If situation (i) occurs, there exist at least two agents that do not satisfy the constraint between them. Let us assume that the agent ranking k-th in the priority order does not satisfy the constraint between the agent ranking j-th (where $j < k$), and all agents ranking higher than k-th satisfy all constraints within them. The only case that the k-th agent waits for incoming messages even though the agent does not satisfy the constraint between the j-th agent is that the k-th agent has sent nogood messages to higher priority agents. This fact contradicts the assumption that higher priority agents satisfy constraints within them. Therefore, situation (i) will not occur.

Also, if the priority values are stable, the asynchronous weak-commitment search algorithm is basically identical to the asynchronous backtracking algorithm. Since the asynchronous backtracking is guaranteed not to fall into an infinite processing loop [13], situation (ii) will not occur.

From the fact that situation (i) or (ii) will not occur, we can guarantee that the asynchronous weak-commitment search algorithm will always find a solution, or find the fact that there exists no solution.

4 Evaluations

In this section, we evaluate the efficiency of algorithms by discrete event simulation, where each agent maintains its own simulated clock. An agent's time

---

[7] To be exact, different agents may find an identical nogood simultaneously.

is incremented by one simulated time unit whenever it performs one cycle of computation. One cycle consists of reading all incoming messages, performing local computation, and sending messages. We assume that a message issued at time t is available to the recipient at time $t + 1$. We analyze performance in terms of the amount of cycles required to solve the problem. Given this model, we compare the following three kinds of algorithms: (a) asynchronous backtracking, in which a variable value is selected randomly from consistent values, and the priority order is determined by alphabetical order, (b) *min-conflict* only, in which the min-conflict heuristic is introduced into the asynchronous backtracking, but the priority order is statically determined by alphabetical order, and (c) asynchronous weak-commitment search[8].

We first applied these three algorithms to the distributed n-queens problem described in the previous section, varying n from 10 to 1000. The results are summarized in Table 1. For each n, we generated 100 problems, each of which had different randomly generated initial values, and averaged the results for these problems. For each problem, in order to conduct the experiments in a reasonable amount of time, we set the bound for the number of cycles to 1000, and terminated the algorithm if this limit was exceeded; we counted the result as 1000. The ratio of problems completed successfully to the total number of problems is also described in Table 1.

Table 1. Required cycles for distributed n-queens problem

n	asynchronous backtracking ratio	cycles	min-conflict only ratio	cycles	asynchronous weak-commitment ratio	cycles
10	100%	105.4	100%	102.6	100%	41.5
50	50%	662.7	56%	623.0	100%	59.1
100	14%	931.4	30%	851.3	100%	50.8
1000	0%	—	16%	891.8	100%	29.6

The second example problem is the distributed graph-coloring problem. The distributed graph-coloring problem is a graph-coloring problem, in which each node corresponds to an agent. The graph-coloring problem involves painting nodes in a graph by k different colors so that any two nodes connected by an arc do not have the same color. We randomly generate a problem with n nodes/agents and m arcs by the method described in [6], so that the graph is connected and the problem has a solution. We evaluate the problem $n = 60, 90,$

---

[8] The amounts of local computation performed in each cycle for (b) and (c) are equivalent. The amounts of local computation for (a) can be smaller since it does not use the min-conflict heuristic, but for the lowest priority agent, the amounts of local computation of these algorithms are equivalent.

and 120, where $m = n \times 2$ and $k=3$. This parameter setting corresponds to the "sparse" problems for which poor performance of the min-conflict heuristic is reported in [6]. We generate 10 different problems, and for each problem, 10 trials with different initial values are performed (100 trials in all). As in the distributed n-queens problem, the initial values are set randomly. The results are summarized in Table 2.

Table 2. Required cycles for distributed graph-coloring problem

n	asynchronous backtracking		min-conflict only		asynchronous weak-commitment	
	ratio	cycles	ratio	cycles	ratio	cycles
60	13%	917.4	12%	937.8	100%	59.4
90	0%	—	2%	994.5	100%	70.1
120	0%	—	0%	—	100%	106.4

Then, in order to examine the applicability of the asynchronous weak-commitment search to real-life problems rather than artificial random problems, we applied these algorithms to the distributed resource allocation problem in a communication network described in [8]. In this problem, there exist requests for allocating circuits between switching nodes of NTT's communication network in Japan (Fig. 5). For each request, there exists an agent assigned to handle it, and candidates for circuits are given. The goal is to find a set of circuits that satisfies the resource constraints. We can formalize this problem as a Distributed CSP by representing each request as a variable and each candidate as a possible value for the variable. We generated problems based on data from the 400 Mbps backbone network extracted from the network configuration management database developed in NTT Optical Network Systems Laboratories [10]. In each problem, there exist 10 circuit allocation requests, and for each request, 50 candidates are given. These candidates represent reasonably short circuits for satisfying the request. The goal is to find the consistent combination of the candidates, i.e., different candidates do not require the same resources.

We generated 10 different sets of randomly generated initial values for 10 different problems (100 trials in all), and averaged the results. As in the previous problems, the limit for the required number of cycles was set to 1000. The results are summarized in Table 3.

We can see the following facts from these results.

- The asynchronous weak-commitment search algorithm can solve problems that can not be solved within a reasonable amount of computation time by other algorithms. By using only the min-conflict heuristic, although the algorithm can obtain a certain amount of speed-up, it fails to solve many problem instances.

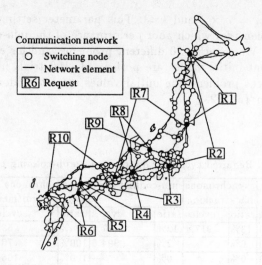

Fig. 5. Example of network resource allocation problem

– When the priority order is static, the efficiency of the algorithm is highly dependent on the selection of initial values, and the distribution of required cycles is quite large. For example, in the network resource allocation problem, when only the min-conflict heuristic is used, the average number of required cycles for 63 successfully completed trials is only 92.8. However, the number of required cycles for 37 failed trials is more than 1000. When the initial values of higher priority agents are good, the solution can easily be found. If some of these values are bad, however, an exhaustive search is required to revise these values; this tends to make the number of required cycles exceed the limit. On the other hand, in the asynchronous weak-commitment search, the initial values are less critical, and a solution can be found even if the initial values are far from the final solution, since the variable values gradually come close to the final solution.

– We can assume that the priority order represents a hierarchy of agent authority, i.e., the priority order of decision making. If this hierarchy is static, the misjudgments (bad value selections) of agents with higher priority are fatal to all agents. On the other hand, when the priority order is changed dynamically and variable values are selected cooperatively, the misjudgments of specific agents do not have fatal effects, since bad decisions will be weeded out, and only good decisions can survive. These results are intuitively natural since they imply that a flexible agent organization performs better than a static and rigid organization.

Table 3. Required cycles for network resource allocation problem

asynchronous backtracking		min-conflict only		asynchronous weak-commitment	
ratio	cycles	ratio	cycles	ratio	cycles
32%	984.8	63%	428.4	100%	17.3

5 Discussions

Since constraint satisfaction is NP-complete in general, the worst-case time complexity of the asynchronous weak-commitment search becomes exponential in the number of variables n. The worst-case space complexity for each agent is determined by the number of recorded nogoods, which is also exponential in n. This result seems inevitable since this algorithm changes the search order flexibly while guaranteeing its completeness.

We can restrict the number of recorded nogoods, i.e., each agent records only a fixed number of the most recently found nogoods. In this case, however, the theoretical completeness can not be guaranteed (the algorithm may fall into an infinite processing loop in which agents repeatedly find identical nogoods). Yet, when the number of recorded nogoods is reasonably large, such an infinite processing loop rarely occurs. Actually, the asynchronous weak-commitment search algorithm can still find solutions for all example problems when the number of recorded nogoods is restricted to 10.

6 Conclusions

In this paper, the asynchronous weak-commitment search algorithm for solving Distributed CSPs is developed. In this algorithm, agents act asynchronously and concurrently based on their local knowledge without any global control, while guaranteeing the completeness of the algorithm. This algorithm can revise a bad decision without an exhaustive search by changing the priority order of agents dynamically. The experimental results indicate that this algorithm can solve problems such as the distributed 1000-queens problem, the distributed graph-coloring problem, and the network resource allocation problem, which can not be solved by asynchronous backtracking algorithm within a reasonable amount of time. These results imply that a flexible agent organization performs better than a static and rigid organization.

Our future work includes showing the effectiveness of the asynchronous weak-commitment search algorithm in more practical application problems, and examining ways of introducing other heuristics (e.g., forward-checking) into this algorithm, and developing iterative improvement algorithms such as the breakout algorithm [7] for solving Distributed CSPs.

Acknowledgments

The author wish to thank N. Fujii and I. Yoda for providing the network configuration management database, and Y. Nishibe for providing the example problems.

References

1. Chandy, K. and Lamport, L.: Distributed Snapshots: Determining Global States of Distributed Systems, *ACM Trans. on Computer Systems*, Vol. 3, No. 1, (1985) 63–75

2. Collin, Z., Dechter, R., and Katz, S.: On the Feasibility of Distributed Constraint Satisfaction, *Proceedings of the Twelfth International Joint Conference on Artificial Intelligence* (1991) 318–324

3. Conry, S. E., Kuwabara, K., Lesser, V. R., and Meyer, R. A.: Multistage Negotiation for Distributed Constraint Satisfaction, *IEEE Transactions on Systems, Man and Cybernetics*, Vol. 21, No. 6, (1991) 1462–1477

4. Dechter, R. and Pearl, J.: Network-based Heuristics for Constraint Satisfaction Problems, *Artificial Intelligence*, Vol. 34, No. 1, (1988) 1–38

5. Huhns, M. N. and Bridgeland, D. M.: Multiagent Truth Maintenance, *IEEE Transactions on Systems, Man and Cybernetics*, Vol. 21, No. 6, (1991) 1437–1445

6. Minton, S., Johnston, M. D., Philips, A. B., and Laird, P.: Minimizing conflicts: a heuristic repair method for constraint satisfaction and scheduling problems, *Artificial Intelligence*, Vol. 58, No. 1–3, (1992) 161–205

7. Morris, P.: The Breakout Method for Escaping From Local Minima, *Proceedings of the Eleventh National Conference on Artificial Intelligence* (1993) 40–45

8. Nishibe, Y., Kuwabara, K., Ishida, T., and Yokoo, M.: Speed-Up of Distributed Constraint Satisfaction and Its Application to Communication Network Path Assignments, *Systems and Computers in Japan*, Vol. 25, No. 12, (1994) 54 – 67

9. Sycara, K. P., Roth, S., Sadeh, N., and Fox, M.: Distributed Constrained Heuristic Search, *IEEE Transactions on Systems, Man and Cybernetics*, Vol. 21, No. 6, (1991) 1446–1461

10. Yamaguchi, H., Fujii, H., Yamanaka, Y., and Yoda, I.: Network Configuration Management Database, *NTT R & D*, Vol. 38, No. 12, (1989) 1509–1518

11. Yokoo, M.: Dynamic Variable/Value Ordering Heuristics for Solving Large-Scale Distributed Constraint Satisfaction Problems, *12th International Workshop on Distributed Artificial Intelligence* (1993) 407–422

12. Yokoo, M.: Weak-commitment Search for Solving Constraint Satisfaction Problems, *Proceedings of the Twelfth National Conference on Artificial Intelligence* (1994) 313–318

13. Yokoo, M., Durfee, E. H., Ishida, T., and Kuwabara, K.: Distributed Constraint Satisfaction for Formalizing Distributed Problem Solving, *Proceedings of the Twelfth IEEE International Conference on Distributed Computing Systems* (1992) 614–621

14. Zhang, Y. and Mackworth, A.: Parallel and distributed algorithms for finite constraint satisfaction problems, *Proceedings of the Third IEEE Symposium on Parallel and Distributed Processing* (1991) 394–397

Optimization-based Heuristics for
Maximal Constraint Satisfaction*

Javier Larrosa and Pedro Meseguer[†]

Universitat Politècnica de Catalunya
Dep. Llenguatges i Sistemes Informàtics
Pau Gargallo 5, 08028 Barcelona, SPAIN
E-mail: {larrosa,meseguer}@lsi.upc.es

Abstract. We present a new heuristic approach for maximal constraint satisfaction of overconstrained problems (MAX-CSP). This approach is based on a formulation of CSP as an optimization problem presented in a previous paper [Meseguer and Larrosa, 95], which has given good results on some classes of solvable CSP. For MAX-CSP, we have developed two heuristics for dynamic variable and value ordering, called highest weight and lowest support respectively, to be used inside the extended forward checking algorithm (P-EFC3). These heuristics are expensive to compute, so we have developed an incremental updating formula to avoid redundant computation. We have tested both heuristics with the P-EFC3 algorithm on several instances of two classes of random CSP. Experimental results show that both heuristics outperform previously used heuristics based on inconsistency counts. In fact, the lowest support heuristic appears as a kind of generalization of these previous heuristics, including extra information about future variables.

1 Introduction

Constraint satisfaction problems (CSP) consider the assignment of values to variables under a set of constraints. When a total assignment satisfying every constraint exists, this assignment is a solution and the problem is said to be solvable. If such an assignment does not exist, the problem is said to be overconstrained or unsolvable, and the best one can obtain is a total assignment satisfying as many constraints as possible. This assignment is called a partial solution satisfying a maximal number of

---

* This research has been supported by the Spanish CICYT under the project #TAP93-0451.

† Current address: Institut d'Investigació en Intel.ligència Artificial, CSIC, Campus UAB, 08193 Bellaterra, SPAIN.

constraints. This specific problem is called the maximal constraint satisfaction problem (usually abbreviated as MAX-CSP), and it is of interest in several areas of application [Fox, 87], [Feldman and Golumbic, 90], [Bakker *et al.*, 93].

The purpose of this paper is to show the applicability of a new heuristic approach to MAX-CSP. This approach is based on an optimization formulation to solve CSP contained in a previous paper [Meseguer and Larrosa, 95], where we formulated the problem of discrete constraint satisfaction as an optimization problem. Specifically, we provided a way to construct, for any binary and discrete CSP, a continuous function A(P) whose global maximum corresponds to the best solution for the CSP. By the best solution we mean either (i) a global solution satisfying every constraint, if the problem is solvable, or (ii) a partial solution satisfying a maximal number of constraints, if the problem is overconstrained. Therefore, the best solution for any CSP can be obtained constructing the function $A(P)$ and computing its global maximum using any kind of standard optimization techniques. Global optimization techniques present several drawbacks: their applicability depends on the kind of function to optimize and they require significant computational resources. On the other hand, local optimization methods can easily compute a maximum but there is no guarantee that it will be a global one. To circumvent all these difficulties, we developed heuristics for variable and value selection which use information from the $A(P)$ function. Using these heuristics in a forward checking algorithm, we obtained good results for several classes of solvable CSP.

Following the same approach for MAX-CSP, in this paper we present two heuristics called *highest weight* and *lowest support*, to be used inside the extended forward checking algorithm (P-EFC3) [Freuder and Wallace, 92]. These heuristics provide dynamic variable and value ordering. They are quite well informed, but expensive to compute. To overcome this drawback, we have developed an incremental updating formula which avoids the repetition of redundant operations. These heuristics with P-EFC3 outperform previously used heuristics based on inconsistency counts on several classes of overconstrained CSP.

The paper is organized as follows. In section 2 we provide a brief summary of previous work on MAX-CSP. We outline our formulation of CSP as optimization problems in section 3. Based on this formulation, we describe the highest weight and lowest support heuristics in section 4. The incremental heuristic computation appears in section 5. Experimental results of the execution of P-EFC3 with and without these heuristics appear in section 6, and we discuss these results in section 7. Finally, section 8 contains the conclusions of this work.

2 Related Work

The simplest algorithm for maximal constraint satisfaction follows a *branch and bound* scheme. This algorithm performs a systematic traversal on the search tree generated by the problem, associating with every —partial or total— assignment of variables a cost function, which is the number of violated constraints caused by this assignment. This cost function is usually called the *distance* from a global solution, that is, the solution satisfying every constraint which does not exist for overconstrained CSP. Branch and bound keeps track of the best solution obtained so far, which is the total assignment with minimal distance in the explored part of the search tree. When a partial solution has a distance greater than or equal to the distance of the current best solution, this line of search is abandoned because it cannot lead to a better solution than the current one. In this way, the distance of the current best solution is used as an *upper bound* of the allowable cost, while the distance of the current partial solution is a *lower bound* of the cost for any solution including this partial solution.

The basic branch and bound can be enhanced with more sophisticated strategies based on previous work on solvable CSP. *Prospective* algorithms look ahead to compute some form of local consistency among future variables. The most common prospective algorithm is *forward checking*, which evaluates the impact of the current partial solution on future variables, recording for each possible value the number of violated constraints with the current partial solution (inconsistency-counts). This improves the lower bound of the current partial solution. *Retrospective* algorithms remember previous actions in order to avoid repeating them in the future and, in this way, they can save redundant constraint checks. The most familiar retrospective algorithms are *backjumping* and *backmarking*. All these algorithms guarantee that the optimal solution will be found. For a detailed description, see [Freuder and Wallace, 92].

Several heuristics for variable and value selection have been developed. For static variable ordering, the most promising heuristic orders variables by decreasing width. This heuristic is enhanced when combined with a second heuristic to break ties, such as minimum domain size, maximum degree, or largest mean ACC (arc consistency counts) in its domain. These combinations are called conjunctive width heuristics [Wallace and Freuder, 93]. For static value ordering, values are ordered by increasing ACC. Regarding dynamic variable ordering in forward checking, variables are ordered either by the largest mean of inconsistency counts in their domains or by minimum domain size. Dynamic value ordering considers values by increasing inconsistency counts [Freuder and Wallace, 92].

Finally, a strategy to improve the computation of the lower bound for the current partial solution with fixed variable order is proposed in [Wallace, 94]. In a preprocessing step, DAC (directed arc consistency counts) are computed for each value following the fixed order. DAC counts are added to other counts (distance and inconsistency counts) to compute a better lower bound for the current partial solution.

3 An Optimization Approach to CSP

A discrete binary CSP is defined by a finite set of variables $\{X_i\}$ taking values on discrete and finite domains $\{D_i\}$ under a set of binary constraints $\{R_{ij}\}$. A constraint R_{ij} is a logical expression which evaluates to true or false on each pair of potential values for X_i and X_j. The number of variables is n and, without loss of generality, we will assume a common domain D for all the variables, m being its cardinality. A global solution of the CSP is an assignment of values to variables satisfying every constraint. If no solution exists the CSP is overconstrained; in this case we are interested in finding solutions satisfying a maximal number of constraints. This problem is usually referred as MAX-CSP.

A solvable or overconstrained CSP can be formulated as an optimization problem as follows. Given a CSP, we define a *weighted labeling* P as a vector of the space K defined by,

$$K = \{ \ P \in R^{nm} \mid P = [p_1,..., p_n]; \ p_i = [p_i[\lambda_1],...,p_i[\lambda_m]] \in R^m;$$

$$0 \leq p_i[\lambda_k] \leq 1 \ ; \ \sum_{k=1}^{m} p_i[\lambda_k] = 1, \ i=1,...,n \ \}$$

P contains n components p_i, each corresponding to a variable X_i. A component p_i is a vector of m components, each corresponding to a different value $\lambda_k \in D$. A single component $p_i[\lambda_k]$ is the weight associated with the value λ_k of variable X_i. A weight can take a value between 0 and 1, and the sum of the weights associated with the values of a variable must be 1. An *unambiguous labeling* is a weighted labeling for which the condition $0 \leq p_i[\lambda_k] \leq 1$ is substituted by $p_i[\lambda_k] \in \{0,1\}$. The space of unambiguous labelings is denoted by K^*. There is a bijection between the set of the total assignments of values to variables and the set of unambiguous labelings: for every variable X_i assigned to a value λ_k the corresponding labeling takes $p_i[\lambda_k]=1$ and $p_i[\lambda]=0$ for all $\lambda \in D$, $\lambda \neq \lambda_k$, and vice versa. For this reason, we will use unambiguous labelings and total assignments as interchangeable. An *ambiguous labeling* is a weighted labeling that is not unambiguous. We define the set $\{r_{ij}\}$ of compatibilities as follows,

$$r_{ij}(\lambda_k,\lambda_l) = 1 \qquad \text{if } R_{ij}(\lambda_k,\lambda_l) = \text{true}$$
$$r_{ij}(\lambda_k,\lambda_l) = -1 \qquad \text{if } R_{ij}(\lambda_k,\lambda_l) = \text{false}$$

Compatibility $r_{ij}(\lambda_k,\lambda_l)$ exists for every pair of variables (X_i, X_j). If X_i does not constrain X_j, $r_{ij}(\lambda_k,\lambda_l) = 1$ for all $\lambda_k, \lambda_l \in D$.

Given a labeling P, the *support* that a value λ_k at variable X_i obtains from variable X_j is,

$$s_i(\lambda_k,X_j) = \sum_{l=1}^{m} r_{ij}(\lambda_k,\lambda_l)p_j[\lambda_l] \tag{1}$$

and the support that a value λ_k at variable X_i obtains from the whole labeling P is,

$$s_i(\lambda_k, P) = \sum_{j=1}^{n} \sum_{l=1}^{m} r_{ij}(\lambda_k, \lambda_l) p_j[\lambda_l]$$

We define the *average local consistency function* $A(P)$ as follows,

$$A(P) = \sum_{i=1}^{n} \sum_{k=1}^{m} \sum_{j=1}^{n} \sum_{l=1}^{m} r_{ij}(\lambda_k, \lambda_l) \, p_i[\lambda_k] \, p_j[\lambda_l] \tag{2}$$

The following result allows us to formulate a CSP as an optimization problem:

Theorem [Meseguer and Larrosa, 95]: Let us consider a binary CSP and let P_0 be an unambiguous labeling. P_0 violates a minimal number of constraints if and only if P_0 is a global maximum of $A(P)$.

This theorem gives a necessary and sufficient condition for the best possible solution one can compute for a CSP: it must be a global maximum of $A(P)$. By best possible solution we mean either (i) a global solution satisfying every constraint, if the problem is solvable, or (ii) an assignment satisfying a maximal number of constraints, if the problem is overconstrained. The previous theorem is restricted to unambiguous labelings; however, maximizing $A(P)$ we can find a global maximum P_0 which is an ambiguous labeling. In this case, there exists a theorem [Sastry and Thathachar, 94] which assures the existence of an unambiguous labeling P_1 such that $A(P_0) = A(P_1)$, that is, P_1 is also a global maximum and it is unambiguous.

The previous theorem allows us to formulate any binary CSP (no matter whether it is solvable or overconstrained) as an optimization problem, and to solve it by standard optimization methods. However, the theorem needs to compute the global maximum of $A(P)$, which is not an easy task for continuous non-convex functions (the case of $A(P)$ in general). There is no standard approach to global optimization: different global optimization methods exist [Horst and Tuy, 93], their applicability depends on specific features of the function to be optimized and they require significant computational resources. Without discarding the possibility of computing the global maximum of $A(P)$ by global optimization methods, which requires further investigation, we considered the applicability of local optimization techniques in the particular case of solvable CSP [Meseguer and Larrosa, 95]. We used the projected gradient algorithm which computes a new point P^{new} from a point P in the following way,

$$P^{new} = P + \alpha \, \text{Proj}(Q) \tag{3}$$

where Q is the gradient of $A(P)$ on P, the operator Proj is the projection on the set K and α is the step size such that $A(P) < A(P^{new})$. We had to use the projected gradient algorithm instead of the pure gradient because this is a case of constrained optimization, where the new generated point should lie on the set K. This approach was feasible for solvable CSP, because solutions can be easily identified when they are found (the number of violated constraints is equal to 0). However, this approach is no longer valid for MAX-CSP because we do not know the value of $A(P)$ on its global maximum, or equivalently, we do not know the number of violated constraints in a maximal consistent solution. To overcome these difficulties, we developed a heuristic approach which is explained in the next section.

4 Dynamic Variable and Value Ordering Heuristics

To circumvent the difficulties of local optimization methods when applied to MAX-CSP, we decided to use a systematic search algorithm —extended forward checking— to guarantee that we will find solutions which will be maximally consistent. To guide the search process, we use information provided by the optimization approach. We have developed two heuristics based on this approach. These heuristics provide advice for dynamic variable and value ordering. They are called the *highest weight* heuristic and the *lowest support* heuristic.

To compute these heuristics, we have to relate systematic search with label updating. At a given time, the current state of past and future variables is reflected in a labeling P in the following form:

if X_i is a past variable $\quad p_i[\lambda^i] = 1, \quad\quad \lambda^i$ is assigned to X_i
$$p_i[\lambda] = 0, \quad\quad \lambda \in D, \lambda \neq \lambda^i$$
if X_i is a future variable $\quad p_i[\lambda] = 1/m_i, \quad \lambda \in feasible(D, X_i),$
$$m_i = card(feasible(D, X_i))$$
$$p_i[\lambda] = 0, \quad\quad \lambda \in D - feasible(D, X_i)$$

where the set $feasible(D, X_i)$ is the set of values that, at that point of the search, are still feasible for the variable X_i. This labeling is unambiguous in past variables and ambiguous in future ones, with a homogeneous weight distribution among the feasible values of future variables.

4.1 The Highest Weight Heuristic

The highest weight heuristic follows a hill-climbing approach. An iteration of the projected gradient algorithm (3) maximizing $A(P)$ causes changes in weights associated with variable-value pairs, producing a new labeling P^{new} such that $A(P) < A(P^{new})$. Those weights of P^{new} which have increased with respect to P correspond to directions in which $A(P)$ locally increases. At this point, we use these weights for variable and value selection. The highest weight heuristic works as follows:

1. Before a variable is assigned, a single iteration of the projected gradient algorithm is performed, starting from the labeling P corresponding to the current search state.

2. P^{new} is used to provide heuristic advice for variable and value selection:

- Variable selection: selects the variable with the highest weight associated with a value of its domain (breaking ties randomly).

- Value selection: selects the value corresponding to the highest weight in the domain of the variable (breaking ties randomly).

This heuristic selects the variable X_i with the "most promising value". The selected variable-value pair defines a direction in which $A(P)$ increases. Once a variable X_i has been selected, all their values will be considered by decreasing weight. This means that the subspace of K^* associated with the variable X_i will be completely explored, considering first those directions in which $A(P)$ increases more.

To compute the new labeling P^{new}, we replace the projected gradient algorithm (3) by the following formula for relaxation labeling [Rosenfeld *et al.*, 76],

$$p_i^{new}[\lambda_k] = \frac{p_i[\lambda_k](2n+q_i[\lambda_k])}{\sum_{k=1}^{m} p_i[\lambda_k](2n+q_i[\lambda_k])} \qquad (4)$$

which has been proved to be an approximation of the projected gradient [Hummel and Zucker, 83], and it is less costly to compute. The elements $q_i[\lambda_k]$ are the components of Q, the gradient vector of $A(P)$ on the point P, which has the following expression [Hummel and Zucker, 83],

$$q_i[\lambda_k] = 2 \sum_{j=1}^{n} \sum_{l=1}^{m} r_{ij}(\lambda_k,\lambda_l)p_j[\lambda_l] = 2\, s_i(\lambda_k,P) \qquad (5)$$

4.2 The Lowest Support Heuristic

The lowest support heuristic is inspired by the fail-first principle. A component $q_i[\lambda_k]$ of Q, the gradient of $A(P)$, is proportional to the support $s_i(\lambda_k,P)$ (5). The support $s_i(\lambda_k,P)$ is an averaged sum of compatibilities between the value λ_k of variable X_i and the labeling P; the lower this support is, the more incompatible appears λ_k for X_i with the labeling P. The sum of gradient components for variable X_i, $\sum q_i[\lambda]$, $\lambda \in feasible(D, X_i)$, is a global measure of the support that the set of feasible values of X_i obtains from all the other variables. The variable with the lowest sum of gradient components appears as the variable with the most incompatible set of values with respect to the labeling P. Following the fail-first principle, this variable is a good candidate to be selected. The lowest support heuristic is based on this fact. This heuristic works as follows,

1. Before a variable is assigned, the gradient Q is computed from the labeling P corresponding to the current search state.

2. Q is used to provide advice for variable and value selection:

- Variable selection: selects the variable with the lowest sum of gradient components (breaking ties randomly).

- Value selection: selects the value corresponding to the highest gradient component (breaking ties randomly).

This heuristic selects a variable with a small denominator in (4), which —depending on the numerator value— can produce a high value for a weight associated with a value of its domain, although it is not necessarily the highest. Once the variable has been selected, values are considered by decreasing gradient component, or equivalently, by decreasing weight.

5 Incremental Heuristic Computation

We have tested the proposed heuristics inside the extended forward checking algorithm P-EFC3 [Freuder and Wallace, 92], because it permits dynamic variable and value ordering. A version of the P-EFC3 algorithm is given in Fig. 1. In addition, P-EFC3 enhanced with dynamic variable ordering (the largest mean of inconsistency counts) and value ordering (increasing inconsistency counts), is considered one of the most efficient algorithms for MAX-CSP, specially for dense constrained problems.

```
procedure P-EFC3 (current_solution, distance, remaining_variables, remaining_domains)
/*   global variables: best_solution  and   best_distance    */

1    v := select-next-variable(remaining_variables); /* depends on variable ordering */
2    values := sort-values(v, remaining_domains);    /* depends on value ordering */
3    while values ≠ Ø do
4         l := first(values);
5         new_distance := distance + inconsistency_count(v, l);
6         if remaining_variables = Ø then
7                   if new_distance < best_distance then
8                             best_distance := new_distance;
9                             best_solution := current_solution + (v, l);
10        endif
11   else
12        if (new_distance + sum_min_inconsistency_counts < best_distance) then
13                  new_remaining_domains := update_inconsistency_counts(domains, v, l);
14                  if (new_distance + sum_min_inconsistency_counts < best_distance) then
15                            P-EFC3 (current_solution + (v, l), new_distance,
16                                          remaining_variables - v, new_remaining_domains);
17                  endif
18        endif
19   endif
20   l := next(values);
21   endwhile
endprocedure
```

Fig. 1. The extended forward checking algorithm.

Regarding the proposed heuristics, both are expensive to compute. To make them useful, their computational cost must not surpass the benefits that they produce in searching. Otherwise, their use would be counterproductive. With this goal, we have developed simpler updating formulas, described below, which supersede (4) and (5) and allow us a much more efficient computation of weights and gradients. However, to employ these new formulas we cannot remove values in variable domains. This is the only difference between our implementation and the pure P-EFC3 algorithm, and its consequences are discussed in section 7. In the following, we provide a detailed explanation about how weights and gradients are computed, assuming that the highest weight heuristic —which requires a more complex calculation— is used for variable and value selection.

5.1 Computing Weights

As we explained in section 4, we have to relate systematic search with label updating. For each state s of the search, we define a labeling $P^{(s)}$ as follows,

if X_i is a past variable, $p_i^{(s)}[\lambda^i] = 1,$ λ^i is assigned to X_i in state s
$\qquad\qquad\qquad\qquad\qquad p_i^{(s)}[\lambda] = 0,$ $\lambda \in D, \lambda \neq \lambda^i$
if X_i is a future variable $p_i^{(s)}[\lambda] = 1/m,$ $\lambda \in D$

where we assume that no value is discarded in future variable domains in any step of the algorithm. We use (4) to compute the new labeling $P^{(s\text{-}new)}$, which will be used to select the next variable. If the new variable is assigned, we move to another state s' defined by the state s plus this variable assignment. Otherwise, if no value can be assigned to the new variable, a backtracking occurs and we return to a previous state.

If X_i is a past variable it is easy to see that (4) does not change its weights, that is, $p_i^{(s\text{-}new)}[\lambda] = p_i^{(s)}[\lambda]$ for every $\lambda \in D$. Therefore, we will execute (4) on future variables only, obtaining the following updating formula,

$$p_i^{(s\text{-}new)}[\lambda_k] = \frac{p_i^{(s)}[\lambda_k](2n+q_i^{(s)}[\lambda_k])}{\displaystyle\sum_{k=1}^{m} p_i^{(s)}[\lambda_k](2n+q_i^{(s)}[\lambda_k])} =$$

$$= \frac{1/m\,(2n+q_i^{(s)}[\lambda_k])}{\displaystyle\sum_{k=1}^{m} 1/m\,(2n+q_i^{(s)}[\lambda_k])} = \frac{2n+q_i^{(s)}[\lambda_k]}{2nm+\displaystyle\sum_{k=1}^{m} q_i^{(s)}[\lambda_k]} \qquad (6)$$

where $q_i^{(s)}[\lambda_k]$ are the components of the vector $Q^{(s)}$, the gradient of $A(P)$ on the point $P^{(s)}$.

5.2 Computing Gradients

From (5), we can express $Q^{(s)}$ as a combination of contributions of past and future variables. Let P and F be the sets of indexes of past and future variables at the state s, the gradient $Q^{(s)}$ can be expressed as,

$$q_i^{(s)}[\lambda_k] = q_i^{P(s)}[\lambda_k] + q_i^{F(s)}[\lambda_k] \qquad (7)$$

$$q_i^{P(s)}[\lambda_k] = 2 \sum_{j \in P} \sum_{l=1}^{m} r_{ij}(\lambda_k, \lambda_l) p_j^{(s)}[\lambda_l]$$

$$q_i^{F(s)}[\lambda_k] = 2 \sum_{j \in F} \sum_{l=1}^{m} r_{ij}(\lambda_k, \lambda_l) p_j^{(s)}[\lambda_l]$$

Components $q_i^{P(s)}[\lambda_k]$ and $q_i^{F(s)}[\lambda_k]$ are called the past and the future components of the gradient, respectively. It is easy to see that,

$$q_i^{P(s)}[\lambda_k] = 2 \sum_{j \in P} r_{ij}(\lambda_k, \lambda^j) \qquad (8)$$

since for a past variable X_j every weight is 0 but the weight associated with the assigned value λ^j which is 1.

After computing $P^{(s\text{-}new)}$ from $Q^{(s)}$ by (6), the algorithm takes a decision in terms of assigning a variable, and it produces a new state s' which has associated the labeling $P^{(s')}$. After this decision, we update $Q^{(s)}$ to obtain the gradient corresponding to s', that is the vector $Q^{(s')}$. In this way, we perform an incremental updating of the gradient vector, computing $Q^{(s')}$ from the previous gradient $Q^{(s)}$ plus the assignment which has occurred between s and s'. We save computational resources, since only those operations strictly needed are performed, in contrast with the computation from scratch of $Q^{(s')}$ using (5).

Gradient updating is as follows. Providing the change from s to s' is the assignment of the value λ^r to the variable X_r, this variable is no longer a future variable and it becomes a past variable. $Q^{(s')}$ can be computed from $Q^{(s)}$ by subtracting from the future component of the gradient the contribution of X_r when it was a future variable, and adding to the past component of the gradient the current contribution of X_r as a past variable,

$$q_i^{F(s')}[\lambda_k] = q_i^{F(s)}[\lambda_k] - 2 \sum_{l=1}^{m} r_{ir}(\lambda_k, \lambda_l) p_r^{(s)}[\lambda_l] = q_i^{F(s)}[\lambda_k] - 2 s_i^{(s)}(\lambda_k, X_r) \qquad (9)$$

$$q_i^{P(s')}[\lambda_k] = q_i^{P(s)}[\lambda_k] + 2 r_{ir}(\lambda_k, \lambda^r) \qquad (10)$$

where $s_i^{(s)}(\lambda_k, X_r)$ is the support that the values of the variable X_r bring to the value

λ_k for the variable X_i in labeling $P^{(s)}$ (see (1)). Therefore, using (9) and (10) we can easily compute $Q^{(s')}$ from $Q^{(s)}$ and the assignment from $P^{(s)}$ to $P^{(s')}$. In terms of the algorithm P-EFC3 of Fig. 1, weight computation is performed in line 1 using (6), inside the function select_next_variable. To compute the gradient, formula (7) is used adding the past and future components which are always kept updated. Thus, after a variable assignment, the gradient components are updated in line 15 before the recursive call, using (9) and (10).

6 Experimental Results

The proposed heuristics have been tested on two classes of randomly generated CSP, to which we will refer as *fixed tightness* and *variable tightness*. A fixed tightness random CSP is characterised by a 4-tuple $<n, m, p_1, p_2>$ [Prosser, 94], where n is the number of variables, m is the common cardinality of their domains, p_1 is the probability of a constraint existing between a pair of variables (connectivity) and p_2 is the probability of a conflict occurring between two values assigned to constrained variables (tightness). Fixed tightness implies constraint homogeneity: every pair of constrained variables has the same expected number of conflicts, $p_2 * m^2$, independently of the variables considered. This homogeneity can be seen as unnatural for the representation of some real CSP.

A variable tightness random CSP is characterised by a 5-tuple $<n, m, p_1, p_2^{inf}, p_2^{sup}>$, where n, m and p_1 are defined as above, and p_2^{inf} and p_2^{sup} are the tightness lower and upper bound, respectively. For each constraint, its tightness is randomly chosen within the interval $[p_2^{inf}, p_2^{sup}]$. Variable tightness allows some diversity in the constraints: every pair of constrained variables does not have the same expected number of conflicts, which varies from $p_2^{inf} * m^2$ to $p_2^{sup} * m^2$.

6.1 Fixed Tightness Random CSP

Our experiments were performed with $<10, 10, p_1, p_2>$ CSP, with p_1 taking values 0.6, 0.8 and 1.0, and p_2 ranging from 0.5 to 0.9. Twenty instances of each parameter setting were created forming a set of 300 problems divided into 15 sets. Because of the values of p_1 and p_2, these problems are typically unsolvable. These problems were solved with the P-EFC3 algorithm on a SUN Sparc 2, using the largest inconsistency mean for variable selection and the lowest inconsistency counts for value selection. We will refer to this version as LM (Largest Mean). Alternatively, we solved the problems using the highest weight heuristic (HW) and the lowest support heuristic (LS). To measure the performance of the different heuristics, we use the number of consistency tests and the CPU time required in the P-EFC3 execution. The number of tests has been widely used as a measure for the computational effort needed for the algorithms to solve MAX-CSP instances. The CPU time is included to check the cost-effectiveness of the extra computation required by HW and LS with respect to the savings they produce in searching. These results are given in Table 1.

It can be observed that HW outperforms LM in all classes of problems, and this improvement increases with the problem difficulty, as p_1 and p_2 increases. The heuristic HW decreases drastically the computational effort needed to solve the problems. Globally, HW gives about a 60% saving in the number of tests with respect to LM. Regarding CPU time, HW clearly outperforms LM, despite the extra computation required to calculate weights. The performance of LS needs some more attention: for connectivities different from 1, the experiments show that LS is between HW and LM regarding both number of tests and CPU time (although closer to HW). However, for full connectivity its performance is similar to LM, with larger CPU times. As we will see in section 7, LS is approaching LM as problem connectivity tends to 1.

		LM		HW		LS	
p_1	p_2	consistency tests	CPU time	consistency tests	CPU time	consistency tests	CPU time
	0.5	14,591	0.13	2,121	0.07	4,072	0.09
	0.6	79,472	0.48	25,049	0.26	36,208	0.33
0.6	0.7	283,185	1.57	77,227	0.67	105,257	0.82
	0.8	870,141	4.75	147,975	1.19	236,862	1.77
	0.9	3,797,692	20.48	554,941	4.20	801,161	5.71
	0.5	111,042	0.69	42,687	0.41	47,815	0.43
	0.6	512,095	2.82	146,414	1.19	190,075	1.46
0.8	0.7	1,019,514	5.70	265,255	2.09	441,612	3.32
	0.8	3,065,557	17.03	589,559	4.54	1,040,506	7.74
	0.9	7,951,244	44.37	1,299,684	9.82	2,244,457	16.72
	0.5	351,871	1.94	167,765	1.34	200,840	1.64
	0.6	973,165	5.33	439,824	3.62	903,770	7.03
1.0	0.7	2,155,926	11.89	903,483	7.31	2,011,695	15.73
	0.8	5,783,030	32.64	2,155,868	17.31	5,053,403	38.90
	0.9	19,247,830	111.67	6,373,465	50.46	15,943,989	124.35

Table 1. Results on fixed tightness random CSP.

6.2 Variable Tightness Random CSP

We suspected that fixed tightness random CSP may be inappropriate to model some real CSP. Therefore, we tested the heuristics with variable tightness random CSP. The values for connectivity were again 0.6, 0.8 and 1. Three widths for the tightness interval were tried: for width = 0.2, we considered the intervals [0.4, 0.6], [0.6, 0.8] and [0.8, 1.0]. For width = 0.4, we considered the intervals [0.2, 0.6] and [0.6, 1.0]. Finally, for width = 1.0, the tightness interval was [0.0, 1.0]. Obviously, the larger the tightness interval is, the more heterogeneous is the problem sample. In order to produce representative results, we increased the number of instances considered for each parameter setting. Thus, for width of 0.2, 0.4 and 1, the number of instances was 40, 60 and 100, respectively, solving 1020 problem instances. Almost all these problems were unsolvable. Again, we report the number of consistency tests and CPU time for the heuristics LM, HW and LS. These results are in Table 2 for width = 0.2, in Table 3 for width = 0.4, and in Table 4 for width = 1.

Results show that HW performs similarly to the fixed tightness case with respect to LM in both number of consistency tests and CPU time. Considering LS, it can be seen a changing behaviour with increasing tightness width. For tightness width = 0.2, LS outperforms HW in problems with low connectivity and tightness, while HW outperforms LS in problems with high connectivity and tightness. For tightness width = 0.4, this behaviour is again observed, but HW can only surpass LS in problems with full connectivity and high tightness. For tightness width = 1, LS

		LM		HW		LS	
$P1$	$p2^{inf} p2^{sup}$	consistency tests	CPU time	consistency tests	CPU time	consistency tests	CPU time
	0.4, 0.6	28,155	0.12	4,378	0.09	3,542	0.08
0.6	0.6, 0.8	394,793	2.10	78,766	0.66	73,881	0.57
	0.8, 1.0	7,657,250	41.23	931,949	7.04	739,405	5.12
	0.4, 0.6	128,683	0.75	42,267	0.42	40,224	0.36
0.8	0.6, 0.8	1,126,827	6.02	273,791	2.21	270,861	2.02
	0.8, 1.0	14,736,931	81.70	2,360,949	18.08	2,703,723	19.42
	0.4, 0.6	431,766	2.32	185,132	1.54	174,265	1.35
1.0	0.6, 0.8	2,337,982	12.69	851,510	6.75	1,114,632	8.27
	0.8, 1.0	31,427,200	181.20	8,488,424	67.27	15,318,073	116.41

Table 2. Results on variable tightness random CSP for width = 0.2.

$P1$	$p_2^{inf} p_2^{sup}$	LM consistency tests	LM CPU time	HW consistency tests	HW CPU time	LS consistency tests	LS CPU time
	0.2, 0.6	2,832	0.05	634	0.06	606	0.06
0.6	0.6, 1.0	2,565,439	13.70	328,493	2.50	237,123	1.70
	0.2, 0.6	21,078	0.16	5,223	0.10	4,562	0.09
0.8	0.6, 1.0	5,750,927	31.44	1,002,846	7.76	1,038,177	7.60
	0.2, 0.6	101,440	0.62	44,307	0.44	38,178	0.37
1.0	0.6, 1.0	9,897,304	55.76	2,773,760	21.78	4,019,892	30.07

Table 3. Results on variable tightness random CSP for width = 0.4.

$P1$	$p_2^{inf} p_2^{sup}$	LM consistency tests	LM CPU time	HW consistency tests	HW CPU time	LS consistency tests	LS CPU time
0.6	0.0, 1.0	688,492	3.98	78,666	0.71	42,969	0.34
0.8	0.0, 1.0	1,477,590	8.12	203,502	1.62	141,404	1.06
1.0	0.0, 1.0	1,629,693	8.77	306,932	2.46	255,381	1.93

Table 4. Results on variable tightness random CSP for width = 1.

outperforms HW in all problems classes. Therefore, LS seems to be a good heuristic for MAX-CSP problems with a high degree of variability on constraint tightness. For a medium degree of variability on constraint tightness, LS works better than HW for low tightness; for high tightness HW surpasses LS in fully connected problems only, showing a similar performance in the rest of the problems.

7 Discussion

Experimental results show that both heuristics, HW and LS, require less consistency tests than LM when used inside the P-EFC3 algorithm, that is, HW and LS are more informed than LM. The improvement that HW provides with respect to LM is approximately homogeneous in all problem classes where it was tested. On the other hand, the improvement that LS provides with respect to LM depends on the connectivity and tightness interval. To explain these facts, we will show that LS follows the same lines than LM, but it goes one step further. Essentially, LS considers more information —the influence of future variables— and, because of that, it is able to guide better the search for a maximal consistent solution. In addition, we will explore the relation between LS and HW.

To analyze the LS heuristic, let us assume first that future variables are not considered in the gradient computation (i.e. $q_i^F[\lambda] = 0$ for all λ). Then, a gradient component for the variable X_i is,

$$q_i[\lambda_k] = q_i^P[\lambda_k] = 2(\text{\#past variables supporting } \lambda_k -$$

$$\text{\#past variables not supporting } \lambda_k) =$$

$$= 2 \ (card(P) - 2 \ inconsistency\_count \ (X_i, \lambda_k))$$

The sum of gradient components is,

$$\sum_{k=1}^{m} q_i[\lambda_k] = 2 \ \{ \ m*card(P) \ - 2 \sum_{k=1}^{m} inconsistency\_count \ (X_i, \lambda_k) \ \}$$

It is easy to see that the variable which minimizes this expression is the variable with the largest mean of inconsistency counts, providing that no values are discarded for any variable by the P-EFC3 algorithm. The same thing applies for value ordering: considering values by increasing number of inconsistency count is equal to order them by decreasing gradient component. Therefore, disregarding the effect of future variables and providing that no values are discarded, LS is equivalent to LM.

If future variables are taken into account, the future gradient component $q_i^F[\lambda_k]$ is,

$$q_i^F[\lambda_k] = 1/m \ \{ \ \sum_{j \in F} \sum_{l=1}^{m} r_{ij}(\lambda_k, \lambda_l) \ \} =$$

$$= 1/m \ \{\text{\#future variables with a value consistent with } \lambda_k -$$

$$\text{\#future variables with a value inconsistent with } \lambda_k \ \}$$

The smaller $q_i^F[\lambda_k]$ is, the less consistent appears λ_k with respect to future variables. The sum of future gradient components provides an estimation of the consistency of the variable values with respect to future variables. Considering both past and future components, the sum of gradient components is,

$$\sum_{k=1}^{m} q_i[\lambda_k] = \sum_{k=1}^{m} q_i^P[\lambda_k] + \sum_{k=1}^{m} q_i^F[\lambda_k]$$

The variable with the lowest sum of gradient components will combine a high number of inconsistencies with past variables with a high estimation of inconsistencies with future variables. In this sense, LS can be seen as a generalization of LM, including extra information from future variables.

According with experimental results, LS improvement with respect to LM is varying with tightness width. This can be explained from the following fact: for fixed tightness random CSP, the contribution of a future variable X_j in the sum of gradient components of any other future variable X_i with which it is constrained is approximately the same. That contribution is,

$$1/m \sum_{k=1}^{m} \sum_{l=1}^{m} r_{ij}(\lambda_k, \lambda_l) \approx m - 2mp_2$$

where $m - 2mp_2$ is the expected value of the contribution of X_j. When connectivity is 1, all future variables are connected with each other, and the sum of their contributions on X_i is,

$$\sum_{k=1}^{m} q_i{}^F[\lambda_k] = 1/m \sum_{j \in F} \sum_{k=1}^{m} \sum_{l=1}^{m} r_{ij}(\lambda_k, \lambda_l) \approx (card(F) - 1) * (m - 2mp_2) \quad (11)$$

where $(card(F) - 1) * (m - 2mp_2)$ is the expected value of the sum of the contributions of future variables. This expected value is the same for each future variable X_i. For fixed tightness fully connected random CSP, the influence of future variables comes from deviations from (11), and typically it is small compared with the influence of past variables. This can be observed in Table 1, where LS approaches LM for $p_1 = 1$. For variable tightness random CSP, (11) is no longer the same for each future variable because constraints do not have a fixed tightness p_2. The wider the tightness interval is, the more informative is the influence of future variables, and the better is LS performance. This can be observed in Tables 2, 3 and 4.

The relation between LS and HW can be seen from the weight updating rule (6). LS selects the variable with the lowest denominator in (6). Typically, this variable will have some values with high weights, although not necessarily the highest. Therefore, in many cases LS will select a variable with high weights associated with values in its domains. These variable-value pairs stand for directions in which $A(P)$ increases. In addition, HW tends to select variables with a high variability in their gradient components, that is, variables in which some values appear as more promising than others (promising uphill directions of $A(P)$).

In summary, LS heuristic appears as a generalization of LM. It is based on the same insights, but it goes one step further by considering the influence that future variables have on selecting the current one. Thus, LS selects the variable with the lowest global support which is a combination of the supports of past and future variables. Regarding HW, it selects a variable with a value where $A(P)$ locally increases. Both LS and HW include information from past and future variables, in contrast with LM which only considers information from past variables. Interestingly, the influence of past and future variables on LS and HW is proportional to their relative number. When no variables have been yet assigned, all the influence comes from future variables; when almost every variable has been assigned, the influence of future variables is very small. It is specially interesting the initial state, when no variable is assigned. LM decides randomly because it has no information (every inconsistency count is zero). This may lead to wrong decisions at early stages of the search, which are critical for search performance.

8. Conclusions

From this work, we extract the following conclusions. First, we have shown that our optimization formulation for CSP is a fruitful approach able to generate new heuristics. These heuristics are not simply "rules of thumb", but they are based on results about the best possible solution for a CSP. This substantiates these new heuristics, which appear to be better justified than other heuristics whose only justification comes from empirical results. Second, our optimization formulation is general (it does not differentiate between solvable and overconstrained CSP), and the heuristics based on it seems to be applicable to both problem types (although more empirical results are needed to qualify precisely this assertion). Third, the proposed approach gives a new perspective of previously applied heuristics, and it can be seen as a step further in the sense that it considers more information and, because of that, it provides better advice. Finally, we notice the practical importance of the incremental approach taken to compute weights in order to make these heuristics competitive against others of simpler computation.

Acknowledgements

We thank Carme Torras for several discussions about the topics of this paper. We thank Richard Cropper for his support in ironing the English. We also thank M. Luisa Romanillos and Romero Donlo for their collaboration on writing this paper.

References

Bakker R., Dikker F., Tempelman F. and Wognum P. (1993). Diagnosing and solving overdetermined constraint satisfaction problems, *Proceedings of IJCAI-93*, 276-281.

Feldman R. and Golumbic M. C. (1990). Optimization algorithms for student scheduling via constraint satisfiability, *Computer Journal*, vol. 33, 356-364.

Fox M. (1987). *Constraint-directed Search: A Case Study on Jop-Shop Scheduling.* Morgan-Kauffman.

Freuder E. C. and Wallace R. J. (1992). Partial constraint satisfaction, *Artificial Intelligence*, 58: 21-70.

Horst R. and Tuy H. (1993). *Global Optimization (2 edition),* Springer-Verlag.

Hummel R. A. and Zucker S. W. (1983). On the Foundations of Relaxation Labeling Processes, *IEEE Trans. Pattern Analysis Machine Intelligence*, vol. 5, no. 3, 267-287.

Meseguer P. and Larrosa J. (1995). Constraint Satisfaction as Global Optimization, *Proceeedings of IJCAI-95*, in press.

Prosser P. (1994). Binary constraint satisfaction problems: some are harder than others, *Proceedings of ECAI-94*, 95-99.

Rosenfeld A., Hummel R. and Zucker S. (1976). Scene Labeling by Relaxation Operators, *IEEE Trans. Systems, Man, Cybernetics*, vol. 6, no.6, 420-433.

Sastry *P.* S. and Thathachar M. A. L. (1994). Analysis of Stochastic Automata Algorithm for Relaxation Labeling, *IEEE Trans. Pattern Analysis Machine Intelligence*, vol. 16, no. 5, 538-543.

Wallace R. J. and Freuder E. C. (1993). Conjunctive width heuristics for maximal constraint satisfaction, *Proceedings of AAAI-93*, 762-778.

Wallace R. J. (1994).Directed Arc Consistency Preprocessing as a Strategy for Maximal Constraint Satisfaction, *ECAI94 Workshop on Constraint Processing*, M. Meyer editor, 69-77.

First-order Definability
over Constraint Databases

(Extended Abstract)

Stéphane Grumbach[*,1] and **Jianwen Su**[**,2]

[1] I.N.R.I.A. and University of Toronto,
I.N.R.I.A. Rocquencourt BP 105, 78153 Le Chesnay, France,
E-mail: stephane.grumbach@inria.fr
[2] Dept. of Computer Science, University of California, Santa Barbara,
CA 93106, USA, E-mail: su@cs.ucsb.edu

Abstract. In this paper, we study the expressive power of first-order logic as a query language over constraint databases. We consider constraints over various domains ($\mathbb{N}, \mathbb{Q}, \mathbb{R}$), and with various operations ($\leqslant, +, \times, x^y$). We first tackle the problem of the definability of parity and connectivity, which are the most classical examples of queries not expressible in first-order logic over finite structures. We prove that these two queries are first-order expressible in presence of (enough) arithmetic. This is in sharp contrast with classical relational databases. Nevertheless, we show that they are not definable with constraints of interest for constraint databases such as linear constraints. We then develop reductions techniques for queries over constraint databases, that allow us to draw conclusions with respect to their undefinability in various constraint query languages.

1 Introduction

Until recently, databases were considered to be finite collections of data items. New applications such as those involving temporal and spatial data (e.g. geographical databases) lead very naturally to more general data models allowing infinite collections of items to be stored in the database.

The *constraint database model*, introduced by Kanellakis, Kuper and Revesz in their seminal paper [KKR90] and convincingly advocated in [KG94], is a powerful generalization of Codd's relational model. In this new paradigm, instead of tuples, queries act on "generalized tuples" expressed as quantifier-free first-order constraints in a decidable theory adequate to definite purposes. A generalized relation is a conjunction of such constraints, interpreted in the domain of a given model of the decidable theory. Interesting constraint query languages are then

---

* Work supported in part by Esprit Project BRA AMUSING, and an NSERC fellowship in Canada.

** Work supported in part by NSF grant IRI-9117094 and NASA grant NAGW-3888. A part of this work was done while visiting I.N.R.I.A.

obtained by coupling the relational calculus (or some version of Datalog) with the theory of dense linear orders without endpoints or the theory of real closed fields for instance.

The expressive power and complexity of first-order logic over such "finitely representable" databases are still far from being clearly understood. In [KKR90], the data complexity of both the relational calculus and inflationary Datalog with negation over dense order constraint databases is studied. Different types of constraints were considered, such as dense linear order inequalities, real polynomial inequalities, etc. These constraints are based on decidable theories which admit the elimination of quantifiers. It is proved that, although the decision problem of the underlying theories may be high, the data complexity of the query languages is tractable. This shows the practical interest of this approach, which has been pursued in [Rev93, Kup93, KG94, GS94, ACGK94, PVV94, CK95, GS95, PVV95, Rev95].

Our goal is to investigate the expressive power of first order logic as a query language over constraint databases. It was shown in [GS94] that the model theory of finitely representable structures, differs strongly from the classical model theory of all structures. In particular, we prove that, like for finite model theory (see the survey by Fagin [Fag93]), most of the classical theorems of logic, such as the compactness and the completeness theorems, fail for finitely representable structures.

The parity of the cardinality of a set, PARITY, and the connectivity of a finite graph, CONNECTIVITY, are the most common examples of queries that are not first-order definable over finite models in a first-order language with equality. They are especially interesting, since they involve two basic primitives, counting and recursion. The undefinability can be shown using various proof techniques, such as locality [Gai81], asymptotic probabilities [Fag74], Ehrenfeucht-Fraïssé games [Fra54, Ehr61], etc. The undefinability results were shown to carry over in the presence of an order relation on the domain [Gur88].

Constraint databases have opened a new area of research on first-order definability. Indeed, constraints generally involve numeric domains with arithmetic. The previous undefinability results were shown for domains allowing at most an order relation. What is particularily challenging is that the previous techniques do not carry over in presence of arithmetic. Ehrenfeucht-Fraïssé games apply, but they lead to inextricable combinatorics [GS94]. Locality and 0/1 laws do not work already in the presence of an order relation.

On the other hand, the queries PARITY and CONNECTIVITY have nothing to do with arithmetic. They are *generic* [CH80], that is they commute with any permutation of the constants of the domain, even permutations violating the order and consequently the arithmetic operations. The increase of the number of relations and arithmetic functions in a first-order language generally results in an increase of its expressive power. This is clear for all classical arithmetics over the natural numbers or the reals for instance with the operations + and ×.

Nevertheless, it is a priori not clear that more generic queries are expressible in a language extended with arithmetic operations. Gurevich ([AHV94], Exercise

17.27, page 162) found an example of a generic query expressible with an order relation, and not expressible without it. We prove that PARITY and CONNECTIVITY are definable over the natural numbers or the rationals with addition and multiplication, and over the reals with exponentiation. On the other hand these queries are not definable with addition only. The results are quite surprising. They shed a new light on the question of the definability of generic queries with arithmetic.

We develop reduction techniques to prove the undefinability of numerous queries under the assumption that parity is not definable. We illustrate these techniques on queries from geometry, topology, computational geometry [Yao90], graph theory, and geographical databases, and we investigate their first-order definability in various contexts.

The paper is organized as follows. In the next section, we analyze the first-order definability of PARITY and CONNECTIVITY. In Section 3, we define real constraint databases, and present interesting examples of queries. In Section 4, we prove reduction theorems, and finally we present more undefinability results in the last section.

2   First-Order Definability of Parity and Connectivity

In this section, we present new results on the definability of PARITY and CON-NECTVITY over numeric domains with arithmetic. Let $\mathcal{L}$ be a first-order language, $\mathcal{D}$ an $\mathcal{L}$-structure of domain D, and $\mathcal{T}$ the theory of $\mathcal{D}$. We further suppose that R is a unary relation symbol not in $\mathcal{L}$. We say that PARITY is $\mathcal{L}$-definable in the context of $\mathcal{D}$ (or simply definable in $\mathcal{D}$) if there is a first-order sentence $\varphi(R)$ in $\mathcal{L} \cup \{R\}$ such that for each finite relation $\overline{R}$,

$$\overline{R} \text{ has even cardinality iff } \mathcal{D}, \overline{R} \models \varphi(R).$$

The definition is similar for the definability of CONNECTIVITY, as well as for any other query. We consider three domains, the natural numbers, $\mathbb{N}$, the rationals, $\mathbb{Q}$, and the reals, $\mathbb{R}$, and various first-order languages with equality involving order over the domain, $\leqslant$, addition, $+$, multiplication, $\times$, and possibly exponentiation, x^y.

The next theorem shows that addition is inadequate to define parity.

Theorem 2.1 [GST94, PVV95] PARITY is definable in none of the following additive context structures: $\langle \mathbb{N}, \leqslant, +, 0, 1 \rangle$, $\langle \mathbb{Q}, \leqslant, +, 0, 1 \rangle$, and $\langle \mathbb{R}, \leqslant, +, 0, 1 \rangle$.

Proof. The result was shown in [GST94] in the case of the rational numbers. The proof exhibits an AC^0 data complexity upper-bound for first order logic with order and addition over rational numbers, over inputs that are finite subsets of $\mathbb{N}^k$. Since PARITY is not in AC^0 [FSS84], it follows that PARITY is not definable. Assume now that there is a sentence φ over $\langle \mathbb{R}, \leqslant, +, 0, 1 \rangle$ which expresses parity of a set of reals. Then, φ is also a sentence over $\langle \mathbb{Q}, \leqslant, +, 0, 1 \rangle$, which also expresses parity of a set of rationals. Therefore parity is not definable in first-order over $\langle \mathbb{R}, \leqslant, +, 0, 1 \rangle$. A different technique was exhibited in [PVV95] for the case of real numbers. $\square$

We next prove a positive result, namely that PARITY is definable over the structure $\langle \mathbb{N}, \leqslant, +, \times, 0, 1 \rangle$. This shows that arithmetic has a strong impact on the expressive power of first-order logic for queries that are *generic*, i.e., independent of the arithmetic.

Theorem 2.2 PARITY is definable in $\langle \mathbb{N}, \leqslant, +, \times, 0, 1 \rangle$.

In order to prove Theorem 2.2, we first prove the following weaker result.

Lemma 2.3 PARITY is definable in $\langle \mathbb{N}, \leqslant, +, \times, x^y, 0, 1 \rangle$.

Proof. Consider the set $\overline{R} = \{a_1, \ldots, a_l\}$, and assume without loss of generality that $a_i < a_{i+1}$. The formula $\varphi(R, n)$ defines *the* natural number $n = 2^{a_1} \times 3^{a_2} \times \ldots \times \alpha_l^{a_l}$, where α_l is the lth prime number.

$$\varphi(R, n) \equiv (\phi(R, n) \wedge \forall n' (\phi(R, n') \Rightarrow n \leqslant n')),$$

where $\phi(R, n)$ is the following formula:

$$div(2^{a_1}, n) \wedge \forall \alpha \, \forall \beta \, \forall a \, \forall b \begin{pmatrix} prime(\alpha) \\ \wedge \ prime(\beta) \\ \wedge \ succ_{prime}(\alpha, \beta) \\ \wedge \ a \in R \ \wedge \ b \in R \\ \wedge \ succ_R(a, b) \end{pmatrix} \Rightarrow (div(\alpha^a, n) \Leftrightarrow div(\beta^b, n)),$$

with the following abbreviations: $div(x, y)$ denotes the relation "x divides y"; $prime(x)$ defines prime numbers; $succ_{prime}(x, y)$ is true if x and y are consecutive primes; $succ_R(x, y)$ is true if x and y are consecutive members of R. All these relations are first-order definable (for first-order definability of relations and functions, see [End72]).

The formula $\varphi'(d, n)$ defines the *biggest* prime divisor d of n. It is easily expressed in first-order.

The formula $\psi(x, y)$ defines the set of pairs of the form (α_k, k), where α_k is the kth prime number. The definition of ψ is given in [End72].

The parity of R is finally expressed by the sentence:

$$\forall n \, \forall d \, \forall k \, ((\varphi(R, n) \wedge \varphi'(d, n) \wedge \psi(d, k)) \Rightarrow div(2, k)). \square$$

The proof of Theorem 2.2 now follows from the fact that the exponentiation function is definable in $\langle \mathbb{N}, \leqslant, +, \times, 0, 1 \rangle$ [End72].

Interestingly, for the domain $\mathbb{N}$, addition is definable in first order using multiplication and the order, or by divisibility (div) and the order [Rob49]. Therefore, PARITY is definable in the structures $\langle \mathbb{N}, \leqslant, \times, 0, 1 \rangle$ and $\langle \mathbb{N}, \leqslant, div, 0, 1 \rangle$.

PARITY is also definable with multiplication over the rational numbers.

Theorem 2.4 PARITY is definable in $\langle \mathbb{Q}, \leqslant, +, \times, 0, 1 \rangle$.

Proof. This follows from the fact that the set of integers, $\mathbb{Z}$, is definable in the rational field [Rob49]. The theory of the rational field is therefore undecidable, and PARITY can be defined in the same way as over the natural numbers. $\square$

For the real field, the situation is different since the theory of $\langle \mathbb{R}, \leqslant, +, \times, 0, 1 \rangle$ is decidable [Tar51]. It is open if PARITY can be defined in this case. Nevertheless, PARITY can be defined over the reals with more operations. Consider for instance the exponentiation function x^y.

Theorem 2.5 PARITY is definable in $\langle \mathbb{R}, \leqslant, +, \times, x^y, 0, 1 \rangle$.

Proof. The technique is similar to the previous cases. The set of integers, $\mathbb{Z}$, is definable by the formula: $\varphi(x) \equiv ((-1)^{2x} = 1)$. $\square$

The exponentiation funnction, x^y, is defined over the complex numbers, and is only partially defined over the real numbers. Indeed, if x is a negative number, x^y may not be defined for some y's. As shown in the previous proof, the function x^y permits the definition of interesting subsets of the reals such as the integers. Other extensions of the language, for instance with trigonometric functions permit also the definition of the integers. This is the case with the function "cos". The set of integers, $\mathbb{Z}$, is definable in this context by $\varphi(x) \equiv (\cos(2\pi x) = 1)$, and the same technique as before apply to define PARITY. (Note that in the later case the constant π is definable with the function cos.)

The previous definability results extend to the CONNECTIVITY query.

Theorem 2.6 CONNECTIVITY is definable in $\langle \mathbb{N}, \leqslant, +, \times, 0, 1 \rangle$.

Proof. Assume a finite graph $G = (V, E)$. We use a standard encoding of pairs of natural numbers into natural numbers in order to be able to quantify over edges in the graph. Consider the pairing function $\mathbb{N} \times \mathbb{N}$ 1-1 onto $\mathbb{N}$, defined by $J(x, y) = \frac{1}{2}((x+y)^2 + 3x + y)$. Let K and L be the corresponding first and second projections. The functions J, K and L are definable in $\{0, 1, \leqslant, +, \times\}$ [End72].

The formula $\varphi(E, n)$ defines the smallest integer, n, which is divisible by the kth prime number if $k = J(x, y)$ and there is a *path* from x to y in G.

$$\varphi(E, n) \equiv (\phi(E, n) \wedge \forall n'(\phi(E, n') \Rightarrow n \leqslant n')),$$

where $\phi(E, n)$ is the formula defined by $\phi(E, n) \equiv$

$$\left[\begin{array}{l} ((k = J(x, y) \wedge G(x, y)) \Rightarrow div(k, n)) \wedge \\ \forall x \, \forall y \, \forall z \, \forall k \, \forall k' \, \forall k'' \left(\left(\begin{array}{l} k = J(x, y) \\ \wedge \, k' = J(y, z) \\ \wedge \, k'' = J(x, z) \end{array} \right) \wedge \left(\begin{array}{l} div(k, n) \wedge \\ div(k', n) \end{array} \right) \right) \Rightarrow div(k'', n) \end{array} \right].$$

	$\leqslant$	$+$	$\times$	x^y
$\mathbb{N}$	no	no	yes	yes
$\mathbb{Z}$	no	no	yes	yes
$\mathbb{Q}$	no	no	yes	yes
$\mathbb{R}$	no	no	?	yes

Fig. 1. Definability of PARITY

Connectivity is then expressible by the sentence:

$$\forall x \, \forall y \, \forall k \, \forall n \, ((V(x) \wedge V(y) \wedge k = J(x,y) \wedge \varphi(E,n)) \Rightarrow div(k,n)).\Box$$

More generally we can prove the following much stronger result.

Theorem 2.7 Every relational recursive query is definable in $\langle \mathbb{N}, \leqslant, +, \times, 0, 1\rangle$.

The proof follows from the fact that any recursive property of the natural numbers is definable in $\langle \mathbb{N}, \leqslant, +, \times, 0, 1\rangle$, and relations of arbitrary arity can be encoded by pairing functions as in the proof of Theorem 2.6. Theorem 2.7 subsumes Theorem 2.2 and Theorem 2.6. We presented the later theorems first to illustrate the encoding techniques.

The previous result extends to all the contexts were we proved that PARITY was definable.

We have been able to prove that PARITY and CONNECTIVITY were definable in structures whose theories are undecidable, such as the natural numbers with arithmetic. We make the following conjecture.

Conjecture: PARITY is not definable in structures admitting a decidable theory.

It follows that we conjecture that PARITY is not definable in $\langle \mathbb{R}, \leqslant, +, \times, 0, 1\rangle$. The same conjecture holds for other queries, such as CONNECTIVITY. This follows from the reductions presented in Section 4.

3 Real Constraint Databases

We assume now a (countable) *first-order language* $\mathcal{L}$ with *equality* ($=$) and *order* ($\leqslant$). Let $\sigma = \{R_1, ..., R_n\}$ be a *signature* (or a *database schema*) such that $\mathcal{L} \cap \sigma = \emptyset$, where $R_1, ..., R_n$ are relation symbols. We distinguish between *logical predicates* (e.g., $=, \leqslant$) in $\mathcal{L}$ and *relations* in σ.

Consider, for instance, the language of the real closed field $\mathcal{R} = \langle \mathbb{R}, \leqslant, +, \times, 0, 1\rangle$. Kanellakis, Kuper, and Revesz [KKR90] introduced the concept of a k-ary generalized tuple, which is a constraint expressed as a conjunction of atomic formulas in $\mathcal{L}$ over k-variables. For instance, $(y + x \geqslant 0 \wedge x \leqslant 0)$ is a binary generalized tuple representing a piece of the rational plane. A k-ary finitely representable relation (or generalized relation in [KKR90]) is then a finite set of k-ary generalized tuples. In this framework, a tuple (a, b) in the classical relational database [Cod70] is an abbreviation for the formula $(x = a \wedge y = b)$ represented using only the equality symbol "$=$" and constants.

Let $\sigma = \{R\}$, where R is a binary relation symbol. A relation of R can be seen as an *expansion* of the real field $\mathcal{R}$ to σ, i.e., a structure over the vocabulary $\{\leqslant, +, \times, 0, 1, R\}$, which coincides with $\mathcal{R}$ on $\{\leqslant, +, \times, 0, 1\}$. The new relation R is the database. R may be infinite, but it has to be representable in a *finite* way with $\{\leqslant, +, \times, 0, 1\}$.

In the remainder of the paper, we focus on constraint databases representable in the first-order language for $\mathcal{R}$.

Definition 3.1 Let $R \subseteq \mathbb{R}^k$ be some k-ary relation. The relation R is *finitely representable over* $\mathcal{R}$ if there exists a quantifier-free formula $\varphi(x_1, ..., x_k)$ in $\mathcal{L}$ with k distinct free variables $x_1, ..., x_k$ such that:

$$\forall a_1, ..., a_k \in \mathbb{R}, \quad (a_1, ..., a_k) \in R \text{ iff } \mathcal{R} \models \varphi(a_1, ..., a_k).$$

We further call φ a *finite representation of R*. Let $\mathcal{A}$ be an expansion of $\mathcal{R}$ to σ. The structure $\mathcal{A}$ is said to be *finitely representable (over $\mathcal{R}$)* if for every relation symbol R in σ, $R^{\mathcal{A}}$ is finitely representable.

If an expansion $\mathcal{A}$ of $\mathcal{R}$ to σ is finitely representable then each finite representation of the restriction $\mathcal{A}|_\sigma$ of $\mathcal{A}$ to σ is called a *(database) instance* over σ. Clearly, the class K_σ of instances over σ is effectively enumerable.

Note that K_σ has interesting closure properties. Indeed, it is closed under finite union and intersection and moreover under complementation. This differs from finite model theory (the complement of a finite model is not finite).

Finally, if φ is a sentence in $\mathcal{L} \cup \sigma$, we denote by K_φ the collection of instances satisfying φ, that is, for each finitely representable expansion $\mathcal{A}$, if $\mathcal{A} \models \varphi$, then every finite representation of $\mathcal{A}|_\sigma$ is in K_φ.

A finite relation is representable using only the equality predicate (and constants). The converse doesn't hold. Nevertheless, a monadic relation is representable with equality only iff it is finite or co-finite.

The notion of a *database query* was introduced by Chandra and Harel [CH80] as a mapping Q from finite structures over a given signature σ to relations of a fixed arity n, which is *partial recursive* and satisfies the following *consistency criterion*: If two structures over σ, $\mathcal{A}$ and $\mathcal{B}$ are isomorphic by an isomorphism μ, then $Q(\mathcal{A})$ and $Q(\mathcal{B})$ are isomorphic by the same isomorphism μ. This criterion was then called "genericity" in the database literature.

In the context of finitely representable databases over the real field $\mathcal{R}$, clearly identity becomes the only isomorphism between the finitely representable extensions of $\mathcal{R}$. Hence the above consistency criterion always holds:

Definition 3.2 A *boolean query* K_σ is a partial recursive collection of instances over σ.

The *data complexity* of first order queries is considered in [KKR90] which measures the time or space complexity of queries with respect to the database size. It was shown that the query language for real constraint databases has an NC data complexity upper bound. More recently, Kanellakis and Goldin [KG94] show that the query language of dense order constraints (without $+, \times$) has an AC^0 data complexity upper bound. The result was then extended further in [GST94], to linear constraints over structures finitely representable in $\{=, \leqslant, +\} \cup \mathbb{Z}$ with the number of occurrences of $+$ in every constraint uniformly bounded.

	$\leqslant$	$+$	$\times$	x^y
$\mathbb{N}$	AC^0	AC^0	arithmetical	arithmetical
$\mathbb{Z}$	AC^0	AC^0	arithmetical	arithmetical
$\mathbb{Q}$	AC^0	NC	arithmetical	arithmetical
$\mathbb{R}$	AC^0	NC	NC	arithmetical

Fig. 2. Data Complexity of First-Order Queries

We next present numerous examples of constraint database queries in the areas of geometry, topology, computational geometry, graph theory, and geographical databases. We also provide reductions among these queries and, in particular, the reduction results establish a hierarchy of equivalence classes of queries.

We consider the mappings corresponding to (i) well studied (boolean) graph queries (parity, majority, etc.), and (ii) spatial queries (e.g., region connectivity). For graph queries, the inputs are finite relations (over, e.g., integer values) defined with equality constraints. For spatial queries, we consider queries over potentially infinite relations. For example, suppose that R is an infinite binary relation. It can be seen as defining an infinite set of points on the real plane. The queries considered here concern topological or geometric properties of the input relations.

More specifically, we consider the following graph queries.

- PARITY, **input**: one finite relation R; **output**: *true* iff $|R|$ is even.
- MAJORITY, **input**: two finite relations, R_1 and R_2, of the same arity; **output**: *true* iff $R_1 \subseteq R_2$, and $|R_2| \leqslant 2|R_1|$.
- HALF, **input**: two relations, R_1 and R_2, of the same arity; **output**: *true* iff $R_1 \subseteq R_2$, and $|R_2| = 2|R_1|$.

The topological and geometric queries considered include the following:

- k-*dimensional* REGION CONNECTIVITY, **input**: one relation R of arity k;

output: *true* iff R is connected, i.e., every pair of points in R can be linked by a curve contained entirely in R.

- *k-dimensional* AT LEAST (EXACTLY) ONE HOLE, **input**: one relation R of arity k; **output**: *true* iff R has at least (exactly) one hole (a connected region non intersecting with R but completely surrounded by points in R).
- EULERIAN TRAVERSAL, **input**: one binary relation R consisting of only line segments; **output**: *true* iff there is a traversal going through each line segment exactly once.
- HOMEOMORPHISM, **input**: two binary relations, R_1 and R_2; **output**: *true* iff the sets of points in R_1 and R_2 are homeomorphic in dimension 2.
- EUCLIDEAN SPANNING TREE, **input**: one binary relation representing a finite set of points in $\mathbb{R}^2$; **output**: one relation with arity four representing a set of pairs of points which are edges of the Euclidean spanning tree.

Note that for $k = 1$, the REGION CONNECTIVITY, AT LEAST and EXACTLY ONE HOLE queries can be easily expressed in first order.

4 Reduction Theorems

We present in the following the notions of "first-order reductions" [Imm87] and establish in the next section reductions among many well known graph and topology/geometry queries.

Let $\mathcal{L}' \subseteq \mathcal{L}$ be a first order language and σ a signature. Suppose Q is an n-ary query over another signature $\sigma' = \{R_1, ..., R_k\}$ and for each $1 \leqslant i \leqslant k$, $\varphi_i(\bar{x}_i, \bar{y}_i)$ is a formula in $\mathcal{L}' \cup \sigma$ with distinct free variables in $\bar{x}$ and $\bar{y}$ where $\bar{x} = x_1, ..., x_{\alpha_i}$ and α_i is the arity of R_i. We view the query Q as a new operator where

$$Q[\lambda\bar{x}_1\varphi_1, ..., \lambda\bar{x}_k\varphi_k]$$

denotes a relation $R(x_1, ..., x_n, \bar{y}_1, ..., \bar{y}_k)$ which is the answer to the query Q on input database I where $I(R_i) = \varphi_i$ ($\bar{y}_i$'s are viewed as "parameters"). We denote the extended language by $(\mathcal{L}' \cup \sigma) + Q$. Intuitively, a formula in $(\mathcal{L}' \cup \sigma) + Q$ can "call" the query Q one or more times. We now present the following definition of a first order reduction.

Definition 4.1 Let Q_1 and Q_2 be two (respectively) n_1-ary and n_2-ary queries over signatures (respectively) σ_1 and σ_2. Let $\mathcal{L}' \subseteq \mathcal{L}$. The query Q_1 is *(first order) $\mathcal{L}'$-reducible* to Q_2 if there exists a formula $\varphi(x_1, ..., x_{n_1})$ in $(\mathcal{L}' \cup \sigma_1) + Q_2$ such that for every database instance I of σ_1:

$$\text{for all } a_1, ..., a_{n_1} \in \mathbb{R}, \quad (a_1, ..., a_{n_1}) \in Q_1(I) \quad \Leftrightarrow \quad \mathcal{R} \models \varphi(a_1, ..., a_{n_1}) .$$

Intuitively, Q_1 is $\mathcal{L}'$-reducible to Q_2 if one can systematically construct from an instance I of σ_1 one or more instances of σ_2, apply the query Q_2 one or more times, and obtain the answer to Q_1. Furthermore, all constructions are done in $\mathcal{L}'$.

In the context of databases over $\mathcal{R}$, $\mathcal{L} = \{\leqslant, +, \times, 0, 1\}$. In particular, the reductions may use the order predicate $\leqslant$, the addition $+$ and the multiplication $\times$. Thus, (informally) if $\mathcal{S}$ is a subset of $\{\leqslant, +, \times\}$, an $\mathcal{S}$-reduction uses only logical symbols in $\mathcal{S}$ in the reduction in addition to the relation symbols, sentential connectives and quantifiers. Especially, we consider $\leqslant$-reductions, $\{\leqslant, +\}$-reductions, and $\{\leqslant, +, \times\}$-reductions. Note that $\leqslant$-reductions are AC^0 reductions. When databases involve only integers, $\{\leqslant, +\}$-reductions are also in AC^0 [GST94]. This is not the case of $\{\leqslant, +, \times\}$-reductions since multiplication is not in AC^0 [FSS84].

Lemma 4.1 Let $\mathcal{L}'' \subseteq \mathcal{L}'\ (\subseteq \mathcal{L})$ be two first order languages. Then the following hold:

(1) $\mathcal{L}'$-reducibility is transitive; and
(2) $\mathcal{L}''$-reducibility implies $\mathcal{L}'$-reducibility.

We now consider the first order reductions among queries.

Theorem 4.2 PARITY is first-order $\leqslant$-reducible to MAJORITY; MAJORITY and HALF are first-order $\leqslant$-reducible to each other.

Proof. Let R be a unary input relation for PARITY. Obviously, if there is a number α such that the set $S = \{x \in R \mid x \leqslant \alpha\}$ satisfies the following conditions:

$$\text{MAJORITY}(S, R) = \text{MAJORITY}(R - S, R) = true$$

then $\text{PARITY}(R) = true$, i.e., $|R|$ is even.

Now let R_1, R_2 be the input database. To prove the reduction from MAJORITY to HALF, one only needs to find a subset S of R_1 such that $2|S| = |R_2|$, when $|R_2|$ is even. When $|R_2|$ is odd, it is sufficient to find a strict subset S of R_1 such that $2|S| = |R_2 - \{\alpha\}|$, where α is the biggest element in $R_2 - R_1$. Similarly, a subset of R_1 can be defined by a number β such that $S = \{b \in R_1 \mid b \leqslant \beta\}$. Subsets and strict subsets can be easily expressed in first order. For the reduction from HALF, notice that $|R_1| = 2|R_2|$ iff $\text{MAJORITY}(R_1, R_2) = \text{MAJORITY}(R_2 - R_1, R_2) = true$.

It is easy to see that the above reductions are first order $\leqslant$-reductions. $\square$

It has already been shown [FSS84, CSV84] that PARITY reduces to (finite graph) CONNECTIVITY. Moreover, several classes of (graph) equivalent problems were presented in [CSV84] under "projection" and "constant-depth truth-table" reductions. The reduction results can also be established in terms of $\leqslant$-reductions. For example, the following shows the $\leqslant$-reduction from MAJORITY to (graph) CONNECTIVITY.

Theorem 4.3 MAJORITY is first-order $\leqslant$-reducible to CONNECTIVITY.

As an interesting aside, Gaifman [Gai81] proved that numerous queries were not definable in first-order logic with only equality using the locality property. This property doesn't carry over in presence of order.

We now consider topological and geometric queries and start with the k-dimensional REGION CONNECTIVITY. Assume that $\sigma = \{R\}$, where R is a k-ary relation symbol. The relation $R \subset \mathbb{R}^k$ defines a *connected region* if every pair of points in R can be linked by a continuous curve lying entirely in R. Note that when $k = 1$, the region connectivity query reduces to checking if the input unary relation defines a single interval, which is first-order definable.

Theorem 4.4 For each $k \geqslant 2$, MAJORITY is first order $\{\leqslant, +\}$-reducible to the k-dimensional REGION CONNECTIVITY query.

Proof. We consider a 2-dimensional subplane in the k-dimensional space. In the following, we use (i, j) to refer to a point in the plane. Let $R_2 = \{a_1, ..., a_n\}$ and $R_1 = \{b_1, ..., b_m\} \subseteq R_2$ be the inputs for MAJORITY. Assume without loss of generality that

$$0 < a_1 < a_2 < \cdots < a_n \text{ and } 0 < b_1 < b_2 < \cdots < b_m .$$

Intuitively, we shall construct line segments within a rectangular area bounded by $(0, 0)$ and $(2b_m, a_n)$ as its lower left and upper right corners (respectively), such that (i) the line segments are connected *iff* (ii) the lower left corner is connected to the upper right corner *iff* (iii) $2|R_1| \geqslant |R_2|$, i.e., the MAJORITY query outputs *true*.

For convenience let $a_0 = b_0 = 0$. We construct the following line segments in the plane:

- from $(0, 0)$ to $(2b_m, 0)$;
- from $(0, a_n)$ to $(2b_m, a_n)$; and
- from (b_{i-1}, a_{j-1}) to (b_i, a_j) and from $(b_m + b_{i-1}, a_{j-1})$ to $(b_m + b_i, a_j)$, for $1 \leqslant i \leqslant m$ and $1 \leqslant j \leqslant n$.

An example of resulting line segments is shown in Fig. 3(a), where $R_2 = \{a_1, ..., a_6\}$ and $R_2 = \{b_1, ..., b_4\} \subseteq R_1$ and $b'_i = b_4 + b_i$ for $1 \leqslant i \leqslant 4$. It is easy to see that the previously defined set of line segments is *connected* if and only if

$$\text{MAJORITY}(R_1, R_2) = true.$$

Indeed, the line starting from the point $(0, 0)$ reaches the "ceiling" segment only in this last case. □

Note that the segments used in the above proof are not definable without $\times$. It suffices, however, to replace each diagonal line by three horizontal and two vertical line segments as shown in Fig. 3(b). It seems that additions are necessary since the input to the MAJORITY query is a pair of arbitrary relations. It is unclear whether an $\leqslant$-reduction exists.

Next we consider the AT LEAST and EXACTLY ONE HOLE queries. Obviously, for one dimensional inputs, both queries are first-order expressible. We prove that for higher dimensions, these queries are analogous to region connectivity.

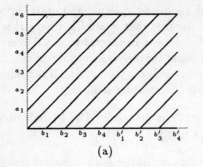 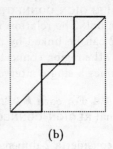

(a)   (b)

Fig. 3. Illustration of reductions

Theorem 4.5

(1) For each $k \geqslant 2$, the MAJORITY query is first-order $\{\leqslant, +\}$-reducible to the k-dimensional AT-LEAST-ONE-HOLE, and EXACTLY-ONE-HOLE queries.

(2) AT-LEAST-ONE-HOLE is first order $\leqslant$-reducible to REGION CONNECTIVITY.

Proof. For (1), the technique is similar to the previous one. For instance, Fig. 4 illustrates the construction for the EXACTLY ONE HOLE query, for $R_2 = \{a_1, ..., a_6\}$ and $R_2 = \{b_1, ..., b_4\} \subseteq R_1$ and $b_i' = b_4 + b_i$ for $1 \leqslant i \leqslant 4$. And for (2), note that a relation R has a hole iff its complement is not region connected. $\square$

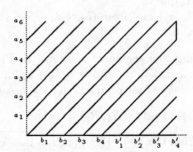

Fig. 4. Reduction to At Least/Exactly One Hole

Next we consider the EULERIAN TRAVERSAL query. The input is a set of line segments and the query returns *true* if there is a traversal which goes through each line segment exactly once continuously. In other words, if we view a line as a set of points, a traversal goes continuously through each point exactly once except for a finite set of points (crossings of lines).

Theorem 4.6 HALF is first order $\{\leqslant, +\}$-reducible to EULERIAN TRAVERSAL.

Proof. The proof of the reduction from the query HALF is similar to the previous reductions. The basic idea of the reduction is to use pairs of parallel line segments in the reduction, similar to that used in Theorem 4.4. An example of the reduction for $R_2 = \{a_1, ..., a_6\}$ and $R_2 = \{b_1, ..., b_4\} \subseteq R_1$, is shown in Fig. 5, where $b_i' = b_4 + b_i$ for $1 \leqslant i \leqslant 4$. Now if HALF returns *true*, the parallel lines originating from $(0, 0)$ go to just below the lowest teeth on the right. Hence a Eulerian traversal exists. Otherwise, if the lines from $(0, 0)$ go too high or too low, the lines are broken into at least two connected parts and Eulerian traversal is impossible. $\square$

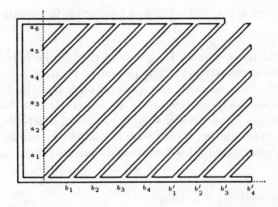

Fig. 5. Reduction to Euler Traversal

In the next example, we consider another topological property — the HOMEOMORPHISM query. Note that two point sets in the real plane are *homeomorphic* if there is a *bi-continuous* bijection on $\mathbb{R}^2$ which maps one to the other. The *homeomorphism* query is defined over databases with two binary relations. The query returns *true* if the two relations are homeomorphic and *false* otherwise.

Theorem 4.7 HALF is first order $\{\leqslant, +\}$-reducible to the HOMEOMORPHISM query.

Proof. The proof uses a similar reduction as in the EULERIAN TRAVERSAL query. The primary differences are that (i) here we use closed areas instead of parallel line segments, and (ii) we need to construct the second relation which is a connected and closed area. $\square$

Finally, we consider EUCLIDEAN SPANNING TREE, whose input is a set of points in $\mathbb{R}^2$ and the output is a set of pairs of points (arity 4) representing the Euclidean spanning tree. We next show that MAJORITY is first order reducible to EUCLIDEAN SPANNING TREE.

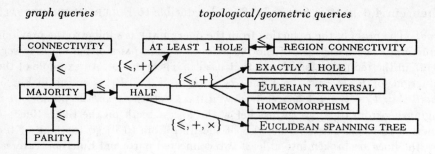

Fig. 6. Summary of Reductions

Theorem 4.8 HALF is first order $\{\leqslant, +, \times\}$-reducible to EUCLIDEAN SPANNING TREE.

Proof. The idea of the reduction is similar to that in the reduction from MAJORITY to REGION CONNECTIVITY. But instead of creating solid line segments, the reduction produces a "dotted" line segments such that the distance between each pair of consecutive points is tiny with respect to the distance between other points, and also much smaller than the minimal difference among the input numbers for HALF. Hence, a Euclidean spanning tree has to use the dotted line segments. These dotted lines form exactly an Euclidean spanning tree iff HALF is *true*. □

Fig. 6 summerizes the reduction results.

5 Conclusion

We have proved that the PARITY and the CONNECTIVITY queries were first-order definable in some contexts, such as the natural numbers with arithmetic. These structures are of little interest to constraint databases, since their theories are not decidable, and we believe, that these two queries are not definable in structures admitting a decidable theory.

Constraint databases and query languages can only be defined over structures with decidable theories (moreover with quantifier elimination and a reasonable data complexity). It follows from our results that, essentially, PARITY and CONNECTIVITY are not first-order queries over constraint databases in general. We proved that many queries of interest for constraint databases, arising in graph theory, computational geometry, or geographical databases are not expressible either, as soon as parity is not expressible using reductions theorems. In particular, REGION CONNECTIVITY, EXACTLY 1 HOLE, AT LEAST 1 HOLE, EULERIAN TRAVERSAL, HOMEOMORPHISM, and EUCLIDEAN SPANNING TREE are not definable over real dense order and linear constraint databases.

The results presented in this paper settle many questions relative to the expressive power of first-order logic with addition. In [KKR90], Kanellakis, Kuper and Revesz made the conjecture that the EUCLIDEAN SPANNING TREE query is not definable with polynomial constraints over the reals, that is in $\mathcal{R} = \langle \mathbb{R}, \leqslant, +, \times, 0, 1 \rangle$. Since we conjecture that parity is not definable in this latter context, we draw the same conjecture, but are unable to provide more evidence.

It follows that from a practical point of view, query languages for constraint databases should support aggregate functions, such as counting, and recursion mechanisms. These issues have been addressed recently in the literature. Inflationary Datalog with negation was used in the context of dense order constraint databases [KKR90], and aggregate functions were discussed in [Kup93, CK95].

Acknowledgments

The authors wish to thank Vassos Hadzilacos, Chee Yap and Scott Weinstein for fruitful discussions; and Leonid Libkin for commenting on an earlier version of the paper.

References

[ACGK94] F. Afrati, S. Cosmadakis, S. Grumbach, and G. Kuper. Expressiveness of linear vs. polynomial constraints in database query languages. In *Second Workshop on the Principles and Practice of Constraint Programming*, 1994.

[AHV94] S. Abiteboul, R. Hull, and V. Vianu. *Foundations of Databases*. Addison-Wesley, 1994.

[CH80] A. Chandra and D. Harel. Computable Queries for Relational Data Bases. *Journal of Computer and System Sciences*, 21(2):156–178, Oct. 1980.

[CK95] J. Chomicki and G. Kuper. Measuring infinite relations. In *Proc. 14th ACM Symp. on Principles of Database Systems*, San Jose, May 1995.

[Cod70] E.F. Codd. A relational model of data for large shared data banks. *Communications of ACM*, 13:6:377–387, 1970.

[CSV84] A. K. Chandra, L. Stockmeyer, and U. Vishkin. Constant depth reducibility. *SIAM J. on Computing*, 13(2):423–439, May 1984.

[Ehr61] A. Ehrenfeucht. An application of games to the completeness problem for formalized theories. *Fund. Math*, 49, 1961.

[End72] H. Enderton. *A Mathematical Introduction to Logic*. Academic Press, 1972.

[Fag74] R. Fagin. Generalized first-order spectra and polynomial-time recognizable sets. *Complexity of Computations, SIAM-AMS Proceedings 7*, pages 43–73, 1974.

[Fag93] R. Fagin. Finite model theory - a personal perspective. *Theoretical Computer Science*, 116:3–31, 1993.

[Fra54] R. Fraïssé. Sur les classifications des systèmes de relations. *Publ. Sci. Univ Alger*, I:1, 1954.

[FSS84] M. Furst, J. B. Saxe, and M. Sipser. Parity, circuits, and the polynomial-time hierarchy. *Mathematical System Theory*, 17:13–27, 1984.

[Gai81]   H. Gaifman. On local and non local properties. In J. Stern, editor, *Proc. Herbrand Symposium Logic Colloquium*, pages 105–135. North Holland, 1981.

[GS94]   S. Grumbach and J. Su. Finitely representable databases. In *13th ACM Symp. on Principles of Database Systems*, pages 289–300, Minneapolis, May 1994.

[GS95]   S. Grumbach and J. Su. Dense order constraint databases. In *Proc. 14th ACM Symp. on Principles of Database Systems*, San Jose, May 1995.

[GST94]   S. Grumbach, J. Su, and C. Tollu. Linear constraint databases. In D. Leivant, editor, *Logic and Computational Complexity Workshop*, Indianapolis, 1994. Springer Verlag. to appear in LNCS.

[Gur88]   Y. Gurevich. *Current Trends in Theoretical Computer Science, E. Borger Ed.*, chapter Logic and the Challenge of Computer Science, pages 1–57. Computer Science Press, 1988.

[Imm87]   N. Immerman. Languages that capture complexity classes. *SIAM J. of Computing*, 16(4):760–778, Aug 1987.

[KG94]   P. Kanellakis and D. Goldin. Constraint programming and database query languages. In *Manuscript*, 1994.

[KKR90]   P. Kanellakis, G Kuper, and P. Revesz. Constraint query languages. In *Proc. 9th ACM Symp. on Principles of Database Systems*, pages 299–313, Nashville, 1990.

[Kup93]   G.M. Kuper. Aggregation in constraint databases. In *Proc. First Workshop on Principles and Practice of Constraint Programming*, 1993.

[PVV94]   J. Paredaens, J. Van den Bussche, and D. Van Gucht. Towards a theory of spatial database queries. In *Proc. 13th ACM Symp. on Principles of Database Systems*, pages 279–288, 1994.

[PVV95]   J. Paredaens, J. Van den Bussche, and D. Van Gucht. First-order queries on finite structures over the reals. In *Proc. IEEE Symposium on Logic In Computer Science*, 1995.

[Rev93]   P. Revesz. A closed form for datalog queries with integer (gap)-order constraints. *Theoretical Computer Science*, 116(1):117–149, 1993.

[Rev95]   P. Revesz. Datalog queries of set constraint databases. In *Proc. Int. Conf. on Database Theory*, 1995.

[Rob49]   J. Robinson. Decidability and decision problems in arithmetic. *Journal of Symbolic Logic*, 14:98–114, 1949.

[Tar51]   A. Tarski. *A Decision method for elementary algebra and geometry*. Univ. of California Press, Berkeley, California, 1951.

[Yao90]   F.F. Yao. *Handbook of Theorical Computer Science*, volume A, chapter 7 Computational Geometry, pages 343–389. J. Van Leeuwen, North Holland, 1990.

On Similarity Queries for Time-Series Data: Constraint Specification and Implementation

Dina Q Goldin * and Paris C Kanellakis *

Department of Computer Science, Brown University
PO Box 1910, Providence RI 02912, USA.
Tel: 1-401-863-7647. Fax: 1-401-863-7657.
Email: dgk@cs.brown.edu and pck@cs.brown.edu.

Abstract. Constraints are a natural mechanism for the specification of similarity queries on time-series data. However, to realize the expressive power of constraint programming in this context, one must provide the matching implementation technology for efficient indexing of very large data sets. In this paper, we formalize the intuitive notions of exact and approximate similarity between time-series patterns and data. Our definition of similarity extends the distance metric used in [2, 7] with invariance under a group of transformations. Our main observation is that the resulting, more expressive, set of constraint queries can be supported by a new indexing technique, which preserves all the desirable properties of the indexing scheme proposed in [2, 7].

1 Introduction

1.1 Approximate Matching of Time-Series Data

Time-series are the principal format of data in many applications, from financial to scientific. Time-series data are sequences of real numbers representing measurements at uniformly-spaced temporal instances. The next generation of database technology, with its emphasis on multimedia, is expected to provide clean interfaces (i.e., declarative specification languages) to facilitate data mining of time-series. However, any proposal of such linguistic facilities must be supported by indexing (i.e., be implementable with reasonable I/O efficiency) for very large data sets. Examples of recent database research towards this goal include [2, 7, 18].

A most basic problem in this area is *First-Occurrence Subsequence Matching*, defined as follows: *given a query sequence Q of length n and a much longer data sequence $\overline{S}$ of length N, find the first occurrence of a contiguous subsequence within $\overline{S}$ that matches Q exactly.*

A wide range of algorithms has been developed for *internal* (i.e., in-core) versions of this question [1] for strings over an alphabet or for values over bounded discrete domains. There are particularly elegant linear-time $O(n+N)$ algorithms

---

* Research supported by ONR Contract N00014-94-1-1153.

(by Knuth-Morris-Pratt and Boyer-Moore) and practical searching utilities for more general patterns instead of query strings Q (e.g., regular patterns in grep). The part of this technology that is most related to our paper is the Rabin-Karp randomized linear-time algorithm [14], which provides an efficient in-core solution based on *fingerprint* functions. Fingerprints are a form of sequence hashing that allow constant-time comparisons between hash values and are incrementally computable.

A variant of the above problem involves finding all occurrences; this is called the *All-Occurrences Subsequence Matching* problem.

The above two problems have variants when the data consists of many sequences of the same length as the query. The *First(All)-Occurrence(s) Whole-Sequence Matching* problem is: *given a query sequence Q of length n and a set of N/n data sequences, all of the same length n, find the first (all) of the data sequences that match Q exactly.*

Since the size of the data in commercial applications of time-series data mining is usually too large to be stored internally, the research in various time-series matching problems has concentrated on the case when storage is *external* (i.e., secondary as opposed to in-core). Here we are interested in:

External solutions to the All-Occurrences Matching problems (either Subsequence or Whole-Sequence), with two additional characteristics:

- the match can be *approximate*;
- the match is up to *similarity*.

We define "approximate" in this subsection and "similar" in the next.

Time-series data in continuous (e.g., real-valued) domains is inherently inexact, due to the unavoidable imprecision of measuring devices and clocking strategies. This forces us to work with the approximate version of the various matching problems.

Given a tolerance $\epsilon \geq 0$ and a distance metric D between sequences, sequences S_1 and S_2 match approximately within tolerance ϵ when $D(S_1, S_2) \leq \epsilon$.

The *All-Occurrences Approximate Matching* problems (either *Subsequence* or *Whole-Sequence*) are defined as before, but with "match approximately within tolerance ϵ" instead of "match exactly".

For external solutions to the All-Occurrence Whole-Sequence Approximate version, we refer to [2, 18]; for the All-Occurrence Subsequence Approximate version, we refer to [7].

A further characteristic of time-series data that is used to advantage, is that they have a *skewed energy spectrum*, to use the terminology borrowed from Discrete Signal Processing [16]. As a result, most of the technology of information retrieval in this area is influenced by signal processing methods.

1.2 Approximately Similar Time-Series Data

The database applications of interest involve queries expressing notions of "user-perceived similarity". Here are some examples of applications for approximate time-series matching that illustrate this notion of similarity:

- find months in the last five years with sales patterns of minivans like last month's;
- find other companies whose stock price fluctuations resembles Microsoft's;
- find months in which the temperature in Paris showed patterns similar to this month's pattern.

In many cases, it is more natural to allow the matching of sequences that are not close to each other in an Euclidean sense. For example, two companies may have identical stock price fluctuations, but one's stock is worth twice as much as the other at all times. For another example, two sales patterns might be similar, even if the sales volumes are different. We shall refer to the difference between these sequences as *scale*. In another example, the temperature on two different days may start at different values but then go up and down in exactly the same way. We shall refer to the difference between these sequences as *shift*. A good time-series data-mining mechanism should be able to find similar sequences, as illustrated by these examples, up to scaling and shifting.

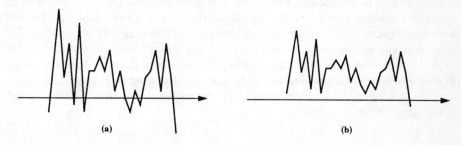

Fig. 1. Sequence (b) is a similarity transformation of (a).

Combinations of scaling and shifting are shape-preserving transformations, known as *similarity transformations* in the mathematical field of Transformational Geometry [15]. We will approach the definition of similarity from this well established geometrical perspective:

Let G be a set of transformations then two sets of points are similar if there exists a transformation, in G, which maps one to the other.

In geometry, a transformation typically belongs to a group. Combinations of scale and shift are affine transformations. In practice, the user may restrict the allowable transformations to a set that may not be group, by imposing constraints on the scaling and shifting factors, or by fixing one or both factors.

Let D be a distance metric between sequences and $\epsilon \geq 0$ a tolerance. Query sequence Q is *approximately similar* within tolerance ϵ to data sequence S when there exists a similarity transformation T so that $D(Q, T(S)) \leq \epsilon$. When ϵ is set to 0, we have *exact similarity*.

Approximate and exact similarity queries can now be defined just like approximate and exact matching queries were defined in the last section.

The *All-Occurrences Approximate Similarity* problems (either *Subsequence* or *Whole-Sequence*) are defined as was Matching, but with "approximately similar within tolerance ϵ" instead of "match approximately within tolerance ϵ". Analogous definitions apply for *All-Occurrences Exact Similarity* problems (either *Subsequence* or *Whole-Sequence*).

When T is restricted to be the identity transformation, the various similarity problems become the matching problems of the last section. In this sense, our work is a generalization of the work of [7]. This generalization is in the direction of [8], which discusses translation and distortion transformations but does not provide the guarantees of [7] and of our indexing scheme.

A general framework for similarity queries is described in [9]. Our work happens to be (an efficiently solvable) special case. The [9] framework for similarity-based queries has three components: a pattern language P, an approximation language (they refer to it as transformation rule language), and a query language. In our case, P is the set of allowable transformations on the query sequence Q. An expression in P specifies a set of data objects; in our case, it is the set of all sequences exactly similar to Q. Approximations have a cost, and the distance between objects is defined as the minimal cost of reaching one object from the other via approximations. In our case, the approximations are the distortions in the time-series data (i.e., the jiggling of individual points); the cost is the distance between the original sequence and the distorted one. Note that membership testing in the [9] framework is at best exponential; thus this framework is too general for our purposes.

1.3 Contributions and Overview

Our main contribution is: *A syntax and semantics for similarity queries, that account for approximate matching, scaling and shifting, and that have efficient indexing support.* We show this using a new indexing technique, which preserves all the desirable properties of the indexing scheme proposed in [2, 7].

In Section 2, we provide a *semantics* for similarity querying where we use the *similarity distance* between Q and S (defined in Section 2.2) as the distance metric. Similarity distance constitutes a *good distance metric* because it is non-negative, symmetric, and effectively computable; it also obeys the triangle inequality. This is not true of the "naive" distance metrics that correspond more closely to the formulation of the problem in the Section 1.2. The semantics of Section 2.2 serves as the basis for the *internal representation* of the query, i.e., our *normal form*.

In Section 3, we show that the semantics of Section 2.2 has several desirable properties, such as *updateability* and *well-behaved trails*, which allow us to provide efficient implementations for similarity querying, both in the internal and external query setting. We first adapt the criteria put forth in [2, 7] (Section 3.1) and satisfy them using fingerprints of the normal form (Section 3.2). We then argue that fingerprints are incrementally computable (Section 3.3), can be used ala Rabin-Karp [14] for internal searching (Section 3.4), and most importantly external indexing (Section 3.5).

This is the implementation technology that is needed to support the internal representation of Section 2. Our new indexing technique combines the MBR structure of [7] with our internal representation. Many spatial data-structures can be used, for examples varieties of R-trees (see [17] for a comprehensive survey of the available external data-structures).

In Section 4, we provide a constraint *syntax* for similarity querying. We show how various query variations can be expressed and translated into the internal representation of Section 2. This translation also clarifies the relationship of the problem as defined in Section 1.2 with the semantics of Section 2.2.

The syntax could be embedded in most constraint logic programming languages [5, 6, 10] or constraint query languages [3, 4, 11, 12]. This completes the connection between high level specification and implementation.

The importance of combining high-level specification with efficient implementation is the common theme of constraint databases (e.g., see [4, 13]) and the main motivation for this work. In Section 5, we close with some open problems and future work.

2 The Semantics of Similarity Queries

2.1 Similarity Transformations and Normal Forms

An *n-sequence* X is a sequence $\{x_1, \ldots, x_n\}$ of real numbers. Each n-sequence X has an *average* $\alpha(X)$ and a *deviation* $\sigma(X)$:

$$\alpha(X) = (1/n) \sum_{1 \leq i \leq n} x_i; \quad \sigma(X) = ((1/n) \sum_{1 \leq i \leq n} (x_i - \alpha(X))^2)^{1/2}.$$

We shall feel free to drop the arguments to α and σ, treating them as constants, when the context is not ambiguous.

A pair of reals (a, b) defines a *similarity transformation* $T_{a,b}$ over n-sequences by mapping each element x_i to $a * x_i + b$. We will assume that all similarity transformations are *non-degenerate*, i.e., that $a \neq 0$. In fact, we will further assume that $a > 0$; this restriction on a implies that a sequence symmetric to X w.r.t. the x-axis is not considered similar to it.

Definition 2.1 We say that X is *similar* to Y if there exist some $(a, b) \in [R^+ \times R]$ such that $X = T_{a,b}(Y)$.

This *similarity relation* is reflexive, symmetric, and transitive:

- **Reflexivity:** for any sequence X, $X = T_{1,0}(X)$ [the *identity* transformation];
- **Symmetry:** if $X = T_{a,b}(Y)$ then $Y = T_{1/a,-b/a}(X) = T_{a,b}^{-1}(X)$ [the *inverse* of $T_{a,b}$];
- **Transitivity:** if $X = T_{a,b}(Y)$ and $Y = T_{c,d}(Z)$, then $X = T_{ac,ad+b}(Z) = (T_{a,b} * T_{c,d})(Z)$ [the non-commutative *product* of $T_{a,b}$ and $T_{c,d}$].

Therefore, the set of all sequences similar to a given one constitutes an equivalence class, which we call a *similarity class*; we shall denote the similarity class of X by X^*. The similarity relation partitions all n-sequences into similarity classes.

To be able to refer to similarity classes, we need a way to compute a unique representative for each class, given any member in it. Towards that end, we now define normal forms of sequences.

Definition 2.2 An n-sequence X is *normal* if $\alpha(X) = 0$ and $\sigma(X) = 1$.

Let X be normal and Y be similar to X, i.e., $Y = T_{a,b}(X)$ for some $(a, b) \in [R^+ \times R]$. Then, $\alpha(Y) = b$ and $\sigma(Y) = a$:

$$\alpha(Y) = (1/n) \sum_{1 \leq i \leq n} y_i = (1/n) \sum_{1 \leq i \leq n} (ax_i + b) = (a/n)\alpha(X) + b = b;$$
$$\sigma^2(Y) = (1/n) \sum_{1 \leq i \leq n} (y_i - \alpha(Y))^2 = (1/n) \sum_{1 \leq i \leq n} (ax_i + b - b)^2 =$$
$$(a^2/n) \sum_{1 \leq i \leq n} (x_i - 0)^2 = a^2 * \sigma^2(X) = a^2.$$

Y is normal only if $\sigma(Y) = a = 1$ and $\alpha(Y) = b = 0$; this is the identity transformation. This means that a similarity class has exactly one normal member; we will call it the *normal form* of all the members of the class.

Given any n-sequence X, $\nu(X)$ denotes the normal form of X^*. If α is the average of X, and σ is the deviation of X, we've shown that $X = \sigma * \nu(X) + \alpha$. Therefore, we can compute $\nu(X)$ from X by the inverse transformation:

$$\nu(X) = T_{\sigma,\alpha}^{-1}(X) = T_{1/\sigma, -\alpha/\sigma}(X).$$

In a transformation $T_{a,b}$, we call a the *scale factor* and b the *shift factor*. If a is 1, the transformation is a pure *shift*; if b is 0, it is a pure *scaling*. The identity transformation is a pure shift; the inverse of a shift is a shift; and the product of two shifts is also a shift. This allows us to conclude that the set of all shifts of a given sequence is an equivalence class. The same is true of the set of all scalings. The normal form for these classes is defined just as for the general case.

2.2 Similarity Distance and Semantics

Given two sequences X and Y, the *similarity distance* between X and Y is the distance between the normal forms of their respective similarity classes:

Definition 2.3
$$D_S(X, Y) = D_E(\nu(X), \nu(Y)),$$

where D_E is the *Euclidean distance*, defined as follows:

Definition 2.4
$$D_E(S_1, S_2) = \left(\sum_{1 \leq i \leq l} (S_1[i] - S_2[i])^2 \right)^{1/2}.$$

Any proper distance metric D for n-sequences can be used instead of D_E. Since we will be using techniques from Discrete Signal Processing (DSP) and the Euclidean distance is a standard distance metric in DSP, we have chosen to use it here.

Note that the similarity distance between any pair of sequences from X^* and Y^* is the same; this gives us a *distance metric for similarity classes*:

Definition 2.5
$$D_S(X^*, Y^*) = D_S(X, Y).$$

A distance metric should be non-negative and symmetric, and it should obey the triangle inequality. A good distance metric should also be effectively computable. It is easy to see that similarity distance satisfies all these criteria.

> **Remark:** Note that there are definitions of distance that correspond more closely to the naive formulation of the problem. For example, given Q and S, we could have used the minimum Euclidean distance between Q and all $S' \in S^*$ (the equivalence class of S); let us denote this distance by $D_m(Q, S^*)$. However, this definition is not symmetric: $D_m(Q, S^*) \neq D_m(S, Q^*)$. Given Q and S, we could have also tried to choose the minimum Euclidean distance between Q' and S' for all $Q' \in Q^*$ (the equivalence class of S) and $S' \in S^*$ (the equivalence class of Q). However, by choosing the members of Q^* and S^* with arbitrarily small deviations, this distance will always approach 0. The normal forms provide a distance metric that does not suffer from any of these defects.

By using similarity distance, we are now ready to define a *similarity semantics* for the *All-Occurrences Subsequence Approximate Similarity* problem.

> Given a query sequence Q, a time-series $\overline{S}$, a tolerance $\epsilon \geq 0$, and a similarity relation [which partitions sequences into equivalence classes with normal forms], find all contiguous subsequences S in the time-series $\overline{S}$ such that $D_S(Q, S) \leq \epsilon$.

Note that these semantics are slightly different from the problem formulation in Section 1.2. The differences will be clarified (and bridged) in Section 4. To conclude this subsection, we want to consider the *All-Occurrences Subsequence Exact Similarity* problem (i.e., when $\epsilon = 0$).

> Given a query sequence Q, a time-series $\overline{S}$, and a similarity relation [which partitions sequences into equivalence classes with normal forms], find all contiguous subsequences S in the time-series $\overline{S}$ such that Q and S are similar [belong to the same equivalence class].

The exact case can be answered using the normal forms, because Q and S are in the same equivalence class if and only if $\nu(Q) = \nu(S)$. Finally, analogous definitions apply to Whole-Sequence problems.

3 Indexing of Similarity Queries

3.1 Sequence Fingerprints: Criteria and Definitions

Computing the similarity distance D_S between any two n-sequences requires $O(n)$ operations. An efficient implementation of similarity querying cannot afford to compute D_S every time for each sequence in the data set (for the Whole-Sequence case), or for each contiguous subsequence in the time-series (for the Subsequence case).

Following the approach of [14], which has gained wide acceptance, we introduce a *fingerprint* function F, together with a fingerprint distance metric D_F. This fingerprint mechanism provides *fast rejection*, filtering out most of the non-similar sequences.

A fingerprint mechanism needs to satisfy the following criteria:

- **Compactness:** The comparison of the fingerprints of two n-sequences can be done in constant time.
- **Validity:** If S is a valid query answer, then the comparison of $F(S)$ and $F(Q)$ should return *TRUE*:

$$D_S(X, Y) \leq \epsilon \Longrightarrow D_F(F(X), F(Y)) \leq \epsilon.$$

- **Accuracy:** If the comparison of $F(S)$ and $F(Q)$ returns *TRUE*, S is highly likely to be a valid query answer.
- **Updateability:** Computing the fingerprints of all subsequences of an N-sequence for N much larger than n can be done in $O(N)$ time, by *updating* the fingerprint value as we move along rather than recomputing it for every subsequence.

We now define the fingerprint function F as well as the fingerprint distance function D_F. These definitions are similar to the ones used for Approximate Matching in [2] and [7].

Definition 3.1 A *fingerprint* $F(X)$ of an n-sequence $X = \{x_1, \ldots, x_n\}$ is the tuple

$$[DFT_1(\nu(X)), \ldots, DFT_l(\nu(X))],$$

where l is a small constant (such as 3), and DFT_m is the m'th coefficient of the *Discrete Fourier Transform* of $\nu(X)$:

$$DFT_m(s_0, \ldots, s_{n-1}) = \frac{1}{\sqrt{n}} \sum_{j=0}^{n-1} (s_j e^{-j(2\pi i)m/n}),$$

where $i = \sqrt{-1}$.

Note that DFT_m is a complex number: $DFT_m = a_m + b_m i$ for some $a_m, b_m \in R$. Thus, F is specified by a sequence of $2l$ real values. Note that we are not including DFT_0 in the fingerprint, since its coefficients are both 0 for normal sequences.

Definition 3.2 The *fingerprint distance* D_F between $F(X)$ and $F(Y)$ is the Euclidean distance between the real-valued sequences for $F(X)$ and $F(Y)$.

By taking l to be a small constant our fingerprint mechanism is compact. In the subsections below, we establish its validity, accuracy, and updateability.

3.2 Validity and Accuracy of Fingerprinting

To establish the validity of fingerprinting, we need to show that

$$D_S(X,Y) \leq \epsilon \implies D_F(F(X), F(Y)) \leq \epsilon.$$

We make use of the fact that the *DFT* is a *linear function*, i.e.,

$$DFT_m(aX + bY) = aDFT_m(X) + bDFT_m(Y)$$

for all scalars a and b. Also, we rely on *Parseval's theorem*, well-known in DSP:

$$\sum_{0 \leq m \leq n-1} |DFT_m(X)|^2 = \sum_{0 \leq i \leq n-1} |x_i|^2.$$

And we make use of the fact that the coefficients of DFT_0 for normal sequences are both 0. First, we show that $D_S(X,Y) \geq D_F(F(X), F(Y))$:

$$D_S(X,Y) = D_E(\nu(X), \nu(Y)) = (\sum_{0 \leq i \leq n-1} |\nu(x_i) - \nu(y_i)|^2)^{1/2} =$$
$$= (\sum_{0 \leq m \leq n-1} |DFT_m(\nu(X) - \nu(Y))|^2)^{1/2} \geq$$
$$\geq (\sum_{0 \leq m \leq l} |DFT_m(\nu(X) - \nu(Y))|^2)^{1/2} = D_F(F(X), F(Y)).$$

It immediately follows that $D_F(F(X), F(Y)) \leq \epsilon$ whenever $D_S(X,Y) \leq \epsilon$.

To establish accuracy, we want to know how likely it is that $D_S(X,Y) \leq \epsilon$ provided that $D_F(F(X), F(Y)) \leq \epsilon$. The cases when $D_F(F(X), F(Y)) \leq \epsilon$ but $D_S(X,Y) \leq \epsilon$ represent *false alarms*, and we want to minimize their occurrence. Therefore, we would like the ratio $D_F(F(X), F(Y))/D_S(X,Y)$ to be close to 1.

The actual ratio strongly depends on the nature of the data sequences. It is worst in the case of white noise, when

$$D_F(F(X), F(Y))/D_S(X,Y) = (l+1)/n.$$

As we mentioned in Section 1.1, time-series data have a *skewed energy spectrum*, which implies that

The amplitude of DFT_m decreases rapidly for increasing values of m.

As shown in [2], 2-3 coefficients are usually sufficient to provide good accuracy. Therefore, we may assume that the length l of the fingerprint is ≤ 3. (Note that, the randomization ala Rabin-Karp [14] makes no assumptions about the spectrum.)

3.3 Updateability of Fingerprinting

When computing fingerprints of all subsequences of length n for a much longer sequence of length N, the efficiency of the algorithm hinges on a property of the fingerprint that we call *updateability*:

Given the fingerprint of a subsequence $\{x_k, \ldots, x_{k+n-1}\}$, it is possible to compute the fingerprint for $\{x_{k+1}, \ldots, x_{k+n}\}$ in constant time.

Let X_k be the first subsequence, and X_{k+1} be the second subsequence. We show how to compute the fingerprint $F(X_{k+1})$ from the fingerprint $F(X_k)$ in constant time. As inputs to the update step, we assume that we have the values of the following expressions:

$$\sum_{k \leq j \leq k+n-1} x_j, \quad \sum_{k \leq j \leq k+n-1} (x_j)^2, \alpha(X_k), \sigma(X_k), DFT_1(X_k), \ldots, DFT_l(X_k), F(X_k).$$

We also assume that all constants (such as $1/n$) are pre-computed. During the update step, we obtain the values for the above expressions with $k + 1$ instead of k; the computation proceeds as follows:

1. Increment k to $k + 1$;
2. Look up x_{k+1}, x_{k+n};
3. Compute $\sum_{k+1 \leq j \leq k+n} x_j$. This involves one subtraction and one addition:

$$\sum_{k+1 \leq j \leq k+n} x_j = (\sum_{k \leq j \leq k+n-1} x_j) - x_k + x_{k+n};$$

4. Compute $\sum_{k+1 \leq j \leq k+n} (x_j)^2$, using two multiplications, one subtraction and one addition:

$$\sum_{k+1 \leq j \leq k+n} x_j^2 = (\sum_{k \leq j \leq k+n-1} x_j^2) - x_k^2 + x_{k+n}^2;$$

5. Compute $\alpha(X_{k+1})$, using one multiplication:

$$\alpha(X_{k+1}) = \alpha_{k+1} = (1/n) \sum_{k+1 \leq j \leq k+n} x_j;$$

6. Compute $\sigma(X_{k+1})$, using two multiplications, one subtraction and one square root:

$$\sigma^2(X_{k+1}) = \sigma_{k+1}^2 = (1/n)(\sum_{k+1 \leq j \leq k+n} x_j^2) - \alpha_{k+1}^2;$$

7. Compute $DFT_1(X_{k+1}), \ldots, DFT_l(X_{k+1})$, using one subtraction, one addition and two multiplications for each index:

$$DFT_m(X_{k+1}) = \frac{1}{\sqrt{n}} \sum_{0 \leq j \leq n-1} (x_{j+k+1} e^{-j(2\pi i)m/n}) =$$

$$= \frac{1}{\sqrt{n}} \sum_{1 \leq j \leq n} (x_{j+k} e^{-(j-1)(2\pi i)m/n}) = e^{(2\pi i)m/n} (DFT_m(X_k) + \frac{x_{n+k} - x_k}{\sqrt{n}});$$

8. Compute the fingerprint of X_{k+1}, using one division for each index. Here, we rely on the linearity of DFT's, and on the fact that $DFT_m(1)$ is 0 when $m > 0$:

$$DFT_m(\nu(X_{k+1})) = DFT_m(X_{k+1}/\sigma_{k+1} - \alpha_{k+1}/\sigma_{k+1}) =$$

$$= (1/\sigma_{k+1})DFT_m(X_{k+1}) - (\alpha_{k+1}/\sigma_{k+1})DFT_m(1) = DFT_m(X_{k+1})/\sigma_{k+1}.$$

Note that the above algorithm is *on-line*, suitable in a situation when the data are streaming past and we can never back over it. In addition, we have shown that the fingerprint of [2] for time-series approximate matching (without similarity) is also updateable.

3.4   Internal Algorithms

In this section, we sketch out the internal implementation of similarity queries, omitting the details that can be found in the works we reference.

The implementation is based on a *unified internal representation* of a similarity query; its definition is given below. We will show in Section 4 how to translate the constraint-based syntax of a user into to the unified internal representation. For the rest of this section, we assume that we have already obtained this internal representation.

Definition 3.3 The *internal representation* of a similarity query consists of: (query sequence Q, the values $\{\epsilon_i, l_\alpha, u_\alpha, l_\sigma, u_\sigma\}$).

This corresponds to the Section 2.2 semantics of All-Occurrences Subsequence Approximate Similarity:

Find all S such that $D_S(Q, S) \leq \epsilon_i$, $l_\alpha \leq \alpha(S) \leq u_\alpha$, $l_\sigma \leq \sigma(S) \leq u_\sigma$.

The updateability results established in Section 3.3 allow us to answer the query for the *in-core case* with an algorithm much like that of [14]. We proceed through the sequences and the subsequences, comparing $D_F(F(Q), F(S))$ to ϵ_i and checking $\alpha(S)$ and $\sigma(S)$ against the bounds. In the case of a potential match, we use the user formulation of the problem (Section 4) to determine if we have a valid query answer, or if it is a *false alarm*.

When we want to avoid run-time linear scanning of the data, we need to create an *index structure* for it. This is the case for any database application of similarity querying. A naive index structure is a list of tuples of the following form:

$[F(X), \alpha(X), \sigma(X),$ location of $X]$.

The algorithm is very similar to the in-core case; we scan the index and look for potential matches:

Is $D_F(F(Q), F(S)) \leq \epsilon_i$, $l_\alpha \leq \alpha(S) \leq u_\alpha$, and $l_\sigma \leq \sigma(S) \leq u_\sigma$?

Whenever one is found, we retrieve X and do the final determination.

3.5   External Indexing

To speed up index searching, we can instead build an indexing mechanism that allows spatial access methods for range queries of multidimensional points. The query point P_Q is computed from the internal query representation:

$$P_Q = (F(Q), m_\alpha, m_\sigma), \text{ where } m_\alpha = (u_\alpha + l_\alpha)/2, \ m_\sigma = (u_\sigma + l_\sigma)/2.$$

The answer to the similarity query is the set of all points $(F(X), \alpha(X), \sigma(X))$ such that:

$F(X)$ is within ϵ of $F(Q)$, $\alpha(X)$ is within $(u_\alpha - l_\alpha)/2$ of m_α, and $\sigma(X)$ is within $(u_\sigma - l_\sigma)/2$ of m_σ.

Though the index structure described above performs well for the whole-sequence case, it is unsuitable in the subsequence setting. This is due to a very simple observation: for a real sequence of length m, the there would be $m - n + 1$ indices with $2l$ reals each. Such space overhead renders indexing less efficient than a direct sequential scan of the data [7].

This problem is overcome with the Minimum Bounding Rectangle (MBR) technique, introduced in [7]. This technique significantly reduces the size of the indexing structure, though introducing some false alarms in the process. Our final indexing method consists of combining the MBR technique with the spatial access approach described above.

The MBR technique relies of the *continuity* of subsequence indices:

– **Continuity:** Given two adjacent subsequences, the difference between the corresponding coefficients of their indices is likely to be small.

We conclude the discussion of indexing by verifying that our indexing possesses the continuity property. This is a "heuristic" statistical argument, that also applies to [7] (where continuity was assumed, but not shown).

Denote adjacent sequences by $X_0 = \{x_0, \ldots, x_{n-1}\}$ and $X_1 = \{x_1, \ldots, x_n\}$; denote the corresponding indices by $(\alpha_0, \sigma_0, F_0)$ and $(\alpha_1, \sigma_1, F_1)$; and Denote the order of the expected value of an expression by $\approx$. Assume that n is reasonably large, so that $1/n$ is considered to be a small constant. Proceed by considering each element of the index separately.

1. The expected value of $|\alpha_1 - \alpha_0|$ is on the order of σ_0/n:

$$|\alpha_1 - \alpha_0| = |x_n - x_0|/n \approx \sigma_0/n.$$

2. The expected value of $|\sigma_1 - \sigma_0|$ is on the order of σ_0/n:

$$|\sigma_1 - \sigma_0|(\sigma_1 + \sigma_0) = |\sigma_1^2 - \sigma_0^2| =$$

$$= \frac{1}{n}|(x_n - \alpha_1)^2 + (x_0 - \alpha_0)^2 + \sum_{1 \le j \le n-1}((x_j - \alpha_1)^2 - (x_j - \alpha_0)^2)| =$$

$$= |(x_n - x_0)(x_n - \alpha_1 + x_0 - \alpha_0)|/n \approx (\sigma_0/n)(\sigma_1 + \sigma_0).$$

3. The expected value of $|DFT_m(\nu(X_1)) - DFT_m(\nu(X_0))|$ is on the order of $|DFT_m(\nu(X_0))|/n + 1/\sqrt{n}$. Here, we use the equations for DFT's derived in Section 3.3, as well as the ones derived above:

$$|DFT_m(\nu(X_1)) - DFT_m(\nu(X_0))| = |DFT_m(X_1)/\sigma_1 - DFT_m(\nu(X_0))| =$$

$$= |\frac{e^{(2\pi i)m/n}}{\sigma_1}(\sigma_0 DFT_m(\nu(X_0)) + \frac{x_n - x_0}{\sqrt{n}}) - DFT_m(\nu(X_0))| =$$

$$= |DFT_m(\nu(X_0))(\frac{\sigma_0}{\sigma_1}e^{(2\pi i)m/n} - 1) + \frac{x_n - x_0}{\sigma_1\sqrt{n}}e^{(2\pi i)m/n}| \approx$$

$$\approx |DFT_m(\nu(X_0))((1 + 1/n)(1 - 2\pi m/n) - 1) + (1 + 1/n)(1 - 2\pi m/n)/\sqrt{n}| \approx$$

$$\approx |DFT_m(\nu(X_0))|/n + O(1/\sqrt{n})$$

4 Constraint Specification of Similarity Queries

In the previous section, we have shown how to provide an efficient database indexing mechanism for queries with similarity semantics. This enables us to answer the following question:

Given Q, ϵ_i, (l_α, u_α) and (l_σ, u_σ),
find all S such that
$D_S(Q, S) \leq \epsilon$, $l_\alpha \leq \alpha(S) \leq u_\alpha$, $l_\sigma \leq \sigma(S) \leq u_\sigma$.

This is based on our *internal representation* of the actual user query, whose syntax may be very different. In particular, the user querying a database of sequences should probably not be expected to refer to normal forms, similarity distance, or even to averages and deviations.

In this section, we provide a *syntax* for similarity queries, based on constraints. Then, we show how to translate from this syntactic formulation to the internal representation.

It is important to note that the translation is not always *bi-directional*. There may be additional *false alarms* retrieved by the indexing mechanism. These will be filtered out via a brute-force comparison prior to returning the query result. The additional filtering indicates a potential performance disadvantage of our approach and is a trade-off to achieve generality.

4.1 Constraint-Based Syntax of Similarity Queries

For the general similarity query, we propose the following constraint-based syntax, which expresses the queries described in Section 1.2:

- **General Case: Given** Q, ϵ, (l_a, u_a), **and** (l_b, u_b),
  find all $[S, a, b]$ **such that**
  $D(Q, aS + b) \leq \epsilon$, $l_a \leq a \leq u_a$ **and** $l_b \leq b \leq u_b$.

We assume that the sequence distance D is the Euclidean distance D_E between sequences. Of course, the user may choose to omit the bounds on a and/or b:

- **Unbounded Case:** Given Q and ϵ,
  find all $[S, a, b]$ such that $D(Q, aS + b) \leq \epsilon$.

In all the following queries, bounds either a or b are optional.

The user may want to query for scaling transformations only, or for shift transformations only:

- **Scaling:** Find all $[S, a]$ such that $D(Q, aS) \leq \epsilon$.
- **Shifting:** Find all $[S, b]$ such that $D(Q, S + b) \leq \epsilon$.

Finally, the user may ask approximate matching queries or exact similarity queries:

- **Approximate Match:** Find all S such that $D(Q, S) \leq \epsilon$.
- **Exact Similarity:** Find all $[S, a, b]$ such that $Q = aS + b$.

For all these variations on similarity queries, it is possible to efficiently find the corresponding values for the variables used in the internal query representation:

$$\{\epsilon_i, l_\alpha, u_\alpha, l_\sigma, u_\sigma\}.$$

We shall show how to do that in the next subsection.

4.2   From Constraint-Based Syntax to Internal Representation

We first reduce the cases of scaling, shifting, alternate matching, and exact similarity to the general case:

Scaling: force b to have the value 0 by specifing an equality constraint $b = 0$:

$$D(Q, aS) \leq \epsilon \Leftrightarrow D(Q, aS + 0) \leq \epsilon \Leftrightarrow D(Q, aS + b) \leq \epsilon \wedge b = 0.$$

Shifting: force a to have the value 1 by specifing an equality constraint $a = 1$:

$$D(Q, S + b) \leq \epsilon \Leftrightarrow D(Q, 1 * S + b) \leq \epsilon.$$

Approximate Matching: by similar reasoning, set a to 1 and b to 0.
Exact Similarity: set ϵ to 0:

$$Q = aS + b \Leftrightarrow D(Q, aS + 0) = 0.$$

Then, we convert the general case to the internal representation. We need to compute the values for $\{\epsilon_i, l_\alpha, u_\alpha, l_\sigma, u_\sigma\}$, so that S is a valid answer to the general similarity query only if

$$D_S(Q, S) \leq \epsilon_i \text{ and } l_\alpha \leq \alpha(S) \leq u_\alpha \text{ and } l_\sigma \leq \sigma(S) \leq u_\sigma.$$

To bridge the difference between Section 1.2 and Section 2.2, we proceed as follows.

Let Q be the given pattern and S an answer for the general case, such that there exist a, b with $D(Q, aS + b) \le \epsilon$, $l_a \le a \le u_a$ and $l_b \le b \le u_b$. Let us denote the minimum distance between Q and S', for all $S' \in S^*$, by $D_m(Q, S^*)$, and $\sigma(Q)$ by σ. It can be shown that:

Lemma: $D_m^2(Q, S^*) = \sigma^2(D_S^2 - D_S^4/4)$, where $D_S = D(\nu(Q), \nu(S))$.

If $D(Q, aS + b) \le \epsilon$ then,

$$D_m(Q, S^*) \le \epsilon \Leftrightarrow D_m^2(Q, S^*) \le \epsilon^2 \Leftrightarrow \sigma^2(D_S^2 - D_S^4/4) \le \epsilon^2 \Leftrightarrow$$

$$\Leftrightarrow D_S^4 - 4D_S^2 + 4\epsilon^2/\sigma^2 \ge 0 \Leftrightarrow (D_S^2 \le 2 - 2\sqrt{1 - \epsilon^2/\sigma^2}) \vee (D_S^2 \ge 2 + 2\sqrt{1 - \epsilon^2/\sigma^2}).$$

We know that $D_S^2 \le 2$, since our similarity transformations do not allow scaling with a negative factor. Therefore, the square root of the first inequality is the desired expression for ϵ_i. Note that ϵ/σ must be less than 1; this does not reduce the expressibility, since the minimal distance $D_m^2(Q, S^*)$ is never greater than $\sigma(Q)$. The above calculation of ϵ_i is bi-directional (iff) when there are no bounds on a, b.

Otherwise, we also need to find "good" bounds for $\sigma(S)$ and $\alpha(S)$. We know that under exact similarity

$$Q = aS + b,$$
$$Q = \sigma(Q) * \nu(Q) + \alpha(Q),$$
$$S = \sigma(S) * \nu(S) + \alpha(S).$$

We solve these equations for a and b:

$$a = \sigma(Q)/\sigma(S),$$
$$b = \alpha(Q) - \alpha(S)\sigma(Q)/\sigma(S).$$

We combine the equation for a with the bounds $l_a \le a \le u_a$ to obtain the bounds for $\sigma(S)$, without any loss in accuracy:

$$l_a \le a \le u_a \Leftrightarrow l_a \le \sigma(Q)/\sigma(S) \le u_a \Leftrightarrow 1/u_a \le \sigma(S)/\sigma(Q) \le 1/l_a \Leftrightarrow$$

$$\Leftrightarrow \sigma(Q)/u_a \le \sigma(S) \le \sigma(Q)/l_a.$$

We combine the equations for b with the bounds $l_b \le b \le u_b$ to obtain the bounds for $\alpha(S)$:

$$l_b \le b \le u_b \Leftrightarrow l_b \le \alpha(Q) - \alpha(S)\sigma(Q)/\sigma(S) \le u_b \Leftrightarrow$$

$$\Leftrightarrow \alpha(Q) - u_b \le \alpha(S)\sigma(Q)/\sigma(S) \le \alpha(Q) - l_b \Leftrightarrow$$

$$\Leftrightarrow \sigma(S)(\alpha(Q) - u_b)/\sigma(Q) \le \alpha(S) \le \sigma(S)(\alpha(Q) - l_b)/\sigma(Q).$$

Since $\sigma(S)$ is not a constant value, we have to eliminate it from the bounds. We accomplish this goal by substituting the lower and upper bounds for $\sigma(S)$, obtained earlier, into the above inequalities:

$$(\sigma(Q)/u_a \le \sigma(S)) \wedge (\sigma(S)(\alpha(Q) - u_b)/\sigma(Q) \le \alpha(S)) \Rightarrow (\alpha(Q) - u_b)/u_a \le \alpha(S);$$

$$(\sigma(S) \le \sigma(Q)/l_a) \wedge (\alpha(S) \le \sigma(S)(\alpha(Q) - l_b)/\sigma(Q)) \Rightarrow \alpha(S) \le (\alpha(Q) - l_b)/l_a.$$

Combining the resulting inequalities, we obtain:

$$(\alpha(Q) - u_b)/u_a \le \alpha(S) \le (\alpha(Q) - l_b)/l_a.$$

The last reduction is not bi-directional. Though we have not forced any false dismissals, we may have generated some false alarms. The inaccuracy introduced when computing the bounds for $\alpha(S)$ is proportional to $u_a - l_a$. Therefore, the expected speed-up from bounding b prior to indexing vs. performing the filtering of b's after the indexing is maximized when there is a very tight bound on a. An ideal candidate is a pure shift query, where $a = 1$.

We summarize the results of this section in a table, providing the values for the internal representation in terms of the user-specified external values.

ϵ_i	$\sqrt{2 - 2\sqrt{1 - \epsilon^2/\sigma^2}}$
l_σ	$\sigma(Q)/u_a$
u_σ	$\sigma(Q)/l_a$
l_α	$(\alpha(Q) - u_b)/u_a$
u_α	$(\alpha(Q) - l_b)/l_a$

Fig. 2. Computing the values for the Internal Representation

5 Conclusion and Open Questions

We have proposed a framework for Time-Series Approximate Similarity Queries that allows the user to pose a wide variety of queries and that preserves desirable indexing properties of Time-Series Approximate Matching. Posssible extensions involve more powerful similarity queries and different distance functions; also indexing of time-series data that is represented using constraints (see [3, 11]).

As with a generalized version of any problem, there is a potential trade-off between a gain in expressibility and a decrease in performance. There should be some slow-down due to the extra keys in the new indexing scheme (as opposed to [7]) and additional slow-down may come from the false alarms generated by our fingerprinting as compared to the specialized cases (without a similarity transformation). We are examining this trade-off through performance evaluation of several versions of similarity querying. The first version is the most general one described here; other versions involve tailoring the internal representation and the corresponding indexing scheme for specialized subsets of similarity queries. This experimental work in progress.

The existence of a fingerprint function for internal similarity querying that is a real hash function but is also distance-preserving and updateable is an interesting open question. *Is there a fingerprint method that gives a provably linear performance for the Rabin-Karp algorithm [14], either for approximate matching or for similarity querying? Can it be truly randomized for any adversary?*

References

1. A. Aho. Algorithms for Finding Patterns in Strings. *Handbook of TCS.*, J. Van Leeuwen editor, volume A, chapter 5, Elsevier, 1990.
2. R. Agrawal, C. Faloutsos, A. Swami. Efficient Similarity Search in Sequence Databases. *FODO Conf.*, Evanston, Ill., Oct. 1993
3. M. Baudinet, M. Niezette, P. Wolper. On the Representation of Infinite Temporal Data and Queries. *Proc. 10th ACM PODS*, 280–290, 1991.
4. A. Brodsky, J. Jaffar, M.J. Maher. Toward Practical Constraint Databases. *Proc. 19th VLDB*, 322–331, 1993.
5. A. Colmerauer. An Introduction to Prolog III. *CACM*, 33:7:69–90, 1990.
6. M. Dincbas, P. Van Hentenryck, H. Simonis, A. Aggoun, T. Graf, F. Berthier. The Constraint Logic Programming Language CHIP. *Proc. Fifth Generation Computer Systems*, Tokyo Japan, 1988.
7. C. Faloutsos, M. Ranganathan, Y. Manolopoulos. Fast Subsequence Matching in Time-Series Databases. *Proc. ACM SIGMOD Conf.*, pp. 419–429, May 1994
8. H.V. Jagadish. A Retrieval Technique for Similar Shapes. *Proc. ACM SIGMOD Conf.*, pp. 208–217, May 1991
9. H. V. Jagadish, A. O. Mendelzon, T. Milo. Similarity-Based Queries. to appear in *Proc. 14th ACM PODS*, 1995
10. J. Jaffar, J.L. Lassez. Constraint Logic Programming. *Proc. 14th ACM POPL*, 111–119, 1987.
11. F. Kabanza, J-M. Stevenne, P. Wolper. Handling Infinite Temporal Data. *Proc. 9th ACM PODS*, 392–403, 1990.
12. P. C. Kanellakis, G. M. Kuper, P. Z. Revesz. Constraint Query Languages. *Proc. 9th ACM PODS*, 299–313, 1990. Full version available as Brown Univ. Tech. Rep. CS-92-50. To appear in JCSS.
13. P. C. Kanellakis, S. Ramaswamy, D. E. Vengroff, J. S. Vitter. Indexing for Data Models with Constraints and Classes. *Proc. 12th ACM PODS*, 233–243, 1993.
14. R. M. Karp and M. O. Rabin. Efficient Randomized Pattern-Matching Algorithms. *IBM J. Res. Develop.*, 31(2), 1987
15. Modenov and Pakhomenko. *Geometric Transformations*, Academic Press, 1965
16. A.V. Oppenheim and R.W. Schafer. *Digital Signal Processing*, Prentice Hall, 1975
17. H. Samet. *The Design and Analysis of Spatial Data Structures.* Addison-Wesley, Reading MA, 1990.
18. P. Sheshadri, M. Livny, R. Ramakrishnan. Sequence Query Processing *Proc. ACM SIGMOD Conf.*, pp. 430–441, May 1994

Safe Stratified Datalog with Integer Order Programs

Peter Z. Revesz

Department of Computer Science and Engineering
and Center for Communication and Information Science
University of Nebraska–Lincoln, Lincoln, NE 68588, USA

Abstract. Guaranteeing termination of programs on all valid inputs is important for database applications. Termination cannot be guaranteed in Stratified Datalog with integer (gap)-order, or $Datalog^{\neg,<z}$, programs on generalized databases because they can express any Turing-computable function [23]. This paper introduces a restriction of $Datalog^{\neg,<z}$ that can express only computable queries. The restricted language has a high expressive power and a non-elementary data complexity.

1 Introduction

Constraint logic programming [14, 15, 27, 12, 10, 9] has a great potential for being adapted for database use. A successful adaptation of constraint logic programming has to meet usual database requirements. In the constraint query languages framework [19] two requirements are identified as especially important: (a) closed-form evaluation and (b) bottom-up processing.

Closed-form evaluation means that all possible tuple answers to a query are represented finitely by an output constraint database that has the same type of constraints as the input constraint database. This is the analogue for the relational database model requirement that relations be finite structures and queries preserve finiteness. The main advantage of closed-form evaluation is that it facilitates composition of queries. In particular, a query may be applied to the *negation* of the output of another query in a natural way. This composition is called *stratified negation* [6, 2] (see Section 2 for further discussion). Closed-form evaluation also allows the addition of aggregate operators as is done recently in [8]. Aggregation is also important in database applications.

Bottom-up processing describes a direction of evaluation of rules within programs. The direction is from known facts to goals. Bottom-up processing can be done in a set-at-a-time way which is faster than the tuple-at-a-time top-down processing done in Prolog. Bottom-up processing requires less access to secondary storage [20] and allows algebraic query optimizations [4, 18].

The good news is that these requirements can be met in a large number of cases. For example, Datalog with rational order constraints can be evaluated bottom-up in closed-form in PTIME data complexity. (Data complexity is the measure of the computational complexity of fixed queries as the size of the input database grows [5, 29]. The rationale behind this measure is that in practice the size of the database typically dominates by several orders of magnitude the size of the query.) Datalog with integer (gap)-order constraints programs and Datalog with $\subseteq$ constraints on set variables are evaluable in closed-form on constraint databases with DEXPTIME-complete data complexity [23, 11, 24]. Datalog$_{1S}$ [7], an extension of Datalog with a successor function applied always to the first argument of relations, can be evaluated in closed-form and has PSPACE-complete data complexity. Datalog with periodicity constraints [26], relational calculus with linear repeating points [17] and temporal constraints [17] can be also evaluated in closed-form.

The bad news is that many other interesting constraint logic programming languages do not guarantee a closed-form evaluation. For example, CLP(R) [16], LIFE [1], the temporal database queries of [3], and stratified Datalog with integer (gap)-order constraints [23] can express any Turing-computable function, hence in these languages termination of query evaluation cannot be guaranteed. In spite of their high expressive power, using these languages for database applications can be difficult.

Developers can translate faster from user specifications to a declarative language than to a procedural language. This is a major advantage of using relational database systems.[1] However, in practice, developers not only have to express the desire of the users as queries, but they also must guarantee that those queries terminate on each possible input. (Obviously, this is important for user satisfaction.) While translating may be easy, guaranteeing termination may be difficult in the above languages. The time saved in translation evaporates rapidly if developers have to prove termination of programs.

It seems ideal if a developer can work in a highly expressive language where however termination is guaranteed. Therefore it seems important to look at restricted cases of the above languages. In this paper, we consider a syntactical restriction of stratified $Datalog^{\neg, <_z}$ programs. Queries expressible in this restricted language are called *safe*. Safe stratified $Datalog^{\neg, <_z}$ queries are guaranteed to be evaluable bottom-up in closed-form on any valid database input. The syntactical restriction is easy to check: it can be done in PTIME in the size of the $Datalog^{\neg, <_z}$ programs. Moreover, this restriction still leaves developers with a highly expressive language: safe stratified $Datalog^{\neg, <_z}$ queries have a non-elementary data complexity.

Section 2 describes basic definitions. Section 3 gives a definition of safety and shows that it can be checked in PTIME in the size of stratified $Datalog^{\neg, <_z}$ programs. Section 4 presents an evaluation algorithm for safe stratified $Datalog^{\neg, <_z}$ queries. It is shown that the evaluation algorithm always terminates in finite time and returns a constraint database representation of the perfect fixpoint model of the query. Section 5 analyzes the computational complexity of safe stratified $Datalog^{\neg, <_z}$ queries. The complexity of these queries is shown to be non-elementary. It is also shown that the level of exponentiation can grow linearly with the number of strata in the programs.

---

[1] In fact, relational database systems also allow so called ad hoc querying by naive users.

2 Basic Concepts

2.1 Definition of Syntax and Semantics

We denote sets of rules by capital letter R and individual rules (predicates) by small case letter r (p) with or without subscripts. We also use small case letters for integer variables.

The syntax of Datalog with integer (gap)-order programs, denoted $Datalog^{<z}$, is that of traditional Datalog (Horn clauses without function symbols) where the bodies of rules can also contain a conjunction of integer (gap)-order constraints. That is, each program is a finite set of rules of form: $A_0 :- A_1, A_2, \ldots, A_l$. The expression A_0 (the rule *head*) must be an atomic formula of the form $p(x_1, \ldots, x_n)$, and the expressions $A_1, \ldots, A_l$ (the rule *body*) must be atomic formulas of the form $x_i = x_j$, $x_i \neq x_j$, $x_i \leq x_j$, $x_i < x_j$, $x_i <_g x_j$ where g is a nonnegative integer, or $p(x_1, \ldots, x_n)$, where p is some predicate symbol.

The definitions below generalize those in [28] to $Datalog^{<z}$ programs and finitely representable relations.

The rules for a predicate p are *rectified* if all their heads are identical and of the form $p(x_1, \ldots, x_k)$ for distinct variables $x_1, \ldots, x_k$.

We call *rule instantiation* a substitution of each variable of a rule by an integer constant.

Let $p_1, \ldots, p_n$ be any set of relation symbols in a language. An *assignment* is a (possibly infinite) set of tuples of proper arity for each p_i where $1 \leq i \leq n$. For any assignment A and rule instantiation, the right hand side is "true" if and only if the argument list of each instantiated subgoal with a relation symbol p appears as a tuple for p in A, and all the instantiated constraints are also satisfied.

Let R be a set of $Datalog^{<z}$ rules. Let $p_1, \ldots, p_n$ be the relation symbols in R that occur only on the right hand sides. We call each assignment to $p_1, \ldots, p_n$ an *extensional database* (EDB) of R and each p_i an EDB relation symbol.

Let R be a set of $Datalog^{<z}$ rules. Let $p_1, \ldots, p_m$ be the EDB relation symbols in R, and let $p_{m+1}, \ldots, p_n$ be the IDB relation symbols (i.e, those relation symbols that occur at least once on the left hand sides). A *model* of R with respect to an extensional database E of R is an assignment M to $p_1, \ldots, p_n$ such that $M = E \cup I$ where I is an assignment to $p_{m+1}, \ldots, p_n$, and the following holds for each $r_i \in R$:

For each instantiation $\sigma = \{x_1 = a_1, \ldots, x_t = a_t\}$ of r_i, where $x_1, \ldots, x_t$ are the variables in r_i, if the right hand side is true, then the left hand side is also true.

Let R be a set of rectified $Datalog^{<z}$ rules with $p_1, \ldots, p_m$ EDB relation symbols and $p_{m+1}, \ldots, p_n$ IDB relation symbols. Let E be an extensional database of R. A *fixpoint model* of R with respect to E is a model M of R with respect to E, such that for each tuple $(a_1, \ldots, a_k)$ for p_j in M where $m + 1 \leq j \leq n$, the following holds:

There is a rule $r_i \in R$ with head $p_j(x_1, \ldots, x_k)$, variables $x_1, \ldots, x_k, \ldots, x_t$, and an instantiation $\sigma = \{x_1 = a_1, \ldots, x_t = a_t\}$ such that the right hand side is true.

Let R be a set of $Datalog^{<z}$ rules and E be an extensional database of R. We say that F is a *least fixpoint model* of R with respect to E, if F is a fixpoint model of R with respect to E, and there is no $F' \subset F$ such that F' is also a fixpoint model of R with respect to E.

The syntax of Stratified Datalog with integer (gap)-order programs, denoted stratified $Datalog^{\neg,<z}$, is that of $Datalog^{<z}$ except in the rule bodies expressions of the form $\neg p(x_1, \ldots, x_n)$ can also occur.

A stratification of a program means the grouping of defined predicates (and the rules defining them) into a set of disjoint subgroups in order $R_1, \ldots, R_n$. A stratification is *correct* if for each rule of the form $p :— \ldots \neg q \ldots$, the predicate p has a higher group number than q has. The intuition here is that during fixpoint computation the lower strata have to be fully evaluated before the higher strata. Each stratified $Datalog^{\neg,<z}$ query is prescribed a unique meaning in terms of a perfect model.

Let $R = R_1 \cup \ldots \cup R_n$ be a set of stratified rules, where stratum i contains rules R_i. Let M_0 be an assignment to the EDB relation symbols in R. The *perfect fixpoint model* of R with respect to M_0 is $M = M_0 \cup I_1 \cup \ldots \cup I_n$ where each I_i is an assignment to the IDB relation symbols in R_i, and for each $1 \leq i \leq n$ the assignment $M_i = M_{i-1} \cup I_i$ is a least fixpoint model of R_i with respect to M_{i-1}. (We also amend the previous definitions by assuming that if $\neg p(a_1, \ldots, a_k)$ is an instantiated predicate on the right hand side, then it is true if and only if $(a_1, \ldots, a_k)$ is not assigned to p.)

In this paper we are not concerned about testing whether a given stratification is correct, or whether a $Datalog^{\neg,<z}$ program can have a correct stratification and how to find a correct stratification if one exists. These questions can be answered by algorithms given in [28]. We will always assume that for each program we already have a correct stratification.

2.2 Definition of Technical Tools

The following definitions and lemmas are either given in or trivially follow from [23].

Definition 2.1 Let x and y be any two integer variables or constants. Given some assignment to the variables, a *gap-order* constraint $x <_g y$ for some gap-value $g \in N$ holds if and only if $g < y - x$ holds in the given assignment. A *gap-order* constraint $x = y$ holds if and only if x and y are equal in the given assignment. □

Definition 2.2 Let $x_1, \ldots, x_n$ be integer variables and $c_1, \ldots, c_m$ be integer constants. Any graph with vertices labeled $x_1, \ldots, x_n, c_1, \ldots, c_m$ and at most one undirected edge labeled by $=$ or at most one directed edge labeled by $<_g$ for some $g \in N$ between any pair of distinct vertices is called a *gap-graph*. □

Remark: It should be clear that each gap-graph represents a set of gap-order constraints. In the case of directed edges the left hand side of the gap-order constraint is the vertex of origin and the right hand side of the gap-order constraint is the vertex of incidence of the directed edge. It is immediate that gap-graphs can represent any set of gap-order constraints S over variables X and constants C if between any two $v, u \in X \cup C$ at most one of $v = u$ or $v <_g u$ for some $g \in \mathbf{N}$ is in S. It is also transparent that gap-graphs can represent any set of gap-order constraints, and disjunctions of gap-graphs can represent any set of $=, \neq, \leq, \geq, <, >, <_g$ constraints.

Definition 2.3 Let $x_1, \ldots, x_n$ be integer variables and l, u be integer constants. Any gap-graph with vertices labeled $x_1, \ldots, x_n, l, u$ is in *(l,u)-standard form*. Furthermore, any set of gap-graphs each with vertices labeled $x_1, \ldots, x_n, l, u$ is in *(l,u)-standard form*. $\square$

Definition 2.4 We say that two gap-graphs G_1 and G_2 are *equivalent* if and only if the following two conditions are both satisfied:
(1) G_1 and G_2 have the same set of non-constant labelled vertices $x_1, \ldots, x_n$.
(2) Any assignment of integers to $x_1, \ldots, x_n$ satisfies the gap-order constraints in G_1 if and only if it satisfies the gap-order constraints in G_2. $\square$

    Remark: We use $\mathcal{A}(G)$ to denote all the assignments that satisfy G. Then an alternative way of stating that G_1 and G_2 are equivalent is to say that $\mathcal{A}(G_1) = \mathcal{A}(G_2)$.

Lemma 2.1 Let G be any gap-graph with smallest constant vertex label $\geq l$ and largest constant vertex label $\leq u$. Then G can be put into an equivalent (l,u)-standard form. Furthermore, let S be any set of gap-graphs each with a (possibly different) smallest constant vertex label $\geq l$ and largest constant vertex label $\leq u$. Then S can be put into an equivalent (l,u)-standard form. $\square$

    We say that a relation r with arity k containing exactly a (finite or infinite) set of tuples $\mathcal{B}$ is representable in gap-graph form if there are $l, u \in \mathbf{N}$ and a finite set of gap-graphs $G_1, \ldots, G_n$ each over the vertices $x_1, \ldots, x_k, l, u$ such that $\mathcal{B} = \bigcup_{1 \leq i \leq n} \mathcal{A}(G_i)$. We say that a database is representable in gap-graph form if each of the relations in it is representable in gap-graph form.

    The main motivation for using gap-graphs is that least models can be computed in gap-graph form. More precisely, the following is shown in [23].

Lemma 2.2 Let P be *Datalog$^{<z}$* program and B be a (possibly infinite) regular relational database. If the database B is representable in gap-graph form, then $L_{P,B}$ the least model of P on B is also representable in gap-graph form. Furthermore, given any gap-graph representation of B a gap-graph representation of $L_{P,B}$ can be computed in finite time.

3   An Algorithm to Test Safety

It is traditional in the relational database literature to define various "safety restrictions" on languages to ensure that queries in the restricted language always yield finite database outputs on finite database inputs [28]. We generalize this notion of safety. Our aim is to ensure that queries in the restricted language always yield finitely representable generalized database outputs on finitely represented generalized database inputs.

In this section we define a syntactic notion of safety that can be tested in PTIME in the size of the programs. In the next section, we show that safe $Datalog^{\neg,<z}$ programs can be evaluated in finite time.

At first let us give an intuition to the problem of computing perfect models. Suppose that we want to evaluate the ith stratum of a stratified $Datalog^{\neg,<z}$ program. What we need intuitively is to find the complement of the negated relations that are either fully evaluated in the previous strata or given in the input database. If we could represent in gap-graph form the complement of each negated relation occurring in the ith stratum, then we could apply Lemma 2.2 and find in finite time a least model of stratum i. The task then is to find those cases when the negated relations are always surely representable in gap-graph form.

We do that in two steps. First, we note that if a relation has a certain simple form, then its negation is representable in gap-graph form. Second, we make a type for each input relation that will tell whether it has a simple form. This will allow calculating the type of each output relation. This essentially can be considered a type checking. Using information about the program syntax, the stratification of the rules in the program, and the type of the input relations, this type checking will approve programs for which termination of evaluation can be guaranteed for any valid input database.

Definition 3.1 A gap-graph is simple if it contains no $<$ or $<_g$ constraint between any pair of variables.

Lemma 3.1 Let p be a relation represented by a set of simple gap-graphs. Then $\neg p$ can be represented as a set of simple gap-graphs. □

Example 3.1 Suppose $p(x) = 20 <_5 x \lor x <_4 7$. Here $l = 7$ and $u = 20$. Then applying De Morgan's laws we have $\neg p(x) = \neg(20 <_5 x \lor x <_4 7) = \neg(25 < x \lor x < 3) = \neg(25 < x) \land \neg(x < 3) = (x \leq 25) \land (3 \leq x) = x < 26 \land 2 < x$. Note that in this rewriting $l = 2$ and $u = 26$. This rewriting makes $u - l$ minimal as in any other rewriting we get either a smaller l or a larger u.

Motivated by the above, we define for each relation a technical tool called a *congraph*. Intuitively, each congraph shows the possible connections via $<$ or $<_g$ constraints among the arguments of a relation. More precisely:

Definition 3.2 Let p be any k-ary predicate. Then the arguments connection graph or *congraph of p* is an assignment of an undirected graph $C(V,E)$ with $V = \{\$1, \ldots, \$k\}$. (We assume that the congraph vertex $\$i$ represents the ith argument of p.)

Let $p(x_1, \ldots, x_k)$ be a k-arity relation and let $C(V,E)$ be any congraph of p. We say that C *pictures* p if the following holds: $(\$i, \$j) \in E$ if there is a path not using l and u from x_i to x_j (or from x_j to x_i) in any gap-graph in p.

We define the congraph of a rule based on the congraphs of the subgoals (atomic formulas on its left hand side).

Definition 3.3 Let r be any rule with variables $x_1, \ldots, x_n$ and of the form $A_0 :- A_1, A_2, \ldots, A_l$. Then the *congraph of* r is the undirected graph $C(V, E)$ with the vertices labeled $x_1, \ldots, x_n$ that has in it an edge between x_i and x_j if and only if some A_j for $1 \leq j \leq l$ is an integer (gap)-order constraint involving both x_i and x_j or it is of the form $p(\ldots, x_i, \ldots, x_j, \ldots)$ and the congraph of p has an edge between \$i' and \$j' where x_i (x_j) is the \$i'th (\$j'th) argument of p.

Our definition of safety is purely syntactic and is based on an algorithm called *CheckSafety*.

Definition 3.4 We say that a program P is safe if and only if algorithm *CheckSafety* returns "yes".

Algorithm CheckSafety
INPUT: A stratified $Datalog^{\neg, <z}$ program P and a congraph for each EDB.
A stratification of program P is also given.
OUTPUT: "Yes" if P is safe if the congraphs picture the EDBs.

FOR each IDB relation p_m with arity k **DO**
    assign to p_m a congraph $C_m(V_m, E_m)$ with $V_m = \{\$1, \ldots, \$k\}$ and $E_m = \emptyset$.
END-FOR
FOR each stratum i **DO**
    WHILE any changes in congraphs **DO**
        FOR each rule r_j with head $p_m(x_1, \ldots, x_k)$ in stratum i **DO**
            Find $C_{r_j}(V_{r_j}, E_{r_j})$ the congraph of rule r_j.
            Let $E_m = E_m \cup \{(\$i, \$j) : x_i$ and x_j are connected in $E_{r_j})\}$.
        END-FOR
    END-WHILE
END-FOR
Output "yes" if in each negated IDBP congraph each vertex is an isolate vertex.

In step (1) of the inner for loop the congraph of rule r_j is found by taking after the appropriate renamings the union of all the vertices and edges in the congraphs of the relations on the right hand side of r_j.

Theorem 3.1 The safety testing algorithm runs in PTIME in the size of the stratified $Datalog^{\neg, <z}$ program. $\square$

Next we give an example of applying algorithm *CheckSafety*.

Example 3.2 Suppose that we know the distance in miles between any pair of cities with a direct road connection on a map and we need to find the length of the shortest path between any pair of cities. The following $Datalog^{\neg, <z}$ program with four rules, r_1, r_2, r_3, r_4 respectively, performs this query.

$$shortest(x, y, s) \qquad :\!- path(x, y, 0, s), \neg not\_shortest(x, y, s).$$

$$not\_shortest(x, y, s_2) :\!- path(x, y, 0, s_1), path(x, y, 0, s_2), s_1 < s_2.$$

$$path(x, y, s_1, s_2) \qquad :\!- path(x, z, s_1, s_3), distance(z, y, s_3, s_2).$$
$$path(x, y, s_1, s_2) \qquad :\!- distance(x, y, s_1, s_2).$$

In the program *path* and *not_shortest* are in the first and *shortest* is in the second stratum. The input relation *distance* describes direct distances between cities in miles using constraint database tuples. For example, to express the fact that city 77 is 60 miles from city 95 we use the constraint tuple:

$$distance(95, 77, s_1, s_2) :\!- s_1 <_{59} s_2.$$

This constraint tuple should be read as follows: if we can reach city 95 within s_1 miles then we can reach city 77 within s_2 miles for any s_1 and s_2 that satisfies $s_1 <_{59} s_2$.

Figure 1 shows the edges in the congraphs of each rule and each relation at the end of each iteration i. For $i = 0$ the congraphs of the input database are shown. The input database relation *distance* will have in its congraph only the edge \$3-\$4, and all the other relations will not have any edge in their congraphs. None of the rule congraphs will have any edge in them either.

After the first iteration, the congraph of rules r_1 and r_3 will have no edges, the congraph of r_2 will have only the edge $s_1 - s_2$ because of the constraint $s_1 < s_2$ occuring in the rule, while the congraph of r_4 will have the edge $s_1 - s_2$ added to it, because on the right hand side the *distance* relation also contains this edge. Because of the change in r_4, the congraph of *path* will also have the edge \$3-\$4 added to it.

After the second iteration, the congraph of rules r_1, r_2 and r_4 will remain unchanged, while the congraph of r_3 will have the edge $s_1 - s_2$ added to it. This change in r_3 however will not cause any change in the congraph of the path relation. Therefore, none of the relation congraphs will change from the end of iteration 1 to the end of iteration 2. Hence the algorithm will terminate and return the congraphs of the last row.

Clearly the only negated relation is *not_shortest*. Since the congraph of *not_shortest* contains no edges, the query must be a safe query. □

iteration	distance	path	not_shortest	shortest	r_1	r_2	r_3	r_4
0	\$3-\$4							
1	\$3-\$4	\$3-\$4				$s_1 - s_2$		$s_1 - s_2$
2	\$3-\$4	\$3-\$4				$s_1 - s_2$	$s_1 - s_2$	$s_1 - s_2$

Fig. 1. The relation and rule congraphs after each iteration

4 An Evaluation Algorithm for Safe $Datalog^{\neg,<z}$ Queries

In this section the operators $\bowtie$ and $\hat{\pi}$ that we use are the extensions of the relational algebra operators of join and project for generalized databases. These operators and their semantics are defined in [23] and for brevity of space we refer to that paper for examples. We also use ρ as a symbol for the renaming operator.

Algorithm EvalQuery
INPUT: A safe stratified $Datalog^{\neg,<z}$ program P and a set of gap-graphs G_i for each p_i. For the defined relations $G_i = \emptyset$. A stratification of program P is also given.
OUTPUT: The perfect fixpoint model of P in gap-graph form.

FOR each stratum i **DO**
  REPEAT
    FOR each relation p_m **DO**
      Let $H_m = G_m$.
    END-FOR
    FOR each r_j of form $p_0(x_1, \ldots, x_k) \leftarrow p_1, \ldots, p_n, \neg p_{n+1}, \ldots, \neg p_{n+l}$ **DO**
      IF stratum$[r_j] = i$ **THEN**
        $T_j = \rho_{j,1}(G_1) \bowtie \ldots \bowtie \rho_{j,n}(G_n) \bowtie (\neg(\rho_{j,n+1}(G_{n+1}))) \bowtie \ldots \bowtie (\neg \rho_{j,n+l}(G_{n+l})))$.
        $F_j = \rho_{x_1/\$1, \ldots, x_k/\$k}(\hat{\pi}_{x_1, \ldots, x_k} T_j)$.
        Delete all inconsistent gap-graphs from F_j.
        Add to G_0 each gap-graph in F_j that does not subsume another in G_0.
      END-IF
    END-FOR
  UNTIL $H_m = G_m$ for each m
END-FOR

The next lemma shows that the query evaluation algorithm always returns relations with a type that conforms to our expectations based on the check safety algorithm.

Lemma 4.1 Let $p_1, \ldots, p_n$ be the input relations and $p_{n+1}, \ldots, p_{n+l}$ be the defined relations of a stratified $Datalog^{\neg,<z}$ program P.
Let $c_{n+1}, \ldots, c_{n+l}$ be the congraphs returned for $p_{n+1}, \ldots, p_{n+l}$ by algorithm *CheckSafety* on P, the stratification of P and congraphs $c_1, \ldots, c_n$ for $p_1, \ldots, p_n$ respectively. Then for any assignment to $p_1, \ldots, p_n$ algorithm *EvalQuery* returns $p_{n+1}, \ldots, p_{n+l}$ such that if each c_i pictures p_i for $1 \leq i \leq n$, then each c_j pictures p_j for $1 \leq j \leq n$. $\square$

Next we prove that for safe programs the query evaluation algorithm returns in finite time the perfect model as expected.

Theorem 4.1 Algorithm *EvalQuery* terminates for any safe stratified *Datalog*$^{\neg,<z}$ program P and valid input database d and returns the perfect fixpoint model of P in gap-graph form.

Proof. We prove the theorem by induction on the number of strata in P. That the first stratum terminates follows by Lemma 2.2 from [23] which shows that any program that adds only gap-graphs with a fixed l and u to the database terminates. Each time the evaluation enters a new stratum and negation is performed the values of l and u may increase but by Lemma 4.1 the complement of the negated relation can be also represented in gap-graph form. The only time l and u may increase is when computing the complement of the relations. Then the evaluation of the next layer terminates as it adds only gap-graphs with a fixed l and u to the database. This shows termination of the computation. The proof that the computation returns the perfect model is similar to the model theory proof in [23] and is omittted here.

Example 4.1 Let's return to Example 3.2. We have seen that it was identified to be a safe query. Now we show how it will be evaluated by *EvalQuery* on the following input database:

$distance(1, 2, s_1, s_2) :\!-\ s_1 <_{19} s_2.$
$distance(1, 3, s_1, s_2) :\!-\ s_1 <_{44} s_2.$
$distance(2, 4, s_1, s_2) :\!-\ s_1 <_{29} s_2.$
$distance(3, 4, s_1, s_2) :\!-\ s_1 <_{14} s_2.$

Let G_R^i and F_j^i denote the set of gap-graphs assigned respectively to IDB relation R and to rule r_j at the end of iteration i of the repeat-until loop.

We have $G_d = \{g_1, g_2, g_3, g_4\}$ where g_1 is the gap-graph for $\$1 = 1, \$2 = 2, \$3 <_{19} \$4$, g_2 is $\$1 = 1, \$2 = 3, \$3 <_{44} \$4$, g_3 is $\$1 = 2, \$2 = 4, \$3 <_{29} \$4$ and g_4 is $\$1 = 3, \$2 = 4, \$3 <_{14} \$4$. We also have $G_p^0 = G_{ns}^0 = G_s^0 = \emptyset$.

Let's see now what happens when algorithm *EvalQuery* enters stratum 1 which contains rules r_2, r_3 and r_4. For each iteration i of the repeat-until loop, the algorithm finds:

$$F_2^i = \rho_{x/\$1, y/\$2, s_2/\$3}(\hat{\pi}_{x,y,s_2}(\rho_{\$1/x, \$2/y, \$3/0, \$4/s_1} G_p^{i-1} \bowtie$$
$$\rho_{\$1/x, \$2/y, \$3/0, \$4/s_2} G_p^{i-1} \bowtie \rho_{\$1/s_1, \$2/s_2} G_<))$$

$$F_3^i = \rho_{x/\$1, y/\$2, s_1/\$3, s_2/\$4}(\hat{\pi}_{x,y,s_1,s_2}(\rho_{\$1/x, \$2/z, \$3/s_1, \$4/s_3} G_p^{i-1} \bowtie$$
$$\rho_{\$1/z, \$2/y, \$3/s_3, \$4/s_2} G_d))$$

$$F_4^i = \rho_{x/\$1, y/\$2, s_1/\$3, s_2/\$4}(\hat{\pi}_{x,y,s_1,s_2}(\rho_{\$1/x, \$2/y, \$3/s_1, \$4/s_2} G_d))$$

Note that $F_4^i = G_d$ because the two renaming operators cancel each other.

In the first iteration of the repeat-until loop, we have $G_p^0 = \emptyset$. Therefore, both F_2^1 and F_3^1 will be empty. As we noted, $F_4^1 = G_d$. This has the net effect of copying each gap-graph in the distance to the path relation. Hence by the end of the first iteration, we have $G_s^1 = G_{ns}^1 = \emptyset$, and $G_p^1 = G_d$. Note that the H variables are used only to detect whether any G changed. Since G_p changed in value, we enter the loop again.

In the second iteration of the repeat-until loop, by substituting into the second of the above equations, we find that F_3^2 is:

$$\rho_{x/\$1,y/\$2,s_1/\$3,s_2/\$4}(\hat{\pi}_{x,y,s_1s_2}(\rho_{\$1/x,\$2/z,\$3/s_1,\$4/s_3}\{g_1,g_2,g_3,g_4\}\bowtie$$

$$\rho_{\$1/z,\$2/y,\$3/s_3,\$4/s_2}\{g_1,g_2,g_3,g_4\}))$$

Here $\rho_{\$1/x,\$2/z,\$3/s_1,\$4/s_3}\{g_1,g_2,g_3,g_4\}$ is

$$\{(x=1,z=2,s_1 <_{19} s_3),(x=1,z=3,s_1 <_{44} s_3),(x=2,z=4,s_1 <_{29} s_3),$$

$$(x=3,z=4,s_1 <_{14} s_3)\}$$

and $\rho_{\$1/z,\$2/y,\$3/s_3,\$4/s_2}\{g_1,g_2,g_3,g_4\}$ is

$$\{(z=1,y=2,s_3 <_{19} s_2),(z=1,y=3,s_3 <_{44} s_2),(z=2,y=4,s_3 <_{29} s_2),$$

$$(z=3,y=4,s_3 <_{14} s_2)\}$$

The join of the above two will be:

$$\{(x=1,z=2,y=4,s_1 <_{19} s_3,s_3 <_{29} s_2),(x=1,z=3,y=4,s_1 <_{44} s_3,s_3 <_{14} s_2)\}$$

and after projection we get: $\{(x=1,y=4,s_1 <_{49} s_2),(x=1,y=4,s_1 <_{59} s_2)\}$

and after renaming we get: $\{(\$1=1,\$2=4,\$3 <_{49} \$4),(\$1=1,\$2=4,\$3 <_{59} \$4)\}$

Both of these gap-graphs will be added to the path relation. Similarly, F_2^2 will be:

$$\{(\$1=1,\$2=2,0 <_{20} \$3),(\$1=1,\$2=3,0 <_{45} \$3),(\$1=2,\$2=4,0 <_{30} \$3),$$

$$(\$1=3,\$2=4,0 <_{15} \$3)\}$$

We find that $G_p^2 = G_d \cup F_3^2$ and $G_{ns}^2 = F_2^2$. Since there are changes in the set of gap-graphs assigned to the IDB relations, we again enter the repeat-until loop.

In the third iteration of the repeat-until loop, similarly to the above, we find that $F_2^3 = F_2^2 \cup \{(\$1=1,\$2=4,0 <_{50} \$3),(\$1=1,\$2=4,0 <_{60} \$3)\}$, $F_3^3 = F_3^2$ and $F_4^3 = G_d$. We also find that $G_{ns}^3 = G_{ns}^2 \cup \{(\$1=1,\$2=4,0 <_{50} \$3),(\$1=1,\$2=4,0 <_{60} \$3)\}$ and $G_p^3 = G_p^2$. Since G_{ns} changed we enter the repeat-until loop again.

In the fourth iteration of the repeat-until loop, none of Fs and Gs will change. We exit the repeat-until loop and enter stratum 2.

In stratum 2 the only relation is *shortest*. To find the value of this relation, we have to enter again the repeat-until loop. Here in each iteration i we have:

$$F_1^i = \rho_{x/\$1,y/\$2,s/\$3}(\hat{\pi}_{x,y,s}(\rho_{\$1/x,\$2/y,\$3/0,\$4/s}\,G_p^{i-1}\bowtie(\neg(\rho_{\$1/x,\$2/y,\$3/s}\,G_{ns}^{i-1}))))$$

Let $S_1 = \rho_{\$1/x,\$2/y,\$3/0,\$4/s}\,G_p^4$. The gap-graphs in S_1 are:
$(x=1,y=2,0 <_{19} s)$
$(x=1,y=3,0 <_{44} s)$

$(x = 2, y = 4, 0 <_{29} s)$
$(x = 3, y = 4, 0 <_{14} s)$
$(x = 1, y = 4, 0 <_{49} s)$
$(x = 1, y = 4, 0 <_{59} s)$

Let $S_2 = \rho_{\$1/x,\$2/y,\$3/s} G_{ns}^4$. The gap-graphs in S_2 are:
$(x = 1, y = 2, 0 <_{20} s)$
$(x = 1, y = 3, 0 <_{45} s)$
$(x = 2, y = 4, 0 <_{30} s)$
$(x = 3, y = 4, 0 <_{15} s)$
$(x = 1, y = 4, 0 <_{50} s)$
$(x = 1, y = 4, 0 <_{60} s)$

We find the negation of S_2 using De Morgan's laws and simplifying:
$(s < 16)$
$(x \neq 3, s < 21)$
$(y \neq 4, s < 21)$
$(x \neq 1, x \neq 3, s < 31)$
$(x \neq 3, y \neq 2, s < 31)$
$(x \neq 2, x \neq 3, y \neq 2, s < 46)$
$(y \neq 2, y \neq 4, s < 46)$
$(x \neq 2, x \neq 3, y \neq 2, y \neq 3, s < 51)$
$(x \neq 1, x \neq 2, x \neq 3)$
$(x \neq 1, y \neq 4)$
$(y \neq 2, y \neq 3, y \neq 4)$

Each of the above constraint tuples can be rewritten into a set of gap-graphs by expanding the $\neq$ constraints into equivalent disjunctions, i.e. $x \neq 3$ into $(x > 3) \lor (x < 3)$. For simplicity we skip this step in the present example. It is already evident that the join of S_1 and the negation of S_2 will be:
$(x = 1, y = 2, s = 20)$
$(x = 1, y = 3, s = 45)$
$(x = 2, y = 4, s = 30)$
$(x = 3, y = 4, s = 15)$
$(x = 1, y = 4, s = 50)$

Note that we get a unique s for each pair of x and y. The s is the length of the shortest path between x and y as we expected. □

5 The Complexity of Safe Stratified $Datalog^{\neg,<z}$ Queries

Although safe stratified $Datalog^{\neg,<z}$ queries can be evaluated in finite time, in this section we show that their evaluation may require a large data complexity. Since the language $Datalog^{<z}$ is included in the language of safe stratified $Datalog^{\neg,<z}$ it is worthwhile to recall the known results about this sublanguage.

(Note: Safe stratified $Datalog^{\neg,<z}$ queries were not considered before in the literature.)

In [23] the data complexity of $Datalog^{<z}$ queries is shown to be in PTIME if the size of each constant in the database is logarithmic in the size of the entire database and to be in DEXPTIME in general. In [11] the expression complexity in general is shown to be DEXPTIME-complete. In [24] the data complexity in general is also shown to be DEXPTIME-complete.

To proceed with the analysis of data complexity, we start with a definition of families of functions F_i of type $N \to N$. Let F_0 be the set of polynomial functions, and let $F_i = \{2^f : f \in F_{i-i}\}$ for $i > 0$. If $\mathcal{F}$ is a family of functions, let $\mathcal{F}$-TIME denote the class of languages that can be accepted within some time $f \in \mathcal{F}$. Now we will show using a Turing machine reduction that evaluation of stratified $Datalog^{\neg,<z}$ queries is $\mathcal{F}$-TIME-hard.

Let d be a database instance and let $\mid d \mid$ denote its size in number of bits representation. Let $\mathcal{D}$ denote the set of possible database instances. We define a function f of type $N \times \mathcal{D} \to N$ as follows. Let $f(0,d) = 2^{|d|}$ and $f(i,d) = 2^{f(i-1,d)}$. (Here $f(i,d) \in \mathcal{F}_i - TIME$.)

We start with a lemma that shows that the successor function on integers from 0 to $f(i,d)$ can be defined using a safe stratified $Datalog^{\neg,<z}$ program with i strata.

Lemma 5.1 There is a safe stratified $Datalog^{\neg,<z}$ program with a single negation that given as inputs a relation that enables counting from 1 to s, and the numbers s and 2^s defines both (1) a relation that enables counting from 1 to 2^s and (2) the numbers 2^s and 2^{2^s}.

Proof. Let us assume that the input relations are $next(0,1), \ldots, next(s-1,s)$ and $no\_digits(s)$, $two\_to\_s(2^s)$. Using a safe stratified $Datalog^{\neg,<z}$ program we will define two output relations, (1) the successor relation $succ(0,1), \ldots, succ(2^s - 1, 2^s)$ and (2) the numbers $two\_to\_two\_to\_s(2^{2^s})$. In this abstract we show only (1) and omit (2).

To show (1): In the reduction it helps to think of each number being written in binary notation. Since the number 2^s has s binary digits, what we really need is given a counter on the digits define a counter from 1 to 2^s.

We start by representing the value of each digit using a constraint interval, where the gap-value is one less than the actual value. That is, for each $1 \leq i \leq s$, we want to represent the value of the ith digit from the right as: $digit(i, x_1, x_2) :\!- x_1 <_{2^i-1} x_2$. The following program P_1 will generate the desired constraint tuples.

$digit(j, x_1, x_2) :\!- next(i,j), digit(j, x_1, x_3), digit(j, x_3, x_2).$
$digit(1, x_1, x_2) :\!- x_1 < x_2.$

Note that we can represent each number i by a pair of constraints: $-1 <_i x$ and $x <_{2^s-(i+1)} 2^s$. Since each number can be expressed as the sum of a subset of the values of the n digits, if we start out from the constraint $-1 < x$ and $x < 2^s$ and choose to increment for each $1 \leq i \leq s$ either the first or the second gap-value by the value of the ith digit, then we will get a single integer between 0 and $2^s - 1$ as output. This gives an idea about how to "build up" any number that we need.

Using this idea, the following program defines all integers between 1 and 2^s. (The program is given here only as an illustration to the above idea, it is not used directly to express the successor function.)

$single\_integer(x) :\!- no\_digits(s), range(x, x, s).$
$range(x_3, x_2, j) \quad :\!- next(i, j), range(x_1, x_2, i), digit(j, x_1, x_3).$
$range(x_1, x_3, j) \quad :\!- next(i, j), range(x_1, x_2, i), digit(j, x_3, x_2).$
$range(x_1, x_2, 0) \quad :\!- -1 < x_1, x_2 < 2^s.$

Technical note: To avoid bad interactions we used a separate x_1 and x_2 in all the rules except the top-most. Intuitively, when computing with constraint tuples [23], in each recursive step, x_1 will be bounded by higher and higher constants from below and x_2 will be bounded by lower and lower constants from above. In the top rule the possible values of x_1 and x_2 will overlap exactly on one integer.

To express the succssor function, we build-up *pairs* of integers. Let x_1 and x_2 represent the first and y_1 and y_2 represent the second integer. Building up pairs at a time is necessary to make sure that when we add a digit to the xs we also add the same digit to the ys the right way.

$succ(x, y) \qquad\qquad :\!- succ2(x, x, y, y, s), no\_digits(s).$

$succ2(x_3, x_2, y_3, y_2, j) :\!- succ2(x_1, x_2, y_1, y_2, i), next(i, j), digit(j, x_1, x_3),$
$\qquad\qquad\qquad\qquad digit(j, y_1, y_3).$
$succ2(x_1, x_3, y_1, y_3, j) :\!- succ2(x_1, x_2, y_1, y_2, i), next(i, j), digit(j, x_3, x_2),$
$\qquad\qquad\qquad\qquad digit(j, y_3, y_2).$
$succ2(x_1, x_3, y_3, y_2, 1) :\!- range(x_1, x_2, y_1, y_2, 1), digit(1, x_3, x_2),$
$\qquad\qquad\qquad\qquad digit(1, y_1, y_3).$
$succ2(x_1, x_3, y_3, y_2, j) :\!- succ3(x_1, x_2, y_1, y_2, i), next(i, j), digit(j, x_3, x_2),$
$\qquad\qquad\qquad\qquad digit(j, y_1, y_3).$

$succ3(x_3, x_2, y_1, y_3, j) :\!- succ3(x_1, x_2, y_1, y_2, i), next(i, j), digit(j, x_1, x_3),$
$\qquad\qquad\qquad\qquad digit(j, y_3, y_2).$
$succ3(x_3, x_2, y_1, y_3, 1) :\!- range(x_1, x_2, y_1, y_2, 1), digit(1, x_1, x_3),$
$\qquad\qquad\qquad\qquad digit(1, y_3, y_2).$
$range(x_1, x_2, y_1, y_2, 0) :\!- -1 < x_1, x_2 < 2^s, -1 < y_1, y_2 < 2^s.$

Theorem 5.1 There is a fixed yes/no program Q in safe stratified $Datalog^{\neg, <z}$ with i negations such that deciding whether $Q(d)$ is yes for variable database d is deterministic $\mathcal{F}_i - TIME$-hard.

Proof. The base case, when $i = 0$, is just the case of $Datalog^{<z}$ programs, which are known to have DEXPTIME-complete data complexity [24]. To prove the theorem for $i > 0$ we will show that we can simulate an $f(i, d)$-time bounded deterministic Turing machine using a safe stratified $Datalog^{\neg, <z}$ program with i negations. $\square$

Theorem 5.1 shows that the data complexity of some stratified $Datalog^{\neg,<z}$ programs can be high. This result of course means nothing about the data complexity of queries that an average user may wish to use. Therefore the high data complexity should not be considered a pessimistic result.

6 Conclusions

This paper considered only stratified $Datalog^{\neg,<z}$ programs. It is still an open problem to find safe subsets of other similarly expressive constraint logic programming languages.

In addition it should be kept in mind that guaranteeing closed-form evaluation and bottom-up processing of queries are just two of the many important features that database systems today should have for enhanced usability and user satisfaction. For example, most current database systems also provide efficient indexing on facts, integrity constraints, built-in aggregate operators, menu-based user interfaces, concurrent access to data, security etc. Many of these problems and related issues have to be rethought in the context of constraint databases (see [22, 18, 13, 25] for some recent papers). The work in this paper is only a part of a bigger context of building a prototype constraint database system. We are in the process of implementing the algorithms presented in the paper and plan to demonstrate them at the conference.

References

1. H. Aït-Kaci, A. Podelski. Towards a Meaing of LIFE. *Journal of Logic Programming*, 16, 195–234,1993.
2. K.R. Apt, H. Blair, A. Walker. Towards a Theory of Declarative Knowledge. In: *Foundations of Deductive Databases in Logic Programming*, Morgan-Kaufmann, 1988.
3. M. Baudinet, M. Niette, P. Wolper. On the Representation of Infinite Temporal Data and Queries. *Proc. 10th ACM PODS*, 280–290, 1991.
4. A. Brodsky, J. Jaffar, M. J. Maher. Toward Practical Constraint Databases, *Proc. VLDB*, 1993.
5. A.K. Chandra, D. Harel. Computable Queries for Relational Data Bases. *Journal of Computer and System Sciences*, 21:156–178, 1980.
6. A.K. Chandra, D. Harel. Structure and Complexityof Relational Queries. *Journal of Computer and System Sciences*, 25:99-128, 1982.
7. J. Chomicki, T. Imielinski. Finite Representation of Infinite Query Answers. *ACM Transactions of Database Systems*, 181–223, vol. 18, no. 2, 1993.
8. J. Chomicki, G. Kuper. Measuring Infinite Relations, *Proc. ILPS Workshop on Constraints and Databases*, 1994.
9. J. Cohen. Constraint Logic Programming Languages. *CACM*, 33 (7): 69–90, 1990.
10. A. Colmerauer. An Introduction to Prolog III, *CACM*, 28 (4): 412–418, 1990.
11. J. Cox, K. McAloon. Decision Procedures for Constraint Based Extensions of Datalog. In: *Constraint Logic Programming*, MIT Press, 1993.

12. M. Dincbas, P. Van Hentenryck, H. Simonis, A. Aggoun, T. Graf, and F. Berthier. The Constraint Logic Programming Language CHIP. *Proc. Fifth Generation Computer Systems*, 1988.

13. S. Grumbach, J Su. Finitely Representable Databases. *Proc. 13th ACM PODS*, 289–300, 1994.

14. J. Jaffar, J.L. Lassez. Constraint Logic Programming. *Proc. 14th ACM POPL*, 111–119, 1987.

15. J. Jaffar, M.J. Maher. Constraint Logic Programming: A Survey. *J.Logic Programming*, 19 & 20, 503–581, 1994.

16. J. Jaffar, S. Michaylov, P.J. Stuckey, R.H. Yap. The CLP(R) Language and System. *ACM Transactions on Programming Languages and Systems*, 14:3, 339-395, 1992.

17. F. Kabanza, J-M. Stevenne, P. Wolper. Handling Infinite Temporal Data. *Proc. 9th ACM PODS*, 392–403, 1990.

18. P.C. Kanellakis, D.Q. Goldin. Constraint Programming and Database Query Languages. *Proc. 2nd TACS*, 1994.

19. P. C. Kanellakis, G. M. Kuper, P. Z. Revesz. Constraint Query Languages. *Proc. 9th ACM PODS*, 299–313, 1990. Final version to appear in *Journal of Computer and System Sciences*.

20. P.C. Kanellakis, S. Ramaswamy, D.E. Vengroff, J.S. Vitter. Indexing for Data Models with Constraints and Classes *Proc. 12th ACM PODS*, 233–243, 1993.

21. M. Koubarakis. Complexity Results for First-Order Theories of Temporal Constraints. *Proc. Int. Conf. on Knowledge Representation and Reasoning*, 1994.

22. *Proc. Post-ILPS Workshop on Constraints and Databases*, P.Z. Revesz, D. Srivastava, P. Stuckey, S. Sudarshan (eds.). Tech. Report, Univ. of Nebraska, CSE-94-025, 1994.

23. P. Z. Revesz. A Closed Form Evaluation for Datalog Queries with Integer (Gap)-Order Constraints, *Theoretical Computer Science*, vol. 116, no. 1, 117-149, 1993.

24. P. Z. Revesz. Datalog Queries of Set Constraint Databases. *Proc. 5th International Conference on Database Theory*, 423–438, 1995.

25. D. Srivastava, R. Ramakrishnan, P.Z. Revesz. Constraint Objects. *Proc. 2nd Workshop on Principles and Practice of Constraint Programming*, 274–284, 1994.

26. D. Toman, J. Chomicki, D.S. Rogers. Datalog with Integer Periodicity Constraints. *Proc. International Logic Programming Symposium*, 189–203, 1994.

27. P. Van Hentenryck. *Constraint Satisfaction in Logic Programming*. MIT Press, 1989.

28. J.D. Ullman. *Principles of Database and Knowledge-Base Systems*, Vols 1&2, Computer Science Press, 1989.

29. M. Vardi. The Complexity of Relational Query Languages. *Proc. 14th ACM Symposium on the Theory of Computing*, 137–145, 1982.

Constrained Dependencies
(Extended Abstract)

Michael J. Maher

IBM - T.J. Watson Research Center
Yorktown Heights, NY 10598, U.S.A.
mjm@watson.ibm.com

1 Introduction

In this paper we study constrained dependencies and, in particular, constrained functional dependencies (CFDs) and constrained finiteness dependencies. CFDs extend the traditional notion of functional dependency by expressing that a functional dependency holds on a subset of a relation, a subset defined by a constraint. For example, the CFD $0 \leq z \leq 9 \Rightarrow x \rightarrow y$ on a relation $p(w, x, y, z)$ expresses that, on the subrelation of p consisting of those tuples whose fourth argument lies in the range between 0 and 9, the value of y is functionally determined by the value of x.

The main advantage of CFDs over FDs is their greater expressiveness. Consequently they provide greater precision in describing and analyzing relations. Furthermore, they have a smooth interaction with semantic knowledge of relations that can be represented as constraints, for example, that lengths must be positive. This information may be available directly from the definition of a relation, from integrity constraints, or from an approximation of the relation. CFDs provide a framework for exploiting this information in the course of analyses that usually simply use FDs. Inference directly from CFDs and constraints is more powerful than the common alternative of representing constraints by the dependencies which hold on them, and then using inference of dependencies only.

CFDs also, naturally, have several applications to query processing in constraint logic programming (CLP) languages and constraint databases (CDBs), where data is represented by constraints (see, for example, [14]). CFDs allow the generalization of results of [19] to CDBs. That generalization uses inferred CFDs in detecting cases where bottom-up execution can omit or limit tests for subsumption and duplication. A modification of the analysis detects cases where top-down execution with tabulation will not reuse tabled answers. Similarly, CFDs can be used to extend the optimizations of [8] to CLP programs. Furthermore, provided the constraint solver is complete in a certain sense, CFDs can be used to determine groundness information as is already done in logic programming [6, 20]. CFDs can be used in detecting query emptiness independent of the underlying database [9], which has applications to transaction scheduling and recomputation of materialized views [10]. There are also applications to semantic query optimization [5], design of database schemas, and knowledge discovery [28]. Finiteness dependencies are used in [15] to define a class of CDB queries for which only trivial constraint solving is needed in computing answers. Constrained finiteness dependencies allow an expansion of this class.

The focus of this paper is on the inference of constrained dependencies and, in particular, the solution of the implication problem. The greater expressiveness of constrained dependencies makes the implication problem correspondingly more difficult. In keeping with the principles of the scheme of [11], we try to develop an approach that is parameterized by the constraint domain. We are able to characterize those constraint domains which admit a polynomial time solution of the implication problem for CFDs (assuming P≠NP) and give an efficient algorithm for these cases, modulo the cost of constraint manipulation. We have slightly weaker results for constrained finiteness dependencies.

There is closely related work on constraint-generating dependencies (CGDs) [2], a general class of dependencies which includes CFDs but not constrained finiteness dependencies. That paper provides an elegant reduction of the implication problem for CGDs to the validity problem of constraint formulas, but does not suggest an efficient algorithm for CFDs. Earlier work on related problems includes that of Klug [16] and Elkan [9]. We give in Section 7 a unifying result on the complexity of the implication problem for CGDs and two classes of CGDs with polynomial time solution of their implication problem.

The next section provides a brief overview of notation and terminology concerning constraints and constraint domains. We then present our inference rules for CFDs, a completeness result and an algorithm for solving the implication problem. The following sections of the paper discuss the inference of finiteness dependencies and CGDs. Finally, we mention some of the applications of CFDs.

2   Constraints and Notation

Notation and definitions concerning constraints follow those of [12]. We write $\tilde{x}$ to denote a collection of distinct variables $x_1, \ldots, x_n$ for an appropriate n determined by the context. We write $\exists_{-\tilde{x}} c$ ($\forall_{-\tilde{x}} c$) to denote the existential (universal) quantification of all variables in c except $\tilde{x}$, and $\tilde{\exists} c$ ($\tilde{\forall} c$) for the existential (universal) closure of c. The expression $\exists^{<k} \tilde{x} \ P(\tilde{x}, \tilde{y})$ is defined to be $\neg \exists \tilde{x}_1 \ldots \tilde{x}_k \ \bigwedge_{i \neq j} \tilde{x}_i \neq \tilde{x}_j \wedge \bigwedge_{i=1}^{k} P(\tilde{x}_i, \tilde{y})$. In particular, $\exists^{<2} \tilde{x} \ P(\tilde{x}, \tilde{y})$ is equivalent to $\forall \tilde{x}, \tilde{x}' \ P(\tilde{x}, \tilde{y}) \wedge P(\tilde{x}', \tilde{y}) \to \tilde{x} = \tilde{x}'$.

In this paper we will make a deliberate confusion between the attributes of a relation p and the variables in an expression $p(x_1, \ldots, x_n)$. We use V for the set of attributes/variables. Consequently, we will equivalently regard a relation as a set of tuples or a set of valuations. When a constraint c holds for every tuple in relation p we write $\mathcal{D} \models p(V) \to c$. If $I \subseteq \tilde{x}$ then we will equivalently write $\tilde{x}_I$ for I.

The constraints under consideration are specified by a constraint domain.

Definition 2.1 *For any signature* Σ, *let* $\mathcal{D}$ *be a* Σ-*structure and* $\mathcal{L}$ *be a class of* Σ-*formulas. The pair* $(\mathcal{D}, \mathcal{L})$ *is called a* constraint domain. $\mathcal{D}$ *is the underlying domain of values and* $\mathcal{L}$ *is the class of constraints. We will assume that the class of constraints contains all equations between terms and is closed under variable renaming and conjunction.*

Generally when dealing with CLP constraints it is convenient to also assume that $\mathcal{L}$ is closed under existential quantification [12], but this is not necessary here since the dependencies we consider do not introduce existential quantification.

We briefly mention some useful constraint domains (for further introduction to these domains, see [12]): the domains of linear arithmetic constraints over the integers, the rational number and the real numbers, are denoted by $\mathcal{Z}_{Lin}$, $\mathbf{Q}_{Lin}$ and $\Re_{Lin}$ respectively; the domain of linear equations over the real numbers is denoted by $\Re_{LinEqn}$; the Herbrand universe with function symbols Σ is denoted by $\mathcal{H}(\Sigma)$ when constraints are equations between terms and $\mathcal{H}^{\exists}(\Sigma)$ when constraints may also incorporate existential quantifiers; similarly, $\mathcal{RT}(\Sigma)$ and $\mathcal{RT}^{\exists}(\Sigma)$ denote corresponding domains over the rational trees; the domain of feature trees is denoted by $\mathcal{FEAT}(\mathcal{S}, \mathcal{F})$ where $\mathcal{S}$ is the set of sorts and $\mathcal{F}$ is the set of features; the two-element Boolean algebra is denoted by $\mathcal{BOOL}$ and the free Boolean algebra generated by an infinite set of generators is denoted by $\mathcal{BOOL}_{\infty}$.

An important property of constraint domains is generally phrased as a form of independence. This property has been investigated in some generality in [17]. The significance of the property for the optimization of bottom-up execution of CDBs and CLP programs is discussed in [18].

Definition 2.2 *A constraint domain* $(\mathcal{D}, \mathcal{L})$ *has the* independence of negative constraints *property if, for all constraints* $c, c_1, \ldots, c_n \in \mathcal{L}$,

$$\mathcal{D} \models \tilde{\exists} \, c \wedge \neg c_1 \wedge \cdots \wedge \neg c_n \;\; \text{iff} \; \mathcal{D} \models \tilde{\exists} \, c \wedge \neg c_i \; \text{for } i = 1, \ldots, n.$$

Of the constraint domains mentioned above, $\Re_{LinEqn}$, $\mathcal{H}(\Sigma)$, $\mathcal{RT}(\Sigma)$ all have the independence of negative constraints property. $\mathcal{H}^{\exists}(\Sigma)$ and $\mathcal{RT}^{\exists}(\Sigma)$ have the property when Σ is infinite, but not when Σ is finite. Similarly, $\mathcal{FEAT}(\mathcal{S}, \mathcal{F})$ has the property when $\mathcal{S}$ and $\mathcal{F}$ are infinite. $\Re_{Lin}$, $\mathbf{Q}_{Lin}$, $\mathcal{Z}_{Lin}$ and $\mathcal{BOOL}$ do not have this property.

We will also need the following property, which requires that every element of $\mathcal{D}$ can be expressed by a constraint.

Definition 2.3 *A constraint domain* $(\mathcal{D}, \mathcal{L})$ *has the* representation of elements by constraints *property if, for every element* $d \in \mathcal{D}$ *there is a constraint* $c(x, \tilde{y}) \in \mathcal{L}$ *such that a valuation* v *satisfies* $\exists \tilde{y} \, c(x, \tilde{y})$ *iff* $v(x) = d$.

For example, $\mathbf{Q}_{Lin}$ has this property, since every positive element $\frac{p}{q}$ is represented by $x + \cdots + x = 1 + \cdots + 1$ where there are p 1's and q x's in the equation (and similarly for the negative rationals). On the other hand, $\Re_{Lin}$ does not have this property since, for example, we cannot define π with finitely many equations and inequalities.

The distinction between relations and constraints is that we assume the existence of algorithms to test properties of constraints, most importantly in this paper to test whether one constraint implies another. The way a relation is defined is not relevant to the results of this paper, although it might be relevant to their application. For concreteness, we have in mind relations defined through constraints by (possibly infinitely many) "generalized tuples" [14], relations defined by formulas which are not constraints (for example, $z = \max\{x * y, x + y\}$), and the composition of these by conjunction and disjunction.

3   Constrained Dependencies

A constrained dependency generalizes traditional dependencies, such as functional dependencies, by expressing that the dependency applies not to an entire relation, but to a subset of the tuples in the relation described by a constraint. We consider a (possibly infinite) relation p on a set of variables (or attributes) V that take values in $\mathcal{D}$.

For simplicity of presentation we assume that the constraints allowed in a constrained dependency are those in the language of constraints $\mathcal{L}$ in the underlying CLP language or CDB. Note, however, that it can be useful to use a different class of constraints in constrained dependencies from that used in the CLP language. We also assume that the only free variables in constraints are those in V.

Definition 3.1 *A constrained functional dependency* over a relation p with variables (or attributes) V on a constraint domain $(\mathcal{D}, \mathcal{L})$ has the form

$$\{p\} \quad c \Rightarrow X \to Y$$

where $X, Y \subseteq V$ and $c \in \mathcal{L}$ is a constraint with free variables from V. Intuitively, such an expression denotes that the functional dependency $X \to Y$ holds on the subset of tuples of p on which c holds. When the relation p is evident from the context we will omit it from the constrained dependency. In conformity with existing notation for FDs, we often will omit the set notation when expressing X or Y by listing the elements. Thus we write $c \Rightarrow x_1 x_2 \to y_1 y_2 y_3$ instead of $c \Rightarrow \{x_1, x_2\} \to \{y_1, y_2, y_3\}$.

Constrained dependencies provide a more expressive and flexible basis for the analysis of constraint logic programs and database queries than traditional dependencies. By taking constraints directly into account, instead of simply abstracting from them any dependency information, we can obtain a more accurate analysis. Furthermore, it often happens that a dependency "almost holds" –

holds with some few exceptions – or holds on some simply-defined sub-relation. Constrained dependencies provide the ability to express and manipulate this information that would otherwise be ignored.

Example 3.1 Consider the relation defined by $x * y = z$. Although the functional dependency $xy \rightarrow z$ holds for this relation, the dependencies $xz \rightarrow y$ and $yz \rightarrow x$ do not hold, since division is not a function. More precisely, when z and x take the value 0 the value of y is not determined (and similarly for the second dependency). However the weaker constrained functional dependency

$$x \neq 0 \vee z \neq 0 \Rightarrow xz \rightarrow y$$

holds. In a situation where there is also a constraint $x > 0$ it is then possible to infer the dependency $xz \rightarrow y$.

For example, in a query fragment

$$travel(JourneyId, Distance, FuelUsed), \; Efficiency = Distance/FuelUsed$$

if we know that, in the *travel* relation, *Distance* and *FuelUsed* are functionally dependent on *JourneyId* and the values of *FuelUsed* are always positive, we can safely infer that *Efficiency* is functionally dependent on *JourneyId*. We cannot make this inference when reasoning only on dependencies. □

Constrained dependencies also can be useful in a conventional database setting where arithmetic and explicit constraints do not occur.

Example 3.2 Consider a database involving students, courses, instructors, etc at a university. The relation describing courses might contain attributes Course Identifier, Level of Instruction (i.e. freshman, sophomore, ...), Room, Time, Instructor, etc. Generally the attributes Room and Instructor, are functionally dependent upon the Course Identifier. However courses in the freshman year often have high attendance and it is not unusual that the university offers more than one class. In this case the functional dependencies might not hold, but the constrained functional dependency

$$LevelofInstruction \neq freshman \Rightarrow CourseId \rightarrow Instructor$$

holds on this relation. □

4 Inference Rules for CFDs

We now enumerate the inference rules for constrained functional dependencies. Let I, J, K range over subsets of V. Let $J' = J - I$ and IJ denote $I \cup J$. For a fixed constraint domain $(\mathcal{D}, \mathcal{L})$ and a fixed relation p, the inference rules are the following:

1. If $I \subseteq J$ then $true \Rightarrow J \rightarrow I$

2. If $c_1 \Rightarrow I \rightarrow J$ and $c_2 \Rightarrow J \rightarrow K$ then $c_1 \wedge c_2 \Rightarrow I \rightarrow K$

3. If $c \Rightarrow I \rightarrow J$ then $c \Rightarrow I \cup K \rightarrow J \cup K$

4. If $c_1 \Rightarrow I \rightarrow J$ and $\mathcal{D} \models c_2 \rightarrow c_1$ then $c_2 \Rightarrow I \rightarrow J$

5. If $\mathcal{D} \models \forall_I \exists_{j'}^{\leq 2} \exists_{-IJ} c$ then $c \Rightarrow I \rightarrow J$

6. Let c_0 denote $c \wedge \bigwedge_{i=1}^{k} \neg c_i$.[1] If $c_i \Rightarrow I \rightarrow J$ for $i = 1, \ldots, k, \ldots, m$, and $\mathcal{D} \models \forall_I \exists_{j'}^{\leq 2} \exists_{-IJ} c_0$ and, for every i and j such that $0 \leq i, j \leq k$,

$$\mathcal{D} \models (\exists_{-I} c \wedge c_i \wedge \exists_{-I} c \wedge c_j) \rightarrow \left((\exists_{j'}^{\leq 2} \exists_{-IJ} c \wedge (c_i \vee c_j)) \vee \bigvee_{l=0}^{m} \forall_{-I} c \wedge (c_i \vee c_j) \rightarrow c_l \right)$$

then $c \Rightarrow I \rightarrow J$

7. If $c_1 \Rightarrow I \rightarrow J$ and $\mathcal{D} \models p(V) \rightarrow c_2$ and $\mathcal{D} \models c_2 \wedge c_3 \rightarrow c_1$ then $c_3 \Rightarrow I \rightarrow J$

Rules 1, 2 and 3 correspond to the Armstrong axioms for functional dependencies. Rule 4 expresses a simple closure property: if a dependency holds under some constraint then it holds under any stronger constraint. Rule 5 generates all CFDs that are independent of the underlying relation: they hold as a consequence of the constraint. For example, from the constraint $x = 2y + 1$ we can see that the functional dependencies $x \rightarrow y$ and $y \rightarrow x$ hold, so that, for example, $x = 2y + 1 \Rightarrow \tilde{x} \rightarrow \tilde{y}$ can be inferred on any relation. Such CFDs are called tautologies. Rule 1 is a special case of rule 5.

Rule 6 allows a constrained functional dependency to be inferred from "fragments". The conditions require that every possible tuple that is addressed by the new CFD is addressed by some fragment, including a possible tautological fragment, and that whenever two fragments overlap on I they are shown to be compatible, either tautologously or by consideration of a single fragment. Rule 4 can be considered the special case of rule 6 where there is a single input CFD, and rule 5 is the special case where there are no input CFDs.

Example 4.1 Consider the relation over the real numbers defined by $y = |x|$. The CFDs $x \geq 0 \Rightarrow x \rightarrow y$ and $x \leq 0 \Rightarrow x \rightarrow y$ can be combined to infer $x \rightarrow y$. We take $c \equiv true$, $I = \{x\}$ and $J = \{y\}$ in rule 6. Then c_0, that is $c \wedge \bigwedge_{i=1}^{k} \neg c_i$, is equivalent to $false$, so $\mathcal{D} \models \forall_I \exists_{j'}^{\leq 2} \exists_{-IJ} c_0$ is satisfied. Moreover $\exists_{-I} c \wedge c_i \wedge \exists_{-I} c \wedge c_j$ is equivalent to $x = 0$, and $c \wedge (c_i \vee c_j)$ is equivalent to $true$. So $\exists_{j}^{\leq 2} \exists_{-IJ} c \wedge (c_i \vee c_j)$ is $false$. However $\mathfrak{R} \models x = 0 \rightarrow \forall y \ (true \rightarrow x \geq 0)$ and thus rule 6 applies.

On the other hand, the CFDs $x \geq 0 \Rightarrow y \rightarrow x$ and $x \leq 0 \Rightarrow y \rightarrow x$ rightly cannot be combined to infer $y \rightarrow x$. Here $c \equiv true$, $I = \{y\}$ and $J = \{x\}$ in rule 6, so that $\exists_{-I} c \wedge c_i \wedge \exists_{-I} c \wedge c_j$ is $\exists x \ x \geq 0 \wedge \exists x \ x \leq 0$, which is equivalent to $true$, and $c \wedge (c_i \vee c_j)$ is also equivalent to $true$. Hence $\exists_{j}^{\leq 2} \exists_{-IJ} c \wedge (c_i \vee c_j)$ is $false$ and $c \wedge (c_i \vee c_j) \rightarrow c_l$ is $false$ for $l = 1, 2$. Thus rule 6 is not applicable. $\square$

---

[1] Note that in general c_0 is not a constraint; the formula is named c_0 purely for notational convenience.

Rule 7 takes into account that some constraints on the variables of p may be known, either explicitly (because the relation was defined using constraints) or implicitly (through integrity constraints, or by approximating the relation with constraints). When there are no such constraints we say p is a *pure* relation. When p is pure, c_2 must be equivalent to *true*, and so, in this case, rule 7 reduces to rule 4.

When a CFD f can be derived from a set F of CFDs using the inference rules 1–6 we write $F \vdash f$. We write $F \vdash_p f$ if f can be derived from F using rules 1–7, where rule 7 uses constraints true of the relation p. Let C be a set of constraints. We say a relation R satisfies C if each tuple in R satisfies every constraint in C. We say a relation R satisfies the CFD $c \Rightarrow I \to J$ if the functional dependency $I \to J$ holds on the set of tuples in R that satisfy c. R satisfies a set of CFDs F if it satisfies every $f \in F$. If every relation R that satisfies C and F also satisfies f, we write $C, F \models f$. When C is empty we write $F \models f$.

The following proposition states the soundness of the inference rules.

Proposition 4.1 *Consider the inference rules for a fixed constraint domain* $(\mathcal{D}, \mathcal{L})$.

- *If* $F \vdash f$ *then* $F \models f$.

- *If* $F \vdash_p f$ *and* C *is the set of constraints true of* p *that are used in applications of rule 7 then* $C, F \models f$.

We use the following notation for restriction by a constraint. $R|_c = \{\tilde{a} \in R \mid c(\tilde{a})$ holds$\}$. $F|_c = \{c \wedge c' \Rightarrow I \to J \mid c' \Rightarrow I \to J$ is a CFD in $F\}$. For a CFD f, say $c \Rightarrow I \to J$, $cons(f)$ denotes c and $fd(f)$ denotes $I \to J$. $fd(F) = \{fd(f) \mid f \in F\}$. We say f is a *tautology* (or is *tautological*) iff f holds for every relation R (containing the variables of f). We have the following properties of tautologies, restriction and the inference rules.

Proposition 4.2 *Let f be the CFD $c \Rightarrow I \to J$ and let F be a set of CFDs. Then*

1. *f is tautological iff f is inferred by rule 5 iff $\emptyset \vdash f$*

2. *If F contains only tautologies and $F \vdash f$ then f is tautological*

3. *For every relation R, R satisfies f iff $R|_c$ satisfies f*

4. *For every relation R, R satisfies $F|_c$ iff $R|_c$ satisfies F iff $R|_c$ satisfies $F|_c$*

5. *$F \vdash f$ iff $F|_c \vdash f$*

6. *If $F \vdash f$ without using rule 6 then, for every CFD g in a minimal derivation of f, $\mathcal{D} \models c \to cons(g)$*

7. *If $F \vdash f$ then there is a derivation of f where each tautology g generated by rule 5 satisfies $\mathcal{D} \models cons(g) \to c$*

5 Completeness

The following theorem expresses the soundness and completeness of the inference rules as a method for inferring CFDs on pure relations when the constraint domain has the independence of negative constraints property.

Theorem 5.1 *Consider the inference rules for a fixed constraint domain $(\mathcal{D}, \mathcal{L})$ which has the independence of negative constraints property. Then, for every CFD f and finite set F of CFDs, $F \vdash f$ iff $F \models f$. Furthermore, completeness still holds when rule 6 is omitted.*

As a simple corollary of this theorem, we can see that rules 2, 3 and 5 form a minimal complete set of inference rules on pure relations when $(\mathcal{D}, \mathcal{L})$ has independence of negative constraints.

In cases where independence holds, we can obtain an efficient algorithm for inferring CFDs, modulo the cost of testing constraint implication. Let the *constraint implication problem* for a constraint domain $(\mathcal{D}, \mathcal{L})$ be the problem of determining that $\mathcal{D} \models c_1 \to c_2$, for $c_1, c_2 \in \mathcal{L}$. Note that the problem of determining whether a CFD is a tautology is a special case of the constraint implication problem.

Theorem 5.2 *If $(\mathcal{D}, \mathcal{L})$ has the independence of negative constraints and the constraint implication problem can be solved in polynomial time then the problem of determining whether $F \models f$ can be solved in polynomial time.*

The algorithm that is the basis of this theorem follows. It can be seen as an extension of the algorithm of [3] for FDs. Let K^+ denote the closure of K with respect to $fd(F')$, that is, $\{v \in V \mid fd(F') \models K \to v\}$. F' is defined in the algorithm.

Algorithm for the Implication Problem

1. Let f be $c \Rightarrow I \to J$.

2. If f is a tautology then return "yes".

3. If $I = \emptyset$ then return "no" else let $T = I$.

4. Let $K = I$.

5. For each $g \in F$, if $\mathcal{D} \not\models c \to cons(g)$ then delete g from F.

6. Let F' be the resulting subset of F.

7. While $J \not\subseteq K$ and $T \neq \emptyset$ do

    (a) Replace K by $(K \cup T)^+$.

    (b) Let $T = \{x \in vars(c) \mid \emptyset \vdash c \Rightarrow K \to x\} - K$.

8. If $J \subseteq K$ then return "yes" else return "no".

The first part of the algorithm (lines 1–4) checks some simple special cases and initializes the variables K and T. The second part (lines 5–6) removes from the set F, CFDs that need not be used in inferring f, by part 6 of Proposition 4.2. By parts 6 and 7 of Proposition 4.2, we need only generate tautologies with constraint c and, by part 5, we can ignore the constraints in all the CFDs. The third part of the algorithm (line 7) computes the closure for rules 2, 3 and 5 by repeatedly taking the closure for rule 5 and then the closure for rules 2 and 3 until $J \subseteq K$ or K is closed. (Note that if $x \notin vars(c)$ then x cannot be the conclusion of a useful tautology.) If, upon exiting the loop, $J \subseteq K$ then $F \vdash f$. Otherwise $F \nvdash f$, by Theorem 5.1.

Let $\gamma(N)$ denote the maximal cost of deciding a constraint implication problem of size N and $\xi(N)$ denote the maximal cost of determining whether a CFD of size N is a tautology. An upper bound for the complexity of this algorithm is $O(N^2 \xi(N) + N\gamma(N))$, where N is the size of $F \cup \{f\}$.

We now turn to the implication problem for constraint domains $(\mathcal{D}, \mathcal{L})$ that do not satisfy the independence of negative constraints. The key lemma concerns the complexity of the *extended constraint implication problem* for $(\mathcal{D}, \mathcal{L})$: the problem of determining that $\mathcal{D} \models c \rightarrow \bigvee_{i=1}^{k} c_i$, for $c, c_1, \ldots, c_k \in \mathcal{L}$.

Lemma 5.1 *Suppose $(\mathcal{D}, \mathcal{L})$ does not have independence of negative constraints. Then the extended constraint implication problem is co-NP-hard.*

A special case of this lemma, for the constraint domain $\Re_{Lin}$, was shown in [24]. Using this lemma, we can establish the intractability of the general implication problem for CFDs.

Proposition 5.1 *Suppose $(\mathcal{D}, \mathcal{L})$ does not have independence of negative constraints. Then the problem of determining whether $F \models f$ is co-NP-hard.*

In view of the intractability of the general problem we must resort to incomplete but more practical algorithms. The algorithm for the implication problem discussed above (modified by replacing "no" on line 8 by "don't know") is one. It represents an approximation that ignores disjunctive reasoning.

In cases where the cost of testing constraint implication and tautologies is too great we can also approximate these operations. That is, we employ a test that is always correct when identifying that $\mathcal{D} \models c_1 \rightarrow c_2$, but does not always detect when this holds. (For example, for linear arithmetic constraints, such a test might eliminate variables in c_1 and c_2 on the basis of equations in c_1 and test whether all resulting constraints in c_2 also occur in c_1.) The same approximation can be applied to testing tautologies since the test for tautology is a form of constraint implication. With this approximation the previous algorithm will delete more CFDs from F on line 5 and accumulate fewer variables on line 7b. We must also replace both occurrences of "no" by "don't know". The resulting algorithm is sound for detecting CFD implication but, of course, not complete.

By using a different approximation we can use the original algorithm as a basis for testing non-implication: that $F \nmodels f$. In this case we must use an approximate test that is always correct when identifying that $\mathcal{D} \nmodels c_1 \rightarrow c_2$ and replace occurrences of "yes" by "don't know". The resulting algorithm proceeds only if the approximate test can detect that f is not a tautology. Compared with the original algorithm, it deletes fewer CFDs from F on line 5 and accumulates more variables on line 7b. This approximate algorithm is sound only for constraint domains with independence of negative constraints.

In summary, when independence of negative constraints holds the implication problem for CFDs is in PTIME iff the constraint implication problem is in PTIME. When independence of negative constraints does not hold the implication problem for CFDs is co-NP-hard. Thus we have

Theorem 5.3 *Suppose* $P \neq NP$.
Then the implication problem for CFDs over constraint domain $(\mathcal{D}, \mathcal{L})$ *is in PTIME iff* $(\mathcal{D}, \mathcal{L})$ *has independence of negative constraints and the constraint implication problem for* $(\mathcal{D}, \mathcal{L})$ *is in PTIME.*

The extension of the inference system (in fact, *any* inference system) for pure relations to arbitrary relations is handled satisfactorily by the addition of rule 7.

Proposition 5.2 *For any inference system* $\vdash$ *that is complete for* $\models$ *on pure relations, the addition of rule 7 produces an inference system* $\vdash_p$ *that is complete for* $\models$.

6   Finiteness Dependencies

We will use the symbol $\rightarrow_{fin}$ for constrained finiteness dependencies, to distinguish such dependencies from constrained functional dependencies. A *constrained finiteness dependency*

$$\{p\} \quad c \Rightarrow X \rightarrow_{fin} Y$$

denotes that, for each fixed valuation of the variables in X, there are only finitely many values of the variables in Y in the tuples of p satisfying c with the valuation for the variables in X.

For unconstrained dependencies, it is well known that the inference rules for functional dependencies are also complete for finiteness dependencies. This fact is no longer true for constrained dependencies.

Example 6.1 Consider the finiteness dependencies $y \geq 0 \Rightarrow x \rightarrow_{fin} y$ and $y < 0 \Rightarrow x \rightarrow_{fin} y$. From them we can validly infer the finiteness dependency $x \rightarrow_{fin} y$. However inferring the functional dependency $x \rightarrow y$ from $y \geq 0 \Rightarrow x \rightarrow y$ and $y < 0 \Rightarrow x \rightarrow y$ is invalid, as the relation $\{\langle 1, -1\rangle, \langle 1, 3\rangle\}$ demonstrates. As a second example, consider the dependency $1 \leq y \leq 3 \Rightarrow x \rightarrow_{fin} y$, where the variables range over integers. This finiteness dependency is a tautology, but the corresponding CFD is not. □

It is necessary to modify rules 5 and 6. The other rules from Section 4 remain the same (except for the replacement of $\rightarrow$ by $\rightarrow_{fin}$). Let c_0 denote $c \wedge \bigwedge_{i=1}^{k} \neg c_i$.

5' If $\mathcal{D} \models \forall_I \bigvee_{n=1}^{\infty} \exists_{j'}^{\leq n} \exists_{-IJ} c$ where $J' = J - I$ then $c \Rightarrow I \rightarrow_{fin} J$

6' If $c_i \Rightarrow I \rightarrow_{fin} J$ for $i = 1, \ldots, k$, $\mathcal{D} \models \forall_I \bigvee_{n=1}^{\infty} \exists_{j'}^{\leq n} \exists_{-IJ} c_0$ and $\mathcal{D} \models c \rightarrow \bigvee_{i=0}^{k} c_i$ then $c \Rightarrow I \rightarrow_{fin} J$

The rule for combining fragmentary constrained finiteness dependencies (rule 6') is considerably simpler than the one for constrained functional dependencies. This is because finiteness of sets has the (very well known) property that it is preserved by finite union. In contrast, the corresponding property for functional dependencies – that a set is empty or singleton – is not preserved under finite union. In that case further conditions are necessary to guarantee that the result of a finite union is either empty or singleton.

The rule for inferring tautologous constrained finiteness dependencies (rule 5') involves a condition that, in general, cannot be expressed as a first-order statement over the underlying domain of values $\mathcal{D}$. Nevertheless, in many of the domains discussed in Section 2 this condition can be decided quite simply.

Once the adjustments to the inference rules are made, the results for finiteness dependencies mirror closely those for functional dependencies. In particular, the algorithm of the previous section extends to finiteness dependencies under the proviso that the tautologies referred to are tautologous finiteness dependencies. One the other hand, the completeness result employs an extra condition in comparison to Theorem 5.1. We summarize the main results as follows.

Theorem 6.1 *The inference rules* $1' - 5'$ *are sound and complete for the inference of finiteness dependencies over pure relations on infinite constraint domains which satisfy independence of negative constraints and representation of elements by constraints.*

Over such constraint domains there is an algorithm for the implication problem for finiteness dependencies of complexity $O(N^2 \xi(N) + N\gamma(N))$, *where* N *is the size of* $F \cup \{f\}$ *and* $\xi(N)$ *refers to the cost of determining that finiteness dependencies are tautologies.*

If the constraint domain is infinite and does not satisfy independence of negative constraints then the implication problem for finiteness dependencies is co-NP-hard.

Finally, we note that inference in a system containing both CFDs and CFinDs is no more difficult than inference in both of the systems separately. Indeed, CFinDs are of no use in inferring CFDs, and CFDs are useful for inferring CFinDs only in that every functional dependency is also a finiteness dependency.

Proposition 6.1 *Fix a constraint domain* $(\mathcal{D}, \mathcal{L})$. *Let* f *and* g *be, respectively, a CFD and a CFinD, and let* F *and* G *be, respectively, a set of CFDs and a set of CFinDs. Let* C *be a conjunction of constraints. Then*

- $C, F, G \models g$ *iff* $C, Fin(F), G \models g$

- $C, F, G \models f$ *iff* $C, F \models f$

where Fin *maps CFDs to the corresponding CFinDs.*

7 Constraint-Generating Dependencies

In [2] the complexity of the implication problem is examined for a large range of dependencies, including constrained functional dependencies (but not the constrained finiteness dependencies), called constraint-generating dependencies.

Definition 7.1 *A constraint-generating dependency (CGD) takes the form*

$$r_1(\tilde{x}_1), \ldots, r_k(\tilde{x}_k), c(\tilde{x}) \to c'(\tilde{x})$$

where c, c' are constraints, the r_i are relations and $\tilde{x}$ contains $\tilde{x}_i$ for $i = 1, \ldots, k$. A CGD such as the above expresses that for each valuation of $\tilde{a}$ for $\tilde{x}$ such that $\tilde{a}_i$ is a tuple in r_i for $i = 1, \ldots, k$ and $c(\tilde{a})$ holds, $c'(\tilde{a})$ must also hold[2].

A constrained functional dependency $c \Rightarrow I \to J$ can be formulated as the following CGD.

$$r(\tilde{x}), r(\tilde{y}), c(\tilde{x}) \wedge c(\tilde{y}) \wedge x_I = y_I \to x_J = y_J$$

A CGD containing k or fewer relation expressions $r_i(\tilde{x}_i)$ is called a *k-dependency*. Those CGDs where $c' \leftrightarrow false$, we call *negative integrity constraints*. Those CGDs where $c \leftrightarrow true$, we call *approximation expressions*.

Let a constraint domain $(\mathcal{D}, \mathcal{L})$ be fixed. The *CGD implication problem* is the problem of determining whether every relation on which a set F of CGDs holds must also satisfy a CGD f (i.e. whether $F \models f$).

It is shown in [2] that $F \models f$ can be expressed as the validity of a formula involving the constraints appearing in F and f. To obtain some complexity results, [2] makes the assumption that the constraint language is closed under negation (among other assumptions). Since this assumption implies that independence of negative constraints does not hold, we can extend some results in that paper as follows, using Lemma 5.1.

Proposition 7.1 *Suppose $(\mathcal{D}, \mathcal{L})$ does not have independence of negative constraints. Then the implication problem for k-dependencies is co-NP-hard. In particular, if $\mathcal{D}$ is any structure and $\mathcal{L}$ is closed under negation and conjunction then the implication problem for k-dependencies is co-NP-hard.*

This result helps to explain why it was necessary in [2] to consider classes of constraints that are not closed under conjunction (by limiting the number of atomic constraints per dependency) to obtain cases in which the implication problem for k-dependencies is in PTIME. It shows that we must find a different, perhaps finer, classification of CGDs than into k-dependencies if we are to find classes of CGDs with a tractable implication problem. We close this section with two such classes. The implication problem for these classes was addressed, for a very narrow range of constraint domains, in [27] and [2] respectively. The proofs of these results use the characterization in [2].

---

[2] $\tilde{a}_i$ is the tuple of values assigned by the valuation to $\tilde{x}_i$.

Proposition 7.2 *Suppose* $(\mathcal{D}, \mathcal{L})$ *has independence of negative constraints and a PTIME algorithm for the constraint implication problem. Let the dependencies of F and f be both negative integrity constraints and k-dependencies, for fixed k.*

Then the implication problem is in PTIME.

Proposition 7.3 *Suppose* $(\mathcal{D}, \mathcal{L})$ *has a PTIME algorithm for the constraint implication problem. Let the dependencies of F and f be both approximation expressions and k-dependencies, for fixed k.*

Then the implication problem is in PTIME.

8 Applications

We have already mentioned the potential use of CFDs in a variety of situations. We now outline some applications in slightly greater detail.

- In the full version of this paper, results of [19] are extended to CLP programs and deductive CDBs. In particular, there is a sufficient condition for the elimination of subsumption tests in bottom-up execution. Use of that condition requires the inference of certain functional dependencies. The combination of CFDs and the constraints in the program is more powerful in inferring FDs. Subsumption tests can be very expensive and, in the case of logic programs, their removal results in significant speedups [19, 22]. We can expect even greater speedups in other constraint domains, where subsumption tests are typically more expensive.

- Some logic programming and database systems employ a top-down execution with memoization (or tabulation) of answers to calls to predicates. XSB [23] is a prime example. In these systems calls are placed in a table with their successful answers, and subsequent calls which are instances of tabled calls are executed by table look-up. Similar techniques can be applied to CLP programs. Clearly memoization is pointless if there are no subsequent calls which are instances. We can detect this situation by applying a magic sets transformation to the original CLP program P so that P^{magic} computes the calling patterns in P [4], and then applying the above analysis to P^{magic}. If P^{magic} is subsumption-free by the analysis above then no call is an instance of another, and memoization can be omitted.

- In [1] an assertional, strongest-postcondition approach to proving the correctness of logic programs is developed, based on first establishing that the program is subsumption-free. It appears that this approach extends to CLP programs. The techniques discussed above apply to many CLP programs in the same way that the techniques for logic programs apply to many logic programs used in practice [19, 1].

- Established CFDs can be used in top-down CLP systems to optimize performance. In the context of logic programs, [8] proposes the use of functionality information to refine backtracking behaviour and to make wise atom selections in systems with dynamic control. These applications extend to CLP programs. Furthermore, the use of CFDs permits a more flexible approach to these applications where the constraint of the CFD can be tested at runtime and, depending on the result, pass control to code with/without refined backtracking.

- Groundness analysis (detecting that variables are bound to a single value in procedure calls) and the very similar determinedness analysis are the basis for important optimizations in the execution of CLP programs and CDB queries. Groundness dependencies, which are used in logic programming [6, 20], are essentially functional dependencies. Thus, in general, the work of this paper applies to constrained groundness dependencies and constrained determinedness dependencies. However, when the constraint solver is weak (for example, incomplete or unable to detect the equivalence of $X \leq 5$, $X \geq 5$ and $X = 5$) constrained groundness dependencies are subtly different from CFDs and the work of this paper is not directly applicable.

- CFDs offer a different approach to horizontal decomposition of relations from that of De Bra and Parendaens [7, 21]. Instead of decomposing a relation into a maximal (in some sense) subrelation on which an FD holds and the remaining tuples, the relation is decomposed according to a simple condition. This approach is less flexible than that of [7], since it requires a characterization by constraints of when a FD will definitely hold on a relation ($Level of Instruction \neq freshman$ in Example 3.2), and it can fail to represent the full collection of tuples that satisfy the FD (all those freshman courses that have only one class). On the other hand, it results in simpler updates of the relation than the method of [7], since there is no necessity to transfer a tuple from one subrelation to another when another tuple is added or deleted from the relation.

- Elkan [9, 10] uses FDs to detect query emptiness without examining the underlying database. CFDs and, more generally, CGDs provide a more powerful and flexible framework in which to approximate queries and thus detect query emptiness.

Finally, note that recent work on functional dependencies for temporal databases [26] appears closely related. In particular, the inference axioms for temporal functional dependencies in [26] appear to be a special case of our inference rules for CFDs, if we regard temporal types as constraints.

9 Conclusion

We have introduced constrained functional and finiteness dependencies and extended the approach of Beeri and Bernstein [3] to solving the implication problem for FDs to these dependencies.

184

For a large class of constraint domains, those satisfying the independence of negative constraints property, the extended Beeri-Bernstein approach provides an efficient solution to the CFD implication problem, modulo the cost of constraint manipulation. For constraint domains not in this class the CFD implication problem is not tractable, but we have outlined some tractable approximations. For constrained finiteness dependencies we have similar results, although for a class of constraint domains it remains open whether the CFinD implication problem is tractable.

Using independence of negative constraints we established a class of constraint domains for which the CGD implication problem is intractable and found two classes of CGDs for which the implication problem is tractable.

We outlined several applications of CFDs, mainly to the analysis and optimization of (relational) database and CDB queries and CLP programs. This work points the way to an extension of other analysis domains: for each domain of elements d we can consider the domain of elements of the form $c \Rightarrow d$, where c is a constraint. Further consideration of this possibility is left as future work.

Acknowledgements

I thank P. Dart, R. Marti, J. Shepherd and some anonymous referees for discussions and/or comments on a version of this paper.

References

[1] K.R. Apt & M. Gabbrielli, Declarative Interpretations Reconsidered *Proc. ICLP*, 1994.

[2] M. Baudinet, J. Chomicki & P. Wolper, Constraint-Generating Dependencies, *Proc. 2nd Principles and Practice of Constraint Programming*, 1994.

[3] C. Beeri & P.A. Bernstein, Computational Problems Related to the Design of Normal Form Relational Schemas, *ACM Transactions on Database Systems* 4, 30–59, 1979.

[4] M. Codish, D. Dams, E. Yardeni, Bottom-Up Abstract Interpretation of Logic Programs, *Theoretical Computer Science* 124, 93–125, 1994.

[5] U.S. Chakravarthy, J. Grant and J. Minker, Foundations of Semantic Query Optimization for Deductive Databases, in: *Foundations of Deductive Databases and Logic Programming*, J. Minker (Ed), Morgan Kaufmann, 243–274, 1988.

[6] P. Dart, On Derived Dependencies and Connected Databases, *Journal of Logic Programming* 11, 163–188, 1991.

[7] P. De Bra & J. Paredaens, Horizontal Decomposition for Handling Exceptions to Functional Dependencies, in: *Advances in Database Theory II*, H. Gallaire, J. Minker, J.M. Nicolas (Eds.), Plenum Press, 1984, 123–141.

[8] S. K. Debray & D.S. Warren, Functional Computations in Logic Programs, *ACM Transactions on Programming Languages and Systems* 11 (3), 451–481, 1989.

[9] C. Elkan, A Decision Procedure for Conjunctive Query Disjointness, *Proc. 8th ACM Symp. on Principles of Database Systems*, 134–139, 1989.

[10] C. Elkan, Independence of Logical Database Queries and Updates, *Proc. 9th ACM Symp. on Principles of Database Systems*, 154–160, 1990.

[11] J. Jaffar & J-L. Lassez, Constraint Logic Programming, *Proc. 14th ACM Symposium on Principles of Programming Languages*, Munich (January 1987), 111–119.

[12] J. Jaffar & M.J. Maher, Constraint Logic Programming: A Survey, *Journal of Logic Programming 19 & 20*, 503–581, 1994.

[13] P. Kanellakis, Elements of Relational Database Theory, in: *Handbook of Theoretical Computer Science, Vol. B*, J. van Leeuwen (Ed), 1073–1156, 1990.

[14] P. Kanellakis, G. Kuper & P. Revesz, Constraint Query Languages, *Journal of Computer and System Sciences*, to appear. Preliminary version appeared in *Proc. 9th ACM Symp. on Principles of Database Systems*, 299–313, 1990.

[15] D. Kemp & P. Stuckey, Analysis based Constraint Query Optimization, *Proc. 10th International Conference on Logic Programming*, 666–682, 1993.

[16] A. Klug, Calculating Constraints on Relational Expressions, *ACM Transactions on Database Systems 5, 3*, 260–290, 1980.

[17] J-L. Lassez & K. McAloon, A Constraint Sequent Calculus, *Proc. of Symp. on Logic in Computer Science*, 52–62, 1990.

[18] M.J. Maher, A Logic Programming View of CLP, *Proc. 10th International Conference on Logic Programming*, MIT Press, 1993, 737–753.

[19] M.J. Maher & R. Ramakrishnan, Déjà Vu in Fixpoints of Logic Programs, *Proc. North American Conference on Logic Programming*, Cleveland, October, 1989, 963–980. Full version next century.

[20] K. Marriott & H. Sondergaard, Notes for a Tutorial on Abstract Interpretation of Logic Programs, distributed at NACLP, 1989.

[21] J. Paredaens, P. De Bra, M. Gyssens & D. Van Gucht, *The Structure of the Relational Database Model*, EATCS Monographs on Theoretical Computer Science, Vol. 17, Springer-Verlag, 1989.

[22] R. Ramakrishnan, personal communication, 1993.

[23] K. Sagonas, T. Swift & D.S. Warren, XSB as an Efficient Deductive Database Engine, *SIGMOD Record*, 1994.

[24] D. Srivastava, Subsumption and Indexing in Constraint Query Languages with Linear Arithmetic Constraints, *Annals of Mathematics and Artificial Intelligence 8*, 315–343, 1993.

[25] M. Vardi, Fundamentals of Dependency Theory, IBM Research Report RJ4858, 1985.

[26] X.S. Wang, C. Bettini, A. Brodsky & S. Jajodia, Logical Design for Temporal Databases with Multiple Granularities, manuscript, 1995.

[27] X. Zhang & Z.M. Ozsoyoglu, On Efficient Reasoning with Implication Constraints, *Proc. Conf. on Deductive and Object-Oriented Databases*, LNCS 760, 236–252, 1993.

[28] W. Ziarko, The discovery, analysis and representation of data dependencies in databases, in: *Knowledge Discovery in Databases*, G. Piatetsky-Shapiro & W. Frawley (Eds), AAAI Press, 1991.

Solving Linear, Min and Max Constraint Systems Using CLP based on Relational Interval Arithmetic

Pierre Girodias, Eduard Cerny
Laboratoire de VLSI, Département d'Informatique et de Recherche Opérationnelle, Université de
Montréal

William J. Older
Computing Research Laboratory, Bell Northern Research, Ottawa

Abstract

Many real problems can be treated as Constraint Satisfaction Problems (CSPs), a type of problem for which efficient tools have been developed. Computing the maximum timing separations between the events of a timing specification falls into this category. CLP (BNR) is a constraint logic programming language which seems well suited to the problem, allowing to draw from the advantages of both CSPs and Logic Programming. Consistency techniques used for solving general CSPs usually produce approximate answers (partial consistency) and the resolution engine for CLP (BNR) behaves in a similar fashion. However, for some specific timing specifications, we show that global consistency can be achieved using CLP (BNR). The timing specifications we consider are systems of strictly linear constraints, systems of either max-only or min-only constraints, and systems where linear and either max or min constraints intermix.

1 Introduction

Many real problems can be treated as Constraint Satisfaction Problems (CSPs), a type of problem for which efficient tools have been developed. A CSP is defined by a set of variables and a set of constraints over these variables; specific domains of possible values are associated with each variable. Consistency techniques are suitable for the analysis of such problems: instead of enumerating all possible solutions, the set of solutions is characterized, often with approximations: there is a trade-off between speed and accuracy. Further gains in efficiency can be realized by imbedding these consistency techniques in the framework of Logic Programming (LP) languages, leading to Constraint Logic Programming (CLP).

Interface timing verification is the problem of verifying that the interfaces of various system components can be connected and operate correctly. Each interface is given as a collection of events and constraints relating the occurrence times of these events. If all these timing constraints are preserved when the specifications are combined to form the connected component, the interfaces are said to be compatible. This problem, in practice, is often reduced to computing the maximum separations between all pairs of events. We define this as the *event separation problem*.

McMillan and Dill [1] have shown that computing maximum separations of events in systems of linear, min and max constraints is a $\mathcal{NP}$-complete problem. Exhaustive simulation is impractical for this purpose: analytical algorithms, through which the process can be automated, are necessary. Indeed, algorithms have been proposed in the past (McMillan and Dill [1], Amon and al. [2], Brozowski and al. [3], Yen and al. [4], etc.) that can efficiently tackle restricted systems of constraints.

A CLP language is a Logic Programming (LP) language in which constraint solving techniques have been substituted for the unification mechanism. The advantages are threefold:

- the user does not need to concern himself with search techniques (black-box concept),
- stating constraints is straightforward,
- programs can be easily modified and extended.

The advantages offered by CLP for the event separation problem have already been explored by Amon and Borriello [5]. However the model developed by Amon and Borriello has limitations: inter-process communications are awkward and the operators defined are semantically weak: it is necessary to define a large number of rules to reason about the constraint system. The CLP language they use relies on an incremental version of the standard simplex linear programming algorithm coupled with a goal-based programming language akin to Prolog.

We have observed affinities between constraint resolution techniques based on relational interval arithmetic used in CLP (BNR) [6], a Prolog language for CLP, and the algorithms of [1]. We will show that, in fact, these are equivalent approaches. It is our belief that CLP (BNR) can be used as a stepping-stone for efficient interface timing verification, based on the event separation problem. Algorithmic considerations put aside, CLP (BNR) offers two immediate advantages: the solving mechanism is event-driven and provides built-in backtracking, and parsing of the problem specifications is not necessary.

Our approach differs from that proposed by Amon in Borriello [5] in the use of a CLP language which in our case exploits relational interval arithmetic and is thus easier to analyze. Furthermore, the system of constraints we analyze is complete in itself: there is no need to define additional constraints (i.e., rules) to solve it.

In the next section, we define formally the event separation problem. In Section 3, we introduce the concepts of constraint satisfaction problems and constraint logic programming. We show, in Section 4, that constraint logic programming based on relational interval arithmetic provides exact solutions to specific event separation subproblems, and, in Section 5, we conclude the presentation.

2   Problem Definition

The problem of timing verification can be defined as one of finding the maximal achievable separation [1]

$$d_{ij} = max(t_j - t_i)$$

between all pairs of events i and j, occurring at times t_i and t_j, respectively. The limits on the occurrence times of these events are specified by a system of linear constraints of the form:

$$t_j - t_i \leq s_{ij} \tag{1}$$

and of non-linear constraints of the form:

$$t_j = min_{i \in preds\ (j)}\ (t_i + \delta_{ij}) \tag{2}$$

$$t_j = max_{i \in preds\ (j)}\ (t_i + \delta_{ij}) \tag{3}$$

where $preds(j)$ is the set of events controlling the occurrence time of j and δ_{ij} is the delay from an event i to an event j. A delay is defined in terms of a lower bound l_{ij} and an upper bound u_{ij} rather than by a single-point value:

$$0 \leq l_{ij} \leq \delta_{ij} \leq u_{ij} \tag{4}$$

Computing only maximal separations is sufficient since minimal separations can be deduced from them:

$$d_{ij} = max\ (t_j - t_i) = -min\ (t_i - t_j)$$

The general event separation problem is concerned with systems in which all three types of constraints are possible simultaneously. Efficient algorithms have been reported for the various restricted systems of constraints. For systems of linear constraints only, a shortest-path algorithm ($O(n^3)$, where n is the number of events) is sufficient to compute the separations between all pairs. Vanbekbergen, Goossens and De Man [7], and McMillan and Dill [1] have proposed algorithms of complexity $O(n^3)$ for max-only (or min-only) systems. Walkup and Borriello [8] and Yen, Ishii, Casavant and Wolf [4], give algorithms conjectured to be of complexity $O(n^6)$ and $O(n^3 \log n)$, respectively, for systems combining either max or min constraints with linear constraints. McMillan and Dill [1] have shown that whenever max and min constraints, or max, min and linear constraints are intermixed, the interface verification problem becomes $\mathcal{NP}$-complete. A branch-and-bound algorithm based on an algorithm for max-only and linear constraints is appropriate for such cases.

We are interested in a new approach to the event separation problem, relying on CSPs and CLP. Both paradigms are introduced more formally in the next section.

3   Constraint Satisfaction Problems and Constraint Logic Programming

"Formally, a CSP can be defined in the following way. Assume the existence of a finite set I of variables $\{X_1, X_2, \dots, X_n\}$, which take respectively their values from their finite domains $D_1, D_2, \dots, D_n$ and a set of constraints. A constraint $c(X_{i1}, X_{i2}, \dots, X_{ik})$ between k variables from I is a subset of the Cartesian product $D_{i1} \times D_{i2} \times \dots \times D_{ik}$, which specifies which values of the variables are compatible with each other. In practice this subset does not need to be given explicitly, but can be defined by equations, inequalities, or programs whatsoever. A solution to a CSP is an assignment of values to all variables, which satisfies all the constraints." [9]

Furthermore, a CSP, $P = (I, D, C)$, where I is the set of variables $\{X_1, X_2, ..., X_n\}$, D is the set of associated domains $\{D_1, D_2, ..., D_n\}$ and, C is the set of constraints, is *globally consistent* if and only if $\forall\ X \in I, \forall\ a \in D_X, X = a$ belongs to a solution of P. Two CSPs, P and P', are *equivalent* if and only if they have the same set of solutions. Solving a CSP P can be defined as the process of finding an equivalent CSP P' which is globally consistent. However, the search for global consistency is a $\mathcal{NP}$-hard problem. Criteria that are not as strict as global consistency are therefore aimed for, e.g., *partial consistency*, where some conditions are guaranteed over all the elements of a domain or over the bounds of a domain [10]. A constraint system is *inconsistent* if it admits no solution.

Various *consistency techniques* have been elaborated for solving CSPs: local propagation of known states, relaxation, propagating degrees of freedom, etc. These techniques rely on removing from a search tree combinations of values that cannot appear together in a solution; the validity of such values is determined dynamically by the constraints. The search is an iterative process: values implied by the constraints are propagated as much as possible after assumptions on the values of some variables have been made. These steps are performed until the system stabilizes.

It should be clear from the preceding that the event separation problem can be treated as a CSP. Furthermore, in timing verification, constraints between events are usually specified as min-max intervals of values, one or more fixed point exact solutions lying somewhere in between; therefore, a model based on interval arithmetic seems natural. Such a system of constraints over intervals can be solved using CLP (BNR) [6].

4   CLP (BNR) and the Event Separation Problem

4.1   Interval Arithmetic

The constraint resolution method of CLP (BNR) is based on interval arithmetic. Some definitions are in order [11].

An *interval* is a closed bounded set of numbers

$$[a, b] = \{x \mid a \le x \le b\}$$

Capital letters are used to denote intervals. Endpoints of an interval X are denoted by $\underline{X}$ and $\check{X}$. Thus, $X = [\underline{X}, \check{X}]$. The interval $[x, x]$ is a *degenerate interval* which we do not distinguish from the number x. Two intervals are *equal* if their corresponding endpoints are equal. If the number x is in the interval X, we write $x \in X$. The *intersection* of two intervals is defined as

$$X \cap Y = [max(\underline{X}, \underline{Y}), min(\check{X}, \check{Y})]$$

Interval addition is defined as

$$[\underline{X}, \check{X}] + [\underline{Y}, \check{Y}] = [\underline{X} + \underline{Y}, \check{X} + \check{Y}]$$

The *negative* of an interval, from which the rules for *interval subtraction* can be deduced, is defined as

$$-X = -[\underline{X}, \check{X}] = [-\check{X}, -\underline{X}] = \{-x \mid x \in X\}$$

The *max* of two intervals (the definition can be generalized for n intervals) is defined as

$$max(X, Y) = [max(\underline{X}, \underline{Y}), max(\check{X}, \check{Y})]$$

4.2 Approximations and the False Positive Problem

Despite attractive features, there are problems to be reckoned with in the use of CLP (BNR). In CLP (BNR), constraints are expressed over interval-valued variables. Systems of constraints are solved, i.e., bounds that respect the constraints are computed for the domain of each variable using interval propagation. One or more variables are originally constrained by finite domains (one variable, for instance, may serve as a reference point, and be set by the user to the value $[0, 0]$). All other interval-valued variables are initialized with the value $[-\infty, \infty]$. An event-driven mechanism repeatedly selects constraints and updates the value of the variables involved by these constraints. Thus, finite values are propagated across the system and eventually replace infinite values. Unfortunately, reasoning on the endpoints of intervals is not sufficient for correctness (partial consistency): it may happen that an impossible value remains hidden within an interval whose bounds are possible values. For example, consider the following constraint system (the example is from [10]):

$$X + Y = 2$$

$$Y \leq X + 1$$

$$Y \geq X$$

Solving these inequalities yields $0.5 \leq X \leq 1$ and $1 \leq Y \leq 1.5$. Yet, interval relational arithmetic will compute $X = [0, 2]$ and $Y = [0, 2]$. The interval propagation mechanism fails to detect that the wider bounds are not possible simultaneously.

Interval propagation leads to a type a partial consistency identified as *arc B-consistency* [10]. A CSP $P = (I, D, C)$ is arc B-consistent if and only if
$(\forall X \in I, D_X = [a_X, b_X], \forall c (X, X_1, ..., X_k) \in C)$ a constraint over X,

   $\exists v_1, ..., v_k \in D_1 \times ... \times D_k | c (a_X, v_1, ..., v_k)$ is satisfied,
   $\exists v_1, ..., v_k \in D_1 \times ... \times D_k | c (b_X, v_1, ..., v_k)$ is satisfied.

In other words, arc B-consistency implies that, given any particular constraint, it is possible to construct a vector of assignments, from the solution set of intervals, that satisfies at least that constraint.

The values returned by CLP (BNR) are therefore approximate. When the solution set is found, it is an upper bound and in fact the system may still be inconsistent. This is known as the *false positive* problem. Only failure to return a satisfying solution set, i.e., one or more interval-valued variables are equal to the empty interval $\varnothing$, can be accepted as a definite exact answer: the constraint system is inconsistent.

4.3 The Event Separation Problem in Terms of CLP (BNR)

We may now reformulate the event separation problem in terms of interval arithmetic and CLP (BNR).

The problem we consider is one of finding the maximum timing separation d_{ij} between all pairs of events i and j. Occurrence times of events i and j are defined by both linear and non-linear constraints (Section 2). Since the event occurrence times are constraints only relative to each other and no absolute time reference is given, it is necessary to designate one event as the reference point for all other events, and set its occurrence time to the value 0. All other event occurrence times are originally considered to lie in the interval $[-\infty, \infty]$. It follows that the event occurrence time intervals computed by the CLP (BNR) resolution mechanism are in fact the timing separations between the reference point event and the other events. If there are n events and event k is the reference point, we have $T_i = [-d_{ki}, d_{ik}]$, where T_i is a variable representing the domain of the occurrence time t_i of event i, $1 \leq i \leq n$. By solving the constraint system for n different reference points, all timing separations can be found.

Definition: Projection of a Constraint

Consider a constraint system defined over n events. Let $T_1, T_2, ..., T_n$ be interval-valued variables representing the domains of $t_1, t_2, ..., t_n$, respectively, where t_j is the occurrence time of an event j, $1 \leq j \leq n$. Let $E = T_1 \times T_2 \times ... \times T_n$. The projection over t_i, $1 \leq i \leq n$, of a constraint $c(t_1, t_2, ..., t_n)$ restricted to domains $T_1, T_2, ..., T_n$, is the interval $\Pi_i(c(t_1, t_2, ..., t_n), E) = \{ t_i \in T_i \mid \exists (t_1, t_2, ..., t_{i-1}, t_{i+1}, ..., t_n) \in T_1 \times T_2 \times ... \times T_{i-1} \times T_{i+1} \times ... \times T_n$ such that $c(t_1, t_2, ..., t_n)$ is satisfied $\}$.

It follows that solving a system of constraints consists of narrowing the bounds of the domains T_j so that the following system of equations is satisfied

$$\forall j, 1 \leq j \leq n, T_j = \bigcap_i^m \Pi_j(c_i(t_1, t_2, ..., t_n), E) \tag{5}$$

where m is the number of constraints in the system.

The question we wish to answer next is under what conditions the bounds of the interval T_j are in fact exact maximal separations as they would be computed by the algorithms in [1] instead of upper bounds only. Namely, we shall examine the following subproblems:

- systems of linear constraints,
- systems of max-only (or min-only) constraints,
- systems of linear constraints and max-only (or min-only) constraints.

We will show in the following that for these specific problems (each in turn defined as a CSP P) the CLP (BNR) resolution mechanism can compute a CSP P' that is

(1) equivalent to the original CSP P,
(2) globally consistent.

In other words, CLP (BNR) will solve the problem exactly.

Proposition (1) is trivially true: interval propagation does not modify the solution space but merely trims the domains of the problem variables.

To prove global consistency, we compare the interval propagation algorithm to known exact algorithms for the three preceding subsets of constraint problems. These algorithms return exact solutions.

Definition: Constraint Graph

It is often useful to present a constraint system of the kind we consider as a *constraint graph*. The constraint graph is constructed by assigning a node to every event occurrence time and an edge to every constraint. If, for instance, the constraint is $t_j - t_i \le s_{ij}$, the direction of the edge is from t_i to t_j and the weight of that edge is s_{ij}; if the constraint is a max constraint $t_j = max_{i \in preds(j)} (t_i + \delta_{ij})$, then there is an edge directed from each t_i to t_j and the weight of this edge is the interval $[l_{ij}, u_{ij}]$.

4.3.1 Systems of Linear Constraints

The constraints are only of form (1) as defined in Section 2. We shall show that the consistency solving technique of CLP (BNR) is equivalent to the simplest all-pairs shortest distance $O(n^4)$ algorithm over constraint graphs (where distances are actually time separations).

All-pairs Shortest Distance Algorithm:

Let t_i and t_j be two event times such that

$$t_j - t_i \le s_{ij}$$

$$t_i - t_j \le s_{ji}$$

A system of such constraints defined over n events can be expressed as a matrix

$$M = \begin{pmatrix} m_{11} & m_{12} & m_{13} & \cdots & m_{1k} & \cdots & m_{1n} \\ m_{21} & m_{22} & m_{23} & \cdots & m_{2k} & \cdots & m_{2n} \\ m_{31} & m_{32} & m_{33} & \cdots & m_{3k} & \cdots & m_{3n} \\ \cdots & \cdots & \cdots & \cdots & \cdots & \cdots & \cdots \\ m_{k1} & m_{k2} & m_{k3} & \cdots & m_{kk} & \cdots & m_{kn} \\ \cdots & \cdots & \cdots & \cdots & \cdots & \cdots & \cdots \\ m_{n1} & m_{n2} & m_{n3} & \cdots & m_{nk} & \cdots & m_{nn} \end{pmatrix}$$

where m_{ij} is the element of this matrix that expresses the time separation from event i to event j ($m_{ij} = -s_{ji}$, as expressed by the original constraint) where $1 \le i, j \le n$. By definition, $m_{kk} = 0, 1 \le k \le n$.

The all-pairs shortest distance algorithm (APSD) operates on this initial matrix M and generates a new matrix M' where m'_{ji} is the shortest separation between events j and i which negative corresponds in turn to the largest separation from i to j satisfying all the constraints. These values are computed by considering all possible paths between two events and discarding all but the shortest.

Symbolically, M' can be expressed as follows:

$$m'_{ji} = min(-s_{ij}, \tag{6}$$

$$min^n_{x_{11}=1}(-s_{x_{11}j} - s_{ix_{11}}),$$

$$min^n_{x_{21}=1}(min^n_{x_{22}=1}(-s_{x_{21}j} - s_{x_{22}x_{21}} - s_{ix_{22}})),$$

$$...,$$

$$min^n_{x_{(n-1)1}=1}(min^n_{x_{(n-1)2}=1}...(min^n_{x_{(n-1)(n-1)}=1}(-s_{x_{(n-1)j}} - s_{x_{(n-1)2}x_{(n-1)1}} - ...$$
$$- s_{x_{(n-1)(n-1)}x_{(n-1)1}} - s_{ix_{(n-1)(n-1)}}))...))$$

The first line represents paths involving two events (direct paths), the second line, paths involving three events (indirect paths through one event), the third line, paths involving four events (indirect paths through two events), etc.

Linear Constraint Systems in CLP (BNR):

Consider the event occurrence times t_i and t_j of two events i and j bound by the constraints:

$$t_i - t_j \leq s_{ji} \tag{7}$$

$$t_j - t_i \leq s_{ij} \tag{8}$$

These constraints (7) and (8) can be expressed as a single constraint $c^*(t_i, t_j)$:

$$t_i - t_j \in [-s_{ij}, s_{ji}]$$

Assuming that T_i and T_j are the domains of t_i and t_j, the projection of this constraint over t_i and t_j yields

$$\Pi_i(c^*(t_i, t_j), T_i \times T_j) = T_j + [-s_{ij}, s_{ji}] \cap T_i = \Delta^i_{ij}(T_i, T_j)$$
$$\Pi_j(c^*(t_i, t_j), T_i \times T_j) = T_i + [-s_{ji}, s_{ij}] \cap T_j = \Delta^j_{ij}(T_j, T_i)$$

$\Delta^i_{ij}(T_i, T_j)$ is read as the projection over t_i of the constraint defined by events i and j, restricted to domains T_i and T_j.

In general, if there are n events, solving a system of constraints with CLP (BNR) consists of finding a solution to the system of equations that the intersection of the projections define (as seen in (5)):

$$(\forall i, 1 \leq i \leq n \qquad T_i = \Delta^i_{1i}(T_i, T_1) \cap \Delta^i_{2i}(T_i, T_2) \cap ... \cap \Delta^i_{ni}(T_i, T_n)) \tag{9}$$

where $\Delta^i_{ji}(T_i, T_j) = [T_j - s_{ij}, T_j + s_{ji}] \cap T_i$ and $\Delta^i_{ii}(T_i, T_i) = T_i$ (since $s_{ii} = 0$). The result of the function $\Delta^i_{ji}(T_i, T_j)$ represents the widest possible interval for T_i with respect to T_j.

As explained in the introduction of Section 4.3, an event k is designated to serve as a reference point. The domain associated to its occurrence time is restricted to the interval $[0, 0]$ ($T_k = [0, 0]$). For all other events i, the original domain is $T_i = [-\infty, \infty]$.

All-pair Shortest Distance Algorithm versus CLP (BNR)

CLP (BNR) uses fixed-point iterations performed over interval-valued variable. Since the right-hand sides of the equations (9) represent monotonic non-increasing functions over intervals, these iterations can be done in any order. CLP (BNR) is an event-driven mechanism but for our purposes, we use the simplest Jacobi iteration

$$T_i^{(m+1)} = F(T_i^{(m)}) = \Delta_{1i}^i(T_i^{(m)}, T_1^{(m)}) \cap \Delta_{2i}^i(T_i^{(m)}, T_2^{(m)}) \cap \dots \cap \Delta_{ni}^i(T_i^{(m)}, T_n^{(m)})$$

with initial values $T_k^{(0)} = [0, 0]$ and $T_i^{(0)} = [-\infty, \infty]$ $\forall\, i \neq k$, and where $T^{(m+1)}$ is the value computed for T_i after $(m + 1)$ iterations.

The propagation of the upper bounds on the intervals throughout the iterations is similar to the propagation of the lower bounds. We only consider the ladder, in order to establish a parallel with the APSD algorithm.

After the first iteration, we have

$$T_j^{(1)} = -s_{ik}$$

The second iteration yields

$$T_j^{(2)} = min(T_j^{(1)}, \min_{x_{11} = 1}^{n} {}^{(-s_{x_{11}k} - s_{ix_{11}})})$$

Similarly, the third one gives

$$T_j^{(3)} = min(T_j^{(2)}, \min_{x_{21} = 1}^{n} (\min_{x_{22} = 1}^{n} {}^{(-s_{x_{21}k} - s_{x_{22}x_{21}} - s_{ix_{22}})}))$$

Etc., until the $(n\text{-}1)^{\text{th}}$ iteration that finally gives

$$T_j^{(n-1)} = min(T_j^{(n-2)}, \min_{x_{(n-1)1} = 1}^{n} (\min_{x_{(n-1)2} = 1}^{n} \dots \min_{x_{(n-1)(n-1)} = 1}^{n} {}^{(-s_{x_{(n-1)1}k}} \tag{10}$$
$$- s_{x_{(n-1)2}x_{(n-1)1}} - \dots - s_{x_{(n-1)(n-1)}x_{(n-1)1}} - s_{ix_{(n-1)(n-1)}}) \dots))$$

By substituting k for i in (10), we can observe that expressions (6) and (10) are equivalent. That is, for one reference point k, CLP (BNR) returns the same values as computed in the kth row and k^{th} column of the matrix M' of the APSD algorithm. By repeatedly solving the constraint equation system for $k = 1, \dots, n$, CLP (BNR) will find all the values computed by the APSD algorithm.

When the system of equations (with either APSD or CLP (BNR)) is consistent, $(n\text{-}1)$ iterations are needed at most. However, the Prolog implementation is event-driven, hence the practical complexity is usually much lower on large problems.

If the system is inconsistent, the APSD algorithm can detect this situation by computing a negative value in a diagonal entry of the matrix (i.e. there is a cycle with negative weight in the constraint graph). CLP (BNR) will detect an inconsistency whenever $\exists\, i, 1 \leq i \leq n, T_i > T_i$. Since the APSD algorithm considers all possible paths (when $(n\text{-}1)$ iterations have been performed), and CLP (BNR) performs the same computation, all paths of $(n\text{-}1)$ nodes from event i to event j are checked.

If the negative cycle in the constraint graph passes through at most c nodes, the iterative implementation of the interval based calculation will detect such a cycle after at most c iterations:

Let k be the action that serves as a reference point and consider the path of minimal weight from k to k. Assuming inconsistency, the weight l of this path is negative. Assume CLP (BNR) is computing the upper limit (lower limit computations are identical) of the interval T_k at the next iteration. By definition, if there were no inconsistencies before, we have $T_k = T_k = 0$; let $T'_k = x$, it follows that $x \geq 0$. We then have $T'_k = T_k + l = l$, and hence, $T'_k = [x, l]$, which is an empty interval since $l < x$.

Note: The APSD algorithm and CLP (BNR) are both monotone processes. When the system is consistent, halting conditions are similar for both algorithms: given n events, the APSD algorithm can go through its maximum of $(n-1)$ iterations systematically or stop its execution when the system stabilizes (stability is guaranteed after $(n-1)$ iterations); similarly CLP (BNR) will terminate when stability is detected. In either case, additional iterations can be performed without affecting the solution.

4.3.2 Systems of Max-only (or Min-only) Constraints

For systems of non-linear constraints (either max-only or min-only), we show that the consistency solving technique used in CLP (BNR) is equivalent to the $O(n^3)$ algorithm (MD1) reported by McMillan and Dill [1]. The corresponding constraint graph is a directed acyclic graph.

MD1 Algorithm for Max-only Constraint Systems:

The algorithm proposed by McMillan and Dill computes the maximum achievable separations between a reference event k and all other events in the constraint system. (We based the following on the revised presentation from [2].) The algorithm consists of two simple steps. First, $m(i)$, the minimum weight path values to event k are computed for all events i:

$$m(i) = min(m(j) - l_{ij}) \tag{11}$$

where $m(k) = 0$. This corresponds to a simple reverse traversal of the constraint graph associated with the constraint system. The value l_{ij} is the minimum weight of the constraints between events i and j. If there is no path from an event i to the event k, then $m(i) = \infty$. Maximal separation from an event j to event k, $U(j)$, is then computed by

$$U(j) = min(m(j), max(U(i) + u_{ij})) \tag{12}$$

where u_{ij} is the maximum weight of the constraint from event i to event j (Section 2). The MD1 algorithm assumes that the constraint graph associated with the constraint system has an unique root (i.e., an event whose occurrence time precedes all others). Evaluation of all $U(i)$ is initiated by setting $U(root) = m(root)$.

By repeating these computations for all possible reference events k, separations between all pairs of events can be obtained.

Max-only Constraint Systems in CLP (BNR):

Consider the max constraint

$$t_j = max_{i \in preds(j)}(t_i + \delta_{ij})$$

where $l_{ij} \le \delta_{ij} \le u_{ij}$. Let T_i and T_j be the domains of t_i and t_j. The possible projections of this constraint become

$$\Pi_j(m(t_1, t_2, ..., t_n), E) = max_{i \in preds(j)}(T_i + [l_{ij}, u_{ij}]) \cap T_j = \omega_j^i(T_j, T_i, \forall i \in preds(j)) \quad (13)$$

$$\forall i \in preds(j) \qquad \Pi_i(m(t_1, t_2, ..., t_n), E) = (T_j + [-\infty, -l_{ij}]) \cap T_i = \omega_j^i(T_i, T_j) \quad (14)$$

where $m(t_1, t_2, ..., t_n)$ is the max constraint and $E = T_1 \times T_2 \times ... \times T_n$. $\omega_j^i(T_i, T_j)$ is read as the projection over t_i of the max constraint defined over event j, restricted to domains T_i and T_j. The second projection (14) is computed from the partial inverse of the max constraint.

In general, if there are n events, the intersection of the projections define the following system of equations:

$$\forall j, 1 \le j \le n \qquad T_j = \omega_j^i(T_j, T_i, \forall i \in preds(j)) \underset{p \in succs(j)}{\cap} \omega_p^j(T_j, T_p) \quad (15)$$

Comparing MD1 and CLP (BNR):

Again we assume that the system defined by (15) is solved using a Jacobi iterative mechanism:

$$T_j' = max_{i \in preds(j)}(T_i + \delta_{ij}) \underset{p \in succs(j)}{\cap} (T_p + [-\infty, -l_{jp}]) \cap T_j,$$

that is

$$T_j' = min(max_{i \in preds(j)}(T_i + u_{ij}), min_{p \in succs(j)}(T_p - l_{jp}), T_j) \quad (16a)$$

$$T_j' = max(max_{i \in preds(j)}(T_i + l_{ij}), -\infty, T_j) \quad (16b)$$

where n is the number of events, $1 \le i, j, k, p \le n$, $\delta_{ij} = [l_{ij}, u_{ij}]$, $succs(j)$ is a function which computes the set of all events whose occurrence times are determined by event j, and, initially, $T_k = [0,0]$ and $\forall j \ne k$, $T_j = [-\infty, \infty]$. The outside min or max in expressions (16a) and (16b) reflect the fact that interval propagation cannot increase the solution space: values computed by previous iterations are preserved or narrowed.

Once the interval propagation is completed, the maximum separation from event k to an event i, d_{ik}, is given by T_i. (The reverse is not always true, i.e., the maximum separation from an event i to event k, d_{ik} is not necessarily given by $-T_i$: there is a loss of information due to partial inverses of max functions. However, this value is obtained when event i becomes the reference point k.)

By combining expressions (11) and (12) we can notice that the same computations are done in expression (16a). We omit the full development of these expressions for the sake of brevity. Expression (11) carries out the equivalent of backward propagation in CLP (BNR) ($min_{p \in succs(j)}(T_p - l_{jp})$). The term $max(U(i) + u_{ij})$ in (12) expresses forward propagation ($max_{i \in preds(j)}(T_i + u_{ij})$). The overall expression (12) is the intersection of forward and backward propagation. The difference lies in the order in which the operations are carried out. However this does not matter because min and max operations are associative and commutative. Furthermore, the min and max operations are performed independently: with the exception of the outer min operation, there is no min operation within the max operations, nor is there any max operation within the min operations.

Note: the MD1 algorithm is defined for system of constraints that has a specific initial event whose occurrence time precedes all others. In fact, any system of constraints can be transformed to respect this property by inserting a virtual event v and defining new constraints $0 \leq t_i - t_v \leq \infty$, for all i.

4.3.3 Systems of Linear Constraints and Max-only (or Min-only) Constraints

For systems of linear and max-only constraints, we show that the consistency solving technique used in CLP (BNR) is equivalent to the algorithm (MD2) of McMillan and Dill [1].

MD2 Algorithm for Systems of Linear and Non-linear (Max-only) Constraints:

McMillan and Dill [1] define a system of non-linear (max-only) and linear constraint as tight if the following inequalities hold:

1. for all $i, j, p, d_{ij} \leq d_{ip} + d_{pj}$ and
2. for all $i, j \in$ preds(i), $d_{ji} \leq -l_{ij}$ and
3. for all $i, j, d_{ij} \leq \max_{p \,\in\, \text{preds}(j)} (d_{ip} + u_{pj})$.

They show that if the constraint system is tight, then all of the maximum separations d_{ij} are achievable. The algorithm for computing these separations is therefore one that tightens a system of constraints:

step 1: for all i, j, let $d_{ij} = \min (s_{ij}, -l_{ji})$
repeat
    step 2: for all i, j, p, let $d_{ij} = \min (d_{ij}, d_{ip} + d_{pj})$
    step 3: for all i, j, let $d_{ij} = \min (d_{ij}, \max_{p \,\in\, \text{preds}(j)} (d_{ip} + u_{pj}))$
until
    condition 1: for some i, $d_{ii} < 0$, or
    condition 2: no change.

Linear and Non-linear Max-only constraint Systems in CLP (BNR):

From the previous two subproblems, more specifically from (9) and (15) we can draw the equation system for the more general case where linear and max constraints are allowed:

$$\forall j, 1 \leq j \leq n \qquad T_j = \omega_j^i(T_i, T_{i, \forall i \in \text{preds}(j)}) \bigcap_{p \,\in\, \text{succs}(j)} \omega_p^j(T_j, T_p) \bigcap_q \Delta_{qj}^j(T_j, T_q) \qquad (17)$$

where q is any event bound by a linear constraint to j (i.e., $-s_{jq} \leq t_j - t_q \leq s_{qj}$).

Comparing MD2 and CLP (BNR):

Assuming a Jacobi iterative mechanism instead of CLP (BNR), an iteration over a system of non-linear constraints is based on the following equation (from (17)):

$$T_j' = \max_{i \,\in\, preds\,(j)} (T_i + \delta_{ij}) \bigcap_{p \,\in\, succs\,(j)} T_p + [-\infty, -l_{jp}] \bigcap_q T_q + [-s_{jq}, s_{qj}] \bigcap T_j,$$

that is

$$T'_j = min\,(max_{i \in preds\,(j)}(T_i + u_{ij}),\ min_{p \in succs\,(j)}(T_p - l_{jp}),\ \forall q,\ T_q + s_{qj},\ T_j) \qquad (18a)$$

$$T'_j = max\,(max_{i \in preds\,(j)}(T_i + l_{ij}),\ -\infty,\ \forall q,\ T_q - s_{jq},\ T_j) \qquad (18b)$$

where n is the number of events, $1 \le i,\ j,\ k,\ p,\ q \le n$, and, initially, $T_k = [0,0]$, $T_j = [-\infty, \infty]$, $\forall\,j \ne k$.

Again, once the interval propagation is completed, the maximum separation from event k to an event j, d_{kj}, is given by T_j, i.e., $t_j - t_k \le T_j$.

As before, we omit the full development of the preceding expressions in our comparison. The basis of this comparison is the fact that in MD2, the outer loops of all "for" (indexed by i) are equivalent to repeated executions in CLP (BNR), each different value of i expressing a new reference point k.

The first step of the algorithm MD2 is thus identical to a first iteration in CLP (BNR) where upper bounds on separations are propagated from the reference event k to events that are directly constrained by it. That is

$$T'_j = min\,(T_p - l_{jp},\ T_q + s_{qj},\ T_j)$$

Other terms in max and in min are dropped since they are constrained by various $T_i = [-\infty, \infty]$ and $T_p = [-\infty, \infty]$, and evaluate to ∞. Substituting either q or p by the reference event k (the other term is dropped), we have $d_{kj} = T'_j$.

Step three of the algorithm expresses the forward propagation of updated values from one iteration to the next. It can be seen in expression (18a) that these computations are the same in CLP (BNR) (see closing remarks of preceding section on systems of max-only constraints).

Termination conditions are identical for both MD2 and CLP (BNR).

The two processes differ when it comes to step 2. While d_{ij} and d_{ip} are expressed in CLP (BNR) by T_j and T_p, d_{pj} has no direct equivalent. However the property $d_{ij} \le d_{ip} + d_{pj}$ is preserved indirectly by the interval propagation mechanism. The proof is by contradiction:

Consider a system of constraints that has already been submitted to the interval propagation mechanism. This system has stabilized. CLP (BNR) is monotone: any extra iteration of the interval propagation will not affect the domain of the interval-valued variables. Let us assume that $\exists\,i,\ j,\ p$ such that $d_{ij} > d_{ip} + d_{pj}$. Three distinct paths of constraints are possible:

- a path from event i to event j, which does not involve event p (path 1),
- a path from event i to event p, which does not involve event j (path 2), and
- a path from event p to event j, which does not involve event i (path 3).

Since $i = k$, the reference event for this system in CLP (BNR), we have $t_i = 0$. The preceding implies that propagating this value along path 1 will produce a first upper bound, x, on the occurrence time of event j. Propagation of the same value along path 2 and path 3 will produce a second upper bound, y, on the occurrence time of event j, where $x > y$ according to our hypothesis. This will narrow the value of the interval-valued variable representing the occurrence time of event j, implying that the system has actually not reached stability which contradicts our initial assumption.

4.3.4 Using CLP to Solve the General Event Separation Problem:

The general event separation problem is concerned with systems of constraints where linear, min and max constraints are allowable simultaneously. As we mentioned before, this problem is $\mathcal{NP}$-complete: an efficient algorithm, i.e., that runs in polynomial time, cannot be expected to solve it. Branch and bound methods for analyzing such systems can be constructed, however. One first approach relies on the observation that min constraints are often present in smaller numbers than max constraints. A simple and exhaustive case analysis based on these min constraints is possible. The general event separation problem is thus reduced to computing separations in systems of linear and max-only constraints problem (Section 4.3.3).

More sophisticated approaches can be conceived by decomposing the min constraints dynamically while the constraint system is submitted to interval propagation. Min constraints are analyzed as they are encountered, allowing some terms to be discarded (e.g., a min node is resolved) and thus reducing the number of possible cases.

4.3.5 Example

The example is taken from [1]. Figure 1 shows the constraint graph of the specification for the read cycle of an Intel 8086 CPU connected via an address decode and an address latch to an Intel 2716 EPROM.

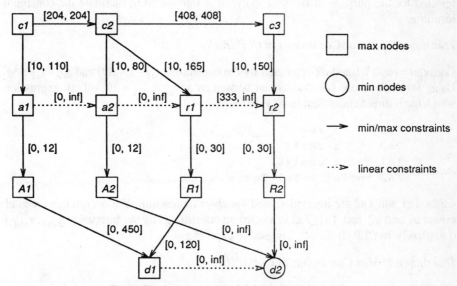

Fig. 1. Timing constraints for 8086/2716 read cycle

Details of the specification can be found in [1] and [12]. Boxes and circles in Figure 1 represent max and min constraints respectively. A solid line with label $[l_{ij}, u_{ij}]$ between two events i and j portrays a delay constraint δ_{ij} where $l_{ij} \leq \delta_{ij} \leq u_{ij}$. A dotted line with label $[-s_{ji}, s_{ij}]$ between two events i and j depicts the linear constraints $t_j - t_i \leq s_{ij}$ and $t_i - t_j \leq s_{ji}$.

We wish compute maximum separations between all pairs of events using CLP (BNR). The example is simple since there is a single min event. A branch-and-bound algorithm is not necessary: only two cases must be analyzed:

- $t_{A2} + \delta_{A2d2} \leq t_{R2} + \delta_{R2d2}$ or
- $t_{R2} + \delta_{R2d2} \leq t_{A2} + \delta_{A2d2}$,

where $0 \leq \delta_{A2d2} \leq \infty$ and $0 \leq \delta_{R2d2} \leq \infty$.

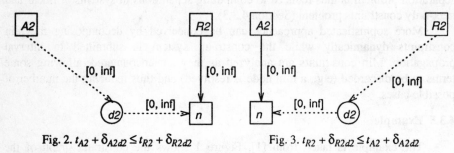

Fig. 2. $t_{A2} + \delta_{A2d2} \leq t_{R2} + \delta_{R2d2}$ Fig. 3. $t_{R2} + \delta_{R2d2} \leq t_{A2} + \delta_{A2d2}$

The graphs in Figures 2 and 3 illustrate the two cases. A virtual event n which represents the occurrence times of either $t_{R2} + \delta_{R2d2}$ or $t_{A2} + \delta_{A2d2}$ (i.e. the value rejected for the purpose of the min analysis) is introduced to facilitate the constraint handling.

Translation of Linear Constraints in CLP (BNR):

Consider events $a1$ and $a2$ separated by the constraints $t_{a1} - t_{a2} \leq 0$ and $t_{a2} - t_{a1} \leq \infty$. Using intervals, those constraints can be written as $t_{a2} = t_{a1} + [0, \infty]$, an expression which has a direct equivalent in CLP (BNR):

```
Ta1      : real(_, _),
Ta2      : real(_, _),
Ta1_Ta2 : real(0, _),
Ta2 == Ta1 + Ta1_Ta2.
```

where Ta1 and Ta2 are interval-valued variables representing the occurrence times of events $a1$ and $a2$, and Ta1_Ta2 is a constant constrained by the interval $[-s_{a2a1}, s_{a1a2}]$ (i.e. $[0, \infty]$). In CLP (BNR), "_" is used to express $\pm\infty$.

Translation of Max Constraints in CLP (BNR):

Consider events $A1$, $R1$ and $d1$ linked by the constraint $t_{d1} = \max(t_{A1} + \delta_{A1d1}, t_{R1} + \delta_{R1d1})$ where $0 \leq \delta_{A1d1} \leq 450$ and $0 \leq \delta_{R1d1} \leq 120$. In CLP (BNR), this becomes:

```
TA1_Td1 : real(0, 450),
TR1_Td1 : real(0, 120),
Td1 == max(TA1 + TA1_Td1, TR1 + TR1_Td1).
```

Translation of Min Constraints:

In this case, there is no direct translation of min constraints. These constraints are converted into linear constraints as illustrated in Figures 2 and 3 and expressed in CLP (BNR) as such. There is therefore one CLP (BNR) program for each case analyzed. (To automate this analysis, when more min constraints appear in a specification, the decomposition of min constraints for case analysis can be handled more efficiently by adding control structures to a single CLP (BNR) program. That is, the min constraints are written directly (in a way similar to the max constraint translation) into the program and the min operator is redefined to perform the case analysis).

The programs that result from the set of constraints given by the original specification are submitted to the CLP (BNR) interpreter (i.e. they are questions: does such a set of constraints admit a solution?). One event must always be initialized to serve as a reference point in time (for example, Ta1 : real(0, 0)). If the system of constraints has a set of solutions, the Prolog interpreter will return the maximum separation for every event to the reference point. By submitting repeatedly the programs with different reference points, maximum separations between all pairs are computed. Since there are two programs, there will be two possibly different sets of results. These sets are combined by selecting the maximum values for all corresponding pairs of results.

j	i	$[-s_{ji}, s_{ij}]$ CLP (BNR)
A1	A2	[92,286]
a2	d1	[0,358]
R1	R2	[303,578]
d1	c3	[40,398]
d1	d2	[0,∞]
c3	d2	[-398,∞]

Table 1: Computed separations

Table 1 shows the separations computed by CLP (BNR). The results obtained are the same as in [1].

5   Conclusions and Future Work

Eliminating uncertainty in CLP (BNR) is only the first step. The brute CLP engine is equivalent to the approaches given in [1] and thus can serve as a basic interface verification tool. However, it also shares with them some undesirable features: systems combining max-only and linear constraints can be solved but at the expense of pseudo-polynomial run-times. Pathological cases are described in [1].

CLP (BNR) is an efficient tool for solving subsets of the general event separation problem. It is in this perspective that we consider CLP (BNR) a stepping-stone for interface timing verification. We believe that the CLP resolution engine can be a powerful addition to, or even the basis of, a more general tool for interface timing verification.

Our task is then to identify and circumvent the limitations of the CLP (BNR) language, to build upon its strengths and also to expand it with advantageous modifications. Vandecasteele and De Schreye have shown in [15] how such improvements can be made. They propose techniques for reducing the amount of checking done in the underlying search tree (specific pruning strategies are associated with each constraint and restrictions made on the range of the domain checking). Further inquiries in this direction seem worthwhile. Similarly, a more efficient algorithm than the one found in [1] is proposed in [4]. The CLP (BNR) resolution mechanism cannot be changed directly but perhaps additional constraints, derived from the algorithm, can be found to improve the speed of the resolution process.

6   References

[1]   K. McMillan and D. Dill, "Algorithms for Interface Timing Verification", Proceedings of the IEEE International Conference on Computer Design, 1992.

[2]   T. Amon, H. Hulgaard, G. Borriello and S. Burns, "Timing Analysis of Concurrent Systems", Proceedings of the Design Automation Conference, 1993.

[3]   J.A. Brozowski, T. Gahlinger and F. Mavaddat, "Consistency and Satisfiability of Waveform Timing Specifications", Networks, Vol. 21, p. 91-107, 1991.

[4]   T.-Y. Yen, A. Ishii, A. Casavant and W. Wolf, "Efficient Algorithms for Interface Timing Verification", Proceedings of the Design Automation Conference, 1994.

[5]   T. Amon and G. Borriello, "An Approach to Symbolic Timing Verification", 29th ACM/IEEE Design Automation Conference, 1992.

[6]   W. Older, and A. Vellino, "Constraint Arithmetic on Real Intervals", Constraints Logic Programming: Selected Research, 1993.

[7]   Vanbekbergen, P. G. Goossens and H. De Man, "Specification and Analysis of Timing Constraints in Signa Transitions Graphs", Proceedings of the European Conference on Design Automation, 1992.

[8]   E.A. Walkup, and G. Borriello, "Interface Timing Verification with Applications to Synthesis", Proceedings of the Design Automation Conference, 1994.

[9]   P. Van Hentenryck, Constraint Satisfaction in Logic Programming, MIT Press, 1989.

[10]   O. Lhomme, "Consistency techniques for numeric CSPs", Proceedings of the 13th IJCAI, 1993.

[11]   R.E. Moore, Methods and Applications of Interval Analysis, SIAM, 1979.

[12]   T. Gahlinger. "Coherence and Satisfiability of Waveform Timing Specifications". Research Report CS-90-11. University of Waterloo. 1990. Ph. D. thesis.

[13]   W. Leler, Constraint Programming Languages : Their Specification and Generation, Addison-Wesley, 1988.

[14]   K. Khordoc, M. Dufresne, E. Cerny, P.-A. Babkine and A. Silburt, "Integrating Behaviour and Timing in Executable Specifications", Proceedings of the IFIP Conference on HDL and their applications, p. 385-402, 1993.

[15]   H. Vandecasteele, and D. De Schreye, "Implementing a Finite-domain CLP-language on Top of Prolog: a Transformation Approach, Lecture Notes in Artificial Intelligence 822, Proceedings of the 5th International Conference Logic Programming and Automated Reasoning, p. 84-98, 1994.

Debugging Constraint Programs

Micha Meier

European Computer Industry Research Centre,
Arabellastr. 17, 81925 Munich, Germany
micha@ecrc.de

Abstract. Constraint programming (CP) is in its substance non-algorithmic programming, not last because it is often being applied to problems for which no efficient algorithms exist. A not immediately obvious consequence of this fact is that debugging CP programs is principally different from debugging algorithmic programs, including imperative, functional or Prolog programs. It is also more difficult. Moreover, it is frequently necessary to apply *performance debugging* to CP programs, which are correct but too slow to be feasible. The whole area of CP debugging is still lacking both methodology and tools to support users in improving their programs.

In this paper, we present a paradigm for tracing constraint programs and the design and implementation of **Grace**, a graphical environment for tracing CLP(FD) programs on top of **ECL^{i}PS^e**.

1 Introduction

Developing CLP applications is a difficult task. This is to a large extent due to the fact that CLP is usually being applied to combinatorial search problems for which no efficient algorithms are known. Instead of following some well-known rules, the users have to experiment with various models, approaches and strategies to solve the problem. Apart from handling the usual *correctness debugging* of their programs, users are also facing the problem of *performance debugging*, i.e. finding a way to execute CLP programs efficiently. To date, there exists no satisfactory methodology for debugging CLP programs. There are basically two ways to approach the problem: either try to apply all available methods exhaustively, last resort being simplification and downscaling of the problem, or to analyse the behaviour of the program and try to understand what is the reason for its poor performance. The current CLP systems unfortunately offer little support for this task and there are no widely available tools which would support tracing and (performance) debugging CLP programs.

Our goal is to contribute to the methodology of performance debugging of constraint programs and to develop an environment to support it. Although much of what we present here applies to the whole CP area, our primary target is performance debugging of CLP(FD) programs and more specifically, programs based on labeling finite domain variables and backtracking search.

In this paper, we first analyse the features of debugging constraint programs as opposed to algorithmic ones and draw the conclusions about the features of a debugging system. Next we present the functionality of the **Grace** system and show some examples of its use. We also discuss implementation issues and show how an advanced debugging environment can be implemented on top of **ECL^{i}PS^e**, using its control features. Finally we discuss the possible extensions of the environment both in the CLP(FD) area and in other areas of constraint programming.

2 Debugging Constraint Programs

To support debugging of constraint programs, we first have to analyse the main features of CP as opposed to more conventional, algorithmic programs.

2.1 Features of Constraint Programs

The constraint programming paradigm is inherently different from imperative, functional or Prolog-type logic programming, since it is *non-algorithmic*. Even in Prolog (without delays), and more so in conventional languages, the program execution follows a fixed scheme which implements a particular algorithm, no matter if the program is declarative or not. CP however, only states constraints and then looks for a solution that satisfies them. The search is rather data-driven than program-driven.

A consequence of these facts is that debugging CP programs is inherently different from debugging algorithmic programs:

- Debugging algorithmic programs is itself also algorithmic, it can follow a particular debugging algorithm, which guarantees success. Even the debugging itself can be automated.
- It is *local*, each program piece, e.g. a function, can be considered and debugged separately and without the execution history.
- It is possible to decide at any execution point if the current state is correct or not.
- Source-level (e.g. for C) or invocation-based (Byrd box for Prolog) debuggers are well suitable for this kind of debugging.

  On the other hand:

- CP debugging, and especially performance CP debugging is not algorithmic and it can hardly be automated.
- It is mostly *global*, it is necessary to consider the whole program and also the execution history.
- Especially for performance debugging it is not possible to decide if a particular execution state is correct or not. The execution state is a point in the search space and we cannot decide if the solution will be quickly found or not.

- Similarly to the search for a solution which is performed by the program, the debugging itself is also a search problem. The debugger to support it must therefore be highly interactive and open. Debugging paradigms for algorithmic languages are not suitable for constraint debugging, it makes little sense to extend source-level or Byrd-box debuggers for constraints.

2.2 Approaches to Debugging

We can divide the debugging approaches into *experimental* and *analytic* ones. A debugging environment must support both of them in a satisfactory way.

Experimental Debugging Experimental debugging does not necessarily assume a deep knowledge of the methods used. All that is needed is a large repository of available methods with which the user can experiment. This approach is quite appropriate for non-expert users or for the first estimation of a given problem and it is of course applicable only to performance debugging.

When we consider the particular area of CLP(FD), we can divide a program into three main parts:

1. The *model*, which, among others, specifies all variables, their domains and their interpretation. It also specifies the conceptual constraints imposed on the variables.
2. The actual *constraints* which are used to express the properties of the solution in the particular model and system.
3. The *labeling strategy* which is used to search for the solution(s). This includes both selection of variables to label and value ordering in the selected variable domains.

Experiments on each of these items should be well supported by the debugging environment:

1. While a debugging environment cannot directly support the user in modelling the problem and switching from one model to another, it should at least be able to compare different models, especially to compare two programs running concurrently with different models.
2. The debugging environment must be able to show the effect of using particular constraints, the amount of propagation achieved, and it also has to allow dynamic adding of new or redundant constraints.
3. The environment should have a large repository of available strategies and heuristics which are easy to use and to combine. Interestingly, CLP(FD) can be used as a unifying framework for various other CP approaches based on finite domains, e.g. local repair or statistical methods and an ideal debugging environment would allow to experiment with various such methods to look for the most suitable combination for the particular application.

Analytic Debugging Analytic debugging assumes a more thorough knowledge of the mechanisms that are involved in the constrained search and it is the only way to perform correctness debugging. An appropriate debugging environment allows to filter and structure the tracing data at various conceptual levels, so that the user is able to infer new information and use it to improve the performance. Some typical analytic debugging approaches are:

- **Looking for redundant constraints.** In most CLP(FD) systems each constraint is considered separately, the only constraint which is used in combination with others is the variable domain itself. It may often happen that some information is not encoded in the constraints because it seems obvious. For instance, from

$$X + Y = 10$$
$$X + Y + Z = 12$$

  a CLP(FD) system is not able to deduce that $Z = 2$. A debugging environment must make it as easy as possible to spot similar cases.
- **Developing new labeling strategies.** When the search path is being displayed in a suitable way, the user may be able to see the reasons for not finding the solution quickly or for not finding a good solution first.
- **Finding the appropriate propagation amount.** A modification of one variable's domain triggers some of the constraints that are attached to this variable. Finding exactly the right amount of constraints to trigger is an important part of performance debugging. If some of the woken constraints make no propagation or only an insignificant one, they only slow down the execution. On the other hand, if the domain update does not trigger enough constraints, the pruning will be insufficient and the search space remains too large.
- **Finding the reason for a failure.** This is important both for correctness and performance debugging. For correctness debugging it helps to find the reason for not finding the correct solution. For performance debugging it helps to find out how some branches in the search space are pruned away. As a result, the user may realise that the reason for pruning is different than expected and that e.g. some constraints which were expected to cause the pruning were not triggered.
- **Finding the reason for a wrong solution.** If the program is about to consider a wrong solution, some of the constraints are wrong or missing. A debugger must assist in fixing this problem.

2.3 Support from the Debugging Environment

The support expected from a CLP(FD) debugging environment can be seen from several different angles.

Display The displayed data is obviously very important for analytic debugging. The debugger must display all necessary information, but it must also apply *display economy*: the information to display is potentially very complex and large and thus the display must contain only the very necessary data so that more information can fit on the screen. In contrast, see the output of the **ECL^{i}PS^e** debugger in a CLP(FD) program:

```
S (61396) 20 RESUME qeq(0, 2575, T_g71094{[0..2575]}) (dbg)?- creep

S (61396) 20 EXIT qeq(0, 2575, 0) (dbg)?- creep

(65874) 20 RESUME 3000 - C_g517524{[19..74]} - C_g518588{[0..560]} - C_g519550{[20..36]}-0 - C_g523442{[22..35]}
- C_g524476{[15..33]} - C_g525540{[9..39]} - C_g526604{[0..510]} - C_g527566{[0..650]} - C_g528528{[15..70]} -
C_g529592{[6..45]} - C_g530634{[8..49]} - C_g531698{[10..61]} - C_g532762{[0..680]} - ... #>=0 (dbg)?- creep

(65878) 20 DELAY 3000 - C_g517524{[19..74]} - C_g518588{[0..560]} - C_g519550{[20..36]} - C_g523442{[22..35]}
- C_g524476{[15..33]} - C_g525540{[9..39]} - C_g526604{[0..510]} - C_g527566{[0..650]} - C_g528528{[15..70]} -
C_g529592{[6..45]} - C_g530634{[8..49]} - C_g531698{[10..61]} - C_g532762{[0..680]} - ... #>=0

(65874) 20 EXIT 3000 - C_g517524{[19..74]} - C_g518588{[0..560]} - C_g519550{[20..36]} - C_g523442{[22..35]}
- C_g524476{[15..33]} - C_g525540{[9..39]} - C_g526604{[0..510]} - C_g527566{[0..650]} - C_g528528{[15..70]} -
C_g529592{[6..45]} - C_g530634{[8..49]} - C_g531698{[10..61]} - C_g532762{[0..680]} - ... #>=0 (dbg)?- creep

(65877) 19 EXIT indomain(0) (dbg)?- creep

(65879) 19 CALL instantiate([D_g5234{[0..10]}, D_g1544{[0..10]}, D_g7284{[0..10]}, D_g4824{[0..10]}, D_g7694{[0..10]},
D_g8514{[0..10]}, D_g8924{[0..10]}, D_g9334{[0..10]}, D_g9744{[0, 1]}, D_g10154{[0, 1]}]) (dbg) ?-
```

Due to the size of problems we are aiming at, it might not be feasible to display the whole constraint network like e.g. [11]; even displaying parts of the network may not necessarily help the user. On the other hand, displaying all of the problem variables is necessary. In case that some data is not or can not be displayed by default, it must be possible to display it on demand.

The debugging environment needs both fixed and user-definable displays. The fixed ones give a structure to the display and to the debugging process itself, the user-definable displays are added to support a particular user and a particular application.

The analytic debugging needs data from different conceptual levels so that more global or more detailed information about the application becomes visible:

- **Solution.** Displays only the solution, its cost, search time, number of backtracks etc. This is also suitable for methods which are not based on backtracking search or which are available only as a black box.
- **Search path.** Displays the path in the search space that leads to the solution. For CLP(FD) this is the sequence of labelled variables and their values.
- **Selected data.** At this level the value of selected variables, expressions and terms is displayed on each step. The expressions must be user-definable, e.g. the current cost estimate, the current value of some particular constraints, number of constraints which are already satisfied and those that are not etc.
- **All data.** Displays the current value of all involved variables.
- **Domain updates.** The sequence of domain updates which are caused by the last labeling step is displayed, either step by step or together as a sequence of events.

- **Constraint propagation.** At this most detailed level the sequence of constraints propagation becomes visible. The environment shows which constraints were triggered and re-evaluated by the most recent labeling step and what was the result of their re-evaluation.

Interaction The debugging environment must be highly flexible and interactive. Most of the user actions should be mouse-oriented, choices supported by buttons and menus. Usual debugger commands like single-stepping through labeling steps, skipping, jumping, retrying, setting breakpoints etc. would be the main vehicle for analytic debugging, choices and comparisons of various strategies would be used for the experimental one. Changing to other conceptual display levels and dynamically modifying the displayed information has to be made easy.

Integration Ideally, the debugging environment would be another process which would control the user application, run and stop it and extract data from it. This is however possible only with a very low-level programming approach and it is completely machine-dependent. On the other hand, the debugging environment which we expect to be most useful has different properties:

- It is *open*, the user can extend it, define new primitives and use new debugging approaches.
- It is easily maintainable and programmed in a high-level language, possibly in CLP(FD) itself.
- It consists of two basic layers: the environment itself is written on top of basic building blocks which allow to access, display and modify data and which are available to the user for extensions.
- Since performance debugging usually handles long programs, the execution overhead caused by debugging must be minimal or, because displays slow down the execution in any case, at least it should depend only on the amount of data displayed.
  Particularly, it must be possible to place breakpoints on variable changes. This is feasible only when the debugger is tightly connected with the object program. Using another process (like in *dbx*) makes efficient variable breakpoints very difficult.

3 Grace Features

The above considerations have led us to the implementation of **Grace**, a graphical constraint tracing environment on top of the **ECL^{i}PS^e** system [5]. The special control primitives available in **ECL^{i}PS^e** [9] make it possible to implement the whole environment in **ECL^{i}PS^e** itself and still to meet most of the requirements stated above. The graphical part was developed using the **ProTcl** [6] interface to the Tcl/Tk toolkit [10]:

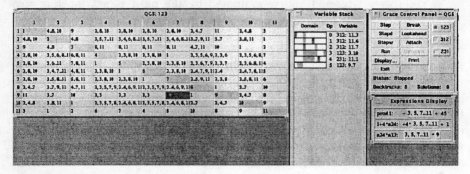

3.1 FD Variable Display

The FD variables in **Grace** are displayed as active fixed-size buttons with the variable domain as button text:

$$3..7, 9, 11$$

To be able to spot different displays of the same variable on the screen, each variable is a *hyperlink*: when the cursor enters the variable display, the button is highlighted and, if there are other displays of the same variable on the screen, they are highlighted as well:

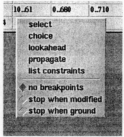

When pressing the first mouse button in the variable display, a menu pops up with various options depending on the window type in which the variable is located:

The middle mouse button causes a separate display of the whole domain and its size, which is useful if the domain is too long to fit into the button:

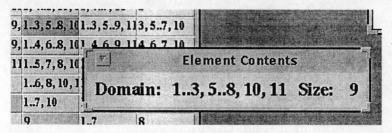

Each variable has an attached *print daemon* which updates the display if the domain of the variable changes and undoes this change on backtracking:

```
% display_handler(Var, OldDomain, VarID)
display_handler(Var, _, ID) :-
    var_domain(Var, D),
    <Display in Tk the domain D at the location ID>
    (var(Var) ->
        % wake when domain of Var changes
        delay(display_handler(Var, D, ID))
    ;
        true
    ).
display_handler(_, Old, ID) :-
    <Display in Tk the domain Old at the location ID>
    fail.
```

In this way, the display can be incrementally updated on both forward and backward execution. This is a well-known CLP(FD) trick to keep the variable display valid, available in languages which can attach a daemon to a FD variable which is triggered on variable domain updates.

3.2 Variable Matrices

The FD variables represent the actual state of the computation and it is therefore important to display them all. **Grace** displays variables in two-dimensional *variable matrices* in a spreadsheet format, because this allows to display a large number of variables in a dense and structured way:

Relocation: d

	1	2	3	4	5	6	7	8	9	10
1	1	0..10	1	0,1	0,1	0,1	1	1	1	0..10
2	0..10	1	1	1	1	0..10	0..10	1	0..10	0..10
3	0..10	0,1	0,1							

Relocation: p

	1	2	3	4	5	6	7	8	9	10
1	1.5	1.5	1.5	1.5	1.5	1.5	1.5	1.5	1.5	1.5
2	1.5	1.5	1.5	1.5	1.5	1.5	1.5	1.5	1.5	1.5
3	1.5	1.5	1.5							

Relocation: c

	1	2	3	4	5	6	7	8	9	10
1	19..74	0.560	20..36	0.39	0..31	0..43	22..35	15..33	9.39	0..510
2	0..650	15..70	6.45	8.49	10..61	0..680	0.710	21..74	0..740	0..510
3	0..580	0..42	0.43	145..5654						

The user can put all variables into one matrix or split them into several matrices. Each matrix can be displayed or hidden independently and when it is resized, the appropriate font is selected.

3.3 Variable Identification

When the user wants to query or modify data attached to a variable, two cases may occur:

- If the data is directly attached to one displayed variable, then the operation can be performed with the mouse. This concerns e.g. modifying the domain of a variable, selecting for the next labeling step, listing constraints attached to a variable etc.
- If the data concerns more than one variable or if it involves typing in additional information, a textual identification of the variable(s) is used [1].

Variables cannot be usually identified by their name because in most CLP(FD) applications they are created dynamically with the same name, e.g. in a recursive predicate. **Grace** therefore uses a different naming scheme, which is shared by the control and the graphics part. Each variable is identified by the name of its matrix and its position, e.g. the highlighted variable in the picture above is a string "d.1.4". Then, for example, the expression $5 * D_{1,4} + 3 * P_{1,4}$ would be typed in as

```
5 * "d.1.4" + 3 * "p.1.4"
```

---

[1] A more mouse-oriented approach would be to type in an expression without variables and when it is displayed, to use a drag and drop operation to insert the appropriate variables. This requires more user actions than typing in, moreover a fully programmable environment needs a textual representation of variables in any case, so that displays can be pre-programmed.

3.4 Search Path Display

Grace uses the *variable stack* to display the current position in the search space and the previous and remaining choices:

Domain	Dp	Variable
	0	312: 13.3
	1	312: 13.6
	2	312: 13.9
	3	123: 3.12
	4	231: 13.1
	5	123: 6.11
	6	231: 6.11
	7	231: 13.2
	8	231: 2.1

Each row in the variable stack represents one variable that has been already labelled. The bar to the left represents the variable domain, to the right there is the depth in the search space and the variable position ('312' etc. happen to be the matrix names). The colours in the domain bar have the following meaning (increasing lightness in black and white display):

red - current variable value,
blue - values in the domain to be still tried,
gray - values that have been already tried (and failed),
white - values already removed from the domain before the variable was selected.

Each row has a popup menu which allows to retry the labeling at this depth, skip to the next value of this variable and fail to the next value of the variable (e.g. to speed up the execution if there is no solution for this label).

3.5 Terms and Expressions Display

Grace displays the value of selected terms and expressions in a separate window. *Terms* are arbitrary Prolog terms which are displayed in their usual form except that the variables in them are displayed as hyperlinks and their display is updated when the variable domain changes. This form can be used e.g. to display the current state of a specified constraint[2]:

---

[2] Note that it does not matter how the constraint is actually implemented. Even if it is compiled into a sequence of machine or abstract instructions, or decomposed into a number of primitive constraints, we only need its structure.

Expressions Display	
##:	1, 4, 5, 7 ## 2, 4, 5
notin:	notin(1, 4, 5, 7 , [4..6 , 1, 4..7 , 3, 1, 5, 7 , 1, 4, 6, 7 , 2])

Constraints attached to a particular variable can be listed from its menu and with a mouse click they are moved to the expression display.

Expressions, on the other hand, are being re-evaluated each time one of their variables becomes instantiated and the display is updated accordingly. For example, the following picture shows a sequence of updates to a cost expression:

Expressions Display
0 #=:   + 19..74 + 15..70 + 6..45 + 8..49 + 10..61 + 21..74 − 162..456 + 83
0 #=:   + 19..74 + 15..70 + 8..49 + 10..61 + 21..74 − 162..417 + 89
0 #=:   + 19..74 + 15..70 + 10..61 + 21..74 − 162..376 + 97
0 #=:   + 19..74 + 15..70 + 21..74 − 162..325 + 107

3.6   Execution and Display Control

Grace is being controlled from the *Control Panel* window. It contains a number of buttons to control the execution, checkbuttons that control display of variable matrices, and several status items. There are two basic modes for the execution, *step* and *run*. In the *step* mode, the execution stops before every labeling step and the whole display is updated. In the *run* mode, the execution stops only on breakpoints or when a solution is found or when the user types Ctrl-C. The display updates in the *run* mode are controlled by Display options in the control panel:

none - the display is not updated at all, the program is running with maximal speed. With this option, the overhead of the debugging environment is minimal (less than 3 %) but whenever the execution stops, the complete execution state can be displayed. This feature alone is extremely helpful for tracing CLP programs.

variable stack - only the display of the variable stack is updated every time a new variable is labeled or when the program backtracks. This is relatively fast and it gives the user an animated view of the execution.

expressions - in addition to the variable stack, the expression display is updated as well. The user has thus the possibility to see the animation of certain variables or expressions which is still faster than to display all variables.

all - on each labeling step, the whole display is updated, including all visible variable matrices. This mode is provided mainly for demonstrations.

The execution can also be traced in fine-grained steps:

− Stepping through domain updates. The execution stops each time a variable is updated, this variable is highlighted and the old domain is printed in the status display. When the propagation fails, the system warns the user and then it waits for the next user command. In this way, the variable configuration directly before failure can be inspected.
− Stepping through woken constraints. All constraints which are triggered and re-evaluated up to the next labeling step are displayed in a separate window in a way which is similar to Prolog debuggers, with the CALL and EXIT or FAIL ports. This display is user-defined, the system may stop at every constraint invocation and update the display, or stop on failure, etc.

At any time, all matrices can also be printed on the printer for a more thorough or off-line analysis of their state.

3.7 Running Two Programs Concurrently

With **Grace** it is possible to compare two different strategies applied to the same problem. Both applications are started with **Grace** and one of them, the *slave*, is then attached to the other one, the *master*, by clicking on the *Attach* button. From now on, most of the control commands executed in the master will be communicated to the slave so that both processes are synchronised. Moreover, the variable selected for labeling in the master will also be selected in the slave. At each labeling step it is then possible to see the comparison of the current values in variable matrices: identical domains are unchanged, smaller domains are displayed in lighter colour whereas larger domains use darker colour. Variables whose domains are not comparable are displayed in a different colour. This mechanism gives the user rudimentary facilities for comparison of two different approaches to solve the problem.

3.8 Interface

The interface between **Grace** and the user CLP(FD) program consists of several predicate calls that have to be inserted into the user program at appropriate places:

− grace_start(Title, MatrixList) - start **Grace** with a given title and a list of variable matrices.
− grace_label(Var, Rest, NewVar, NewRest) is inserted into the labeling predicate just before labeling the variable **Var**. Since the selected variable can be modified by the user, this predicate returns the newly selected variable and the rest as separate arguments. The labeling predicate then looks for instance as follows:

```
labeling([]).
labeling(Vars) :-
    deleteff(Var, Vars, Rest),
    grace_label(Var, Rest, NewVar, NewRest),
    indomain(NewVar),
    labeling(NewRest).
```

- **grace_display_term(Term, Name)** displays the given term in the Expression display.
- **grace_solution** is called when a solution has been found. It stops and displays the execution state.

4   Implementation Issues

The implementation of an efficient and flexible debugging environment is a challenging task. The more functionality is required from the system, the more of complex and low-level coding is necessary to implement it. Low-level coding, however, is not compatible with flexibility, maintainability and extensibility. High-level coding, on the other hand, usually causes an unacceptable execution overhead. For example, the otherwise excellent OPIUM system [2] gives the user a wide spectrum of ways to debug Prolog programs, however it can hardly be used for real-time debugging, due to the time and space overhead.

The **ECL^{i}PS^e** system [4, 3] based on Sepia [8] is a logic programming system which has been designed to support a wide range of extensions. To implement the extensions in an efficient way, the system provides high-level interfaces to low-level kernel primitives so that the whole extension code can be written in **ECL^{i}PS^e** itself. **ECL^{i}PS^e** also provides several CLP libraries for various domains.

Grace has been fully implemented in **ECL^{i}PS^e** and in Tcl/Tk and its implementation has benefited to a large extent from the special control and extension primitives available in **ECL^{i}PS^e**. In this section, we will list the most interesting features of the implementation and the **ECL^{i}PS^e** primitives which were exploited. We will at the same time refrain from describing the complex issues of display and events handling which were tedious to implement but are not of particular interest for the CP community.

4.1   Logical vs. Extralogical Primitives

Although a CLP program is declarative, a CLP debugger cannot be completely declarative, otherwise all user actions would be undone on backtracking and some features would be difficult or impossible to implement. On the other hand, some user actions, like setting a breakpoint on a variable update, can be undone on backtracking without much harm. We have therefore decided to implement **Grace** as declaratively as possible, without defining special primitives to support imperative actions of the debugger.

4.2 Global Data

ECL^{i}PS^e provides two kinds of global data: *global variables* which are in fact destructively updatable arrays and which can be used to store ground terms, and *global references* which can also be updated but their value is restored on backtracking and they can contain terms with variables. All permanent debugger data have been implemented with the former type, for instance the current execution mode, current execution priority and breakpoints not related to variables (e.g. search depth or goal number).

The backtrackable global references have been used to store all variable matrices. In this way, the matrices are accessible everywhere in the program without having to pass them as arguments to all predicates. The current search depth is also implemented using this mechanism, because it has to be restored on backtracking.

4.3 Variable Attributes

The attributed variables available in ECL^{i}PS^e [5] make it possible to associate transparently attributes to variables. **Grace** uses this mechanism for several purposes:

- to associate the variable identification (i.e. matrix name and position) with the variable,
- to remember the initial variable domain which is necessary for the display in the variable stack
- implicitly, to associate daemons with variables; this was done using the coroutining primitives which are themselves built on top of the attribute scheme. The system uses various daemons: to update the display of variables, to recompute and redisplay expressions, to set a breakpoint on a variable and to step through domain updates.

4.4 Execution Priority

A major issue in implementing **Grace** was the question of minimal execution overhead. With our scheme of associating print daemons with each variable it is not straightforward to suppress their execution in case we want to run the program with maximum possible speed. Fortunately, the new waking scheme in ECL^{i}PS^e which is based on suspension priorities [9] could be used for this purpose. Every suspended goal in ECL^{i}PS^e (suspension) has an associated priority. When the goal is woken, e.g. by updating the domain of a variable, it is not immediately executed, but it is passed to the *waking scheduler* instead. The scheduler takes care that all woken suspensions are executed in their priority order and that a suspension with lower priority does not interrupt the execution of predicates with higher priority.

This scheme could be directly exploited in **Grace**: the various daemons have different priorities and the program is also assigned a given priority depending on the amount of display updates which are required. When no updates and maximum speed is required, the program priority is set to a value which is higher than that of any display daemon. Whenever a domain variable is updated, its associated print daemon is woken and passed to the waking scheduler, but since its priority is not high enough, it is never actually executed, the display is not updated and also no new daemon is placed on the variable from its body. The overhead is therefore reduced to the first waking of the daemon of each variable, which is a simple operation. By setting the program priority to different values the amount of display updates can be controlled.

4.5 Stepping through Domain Updates

Showing the successive changes of variable domains is also implemented using the waking priority scheme. When this execution mode is first entered, the system places another display daemon with a very high priority on each variable. When a domain variable is updated, this daemon will be the first attached suspension to be woken (before all the constraints). It will update the display and then wait for user action, i.e. clicking on a button. Then it places a new daemon on the variable and exits. In this way, all domain updates can be successively traced no matter how many constraints are invoked inbetween.

4.6 Breakpoints on Variables

The **ECL^{i}PS^e** finite domain constraint solver [5] allows to set up suspensions which are woken when a variable is constrained in various ways:

- the minimum or maximum of its domain changes,
- any element is removed from the domain
- variable is instantiated
- variable is bound to another constrained variable

This mechanism is used to set breakpoints on these events for a particular variable: when the suspension is woken (its priority is higher than that of the *run* mode), it changes the mode to *step* and prints information about the break into the status line. Note that this approach imposes no execution overhead.

4.7 Interrupting the Execution

When the program executes in the *run* mode, no X events are served (because of efficiency) and thus it cannot be stopped by clicking on a button. Instead, the handler for the keyboard interrupt signal is modified to set the *step* mode so that the execution stops on the next labeling step.

4.8 Stepping through Woken Constraints

Constraints are implemented in **ECLⁱPS^e** as suspensions which wait for a modification of one of their variables. When the variable is modified, the suspension is woken and the constraint is thus re-evaluated. As we said before, the waking does not happen directly, but through the waking scheduler. When stepping through woken constraints is required, **Grace** redefines the built-in waking scheduler with a predicate which is equivalent, but enhanced with printing the debugging information before and after calling the woken suspension. When this stepping is no longer required, the built-in waking scheduler is restored again.

The waking is thus temporarily enhanced and slowed down, which is exactly what is needed. Moreover, the user can define her own way to trace the woken constraints.

4.9 Listing Constraints Attached to a Variable

The constraints mechanism in **ECLⁱPS^e** is fully accessible to the user and it is thus possible to obtain the list of constraints attached to a particular domain variable using available primitives.

4.10 Restoring a Previous State

For the *retry* command it is necessary to restore a previous execution state and restart it. **Grace** creates an additional choice point on each labeling step, which is used to count the number of backtracks. This choice point can also be exploited to restore a previous state, if the execution fails up to this point. This failure, however, is not always easy to enforce: **Grace** can of course force the current labeling step to fail and to fail each time it obtains control until the target depth is reached, however the user program obtains control after each labeling step and after failure it retries another value in the domain of the labeled variable (see the **labeling/1** predicate on p. 12). This means that when executed declaratively, the program would perform a potentially large number of backtracks before it fails to the right choice point. Experiments have shown that this overhead is not acceptable and we thus had to use an impure primitive, *nonlocal cut* to handle this case. **ECLⁱPS^e** offers two primitives, **get_cut/1** and **cut_to/1** which implement a nonlocal cut. **get_cut/1** marks the current execution state and returns this mark, whereas **cut_to/1** removes all choice points up to a specified mark. This mechanism is used to remove all user choice points in each labeling step so that retrying is an operation which is only proportional to the depth in the search space, but not to the size of involved domains.

4.11 Comparing Two Grace Processes

The Tk toolkit has a *send* command which allows one Tk application to communicate with another Tk process. This mechanism has been used to attach one **Grace** process to another and to synchronise their labeling.

4.12 Handling Window Events

Most of the GUI events are handled in **ECL^{i}PS^e**. When the execution stops, the system blocks and waits for an X event. When it arrives, it is served by the **ECL^{i}PS^e** code and, depending on its type, the execution either continues, possibly in new mode, or it waits for another event.

The events which have no influence on the CLP data or execution (e.g. highlighting a variable when the cursor enters it) are handled by the Tk toolkit itself, so that the Prolog and Tcl code is cleanly separated.

5 Conclusions and Future Work

We have presented some basic principles for debugging CLP programs and from them we have concluded the properties of a system to support them. The design and implementation of **Grace** was surprisingly easy, taken into account the expected functionality and complexity. On preliminary tests [7] it showed to be quite useful and helpful for CLP tracing and debugging. As soon as the system is stable and foolproof enough, it will be released for public use.

There are many possible ways to enhance the current version of **Grace**, ranging from cosmetic ones to significant extensions. The most interesting ones are:

- Support for conditional breakpoints and user-definable breakpoints.
- Save/restore facility.
- Display the propagation steps in a graph format, similar to the Causality Graphs of [1]. It might also be interesting to explore the possibility of displaying selected parts of the constraint network as a graph. Since the actual constraints used to implement the application may be at a too low conceptual level, we see a need for more global and generalised representation of the constraint network which would give the user a good overview at the required conceptual level.
- Create a sophisticated repository of evaluation and labeling strategies and integrate them seamlessly into the **Grace** tracing paradigm.
- Support for parallel execution. The **ECL^{i}PS^e** system is able to perform OR-parallel search on shared-memory multiprocessors and in its next version it will be able to perform parallel search also on a network of workstations. The search paradigm in this context is slightly different from the sequential one - variables no longer have one value, because different processes explore different search paths in parallel and give the variables different values. On the other hand, the variable stack could be enhanced to visualise the search in all processes concurrently.
- With support for parallel execution it becomes very interesting to run several different strategies in parallel, possibly with some limited communication among the parallel processes. Rapid prototyping or experimental debugging in this context is an important area to explore.

– Inclusion of other methods than labeling based on backtracking search. Ideally, the debugging environment would also provide a number of other methods, e.g. local repair or statistical methods and it would allow to combine them into new and possibly very powerful strategies.

References

1. Michael Dahmen. A Debugger for Constraints in Prolog. Technical Report ECRC-91-11, ECRC, 1991.
2. M. Ducassé. Opium+, a meta-debugger for Prolog. In *Proceedings of the European Conference on Artificial Intelligence*, Munich, August 1988.
3. ECLiPSe.
   URL http://www.ecrc.de/eclipse/eclipse.html, 1995.
4. *ECLiPSe 3.5 User Manual*, 1995.
   URL http://www.ecrc.de/eclipse/html/umsroot/umsroot.html.
5. *ECLiPSe 3.5 Extensions User Manual*, 1995.
   URL http://www.ecrc.de/eclipse/html/extroot/extroot.html.
6. Micha Meier. ProTcl, the Prolog interface to the Tcl/Tk toolkit.
   URL http://www.ecrc.de/eclipse/html/protcl.html.
7. Micha Meier. Visualizing and solving finite algebra problems. In *Workshop on Finite Algebras*, ECRC, Munich, March 1994.
8. Micha Meier, Abderrahmane Aggoun, David Chan, Pierre Dufresne, Reinhard Enders, Dominique Henry de Villeneuve, Alexander Herold, Philip Kay, Bruno Perez, Emmanuel van Rossum, and Joachim Schimpf. SEPIA - an extendible Prolog system. In *Proceedings of the 11th World Computer Congress IFIP'89*, pages 1127–1132, San Francisco, August 1989.
9. Micha Meier and Joachim Schimpf. Control in ECLiPSe. Technical Report ECRC-95-07, ECRC, February 1995.
   URL http://www.ecrc.de/eclipse/html/reports.html.
10. John K. Ousterhout. *Tcl and the Tk Toolkit*. Addison-Wesley, 1994.
11. Michael Sanella. Analyzing and debugging hierarchies of multi-way local propagation constraints. In *Proceedings of the 1994 Workshop on Principles and Practice of Constraint Programming*, 1994.

An Optimizing Compiler for CLP($\mathcal{R}$)

Andrew D. Kelly[1], Andrew Macdonald[2], Kim Marriott[1], Harald Søndergaard[2], Peter J. Stuckey[2], Roland H.C. Yap[1,2]

[1] Dept. of Computer Science, Monash University, Clayton 3168, Australia.
[2] Dept. of Computer Science, The University of Melbourne, Parkville 3052, Australia.

Abstract. The considerable expressive power and flexibility gained by combining constraint programming with logic programming is not without cost. Implementations of constraint logic programming (CLP) languages must include expensive constraint solving algorithms tailored to specific domains, such as trees, Booleans, or real numbers. The performance of many current CLP compilers and interpreters does not encourage the widespread use of CLP. We outline an optimizing compiler for CLP($\mathcal{R}$), a CLP language which extends Prolog by allowing linear arithmetic constraints. The compiler uses sophisticated global analyses to determine the applicability of different program transformations. Two important components of the compiler, the *analyzer* and the *optimizer*, work in continual interaction in order to apply semantics-preserving transformations to the source program. A large suite of transformations are planned. Currently the compiler applies three powerful transformations, namely "solver bypass", "dead variable elimination" and "nofail constraint detection". We explain these optimizations and their place in the overall compiler design and show how they lead to performance improvements on a set of benchmark programs.

1 Introduction

CLP($\mathcal{R}$) is an extension of Prolog incorporating arithmetic constraints over the real numbers, with applications in a variety of areas, for example financial planning, options trading, electrical circuit analysis, synthesis and diagnosis, civil engineering, and genetics. As with many other constraint logic programming languages, CLP($\mathcal{R}$) has so far mainly been considered a research system, useful for rapid prototyping, but not really competitive with more conventional programming languages when performance is crucial. In general, performance is probably the main current obstacle to the widespread use of CLP. This situation is not surprising, as current CLP systems are offshoots of first-generation research systems.

In this paper we present an optimizing compiler for CLP($\mathcal{R}$). We are working towards a second generation implementation which overcomes the efficiency problems of current technology. The main innovation in the compiler is the incorporation of powerful program transformations and associated sophisticated global analysis which determines information about various kinds of interaction among constraints. Our earlier studies [10, 8, 15, 12, 14] have indicated that a suite of transformation techniques can lead to an order of magnitude improvement in execution time or space for particular classes of programs. Our implementation verifies this.

Our compiler also continues a line of experimental Prolog compilers which have made use of global program analysis to great advantage, see Taylor [18] and van Roy [19]. However, we achieve even larger performance improvements because linear arithmetic constraint solving is significantly more expensive than unification, and the scope for improvement in the handling of constraints is correspondingly greater. The most powerful analyses and program transformations employed by our CLP($\mathcal{R}$) compiler have no parallel in other programming language paradigms but are specific to linear real number constraint solving.

We assume the reader is familiar with constraint logic programming in general and with constraint logic programming over real arithmetic constraints in particular. A good introduction to CLP is to be found in [7] and a detailed introduction to CLP($\mathcal{R}$) can be found in [9]. In Section 2 we discuss the existing compiler and abstract machine CLAM. Section 3 presents three program transformations, "solver bypass," "dead variable elimination," and "nofail constraint detection." Section 4 covers the structure of the highly optimizing compiler and its three major components: the optimizer, the analyzer, and the code generator. In Section 5 we present our empirical results on a set of benchmarks. Section 6 contains a summary.

2 Compilation of CLP($\mathcal{R}$)

Execution of CLP($\mathcal{R}$) programs involves repeatedly adding a constraint to the constraint store and checking that the store remains satisfiable. Thus a successful execution path involves a growing number of constraints in the store, and the key issues in implementation are incremental constraint solving and dealing with a growing constraint store. While the constraint solvers in CLP($\mathcal{R}$) are specialized for incremental solving, adding a single new constraint may in the worst case they require processing virtually the entire constraint store. The number of constraints in the constraint store can therefore have a major impact on run-time speed.

The first CLP($\mathcal{R}$) implementation was based on an interpreter which consisted of a Prolog-like rewriting engine and a set of constraint solvers: a unification solver, a linear equation solver, a linear inequality solver, and a non-linear solver, together with an interface which translates constraints into a canonical form suitable for the constraint solvers. The constraint solvers are organized in a hierarchy: unification solver, direct evaluation/testing, linear equation solver and linear inequality solver, where the later solvers are more expensive to invoke than earlier ones. The interface sends constraints to the earliest solver in the hierarchy that can deal with the constraint. Thus a more expensive solver is only invoked when the previous solver in the hierarchy is not applicable. For example, when solving a linear equation, the linear equation solver is often sufficient and only when all the variables in the equation are involved in inequalities is it necessary to also use the inequality solver.

The current implementation of CLP($\mathcal{R}$) is a compiler. It translates into code for an abstract machine, the CLAM. This machine is an extension of the Prolog WAM architecture (see for example Aït-Kaci [1]) to deal with arithmetic constraints. Because the constraint solvers deal principally with linear constraints, the main arithmetic instructions in the CLAM construct the data structures representing linear arithmetic forms. These data structures are in a form which can be used directly by the constraint solvers. The constraint solving hierarchy used in the interpreter is retained but is more effective since some run-time decisions in the interpreter can now be shifted to compile-time.

To give a flavor of the CLAM (see [8] for details), let us describe the compilation of the constraint $5 + X = Y$. Assume that X is a new variable and the equation store contains $Y = Z + 3.14$. The following CLAM code could be generated:

```
initpf    5       lf :5
addpf_var 1,X     lf :5 + X
addpf_val -1,Y    lf :1.86 + X - Z
solve_eq0         solve :1.86 + X - Z = 0
```

On the left are the CLAM instructions while the right shows the effect on the constructed "linear form" (lf). The original constraint is rewritten into a linear canonical form, $5 + X - Y = 0$ to compile. The CLAM code executes as follows: First a new linear form is initialized to 5, and X, being a new variable, is added directly. Then Y is added which entails adding its linear form, $Z + 3.14$. After the first three instructions have constructed a linear form, the last solve_eq0 instruction is used to represent the equation $lf = 0$. In general the solve_eq0 may reduce to an assignment, a test or a call to the equation solver.

CLAM instructions operate below the level of a single constraint and can be optimized and combined in various ways. The highly optimizing compiler extends the earlier work on a *core CLAM* instruction set which is sufficient to execute a CLP($\mathcal{R}$) program together with some peephole optimizations and some rule level optimizations. For example, when we know that a constraint is always satisfiable, it may be possible to decide at compile-time how the constraint is to be represented in the constraint store at run-time and simply add that data structure.

3   Three Optimizations

In this section we present three powerful optimizations for CLP($\mathcal{R}$) programs using a worked example. Though we only informally justify the correctness of each of the optimization methods, global analysis methods (see Section 4) can be used to determine the applicability of each method. Consider the following CLP($\mathcal{R}$) program defining the relation *mortgage* where *mortgage*(p, t, r, mp, b) holds when p, t, r, mp, b respectively represent the principal, number of time periods, interest rate, payment and final balance of a loan.

```
(MG)                                  mortgage(P, T, R, MP, B) :-
                                         T >= 1,
                                         NT = T - 1,
mortgage(P, T, R, MP, B) :-              I = P * R,
   T = 0,                                NP = P + I - MP,
   P = B.                                mortgage(NP, NT, R, MP, B).
```

Solver Bypass. Often, by the time a constraint is encountered, it is a simple Boolean test or assignment. In that case a call to the solver can be replaced by the appropriate test or assignment. This both decreases the size of the constraint store and removes expensive calls to the solver. The optimization requires determining when variables are constrained to a unique value and when they are new to the solver.

Consider the execution of the goal $mortgage(p, t, r, mp, B)$ where p, t, r, mp are all fixed values. By replacing constraints with tests and assignments we can in fact remove all access to the constraint solver. This results in the following program:

```
(BYP)                                 mortgage(P, T, R, MP, B) :-
                                         test(T >= 1),
                                         assign(NT = T - 1),
mortgage(P, T, R, MP, B) :-              assign(I = P * R),
   test(T = 0),                          assign(NP = P + I - MP),
   assign(B = P).                        mortgage(NP, NT, R, MP, B).
```

Here the *test* wrapper causes the generation of code to evaluate the constraint, given values for all the variables and to check whether the appropriate relationship holds, while *assign* causes evaluation of the right-hand side as well as its assignment to the variable on the left. This may require equations to be re-arranged; here $P = B$ became $B = P$.

Removal of Dead Variables. A common source of redundancy in the constraint solver are variables which will never be referred to again, so-called *dead* variables. Execution can be improved by adding instructions that remove variables from the constraints currently in the store. This optimization requires determining which variables are still alive, that is, can be accessed later in the computation. One feature of the optimization is that usually it will not apply for all calling patterns of a predicate and thus the predicate definition has to be split, to utilize the benefits of variable removal.

Consider the original program (MG) and the variable P in the second clause. After the constraint $NP = P + I - MP$, the variable is never again referred to within the clause. If it is not required after the call, it can be removed at this point. Examining the recursive call $mg(NP, NT, R, MP, B)$, we note that the variable NP is never referred to again. Similar arguments apply to the variable NT. Hence we can optimize the program by giving two versions of the clauses— one for when the variables P and T may be referred to later (mortgage), and one when they are not (`mortgage_1`). For the second set of clauses we can remove the variables *P* and *T* from the solver after their last occurrence. This is indicated by the wrappers of the form *dead(var)*. This reduces the number of variables and constraints in the solver.

(REV)

```
mortgage(P, T, R, MP, B) :-        mortgage_1(P, T, R, MP, B) :-
    T = 0,                             dead(T)(T = 0),
    P = B.                             dead(P)(P = B).
mortgage(P, T, R, MP, B) :-        mortgage_1(P, T, R, MP, B) :-
    T >= 1,                            T >= 1,
    NT = T - 1,                        dead(T)(NT = T - 1),
    I = P * R,                         I = P * R,
    NP = P + I - MP,                   dead(P)(NP = P + I - MP),
    mortgage_1(NP, NT, R, MP, B).      mortgage_1(NP, NT, R, MP, B).
```

Nofail Constraint Detection. Sometimes, when a new constraint is encountered, it can be guaranteed not to fail because of the presence of new variables. The solver can use this to solve the constraint quickly, but there is still an overhead in detecting the possibility and manipulating the constraint into the required form. If the information about new variables is collected at compile-time, we can produce specialized CLAM instructions that reduce the overhead. Consider the example equation from Section 2, $5 + X = Y$. If X is new, the equation can never cause failure and we can produce more efficient code.

For the mortgage program there are several cases of "nofail" behaviour. Adding *nofail* wrappers for these cases yields the following program, optimized for any possible goal:

(NOF)

```
                                   mortgage(P, T, R, MP, B) :-
                                       T >= 1,
                                       nofail(NT = T - 1),
mortgage(P, T, R, MP, B) :-            nofail(I = P * R),
    T = 0,                             nofail(NP = P + I - MP),
    P = B.                             mortgage(NP, NT, R, MP, B).
```

Combining the Optimizations. The three optimizations may interact. Sometimes two optimizations may be available on a single constraint, so an overall strategy is needed for their application. As an example, when a variable has a fixed value then its removal from the constraint solver is less important since there is no overhead in further constraint solving. Nofail optimizations can be replaced by assignments when the appropriate variables are fixed. Similarly the splitting caused by dead variable removal can often allow more solver bypass optimizations.

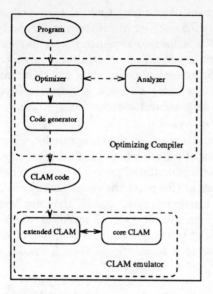

Fig. 1. The optimizing compiler

4　The Compiler

In the previous section we indicated how the key to faster execution of constraint logic languages lies with sophisticated compile-time optimizations. We now sketch the implementation of the optimizing CLP($\mathcal{R}$) compiler which performs these optimizations. The system currently consists of about 45,000 lines of C++ code.

The optimizing compiler has four distinct components : a *parser* which performs normalization and syntax analysis, an *optimizer* which takes a program as input and performs high-level optimizations, an *analyzer* which is used by the optimizer to determine applicability of the various optimizations, and a *code generator* which takes the output of the optimizer and translates it into CLAM code. One reason for this architecture is that it allows us to leverage from existing technologies and software. In particular, the CLAM emulator is an extension of that used in the first-generation CLP($\mathcal{R}$) compiler. We now discuss the three main components of the compiler (see also Figure 1).

The Analyzer

Analysis is formalized in terms of abstract interpretation [4]. Consider the idea of a constraint logic program interpreter which answers goals by returning not only a set of answer constraints, but also a thoroughly annotated version of the program: For each program point it lists the current constraint store for each time that point was reached during evaluation of the given query. Since control may return to a program point many times during evaluation, each annotation is naturally a (possibly infinite) set of constraints. Properly formalized, this idea leads to the notion of a *collecting semantics* which gives very precise dataflow information, but which is not finitely computable in general. However, if we replace the possibly infinite sets of constraints by conservative "approximations" or "descriptions" then we may obtain a dataflow analysis which works in finite time. This is the idea behind abstract interpretation of logic programs and constraint logic programs [5, 13].

As an example consider the mortgage program from Section 3. If this program is analyzed for the class of calls in which the first three arguments are bound to a number then the following annotated program results. The constraint description $\{X, Y, Z, \ldots\}$ is read as: at this point the constraint store constrains the variables X, Y, Z, $\ldots$ to take a unique value, that is, they are bound to a number. The two columns to the right give the set of variables which are ground after the corresponding statement in the program. The different columns occur because of different calling patterns to mortgage. The first annotation column results from the initial call.

	First Call	*Other Calls*
`mortgage(P, T, R, MP, B) :-`	$\{P, T, R\}$	$\{T, R\}$
`  T = 0,`	$\{P, T, R\}$	$\{T, R\}$
`  P = B.`	$\{P, T, R, B\}$	$\{T, R\}$
`mortgage(P, T, R, MP, B) :-`	$\{P, T, R\}$	$\{T, R\}$
`  T >= 1,`	$\{P, T, R\}$	$\{T, R\}$
`  NT = T - 1,`	$\{P, T, R, NT\}$	$\{T, R, NT\}$
`  I = P * R,`	$\{P, T, R, NT, I\}$	$\{T, R, NT\}$
`  NP = P + I - MP,`	$\{P, T, R, NT, I\}$	$\{T, R, NT\}$
`  mortgage(NP, NT, R, MP, B).`	$\{P, T, R, NT, I\}$	$\{T, R, NT\}$

For example, initially, when the second clause is entered, P, T, and R are ground. The statement `T >= 1` does not change this. After the statement `NT = T - 1`, as T is ground, NT becomes ground. Similarly, after `I = P * R`, I becomes ground. Nothing is changed by executing `NP = P + I - MP`. To analyze the effect of `mortgage(NP,NT,R,MP,B)` we need to know its effect for the new calling pattern in which only the second and third arguments are ground. This is detailed in the second column. This second calling pattern leads to a call with the same calling pattern, so the analysis stops. The analyzer implicitly returns this information as a *calling pattern graph*. The analyzer used in the compiler actually uses a more powerful description domain for determining groundness but we have used this simple domain to clarify the exposition.

To facilitate the rich variety of analyses required in the compiler, the analyzer is a generic tool similar to other analysis engines, such as PLAI [16] and GAIA [11] developed for Prolog. The core of the analyzer is an algorithm for efficient fixpoint computation. Efficiency is obtained by keeping track of which parts of a program must be reexamined when a success pattern is updated.

The role of the analyzer is to provide information which determines applicability of optimizations such as solver bypass, dead variable removal and nofail constraint removal. The main interface to the optimizer is by way of five functions which provide information for a given program point in some clause either for a single calling pattern to that clause, or for all such calling patterns. The functions respectively return: the list of *ground* variables (those constrained to take a unique value); the list of variables which are definitely *free* in the sense that they are only constrained to be equal to another variable; the list of variables which are *nofail* for a particular constraint in the sense that if this constraint is added to the solver then it cannot cause failure (they are free and not aliased to any other variable in the following constraint); the list of variables which are *dead* in the sense that they will not be referenced directly or indirectly in the future after the next constraint; the list of variables that are possibly *Herbrand*, and therefore, not candidates for arithmetic constraint optimisations. Groundness and freeness information is for determining applicability of the solver bypass optimization while nofail and dead variable information is used for nofail detection and dead variable removal respectively.

Another function in the interface of the analyzer is to split rules. For example after the preceding analysis, the optimizer might split mortgage into two different versions, one for each calling pattern. An important feature of the analyzer is that it is incremental in the sense that when a rule is split, the program is not reanalyzed from scratch, but rather analysis information for the original rule is used to give information for the new rule. This is unlike most generic Prolog analyzers which are non-incremental.

Details of the description domains used by the analyzer to provide information about freeness, groundness, nofailness and deadness are deliberately kept insulated from the optimizer, so as to make it easier to change these. Currently the analyzer works on descriptions which are tuples of 6 different domains.

The first description domain, *Pos*, consists of Boolean functions which capture groundness information about variables and definite dependencies among variables, see for example [2]. For example the function $X \wedge (Y \rightarrow Z)$ indicates that the variable X is constrained to take a unique value, and that if Y is ever constrained to a unique value, then so is Z. Our implementation uses ROBDDs to represent the Boolean functions.

The second description domain, *Free*, captures information about "freeness". It is based on the descriptions used by Debray [6] for the optimization of Prolog unification. Each description consists of a list of definitely free variables and an equivalence relation which captures possible "aliasing" between free variables. For example, the description after processing the constraints $X = Y \wedge Z = W$ is that X, Y Z and W are free and that X and Y are possibly aliases and Z and W are possibly aliases. If $Z = f(Y)$ is now encountered, the description is that X and Y are free and that they are possibly aliases. The implementation uses a Boolean matrix to represent the alias relation.

The third description domain, *CallAlive*, consists of lists of variables which are possibly still "textually alive". For example, in the goal $X = 1, p(X, Y), q(Y)$, both X and Y are initially textually alive, for the call $p(X, Y)$ only Y is alive. For the call $q(Y)$ no variables are textually alive.

Unfortunately, not being textually alive may not mean a variable is dead, for two reasons. The first reason is "structure sharing" between terms. If a textually non-alive variable shares with a term that contains textually alive variables, then it may not be dead. For example, consider the variable X in the goal $Y = f(X), p(X), Y = f(Z), q(Z)$. Here the variable X may be accessed in the call to $q(Z)$ by means of Z. The second reason is that "hard" constraints such as non-linear equations are delayed by the constraint solver until they become simple enough to solve. This means that variables in hard constraints may be alive until the time we can guarantee the constraint is simple enough to be solved in the linear constraint solver. For example, consider X in goal $X = Y * Z, Y = 1$. Even though X does not appear after $X = Y * Z$ it will be accessed in the linear constraint solver after processing $Y = 1$ as when Y is grounded, essentially the constraint $X = 1 * Z$ is added to the linear solver. For these reasons the analyzer has two more description domains which provide information about dead variables.

The fourth description domain, $Shar$, captures information about possible sharing of variables between Prolog terms. It is based on descriptions introduced by Søndergaard [17] for eliminating occur checks in Prolog. The description consists of a possible sharing relation for variables. Consider again the goal $Y = f(X), p(X), Y = f(Z), q(Z)$. After $Y = f(X)$, X and Y possibly share, but Z does not share with anything else. After $Y = f(Z)$, all variables possibly share. Note that arithmetic constraints do not cause sharing to take place. A special variable $\perp$ represents "hidden" alive variables. Thus if a variable shares with $\perp$ it cannot be dead.

The fifth description domain, $NonLin$, consists of lists of variables which are possibly contained in a delayed non-linear. When a non-linear is first encountered, groundness information is used to check if it is definitely linear. If it is not, then the analyzer assumes it is non-linear and adds its variables to the $NonLin$ list. For instance, in mortgage, when the statement I = P * R is reached with R ground, the analyzer will determine that I = P * R is linear, so no variables will be added. If none of I, P or R were ground then all three variables would be added to the $NonLin$ list. A variable in the $NonLin$ list is never dead[3].

The sixth description domain, $Type$, captures information about whether a variable is definitely arithmetic or possibly Herbrand. The implementation maintains two lists of variables. More accurate type information can be obtained by keeping track of aliasing between variables for cases like X = Y when no type information is known about X or Y. It is expected that this can be done efficiently by integrating type analysis with freeness analysis.

As a real example of the analyzer's use, consider the analysis of the mortgage program for queries of the form

P = α, T = β, R = γ, MP <= δ, mortgage(P,T,R,MP,B).

where α, β, γ and δ are constants. The description consists of a tuple of the four descriptions: Pos, $Free$, $CallAlive$ and $Shar$. The descriptions $NonLin$

---

[3] Note that this is a simplification of the approach of [12]

and *Type* have been omitted for simplicity as they are not significant for this example. The initial calling pattern, CP_0, is:

$$\langle P \wedge T \wedge R, \{B\}, \{P, T, R, MP, B\}, \emptyset, \emptyset \rangle$$

where $P \wedge T \wedge R$ indicates that P, R, T are ground, $\{B\}$ that B is free, $\{P, T, R, MP, B\}$ that P, T, R, MP, and B are textually alive and the last two components that there is no sharing and that no variables are involved in non-linears. The annotated program points in mortgage for calling pattern CP_0 are:

```
mortgage(P,T,R,MP,B) :-                 ⟨P ∧ T ∧ R, {B}, {P, T, R, MP, B}, ∅⟩
   T = 0,                               ⟨P ∧ T ∧ R, {B}, {P, T, R, MP, B}, ∅⟩
   P = B.                          ⟨P ∧ T ∧ R ∧ B, ∅, {P, T, R, MP, B}, {(B, P)}⟩
```

```
mortgage(P,T,R,MP,B) :-   ⟨P ∧ T ∧ R, {B, NT, NP, I}, {P, T, R, MP, NT, NP, B, I}, ∅⟩
   T >= 1,                ⟨P ∧ T ∧ R, {B, NT, NP, I}, {P, T, R, MP, NT, NP, B, I}, ∅⟩
   NT = T - 1,            ⟨P ∧ T ∧ R ∧ NT, {B, NP, I}, {P, T, R, MP, NT, NP, B, I}, ∅⟩
   I = P * R,             ⟨P ∧ T ∧ R ∧ NT ∧ I, {B, NP}, {P, T, R, MP, NT, NP, B, I}, ∅⟩
   NP = P + I - MP,    ⟨P ∧ T ∧ R ∧ NT ∧ I ∧ (MP ↔ NP), {B}, {P, T, R, MP, NT, NP, B}, ∅⟩
   mortgage(NP,NT,R,MP,B).  ⟨P ∧ T ∧ R ∧ (MP → B), ∅, {P, T, R, MP, B}, {(B, P), (B, ⊥)}⟩
```

At the end of a clause, local variables are uninteresting, so we have restricted the last annotation accordingly. From the annotation immediately before the last, we see that the calling pattern CP_0 generates a new calling pattern CP_1:

$$\langle T \wedge R \wedge (MP \leftrightarrow P), \{B\}, \{R, MP, B\}, \emptyset, \emptyset \rangle.$$

In turn, CP_1 generates the calling pattern CP_2:

$$\langle T \wedge R \wedge (MP \rightarrow P), \{B\}, \{R, MP, B\}, \emptyset, \emptyset \rangle$$

which generates itself. We will not go through details of the analysis for these subsequent calling patterns. After the analysis terminates it stores information about the relationship between calling patterns for the head of a clause and the calling patterns for each body atom in the clause. This defines a calling pattern graph similar to the predicate call graph of the program, but containing calling pattern information. The optimizer will use this graph to order the processing of predicates and calling patterns. In particular the optimizer will examine entire strongly connected components (SCCs) of this graph one by one. The call graph and calling pattern graph for the example are shown in Figure 2.

The Optimizer

The optimizer examines the clauses of the program and where possible performs optimizations upon them. It finds where this is possible by querying the analyzer about which variables are free, ground, dead, and nofail at the various program points for the calling patterns of interest. The optimizations are performed by re-writing the clauses to include specialized rather than generic primitives.

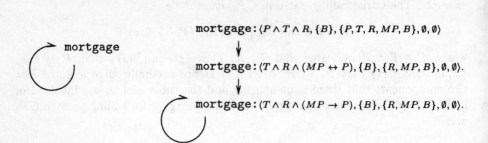

Program Call Graph   Calling Pattern Graph

mortgage: $\langle P \wedge T \wedge R, \{B\}, \{P, T, R, MP, B\}, \emptyset, \emptyset\rangle$

mortgage: $\langle T \wedge R \wedge (MP \leftrightarrow P), \{B\}, \{R, MP, B\}, \emptyset, \emptyset\rangle.$

mortgage: $\langle T \wedge R \wedge (MP \rightarrow P), \{B\}, \{R, MP, B\}, \emptyset, \emptyset\rangle.$

Fig. 2. Call graph and calling pattern graph for mortgage

The modified program is written in an intermediate language called CLIC, for Constraint Logic Intermediate Code. This language is a superset of CLP($\mathcal{R}$) which allows for non-logical commands, including the wrappers already introduced. Thus, the compiler is in fact a CLIC source-to-source transformer with a CLAM-generating back-end. CLIC can be considered a hybrid imperative-logic programming language which could be useful (if dangerous) for writing efficient constraint programs.

The optimizer examines and optimizes each strongly connected component (SCC) in the program call graph in turn. SCCs are examined from the bottom up, so that predicates at the bottom of the call graph are optimized first. This decision implements the heuristic that optimizations at a lower level are likely to be more important than at a higher level since low level predicates are (in general) executed more frequently. In general, optimizations made for one predicate may prevent optimizations in other predicates, but for the optimizations currently implemented in the compiler this is not the case since none of the optimizations can change calling patterns.

When optimizing the clauses in a single SCC, the optimizer first performs optimizations which are valid for all calling patterns of each predicate. It scans each clause, examining each constraint for possible optimizations. Also if an atom (defined in a lower SCC) is present in the clause which is always called using a calling pattern for which the optimizer has created a specialized version, the atom is replaced by a call to the specialized version. Where competing optimizations are available they are currently handled as follows: *assign* and *test* are preferred to *nofail* and *dead*. Thus for example a *dead* wrapper will not be added in cases where the dead variable is always ground. This decision is based on the effects of the optimizations in the run-time system. Removing a fixed dead variable will not increase the speed of future constraint solving, but will cause extra overhead if backtracking occurs, and using assignment is preferable to *nofail* since assignment does not involve the solver at all.

We now detail how mortgage is optimized for queries of the form

`P = α, T = β, R = γ, MP <= δ, mortgage(P,T,R,MP,B).`

where α, β, γ and δ are constants. We first perform optimizations which are valid for all three calling patterns. Information from the analyzer tells the optimizer that T is ground before the constraint `T = 0`. Hence it can be made a test. Similarly, `T >= 1` can be made a test. In general, any constraint in which all variables are ground, can be made into a test. Next the constraint `NT = T - 1` is considered. It can be made into an assignment because the analyzer gives the information that NT is free in all calling patterns and T is ground in all calling patterns. In general, for an equation to be made an assignment it must have one free variable that can be put on the left-hand side, and all other variables ground. The optimizer can re-arrange linear equalities, so that the optimization is applicable when any one variable is free. For multiplication the variable on the left must be free to start with, as they have a standard form $Y = X * Z$. The analyzer gives the information that NP is nofail for the constraint `NP = P + I - R`. This is because NP is free and shares with no other variables in the constraint. Similarly the constraint `B = P` is found to be a nofail[4]. The resulting program is

(OPT-ALL)

```
mortgage(P, T, R, MP, B) :-
    test(T = 0),
    nofail(B = P).
```

```
mortgage(P, T, R, MP, B) :-
    test(T >= 1),
    assign(NT = T - 1),
    I = P * R,
    nofail(NP = P + I - MP),
    mortgage(NP, NT, R, MP, B).
```

Next the calling pattern graph is examined. If there are multiple calling patterns for any predicates in the SCC of the call graph under consideration, the optimizer examines each SCC of the calling pattern graph in turn, again bottom up. If, for the particular calling pattern, new optimizations are available, either because a new constraint optimization is possible, or an atom may be replaced with a more specific version, the optimizer creates a new version of the predicate for this specific calling pattern. This operation will be performed whenever any new optimization is made possible by splitting. This means optimization of one constraint can cause many splits, as the divergence in calling patterns that allow the optimization may be some way up the call graph.

Once the optimizer has determined that a predicate must be split, it constructs a new copy of the code — containing the optimizations already made for all calling patterns — and optimizes this code further. Analysis information for the new code is extracted from the original. In general some reanalysis may be required, but for the optimizations dealt with by the current compiler, no new analysis is required. New split predicates may allow new optimizations of other predicates, so for maximum improvement we should continue the process

---

[4] Note that the equation `I = P * R` could be made a nofail constraint except the run-time system does not currently support nofail non-linear constraints.

of splitting and optimizing until a fixpoint is reached. However, for simplicity, the optimizer presently examine each calling pattern once only.

In our example, the initial call has given the calling pattern SCC detailed in the last subsection. Examining the SCC for the lowest calling pattern and the first clause, the analyzer will give the information that for this calling pattern, P is dead. This means the optimizer can modify the constraint *nofail*(B = P) to *dead*(P)(*nofail*(B=P)). Hence it will split a new copy of the code for this calling pattern. After optimization, the optimizer gives

(OPT-CP2)

```
mortgage$CP2(P, T, R, MP, B) :-     mortgage$CP2(P, T, R, MP, B) :-
  test(T = 0),                        test(T >= 1),
  dead(P)(nofail(B = P)).             assign(NT = T - 1),
                                      I = P * R,
                                      dead(P)(nofail(NP = P + I - MP)),
                                      mortgage$CP2(NP, NT, R, MP, B).
```

Note that the recursive call is updated to call mortgage$CP2 since when it is examined the clause, the more specific version has been created.

Next the SCC for the middle calling pattern, CP1, is examined. It gives a new version identical to **(OPT-CP2)**, except that the head predicates are called mortgage$CP1. At present the compiler will not collapse these two versions, however in the future it will do so.

Now the SCC for the top calling pattern is examined. The analyzer gives the information that for the top calling pattern, P is ground. Therefore the optimizer further optimizes both B = P and I = P * R. Similarly, the call to mortgage in the body now has a specialized version that can be used. The resulting code is

(OPT-CP0)

```
mortgage$CP0(P, T, R, MP, B) :-     mortgage$CP0(P, T, R, MP, B) :-
  test(T = 0),                        test(T >= 1),
  assign(B = P).                      assign(NT = T - 1),
                                      assign(I = P * R),
                                      nofail(NP = P + I - MP),
                                      mortgage$CP1(NP, NT, R, MP, B).
```

Note that *nofail* and *dead* wrappers have been replaced by *assign* in the first clause, and a *dead* declaration removed in the second clause, since the variable P is now always ground.

The final step in the optimization of the program is to examine the goal which can now be specialized to execute using mortgage$CP0.

$$P = \alpha, \ T = \beta, \ R = \gamma, \ MP <= \delta, \ \text{mortgage\$CP0(P,T,R,MP,B)}.$$

where α, β, γ and δ are constants.

There are many more interesting and valuable optimizations that we plan to incorporate in the compiler, requiring more analysis domains and considerable implementation effort, among them future redundancy, constraint removal, mutual exclusion and determinacy [15].

Code Generator and Emulator

The code generator maps the CLIC code into CLAM [8] instructions which are executed by the CLAM emulator. The original CLP($\mathcal{R}$) compiler also produced CLAM code, but used only a core set. The new compiler makes use of extended CLAM instructions for achieving the optimizations that are made possible by global analysis. The CLAM architecture is suited to this as it operates below the level of a constraint and the optimizations described all require modifying the operation of constraint solving to be effective and thus slot neatly with the rest of the CLAM architecture.

We will give an overview of what the extended CLAM instructions look like rather than describe them in detail. Solver bypass adds instructions which are like traditional arithmetic and conditional instructions on conventional architectures. These operate directly on "unboxed" floating point values, called fp_vals, whereas most of the values in the CLAM (like the WAM) are tagged and may represent bindings. The core instruction set for solver bypass is as follows:

getf[5] V, FP	Convert a solver variable V to an fp_val FP, where V must be fixed.
putf FP, V	Convert an fp_val FP to a solver variable V
mvf FP_1, FP_2	Move one fp_val to another: $FP_2 := FP_1$
addf FP_1, FP_2, FP_3	Add fp_vals: $FP_3 := FP_1 + FP_2$
subf, mulf, divf	Similar: subtract, multiply, divide
addcf FP_1, c, FP_2	Add a constant to an fp_val: $FP_2 := FP_1 + c$
mulcf	Similar, for multiplication
jeqf FP, L	Jump to label L if FP is zero
jgtf, jgef, jltf, jlef	Similar jumps

Dead variable removal is handled by the emulator by a number of different kinds of instructions indicating a variable can be removed. All of them are only advisory to the run-time system, so it is not guaranteed that a variable is removed when an instruction indicates it. Depending upon the internal form of constraints in the solver, a variable may be *non-parametric*, that is, present in exactly one equation, or *parametric*, present in many equations. In the first case removing the variable is easy and inexpensive, simply consisting of removing the equation from the constraint store. In the second case the removal may incur significant extra overhead, in some cases as much as adding a new equation. In the current implementation we only perform non-parametric removal.

There are several possibilities for removing dead variables, using different CLAM instructions. Removing variable V is accomplished by dead_var_elim V. More efficient execution can be achieved by removing a dead variable while constructing the last constraint in which it appears. In order to do this, new constraint construction CLAM instructions have been added that also remove

---

[5] Presently the code generator does not make use of a special representation for fp_vals, hence the solver bypass optimizations do not gain as much as they should, and getf and putf are not used.

the variable, for example, addpf_val_elim c, V which adds $c \times V$ to the linear form accumulator and then deletes V. Even more efficiency can be gained if a variable V can be deleted and its equation used as the basis for constructing a new constraint. To do so we add an instruction initpf_var_elim c_0, c_1, V. If V is non-parametric appearing in an equation $V := t$, this instruction initializes the linear form accumulator to contain $c_0 + c_1 \times t$ using a destructive update of the linear form t. If V is parametric it acts like initpf c_0, addpf_val c_1, V.

Nofail constraints are compiled into CLAM instructions that simply build a linear form and add it to the solver without expensive substitution steps. Consider the example equation from Section 2, $5 + X = Y$. If X is a new variable the optimizer re-writes the equation to $nofail(X = -5 + Y)$ and generates the following code:

```
initpf          -5      lf: -5
addpf_val        1, Y   lf: -1.86 + Z
solve_nofail_eq0 X      sets : X = -1.86 + Z
```

The right-hand side shows how the CLAM instructions on the left execute, assuming the solver contains the equation $Y = Z + 3.14$. The first two instructions build the linear form equivalent to $-5 + Y$, while the last instruction simply adds the equation to the solver. As X does not appear elsewhere in the solver, no further actions are required to maintain the solved form.

5   Empirical Results

To illustrate the effect of the optimizations, we show the effect on a number of different programs and goals. Execution times are in CPU seconds using a modified version of CLP($\mathcal{R}$) v1.1 on a Sparc 1000. The speedup ratios are given with respect to the original unoptimized program. The space originally used by the constraint solver (measured in solver nodes = 6 words) is given together with the percentage used by the optimised programs. The set of benchmarks programs and goals are shown in Table 1.

Table 2 shows some of the characteristics of these programs. The programs have been used a number of different goals which execute and optimize differently.

Table 3 shows the effect of the optimizations, comparing the optimized code with and without splitting versus unoptimised code. We see across-the-board improvements in time and space. In the best case (sumlist-var) the results can be asymptotically better. The table also shows the advantage of splitting predicate definitions. In particular, whenever significant dead variable optimizations are applicable, the split version is markedly better. Note that the increase in code size, even with the current naive splitting strategy, is acceptable.

mg-*work*	The worked mortgage example of the paper
mg-*gnd*	The ground mortgage example of Section 3
fib-*forw*	Naively computes Fibonacci numbers forward
fib-*back*	and backward
sumlist-*gnd*	Adds up numbers from a list
sumlist-*var*	Adds up variables from a list (300 elements), then grounds them
mg-extend	Handles complex mortgages with provisions for a number of payments per month and special initial conditions and provisos
matmul	Multiplying matrices
ladder	Analyzes electrical ladder circuits
ode	A simple ordinary differential equation solver
circuit	Performs simple circuit analysis
neural	A neural net training program
bridge	Generates a finite element model of a bridge

Table 1. Benchmark descriptions

	Clauses	Literals	Max vars in a clause	Total vars in program
mg-*work*	3	16	7	17
mg-*gnd*	3	15	7	16
fib-*forw*	5	18	5	11
fib-*back*	5	17	5	11
sumlist-*gnd*	7	23	4	15
sumlist-*var*	9	24	4	17
mg-extend	11	48	15	64
matmul	13	45	9	55
ladder	22	140	22	173
ode	31	111	20	173
circuit	34	102	20	138
neural	81	259	13	258
bridge	89	446	22	549

Table 2. Characteristics of programs in the test suite

6   Conclusion

The current compiler is a partial implementation of the compiler proposed in [14]. The results demonstrate that global analysis and optimization can significantly improve the performance of CLP languages. Even without complete run-time support for the optimizations we gain considerably in terms of space and time of execution. We expect to improve these results significantly in the near future.

Query	Original space use	Without splitting		With splitting		
		Speedup	Space (%)	Literals	Speedup	Space (%)
mg-*work*	3626	1.7	70	23 (1.4)	1.7	70
mg-*gnd*	2169	1.9	100	22 (1.5)	2.2	100
fib-*forw*	62608	2.4	54	38 (2.1)	2.6	46
fib-*back*	60840	1.2	100	57 (3.2)	1.7	61
sumlist-*gnd*	18005	1.1	100	33 (1.4)	1.6	56
sumlist-*var*	137559	1.0	100	63 (2.6)	49.2	2
mg-extend	36392	1.5	64	79 (1.6)	1.5	64
matmul	60840	1.8	100	68 (1.5)	1.8	61
ladder	8075	1.2	70	174 (1.2)	1.2	70
ode	22013	1.4	100	136 (1.2)	1.4	100
circuit	1346	1.5	68	211 (2.1)	1.6	66
neural	9319	1.2	90	426 (1.6)	1.3	75
bridge	33690	2.2	100	446 (1.0)	2.2	100

Table 3. Impact of optimizations (time in seconds, space in solver nodes)

This is the first implementation of a constraint logic programming system that makes use of global analysis and performs optimizations of arithmetic constraint solving. Only one other logic programming compiler that we are aware of uses such complex analysis domains and transformations (the &-Prolog compiler [3]). It is also the only system we are aware of which splits predicate definitions to allow more optimization, although using a completely different splitting strategy.

The proposed compiler includes several optimizations which the current implementation does not provide and which we intend to implement. These include transforming mutually exclusive rules into if-then-else statements if the arithmetic tests are mutually exclusive or into indexing instructions for mutually exclusive Prolog terms. We also plan to provide removal of arithmetic inequality constraints and reordering of constraints in rule bodies. Finally we plan to improve the optimizer's handling of splitting, so that it will generate all appropriate versions, and collapse versions when they are indistinguishable.

References

1. H. Aït-Kaci. *Warren's Abstract Machine: A Tutorial Reconstruction.* MIT Press, 1991.
2. T. Armstrong, K. Marriott, P. Schachte and H. Søndergaard. Boolean functions for dependency analysis: Algebraic properties and efficient representation. In B. Le Charlier, editor, *Static Analysis: Proc. First Int. Symp.* (Lecture Notes in Computer Science 864), pages 266–280. Springer-Verlag, 1994.

3. F. Bueno, M. García de la Banda and M. Hermenegildo. Effectiveness of global analysis in strict independence-based automatic parallelization. In *Logic Programming: Proc. 1994 Int. Symp.*, pages 320–336. MIT Press, 1994.

4. P. Cousot and R. Cousot. Abstract interpretation: A unified lattice model for static analysis of programs by construction or approximation of fixpoints. In *Proc. Fourth Ann. ACM Symp. Principles of Programming Languages*, pages 238–252. ACM Press, 1977.

5. P. Cousot and R. Cousot. Abstract interpretation and application to logic programs. *Journal of Logic Programming* **13** (2&3): 103–179, 1992.

6. S. Debray. Static inference of modes and data dependencies in logic programs. *ACM Transactions on Programming Languages and Systems* **11** (3): 418–450, 1989.

7. J. Jaffar and M. Maher. Constraint logic programming: A survey. *Journal of Logic Programming* **19/20**: 503–581, 1994.

8. J. Jaffar, S. Michaylov, P. Stuckey and R. Yap. An abstract machine for CLP($\mathcal{R}$). *Proc. ACM Conf. Programming Language Design and Implementation*, pages 128–139. ACM Press, 1992.

9. J. Jaffar, S. Michaylov, P. Stuckey and R. Yap. The CLP($\mathcal{R}$) language and system. *ACM Transactions on Programming Languages and Systems* **14** (3): 339–395, 1992.

10. N. Jørgensen, K. Marriott and S. Michaylov. Some global compile-time optimizations for CLP($\mathcal{R}$). In V. Saraswat and K. Ueda, editors, *Logic Programming: Proc. 1991 Int. Symp.*, pages 420–434. MIT Press, 1991.

11. B. Le Charlier and P. Van Hentenryck. Experimental evaluation of a generic abstract interpretation algorithm for Prolog. *ACM Transactions on Programming Languages and Systems* **16** (1): 35–101, 1994.

12. A. Macdonald, P. Stuckey and R. Yap. Redundancy of variables in CLP($\mathcal{R}$). In *Logic Programming: Proc. 1993 Int. Symp.*, pages 75–93. MIT Press, 1993.

13. K. Marriott and H. Søndergaard. Analysis of constraint logic programs. In S. Debray and M. Hermenegildo, *Logic Programming: Proc. North American Conf. 1990*, pages 531–547. MIT Press, 1990.

14. K. Marriott, H. Søndergaard, P. Stuckey and R. Yap. Optimizing compilation for CLP($\mathcal{R}$). In G. Gupta, editor, Proc. Seventeenth Australian Computer Science Conf., *Australian Computer Science Comm.* **16** (1): 551–560, 1994.

15. K. Marriott and P. Stuckey. The 3 R's of optimizing constraint logic programs: Refinement, removal and reordering. *Proc. Twentieth ACM Symp. Principles of Programming Languages*, pages 334–344. ACM Press, 1993.

16. K. Muthukumar and M. Hermenegildo. Compile-time derivation of variable dependency using abstract interpretation. *Journal of Logic Programming* **13** (2&3): 315–347, 1992.

17. H. Søndergaard. An application of abstract interpretation of logic programs: Occur check reduction. In B. Robinet and R. Wilhelm, editors, *Proc. ESOP 86* (Lecture Notes in Computer Science 213), pages 327–338. Springer-Verlag, 1986.

18. A. Taylor. LIPS on a MIPS: Results from a Prolog compiler for a RISC. In D. Warren and P. Szeredi, editors, *Logic Programming: Proc. Seventh Int. Conf.*, pages 174–185. MIT Press, 1990.

19. P. van Roy and A. Despain. The benefits of global dataflow analysis for an optimizing Prolog compiler. In S. Debray and M. Hermenegildo, editors, *Logic Programming: Proc. North American Conf. 1990*, pages 501–515. MIT Press, 1990.

Local and Global Relational Consistency

Rina Dechter[1] and Peter van Beek[2]

[1] Department of Information and Computer Science
University of California, Irvine
Irvine, California, USA 92717
dechter@ics.uci.edu
[2] Department of Computing Science
University of Alberta
Edmonton, Alberta, Canada T6G 2H1
vanbeek@cs.ualberta.ca

Abstract. Local consistency has proven to be an important concept in the theory and practice of constraint networks. In this paper, we present a new definition of local consistency, called *relational consistency*. The new definition is *relation-based,* in contrast with the previous definition of local consistency, which we characterize as variable-based. It allows the unification of known elimination operators such as resolution in theorem proving, joins in relational databases and variable elimination for solving linear inequalities. We show the usefulness and conceptual power of the new definition in characterizing relationships between four properties of constraints— domain tightness, row-convexity, constraint tightness, and constraint looseness—and the level of local consistency needed to ensure global consistency. As well, algorithms for enforcing relational consistency are introduced and analyzed.

1   Introduction

Constraint networks are a simple representation and reasoning framework. A problem is represented as a set of variables, a domain of values for each variable, and a set of constraints between the variables. A central reasoning task is then to find an instantiation of the variables that satisfies the constraints.

In general, what makes constraint networks hard to solve is that they can contain many local inconsistencies. A local inconsistency is a consistent instantiation of $k - 1$ of the variables that cannot be extended to a kth variable and so cannot be part of any global solution. If we are using a backtracking search to find a solution, such an inconsistency can lead to a dead end in the search. This insight has led to the definition of conditions that characterize the level of local consistency of a network [17, 20] and to the development of algorithms for enforcing local consistency conditions by removing local inconsistencies (e.g., [3, 7, 11, 17, 20]).

In this paper, we present a new definition of local consistency called *relational consistency*, introduced recently [24]. We show the usefulness and conceptual power of the new definition in generalizing results for binary networks to non-binary networks on the relationships between four properties of constraints— row-convexity, domain sizes, constraint tightness, and constraint looseness— and the level of local consistency needed to ensure global consistency. As well, algorithms for enforcing relational consistency are introduced and analyzed.

The virtue of the new definition of local consistency is that, firstly, it allows expressing the relationships between the properties of the constraints and local consistency in a way that avoids an explicit reference to the arity of the constraints. Secondly, it is operational, thus generalizing the concept of the composition operation defined for binary constraints, and can be incorporated naturally in algorithms for enforcing desired levels of relational consistency. Thirdly, it unifies known operators such as resolution in theorem proving, joins in relational databases, and variable elimination for solving equations and inequalities. In particular it allows the formulation of an elimination algorithm that generalizes algorithms appearing in each of these areas. Finally, it allows identifying those formalisms for which consistency can be decided by enforcing a bounded level of consistency, like propositional databases and linear equalities and inequalities, from general databases requiring higher levels of local consistency. For space considerations almost all proofs are omitted.

2 Definitions and Preliminaries

Definition 1 constraint network. A *constraint network* $\mathcal{R}$ is a set X of n variables $\{x_1, \ldots, x_n\}$, a domain D_i of possible values for each variable, and a set of relations $R_{S_1}, \ldots, R_{S_t}$, each defined on a subset of the variables $S_1, \ldots, S_t$, respectively. A *constraint* or relation R_S over a set of variables $S = \{x_1, \ldots, x_r\}$ is a subset of the product of their domains (i.e., $R_S \subseteq D_1 \times \cdots \times D_r$). The set of subsets $\{S_1, \ldots, S_t\}$ on which constraints are specified is called the *scheme* of $\mathcal{R}$. A *binary constraint network* is the special case where all constraints are over pairs of variables. An *instantiation* of the variables in X, denoted X_I, is an n-tuple $(a_1, \ldots, a_n)$, representing an assignment of $a_i \in D_i$ to x_i. A *consistent instantiation* of a network is an instantiation of the variables such that the constraints between variables are satisfied. A consistent instantiation is also called a *solution*.

The notion of a consistent instantiation of a subset of the variables can be defined in several ways. We use the following definition: an instantiation is consistent if it satisfies all of the constraints that have no uninstantiated variables.

Definition 2 consistent instantiation of subsets of variables. Let Y and S be sets of variables, and let Y_I be an instantiation of the variables in Y. We denote by $Y_I[S]$ the tuple consisting of only the components of Y_I that correspond to the variables in S. An instantiation Y_I is *consistent* relative to a network $\mathcal{R}$ iff for all S_i in the scheme of $\mathcal{R}$ such that $S_i \subseteq Y$, $Y_I[S_i] \in R_{S_i}$. The set of all consistent instantiations of the variables in Y is denoted $\rho(Y)$. One can view $\rho(Y)$ as the set of all solutions of the subnetwork defined by Y.

Definition 3 operations on constraints. Let R be a relation on a set S of variables, let $Y \subseteq S$ be a subset of the variables, and let Y_I be an instantiation of the variables in Y. We denote by $\sigma_{Y_I}(R)$ the selection of those tuples in R that agree with Y_I. We denote by $\Pi_Y(R)$ the projection of the relation R on the subset Y; that is, a tuple over Y appears in $\Pi_Y(R)$ if and only if it can be extended to a full tuple in R. Let R_{S_1} be a relation on a set S_1 of variables and let R_{S_2} be a relation on a set S_2 of variables. We denote by $R_{S_1} \bowtie R_{S_2}$ the join of the two relations. A tuple t is in the join of R_{S_1} and R_{S_2} if it can be constructed by the following steps: (i) take a tuple r from R_{S_1}, (ii) select a tuple s from R_{S_2} such that the components of r and s agree on the variables that R_{S_1} and R_{S_2} have in common (that is, on the variables $S_1 \cap S_2$), and (iii) form the tuple t by combining the components of r and s, keeping only one copy of components that correspond to variables that the original relations R_{S_1} and R_{S_2} have in common. The resulting relation is on the set of variables given by $S_1 \cup S_2$.

A binary relation R_{ij} between variables x_i and x_j can be represented as a $(0,1)$-matrix with $|D_i|$ rows and $|D_j|$ columns by imposing an ordering on the domains of the variables. A zero entry at row a, column b means that the pair consisting of the ath element of D_i and the bth element of D_j is not permitted; a one entry means that the pair is permitted.

Four properties of constraints central to this paper are domain-tightness, row-convexity, constraint tightness, and constraint looseness.

Definition 4 k-valued domains. A network of constraints is k-valued if the domain sizes of all variables are bounded by k.

Definition 5 row convex constraints. A binary constraint is *row convex* if in every row of the $(0,1)$-matrix representation of the constraint, all of the ones are consecutive; that is, no two ones within a single row are separated by a zero in that same row. A binary constraint network is row convex if all its binary constraints are row convex.

Definition 6 m-tight binary constraints. A binary constraint is *m-tight* if every row and every column of the $(0,1)$-matrix representation of the constraint has at most m ones, where $0 \leq m \leq |D| - 1$. Rows and columns with exactly $|D|$ ones are ignored in determining m. A binary constraint network is m-tight if all its binary constraints are m-tight.

Definition 7 m-loose binary constraints. A binary constraint is *m-loose* if every row and every column of the $(0,1)$-matrix representation of the constraint has at least m ones, where $0 \leq m \leq |D| - 1$. A binary constraint network is m-loose if all its binary constraints are m-loose.

Definition 8 row convex, m-tight, and m-loose general constraints. An r-ary relation R on a set S of variables $\{x_1, \ldots, x_r\}$ is *row convex* (*m-tight, m-loose*, respectively) if for every subset of $r - 2$ variables $Y \subseteq S$ and for every instantiation Y_I of the variables in Y, the binary relation $\Pi_{(S-Y)}(\sigma_{Y_I}(R))$ is row convex (m-tight, m-loose, respectively).

Example 1. We illustrate the definitions using the following network $\mathcal{R}$ over the set X of variables $\{x_1, x_2, x_3, x_4\}$. The network is 3-valued. The domains of the variables are $D_i = \{a,b,c\}$ and the relations are given by,

$$R_{S_1} = \{(a,a,a),\ (a,a,c),\ (a,b,c),\ (a,c,b),\ (b,a,c),$$
$$(b,b,b),\ (b,c,a),\ (c,a,b),\ (c,b,a),\ (c,c,c)\},$$
$$R_{S_2} = \{(a,b),\ (b,a),\ (b,c),\ (c,a),\ (c,c)\},$$
$$R_{S_3} = \{(a,b),\ (a,c),\ (b,b),\ (c,a),\ (c,b)\},$$

where $S_1 = \{x_1, x_2, x_3\}$, $S_2 = \{x_2, x_4\}$, and $S_3 = \{x_3, x_4\}$. The set of all solutions of the network is given by,

$$\rho(X) = \{(a,a,a,b),\ (a,a,c,b),\ (a,b,c,a),\ (b,a,c,b),$$
$$(b,c,a,c),\ (c,a,b,b),\ (c,b,a,c),\ (c,c,c,a)\}.$$

Let $Y = \{x_2, x_3, x_4\}$ be a subset of the variables and let Y_I be an instantiation of the variables in Y. The tuple $Y_I = (a,c,b)$ is consistent relative to $\mathcal{R}$ since $Y_I[S_2] = (a,b)$ and $(a,b) \in R_{S_2}$, and $Y_I[S_3] = (c,b)$ and $(c,b) \in R_{S_3}$. The tuple $Y_I = (c,a,b)$ is not consistent relative to $\mathcal{R}$ since $Y_I[S_2] = (c,b)$, and $(c,b) \notin R_{S_2}$. The set of all consistent instantiations of the variables in Y is given by,

$$\rho(Y) = \{(a,a,b),\ (a,b,b),\ (a,c,b),\ (b,a,c),\ (b,c,a),\ (c,a,c),\ (c,a,a)\}.$$

If we order the domains of the variables according to the natural lexicographic ordering, the $(0,1)$-matrix representation of the binary constraint R_{S_2} between x_2 and x_4 is given by,

$$R_{S_2} = \begin{bmatrix} 0 & 1 & 0 \\ 1 & 0 & 1 \\ 1 & 0 & 1 \end{bmatrix}.$$

For example, the entry at row 3 column 1 of R_{S_2} is 1, which states that the tuple (c,a) corresponding to the third element of D_2 and the first element of D_4 is allowed by the constraint. It can be seen that the constraint is 2-tight, 1-loose, and not row convex. It can also be verified that the other constraints are 2-tight and 1-loose, and therefore the network is 2-tight and 1-loose. As a partial verification of the ternary constraint R_{S_1}, let $Y = \{x_1\}$ and let $Y_I = (a)$ in the definition. Then, $\sigma_{Y_I}(R_{S_1}) = \{(a,a,a),\ (a,a,c),\ (a,b,c),\ (a,c,b)\}$, and $\Pi_{(S_1-Y)}(\sigma_{Y_I}(R_{S_1})) = \{(a,a),\ (a,c),\ (b,c),\ (c,b)\}$, which is a 2-tight and 1-loose binary relation.

3 Local Consistency

Local consistency has proven to be an important concept in the theory and practice of constraint networks. In this section we first review previous definitions of local consistency, which we characterize as variable-based. We then present new definitions of local consistency that are *relation-based* and present algorithms for enforcing these local consistencies.

3.1 Variable-based consistency

Mackworth [17] defines three properties of networks that characterize local consistency of networks: *node, arc,* and *path consistency.* Freuder [11] generalizes this to k-consistency.

Definition 9 k-consistency; Freuder [11, 12]. A network is k-*consistent* if and only if given any instantiation of any $k - 1$ distinct variables satisfying all of the direct relations among those variables, there exists an instantiation of any kth variable such that the k values taken together satisfy all of the relations among the k variables. A network is *strongly k-consistent* if and only if it is j-consistent for all $j \leq k$.

Node, arc, and path consistency correspond to one-, two-, and three-consistency, respectively. A strongly n-consistent network is called *globally consistent.* Globally consistent networks have the property that any consistent instantiation of a subset of the variables can be extended to a consistent instantiation of all of the variables without backtracking [5]. It is frequently enough to have a globally consistent network along a single ordering of the variables as long as this ordering is known in advance.

Definition 10 globally solved. We say that a problem is globally solved if it is consistent, and if there is a known ordering of the variables along which solutions can be assembled without encountering deadends. An algorithm *globally solves* a problem if it generates a globally solved network.

3.2 Relation-based consistency

In [25], we extended the notions of arc and path consistency to non-binary relations, and used it to specify an alternative condition under which row-convex non-binary networks are globally consistent. The new local consistency conditions were called relational arc- and path-consistency. In [24] we generalized relational arc- and path-consistency to *relational m-consistency.* In the definition of *relational-consistency,* the relations rather than the variables are the primitive entities. This allows expressing the relationships between properties of the constraints and local consistency in a way that avoids an explicit reference to the arity of the constraints. In this section we revisit the definition of relational consistency and provide algorithms for enforcing such conditions.

Definition 11 relational arc, and path-consistency. Let $\mathcal{R}$ be a constraint network over a set of variables X, and let R_S and R_T be two distinct relations in $\mathcal{R}$, where $S, T \subseteq X$. We say that R_S is *relationally arc-consistent relative to variable* x iff any consistent instantiation of the variables in $S - \{x\}$, has an extension to x that satisfies R_S; that is, iff

$$\rho(S - \{x\}) \subseteq \Pi_{S-\{x\}}(R_S).$$

(Recall that $\rho(A)$ is the set of all consistent instantiations of the variables in A.) A relation R_S is *relationally arc-consistent* iff it is relationally arc-consistent relative to each variable in S. A network is relationally arc-consistent iff every relation is relationally arc-consistent. We say that R_S and R_T are *relationally path-consistent relative to variable x* iff any consistent instantiation of the variables in $(S \cup T) - \{x\}$, has an extension to x that satisfies R_S and R_T simultaneously; that is, iff

$$\rho(A) \subseteq \Pi_A(R_S \bowtie R_T),$$

where $A = (S \cup T) - \{x\}$. A pair of relations R_S and R_T is *relationally path-consistent* iff it is relationally path-consistent relative to each variable in $S \cap T$. A network is relationally path-consistent iff every pair of relations is relationally path-consistent.

Note that the definition of relational path-consistency subsumes relational arc-consistency if in the above definition we do not assume distinct pairs of relations. For simplicity, we will assume that relational path-consistency includes relational arc-consistency.

Definition 12 relational m-consistency. Let $\mathcal{R}$ be a constraint network over a set of variables X, and let $R_{S_1}, \ldots, R_{S_{m-1}}$ be $m - 1$ distinct relations in $\mathcal{R}$, where $S_i \subseteq X$. We say that $R_{S_1}, \ldots, R_{S_{m-1}}$ are *relational m-consistent relative to variable x* iff any consistent instantiation of the variables in A, where $A = \bigcup_{i=1}^{m-1} S_i - \{x\}$, has an extension to x that satisfies $R_{S_1}, \ldots, R_{S_{m-1}}$ simultaneously; that is, if and only if

$$\rho(A) \subseteq \Pi_A(\bowtie_{i=1}^{m-1} R_{S_i}).$$

A set of relations $\{R_{S_1}, \ldots, R_{S_{m-1}}\}$ is *relationally m-consistent* iff it is relationally m-consistent relative to each variable in $\bigcap_{i=1}^{m-1} S_i$. A network is relationally m-consistent iff every set of $m - 1$ relations is relationally m-consistent. A network is strongly relational m-consistent if it is relational i-consistent for every $i \leq m$. Relational arc- and path-consistency correspond to relational two- and three-consistency, respectively.

Definition 13 directional relational consistency. Given an ordering of the variables, a network is m-*directional relational consistent* iff for every set of relations $\{R_{S_1}, \ldots, R_{S_{m-1}}\}$ it is relationally m-consistent relative to the largest indexed variable in $\bigcap_{i=1}^{m-1} S_i$.

Example 2. Consider the constraint network over the set of variables $\{x_1, x_2, x_3, x_4, x_5\}$, where the domains of the variables are all $D = \{a, b, c\}$ and the relations are given by,

$R_{2,3,4,5} = \{$ (a,a,a,a), (b,a,a,a), (a,b,a,a), (a,a,b,a), (a,a,a,b) $\}$,
$R_{1,2,5} = \{$ (b,a,b), (c,b,c), (b,a,c) $\}$.

The constraints are not relationally arc-consistent. For example, the instantiation $x_2 = a$, $x_3 = b$, $x_4 = b$ is a consistent instantiation as it satisfies all the applicable constraints (trivially so, as there are no constraints defined strictly over $\{x_2, x_3, x_4\}$ or over any subset), but it does not have an extension to x_5 that satisfies $R_{2,3,4,5}$. Similarly, the constraints are not relationally path-consistent. For example, the instantiation $x_1 = c$, $x_2 = b$, $x_3 = a$, $x_4 = a$ is a consistent instantiation (again, trivially so), but it does not have an extension to x_5 that satisfies $R_{2,3,4,5}$ and $R_{1,2,5}$ simultaneously. If we add the constraints $R_2 = R_3 = R_4 = \{a\}$ and $R_1 = R_5 = \{b\}$, the set of solutions of the network does not change, and it can be verified that the network is both relationally arc- and path-consistent.

When all of the constraints are binary, relational m-consistency is identical (up to minor preprocessing) to variable-based m-consistency; otherwise the conditions are different. The virtue in our definition (relative to the one based on the dual graph [14]), is that it can be incorporated naturally into algorithms for enforcing desired levels of relational m-consistency, it allows a simple generalization of local consistency relationships, and it unifies several operators of variable elimination.

One disadvantage is that verifying relational m-consistency can be exponential even for relational arc-consistency, if the arity of the constraints is not bounded. In general, however, we will never be interested in verifying relational consistency, but rather in *enforcing* that condition. Below we present algorithm RELATIONAL-CONSISTENCY or RC_m, a brute-force algorithm for enforcing strong relational m-consistency on a network $\mathcal{R}$. Note that R_A stands for the current unique constraint specified over a subset of variables A. If no constraint exists, then R_A is the universal relation over A.

RELATIONAL-CONSISTENCY$(\mathcal{R}, m)$

1. **repeat**
2. $Q \leftarrow \mathcal{R}$
3.   **for** every $m - 1$ relations $R_{S_1}, \ldots, R_{S_{m-1}} \in Q$
      and every $x \in \bigcap_{i=1}^{m-1} S_i$
4.   **do** $A \leftarrow \bigcup_{i=1}^{m-1} S_i - \{x\}$
5. $R_A \leftarrow R_A \cap \Pi_A(\bowtie_{i=1}^{m-1} R_{S_i})$
6.   **if** R_A is the empty relation
7.   **then** exit and return the empty network
8. **until** $Q = \mathcal{R}$

We call the operation in Step 5 *extended m-composition*, since it generalizes the composition operation defined on binary relations. Algorithm RC_m computes the closure of $\mathcal{R}$ with respect to extended m-composition.

Algorithm RC_m is clearly computationally expensive though it can be improved in a manner parallel to the improvements of path-consistency algorithms [18]. Such improvements are not of much interest since enforcing relational consistency is likely to remain exponential for $m \geq 3$, unless the constraints are binary. We will see that even for $m = 3$, RC_3 solves the NP-complete problem of propositional satisfiability.

As with variable-based local-consistency, we can improve the efficiency of enforcing relational consistency by enforcing it only along a certain direction. Below we present algorithm DIRECTIONAL-RELATIONAL-CONSISTENCY or DRC_m, which enforces strong directional relational m-consistency on a network $\mathcal{R}$, relative to a given ordering $o = x_1, x_2, \ldots, x_n$. We call the network generated by the algorithm the *directional extension of* $\mathcal{R}$, denoted $E_m(R)$.

DIRECTIONAL-RELATIONAL-CONSISTENCY$(\mathcal{R}, m, o)$

1. Initialize: generate an ordered partition of the constraints, $bucket_1, \ldots,$ $bucket_n$, where $bucket_i$ contains all constraints whose highest variable is x_i.

2. **for** $p \leftarrow n$ **downto** 1

3.   **do** (simplify $bucket_p$:) **for** every $S_i, S_j \in bucket_p$, s.t. $S_i \supseteq S_j$
        do $R_{S_i} \leftarrow R_{S_i} \cap \Pi_{S_i}(R_{S_i} \bowtie R_{S_j})$

4. $j \leftarrow \min\{$cardinality of $bucket_p$, $m - 1\}$

5.   **for** every j relations $R_{S_1}, \ldots, R_{S_j}$ in $bucket_p$,

6.   **do** $A \leftarrow \bigcup_{i=1}^{j} S_i - \{x_p\}$

7. $R_A \leftarrow R_A \cap \Pi_A(\bowtie_{i=1}^{j} R_{S_i})$

8.   **if** R_A is not the empty relation

9.   **then** add R_A to its appropriate bucket

10.   **else** exit and return the empty network

11. **return** $E_m(R) = \bigcup_{j=1}^{n} bucket_j$

Step 3 of simplifying each bucket is optional. It ensures that there is no relation in a bucket whose variables are contained in another relation's subset.

Although algorithm DRC_m enforces extended m-composition only, it generates a *strong* directional relational m-consistent network in the following sense.

Theorem 14. *The closure under DRC_m along ordering $o = x_1, \ldots, x_n$, is a network such that all the relations in the same bucket are strong directional relational m-consistent.*

Like similar algorithms for enforcing directional consistency, the worst-case complexity of DIRECTIONAL-RELATIONAL-CONSISTENCY can be bounded as a function of the topological structure of the problem via parameters like the *induced width* of the graph [7], also known as *tree-width* [1].

Definition 15 width, tree-width. A constraint network $\mathcal{R}$ can be associated with a constraint graph, where each node is a variable and two variables that appear in one constraint are connected. A general graph can be embedded in a *clique-tree* namely, in a graph whose cliques form a tree-structure. The induced width w^* of such an embedding is its maximal clique size and the induced width w^* of an arbitrary graph is the minimum induced width over all its tree-embeddings.

It is known that finding the minimal width embedding is NP-complete [1], nevertheless every ordering of the variables o, yields a simple to compute upper bound denoted $w^*(o)$ (see [8]). The complexity of DRC_m along o can be bounded as a function of $w^*(o)$ of its constraint graph. Specifically [8],

Theorem 16. *The time complexity and size of the network generated by DRC_m along ordering o is $O(\exp(mw^*(o)))$. In particular, the time complexity of DRC_3 is $O(\exp(w^*(o) + 1))$.*

The complexity of DRC_2 is polynomial.

Lemma 17. *The complexity of DRC_2 is $O(n \cdot e^2 \cdot t^2)$ when e is the number of input relations, and t bounds the number of tuples in each relation.*

Example 3. Crossword puzzles have been used experimentally in evaluating backtracking algorithms for solving constraint networks [13]. We use an example puzzle to illustrate algorithm DRC_3 (see Figure 1). One possible constraint network formulation of the problem is as follows: there is a variable for each square that can hold a character, $x_1, \ldots, x_{13}$; the domains of the variables are the alphabet letters; and the constraints are the possible words. For this example, the constraints are given by,

$$R_{1,2,3,4,5} = \{(H,O,S,E,S), (L,A,S,E,R), (S,H,E,E,T), (S,N,A,I,L), (S,T,E,E,R)\}$$
$$R_{3,6,9,12} = \{(H,I,K,E), (A,R,O,N), (K,E,E,T), (E,A,R,N), (S,A,M,E)\}$$
$$R_{5,7,11} = \{(R,U,N), (S,U,N), (L,E,T), (Y,E,S), (E,A,T), (T,E,N)\}$$
$$R_{8,9,10,11} = R_{3,6,9,12}$$
$$R_{10,13} = \{(N,O), (B,E), (U,S), (I,T)\}$$
$$R_{12,13} = R_{10,13}$$

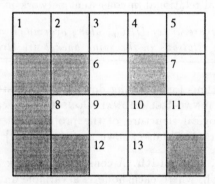

Fig. 1. A crossword puzzle

Let us perform three iterations of DRC_3 with the ordering of variables $o = x_{13}, x_{12}, \ldots, x_1$. Processing bucket$_1$ adds the relation,

$$R_{2,3,4,5} = \Pi_{2,3,4,5}(R_{1,2,3,4,5})$$
$$= \{(O,S,E,S), (A,S,E,R), (H,E,E,T), (N,A,I,L), (T,E,E,R)\},$$

to the bucket of variable x_2 which is processed next. The bucket for x_2 contains the single relation $R_{2,3,4,5}$. Processing $bucket_2$ adds the relation,

$$R_{3,4,5} = \Pi_{3,4,5}(R_{2,3,4,5})$$
$$= \{(S,E,S), (S,E,R), (E,E,T), (A,I,L), (E,E,R)\},$$

to the bucket of variable x_3 which is processed next. The bucket for x_3 contains the relations $R_{3,4,5}$ and $R_{3,6,9,12}$. Processing $bucket_3$ adds the relations,

$$R_{4,5} = \Pi_{4,5}(R_{3,4,5})$$
$$= \{(E,S), (E,R), (E,T), (I,L), (E,R)\},$$

$$R_{6,9,12} = \Pi_{6,9,12}(R_{3,6,9,12})$$
$$= \{(I,K,E), (R,O,N), (E,E,T), (A,R,N), (A,M,E)\},$$

$$R_{4,5,6,9,12} = \Pi_{4,5,6,9,12}(R_{3,4,5} \bowtie R_{3,6,9,12})$$
$$= \{(E,S,A,M,E), (E,R,A,M,E), (E,T,A,R,N), (I,L,R,O,N), (E,R,A,R,N)\},$$

to the buckets of variables x_4 (relations $R_{4,5}$ and $R_{4,5,6,9,12}$) and x_6 (relation $R_{6,9,12}$). Continuing in this manner, at iteration 10 the empty relation is derived and thus the algorithm can stop and report that the network is inconsistent. It can be shown that crossword puzzles can be globally solved by DRC_3.

Finally, we propose algorithm ADAPTIVE-RELATIONAL-CONSISTENCY (ARC) which is the relational counter-part of algorithm adaptive-consistency [7]. Like algorithm DRC_m, it process the buckets in order from last to first. When processing the bucket of x_j, it applies extended composition relative to x_j to *all* the relations in that bucket, and then places the resulting relation in its appropriate bucket. It can be shown that ARC can *globally solve* any constraint network.

ADAPTIVE-RELATIONAL-CONSISTENCY($\mathcal{R}, o$)

1. Initialize: generate an ordered partition of the constraints, $bucket_1, \ldots,$ $bucket_n$, where $bucket_i$ contains all constraints whose highest variable is x_i.

2. **for** $p \leftarrow n$ **downto** 1

3.   **do for** all the relations $R_{S_1}, \ldots, R_{S_j}$ in $bucket_p$,

4.   **do** $A \leftarrow \bigcup_{i=1}^{j} S_i - \{x_p\}$

5. $R_A \leftarrow R_A \cap \Pi_A(\bowtie_{i=1}^{j} R_{S_i})$

6.   **if** R_A is not the empty relation

7.   **then** add R_A to its appropriate bucket

8.   **else** exit and return the empty network

9. **return** $E_o(R) = bucket_1 \cup bucket_2 \cup \cdots \cup bucket_n$

Theorem 18. *Algorithm* ADAPTIVE-RELATIONAL-CONSISTENCY *(ARC) globally solves any constraint network. The complexity of the algorithm when processed along ordering o is bounded by $O(n \cdot exp((n + e) \cdot w^*(o)))$, where e is the number of relations in the input network.*

4 Variable Elimination Operators

The extended m-composition operator unifies known operators such as resolution in theorem proving, joins in relational databases, and variable elimination for solving equations and inequalities. It is easy to see that pair-wise resolution is equivalent to extended 3-composition.

4.1 Variable elimination in propositional CNF theories

We denote propositional symbols, also called *variables*, by uppercase letters $P, Q, R, ...$, propositional literals (i.e., $P, \neg P$) by lowercase letters $p, q, r, ...$, and disjunctions of literals, or *clauses*, by $\alpha, \beta, ...$ A *unit clause* is a clause of size 1. The notation $(\alpha \vee T)$ is a shorthand for the disjunction $(P \vee Q \vee R \vee T)$, and $\alpha \vee \beta$ denotes the clause whose literal appears in either α or β. The *resolution* operation over two clauses $(\alpha \vee Q)$ and $(\beta \vee \neg Q)$ results in a clause $(\alpha \vee \beta)$, thus eliminating Q. A formula φ in conjunctive normal form (CNF) is a set of clauses $\varphi = \{\alpha_1, ..., \alpha_t\}$ that denotes their conjunction. The set of *models* of a formula φ, denoted $models(\varphi)$, is the set of all satisfying truth assignments to all its symbols. A Horn formula is a CNF formula whose clauses all have at most one positive literal. Let $EC_Q(R_A, R_B)$ denote the relation generated by extended 3-composition of R_A and R_B relative to Q, $Q \in A \cap B$.

Lemma 19. *The* resolution *operation over two clauses* $(\alpha \vee Q)$ *and* $(\beta \vee \neg Q)$, *results in a clause* $(\alpha \vee \beta)$ *satisfying:* $models(\alpha \vee \beta) = EC_Q(models(\alpha), models(\beta))$.

Incorporating resolution into DRC_3 results in algorithm *Directional Resolution* which is the core of the well known Davis Putnam algorithm for satisfiability [4, 10]. As is well known, and as will follow from our theory, the algorithm globally solves any CNF theory.

DIRECTIONAL-RESOLUTION (φ, o)

1. Initialize: generate an ordered partition of clauses to buckets.

2. **for** $i \leftarrow n$ **downto** 1

3.   **do** resolve each pair $\{(\alpha \vee Q_i), (\beta \vee \neg Q_i)\} \subseteq bucket_i$. If $\gamma = \alpha \vee \beta$ is empty, return $E_o(\varphi) = \{\}$, the theory is not satisfiable; else, determine the index of γ and add it to the appropriate bucket.

4. **return** $E_o(\varphi) \leftarrow \bigcup_i bucket_i$

It is easy to see that DRC_2 *with the simplification step*, when applied to CNF theories is a slight extension of unit-resolution. It allows resolution involving non-unit clauses as long as the variables appearing in one clause are contained in the other clause. Consequently,

Lemma 20. *Algorithm* DRC_2 *decides the satisfiability of Horn theories.*

4.2 Variable elimination in linear inequalities

Let us now consider the class of linear inequalities over finite subsets[3] of the integers and let a constraint between r variables or less be a conjunction of linear equalities and inequalities of the form $\sum_{i=1}^{r} a_i x_i \leq c$, where a_i, and c are integer constants. For example, the conjunction $(3x_i + 2x_j \leq 3) \wedge (-4x_i + 5x_j < 1)$ is an allowed constraint between variables x_i and x_j. A network with constraints of this form can be formulated as an integer linear program where each constraint is on r variables and the domains of the variables are finite subsets of integers that may be restricted by unary linear inequalities. It can be shown that the standard operation of eliminating variables between pairs of inequality is almost equivalent to extended 3-composition. Let us denote by $sol(\alpha)$ the finite set of solutions over the integers of one inequality α. $sol(\alpha)$ is the relational representation of the inequality. We define the elimination operation as follows:

Definition 21 linear elimination. Let $\alpha = \sum_{i=1}^{(r-1)} a_i x_i + a_r x_r \leq c$, and $\beta = \sum_{i=1}^{(r-1)} b_i x_i + b_r x_r \leq d$. Then $elim_r(\alpha, \beta)$ is applicable only if a_r and b_r have opposite signs, in which case $elim_r(\alpha, \beta) = \sum_{i=1}^{r-1} (-a_i \frac{b_r}{a_r} + b_i) x_i \leq -\frac{b_r}{a_r} c + d$. If a_r and b_r have the same sign the elimination implicitly generates the universal constraint.

Lemma 22. $sol(elim_r(\alpha, \beta)) \supseteq EC_r(sol(\alpha), sol(\beta))$

Proof. Assume now that a_r and b_r contain opposite signs. Multiplying α by $-\frac{b_r}{a_r}$ and summing the resulting inequality with β yields the inequality

$$\sum_{i=1}^{r-1} (-a_i \frac{b_r}{a_r} + b_i) x_i \leq -\frac{b_r}{a_r} c + d.$$

In other words, any tuple satisfying this inequality can be extended to a *real value* of x_r in a way that satisfies both α and β. It is unclear, though, that there is an integer extension to x_r which is the reason for partial containment. $\square$

Incorporating linear elimination into DRC_3 results in algorithm *Directional Linear Elimination* (abbreviated DLE) which is the well known Fourier elimination algorithm (see [16]). It was shown that the algorithm decides the solvability of any set of linear inequalities over the Reals.

DIRECTIONAL-LINEAR-ELIMINATION (φ, o)

1. Initialize: generate an ordered partition of the inequalities into buckets.

2. **for** $i \leftarrow n$ **downto** 1

3.   **do** for each pair $\{\alpha, \beta\} \subseteq bucket_i$, compute $\gamma = elim_i(\alpha, \beta)$. If γ has no solutions, return $E_o(\varphi) = \{\}$, the theory is not satisfiable; else, add γ to the appropriate bucket.

---

[3] Our treatment can be extended to non-finite domains. However to simplify we will assume that the domains are integers bounded between [-M,M] for very large M, whenever other bounds are not explicitly given.

4. **return** $E_o(\varphi) \leftarrow \bigcup_i bucket_i$

If DLE is processed over the relational representation of the linear inequalities, (in which case it becomes DRC_3), we will be able to bound its complexity using the notion of induced width. However, when DLE uses inequality representation only (the only option for infinite domains) its complexity may be worst-case exponential even when the induced width $w*$, is bounded. The reason is that an exponential number of inequalities may be recorded, even on one or two variables. We cannot "intersect" two inequalities and replace them by one. Even for binary inequalities the algorithm may be exponential, unless we use relational representation and DRC_3. In summary,

Theorem 23. *Algorithm DLE is exponential even for binary inequalities and even for bounded induced width. For finite domains DRC_3 is applicable and its complexity is polynomial for binary constraints and bounded induced width.*

Propositional CNFs as well as linear inequalities share an interesting syntactic property: It is easy to recognize whether applying extended-3-composition relative to variable x_i results in a universal constraint. Both resolution and linear elimination relative to x_i are effective only when the variable to be eliminated appears with opposite signs. This leads to a simple-to-identify tractable class for both these languages. If there exists an ordering of the variables, such that in each of its $bucket_i$, x_i appears with the same sign, then the theory is already globally solved relative to that ordering. We called in [10] such theories as "zero diversity" and we showed that they can be recognized in linear time.

5   From Local to Global Consistency

Much work has been done on identifying relationships between properties of constraint networks and the level of local consistency sufficient to ensure global consistency. This work falls into two classes: identifying topological properties of the underlying graph of the network and identifying properties of the constraints.

For work on identifying topological properties, Freuder [12] identifies a relationship between the *width* of a constraint graph and the level of local consistency needed to ensure a solution can be found without backtracking. Dechter and Pearl [7] provide an adaptive scheme where the level of local consistency is adjusted on a node-by-node basis. Dechter and Pearl [8] generalize the results on trees to hyper-trees which are called acyclic databases in the database community [2].

For work on identifying properties of the constraints, Montanari [20] shows that path consistency is sufficient to guarantee that a binary network is globally consistent if the relations are monotone. Dechter [5] identifies a relationship between the size of the domains of the variables, the arity of the constraints, and the level of local consistency sufficient to ensure the network is globally consistent. These results were extended recently by van Beek and Dechter to the property of tightness and looseness of the constraint networks [24, 23]. Van

Hentenryck, Deville, and Teng [26] show that arc consistency is sufficient to test whether a network is satisfiable if the relations are from a restricted class of functional and monotone constraints. These properties were generalized recently to the property of row-convexity [25].

Finally, for work that falls into both classes, Dechter and Pearl [9] present effective procedures for determining whether a constraint network can be formulated as a *causal theory* and thus a solution can be found without backtracking. Whether a constraint network can be so formulated depends on the topology of the underlying constraint graph and the type of the constraints.

In this section we show the power of relational consistency in generalizing some recently identified relationships between properties of the constraints and the level of local consistency sufficient to ensure that a network is globally consistent. This formulation leads to a characterization of classes of problems that can be solved by a restricted level m of DRC_m. The general pattern we will see is as follows. We present a sufficient condition showing that a network satisfying a property p, and having a corresponding level of local consistency $l(p)$, is globally consistent. This implies that whenever the property p is maintained under extended $l(p) - composition$, those networks (satisfying p) can be globally solved by $DRC_{l(p)}$. Furthermore, it is sufficient for condition $l(p)$ to hold only relative to the particular ordering on which the algorithm is applied.

5.1 Domain tightness and global consistency

In [5], we have shown that:

Theorem 24. *[5] If $\mathcal{R}$ is a k-valued binary constraint network that is $k+1$ consistent then it is globally consistent. If $\mathcal{R}$ is a k-valued r-ary constraint network that is $k(r-1)+1$ consistent then it is globally consistent.*

We now show that by using the notion of relational consistency the above relationship for r-ary networks (as well as its proof), are simplified. Moreover, the implied algorithm can be stated more coherently.

Theorem 25. *A k-valued constraint network $\mathcal{R}$, that is $k+1$-relational-consistent is globally consistent.*

Since the domains do not increase by extended $(k+1)$-composition we get:

Theorem 26. *Any k-valued network $\mathcal{R}$ can be globally solved by DRC_{k+1}.*

Example 4. From Theorem 26, bi-valued networks can be globally solved by DRC_3. In particular, propositional *CNFs* can be globally solved by DRC_3. As we have seen, in this case, the operator of extended 3-composition takes the form of pair-wise resolution yielding algorithm directional resolution [10].

5.2 Row-convexity and global consistency

In [22], we have shown that:

Theorem 27. *[22] Let $\mathcal{R}$ be a path-consistent binary constraint network. If there exists an ordering of the domains $D_1, \ldots, D_n$ of $\mathcal{R}$ such that the relations are row convex, the network is globally consistent.*

The result for binary networks was generalized to constraints of arbitrary arity, using relational path consistency.

Theorem 28. *[25]. Let $\mathcal{R}$ be a relational path consistent constraint network. If there exists an ordering of the domains $D_1, \ldots, D_n$ of $\mathcal{R}$ such that the relations are row convex, the network is globally consistent.*

We can conclude that:

Theorem 29. *If $\mathcal{R}$ is a network whose closure under extended 3-composition is row convex then $\mathcal{R}$ can be globally solved by DRC_3.*

Example 5. Consider a set of linear equalities and inequalities over finite subsets of integers of the form: $\sum_{i=1}^{r} a_i x_i \leq c$ where a_i, c are integers. It can be shown that the $(0, 1)$ matrices of such relations are row convex and, when the constraints are binary, their row-convexity is invariant to extended 3-composition. It is also easy to see that any bi-valued relation is row-convex. Consequently,

Theorem 30. *A set of linear inequalities over finite set of integers can be globally solved by DRC_3. A CNF formula can be globally solved by DRC_3.*

Two special cases are a restricted and discrete version of Dechter, Meiri, and Pearl's [6] continuous, bounded difference framework for temporal reasoning and a restricted and discrete version of Vilain and Kautz's [27] qualitative framework for temporal reasoning. Another known class that can be shown to be row-convex is implicational constraints [15]. For more details see [25].

5.3 Constraint tightness and global consistency

For some networks, Theorem 24 is tight in that the level of local consistency specified by the theorem is really required (graph coloring problems formulated as constraint networks are an example). For other networks, Theorem 24 overestimates. In [24], we refined that relationship by extending the notion of tightness to the constraints themselves.

Theorem 31. *[24]. If a binary constraint network $\mathcal{R}$ is m-tight, and if the network is strongly $(m + 2)$-consistent, then the network is globally consistent.*

Theorem 32. *[24] If a general constraint network $\mathcal{R}$ is m-tight, and relationally $(m + 2)$-consistent, then the network is globally consistent.*

Theorems 31 & 32 always specify a level of strong consistency that is less than or equal to the level of strong consistency required by Theorem 24. The level of required consistency is equal only when $m = d - 1$ and is less when $m < d - 1$. As well, the theorem can sometimes be usefully applied if $d \geq n - 1$, whereas Theorem 24 cannot.

Example 6. Nadel [21] introduces a variant of the n-queens problem called confused n-queens and uses it to empirically compare backtracking algorithms. In [24], we use Theorem 31 to show that these problems are quite easy (as they require a low level of local consistency to ensure global consistency) and that any empirical results on these problems should be interpreted in this light.

5.4 Constraint looseness and local consistency

In [23], we presented a simple sufficient condition that estimates the inherent level of strong k-consistency of a binary constraint network.

Theorem 33. *[23] If a binary constraint network $\mathcal{R}$ is m-loose and all domains are of size d or less, then the network is strongly $\left(\left\lceil \frac{d}{d-m} \right\rceil\right)$-consistent.*

We now generalize the result to networks with constraints of arbitrary arity.

Theorem 34. *If a general constraint network $\mathcal{R}$ is m-loose and all domains are of size d or less, then the network is relational $\left(\left\lceil \frac{d}{d-m} \right\rceil\right)$-consistent.*

Theorems 33 & 34 provide a lower bound on the actual level of inherent local consistency of a constraint network. Graph coloring problems provide examples where the bound is exact, whereas n-queens problems provide examples where the bound underestimates the true level of local consistency [23].

5.5 Acyclic and causal networks and global consistency

Relational consistency and the DRC_m algorithms can also easily capture the tractable classes of acyclic and causal networks. It is well known that acyclic networks are tractable [19, 8].

Lemma 35. *If a network is acyclic then there exists an ordering of the variables for which each bucket has a single relation.*

Single-bucket networks contain the class of acyclic networks and causal networks. It was shown in [9] that it is possible to discover an ordering of the variables for which each bucket contains a single relation, whenever such an ordering exist. We conclude:

Theorem 36. *Single-bucket networks that are closed under DRC_2 are tractable.*

6 Conclusions

We have shown that different levels of DRC can globally solve different classes of constraint networks:

1. DRC_2 globally solves acyclic and single-bucket, causal relations in polynomial time. It solves, (not globally solves) Horn CNF theories.
2. DRC_3 globally solves closed row-convex networks, bi-valued domain networks, closed 1-tight networks, crossword puzzles, and linear inequalities over finite subsets of the integers. The algorithm is polynomial for binary constraints over finite domains in relational form, and can be exponential otherwise. Algorithm DLE is a linear elimination algorithm that approximates DRC_3 over integers.
3. Algorithm DRC_m globally solves $(m-1)$-valued networks, and closed $(m-2)$-tight networks. The algorithm is polynomial for binary constraints.
4. Algorithm ARC globally solves all networks and is exponential.
5. The complexity of both DRC_m and ARC is exponentially bounded by $w*$, the tree-width of the network over finite domains.

Acknowledgement. We would like to thank Simon Kasif for mentioning Fourier's elimination algorithm to us. This work was partially supported by NSF grant IRI-9157636, by the Electrical Power Research Institute (EPRI) and by grants from Xerox, Northrop and Rockwell. This work was also supported in part by the Natural Sciences and Engineering Research Council of Canada.

References

1. S. Arnborg, D. G. Corneil, and A. Proskurowski. Complexity of finding an embedding in k-trees. *SIAM Journal of Algebraic Discrete Methods*, 8:177–184, 1987.
2. C. Beeri, R. Fagin, D. Maier, and M. Yannakakis. On the desirability of acyclic database schemes. *J. ACM*, 30:479–513, 1983.
3. M. C. Cooper. An optimal k-consistency algorithm. *Artif. Intell.*, 41:89–95, 1989.
4. M. Davis and H. Putnam. A computing procedure for quantification theory. *J. ACM*, 7:201–215, 1960.
5. R. Dechter. From local to global consistency. *Artif. Intell.*, 55:87–107, 1992.
6. R. Dechter, I. Meiri, and J. Pearl. Temporal constraint networks. *Artif. Intell.*, 49:61–95, 1991.
7. R. Dechter and J. Pearl. Network-based heuristics for constraint satisfaction problems. *Artif. Intell.*, 34:1–38, 1988.
8. R. Dechter and J. Pearl. Tree clustering for constraint networks. *Artif. Intell.*, 38:353–366, 1989.
9. R. Dechter and J. Pearl. Directed constraint networks: A relational framework for causal modeling. In *Proc. of the 12th Int'l Joint Conf. on AI*, pages 1164–1170, 1991.
10. R. Dechter and I. Rish. Directional resolution: The Davis-Putnam procedure, revisited. In *Proc. of the 4th Int'l Conf. on Principles of KR&R*, 1994.

11. E. C. Freuder. Synthesizing constraint expressions. *Comm. ACM*, 21:958–966, 1978.

12. E. C. Freuder. A sufficient condition for backtrack-free search. *J. ACM*, 29:24–32, 1982.

13. M. L. Ginsberg, M. Frank, M. P. Halpin, and M. C. Torrance. Search lessons learned from crossword puzzles. In *Proc. of the 8th Nat'l Conf. on AI*, pages 210–215, 1990.

14. P. Jégou. On the consistency of general constraint satisfaction problems. In *Proc. of the 11th National Conf. on AI*, pages 114–119, 1993.

15. L. M. Kirousis. Fast parallel constraint satisfaction. *Artif. Intell.*, 64:147–160, 1993.

16. J-L Lassez and M. Mahler, "On Fourier's algorithm for linear constraints" *Journal of Automated Reasoning*, Vol 9, 1992.

17. A. K. Mackworth. Consistency in networks of relations. *Artif. Intell.*, 8:99–118, 1977.

18. A. K. Mackworth and E. C. Freuder. The complexity of some polynomial network consistency algorithms for constraint satisfaction problems. *Artif. Intell.*, 25:65–74, 1985.

19. D. Maier. *The Theory of Relational Databases*. Computer Science Press, 1983.

20. U. Montanari. Networks of constraints: Fundamental properties and applications to picture processing. *Inform. Sci.*, 7:95–132, 1974.

21. B. A. Nadel. Constraint satisfaction algorithms. *Comput. Intell.*, 5:188–224, 1989.

22. P. van Beek. On the minimality and decomposability of constraint networks. In *Proc. of the 10th National Conf. on AI*, pages 447–452, 1992.

23. P. van Beek. On the inherent level of local consistency in constraint networks. In *Proc. of the 12th National Conf. on AI*, pages 368–373, 1994.

24. P. van Beek and R. Dechter. Constraint tightness versus global consistency. In *Proc. of the 4th Int'l Conf. on Principles of KR&R*, pages 572–582, 1994.

25. P. van Beek and R. Dechter. On the minimality and global consistency of row-convex constraint networks. *To appear in J. ACM*, 1995.

26. P. Van Hentenryck, Y. Deville, and C.-M. Teng. A generic arc consistency algorithm and its specializations. *Artif. Intell.*, 57:291–321, 1992.

27. M. Vilain and H. Kautz. Constraint propagation algorithms for temporal reasoning. In *Proc. of the 5th National Conf. on AI*, pages 377–382, 1986.

Dynamic Variable Ordering in CSPs

Fahiem Bacchus[1] and Paul van Run[2]

[1] Dept. of Computer Science, University of Waterloo, Waterloo, Ontario, Canada,
N2L 3G1, (fbacchus@logos.uwaterloo.ca)
[2] NN Financial, 1 Concorde Gate, Toronto, Ontario, Canada, M3C 3N6,
(pvanrun@idirect.com)

Abstract. We investigate the *dynamic variable ordering* (DVO) technique commonly used in conjunction with tree-search algorithms for solving constraint satisfaction problems. We first provide an implementation methodology for adding DVO to an arbitrary tree-search algorithm.
Our methodology is applicable to a wide range of algorithms including
those that maintain complicated information about the search history,
like backmarking. We then investigate the popular reordering heuristic
of next instantiating the variable with the minimum remaining values
(MRV). We prove some interesting theorems about the MRV heuristic which demonstrate that if one wants to use the MRV heuristic one
should use it with forward checking. Finally, we investigate the empirical performance of 12 different algorithms with and without DVO. Our
experiments and theoretical results demonstrate that forward checking
equipped with dynamic variable ordering is a very good algorithm for
solving CSPs.

1 Introduction

Despite being in the class of NP-complete problems, many practical constraint
satisfaction problems (CSPs) can be solved by tree-search algorithms that are
derivatives or variants of backtracking. Naive backtracking (BT) is not a particularly useful method as the class of problems that it can solve within practical
resource limits is small. A number of improvements to BT have been developed in
the literature. None of these improvements can, of course, escape from behaving
badly on certain inputs, given that NP $\neq$ P. Nevertheless, these improvements
are often able to solve wider, or perhaps different, classes of problems.

Tree-search algorithms try to construct a solution to a CSP by sequentially
instantiating the variables of the problem. The order in which the algorithm instantiates the variables is known to have a potentially profound effect on its efficiency, and various heuristics have been investigated for choosing good orderings.
Dynamic variable ordering (DVO) is technique that has been shown empirically
to be even more effective than choosing a good static ordering [Pur83, DM94a].
With DVO the order in which the variables are instantiated during tree-search

---

* This research was supported by the Canadian Government through their IRIS project
and NSERC programs.

can vary from branch to branch in the search tree. In this paper we will study in more detail dynamic variable ordering, in the context of binary constraint satisfaction problems.

The first issue we address is how the various CSP tree-search algorithms can be modified so as to utilize dynamic variable ordering. It is not immediately obvious how to do this, as some of these algorithms, e.g., backmarking (BM), maintain complicated information about the search history. How can the integrity of this information be maintained when the variable ordering is changing from path to path? Our first contribution is to describe a systematic methodology for modifying a tree-search algorithm so that it can use DVO. This methodology is described in Section 2, where we also present a brief description of the components of a CSP.

Given an algorithm capable of using DVO, the next question is how do we dynamically select the variable ordering. In Section 3 we examine the most popular DVO heuristic: instantiate next the variable that has the fewest values compatible with the previous instantiations. We call this heuristic the minimum remaining values heuristic (MRV). It turns out that MRV has some very strong properties, and we prove some key results about MRV in this section.

Our theoretical examination of the MRV heuristic does not tell the entire story, so we turn next to experimental evaluations to gather more information. In Section 4, we show the results of some of the experiments we have run using 12 different CSP algorithms with and without DVO using the MRV heuristic. Our experiments allow us to make a number of additional observations about the effectiveness of these algorithms and the effect of DVO using the MRV heuristic. Finally, we close with a summary of the main conclusions arising from our study.

2 A methodology for adding DVO

We assume some familiarity with CSPs in this paper (see, e.g., [Mac87]), but the basics can be easily described. Here we give a description of CSPs that is designed to make our subsequent description of the mechanics of certain CSP algorithms easier.

A *binary* CSP is a finite set of variables, each with a finite domain of potential values, and a collection of pairwise constraints between the variables. The goal is to assign a value to each variable so that all of the constraints are satisfied. Depending on the application the goal may be to find all consistent solutions, or to find just one. Formally:

Definition 1. A binary constraint satisfaction problem $\mathcal{P}$ consists of:

- A finite collection of N *variables*, $V[1], \ldots, V[N]$.
- For each variable $V[i]$, a finite domain $D[1]$ containing $\#D[i]$ *values*: $D[i] = \{v[i, 1], v[i, 2], \ldots, v[i, \#D[i]]\}$.
- For each pair of variables $\{V[i], V[j]\}$, a *constraint* $C[i, j]$ between $V[i]$ and $V[j]$ which is simply a subset (not necessarily proper) of $D[i] \times D[j]$. The constraints must be symmetric, i.e., $(x, y) \in C[i, j]$ iff $(y, x) \in C[j, i]$.

The *assignment* of the value $v \in D[i]$ to the variable $V[i]$ is written $V[i] \leftarrow v$. If $(v, v') \in C[i, j]$ we say that the pair of assignments $\{ V[i] \leftarrow v, V[j] \leftarrow v' \}$ is *consistent*. A *partial solution* for $\mathcal{P}$ is a set of assignments such that every pair in the set is consistent. A *solution* to $\mathcal{P}$ is a partial solution that contains an assignment for every variable. ∎

Tree-search algorithms generate search trees during their operation. The search tree consists of nodes which we take in this paper to be an assignment of a particular value to a particular variable. Each node in the search tree has an associated depth. Tree-search algorithms explore paths in the search tree. At any point during search the current path consists of a series of nodes from the root to the current node, and a set of as yet uninstantiated variables. We use the following notational conventions:

- $Nd[i]$ denotes the node at depth i in the current path.
- $Nd[i].Var$ denotes the *index* of the variable assigned at node $Nd[i]$. Hence, $V[Nd[i].Var]$ is the variable itself.[3]
- $Nd[i].val$ denotes the value assigned to the variable associated with node $Nd[i]$. It should be a member of this variable's domain; i.e., we should have $Nd[i].val \in D[Nd[i].Var]$.
- $Incon(Nd[i], Nd[j])$ denotes that the assignments associated with the i'th and j'th nodes are inconsistent. This corresponds to the condition:

$$(Nd[i].val, Nd[j].val) \notin C[Nd[i].Var, Nd[j].Var]$$

- Finally, we consider $Nd.Var$ and $Nd.val$ to be fields that can be assigned to.

With this notation we can now describe our methodology for adding dynamic variable ordering to any particular tree-search algorithm quite easily. The methodology is very simple. All that is required is to maintain a clear distinction between the *nodes* of the search tree and the *variables*. Both the nodes of the current path $Nd[i]$ and the variables $V[j]$ are indexed sets. When a static ordering is used there is a constant mapping between the depth of a node and the index of the variable that is assigned at that node. This often leads to a blurring of the distinction between the node index (the node's depth) and the variable index. With DVO there is no longer a static mapping between these two indices, and a failure to distinguish between them leads to confusion.

Once this distinction is maintained it becomes relatively straightforward to modify a tree-search algorithm to allow it to use DVO. One need only be careful about whether or not each step of the algorithm is indexing a node or a variable. A few examples should make the mechanics of the methodology clear.

First, consider simple backtracking (BT). In BT we assign a variable at the current *node*, selecting the variable to be assigned from the current set of uninstantiated variables. We then test the consistency of this assignment against the assignments of the previous *nodes*. This occurs with both static and dynamic

---

[3] We let $Nd[i].Var$ be an index instead of a variable so that it can also index into the variable's domain $D[Nd[i].Var]$ and the variable's domain size $\#D[Nd[i].Var]$.

variable orderings, but with a static order one might be tempted to state this as "test the assignment of the current *variable* against the assignments of the previous *variables*", a notion that does not apply in the dynamic case.

Second, consider forward checking (FC). In FC we do not check the assignment of the current node against the previous nodes, rather we use it to prune the domains of the as yet uninstantiated *variables*. FC needs to maintain information about when domain values are pruned, so that it can correctly restore those values when backtracking. Clearly, the domain values are associated with the variables, but the pruning of the values arises from particular nodes (specifically, from the assignment made at those nodes).

A common way of implementing FC is to associate with each variable an array of flags, one for each domain value. Let Domain be a two-dimensional array such that Domain$[i, k]$ contains the flag for the k-th value of the i-th variable. If this flag is set to 0 it indicates that this value has not yet been pruned, while if the flag is set to some number j it indicates that this value has been pruned by the *node* at depth j. Thus the Domain array is indexed by a variable-value pair, but it stores a node index. When we change the assignment associated with the node at level j, we can scan the Domain array restoring all variable values that were pruned by that node. In the context of a static ordering, the Domain$[i, k]$ array is commonly described as storing the *variable* that pruned the k-th value of the i-th variable.

One of the most powerful demonstrations of the simplicity of our methodology comes from its application to Gashnig's backmarking (BM) algorithm [Gas77]. BM is one of the more complex tree-search algorithms, and implementing DVO with BM seems to be difficult because of all of the bookkeeping information that BM maintains. In fact, some authors have mistakenly claimed that BM and dynamic variable ordering are incompatible [Pro93].[4]

BM is standardly described in a manner that confuses between nodes and variables. A standard description that relies implicitly on a static ordering is as follows. When an assignment $V[i] \leftarrow k$ of $V[i]$ is made, BT checks the consistency of this assignment against all of the previous assignments $\{ V[1] \leftarrow s_1, \ldots, V[i-1] \leftarrow s_{i-1} \}$, where s_i are the values assigned in the current path. If any of these consistency checks fail, BM takes the additional step of remembering the first point of failure in an array Mcl$[i, k]$ (the maximum check level array). This information is used to save subsequent consistency checks. Say that later we backtrack from $V[i]$ up to $V[j]$, assign $V[j]$ a new value, and then progress down the tree, once again reaching $V[i]$. At $V[i]$ we might again attempt the assignment $V[i] \leftarrow k$. The assignments $\{ V[1] \leftarrow s_1, \ldots, V[j-1] \leftarrow s_{j-1} \}$ have not changed since we last tried $V[i] \leftarrow k$, so there is no point in repeating these checks. Furthermore, if $V[i] \leftarrow k$ had failed against one of these assignments, we need not make any checks at all; the assignment will fail again, so we can immediately reject it. To realize these savings, Mcl is by itself insufficient. We

---

[4] It is worth noting that Haralick and Elliot [HE80] had in fact implemented DVO with BM and reported on its empirical performance. However, they never described the manner in which BM was altered to accommodate DVO.

```
procedure BMvar(i)
%Tries to instantiate node at level i
%Then recurses
    Cur ← NextVar()
    Nd[i].Var ← Cur
    for k = 1 to #D[Cur]
        Nd[i].val ← v[Cur, k]
        if Mcl[Cur, k] ≥ Mbl[Cur] then
            ok ← true
            for j = Mbl[Cur] to i − 1 and while ok
                Mcl[Cur, k] ← j
                if Incon(Nd[i], Nd[j],) then
                    ok ← false
            if ok then
                V[Cur] ← v[Cur, k]
                if i = N then
                    print V[1], ..., V[N]
                else
                    BMvar(i + 1)
    Mbl[Cur] ← i−1
    Restore(i)
```

```
procedure Restore(i)
%Updates Mbl
    for j = 1 to N
        if Mbl[j] = i then
            Mbl[j] ← i−1
```

Fig. 1. Backmarking with dynamic variable ordering

also need to know how far up the tree we have backtracked since last trying to instantiate $V[i]$, so that we know what checks we can save given the information in Mcl. Hence, BM uses an additional array Mbl (the minimum backtrack level) which for each variable keeps track of how far we have backtracked since trying to instantiate this variable. (In the example above, Mbl[i] will store the information that we have only backtracked to $V[j]$ since last visiting $V[i]$).

To apply our methodology we must distinguish between nodes and variables. Clearly, Mcl[i, k] is not the deepest variable, but rather the deepest node that the assignment $V[i] ← k$ checked against. And similarly, Mbl[i] is the shallowest node whose assignment has been changed since the i-th variable was the variable associated with the current node. So Mcl and Mbl are both indexed by variable indices, but store node indices. This distinction allows us implement a correct version of BM that can use dynamic variable ordering. Figure 1 gives the resulting algorithm in more detail. To our knowledge, a DVO version of BM has not previously appeared in the literature.

In the code the procedure *NextVar*() returns the index of the next variable to be assigned. It computes which of the uninstantiated variables should be assigned next by some heuristic measure. Backmarking is invoked, after initialization, with the call BM(1) and it will subsequently print all solutions. The only differences between this code and the standard static order BM algorithm are (1) a dynamic choice of the variable to instantiate next, (2) the indirection of consistency checks through the node structures, and (3) the restore function must scan all variables, not just $V[i]$ to $V[N]$ (these may not be the uninstantiated variables at this point in the search tree).

A large number of tree-search algorithms have been implemented by Manchak and van Beek as a library of C routines [MvB94]. These include the traditional algorithms of backtracking (BT) [BE75], backjumping (BJ) [Gas78], backmarking (BM) [Gas77], and forward checking (FC) [HE80]. They have also implemented all of Prosser's hybrid algorithms [Pro93], conflict-directed backjumping (CBJ), backmarking with backjumping (BMJ), backmarking with conflict-directed backjumping (BM-CBJ), forward checking with backjumping (FC-BJ), and forward checking with conflict-directed backjumping (FC-CBJ); Dechter's graph-based backjumping (GBJ) [Dec90]; forward checking that uses full arc consistency to prune the future domains (FCarc); and forward checking that uses full path consistency to prune the future domains (FCpath).

We have applied our methodology to all of these algorithms, implementing a DVO version of each. In Section 4 we will report on the performance of these algorithms with and without DVO.

3 The MRV Heuristic

In the previous section we demonstrated how a tree-search algorithm can be modified so as to use DVO. It has long been known that DVO can yield a considerable performance speedup [HE80, DM94a]. However, the notion of using DVO is quite distinct from the method by which the ordering is chosen. In previous work attention has focused almost exclusively on the heuristic of choosing at every point in the search, the next variable to be that which has the minimal number of remaining values, i.e., the minimal number of values compatible with all of the previous assignments [HE80, Pur83, DM94a]. We call this the minimum remaining values heuristic (MRV). Previous authors have called this heuristic dynamic variable ordering [FD94], and dynamic search rearrangement [Pur83]. But such names confuse the specific heuristic MRV with the general technique DVO. As we will see in this section, MRV has some very particular properties that might not be shared by other ordering heuristics. Other authors have also called the MRV heuristic the fail first (FF) heuristic. But this also is a somewhat ambiguous name.

An immediate question is how do we implement MRV in a domain independent manner? First, we should note that for algorithms that do all of their constraint checks backwards against previous assignments, computing the MRV heuristic will require additional constraint checks. If all we have access to is the set of constraint relations, then there is an obvious but inefficient strategy. The tree-search algorithm calls the MRV procedure when it has descended to the next level and needs to choose a variable to assign at this level.[5] When it is invoked, the MRV procedure can check each value in the domain of each uninstantiated variable to see if that value is consistent with the current set of assignments. By cycling through all the values in the variable domains it can count the number

---

[5] For example, in the BM code of Figure 1, the call to *NextVar* would be a call to a procedure that computes the MRV heuristic.

of remaining compatible values each variable has, and return a variable with the minimum such number.

However, as pointed out by Dechter and Meiri [DM94a], with this implementation computing the MRV heuristic will consume many redundant constraint checks. For example, consider the following scenario. We make the assignment $V[1] \leftarrow 1$ at $Nd[1]$. Then we call MRV and it discovers that $V[3] \leftarrow 1$ is incompatible with this assignment, but it also finds that $V[2]$ is the variable with fewest remaining values. The tree-search algorithm then makes the assignment $V[2] \leftarrow 1$ at $Nd[2]$. Upon calling MRV again, our naive strategy will again check $V[3] \leftarrow 1$ against $V[1] \leftarrow 1$, even though it had already determined at a previous level that this pair was incompatible. This constraint check is redundant.

A superior implementation strategy for MRV is to use the same procedure as FC. Basically, we allow the MRV procedure to maintain a set of pruned domains for all the uninstantiated variables. Whenever the tree-search algorithm instantiates a variable, it can call MRV to allow it to prune the remaining variable domains using the new instantiation. And whenever the tree-search algorithm uninstantiates a variable it can call MRV to allow it to restore the values pruned by that instantiation. Now the MRV procedure can simply count the number of remaining elements in each of the pruned domains to determine the next variable. In the example above, when we make the assignment $V[1] \leftarrow 1$, MRV will prune the value 1 from the domain of $V[3]$. Hence, when we make the next assignment $V[2] \leftarrow 1$, MRV does not have to do any checks against $V[3] \leftarrow 1$: that value has been pruned from $V[3]$'s domain. Note that the tree-search algorithm is still using MRV as a heuristic. In particular, the structures containing the pruned domains remain local to the MRV procedure. All the MRV procedure does is to return the next variable, it *communicates no other information* to the tree-search algorithm. Let us call the MRV heuristic computed using the forward checking procedure MRV$_{FC}$.

In FC algorithms, on the other hand, the pruned domains are maintained as part of the algorithm itself. For these algorithms, the MRV procedure does not need to do any extra constraint checks. It can simply count the number of values in the pruned domains, and rely on the FC algorithm to maintain these structures.

Since MRV$_{FC}$ is computed using the same procedure used by forward there is a close relationship between tree-search algorithms that use MRV$_{FC}$ and FC itself. This relation is characterized by the following theorems. Let *checks*(A) be the number of constraint checks performed by algorithm A. This is actually a function from problem instances to number of constraint checks. When we write *checks*$(A) <$ *checks*(B) we mean that the "$<$" relation holds for *all* problem instances, similarly for the other binary relations.

Theorem 2. *MRV makes standard backjumping redundant.*[6] *Specifically, we have*

$$checks(\text{BT+MRV}) = checks(\text{BJ+MRV}), \text{ and}$$
$$checks(\text{BM+MRV}) = checks(\text{BMJ+MRV}).$$

Proof. Note that this theorem holds for the more general MRV, not only for MRV_{FC}. Backjumping operates when search hits a dead end. Say that the variable associated with the dead end node is $V[j]$. Instead of stepping back to the previous node, backjumping jumps back to the deepest previous node, say node i, that had a conflict with some value of $V[j]$; i.e., none of the nodes deeper than i had any conflicts with $V[j]$. This means that if the tree-search algorithm is using MRV, at the time that node i's assignment was made, $V[j]$ must have had zero remaining compatible domain values. Hence, it must have been chosen by MRV to be the next variable,[7] and the dead end must in fact have occured at level $i + 1$. That is, the backjump must have been simply a chronological backstep, and the search process without backjumping would have been identical. ∎

This theorem does not hold for more sophisticated forms of backjumping such as CBJ, or GBJ. CBJ and GBJ do not perform standard backjumping. Rather they use a backjumping technique that passes information further up the tree allowing multiple backjumps. Prosser's FC-BJ algorithm [Pro93] is presented as a combination of FC and standard BJ, and one might suspect that the above theorem implies that $checks(\text{FC}) = checks(\text{FC-BJ})$. However, the backjumping in FC-BJ is not standard backjumping. Rather, it can be considered to be a "one-step" version of CBJ. In particular, it uses information gathered from a future variable (the variable whose domain has wiped out), plus information from the current node to decide where to jump back to. Standard backjumping only uses information from the current node in determining where to jump back to. Hence, the theorem does not apply to FC-BJ either.

Theorem 3. *The number of consistency checks performed by each of the algorithms* $\text{BT+MRV}_{\text{FC}}$, $\text{BJ+MRV}_{\text{FC}}$, $\text{BM+MRV}_{\text{FC}}$, *and* $\text{BMJ+MRV}_{\text{FC}}$, *lie in the range*

$$[checks(\text{FC+MRV}), 2KN\, checks(\text{FC+MRV})],$$

where N is the number of variables and K is the maximum of the variable domain sizes, and assuming that the MRV heuristics break ties in the same way,

Proof. To conserve space we provide only parts of the proof. Also in our discussion we drop the $+\text{MRV}_{\text{FC}}$ suffix on the algorithm names.

---

[6] This result is very closely related to (and, in fact, can be viewed as being a corollary of) Kondrak and van Beek's result that FC visits fewer nodes than BJ [KvB95]. To see the similarly note that in our proof FC would have detected a domain wipeout at node i and would never had descended below that node.

[7] If there was more than one variable with zero remaining domain values, MRV would still have chosen $V[j]$. Otherwise $V[j]$ would not have been the variable associated with the dead end node.

The key to understanding this theorem is to realize that the MRV heuristic acts much like the domain wipeout (DWO) detection that FC performs. Recall that FC checks forward from the current node and backtracks immediately if it detects that some future variable has no remaining consistent values. Such a variable is said to have had a domain wipeout. Now consider the search tree explored by FC. All leaf nodes are either solutions or nodes where DWO was detected. At these DWO nodes any algorithm equipped with MRV reordering would at the next level try to assign a value to a variable with zero remaining compatible values. Hence, MRV will allow the algorithm to fail at the very next level anyway.

BT and BM visit all of the nodes visited by FC [KvB95], and in the same order as FC. (The ordering follows from our requirement that ties are broken identically). The above argument can be made sufficiently precise to show that besides these nodes, BT and BM (with MRV) visit at most $K - 1$ additional siblings of each of these nodes (the assignments that were pruned by FC), and at the leaf nodes of FC's search tree they can descend at most one level deeper, visiting at most K additional children nodes. Hence, we can identify three different types of nodes visited by BT and BM: (1) nodes also visited by FC, (2) children nodes of a FC leaf node, and (3) siblings of FC nodes not visited by FC.

With this in hand all we need to do is to examine the number of checks that BT and BM perform at each type of node. Consider BT. For a node also visited by FC, it must check that node's assignment against all previous assignments, consuming at most N checks. These checks must succeed (else FC would have pruned this value and would never have visited this node). Hence, BT must descend to the next level and it will invoke the MRV_{FC} procedure. This procedure consumes the same number of checks as FC's forward checking phase. FC, on the other hand, consumes no checks to determine the node's consistency with the previous assignments (all of these checks were performed earlier), and then it performs forward checking, consuming the same number of checks as BT's invocation of MRV_{FC}. Hence, for these nodes BT performs at most N more checks. For nodes that are children nodes of a FC leaf node, BT performs at most N more checks. These checks must fail as the variable at this level (selected by MRV) has no values compatible with the previous assignments. Every leaf node in FC's search tree can have at most K children, so BT can consume at most NK additional checks in searching the children of FC leaf nodes. Note that because these children nodes fail against previous assignments, BT does not need to compute the MRV heuristic at these nodes. Finally, for nodes that are siblings of FC nodes not visited by FC, BT will again perform up to N additional checks, and again will not need to compute the MRV heuristic since some of these checks must fail. Each node in the FC search tree can have at most $K - 1$ unvisited siblings. Putting this all together, we see that the worst case are the FC leaf nodes. There BT can perform N more checks at the node itself, NK more checks visiting its children, and $N(K - 1)$ more checks visiting its unvisited siblings. This gives the $2NK$ upper bound of the theorem. At no node does BT perform fewer checks than FC (due to its MRV computation). This gives the lower bound.

The result for BM follows the same argument. BM will save a number of checks over BT, so for BM the upper bound becomes looser. Nevertheless, the lower bound is clearly the same. The result for BMJ and BJ follow from Theorem 2. ∎

Intuitively what is occuring here, is that in computing the MRV heuristic these algorithms are forced to consume at least as many checks as FC. Plain BT may in certain cases perform fewer checks than FC, but once we add MRV_{FC} this is no longer possible. Furthermore, MRV_{FC} has the property of promoting future failures to the next variable. This means that with MRV, algorithms like BT cannot consume an exponential amount of extra checks prior to reaching the level at which a domain wipeout occurs. Plain BT, on the other hand, often falls prey to this behavior. MRV makes the BT, BM, and BJ search spaces very similar to that of FC+MRV.

Two obvious questions arise. First, since computing the MRV heuristic causes BT and its variants to consume as many checks as FC, is it worthwhile? And second, why have we placed such strong restrictions on the information that the MRV computation can communicate to the tree-search algorithm?

The first question can only be answered experimentally. DVO using MRV is a heuristic technique, and there is no guarantee its costs are worthwhile. Nevertheless, the experimental evidence is unequivocal, DVO using MRV generates net speedups of can be orders of magnitude in size. Significant performance gains occurred in all of the experiments we performed, and such gains confirmed the results found in previous work [HE80, Pur83, DM94a].

As for the second question, indeed other information could be returned from the MRV computation. For example, the MRV procedure could tell the algorithm about pruned domain values, or about domain wipeout. However, if one follows this strategy, sharing more and more information between the MRV procedure and the tree-search algorithm, one is lead naturally to a combined algorithm that is identical to FC! In fact, our theorem shows that if one wants to do DVO with MRV, one should adopt the FC algorithm from the onset. Unless, of course, one has a much more efficient method of implementing MRV than MRV_{FC}.[8]

Theorem 3 does not cover the algorithms that perform more sophisticated backjumping. One result that can be proved for these algorithms is the following (the proof is omitted due to space considerations):

Theorem 4. *The number of consistency checks performed by the algorithms* $CBJ + MRV_{FC}$, $BM\text{-}CBJ+MRV_{FC}$ *lie in the range*

$$[checks(\text{FC-CBJ+MRV}), 2KN\,checks(\text{FC-CBJ+MRV})]$$

---

[8] A more efficient method for computing the MRV heuristic has recently been developed by Bacchus and Grove [BG95] using "lazy" computation. However this improvement, and probably any others, can be applied to improve FC in such a way that it continues to be the superior algorithm.

	First Solution				All Solutions			
Algorithm	Mean	Stan. Dev	Min	Max	Mean	Stan. Dev	Min	Max
FC-CBJvar	502.3	394	236	2162	2921	331	2184	4186
FC-BJvar	502.9	396	236	2162	2925	333	2184	4186
FCvar	504	398	236	2162	2928	336	2184	4186
BM-CBJvar	863	665	391	3586	5328	538	4101	7344
BMvar	867	675	391	3610	5357	550	4101	7389
BMJvar	867	675	391	3610	5357	550	4101	7389
CBJvar	1078	981	391	5187	7824	913	5814	11077
GBJvar	1078	981	391	5187	7854	914	5819	11086
BJvar	1095	1012	391	5334	7933	946	5819	11290
BTvar	1095	1012	391	5334	7933	946	5819	11290
FCarcvar	1624	228	1350	2391	5786	321	4749	6562
FCarc	5581	7203	1069	47390	36155	29314	6551	202868
FC-CBJ	10361	16383	262	119767	69982	74195	9370	560479
FC-BJ	16840	29977	262	280302	101824	107137	9779	777805
BM-CBJ	25471	72004	297	1237283	160114	240352	11690	2249471
FC	35582	71012	262	802069	181985	226318	13376	1891452
CBJ	63212	193846	339	3297304	397341	638772	23915	5877579
BMJ	125474	361595	300	5214608	557189	963154	15023	8642938
BM	396945	1276415	401	18405514	1607926	3110485	16504	29840296
BJ	503324	1524191	358	19324081	2225701	4084082	39269	34453199
FCpathvar	644651	54488	493703	834143	1471904	82555	1238546	1737179
GBJ	713603	2774915	870	46480727	2888529	6363137	46921	75012744
FCpath	844474	417441	377603	3138981	3183214	1265627	1479863	9649464
BT	3858989	9616408	1773	102267383	16196384	33354822	109317	417147956

Table 1. Number of consistency checks for the Zebra Problem

assuming that the MRV heuristics break ties in the same way, and that in the case of DWO the MRV$_{FC}$ *heuristics return as the next variable the first variable at which* FC-CBJ *detected DWO.*

4 Experiments

Our theoretical results give some valuable insight into the relative performance of various CSP algorithms when equipped with DVO using the MRV heuristic. However, they do not answer all of the questions. So we turn now to the results of a series of experiments we ran using the 12 different algorithms mentioned in Section 2 (BT, BM, BJ, FC, CBJ, BMJ, BM-CBJ, FC-BJ, FC-CBJ, FCarc, FCpath, and GBJ). We experimented with these algorithms using both static and dynamic variable orderings, for a total of 24 different algorithms tested. The

DVO equipped algorithms are all indicated with a "var" suffix: BTvar, BMvar, etc. The MRV heuristic was used throughout, with the non-FC algorithms using MRV_{FC}. In our tests we included the number of constraint checks consumed by the MRV computation.

Table 1 shows experimental results from Prosser's version of the Zebra problem [Pro93]. This version of the problem has 11 solutions. Prosser used 450 different static variable orderings, of varying bandwidths, and computed the average number of consistency checks required to find the first solution. We used the same orderings and repeated Prosser's original tests, extending them to test all of our algorithms and to test finding all solutions. We also used these tests as a "sanity" check on our implementation: we checked that we obtained exactly the same results as Prosser on the tests he performed, and we checked the correctness of every solution found during all of the runs of each algorithm. The table shows the mean, standard deviation, minimum, and maximum number of consistency checks consumed by each algorithm when computing both the first solution and all solutions.

Table 2 and 3 shows experimental results from the n-Queens problem, for finding the first and all solutions respectively. Blank entries indicate that the algorithm was unable to solve that size problem within a preset check limit of 40,000,000 checks. For those algorithms that have blank entries the last non-blank entry also indicates the maximum sized problem the algorithm could solve (within the aforementioned resource bounds).[9] For example, when finding the first solution (Table 2) FC is able to solve the 27-Queen problem, but failed on the 28-Queen problem.

Table 4 shows experimental results from random hard CSP problems. These problems are drawn from the range of 50% solvable classes computed by Frost and Dechter [FD94]. The problem classes are defined by four parameters: N the number of variables; K the number of values in each variable's domain; T the number of incompatible value pairs in each non-trivial constraint (i.e., the tightness of each constraint); and C the number of non-trivial constraints. The columns of Table 4 are labeled by the four numbers $K/N/T/C$. For example the first column indicates experiments run from the class $K = 3$, $N = 25$, $T = 1$, and $C = 199$. The value for C that gives rise to approximately 50% solvable problems, given the values for the other parameters, was computed by Frost and Dechter for a range of setting of the other parameters. The entries show the average number of checks needed to solve a sample of 100 random problems using Frost and Dechter's distribution.[10] Blank entries indicate that the algorithm was

---

[9] Actually, the last non-blank entry indicates that the algorithm failed on the next size test, at which point its execution was terminated. However, the variance in the number of checks required when finding the first solution in n-Queens is so high that these algorithms may well be able to find solutions for much larger n-Queen problems: the larger problems can be much easier. For example, in other tests we ran FCvar fails to solve the 94-Queens problem (first solution), but finds 1000-Queens easy!

[10] Specifically, the distribution is as follows: out of all possible sets of C variable pairs choose any particular set with uniform probability, and for each constrained pair out of all possible sets of T value pairs choose any particular set with uniform probability.

Algorithm	17 Queens	20 Queens	21 Queens	27 Queens	29 Queens	50 Queens
FC-CBJvar	1959	4144	2572	5602	6353	73497
FC-BJvar	1959	4144	2572	5602	6352	74478
FCvar	1959	4144	2572	5602	6352	74478
BM-CBJvar	3348	7048	4404	9744	10228	116483
BMvar	3354	7031	4404	9744	10228	117720
BMJvar	3354	7031	4404	9744	10228	117720
CBJvar	6782	21918	6887	17746	12338	1766530
GBJvar	6830	22064	6887	17746	12338	1832429
BJvar	6830	22064	6887	17746	12338	1832429
BTvar	6830	22064	6887	17746	12338	1832429
FCarcvar	17311	35721	37502	104063	137140	1341257
BM	37901	1343970	57268	2827027	9339790	
BMJ	39328	1390002	59803	2977455	9739637	
BM-CBJ	40292	1422246	61081	3051718	9956436	
FC-CBJ	67090	2383500	114612	7370008		
FC-BJ	67218	2386695	114757	7389632		
FC	67329	2398022	115120	7448781		
FCarc	251009	8114120	458113			
CBJ	428645	21113299	949128			
BJ	436340	21882531	972065			
GBJ	485597	25428842	1156015			
BT	485597	25428842	1156015			
FCpathvar	13025412	35489731				
FCpath	21751599					

Table 2. Number of consistency checks for finding the First Solution in n-Queens

unable to solve all random instances within a limit of 40,000,000 checks for each instance.

Discussion. The most important result of our tests is that the three algorithms FC-CBJvar, FC-BJvar, and FCvar prove themselves to one-two-three in all of the tests we ran (including other random tests not reported here). FC-CBJvar seems to be the fastest algorithm among those tested, and we know of only one other algorithm that beats it. This algorithm is minimal forward checking, which was developed by Dent and Mercer [DM94b] and adapted to use the MRV heuristic by Bacchus and Grove [BG95]).

However, the performance gain obtained by adding conflict directed back-jumping hardly seems worthwhile when DVO is being used. At least this was the case in the range of experiments we performed. A 5% gain over FCvar was the largest we found in any of our tests (the tables shows at most a 2% gain). Given

Algorithm	8 Queens	9 Queens	10 Queens	11 Queens	12 Queens	13 Queens
FC-CBJvar	12066	49903	204907	934630	4632066	24367856
FC-BJvar	12066	49903	204909	934866	4633478	24376345
FCvar	12066	49914	204954	935124	4634624	24384172
BM	12308	50866	220052	1026576	5224512	28405086
BM-CBJ	12519	52132	225086	1046235	5306272	28808758
BMJ	12419	52005	224648	1046427	5309340	28857934
FC-CBJ	13003	55132	241107	1148115	5915759	32293528
FC-BJ	13003	55134	241213	1149081	5923788	32355595
FC	13024	55326	242174	1154984	5958644	32592662
BMvar	22878	93526	375380	1700864	8383142	
BMJvar	22878	93526	375380	1700864	8383142	
BM-CBJvar	22901	93590	375582	1701208	8384896	
FCarcvar	37476	157531	648781	2987019	14851673	
FCarc	37953	163227	697024	3313549	17015768	
CBJ	41128	214510	1099796	6129447	36890689	
BJ	41862	219997	1131942	6364834	38511567	
CBJvar	42463	202849	913098	4699863	26413881	
GBJvar	42540	203763	917408	4725855	26582134	
BJvar	42540	203763	917408	4725855	26582134	
BTvar	42540	203763	917408	4725855	26582134	
GBJ	46752	243009	1297558	7416541		
BT	46752	243009	1297558	7416541		
FCpathvar	1877331	9823035	38825419			
FCpath	1881899	9843276	39316475			

Table 3. Number of consistency checks for finding the All Solutions in n-Queens

the simplicity of FCvar (it is FC with a simple domain counting implementation of MRV) it would seem that this is the algorithm of choice.

In fact, a plausible argument can be given as to why adding CBJ to an algorithm is unlikely to yield much improvement when the MRV heuristic is being used. With MRV, variables that have conflicts with past assignments (i.e., that have values eliminated from their domain by these assignments) are likely to be instantiated sooner. Thus, MRV will tend to cluster conflicted variables together. Hence, CBJ is unlikely to generate large backjumps, and its savings are likely to be minimal.[11] In essence what is happening with plain backjumping (the tables show that the results for BTvar, BJvar and BMvar, BMJvar are as predicted by Theorem 2) is also happening with CBJ, but to a lesser extent.

---

[11] Prosser (personal communication) has pointed out that CBJ might still yield significant benefits when the variables have very different domain sizes (as the MRV heuristic may then be fooled by this initial difference in domain sizes). In all of the tests we have performed the variables have identical domain sizes. We hope to do some additional tests in the future to test this conjecture.

Class	3/25/1/199	6/35/4/500	6/50/4/710	9/15/27/79	9/35/27/178
FC-CBJvar	2355.2	750696.4	10704412.1	14482.0	682625.1
FC-BJvar	2413.0	757654.9	10951900.4	14499.9	696165.8
FCvar	2413.0	757717.0	10953565.3	14500.5	697224.1
BM-CBJvar	3262.6	952415.4	13239561.0	20711.4	896761.5
BMvar	3330.8	959341.4	13452497.5	20748.4	918496.8
BMJvar	3330.8	959341.4	13452497.5	20748.4	918496.8
CBJvar	3456.5	1237790.1	17666604.5	25911.0	1192841.5
GBJvar	3569.3	1264438.4	18261854.0	26062.4	1218423.4
BTvar	3571.8	1264642.3	18290211.4	26079.4	1241074.3
BJvar	3571.8	1264642.3	18290211.4	26079.4	1241074.3
FCarcvar	6079.1	2613758.9		57826.9	2211137.4
FCarc	8594.9			80780.5	
FC-CBJ	12502.5			66323.1	
BM-CBJ	17454.9			72914.1	
FC-BJ	19205.8			67937.2	
FC	25864.3			72742.2	
CBJ	30900.3			271248.0	
BMJ	46788.2			85266.5	
BM	62395.8			111088.7	
BJ	140487.8			392578.0	
GBJ	363117.4			876196.4	
BT	395590.0			954209.0	
FCpathvar	626680.4				
FCpath	631379.1				

Table 4. Number of consistency checks for finding the first solution for random problems drawn from various 50% solvable classes.

Our results also show that DVO using MRV is generally a great win. The only case where static order algorithms beat their DVO counterparts is in the case of finding all solutions to n-Queens. There, BM was the fourth best algorithm. Nevertheless, it was still beaten by FCvar by about 15%. In the other tests the DVO algorithms display much greater performance gains over their static order counterparts. Our results for the Zebra problem also show that DVO using MRV leads to a significant increase in the robustness of performance in the face of varying initial orderings. That is, the variance of the number of checks performed over the 450 different orderings is significantly lower for the MRV versions. The reader might think that since variable ordering is done dynamically there should be no dependence on the initial ordering. However, in our implementation the initial ordering affects the way in which ties are broken when the MRV heuristic decides upon the next variable to instantiate. Tie breaking can have a tremendous effect on performance, as is indicated by the range between the minimum and maximum number of checks performed by the DVO algorithms.

These performance gains show that the forward checking algorithm is a very powerful CSP solution technique. Frost and Dechter suggest, in a recent paper [FD94], that "FC should be recognized as a more valuable variable ordering heuristic than as a powerful algorithm". We disagree. Even without variable reordering, FC is one of the most powerful static order algorithms. FC and its variants along with BM and its variants generally display significantly better performance than any of the other static order algorithms.[12] Where FC gains its greatest superiority is that the data structures it maintains allow for a *check-free* implementation of the powerful MRV heuristic. FC and its variants with the MRV heuristic performed better in our experiments than any of the other algorithms we tested. Furthermore, we have *proved* that it will always have better performance than a number of other algorithms. It is true that the process of forward checking can be used to implement the MRV heuristic (as pointed out by Dechter and Meiri [DM94a]), but it is misleading to categorize FC as simply a method for computing this heuristic.

The Frost and Dechter study [FD94] also reported a number of empirical results that are contradicted by the theorems and empirical results of our study. First, they reported that BJ when equipped with DVO using MRV outperforms a similarly equipped BT algorithm. Theorem 2 shows that this is not possible. Furthermore, our empirical results show exact agreement with the theorem. Additional support for the correctness of our empirical results comes from our exact agreement with Prosser's results on the Zebra problem and with Nadel on his n-Queens results [Nad89]. Second, they reported that BT with DVO using MRV slightly outperforms a similarly equipped FC algorithm. This possibility is contradicted by Theorem 3 which once again is in agreement with our empirical results. Finally, for the random classes on which we duplicated their tests, e.g., 3/25/1/199, none of our algorithms matched their results; even our best algorithm FC-CBJvar required more checks than their implementation of BT with DVO using MRV.[13]

In view of these discrepancies, we must conclude that Frost and Dechter's implementation of BT+DVO and BJ+DVO differ quite significantly from ours (and thus also Nadel's and Prosser's). Hence, we cannot meaningfully compare their empirical results with ours.[14]

There is one final point that is worth making here. It has often been claimed that static order FC performs the "optimal" amount of forward checking [Nad89]. Our results dispute this claim. Static order FCarc (which uses full arc consistency to prune the future domains) often beats static order FC, in the Zebra and in

---

[12] Bacchus and Grove [BG95] demonstrate that there is actually a close relationship between BM and FC in the manner in which they optimize their checks.

[13] Table 4 shows results for a sample of only 100 problems, while Frost and Dechter used samples of size 1000. Nevertheless, when we repeated some of these tests with 1000 problems we obtained very similar results, indicating that sample size is not the issue here.

[14] We have communicated with them about some of these discrepancies and in the case of the inferior performance of FC they have agreed that there might be some anomaly in their implementation.

many of the random tests.[15] However, with the extra edge provided by DVO, FC once again seems to be the "right amount" of forward checking. FCpath (which uses full path consistency to prune the future domains), on the other hand, is definitely doing too much forward checking in all of these tests.

In conclusion, in this paper we have (1) provided a methodology for implementing dynamic variable ordering that can be applied to a range of CSP tree-search algorithms; (2) have implemented a range of DVO algorithms and tested them empirically; and (3) have provided some useful theoretical insights into the popular MRV heuristic. The main practical lesson of our study is that forward checking with variable reordering is both empirically and theoretically a very good algorithm for CSPs. Its main limitation seems to be its application to very large but "easy" problems (i.e., problems were there are an exponential number of solutions). For large problems the forward checking phase of FC can be quite expensive. Guided "random" guesses in the solution space, e.g., the GSAT technique [SLM92], seems to be a superior method for such problems. However, FC with variable reordering (or some variant of FCvar) may well be the best algorithm for small "hard" problems (i.e., problems with fewer variables and values that have only a few solutions scattered in an exponentially sized search space).

References

[BE75] J. R. Bitner and Reingold E. Backtracking programming techniques. *Communications of the ACM*, 18(11):651–656, 1975.

[BG95] Fahiem Bacchus and Adam Grove. On the Forward Checking algorithm. In *First International Conference on Principles and Practice of Constraint Programming (CP95)*, 1995.

[Dec90] R. Dechter. Enhancement schemes for constraint processing: Backjumping, learning and cutset decomposition. *Artificial Intelligence*, 41:273–312, 1990.

[DM94a] R. Dechter and Itay Meiri. Experimental evaluation of preprocessing algorithms for constraint satisfaction problems. *Artificial Intelligence*, 68:211–241, 1994.

[DM94b] M. J. Dent and R. E. Mercer. Minimal forward checking. In *6th IEEE International Conference on Tools with Artificial Intelligence*, pages 432–438, New Orleans, 1994. Available via anonymous ftp from ftp://csd.uwo.ca/pub/csd-technical-reports/374/tai94.ps.Z.

[FD94] Daniel Frost and Rina Dechter. In search of the best constraint satisfaction search. In *Proceedings of the AAAI National Conference*, pages 301–306, 1994.

[Gas77] J. Gaschnig. A general Backtracking algorithm that eliminates most redundant tests. In *Procceedings of the International Joint Conference on Artifical Intelligence (IJCAI)*, page 457, 1977.

[Gas78] J. Gaschnig. Experimental case studies of backtrack vs. Waltz-type vs. new algorithms for satisficing assignment problems. In *Proceedings of the Canadian Artifical Intelligence Conference*, pages 268–277, 1978.

---

[15] The superiority of FCarc over FC in the static order case in some situations was first pointed out to us by Peter van Beek (personal communication).

[HE80] R. M. Haralick and G. L. Elliott. Increasing tree search efficiency for constraint satisfaction problems. *Artificial Intelligence*, 14:263–313, 1980.

[KvB95] Grzegorz Kondrak and Peter van Beek. A theoretical evaluation of selected backtracking algorithms. In *Procceedings of the International Joint Conference on Artifical Intelligence (IJCAI)*, 1995.

[Mac87] A. K. Mackworth. Constraint satisfaction. In S. C. Shapiro, editor, *Encyclopedia of Artificial Intelligence*. John Wiley and Sons, New York, 1987.

[MvB94] D. Manchak and P. van Beek. A 'C' library of constraint satisfaction techniques, 1994. Available by anonymous ftp from: ftp.cs.ualberta.ca:pub/ai/csp.

[Nad89] Bernard A. Nadel. Constraint satisfaction algorithms. *Computational Intelligence*, 5:188–224, 1989.

[Pro93] P. Prosser. Hybrid algorithms for the constraint satisfaction problem. *Computational Intelligence*, 9(3), 1993.

[Pur83] P. W. Jr. Purdom. Jr. Search rearrangement backtracking and polynomial average time. *Artificial Intelligence*, 21:117–133, 1983.

[SLM92] B. Selman, H. J. Levesque, and D. G. Mitchell. A new method for solving hard satisfiability problems. In *Proceedings of the AAAI National Conference*, pages 440–446, 1992.

A Unifying Framework
for
Tractable Constraints

Peter Jeavons[1], David Cohen[1] and Marc Gyssens[2]

[1] Department of Computer Science, Royal Holloway, University of London, UK
[2] Department WNI, University of Limburg, B-3590 Diepenbeek, Belgium

Abstract. Many combinatorial search problems may be expressed as *constraint satisfaction problems*, and this class of problems is known to be NP-complete in general. In this paper we examine restricted classes of constraints which lead to tractable problems. We show that all known classes with this property may be characterized by a simple algebraic closure condition. Using this condition provides a uniform test to establish whether a given set of constraints falls into any of the known tractable classes, and may therefore be solved efficiently.

1 Introduction

Many combinatorial search problems may be expressed as constraint satisfaction problems. Unfortunately, finding solutions to a constraint satisfaction problem is known to be an NP-complete problem in general [12] even when the constraints are restricted to binary constraints. However, many of the problems which arise in practice have special properties which allow them to be solved efficiently. The question of identifying restrictions to the general problem which are sufficient to ensure tractability is important from both a practical and a theoretical viewpoint, and has been extensively studied.

Such restrictions may either involve the structure of the constraints, in other words which variables may be constrained by which other variables, or they may involve the nature of the constraints, in other words which combinations of values may be allowed for variables which are mutually constrained. Examples of the first approach may be found in [6, 7, 8, 13, 14] and examples of the second approach may be found in [2, 3, 10, 13, 18, 19].

In this paper we take the second approach, and investigate those classes of constraints which ensure tractability in whatever way they are combined. We bring together all currently known examples of such tractable classes, which may be described informally as follows (precise definitions are given later in the paper):

Class 0 Any set of constraints which all allow some constant value d to be assigned to every variable.

Class I Any set of binary constraints which are "0/1/all," as defined in [2]. (This class was described independently in [10]).

Class II Any set of constraints on an ordered domain in which each constraint is "max-closed," as defined in [3]. (This class includes any set of logical relations which are defined by Horn sentences [5]. It also includes the "basic" arithmetic constraints allowed by the CHIP programming language [19].)

Class III Any set of constraints in which each constraint corresponds to a system of linear equations (over some appropriate field).

We establish in this paper that each of these classes may be characterized by a simple algebraic closure condition. This provides a unifying theoretical framework for all known families of tractable constraints, and suggests that tractability is very closely linked to algebraic properties.

Using this algebraic closure condition provides a simple uniform test to establish whether a given set of constraints falls into any of the known tractable classes, and may therefore be solved efficiently using an appropriate algorithm. It has recently been established that any set of constraints which does not satisfy any (non-trivial) algebraic closure condition will generate a class of problems which is NP-complete [9]. Hence, in these cases there is unlikely to be an efficient general algorithm, and it may be more appropriate to employ heuristic solution strategies.

The work described in this paper represents a generalization of earlier results concerning tractable subproblems of the SATISFIABILITY problem. Schaefer [16] describes all possible tractable classes of constraints for this problem, which corresponds to the special case of the constraint satisfaction problem in which the variables are Boolean. The tractable classes described in [16] correspond precisely to the four tractable classes described here, in the special case of Boolean variables.

A different approach to identifying tractable constraints is taken in [18], where it is shown that a property of constraints referred to as "row-convexity," together with path-consistency, is sufficient to ensure tractability in binary constraint satisfaction problems. It should be noted, however, that because of the additional requirement for path-consistency row-convex constraints do *not* constitute a tractable class in the sense defined in this paper. In fact, the class of problems which contain only row-convex constraints is NP-complete [2].

The paper is organized as follows. In Section 2, we give the basic definitions, and describe the general form of the algebraic closure conditions for constraints which will be used to characterize each tractable class. In Sections 3 to 6, we describe the particular form of closure condition which applies to each tractable class listed above. Finally, in Section 7, we draw some conclusions from the results presented and identify open problems.

2 Definitions

2.1 The constraint satisfaction problem

We now define the (finite) *constraint satisfaction problem* which has been widely studied in the Artificial Intelligence community [13, 12, 11]

Definition 1. An instance of a *constraint satisfaction problem* consists of the following:

- a finite set of variables, N, identified by the natural numbers $1, 2, \ldots, n$;
- a finite domain of values, D; and
- a set of constraints $\{C(S_1), C(S_2), \ldots, C(S_c)\}$, where, for $i = 1, \ldots, c$, S_i is an ordered subset of the variables, and $C(S_i)$ is a set of tuples indicating the mutually consistent values for the variables in S_i.

The length of the tuples in a given constraint will be called the *arity* of that constraint. In particular, unary constraints specify the allowed values for a single variable, and binary constraints specify the allowed combinations of values for a pair of variables.

A *solution* to a constraint satisfaction problem is an assignment of values to the variables which is consistent with all of the constraints.

Deciding whether or not a given problem instance has a solution is NP-complete in general [12], even when the constraints are restricted to binary constraints. In this paper, we shall consider how restricting the allowed constraints to some fixed subset of all the possible constraints affects the complexity of this decision problem. We therefore make the following definition:

Definition 2. Let Γ be a set of sets of tuples. Then $CSP(\Gamma)$ is the class of decision problems with

INSTANCE: A constraint satisfaction problem $\mathcal{P}$ in which all constraints are elements of Γ.

QUESTION: Does $\mathcal{P}$ have a solution?

If every problem in $CSP(\Gamma)$ is solvable in polynomial time, then Γ is called a *tractable* set of constraints.

Example 1. We now describe four constraints which will be used as running examples throughout the paper. Each of these constraints is a set of 4-tuples:

$$C_0 = \{ (1,1,1,1), \qquad C_1 = \{ (0,1,1,1),$$
$$(1,0,0,1), \qquad\qquad (1,0,0,1),$$
$$(1,0,1,0), \qquad\qquad (1,0,1,0),$$
$$(0,1,1,0) \} \qquad\qquad (1,0,1,1),$$
$$(0,1,1,0) \}$$

$$C_2 = \{ (0,0,1,1), \qquad C_3 = \{ (0,1,1,1),$$
$$(1,0,0,1), \qquad\qquad (0,0,0,1),$$
$$(1,0,1,0), \qquad\qquad (0,0,1,0),$$
$$(1,0,1,1), \qquad\qquad (0,1,0,0) \}$$
$$(0,0,1,0),$$
$$(1,0,0,0),$$
$$(0,0,0,1) \}$$

$CSP(\{C_0, C_1, C_2, C_3\})$ contains all constraint satisfaction problems in which the constraints are all equal to C_0, C_1, C_2, or C_3.

2.2 Operations on constraints

Since constraints are simply relations, it is convenient to make use of the following operations from relational algebra [1]:

Definition 3. Let S be any ordered set of r variables and let $C(S)$ be a constraint on S. For any ordered subset $S' \subseteq S$, of size $r' \leq r$, the *projection* of $C(S)$ onto S', denoted $\pi_{S'}(C(S))$, is the r'-ary set of tuples obtained by restricting each tuple of $C(S)$ to the positions corresponding to variables of S'.

Definition 4. For any constraints $C(S_1)$ and $C(S_2)$, the *join* of $C(S_1)$ and $C(S_2)$, denoted $C(S_1) \bowtie C(S_2)$, is the constraint on $S_1 \cup S_2$ containing all tuples t whose restrictions to the index positions of S_1 and S_2 are contained in $C(S_1)$ and $C(S_2)$, respectively.

For simplicity, and without loss of generality, we shall assume that each variable is subject to at least one constraint. Hence, the set of all solutions to a constraint satisfaction problem $\mathcal{P}$, denoted $\mathrm{Sol}(\mathcal{P})$, is simply the join of all the constraints [8]:

$$\mathrm{Sol}(\mathcal{P}) = C(S_1) \bowtie C(S_2) \bowtie \cdots \bowtie C(S_c).$$

The decision problem for $\mathcal{P}$ is to determine whether or not this join is empty.

2.3 Operations on tuples

Any operation on the elements of the domain may be extended to an operation on tuples by applying the operation in each coordinate position separately. Hence, any operation defined on the domain of values may be used to define an operation on the elements of a constraint, as follows:

Definition 5. Let D be a set and let $\otimes : D^k \to D$ be a k-ary operation on D. For any collection of k tuples, $t_1, t_2, \ldots, t_k \in D^r$ (not necessarily all distinct), where $t_i = (x_{i1}, x_{i2}, \ldots, x_{ir})$, we define $\otimes(t_1, t_2, \ldots, t_k)$ to be the r-ary tuple

$$\big(\otimes(x_{11}, x_{21}, \ldots, x_{k1}), \otimes(x_{12}, x_{22}, \ldots, x_{k2}), \ldots, \otimes(x_{1r}, x_{2r}, \ldots, x_{kr})\big).$$

We now define the following closure property of constraints:

Definition 6. Let C be a constraint over domain D, and let $\otimes : D^k \to D$ be a k-ary operation on D. The constraint C is said to be $\otimes$-*closed* if, for all $t_1, t_2, \ldots, t_k \in C$ (not necessarily all distinct), $\otimes(t_1, t_2, \ldots, t_k) \in C$.

Example 2. Let $\triangle$ denote the ternary operation which returns the first repeated value of its three arguments, or the first value if they are all distinct. The constraint C_1 defined in Example 1 is $\triangle$-closed, since applying the $\triangle$ operation to any 3 elements of C_1 yields an element of C_1. For example,

$$\triangle((0,1,1,1),(1,0,0,1),(1,0,1,0)) = (1,0,1,1) \in C_1.$$

The constraint C_2 defined in Example 1 is *not* $\triangle$-closed, since applying the $\triangle$ operation to the last 3 elements of C_2 yields a tuple which is not an element of C_2:

$$\triangle((0,0,1,0),(1,0,0,0),(0,0,0,1)) = (0,0,0,0) \notin C_2.$$

If Γ is a set of constraints and $\otimes$ is an operation such that every constraint in Γ is $\otimes$-closed, then Γ is said to be $\otimes$-closed.

The following properties of closed constraints follow immediately from Definitions 3 and 4:

Proposition 7. *Let $C(S_1)$ and $C(S_2)$ be constraints which are $\otimes$-closed, for some operation $\otimes$, and let $S \subseteq S_1$. Then $\pi_S(C(S_1))$ and $C(S_1) \bowtie C(S_2)$ are also $\otimes$-closed.*

Note that this result implies that if all the constraints in some problem instance are $\otimes$-closed, then the set of solutions is also $\otimes$-closed.

3 Class 0: Constant operations

In this section, we consider constant operations, and show that these may be used to characterize the class of tractable constraint sets which we have called **Class 0** above.

Definition 8. *Let C be a constraint over domain D, and let $d \in D$. Then C is said to be d-uniform if it is either empty or contains the tuple $(d, d, \ldots, d)$.*

A set of constraints Γ over domain D is said to fall in **Class 0** if there is some $d \in D$ such that every constraint in Γ is d-uniform.

Example 3. The constraint C_0 defined in Example 1 is 1-uniform since it contains the tuple $(1, 1, 1, 1)$.

The set of constraints $\{C_0\}$ therefore falls into **Class 0**.

If Γ is in **Class 0** then the decision problem of a constraint satisfaction problem $\mathcal{P}$ in CSP(Γ) is clearly trivial to solve, since it either contains an empty constraint, in which case it does not have a solution, or it allows the solution in which every variable is assigned the value d.

Here, we simply point out that this rather trivial class may be characterized by an algebraic closure condition, and so fits into the general theory we are developing. The proof is immediate.

Proposition 9. *A constraint C over domain D is d-uniform for some $d \in D$ if and only if C is $\otimes$-closed for the constant operation $\otimes : D \to D : x \mapsto d$.*

Example 4. Let $\top$ denote the unary operation on the domain $D = \{0, 1\}$ which returns the constant value 1. The constraint C_0 defined in Example 1 is $\top$-closed, since applying the $\top$ operation to any element of C_0 yields the tuple $(1, 1, 1, 1)$, which is an element of C_0. The constraint C_1 defined in Example 1 is *not* $\top$-closed, since applying the $\top$ operation to any element of C_1 yields the tuple $(1, 1, 1, 1)$, which is not an element of C_1. In fact, C_1 is clearly not $\otimes$-closed for any constant operation $\otimes$.

4 Class I: A majority operation

In this Section we consider the ternary operation, $\triangle$, which returns the first of its argument values which is repeated, or the first argument value if they are all distinct:

$$\triangle(x, y, z) = \begin{cases} y \text{ if } y = z; \\ x \text{ otherwise.} \end{cases}$$

We will show that the $\triangle$ operation may be used to characterize the class of tractable constraint sets which we have called Class I above.

We first establish an important property of $\triangle$-closed constraints.

Proposition 10. *For any constraint $C(S)$ which is $\triangle$-closed we have*

$$C(S) = \underset{i,j \in S}{\bowtie} \pi_{(i,j)}(C(S)).$$

Hence $C(S)$ is equivalent to a set of binary constraints on S.

Proof. It is clear that $C(S) \subseteq \underset{i,j \in S}{\bowtie} \pi_{(i,j)}(C(S))$, since any relation is contained in the join of all of its binary projections.

Now let t be any element of $\underset{i,j \in S}{\bowtie} \pi_{(i,j)}(C(S))$. We shall prove, by induction on $|S|$, that $t \in C(S)$, thereby establishing the reverse inclusion.

For $|S| < 3$ the result holds trivially, so assume that $|S| \geq 3$, and that the result holds for all smaller values. Choose $s_1, s_2, s_3 \in S$. By Proposition 7 and the inductive hypothesis, applied to $\pi_{S \setminus \{s_i\}}(C(S))$, there is some $t_i \in C(S)$ which agrees with t on all variables except s_i, for $i = 1, 2, 3$. Since $C(S)$ is $\triangle$-closed, it follows that $t = \triangle(t_1, t_2, t_3) \in C(S)$.

In the light of Proposition 10, it is sufficient to consider *binary* $\triangle$-closed constraints.

Example 5. Reconsider the constraint C_1 defined in Example 1. The binary projections of C_1 are as follows:

- $\pi_{(1,2)}(C_1) = \{(0,1), (1,0)\}$
- $\pi_{(1,3)}(C_1) = \{(0,1), (1,0), (1,1)\}$
- $\pi_{(1,4)}(C_1) = \{(0,1), (1,0), (1,1)\}$
- $\pi_{(2,3)}(C_1) = \{(0,0), (0,1), (1,1)\}$
- $\pi_{(2,4)}(C_1) = \{(0,0), (0,1), (1,0), (1,1)\}$
- $\pi_{(3,4)}(C_1) = \{(0,1), (1,0), (1,1)\}$

It was shown in Example 2 that C_1 is $\triangle$-closed. Hence, by Proposition 10 we know that C_1 is equal to the join of these binary projections, and so may be replaced by this collection of binary constraints.

It is, of course, not always the case that a constraint may be replaced by its binary projections, as the following example demonstrates.

Example 6. Reconsider the constraint C_2 defined in Example 1. It was shown in Example 2 that C_2 is not $\triangle$-closed. The binary projections of C_2 are as follows:

- $\pi_{(1,2)}(C_2) = \{(0,0),(1,0)\}$
- $\pi_{(1,3)}(C_2) = \{(0,0),(0,1),(1,0),(1,1)\}$
- $\pi_{(1,4)}(C_2) = \{(0,0),(0,1),(1,0),(1,1)\}$
- $\pi_{(2,3)}(C_2) = \{(0,0),(0,1)\}$
- $\pi_{(2,4)}(C_2) = \{(0,0),(0,1)\}$
- $\pi_{(3,4)}(C_2) = \{(0,0),(0,1),(1,0),(1,1)\}$

The join of these binary projections contains the tuple $(0,0,0,0)$ which is not an element of C_2. Hence, C_2 cannot be replaced by a set of binary constraints.

We now show that binary $\triangle$-closed constraints correspond precisely to the *0/1/all constraints* defined in [2] (see also [10]). This result is rather unexpected, in view of the fact that 0/1/all constraints were originally defined purely in terms of syntactic structure.

Definition 11 [2]. A binary constraint $C(i,j)$ over domain D is said to be a *directed 0/1/all constraint* if $C(i,j)$ allows every value in D at variable i with zero, one, or all of the values in $\pi_j(C(i,j))$.

If $C(i,j)$ and $C(j,i)$ are both directed 0/1/all constraints, then $C(i,j)$ is said to be a *0/1/all constraint*.

Proposition 12. *A binary constraint $C(i,j)$ is $\triangle$-closed if and only if it is a 0/1/all constraint.*

Proof. (only if) Assume that $C(i,j)$ is a binary constraint over domain D which is $\triangle$-closed. Let (d,d') be any element of $C(i,j)$. Choose any value $d_0 \in D$. If C contains two distinct tuples (d_0,d_1) and (d_0,d_2), then it must contain the tuple

$$\triangle((d,d'),(d_0,d_1),(d_0,d_2)) = (d_0,d').$$

Hence, if d_0 is allowed with two distinct values in $\pi_j(C(i,j))$, then it is allowed with all of the values in $\pi_j(C(i,j))$, so $C(i,j)$ is a directed 0/1/all constraint. Similarly, $C(j,i)$ is a directed 0/1/all constraint.

(if) Assume that $C(i,j)$ is a 0/1/all constraint over domain D. Choose any 3 elements of $C(i,j)$, (d_1,d_1'), (d_2,d_2'), and (d_3,d_3'), and consider the tuple $t = \triangle((d_1,d_1'),(d_2,d_2'),(d_3,d_3'))$. By the definition of $\triangle$, we know that either $t = (d_1,d_1')$ or $d_2 = d_3$ or $d_2' = d_3'$. If $d_2 = d_3$ then either $d_2' = d_3'$ or $(d_2,d_1') \in C(i,j)$, since $C(i,j)$ is 0/1/all. Similarly, if $d_2' = d_3'$, then either $d_2 = d_3$ or $(d_1,d_2') \in C(i,j)$. Hence, in all cases, $t \in C(i,j)$, so $C(i,j)$ is $\triangle$-closed.

Hence, a set of binary constraints belongs to **Class I** if and only if it is $\triangle$-closed.

Theorem 13. *Let Γ be any set of constraints which are $\triangle$-closed. The decision problem for any constraint satisfaction problem $\mathcal{P} \in \mathrm{CSP}(\Gamma)$ may be solved in polynomial time.*

Proof. By Proposition 10, every constraint $C \in \Gamma$ may be replaced by an equivalent set of binary constraints, which are also $\triangle$-closed, by Proposition 7. By Proposition 12, these binary constraints are all 0/1/all constraints. Hence, by using the algorithm described in Section 4 of [2], any problem involving these constraints may be solved in polynomial time.

The time complexity of the algorithm for solving problems involving 0/1/all constraints, described in [2], is $O(c|D|(|D|+n))$, where c is the number of binary constraints and n is the number of variables.

5 Class II: ACI operations

In this section, we consider binary operations which are associative, commutative, and idempotent (ACI).

Definition 14. Let $\sqcup : D^2 \to D$ be a binary operation on the set D such that, for all $d_1, d_2, d_3 \in D$,

- $\sqcup(\sqcup(d_1, d_2), d_3) = \sqcup(d_1, \sqcup(d_2, d_3))$;   (associativity)
- $\sqcup(d_1, d_2) = \sqcup(d_2, d_1)$; and   (commutativity)
- $\sqcup(d_1, d_1) = d_1$ (idempotency)

Then $\sqcup$ is said to be an *ACI operation*.

We will show that these operations may be used to characterize a class of tractable constraint sets, including the class we have called **Class II** above.

The following result about ACI operations is well-known from elementary algebra [4].

Lemma 15. *Let $\sqcup$ be an ACI operation on the set D. The binary relation R on D defined by*

$$R(d_1, d_2) \iff \sqcup(d_1, d_2) = d_2$$

is a partial order on D in which any two elements d_1, d_2 have a least upper bound given by $\sqcup(d_1, d_2)$.

Example 7. When $D = \{\text{true}, \text{false}\}$, there are only two possible ACI operations on D, corresponding to the logical AND operation and the logical OR operation. These two operation correspond to the two possible orderings on D.

It is shown in [5] that a logical relation is AND-closed if and only if it may be defined by a Horn sentence (that is, a conjunction of clauses each of which contains at most one unnegated literal). Hence, if a set of constraints Γ is AND-closed, then $\text{CSP}(\Gamma)$ is equivalent to the Horn clause satisfiability problem, HORNSAT [15].

Similarly, a logical relation is OR-closed if and only if it may be defined by a conjunction of clauses each of which contains at most one negated literal.

Example 8. If we identify the logical value **true** with the value 1 and the logical value **false** with the value 0, then the constraint C_2 defined in Example 1 is OR-closed, since applying the OR operation to any 2 elements of C_2 yields an element of C_2. For example,

$$\text{OR}((1, 0, 0, 1), (0, 0, 1, 0)) = (1, 0, 1, 1) \in C_2.$$

The constraint C_3 defined in Example 1 is *not* OR-closed, since applying the OR operation to the last 2 elements of C_3 yields a tuple which is not an element of C_3:

$$\text{OR}((0,0,1,0),(0,1,0,0)) = (0,1,1,0) \notin C_3.$$

Similarly, C_3 is not AND-closed. Hence, by the remarks in Example 7, C_3 is not $\sqcup$-closed for any ACI operation $\sqcup$.

It follows from Lemma 15 that any (finite) non-empty set $D' \subseteq D$ which is $\sqcup$-closed contains a least upper bound with respect to the partial order R. This upper bound will be denoted $\sqcup(D')$.

Using Lemma 15, we now show that constraints which are closed under some arbitrary ACI operation form a tractable class.

Theorem 16. *Let $\sqcup$ be an ACI operation, and let Γ be any set of constraints which are $\sqcup$-closed. The decision problem for any $\mathcal{P} \in \text{CSP}(\Gamma)$ may be solved in polynomial time.*

Proof. Let $\mathcal{P} \in \text{CSP}(\Gamma)$. Let $\mathcal{P}'$ be a constraint satisfaction problem with the same set of solutions, such that for any variable v, and any constraints $C(S_1)$ and $C(S_2)$ of $\mathcal{P}'$ with $v \in S_1$ and $v \in S_2$, we have $\pi_{\{v\}}(C(S_1)) = \pi_{\{v\}}(C(S_2))$. (This is a generalization of the notion of "arc-consistency" [12] to non-binary problems.) Such a problem $\mathcal{P}'$ may be obtained by forming the join of every pair $C(S_i), C(S_j)$ of constraints in $\mathcal{P}$, replacing these constraints with the (possibly smaller) constraints $\pi_{S_i}(C(S_i) \bowtie C(S_j))$ and $\pi_{S_j}(C(S_i) \bowtie C(S_j))$, and then repeating this process until there are no further changes in the constraints. The time complexity of this procedure is polynomial in the size of $\mathcal{P}$, and the resulting problem $\mathcal{P}'$ is also a member of $\text{CSP}(\Gamma)$, by Proposition 7.

Now let $D(v)$ denote the set of values allowed for variable v by every constraint in $\mathcal{P}'$. Since $D(v)$ equals the projection of some $\sqcup$-closed constraint onto v, it must be $\sqcup$-closed, by Proposition 7. There are two cases to consider.

If any of the sets $D(v)$ is empty then $\mathcal{P}'$ has no solutions, so the decision problem is trivial.

On the other hand, if all these sets are non-empty, then we claim that assigning the value $\sqcup(D(v))$ to each variable v gives a solution to $\mathcal{P}'$, so the decision problem is again trivial. To establish this claim, consider any constraint $C(S)$ in $\mathcal{P}'$, where S is the ordered set $(v_1, v_2, \ldots, v_r)$. For each $v_i \in S$, there must be some tuple $t_{v_i} \in C(S)$ such that $\pi_{\{v_i\}}(\{t_{v_i}\}) = \{\sqcup(D(v_i))\}$, by the definition of $D(v_i)$. Now consider the tuple $t = \sqcup(t_{v_1}, \sqcup(t_{v_2}, \ldots, \sqcup(t_{v_{r-1}}, t_{v_r})) \cdots)$. We know that $t \in C(S)$, since $C(S)$ is $\sqcup$-closed. Furthermore, for each $v_i \in S$, $\pi_{\{v_i\}}(\{t\}) = \sqcup(D(v_i))$, because $\sqcup(D(v_i))$ is an upper bound of $D(v_i)$, so

$$\sqcup(d, \sqcup(D(v_i))) = \sqcup(D(v_i))$$

for all $d \in D(v_i)$. Hence the constraint $C(S)$ allows the assignment of $\sqcup(D(v))$ to each variable. Since $C(S)$ was arbitrary, we have shown that this assignment is a solution to $\mathcal{P}'$.

Example 9. Let D be a finite subset of the natural numbers. The operation MAX : $D^2 \to D$ which returns the larger of any pair of numbers is an ACI operation. The following types of arithmetic constraints (amongst many others) are closed under this operation:

- $aX \neq b$
- $aX = bY + c$
- $aX \leq bY + c$
- $aX \geq bY + c$
- $a_1X + a_2Y + \cdots + rZ \geq c$
- $aXY \geq c$

where upper-case letters represent variables and lower-case letters represent positive constants. Hence, by Theorem 16 it is possible to determine efficiently whether any collection of constraints of these types has a solution. These constraints include the 'basic' arithmetic constraints allowed by the CHIP programming language [19].

The *max-closed constraints*, defined in [3], correspond to $\sqcup$-closed constraints in the special case when the partial order R, defined in Lemma 15, is a total ordering of D. Hence, a set of constraints belongs to **Class II** if and only if it is $\sqcup$-closed, for a specialized ACI operation of this kind (see, for example, Example 9).

However, the class of tractable sets defined by ACI operations is a true generalization of the class containing all sets of max-closed constraints. In other words, there exist constraints which are $\sqcup$-closed for some ACI operation $\sqcup$ but are not max-closed for any (total) ordering of the domain.

Example 10. Consider, for example, the constraint C_2' over domain $D = \{0, 1, 2\}$ defined by

$$C_2' = \{ (0, 0, 2, 2),$$
$$(2, 0, 0, 2),$$
$$(2, 0, 2, 0),$$
$$(2, 0, 2, 2),$$
$$(0, 0, 1, 0),$$
$$(1, 0, 0, 0),$$
$$(0, 0, 0, 1) \}$$

The constraint C_2' is $\sqcup$-closed for the ACI operation $\sqcup$ defined by

$$\sqcup(x, y) = \begin{cases} x \text{ if } x = y \\ 2 \text{ otherwise.} \end{cases}$$

Hence, any problem in $\text{CSP}(\{C_2'\})$ may be solved in polynomial time. However, C_2' is not max-closed for any (total) ordering of D.

6 Class III: Affine operations

In this section, we consider ternary affine operations, which are defined as follows:

Definition 17. Let $\otimes : D^3 \to D$ be a ternary operation on the set D such that, for all $x, y, z, u \in D$

- $\otimes(\otimes(x, y, z), z, u) = \otimes(x, y, u)$;
- $\otimes(x, y, z) = \otimes(z, y, x)$; and
- $\otimes(x, x, y) = y$.

Then $\otimes$ is said to be an *affine operation*.

Any constraint which is $\otimes$-closed for some affine operation $\otimes$ will be called an *affine constraint*.

We will show that, when $|D|$ is prime, any affine operation may be used to characterize the class of tractable constraint sets which we have called **Class III** above.

First, we define a special type of affine operation, which will play a central role in what follows.

Definition 18. Let $D = \{0, 1, 2, \ldots, n-1\}$.

Define the operation $\nabla : D^3 \to D$ as follows. For all $x, y, z \in D$,

$$\nabla(x, y, z) = x - y + z \pmod{n}.$$

Example 11. Let $D = \{0, 1\}$. The constraint C_3 over D defined in Example 1 is ∇-closed, since applying the ∇ operation to any 3 elements of C_3 yields an element of C_3. For example,

$$\nabla((0, 1, 1, 1), (0, 1, 0, 0), (0, 0, 1, 0)) = (0, 0, 0, 1) \in C_3.$$

The constraint C_0 over D defined in Example 1 is *not* ∇-closed, since applying the ∇ operation to the first 3 elements of C_0 yields a tuple which is not an element of C_0:

$$\nabla((1, 1, 1, 1), (1, 0, 0, 1), (1, 0, 1, 0)) = (1, 1, 0, 0) \notin C_0.$$

We now show that for certain types of constraints, which we call *functional constraints*, ∇-closure corresponds to a simple linearity property.

Definition 19. Let C be a constraint of arity r over D. The constraint C is said to be a *functional constraint* if there exists some function $f : D^{r-1} \to D$ such that, for some i, $1 \leq i \leq r$,

$$C = \{(x_1, x_2, \ldots, x_r) \in D^r \mid x_i = f(x_1, \ldots, x_{i-1}, x_{i+1}, \ldots, x_r)\}.$$

Proposition 20. *Let $D = \{0, 1, 2, \ldots, n-1\}$, and let C be a functional constraint of arity r over D. Then C is ∇-closed if and only if*

$$C = \{(x_1, x_2, \ldots, x_r) \in D^r \mid \sum_{i=1}^{r} a_i x_i \equiv a \pmod{n}\}$$

for some $a, a_1, a_2, \ldots, a_r \in D$.

Proof. Since the "if" is immediate, we limit ourselves to the "only if." Thus assume that C is ∇-closed. Without loss of generality, we can assume that C is functional at the first index position. Thus let $f : D^{r-1} \to D$ be the function such that $C = \{(x_1, x_2, \ldots, x_r) \in D^r \mid x_1 = f(x_2, x_3, \ldots, x_r)\}$.

Since C is ∇-closed, we have, for all $x_2, \ldots, x_r, y_2, \ldots, y_r, z_2, \ldots, z_r \in D$, that

$$f(x_2 - y_2 + z_2, x_3 - y_3 + z_3, \ldots, x_r - y_r + z_r) =$$
$$f(x_2, x_3, \ldots, x_r) - f(y_2, y_3, \ldots, y_r) + f(z_2, z_3, \ldots, z_r) \pmod{n}.$$

In particular,

$$f(x_2 + z_2, x_3 + z_3, \ldots, x_r + z_r) =$$
$$f(x_2, x_3, \ldots, x_r) - f(0, 0, \ldots, 0) + f(z_2, z_3, \ldots, z_r) \pmod{n}.$$

So, if we define the function f^0 by setting

$$f^0(x_2, x_3, \ldots, x_r) = f(x_2, x_3, \ldots, x_r) - f(0, 0, \ldots, 0),$$

we have that

$$f^0(x_2 + z_2, x_3 + z_3, \ldots, x_r + z_r) = f^0(x_2, x_3, \ldots, x_r) + f^0(z_2, z_3, \ldots, z_r) \pmod{n}.$$

Thus we have shown that f_0 is a *linear* function modulo n, whence

$$f^0(x_2, x_3, \ldots, x_r) \equiv \sum_{i=2}^{r} f^0(\underbrace{0, 0, \ldots, 0}_{i-2}, 1, 0, \ldots, 0)\, x_i \pmod{n}.$$

Setting $a_1 = 1$,

$$a_i = -f^0(\underbrace{0, 0, \ldots, 0}_{i-2}, 1, 0, \ldots, 0),$$

for $i = 2, 3, \ldots, r$, and $a = f(0, 0, \ldots, 0)$, yields the desired result.

The next result shows that, when $D = \{0, 1, 2, \ldots, p-1\}$ and p is prime, *any* constraint over D which is ∇-closed may be expressed as a system of linear equations.

Proposition 21. *Let $D = \{0, 1, 2, \ldots, p-1\}$, for some prime p, and let C be a constraint over D. Then C is ∇-closed if and only if it is the set of solutions to a system of simultaneous linear equations over the integers modulo p.*

Proof. Since, again, the "if" is immediate, we limit ourselves to the "only if." Thus assume that C is ∇-closed, and C has arity r. The proof will be by induction on r.

Consider first the case when $r = 1$. For $i = 0, \ldots, p-1$, we define the binary operation ∇_i by

$$\nabla_i(x, y) = ix + (1 - i)y \pmod{p}.$$

Since $\nabla_0(x, y) = \nabla(x, x, y)$ and $\nabla_i(x, y) = \nabla(x, y, \nabla_{i-1}(x, y))$, and since C is ∇-closed, C is also ∇_i-closed. Hence, if C contains at least two elements, say (d_1) and (d_2), then C also contains $\{(d_2 + i(d_1 - d_2) \pmod{p})) \mid i = 0, 1, 2, \ldots, p-1\}$. Since p is prime, this set equals $\{(x) \mid x \in D\}$. Hence, if $r = 1$, then either $|C| = 1$ or else $C = D^1$. If $|C| = 1$, then $C = \{(d)\}$, for some $d \in D$, so C is the set of solutions to the linear equation $x = d$. Alternatively, if $C = D^1$, then C is the set of solutions to the empty set of linear equations.

Now assume that $r = m$ for some $m > 1$, and the result holds for all smaller values of r. If $C = D^m$ then C is the set of solutions to the empty set of linear equations and we are done. Otherwise, there must be a minimal sequence of distinct indices, $I = (i_1, i_2, \ldots, i_s)$, such that $\pi_I(C) \neq D^s$. Clearly, $1 < s \leq m$. By Proposition 7, $\pi_I(C)$ is also ∇-closed. We claim that $\pi_I(C)$ is a functional constraint.

To establish this claim, first note that, by the minimality of I, $\pi_{I \setminus \{i_j\}}(C) = D^{s-1}$. Hence,

$$p^{s-1} \leq |\pi_I(C)| < p^s.$$

This inequality can only be satisfied if there exists some $a \in D$ such that $(a, 0, 0, \ldots, 0) \in \pi_I(C)$. Now consider the mapping $\psi : \pi_I(C) \to D^s$ defined as follows:

$$\psi((x_{i_1}, x_{i_2}, \ldots, x_{i_s})) = (x_{i_1} - a, x_{i_2}, \ldots, x_{i_s}).$$

The image of $\pi_I(C)$ under ψ, $\psi(\pi_I(C))$, is ∇-closed and contains the tuple $(0, 0, \ldots, 0)$, so it is closed under (vector) addition, and hence is a vector subspace of $(GF(p))^s$ (where $GF(p)$ is the Galois Field of order p). This implies that $|\psi(\pi_I(C))|$ is a power of p. Since ψ is injective, $|\psi(\pi_I(C))| = |\pi_I(C)|$, whence $|\pi_I(C)| = p^{s-1}$. This means that given any sequence of values $x_{i_2}, x_{i_3}, \ldots, x_{i_s}$ there must be a unique value of x_{i_1} such that $(x_{i_1}, x_{i_2}, \ldots, x_{i_s}) \in \pi_I(C)$. Hence, $\pi_I(C)$ is a functional ∇-closed constraint, so by Proposition 20, $\pi_I(C)$ must be the set of solutions to a linear equation.

Now let $I' = \{\{1, \ldots, i_1 - 1, i_1 + 1, \ldots, m\}$ and consider the constraint $\pi_{I'}(C)$. Since the arity of $\pi_{I'}(C)$ is $m - 1$, we know by the inductive hypothesis that $\pi_{I'}(C)$ is also the set of solutions to a system of linear equations. Finally, since we have established a functional dependency between the value at coordinate position i_1 and the values at some subset of the remaining coordinate positions, we know that C may be written as follows:

$$C = \{(x_1, x_2, \ldots, x_m) \in D^m \mid (x_{i_1}, x_{i_2}, \ldots, x_{i_s}) \in \pi_I(C)\} \cap$$
$$\{(x_1, x_2, \ldots, x_m) \in D^m \mid (x_1, \ldots, x_{i_1-1}, x_{i_1+1}, \ldots, x_m) \in \pi_{I'}(C)\}.$$

Hence, C is the set of solutions to the system of simultaneous linear equations which is obtained by combining the equation for $\pi_I(C)$ and the equations for $\pi_{I'}(C)$.

Example 12. The constraint C_3 over $D = \{0, 1\}$ defined in Example 1 was shown to be ∇-closed in Example 11. Hence, by Proposition 21, C_3 must be the set of solutions to some system of linear equations over the integers modulo 2. In fact, we have

$$C_3 = \{(x_1, x_2, x_3, x_4) \mid (x_1 = 0) \wedge (x_2 + x_3 + x_4 \equiv 1 \pmod{2})\}.$$

Finally, we show that, when D is prime, *any* affine constraint is isomorphic to a constraint over $\{0, 1, 2, \ldots, |D| - 1\}$ which is ∇-closed. We make use of the following algebraic property of affine operations which was established in [17].

Lemma 22 [17]. *The ternary operation* $\otimes : D^3 \to D$ *is an affine operation if and only if there is an Abelian group* $(D, +)$ *such that, for all* $x, y, z \in D$,

$$\otimes(x, y, z) = x - y + z.$$

As a consequence of Lemma 22, we have the following

Lemma 23. *If* $|D|$ *is prime, and* $\otimes : D^3 \to D$ *is an affine operation, then there is a bijection* $\varphi : D \to \{0, 1, 2, \ldots, |D| - 1\}$ *such that, for all* $x, y, z \in D$,

$$\varphi(\otimes(x, y, z)) = \varphi(x) - \varphi(y) + \varphi(z) \pmod{|D|}.$$

Proof. If $|D|$ is prime, every Abelian group $(D, +)$, is isomorphic to the group of integers modulo $|D|$.

Lemma 23 yields that Proposition 21 may be applied to *arbitrary* affine constraints, to give the following result:

Theorem 24. *Let* Γ *be any set of constraints over some domain with a prime number of elements. If* Γ *is* $\otimes$-*closed for some affine operation* $\otimes$, *then the decision problem of any* $\mathcal{P} \in CSP(\Gamma)$ *may be solved in polynomial time.*

Recall that the decision problem for any system of linear equations over a field may be solved in polynomial time using well-known techniques of linear algebra (e.g. Gaussian elimination, which requires $O(n^3)$ arithmetic operations, where n is the number of variables).

7 Conclusion

We have now described a variety of operations which give rise to tractable sets of constraints. Furthermore, we have demonstrated that the sets of constraints in all known tractable classes are characterized by being closed under one of these operations.

Example 13. Reconsider the constraints C_0, C_1, C_2, C_3 over $D = \{0, 1\}$ defined in Example 1. We have shown that

- $\{C_0\}$ is in **Class 0** (Example 4);
- $\{C_1\}$ is in **Class I** (Example 2);
- $\{C_2\}$ is in **Class II** (Example 8); and
- $\{C_3\}$ is in **Class III** (Example 11).

Hence, any problem in $\mathrm{CSP}(\{C_0\})$, $\mathrm{CSP}(\{C_1\})$, $\mathrm{CSP}(\{C_2\})$, or $\mathrm{CSP}(\{C_3\})$ may be solved in polynomial time.

We have also shown that

- C_1 is not $\otimes$-closed for any constant operation $\otimes$ (Example 4);
- C_2 is not $\triangle$-closed (Example 2);
- C_3 is not $\sqcup$-closed for any ACI operation $\sqcup$ (Example 8);
- C_0 is not ∇-closed (Example 11).

Hence, the set of constraints $\Gamma = \{C_0, C_1, C_2, C_3\}$ does *not* fall into any known tractable class. In fact, it can be shown using the results in [9] that $\mathrm{CSP}(\Gamma)$ is NP-complete.

For each of the operations described in Sections 3, 4 and 5, it can be shown using the results of [9] that the set, Γ, containing all constraints which are closed under that operation is a maximal set of tractable constraints. In other words, the addition of *any* other constraint which is not closed under the same operation changes $\mathrm{CSP}(\Gamma)$ from a tractable problem class into an NP-complete problem class. Hence, the tractable classes which correspond to these operations are defined in the most general way possible.

We believe that the close connection between tractability and algebraic properties which has been demonstrated in this paper will lead to considerable further progress in understanding the boundary between tractable and intractable constraint satisfaction problems. For example, it may be possible to show, using known results about the structure of finite algebras, that no further tractable constraint classes exist. This question is currently being investigated.

Acknowledgments

The authors were supported by a grant from the "British-Flemish Academic Research Collaboration Programme" of the Belgian National Fund for Scientific Research and the British Council which enabled them to make mutual visits during which this research was carried out.

References

1. Codd, E.F., "A Relational Model of Data for Large Shared Databanks," *Communications of the ACM 13* (1970), pp. 377–387.
2. Cooper, M.C., Cohen, D.A., Jeavons, P.G., "Characterizing tractable constraints," *Artificial Intelligence 65* (1994), pp. 347–361.
3. Cooper, M.C., & Jeavons, P.G., "Tractable constraints on ordered domains," Technical Report, Dept of Computer Science, Royal Holloway, University of London (1994) and submitted to *Artificial Intelligence*.
4. Davey B.A. & Priestley, H.A., *Introduction to Lattices and Order*, Cambridge University Press (1990).
5. Dechter, R., & Pearl, J., "Structure identification in relational data," *Artificial Intelligence 58* (1992), pp. 237–270.
6. Dechter, R. & Pearl J. "Network-based heuristics for constraint-satisfaction problems," *Artificial Intelligence 34* (1988), pp. 1–38.
7. Freuder, E.C., "A sufficient condition for backtrack-bounded search," *Journal of the ACM 32* (1985), pp. 755–761.
8. Gyssens, M., Jeavons, P., Cohen, D., "Decomposing constraint satisfaction problems using database techniques," *Artificial Intelligence 66* (1994), pp. 57–89.
9. Jeavons, P.G., "An algebraic characterization of tractable constraints," Technical Report CSD-TR-95-05, Royal Holloway, University of London (1995).
10. Kirousis, L., "Fast parallel constraint satisfaction," *Artificial Intelligence 64* (1993), pp. 147–160..
11. Ladkin, P.B., & Maddux, R.D., "On binary constraint problems," *Journal of the ACM 41* (1994), pp. 435–469.
12. Mackworth, A.K. "Consistency in networks of relations," *Artificial Intelligence 8* (1977), pp. 99–118.
13. Montanari, U., "Networks of constraints: fundamental properties and applications to picture processing," *Information Sciences 7* (1974), pp. 95–132.
14. Montanari, U., & Rossi, F., "Constraint relaxation may be perfect," *Artificial Intelligence 48* (1991), pp. 143–170.
15. Papadimitriou, C.H., *Computational Complexity*, Addison-Wesley (1994).
16. Schaefer, T.J., "The complexity of satisfiability problems," *Proc 10th ACM Symposium on Theory of Computing (STOC)* (1978), pp. 216–226.
17. Szendrei, A., *Clones in Universal Algebra*, Séminaires de Mathématiques Supérieures 99, Université de Montréal (1986).
18. van Beek, P., "On the Minimality and Decomposability of Row-Convex Constraint Networks," *Proceedings of the Tenth National Conference on Artificial Intelligence, AAAI-92*, MIT Press (1992), pp. 447–452.
19. Van Hentenryck, P., Deville, Y., Teng, C-M., "A generic arc-consistency algorithm and its specializations," *Artificial Intelligence 57* (1992), pp. 291–321.

On the Forward Checking Algorithm

Fahiem Bacchus[1] and Adam Grove[2]

[1] Dept. of Computer Science, University of Waterloo, Waterloo, Ontario, Canada,
N2L 3G1, (fbacchus@logos.uwaterloo.ca)
[2] NEC Research Institute, 4 Independence Way, Princeton NJ 08540, USA,
(grove@research.nj.nec.com)

Abstract. The *forward checking* algorithm for solving constraint satisfaction problems is a popular and successful alternative to backtracking. However, its success has largely been determined empirically, and there has been limited work towards a real understanding of why and when forward checking is the superior approach.

This paper advances our understanding by showing that forward checking is closely related to *backmarking*, which is a widely used improvement of ordinary backtracking. This result is somewhat surprising, because (as their names suggest) forward checking is superficially quite different from backtracking and its variants. The result may also help in predicting when forward checking will be the best method.

Finally, the paper shows how the relationship to backmarking helps in understanding a recently introduced improvement to the forward checking algorithm, known as *minimal forward checking*. We argue that the new algorithm is best viewed as a hybrid combination of backmarking and forward checking.

1 Introduction

Constraint satisfaction problems (CSPs) [Mac87] are typical of the NP-complete combinatorial problems that are so pervasive in AI. Plain *backtracking* (BT) is an algorithm for solving CSPs that has been known for at least a century [BE75], but it is far from the best. There are easy improvements to backtracking such as backjumping (BJ) [Gas78] and backmarking (BM) [Gas77], which never do worse than backtracking [KvB95], and generally do much better. There are also simple alternatives to backtracking, notably *forward checking* (FC) and its variants [HE80].

The main purpose of this paper is to further our understanding of forward checking, which has extensive empirical but limited theoretical support as one of the very best among the class of simple, general, CSP algorithms [Nad89]. Because of its demonstrated practical success, it is important to discover as much as possible about when and why FC is superior to other approaches.

It can be argued that since the general class of CSPs are NP-complete, there are unlikely to be any major distinctions between the various algorithms. But this is too pessimistic. While any NP-complete family must contain impractically hard problems, it is also likely to contain large subclasses of simpler problems.

Indeed, the "region" of truly hard classes can be rather small [CKT91], and the particular instances we encounter in practice may well be outside of this region. Ideally we would identify the simple classes and develop special purpose fast algorithms to solve them, but this is usually impractical. Instead, we can search for better general techniques that less often display exponential behavior. Backmarking, backjumping, and forward checking have all shown themselves to be practical improvements over backtracking: they are all able to solve problems that defeat plain backtracking.

All these CSP algorithms examine partial solutions, which are assignments to a subset of the variables, and try to extend these until all variables are assigned. BM is a variant of BT that saves a number of redundant consistency checks by some straightforward bookkeeping. BJ is another variant of BT that saves a distinct set of consistency checks from BM, this time by detecting and avoiding parts of the search tree that cannot contain any solutions. FC, on the other hand, is quite different from BT. In particular, it orders its consistency checks in a completely different way. BT and its variants do all of their checks backwards: whenever a new assignment is make, it is checked for compatibility against all previous assignments. FC does all of its checks forward: whenever a new assignment is made, it checks that assignment against all future, as yet uninstantiated, variables, keeping track of the implications of these checks. In Section 2 we discuss the FC algorithm in detail and present some additional background. FC can do exponentially better than BT and its variants, but it can also do worse. However, in Section 3 we observe that there is a tight polynomial bound on how much worse it can do. The seemingly very different nature of FC, coupled with the known fact that it can do worse, appears to have hindered a serious study of its relationship to the other algorithms. However, as we show, there are in fact important connections between FC and BT, BM, and BJ.

There seem to be a couple of different ways in which FC can be beaten by BT and its variants, and both lead to important insights about their relationship. We examine one example in Section 3, where we present the first of our main results. Roughly speaking, this is as follows. FC achieves its success (or otherwise) over the backward checking algorithms in two ways. First, it optimizes checks over its search tree in *exactly* the same way that BM does. And second, it performs other checks that work as an "early-warning-system" of inconsistency. Our result requires some care in formulation, but it essentially says that, were one to provide BM with an oracle that provides the same warnings, and simultaneously ignore the cost that FC incurs in finding these warnings, the two algorithms would have equivalent complexity.

So we see that there is a particular cost/benefit tradeoff that must be considered when comparing FC to BM, and in specific types of problem the net effect of this tradeoff may be apparent. While it is hard to make many further generalizations about the value of FC, another interesting result is due to Kondrak and van Beek [KvB95]. They show that every node that BJ avoids searching (over BM or BT) is also avoided by FC. In a sense, then, FC always includes the specific savings of *both* BM and BJ, but it also incurs some additional cost in the hope of being even more efficient than either. The connection between BM and FC that we derive here has, to the best of our knowledge, never been noticed before. Prosser [Pro95] has previously presented a modification of FC that allows it to realize some *additional* BM-type savings. But his modification is distinct from the results we prove here. We will discuss Prosser's work again in Section 3.

In Section 4 we examine an improved version of forward checking first proposed by Zweben and Eskey [ZE89], and subsequently presented independently, and in greater detail, by Dent and Mercer [DM94]. Dent and Mercer call their improved algorithm *minimal forward checking* (MFC). MFC was proposed as a "lazy" version of forward checking which avoids doing checks until they are absolutely necessary. MFC provably never does worse than the original FC algorithm. Its gains over plain FC are typically modest (10-40% in our own experiments, which seems to be in fair agreement with [DM94]), but are nevertheless worthwhile.

We re-discovered this algorithm not by thinking about lazy evaluation, but instead as a corollary of our results connecting backmarking and forward checking. As we show, there is a strong and precise sense in which minimal forward checking is a logical hybrid of regular forward checking and backmarking that benefits from the advantages of both. Thus the algorithm that Zweben and Eskey, and Dent and Mercer, present as essentially a clever optimization of regular forward-checking has what is arguably quite a deep foundation.

In Section 4 we also show how MFC can be combined with dynamic variable reordering heuristics in a manner that preserves its performance edge over plain FC (with variable reordering). In fact, MFC in combination with dynamic variable reordering showed itself to be one of the most effective algorithms when tested against a wide range of other algorithms.

2 Preliminaries

A *binary* CSP is a finite set of variables, each with a finite domain of potential values, and a collection of pairwise constraints between the variables. The goal is to assign a value to each variable so that all of the constraints are satisfied. Depending on the application the goal may be to find all consistent assignments, or to find just one. Formally:

Definition 1. A binary constraint satisfaction problem, $\mathcal{P}$, consists of:

- A finite collection of N *variables*, $V_1, \ldots, V_N$.
- For each variable V_i, a finite domain of k_i *values*, $D_i = \{v_1^i, v_2^i, \ldots, v_{k_i}^i\}$.
- For each pair of variables $\{V_i, V_j\}$, a *constraint* $C_{\{i,j\}}$ between D_i and D_j which is simply a subset of $D_i \times D_j$. If $(v_l^i, v_m^j) \in C_{\{i,j\}}$ we say that the assignment $\{V_i \leftarrow v_l^i, V_j \leftarrow v_m^j\}$ is *consistent*.

A *solution* to $\mathcal{P}$ is an assignment $\{V_1 \leftarrow v_{s_1}^1, \ldots, V_i \leftarrow v_{s_i}^i, \ldots, V_N \leftarrow v_{s_N}^N\}$ such that for all i, j, $\{V_i \leftarrow v_{s_i}^i, V_j \leftarrow v_{s_j}^j\}$ is consistent. ∎

```
procedure FC(i)                          function Check-Forward(i)
%Tries to instantiate V_i, then recurses  %Checks s_i against future variables
    for each v_l^i ∈ D_i                     for j = i + 1 to N
        s_i ← v_l^i                             dwo = true
        if Domain_l^i = 0 then                  for each v_m^j ∈ D_j
            if i = N then                           if Domain_m^j = 0 then
                print s_1, ..., s_N                     if (s_i, v_m^j) ∈ C_{i,j} then
            else                                            dwo = false
                if Check-Forward(i) then             else
                    FC(i+1)                              Domain_m^j ← i
                Restore(i)                      if dwo then return(false)
                                             return(true)
procedure Restore(i)
%Returns Domain to previous state
    for j = i + 1 to N
        for each v_m^j ∈ D_j
            if Domain_m^j = i then
                Domain_m^j ← 0
```

Fig. 1. Pseudo-code for Forward Checking

The forward checking algorithm [HE80] constructs solutions by considering assignments to variables in a particular order, which for concreteness we take to be $V_1, V_2, V_3, \ldots, V_N$.[3] Suppose that we have found a consistent assignment to the first $i-1$ variables, which means that all pairwise comparisons involving only these $i-1$ variables are satisfied. At this point, we call $V_1, \ldots, V_{i-1}$ the *past* variables, V_i the *current variable*, and the others the *future* variables. The characteristic data structure of the FC algorithm is a two dimensional array Domain. The idea is that $Domain_m^j$ will contain 0 if and only if the assignment $V_j \leftarrow v_m^j$ is consistent with the assignments chosen for all the past variables. Otherwise, it contains the index of the first (i.e., the lowest) assigned variable with which $V_j \leftarrow v_m^j$ is inconsistent.

It follows that, when we are considering a possible value v_l^i for the current variable V_i, it is sufficient to look for a zero in $Domain_l^i$. Any such value is guaranteed to be consistent with all past choices. Hence, we do not need to do the backwards consistency checks that are characteristic of BT and its variants. The price, of course, is that when we make a successful assignment to the current variable, we must check it against all outstanding values of the future variables, updating Domain as necessary. Figure 1 gives the important parts of the algorithm in more detail; after initialization, the call FC(1) will print all solutions. Note that the current partial assignment is remembered in program variables $s_1, \ldots, s_N$. An assignment to s_i fails if there is a "domain wipe-out" (DWO), which means that we have discovered that every value of some future variable

---

[3] That is, we assume a static ordering in this paper. But see Section 4 for a discussion of dynamic variable orderings.

is inconsistent with our choices so far. DWO means, of course, that no solution can exist in the subtree below this assignment. Note also that, after we finish considering a choice for s_i, we must undo any changes made to the Domain array before continuing.[4]

It may seem as if FC can end up doing many redundant checks, as it checks against future variables that may never be visited. For example, checking V_1 against V_N is wasted work if the assignment to V_1 ends up forcing V_2 and V_3 to be completely inconsistent with each other. But balanced against this is the chance that it can detect domain wipe-outs and avoid parts of the search tree explored by the backward checking algorithms.

Our own experiments and those of Haralick and Elliot [HE80], Nadel [Nad89], Prosser [Pro93] and van Run [vR94], have shown that the work expended by FC to perform DWO detection generally results in a net gain. In the n-Queens problem FC is slightly outperformed by BM, but in Nadel's confused queens, Prosser's version of the Zebra problem, and in a number of random tests (including extensive tests from Frost and Dechter's table of 50% solvable classes [FD94]) FC outperforms BM, is generally much better than BJ, and always totally out classes BT. In most of these tests the measure of complexity was taken to be the number of consistency checks. Several other complexity measures have been considered in the literature, the most popular being the number of nodes visited and CPU time. Counting the nodes visited is not an appropriate measure for comparing the performance of FC and the backward checking algorithms, as the amount of work FC does at each node is completely different from the other algorithms.[5] CPU time, on the other hand, is a very difficult measure to evaluate correctly as it is extremely implementation dependent. For this reason we also will focus on counting the number of consistency checks in our theoretical and experimental results.

Another major advantage of FC is that the number of remaining consistent values for each of the future variables can be computed without any additional constraint checks. This means that the highly effective minimal remaining values (MRV) heuristic, in which we instantiate next that variable with fewest remaining values (also known as the fail-first (FF) heuristic), can be used "for free" to perform dynamic variable reordering. Bacchus and van Run [BvR95] have shown that FC and its variant FC-CBJ, when equipped with dynamic variable reordering using the MRV heuristic, outperform a wide range of similarly equipped backwards checking algorithms.

---

[4] We have designed this code for clarity; there are many alternatives that are more efficient. The Restore procedure could be improved, and a common presentation of the FC algorithm [HE80] uses a loop over V_i's current domain, i.e., the elements of Domain^i that are zero, instead of over D_i. (The latter "improvement" may or may not be more efficient in practice as it requires maintaining a data structure containing the current domain.)

[5] Nodes visited can be a useful measure for comparing features other than performance.

```
procedure BM(i)                          procedure Restore(i)
%Tries to instantiate Vᵢ, then recurses  %Updates Mbl
    for each vⱼⁱ ∈ Dᵢ                        for j = i + 1 to N
        sᵢ ← vₗⁱ                                 if Mblʲ = i then Mblʲ ← i−1
        if Mclᵢ ≥ Mblⁱ then
            ok ← true
            for j = Mblⁱ to i − 1 and while ok
                Mclⱼⁱ ← j
                if (sⱼ, sᵢ) ∉ C₍ᵢ,ⱼ₎ then
                    ok ← false
*       if ok then
            if i = N then
                print s₁, . . . , sₙ
            else
                BM(i+1)
    Mblⁱ ← i−1
    Restore(i)
```

Fig. 2. Backmarking

3 Forward checking—some theoretical results

Gashnig's backmarking algorithm [Gas77] improves backtracking by eliminating some redundant consistency checks. Recall that when an assignment $V_i \leftarrow v_l^i$ of the current variable V_i is made, BT checks the consistency of this assignment against all of the previous assignments $\left\{ V_1 \leftarrow v_{s_1}^1, \ldots, V_{i-1} \leftarrow v_{s_{i-1}}^{i-1} \right\}$. If any of these consistency checks fail, BM takes the additional step of remembering the first point of failure in an array Mcl_l^i ("maximum check level"). This information is used to save later consistency checks. Say that later we backtrack from V_i up to the variable V_j, assign V_j a new value, and then progress down the tree, once again reaching V_i. At V_i we might again attempt the assignment $V_i \leftarrow v_l^i$. The assignments $\left\{ V_1 \leftarrow v_{s_1}^1, \ldots, V_{j-1} \leftarrow v_{s_{j-1}}^{j-1} \right\}$ have not changed since we last tried $V_i \leftarrow v_l^i$, so there is no point in repeating these checks. Furthermore, if $V_i \leftarrow v_l^i$ had failed against one of these assignments, we need not make any checks at all; the assignment will fail again, so we can immediately reject it. To realize these savings, the Mcl array is not quite enough by itself, because its entries are not necessarily up to date. Thus BM uses an additional array Mbl ("minimum backtrack level") which for each variable keeps track of how far we have backtracked since trying to instantiate this variable. (In the example above, Mbl^i will store the information that we have only backtracked to V_j since last visiting V_i. Thus we know to ignore any information in Mcl_l^i that pertains to variable V_j or later.) Figure 2 gives the backmarking algorithm in more detail.

As we have mentioned, in empirical tests BM and FC often vie for top honors. But the differences can be enormous. It is easy to see that FC can do much better. For example, if the first and last variables are incompatible with each other FC will realize this almost immediately, whereas BM might search the entire search tree—which can be exponentially large—before declaring failure. Kondrak and van Beek [KvB95] have shown that FC always explores a subset (not necessarily proper) of the nodes (i.e., partial instantiations) that BT, BM, and BJ visit. Nevertheless, since FC can perform more checks per node, FC may perform more consistency checks.

Example 1. Suppose V_2 and V_3 are mutually inconsistent. The backward checking algorithms can discover this quickly, only searching three variables deep (thus making at most $k_1 k_2 + k_1 k_3 + k_2 k_3$ consistency checks). Forward checking can take much longer. For each assignment to V_1, it checks against all subsequent variables, so that it does as many as $k_1 \sum_{i=4}^{N} k_i$ additional checks over the backward checking algorithms. These extra checks do not reveal the inconsistency between V_2 and V_3 and hence are wasted work. ∎

The problem is, of course, that FC delves deeply into the search tree to find DWO, and this does not always pay off. But the cost is never exponential in the size of the problem. The following simple corollary of Kondrak and van Beek's result is worth making explicit.

Remark. Let K be the largest domain size. FC never performs more than NK times as many consistency checks as BT, BJ or BM, but the performance loss can be arbitrarily close to this bound. On the other hand, there are families of problems in which BT, BJ and BM all perform $e^{\Omega(N \ln K)}$ more checks than FC.

Proof. Reasoning as in Example 1, we see that forward checking from a node costs at most NK checks. The example can be arranged (by choosing N large enough, $k_2 = k_3 = 1$, and $k_i = K$ for $i > 3$) so that the actual number of checks divided by NK is arbitrarily close to one. Our first claim now follows from Kondrak and van Beek's result showing that FC explores no more nodes than BT, BM or BJ. There is a slight subtlety in the case of BM, as at some nodes BM does not perform any consistency checks. However, these nodes correspond to inconsistent assignments to the current variable so FC does no work at these nodes either.

For our second claim, simply consider a CSP problem in which BM, BJ, and BT do an exponential amount of work without finding a solution. Modify the problem by adding a new variable V_{N+1} that is incompatible with all assignments to V_1. In the new tree FC will detect that no solution exists in no more than NK^2 checks, while BT, BM and BJ will still require an exponential amount of work. ∎

It is obvious that the important feature of FC is that it can use DWO detection to prune large amounts of the search space, and in doing so save itself a considerable amount of work over BT (as well as over BJ and BM). However, it turns out that FC improves over BT in another way as well. In particular, FC avoids many redundant checks in a manner that is *exactly* the same as BM. This connection between FC and BM has, to our knowledge, never been made before, and the main result in this section is to make precise this connection. Taking account of the similarity between FC and BM allows us to make the difference— which is exactly DWO detection—clear. Our first definition partitions the work (i.e., the consistency checks) that FC performs into two groups.

Definition 2. A particular consistency check $(s_i, v_\ell^j) \in C_{\{i,j\}}$ performed during the execution of the FC algorithm (Figure 1) is called a *tree-check* if the algorithm later attempts the partial assignment $s_j \leftarrow v_\ell^j$,[6] while $s_1, \ldots, s_i$ remain the same as at the time the check was made. (That is, $s_j \leftarrow v_\ell^j$ is later attempted in the subtree below the node where the check was make). ∎

Example 2. Consider the example shown in Figure 3. The diagram shows a backtracking tree explored by FC. In the CSP there are four variables each with the two element domain $\{a, b\}$. At the top level of the tree the variable V_1 is instantiated with the value a. Then the domains of the future variables are checked against this instantiation. The checks performed at this stage are shown in the box below the assignment statement. Six constraints are checked: all possible values of the future variables against the assignment $V_1 \leftarrow a$. The search trees show no node making an assignment to V_4 is ever visited. Hence, the checks against $V_4 = a$ and $V_4 = b$ are non-tree checks. The other four checks are, on the other hand all tree checks, as is indicated by the label "T" that follows them. In these cases a node that "attempts" that instantiation is later visited by the search process.

It should be noted that the node $V_3 = b$ is in a sense never visited by the search process, since this value for V_3 has been pruned prior to arriving at this node. Nevertheless, we consider FC to have visited that node, as it executes the assignment $s_3 \leftarrow v_l^3$ (line 4 in FC procedure) prior to checking to see if the value v_l^3 has already been pruned. Hence, we show this node as being connected via a dotted line, and we count the check against $V_3 = b$ to be a tree check.

Many of the checks are non-tree checks. For example, all the checks performed at a node where DWO is detected are non-tree checks. More generally, all checks against a variable that is never visited in the subtree below are non-tree checks. ∎

Non-tree-checks have the *sole* purpose of looking for DWO's, and if no DWO is found they are, in a sense, wasted. A tree-check may help in finding a DWO, but it is also used at least once in evaluating the correctness of a proposed instantiation to the current variable (in a sense, it directly helps in "building" the search tree). This distinction is an natural one, although it has the practical disadvantage that it can only be made after the fact.[7]

---

[6] We consider an assignment to be attempted as soon as FC executes the code $s_i \leftarrow v_l^i$ (line 4 in FC procedure), even if the subsequent code immediately discovers that this value has already been pruned from the current domain of V_i.

[7] That is, we do not know whether or not a particular consistency check is a tree-check until somewhat later in the search process. However, should one wish to, it is quite easy to code the FC algorithm so that it keeps an accurate count of the tree-checks.

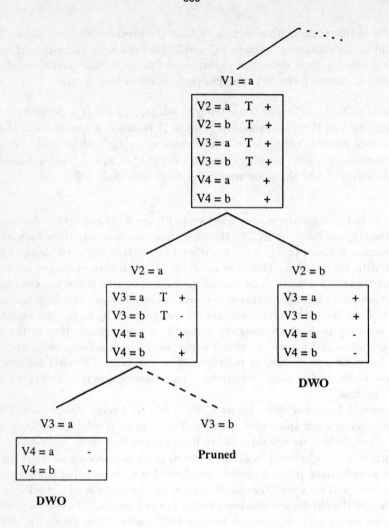

Fig. 3. Tree Checks: only the checks labeled with "T" are tree checks. Checks labeled with a "+" are successful checks, failed checks are marked with a "-".

The concept of tree-checks is not the only idea we need. The other issue that makes a direct comparison between BM and FC impossible is simply that BM explores a different set of nodes: it does not detect DWO. To overcome this, we must imagine that BM is supplied with an "oracle" that, given any partial assignment, can tell whether there is DWO at some future variable. We can imagine line (∗) in Figure 2 being replaced by:

∗   **if** ok **and not**(DWO(i)) **then**

where DWO(i) is a call to an oracle testing for DWO at some variable in the future of V_i. This change now makes the comparison between BM and FC fair. The surprising result is that, after accounting for this change, FC and BM are essentially identical algorithms.

Theorem 3. *BM, supplied with an oracle as described above, explores exactly the same nodes as FC. Furthermore, the number of consistency checks it makes is the same as the number of tree-checks FC makes.*

Proof. (Sketch.) FC fails to reach a partial assignment $s_1, \ldots, s_j$, if and only if DWO was detected at some point prior to s_j (that is, while instantiating s_i where $i < j$) or if the assignment $s_1, \ldots, s_{j-1}$ was not internally consistent. It is easy to verify that this is exactly the same condition under which BM equipped with a DWO oracle fails to visit a node. Thus these two algorithms explore exactly the same nodes.

Next, consider the set of pairs $(< s_1, \ldots, s_i >, s_j)$ for $j > i$, where the first component is a consistent assignment to the first i variables, s_j is an assignment to the j'th variable such that some node $< s_1, \ldots, s_i, s_{i+1}, \ldots, s_{j-1}, s_j >$ is actually reached by the algorithms, and finally, where s_j is consistent with each of $s_1, \ldots, s_{i-1}$. Note that many different nodes can lead to the same pair, because we do not care about the values of $s_{i+1}, \ldots, s_{j-1}$. We know that the set of pairs thus defined is the same for the two algorithms. The result follows once we show that the (for FC, tree-) checks made by each of the two algorithms is in one-to-one correspondence with the set of these pairs. This is fairly straightforward. For FC, we assign to $(< s_1, \ldots, s_i >, s_j)$ the check s_i against s_j made when we were forward checking ahead from the partial assignment $< s_1, \ldots, s_i >$. In this way, every pair corresponds to a particular tree check, and it is easy to verify that each tree check corresponds to a unique pair. For BM, we map $(< s_1, \ldots, s_i >, s_j)$ to the first check s_i against s_j that we perform while instantiating s_j and while the current assignment includes $< s_1, \ldots, s_i >$. However, the whole point of the BM bookkeeping is that there is only one such check. Thus, this correspondence includes all the checks that BM ever makes and the result now follows. Note that although it is possible to compare checks this way, BM and FC nevertheless do their checks in very different orders. ∎

That BM, when equipped with a DWO oracle should visit exactly the same nodes as FC is not surprising. However, that BM does no fewer checks than the tree-checks of FC is. It must be remembered that BM utilizes some subtle bookkeeping in order to eliminate many redundant checks over BT. FC, on the other hand, simply prunes its future domains, a process that is, on the surface, quite distinct from BM's bookkeeping. It would seem that except for DWO detection FC would simply be doing its checks in the same manner as BT. Our theorem show that this is not the case. FC's domain pruning allows it to achieve all of the savings of BM's sophisticated bookkeeping; it is doing its checks in a much more "intelligent" manner than plain BT.

This theorem aids our understanding of these algorithms by getting to the heart of their similarities and differences. It also has some practical implications.

For instance, for some CSPs it may be clear that few DWO's will occur for distant future variables, in which case we now *know* (as contrasted to merely having a vague intuition) that FC will be outperformed by BM: BM does its checks as efficiently as FC without expending extra checks on the gamble of DWO detection. Perhaps deeper analysis will help us get a more quantitative understanding of the cost/benefit tradeoff of DWO detection in various problems. This result also helps us explain the empirical effectiveness of FC; BM's savings over BT can be very substantial in practice, so FC's ability to capture all of these savings can make it very efficient even in cases where not much is saved by its DWO detection. This suggests that on some problems, the "forward looking" aspect of FC might be a misleading explanation for its success and that what is really important is its embedding of backmarking savings. Finally, we present another practical application of our result in the next section, where it is used to motivate an improvement to FC. Not coincidentally, the improvement makes the connection to BM more apparent.

Besides optimizing its tree-checks in exactly the same manner as BM, FC's DWO detection allows FC to achieve BJ savings. This observation is essentially a corollary of Kondrak and van Beek's result, but we present a different proof that serves to make our point more clearly.

Theorem 4. *Let n be a node visited by BT that is skipped by BJ. Then any algorithm that uses DWO detection would never visit n either.*

Proof. [8] BJ can skip nodes only when it backjumps from some node n_1 (which is a partial assignment to the variables $V_1, \ldots, V_i$), to a lower level node n_0 (which is a partial assignment to the variable $V_1, \ldots, V_j$, $j < i$). Any skipped node n will be a node in the subtree under some such n_0. For the backjump to have occurred from n_1 directly to n_0, every value of V_i must have been inconsistent with the partial assignment at n_0. But then DWO detection would have discovered that V_i had a domain wipe-out at n_0. Hence, any algorithm that used DWO detection would never have explored *any* node in the subtree under n_0, and in particular would not have visited n. ∎

A very similar argument can be used to show that, if all algorithms are supplied with a DWO oracle, then BT becomes equivalent to BJ, and BM becomes equivalent to BMJ (Prosser's [Pro93] backmark-jumping algorithm). So Theorem 3 also holds for BMJ supplied with an oracle.

Theorem 3 demonstrates that FC optimizes its tree-checks in the same manner as BM. In particular, it realizes all of the BM savings in doing these checks. Prosser, in [Pro95], has developed a technique whereby FC can achieve even more BM-type savings by maintaining information gathered whenever a domain wipe-out occurs. This information and the savings that can be realized from it are orthogonal to the BM savings already embedded within FC. That FC already embeds the savings of standard BM was not noticed by Prosser. Interestingly,

---

[8] Here we assume some familiarity with details of the BJ algorithm which, due to space limitations, we are unable to provide in the text.

it would appear that Prosser's technique can easily added to the minimal forward checking technique described below. Such a combination would be worth exploring.

4 Minimal Forward checking

The simplest example for which plain backtracking outperforms FC is where the assignments $V_i \leftarrow v_1^i$ (i.e., each variable is assigned the first value in its domain) are consistent, and where we are content to find a single solution. In this case, backtracking can descend immediately to a solution (the leftmost branch of the backtrack tree), while forward checking is held up checking each variable on that branch against all possible values of future variables. This example of BT outperforming FC is often mentioned in the literature, e.g., [Pro93].

However, it is possible to improve the behavior of forward checking in such cases. The technique has been noted by Zweben and Eskey in [ZE89] and in more detail by Dent and Mercer in [DM94]. The idea motiving this technique is that of lazy evaluation, i.e., the notion of delaying computation until absolutely necessary.

Standard FC checks every value in the remaining domains of the future variables, pruning those values that are inconsistent with the current assignment. If during this pruning phase it detects DWO it retracts the current assignment. Hence, we see that to apply the notion of lazy evaluation, all we need to compute immediately is whether or not DWO occurs. We do not need to check every value in the future domains at this stage, and we can delay these checks until we absolutely need it. By delaying these checks it may turn out that a DWO is detected before we need to perform them, hence a lazy version of FC can avoid performing some of the checks standard FC performs.

In the example, we only need to check forward against the first value of each subsequent variable's domain. In general, it is enough to find a single consistent value in the domain of each future variable to determine whether or not DWO occurs. In delaying the other consistency checks, however, when we backtrack, and need to re-instantiate a variable, we are no longer guaranteed that all relevant backward consistency checks have been performed. But whenever this happens, we can simply "catch up" by performing the appropriate checks. That is, we reach a stage where we must complete the delayed computations. If these tree checks are performed only "on demand" we can end up doing far fewer than if all *potentially* useful checks had been done during the forward checking phase. The overhead needed to keep track of what checks have been done is negligble, and so this idea leads to worthwhile gains.

The results of Section 3 led us to rediscover the MFC algorithm, but from notions quite different from lazy evaluation. Consider Theorem 3, which we can roughly paraphrase as saying that FC is essentially BM with DWO detection added. Our idea was to take this literally; i.e., implement BM and then enhance it with DWO detection. The point of this is that it becomes quite clear that we have the freedom to implement DWO detection as efficiently as possible—in particular, we can stop checking a future variable as soon as we have found a consistent value. In the regular presentation of forward checking, the forward consistency checks are doing several different things at once, and so it takes more insight to notice safe optimizations. Given our theorem, the situation is much more obvious.

Admittedly, some care is necessary. If we were to implement BM and DWO detection entirely independently, we may end up repeating checks. In particular, the DWO detection phase will perform some checks that BM also needs to perform. One feature of FC is that it can avoid repeating these checks. Nevertheless, it is easy to arrange things so that relevant checks in the DWO (forward checking) stage are remembered, and made available to the backmarking component. With this modification the hoped for gains do appear.

In our implementation of this idea, the main step is to modify the interpretation and use of the Domain array slightly. Now, we will use a *negative* value to note that a domain value was inconsistent with some past assignment. That is, $\text{Domain}_l^i = -j$ will signify that $V_i \leftarrow v_l^i$ was consistent with the current assignments up to s_{j-1}, but failed against s_j. We do this because the algorithm no longer checks every future value right up to the current assignment, even if it is consistent to that point. Furthermore, we wish to use positive values to remember the latest variable successfully checked against. Thus, $\text{Domain}_l^i = j$ means that $V_i \leftarrow v_l^i$ is consistent up to *and including* s_j. In particular, the initial value $\text{Domain}_l^i = 0$ means that $V_i \leftarrow v_l^i$ has not yet been checked against anything at all. We note that this is a different "accounting scheme" than that used by Dent and Mercer, who keep track of exactly which checks have been performed against earlier variables (rather than just the (signed) index of the last variable). Our scheme is more efficient as it requires $O(NK)$ space as compared to the $O(NK^2)$ space required by Dent and Mercer's scheme (where N is the number of variables and K is the size of the largest domain). More importantly, however, it makes the connection to BM much clearer. Nevertheless, we emphasize that this is a relatively minor implementation detail and the algorithm we were lead to by Theorem 3 is identical with Dent and Mercer's in all important respects.

Figure 4 shows the pseudo-code for the algorithm. The changes over FC have been marked and in addition the Update procedure is completely new. Procedure Check-Forward implements DWO, in the efficient fashion discussed above. In the main procedure MFC, we can no longer automatically assign values to s_i, as we did in FC. Rather, we must first catch up on any of the consistency checks that have been omitted. Catch up occurs in Update, which performs backwards checks. Note that it only checks the value v_m^j against the assignments it has not yet been checked against (i.e., the assigned values after the Domain_m^j'th). Furthermore, if Domain_m^j is initially negative we perform no checks at all, as we know that this value is still inconsistent. This corresponds precisely to BM rejecting a value without incurring any checks when $\text{Mcl}_m^j < \text{Mbl}^j$. The only real difference between Update and BM is that the forward checking phase may have done more work than plain BM. That is, Domain_m^j, which plays a similar but more flexible role to the Mbl array in BM, may have a value greater than Mbl^j in

```
procedure MFC(i)                              function Check-Forward(i)
%Tries to instantiate Vᵢ                      %Checks sᵢ against future variables
    for each vⱼⁱ ∈ Dᵢ                         %Only does enough work to find DWO
        sᵢ ← vⱼⁱ                                   for j = i + 1 to N
!       if Update(i,l,i−1) then                        DWO = true
            if i = N then                     !            for vₘʲ ∈ Dⱼ and while DWO
                print s₁,...,sₙ                !                if Update(j,m,i) then
            else                                              DWO = false
                if Check-Forward(i) then               if DWO then return(false)
                    MFC(i+1)                      return(true)
                Restore(i)
                                              function Update(j,m,i)
procedure Restore(i)                          %Checks vₘʲ against s₁ to sᵢ
%Returns Domain to previous state             %Updates Domainₘʲ appropriately
    for j = i + 1 to N                            if Domainₘʲ ≥ 0 then
        for each vₘʲ ∈ Dⱼ                             ok ← true
!           if Abs(Domainₘʲ) = i then                else
                Domainₘʲ ← i−1                            ok ← false
                                                      for p = Domainₘʲ + 1 to i and while ok
                                                          if (sₚ, vₘʲ) ∉ C₍ₚ,ⱼ₎ then
                                                              ok ← false
                                                              Domainₘʲ ← −p
                                                      if ok then
                                                          Domainₘʲ ← i
                                                  return(ok)
```

$$\textbf{Fig. 4.}\ \text{``Minimal'' Forward Checking}$$

BM. This allows MFC to avoid repeating checks performed during the forward checking phase. Our purpose in presenting this pseudo-code is to highlight the Update procedure and its connection to BM. Of course, our whole point is that this is not a coincidence: the update code essentially *is* doing backmarking. Clearly MFC performs no more checks than regular FC. Furthermore, as might be expected from the argument we gave, the relation that FC has to BM still holds:

Theorem 5. *BM with an oracle as in Section 3 explores the same nodes as MFC, and the number of consistency checks it makes is equal to the number of tree checks MFC makes.*

Thus, as should be expected from our description of the algorithm, MFC gains solely by performing fewer non-tree checks.

We have tested MFC on various problems, including n-Queens, Prosser's version of the Zebra problem [Pro93], and many random CSPs drawn from Frost and Dechter's table of 50% solvable classes [FD94]. As can be seen in Figure 5, MFC results in modest gains over FC, typically in the range of 10–30%. But in view of the fairly small changes over forward checking this is surely worthwhile.

Figure 6 gives a comparison of the number of non-tree checks for both FC and MFC, to give some idea of the size of the savings here (which are surprisingly uniform across problem type). These results are in agreement with those of [DM94].

For the 10, 11, and 12 Queen problems we see that FC and MFC perform fewer tree checks than the number of checks performed by plain BM. Subtracting these numbers of tree checks from the corresponding number of checks performed by plain BM gives us the amount of savings that DWO detection yields. The data indicates that for these problems we do get savings from DWO detection, but looking at the non-tree checks we see that these savings are approximately equal to their costs. Hence, there is very little benefit, for n-Queens, in doing DWO detection. The main reason then, that FC performs about as well as BM in n-Queens is that FC optimizes its tree-checks just like BM.

	MFC	FC	BM	BT	MFCvar	FC-CBJvar[9]
10 Q[10]	220	242	220	1298	192	204
11 Q	1038	1155	1027	7417	868	935
12 Q	5298	5959	5225	—	4282	4635
Zebra[11]	129	182	1608	16196	2.8	2.9
R1[12]	11.6	15.1	73.8	511.1	0.78	0.86
R2	439	685	2447	—	20.7	27.7
R3	311	469	5753	—	3.3	3.9
R4	54	80	115	908	10.6	14.3

Fig. 5. Number of consistency checks (thousands) for various algorithms

	10 Queens	11 Queens	12 Queens	Zebra	R1	R2
Tree checks	134	616	3127	30	2.9	82.2
FC non-tree	108	539	2832	152	12.2	602
MFC non-tree	86	422	2171	99	8.7	357

Fig. 6. Tree and non-tree checks (thousands)

---

[9] FC with conflict directed backjumping and dynamic variable reordering.

[10] 10, 11, and 12 Queen problems. Number of checks to find *all* solutions.

[11] Prosser's Zebra problem. The number given is for finding all solutions, averaged over Prosser's original set of 450 different orderings of the problem variables [Pro93].

[12] R1, R2, R3, and R4 are averages computed over 30 randomly generated problems drawn from Frost and Dechter's table of 50% solvable classes [FD94]. R1 consists of $N = 25$ (number of variables), $k = 3$ (domain size for each variable), $C = 89$ (number of variable pairs among the $N(N-1)/2$ possible pairs that are non-trivially

We have also implemented and tested MFC using dynamic variable reordering (labeled MFCvar in the tables). The reordering heuristic we used was the minimum-remaining-values heuristic, whereby the next variable instantiated is that variable with fewest remaining consistent values (sometimes called a "fail-first" heuristic). Because MFC delays performing consistency checks on the future variables, it does not provide an accurate count of the real number of remaining consistent values. Some of the values in the future domains will have been eliminated in MFC's search for the first consistent value, so the number of unpruned values can be used as a rough estimate of the true number of remaining values. This is the estimate used by Dent and Mercer [DM94]. However, they found that since they were only using an estimate, this technique was often inferior to FCvar (which has the exact values).[13]

In contrast, our MFCvar is guaranteed to instantiate variables in the identical order to FCvar, and to perform the same or fewer checks. The key idea is, again, lazy evaluation. Although we must locate that future domain with the fewest remaining values, it is generally not necessary to discover all the remaining domain sizes exactly to do this. All we need to discover is the smallest domain, and do enough checks to find out that the others are larger (but we do not care how much larger). This idea allows several distinct implementations. One efficient technique is to search all future variable domains, one at a time, attempting to find a single consistent value in each. So far, this is just like MFC. But if we succeed, we then try to find a second consistent value in each domain, and then a third, and so on. That is, we repeatedly scan the future variables in sequence, and in each iteration try to find a single new consistent value for each variable. We stop as soon as we fail to find a new consistent value in some domain: this domain is then guaranteed to be the smallest (or the first among the smallest, if there is a tie).[14]

This procedure, Next-Variable, is given in Figure 7. Note the great similarity to the Check-Forward procedure in Figure 4 (which it essentially replaces). This is not a coincidence, because the minimum-remaining-value heuristic subsumes DWO detection [BvR95]. If there is a DWO then the inconsistent domain, having no consistent values at all, will be selected as the next variable. But when we try to instantiate it we will fail immediately and backtrack, just as if we were to have made an explicit check for DWO. See [BvR95] for more details.

---

constrained), and $T = 2$ (the number of incompatible value pairings among the K^2 possible pairings in each of the nontrivial constraint matrices, i.e., the tightness of each constraint). R2 is $N = 25$, $k = 6$, $C = 165$ and $T = 8$. R3 is $N = 25$, $k = 6$, $C = 65$, and $T = 16$. R4 is $N = 15$, $k = 9$, $C = 79$ and $T = 27$.

[13] Dent (personal communication, May 1995) has told us that he has recently been experimenting with other combinations of MFC and variable reordering, including some methods that can always find the smallest future domain with certainty. This would appear to be closely related to the work we report here.

[14] Note that when comparing algorithms with variable reordering, it is important to break ties in consistent fashion. Otherwise, the variation due simply due to the use of slightly different orderings can dominate more interesting distinctions between algorithms.

```
function Next-Variable(i)
%Checks s_i against future variables
%Finds and returns the smallest future domain
        while true
            for each future variable j
                FOUND-CONSISTENT = false
                for each unchecked v_m^j ∈ D_j and while not FOUND-CONSISTENT
                    if Update(j,m,i) then
                        FOUND-CONSISTENT = true
                if not FOUND-CONSISTENT then return(j);
```

Fig. 7. Variable reordering for MFC.

In *all* of our experiments, MFCvar performed the fewest checks when compared with 24 other algorithms; see [BvR95] for details. The second best algorithm (which is usually close in performance) was FC-CBJvar, forward checking with conflict directed backjumping [Pro93] and dynamic variable reordering. It appears feasible to combine MFC with conflict directed backjumping, and with Prosser's additional BM savings [Pro95]. We intend to examine these combinations in future work.

5 Conclusion

Strictly speaking, forward checking and backtracking, or backmarking, are incomparable by worst-case complexity measures. This, coupled with the seemingly radical difference between looking forward and looking into the past, might lead to the view that no interesting formal comparison is possible.

On the contrary, there is as much similarity as there is difference. To stretch a point, we may say that forward-checking *is* backmarking augmented by a scheme to detect certain "obvious" wastes of time. The relative merits of the two depends only on whether or not the scheme pays off enough to be worth its cost, and simply knowing this may be sufficient to determine which will be better in a particular application.

Ordinary forward checking is not as efficient as it might be, and removing the inefficiency reveals its connection to backmarking even more clearly. This leads directly to the previously known idea of "minimal forward checking". Our reconstruction of MFC is interesting for two reasons, however. First, it emphasizes that MFC is a natural algorithm—a mixture of BM and FC—rather than an *ad hoc* optimization. Second, it is a good illustration of how greater understanding of the connections between various CSP algorithms can lead directly to even better techniques.

References

[BE75]   J. R. Bitner and Reingold E. Backtracking programming techniques. *Communications of the ACM*, 18(11):651–656, 1975.

[BvR95] Fahiem Bacchus and Paul van Run. Dynamic variable reordering in CSPs. In *First International Conference on Principles and Practice of Constraint Programming (CP95)*, 1995.

[CKT91] Peter Cheeseman, Bob Kanefsky, and Willian M. Taylor. Where the really hard problems are. In *Procceedings of the International Joint Conference on Artifical Intelligence (IJCAI)*, pages 331–337, 1991.

[DM94] M. J. Dent and R. E. Mercer. Minimal forward checking. In *6th IEEE International Conference on Tools with Artificial Intelligence*, pages 432–438, New Orleans, 1994. Available via anonymous ftp from ftp://csd.uwo.ca/pub/csd-technical-reports/374/tai94.ps.Z.

[FD94] Daniel Frost and Rina Dechter. In search of the best constraint satisfaction search. In *Proceedings of the AAAI National Conference*, pages 301–306, 1994.

[Gas77] J. Gaschnig. A general Backtracking algorithm that eliminates most redundant tests. In *Procceedings of the International Joint Conference on Artifical Intelligence (IJCAI)*, page 457, 1977.

[Gas78] J. Gaschnig. Experimental case studies of backtrack vs. Waltz-type vs. new algorithms for satisficing assignment problems. In *Proceedings of the Canadian Artifical Intelligence Conference*, pages 268–277, 1978.

[HE80] R. M. Haralick and G. L. Elliott. Increasing tree search efficiency for constraint satisfaction problems. *Artificial Intelligence*, 14:263–313, 1980.

[KvB95] Grzegorz Kondrak and Peter van Beek. A theoretical evaluation of selected backtracking algorithms. In *Procceedings of the International Joint Conference on Artifical Intelligence (IJCAI)*, 1995.

[Mac87] A. K. Mackworth. Constraint satisfaction. In S. C. Shapiro, editor, *Encyclopedia of Artificial Intelligence*. John Wiley and Sons, New York, 1987.

[Nad89] Bernard A. Nadel. Constraint satisfaction algorithms. *Computational Intelligence*, 5:188–224, 1989.

[Pro93] P. Prosser. Hybrid algorithms for the constraint satisfaction problem. *Computational Intelligence*, 9(3), 1993.

[Pro95] P. Prosser. Forward checking with backmarking. In M. Meyer, editor, *Constraint Processing*, LNCS 923, pages 185–204. Springer-Verlag, New York, 1995.

[vR94] Paul van Run. Domain independant heuristics in hybrid algorithms for CSPs. Master's thesis, Dept. of Computer Science, University of Waterloo, Waterloo, Ontario, Canada, 1994. Available via anonymous ftp at "logos.uwaterloo.ca" in the file "/pub/bacchus/vanrun.ps.Z".

[ZE89] Monte Zweben and Megan Eskey. Constraint satisfaction with delayed evaluation. In *Procceedings of the International Joint Conference on Artifical Intelligence (IJCAI)*, pages 875–880, 1989.

A Confluent Calculus for Concurrent Constraint Programming with Guarded Choice

Kim Marriott

Monash University
Clayton 3168, Victoria, Australia
marriott@cs.monash.edu.au

Martin Odersky

Universität Karlsruhe
76128 Karlsruhe, Germany
odersky@ira.uka.de

Abstract. Confluence is an important and desirable property as it allows the program to be understood by considering any desired scheduling rule, rather than having to consider all possible schedulings. Unfortunately, the usual operational semantics for concurrent constraint programs is not confluent as different process schedulings give rise to different sets of possible outcomes. We show that it is possible to give a natural confluent calculus for concurrent constraint programs, if the syntactic domain is extended by a blind choice operator and a special constant standing for a discarded branch. This has application to program analysis.

1 Introduction

Concurrent constraint programming (ccp) [16, 15] is a recent paradigm which elegantly combines logical concepts and concurrency mechanisms. The computational model of ccp is based on the notion of a *constraint system*, which consists of a set of constraints and an *entailment* relation. Processes interact through a common *store*. Communication is achieved by *telling* (adding) a given constraint to the store, and by *asking* (checking whether the store entails) a given constraint. Standard ccp provides a non-deterministic guarded choice operator. In the operational semantics of ccp, non-determinism arises in two different ways. First, if the guards of two branches in a committed choice construct are both entailed by the store either branch can be picked. Second, different process schedulings (that is, interleavings of transitions) can lead to different results since a given process scheduling can prune the decision space by selecting a branch in a committed choice before strengthening the store. In this way, some branches that would be entailed by the stronger store might be excluded by the weaker one. This second source of non-determinism means that to find the possible outcomes of a program all process schedulings must be considered in the operational semantics. This need to consider all process schedulings also holds for the denotational semantics of ccp, which expresses parallel composition by interleaving.

Because of the combinatorial explosion of reduction sequences, an interleaving semantics makes reasoning about possible evaluations cumbersome. Yet such reasoning is necessary for many tasks in program analysis, verification and transformation. This contrasts to the situation in both the lambda calculus and (idealised) Prolog. The semantics for both have confluence properties that make it unnecessary to consider different process schedulings. In the lambda calculus, confluence is embodied in the Church-Rosser theorem [1], which says that different reduction sequences starting from the same term can always be re-joined in a common reduct. As a consequence, evaluation in the lambda calculus is deterministic. In Prolog, confluence is embodied in the Switching Lemma [10], which ensures that different literal selection strategies give rise to the same set of answers.

In the context of concurrency, confluence is an even more desirable property since concurrent programs are notoriously difficult to reason about and to analyse. Unfortunately, as we have seen, despite monotonicity of communication, the standard operational semantics for ccp languages is not confluent in the sense that different process schedulings can give rise to different outcomes. This is because of the guarded choice. Indeed, it has become part of the programming language folklore that it is impossible to have both guarded choice and confluence.

We present here a calculus for ccp that is equivalent to ccp's standard semantics in that both lead to the same observations, yet is confluent. Actually we give a calculus for a slightly larger language, ccp_{+0}, which extends ccp by providing a *blind choice* construct and a *failure* constant 0. The main difference between our calculus for ccp_{+0} and the standard operational semantics for ccp lies in the treatment of guarded choice. In ccp, once a choice is made, all other alternatives of a choice construct are discarded. In ccp_{+0}, the other alternatives are kept around, but extended with a guarded branch which reduces to 0 on termination, indicating that this alternative is only valid if another branch in the guard does not suspend. The calculus distinguishes between the two forms of non-determinism in ccp. Non-determinism arising from multiple guards being enabled is expressed by the blind choice operator in the term language. Process scheduling non-determinism is reflected by a choice among different reduction sequences, analogous to the situation in the lambda calculus. Our main result is a confluence theorem for this calculus, which essentially says that the choice of process scheduling has no influence on the observable behaviour. This is equivalent to the Church-Rosser theorem for the lambda calculus or the Switching Lemma for Prolog. Our result thus refutes the folklore that is impossible to have both guarded choice and confluence. Monotonicity of communication is crucial to our result.

Besides its theoretical interest, our confluent calculus has practical applications in static analysis of ccp. Lack of confluence in the usual operational semantics and denotational semantics means that program analysis cannot be directly based on these semantics, as the cost of considering all process schedulings in an analysis is prohibitive. There have been two main approaches to overcome this difficulty. The first is to use a fixed process scheduling, but then to "re-execute" the program until a fixpoint is reached. This was suggested in [4] for concurrent logic programs and extended in [5] to ccp. This may be expensive and is inherently imprecise because re-execution confuses the behaviour of different branches. The second approach is to give a non-standard operational semantics for ccp which is confluent but which approximates the usual ccp operational semantics by allowing more reductions. Analyses are then proved correct with respect to this approximate operational semantics. This was suggested in [2, 3] for concurrent logic programs and couched in [17, 6] in the slightly different context of ccp as a transformation from a program written in full ccp to an approximating program written in a subset of ccp for which the usual operational semantics is confluent. The disadvantage of this approach is an inherent loss of precision in the analysis because of the approximation introduced in the new semantics or in the program transformation. Our calculus, therefore, provides a better basis for analysis for two reasons. First, because the calculus is confluent, there is no need to introduce complex artificial semantics or transformations as efficient analysis can be directly based on the calculus. Second, because the calculus gives the same observational behaviour as the usual operational semantics, there is no inherent loss of precision and the analysis can be more accurate.

Our result showing that the ccp_{+0} programs are confluent generalizes confluence results of Maher [11] and Saraswat et al [15] about deterministic ccp subsets and Falaschi et al [6] identification of subclasses of ccp for which the usual operational semantics is confluent. Montanari et al [12] give a confluent operational semantics for a variant of ccp with both indeterminism (blind choice) and nondeterminism (angelic choice), however they do not consider guarded choice. Niehren and Smolka have introduced the δ [13] and ρ [14] calculi which have strong connections to the π-calculus and deterministic ccp respectively. They have shown that both of these calculi are confluent. However, unlike our calculus neither the ρ nor the δ calculus has a non-deterministic guarded choice operator.

The rest of this paper is organized as follows. Section 2 introduces the standard operational semantics of the ccp languages. Section 3 presents our calculus. Section 4 shows that reduction in our calculus is confluent and Section 5 shows that the calculus and operational semantics of ccp are observationally equivalent. Section 6 sketches an application of our calculus to the analysis of ccp programs. Section 7 concludes.

2 Concurrent Constraint Programming

Concurrent constraint programming was proposed by Saraswat [16, 15]. We follow here the definition given in [15], which is based on the notion of cylindric constraint system.

A *cylindric constraint system* [7] is a structure $C = \langle \mathcal{C}, \leq, \sqcup, true, false, \exists \rangle$ such that:

1. $\langle \mathcal{C}, \leq \rangle$ is a complete algebraic lattice, where $\sqcup$ is the lub operation (representing logical and), and *true*, *false* are the least and the greatest elements of $\mathcal{C}$, respectively;

2. For each $x \in Vars$ the function $\exists_x : \mathcal{C} \to \mathcal{C}$ is a *cylindrification operator*:
   (E1) $\exists_x c \leq c$,

(E2) $c \leq c'$ implies $\exists_x c \leq \exists_x c'$,

(E3) $\exists_x (c \sqcup \exists_x c') = \exists_x c \sqcup \exists_x c'$,

(E4) $\exists_x \exists_y c = \exists_y \exists_x c$;

3. For each $x, y \in Vars$, C contains the *diagonal element*, d_{xy}, which satisfies:

(D1) $d_{xx} \leq true$,

(D2) if $z \neq x, y$ then $d_{xy} = \exists_z (d_{xz} \sqcup d_{zy})$,

(D3) if $x \neq y$ then $c \leq d_{xy} \sqcup \exists_x (c \sqcup d_{xy})$.

As usual, we take $c = c'$ iff $c \leq c' \wedge c' \leq c$. The cylindrification operators essentially model existential quantification and so are useful for defining a hiding operator in the language. Note that if C models the equality theory, then the diagonal element d_{xy} can be thought of as the formula $x = y$.

Deviating slightly from the treatment of [15], we will base our exposition of ccp on renamings instead of diagonal elements. Renamings can be defined in terms of diagonal elements as follows.

Definition. Let x and y be variables and let $c \in C$. Then the *renaming* $[y/x]c$ of y for x in c is the constraint $\exists_x (d_{xy} \sqcup c)$.

Definition. The *free variables* fv(c) of $c \in C$ is the set $\{x \mid \exists_x c \neq c\}$.

The following proposition shows that we can consistently rename the free variables of a constraint.

Proposition 2.1 Let $c \in C$ and let x and y be variables such that $y \notin$ fv(c). Then $\exists_y [y/x]c = \exists_x c$.

The description and semantics of the ccp class of languages is parametric with respect to an underlying cylindric constraint system C. The syntax of agents M and programs P is given by the grammar:

$$
\begin{array}{lll}
\text{(Agent)} & M ::= c \mid R \mid p\overline{y} \mid M \cdot M \mid \exists_x M \\
\text{(Choice)} & R ::= R \parallel R \mid c \mapsto M \\
\text{(Program)} & P ::= D \; ; \; M \\
\text{(Declarations)} & D ::= D, D \mid p\overline{x} := M
\end{array}
$$

Two fundamental agents are the *tell* operation c which adds the constraint c to the store and the guarded choice among *ask* operations $\parallel_{i=1}^{n} c_i \mapsto M_i$ which evaluates some M_i, provided the corresponding *guard* c_i is entailed by the store. An agent can also be a *procedure call* $p\overline{y}$, where $\overline{y}$ is a vector of parameters $(y_1, \ldots, y_n)$. We assume that every procedure identifier p has exactly one declaration of the form $p(x_1, \ldots, x_n) := M$ in a program and that the lengths of actual and formal argument lists match. Agents can be combined using parallel composition $(\cdot)$. The quantifier $\exists_x M$ hides the use of variable x inside the agent M. We will often use the word *term* as a synonym for *agent*.

Free variables fv(M) and *renamings* $[x/y]M$ have their usual inductive definitions, where the cases where M is a constraint are as defined previously. Following the usual convention for reduction systems, we identify α-renamable terms. That is, $\exists_x M$ and $\exists_x [y/x]M$ are regarded as the same term, provided

$$\textbf{R1} \ \langle c, d \rangle \xrightarrow{ccp} \langle true, c \sqcup d \rangle \qquad\qquad \text{where } c \neq true$$

$$\textbf{R2} \ \langle \ [\ ]_{i=1}^{n} c_i \mapsto M_i, d \rangle \xrightarrow{ccp} \langle M_j, d \rangle \quad \text{where } j \in [1, n] \text{ and } c_j \leq d$$

$$\textbf{R3} \ \frac{\langle M, c \rangle \xrightarrow{ccp} \langle M', c' \rangle}{\langle M \cdot N, c \rangle \xrightarrow{ccp} \langle M' \cdot N, c' \rangle}$$
$$\langle N \cdot M, c \rangle \xrightarrow{ccp} \langle N \cdot M', c' \rangle$$

$$\textbf{R4} \ \frac{\langle M, d \sqcup \exists_x c \rangle \xrightarrow{ccp} \langle N, d' \rangle}{\langle \exists_x^d M, c \rangle \xrightarrow{ccp} \langle \exists_x^{d'} N, c \sqcup \exists_x d' \rangle}$$

$$\textbf{R5} \ \langle p\overline{y}, c \rangle \xrightarrow{ccp} \langle [\overline{y}/\overline{x}]M, c \rangle \qquad\qquad \text{where } (p\overline{x} := M) \in D$$

Fig. 1. The transition system T_D.

that $y \notin \mathrm{fv}\, M$. Proposition 2.1 shows that this identification is consistent with our definition of a constraint system.

The standard operational model of ccp is given as a transition system over *configurations*. A configuration consists of a ccp agent and a constraint representing the current store. The transition system T_D is specified with respect to a set of procedure declarations D. Figure 1 gives the rules in the transition system. Constraints are added to the store (R1). A guarded choice is reduced non-deterministically by choosing a branch whose guard is enabled (R2). (R3) describes parallelism as interleaving. To describe locality (R4) the syntax of existentially quantified agents is extended by allowing agents of the form $\exists_x^d M$. This represents an agent in which x is local to M and d is the "hidden" store that has been produced locally by M on x. Initially the local store is empty, that is, $\exists_x M = \exists_x^{true} M$. The execution of a procedure call is modelled by (R5). We write $\xrightarrow{ccp}$ for the reflexive and transitive closure of $\xrightarrow{ccp}$.

The standard observable behavior of a ccp agent is the set of possible constraint stores which can result when the agent is reduced to a normal form. A configuration S is in *normal form* if it cannot be reduced further. Infinite reduction sequences are equated to the constraint *false*.

Definition. Let P be the ccp program D ; M. Then $P \Downarrow_{ccp} c$ if there is a normal form $\langle N, c \rangle$ such that $\langle M, true \rangle \xrightarrow{ccp} \langle N, c \rangle$ in the transition system T_D. P *diverges*, written $P \Uparrow_{ccp}$ iff there is an infinite T_D-transition sequence starting with $\langle M, true \rangle$.

Definition. The set of *observations* of a program P, $Obs(\xrightarrow{ccp}, P)$ is

$$\{c \mid M \Downarrow_{ccp} c\} \cup \{false \mid M \Uparrow_{ccp}\}.$$

Example 2.1 The following declaration D defines an agent *merge*, which non-deterministically merges its two input streams x and y into an output stream z. The constraint domain is equations over finite terms. We use $[]$ to denote the empty stream, and $[u \mid v]$ to denote the stream with head u and tail v.

$$merge(x, y, z) :=$$
$$\exists_{x'} \exists_u \; x = [u \mid x'] \mapsto \exists_{x'} \exists_u \exists_{z'} (x = [u \mid x'] \cdot z = [u \mid z'] \cdot merge(x', y, z'))$$
$$[] \; \exists_{y'} \exists_u \; y = [u \mid y'] \mapsto \exists_{y'} \exists_u \exists_{z'} \; (y = [u \mid y'] \cdot z = [u \mid z'] \cdot merge(x, y', z'))$$
$$[] \; x = [] \mapsto z = y$$
$$[] \; y = [] \mapsto z = x.$$

Let P be the program $D \; ; \; x = [a] \cdot merge(x, y, z) \cdot y = [b]$. A reduction sequence using left-most agent scheduling is:

$$\langle x = [a] \cdot merge(x, y, z) \cdot y = [b], true \rangle$$
$$(R1) \xrightarrow{ccp} \langle merge(x, y, z) \cdot y = [b], x = [a] \rangle$$
$$(R5) \xrightarrow{ccp} \langle M \cdot y = [b], x = [a] \rangle$$
$$(R2) \xrightarrow{ccp} \langle \exists_{x'} \exists_u \exists_{z'} \; (x = [u \mid x'] \cdot z = [u \mid z'] \cdot merge(x', y, z')) \cdot y = [b], x = [a] \rangle$$
$$(R1) \xrightarrow{ccp} \langle \exists_{x'}^{x'=[]} \exists_u^{u=a} \exists_{z'}, \; z = [u \mid z'] \cdot merge(x', y, z')) \cdot y = [b], x = [a] \rangle$$
$$(R1) \xrightarrow{ccp} \langle \exists_{x'}^{x'=[]} \exists_u^{u=a} \exists_{z'}, \; merge(x', y, z') \cdot y = [b], x = [a] \sqcup \exists_{z'} \, z = [a \mid z'] \rangle$$
$$(R5) \xrightarrow{ccp} \langle \exists_{x'}^{x'=[]} \exists_u^{u=a} \exists_{z'}, \; M' \cdot y = [b], x = [a] \sqcup \exists_{z'} \, z = [a \mid z'] \rangle$$
$$(R2) \xrightarrow{ccp} \langle \exists_{x'}^{x'=[]} \exists_u^{u=a} \exists_{z'}, \; y = z' \cdot y = [b], x = [a] \sqcup \exists_{z'} \, z = [a \mid z'] \rangle$$
$$(R1) \xrightarrow{ccp} \langle true \cdot y = [b], x = [a] \sqcup z = [a \mid y] \rangle$$
$$(R1) \xrightarrow{ccp} \langle true \cdot true, y = [b] \sqcup x = [a] \sqcup z = [a, b] \rangle$$

where M and M' are appropriate renamings of the definition of $merge(x, y, z)$ and $merge(x', y, z')$ respectively. This reduction sequence gives the observable behavior $y = [b] \sqcup x = [a] \sqcup z = [a, b]$.

In fact this is the only reduction sequence possible with a leftmost agent scheduling. With rightmost agent scheduling, however, the only observation is $y = [b] \sqcup x = [a] \sqcup z = [b, a]$. Thus

$$Obs(\xrightarrow{ccp}, P) \supseteq \{y = [b] \sqcup x = [a] \sqcup z = [b, a], y = [b] \sqcup x = [a] \sqcup z = [a, b]\}.$$

In fact, examination of the (large number of) other agent schedulings shows that these are the only observable behaviours. A more efficient way to show that these are the only observable behaviours will be discussed in the next section.

This example clearly shows the non-confluence of the standard operational semantics, as different agent schedulings give different results.

3   The Concurrent Constraint Calculus

In this section, we develop a calculus for concurrent constraint programming which has the same observable behavior as the operational semantics defined in the last section. The calculus is formulated as a reduction system modulo a set of structural congruences.

The calculus describes a slightly larger language than ccp, adding a blind choice operator $(+)$ and a failure operator 0, which is an identity for $(+)$. Informally, using $(+)$ one can collect all possible execution paths of an agent. We also admit a new form of guarded branch in an ask agent, written $\sqrt{} \rightarrow 0$, which stands for failure upon termination. Hence, a guard g is now a constraint c or the symbol $\sqrt{}$. Informally, once an alternative in a guarded choice is selected, the branch that corresponds to taking some other alternative is marked with a $\sqrt{}$-guard, which causes the branch to be discarded upon termination.

Example 3.1 To see the essential idea for obtaining confluence, consider the agent

$$A \stackrel{def}{=} d \mapsto M \parallel e \mapsto N,$$

run in a context where the store entails d. If the store does not also entail e this should rewrite to M. On the other hand, if the store entails both d and e, A should rewrite to $M + N$. The problem is that the property "the store does not imply e" is not monotonic – in fact it is anti-monotonic since the store increases monotonically during execution. Therefore, it is not possible to make a choice between the two reductions uniformly for all process schedulings. One solution to the problem is to consider each possible process scheduling individually, using an interpretation of parallel composition as interleaving. The resulting calculus is unsuitable for program analysis, however, due to the state space explosion incurred by the interleaving semantics.

In our calculus, A reduces instead to

$$M + (e \mapsto N \parallel \sqrt{} \mapsto 0) \stackrel{def}{=} B.$$

In effect this defers the decision whether or not to drop the "$e \mapsto N$" branch until program termination. If further reductions determine that the store also entails e, this term could further reduce to

$$M + N + (\sqrt{} \mapsto 0 \parallel \sqrt{} \mapsto 0),$$

which is observationally equivalent to $M + N$. On the other hand, if the store never entails e, we end with agent B, which produces the same observations as M. We thus get a confluent calculus that is observationally equivalent to the transition system presented in the last section.

We now make these intuitions precise by defining a reduction system over an extended concurrent constraint language, called ccp_{+0}. Terms in ccp_{+0} are produced by the grammar.

| Agent | $M ::= c \mid R \mid p\overline{y} \mid M \cdot M \mid \exists_x M \mid M + M \mid 0$ |
| Choice | $R ::= R \parallel R \mid c \mapsto M \mid \sqrt{} \mapsto 0$ |

The definitions of renaming and free variables carry over in the obvious way.

The operators have the natural precedence rules: $\exists_x$ binds strongest, followed by $(\cdot)$, followed by $(\parallel)$, followed by $(+)$ which binds weakest. Guard prefixes $g \mapsto$ extend as far to the right as possible.

The ccp calculus has a rich set of structural equivalences ($\equiv$). If $M \equiv N$, then M and N are generally identified. If we want to avoid this identification, speaking only of the concrete term syntax, we will explicitly talk about pre-agents or pre-programs. Structural equivalence ($\equiv$) is the least congruence that satisfies the laws below.

1. ($+$) is associative and commutative, with identity 0.

$$(L + M) + N \equiv L + (M + N)$$
$$M + N \equiv N + M$$
$$M + 0 \equiv M$$

2. ($\cdot$) is associative and commutative, with identity $true$ and zero 0.

$$(L \cdot M) \cdot N \equiv L \cdot (M \cdot N)$$
$$M \cdot N \equiv N \cdot M$$
$$M \cdot true \equiv M$$
$$M \cdot 0 \equiv 0$$

3. ($\cdot$) distributes through ($+$).

$$M \cdot (N_1 + N_2) \equiv M \cdot N_1 + M \cdot N_2$$

4. ($\parallel$) is associative and commutative.

$$(L \parallel M) \parallel N \equiv L \parallel (M \parallel N)$$
$$M \parallel N \equiv N \parallel M$$

5. Parallel composition of constraints equals least upper bound.

$$c \cdot c' \equiv c \sqcup c'$$

6. The following laws govern existential quantification:

$$\exists_x (M + N) \equiv \exists_x M + \exists_x N$$
$$M \cdot \exists_x N \equiv \exists_x (M \cdot N) \qquad \text{if } x \notin \mathrm{fv}(M)$$
$$\exists_x M \equiv M \qquad \text{if } x \notin \mathrm{fv}(M)$$
$$\exists_x M \equiv \exists_y [y/x] M \qquad \text{if } y \notin \mathrm{fv}(M)$$
$$\exists_x \exists_y M \equiv \exists_y \cdot \exists_x M$$

Reduction $\rightarrow$ is a binary relation between agents that is parameterized by a procedure environment D. We write $M \rightarrow_D N$ if M reduces to N in one step in the procedure environment D. We sometimes leave out the D-suffix if the environment is clear from the context.

In essence there are two reduction rules, one for communication, and one for procedure unfolding. The rule for procedure unfolding is:

$$p\overline{y} \xrightarrow{P}_D [\overline{y}/\overline{x}] M \qquad (p\overline{x} := M \in D).$$

The rule for communication comes in two variants. The first variant handles the deterministic case, where no choice operator is present:

$$c \cdot (d \mapsto M) \xrightarrow{cc}_D c \cdot M \qquad (d \leq c)$$

The second variant handles the case where the ask agent is part of a guarded choice:

$$c \cdot (d \mapsto M \parallel R) \xrightarrow{\ cc\ }_D c \cdot M + c \cdot (\sqrt{} \mapsto \mathbf{0} \parallel R) \qquad (d \leq c)$$

The standard semantics of ccp captures the idea that once a guard in one of the guarded choice branches is enabled then that branch can be chosen and the other branches can be discarded. By contrast, our rule does not discard any branches. Instead, we also keep the original ask agent as a $(+)$-alternative, but with the taken branch replaced by the branch $(\sqrt{} \mapsto \mathbf{0})$. Essentially this indicates that the alternative cannot lead to suspension, but that other branches in the alternative can still be taken if their guards are enabled.

Reduction can only occur in the top-level agents, it cannot occur inside the branches of a guarded choice. That is, our reduction relation, $\rightarrow$, is given by

$$\frac{M \xrightarrow{\ p \cup cc\ }_D M'}{\exists_{\overline{x}}(M \cdot N) + N' \rightarrow_D \exists_{\overline{x}}(M' \cdot N) + N'}.$$

We write $\twoheadrightarrow$ for the reflexive and transitive closure of $\rightarrow$.

We now define the set of possible observations of a ccp-term M. Since we express non-determinism by the $(+)$ operator, we might expect that each $(+)$-alternative in a reduct would contribute to the set of possible observations. However, we have to disregard those alternatives that contain a guard of the form $\sqrt{} \mapsto \mathbf{0}$ at top-level, since they represent untaken branches in a committed choice. Upon termination such alternatives are identified with failure, as is formalized below.

Definition. Let *terminal equivalence* $\approx$ be the least congruence that contains $\equiv$ and the equality

$$R \parallel \sqrt{} \mapsto \mathbf{0} \approx \mathbf{0}.$$

Definition. The *constraint part* $Con(M)$ of a term M is $\bigsqcup \{c \mid \exists N . M \equiv c \cdot N\}$.

Definition. A term M is in *normal form* if it cannot be reduced by $\rightarrow_D$.

Definition. Let P be the ccp_{+0} program $D \; ; \; M$. Then $P \Downarrow_{\text{ccp}_{+0}} c$ if there is a normal form N and a term M' such that $M \twoheadrightarrow_D N + M'$, $N \not\approx \mathbf{0}$ and $c = Con(N)$. P *diverges*, written $P \Uparrow_{\text{ccp}_{+0}}$ if there is an infinite $\rightarrow_D$-transition sequence starting with M.

The set of *observations* of a program P, $Obs(\rightarrow, P)$ is defined as in the ccp case.

$$Obs(\rightarrow, P) = \{c \mid M \Downarrow_{\text{ccp}_{+0}} c\} \cup \{\text{false} \mid M \Uparrow_{\text{ccp}_{+0}}\}.$$

Thus, the possible observations of a program P are the constraint parts of all non-zero normal form alternatives of P. In addition, we add *false* to the observations of P if there is a possibility that evaluation of P does not terminate. We often abbreviate $Obs(\rightarrow, P)$ to $Obs(P)$.

As usual, we define *observational equivalence* ($\cong$) to be the largest congruence on terms and programs such that $P \cong Q$ implies $Obs(P) = Obs(Q)$, for all programs P, Q.

An equivalent, but more constructive definition of $\cong$ for terms is based on a *program context*, C, which is a program with a hole [ ] in it. Let $C[M]$ denote the term that results from filling out the hole in C. Then $M \cong N$ iff for all program contexts C such that $C[M]$ and $C[N]$ are well-formed programs,

$$Obs(C[M]) = Obs(C[N]).$$

Proposition 3.1 The following are observational equivalences in ccp_{+0}.

$$M + M \cong M$$
$$M_1 + M_2 \cong true \mapsto M_1 \parallel true \mapsto M_2$$
$$R \parallel R \cong R$$
$$c \cdot (d \mapsto M \parallel R) \cong c \cdot R \qquad\qquad (c \sqcup d = false)$$
$$c \cdot (d \mapsto M \parallel R \parallel \sqrt{} \mapsto 0) \cong c \cdot (d \mapsto M \parallel R) \qquad (d \leq c)$$

Note that the second observational equivalence means that the explicit blind choice construct does not add to the expressiveness of ccp.

Example 3.2 A reduction sequence in ccp_{+0} using left-most agent scheduling from the program given in Example 2.1 is given in Figure 2, where M, M' and M'' are appropriate renamings of the definition of $merge(x, y, z)$, $merge(x', y, z')$ and $merge(x, y', z')$ respectively and R' and R'' are the remaining branches in the guarded choices in M' and M''. This reduction sequence gives the observable behavior

$$\{y = [b] \sqcup x = [a] \sqcup z = [b, a], y = [b] \sqcup x = [a] \sqcup z = [a, b]\}.$$

This is exactly the observable behaviour with the ccp operational semantics, but is obtained with a single reduction scheduling.

4 Confluence

In this section we show that $\rightarrow$ is confluent. The confluence proof has to overcome the difficulty that agents do not form a free algebra (modulo α-renaming), but are equivalence classes of pre-agents. Hence, standard techniques such as studied in [8] or [9] are not applicable.

Instead we adopt the following strategy: We define a *canonical form* $[\![M]\!]$ of a term M, together with a reduction relation on canonical forms. We show that the canonical form mapping has an inverse, and that both it and its inverse commute with equivalences and multi-step reductions. We then show that reduction on canonical forms is confluent, using standard techniques. By the properties of the canonical form mapping, this gives us then confluence of the original ccp_{+0} calculus. A similar technique has been used by Niehren and Smolka in their confluence proofs for the δ and ρ calculi [13, 14].

$$x = [a] \cdot merge(x, y, z) \cdot y = [b]$$
$$\xrightarrow{p} \; y = [b] \sqcup x = [a] \cdot M$$
$$\xrightarrow{cc} \; y = [b] \sqcup x = [a] \cdot$$
$$(\; \exists_{x'} \exists_u \exists_{z'} \; (x = [u \mid x'] \cdot z = [u \mid z'] \cdot merge(x', y, z'))$$
$$+ \exists_{y'} \exists_u \exists_{z'} \; (y = [u \mid y'] \cdot z = [u \mid z'] \cdot merge(x, y', z'))$$
$$+ \sqrt{} \mapsto 0 \; [\![\; x = [\,] \mapsto z = y \; [\![\; y = [\,] \mapsto z = x$$
$$)$$
$$\cong \; y = [b] \sqcup x = [a] \cdot$$
$$(\; \exists_{x'} \exists_u \exists_{z'} \; (x = [u \mid x'] \cdot z = [u \mid z'] \cdot merge(x', y, z'))$$
$$+ \exists_{y'} \exists_u \exists_{z'} \; (y = [u \mid y'] \cdot z = [u \mid z'] \cdot merge(x, y', z'))$$
$$)$$
$$\xrightarrow{p} \; y = [b] \sqcup x = [a] \cdot$$
$$(\; \exists_{x'} \exists_u \exists_{z'} \; (x = [u \mid x'] \sqcup z = [u \mid z'] \cdot M')$$
$$+ \exists_{y'} \exists_u \exists_{z'} \; (y = [u \mid y'] \sqcup z = [u \mid z'] \cdot M'')$$
$$)$$
$$\xrightarrow{cc} \; y = [b] \sqcup x = [a] \cdot$$
$$(\; \exists_{x'} \exists_u \exists_{z'} \; (x = [u \mid x'] \sqcup z = [u \mid z'] \cdot (z' = y + \sqrt{} \mapsto 0 \; [\![\; R'))$$
$$+ \exists_{y'} \exists_u \exists_{z'} \; (y = [u \mid y'] \sqcup z = [u \mid z'] \cdot (z' = x + \sqrt{} \mapsto 0 \; [\![\; R''))$$
$$)$$
$$\cong \; y = [b] \sqcup x = [a] \cdot$$
$$(\; \exists_{x'} \exists_u \exists_{z'} \; (x = [u \mid x'] \sqcup z = [u \mid z'] \sqcup z' = y)$$
$$+ \exists_{y'} \exists_u \exists_{z'} \; (y = [u \mid y'] \sqcup z = [u \mid z'] \sqcup z' = x)$$
$$)$$
$$\equiv \; y = [b] \sqcup x = [a] \sqcup z = [a, b] + y = [b] \sqcup x = [a] \sqcup z = [b, a].$$

Fig. 2. Example reduction in ccp_{+0}.

Definition. A *canonical form* X is a multi-set of *alternatives*. Each alternative A is a quadruple (xs, c, ps, rs), where

- xs is a set of variables (the bound variables of the alternative).
- c is a constraint.
- ps is a multi-set of procedure calls $p\overline{y}$.
- rs is a multi-set of *readers*, where each reader is itself a non-empty multi-set of pairs (g, X), with g a guard and X a canonical form. We assume that the termination guard $\sqrt{}$ appears only in conjunction with the empty set (which represents 0).

Let letters X, Y, Z range over canonical forms.

The set of free variables $fv(X)$ of a canonical form X is the union of the sets of free variables of its alternatives. The free variables of an alternative (xs, c, ps, rs) is the union of the free variables of its components, minus all variables that occur in xs. We assume that for each alternative (xs, c, ps, rs) in a canonical form it holds that $xs \subseteq fv(\emptyset, c, ps, rs)$.

Two alternatives $A \stackrel{def}{=} (xs, c, ps, rs)$ and $B \stackrel{def}{=} (ys, d, qs, ss)$ are considered identical if $xs \cap fv(B) = ys \cap fv(A) = \emptyset$ and there exists a renaming ρ from xs to ys such that $B = \rho A$.

$$[\![c]\!] = \{(\emptyset, c, \emptyset, \emptyset)\}$$
$$[\![p\overline{y}]\!] = \{(\emptyset, true, \{p\overline{y}\}, \emptyset)\}$$
$$[\![\exists_x M]\!] = \{\exists_x A \mid A \in [\![M]\!]\}$$
$$[\![M \cdot N]\!] = \{A \sqcup B \mid A \in [\![M]\!], B \in [\![N]\!]\}$$
$$[\![M + N]\!] = [\![M]\!] \cup [\![N]\!]$$
$$[\![0]\!] = \emptyset$$
$$[\![g \mapsto M]\!] = \{(\emptyset, true, \emptyset, \{\{(g, [\![M]\!])\}\})\}$$
$$[\![R \mathbin{[\![} S]\!] = \{A \uplus B \mid A \in [\![R]\!], B \in [\![S]\!]\}$$

$$[\![\emptyset]\!]^{-1} = 0$$
$$[\![\{A_1, ..., A_n\}]\!]^{-1} = [\![A_1]\!]^{-1} + ... + [\![A_n]\!]^{-1} \qquad (n \geq 1)$$
$$[\![(\overline{x}, c, \{p_1\overline{y_1}, ..., p_j\overline{y_j}\}, \{r_1, ..., r_k\})]\!]^{-1} = \exists_{\overline{x}}(c \cdot p_1\overline{y_1} \cdot \ldots \cdot p_j\overline{y_j} \cdot [\![r_1]\!]^{-1} \cdot \ldots \cdot [\![r_k]\!]^{-1})$$
$$[\![\{(g_1, X_1), \ldots, (g_m, X_m)\}]\!]^{-1} = g_1 \mapsto [\![X_1]\!]^{-1} \mathbin{[\![} \ldots \mathbin{[\![} g_m \mapsto [\![X_m]\!]^{-1}$$

Fig. 3. Mapping a term to its canonical form and back.

Definition. A *canonical form environment* is a set of procedure definitions $\{p\overline{x} = X\}$ that associate a procedure name p and formal arguments $\overline{x}$ with a canonical form X. We use the letter E for canonical form environments.

We now define some useful operations on canonical forms and alternatives. Let

$$A \stackrel{def}{=} (xs, c, ps, rs)$$
$$B \stackrel{def}{=} (ys, d, qs, ss)$$

be two alternatives such that $xs \cap ys = xs \cap fv(B) = ys \cap fv(A) = \emptyset$. Then their least upper bound is given by

$$A \sqcup B = ((xs \cup ys) \cap fv(\emptyset, c \sqcup d, ps \cup qs, rs \cup ss), c \sqcup d, ps \cup qs, rs \cup ss).$$

Existential quantification $\exists_x A$ of an alternative A is defined as follows.

$$\exists_x(xs, c, ps, rs) = \begin{cases} (xs, c, ps, rs) & \text{if } x \notin fv(xs, c, ps, rs) \\ (xs, \exists_x c, ps, rs) & \text{if } x \in fv(c) \wedge x \notin fv(xs, true, ps, rs) \\ (xs \cup \{x\}, c, ps, rs) & \text{otherwise.} \end{cases}$$

Another useful operation is the merge $\uplus$ of two alternatives with a single reader each into an alternative where both readers are combined.

$$(xs, c, ps, \{r_1\}) \uplus (xs, c, ps, \{r_2\}) = (xs, c, ps, \{\bigcup(r_1 \cup r_2)\}).$$

Figure 3 presents a mapping $[\![\cdot]\!]$ that maps a pre-term to its canonical form, together with its right inverse, $[\![\cdot]\!]^{-1}$.

Lemma 4.1 For all pre-terms M, N, we have $M \equiv N$ iff $[\![M]\!] = [\![N]\!]$.

We now define a notion of reduction $\Rightarrow$ on canonical forms that simulates reduction $\rightarrow$ on ccp_{+0} terms. Analogous to $\rightarrow$, $\Rightarrow$ is parameterized by a normal form environment. There are three different ways a canonical form X can reduce.

1. If $(p\overline{x} = Y) \in E$ and X is $X' \cup \{(xs, c, \{p\overline{y}\} \cup ps, rs)\}$ then

$$X \Rightarrow_E X' \cup \{(xs, c, ps, rs) \sqcup A \mid A \in [\overline{y}/\overline{x}]Y\}.$$

2. If $d \leq c$ and X is $X' \cup \{(xs, c, ps, \{\{(d, Y)\}\} \cup rs)\}$ then

$$X \Rightarrow_E X' \cup \{(xs, c, ps, rs) \sqcup A \mid A \in Y\}.$$

3. If $r \neq \emptyset$, $d \leq c$ and X is $X' \cup \{(xs, c, ps, \{\{(d, Y)\} \cup r\} \cup rs)\}$ then

$$X \Rightarrow_E X' \cup \{(xs, c, ps, rs) \sqcup A \mid A \in Y\} \cup \{(xs, c, ps, \{\{(\sqrt{}, 0)\} \cup r\} \cup rs\})\}.$$

We now show that multi-step $\Rightarrow$ reduction can simulate $\rightarrow$.

Lemma 4.2 For all terms M, N, procedure environments D, if $M \rightarrow_D N$, then $[\![M]\!] \Rightarrow_{[D]} [\![N]\!]$.

The reverse of Lemma 4.2 also holds.

Lemma 4.3 For all canonical forms X, Y, canonical form environments E, if $X \Rightarrow_E Y$, then $[\![X]\!]^{-1} \rightarrow_{[E]^{-1}} [\![Y]\!]^{-1}$.

We now establish that reduction $\Rightarrow$ is confluent.

Definition. Let $\xrightarrow{p}$ be the reduction relation generated by the first rule (the unfolding rule) in the definition of $\Rightarrow$. Let $\xrightarrow{cc}$ be the reduction relation generated by the second and third rule (the communication rules) in the definition of $\Rightarrow$.

Lemma 4.4 $\xrightarrow{p}$ is Church-Rosser: If $X \xrightarrow{p}_E X_1$ and $X \xrightarrow{p}_E X_2$ then there is a canonical form X_3 s.t. $X_1 \xrightarrow{p}_E X_3$ and $X_2 \xrightarrow{p}_E X_3$.

Lemma 4.5 $\xrightarrow{cc}$ is Church-Rosser.

Lemma 4.6 $\Rightarrow$ is Church-Rosser.

Proof: By Lemma 4.4 and Lemma 4.5, $\xrightarrow{p}$ and $\xrightarrow{cc}$ are both Church-Rosser. An analysis of reduction sequences shows that $\xrightarrow{p}$ and $\xrightarrow{cc}$ commute. By the Lemma of Hindley and Rosen [1, Prop. 3.3.5], it follows that $\Rightarrow = \xrightarrow{p} \cup \xrightarrow{cc}$ is Church-Rosser.

We are finally in a position to show confluence for the original notion of reduction $\rightarrow$ on ccp_{+0} terms.

Theorem 4.7 $\rightarrow$ is Church-Rosser. For all terms M, M_1, M_2, environments D, if $M \twoheadrightarrow_D M_1$ and $M \twoheadrightarrow_D M_2$ then there is a term M_3 s.t. $M_1 \twoheadrightarrow_D M_3$ and $M_2 \twoheadrightarrow_D M_3$.

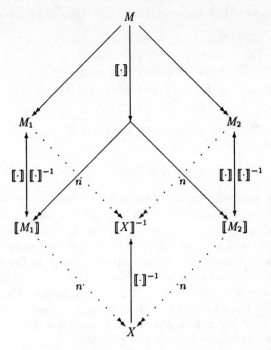

Fig. 4. Strategy of the CR proof

Proof: The proof strategy is depicted in Figure 4. Assume that $M \twoheadrightarrow_D M_1$ and $M \twoheadrightarrow_D M_2$. By an induction on the length of the two reduction sequences from M to M_1 and M_2, using Lemma 4.1 and Lemma 4.2 at each step, we have that $[\![M]\!] \Rightarrow_{[D]} [\![M_1]\!]$ and $[\![M]\!] \Rightarrow_{[D]} [\![M_2]\!]$. Since by Lemma 4.6 $\Rightarrow$ is confluent, this implies the existence of a canonical form X such that $[\![M_1]\!] \Rightarrow_{[D]} X$ and $[\![M_2]\!] \Rightarrow_{[D]} X$. As $[\![\cdot]\!]^{-1}$ is an inverse of $[\![\cdot]\!]$, $[\![[\![M_i]\!]]\!]^{-1} \equiv M_i$ for $i = 1, 2$. Then by induction on the length of the two reduction sequences from $[\![M_1]\!]$ and $[\![M_2]\!]$ to X, using Lemma 4.3 at each step, we have that $M_i = [\![[\![M_i]\!]]\!]^{-1} \twoheadrightarrow [\![X]\!]^{-1}$, $(i = 1, 2)$. This implies the proposition with $M_3 = [\![X]\!]^{-1}$.

5 Relationship to ccp

In this section we show that the observational behaviour of our calculus is identical to the observational behaviour of ccp in its standard transition system semantics. To do this we extend $[\![\cdot]\!]$ so that it maps a ccp configuration to a subset of the canonical forms given in the previous section, together with a reduction relation $\overset{ccp}{\Longrightarrow}$ on this canonical form and a notion of observables. We show that for a given program $\overset{ccp}{\longrightarrow}$, $\overset{ccp}{\Longrightarrow}$, $\Rightarrow$ and $\rightarrow$ all give rise to the same observations.

In order to extend $[\![\cdot]\!]$, we first give a mapping $pa()$ from ccp agents in a configuration to a ccp$_{+0}$ pre-agent. This is needed because ccp agents in a configuration may have hidden stores which are not allowed in pre-agents.

$$
\begin{aligned}
pa(c) &= c \\
pa(p\overline{y}) &= p\overline{y} \\
pa(\exists^d_x M) &= \exists_x(d \cdot pa(M)) \\
pa(M \cdot N) &= pa(M) \cdot pa(N) \\
pa(g \mapsto M) &= g \mapsto M.
\end{aligned}
$$

Note that terms in the range of pa never contain 0, $+$ or $\sqrt{}$. The *canonical form* of a ccp configuration $\langle A, c \rangle$ is given by

$$
[\![\langle A, c \rangle]\!] = [\![pa(A) \cdot c]\!].
$$

As ccp agents and programs do not contain blind choice, the canonical form of a ccp configuration will always consist of a single alternative. Because there is no need to distribute blind choice over the parallel operator, there is a bijection between the readers and the procedure calls in the ccp configuration and the canonical form. We will make use of this correspondence in the proofs below.

We now define a notion of reduction $\xrightarrow{ccp}$ on the canonical form of a ccp agent that simulates reduction $\xrightarrow{ccp}$ on ccp configurations. Like $\xrightarrow{ccp}$, $\xrightarrow{ccp}$ is parameterized by an environment E of definitions, i.e., associations between ccp procedure names with formal arguments and canonical forms. There are two different ways a ccp canonical form X can reduce:

1. If $(p\overline{x} = \{A\}) \in E$ then

$$
\{(xs, c, \{p\overline{y}\} \cup ps, rs)\} \qquad \xLongrightarrow{ccp}_E \{(xs, c, ps, rs) \sqcup A\}.
$$

2. If $d \leq c$ then

$$
\{(xs, c, ps, \{\{(d, \{A\})\}\} \cup rs)\} \xLongrightarrow{ccp}_E \{(xs, c, ps, rs) \sqcup A\}.
$$

Definition. A canonical form is in *normal form* if it cannot be reduced. $Con(A)$ is the constraint component of A. We write $\xLongrightarrow{ccp}$ for the reflexive and transitive closure of $\xrightarrow{ccp}$.

Analogous to the cases for $\to$ reductions and ($\xrightarrow{ccp}$) transitions, we now define two notions of observables for canonical form reductions.

Definition. Let the notion of reduction $\hookrightarrow$ be one of $\Rightarrow$, $\xLongrightarrow{ccp}$. Let P be the ccp program $D \; ; \; M$. Then the set of possible observations of P wrt $\hookrightarrow$ is given by

$$
Obs(\hookrightarrow, P) = \bigcup \{Obs([\![A]\!]^{-1}) \mid P \hookrightarrow \{A\} \cup X \ \wedge \ \{A\} \text{ is in } \hookrightarrow\text{-normal form}\}.
$$

The following two lemmas are shown by an analysis of $\xrightarrow{ccp}$ transitions and $\xLongrightarrow{ccp}$ reductions.

Lemma 5.1 If $S \xrightarrow{ccp} S'$ in the transition system T_D, then either $[\![S]\!] = [\![S']\!]$ or $[\![S]\!] \xLongrightarrow{ccp}_{[D]} [\![S']\!]$.

Lemma 5.2 Let S be a ccp configuration and D be a set of ccp definitions. If $[\![S]\!] \overset{ccp}{\Longrightarrow}_{[D]} X$ then there is a configuration S' such that $X = [\![S']\!]$ and $S \overset{ccp}{\longrightarrow} S'$ in the transition system T_D.

Thus:

Lemma 5.3 For any ccp program P, $Obs(\overset{ccp}{\longrightarrow}, P) = Obs(\overset{ccp}{\Longrightarrow}, P)$.

We also have that:

Lemma 5.4 For any ccp program P, $Obs(\overset{ccp}{\Longrightarrow}, P) = Obs(\Rightarrow, P)$.

Lemma 5.5 For any program P, $Obs(\Rightarrow, P) = Obs(P)$.

The main result of this section follows from Lemma 5.3, Lemma 5.4 and Lemma 5.5 – the confluent calculus is observationally equivalent to the operational semantics of ccp.

Theorem 5.6 For any ccp program P, $Obs(P) = Obs(\overset{ccp}{\longrightarrow}, P)$.

6 Application to Program Analysis

One application of our confluent semantics is to the static analysis of ccp programs. Codish *et al* [3, 2] propose a generic approach to the analysis of concurrent logic and constraint programs. They introduce a confluent semantics which approximates the standard (non-confluent) semantics of the concurrent constraint logic languages and use this as a basis for program analysis. Correctness of their analysis holds because the confluent semantics approximates the standard semantics in the sense that any successful reduction sequence in the usual semantics is also a valid reduction sequence in the confluent semantics, and suspension in the usual semantics implies suspension in the confluent semantics. The reason for requiring confluence is so that an analysis based on this semantics need only be proven correct for a single scheduling rule. This provides for accuracy as the analysis can choose a scheduling which gives the most precise answer and also provides for efficiency as there is no need to examine the potentially exponential or even infinite number of different but "isomorphic" reduction sequences corresponding to other schedulings. Zaffanella et al [17] and Falaschi et al [6] have given a modification of this idea for the slightly different context of ccp. They formalize the analysis as a transformation from a program written in full ccp to a an approximating program written in a subset of ccp for which the usual operational semantics is confluent.

Our calculus provides an alternative semantic basis for program analysis. Because the calculus is Church-Rosser it has all of the advantages of the approximate confluent semantics or program transformation. Yet it is inherently more precise because programs have exactly the same observable behaviour as in the usual operational semantics and the calculus does not introduce extra reductions. For example, consider the ccp agent

$$p(x) \cdot choose(x, y, z) \cdot c(z)$$

with the following ccp definitions.

$$p(x) \qquad := x = a$$
$$choose(x, y, z) := x = a \mapsto z = x \; [\!] \; y = a \mapsto true$$
$$c(z) \qquad := z = a \mapsto true$$

No analysis based on the approximate confluent semantics or transformed program approach can ever prove that this agent is suspension free as the approximate operational semantics and program transformation introduce a reduction sequence which leads to suspension. However, an analysis based on our calculus can show that this agent does not lead to suspension.

7 Conclusion

We have given a calculus for a class of languages, ccp_{+0}, which generalize concurrent constraint programs (ccp). However, unlike the usual operational semantics for ccp, the calculus is confluent in the sense that different process schedulings give rise to exactly the same set of possible outcomes. This disproves the folklore that it is impossible to give a confluent semantics for languages with non-deterministic guarded choice.

The calculus has application to static analysis of ccp programs. As the calculus is confluent, it provides a good basis on which develop analyses. Confluence means that not all process schedulings need to be considered in an analysis, allowing for efficiency, and that an analysis can choose a process scheduling which gives better information, allowing for accuracy.

Acknowledgements

We thank the referees for their detailed comments.

References

1. H. P. Barendregt. *The Lambda Calculus: its Syntax and Semantics*, volume 103 of *Studies in Logic and the Foundations of Mathematics*. North-Holland, Amsterdam, revised edition, 1984.
2. M. Codish, M. Falaschi, and K. Marriott. Suspension analyses for concurrent logic programs. *ACM Transactions on Programming Languages and Systems*, 16(3):649–686, 1994.

3. M. Codish, M. Falaschi, K. Marriott, and W. Winsborough. Efficient analysis of concurrent constraint logic programs. In *Proc. 20th International Colloquium on Automata, Languages, and Programming*, pages 633–644. Springer Verlag, 1993. LNCS 700.

4. C. Codognet, P. Codognet, and M. Corsini. Abstract interpretation for concurrent logic languages. In *Proc. North American Conf. on Logic Programming*, pages 215–232, 1990.

5. M. Falaschi, M. Gabbrielli, K. Marriott, and C. Palamidessi. Compositional analysis for concurrent constraint programming. In *Proc. 8th IEEE Symposium on Logic In Computer Science*, pages 210–221, 1993.

6. M. Falaschi, M. Gabbrielli, K. Marriott, and C. Palamidessi. Confluence and concurrent constraint programming. In *to appear in Proc. AMAST*, 1995.

7. Leon Henkin, J.Donald Monk, and Alfred Tarski. *Cylindric Algebras*, volume 64 of *Studies in Logic and the Foundations of Mathematics*. North Holland, 1971.

8. Gérard Huet. Confluent reductions: Abstract properties and applications to term rewriting systems. *Journal of the ACM*, 27(4):797–821, 1980.

9. Jan Willem Klop. *Combinatory Reduction Systems*. PhD thesis, Mathematisch Centrum, Kruislaan 413, 1098 SJ Amsterdam, 1980. Mathematical Centre Tracts n. 127.

10. J. W. Lloyd. *Foundations of Logic Programming*. Springer-Verlag, Berlin, second edition, 1987.

11. M. Maher. Logic semantics for a class of committed-choice programs. In *Proc. Fouth Int. Conf. on Logic Programming*, pages 858–876, 1987.

12. U. Montanari, F. Rossi, and V. Saraswat. CC programs with both in- and nondeterminism: A concurrent semantics. In *Second Int. Workshop on Principles and Practice of Constraint Programming (PPCP'94)*, pages 151–161. Springer Verlag, 1994. LNCS 874.

13. Joachim Niehren. *Funktionale Berechnung in einem uniform nebenläufigen Kalkül mit logischen Variablen*. PhD thesis, Universität des Saarlandes, 1994.

14. Joachim Niehren and Gert Smolka. A confluent relational calculus for higher-order programming with constraints. In Jean-Pierre Jouannaud, editor, *1st International Conference on Constraints in Computational Logics*, Lecture Notes in Computer Science, vol. 845, pages 89–104, München, Germany, 7–9 September 1994. Springer-Verlag.

15. Vijay Saraswat, Martin Rinard, and Prakash Panangaden. The semantic foundations of concurrent constraint programming. In *Conference Record of the Eighteenth Annual ACM Symposium on Principles of Programming Languages, Orlando, Florida*, pages 333–352. ACM Press, January 1991.

16. Vijay A. Saraswat and Martin Rinard. Concurrent constraint programming. In *Proceedings of the Seventeenth Annual ACM Symposium on Principles of Programming Languages*, pages 232–245, San Francisco, California, January 1990.

17. E. Zaffanella, G. Levi, and R. Giacobazzi. Abstracting synchronization in concurrent constraint programming. In *Proc. 5th Int'l Symposium on Programming Language Implementation and Logic Programming*. Springer Verlag, 1994. LNCS 844.

Situated Simplification

Andreas Podelski[1] and Gert Smolka[2]

[1] Max-Planck-Institut für Informatik, Im Stadtwald, D-66123 Saarbrücken, Germany
[2] German Research Center for Artificial Intelligence (DFKI), Stuhlsatzenhausweg 3, D-66123 Saarbrücken, Germany

Abstract. Testing satisfaction of guards is the essential operation of concurrent constraint programming (CCP) systems. We present and prove correct, for the first time, an incremental algorithm for the simultaneous tests of entailment and disentailment of rational tree constraints to be used in CCP systems with deep guards (*e.g.*, AKL or Oz). The algorithm is presented as the *simplification* of the constraints which form the (possibly deep) guards and which are *situated* at different nodes (or, local computation spaces) in a tree (of arbitrary depth). In this algorithm, each variable may have multiple bindings (representing multiple constraints on the same variable in different nodes). These may be realized by re- and de-installation upon each newly resumed check of the guard in the corresponding node (as done, *e.g.*, in AKL or Oz), or by using look-up tables (with entries indexed by the nodes). We give a simple fixed-point algorithm and use it for proving that the tests implemented by another, practical algorithm are correct and complete for entailment and disentailment. We formulate the results in this paper for rational tree constraints; they can be adapted to finite and feature trees.

1 Introduction

One idea behind concurrent constraint programming (CCP) is to base the satisfaction of guards (which is the condition driving the synchronization mechanism) on constraints. In this model, a constraint store is connected with several nodes α. Each of them is associated with a constraint φ_α (its guard) and with a guard check. The guard check consists of the tests of entailment and disentailment of φ_α by the constraint store. (If one of the two tests succeeds, an action may be triggered from that node.) The constraint store grows monotonically; upon each augmentation, the tests are repeated until one of the two tests succeeds. In the deep-guard model, each constraint φ_α may itself be a constraint store which also grows monotonically and which is itself connected with "lower" nodes, and so on. That is, at each instance one has a tree of nodes (or, *local computation spaces*) with constraints; a constraint in a node α is visible in all nodes lower than α. The problem is to determine which of these nodes are entailed [disentailed] by their parent node. At every next instance, this test will be repeated for a tree with augmented constraint stores in the nodes. Thus, an algorithm implementing the test has to be incremental. In this paper, we will introduce *situated simplification*, a general implementation scheme for such an algorithm, and instantiate the scheme with an algorithm for the case of constraints over rational trees.

CCP [16] comes out of concurrent and constraint logic programming, which originated with the Relational Language [4] and with Prolog-II [5], respectively. The computation model of concurrent logic programming languages [17] is based on committed-choice, a particular guard operator. In [10], the commit condition was analyzed as logical entailment. The delay mechanism in Prolog-like languages as MuProlog [13, 12] and functional residuation in LIFE [1, 2] are based on entailment as well; for a formal operational semantics of these languages see [15]. AKL [7] and Oz [8, 9] are two practical systems providing both for concurrent (as in multi-agent) and constraint logic programming in one uniform framework. Here, deep guards constitute the central mechanism to combine processes and ("encapsulated") search for problem-solving.

The first formal account (with proof of correctness) of an incremental algorithm for the simultaneous tests of entailment and disentailment is given in [3], for flat guards and a constraint system over feature trees. This algorithm is an instance of a general scheme called relative simplification. An abstract machine for the check of flat guards for constraint systems over trees is given (and proven correct) in [18]. It reflects the present implementations in AKL and Oz. The algorithm is guard-based in the sense that for every guard to be revisited (*i.e.*, whose test is resumed), the entire local binding environment is re-installed (and removed afterwards, if the test still suspends). Its on-line complexity is quadratic, whereas it is quasi-linear for the Beauty&Beast algorithm given in [14]. That algorithm is variable-based in the sense that the bindings are installed for each variable independently and only when needed. The bindings are indexed by the guard; thus, they may remain being installed (*i.e.*, this avoids re-installing/removing the local binding environment each time the test of the guard is resumed). The algorithm given in this paper picks up that idea, namely of indexing the bindings of the same variable by the different nodes (where each of the bindings represents a constraint on the variable in a different node). This provides for a high-level presentation. It now remains a matter of implementation how a variable's multiple bindings are realized. This may be done, for example, by re-installing/removing the guard environment as mentioned above, or "permanently" by using lookup tables, which seems more efficient. In a very recent, parallel implementation of AKL [11], the binding of a variable x in a local computation space α is also stored permanently, namely in a table local to α which uses the variable x as the index (*i.e.*, in record notation, the binding's value would be $\alpha.x$). The algorithm used there is not fully described, but it seems that it could be presented as an instance of the algorithm given in this paper (which would refer to the binding's value as $x.\alpha$).

In this section, we have stated the problem informally and put it into a general context. In Section 3, we formalize it and give the general implementation scheme called situated simplification for incremental algorithms solving the problem. Before that, however, we discuss a motivating example informally, in Section 2. Section 4 collects those properties of rational trees that we need here. We also give their proofs in a simple, self-contained form (to our knowledge, for the first time). In Section 5 we give a simple algorithm which is straightforward once the problem is stated formally and the idea of multiple bindings is there. This algorithm is given on a high level and uses a fixed-point iteration, which is not practical. It is useful, however, for didactic reasons and for proving correct the practical algorithm given in Section 6. We close with a conclusion section.

```
1    X=f(a Y)
2    or
3        Z in X=f(Z Z)
4        or
5            Y=Z
6        []
7            Y=b
8        ro
9    []
10       Y=c
11   ro
```

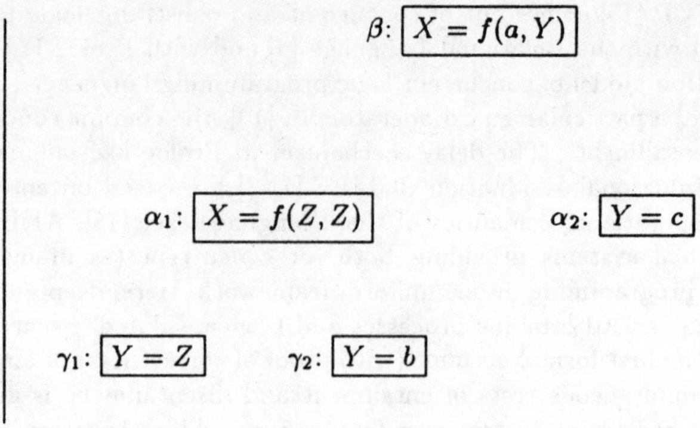

$\beta:\ \boxed{X = f(a, Y)}$

$\alpha_1:\ \boxed{X = f(Z, Z)}$ $\qquad$ $\alpha_2:\ \boxed{Y = c}$

$\gamma_1:\ \boxed{Y = Z}$ $\qquad$ $\gamma_2:\ \boxed{Y = b}$

Fig. 1. Oz program and corresponding tree of 5 computation spaces

2 Motivating example

The execution of the Oz program given in Figure 1 will build up a tree of 5 computation spaces. The constraints are equations between terms, interpreted over the domain of rational trees. The effect of line 1 is to put the constraint $X = f(a, Y)$ into the ("global") constraint store at the root of the tree; we note this node β. Lines 2 to 11 code a disjunction consisting of two disjuncts. These have to be tested simultaneously for entailment and disentailemt (the disjunction is suspended until one of the disjuncts is entailed or disentailed, *i.e.*, "determined"). In this section, we will use "determine" as a synonym of "entail or disentail." The tests of the two disjuncts are done in the two local computation spaces α_1 and α_2 which are directly below β.

The constraint $X = f(a, Y)$ does not determine the constraint $Y = c$. That is, the constraints in the computation spaces above α_2 (here, only β) do not determine the constraint in α_2 (which forms the second of the two disjuncts, given in line 10). This might change during the execution of other, not shown parts of the program, say, if $Y = c$ was added to β (then α_2 would be entailed), or if $Y = d$ was added to β (then α_2 would be disentailed).

The first of the two disjuncts (coded by lines 3 to 8) is a conjunction of the constraint $X = f(Z, Z)$ and another disjunction. The variable Z is quantified existentially over this conjunction, or: α_1 is the "home" of Z (whereas β is the home of X and Y). The computation space α_1 is above the two computation spaces γ_1 and γ_2 for the tests of the disjuncts $Y = Z$ and $Y = b$, respectively.

Now, γ_2 is disentailed since the conjunction $X = f(a, Y) \wedge X = f(Z, Z)$ of the constraints in computation spaces above γ_2, here α_1 and β, disentails the constraint $Y = b$. On the other hand, γ_1 is entailed since the conjunction $X = f(a, Y) \wedge X = f(Z, Z)$ of the constraints in computation spaces above γ_1, here also α_1 and β, entails the constraint $Y = Z$.

Finally, we observe that α_1 itself is not determined. The constraint $X = f(a, Y)$ does not determine $\exists Z\ X = f(Z, Z)$. This might change, for example, if the constraint $Y = a$ was added to β. This last case touches the issue of detecting "implicit equalities," here, between the first and second argument of the term $f(a, Y)$.

How does our algorithm perform a test on the five computation spaces? It will simplify the constraint in each computation space to a new constraint, hereby taking into account the constraints in *all* the computation spaces above. This simplified constraint signals (by its syntactic form) whether the computation space is entailed or disentailed or neither.

For example, the simplified constraint in γ_1 is $\top$ (for *true*) and thus signals entailment ($\top$ is a special case of a constraint signaling entailment). The one in γ_2 is $\bot$ (for *false*) and thus signals disentailment. The one in α_1 is $Z = Y \wedge Y = a$ and, since it binds a variable (here Y) from a computation space above, it does not determine α_1. (It would be further simplified to $Z = Y$ if the constraint $Y = a$ was added to β, and this would signal entailment; note that $\exists Z \; Z = Y$ is equivalent to $\top$.) Finally, the simplified constraint in α_2 would be $Y = c$ and thus signals "not determined." (It would be further simplified to $\bot$ if $Y = a$ was added to β, and then signal disentailment.)

Intrinsic difficulties of tree-ordered constraint stores. The algorithm will compute with suitable representations of the constraints, namely by bindings on variables. These representations must specify to which node the binding belongs. Also, there might be several bindings on the same variable (in the example, two on X and three on Y). This will be handled by allowing multiple bindings and by indexing the bindings with the nodes. For a fixed node, the algorithm must accumulate the constraints in *all* the computation spaces above; *i.e.*, it must represent their conjunction. What if there are several bindings on the same variable in this conjunction (in the example, if we take either of γ_1 or γ_2 as the fixed node, there are two bindings on X)? Could they be contradictory? Which one to choose? Also, if the test on a node depends on all nodes above it, then this means that each modification of the constraints of a node (by incremental adding of a conjunct) concerns potentially all the nodes below it. That is, their suspending tests may have to be resumed. Furthermore, acyclicity of bindings going through nodes above *and below* has to be re-checked. An additional difficulty comes from the well-known fact that for rational trees, the detection of implicit equalities can become involved (as in the proof that $X = f(Y)$, $Y = f(X)$ and $Z = f(Z)$ together entail $X = Z$). In the next sections we will present how we can solve these problems in an efficient manner.

3 Situated Simplification

In this section we will introduce some notions whose context is as follows. The algorithm to be presented in this paper is an instance of a new general scheme (called *situated simplification*) which is parameterized by the *constraint system*. An algorithm in this scheme will take a *constraint tree* as input. For each of the *nodes* of the constraint tree, the algorithm will decide whether the node has one of two properties called *inconsistent* or *entailed*, or none of both. It will do this by transforming the constraint tree into a *normal* one.

We assume a *constraint system*, *i.e.*, a first-order theory Δ (the theory can be given as the set of all sentences valid in a given structure; *e.g.*, of rational trees) and a set Con of first-order formulae called constraints. The set Con must be closed wrt. conjunction.[3] The set of variables is Var. For $\varphi \in$ Con, free_var(φ) is the set of all free variables of φ.

---

[3] As usual, we identify a conjunction with the multiset of its conjuncts (and $\wedge$ with $\cup$) in our notation. Thus, $X = t \in \varphi$ means that $X = t$ is a conjunct in φ, and $\bigcup\{\varphi \mid \varphi \in M\}$ is the conjunction of all constraints φ in the set M.

We also assume a finite tree-ordered set[4] Nodes whose elements we refer to as *nodes* (or, local computation spaces). We note the tree-order "$\leq$". We read $\beta < \alpha$ as "β is above α" (which means, β is closer to the root in the tree order). In the notation in this paper, we will try to keep the order $\beta \leq \alpha \leq \gamma$ when we choose letters α, β, γ to name nodes.

Finally, we assume a function home : Var $\mapsto$ Nodes which assigns each variable x one node α as its "home." We call the variables in home$^{-1}(\alpha)$ the *local* variables of the node α. We often write them in a tuple $\bar{x}_\alpha$. Thus,

$$\bar{x}_\alpha = \{\text{local variables of } \alpha\} = \text{home}^{-1}(\alpha).$$

The variables x with home in nodes strictly above α are the *global* variables of α. Thus,

$$\{\text{global variables of } \alpha\} = \bigcup\{\text{home}^{-1}(\beta) \mid \beta < \alpha\}.$$

We may use "global" and "local" referring only implicitly to a fixed node α. The local and the global variables are the ones "visible in α." Thus,

$$\{\text{variables visible in } \alpha\} = \bigcup\{\text{home}^{-1}(\beta) \mid \beta \leq \alpha\}.$$

The set Nodes and the assignment home of variables to their "home" nodes are fixed throughout the rest of this paper. We are interested in labelings of the nodes by constraints (hence the name "constraint tree") which respect the partition of the variables according to their home nodes in the following sense.

We define that a *constraint tree* T is a mapping

$$T : \text{Nodes} \mapsto \text{Con}, \ \alpha \mapsto \varphi_\alpha$$

where the free variables of each constraint φ_α are visible in its home node α; *i.e.*,

$$\text{free\_var}(\varphi_\alpha) \subseteq \bigcup\{\text{home}^{-1}(\beta) \mid \beta \leq \alpha\}.$$

We will write T also as $(\varphi_\alpha)_{\alpha \in \text{Nodes}}$.

We refer to the constraint φ_α as the "constraint situated in α." We define the "context of α" as the constraint $\varphi_{<\alpha}$ which is the conjunction of the constraints situated in nodes strictly above α; *i.e.*,

$$\varphi_{<\alpha} = \bigcup\{\varphi_\beta \mid \beta < \alpha\}.$$

The constraint "visible in α" is noted $\varphi_{\leq\alpha}$ and defined accordingly.

The node α is *inconsistent* (or, disentailed) if $\varphi_{\leq\alpha}$ is unsatisfiable, which is the same as

$$\Delta \models \varphi_{<\alpha} \rightarrow \neg \exists \bar{x}_\alpha \varphi_\alpha.$$

Note that this may also be expressed by $\Delta \models \varphi_{<\alpha} \rightarrow (\exists \bar{x}_\alpha \varphi_\alpha \leftrightarrow \bot)$.

The node α is *entailed* if (1) it is consistent and (2) the constraint situated in α is entailed (modulo local variables) by the context of α. Condition (2) is formally:

$$\Delta \models \varphi_{<\alpha} \rightarrow \exists \bar{x}_\alpha \varphi_\alpha.$$

Note that condition (2) may also be expressed by $\Delta \models \varphi_{<\alpha} \rightarrow (\exists \bar{x}_\alpha \varphi_\alpha \leftrightarrow \top)$.

The constraint tree $(\varphi_\alpha)_{\alpha \in \text{Nodes}}$ is *normal* if it satisfies conditions 1. and 2. below.

---

[4] A tree-ordered set is isomorphic to a prefix-closed subset of some free monoid, where "$\leq$" corresponds to the relation "is prefix of".

1. If α is inconsistent, then the constraint φ_α is the constraint *false*.

2. If α is entailed, then the constraint $\exists \bar{x}_\alpha \, \varphi_\alpha$ is equivalent to *true*.

Formally, this means the same as the following.

1. If $\Delta \models \varphi_{<\alpha} \to \neg \exists \bar{x}_\alpha \, \varphi_\alpha$, then $\varphi_\alpha = \bot$.

2. If $\Delta \models (\exists) \varphi_{<\alpha}$ and $\Delta \models \varphi_{<\alpha} \to \exists \bar{x}_\alpha \, \varphi_\alpha$, then $\Delta \models \exists \bar{x}_\alpha \, \varphi_\alpha$.

Two constraint trees are *equivalent* if for every node α, the two constraints visible in α in each constraint tree are equivalent. Formally, for two constraint trees $(\varphi_\alpha)_{\alpha \in \mathsf{Nodes}}$ and $(\varphi'_\alpha)_{\alpha \in \mathsf{Nodes}}$, if

$$\Delta \models \varphi_{\leq \alpha} \leftrightarrow \varphi'_{\leq \alpha}.$$

Note that the two constraint trees have the same set of nodes, namely Nodes, which is fixed (as is the home mapping on variables).

We name *situated simplification* a procedure which transforms a constraint tree into an equivalent normal constraint tree.

Situated Simplification implements the simultaneous tests of entailment and disentailment of φ_α by the context of α for every $\alpha \in \mathsf{Nodes}$.

4 Rational-tree constraints

In Sections 5 and 6, we will instantiate the constraint system in the situated simplifiaction scheme with the one over rational trees (*i.e.*, the scheme will work over "rational-tree-constraint trees"). Here, we will introduce it formally and state the properties that are important for the tests of satisfiability and entailment. We also give their proofs in a simple (and, as we think, minimal) way.

We assume a signature containing the function symbols (or constructor symbols) which we note f, g, h, a, b, c, *etc.* (we assume at least two different symbols). We call *constructions* the terms of the form $f(\bar{x})$ and note Struct the set that they form. Here, $\bar{x}$ denotes an ordered tuple $(x_1, \ldots, x_n)$ of length n according to the arity of the function symbol f, with *pairwise different* variables $x_1, \ldots, x_n$.

The set of constraints Con is the set of possibly existentially quantified conjunctions φ of equations between variables $x \in \mathsf{Var}$ and terms $t \in \mathsf{Var} \cup \mathsf{Struct}$ (thanks to the existential quantification, the restriction to terms of depth at most one is not a proper one). Formally, we have the following abstract syntax for constraints.[5]

$$\varphi \; ::= \; x = y \; \mid \; y = f(\bar{x}) \; \mid \; \exists x \, \varphi \; \mid \; \top \; \mid \; \bot$$

Given a constraint φ, we say that the variable x is *determined* if φ contains an equation between x and a construction. A constraint $\varphi = \{x_i = f_i(\bar{u}_i) \mid i = 1, \ldots, n\}$ where the determined variables $x_1, \ldots, x_n$ are pairwise different is called a *linear system*.

From now on, Δ is the theory of rational trees over the given signature of function symbols. We will use the following three facts about trees, the first one for the consistency test and the other two for the entailment test. The first one is *the* characteristic property of rational trees (*cf.*, for example, [6]); this is what God made them for.

Fact 1. *A linear system φ is satisfiable; i.e., $\Delta \models (\exists) \, \varphi$.*

---

[5] We use $=$ for both the logical equality symbol and the meta-level identity; no ambiguity will arise.

The first fact is a logical consequence of the next one. (On the other hand, given a proof of the first fact, the second fact could have been proven from the first. Namely, the value of a non-determined variable never contains an occurrence of the value of a determined variable and, thus, may be chosen arbitrarily in any solution for φ.)

Fact 2. *For all values of the non-determined variables in a linear system φ there exist values for its determined variables $x_1, \ldots, x_n$ such that φ holds, i.e.,* $\Delta \models (\forall) \exists (x_1, \ldots, x_n) \varphi$.

Proof. A tree τ may be represented as a set of pairs (w, f) where the function symbol f is the labeling of the node with the path $w \in \{1, 2, \ldots\}^*$. The tree τ is rational iff it has only finitely many subtrees, which are the trees $w^{-1}\tau = \{(v, f) \mid (wv, f) \in \tau\}$ for some path w.

Given φ, we define the relation $x \leadsto_w y$ ("x leads to y") by: $x \leadsto_\epsilon x$, and if $x \leadsto_w y$ and $y = f(y_1, \ldots, y_k, \ldots, y_n) \in \varphi$ then $x \leadsto_{wk} y_k$. We extend any valuation ν defined on the non-determined variables of φ by setting

$$\nu(x) = \begin{array}{l} \{\ (w, f) \mid x \leadsto_w y,\ y = f(\bar{u}) \in \varphi\}\ \cup \\ \{(wv, f) \mid x \leadsto_w y,\ y \text{ is non-determined},\ (v, f) \in \nu(y)\}. \end{array}$$

For all determined variables x, every subtree of $\nu(x)$ is of the form $w^{-1}\nu(x) = \nu(z)$ where z is the variable occuring in φ such that $x \leadsto_w z$. Thus, $\nu(x)$ is a rational tree, and ν satisfies all equations $x = f(\bar{u}) \in \varphi$. □

The next fact says when equations between determined variables are entailed.[6]

Fact 3. *The constraint φ entails the conjunction ψ of variable-variable equations if for every conjunct $x = y$ of ψ there exist determining equations $x = f(u_1, \ldots, u_m)$ and $y = f(v_1, \ldots, v_m)$ in φ such that the variables u_j and v_j are equated in φ or in ψ or they are the same variable (i.e., $u_j = v_j \in \varphi \cup \psi$ or $u_j = v_j$ for $j = 1, \ldots, m$).*

Proof. We first note that two rational (or infinite, or finite) trees τ_1 and τ_2 are equal iff for all n they are equal up to depth n.[7] Given a valuation ν which satisfies φ (i.e., $\Delta, \nu \models \varphi$), we prove, by induction over n,

$$\text{for all } x = y \in \psi,\ \nu(x) \text{ and } \nu(y) \text{ are equal up to depth } n. \tag{1}$$

We assume (1) for n' with $n' < n$ and $x = y \in \psi$. Then there exist $x = f(u_1, \ldots, u_m)$, $y = f(v_1, \ldots, v_m) \in \varphi$ as in the formulation of Fact 3. Thus, if $n = 0$ then (1) holds. Otherwise, for $j = 1, \ldots, m$, $u_j = v_j$ or $u_j = v_j \in \varphi$ or $u_j = v_j \in \psi$. In any of the three cases (in the last one by induction), $\nu(u_j)$ and $\nu(v_j)$ are equal up to depth $n - 1$, and hence, (1) holds for n. □

---

[6] This is a simple fact about rational trees, and finite trees as well. It is orthogonal to the algorithmic problem of the entailment test for rational trees which is caused by cycles in the determining equations.

[7] Formally, one may define the restriction of a tree τ to depth n inductively by $f(\tau_1, \ldots, \tau_m)|_0 = f(a, \ldots, a)$ and $f(\tau_1, \ldots, \tau_m)|_{n+1} = f(\tau_1|_n, \ldots, \tau_m|_n)$, for some constant symbol a.

5 Fixed-Point Algorithm

In this section, we will represent the two kinds of rational-tree constraints by bindings (either to a variable or to a construction) which are marked by the node to which the constraint belongs. We call the corresponding representation of a whole constraint tree a *decoration*. Then we will describe an algorithm which works by generating many new bindings (a lot of which will be "redundant"). Since it will never remove a binding (and not use new constructions), however, the termination follows from the finiteness of all possible bindings. The successive generations of bindings are justified by either the logical properties of equality, or by the fact that a constraint is visible in all nodes below the one to which it belongs, or by one logical property of the rational-tree constraint system (namely, the injectivity of function symbols). If there are no more justified generations of bindings possible, then the bindings (reduced to a non-redundant subset) represent a constraint tree which is *normal* (and, thus, exhibits which nodes are inconsistent or entailed). This follows from Theorem 5, which states how the bindings exhibit directly which nodes are inconsistent or entailed.

We will next define a representation for rational-tree constraint trees.

A *decoration* D is a labeling of nodes α by relations $\stackrel{\alpha}{=} \subseteq \mathsf{Var} \times (\mathsf{Var} \cup \mathsf{Struct})$ such that all variables occurring in $\stackrel{\alpha}{=}$ are visible in the node α. We write the relationship as $x \stackrel{\alpha}{=} y$ or $x \stackrel{\alpha}{=} f(\bar{x})$, respectively. For each node α, we define its "context relation"

$$\stackrel{\leq \alpha}{=} = \bigcup \{ \stackrel{\beta}{=} \mid \beta < \alpha \}.$$

A decoration D defines a constraint tree $(\varphi_\alpha)_{\alpha \in \mathsf{Nodes}}$ by $\varphi_\alpha = \{ x = t \mid x \stackrel{\alpha}{=} t \}$.

For decorations, the notions of equivalence and of inconsistent [entailed] nodes and of determined variables are obtained by referring to the defined constraint trees.

A decoration D is *complete* if for all variables x, y, constructions $f(\bar{u}), f(\bar{v})$ and nodes α,

1. $\stackrel{\alpha}{=} \cap (\mathsf{Var} \times \mathsf{Var})$ is an equivalence relation,
2. $\stackrel{\leq \alpha}{=} \subseteq \stackrel{\alpha}{=}$,
3. $x \stackrel{\alpha}{=} y$, $x \stackrel{\alpha}{=} f(\bar{u})$ implies $y \stackrel{\alpha}{=} f(\bar{u})$,
4. $x \stackrel{\alpha}{=} f(\bar{u})$, $x \stackrel{\alpha}{=} f(\bar{v})$ implies $\bar{u} \stackrel{\alpha}{=} \bar{v}$.

Given any decoration D, each of the conditions above can be made to be satisfied by adding pairs to the relations $\stackrel{\alpha}{=}$ (which is an equivalence transformation on the defined constraint tree). Going iteratively through the four conditions yields a monotonically growing family of relations. Since for each α, $\stackrel{\alpha}{=}$ is a subset of $\mathsf{Var} \times (\mathsf{Var} \cup \mathsf{Struct})$ ranging only over the variables occurring in D, the iteration reaches a fixed point in finitely many steps.[8] We have given an algorithm which proves:

Proposition 4. *For every decoration D there exists a least complete decoration D' containing D (i.e., $D \subseteq D'$). Moreover, such a decoration D' is equivalent to D.*

A complete decoration is interesting because it exhibits which nodes of the defined constraint tree are inconsistent and which are entailed.

---

[8] Note that the fixed set Nodes is finite.

Theorem 5. *If D is a complete decoration, then:*

1. *The node α is inconsistent iff $x \stackrel{\alpha}{=} f(\bar{u})$ and $x \stackrel{\alpha}{=} g(\bar{v})$ and $f \neq g$ for some variable x and constructions $f(\bar{u})$, $g(\bar{v})$;*
2. *The node α is entailed iff α is consistent and the following two conditions hold.*
   (a) *If x is global and $x \stackrel{\alpha}{=} f(\bar{u})$ then there exists a variable y and a construction $f(\bar{v})$ with $x \stackrel{\alpha}{=} y$ and $y \stackrel{\leq \alpha}{=} f(\bar{v})$ (i.e., y is determined in the context of α).*
   (b) *If x and y are global and $x \stackrel{\alpha}{=} y$ then either $x \stackrel{\leq \alpha}{=} y$ or $x \stackrel{\leq \alpha}{=} f(\bar{u})$ and $y \stackrel{\leq \alpha}{=} f(\bar{v})$ for some constructions $f(\bar{u})$, $f(\bar{v})$ (i.e., both x and y are determined in the context of α).*

Proof. Given a complete decoration and a node α fixed, we may construct a function $r : \mathsf{Var} \mapsto \mathsf{Var}$ such that (1) $r(x) = r(y)$ iff $x \stackrel{\alpha}{=} y$, and (2) $r(x)$ is local only if x is local. That is, r assigns each variable a—with preference global—representative of its equivalence class, the equivalence being $\stackrel{\alpha}{=} \cap (\mathsf{Var} \times \mathsf{Var})$. The constraint

$$\varphi_\alpha^r = \{r(x) = f(r(\bar{u})) \mid x \stackrel{\alpha}{=} f(\bar{u})\} \cup \{x = r(x) \mid x \stackrel{\alpha}{=} r(x),\ x \neq r(x)\}$$

is equivalent to φ_α (in the empty theory, by the laws for equality),

$$\models \varphi_\alpha \leftrightarrow \varphi_\alpha^r.$$

If the condition in *Statement 1* of the theorem holds, then clearly φ_α^r is unsatisfiable. Otherwise, we can write φ_α^r in the form

$$\varphi_\alpha^r = \{x_1 = f_1(\bar{u}_1), \ldots, x_n = f_n(\bar{u}_n)\} \cup \{x_{n+1} = y_{n+1}, \ldots, x_m = y_m\} \tag{2}$$

where the variables $x_1, \ldots, x_m$ are pairwise different and different from the variables $y_{n+1}, \ldots, y_m$. The first part is a linear system and, by **Fact 1**, has a solution over rational trees. Again by the laws for equality, this solution may be completed to be one for the second part too. This proves *Statement 1*.

If the condition *(a)* in *Statement 2* is violated, then $\varphi_{<\alpha} \wedge x = g(\bar{v})$ is satifiable and disentails $x = f(\bar{u})$ and, hence, φ_α. If condition *(b)* is violated, then $\varphi_{<\alpha} \wedge x = f(\bar{u}) \wedge y = g(\bar{v})$ is consistent and disentails $x = y$ and, hence, φ_α. Thus, $\varphi_{<\alpha}$ does not entail φ_α.

If conditions *(a)* and *(b)* hold, then **Fact 3** says that $\varphi_{<\alpha} \wedge \varphi_\alpha$ is equivalent to $\varphi_{<\alpha} \wedge \varphi_{\alpha,\mathsf{local}}^r$, where

$$\varphi_{\alpha,\mathsf{local}}^r = \{x = t \in \varphi_\alpha^r \mid x \text{ local}\}.$$

But **Fact 2** says that $\exists \bar{x}_\alpha \varphi_{\alpha,\mathsf{local}}^r$ is valid. This proves *Statement 2*. $\qquad \square$

Remark. In the theorem above, *Statement 2* holds with respect to finite trees too. Thus, the algorithm can be adapted to finite trees simply by adding the occurs-check to the test of a node's consistency.

In fact, the description above yields that if each of two constraints is satisfiable over finite trees (and hence, also over rational trees), then the entailment relation between them is the same for finite and for rational trees.

The theorem above expresses that the fixed-point algorithm implements situated simplification. Namely, a complete decoration D can be assigned a constraint tree $(\psi_\alpha)_{\alpha \in \mathsf{Nodes}}$ (which is equivalent to the one defined by D and which is normal) as follows. If there exist $x \stackrel{\alpha}{=} f(\bar{u})$ and $x \stackrel{\alpha}{=} g(\bar{v})$ with $\neq g$, then $\psi_\alpha = \bot$. Otherwise,

$$\psi_\alpha = \varphi_\alpha^r - \varphi_{<\alpha} - \{x = y \mid x \text{ and } y \text{ are determined in } \varphi_{<\alpha}\}.$$

6 Practical Algorithm

We will first define an efficient (*i.e.*, non-redundant) representation for the equations visible in the nodes of a constraint tree and then investigate a "solved form" for such a representation, *i.e.*, a form for consistent nodes exhibiting which of them are entailed. We next define a representation of a constraint tree specifying the constraint tree as a triple of (yet) unsolved equations, solved ones and inconsistent nodes. Naturally, the operational service of the practical algorithm is to "solve" such a representation of a constraint tree, namely, to transform it into an equivalent one where all consistent nodes are represented by equations in solved form. We will finally give such an algorithm and prove it correct.

6.1 Sets of Situated Bindings

A *set of situated bindings* B is a set of elements $(x, \alpha, t) \in \mathsf{Var} \times \mathsf{Nodes} \times (\mathsf{Var} \cup \mathsf{Struct})$, where x and the variables of t are visible in α, which satisfies the following conditions.

1. ("No cycles on the same path")
   If $\alpha_1, \dots, \alpha_n \leq \alpha$ and $\{(x_1, \alpha_1, x_2), \dots, (x_n, \alpha_n, x_{n+1})\} \subseteq B$, then $x_1 \neq x_{n+1}$.
2. ("No binding of global to local variable")
   If $(x, \alpha, y) \in B$ and x is global, then y is global too.
3. ("No two bindings of the same variable in the same node")
   If $(x, \alpha, s), (x, \alpha, t) \in B$, then $s = t$.
4. ("If two bindings of the same variable are on the same path, then the above one to a construction and the lower one to a variable")
   If $\beta < \alpha$ and $(x, \beta, s), (x, \alpha, t) \in B$, then $s \in \mathsf{Struct}$ and $t \in \mathsf{Var}$.

A set of situated bindings B defines a constraint tree by $\varphi_\alpha = \{x = t \mid (x, \alpha, t) \in B\}$ and thereby the notions of inconsistent and of entailed nodes.

Thanks to the first condition above, the following definition is well-founded.[9]

$$\mathsf{vderef}(x, \alpha, B) = \begin{cases} \mathsf{vderef}(y, \alpha, B) & \text{if there exists } (x, \beta, y) \in B \text{ with } \beta \leq \alpha, \\ x & \text{otherwise.} \end{cases}$$

A set of situated bindings B defines a decoration $\left(\frac{\alpha}{B}\right)_{\alpha \in \mathsf{Nodes}}$ by

$$x \stackrel{\alpha}{\underset{B}{=}} y \quad \text{iff } \mathsf{vderef}(x, \alpha, B) = \mathsf{vderef}(y, \alpha, B), \text{ and}$$

$$x \stackrel{\alpha}{\underset{B}{=}} f(\bar{u}) \quad \text{iff } (\mathsf{vderef}(x, \alpha, B), \beta, f(\bar{u})) \in B \text{ for some } \beta \leq \alpha.$$

This decoration satisfies the first two, but generally not the last two conditions for a complete decoration (defined on page 8).

We call a set B of situated bindings *complete* if the following two conditions hold.

1. If $(x, \alpha, y), (x, \beta, f(\bar{u})) \in B$ and $\beta \leq \alpha$ then $y \stackrel{\alpha}{\underset{B}{=}} f(\bar{u})$.
2. If $(x, \beta_1, f(\bar{u})), (y, \beta_2, f(\bar{v})) \in B$ and $x \stackrel{\alpha}{\underset{B}{=}} y$ and $\beta_1, \beta_2 \leq \alpha$ then $\bar{u} \stackrel{\alpha}{\underset{B}{=}} \bar{v}$.

---

[9] Note that the function vderef always yields a variable (and never a construction). This allows us to express, in the definition of $\stackrel{}{\underset{B}{=}}$, an "explicit equality" between two variables. (An "implicit equality" is one between two variables bound to equal constructions; *e.g.*, between x and y when $(x, \alpha, f(\bar{u})), (y, \alpha, f(\bar{u})) \in B$, or when $(x, \alpha, f(x)), (y, \alpha, f(y)) \in B$, and so on.)

We now have the following characterization.

Proposition 6. *B is a complete set of situated bindings iff $\left(\frac{\alpha}{B}\right)_{\alpha \in \mathsf{Nodes}}$ is a complete decoration.*

Given a set of situated bindings B, we obtain B^- by removing "secondary bindings" in B, *i.e.*,

$$B^- = B - \{(x, \alpha, y) \mid \text{exists } (x, \beta, f(\bar{u})) \in B, \ \beta \leq \alpha\}.$$

Theorem 5 and Proposition 6 immediately yield the following characterization of entailed nodes.

Proposition 7. *Given a complete set of situated bindings B, a node α is entailed iff all bindings $(x, \alpha, t) \in B^-$ are on local variables x only. All nodes are consistent.*

With respect to situated simplification, the statement above means the following.

Corollary 8. *If B is a complete set of situated bindings, then B^- defines an equivalent normal constraint tree (with consistent nodes only).*

6.2 Configurations

A *configuration* is a triple (E, B, I) where

- E is a multiset of "situated equations" $(x, \alpha, t) \in \mathsf{Var} \times \mathsf{Nodes} \times (\mathsf{Var} \cup \mathsf{Struct})$,
- B is a set of situated bindings, and
- I is a set of *inconsistent nodes* $\alpha \in \mathsf{Nodes}$.

We moreover require that I never contains a node occurring in either B or E and that I is downward closed (*i.e.*, if $\beta \leq \alpha$ and $\beta \in I$ then $\alpha \in I$).

A configuration defines a rational-tree-constraint tree by

$$\varphi_\alpha = \begin{cases} \perp & \text{if } \alpha \in I, \\ \{x = t \mid (x, \alpha, t) \in B \cup E\} & \text{otherwise.} \end{cases}$$

Given a configuration, the notions of equivalence and of inconsistent and entailed nodes refer to the defined constraint tree.

We call a configuration (E, B, I) *normal* if $E = \emptyset$ and B is a complete set of situated bindings.

The operational service to be provided by our algorithm is indicated by the following characterization (namely, to transform a configuration into a normal one).

Proposition 9. *Given a normal configuration (E, B, I), a node α is*

1. *inconsistent iff $\alpha \in I$, and*
2. *entailed iff all variables x with a binding $(x, \alpha, t) \in B^-$ are local variables of α.*

The next remark says that the algorithm implements situated simplification; it is a reformulation of Corollary 8.

Corollary 10. *Given a normal configuration (E, B, I), the equivalent configuration (B^-, E, I) obtained by removing secondary bindings in B defines a normal constraint tree.*

```
1    while E ≠ ∅
2        choose (x, α, t) ∈ E
3        x := vderef(x, α, B)
4        if t = y (i.e., t ∈ Var) then
5            y := vderef(y, α, B)
6            if x = y then
7                skip
8            [] x ≠ y then
9                if x global and y local for α then swap(x,y) fi
10               for all (x, γ, s) ∈ B with α ≤ γ
11                   remove (x, γ, s) from B, add (y, γ, s) to E
12               for all (y, γ, z) ∈ B with α < γ
13                   if vderef(z, γ, B) = x then remove (y, γ, z) from B fi
14               if exists (x, β, s) ∈ B with β < α then add (y, α, s) to E fi
15               add (x, α, y) to B
16           fi
17       [] t = f(ū) (i.e., t ∈ Struct) then
18           if exists (x, β, g(v̄)) ∈ B with β ≤ α, f ≠ g then
19               for all (z, γ, s) ∈ B ∪ E with α ≤ γ
20                   remove (z, γ, s) from B and E, add γ to I
21           [] exists (x, β, f(v̄)) ∈ B with β ≤ α, then
22               add (ū, α, v̄) to E
23           [] not exists (x, β, g(v̄)) ∈ B with β ≤ α (f = g or f ≠ g), then
24               for all (x, γ, s) ∈ B with α ≤ γ
25               remove (x, γ, s) from B and add to E
26               add (x, α, f(ū) to B
27           fi
28       fi
29       remove (x, α, t) from E
30   end
```

Fig. 2. The algorithm transforming a configuration into a normal one

6.3 Normalization of Configurations

We consider the procedure given in Figure 2.

Starting with an initial configuration (E_0, B_0, I_0), each execution of the body of the while loop yields a new triple (E_i, B_i, I_i), for $i = 1, \ldots, N$ where $N \leq \omega$. It might be a useful exercise for the reader to reformulate the algorithm using configuration-rewrite rules.

It is important to note that the algorithm can start with any configuration (and not just with one where B and I are empty). The algorithm is to be used on-line, *i.e.*, where the computation tree and the set of situated equations E are augmented incrementally. The algorithm is incremental since B and I grow then incrementally too.

We will next explain some lines of the algorithm. In line 3, the result of vderef applied to x is again a variable, by the definition of vderef. This variable might itself be bound to a construction. If the binding lies in α, line 10 will take care of that case. If the binding lies in a node β above α, line 14

If the term t is a variable, then its deref value is a variable too (again, by the definition of **vderef**). Line 9 ensures that we don't bind a global to a local variable. This corresponds to condition 2. in the definition of a set of situated bindings in Section 6.1 (which plays a role for the entailment condition).

Lines 10-11 ensure conditions 3. and the part of 4. which concerns the lower parts of paths through α.

Lines 12-13 ensure that condition 1. holds even after line 15 has been executed. Namely, one has to avoid cyclic references which go through nodes above *and below* α. It is important to note that we can restrict ourselves to removing bindings (y, γ, z) where $\alpha < \gamma$, and not $\alpha \leq \gamma$. This reason is that y is the result of applying the function $\mathsf{vderef}(\_, \alpha, B)$. Thus, there cannot be a binding (y, α, z).

In line 14, the term s is necessarily a construction (if it were a variable, the value of **vderef** could not be x). Thus, condition 4. holds even after line 15 has been executed. We need, however, ensure that condition 1. of the definition of a *complete* set of situated bindings will hold (which plays a role for the disentailment test).

If the term t is a construction, then there are three cases. All of them are easy to deal with. Case 1 (lines 18-20). The variable x is bound to a construction with a different function symbol. Then the node α and all nodes below it are inconsistent. We need remove their bindings according to the definition of a configuration in Section 6.2. Case 2 (lines 21-22). The variable x is bound to a construction with the same function symbol. Then we need ensure that condition 2. of the definition of a complete set of situated bindings will hold. Case 3. (lines 23-26). The variable x is not bound to any construction ("x is free"). Then we only need to ensure conditions 3. and 4. in the definition of a set of situated bindings in Section 6.1.

Example from Section 2. The initial configuration (B_0, E_0, I_0) which corresponds to the execution of the Oz program given in Section 2 is given by $B_0 = \emptyset$, $I_0 = \emptyset$, and

$$
\begin{aligned}
E_0 = \{\, & (x, \beta, f(y_1, y)), (y_1, \beta, a), \\
& (x, \alpha_1, f(z_1, z)), (z_1, \alpha_1, z), \\
& (y, \gamma_1, z), (y, \gamma_2, b), \\
& (y, \alpha_2, c) \qquad\qquad\qquad \}.
\end{aligned}
$$

Note that we need introduce auxiliary (existentially quantified) variables y_1 and z_1 because constructions are of the form $f(\bar{x})$ where the variables in the tuple $\bar{x} = (x_1, \ldots, x_n)$ are pairwise different.

We will choose (and remove) and add elements of E in a stack-like manner. That is, the algorithm will first move $(x, \beta, f(y_1, y))$ and (y_1, β, a) from E to B (using lines 23-26). Then it will remove $(x, \alpha_1, f(z_1, z))$ from E and add (z_1, α_1, y_1) and (z, α_1, y) to B (after adding the two bindings temporarily to E, using lines 21–22).

After applying **vderef** twice, the binding (z_1, α_1, z) gets installed in B as (y_1, α_1, y). Here, line 14 is applied; *i.e.*, (y, α_1, a) is put into E and eventually installed in B.

After applying **vderef** on z, the binding (y, γ_1, z) is simply removed from E (using lines 6-7). So the node γ_1 does not contain any bindings. Thus, in the constraint tree, the constraint in the node γ_1 is the empty conjunction, which is T (for *true*).

Using lines 18-20, we remove the binding (y, γ_2, b) from E and add γ_2 to I.

Finally, the binding (y, α_2, c) is moved from E to B, by use of lines 23-26.

Then, the outcome of the algorithm is the configuration (E, B, I) where $E = \emptyset$, $I = \{\gamma_2\}$, and

$$B = \{ (x, \beta, f(y_1, y)), (y_1, \beta, a),$$
$$(z_1, \alpha_1, y_1), (z, \alpha_1, y), (y_1, \alpha_1, y), (y, \alpha_1, a),$$
$$(y, \alpha_2, c) \qquad\qquad \}.$$

If we eliminate the existentially quantified variables y_1 and z_1, then $x = f(a, y)$ is the constraint of the node β, $z = y \wedge y = a$ the one of α_1, $\top$ the one of γ_1, $\bot$ the one of γ_2, and $y = c$ the one of α_2.

Other examples. We will now give some examples in order to motivate particular lines of the algorithm. Always, we assume $\beta \leq \alpha \leq \gamma$.

The configuration with $B = \{(x, \beta, f(x)), (y, \beta, f(y))\}$ and $E = \{(x, \alpha, y)\}$ will lead to applications of lines 14-15 (add (x, α, y) to B and $(y, \alpha, f(y))$ to E) and lines 21-22 (add (x, α, y) to E) and lines 6-7 and then terminate. The node α is entailed since both x and y are bound to constructions.

The configuration with $B = \{(x, \beta, f(u))\}$, $\{(x, \alpha, y)$ and $E = \{(y, \beta, g(v))\}$ will lead to applications of lines 14-15 (add (x, α, y) to B and $(y, \alpha, f(u))$ to E and afterwards to B) and line 25 (move $(y, \alpha, f(u))$ from B to E) and then to line 18 (add α to I).

The configuration with $B = \{(y, \beta, f(v)), (x, \alpha, f(u))\}$ and $E = \{(y, \alpha, x)\}$ where home(x) $= \alpha$ will lead to applications of line 9 (swap x and y), and then line 10-11 (remove $(x, \alpha, f(u))$ from B, add $(y, \alpha, f(u))$ to E). After adding (u, α, v) to E (by application of line 21) and then moving the binding from E to B, the algorithm terminates. The node α is not determined.

The configuration with $B = \{(w, \beta, u), (u, \alpha, v)\}$ and $E = \{(v, \beta, w)\}$ will lead to an application of lines 12-13 (that is, (u, α, v) is removed from B) before the installation of (v, β, w) in B.

Thus, if we put the two preceding examples together, the configuration with $B = (\{(y, \beta, f(v)), (x, \alpha, f(u)), (w, \beta, u)\}$ and $E = \{(y, \alpha, x), (v, \beta, w)\}$ where home(x) $= \alpha$ will lead to a configuration without a binding on α. That is, α is entailed.

6.4 Correctness and Termination

We consider any sequence $((E_i, B_i, I_i))_{i=0,\ldots,N}$ starting in a configuration (E_0, B_0, I_0) and obtained by successive execution of the body of the while loop. The proofs of the next three propositions are done by analysis of the algorithm.

Proposition 11. *Each triple (E_i, B_i, I_i) is a configuration.*

Proposition 12. *If the procedure terminates in (E_N, B_N, I_N) then (E_N, B_N, I_N) is a normal configuration.*

Proposition 13. *The step from (E_i, B_i, I_i) to $(E_{i+1}, B_{i+1}, I_{i+1})$ is an equivalence transformation on the defined constraint trees.*

Theorem 14. *The sequence $((E_i, B_i, I_i))_{i=0,\ldots,N}$ must be finite; i.e., the procedure given in Figure 2 always terminates.*

Proof. Every configuration $(E_{i+1}, B_{i+1}, I_{i+1})$ is obtained from (E_i, B_i, I_i) by one of five cases inside the body of the while loop. Hence, we have one of the following possibilities.

1. $(E_{i+1}, B_{i+1}, I_{i+1}) = (E_i - \{(x, \alpha, x)\}, B_i, I_i)$ for some variable x
2. $I_{i+1} = I_i$, and

   $B_{i+1} = B_i \cup \{(x, \alpha, y)\} - B$ where $B \subseteq \{(x, \alpha, f(\bar{u}))\} \cup \{(z, \gamma, t) \mid \alpha < \gamma\}$
3. $I_{i+1} = I_i \uplus I$ where $I \neq \emptyset$
4. $(E_{i+1}, B_{i+1}, I_{i+1}) = (E_i - \{(x, \alpha, f(\bar{u}))\} \cup E, B_i, I_i)$ where $E \subseteq \{(u, \gamma, v) \mid \alpha \leq \gamma\}$
5. $I_{i+1} = I_i$, and $B_{i+1} = B_i \cup \{(x, \alpha, f(\bar{u}))\} - B$ where $B \subseteq \{(x, \gamma, t) \mid \alpha < \gamma\}$

In each of these cases, $(E_{i+1}, B_{i+1}, I_{i+1}) \prec (E_i, B_i, I_i)$ where $\preceq$ is the lexicographic ordering on reversed configuration-triples, with, component-wise,

1. $I \leq I'$ if $I \supseteq I'$,
2. $B \leq B'$ if $B \sqsupseteq B'$, where $\sqsupseteq$ is the multiset ordering induced by

$$(x, \alpha, y) > (x, \alpha, f(\bar{u})) > (x, \gamma, t) \text{ if } \alpha < \gamma,$$

3. $E \leq E'$ if $E \sqsubseteq E'$, where $\sqsubseteq$ is the multiset ordering induced by

$$(z, \gamma, t) < (u, \alpha, v) < (x, \alpha, f(\bar{u})) \text{ if } \alpha < \gamma.$$

Since there are no infinitely decreasing $\prec$-chains, the sequence $((E_i, B_i, I_i))_{i=0,\dots,N}$ is finite. □

7 Conclusion and Future Work

We have given the first formal account of an algorithm for checking entailment and disentailment of deep guards. We have formulated the results in this paper for rational tree constraints; they can be adapted to finite and to feature trees.

A first conclusion one may draw is that the machinery needed for deep guards is principally not more complicated than for flat guards. The sole difference lies in the administration of the tree order for (1) the implementation of the function vderef(x, α, B), which goes over at most two levels of the computation tree in the case of flat guards, but arbitrarily many in the case of deep guards, and (2) the removal of situated bindings (x, γ, s) from nodes γ below a given node α, thus, essentially, for the test of $\leq$-comparison between nodes.

This work is the preliminary for (on-line) complexity analysis and for comparing different realizations of our algorithm. The difficulty seems here to determine the complexity of finding all situated bindings (x, γ, s) with $\gamma \leq \alpha$. It will be interesting to measure the performance of the implementations already existing in AKL and in Oz, which are guard-based, against a variable-based implementation using hash-tables for the lists of situated bindings of each variable. The theoretical on-line complexity seems better for the latter which avoids re-installing multiple bindings. In the case of flat guards over rational trees, this has been shown in [14]: It has quasi-linear as opposed to quadratic cost. Interesting, though mainly theoretically, is also the problem of the optimal amortized-time complexity of the vderef(x, α, B) function, which is about path-compression for bindings which go through several nodes.

Acknowledgements

We thank Peter Van Roy for discussion and suggestions to improve this presentation. This work is partially supported by the ESPRIT project ACCLAIM (EP 7195). Gert Smolka has also been supported by the BMBF Project Hydra (contract ITW 9105) and the Esprit Project CCL (contract EP 6028).

References

1. Hassan Aït-Kaci and Andreas Podelski. Towards a meaning of LIFE. In J. Maluszyński and M. Wirsing, editors, *Proceedings of the 3rd International Symposium on Programming Language Implementation and Logic Programming*, Springer LNCS vol. 528, pages 255–274. Springer-Verlag, 1991.

2. Hassan Aït-Kaci and Andreas Podelski. Functions as passive constraints in life. *ACM Transactions on Programming Languages and Systems (TOPLAS)*, 16(4):1279–1318, July 1994.

3. Hassan Aït-Kaci, Andreas Podelski, and Gert Smolka. A feature-based constraint system for logic programming with entailment. *Theoretical Computer Science*, 122(1-2):263–283, January 1994.

4. K.L. Clark and S. Gregory. A relational language for parallel programming. In *Proc. of the ACM Conference on Functional Programming Languages and Computer Architecture*, pages 171–178, 1981.

5. Alain Colmerauer. Prolog II reference manual and theoretical model. Technical report, Groupe Intelligence Artificielle, Université Aix – Marseille II, October 1982.

6. Bruno Courcelle. Fundamental properties of infinite trees. *Theoretical Computer Science*, 25(2):95–169, 1983.

7. S. Haridi and S. Janson. Kernel Andorra Prolog and its computation model. In D.H.D. Warren and P. Szeredi, editors, *Proceedings of the 7th International Conference on Logic Programming*, pages 31–48. MIT Press, June 1990.

8. M. Henz, M. Mehl, M. Müller, T. Müller, J. Niehren, R. Scheidhauer, C. Schulte, G. Smolka, R. Treinen, and J. Würtz. The Oz Handbook. Research Report RR-94-09, Deutsches Forschungszentrum für Künstliche Intelligenz, Stuhlsatzenhausweg 3, D-66123 Saarbrücken, Germany, 1994. Available through anonymous ftp from `duck.dfki.uni-sb.de`.

9. Martin Henz, Gert Smolka, and Jörg Würtz. Oz—a programming language for multi-agent systems. In Ruzena Bajcsy, editor, *13th International Joint Conference on Artificial Intelligence*, volume 1, pages 404–409, Chambéry, France, 30 August–3 September 1993. Morgan Kaufmann Publishers.

10. Michael J. Maher. Logic semantics for a class of committed-choice programs. In Jean-Louis Lassez, editor, *Proceedings of the Fourth International Conference on Logic Programming*, pages 858–876. MIT Press, 1987.

11. Johan Montelius and Khayri A. M. Ali. An and/or-parallel implementation of AKL. *New Generation Computing*, 13(4), December 1995.

12. Lee Naish. Automating control for logic programs. *The Journal of Logic Programming*, 2(3):167–184, October 1985.

13. Lee Naish. The Mu-Prolog 3.2db reference manual. Technical report, Department of Computer Science, University of Melbourne, Victoria, Australia, 1985.

14. Andreas Podelski and Peter Van Roy. The Beauty and the Beast algorithm: Quasi-linear incremental tests of entailment and disentailment. In Maurice Bruynooghe, editor, *Proceedings of the International Symposium on Logic Programming (ILPS)*, pages 359–374. MIT Press, November 1994.
15. Andreas Podelski and Gert Smolka. Operational semantics of constraint logic programming with coroutining. In Leon Sterling, editor, *Proceedings of the 12th International Conference on Logic Programming*, pages 449–463, Kanagawa, Japan, 1995. The MIT Press.
16. Vijay Saraswat and Martin Rinard. Concurrent constraint programming. In *Proceedings of the 17th ACM Conference on Principles of Programming Languages*, pages 232–245, San Francisco, CA, January 1990.
17. Ehud Shapiro. The family of concurrent logic programming languages. *ACM Computing Surveys*, 21(3):413–511, September 1989.
18. Gert Smolka and Ralf Treinen. Records for logic programming. *The Journal of Logic Programming*, 18(3):229–258, April 1994.

Guarded Constructive Disjunction :
Angel or Demon ?

Christian Codognet
LIENS / University of Paris XIII
45 rue d'Ulm, 75005 Paris, FRANCE
Christian.Codognet@ens.fr

Philippe Codognet
INRIA-Rocquencourt
B. P. 105, 78153 Le Chesnay, France
Philippe.Codognet@inria.fr

*Quoniam sepe, ut mihi videtur, expertus sum, quod cum rationes viderem
ad utramque partem probabiles, tamen ad neutram partem iudicii deter-
minabam me (...) sed in suspenso tenebam me.*

Jean Buridan. Quaestiones super decem libros Ethicorum.

*Jean Buridan (1300-1358) studied logic, ethics and physics. He taught at
the university of Paris. (...) Buridan was known as a student of Ockham
and was an intellectual determinist: in choosing one of several possible
decisions, the "will" is controlled by reason. It acts only when the reason
decides that one of the possibilities is the best (the will also chooses this
possibility). But if reason decides that several possibilities are equivalent,
the will does not act. This is the source of the well-known example of
"Buridan's ass", which died while standing between two identical hand-
fuls of grass.*

N. I. Styazhkin. History of Mathematical Logic from Leibniz to Peano.

Abstract. We propose a new operator for Concurrent Constraint (cc)
programming, called guarded constructive disjunction, in order to avoid
indeterminism, aka demonic non-determinism, aka don't care non-deter
minism. This operator is deterministic, avoiding thus confluence problems, and extends constructive disjunction by guarding each alternative
branch. Our framework is based on a denotational semantics of concurrent constraint languages, where each agent, including the guarded constructive disjunction operator, is seen as a closure operator over the lattice defined by the constraint system. We investigate the interest of this
semantics for program analysis in the abstract interpretation paradigm,
thanks to the notion of abstraction between constraint systems. We illustrate with some programming examples how suspension analysis can
be performed within this framework.

1   Introduction

Concurrent Constraint (cc) languages have been proposed originally by [23] [24]; they extend Constraint Logic Programming (CLP) with concurrency features that have emerged from the domain of Concurrent Logic Programming. The key idea underlying the family of cc languages is to use constraints to extend the synchronization and control mechanisms of concurrent logic languages. Briefly, multiple agents (processes) run concurrently and interact by means of a shared *store*, i.e. a global set of constraints. Each agent can either add a new constraint to the store (*Tell* operation) or check whether or not the store entails a given constraint (*Ask* operation). Synchronization is achieved through a *blocking ask* : an asking agent may block and suspend if one cannot state if the asked constraint is entailed nor its negation is entailed. Thus nothing prevents the constraint to be entailed later in the execution, but the store does not yet contain enough information. The agent is suspended until other concurrently running agents add (*Tell*) new constraints to the store to make it strong enough to decide.

The general cc framework makes room for both angelic non-determinism and demonic non-determinism (indeterminism). However if angelic nondeterminism causes no problem from the semantical point of view, indeterminism is more problematic to incorporate because it gives rise to non-confluent semantics. Observe also that indeterminism requires, from a pragmatic programming point of view, guarding each alternative with some condition, as originally proposed by [11]. Non-confluency is an important problem and particularly hampers the design of program analysis frameworks. It notably prevents, together with the problem of *Ask* approximation [31, 32], to directly lift CLP analysis frameworks to cc analysis. It seems therefore natural to base an analysis framework on confluent semantics. This kind of approach has been taken in [13], which nevertheless only leads to the definition of an obvious class of indeterministic cc programs ensured to be confluent : when for all indeterministic choices either all guards are mutually exclusive or all guards are reduced to true. Our approach is also to propose a confluent semantics and, in order to avoid indeterminism, we choose to design a new operator for cc languages called *guarded constructive disjunction (GCD)*. This operator is deterministic, thus avoiding confluency problems, and extends constructive disjunction by guarding each alternative branch. We therefore move from an irreversible choice construct (i.e. indeterminism) to a refinable non-choice construct (i.e. GCD operator). The interest of defining a new operator in the language makes it possible to analyze a larger class of programs than in [13], because non mutually-exclusive guards can be handled and common information extracted from the corresponding branches.

Indeed, the GCD operator generalizes the ∇ operator, a particular form of constructive disjunction, introduced in [30] in the case of finite domain constraints. Note that constructive disjunction is very close to the generalized propagation method of [19], which attempts, in the constraint logic programming framework, to extract common information from disjunctive branches. The interest of constructive disjunction for improving efficiency in constraint logic programming with disjunctive constraints has been assessed by [16] and [20]. The

GCD operator can somehow be seen as a minimal generalization of those constructs for cc programming, obtained on the one hand by the introduction of guards and on the other hand by considering the disjunction of agents and not only constraints.

Our framework is based on a denotational semantics of concurrent constraint languages. The denotational semantics of cc languages [25] consists in interpreting the basic operations in cc languages and the agents as *closure operators* over the underlying constraint system. A constraint system is a pair $(D, \vdash)$ where D is the constraint domain and $\vdash$ an entailment relation over D satisfying some simple conditions, and can be seen as a first-order generalization of Scott's *information systems* [28]. The denotational semantics we propose is inspired by [25] but different in several features. Closure operators are defined directly as functions over stores instead of defining them via the set of their fixpoints. This formulation has a more natural intuitive meaning and makes it possible to smoothly integrate the GCD operator as a closure operator over stores.

We also investigate the interest of this semantics, and of the GCD operator in particular, for program analysis in the abstract interpretation paradigm. Abstract interpretation is defined for cc languages in a way similar to what was done for CLP programs in [7], by introducing a notion of abstraction (i.e. approximation) between constraint systems. If C' abstracts C, then for each program P computing on C, P can be syntactically transformed into a program P' computing on C' such that the computation of P' is an abstraction of that of P, and thus the static analysis of P is obtained in executing P'. Of course, one should ensure that the execution of P' terminates.

For abstract interpretation purposes, it is very interesting to have a confluent denotational semantics, as it avoids the scheduling policy problems of an operational semantics. Our denotational semantics also makes it possible to derive a generic (fixpoint) algorithm that computes the functions defined by the semantic equations, in a way similar to what is done for Prolog (see [9] for a survey on that topic), but using reexecution to simulate concurrent execution, cf. [6]. Remark that those practical considerations are not investigated in other frameworks of abstract interpretation for cc languages [12, 3]. The main contribution of [3] is the definition of a confluent (w.r.t. scheduling) operational semantics, close to the original proposal of [6] for languages with monotonic guards. It is however not so clear how to derive an efficient algorithm from that operational semantics. [12] defines a denotational semantics in terms of input-output relations on stores which is very close to those of [25, 15] but unfortunately does not lead to a practical analysis algorithm.

We illustrate with some programming examples how suspension analysis can be performed within this framework. Suspension analysis for concurrent logic languages has been first investigated in [6] under the name of deadlock analysis, and also developed in [2, 3]. The purpose of this analysis is to prove statically that the execution of a concurrent program will lead to a final state where all processes are terminated, i.e. none of them is suspended forever. One of the main advantages of using the GCD operator in the analysis framework lies in the possibility of taking the simple *Prop* domain for groundness analysis as a basis for suspension analysis.

The rest of this paper is organized as follows. Section 2 defines constraint systems. The syntax of cc languages is presented in section 3 while their semantics is given in section 4. Abstract interpretation is introduced in section 5, and section 6 details two simple programming examples in diagnosis reasoning. A short conclusion ends the paper.

2 Constraint Systems

The simplest way to define constraints is to consider them as first-order formulas interpreted in some structure, [14] in order to take into account the peculiar semantics of the constraint system. However a more general formalization was recently proposed by [26], which can be seen as a first-order generalization of Scott's *information systems* [28]. The emphasis is put on the definition of an *entailment* relation (noted ⊢) between constraints, which suffices to define the overall constraint system.

Definition [26]

A constraint system is a pair $\mathcal{C} = (D, \vdash)$ satisfying the following conditions :

1. D is a set of first-order formulas (over a vocabulary containing at least an equality predicate "=" and the constant false) closed under conjunction and existential quantification.

2. ⊢ is an *entailment* relation between a finite set of formulas and a single formula satisfying the following inference rules (where Γ, Γ_1 and Γ_2 denote finite sets of formulas and d, e and f denote formulas):

$$\Gamma, d \vdash d \text{ (Struct)} \qquad \frac{\Gamma_1 \vdash d \ \Gamma_2, d \vdash e}{\Gamma_1, \Gamma_2 \vdash e} \text{ (Cut)}$$

$$\frac{\Gamma, d, e \vdash f}{\Gamma, d \wedge e \vdash f} \ (\wedge \vdash) \qquad \frac{\Gamma \vdash d \ \Gamma \vdash e}{\Gamma \vdash d \wedge e} \ (\vdash \wedge)$$

$$\frac{\Gamma, d \vdash e}{\Gamma, \exists X. d \vdash e} \ (\exists \vdash) \qquad \frac{\Gamma \vdash d[t/X]}{\Gamma \vdash \exists X. d} \ (\vdash \exists)$$

In $(\exists \vdash)$, X is assumed not free in Γ, e.

3. ⊢ is *generic*: that is $\Gamma[t/X] \vdash d[t/X]$ whenever $\Gamma \vdash d$, for any term t.

Constraint systems can nevertheless be built very simply in a straightforward way from any first-order theory, i.e. any set of first-order formulas [26]. Consider a theory T and take for D the closure of the subset of formulas in the vocabulary of T under existential quantification and conjunction. Then one defines the entailment relation $\vdash_T$ as follows. $\Gamma \vdash_T d$ iff Γ entails d in the logic, *with the extra axioms of* T. Then $(D, \vdash_T)$ can be easily verified to be a constraint system.

Observe that this definition of constraint systems thus naturally encompasses the traditional view of constraints as interpreted formulas.

Definition

For a constraint system $\mathcal{C} = (D, \vdash)$, let us denote by $|D|$ the set of *stores* of constraints of $\mathcal{C}$, i.e. sets of elements of D closed under $\vdash$.

For a given set V of variables, we will note $|D|_V$ the set of stores of $|D|$ using only variables of V.

Observe that constraints can be naturally embedded in $|D|$ by considering for each constraint c the store equal to the closure of c under $\vdash$. Let us now state some interesting properties of stores.

Propositions [26]

For a constraint system $(D, \vdash)$, $|D|$ can be given a structure of complete lattice with lub (noted $\sqcup$) defined as closure (by $\vdash$) of union and glb (noted $\sqcap$) defined as intersection.

For a given finite set V of variables (those of a given program, as will be seen later), $|D|_V$ is a complete ω-algebraic lattice.

Observe then that $\sqcup$ represents the conjunction of two constraints, whereas $\sqcap$ represents the information common to both. This last operator will be useful for defining the GCD construct.

3 Syntax of cc programs

We will give an "algebraic" syntax[1] for cc programs over a constraint system $\mathcal{C} = (D, \vdash)$ defined by Table 1 below.

Programs are sequences of definitions, associating an atomic formula with an *agent*. An agent is either a primitive constraint, a simple conditional (ask) agent, a conjunction (parallel composition), a disjunction (angelic non-determinism), a *guarded constructive disjunction (GCD)*, an existential quantification (local hiding), or an atomic formula (procedure call), where $\overline{X}$ denotes a vector of variables.

Observe that the GCD operator represents a new form of non-determinism, somewhere between the angelic non-determinism of [15, 30] and the demonic non-determinism (indeterminism) of [12, 3], see section 4.2

---

[1] somewhat different from the usual clausal syntax, but better emphasizing the basic operators of the language

Programs $P ::=$	$D.A$	(Declarations and initial agent)
Declarations $D ::=$	ϵ	(Empty declaration)
	$\mid D.D$	(Sequence of declarations)
	$\mid p(\overline{X}) : -\, A$	(Procedure declaration)
Agents $A ::=$	c	(Tell)
	$\mid c \rightarrow A$	(Ask)
	$\mid A \wedge A$	(Conjunction)
	$\mid A \vee A$	(Disjunction)
	$\displaystyle\mid \sum_{i=1}^{n} c_i \rightarrow A_i$	(GCD)
	$\mid \exists X . A$	(Local variables)
	$\mid p(\overline{X})$	(Procedure call)

Table 1 : *Syntax*

4 Semantics of cc languages

cc languages can been given simple denotational semantics, as proposed by [25]: agents are given denotations as closure operators[2] over the underlying constraint system. The most important property of closure operators is that they can be completely characterized by the set of their fixpoints. However, we will not in this paper define denotations of operators by the set of their fixpoints as in [25], but rather give direct functional definitions. This formulation has a more natural intuitive operational meaning and makes it possible to derive a generic fixpoint algorithm that computes the functions defined by the semantic equations, in a way similar to that of [17] for Prolog.

Let $\mathcal{C} = (D, \vdash)$ be a constraint system, and P a cc program over $\mathcal{C}$. Let $\mathcal{V}$ be the union of the set of variables appearing in P and $\{\alpha_1, ..., \alpha_{\rho(p)}\}$ where $\rho(p)$ is the arity of a predicate p of maximal arity in P. Those last variables will be used for defining parameter passing and can be seen, using an implementation metaphor, as a bank of registers. We will note $\overline{\alpha}_i$ the vector of variables $(\alpha_1, ..., \alpha_i)$.

---

[2] i.e. monotonic, extensive and idempotent operators.

4.1 Determinate subset

The denotation of an agent A is $[\![\,A\,]\!]$, and has type $Env \to |D|_V \to |D|_V$, where Env is a domain of environments (that of mappings from procedure names to agents). The denotation of a declaration K is noted $[\![\,K\,]\!]_{dec}$, and has type $Env \to Env$, while that of a program P (including the initial agent) is noted $[\![\,P\,]\!]_{prog}$ and has type $|D|_V$.

The semantic equations are then derived from the syntax of Table 1, as shown in Table 2 below (where μ is the least fixpoint operator).

(1) defines an eventual Tell, as usual. (2) presents an Ask operator as defined in [23] : if the constraint c is entailed the computation reduces to that of agent A, if $\neg c$ is entailed then the computation succeeds immediately, otherwise it suspends. Defining this behavior as a function from stores to stores, these two last cases coincide in returning the input store as output. (3) describes the And-parallel conjunction as defined in [4]. In (4), the existential quantification has been extended to finite stores in an obvious way, and hiding works as follows: A is first executed in a store were X is hidden, and X is again hidden in the resulting store. In (5) and (7), the variables $\overline{\alpha}_{\rho(p)}$ are used for parameter passing. They are equated with the call variables $\overline{X}$ in (5) (and obviously hidden outside the call), and equated with the variables $\overline{Y}$ of the procedure declaration in (7) (themselves also hidden).

$$[\![\,c\,]\!]\,e = \lambda s\,.\,s \sqcup c \tag{1}$$

$$[\![\,c \to A\,]\!]\,e = \lambda s.\ \text{if}\quad s \vdash c\ \ \text{then}\quad [\![\,A\,]\!]\,e\,s\ \ \text{else}\quad s \tag{2}$$

$$[\![\,A_1 \wedge A_2\,]\!]\,e = \lambda s\,.\,\mu c\,.\,([\![\,A_1\,]\!]\,e\,c) \sqcup ([\![\,A_2\,]\!]\,e\,c) \sqcup s \tag{3}$$

$$[\![\,\exists X.A\,]\!]\,e = \lambda s\,.\,s \sqcup \exists X.[\![\,A\,]\!]\,e\,(\exists X\,.s) \tag{4}$$

$$[\![\,p(\overline{X})\,]\!]\,e = \lambda s\,.\,(\exists\,\overline{\alpha}_{\rho(p)}.[\![\,e\,p\,]\!]\,e\,(\overline{X} = \overline{\alpha}_{\rho(p)} \sqcup s)) \tag{5}$$

$$[\![\,\epsilon\,]\!]_{dec}\,e = e \tag{6}$$

$$[\![\,p(\overline{Y}) : - A\,]\!]_{dec}\,e = e[p \mapsto \exists \overline{Y}.(\overline{Y} = \overline{\alpha}_{\rho(p)} \wedge A)] \tag{7}$$

$$[\![\,D_1.D_2\,]\!]_{dec}\,e = [\![\,D_1\,]\!]_{dec}\,e \cup [\![\,D_2\,]\!]_{dec}\,e \tag{8}$$

$$[\![\,D.A\,]\!]_{prog} = [\![\,A\,]\!]\,([\![\,D\,]\!]_{dec}\,[\,]\,)\,\emptyset \tag{9}$$

Table 2 : *Semantics*

4.2 Guarded Constructive Disjunction

The semantics of the GCD operator is as follows :

$$
[\![\sum_{i=1}^{n} c_i \to A_i]\!] \, e = \lambda s \, . \, \mu c \, . \, s \sqcup \text{ if } \exists i \in [1,n], \, c \vdash c_i
$$

$$
\text{then } \sqcap_{i \in \{j \in [1,n] / c \sqcup c_j \nvdash false\}} [\![A_i]\!] \, e \, c
$$
$$
\text{else } true
$$

(10)

Intuitively, a GCD agent will suspend until one of its guards is entailed by the current store or all are disentailed. Then it will tell the constructive disjunction (using the $\sqcap$ operator) of all branches whose guards are not inconsistent with the current store. An encapsulating fixpoint computation is needed because such a tell can (pathologically) produce a store where some guards are now disentailed. Therefore a second iteration can produce a different (stronger) store, etc. Observe that in the degenerated case of one single branch, the GCD reduces to an *Ask* operation, cf. equation (2).

In our denotational semantics, it is not possible however to distinguish between suspension and termination as they both amount for a process to return its input as output. The store is the only observable of our semantics. We will show in section 5.3 how to instrument this semantics in order to "observe" suspension.

Proposition
The GCD operator is a closure operator.

Proof

- Idempotency: ensured by the outer fixpoint computation.
- Extensivity: because of union with input store.
- Monotonicity: given some store, a stronger store can either :
  1. entail a guard whereas previously none were entailed and then the GCD will obviously produce a stronger output store.
  2. be inconsistent with more guards (never less) and then the GCD will produce a stronger output : the intersection of (the result of) fewer branches, the (relatively) consistent ones.

Observe that the GCD operator generalizes the ∇ operator, a particular form of constructive disjunction, introduced in [30] in the case of finite domain constraints and noted $c_1 \nabla c_2$. This latter construction is only possible in a constraint system closed under negation, such as for instance finite domains or reals/rationals with arithmetic constraints (equations, inequations and disequations). $c_1 \nabla c_2$ can then be simulated as follows :

$$
(true \to c_1 + true \to c_2) \wedge (\neg c_1 \to c_2) \wedge (\neg c_2 \to c_1)
$$

The first agent will produce the constructive disjunction of c_1 and c_2, and the second (resp. third) will tell c_2 (resp. c_1) as soon as c_1 (resp. c_2) is disentailed.

4.3 Angelic Non-determinism

For introducing classical[3] disjunction, we have to consider sets of stores instead of stores as inputs and outputs of agents. $2^{|D|_v}$ can be given a structure of complete lattice by considering the Smyth order on $2^{|D|_v}$ as in the standard powerdomain constructions [22], see [15] for a complete and straightforward treatment. The type of the denotation $[\![A]\!]$ of an agent A is thus $Env \rightarrow 2^{|D|_v} \rightarrow 2^{|D|_v}$.

The disjunction operator is then simply treated as follows:

$$[\![A_1 \vee A_2]\!] \, e = [\![A_1]\!] \, e \cup [\![A_2]\!] \, e$$

5 Abstract Interpretation

5.1 Abstraction between constraint systems

We can now introduce the notion of abstraction between constraint systems and that of abstract programs that will make it possible to perform abstract interpretation of cc programs, as originally proposed in [4]. As the semantics defined above is parametric w.r.t. the constraint system, it works for both concrete and abstract programs.

Definition

A constraint system $(D', \vdash')$ *abstracts* a constraint system $(D, \vdash)$ w.r.t. a concretization function γ from D' to 2^D iff

(i) γ is monotonic
(ii) $\forall c \in D, \ \exists c' \in D', \ c \in \gamma(c')$
(iii) $\forall c'_1, c'_2 \in D', \ \forall c_1, c_2 \in D,$
       $c_1 \in \gamma(c'_1), \ c_2 \in \gamma(c'_2) \ \Rightarrow \ c_1 \wedge c_2 \in \gamma(c'_1 \wedge c'_2,)$
(iv) $\forall S' \in D', \ \forall c' \in D',$
       $S' \vdash' c' \ \Rightarrow \ (\forall S \in \gamma(S'), \ \forall c \in \gamma(c'), \ S \vdash c)$

Point *(i)* is a basic requirement for abstractions, *(ii)* states that each concrete element is the concretization of some abstract one, *(iii)* ensures that conjunction is safe, and *(iv)* guaranties that entailment checking is also safe. Note that condition *(iv)* is fairly strong. Nevertheless it is enjoyed by some non-trivial abstract domains such as k-depth abstraction for first-order terms with unification constraints [27] used for pattern analysis. Moreover we will show how to weaken this condition in the next section.

Observe that γ can be naturally extended to stores as a (monotonic) function from $|D'|$ to $2^{|D|}$ defined by :
$\gamma(s) = \{c' \ / \ \exists c \in s, \gamma(c) \vdash c'\}$

Definitions

Consider two constraint systems $\mathcal{C} = (D, \vdash)$ and $\mathcal{C}' = (D', \vdash')$ such that $\mathcal{C}'$ abstracts $\mathcal{C}$ w.r.t. a concretization function γ, and a program P over $\mathcal{C}$.

---

[3] i.e., non constructive.

An *abstract program* P' over C' corresponding to P is a program formed by replacing all constraints c_i in P by constraints c'_i such that $c_i \in \gamma(c'_i)$
A store c' of $|D'|$ *safely abstracts* a store c of $|D|$ iff $\exists c_0 \in \gamma(c'), c \vdash c_0$.

It is indeed easy to see that the computation of an abstract program P' abstracts the computation of P in the sense that the output constraints of P are contained in the concretization of the output constraints of P'.

Theorem 1
Let C' be a constraint system abstracting another constraint system C , P be a program over C and P' a corresponding abstract program over C' . Then :
$$\forall s \in [\![P]\!]_{prog}, \exists s' \in [\![P']\!]_{prog} \text{ such that } s' \text{ safely abstracts } s$$

Proof
This is ensured by a step by step comparison of the concrete computation with the abstract one. The only points where the computations differ are when constraints appear : Ask, Tell and GCD operations. For Tell, inclusion is ensured (as in [7]) by point *(iii)* of the definition of abstractions. For Ask and GCD, the abstract computation may stop producing new ouput while the concrete one would (as in [6]), i.e. in operational terms the former would suspend while the latter would proceed. In this case the output of the abstract computation safely abstract (thanks to monotonicity) the concrete one. Also for GCD, one has to take care that the information added by the constructive disjunction in the abstract case safely abstracts that of the concrete one: this is true because all (relatively) inconsistent abstract branches are also (relatively) inconsistent in the concrete computation (thanks to points *(iii)* and *(iv)*), and then the disjunction of the (results of the) consistent branches in the abstract computation safely abstracts the disjunction of the concrete ones.

5.2   Abstraction w.r.t. a program

The notion of abstraction defined above is sometimes too strong and can be weakened. For instance the classical *Prop* domain [8] used for groundness analysis of clp(Herbrand) (read: Prolog) does not satisfy point *(iv)* above. The idea is to consider, instead of abstraction between constraint systems in general, abstraction between particular constraints appearing in a given program. This will be done by discriminating the required conditions of abstraction according to the operators under which the constraints appear in the program.

Definition
Let C and C' be two constraint systems, let γ be a function satisfying points *(i)*, *(ii)* and *(iii)* above, let P be a program over C and let P' be a program over C' formed by replacing all constraints c_i in P by constraints c'_i such that $c_i \in \gamma(c'_i)$. Then, P' *abstracts* P iff:

1. for each *Ask* agent $c' \to A'$ in P' corresponding to $c \to A$ in P :
   $$\forall S' \in D', (S' \vdash' c' \Rightarrow \forall S \in \gamma(S'), S \vdash c)$$

2. for each GCD agent $\sum_{i=1}^{n} c_i' \to A_i'$ in P' corresponding to $\sum_{i=1}^{n} c_i \to A_i$ in P :

$$\forall S' \in D', (\exists i \in [1,n] \ S' \vdash' c_i' \ \Rightarrow \ \forall S \in \gamma(S'), \exists j \in [1,n], S \vdash c_j)$$

Observe that point (1) is a reformulation of point (iv) in the definition of abstraction between constraint systems, and that point (2) ensures that, whenever an abstract GCD may produce new output (i.e., operationally speaking, it is not suspended), then the corresponding concrete GCD may do so. Note that this was previously ensured by (structural) property (iv) which was stronger. The following property is obvious.

Proposition
Let C' be a constraint system abstracting another constraint system C , P be a program over C and P' a corresponding abstract program over C' .
Then P' abstracts P.

In this context, we can now state a result analogous to Theorem 1.

Theorem 2
Let C and C' be two constraint systems, let γ be a function satisfying points (i), (ii) and (iii) above, let P be a program over C and let P' be a program over C' abstracting P. Then :
$\forall s \in \llbracket P \rrbracket_{prog}, \exists s' \in \llbracket P' \rrbracket_{prog}$ *such that s' safely abstracts s*

Proof
Identical to that of Theorem 1, the point (1) of the definition of abstraction of P by P' is the one already seen for *Ask* operators, and point (2) is enough to take care of GCD operators.

5.3 Suspension analysis

The main interest of substituting abstraction between constraint systems by abstraction w.r.t. programs is that for programs with only GCD operators and no *Ask* operators, such as the examples below, the *Prop* domain (a subset of propositional formulas [8]) can be used for groundness analysis. *Prop* is easily formalized as a constraint system by considering implication between boolean formulas as entailment relation. On these grounds, let us see now how to perform suspension analysis, whose purpose is to prove statically that the execution of a concurrent program will lead to a final state where all processes are terminated, i.e. none of them is suspended forever.

One of the main disadvantages of denotational frameworks w.r.t. operational ones is that the only observable of a computation is the final store, whereas an operational framework can observe both the final store and the final state of agents (e.g. terminated or suspended). It is therefore not surprising that suspension analysis of concurrent logic or constraint languages has only be tackled in operational frameworks such as [6, 3]. We will present in the following a simple extension of our denotational semantics which makes it possible to perform suspension analysis. We simply have to introduce special variables in the store (one for each suspendible agent – *Ask* or *GCD*) that will be unbound as long as the corresponding process is suspended and bound to some constant value when the process terminates. Determining suspension freeness of a program will therefore amount to inspect the final store and check that none of those special variables is unbound. Let us denote by $(\rho_i)_{i>0}$ the set of those variables and let us use a new constant *fired* to denote that a process is not suspended, we need to modify the semantic equations (2) and (10) as follows :

$$
\begin{aligned}
[\![\, c \to A \,]\!]\, e = \lambda s.\ &\textbf{if}\quad s \vdash c\ \textbf{then}\quad [\![\, A \,]\!]\, e\, s\ \textbf{else}\quad s \\
&\sqcup \\
&\textbf{if}\quad s \vdash c\ \textbf{or}\ s \sqcup c \vdash false \\
&\textbf{then}\quad \rho_i = fired \\
&\textbf{else}\quad \rho_i = \rho_i
\end{aligned}
\tag{2'}
$$

$$
\begin{aligned}
[\![\, \sum_{i=1}^{n} c_i \to A_i \,]\!]\, e = \lambda s.\ \mu c.\ s \sqcup\ &\textbf{if}\ \ \exists i \in [1,n],\, c \vdash c_i \\
&\textbf{then}\quad \sqcap_{i \in \{j \in [1,n]\,/\,c \sqcup c_j \not\vdash\, false\}}\ [\![\, A_i \,]\!]\, e\, c \\
&\textbf{else}\quad true \\
\sqcup\ & \\
&\textbf{if}\ \ \forall i \in [1,n],\, c \vdash c_i\ \textbf{or}\ c \sqcup c_i \vdash false \\
&\textbf{then}\quad \rho_i = fired \\
&\textbf{else}\quad \rho_i = \rho_i
\end{aligned}
\tag{10'}
$$

Those equations make it possible to observe process termination in the store : there exists some unbound ρ_i variable in the store iff there is some suspended process.

Let us now introduce another notion that will be useful for suspension analysis.

Definition
A constraint system $\mathcal{C} = (D, \vdash)$ is said to be *ground-decidable* iff
$\forall c \in D,\ \textbf{var}(c) = \emptyset \Rightarrow (c \dashv\vdash true \vee c \dashv\vdash false)$
where $\dashv\vdash$ means constraint equivalence, i.e. entailment in both directions.

Therefore in such constraint systems groundness is enough to make entailment decidable. Observe that this property obviously holds for usual constraint systems such as for instance reals/finite domains with linear (in/dis)equations or first-order terms with unification constraints, but does not hold for Scott's propositional information systems.

Proposition
Let $\mathcal{C}$ be a ground-decidable constraint system, let γ be a function from $\mathcal{C}$ to Prop satisfying points (i), (ii) and (iii) above, let P be a program over $\mathcal{C}$, and let P' be a program over Prop abstracting P. Consider a GCD operator $\sum_{i=1}^{n} c_i' \to A_i'$

in P' satisfying point (2) of the definition of abstraction between programs. Then, given a store S' such that all the variables of all c_i' are ground, the GCD operator in P will not suspend in any store S concretizing S'.

Proof
If all variables are ground, then the guards c_i' are either entailed or disentailed and therefore there exists some concrete guard c_j that is entailed or all guards are disentailed. In any case the concrete GCD does not suspend.

We can state how to derive suspension analysis from groundness analysis:

Proposition
Let C be a constraint system, let γ be a function from C to Prop satisfying points (i), (ii) and (iii) above, let P be a program over C without Ask operators, and let P' be a program over Prop abstracting P.
If, for all predicates of P', all variables in the guards of all GCD operators are statically known to be ground, then P is suspension free.

Proof
Obvious application of the previous proposition.

6 Examples

Let us now consider a few cc programs written using the GCD operator and see also how to perform simple but accurate suspension analysis. We will use two classical diagnosis problems adapted from [29] and [21] that will be solved in a natural way in our framework, using boolean or finite domain constraints. For simplicity, we will also assume that the underlying constraint system also contains unification of first-order terms (as Prolog) as terms (in particular lists) improve the clarity of programs by making it possible to encapsulate several variables together. This is indeed the case in all CLP languages with finite domain constraints such as clp(FD) [10], cc(FD) [30] or AKL(FD) [1].

6.1 Electrical circuit

Let us now describe a simple fault diagnosis problem and its formulation in our scheme. This example is rephrased from [29] and deals with a simple electrical circuit consisting of three bulbs connected in parallel to a battery by wires. Observation shows that only the third bulb is lit and an explanation of this phenomenon is sought.

The program will consist in defining an agent for each circuit component, reflecting the different possibilities of the artifact. The *State* argument of a component will indicate if the component is working (value 1) or not (value 0). Other arguments will be used to represent the connections in the circuit; those variables will have value 1 if some current is going through them, or value 0 otherwise. Also the *bulb* predicate has an extra *Light* argument to indicate if the light is on (value 1) or off (value 0).

$battery(State, Left, Right)$:- $State=0 \rightarrow (Left=0, Right=0)$
  $+$ $\qquad\qquad\qquad State=1 \rightarrow (Left=1, Right=1)$

$wire(State, In, Out)$:- $State=1 \rightarrow In=Out$
  $+$ $\qquad\qquad State=0 \rightarrow Out=0$

$bulb(State, Light, Left, Right)$:- $(State=1, Left=1, Right=1) \rightarrow Light=1$
  $+$ $\qquad\qquad\qquad\qquad Left=0 \rightarrow Light=0$
  $+$ $\qquad\qquad\qquad\qquad Right=0 \rightarrow Light=0$
  $+$ $\qquad\qquad\qquad\qquad State=0 \rightarrow Light=0$

$circuit(L, Light1, Light2, Light3)$:-
  $L = [S, B1, B2, B3, W1, W2, W3, W4, W5, W6]$,
  $battery(S, Sw1, Sw2)$,
  $wire(W1, Sw1, B1w1)$,
  $wire(W2, Sw2, B1w2)$,
  $bulb(B1, Light1, B1w1, B1w2)$,
  $wire(W3, B1w1, B2w1)$,
  $wire(W4, B1w2, B2w2)$,
  $bulb(B2, Light2, B2w1, B2w2)$,
  $wire(W5, B2w1, B3w1)$,
  $wire(W6, B2w2, B3w2)$,
  $bulb(B3, Light3, B3w1, B3w2)$

Let us begin by the concrete execution.
By running the query :- $circuit(L, 0, 0, 1)$, $labeling(L)$
denoting that the first two bulbs are off while the third is lit, we obtain the answer: $[1, 0, 0, 1, 1, 1, 1, 1, 1, 1]$
meaning that everything is working fine except the first two bulbs.
Observe that we use in the query the traditional *labeling* predicate of finite domain constraints, that is defined trivially using the angelic non-deterministic operator, in order to generate the different values of the (finite) domain.

Let us show that this program is suspension-free. A simple groundness analysis, e.g. using the *Prop* domain and the framework of section 5, reveals that for any query as above (containing the *labeling* predicate) all the predicates of the program will eventually have their arguments ground. Then the last proposition of section 5.3 will ensure that the execution of this program is suspension-free.

Full Adder Now consider the following program, adapted from [21], which describes a basic ripple-carry adder circuit made of *and*, *or* and *xor* gates. It is possible to give system descriptions and to obtain abductive diagnoses of combinatorial digital circuits in a straightforward way in $cc(\mathcal{B} \times \mathcal{L})$. Observe in particular the *table* definition which is much more simple than that of [5] or [21], thanks to boolean constraints.

The program has roughly the same structure than the previous one. *State* arguments are used to represent the state of the component (ok, stuck at 0 or stuck at 1), observe that now we cannot stick to cc(B) but have to "upgrade" to cc(FD) : value 0 will denote that the gate is stuck at 0, value 1 that it is stuck at 1, and value 2 that it is working fine. We also have a *Type* argument to indicate the types of the gates (and, or, xor). The program is as follows :

$$gate(State, Type, In1, In2, Out) :- State=2 \rightarrow table(Type, In1, In2, Out)$$
$$+ \qquad\qquad\qquad State=0 \rightarrow Out=0$$
$$+ \qquad\qquad\qquad State=1 \rightarrow Out=1$$

$$table(Type, X, Y, Z) :- Type=and \rightarrow Z = X \wedge Y$$
$$+ \qquad\qquad Type=or \rightarrow Z = X \vee Y$$
$$+ \qquad\qquad Type=xor \rightarrow Z = (X \wedge \neg Y) \vee (Y \wedge \neg X)$$

$$adder(L, In1, In2, In3, Out1, Out2) :-$$
$$L = [Sx1, Sa1, Sx2, Sa2, So],$$
$$gate(Sx1, xor, In1, In2, X1),$$
$$gate(Sa1, and, In1, In2, A1),$$
$$gate(Sx2,, xor, X1, In3, Out1),$$
$$gate(Sa2,, and, In3, X1, A2),$$
$$gate(So, or, A1, A2, Out2)$$

The concrete execution is as follows.
By running the query $:- adder(L,0,1,0,0,0), adder(L,1,1,1,1,1), labeling(L)$
denoting that we have two experimental observations relating inputs and outputs (remark that the list L representing the states of the components is shared between the two observations), we obtain the answer: $L=[0, 2, 2, 2, 2]$
meaning that the first xor gate x1 is stuck at 0 while all other components are working fine.

Let us show that this program is suspension-free for any query as above. Again, a simple groundness analysis reveals that in this case all the predicates of the program will eventually have their arguments ground. Again, the last proposition of section 5.3 will ensure that the execution of this program is suspension-free.

7 Conclusion

In this paper, we have introduced a new operator for cc languages called *guarded constructive disjunction*, in order to avoid indeterminism and its subsequent confluency problems. This operator generalizes the idea of constructive disjunction introduced in constraint logic programming a few years ago by guarding each alternative and considering disjunction of agents and not only of constraints. Our framework is based on a denotational semantics of concurrent constraint languages, as it is simple and elegant and makes it possible to smoothly integrate the guarded constructive disjunction operator.

We have investigated the interest of this semantics, and of the guarded constructive disjunction operator in particular, for program analysis in the abstract interpretation paradigm. We have studied suspension analysis of cc programs and presented two simple but realistic programming examples.

Future work will consist in using the GCD operator to approximate indeterministic choices and extend the scope of these analysis techniques.

Acknowledgements

We are grateful to the anonymous referees for many useful comments and suggestions.

References

1. B. Carlson, S. Haridi and S. Janson. AKL(FD) : finite domain constraints in AKL. In *International Logic Programming Symposium*, Ithaca, USA, MIT Press 1994.
2. M. Codish, M. Falaschi and K. Marriott. Suspension Analyses for Concurrent Logic Programs. In *proc. ICLP 91*, Paris, France, MIT Press 1991.
3. M. Codish, M. Falaschi, K. Marriott and W. Winsborough. Efficient Analysis of Concurrent Constraint Logic Programs. In *proc. ICALP 93*, Springer Verlag 1993.
4. C. Codognet and P. Codognet. A generalized semantics for concurrent constraint languages and their abstract interpretation. *In: Constraint Processing*, M. Meyer (Ed.), LNCS 923, Springer Verlag, 1995.
5. C. Codognet and P. Codognet. Abduction and Concurrent Logic Languages. *In: proceedings of ECAI'94, European Conference on Artificial Intelligence*, Amsterdam, Netherlands, August 1994.
6. C. Codognet, P. Codognet and M-M. Corsini. Abstract Interpretation for Concurrent Logic Languages. In *proc. North American Conference on Logic Programming*, Austin, Texas, MIT Press 1990.
7. P. Codognet and G. Filé. Computation, abstractions and Constraints in Logic Programs. In *proc. IEEE International Conference on Computer Languages*, IEEE Press 1992.
8. A. Cortesi, G. Filé and W. Winsborough. Prop revisited : propositional formulas as abstract domain for groundness analysis. In *proc. LICS 91, IEEE symposium on Logic In Computer Science*, Amsterdam, IEEE Press 1991.
9. P. Cousot and R. Cousot. Abstract Interpretation and Application to Logic Programs. *Journal of Logic Programming 13(2)*, 1992.
10. D. Diaz and P. Codognet. A minimal extension of the WAM for clp(FD). In *proc. ICLP'93, 10th International Conference on Logic Programming*, Budapest, Hungary, MIT Press 1993.
11. E. W. Dijkstra. Guarded commands, nondeterminacy and formal derivation of programs. *Communications of the ACM 21 (11)* , 1975.
12. M. Falaschi, M. Gabbrielli, K. Marriott and C. Palamidessi. Compositional Analysis for Concurrent Constraint Programming. In *proc. LICS 93*, IEEE Press 1993.
13. M. Falaschi, M. Gabbrielli, K. Marriott and C. Palamidessi. Confluence and CC programming. In proc. GULP+PRODE 94, Peniscola, Spain, 1994.

14. J. Jaffar and J-L. Lassez. Constraint Logic Programming. Research Report, University of Melbourne, June 1986. Short version in *proc. 14th ACM conference on Principles Of Programming Languages, POPL'87*, ACM Press 1987.

15. R. Jagadeesan, V. Saraswat and V. Shanbhogue. Angelic non-determinism in concurrent constraint programming. Technical Report, Xerox PARC, 1991.

16. J. Jourdan and T. Sola. The Versatility of Handling Disjunctions as Constraints. in *proc. PLILP'93, Programming Language Implementation and Logic Programming, Lecture Notes in Computer Science*, Springer Verlag.

17. B. Le Charlier K. Musumbu and P. Van Hentenryck. A generic abstract interpretation algorithm and its complexity analysis. In *8th International Conference on Logic Programming*, Paris, MIT Press 1991.

18. B. Le Charlier and P. Van Hentenryck. Reexecution in Abstract Interpretation of Prolog. In *proc. Joint International Conference and Symposium on Logic Programming*, Washington, MIT Press 1992.

19. T. Le Provost and M. Wallace. Domain Independent Propagation. In *proc. FGCS 92*, Tokyo, Japan, ICOT Press 1992.

20. A. V. Mantsivoda. Disjunctive Constraints and Finite Domains. Technical Report 25-07/93, Irkutsk State University, CEI, 1993.

21. S. Morishita, M. Numao and S. Hirose. Symbolical construction of truth value domain for logic programs. In *proceedings of the 4th International Conference on Logic Programming*, Sidney, Australia, MIT Press 1987.

22. G. Plotkin. Domains. University of Edinburgh, 1983.

23. V. A. Saraswat. *Concurrent Constraint Programming Languages*. Research Report CMU-CS-89-108, Carnegie Mellon University, 1989. Revised version MIT Press 93.

24. V.A. Saraswat and M. Rinard. Concurrent Constraint Programming. In *Proceedings of Seventeenth ACM Symposium on Principles of Programming Languages*, San Francisco, CA, January 1990.

25. V.A. Saraswat, M. Rinard, and P. Panangaden. Semantic Foundations of Concurrent Constraint Programming. In *Proceedings of Ninth ACM Symposium on Principles of Programming Languages*, Orlando, FL, January 1991.

26. V. Saraswat. The Category of Constraint Systems is Cartesian-Closed. In *proc. LICS'92, Logic In Computer Science*, IEEE Press 1992.

27. T. Sato and H. Tamaki. Enumeration of success patterns in logic programs. *Theoritical Computer Science*, vol. 34:227-240, 1984.

28. D. S. Scott Domains for denotational semantics. In *proc. ICALP'82, International Colloquium on Automata, Languages and Programming*, Springer Verlag 1982.

29. P. Struss and O. Dressler. Physical negation - integrating fault models into the General Diagnostic Engine. In *proceedings of IJCAI 89*, Detroit, 1989.

30. P. Van Hentenryck, V. Saraswat and Y. Deville. Constraint processing in cc(FD). Research Report, Brown University, 1991.

31. E. Zaffanella, G. Levi and R. Giacobazzi. Abstracting Synchronization in Concurrent Constraint Programming. In *proceedings of PLILP 94*, Madrid, LNCS 844, Springer Verlag 1994.

32. E. Zaffanella. Domain Independent Ask Approximation in CCP. *This volume*.

Domain Independent
Ask Approximation in CCP*

Enea Zaffanella

Dipartimento di Informatica
Università di Pisa
Corso Italia 40, 56125 Pisa, Italy
zaffanel@di.unipi.it

Abstract. The main difficulty in the formalization of a static analysis framework for CC programs is probably related to the correct approximation of the entailment relation between constraints. This approximation is needed for the abstract evaluation of the ask guards and directly influences the overall precision of the analysis. In this paper we provide a solution to this problem by stating reasonable correctness conditions relating the abstract and the concrete domains of computation. The solution is domain independent in the sense that it can be applied to the class of *downward closed* observables. Properties falling in this class have already been studied in the context of the analysis of sequential (constraint) logic programs. As an example, we consider an abstract domain designed for the analysis of *freeness* in CLP programs and we show how it can be usefully applied in the CC context to discover undesired data dependencies between concurrent processes.

1 Introduction

Abstract interpretation is intended to formalize the idea of approximating program properties by evaluating them on suitable non-standard domains. The standard domain of values is replaced by a domain of descriptions of values and the basic operators are provided with a corresponding non-standard interpretation. In the classical framework of abstract interpretation [7], the relation between abstract and concrete semantic objects is provided by a pair of adjoint functions referred to as *abstraction* α and *concretization* γ. The idea is to describe data-flow information about a program P by evaluating the program by means of an abstract interpreter $\mathcal{I}$. The abstract interpretation $\mathcal{I}(P)$ is *correct* if any possible concrete computation is described by $\gamma(\mathcal{I}(P))$.

Concurrent Constraint (CC) programming [26] arises as a generalization of both concurrent logic programming and constraint logic programming (CLP). In the CC framework processes are executed concurrently in a shared *store*, which is a constraint representing the global state of the computation. Communication

---

* This work has been supported by the "PARFORCE" (Parallel Formal Computing Environment) BRA-Esprit II Project n. 6707.

is achieved by ask and tell basic actions. A process telling a constraint simply adds it to the current store, in a completely asynchronous way. Synchronization is achieved through *blocking asks*. Namely the process is suspended when the store does not entail the ask constraint and it remains suspended until the store entails it. While being elegant from a theoretical point of view, this synchronization mechanism turns out to be very difficult to model in the context of static analysis. The reason for such a problem lies in the anti–monotonic nature of the ask operator wrt the asked constraint: if we replace this constraint with a weaker one we obtain stronger observables. As a consequence, the approximation theory developed to correctly characterize the *upward closed* properties (i.e. properties closed wrt entailment) becomes useless when we are looking for a domain independent solution to the ask approximation problem [28].

In this paper we thus consider the *downward closed* properties and we specify suitable domain independent correctness conditions that allow to overcome the problem of a safe abstraction of ask constraints. In particular we develop an approximation theory that correctly detects the definite suspension of an ask guard. This information can be used in many ways, e.g. for the debugging of CC programs as well as to identify processes that are definitely serialized (so that we can avoid their harmful parallel execution). Moreover, the same information can improve the precision of the static analysis framework, as it allows to cut the branches of code that will not be considered in the concrete computation.

This (partial) classification of CC program's observables is not new. See [19] for an interesting discussion about *safety* and *liveness* properties in CCP, being downward closed and upward closed respectively. As a matter of fact, in the literature there already exist abstract domains developed for the static analysis of sequential (constraint) logic languages dealing with downward closed observables, e.g. freeness in the Herbrand constraint system [23, 6, 3] as well as in arithmetic constraint systems [13, 20]. It is our opinion that these abstract domains can be usefully applied to the CC context and provide meaningful ask approximations. We indeed show an example where the abstract domain formalized in [13] is applied to detect an *undesired* data dependency between two concurrent processes.

2 Preliminaries

Throughout the paper we will assume familiarity with the basic notions of lattice theory [2] and abstract interpretation [7, 9].

A set P equipped with a partial order $\leq$ is said to be *partially ordered*. Given a partially ordered set $\langle P, \leq \rangle$ and $X \subseteq P$, the set $\uparrow X = \{ y \in P \mid \exists x \in X . x \leq y \}$ is the *upward closure* of X. In particular X is an upward closed set iff $X = \uparrow X$. The *downward closure* $\downarrow X$ and downward closed sets are defined dually.

We write $f : A \to B$ to mean that f is a total function of A into B. Functions from a set to the same set are usually called *operators*. The identity operator $\lambda x.x$ is denoted by id. Given the partially ordered sets $\langle A, \leq_A \rangle$ and $\langle B, \leq_B \rangle$, a function $f : A \to B$ is *monotonic* if for all $x, x' \in A$. $x \leq_A x'$ implies $f(x) \leq_B f(x')$.

f is *continuous* iff for each non-empty chain $X \subseteq A$: $f(\sqcup_A X) = \sqcup_B f(X)$. A function f is *additive* iff the previous conditions are satisfied for each non-empty set $X \subseteq A$ (f is also called *complete join-morphism*). A *retraction* ϱ on a partially ordered set $\langle L, \leq \rangle$ is a monotonic operator such that for all $x \in L$. $f(f(x)) = f(x)$ (idempotent). An *upper closure operator* (uco) on L is a retraction ρ such that $\forall x \in L$. $x \leq \rho(x)$ (extensive); a *lower closure operator* (lco) on L is a retraction δ such that $\forall x \in L$. $\delta(x) \leq x$ (reductive). More on closure operators can be found in [8].

Let $\langle L, \leq, \bot, \top, \vee, \wedge \rangle$ and $\langle L', \leq', \bot', \top', \vee', \wedge' \rangle$ be complete lattices. An *upper Galois connection* between L and L' is a pair of functions (α, γ) such that

1. $\alpha : L \to L'$ and $\gamma : L' \to L$
2. $\forall x \in L. \forall y \in L'. \alpha(x) \leq' y \Leftrightarrow x \leq \gamma(y)$.

An upper Galois *insertion* between L and L' is an upper Galois connection such that α is surjective (equivalently, γ is one-to-one). Both α (the abstraction function) and γ (the concretization function) are monotonic. α is a *complete join-morphism* and γ is a *complete meet-morphism* and each one determines the other; i.e. $\alpha(x) = \wedge' \{ y \in L' \mid x \leq \gamma(y) \}$ and $\gamma(y) = \vee \{ x \in L \mid \alpha(x) \leq' y \}$.

3 The language

CC is not a language, it is a class of languages parametric wrt the constraint system, a semantic domain formalizing the gathering and the management of partial information. Starting from Scott's partial information systems [27], describing the basic notion of entailment in a constructive fashion, the domains of [26] enclose typical cylindric algebras' operators [17].

Definition 1 (partial information system).
A *partial information system* is a quadruple $\langle D, \Delta, Con, \vdash \rangle$ where D is a denumerable set of elementary assertions (tokens), $\Delta \in D$ is a distinguished assertion (the least informative token), Con is a family of *finite* subsets of D (the consistent subsets of tokens) and $\vdash \subseteq Con \times Con$ is a (compact) entailment relation satisfying (for $u, v, w \in Con$, $P \in D$):

$$\emptyset \vdash \{\Delta\}$$
$$u \vdash \{P\} \text{ if } P \in u$$
$$u \vdash w \quad \text{if } u \vdash v \text{ and } v \vdash w$$

Entailment closed sets of tokens are called *constraints* and provide representatives for the equivalence classes induced by the entailment relation; in particular, *true* denotes the set of the trivial tokens. The *simple constraint system* generated by the partial information system is the set of all the constraints together with the partial order induced on them by the reverse of the entailment relation (which we will denote $\dashv$). We write $\otimes$ to denote the constraint composition operator (the *lub*) which is obtained by taking the entailment closure of the set theoretical union. We refer to [27] and [26] for a more detailed presentation.

$$
\begin{array}{ll}
\text{Progr} & ::= \text{Dec. Agent} \\[2mm]
\text{Dec} & ::= \epsilon \\
& \mid \text{p(x):-Agent. Dec} \\[2mm]
\text{Agent} & ::= \text{Stop} \\
& \mid \text{tell}(c) \\
& \mid \exists\, \text{x in Agent} \\
& \mid \text{Agent} \parallel \text{Agent} \\
& \mid \sum_{i=1}^{n} \text{ask}(c_i)\text{->Agent}_i \\
& \mid \text{p(y)}
\end{array}
$$

Table 1. The syntax

Definition 2 (constraint system).
A (cylindric) *constraint system* $C^{\top} = \langle\, C \cup \{false\}, \dashv, true, false, \otimes, \sqcap, V, \exists_x, d_{xy}\,\rangle$
is an algebraic structure where

- $\langle C, \dashv, true, \otimes, \sqcap \rangle$ is a simple constraint system
- *false* is the top element
- V is a denumerable set of variables
- $\forall x, y \in V$, $\forall c, d \in C$, the cylindric operator $\exists_x$ satisfies
  1. $\exists_x false = false$
  2. $\exists_x c \dashv c$
  3. $c \dashv d$ implies $\exists_x c \dashv \exists_x d$
  4. $\exists_x(c \otimes \exists_x d) = \exists_x c \otimes \exists_x d$
  5. $\exists_x(\exists_y c) = \exists_y(\exists_x c)$
- $\forall x, y, z \in V$, $\forall c \in C$, the diagonal element d_{xy} satisfies
  1. $d_{xx} = true$
  2. $z \not\equiv x, y$ implies $d_{xy} = \exists_z(d_{xz} \otimes d_{zy})$
  3. $x \not\equiv y$ implies $c \dashv d_{xy} \otimes \exists_x(c \otimes d_{xy})$

Note that we are distinguishing between the consistent constraints C and the top element *false* representing inconsistency. In the following we will write $\mathcal{C}$ to denote the subalgebra of consistent constraints, namely the set C together with the constraint system's operators restricted to work on C. We will denote operators and their restrictions in the same way and we will often refer to $\mathcal{C}$ as a "constraint system".

Tables 1 and 2 introduce the syntax and the operational semantics of CC languages. For notational convenience, we consider processes having one variable only in the head. We also assume that for all the procedure names occurring in the program text there is a corresponding definition. The operational model is

R1	$\langle \text{tell}(c), d \rangle \longrightarrow \langle \text{Stop}, d \otimes c \rangle$
R2	$\dfrac{\langle A, c \otimes \exists_x d \rangle \longrightarrow \langle A', c' \rangle}{\langle \exists(\mathbf{x}, c) \text{ in } A, d \rangle \longrightarrow \langle \exists(\mathbf{x}, c') \text{ in } A', d \otimes \exists_x c' \rangle}$
R3	$\dfrac{\langle A, c \rangle \longrightarrow \langle A', d \rangle}{\begin{array}{c}\langle A \parallel B, c \rangle \longrightarrow \langle A' \parallel B, d \rangle \\ \langle B \parallel A, c \rangle \longrightarrow \langle B \parallel A', d \rangle\end{array}}$
R4	$\dfrac{j \in \{1, \ldots, n\} \ \wedge \ d \vdash c_j}{\langle \sum_{i=1}^{n} \text{ask}(c_i) \text{->} A_i, d \rangle \longrightarrow \langle A_j, d \rangle}$
R5	$\dfrac{\text{p}(\mathbf{x}) \text{:-} A \in P}{\langle \text{p}(\mathbf{y}), d \rangle \longrightarrow \langle \Delta_{\mathbf{x}}^{\mathbf{y}} A, d \rangle}$

Table 2. The transition system T

described by a transition system $T = (Conf, \longrightarrow)$. Elements of $Conf$ (configurations) consist of an agent and a constraint, representing the residual computation and the global store respectively. $\longrightarrow$ is the (minimal) transition relation satisfying axioms **R1-R5**.

The execution of an elementary tell action simply adds the constraint c to the current store d (no consistency check). Axiom **R2** describes the hiding operator. The syntax is extended to deal with a local store c holding information about the hidden variable x. Hence the information about x produced by the external environment does not affect the process behaviour and conversely the external environment cannot access the local store. Initially the local store is empty, i.e. $\exists \mathbf{x} \text{ in } A \equiv \exists(\mathbf{x}, true) \text{ in } A$. Parallelism is modelled as *interleaving* of basic actions. In a guarded choice operator, a branch A_i is enabled in the current store d iff the corresponding guard constraint $\text{ask}(c_i)$ is entailed by the store, i.e. $d \vdash c_i$. The guarded choice operator indeterministically selects one enabled branch A_i and behaves like it. If there is no enabled branch then it suspends, waiting for other processes to add the desired information to the store. Finally, when executing a procedure call, rule **R5** models parameter passing without variable renaming, where $\text{p}(\mathbf{x}) \text{:-} A \in P$ and $\Delta_{\mathbf{x}}^{\mathbf{y}} A = \exists \mu \text{ in } (\text{tell}(d_{\mu y}) \parallel \exists \mathbf{x} \text{ in } (\text{tell}(d_{x\mu}) \parallel A))^2$.

Definition 3 (c-computations semantics).
A c-computation for program $D.A$ is a sequence $s = \langle A_0, c_0 \rangle \ldots \langle A_i, c_i \rangle \ldots$ of configurations such that $A_0 = A$ and $c_0 = c$ and for all $0 < i < |s|$

---

[2] Here μ is a variable not occurring in the program [26].

$\langle A_{i-1}, c_{i-1} \rangle \longrightarrow \langle A_i, c_i \rangle^3$. The c-computations semantics of a program is the set of all its c-computations.

Let $\not\longrightarrow$ denote the absence of admissible transitions. Computations reaching configuration $\langle A_n, c_n \rangle$ such that $\langle A_n, c_n \rangle \not\longrightarrow$ are called *finite* computations. If the residual agent A_n contains some choice operators then the corresponding computation is *suspended*, otherwise it is a *successful* computation and in this case we denote A_n by ϵ.

Definition 4 (c.a.c. semantics).
The c.a.c. (computed answer constraints) semantics for program $P = D.A$ in the store c is

$$\mathcal{O}[\![D.A]\!]c = \left\{ d \in C \;\middle|\; \langle A, c \rangle \xrightarrow{*} \langle B, d \rangle \not\longrightarrow \right\}$$

$$\bigcup \left\{ d \in C \;\middle|\; \begin{array}{ll} A_0 = A, & c_0 = c, \quad d = \bigotimes_{i < \omega} c_i, \\ \langle A_0, c_0 \rangle \longrightarrow \ldots \longrightarrow \langle A_i, c_i \rangle \longrightarrow \ldots \end{array} \right\}$$

Note that this semantics collects the limit constraints of infinite fair computations as well as the answer constraints associated to finite computations, regardless of whether the latter are successful or suspended. In any case we are considering consistent constraints only, i.e. we disregard all computations delivering *false*.

4 Program properties and approximations

As we have seen, the c.a.c. semantics of a CC program associates each initial store c to the set of all the consistent constraints that we obtain by executing $P = D.A$ at c. In a similar way we define a *semantic property* ϕ as a subset of C, namely the set of consistent constraints that satisfy the property. Therefore a program satisfies a semantic property ϕ at c iff the observables of the program are a *subset* of the property, i.e. $\mathcal{O}[\![P]\!]c \subseteq \phi$. Following this general view[4], the static analysis of a CC program can be formalized as a finite construction of an approximation (a superset) of the program denotation. If the approximation satisfies the semantic property, then we can correctly say that our program satisfies the property too. Abstract interpretation [9] formalizes the approximation construction process by mapping concrete semantic objects and operators into corresponding abstract semantic objects and operators.

Let us define a program property to be *ordering closed* iff it is downward closed or upward closed wrt entailment. As an example, consider the Herbrand constraint system $\mathcal{C}_H$. If the constraint $c \in \mathcal{C}_H$ binds variable x to a ground term, then all the constraints $d \in \mathcal{C}_H$ such that $d \vdash c$ will bind x to a ground term; therefore *groundness* is an upward closed property. On the other hand,

---

[3] As usual, if $|s| = \omega$ we also require that s is *fair* wrt the parallel operator.
[4] The same reasoning can be lifted in order to consider the c-computations semantics.

freeness is a downward closed property. A variable x is free in $c \in C_H$ iff there does not exist a term functor f/n such that $c \vdash (\exists_{y_1} \ldots \exists_{y_n} x = f(y_1, \ldots, y_n))$. Thus, if x is free in c then it will be free in all the constraints $d \in C_H$ such that $c \vdash d$. However, there obviously exist properties falling in none of these two classes, e.g. *independence*. Let us say that variables x and y share in $c \in C_H$ iff c binds x and y to the terms t_x and t_y such that $var(t_x) \cap var(t_y) \neq \emptyset$. Variables x and y are independent in c if they do not share in c. Now, if x and y share in c, we can choose constraints $d_1, d_2 \in C_H$ such that $d_1 \vdash c \vdash d_2$ and x and y are independent in both d_1 and d_2.

Ordering closed properties are very common in the static analysis of logic languages and furthermore they are easier to verify, because correctness of the abstract interpretation can be based on a semantics returning ordering closed observables. In [28] entailment closed[5] properties are considered. The main result is that it is impossible to develop a meaningful generalized semantics for CC languages in the style of [16], namely the only way to correctly abstract ask constraints in a domain independent fashion is a trivial approximation.

In this work we turn our interest upon downward closed properties and we show that a (carefully chosen but natural) notion of correctness of the abstract domain wrt the concrete one allows to automatically derive a correct approximation of all the asks occurring in the program. Dealing with such a class of properties, the collecting semantics can be defined naturally as the downward closure of the operational semantics, as there is no benefit in considering a stronger one [28].

Remark. If ϕ is downward closed then $\mathcal{O}[\![P]\!]c \subseteq \phi \Leftrightarrow \downarrow(\mathcal{O}[\![P]\!]c) \subseteq \phi$.

As we are observing infinite computations also, we have to be careful when defining the downward closed properties that we are interested in. In particular we have to remember that usually the correctness of our abstract semantic construction is based on the Scott's induction principle; this principle is only valid for *admissible* properties.

Definition 5. A property $\phi \subseteq C$ is *admissible* iff ϕ is closed under directed *lub*'s.

This definition means that whenever an admissible property is satisfied by all the finite approximations of the semantics, then *the* semantics will satisfy the property too. As an example of a downward closed property that is not admissible, consider the following definition of *nongroundness*: a variable x is nonground in $c \in C_H$ iff c binds x to a term t such that $var(t) \neq \emptyset$. Given the infinite chain of constraints $c_i \equiv (\exists_y x = f^i(y)) \in C_H$, for every $i < \omega$ we have that x is nonground in c_i. However, considering the limit constraint $c \equiv \bigotimes_{i < \omega} c_i = (x = f^\omega)$ one observes that x is *not* nonground in c. In order to grant the correctness of

---

[5] Due to a dual definition of the ordering on the constraint system, in [28] entailment closed properties are the downward closed ones. The choice of turning the domain upside–down was influenced by the standard theory of semantic approximation by means of upper Galois insertions [9].

this analysis, we have to redefine the property, e.g. by stating that if c binds x to an infinite term then x is nonground in c.

Hence, in this work we are interested in downward closed and admissible program properties. The Hoare's powerdomain construction [24, 27] over the constraint system characterizes this kind of observables.

Definition 6. The Hoare's powerdomain of the constraint system C is

$$\mathcal{H}(C) = \langle \mathcal{P}{\downarrow}(C), \subseteq, \{true\}, C, \uplus, \cap \rangle$$

where $\mathcal{P}{\downarrow}(C)$ is the set of all the nonempty, downward closed and admissible subsets of C; $\uplus$ is the closure under directed C-lub's of the set theoretical union; $:\{\cdot\}: : C \to \mathcal{P}{\downarrow}(C)$ defined as $:\{c\}: = {\downarrow}\{c\}$ is the singleton embedding function.

The alert reader would observe that this collecting semantics models nonempty observables only. From a semantic construction point of view, this is not completely satisfactory as we cannot describe the behaviour of a program having inconsistent computations only. However, the alternative choice of considering failed computations would imply some negative consequences. Firstly, it would complicate the formalization of the correctness conditions, requiring a special treatment for inconsistency. Moreover it would degrade the precision of our static analysis, adding very little to the understanding of the program. To see this, observe that when considering downward closed observables a failed computation has to be interpreted as "the program *may* fail", meaning that anything can happen. Also consider that there are CC languages explicitly designed to statically avoid the possibility of a failing computation (see [25] for a discussion of this topic in the distributed programming context).

From now on, $\tilde{\otimes}$ and $\tilde{\exists}_x$ will denote the additive extensions of $\otimes$ and $\exists_x$ over $\mathcal{H}(C)$. Thus, for all $S, T \in \mathcal{P}{\downarrow}(C)$, we have

$$S \tilde{\otimes} T = \uplus \{ :\{c \otimes d\}: \mid c \in S, d \in T, c \otimes d \in C \}$$
$$\tilde{\exists}_x S = \uplus \{ :\{\exists_x c\}: \mid c \in S \}$$

Note that the *merge over all paths* operator [9] is provided by $\uplus$ (the *lub* of $\mathcal{H}(C)$). Also note that in general the (lifted) constraint composition operator $\tilde{\otimes}$ is not idempotent, while being extensive.

5 Correctness

In this section we formalize the notion of *correctness* of an abstract domain wrt a concrete constraint system when downward closed properties are observed.

Definition 7. An abstract domain $\mathcal{A} = \langle L, \sqsubseteq^\sharp, \perp^\sharp, \top^\sharp, \sqcup^\sharp, \sqcap^\sharp, \otimes^\sharp, V, \exists_x^\sharp, d_{xy}^\sharp \rangle$ is a complete lattice $\mathcal{L} = \langle L, \sqsubseteq^\sharp, \perp^\sharp, \top^\sharp, \sqcup^\sharp, \sqcap^\sharp \rangle$ together with a binary operator $\otimes^\sharp$, a family of unary operators $\exists_x^\sharp$ for $x \in V$ and a family of distinguished elements $d_{xy}^\sharp \in L$ for $x, y \in V$.

As outlined in the previous section, we have to grant the existence of an upper Galois insertion relating the Hoare's powerdomain of the concrete constraint system and the abstract domain of descriptions, together with suitable correctness conditions regarding the domain's operators.

Definition 8. An abstract domain $\mathcal{A} = \langle L, \sqsubseteq^{\natural}, \perp^{\natural}, \top^{\natural}, \sqcup^{\natural}, \sqcap^{\natural}, \otimes^{\natural}, V, \exists_x^{\natural}, d_{xy}^{\natural} \rangle$ is *down-correct* wrt the constraint system $\mathcal{C} = \langle C, \dashv, true, \otimes, \sqcap, V, \exists_x, d_{xy} \rangle$ using α iff there exists an upper Galois insertion (α, γ) relating $\mathcal{H}(\mathcal{C})$ and $\mathcal{L}$ and $\forall S, T \in \mathcal{P}{\downarrow}(C), \forall x, y \in V$

$$\alpha(S \tilde{\otimes} T) \sqsubseteq^{\natural} \alpha(S) \otimes^{\natural} \alpha(T)$$
$$\alpha(\tilde{\exists}_x S) \sqsubseteq^{\natural} \exists_x^{\natural} \alpha(S)$$
$$\alpha(:\{d_{xy}\}:) \sqsubseteq^{\natural} d_{xy}^{\natural}$$

By assuming that the abstract domain $\mathcal{A}$ is *down-correct* wrt the constraint system $\mathcal{C}$ using α, we are able to prove the correctness of any abstract semantic construction based on the abstract interpretation theory. This means that the proof is valid for any abstract semantics that systematically mimics the basic concrete semantic operators ($\uplus, \otimes, \exists_x, d_{xy}$) and the relation $\dashv$ by using the corresponding abstract operators ($\sqcup^{\natural}, \otimes^{\natural}, \exists_x^{\natural}, d_{xy}^{\natural}$) and the relation $\sqsubseteq^{\natural}$. For the purposes of the present work it is sufficient to consider the operational semantics.

Definition 9. Given the concrete agent (resp. program, configuration) A, the corresponding abstract agent (resp. program, configuration) $\alpha(A)$ is obtained by replacing all the concrete constraints $c \in C$ occurring in A by the corresponding abstractions $\alpha(:\{c\}:) \in L$. Abstract agents (resp. programs, configurations) are partially ordered by writing $A^{\natural} \sqsubseteq^{\natural} B^{\natural}$ iff $B^{\natural}$ is obtained from $A^{\natural}$ by replacing each abstract constraint $c^{\natural}$ by another abstract constraint $d^{\natural}$ such that $c^{\natural} \sqsubseteq^{\natural} d^{\natural}$.

The following lemma shows that the abstract program correctly mimics each transition of the concrete one. This also means that if the abstract program suspends, then the concrete program suspends too.

Lemma 10 (correctness).

$$\text{If} \begin{cases} \langle A, c \rangle \longrightarrow \langle B, d \rangle \\ \quad and \\ \alpha(\langle A, c \rangle) \sqsubseteq^{\natural} \langle A^{\natural}, c^{\natural} \rangle \end{cases} \text{then} \begin{cases} \langle A^{\natural}, c^{\natural} \rangle \longrightarrow \langle B^{\natural}, d^{\natural} \rangle \\ \quad and \\ \alpha(\langle B, d \rangle) \sqsubseteq^{\natural} \langle B^{\natural}, d^{\natural} \rangle \end{cases}$$

The following proposition is proved by induction on the number of transitions.

Proposition 11 (c-computations correctness).
For every concrete c-computation $s = \{\langle A_i, c_i \rangle\}_{i < |s|}$ of P there exists a corresponding abstract $\alpha(:\{c\}:)$-computation $s^{\natural} = \{\langle A_i^{\natural}, c_i^{\natural} \rangle\}_{i < |s^{\natural}|}$ of $\alpha(P)$ such that $|s| = |s^{\natural}|$ and for all $0 \le i < |s|$ we have $\alpha(\langle A_i, c_i \rangle) \sqsubseteq^{\natural} \langle A_i^{\natural}, c_i^{\natural} \rangle$.

Corollary 12 (c.a.c. correctness).
$$\alpha({\downarrow}(\mathcal{O}[\![D.A]\!] c)) \sqsubseteq^{\natural} \bigsqcup^{\natural} (\mathcal{O}[\![\alpha(D.A)]\!] \alpha(:\{c\}:))$$

Note that in general the converse of Lemma 10 does not hold; in particular the concrete program may suspend while the abstract one has a transition. As a consequence, a finite concrete computation can be mapped into a diverging abstract computation, i.e. this approximation of the semantics does not preserve the termination's modes. Nonetheless, Proposition 11 ensures that every *finite* concrete computation is correctly approximated by a *partial* abstract computation of the same finite length.

Definition 7 and 8 do not require that the abstract domain is a constraint system and neither that it can be obtained as the Hoare's powerdomain of a constraint system. In the latter case we are in an *ideal situation* where a simpler notion of correctness can be used instead.

Definition 13.
An abstract constraint system $\mathcal{A}^\top = \langle L, \dashv^\sharp, \bot^\sharp, \top^\sharp, \otimes^\sharp, \sqcap^\sharp, V, \exists^\sharp_x, d^\sharp_{xy} \rangle$ is *correct* wrt the constraint system $\mathcal{C} = \langle C, \dashv, \mathit{true}, \otimes, \sqcap, V, \exists_x, d_{xy} \rangle$, using a surjective and monotonic function $\alpha : C \to L$, iff for each $c, d \in C$ (s.t. $c \otimes d \in C$), $x, y \in V$

$$\alpha(c \otimes d) \dashv^\sharp \alpha(c) \otimes^\sharp \alpha(d)$$
$$\alpha(\exists_x c) \dashv^\sharp \exists^\sharp_x \alpha(c)$$
$$\alpha(d_{xy}) = d^\sharp_{xy}$$

Let $\mathcal{A}^\top$ be an abstract constraint system which is correct wrt the constraint system $\mathcal{C}$ using α. Observe that $\otimes^\sharp$ is the *lub* over $\mathcal{A}^\top$.

Proposition 14.
1. $\mathcal{H}(\mathcal{A}^\top)$ *is* down–correct *wrt* $\mathcal{H}(\mathcal{C})$ *using* $\tilde{\alpha}$ *(the additive extension of* α*)*
2. α *is a* $\otimes$*–morphism between* C *and* L
3. $\tilde{\alpha}$ *is a complete* $\tilde{\otimes}$*–morphism between* $\mathcal{P}{\downarrow}(C)$ *and* $\mathcal{P}{\downarrow}(L)$

Defining abstract domains based on correct abstract constraint systems is a very difficult task. The previous proposition gives an explanation to this assertion: these domains have to satisfy properties that usually are too strong.

6 Examples

As a first example, we present the (somehow trivial) abstract constraint system of *untouched variables*[6] $\mathcal{V} = \langle \mathcal{P}(V), \subseteq, \emptyset, V, \otimes^\sharp, \cap, V, \exists^\sharp_x, d^\sharp_{xy} \rangle$, where

$$S \otimes^\sharp T = S \cup T \qquad\qquad d^\sharp_{xy} = \begin{cases} \{x, y\} & \text{if } x \not\equiv y \\ \emptyset & \text{otherwise} \end{cases}$$
$$\exists^\sharp_x S = S \setminus \{x\}$$

Let us assume that $\mathcal{C}$ is a concrete constraint system having variables in V and satisfying the following axiom [12]: $\forall c, d \in C \,.\, \exists_x c \vdash d \Rightarrow \exists_x d = d$. Note that even if this axiom is not a consequence of Definition 2, it is true in almost all the "real" constraint systems.

---

[6] To our knowledge, this domain has been firstly introduced in [15].

Proposition 15. *Let $\alpha : C \rightarrow \mathcal{P}(V)$ being defined as $\alpha(c) = \{x \in V \mid \exists_x c \neq c\}$. The abstract constraint system V is correct wrt C by using α.*

Therefore, we are in the ideal situation of Definition 13 and we can define our abstract domain as the Hoare's powerdomain of V. Having stated correctness, we can approximate every concrete ask evaluation (i.e. entailment check) by the corresponding abstract ask evaluation. Whenever the abstract computation suspends, we definitely know that every concrete constraint described by the abstract store contains no information about one (or more) of the variables touched by the ask. As a consequence all the associated concrete computations will suspend too and we are safe.

Remark. This abstract domain is very weak: every time we perform an abstract procedure call we lose all the information about the actual parameter. This is due to the interaction between the abstract cylindric operator and the abstract diagonal element, namely when performing the parameter passing we compute $\exists_x^\sharp d_{xy}^\sharp = \{y\}$. As a consequence the usefulness of this domain is restricted to local (i.e. intra-procedural) analyses. However the solution of such a problem is well known: we have to consider a richer abstract domain (e.g. one of the domains for freeness analysis given in the literature), where also some information about *variable sharing* is taken into account.

6.1   Abstracting the constraint system $\mathcal{R}_{LinEq}$

Even if previous example is not very involved, the same approach is valid for any admissible downward closed property of any constraint system. Some examples of this kind of abstract domains can be found in the literature.

[13] describes an abstract domain for the static analysis of CLP programs that is useful for the detection of *definitely free* variables in the presence of both Herbrand constraints as well as systems of linear equations. Let us consider the latter case. Given a linear equation system

$$ E = \begin{cases} a_{11}X_1 + a_{12}X_2 + \ldots + a_{1n}X_n = b_1 \\ \cdots \qquad \cdots \qquad \cdots \qquad \cdots \ \cdots \\ a_{m1}X_1 + a_{m2}X_2 + \ldots + a_{mn}X_n = b_m \end{cases} $$

where $X_1, \ldots, X_n$ are variables and a_{ij} and b_j are numbers, variable X_i is definitely free if there does not exist a linear combination of the equations in E having the form $X_i = b$. Denoting $lc(E)$ the infinite set of linear combinations of equations in E, [13] defines the following abstraction function.

$$ \alpha(E) = \left\{ \{X_1, \ldots, X_k\} \ \middle| \ \begin{matrix} (a_1 X_1 + \ldots + k X_k = b) \in lc(E) \\ a_i \neq 0 \quad i = 1, \ldots, k \quad k > 0 \end{matrix} \right\} $$

Thus, the abstract domain is $\mathcal{A} = \langle \mathcal{P}(\mathcal{P}(V) \backslash \emptyset), \subseteq, \cup, \cap, \otimes^\sharp, V, \exists_x^\sharp, d_{xy}^\sharp \rangle$ where

$$ S_1 \otimes^\sharp S_2 = S_1 \cup S_2 \cup \left\{ A \ \middle| \ \begin{matrix} A = (A_1 \cup A_2) \backslash D, \quad A \neq \emptyset \\ A_1 \in S_1, \ A_2 \in S_2, \ D \subseteq A_1 \cap A_2 \end{matrix} \right\} $$

$$ \exists_x^\sharp S = \{A \in S \mid x \notin A\} \qquad d_{xy}^\sharp = \begin{cases} \{\{x, y\}\} & \text{if } x \neq y \\ \emptyset & \text{otherwise} \end{cases} $$

We refer to [13] for a complete definition of the domain and for the proofs of the abstract operators' correctness. Intuitively, the correctness conditions ensure that all the possible linear combinations of concrete equations are described by the computed abstract element. The abstract entailment is a containment test; as a particular case, if the abstract linear combination $\{X_i\}$ is not a member of the abstract store description, we can safely say that variable X_i is free.

In [13] it is also shown that inequalities and disequations can be correctly abstracted in the same way, namely by reading them as equations.

Example 1. Consider this definition of the process length, computing the length of a list, together with the following initial configuration.

```
length(L,N) :-
  ask(L=[]) -> tell(N=0)
  +
  ask(L=[_|_]) -> ∃L1,N1 in
                  tell(L=[_|L1],N=N1+1) || length(L1,N1).

⟨ produce(L) || length(L,N) || ask(N>20) -> consume(L) , true ⟩
```

By substituting each concrete constraint by its abstraction, we obtain the corresponding abstract program and initial agent; note that Herbrand constraints are mapped into the least abstract element $\emptyset$, while the disequation N>20 is treated as N=20.

```
length(L,N) :-
  ask(∅) -> tell({{N}})
  +
  ask(∅) -> ∃L1,N1 in tell({{N,N1}}) || length(L1,N1).

⟨ produce(L) || length(L,N) || ask({{N}}) -> consume(L) , ∅ ⟩
```

By considering the possible abstract transitions of this program, we can easily make the following observations.

1. The abstract ask guard associated to the process consume is initially suspended (i.e. the abstract entailment test $\emptyset \supseteq \{\{N\}\}$ is not satisfied);
2. as long as we reduce the process length by selecting the *second* branch of its definition, the abstract global store will not change; namely we compute the store $\exists_{N1}^{\sharp}\{\{N, N1\}\} = \emptyset$, going back to the initial situation; therefore the ask guard associated to the process consume keeps suspending;
3. when reducing the process length by selecting the *first* branch of its definition, the global store changes to $\{\{N\}\}$ and the abstract ask synchronization succeeds.

Therefore, processes produce and length can be executed concurrently, while process consume has to wait for the process length to reach the end of the list L, i.e. to terminate. Indeed, this is actually what happens in any concrete computation. Consider the sequence of *concrete* constraints c_i obtained by restricting on variable N the stores generated by the process length. Note that $|L| > i$ implies $c_i \equiv (\exists_M N = M + i)$ but, since the variable M is unconstrained, c_i cannot entail the concrete guard N>20. This behaviour is not very satisfactory and probably it does not correspond to our intended semantics, as we could prefer a situation where all of these processes can execute concurrently.

To conclude, in this example our approximation is able to detect an *undesired data dependency* between the process length and the ask guard associated to consume[7].

7   Toward an abstract semantics

In this section we will informally consider the problems related to the construction of an abstract semantics that correctly approximates the concrete one in the case of downward closed observables.

It is known that, in the general case, the c.a.c. semantics of a CC program is not invariant wrt different schedulings of parallel processes, i.e. it is not *confluent*. In principle, confluence is not needed to correctly define a static analysis framework. However, in order to be really useful, a static analysis must be correct wrt all the possible scheduling and must not be too inefficient. Therefore, when considering real programs, confluence becomes as desirable as correctness [15]. As a matter of fact, almost all the literature concerning the static analysis of CC languages [4, 5, 14, 15, 28] considers a two-steps approximation; in the first step the standard semantics is replaced by a confluent non-standard semantics, which is then abstracted in the second step. These intermediate semantics are correct wrt the standard one, but usually *must pay* in terms of accuracy of the results.

This is not the case when considering downward closed properties, because we can base our static analysis on a confluent semantics being as precise as the c.a.c. semantics. Confluence is easily obtained by reading the CC indeterministic program as a nondeterministic program (an *angelic* program, using the terminology of [18]), that is by interpreting all the *don't care* choice operators of the program as *don't know* choice operators. In the nondeterministic case, when considering a choice operator we split the control and consider all the branches. In the transition system this difference is captured by replacing rule **R4** of Table 2 with the following.

$$\textbf{R4}' \; \frac{d \vdash c}{\langle\, \text{ask}(c)\text{->}A, d\,\rangle \longrightarrow \langle\, A, d\,\rangle} \qquad \textbf{R4}'' \; \frac{j \in \{1, \dots, n\}}{\langle\, \sum_{i=1}^{n} A_i, d\,\rangle \longrightarrow \langle\, A_j, d\,\rangle}$$

Observe that the only difference between the two programs is that the indeterministic program has less suspensions; however, due to the monotonic nature of CC computations, for every suspended computation of the nondeterministic

---

[7] This data dependency can be avoided by telling the constraint N1>=0 (or equivalently N>0) in the second branch of the definition of the process length.

program there exists a (terminated or suspended or infinite) computation in the original program that computes a stronger store. Let $\mathcal{O}'$ be the c.a.c. semantics based on the confluent transition system.

Proposition 16. *For all $c \in C$. $\downarrow(\mathcal{O}[\![P]\!]c) = \downarrow(\mathcal{O}'[\![P]\!]c)$.*

Technical problems related to termination can be solved essentially in the same way as it was done in [4].

Let us now consider some of the *denotational* semantics proposed in the literature. In [26] deterministic CC processes are elegantly modelled as upper closure operators (uco's) over the constraint system. The main property of this kind of representation is that any uco is fully determined by the set of its fixpoints. Moreover all the semantic operators on processes are naturally mapped into simple set theoretic operations over their representations, e.g. the parallel composition of two processes is obtained by intersecting their sets of fixpoints. [18] extends such a semantics to nondeterministic CC languages. When upward closed observables are considered, each (nondeterministic) process can be mapped into a *linear* uco over the Smyth's powerdomain of the constraint system. These functions can be coded as sets of (singleton) fixed point, essentially in the same way as it was done in [26] for the deterministic case. In [18] it is also shown that these processes can be alternatively modelled as *sets* of uco's on the (simple) constraint system. Different sets of closure operators may in general denote the same nondeterministic process and therefore the Smyth's powerdomain construction is applied onto the (extensionally ordered) domain of uco's. Such an alternative semantics definition can be easily adapted to model the abstract case, provided that we are dealing with an abstract constraint system (see Definition 13). However, as we are observing downward closed properties, we should consider the Hoare's powerdomain of the domain of uco's.

Definition 17. The Hoare's powerdomain of uco's on the constraint system C is

$$\mathcal{H}(uco(C)) = \langle \mathcal{P}\downarrow(uco(C)), \subseteq, \perp_H, \top_H, \uplus, \cap \rangle$$

where $\mathcal{P}\downarrow(uco(C))$ is the set of all the non–empty subsets of uco's on C that are downward closed and admissible wrt the extensional ordering; $\{\!| \cdot |\!\} : uco(C) \to \mathcal{P}\downarrow(uco(C))$ is defined as $\{\!| f |\!\} = \{ g \in uco(C) \mid \forall c \in C . g(c) \dashv f(c) \}$; $\uplus$ is the closure of the union, $\perp_H = \{\!| C |\!\} = \{ id \}$ is the bottom element and $\top_H = uco(C)$ is the top element.

The equations modelling the semantic functions look essentially the same as those given in [18] (see Table 3, where Π is the set of process names and $\Im = \Pi \to \mathcal{P}\downarrow(uco(C))$ is the domain of environments). The only difference is the definition of the singleton embedding operator.

Unfortunately, most of the abstract domains modelling downward closed properties are not constraint systems. In these cases, if we are interested in a denotational abstract semantic construction, we can consider a suitable variant of the approach based on ask/tell traces developed in [10, 11]. Here the first

$$\mathcal{N} : \text{Progr} \to \mathcal{P}{\downarrow}(uco(C))$$

$$\mathcal{N}[\![D.\ A]\!] = \mathcal{E}[\![A]\!](lfp\ \mathcal{D}[\![D]\!])$$

$$\mathcal{D} : \text{Dec} \times \Im \to \Im$$

$$\mathcal{D}[\![\epsilon]\!]I = I$$

$$\mathcal{D}[\![\text{p}(\text{x}):\text{-}A.\ D]\!]I = \mathcal{D}[\![D]\!](I[\text{p} \mapsto \mathcal{E}[\![\exists\, \text{x in}\, (\text{tell}(d_{x\mu})\ \|\ A)]\!]I])$$

$$\mathcal{E}[\![\cdot]\!] : \text{Agent} \times \Im \to \mathcal{P}{\downarrow}(uco(C))$$

$$\mathcal{E}[\![\text{Stop}]\!]I = \{\!|C|\!\}$$

$$\mathcal{E}[\![\text{tell}(c)]\!]I = \{\!|\uparrow c|\!\}$$

$$\mathcal{E}[\![\text{ask}(c)\text{->}A]\!]I = \biguplus\big\{\{\!|\overline{\uparrow c}\cup(\uparrow c\cap f)|\!\}\ \big|\ f\in\mathcal{E}[\![A]\!]I\big\}$$

$$\mathcal{E}[\![\exists\, \text{x in}\, A]\!]I = \biguplus\big\{\{\!|\exists_x f|\!\}\ \big|\ f\in\mathcal{E}[\![A]\!]I\big\}$$

$$\mathcal{E}[\![A\ \|\ B]\!]I = \biguplus\big\{\{\!|f\cap g|\!\}\ \big|\ f\in\mathcal{E}[\![A]\!]I,\ g\in\mathcal{E}[\![B]\!]I\big\}$$

$$\mathcal{E}[\![\sum_{i=1}^n A_i]\!]I = \biguplus_{i=1}^n \mathcal{E}[\![A_i]\!]I$$

$$\mathcal{E}[\![\text{p}(\text{y})]\!]I = \biguplus\big\{\{\!|\exists_\mu(\uparrow d_{\mu y}\cap f)|\!\}\ \big|\ f\in I[p]\big\}$$

where

$$\exists_x f = \{d\in C\ |\ \exists_x d = \exists_x c,\ c\in f\}$$

Table 3. The generalized semantics

problem to solve is termination, because a trace can be infinite even if it is defined over a finite abstract domain. We think that a notion of *canonical form* for traces (similar to the one developed in [26] for bounded trace operators) would suffice.

It is worth pointing out that the approximation theory developed in this work can be applied to any kind of semantic construction dealing with the basic mechanism of blocking ask. As a matter of fact, note that we already proved the correctness result for (the abstract version of) the c-computations semantics (see Proposition 11), which observes all the intermediate steps of the concrete computations; we also implicitly used this semantics in Example 1. Therefore, our technique can be also applied to semantics observing *the way* the answer constraints are actually computed. We believe that such a correctness result can be easily lifted to the case of a non-interleaving semantics, e.g. by considering a variant of the *true concurrent* semantics developed in [21, 22]. In this case the definite suspension information could be useful to obtain upper bounds to the degree of parallelism of the program.

8 Conclusions and related works

The static analysis of CC languages is a relatively new but very active area of research. To our knowledge, this is the first work on this topic in which a domain independent correct approximation of ask constraints is identified. Almost all the previous works about the static analysis of CC programs [4, 14, 15, 28] either consider a specific constraint system or *assume* that a correct ask approximation has already been found. [5] claims that it is possible to abstract ask constraints in a domain independent way even when considering entailment closed properties (e.g. groundness). This result contrasts with a *negative* result established in [28] and simple counterexamples can be shown that prove the uncorrectness of such an approach in the general case.

The approximation described in our work can be applied to a wide class of program properties, namely the downward closed ones. Several properties falling in this class (e.g. freeness) have already been studied in the context of the static analysis of sequential (constraint) logic languages. In our opinion the same abstract domains can be used in the CC case, provided that a suitable abstract semantic construction is identified. At the same time, we strongly believe that such a general result can motivate the study of "new" downward closed properties. This approximation theory allows to detect definitely suspended branches of the computation. Such an information can be usefully applied to the debugging and specialization of CC programs. Another area of application could be the compile-time (partial) scheduling of concurrent processes; whenever our analysis can prove that two or more processes are definitely serialized, we can avoid their costly and harmful parallel execution.

The definition of "the right" abstract semantics is an open problem. We have shown that if we are only interested in the downward closed properties obtainable from the c.a.c. semantics, then we can assume that all the choice operators in our program are local, thus achieving the confluence of the computation without any loss of precision. In our opinion, however, an extensive study of the cost/precision tradeoffs of the different abstract semantics proposals is strongly needed.

It has been recently shown that *delay* mechanisms in both sequential constraint languages and constraint solvers can be formalized as asks primitives on an underling domain (see [1] for the definition of ask&tell constraint systems and some related issues). This connection is currently being further investigated from the point of view of ask approximation.

Acknowledgements: The author would like to thank Catuscia Palamidessi for her valuable comments and suggestions on a previous version of this work.

References

1. R. Bagnara. Constraint Systems for Pattern Analysis of Constraint Logic–Based Languages. Presented at the *First Int'l Workshop on Concurrent Constraint Programming*, Venice, Italy, 1995.
2. G. Birkhoff. Lattice Theory. In *AMS Colloquium Publication, third ed.*, 1967.
3. M. Codish, D. Dams, G. Filé, and M. Bruynooghe. Freeness Analysis for Logic Programs - And Correctness? In D. S. Warren, editor, *Proc. Tenth Int'l Conf. on Logic Programming*, pages 116–131. The MIT Press, Cambridge, Mass., 1993.
4. M. Codish, M. Falaschi, K. Marriott, and W. Winsborough. Efficient Analysis of Concurrent Constraint Logic Programs. In A. Lingas, R. Karlsson, and S. Carlsson, editors, *Proc. of the 20th International Colloquium on Automata, Languages, and Programming*, volume 700 of *Lecture Notes in Computer Science*, pages 633–644, 1993.
5. C. Codognet and P. Codognet. A general semantics for Concurrent Constraint Languages and their Abstract Interpretation. In M. Meyer, editor, *Workshop on Constraint Processing at the International Congress on Computer Systems and Applied Mathematics, CSAM'93*, 1993.
6. A. Cortesi and G. Filè. Abstract Interpretation of Logic Programs: an Abstract Domain for Groundness, Sharing, Freeness and Compoundness Analysis. In *Proc. ACM Symposium on Partial Evaluation and Semantics-based Program Transformation*, pages 52–61. ACM Press, 1991.
7. P. Cousot and R. Cousot. Abstract Interpretation: A Unified Lattice Model for Static Analysis of Programs by Construction or Approximation of Fixpoints. In *Proc. Fourth ACM Symp. Principles of Programming Languages*, pages 238–252, 1977.
8. P. Cousot and R. Cousot. A constructive characterization of the lattices of all retracts, pre-closure, quasi-closure and closure operators on a complete lattice. *Portugaliæ Mathematica*, 38(2):185–198, 1979.
9. P. Cousot and R. Cousot. Systematic Design of Program Analysis Frameworks. In *Proc. Sixth ACM Symp. Principles of Programming Languages*, pages 269–282, 1979.
10. F.S. de Boer and C. Palamidessi. A Fully Abstract Model for Concurrent Constraint Programming. In S. Abramsky and T. Maibaum, editors, *Proc. TAP-SOFT'91*, volume 493 of *Lecture Notes in Computer Science*, pages 296–319. Springer-Verlag, Berlin, 1991.
11. F.S. de Boer and C. Palamidessi. A process algebra for concurrent constraint programming. In K. Apt, editor, *Proc. Joint Int'l Conf. and Symposium on Logic Programming*, Series in Logic Programming, pages 463–477, Washington, USA, 1992. The MIT Press, Cambridge, Mass.
12. F.S. de Boer, C. Palamidessi, and A. Di Pierro. Infinite Computations in Nondeterministic Constraint Programming. *Theoretical Computer Science*. To appear.
13. V. Dumortier, G. Janssens, M. Bruynooghe, and M. Codish. Freeness analysis in the presence of numerical constraints. In D. S. Warren, editor, *Proc. Tenth Int'l Conf. on Logic Programming*, pages 100–115. The MIT Press, Cambridge, Mass., 1993.
14. M. Falaschi, M. Gabbrielli, K. Marriott, and C. Palamidessi. Compositional Analysis for Concurrent Constraint Programming. In *Proc. of the Eight Annual IEEE Symposium on Logic in Computer Science*, pages 210–221. IEEE Computer Society Press, 1993.

15. M. Falaschi, M. Gabbrielli, K. Marriott, and C. Palamidessi. Confluence and Concurrent Constraint Programming. In *Proc. of the Fourth International Conference on Algebraic Methodology and Software Technology (AMAST'95)*, Montreal, Canada, 1995.

16. R. Giacobazzi, S. K. Debray, and G. Levi. A Generalized Semantics for Constraint Logic Programs. In *Proc. of the International Conference on Fifth Generation Computer Systems 1992*, pages 581–591, 1992.

17. L. Henkin, J.D. Monk, and A. Tarski. *Cylindric Algebras. Part I and II.* North-Holland, Amsterdam, 1971.

18. R. Jagadeesan, V. Shanbhogue, and V. Saraswat. Angelic non-determinism in concurrent constraint programming. Technical report, System Science Lab., Xerox PARC, 1991.

19. M. Z. Kwiatkowska. Infinite Behaviour and Fairness in Concurrent Constraint Programming. In J.W. de Bakker, W.P. de Roever, and G. Rozenberg, editors, *Semantics: Foundations and Applications*, volume 666 of *Lecture Notes in Computer Science*, pages 348–383, Beekbergen The Netherlands, 1992. REX Workshop, Springer-Verlag, Berlin.

20. K. Marriott and P. J. Stuckey. Approximating Interaction between Linear Arithmetic Constraints. In M. Bruynooghe, editor, *Proc. 1994 Int'l Logic Programming Symposium*, pages 571–585. The MIT Press, Cambridge, Mass., 1994.

21. U. Montanari and F. Rossi. Contextual Occurrence Nets and Concurrent Constraint Programming. In *Proc. Dagstuhl Seminar on Graph Transformations in Computer Science*, volume 776 of *Lecture Notes in Computer Science*. Springer-Verlag, Berlin, 1994.

22. U. Montanari and F. Rossi. A Concurrent Semantics for Concurrent Constraint Programming via Contextual Nets. In *Principles and Practice of Constraint Programming*. The MIT Press, Cambridge, Mass., 1995.

23. K. Muthukumar and M. Hermenegildo. Combined Determination of Sharing and Freness of Program Variables through Abstract Interpretation. In K. Furukawa, editor, *Proc. Eighth Int'l Conf. on Logic Programming*, pages 49–63. The MIT Press, Cambridge, Mass., 1991.

24. G.D. Plotkin. Pisa lecture notes. Unpublished notes, 1981-82.

25. V. A. Saraswat, K. Kahn, and J. Levy. Janus: A step towards distributed constraint programming. In S. K. Debray and M. Hermenegildo, editors, *Proc. North American Conf. on Logic Programming'90*, pages 431–446. The MIT Press, Cambridge, Mass., 1990.

26. V. A. Saraswat, M. Rinard, and P. Panangaden. Semantic Foundation of Concurrent Constraint Programming. In *Proc. Eighteenth Annual ACM Symp. on Principles of Programming Languages*, pages 333–353. ACM, 1991.

27. D. Scott. Domains for Denotational Semantics. In M. Nielsen and E. M. Schmidt, editors, *Proc. Ninth Int. Coll. on Automata, Languages and Programming*, volume 140 of *Lecture Notes in Computer Science*, pages 577–613. Springer-Verlag, Berlin, 1982.

28. E. Zaffanella, G. Levi, and R. Giacobazzi. Abstracting Synchronization in Concurrent Constraint Programming. In M. Hermenegildo and J. Penjam, editors, *Proc. Sixth Int'l Symp. on Programming Language Implementation and Logic Programming*, volume 844 of *Lecture Notes in Computer Science*, pages 57–72. Springer-Verlag, 1994.

On the Combination of Symbolic Constraints, Solution Domains, and Constraint Solvers*

Franz Baader[1] and Klaus U. Schulz[2]

[1] Lehr- und Forschungsgebiet Theoretische Informatik, RWTH Aachen
Ahornstraße 55, 52074 Aachen, Germany
e-mail: baader@informatik.rwth-aachen.de
[2] CIS, Universität München
Wagmüllerstraße 23
80538 München, Germany
e-mail: schulz@cis.uni-muenchen.de

Abstract. When combining languages for symbolic constraints, one is typically faced with the problem of how to treat "mixed" constraints. The two main problems are (1) how to define a combined solution structure over which these constraints are to be solved, and (2) how to combine the constraint solving methods for pure constraints into one for mixed constraints. The paper introduces the notion of a "free amalgamated product" as a possible solution to the first problem. Subsequently, we define so-called *simply-combinable structures* (SC-structures). For SC-structures over disjoint signatures, a canonical amalgamation construction exists, which for the subclass of *strong* SC-structures yields the free amalgamated product. The combination technique of [BaS92, BaS94a] can be used to combine constraint solvers for (strong) SC-structures over disjoint signatures into a solver for their (free) amalgamated product. In addition to term algebras modulo equational theories, the class of SC-structures contains many solution structures that have been used in constraint logic programming, such as the algebra of rational trees, feature structures, and domains consisting of hereditarily finite (well-founded or non-wellfounded) nested sets and lists.

1 Introduction

Many CLP dialects, and some of the related formalisms used in computational linguistics, provide for a combination of several "primitive" constraint languages. For example, in Prolog III [Col90], mixed constraints can be used to express lists of rational trees where some nodes can again be lists etc.; Mukai [Muk91] combines rational trees and record structures, and a domain that integrates rational trees and feature structures has been used in [SmT94]; Rounds [Rou88]

---

* This work was supported by a DFG grant (SSP Deduktion) and by the EC Working Group CCL, EP6028.

introduces set-valued feature structures that inter-weave ordinary feature structures and non-wellfounded sets, and many other suggestions for integrating sets into logic programming exist [DOP91, DoR93].

In this paper, we study techniques for combining symbolic constraints from a more general point of view. On the practical side, these considerations may facilitate the design and implementation of new combined constraint languages and solvers. On the theoretical side, we hope to obtain a better understanding of the principles underlying existing combination methods. This should show their essential similarities and differences, and clarify their limitations.

When combining different constraint systems, at least three problems must be solved. The first problem, namely how to define the set of "mixed" constraints, is usually relatively trivial. The two remaining problems—which will be addressed in this paper—are

(1) how to define the *combined solution structure* over which the mixed constraints are to be solved, and
(2) once this combined structure is fixed, how to *combine constraint solvers* for the single languages in order to obtain a constraint solver for the mixed language.

The first part of this paper is concerned with the first aspect. So far, the problem of combining solution domains has not been discussed in a general and systematic way. The reason is that most of the general combination results obtained until now were concerned with cases where the solution structures are defined by logical theories. In this case, the combined structures are defined by the union of the theories. For example, in unification modulo equational theories, the single solution structures are term algebras $\mathcal{T}(\Sigma_1, X)/_{=_{E_1}}$ and $\mathcal{T}(\Sigma_2, X)/_{=_{E_2}}$ modulo equational theories E_1 and E_2. Thus, the obvious candidate for the combined structure is $\mathcal{T}(\Sigma_1 \cup \Sigma_2, X)/_{=_{E_1 \cup E_2}}$, the term algebra modulo the union $E_1 \cup E_2$ of the theories. It is, however, easy to see that feature structures and the "nonwellfounded" solution domains (such as rational trees) mentioned above cannot be described as such quotient term algebras. For this reason, it is not a priori clear whether there is a canonical way of combining such structures. The same problem also arises for other solution domains of symbolic constraints.

As a possible solution to this problem, we introduce the abstract notion of a "free amalgamated product" of two arbitrary structures in Section 3. Whenever the free amalgamated product of two given structures $\mathcal{A}$ and $\mathcal{B}$ exists, it is unique up to isomorphism, and it is the most general element among all structures that can be considered as a reasonable combination of $\mathcal{A}$ and $\mathcal{B}$. For the case of quotient term algebras $\mathcal{T}(\Sigma_1, X)/_{=_{E_1}}$ and $\mathcal{T}(\Sigma_2, X)/_{=_{E_2}}$, the free amalgamated product yields the combined term algebra $\mathcal{T}(\Sigma_1 \cup \Sigma_2, X)/_{=_{E_1 \cup E_2}}$. This indicates that it makes sense to propose the free amalgamated product of two solution structures as an adequate combined solution structure.

With respect to the second problem—the problem of combining constraint solvers—rather general results have been obtained for unification in the union of equational theories over disjoint signatures [ScS89, Bou90, BaS92].[3] These results have been generalized to the case of signatures sharing constants [Rin92, KiR94], and to disunification [BaS93]. Prima facie, such an extension of results seems to be mainly an algorithmic problem. The difficulty, one might think, is to find the correct combination method. A closer look at the results reveals, however, that most of the recent combination algorithms use, modulo details, the same transformation steps.[4] In each case, the real problem is to show correctness of the "old" algorithm in the new situation. In [BaS94a] we have tried to isolate the essential algebraic and logical principles that guarantee that the—seemingly universal—combination scheme works. We found a simple and abstract algebraic condition—called combinability—that guarantees correctness of the combination scheme, and allows for a rather simple proof of this fact. In addition, it was shown that this condition characterizes the class of quotient term algebras (i.e., free algebras), or more generally (if additional predicates are present), the class of free structures. In the above mentioned proof, an explicit construction was given that can be used to amalgamate two quotient term algebras over disjoint signatures, and which yields the combined quotient term algebra as result.

In the second part of this paper it is shown that the concept of a combinable structure and the amalgamation construction can considerably be generalized. This yields combination results that apply to most of the structures mentioned above, and which go far beyond the level of quotient term algebras. To this purpose, a weakened notion of "combinability" is introduced (Section 4). Structures that satisfy this weak form of combinability will be called *simply-combinable structures* (SC-structures).[5] The algebra of rational trees [Mah88], feature structures [APS94, SmT94], but also domains over hereditarily finite (wellfounded or non-wellfounded) nested sets and lists turn out to be SC-structures. The main difference between free structures (treated in [BaS94a]) and SC-structures is that free structures are generated by a (countably infinite) set of (free) generators, whereas this need not be the case for SC-structures (e.g., an infinite rational tree is not generated—in the algebraic sense—by its leaf nodes). This difference makes it necessary to give rather involved proofs [BaS94b] for facts that are trivial for the case of free structures. Nevertheless, a variant of the amalgama-

---

[3] It should be noted that the problem of combining constraint solvers considered in unification theory and in the present paper differs from the combination problems investigated in [NeO79] in at least two respects. In [NeO79], techniques for deciding *validity* of quantifier-free formulae over a mixed logical alphabet are discussed. Thus, all variables are (implicitly) *universally* quantified, but there is no restriction on the occurrence of *negation*. In contrast, in unification one is interested in validity of *existentially* quantified *positive* (equational) formulae, and we shall consider validity (in a fixed solution domain) of *positive* formulae with *arbitrary quantifier prefix*.

[4] Sometimes, additional steps are introduced just to adapt the general scheme to special situations (e.g., [KiR94, BaS93]). For optimization purposes, steps may be applied in different orders, and delay mechanisms are employed (e.g., [Bou90]).

[5] It has turned out that the notion of an SC-structure is closely related to the concept of a "unification algebra" [ScS88], and to the notion of an "instantiation system" [Wil91].

tion construction of [BaS94a] can be used to combine arbitrary SC-structures $\mathcal{A}$ and $\mathcal{B}$ over disjoint signatures Σ and Δ (Section 5). As a Σ-structure (resp. Δ-structure), the amalgam $\mathcal{A} \otimes \mathcal{B}$ is isomorphic to $\mathcal{A}$ (resp. $\mathcal{B}$). Consequently, pure Σ-constraints (resp. Δ-constraints) are solvable in $\mathcal{A}$ (resp. $\mathcal{B}$) iff they are solvable in $\mathcal{A} \otimes \mathcal{B}$. If $\mathcal{A}$ and $\mathcal{B}$ belong to the subclass of strong SC-structures, then it can be shown that $\mathcal{A} \otimes \mathcal{B}$ is in fact the free amalgamated product of $\mathcal{A}$ and $\mathcal{B}$ as defined in Section 3. In this case, the amalgamation construction can be applied iteratedly since $\mathcal{A} \otimes \mathcal{B}$ is again a strong SC-structure.

The combination scheme, in the form given in [BaS92, BaS94a], can be used to combine constraint solvers for two arbitrary SC-structures $\mathcal{A}$ and $\mathcal{B}$ over disjoint signatures into a solver for $\mathcal{A} \otimes \mathcal{B}$ (Section 6). In this general setting, the scheme reduces the problem of deciding validity of *existential positive sentences* in the combined solution structure to validity of (not necessarily existential) positive sentences in the component structures. Thus, decidability of the *existential* positive theory of $\mathcal{A} \otimes \mathcal{B}$ can be reduced to decidability of the positive theories of $\mathcal{A}$ and $\mathcal{B}$. For the case of strong SC-structures $\mathcal{A}$ and $\mathcal{B}$, the combination method can also treat *general positive sentences*. Thus, in this case, decidability of the *full* positive theory of $\mathcal{A} \otimes \mathcal{B}$ can be reduced to decidability of the positive theories of $\mathcal{A}$ and $\mathcal{B}$. As one concrete application we show that validity of positive sentences is decidable in domains that inter-weave (finite or rational) trees with hereditarily finite (wellfounded or non-wellfounded) sets and lists. For reasons of space limitation, the rather long and technical proofs had to be omitted here. An internal report, providing complete proofs, is available via ftp [BaS94b].

2 Formal Preliminaries

A signature Σ consists of a set Σ_F of function symbols and a disjoint set Σ_P of predicate symbols (not containing "="), each of fixed arity. Atomic Σ-formulae are built with equality "=" or with predicate symbols $p \in \Sigma_P$ as usual. A *positive* Σ-formula has the form $Q_1 u_1 \ldots Q_k u_k \ \varphi$, where $Q_i \in \{\forall, \exists\}$ and φ is a quantifier-free positive matrix, i.e., built from atoms using conjunction and disjunction only. An *existential positive* Σ-formula is a positive formula where the prefix contains only existential quantifiers. Expressions $\mathcal{A}^{\Sigma}$ ($\mathcal{A}^{\Delta}$, ...) denote Σ-structures (Δ-structures, ...) over the same carrier set A, and $f_\mathcal{A}$ ($p_\mathcal{A}$) stands for the interpretation of $f \in \Sigma_F$ ($p \in \Sigma_P$) in $\mathcal{A}^{\Sigma}$. If Δ is a subset of the signature Σ, then any Σ-structure $\mathcal{A}^{\Sigma}$ can also be considered as a Δ-structure, $\mathcal{A}^{\Delta}$, by just forgetting about the interpretation of the additional symbols.

Usually, "constraints" are formulae $\varphi(v_1, \ldots, v_n)$ with free variables. The constraint $\varphi(v_1, \ldots, v_n)$ is solvable in $\mathcal{A}^{\Sigma}$ iff there are $a_1, \ldots, a_n \in A$ such that $\mathcal{A}^{\Sigma} \models \varphi(a_1, \ldots, a_n)$. Thus, solvability of φ in $\mathcal{A}^{\Sigma}$ is equivalent to validity of the sentence $\exists v_1 \ldots \exists v_n \ \varphi(v_1, \ldots, v_n)$ in $\mathcal{A}^{\Sigma}$. In this paper we shall always use this logical point of view. As constraints we consider positive and existential positive sentences. A constraint is "mixed" if it is built over a mixed signature $\Sigma \cup \Delta$.

A Σ-homomorphism between two structures $\mathcal{A}^{\Sigma}$ and $\mathcal{B}^{\Sigma}$ (also called homomorphic embedding of $\mathcal{A}^{\Sigma}$ into $\mathcal{B}^{\Sigma}$ in the following) is a mapping $h : A \to B$ such that $h(f_A(a_1,\ldots,a_n)) = f_B(h(a_1),\ldots,h(a_n))$ and $p_A[a_1,\ldots,a_n]$ implies that $p_B[h(a_1),\ldots,h(a_n)]$ for all $f \in \Sigma_F, p \in \Sigma_P$, and $a_1,\ldots,a_n \in A$. Letters $h, g,\ldots,$ possibly with subscript, denote homomorphisms. Whenever the signature Σ is not clear from the context, expressions $h^\Sigma, g^\Sigma, \ldots$ will be used. A Σ-isomorphism is a bijective Σ-homomorphism $h : \mathcal{A}^\Sigma \to \mathcal{B}^\Sigma$ such that $p_A[a_1,\ldots,a_n]$ if, and only if, $p_B[h(a_1),\ldots,h(a_n)]$, for all $p \in \Sigma_P$, and $a_1,\ldots,a_n \in A$. We write $\mathcal{A}^\Sigma \cong \mathcal{B}^\Sigma$ to indicate that $\mathcal{A}^\Sigma$ and $\mathcal{B}^\Sigma$ are isomorphic. A Σ-endomorphism of $\mathcal{A}^\Sigma$ is a homomorphism $h^\Sigma : \mathcal{A}^\Sigma \to \mathcal{A}^\Sigma$. With End_A^Σ we denote the monoid of all endomorphisms of the Σ-structure $\mathcal{A}^\Sigma$, with composition as operation. The notation $\mathcal{M} \leq End_A^\Sigma$ expresses that $\mathcal{M}$ is a submonoid of End_A^Σ. If $g : A \to B$ and $h : B \to C$ are mappings, then $g \circ h : A \to C$ denotes their composition.

3 Combination of Structures

Let $\mathcal{B}_1^\Sigma$ and $\mathcal{B}_2^\Delta$ be two structures. In this section we shall discuss the following question: What conditions should a $(\Sigma \cup \Delta)$-structure $\mathcal{C}^{\Sigma \cup \Delta}$ satisfy to be called a "combination" of $\mathcal{B}_1^\Sigma$ and $\mathcal{B}_2^\Delta$? The central definition of this section will be obtained after three steps, each introducing a restriction that is motivated by the example of the combination of term algebras modulo equational theories. The structures $\mathcal{B}_1^\Sigma$ and $\mathcal{B}_2^\Delta$ will be called the *components* in the sequel.

Restriction 1: Homomorphisms that "embed" the components into the combined structure must exist. If the components share a common substructure, then the homomorphisms must agree on this substructure.

It would be too restrictive to demand that the components are substructures of the combined structure. For the case of consistent equational theories E, F over disjoint signatures Σ, Δ, there exist injective homomorphisms of $\mathcal{T}(\Sigma, V)/=_E$ and $\mathcal{T}(\Delta, V)/=_F$ into $\mathcal{T}(\Sigma \cup \Delta, V)/=_{E \cup F}$. For non-disjoint signatures, however, these "embeddings" need no longer be 1–1. Note that even for disjoint signatures Σ and Δ there is a common part, namely the trivial structure represented by the set V of variables. Restriction 1 motivates the following definition.

Definition 1. Let Σ and Δ be signatures, let $\Gamma \subseteq \Sigma \cap \Delta$. A triple $(\mathcal{A}^\Gamma, \mathcal{B}_1^\Sigma, \mathcal{B}_2^\Delta)$ with given homomorphic embeddings $h_{A-B_1}^\Gamma : \mathcal{A}^\Gamma \to \mathcal{B}_1^\Sigma$ and $h_{A-B_2}^\Gamma : \mathcal{A}^\Gamma \to \mathcal{B}_2^\Delta$ will be called an *amalgamation base*. The structure $\mathcal{D}^{\Sigma \cup \Delta}$ *closes* the amalgamation base $(\mathcal{A}^\Gamma, \mathcal{B}_1^\Sigma, \mathcal{B}_2^\Delta)$ iff there are homomorphisms $h_{B_1-D}^\Sigma : \mathcal{B}_1^\Sigma \to \mathcal{D}^\Sigma$ and $h_{B_2-D}^\Delta : \mathcal{B}_2^\Delta \to \mathcal{D}^\Delta$ such that $h_{A-B_1}^\Gamma \circ h_{B_1-D}^\Sigma = h_{A-B_2}^\Gamma \circ h_{B_2-D}^\Delta$. We call $(\mathcal{D}^{\Sigma \cup \Delta}, h_{B_1-D}^\Sigma, h_{B_2-D}^\Delta)$ an *amalgamated product* of $(\mathcal{A}^\Gamma, \mathcal{B}_1^\Sigma, \mathcal{B}_2^\Delta)$.

Restriction 2: The combined structure should share "relevant" structural properties with the components.

This principle accounts for the fact that there must be some kind of (logical, algebraic, algorithmic) relationship between the components and the combined structure. In the case of quotient term algebras $\mathcal{T}(\Sigma, V)/=_E$ and $\mathcal{T}(\Delta, V)/=_F$, the combined algebra $\mathcal{T}(\Sigma \cup \Delta, V)/=_{E \cup F}$ satisfies $E \cup F$. In general, we cannot use this as a condition on the structures that close the amalgamation base since

B_1^Σ and B_2^Δ are not necessarily defined by logical theories. However, for the case of term algebras there is an equivalent algebraic reformulation:

Proposition 2. *For a* $(\Sigma \cup \Delta)$*-algebra* $C^{\Sigma \cup \Delta}$ *and a countably infinite set (of variables)* V*, the following conditions are equivalent:*

- *The structure* $C^{\Sigma \cup \Delta}$ *satisfies all axioms of* $E \cup F$.
- *For every mapping* $g_{V-C} : V \to C$ *there exist unique homomorphisms* $h_E^\Sigma :$ $\mathcal{T}(\Sigma, V)/_{=_E} \to C^\Sigma$ *and* $h_F^\Delta : \mathcal{T}(\Delta, V)/_{=_F} \to C^\Delta$ *extending* g_{V-C}.

In Section 5, where we consider amalgamation of a particular type of structures, we shall restrict the admissible structures for closing an amalgamation base $(A^\Gamma, B_1^\Sigma, B_2^\Delta)$ to structures satisfying the second condition of the proposition (with B_1^Σ, B_2^Δ in place of the term algebras). In the remainder of this section it is sufficient to assume that some class of admissible structures $Adm(B_1^\Sigma, B_2^\Delta)$ for closing the amalgamation base has been fixed.

Definition 3. Let $(A^\Gamma, B_1^\Sigma, B_2^\Delta)$ be an amalgamation base, let $Adm(B_1^\Sigma, B_2^\Delta)$ be a class of $(\Sigma \cup \Delta)$-structures, to be called *admissible structures*. An amalgamated product $(\mathcal{D}^{\Sigma \cup \Delta}, h_{B_1-D}^\Sigma, h_{B_2-D}^\Delta)$ of $(A^\Gamma, B_1^\Sigma, B_2^\Delta)$ is called *admissible with respect to* $Adm(B_1^\Sigma, B_2^\Delta)$ (or simply *admissible*, if the class of admissible structures is clear from the context) iff $\mathcal{D}^{\Sigma \cup \Delta} \in Adm(B_1^\Sigma, B_2^\Delta)$.

Restriction 3: Whenever possible, we want to obtain a most general element among all admissible amalgamated products of the components.
In the case of term algebras, the combined algebra $\mathcal{T}(\Sigma \cup \Delta, V)/_{=_{E \cup F}}$ is not just any algebra satisfying $E \cup F$: it is the free algebra.

Definition 4. Let $(A^\Gamma, B_1^\Sigma, B_2^\Delta)$ be an amalgamation base and let $Adm(B_1^\Sigma, B_2^\Delta)$ be a class of admissible $(\Sigma \cup \Delta)$-structures. The admissible amalgamated product $(C^{\Sigma \cup \Delta}, h_{B_1-C}^\Sigma, h_{B_2-C}^\Delta)$ of B_1^Σ and B_2^Δ over A^Γ is called a *free amalgamated product with respect to* $Adm(B_1^\Sigma, B_2^\Delta)$ iff for every admissible amalgamated product $(\mathcal{D}^{\Sigma \cup \Delta}, h_{B_1-D}^\Sigma, h_{B_2-D}^\Delta)$ of B_1^Σ and B_2^Δ over A^Γ there exists a *unique* homomorphism $h_{C-D}^{\Sigma \cup \Delta} : C^{\Sigma \cup \Delta} \to \mathcal{D}^{\Sigma \cup \Delta}$ such that $h_{B_1-D}^\Sigma = h_{B_1-C}^\Sigma \circ h_{C-D}^{\Sigma \cup \Delta}$ and $h_{B_2-D}^\Delta = h_{B_2-C}^\Delta \circ h_{C-D}^{\Sigma \cup \Delta}$.

Free amalgamated products need not exist, but if they exist they are unique up to isomorphism.

Theorem 5. *Let* $(A^\Gamma, B_1^\Sigma, B_2^\Delta)$ *be an amalgamation base with fixed homomorphic embeddings* $h_{A-B_1}^\Gamma : A^\Gamma \to B_1^\Sigma$ *and* $h_{A-B_2}^\Gamma : A^\Gamma \to B_2^\Delta$. *The free amalgamated product of* B_1^Σ *and* B_2^Δ *over* A^Γ *with respect to a given class* $Adm(B_1^\Sigma, B_2^\Delta)$ *is unique up to* $(\Sigma \cup \Delta)$*-isomorphism.*

In Section 5 we shall give an explicit construction of the free amalgamated product for the class of "strong SC-structures." For our standard example, term algebras modulo equational theories, the free amalgamated product yields the combined quotient term algebra, which shows that the above definition makes sense:

Proposition 6. *Let $B_1^\Sigma = \mathcal{T}(\Sigma, V)/_{=E}$ and $B_2^\Delta = \mathcal{T}(\Delta, V)/_{=F}$ for consistent equational theories E and F. Let $\text{Adm}(B_1^\Sigma, B_2^\Delta)$ be the class of algebras satisfying (one of) the conditions of Proposition 2. For the amalgamation base $(\mathcal{T}(\Sigma \cap \Delta, V), B_1^\Sigma, B_2^\Delta)$, the free amalgamated product with respect to $\text{Adm}(B_1^\Sigma, B_2^\Delta)$ is isomorphic to the combined algebra $\mathcal{T}(\Sigma \cup \Delta, V)/_{=E \cup F}$.*

Free amalgamation is obviously commutative if the class of admissible structures satisfies $\text{Adm}(B_1^\Sigma, B_2^\Delta) = \text{Adm}(B_2^\Delta, B_1^\Sigma)$. Some of our results concerning combination of constraint solvers depend on the assumption that free amalgamation is *associative* as well. In order to guarantee associativity, some conditions on the classes of admissible structures have to be imposed (see [BaS94b] for details).

It should be noted that notions of "amalgamated product," similar to the one given above, can be found in universal algebra, model theory, and category theory ([Mal73, Che76, DrG93]). There, however, amalgamation is typically studied for structures over the same signature. Moreover, in most cases these structures satisfy a fixed set of axioms (e.g., those for groups, fields, skew fields, etc.).

4 Simply Combinable Structures

In this section we shall introduce the concept of a simply combinable (SC-) structure. This purely algebraic notion yields a large class of structures for which an amalgamated product can be obtained by an explicit construction, provided that the components have disjoint signatures. In this case, general techniques exist that can be used to combine constraint solvers for the components in order to obtain a constraint solver for the amalgamated structure. Many typical domains for constraint-based reasoning turn out to be SC-structures. Quotient term algebras will serve as illustrating and motivating example for the abstract definitions. In the sequel, let $\mathcal{T} := \mathcal{T}(\Sigma_F, V)/_{=E}$ be such an algebra.

Two endomorphisms of $\mathcal{T}$ that coincide on a set $U \subseteq V$ of variables also coincide on all terms that are built over U. Abstracting this property, we arrive at the following two definitions.

Definition 7. *Let A_0, A_1 be subsets of the Σ-structure $\mathcal{A}^\Sigma$, and let $\mathcal{M} \leq \text{End}_{\mathcal{A}}^\Sigma$. Then A_0 stabilizes A_1 with respect to $\mathcal{M}$ iff all elements h_1 and h_2 of $\mathcal{M}$ that coincide on A_0 also coincide on A_1.*

The reason for considering submonoids of $\text{End}_{\mathcal{A}}^\Sigma$ is that in some cases (such as for feature structures) not all endomorphisms will be of interest in our context. In the sequel, we consider a fixed Σ-structure $\mathcal{A}^\Sigma$; $\mathcal{M}$ always denotes a submonoid of $\text{End}_{\mathcal{A}}^\Sigma$.

Definition 8. *For $A_0 \subseteq A$ the stable hull of A_0 with respect to $\mathcal{M}$ is the set*

$$SH_{\mathcal{M}}^{\mathcal{A}}(A_0) := \{a \in A; \ A_0 \text{ stabilizes } \{a\} \text{ with respect to } \mathcal{M}\}.$$

The stable hull of a set A_0 has properties that are similar to those of the subalgebra generated by A_0: (1) $SH_{\mathcal{M}}^{\mathcal{A}}(A_0)$ is a Σ-substructure of $\mathcal{A}^\Sigma$, and (2) $A_0 \subseteq SH_{\mathcal{M}}^{\mathcal{A}}(A_0)$. In general, however, the stable hull can be larger than the generated subalgebra.

Definition 9. The set $X \subseteq A$ is an *M-atom set for* $\mathcal{A}^\Sigma$ if every mapping $X \to A$ can be extended to an endomorphism in $\mathcal{M}$. If $\mathcal{M} = End_\mathcal{A}^\Sigma$, then X is simply called an *atom set* for $\mathcal{A}^\Sigma$.

For $\mathcal{T}$, the set of variables V is an atom set. Two subalgebras generated by subsets V_0, V_1 of V of the same cardinality are isomorphic. The same holds for atom sets and their stable hulls.

Lemma 10. *Let* X_0, X_1 *be two* $\mathcal{M}$-*atom sets of* $\mathcal{A}^\Sigma$ *of the same cardinality. Then every bijection* $h_0 : X_0 \to X_1$ *can be extended to an isomorphism between* $SH_\mathcal{M}^A(X_0)$ *and* $SH_\mathcal{M}^A(X_1)$.

We are now ready to introduce the main concept of this paper.

Definition 11. A countably infinite Σ-structure $\mathcal{A}^\Sigma$ is an *SC-structure* iff there exists a monoid $\mathcal{M} \leq End_\mathcal{A}^\Sigma$ such that $\mathcal{A}^\Sigma$ has an infinite $\mathcal{M}$-atom set X where every $a \in A$ is stabilized by a finite subset of X with respect to $\mathcal{M}$. We denote this SC-structure by $(\mathcal{A}^\Sigma, \mathcal{M}, X)$. If $\mathcal{M} = End_\mathcal{A}^\Sigma$, then $(\mathcal{A}^\Sigma, End_\mathcal{A}^\Sigma, X)$ is called a *strong SC-structure*.

Examples 12 The following examples show that many solution domains for symbolic constraints are indeed SC-structures.

- Let Σ_F be a finite set of function symbols. The free algebra $\mathcal{T}(\Sigma_F, V)/_{=E}$ modulo the equational theory E with countably infinite generator set V is a strong SC-structure with atom set V. The same holds for free structures, as considered in [BaS94a].
- Let K be a field, let $\Sigma_K := \{+\} \cup \{s_k; k \in K\}$. The K-vector space spanned by a countably infinite basis X is a strong SC-structure over the atom set X. Here "+" is interpreted as addition of vectors, and s_k denotes scalar multiplication with $k \in K$.
- Let Σ_F be a finite set of function symbols, and let $\mathcal{R}^{\Sigma_F}$ be the algebra of rational trees where leaves are labelled with constants from Σ_F or with variables from the countably infinite set (of variables) V. It is easy to see that every mapping $V \to R$ can be extended to a unique endomorphism of $\mathcal{R}^{\Sigma_F}$, and that $(\mathcal{R}^{\Sigma_F}, End_\mathcal{R}^{\Sigma_F}, V)$ is a strong SC-structure. Note, however, that $\mathcal{R}^{\Sigma_F}$ is not generated by V.
- Let $V_{hfs}(Y)$ be the set of all nested, hereditarily finite (standard, i.e., well-founded) sets over the countably infinite set of "urelements" Y. Thus, each set $M \in V_{hfs}(Y)$ is finite, and the elements of M are either atomic elements in Y or sets in $V_{hfs}(Y)$, the same holds for elements of elements etc. There are no infinite descending membership sequences. Since union is not defined for the urelements $y \in Y$, the urelements will not be treated as sets here. Let $X := \{\{y\} \mid y \in Y\}$. Let $h : X \to V_{hfs}(Y)$ be an arbitrary mapping. We want to show that there exists a unique extension of h to a mapping $\hat{h} : V_{hfs}(Y) \to V_{hfs}(Y)$ that is homomorphic with respect to union "$\cup$" and (unary) set construction $\{\cdot\}$. Each $M \in V_{hfs}(Y)$ can uniquely be represented in the form $M = x_1 \cup \ldots \cup x_k \cup \{M_1\} \cup \ldots \cup \{M_l\}$ where $x_i \in X$, for $1 \leq i \leq k$,

and where the M_i are the elements of M that belong to $V_{\text{hfs}}(Y)$. By induction (on nesting depth), we may assume that $\hat{h}(M_i)$ is already defined $(1 \leq i \leq l)$. Obviously $\hat{h}(M) := h(x_1) \cup \ldots \cup h(x_k) \cup \{\hat{h}(M_1)\} \cup \ldots \cup \{\hat{h}(M_l)\}$ is one and the only way of extending $\hat{h}$ in a homomorphic way to the set M of deeper nesting. For $M = x \in X$ we obtain $\hat{h}(x) = h(x)$, thus $\hat{h}$ is an extension of h. Moreover, each mapping $\hat{h}$ is in fact homomorphic with respect to union "$\cup$" and set construction "$\{\cdot\}$". It follows easily that $\hat{h}_1 \circ \hat{h}_2$ is the unique extension of $h_1 \circ \hat{h}_2 : X \to V_{\text{hfs}}(Y)$, for all mappings $h_1, h_2 : X \to V_{\text{hfs}}(Y)$, which implies that $\mathcal{M} := \{\hat{h} \mid h : X \to V_{\text{hfs}}(Y)\}$ is closed under composition. Obviously, identity on $V_{\text{hfs}}(Y)$ belongs to $\mathcal{M}$. Thus $V_{\text{hfs}}(Y)$, with union "$\cup$" and set construction "$\{\cdot\}$", is a strong SC-structure with atom set X.

- Similarly it can be seen that the domain of hereditarily finite *non-wellfounded* sets[6] over a countably infinite set of urelements Y, with union "$\cup$" and set construction "$\{\cdot\}$", is a strong SC-structure over the atom set $X = \{\{y\}; y \in Y\}$.

- The two domains of nested, hereditarily finite (1) wellfounded or (2) non-wellfounded lists over the countably infinite set of urelements Y, with concatenation "$\circ$" as binary operation and with (unary) list construction $\langle \cdot \rangle : l \mapsto \langle l \rangle$, are strong SC-structures over the atom set $X = \{\langle y \rangle; y \in Y\}$ of all lists with one element $y \in Y$. Formally, these domains can be described as the set of all (1) finite or (2) rational trees where the topmost node has label "$\langle \; \rangle$" (representing a list constructor of varying finite arity), nodes with successors have label "$\langle \; \rangle$", and leaves have labels $y \in Y$.

- Let *Lab*, *Fea*, and X be mutually disjoint infinite sets of labels, features, and atoms respectively. Following [APS94], a feature tree is a partial function $t : Fea^* \to Lab \cup X$ whose domain is prefix closed (i.e., if $pq \in dom(t)$ then $p \in dom(t)$ for all words $p, q \in Fea^*$), and in which atoms do not label interior nodes (i.e., if $p(t) = x \in X$ then there is no $f \in Fea$ with $pf \in dom(t)$). As usual, *rational* feature trees are required to have only finitely many subtrees. In addition, they must be finitely branching.

  We use the set R of all rational feature trees as carrier set of a structure $\mathcal{R}^\Sigma$ whose signature contains a unary predicate L for every label $L \in Lab$, and a binary predicate f for every $f \in Fea$. The interpretation $L_\mathcal{R}$ of L in $\mathcal{R}$ is the set of all rational feature trees having root label L. The interpretation $f_\mathcal{R}$ of f consists of all pairs $(t_1, t_2) \in R \times R$ such that $t_1(f)$ is defined and t_2 is the subtree of t_1 at f. The structure $\mathcal{R}^\Sigma$ defined this way can be seen as a non-ground version of the solution domain used in [APS94].

  Each mapping $h : X \to R$ has a unique extension to an endomorphism of $\mathcal{R}^\Sigma$ that acts like a substitution, replacing each leaf with label $x \in X$ by the feature tree $h(x)$. With composition, the set of these substitution-like endomorphisms yields a monoid $\mathcal{M}$. Thus $(\mathcal{R}^\Sigma, \mathcal{M}, X)$ is an SC-structure. In

---

[6] Non-wellfounded sets, sometimes called hypersets, became prominent through [Acz88]. They can have infinite descending membership sequences. The hereditarily finite non-wellfounded sets are those having a "finite picture;" see [Acz88] for details.

this case, we do not have a strong SC-structure since $\mathcal{R}^\Sigma$ has endomorphisms that modify non-leaf nodes (e.g., by introducing new feature-edges for such internal nodes).

Now suppose that we introduce, following [SmT94], additional arity predicates F for every finite set $F \subseteq Fea$. The interpretation $F_\mathcal{R}$ of F consists of all feature trees t where the root of t has a label $L \in Lab$ and where F is (exactly) the set of all features departing from the root of t. Let Δ be the extended signature. Then $(\mathcal{R}^\Delta, End_\mathcal{R}^\Delta, X)$ is a strong SC-structure.

Let us now establish some useful properties of SC-structures.

Lemma 13. *Let* $(\mathcal{A}^\Sigma, \mathcal{M}, X)$ *be an SC-structure.*

1. $\mathcal{A}^\Sigma = SH_\mathcal{M}^\mathcal{A}(X)$ *and every mapping* $X \to A$ *has a* unique *extension to an endomorphism of* $\mathcal{A}^\Sigma$ *in* $\mathcal{M}$.
2. *For all finite sets* $\{a_1, \ldots, a_n\} \subseteq A$ *there exists a* smallest *(w.r.t. set inclusion) finite subset* Y *of* X *such that* $\{a_1, \ldots, a_n\} \subseteq SH_\mathcal{M}^\mathcal{A}(Y)$. *This set will be called the* stabilizer $Stab_\mathcal{M}(a_1, \ldots, a_n)$ *of* $\{a_1, \ldots, a_n\}$ *with respect to* $\mathcal{M}$.

Using this notion of stabilizers, the validity of positive formulae in SC-structures can be characterized in an algebraic way. This characterization is essential for proving correctness of our combination method for constraint solvers over SC-structures. In the following lemma, letters of the form $\vec{u}$ and $\vec{v}$ ($\vec{e}$ and $\vec{x}$) denote sequences of variables (elements) of arbitrary finite length.

Lemma 14. *Let* $(\mathcal{A}^\Sigma, \mathcal{M}, X)$ *be an SC-structure, and let*

$$\forall \vec{u}_1 \exists \vec{v}_1 \ldots \forall \vec{u}_k \exists \vec{v}_k \; \varphi(\vec{u}_1, \vec{v}_1, \ldots, \vec{u}_k, \vec{v}_k)$$

be a positive Σ-sentence. Then the following conditions are equivalent:

1. $\mathcal{A}^\Sigma \models \forall \vec{u}_1 \exists \vec{v}_1 \ldots \forall \vec{u}_k \exists \vec{v}_k \; \varphi(\vec{u}_1, \vec{v}_1, \ldots, \vec{u}_k, \vec{v}_k)$,
2. *there exist* $\vec{x}_1 \in \vec{X}, \vec{e}_1 \in \vec{A}, \ldots, \vec{x}_k \in \vec{X}, \vec{e}_k \in \vec{A}$ *such that*
   (a) $\mathcal{A}^\Sigma \models \varphi(\vec{x}_1, \vec{e}_1, \ldots, \vec{x}_k, \vec{e}_k)$,
   (b) *all $\mathcal{M}$-atoms in the sequences* $\vec{x}_1, \ldots, \vec{x}_k$ *are distinct,*
   (c) *for all* $j, 1 \leq j \leq k$, *the components of* $\vec{x}_j$ *are not contained in* $Stab_\mathcal{M}(\vec{e}_1) \cup \ldots \cup Stab_\mathcal{M}(\vec{e}_{j-1})$.

The role of the second condition is very similar to one that *linear constant restrictions* played in our work on combining unification algorithms [BaS92]. To see this, consider a prefix $\vec{x}_1, \vec{e}_1, \ldots, \vec{x}_{i-1}, \vec{e}_{i-1}, \vec{x}_i$ of the sequence in Condition 2. Condition (c) makes sure that the atoms in $\vec{x}_i$ do not occur in the stabilizers of the elements $\vec{e}_1, \ldots, \vec{e}_{i-1}$ preceding $\vec{x}_i$ in the order of the enumeration. In a solution σ of a unification problem with linear constant restrictions, a constant c (corresponding to an atom x above) my not occur (corresponding to "is not in the stabilizer" above) in the image $v\sigma$ (corresponding to an element e above) if v comes before c in the linear order of the restriction.

In Section 5, where we describe how to construct amalgamated products of SC-structures, we will have to embed a given SC-structure $(\mathcal{A}^\Sigma, \mathcal{M}, X)$ into a larger SC-structure $(\mathcal{A}_\infty^\Sigma, \mathcal{M}_\infty, X_\infty)$. The amalgamated product will be obtained from $\mathcal{A}_\infty^\Sigma$ by adding appropriate interpretations for the symbols in Δ. The following, rather technical lemma collects all the conditions that are necessary for establishing a collection of "nice" properties for the resulting structure $\mathcal{A}_\infty^{\Sigma \cup \Delta}$. For example, (a0) makes sure that pure Σ-constraints are solvable in $\mathcal{A}^\Sigma$ iff they are solvable in $\mathcal{A}_\infty^\Sigma$, and thus in $\mathcal{A}_\infty^{\Sigma \cup \Delta}$. The properties (a3) and (a4) are necessary for proving that, in the case of strong SC-structures, $\mathcal{A}_\infty^{\Sigma \cup \Delta}$ is in fact the free amalgamated product.

Lemma 15. *For any SC-structure* $(\mathcal{A}^\Sigma, \mathcal{M}, X)$, *there exists an SC-structure* $(\mathcal{A}_\infty^\Sigma, \mathcal{M}_\infty, X_\infty)$ *such that:*

(a0) $\mathcal{A}^\Sigma$ *and* $\mathcal{A}_\infty^\Sigma$ *are isomorphic.*

(a1) $\mathcal{A}^\Sigma = SH_{\mathcal{M}_\infty}^{A_\infty}(X)$, $X \subset X_\infty$, *and* $X_\infty \setminus X$ *is infinite.*

(a2) $(\mathcal{A}_\infty^\Sigma, \mathcal{M}_\infty, X_\infty)$ *is strong iff* $(\mathcal{A}^\Sigma, \mathcal{M}, X)$ *is strong.*

(a3) *If* $(\mathcal{A}^\Sigma, \mathcal{M}, X)$ *is a strong SC-structure, then every mapping* $X \to A_\infty$ *has a unique extension to a homomorphism* $h_{A-A_\infty}^\Sigma : \mathcal{A}^\Sigma \to \mathcal{A}_\infty^\Sigma$.

(a4) *If* $(\mathcal{A}^\Sigma, \mathcal{M}, X)$ *is a strong SC-structure, and if* $X \subseteq X' \subseteq X_\infty$, *then every bijection* $g_0 : X \to X'$ *has a unique extension to an isomorphism between* $SH_{\mathcal{M}_\infty}^{A_\infty}(X)$ *and* $SH_{\mathcal{M}_\infty}^{A_\infty}(X')$.

For the case of a term algebra modulo an equational theory, the statement of the lemma trivially holds. In fact, if V_∞ is any countable superset of the countably infinite set V, then $\mathcal{T}(\Sigma_F, V)/=_E$ is isomorphic to $\mathcal{T}(\Sigma_F, V_\infty)/=_E$. In the case of SC-structures, the proof is much more involved.

5 Amalgamation of Simply Combinable Structures

We describe an explicit construction that may be used to close any amalgamation base where the two components are SC-structures over disjoint signatures. If both components are strong SC-structures, then this construction yields the free amalgamated product of these structures. In the general case, the resulting structure also seems to play a unique role, but a precise characterization of this intuition has not yet been obtained. The construction is almost identical to the amalgamation construction given in [BaS94a] for the case of free structures. There is just one essential difference. In [BaS94a], substructures that are generated by increasing sets of free generators are used in each step of the construction. Here, in the case of SC-structures, stable hulls (as defined in Definition 8) of increasing sets of atoms must be used instead.

Let $(\mathcal{A}^\Sigma, \mathcal{M}, X)$ and $(\mathcal{B}^\Delta, \mathcal{N}, X)$ be two SC-structures over disjoint signatures Σ and Δ. We consider the amalgamation base $(X, \mathcal{A}^\Sigma, \mathcal{B}^\Delta)$, where the common part is just the set of atoms X. Thus, the embedding "homomorphisms" $h_{X-A} : X \to A^\Sigma$ and $h_{X-B} : X \to B^\Delta$ are given by Id_X, i.e., the identity mapping on X. In order to close this amalgamation base, we shall first embed $\mathcal{A}^\Sigma$ and $\mathcal{B}^\Delta$ into isomorphic superstructures. Let $(\mathcal{A}_\infty^\Sigma, \mathcal{M}_\infty, X_\infty)$ be an SC-superstructure of $(\mathcal{A}^\Sigma, \mathcal{M}, X)$ satisfying conditions (a0)–(a4) of Lemma 15.

Analogously, there exists an SC-superstructure $(\mathcal{B}^\Delta_\infty, \mathcal{N}_\infty, Y_\infty)$ of $(\mathcal{B}^\Delta, \mathcal{N}, X)$ such that the corresponding properties (b0)–(b4) hold.

Starting from $\mathcal{A}^\Sigma_0 := \mathcal{A}^\Sigma$ and $\mathcal{B}^\Delta_0 := \mathcal{B}^\Delta$, we shall make a zig-zag construction that defines an ascending tower of Σ-structures $\mathcal{A}^\Sigma_n$, and similarly an ascending tower of Δ-structures $\mathcal{B}^\Delta_n$. These structures are connected by bijective mappings h_n and g_n. The combined structure is obtained as the limit structure, which obtains its functional and relational structure from both towers by means of the limits of the mappings h_n and g_n. Let $X_0 := Y_0 := X$.

$n = 0$: Consider $\mathcal{A}^\Sigma_0 = \mathcal{A}^\Sigma = SH^{A_\infty}_{\mathcal{M}_\infty}(X_0)$. We interpret the "new" elements in $A_0 \setminus X_0$ as atoms in $\mathcal{B}^\Delta_\infty$. For this purpose, select a subset $Y_1 \subseteq Y_\infty$ such that $Y_1 \cap Y_0 = \emptyset$, $|Y_1| = |A_0 \setminus X_0|$, and the remaining complement $Y_\infty \setminus (Y_0 \cup Y_1)$ is countably infinite. Choose any bijection $h_0 : Y_0 \cup Y_1 \to A_0$ where $h_0|_{Y_0} = Id_{Y_0}$.

Consider $\mathcal{B}^\Delta_0 = \mathcal{B}^\Delta = SH^{B_\infty}_{\mathcal{N}_\infty}(Y_0)$. As for A_0, we interpret the "new" elements in $B_0 \setminus Y_0$ as atoms in $\mathcal{A}^\Sigma_\infty$. Select a subset $X_1 \subseteq X_\infty$ such that $X_1 \cap X_0 = \emptyset$, $|X_1| = |B_0 \setminus Y_0|$ and the remaining complement $X_\infty \setminus (X_0 \cup X_1)$ is countably infinite. Choose any bijection $g_0 : X_0 \cup X_1 \to B_0$ where $g_0|_{X_0} = Id_{X_0}$.

$n \to n + 1$: Suppose that the structures $\mathcal{A}^\Sigma_n = SH^{A_\infty}_{\mathcal{M}_\infty}(\bigcup_{i=0}^n X_i)$ and $\mathcal{B}^\Delta_n = SH^{B_\infty}_{\mathcal{N}_\infty}(\bigcup_{i=0}^n Y_i)$ and the atom sets $X_{n+1} \subset (X_\infty \setminus \bigcup_{i=0}^n X_i)$ and $Y_{n+1} \subset (Y_\infty \setminus \bigcup_{i=0}^n Y_i)$ are already defined. We assume that the complements $X_\infty \setminus \bigcup_{i=0}^{n+1} X_i$ and $Y_\infty \setminus \bigcup_{i=0}^{n+1} Y_i$ are infinite. In addition, we assume that bijections $h_n : B_{n-1} \cup Y_n \cup Y_{n+1} \to A_n$ and $g_n : A_{n-1} \cup X_n \cup X_{n+1} \to B_n$ are defined such that

$(*)$ $g_n(h_n(b)) = b$ for $b \in B_{n-1} \cup Y_n$ and $h_n(g_n(a)) = a$ for $a \in A_{n-1} \cup X_n$,
$(**)$ $h_n(Y_{n+1}) = A_n \setminus (A_{n-1} \cup X_n)$ and $g_n(X_{n+1}) = B_n \setminus (B_{n-1} \cup Y_n)$.

We define $\mathcal{A}^\Sigma_{n+1} := SH^{A_\infty}_{\mathcal{M}_\infty}(\bigcup_{i=0}^{n+1} X_i)$ and $\mathcal{B}^\Delta_{n+1} = SH^{B_\infty}_{\mathcal{N}_\infty}(\bigcup_{i=0}^{n+1} Y_i)$ and select subsets $Y_{n+2} \subseteq Y_\infty$ and $X_{n+2} \subseteq X_\infty$ such that $Y_{n+2} \cap \bigcup_{i=0}^{n+1} Y_i = \emptyset = X_{n+2} \cap \bigcup_{i=0}^{n+1} X_i$. In addition, the cardinalities must satisfy $|Y_{n+2}| = |A_{n+1} \setminus (A_n \cup X_{n+1})|$ and $|X_{n+2}| = |B_{n+1} \setminus (B_n \cup Y_{n+1})|$, and the remaining complements $Y_\infty \setminus \bigcup_{i=0}^{n+2} Y_i$ and $X_\infty \setminus \bigcup_{i=0}^{n+2} X_i$ must be countably infinite. Let

$$\upsilon_{n+1} : Y_{n+2} \to A_{n+1} \setminus (A_n \cup X_{n+1}) \quad \text{and} \quad \xi_{n+1} : X_{n+2} \to B_{n+1} \setminus (B_n \cup Y_{n+1})$$

be arbitrary bijections. We define $h_{n+1} := \upsilon_{n+1} \cup g_n^{-1} \cup h_n$ and $g_{n+1} := \xi_{n+1} \cup h_n^{-1} \cup g_n$.

Without loss of generality we may assume (for notational convenience) that the construction eventually covers all atoms in X_∞ and Y_∞; in other words, we assume that $\bigcup_{i=0}^\infty X_i = X_\infty$ and $\bigcup_{i=0}^\infty Y_i = Y_\infty$, and thus $\bigcup_{i=0}^\infty A_i = A_\infty$ and $\bigcup_{i=0}^\infty B_i = B_\infty$. We define the limit mappings $h_\infty := \bigcup_{i=0}^\infty h_i : B_\infty \to A_\infty$ and $g_\infty := \bigcup_{i=0}^\infty g_i : A_\infty \to B_\infty$. It is easy to see that h_∞ and g_∞ are bijections that are inverse to each other. They may be used to carry the Δ-structure of $\mathcal{B}^\Delta_\infty$ to $\mathcal{A}^\Sigma_\infty$, and to carry the Σ-structure of $\mathcal{A}^\Sigma_\infty$ to $\mathcal{B}^\Delta_\infty$: Let f (f') be an n-ary function symbol of Δ (Σ), let p (p') be an n-ary predicate symbol of Δ (Σ), and let $a_1, \ldots, a_n \in A_\infty$ ($b_1, \ldots, b_n \in B_\infty$). We define

$$f_{A_\infty}(a_1, \ldots, a_n) := h_\infty(f_{B_\infty}(g_\infty(a_1), \ldots, g_\infty(a_n))),$$

$$f'_{\mathcal{B}_\infty}(b_1,\ldots,b_n) \quad := \quad g_\infty(f'_{\mathcal{A}_\infty}(h_\infty(b_1),\ldots,h_\infty(b_n))),$$
$$p_{\mathcal{A}_\infty}[a_1,\ldots,a_n] :\iff p_{\mathcal{B}_\infty}[g_\infty(a_1),\ldots,g_\infty(a_n)],$$
$$p'_{\mathcal{B}_\infty}[b_1,\ldots,b_n] :\iff p'_{\mathcal{A}_\infty}[h_\infty(b_1),\ldots,h_\infty(b_n)].$$

With this definition, the mappings h_∞ and g_∞ are inverse isomorphisms between the $(\Sigma \cup \Delta)$-structures $\mathcal{A}_\infty^{\Sigma\cup\Delta}$ and $\mathcal{B}_\infty^{\Sigma\cup\Delta}$. We take $\mathcal{A}_\infty^{\Sigma\cup\Delta}$ as the result of the construction.

Lemma 16. $\mathcal{A}_\infty^{\Sigma\cup\Delta}$ *closes the amalgamation base* $(X, \mathcal{A}^\Sigma, \mathcal{B}^\Delta)$.

In order to obtain a better algebraic characterization of what the above construction generates, we restrict our attention to strong SC-structures. First, we must define a class of admissible structures. To this purpose we use the algebraic condition of Proposition 2:

Definition 17. For strong SC-structures $(\mathcal{A}^\Sigma, \mathcal{M}, X)$ and $(\mathcal{B}^\Delta, \mathcal{N}, X)$, the class of admissible structures, $Adm(\mathcal{A}^\Sigma, \mathcal{B}^\Delta)$, consists of all structures $\mathcal{C}^{\Sigma\cup\Delta}$ such that for every mapping $g_{X-C} : X \to C$ there exist unique homomorphisms $g_{A-C}^\Sigma : \mathcal{A}^\Sigma \to \mathcal{C}^\Sigma$ and $g_{B-C}^\Delta : \mathcal{B}^\Delta \to \mathcal{C}^\Delta$ extending g_{X-C}.

We may now formulate our central result concerning amalgamation of strong SC-structures. In the proof, the conditions $(a_1) - (a_4)$ and $(b_1) - (b_4)$ that have been imposed on $\mathcal{A}_\infty^\Sigma$ and $\mathcal{B}_\infty^\Delta$ at the beginning of the amalgamation construction become relevant.

Theorem 18. *If* $(\mathcal{A}^\Sigma, \mathcal{M}, X)$ *and* $(\mathcal{B}^\Delta, \mathcal{N}, X)$ *are strong SC-structures over disjoint signatures, then* $\mathcal{A}_\infty^{\Sigma\cup\Delta}$ *is the free amalgamated product of* $\mathcal{A}^\Sigma$ *and* $\mathcal{B}^\Delta$ *over* X *with respect to the class* $Adm(\mathcal{A}^\Sigma, \mathcal{B}^\Delta)$ *of admissible structures defined above.*

For strong SC-structures, the amalgamation construction can be applied iteratedly because the obtained structure is again a strong SC-structure:

Theorem 19. *The free amalgamated product of two strong SC-structures with common atom set* X *is a strong SC-structure with atom set* X.

The following theorem is an important prerequisite for proving correctness of our method for deciding the (full) positive theory of the free amalgamated product of two strong SC-structures (over disjoint signatures) with decidable positive theories (Theorem 23).

Theorem 20. *Free amalgamation of strong SC-structures with disjoint signatures over the same atom set is associative.*

6 Combining Constraint Solvers for SC-Structures

Let $(\mathcal{A}^\Sigma, \mathcal{M}, X)$ and $(\mathcal{B}^\Delta, \mathcal{N}, X)$ be two SC-structures over disjoint signatures Σ and Δ; let $\mathcal{A}^\Sigma \otimes \mathcal{B}^\Delta \cong \mathcal{A}_\infty^{\Sigma\cup\Delta}$ denote the result of the amalgamation construction described in the previous section.

Lemma 21. *There exists a decomposition algorithm that decomposes a positive existential* $(\Sigma \cup \Delta)$*-sentence* φ_0 *into a finite set of output pairs* (α, β)*, where* α *is a positive* Σ*-sentence, and* β *is a positive* Δ*-sentence, such that* $\mathcal{A}^\Sigma \otimes \mathcal{B}^\Delta \models \varphi_0$ *iff* $\mathcal{A}^\Sigma \models \alpha$ *and* $\mathcal{B}^\Delta \models \beta$ *for some output pair* (α, β)*.*

A brief description of the algorithm is given in the Appendix. A detailled description of all steps can be found in [BaS94a], where the same algorithm has been used in the restricted context of constraint solvers for free structures.

Theorem 22. *The existential positive theory of* $\mathcal{A}^\Sigma \otimes \mathcal{B}^\Delta$ *is decidable, provided that the positive theories of* $\mathcal{A}^\Sigma$ *and of* $\mathcal{B}^\Delta$ *are decidable.*

Recall that, for strong SC-structures $(\mathcal{A}^\Sigma, \mathcal{M}, X)$ and $(\mathcal{B}^\Delta, \mathcal{N}, X)$, the structure $\mathcal{A}^\Sigma \otimes \mathcal{B}^\Delta$ is the free amalgamated product of $\mathcal{A}^\Sigma$ and $\mathcal{B}^\Delta$ over X with respect to $Adm(\mathcal{A}^\Sigma, \mathcal{B}^\Delta)$. In this case, our combination method is not restricted to *existential* positive sentences. The main idea is to transform positive sentences (with arbitrary quantifier prefix) into existential positive sentences by Skolemizing the universally quantified variables. In principle, the decomposition algorithm for positive sentences is now applied twice to decompose the input sentence into three positive sentences α, β, ρ, whose validity must respectively be decided in $\mathcal{A}^\Sigma$, $\mathcal{B}^\Delta$, and the absolutely free term algebra over the Skolem functions (here Theorem 20 becomes relevant).

Theorem 23. *If* $(\mathcal{A}^\Sigma, \mathcal{M}, X)$ *and* $(\mathcal{B}^\Delta, \mathcal{N}, X)$ *are strong SC-structures then the (full) positive theory of the free amalgamated product* $\mathcal{A}^\Sigma \otimes \mathcal{B}^\Delta$ *is decidable, provided that the positive theories of* $\mathcal{A}^\Sigma$ *and of* $\mathcal{B}^\Delta$ *are decidable.*

In connection with the Theorems 19 and 20, this provides the basis for constraint solving in the combination of any finite number of strong SC-structures.

Theorems 22 and 23 show that the prerequisite for combining constraint solvers with the help of our decomposition algorithms is that validity of arbitrary positive sentences is decidable in both components. If we leave the realm of free structures, not many results are known that show that the positive theory of a particular SC-structure is decidable. One example is the algebra of rational trees: its full first order theory—like the theory of the algebra of finite trees—is known to be decidable [Mah88].[7] In general, the problem of deciding validity of existential positive sentences and the problem of deciding validity of arbitrary positive sentences in a given structure can be quite different. For the case of SC-structures, however, the following variant of Lemma 14 shows that the difference is not drastic.

Lemma 24. *Let* $(\mathcal{A}^\Sigma, \mathcal{M}, X)$ *be an SC-structure, let*

$$\forall \vec{u}_1 \exists \vec{v}_1 \dots \forall \vec{u}_k \exists \vec{v}_k \; \varphi(\vec{u}_1, \vec{v}_1, \dots, \vec{u}_k, \vec{v}_k)$$

be a positive Σ*-sentence, and let, for each* $i, 1 \leq i \leq k$*,* $\vec{x}_i$ *be an arbitrary (but fixed) sequence of length* $|\vec{u}_i|$ *of distinct atoms such that distinct sequences* $\vec{x}_i$ *and*

---

[7] Maher considers ground tree algebras, but over possibly infinite signatures. Therefore his result can be lifted to the non-ground case by treating variables as constants.

$\vec{x}_j$ do not have common elements. Let $X_{1,i}$ denote the set of all atoms occurring in the sequences $\vec{x}_1, \ldots, \vec{x}_i$ $(i = 1, \ldots, k)$. Then the following conditions are equivalent:

1. $\mathcal{A}^\Sigma \models \forall \vec{u}_1 \exists \vec{v}_1 \ldots \forall \vec{u}_k \exists \vec{v}_k \; \varphi(\vec{u}_1, \vec{v}_1, \ldots, \vec{u}_k, \vec{v}_k)$,
2. there exist $\vec{e}_1 \in SH_\mathcal{M}^A(X_{1,1}), \ldots, \vec{e}_k \in SH_\mathcal{M}^A(X_{1,k})$ such that $\mathcal{A}^\Sigma \models \varphi(\vec{x}_1, \vec{e}_1, \ldots, \vec{x}_k, \vec{e}_k)$.

Looking at the second condition of the lemma, one sees that a positive sentence can be reduced to an *existential* positive sentence where the universally quantified variables are replaced by atoms (i.e., free constants), and additional restrictions are imposed on the values of the existentially quantified variables. For this reason, it is often not hard to extend decision procedures for the existential positive theory of an SC-structure to a decision procedure for the full positive theory. This way of proceeding can, for example, be used to prove that the positive theories of the four domains of nested, hereditarily finite wellfounded or non-wellfounded sets or lists, as introduced in Example 12, are decidable.

Corollary 25. *Simultaneous free amalgamated products have a decidable positive theory if the components are finite or rational tree algebras, or nested, hereditarily finite wellfounded or non-wellfounded sets or lists, and if the signatures of the components are disjoint.*

7 Conclusion

This paper should be seen as a first step to provide an abstract framework for the combination of constraint languages and constraint solvers. We have introduced the notion "admissible amalgamated product" in order to capture—in an abstract algebraic setting—our intuition of what a combined solution structure should satisfy. It was shown that in certain cases there exists a canonical structure—called the free amalgamated product—that yields a most general admissible amalgamated product of a given amalgamation base.

We have introduced a class of structures—called SC-structures—that are equipped with structural properties that guarantee (1) that a canonical amalgamation construction can be applied to SC-structures over disjoint signatures, and (2) that validity of positive existential formulae in the amalgamated structure obtained by this construction can be reduced to validity of positive formulae in the component structures. For the subclass of strong SC-structures we have obtained stronger results. Interestingly, a very similar class of structures has independently been introduced in [ScS88, Wil91] in order to characterize a maximal class of algebras where equation (and constraint) solving essentially behaves like unification.[8]

---

[8] The notion of an SC-structure can be considered as a sort-free version of the concepts that have been discussed in [ScS88, Wil91].

It is interesting to compare the concrete combined solution domains that can be found in the literature with the combined domains obtained by our amalgamation construction. It turns out that there can be differences if the elements of the components have a tree-like structure that allows for infinite paths (as in the examples of non-wellfounded lists/sets and rational trees). In these cases, frequently a combined solution structure is chosen where an infinite number of "signature changes" may occur when following an infinite path in an element of the combined domain ([Col90, Rou88]). In contrast, our amalgamation construction yields a combined structure where elements allow for a finite number of signature changes only. This indicates that the free amalgamated product, even if it exists, is not necessarily the only interesting combined domain. It remains to be seen which additional natural ways to combine structures exist, and how different ways of combining structures are formally related.

It should be noted that for most of the results presented in the paper the presence of countably many atoms ("variables") in the structures to be combined is an essential precondition. On the other hand, many constraint-based approaches consider ground structures as solution domains. In most cases, however, a corresponding non-ground structure containing the necessary atoms exists. Thus, our combination method can be applied to these non-ground variants. Of course, the combined structure obtained in this way is again non-ground. However, in the context of constraint solving this distinction is rather irrelevant: typically, "constraints" are *existential* positive formulae, and for existential positive formulae, validity in the non-ground combined structure is equivalent to validity in the ground variant of the combined structure.[9] This observation has the following interesting consequence. Even in cases where the (full) positive theory of a ground component structure is undecidable, our combination methods can be applied to show decidability of the existential positive theory for the *ground* combined structure, provided that the (full) positive theories of the non-ground component structures are decidable. Our remark following Lemma 24 shows that decidability of the full positive theory of such a non-ground structure can sometimes be obtained by an easy modification of the decision method for the existential positive case. Free semigroups are an example for this situation: the positive theory of a free semigroup with a finite number $n \geq 2$ of generators is undecidable, whereas the positive theory of the countably generated free semigroup (which corresponds to our non-ground case) is decidable [VaR83].

References

[Acz88] P. Aczel, "Non-well-founded Sets," *CSLI* Lecture Notes 14, Stanford University, 1988.

[APS94] H. Ait-Kaci, A. Podelski, and G. Smolka, "A feature-based constraint system for logic programming with entailment," *Theoretical Comp. Science* 122, 1994, pp.263–283.

---

[9] We assume here that the ground structure is a substructure of the non-ground structure and that "substitution" of ground elements for atoms is homomorphic.

[BaS92] F. Baader and K.U. Schulz, "Unification in the union of disjoint equational theories: Combining decision procedures," in: *Proc. CADE-11*, LNAI 607, 1992, pp.50-65.

[BaS93] F. Baader and K.U. Schulz, "Combination techniques and decision problems for disunification," in: *Proc. RTA-93*, LNCS 690, 1993.

[BaS94a] F. Baader and K.U. Schulz, "Combination of Constraint Solving Techniques: An Algebraic Point of View," Research Report CIS-Rep-94-75, University Munich, 1994; short version in: Proc. RTA'95, Springer LNCS 914, 1995.

[BaS94b] F. Baader and K.U. Schulz, "On the Combination of Symbolic Constraints, Solution Domains, and Constraint Solvers," Research Report CIS-Rep-94-82, University Munich, 1994. Long version of this paper, available via anonymous ftp from ftp.cis.uni-muenchen.de, directory "schulz", file name "SCstructures.ps.Z".

[Bou90] A. Boudet, "Unification in a combination of equational theories: An efficient algorithm," in: *Proc. CADE-10*, LNCS 449, 1990, pp.292-307.

[Che76] G. Cherlin, "Model Theoretic Algebra: Selected Topics," Springer Lecture Notes in Mathematics 521, 1976.

[Col90] A. Colmerauer, "An introduction to PROLOG III," *C. ACM* **33**, 1990, pp.69-90.

[DOP91] A. Dovier, E.G. Omodeo, E. Pontellio, G.F. Rossi, "{log}: A Logic Programming language with finite sets," in: *Logic Programming: Proc. 8th International Conf.*, The MIT Press, 1991.

[DoR93] A. Dovier, G. Rossi, "Embedding extensional finite sets in CLP," in: *Proc. International Logic Programming Symposium*, 1993, pp. 540-556.

[DrG93] M. Droste, R. Göbel, "Universal domains and the amalgamation property," *Math. Struct. in Comp. Science* **3**, pp. 137-159, 1993.

[KiR94] H. Kirchner and Ch. Ringeissen, "Combining symbolic constraint solvers on algebraic domains," *J. Symbolic Computation*, 18(2), 1994, pp. 113-155.

[Mah88] M.J. Maher, "Complete axiomatizations of the algebras of finite, rational and infinite trees," in: *Proceedings of Third Annual Symposium on Logic in Computer Science, LICS'88*, pp.348-357, Edinburgh, Scotland, 1988. IEEE Computer Society.

[Mal73] A.I. Mal'cev, "Algebraic Systems," Volume 192 of *Die Grundlehren der mathematischen Wissenschaften in Einzeldarstellungen*, Springer-Verlag, Berlin, 1973.

[Muk91] K. Mukai, "Constraint Logic Programming and the Unification of Information," doctoral thesis, Dept. of Comp. Science, Faculty of Engineering, Tokyo Institute of Technology, 1991.

[NeO79] G. Nelson, D.C. Oppen, "Simplification by Cooperating Decision Procedures," ACM TOPLAS, Vol. 1, No. 2, October 1979, 245-257.

[Rin92] Ch. Ringeissen, "Unification in a combination of equational theories with shared constants and its application to primal algebras," in: *Proc. LPAR'92*, LNCS 624, 1992.

[Rou88] W.C. Rounds, "Set Values for Unification Based Grammar Formalisms and Logic Programming," Research Report CSLI-88-129, Stanford, 1988.

[ScS88] M. Schmidt-Schauß, "Unification Algebras: An Axiomatic Approach to Unification, Equation Solving and Constraint Solving," *SEKI-Report*, SR-88-23, University of Kaiserslautern, 1988.

[ScS89] M. Schmidt-Schauß, "Unification in a combination of arbitrary disjoint equational theories," *J. Symbolic Computation* **8**, 1989, pp.51-99.

[SmT94] G. Smolka, R. Treinen, "Records for Logic Programming," *J. of Logic Programming* 18(3) (1994), pp. 229-258-556.

[VaR83] Y.M. Vazhenin and B.V. Rozenblat, "Decidability of the positive theory of a free countably generated semigroup," *Math. USSR Sbornik* 44 (1983), pp.109–116.

[Wil91] J.G. Williams, "Instantiation Theory: On the Foundation of Automated Deduction," Springer LNCS 518, 1991.

Appendix: The Decomposition Algorithm Let φ_0 be a positive existential $(\Sigma \cup \Delta)$-sentence, the *input*. We may assume that φ_0 has the form $\exists \vec{u}_0 \ \gamma_0$, where γ_0 is a conjunction of atomic formulae.

Step 1. An equivalent positive existential $(\Sigma \cup \Delta)$-sentence φ_1 is generated where all atomic subformulae are pure, i.e., they are built over one signature (Σ or Δ) only.

Step 2. All equations $u = v$ between variables are removed after replacing every occurrence of u in φ_1 by v. Let φ_2 be the new sentence obtained this way. The matrix of φ_2 can be written as a conjunction $\gamma_{2,\Sigma} \wedge \gamma_{2,\Delta}$, where $\gamma_{2,\Sigma}$ is the conjunction of all atomic Σ-subformulae, and $\gamma_{2,\Delta}$ is the conjunction of all atomic Δ-subformulae. There are three different types of variables occurring in φ_2: shared variables occur both in $\gamma_{2,\Sigma}$ and in $\gamma_{2,\Delta}$; Σ-variables (Δ-variables) occur only in $\gamma_{2,\Sigma}$ (in $\gamma_{2,\Delta}$). Let $\vec{u}_{2,\Sigma}$ ($\vec{u}_{2,\Delta}$) be the tuple of all Σ-variables (Δ-variables), let $\vec{u}_2$ be the tuple of all shared variables. Obviously, φ_2 is equivalent to the sentence $\exists \vec{u}_2 (\exists \vec{u}_{2,\Sigma} \ \gamma_{2,\Sigma} \wedge \exists \vec{u}_{2,\Delta} \ \gamma_{2,\Delta})$.

Step 3 (non-deterministic). We choose a partition of the set of *shared* variables. For each class of the partition, a representative is selected, and all variables of the class are replaced by the representative. Quantifiers for replaced variables are removed. Let $\exists \vec{u}_3 (\exists \vec{u}_{2,\Sigma} \ \gamma_{3,\Sigma} \wedge \exists \vec{u}_{2,\Delta} \ \gamma_{3,\Delta})$ denote a sentence obtained by Step 3.

Step 4 (non-deterministic). We choose a label Σ or Δ for each component of $\vec{u}_3$, and a linear ordering $<$ on the set of these variables.

Step 5. The sentence $\exists \vec{u}_3 (\exists \vec{u}_{2,\Sigma} \ \gamma_{3,\Sigma} \wedge \exists \vec{u}_{2,\Delta} \ \gamma_{3,\Delta})$ is split into two sentences

$$\alpha = \forall \vec{v}_1 \exists \vec{w}_1 \ldots \forall \vec{v}_k \exists \vec{w}_k \exists \vec{u}_{2,\Sigma} \ \gamma_{3,\Sigma}, \quad \text{and} \quad \beta = \exists \vec{v}_1 \forall \vec{w}_1 \ldots \exists \vec{v}_k \forall \vec{w}_k \exists \vec{u}_{2,\Delta} \ \gamma_{3,\Delta}.$$

Here $\vec{v}_1 \vec{w}_1 \ldots \vec{v}_k \vec{w}_k$ is the unique re-ordering of $\vec{u}_3$ along $<$. The variables $\vec{v}_i$ ($\vec{w}_i$) are the variables with label Δ (label Σ). The *output sentences* α and β are (not necessarily existential) positive formulae.

Constraint Propagation in Model Generation*

Jian Zhang and Hantao Zhang

Department of Computer Science, University of Iowa
Iowa City, IA 52242, USA
{ jzhang | hzhang }@cs.uiowa.edu

Abstract. Model generation refers to the automatic construction of models of a given logical theory. It can be regarded as a special case of constraint satisfaction where the constraints are a set of clauses with equality and functions. In this paper, we study various constraint propagation rules for finite model generation. We implemented these rules in a prototype system called SEM (a System for Enumerating Models). By experimenting with SEM, we try to identify a set of transformation rules that are both efficient and easy to implement. We also compare several existing model generation systems that are based on different logics and strategies.

1 Introduction

Many problems in computer science and AI can be formulated as constraint satisfaction problems (CSPs), that is, finding suitable values for a set of variables such that some constraints hold. However, the notion of "constraints" is somehow vague. In general, the CSP paradigm in AI can be regarded as a restricted logical calculus [1, 10] and various logical formalisms can be used to express the constraints. In this paper, we study a class of CSPs that are different from the conventional CSP paradigm [8, 10] or the constraint logic programming (CLP) paradigm [6]. Here we are concerned with finding structures satisfying a set of clauses in first order logic. That is, instead of finding values for variables, our goal is to define functions (and predicates) in a suitable way such that all the clauses hold. Such a problem is often called *model generation* (or *model finding*).

The conventional CSP can be expressed by the formula $\exists \mathbf{x}.C(\mathbf{x})$, where $\mathbf{x}$ is a finite set of variables (with each variable $x \in \mathbf{x}$ bounded to a specific domain) and C is a first order formula (or a conjunction of clauses). In contrast, the model generation problem can be expressed by $\forall \mathbf{x}.\exists \mathbf{f}.C(\mathbf{f}, \mathbf{x})$, where $\mathbf{f}$ is a finite set of function symbols appearing in C. In other words, we view C as a special case of second-order formula. When the domain of each variable is finite, we may remove the universal quantifier by instantiating $\mathbf{x}$ with its all possible values. For instance, suppose f is a binary function over the domain $D = \{0, 1, ..., n-1\}$ and C is $f(y, f(x, y)) = x$. To eliminate x and y, we may use the n^2 instances of C, i.e, $f(0, f(0, 0)) = 0$, $f(1, f(0, 1)) = 0$, etc.

* Partially supported by the National Science Foundation under Grants CCR-9202838 and CCR-9357851.

Model generation is clearly very important. In fact, many open questions in mathematics have recently been solved by various model finding programs, such as FALCON [20], FINDER [14], MGTP [4, 5], LDPP [19, 15], SATO [19] and MACE [13]. These programs successfully found mathematical objects having certain properties. Besides such uses, model generators also have other applications. For example, the existence of a model implies the consistency of a theory. And, suitable models may serve as counterexamples refuting conjectures. In this sense, model generation is complementary to conventional theorem proving.

Currently, there exist a number of different approaches to generating models of first order theories, see for example, [2, 9, 15, 16]. Some of them are closely related to automated deduction, while others rely heavily on constraint satisfaction techniques. Some deal only with a certain type of logical formulas, and some can only find finite models.

The formulas considered in this paper are arbitrary clauses, but the models are restricted to *finite* ones. In such cases, decidability or completeness is guaranteed. A model can be found by exhaustive search, if it exists. However, efficiency is an important issue, because in general, the problems involve huge search spaces.

Like conventional CSPs, finite model generation problems can be solved with backtracking procedures and other algorithms (like constraint propagation) [8]. To define a function over finite domains, we can define its "multiplication table", or equivalently, determine the values for all the cells (or entries) in the table. This can be done one cell at a time. For each cell, we choose a value from a finite set of possible values; then we propagate the effects of this choice; if it does not result in contradiction, we accept it and consider the next cell; otherwise we try other values or go back to the previous cell. Just as in the case of ordinary constraint satisfaction, many issues arise here. For example, in what order shall we choose the next cell? When shall we do the propagation? How can we propagate the effect of a choice? What kind of propagation is complete or inexpensive? How much propagation is necessary? Of course, the answers to these questions depend largely on the application domains.

The purpose of this paper is to describe and analyze some rules for constraint propagation and entailment, in the context of finite model generation. To the best of our knowledge, there is little formal study of constraint satisfaction when the constraints are expressed as arbitrary clauses. In general, many notions of CSP such as k-variable constraints and arc-consistency do not apply here.

As we mentioned earlier, there exist several model generation systems. But their performances on some problems are quite different. For instance, Slaney, Stickel and Fujita [15] observed that, on the quasigroup identity problems, there is a "large difference between DDPP and FINDER in the matter of branching: DDPP generates far fewer branches than FINDER, but takes from 5 to 66 times longer to explore each one." However, no reasons were given why there exists such a big difference. We believe that our experimental results and analysis will provide some hint on this issue.

The rest of this paper is organized as follows. In the next section, we describe some basic concepts and notations which will be used later, e.g. cells, elements and some special forms of clauses. In §3, we give some rules for transforming the constraints. Then we briefly describe our model finding program SEM, and its constraint solving mechanism. In §5, several similar systems are compared on some benchmark problems, and their differences in performances are analyzed. Finally, we discuss some of the related work and conclude the paper.

2 Basic Concepts and Notations

For the basic concepts in predicate calculus, automated theorem proving and the clausal representation language, the reader is referred to standard textbooks or the book [17] (Chap. 4). In the sequel, we use s, t (and s_i, t_j) to denote arbitrary terms; C and M to denote a set of clauses and a disjunction of literals, respectively. A positive equality literal is represented by $t_1 = t_2$ and a negative equality literal is by $t_1 \neq t_2$, where t_1 and t_2 are well-formed terms. We also use $L[t]$ to denote a literal which contains the subterm t.

Simply stated, the model generation problem is, given a set of first order clauses, find an interpretation of all the function symbols appearing in them such that all the clauses become true. Such an interpretation is called a *model*. Predicate symbols can be regarded as function symbols of the Boolean sort in a many-sorted language. For simplicity, we shall only consider the uni-sorted case with the special predicate "equality". We assume that the size of the model is a fixed finite positive number, denoted by n.

When the involved domain is finite, an interpretation can be represented by a set of *multiplication tables*, one for each function. Without loss of generality, an n-element domain is assumed to be $D_n = \{ 0, 1, \ldots, n-1 \}$. From now on, we use e_i to denote an element of a domain. Syntactically it can be regarded as a constant symbol. For any two distinct elements e_i and e_j $(i \neq j)$, it is assumed that the inequality $e_i \neq e_j$ always holds.

For an m-ary function f, each entry of its multiplication table can be represented by a ground term of the form $f(e_1, e_2, \ldots, e_m)$. Such a term is called a *cell term* or simply a *cell*, and will be denoted by ce or ce_i.

To find the models, we have to assign suitable values (i.e. elements) to the cells. For this purpose, we are interested in certain relationships between cells and elements. In particular, we distinguish the following three types of clauses:

- possible values (PV) clause: $ce = e_1 \lor \ldots \lor ce = e_i \lor \ldots \lor ce = e_k$
- value assignment (VA) clause: $ce = e_i$
- value elimination (VE) clause: $ce \neq e_i$

These clauses tell us what values a cell can take during the search. Note that, in a PV clause, all the cell terms are the same, and a VA clause is a special case of a PV clause. The left-hand side and the right-hand side of an equation (or inequality) are interchangeable. So, $e_i = ce$ is also a VA clause, and $e_j \neq ce$ is also a VE clause.

A finite model can be represented by a set of VA clauses. As a simple example, let us consider quasigroups.

Example. A quasigroup has one binary operation whose multiplication table forms a Latin square, i.e. each row and each column is a permutation of the elements. Let us denote the operation by f. A 3-element quasigroup is shown below.

$$
\begin{array}{c|ccc}
f & 0 & 1 & 2 \\
\hline
0 & 0 & 2 & 1 \\
1 & 1 & 0 & 2 \\
2 & 2 & 1 & 0 \\
\end{array}
$$

This table is equivalent to the following set of VA clauses:

$$
\begin{array}{lll}
f(0,0) = 0, & f(0,1) = 2, & f(0,2) = 1, \\
f(1,0) = 1, & f(1,1) = 0, & f(1,2) = 2, \\
f(2,0) = 2, & f(2,1) = 1, & f(2,2) = 0.
\end{array}
$$

In general, the constraint of a (finite) model generation problem is a set of clauses, called *axioms*. For example, quasigroups can be axiomatized by the following two clauses:

$$f(x,y) \neq f(x,z) \vee y = z, \tag{1}$$

$$f(x,z) \neq f(y,z) \vee x = y, \tag{2}$$

where all the three variables, x, y, and z, are universally quantified. One can easily verify that the above 3-element quasigroup satisfies the two axioms, by substituting i, j, k $(0 \leq i, j, k \leq 2)$ for x, y, z, respectively.

Usually the axioms contain some free variables which are assumed to be universally quantified. When the size of each domain is finite and fixed beforehand, we may consider the instantiated clauses as the constraints, instead of the original axioms. For example, to find a 3-element quasigroup, we should satisfy $3^3 \times 2 = 54$ ground (i.e. variable-free) clauses. The benefit of this instantiation is that unification is avoided in the rules for constraint propagation, and the computational costs of many inferences are reduced.

In short, when the domain is finite, both the constraint and the solution (i.e. the model) can be expressed by a set of first-order ground clauses. In the remainder of this paper, we shall assume that all the terms, literals and clauses are ground (i.e., free of variables). And, when saying a set of clauses is *satisfiable*, we mean that it has a model whose domain is D_n.

3 Rules for Constraint Transformation

To find an n-element model of a set of axioms, we start from a set of ground clauses which includes all the instantiations of the axioms (by substituting elements of D_n for the variables), and exactly one PV clause for each cell ce:

$$ce = 0 \vee ce = 1 \vee \ldots \vee ce = n - 1.$$

For convenience, let us call such a set of ground clauses *n-complete*. Our goal is to derive a set of VA clauses such that all the clauses are true. Essentially this can be achieved through a sequence of transformations.

In this section, we describe some rules for transforming the clause set. These rules can be classified into the following three categories:

- **simplification rules:** A current clause is simplified or removed from the clause set. Tautology deletion and subsumption are such rules.
- **inference rules:** A new clause is generated and added into the clause set. For instance, resolution and paramodulation [17] are two well-known inference rules.
- **splitting rules:** The current clause set is split into several clause sets. Such rules are used in case-analysis reasoning.

3.1 Simplification Rules

Most simplification rules in first order theorem proving, such as tautology deletion, subsumption, and rewriting, can be used to simplify constraints. Let us start with the simplest ones.

equality resolution:

$$(\textbf{ER1}) \ \frac{C \cup \{t \neq t \vee M\}}{C \cup \{M\}} \qquad (\textbf{ER2}) \ \frac{C \cup \{e_i = e_j \vee M\}}{C \cup \{M\}} \ (i \neq j)$$

equality subsumption:

$$(\textbf{ES1}) \ \frac{C \cup \{t = t \vee M\}}{C} \qquad (\textbf{ES2}) \ \frac{C \cup \{e_i \neq e_j \vee M\}}{C} \ (i \neq j)$$

The above rules are sound, because we have, for all x, $x = x$; and $e_i \neq e_j$ is assumed to be true for any two distinct elements e_i and e_j in the domain.

Next we consider unit resolution, which is a well-known inference rule in theorem proving. In the ground case, it can be used as a simplification rule. When an empty clause is produced by either equality resolution or unit resolution, the entire set of clauses is unsatisfiable.

unit resolution:

$$(\textbf{UR1}) \ \frac{C \cup \{t_1 \neq t_2 \vee M, \ t_1 = t_2\}}{C \cup \{M, \ t_1 = t_2\}} \qquad (\textbf{UR2}) \ \frac{C \cup \{t_1 = t_2 \vee M, \ t_1 \neq t_2\}}{C \cup \{M, \ t_1 \neq t_2\}}$$

Because it is expensive to perform full subsumption in model generation, only unit subsumption is considered in our experimentation. Actually, in our experiments, we find that when splitting rule is used, the performance of the system is often better if we impose further restrictions on unit resolution and unit subsumption that the involved unit clause must be either a VA or VE clause.

unit subsumption:

(US1) $\dfrac{C \cup \{t_1 = t_2 \vee M, \ t_1 = t_2\}}{C \cup \{t_1 = t_2\}}$ (US2) $\dfrac{C \cup \{t_1 \neq t_2 \vee M, \ t_1 \neq t_2\}}{C \cup \{t_1 \neq t_2\}}$

Rewriting is a powerful simplification rule for theorem proving. It can also be used in constraint propagation.

rewriting:

$$\frac{C \cup \{L[t_1] \vee M, \ t_1 = t_2\}}{C \cup \{L[t_2] \vee M, \ t_1 = t_2\}}$$

The effect of this rule is to replace t_1 in the clause $L[t_1] \vee M$ by t_2. In our experimentation, we require that t_2 be an element and t_1 be a non-element term, so that the termination of rewriting is guaranteed. In fact, it is often simple and efficient if we require that t_1 be a cell, i.e., $t_1 = t_2$ is a VA clause.

After the simplification rules are applied, some of the clauses may be reduced to VA or VE clauses, so that further simplification can be performed.

Let us consider the quasigroup example in §2. Substituting 0, 1, 2 for x, y, z respectively in clause (1), we get the following clause:

$$f(0,1) \neq f(0,2) \vee 1 = 2$$

This may be reduced by the rule (**ER2**) to:

$$f(0,1) \neq f(0,2)$$

Suppose during the search we choose $f(0,1) = 2$, then we can infer a VE clause $2 \neq f(0,2)$ by rewriting.

3.2   Inference Rules

The first inference rule we consider here is paramodulation, which is defined as follows (assuming C is a set of ground clauses):

paramodulation:

$$\frac{C \cup \{L[t_1] \vee M_1, \ t_1 = t_2 \vee M_2\}}{C \cup \{L[t_1] \vee M_1, \ t_1 = t_2 \vee M_2, \ L[t_2] \vee M_1 \vee M_2\}}$$

This rule, together with equality resolution, provides a decision procedure for the unsatisfiability of a set of clauses. However, our experiences show that it is not practical to apply paramodulation in its general form, because it may generate too many new clauses. Imposing an ordering on literals can help but the problem of explosion remains. However, if we impose more restrictions on this rule, we may obtain various simplification rules such as rewriting or unit resolution.

Another inference rule involving the equality predicate is called **dismodulation:**

$$\frac{C \cup \{f(t_1, ..., t_m) = t_0 \vee M_1, \quad f(s_1, ..., s_m) \neq s_0 \vee M_2\}}{C \cup \{f(t_1, ..., t_m) = t_0 \vee M_1, \quad f(s_1, ..., s_m) \neq s_0 \vee M_2, \quad \bigvee_{i=0}^{m}(t_i \neq s_i) \vee M_1 \vee M_2\}}$$

The soundness of this rule can be easily established. Suppose the derived clause, $\bigvee_{i=0}^{m}(t_i \neq s_i) \vee M_1 \vee M_2$, is false in an interpretation, then both M_1 and M_2 are false, and for each i ($0 \leq i \leq m$), $t_i = s_i$ holds. So one of the parent clauses must be false in the interpretation, since $f(t_1, ..., t_m) = f(s_1, ..., s_m)$ and $t_0 = s_0$.

The above rule is quite similar to negative paramodulation [18], in that new information is derived from inequalities. However, since we consider only ground clauses, the function f in our rule need not have any special property (e.g. the cancellation property).

The dismodulation rule in its general form has the similar problem as the paramodulation rule, i.e., it may generate too many new clauses. From our experiments, we find that it is often beneficial if the above rule produces only VE clauses. In this case, M_1 and M_2 are empty, one of the terms $t_1, ..., t_m, s_1, ..., s_m$ is a cell, and the rest t_i's and s_i's (including t_0 and s_0) are elements. So we have the following two rules.

VE generation:

(**VEG1**) $\dfrac{C \cup \{f(e_1, .., e_i, .., e_m) = e_0, \quad f(e_1, .., ce, ..., e_m) \neq e_0\}}{C \cup \{f(e_1, .., e_i, .., e_m) = e_0, \quad f(e_1, .., ce, ..., e_m) \neq e_0, \quad ce \neq e_i\}}$

(**VEG2**) $\dfrac{C \cup \{f(e_1, .., ce, .., e_m) = e_0, \quad f(e_1, .., e_i, ..., e_m) \neq e_0\}}{C \cup \{f(e_1, .., ce, .., e_m) = e_0, \quad f(e_1, .., e_i, ..., e_m) \neq e_0, \quad ce \neq e_i\}}$

Note that, to apply each of the VE generation rules, one parent must be a VA or VE clause, and the complex terms in the two parents differ only in one argument. The resulting new clause is a VE clause.

Actually, the above rules of VE generation can be generalized. Let us call a complex term *nearly evaluable* if all but one of its arguments are elements in the domain. For example, $h(1, g(f(2, 4)), 3)$ is a nearly evaluable term, while $h(1, f(2, 4), g(3))$ is not. We may replace the cell ce in the above rules by a nearly evaluable term t. The deduced inequality $t \neq e_i$ can participate in further similar inferences, until a VE clause is produced. The new rule can be decomposed into a sequence of VE generation steps, just as hyperresolution can be decomposed into a sequence of resolution steps. For example, suppose we have the following three clauses:

$$h(1, g(f(2, 4)), 3) \neq 5$$
$$h(1, 2, 3) = 5$$
$$g(1) = 2$$

Then we can conclude that $f(2, 4) \neq 1$ by applying (**VEG1**) twice: from the first two clauses, derive $g(f(2, 4)) \neq 2$; and then from this new inequality and the third clause, derive the VE clause $f(2, 4) \neq 1$.

3.3   Splitting

Since we do not use paramodulation in its full version, to compensate the incompleteness resulted from this restriction, we use splitting (or equivalently, case analysis). The effect of this rule is that the current set of clauses is split into several sets of clauses. The completeness of a splitting rule requires that the original set of clauses is satisfiable iff one of the resulting set of clauses is satisfiable. Below we give two forms of splitting rules which are often used. In each case, a non-unit PV clause is chosen to split. If there is no such a PV clause, the search is completed.

splitting:

$$\textbf{(SP1)} \quad \frac{C \cup \{ce = e_1 \vee ce = e_2 \vee \ldots \vee ce = e_k\}}{C \cup \{ce = e_1\} \qquad C \cup \{ce \neq e_1, \ ce = e_2 \vee \ldots \vee ce = e_k\}} \ (k > 1)$$

$$\textbf{(SP2)} \quad \frac{C \cup \{ce = e_1 \vee ce = e_2 \vee \ldots \vee ce = e_k\}}{C \cup \{ce = e_1\} \qquad C \cup \{ce = e_2\} \qquad \cdots \qquad C \cup \{ce = e_k\}} \ (k > 1)$$

In the first rule, two sets of clauses are generated such that the VA clause $ce = e_1$ is in one set and the VE clause $ce \neq e_1$ is in the other. In the second rule, k sets of clauses are generated, each containing a unique VA clause $ce = e_i$. The two rules are logically equivalent but may result in different performances. We shall discuss this issue in §5.3.

The soundness and completeness of the simplification rules, inference rules and the splitting rules can be easily established. Specifically, let $C \Rightarrow C'$ denote that C' is derived from C by either of equality resolution, unit resolution, rewriting by VA clause, VE generation or splitting, and let $\Rightarrow^*$ be the reflexive and transitive closure of $\Rightarrow$, then we have the following

Theorem   *A set C of n-complete ground clauses has a model over D_n iff $C \Rightarrow^* C'$ in a finite number of steps, where C' is satisfiable and contains a VA clause $ce = e$ for every cell ce.*

Note that the satisfiability of C' is very easy to check when it contains a VA clause $ce = e$ for every cell ce.

4   A Prototype System

We have developed a prototype System for Enumerating finite Models of first order theories, called SEM. It accepts a set of many-sorted clauses, and produces finite models of fixed sizes, if they exist. The system is implemented in C. Internally it uses ground clauses to represent the constraints of a problem, as described in §2.

In SEM, we implemented the rules **(SP2)**, **(ER2)**, **(ES2)** and the VE generation rules. We also implemented restricted forms of other simplification rules which include: rewriting by VA clauses, **(ER1)** and **(ES1)** when the term t is an element, unit resolution and unit subsumption when one term is a cell and the other is an element. The execution mechanism of the system is as follows. Through splitting, we get some VA clauses. With such clauses, the resolution and rewriting rules can be applied to simplify the constraints. After the simplification, some new VA (or VE) clauses might be generated, which can be used again. A VE clause may be propagated in two ways. Firstly, it reduces the number of possible values for the cell, thus simplifying the corresponding PV clause; secondly, VE generation rules might be applied to produce new VE clauses.

The overall process can be described as a search tree whose internal nodes correspond to the applications of the splitting rule. As the search proceeds, the number of VA and VE clauses increases, while the constraint clauses become simpler or even disappear. Each branch of the search tree ends in two possible states: (1) the clause set contains one VA clause for each cell, and a model is found successfully; or (2) the empty clause is generated, which means the clause set is unsatisfiable.

Let us give a simple example to illustrate the use of SEM. The problem is to decide how to color the Canadian flag with two colors, satisfying certain constraints [10]. The problem can be specified in SEM as follows. (A comment begins with '%' and extends to the end of the line.)

```
%% Sorts

( color  : red, white )
( region : X, Y, Z, U )

%% Functions

{ ne : region region -> BOOL }     % the neighborhood relation
{ f  : region -> color }

%% Variables

< x1, x2 : region >

%% Clauses

[ -ne(x1,x2) | ne(x2,x1) ]          % commutativity of 'ne'
[ -ne(x1,x2) | f(x1) != f(x2) ]     % different colors for neighbors
[ ne(X,Y) ]
[ ne(Y,Z) ]
[ ne(Y,U) ]
[ f(U) = red ]
```

With this as input, SEM will produce a model of the clauses in which $f(X) = f(Z) = f(U) = red, f(Y) = white$.

In contrast to most constraint logic programming systems [6], SEM is not restricted to Horn clauses. Lee and Plaisted give solutions to some non-Horn problems in [9]. These problems can be solved easily with our system. For example, Lee and Plaisted's prover, which was implemented in C Prolog and runs on a DEC workstation 5000/125, spent 31.5 seconds solving the so-called "salt and mustard" problem. SEM used the same clauses as given in [9] and found a solution in 0.06 seconds, running on a SPARCstation 2.

Our system also allows the use of function symbols. Let us give one example of its uses in solving mathematical problems. In [12], McCune gives some single (equational) axioms for group theory. (A single axiom is an equation from which all the group theorems can be derived.) He reports that the search for simpler axioms (by taking instances of the known axioms) failed. There can be two reasons for such failures. One is that the equation is too weak, the other is that the proof is difficult to find. Model generators may play a role here. Consider the equation

$$f(y, g(f(y, f(f(f(z, g(z)), g(f(u, y))), y)))) = u$$

which is an instance of the single axiom (3.1) in [12]. SEM found a 4-element model of it which is not a group. Thus we know that it is *impossible* for this equation to be a single axiom.

5 Experiments and Analysis

SEM can solve a wide range of problems efficiently. Its performance is very competitive, compared with other similar systems. In this section, we describe some experiments with various rules on solving sample problems from discrete mathematics. Some issues will be discussed, based on the analysis of the results.

Besides SEM, we used the following three programs in our experiments: FINDER 3.0.1 [14], MACE 1.0.0 [13], and SATO 2.0 [19]. All of them were implemented in C, and are available to the public. Moreover, each has solved nontrivial previously open questions from mathematics.

Like SEM, FINDER also uses first-order ground clauses. Its rules include unit resolution and negative hyper-resolution, in addition to case analysis. On the other hand, MACE and SATO, as well as DDPP [19] which is written in LISP, are based on the Davis-Putnam algorithm [3] for testing satisfiability of propositional formulas. These three programs rely heavily on the unit propagation rule. But they use different data structures and search strategies.

5.1 Test Problems

Our focus is on the applications to some branches of mathematics. Two representative problems are chosen to test the aforementioned programs. The first one is to find quasigroups satisfying some additional constraints, called the QG5 problem in [4, 15].

The QG5 problem. The axioms for this problem are[2]:

$$f(x,y) \neq f(x,z) \lor y = z$$
$$f(x,z) \neq f(y,z) \lor x = y$$
$$f(x,x) = x$$
$$f(f(f(y,x),y),y) = x$$
$$f(y,f(f(x,y),y)) = x$$
$$f(f(y,f(x,y)),y) = x$$

The second problem asks to find finite noncommutative groups. It is suggested in [17] that, to test the performance of automated theorem provers, one may let them prove certain properties (e.g. commutativity) of finite groups. Such problems are good candidates for model generators.

The NCG problem. The axioms are:

$$f(0,x) = x$$
$$f(x,0) = x$$
$$f(g(x),x) = 0$$
$$f(x,g(x)) = 0$$
$$f(f(x,y),z) = f(x,f(y,z))$$
$$f(1,2) \neq f(2,1)$$

Here f and g denote respectively the multiplication and inverse operations of groups. Without loss of generality, we choose 0 as the identity element of the group. It can be proved that, in a noncommutative group, if there are two elements, a and b, for which $f(a,b) \neq f(b,a)$, then a and b should be different from each other, and neither of them can equal the identity. Thus we assume the two elements are 1 and 2.

We shall use QG5.n and NCG.n to denote the problem of finding n-element models of QG5, and n-element non-commutative groups, respectively. It should be noted that, in experimenting with the different programs, we use the same representation for the same problem. On the NCG problem, we do not use any method for rejecting isomorphism[3]. For each problem, the programs are asked to search for all solutions. Table 1 gives the numbers of models of different sizes.

5.2 Experimental Results

The following four tables show the performances of the four programs on the test problems. The columns of these tables are explained as follows.

– c: number of propositional clauses (for MACE and SATO)

---

[2] An additional clause for eliminating some isomorphic models is not shown here. See [4, 15].

[3] With the least number heuristic [20] for isomorphism elimination, SEM's performance is much better than described in this paper. On the QG5 problem, FINDER also has a more elaborate method for dealing with isomorphism [14].

QG5	order	7	8	9	10	11	12
	models	3	1	0	0	5	0
NCG	order	4	5	6	7	8	9
	models	0	0	18	0	480	0

Table 1. Number of Models

- v: number of propositional variables (for MACE and SATO)
- b: number of branches of the search tree, or,
    number of backtracks (for FINDER)
- t_1: time spent on generating the clauses
- t_2: time spent on search
- m: memory used (for MACE and SEM)

In addition, b' and t_2' denote respectively the number of branches and the search time, when SEM does not use the VE generation rules. The execution times are measured in seconds, and the memory is in K bytes. The data were obtained on a SPARCstation 2. FINDER did not complete the search for NCG.8 within an hour, and MACE aborted the search for NCG.9 due to the limit of memory.

	b	t_1	t_2
QG5.7	3	0.53	0.07
.8	13	1.07	0.10
.9	46	1.98	0.33
.10	341	3.42	3.70
.11	1728	5.53	20.27
.12	11047	19.98	139.92
NCG.4	5	0.01	0.03
.5	44	0.02	0.43
.6	727	0.10	12.23
.7	24237	1.83	539.02

Table 2. Performance of FINDER

5.3 First-Order vs. Propositional Clauses

Finite model generation problems in first-order logic, as well as many finite constraint satisfaction problems, can be transformed to problems in propositional logic. (See, for example, [10, 7].) In this approach, we introduce some propositional variables to represent the values of the cells. For example, if f is a binary

	b	b'	t_1	t_2	t_2'	m
QG5.7	6	12	0.03	0.02	0.02	95
.8	11	66	0.04	0.03	0.06	127
.9	29	509	0.05	0.06	0.32	159
.10	250	2329	0.06	0.62	2.48	223
.11	1231	20351	0.08	2.71	18.96	287
.12	8636	381787	0.13	20.08	365.24	351
NCG.4	30	30	0.01	0.00	0.00	31
.5	123	123	0.01	0.03	0.03	63
.6	734	734	0.03	0.22	0.19	63
.7	4893	4893	0.05	1.89	1.87	95
.8	54288	54288	0.06	24.58	25.07	159
.9	598871	598871	0.10	347.66	343.24	191

Table 3. Performance of SEM

	v	c	b	t_1	t_2	m
QG5.7	392	10508	4	0.39	0.08	300
.8	576	17949	8	0.65	0.12	596
.9	810	28792	14	1.09	0.24	894
.10	1100	43946	37	1.63	0.58	1193
.11	1452	64428	112	2.45	2.38	1786
.12	1872	91363	369	3.52	7.25	2674
NCG.4	108	8976	1	0.37	0.00	294
.5	190	32921	2	1.34	0.05	295
.6	306	96471	18	4.13	1.08	884
.7	462	240771	120	10.44	3.04	2645
.8	664	533162	1110	23.51	175.57	6751
.9	918	1076541		47.12		>16000

Table 4. Performance of MACE

	n	v	c	b	t_1	t_2
QG5.7	343	10461	5	0.16	0.06
.8	512	17887	8	0.32	0.09
.9	729	28714	11	0.55	0.17
.10	1000	43849	21	0.91	0.39
.11	1331	64311	43	1.41	1.06
.12	1728	91223	277	2.18	4.97

Table 5. Performance of SATO

function symbol, then we may use the propositional variable f_{ijk} to denote that $f(i,j) = k$. And, a first-order ground clause like $f(2, f(0,1)) = 0$ can be translated into a set of propositional clauses, i.e., $\{ \neg f_{01k} \vee f_{2k0} \mid 0 \leq k < n \}$.

Thus decision procedures for propositional logic (like the Davis-Putnam procedure [3]) may be used to find finite models of first-order theories. But in some cases, a large number of propositional clauses are needed to represent the problem. (See Table 4 and Table 5.) The memory requirements restrict the uses of propositional clauses in model generation. However, when the number of clauses is not too large, programs based on this approach are very efficient.

One can see from the four tables that, the search trees of MACE and SATO have much fewer branches than those of FINDER and SEM. This is because different splitting rules are used (see §3.3). Let us compare SEM with SATO. The former uses (**SP2**) for splitting, while the latter uses (**SP1**). Suppose during the search, there are k possible values e_i $(1 \leq i \leq k)$ for the cell ce. Then SEM divides the search space into k subspaces, each containing a different assignment $ce = e_i$. In contrast, SATO first considers the case $ce = e_1$; if this assignment leads to a contradiction, then we know $ce \neq e_1$, and the program propagates the effect of this negative unit clause. Such a propagation may reveal the unsatisfiability immediately, eliminating the need for considering the cases $ce = e_2, \ldots, ce = e_k$.

The difference can be illustrated with a simple example. Suppose we want to find QG5.6, and assume that the multiplication table is constructed row by row. After making three choices, both SEM and SATO can determine all the values at the first row, which are:

$$f(0,0) = 0, \ f(0,1) = 2, \ f(0,2) = 1, \ f(0,3) = 4, \ f(0,4) = 5, \ f(0,5) = 3.$$

The next cell is $f(1,0)$ which has three possible values: 3, 4, or 5. SEM assigns each value to the cell, then deduces contradiction from each assignment. On the contrary, SATO first assumes $f(1,0) = 3$ and then assumes $f(1,0) \neq 3$. In each case, contradiction results.

Now let us compare SEM and SATO on constraint propagation. The unit propagation rules in propositional logic are flexible enough to simulate many rules discussed in this paper. However, there are still some differences between the behaviors of the two programs. Suppose we have an assignment $f(1,0) = 3$, then SEM simply replaces all occurrences of $f(1,0)$ by 3. SATO not only performs such propagations, but also propagate the negative unit clauses $f(1,0) \neq k$, for every $k \neq 3$.

In general, it is important to eliminate as many candidate values as possible, before the splitting rule is used. This is crucial for some problems which have many negative constraints (like QG5). From Table 3, we can see the difference in performances when SEM uses and does not use the VE generation rules. For problems like NCG in which most of the clauses are positive equalities, using VE rules has some overhead, but that is negligible.

When choosing the next cell for splitting, a good heuristic is to choose the cell with the fewest possible values. Our experiments confirm that it is indeed helpful. But this is not the focus of this paper.

6 Related Work

Many researchers have worked on constraint satisfaction problems, and a number of algorithms and heuristics have been proposed. (See for example, [8].) Some authors have also discussed them from the deductive point of view [1, 10, 15]. But the constraints studied in this paper are more complicated than those of conventional CSPs. On the other hand, most work on constraint logic programming [6] focus on such specialized domains as Boolean algebra and linear arithmetic.

Bourely, Caferra and Peltier [2] proposed some inference rules for building Herbrand models. Their method is based on constrained formulas which usually contain variables. Infinite models as well as finite ones can be found. The rules discussed in this paper are restricted to ground clauses. But they are very simple, computationally inexpensive and easy to implement.

Slaney, Stickel and Fujita [15] described some experiments with three model generation programs, i.e. FINDER, MGTP, and DDPP, on solving the quasi-group problems. Since the three programs are based on different approaches, implemented in different languages, and accept different specifications, it is hard to compare the constraint propagation mechanisms of these systems.

FINDER and SEM are quite similar in that both of them reason with first-order ground clauses. But there are also some differences. For example, SEM keeps only a limited amount of information. In contrast, one feature of FINDER is that, it derives (using negative hyper-resolution) and stores secondary constraints during the search process, so that the program does not backtrack twice for the same reason [4, 14, 15]. This may be beneficial on some problems. But unrestricted use of such a strategy can result in too many clauses. We believe this is one reason why FINDER is not so efficient on the NCG problem.

The program MGTP [5, 15] uses (range-restricted) clauses with variables. One benefit of such a formalism is that less memory is required. But our experiences tell us, even though ground clauses are used, memory is not a serious problem in most applications.

DDPP, like SATO, is an implementation of the Davis-Putnam algorithm [19]. From the comparison of SEM and SATO made in §5.3, we may see why there is a "large difference between DDPP and FINDER in the matter of branching" [15].

7 Conclusion

The subject of this paper is to study constraint propagation rules for finding finite models. Our experiments show that first-order ground clauses are suitable to represent the constraints in such applications as finding finite algebras. For the purpose of model generation, we defined several special forms of clauses, and studied some rules for transforming the ground clauses. These rules have been implemented in our model generation system SEM. Experiments with SEM show that the transformation rules are quite effective. For example, the VE generation rules help to prune the search tree in some applications.

We also made some comparison between several existing model generators. Our experimental results exhibit the differences between systems based on the propositional logic (like DDPP, SATO and MACE) and those based on first-order ground clauses (like FINDER and SEM). Comparing SEM with FINDER, we find that, it is often beneficial to use a limited number of rules in a restricted manner. This is similar to the case of propositional logic. For example, in practical implementations of the Davis-Putnam algorithm, the pure literal rule is rarely used, and the subsumption rule turns out to be expensive in most cases [13, 19].

Our experimental evaluation is by no means complete. We will investigate which rules and which data structures work best for which problems. We intend to conduct additional experiments with more problems, and compare SEM with more systems, such as SATCHMO [11] and MGTP [5].

References

1. Bibel, W., "Constraint satisfaction from a deductive viewpoint," *Artificial Intelligence* 35 (1988) 401–413.
2. Bourely, C., Caferra, R., and Peltier, N., "A method for building models automatically: Experiments with an extension of OTTER," *Proc. 12th Conf. on Automated Deduction (CADE-12)*, Springer *LNAI* 814 (1994) 72–86.
3. Davis, M., and Putnam, H., "A computing procedure for quantification theory," *J. ACM* 7 (1960) 201–215.
4. Fujita, M., Slaney, J., and Bennett, F., "Automatic generation of some results in finite algebra," *Proc. 13th IJCAI* (1993) 52–57.
5. Hasegawa, R., Koshimura, M., and Fujita, H., "MGTP: A parallel theorem prover based on lazy model generation," *Proc. 11th Conf. on Automated Deduction (CADE-11)* Springer *LNAI* 607 (1992) 776–780.
6. Jaffar, J., and Maher, M.J., "Constraint logic programming: A survey," *J. of Logic Programming* 19/20 (1994) 503–581.
7. Kim, S., and Zhang, H., "ModGen: Theorem proving by model generation," *Proc. AAAI-94*, Seattle (1994) 162–167.
8. Kumar, V., "Algorithms for constraint satisfaction problems: A survey," *AI Magazine* 13 (1992) 32–44.
9. Lee, S.-J., and Plaisted, D. A., "Problem solving by searching for models with a theorem prover," *Artificial Intelligence* 69 (1994) 205–233.
10. Mackworth, A.K., "The logic of constraint satisfaction," *Artificial Intelligence* 58 (1992) 3–20.
11. Manthey, R., and Bry, F., "SATCHMO: A theorem prover implemented in Prolog," *Proc. 9th Conf. on Automated Deduction (CADE-9)*, LNCS 310 (1988) 415–434.
12. McCune, W., "Single axioms for groups and Abelian groups with various operations," *J. of Automated Reasoning* 10 (1993) 1–13.
13. McCune, W., "A Davis-Putnam program and its application to finite first-order model search: Quasigroup existence problems," Technical Report ANL/MCS-TM-194, Argonne National Laboratory (1994).
14. Slaney, J., "FINDER: Finite domain enumerator. Version 3.0 notes and guide," Australian National University (1993).

15. Slaney, J., Stickel, M., and Fujita, M., "Automated reasoning and exhaustive search: Quasigroup existence problems," *Computers and Mathematics with Applications* 29 (1995).

16. Tammet, T., 'Using resolution for deciding solvable classes and building finite models,' *Baltic Computer Science: Selected Papers*, Springer *LNCS* 502 (1991) 33–64.

17. Wos, L., *Automated Reasoning: 33 Basic Research Problems*, Prentice-Hall, Englewood Cliffs, New Jersey (1988).

18. Wos, L., and McCune, W., "Negative paramodulation," *Proc. 8th Conf. on Automated Deduction (CADE-8)*, Springer *LNCS* 230 (1986) J.H. Siekmann (ed.) 229–239.

19. Zhang, H. and Stickel, M., "Implementing the Davis-Putnam algorithm by tries," Technical Report, University of Iowa (1994).

20. Zhang, J., "Constructing finite algebras with FALCON," *J. of Automated Reasoning,* to appear.

Normalizing Narrowing for Weakly Terminating and Confluent Systems[*]

Andreas Werner

ILKD, University of Karlsruhe, D-76128 Karlsruhe, werner@ira.uka.de

Abstract. In this paper we show that narrowing strategies based on normalizing narrowing are complete for weakly terminating and confluent systems. Usually, in completeness results rewriting systems are assumed to be noetherian (and confluent) and this property is essential for the proof. We develop a new method to prove completeness where weak termination (and confluence) suffices. Basic narrowing is known to be incomplete for these systems. We prove that normalizing basic narrowing and its refinements are complete. Using our proof method we also obtain new results for narrowing modulo a (term finite) equational theory. Narrowing modulo equational theories allows us to use efficient built-in E-unification algorithms.

1 Introduction

Narrowing allows us to solve equations in equational theories defined by canonical term rewrite systems. It is also the operational semantics of various logic and functional programming languages [Han94a]. Since narrowing is in its original form extremely inefficient, many optimizations have been proposed during the last years.

Besides developing strategies it is desirable to make them accessible to a large class of rewriting systems by providing completeness results. Relaxing the confluence condition requires to incorporate completion steps into narrowing or to use an E-unification algorithm. We consider in this paper non-terminating systems. Whereas results are already available for some narrowing strategies [Yam88, Han94a, MH94], normalizing narrowing only has been investigated for weakly orthogonal systems [Han94b]. We require the systems to be weakly terminating and confluent. For normalizing narrowing, these are reasonable restrictions: weak termination ensures that each term has a normal form, whereas confluence guarantees that this normal form is unique. In contrast to noetherian systems, there still may exist infinite rewriting derivations.

For example, in [DHK94] higher-order unification is reduced to first-order equational unification. The used term rewriting system $\lambda\sigma$ is not noetherian, but it is weakly normalizing. So the technique developed in this paper can be used to show the completeness of [DHK94].

---

[*] This work was supported by the *Deutsche Forschungsgemeinschaft* as part of the SFB 314 (project S2).

Normalizing narrowing allows us to separate rewriting steps from proper narrowing steps. Whereas rewriting steps preserve solutions each narrowing step leads to a new path in the search space. On the other side, the normalization of goals supports the detection of unsolvable goals [Han94b].

Usually, the completeness of normalizing narrowing is shown by noetherian induction on the rewriting relation. Since the systems we consider in this paper are not necessarily noetherian, this method is not applicable here. We observe that each normalizing narrowing step instantiates at least one variable. Therefore, given a solution σ and a branch that computes σ the size of the substitution that remains to be computed decreases with each step. Using this observation we are able to show the completeness of normalizing narrowing, normalizing basic narrowing and its refinements for weakly terminating and confluent systems. This is surprising since basic narrowing is known to be incomplete for this class of rewriting systems [MH94].

From a practical point of view normalizing basic narrowing allows us to combine basic and normalizing narrowing. Basic narrowing excludes occurrences from narrowing that have been introduced by a narrowing substitution whereas normalizing narrowing separates rewritings steps from proper narrowing steps. A comparison between these strategies based on empirical results can be found in [BKW93].

The method we develop is also applicable to narrowing modulo a term finite equational theory. The class of term finite theories (cf. below) includes important theories like associativity and commutativity. Narrowing modulo equational theories allows us to use efficient built-in E-unification algorithms. This may reduce the search space and lead to more efficient computations [Boc90, Boc93]. A built-in theory may also be considered as a special kind of constraints.

The paper is organized as follows. After some preliminaries on rewriting and narrowing in Section 2 we introduce in Section 3 an ordering on substitutions and give conditions for its well-foundedness. Then, we show the completeness of normalizing narrowing by induction on this ordering (Section 4). Section 5 contains completeness results for strategies based on normalizing narrowing. Finally, we extend our results to equational narrowing (Section 6).

2 Preliminaries

2.1 Rewriting

Throughout this paper, we use the standard terminology of term rewriting [HO80, DJ90, Klp92]. An *occurrence* in a *system of equations* $G : t_1 \doteq u_1 \wedge \ldots \wedge t_n \doteq u_n, n \geq 0$ has the form $m.\omega$ where m is the number of an equation and ω is an occurrence in the equation. $FuOcc(T)$ denotes the set of non-variable occurrences of a system or a term T. An occurrence v is *left* of an occurrence v', denoted $v \lhd v'$, iff there are occurrences o, u, u' and natural numbers i, i' such that $i < i', v = o.i.u$ and $v' = o.i'.u'$. An occurrence v is *below* an occurrence v', denoted $v \succ v'$, iff there exists an occurrence $u \neq \epsilon$ such that $v = v'.u$.

A *substitution* is a mapping σ from variables to terms such that the *domain* $Dom(\sigma) \stackrel{def}{=} \{x \mid \sigma(x) \neq x\}$ is finite. $Im(\sigma) \stackrel{def}{=} \bigcup_{x \in Dom(\sigma)} Var(\sigma(x))$ denotes the set of *variables introduced* by σ. We do not distinguish σ from its canonical extension to terms. Given a set of variables V a substitution σ with $Dom(\sigma) \subseteq V$ is called *variable renaming on* V, if there exists a substitution τ with $\tau \circ \sigma = id_V[V]$. Note that each variable renaming replaces variables by variables. On the other hand, an arbitrary substitution that replaces variables by variables is not necessarily a variable renaming (e.g., consider the substitution $\{x \mapsto z, y \mapsto z\}$).

Let E be an equational theory. Equality with respect to E is denoted by $=_E$. E is called *term finite* iff every equivalence class with respect to $=_E$ on the term algebra is finite, *simple* iff there does not exist an E-unifier for equations of the form $x = t$ where x is a variable that occurs in the non-variable term t, and *regular* iff $s =_E t$ implies $Var(s) = Var(t)$. Each term finite equational theory is simple and each simple equational theory is regular [BHS89]. We identify an equational theory with a set of equations that generates it. If E is the syntactical identity, represented by the set $\emptyset$, then we usually drop the index E.

A term *rewriting system* $\mathcal{R}$ is a set of rules $l \to r$ where $Var(r) \subseteq Var(l)$. For technical reasons we assume that each rewriting system contains the rule $x \doteq x \to true$ which does not have any influence on confluence or (weak) termination of the systems. An *equational rewriting system* $\mathcal{R}, E$ consists of a rewriting systems $\mathcal{R}$ and an equational theory E. *Trivial* systems of equations have the form $true \wedge \ldots \wedge true$.

A term s rewrites to a term t, denoted by $s \to_{\mathcal{R},E} t$, if there is an occurrence $v \in Occ(s)$, a rule $l \to r \in \mathcal{R}$ and a substitution σ such that $s/v =_E \sigma(l)$, $t = s[v \leftarrow \sigma(r)]$. We call a sequence of rewriting steps a *rewriting derivation* or a *reduction*. A term t is *irreducible*, *normalized* or in *normal form*, if there does not exist a term t' with $t \to_{\mathcal{R},E} t'$. A substitution σ is normalized, if $\sigma(x)$ is irreducible for all variables x. A normal form of a term t is a normalized term t' such that $t \stackrel{*}{\to}_{\mathcal{R},E} t'$. A binary relation $\to$ (or the corresponding rewriting system) is called *noetherian* or *terminating* if there are no infinite sequences $t_1 \to t_2 \to \ldots$. The relation is said to be *weakly terminating* if each term t has at least one normal form $t\downarrow$.

2.2 Narrowing

Let $\mathcal{R}, E$ be an equational rewriting system. A system of equations G is *narrowable* to a system of equations G' with *narrowing substitution* δ, denoted by $G \rightsquigarrow_{\mathcal{R},E\,[v,\pi,\delta]} G'$, iff there exist a non-variable occurrence $v \in FuOcc(G)$ and a rule $\pi : l \to r$ in $\mathcal{R}$ such that δ is an element of a complete set of E-unifiers of G/v and l, and $G' = \delta(G)[v \leftarrow \delta(r)]$. If $E = \emptyset$ then we require that δ is the most general unifier of G/v and l. We always assume that G and $l \to r$ have no variables in common. A *narrowing derivation* $G_0 \rightsquigarrow^*_\sigma G_n$ with *narrowing substitution* σ is a sequence of narrowing steps $G_0 \rightsquigarrow_{\delta_1} G_1 \rightsquigarrow_{\delta_2} \ldots \rightsquigarrow_{\delta_n} G_n$, where $\sigma \stackrel{def}{=} (\delta_n \circ \ldots \circ \delta_1) \mid_{Var(G_0)}$ and $n \geq 0$. The narrowing substitution leading from

G_i to G_j, for $0 \leq i \leq j \leq n$, will be denoted by $\lambda_{i,j} \overset{\text{def}}{=} \delta_j \circ \ldots \circ \delta_{i+1}$. In particular, $\lambda_{i,i} = id$, for $i = 0, \ldots, n$.

Given a weakly terminating and confluent equational term rewriting system $\mathcal{R}, E$ and a normalized system of equations G, a *normalizing narrowing step* $G \leadsto_{\mathcal{R},E\,[v,\pi,\delta]}^{\downarrow} G'\!\downarrow$ consists of a narrowing step $G \leadsto_{\mathcal{R},E\,[v,\pi,\delta]} G'$ followed by a normalization $G' \overset{*}{\to}_{\mathcal{R},E} G'\!\downarrow$ with $G'\!\downarrow$ normalized. Note that each normalizing narrowing step can also be considered as a sequence of ordinary narrowing steps.

3 Comparing Solutions

Usually, the completeness of normalizing narrowing is shown by noetherian induction on the rewriting relation [Rét88]. Since the rewriting systems that we consider are not necessarily noetherian this method is not applicable here. We solve this problem using the following observation. Each normalizing narrowing step instantiates some goal variables. Since the goal is normalized this instantiation is not a renaming. Therefore, given a solution σ and a branch that computes σ the size of the substitution that remains to be computed decreases with each step. In the following we therefore introduce an ordering on substitutions and give conditions for its well-foundedness. In Section 4, the completeness of normalizing narrowing will be shown by noetherian induction on this ordering.

Definition 1. Let E be an equational theory, σ, σ' be substitutions, and V, V' be finite set of variables such that $Dom(\sigma) \subseteq V$, $Dom(\sigma') \subseteq V'$. We write $[\sigma, V] \unrhd_{\lambda'}^{E} [\sigma', V']$ or simply $[\sigma, V] \unrhd [\sigma', V']$ iff there exists a substitution λ' such that

(1) $Dom(\lambda') \subseteq V$
(2) $\sigma =_E \sigma' \circ \lambda' \, [V]$
(3) $V' = (V \setminus Dom(\lambda')) \cup Im(\lambda')$.

In the completeness proof σ will be a substitution that has to be computed by narrowing, λ' the substitution of a narrowing step and σ' the (remaining) substitution that has to be computed after the narrowing step. The variable sets are only needed for technical reasons. For example, they ensure that the relation is transitive. Note that this relation is the counterpart to E-subsumption. Whereas E-subsumption allows us to compare σ and λ', $\unrhd$ is a relation between σ and σ'.

Proposition 2. $\unrhd$ *is a quasi ordering.*

Proof. Reflexivity: obviously $[\sigma, V] \unrhd_{id_V} [\sigma, V]$ where id_V is the identity on V. Transitivity: if $[\sigma_1, V_1] \unrhd_{\lambda_{12}} [\sigma_2, V_2]$ and $[\sigma_2, V_2] \unrhd_{\lambda_{23}} [\sigma_3, V_3]$ then $[\sigma_1, V_1] \unrhd_{\lambda_{13}} [\sigma_3, V_3]$ where $\lambda_{13} = (\lambda_{23} \circ \lambda_{12})|_{V_1}$. $\qquad\square$

Definition 3. The ordering generated by $\unrhd$ is denoted by $\rhd$: $[\sigma, V] \rhd [\sigma', V']$ iff $[\sigma, V] \unrhd [\sigma', V']$ and not $[\sigma', V'] \unrhd [\sigma, V]$.

Lemma 4. $\rhd^\emptyset$ *is well-founded.*

Proof. We assign to each pair $[\sigma, V]$ the pair $(|\sigma|_{NV}, |V|)$ where $|t|_{NV}$ denotes the number of non-variable occurrences in t, $|\sigma|_{NV} \stackrel{\text{def}}{=} \sum_{x \in Dom(\sigma)} |\sigma(x)|_{NV}$ denotes the number of non-variable occurrences in the image of σ and $|V|$ is the number of elements in V. We show that $[\sigma, V] \rhd^\emptyset_{\lambda'} [\sigma', V']$ implies $(|\sigma|_{NV}, |V|) > (|\sigma'|_{NV}, |V'|)$ where $(n, m) > (n', m')$ if $n > n'$ or both $n = n'$ and $m > m'$.

Due to the conditions on the substitutions and since $|\rho(x)|_{NV} = 0$ for all substitutions ρ and all variables $x \notin Dom(\rho)$, we have

$$
\begin{aligned}
|\sigma|_{NV} &= \sum_{x \in Dom(\sigma)} |\sigma(x)|_{NV} \\
&= \sum_{x \in V} |\sigma(x)|_{NV} \\
&= \sum_{x \in Dom(\lambda')} |\sigma'(\lambda'(x))|_{NV} + \sum_{x \in V \setminus Dom(\lambda')} |\sigma'(x)|_{NV} \\
&\geq \sum_{x \in Dom(\lambda')} |\lambda'(x)|_{NV} + \sum_{y \in Im(\lambda')} |\sigma'(x)|_{NV} \\
&\quad + \sum_{x \in V \setminus Dom(\lambda')} |\sigma'(x)|_{NV} \\
&= \sum_{x \in Dom(\lambda')} |\lambda'(x)|_{NV} + \sum_{x \in Dom(\sigma')} |\sigma'(x)|_{NV} \\
&= |\sigma'|_{NV} + |\lambda'|_{NV}.
\end{aligned}
$$

Hence, the cases $|\lambda'|_{NV} \neq 0$ or $|\sigma|_{NV} > |\sigma'|_{NV}$ are trivial. Assume $|\lambda'|_{NV} = 0$ and $|\sigma|_{NV} = |\sigma'|_{NV}$. Thus, $\lambda'(x)$ is a variable for all variables x. Hence, $|V| \geq |V'|$. Since the case $|V| > |V'|$ is trivial, we assume $|V| = |V'|$. Due to the third condition of Definition 1, λ' is injective on $Dom(\lambda')$. Thus, the substitution $\lambda \stackrel{\text{def}}{=} \{\lambda'(x) \mapsto x \mid x \in Dom(\lambda')\}$ is well-defined. Furthermore, we have $Dom(\lambda) \subseteq V'$. Since $|V| = |V'|$ and $V' = (V \setminus Dom(\lambda')) \cup Im(\lambda')$ it follows $V = (V' \setminus Dom(\lambda)) \cup Im(\lambda)$. Let $x \in V' = (V \setminus Dom(\lambda')) \cup Im(\lambda')$.

- If $x \in V \setminus (Dom(\lambda') \cup Im(\lambda'))$ then $\sigma(x) = (\sigma' \circ \lambda')(x)$ and $x \notin Im(\lambda') = Dom(\lambda)$ implies $\sigma(\lambda(x)) = \sigma'(x)$.
- Otherwise, $x \in Im(\lambda')$. Hence, there is $y \in V$ with $\lambda'(y) = x$. Thus, $\sigma(\lambda(x)) = \sigma(y) = \sigma'(\lambda'(y)) = \sigma'(x)$.

We conclude $[\sigma', V'] \unrhd^\emptyset [\sigma, V]$ in contradiction to the definition of $\rhd^\emptyset$. $\square$

Using the well-foundedness of $\rhd^\emptyset$ we are able to show that $\rhd^E$ is well-founded for term finite equational theories E.

Lemma 5. *If E is term finite then $\rhd^E$ is well-founded.*

Proof. Let E be term finite and assume there is an infinite sequence $[\sigma_1, V_1] \rhd^E_{\lambda_1}$ $[\sigma_2, V_2] \rhd^E_{\lambda_2} \dots$. Since E is term finite, obviously, the equivalence class of $t_1 \stackrel{\text{def}}{=} \sigma_1(k(x_1, \dots, x_n))$ where $V_1 = \{x_1, \dots, x_n\}$ and k is a new symbol not occurring in E is finite. Let $t_i \stackrel{\text{def}}{=} (\sigma_i \circ \lambda_{i-1} \circ \dots \circ \lambda_1)(k(x_1, \dots, x_n))$ for $i = 1, 2 \dots$. Then we obtain by induction that $t_1 =_E t_i$ for $i = 1, 2 \dots$. Since the equivalence class of t_1 is finite there is an infinite sequence of terms $t_{i_1}, t_{i_2}, \dots$ such that $i_j < i_{j+1}$ and $t_{i_j} = t_{i_{j+1}}$ for $j = 1, 2, \dots$. By construction we have $[\sigma_{i_j}, V_{i_j}] \rhd^\emptyset [\sigma_{i_{j+1}}, V_{i_{j+1}}]$ for $j = 1, 2, \dots$. Hence, $\rhd^\emptyset$ is not well-founded in contradiction to Lemma 4. $\square$

The following result will later guarantee that the substitutions in the completeness proof are comparable with respect to $\rhd$.

Lemma 6. *The following properties are equivalent:*

- *E is simple.*
- *For all substitutions σ, σ', λ, λ' and for all sets of variables V, V', if $[\sigma, V] \unrhd^E_{\lambda'} [\sigma', V']$ and $[\sigma', V'] \unrhd^E_\lambda [\sigma, V]$ then λ' is a renaming substitution on V.*

Proof. Let E be simple and assume $[\sigma, V] \unrhd^E_{\lambda'} [\sigma', V']$ and $[\sigma', V'] \unrhd^E_\lambda [\sigma, V]$.

- First case: there is a $x \in Dom(\lambda')$ such that $\lambda'(x)$ is not a variable. We show that this contradicts the assumption that E is simple.
  Since
  - $\sigma =_E \sigma' \circ \lambda'[V]$,
  - $\sigma' =_E \sigma \circ \lambda[V']$ and
  - $V' = (V \setminus Dom(\lambda')) \cup Im(\lambda')$

  we obtain $\sigma =_E \sigma \circ \lambda \circ \lambda'[V]$. Hence, σ is an E-unifier of all equations in the system $x_1 \doteq \lambda(\lambda'(x_1)) \wedge \ldots \wedge x_n \doteq \lambda(\lambda'(x_n))$ where $Dom((\lambda \circ \lambda')|_V) = \{x_1, \ldots, x_n\}$. Since
  - $x_i \in V$,
  - $V = (((V \setminus Dom(\lambda')) \cup Im(\lambda')) \setminus Dom(\lambda)) \cup Im(\lambda)$,
  - $Dom(\lambda') \subseteq V$ and
  - $Dom(\lambda) \subseteq (V \setminus Dom(\lambda')) \cup Im(\lambda')$

  we also get $x_i \in \bigcup_{j=1}^n Var(\lambda(\lambda'(x_j)))$ for $i = 1, \ldots, n$.
  We show by induction on n that if there is an E-unifier ρ of a system

  $$G_n \stackrel{\text{def}}{=} x_1 \doteq t_1 \wedge \ldots \wedge x_n \doteq t_n$$

  where $x_i \in \bigcup_{j=1}^n Var(t_j)$ for $i = 1, \ldots, n$, $x_i \neq x_j$ for $i \neq j$, and t_{i_0} is not a variable for some $i_0 \in \{1, \ldots, n\}$ then E is not simple.
  - The case $n = 0$ is impossible. If $n = 1$ then there exists an E-unifier for $x_1 \doteq t_1$ where t_1 is not a variable and where x_1 occurs in t_1. Hence E is not simple.
  - Let $n > 1$ and assume without restriction $i_0 = 1$. If x_1 occurs in t_1 then we again immediately conclude that E is not simple. Hence x_1 occurs in t_{i_1} for some $i_1 \neq 1$. Consider the system

    $$G_{n-1} \stackrel{\text{def}}{=} \tau(x_2 \doteq t_2 \wedge \ldots \wedge x_n \doteq t_n)$$

    where $\tau \stackrel{\text{def}}{=} \{x_1 \mapsto t_1\}$. Since $\rho(x_1) =_E \rho(t_1)$ we conclude that ρ is an E-unifier of G_{n-1}. Trivially, $x_i \in \bigcup_{j=2}^n Var(\tau(t_j))$ for $i = 2, \ldots, n$, and $\tau(t_{i_1})$ is not a variable. Hence, by induction hypothesis E is not simple.
- Second case: $\lambda'(x)$ is a variable for all $x \in Dom(\lambda')$. We may also assume that $\lambda(x)$ is a variable for all $x \in Dom(\lambda)$ since otherwise E is not simple by the first case. Hence $\lambda(\lambda'(x))$ is a variable for all $x \in Dom(\lambda) \cup Dom(\lambda')$.

Since

- $V' = (V \setminus Dom(\lambda')) \cup Im(\lambda')$,
- $V = (V' \setminus Dom(\lambda)) \cup Im(\lambda)$,
- $Dom(\lambda') \subseteq V$,
- $Dom(\lambda) \subseteq V'$

we conclude $Dom((\lambda \circ \lambda')|_V) = Im((\lambda \circ \lambda')|_V) = \bigcup_{x \in Dom((\lambda \circ \lambda')|_V)} \{\lambda(\lambda'(x))\}$.

Hence, the substitution $\rho \stackrel{\text{def}}{=} \{\lambda(\lambda'(x)) \mapsto x \mid x \in Dom((\lambda \circ \lambda')|_V)\}$ is well-defined and $\rho \circ \lambda \circ \lambda' = id_V[V]$ holds. Therefore, we define $\tau \stackrel{\text{def}}{=} \rho \circ \lambda$.

Now assume that E is not simple. Let σ be an E-unifier of $x \doteq t$ where x in $Var(t)$. If we define

- $V \stackrel{\text{def}}{=} Dom(\sigma) \cup Var(t) \cup \{x\}$,
- $V' \stackrel{\text{def}}{=} V$,
- $\sigma' \stackrel{\text{def}}{=} \sigma$,
- $\lambda' \stackrel{\text{def}}{=} \{x \mapsto t\}$ and
- $\lambda \stackrel{\text{def}}{=} id_{V'}$

we obtain $[\sigma, V] \geq^E_{\lambda'} [\sigma', V']$ and $[\sigma', V'] \geq^E_\lambda [\sigma, V]$. However, λ' is not a variable renaming. $\qquad \square$

4 Completeness of Normalizing Narrowing

In this section we use the ordering introduced in the previous one to prove the completeness of normalizing narrowing for weakly terminating and confluent rewriting system. For the reason of simplicity we consider in the following sections only $E = \emptyset$ and explain how to drop this restriction in Section 6.

When we prove the completeness of some strategies based on normalizing narrowing we assume that the rewriting derivation that we construct below has a special form. We assume that the rules in $\mathcal{R}$ are ordered by a total well-founded ordering $<$.

Definition 7. A rewriting step $G \to_{[v, \pi, \tau]} G'$ is called a *left reduction step* iff

- all subterms G/ω with ω left of v are irreducible ("leftmost")
- all subterms G/ω with ω below v are irreducible ("innermost")
- G cannot be reduced at occurrence v by a rule π' with $\pi' < \pi$ ("minimal rule").

A rewriting derivation is called a *left reduction* iff all steps are left reduction steps.

If the rewriting system is terminating and confluent then for each term there exists a unique left reduction to its normal form [BKW93]. Since in this paper we only require weak termination and confluence, it may happen that left reductions do not terminate. For example, given the rules $a \to f(a)$ and $f(x) \to b$, the term $f(a)$ has a normal form, but we do not reach it by a left reduction. However, left reduction steps still exist and are unique.

Proposition 8. *Let $\mathcal{R}$ be a weakly terminating and confluent rewriting system, T be a system of equations and $T\!\!\downarrow$ be the normal form of T such that $T \neq T\!\!\downarrow$. Then there exists a unique left reduction step $T \to T'$ such that $T' \overset{*}{\to} T\!\!\downarrow$.*

Proof. Similar to the proof of Proposition 10 in [BKW92]. $\qquad\qquad\Box$

We use the standard method to prove completeness of narrowing and its strategies. Since the rewriting system is confluent a substitution μ is a $\mathcal{R}$-unifier of a system G iff $\mu(G) \overset{*}{\to} true \wedge \ldots \wedge true$. Therefore, is suffices to show that if there is a derivation $\mu(G) \overset{*}{\to} true \wedge \ldots \wedge true$ then there exists one with a corresponding narrowing derivation $G \leadsto \overset{*}{\to}_\sigma true \wedge \ldots \wedge true$ that uses the same rules at the same occurrences such that $\sigma \leq_\mathcal{R} \mu[V]$. Strategies usually require that the narrowing derivation and the rewriting derivation have special properties.

Lemma 9. *Let R be a rewriting system and let G be a system of equations. If μ is a normalized substitution and V a set of variables such that $Var(G) \cup Dom(\mu) \subseteq V$, then for every rewriting step*

$$H_0 \overset{\mathrm{def}}{=} \mu(G) \to_{[v_1, l_1 \to r_1, \tau_1]} H_1$$

there exist a normalized substitution τ and a narrowing step

$$G_0 \overset{\mathrm{def}}{=} G \leadsto_{[v_1, l_1 \to r_1, \delta_1]} G_1$$

using the same rewriting rule at the same occurrence such that $\mu = \tau \circ \delta_1 \,[V]$ and $H_0 = \tau(\delta_1(G_0))$, $H_1 = \tau(G_1)$.

Proof. The lemma is an immediate consequence of the Lifting Lemma of Hullot (see for example Theorem 6 in [BKW93]) and its proof. $\qquad\qquad\Box$

Theorem 10. *Let $\mathcal{R}$ be a weakly terminating and confluent rewriting system. Consider a normalized system of equations G, a normalized substitution μ and a set of variables V such that $Var(G) \cup Dom(\mu) \subseteq V$. If there is a derivation $H \overset{\mathrm{def}}{=} \mu(G) \overset{*}{\to} Triv$ to some trivial system $Triv$, then there exist a rewriting derivation*

$$H = H_0' \to_{[v_1, \pi_1]} H_1 \overset{*}{\to} H_1' \to \; \cdots \; \to_{[v_n, \pi_n]} H_n \overset{*}{\to} H_n' = Triv,$$

where the rewrite steps $H_i' \to_{[v_{i+1}, \pi_{i+1}]} H_{i+1}$, $i = 0, \ldots, n-1$, are left reduction steps, and a normalizing narrowing derivation

$$G = G_0\!\!\downarrow \leadsto_{[v_1, \pi_1, \delta_1]} G_1 \overset{*}{\to} G_1\!\!\downarrow \leadsto \; \cdots \; \leadsto_{[v_n, \pi_n, \delta_n]} G_n \overset{*}{\to} G_n\!\!\downarrow = Triv$$

which uses the same rules at the same occurrences. Furthermore, there is a normalized substitution λ such that

- $\lambda \circ \delta_n \circ \ldots \circ \delta_1 = \mu \,[V]$
- $H_i = (\lambda \circ \delta_n \circ \ldots \circ \delta_{i+1})\,(G_i), i = 1, \ldots, n$

$$- H_i' = (\lambda \circ \delta_n \circ \ldots \circ \delta_{i+1})(G_i\downarrow), i = 0, \ldots, n.$$

Proof. By noetherian induction on the ordering $\rhd$.

If $H = \mu(G)$ is trivial, then G is trivial and the theorem holds with $\lambda = \mu$ and $Triv = H$. Otherwise, by Proposition 8 there exists a left reduction step $H \to_{[v_1,\pi_1]} H_1$ such that $H_1 \overset{*}{\to} Triv$. Lemma 9 allows us to lift the first step in this reduction to a narrowing step $G \leadsto_{[v_1,\pi_1,\delta_1]} G_1$. Furthermore, there is a normalized substitution τ with $\mu = \tau \circ \delta_1 \ [V]$ and $H_1 = \tau(G_1)$. We may assume $Dom(\tau) \subseteq V \cup Im(\delta_1|_V)$. Let $G_1 \overset{*}{\to} G_1\downarrow$. Since $\to$ is stable under substitutions we get a corresponding rewriting derivation $H_1 = \tau(G_1) \overset{*}{\to} \tau(G_1\downarrow) = H_1'$. Since $\to$ is confluent, we have $H_1' \overset{*}{\to} Triv$.

Let $V' \overset{\text{def}}{=} (V \setminus Dom(\delta_1)) \cup Im(\delta_1|_V)$. Thus, we obtain $[\sigma, V] \unrhd_{\delta_1|_V}^\emptyset [\tau, V']$. Assume $[\tau, V'] \unrhd^\emptyset [\sigma, V]$. From $G \leadsto_{[v_1,\pi_1,\delta_1]} G_1$ we conclude $\delta_1(G) \to G_1$. Since $E = \emptyset$ is simple, by Lemma 6 there exists a substitution ψ such that $G = \psi(\delta_1(G)) \to \psi(G_1)$ in contradiction to the assumption that G is normalized. Thus, $[\sigma, V] \rhd_{\delta_1|_V}^\emptyset [\tau, V']$. By applying the induction hypothesis to H_1', we obtain a derivation

$$H_1' \to_{[v_2,\pi_2]} H_2 \overset{*}{\to} H_2' \to \ldots \to_{[v_n,\pi_n]} H_n \overset{*}{\to} H_n' = Triv,$$

with left reduction steps $H_i' \to_{[v_{i+1},\pi_{i+1}]} H_{i+1}$, $i = 1, \ldots, n-1$, and a corresponding normalizing narrowing derivation

$$G_1\downarrow \leadsto_{[v_2,\pi_2,\delta_2]} G_2 \overset{*}{\to} G_2\downarrow \leadsto \ldots \leadsto_{[v_n,\pi_n,\delta_n]} G_n \overset{*}{\to} G_n\downarrow = Triv.$$

Furthermore, there is a normalized substitution λ such that

- $\lambda \circ \delta_n \circ \ldots \circ \delta_2 = \tau \ [V']$,
- $H_i = (\lambda \circ \delta_n \circ \ldots \circ \delta_{i+1})(G_i)$, for $i = 2, \ldots, n$, and
- $H_i' = (\lambda \circ \delta_n \circ \ldots \circ \delta_{i+1})(G_i\downarrow)$, for $i = 1, \ldots, n$.

From $\mu = \tau \circ \delta_1 \ [V]$ and $\tau = \lambda \circ \delta_n \circ \ldots \circ \delta_2 \ [V']$, we get $\lambda \circ \delta_n \circ \ldots \circ \delta_1 = \mu \ [V]$. $\square$

Theorem 11. *Normalizing narrowing is complete for confluent and weakly terminating rewrite systems.*

Proof. It suffices to consider normalized goals since a goal and its normal form have the same $\mathcal{R}$-unifiers. A substitution τ is a $\mathcal{R}$-unifier of a system of equations G iff $\mu(G) \overset{*}{\to} true \wedge \ldots \wedge true$ where $\mu \overset{\text{def}}{=} \{\tau(x)\downarrow \mid x \in Dom(\tau)\}$ is the normal form of τ. Since $\mu(G) \overset{*}{\to} true \wedge \ldots \wedge true$ implies there is a normalizing narrowing derivation $G \leadsto_\sigma^{\downarrow *} true \wedge \ldots \wedge true$ such that $\sigma \leq \mu =_\mathcal{R} \tau[V]$ where $Dom(\mu) \cup Var(G) \subseteq V$, normalizing narrowing is complete. $\square$

Normalizing narrowing is correct since $G \leadsto_\sigma^{\downarrow *} true \wedge \ldots \wedge true$ implies $\sigma(G) \overset{*}{\to} true \wedge \ldots \wedge true$.

Extensions

Now we know that ordinary and normalizing narrowing are complete for confluent and weakly terminating systems. In the first case we do not reduce the obtained goal after pure narrowing steps, in the second case we reduce it to its normal form. The following example shows that we lose completeness if we arbitrarily rewrite goals after a narrowing step.

Example 1. Consider the following rewriting system $\mathcal{R}$:

$$f(g(x)) \rightarrow g(f(x)) \qquad f(g(x)) \rightarrow c$$
$$g(f(x)) \rightarrow f(g(x))$$

Obviously, $\mathcal{R}$ is confluent and weakly terminating. The substitution $\{y \mapsto f(x)\}$ is a $\mathcal{R}$-unifier of the goal $g(y) \doteq c$. However, there only exists one (non-terminating) narrowing derivation:

$$g(y) \doteq c \leadsto_{\{y \mapsto f(x)\}} f(g(x)) \doteq c \xrightarrow{*} g(f(x)) \doteq c$$
$$\leadsto_{id_V} \qquad f(g(x)) \doteq c \xrightarrow{*} g(f(x)) \doteq c$$
$$\dots$$

In this example there exists a non-trivial critical pair. If the system is weakly orthogonal then it is possible to simplify goals without losing completeness (see [Han94b, LW91] for details). Another possibility to ensure completeness is to require termination instead of weak termination.

In [Höl 89] it is stated that normalizing narrowing is complete for confluent and terminating *conditional* term rewriting systems without extra variables (i.e. $Var(c) \cup Var(r) \subseteq Var(l)$ for all rules $l \rightarrow r \Leftarrow c$). However, this is not true. We observed that each unconditional normalizing narrowing step instantiates at least one variable and used this to prove the completeness of normalizing narrowing. In the conditional case there may be normalizing narrowing steps which do not instantiate any goal variable but which are also not rewriting steps. This is the reason why normalizing narrowing is not complete for conditional systems, even if they are confluent, terminating and do not contain extra variables.

Example 2. Consider the following rules:

$$b \rightarrow a \qquad f(d, b) \rightarrow c \qquad f(x, a) \rightarrow c \Leftarrow f(x, b) \doteq c$$

This system is noetherian and confluent. Although the substitution $\mu \overset{\text{def}}{=} \{x \mapsto d\}$ is a solution of the goal $f(x, a) \doteq c$ there is only one (non-terminating) normalizing narrowing derivation

$$f(x, a) \doteq c \leadsto f(x, b) \doteq c \wedge c \doteq c \xrightarrow{*} f(x, a) \doteq c \wedge true \leadsto \dots$$

If the rewriting relation is *almost unconditional* (i.e. a term is irreducible iff it is irreducible when we neglect the conditions) then the techniques developed in the previous sections can be used to obtain completeness results. In [BW94] we required decreasing and confluent rewriting systems to restore completeness.

5 Strategies Based on Normalizing Narrowing

In the following we obtain completeness results for refinements of normalizing narrowing. After an introduction to the strategies we explain why they are not complete for non-normalizing narrowing. Then we illustrate that these problems do not occur if we normalize the goals after each narrowing step. Finally, we give the completeness proofs.

The necessity to develop strategies for narrowing emerged from the observation that in its original form narrowing is too inefficient since there are many redundant derivations [BKW93]. Basic narrowing [Hul80, Rét87] restricts the application of narrowing steps to occurrences that do not have been introduced by a narrowing substitution. Left-to-right basic narrowing additionally excludes occurrences left of narrowing occurrences [Her86]. It can be shown that each leftmost-innermost rewriting derivation generates a corresponding left-to-right basic narrowing derivation (similar to Section 4).

Definition 12. Given a rewriting step $T \to_{[v,l \to r]} T'$, we call an occurrence ω in T an *antecedent* of the occurrence ω' in T' iff

- $\omega = \omega'$ and neither $\omega \succeq v$ nor $v \preceq \omega$ or
- there exists an occurrence ρ' of a variable x in r such that $\omega' = v.\rho'.o$ and $\omega = v.\rho.o$ where ρ is an occurrence of the same variable x in l.

Definition 13. Let G be a system of equations, U a set of occurrences of G, and $\pi : l \to r$ a rewriting rule. For a narrowing or rewriting step we define

$$LB(U, G \leadsto_{[v,\pi,\delta]} G') \stackrel{\text{def}}{=} (U \setminus \{u \mid u \triangleleft v \text{ or } u \succeq v\}) \cup \{v.o \mid o \in FuOcc(r)\}$$

$$LB(U, G \to_{[v,\pi,\delta]} G') \stackrel{\text{def}}{=} (U \setminus \{u \mid u \succeq v\}) \cup \{v.o \mid o \in FuOcc(r)\}$$
$$\cup \{v.o \mid o \in FuOcc(\delta(r)) \setminus FuOcc(r) \text{ and all antecedents of } v.o \text{ are in } U\}$$

respectively. Given an ordinary or a normalizing narrowing derivation of the form

$$G'_0 \quad \leadsto_{[v_1,l_1 \to r_1,\delta_1]} \quad G_1 = G_{10} \to \ldots \to G_{1k_1} = G'_1$$
$$\vdots$$
$$G'_{n-1} \leadsto_{[v_n,l_n \to r_n,\delta_n]} G_n = G_{n0} \to \ldots \to G_{nk_n} = G'_n$$

the sets of *left-to-right basic occurrences* are inductively defined by

$$LB'_0 \stackrel{\text{def}}{=} FuOcc(G'_0)$$
$$LB_i \stackrel{\text{def}}{=} LB(LB'_{i-1}, G'_{i-1} \leadsto_{[v_i,\pi_i,\delta_i]} G_i)$$
$$LB_{ij} \stackrel{\text{def}}{=} LB(LB_{i,j-1}, G_{i,j-1} \to_{[v_{ij},\pi_{ij},\delta_{ij}]} G_{i,j})$$

with $LB_{i0} = LB_i$ and $LB'_i = LB_{i,k_i}$, for $i = 1, \ldots n$ and $j = 1, \ldots, k_i$. For a *left-to-right basic derivation* we require that $v_i \in LB'_{i-1}$, for all $i = 1, \ldots, n$, and $v_{ij} \in LB_{i,j-1}$, for all $i = 1, \ldots, n$ and $j = 1, \ldots, k_i$.

Example 3 [MH94]. Consider the following rewriting system:

$$f(x) \rightarrow g(x,x) \qquad g(a,b) \rightarrow c$$
$$a \rightarrow b \qquad g(b,b) \rightarrow f(a)$$

This rewriting system is confluent and weakly terminating. Figure 1, given in [MH94], illustrates that although there are solutions for the goals $f(a) \doteq c$ and $g(x,x) \doteq c$ they cannot be obtained by left-to-right basic narrowing. Occurrences that are not left-to-right basic are underlined, non-left-to-right-basic narrowing steps are marked with $*$.

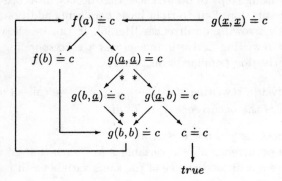

Fig. 1. Narrowing derivations starting from $f(a) \doteq c$ and $g(x,x) \doteq c$.

However, *normalizing* left-to-right narrowing is able to solve these goals. The normal form of the goal $f(a) \doteq c$ is the trivial goal *true*. Therefore, solving it only requires normalizing it which is done before the first narrowing step. On the other-hand, the goal $g(x,x) \doteq c$ is normalized. If we perform a pure narrowing step using the last rule, we obtain the narrowing substitution $\{x \mapsto b\}$ and the goal $f(a) \doteq c$ which can be normalized to the trivial goal *true*. This derivation is left-to-right basic, it is even LSE (see below). The underlined occurrences are left-to-right basic if we obtain the corresponding equations by rewriting steps instead of narrowing steps. Note that the formulas for left-to-right basic occurrences are different for rewriting and narrowing steps.

This example explains why normalizing the goals solves the incompleteness problem. Steps that are not adequate for the strategy but which are necessary to solve a goal are performed by normalization instead of narrowing. For example, the step from $f(a) \doteq c$ to $g(a,a) \doteq c$ is not innermost in the corresponding (identical) rewrite derivation. Thus, performing it as a narrowing step excludes further steps whereas this does not happen if we perform it as a rewriting step.

In [BKW92, BKW93, BW94] we introduced LSE narrowing as a refinement of left-to-right basic narrowing. LSE narrowing derivations are just the narrowing derivations corresponding to left reductions. The substitution $\lambda_{i,n}$ used in the LSE-Tests is the narrowing substitution leading from $G_i\downarrow$ to $G_n\downarrow$ (cf. Preliminaries).

Definition 14. In a normalizing narrowing derivation

$$G_0\downarrow \quad \leadsto_{[v_1,\pi_1,\delta_1]} \quad G_1 \overset{*}{\to} G_1\downarrow$$
$$\vdots$$
$$G_{n-1}\downarrow \leadsto_{[v_n,\pi_n,\delta_n]} G_n \overset{*}{\to} G_n\downarrow$$

the step $G_{n-1}\downarrow \leadsto G_n \overset{*}{\to} G_n\downarrow$ is called a *LSE step* iff the following three conditions are satisfied for all $i \in \{0,\ldots,n-1\}$:

(Left-Test) The subterms of $\lambda_{i,n}(G_i\downarrow)$ which lie left of v_{i+1} are irreducible.
(Sub-Test) The subterms of $\lambda_{i,n}(G_i\downarrow)$ which lie below v_{i+1} are irreducible.
(Epsilon-Test) The term $\lambda_{i,n}(G_i\downarrow/v_{i+1})$ is not reducible at occurrence ϵ by a rule π with $\pi < \pi_{i+1}$.

A normalizing narrowing derivation is called a *normalizing LSE narrowing derivation* iff all steps are LSE steps.

Theorem 15. *Normalizing LSE narrowing is complete for weakly terminating and confluent rewriting systems.*

Proof. We show that the narrowing derivation constructed in Theorem 10 is LSE. Assume that the step $G_{m-1}\downarrow \leadsto_{[v_m,\pi_m,\delta_m]} G_m\downarrow$ is not LSE, for m in $\{1,\ldots,n\}$. Then there exists a $i \in \{0,\ldots,m-1\}$ such that

(1) $\lambda_{i,m}(G_i\downarrow)$ is reducible at an occurrence v left of v_{i+1} or
(2) $\lambda_{i,m}(G_i\downarrow)$ is reducible at an occurrence v below v_{i+1} or
(3) $\lambda_{i,m}(G_i\downarrow)$ is reducible at occurrence v_{i+1} with a rule smaller than π_{i+1}.

Since we have $H_i' = (\lambda \circ \lambda_{m,n} \circ \lambda_{i,m})(G_i\downarrow)$ and $\to$ is stable under substitutions we conclude that one of the properties (1) to (3) must hold with H_i' in place of $\lambda_{i,m}(G_i\downarrow)$. This means that $H_i' \to_{[v_{i+1},\pi_{i+1}]} H_{i+1}$ is not a left reduction step in contradiction to Theorem 10. $\square$

Theorem 16. *Let $\mathcal{R}$ be a weakly terminating and confluent rewriting system. Any normalizing LSE narrowing derivation $G \leadsto^{\downarrow*} Triv$ to a trivial system $Triv$ is also a normalizing left-to-right basic narrowing derivation.*

Corollary 17. *Let $\mathcal{R}$ be a weakly terminating and confluent rewriting system. Then normalizing left-to-right basic narrowing is complete.*

For Theorem 16 and Corollary 17 we require in [BKW93] termination and confluence. However the proofs are still valid for weakly terminating and confluent systems. The same holds for the following optimality results of LSE narrowing. The narrowing substitution of any LSE derivation is normalized. Furthermore, we obtain that two arbitrary normalizing LSE derivations cannot compute the same narrowing substitution.

An advantage of our method to prove completeness is that is was possible to show the completeness of strategies by slight modifications of the well-known proofs for noetherian and confluent systems. As a consequence of these results it is possible to restore the completeness of (non-normalizing) basic narrowing and its refinements by treating narrowing steps that do not instantiate any variable in the goal as rewriting step with respect to the strategy.

6 Narrowing Modulo an Equational Theory

In the following we extend the obtained results to narrowing modulo an equational theory. It is possible to use similar arguments as in the previous sections. However, the presence of an equational theory leads to more complicated proofs.

Theorem 18 [Wer95]. *Let $\mathcal{R}$ be a rewriting system and let E be a term finite equational theory such that $\mathcal{R}, E$ is Church-Rosser modulo E and coherent modulo E, and $\rightarrow_{\mathcal{R},E}$ is weakly terminating. Then normalizing narrowing and normalizing LSE narrowing are complete.*

The proofs in [JKK83] for unconditional narrowing modulo an equational theory and in [Boc90, Boc93] for decreasing equational conditional rewriting systems use well-founded orderings on goals. In contrast, our proof is based on the ordering $\triangleright$, which is an ordering on substitutions.

Similar to Proposition 8 it is possible to show that there exist left reduction steps. However, due to the presence of an equational theory, they may not be unique.

Example 4. Consider the following equational rewriting system:

$$E : \quad x + y \quad \dot{=} \quad y + x$$

$$\mathcal{R} : \quad s(x) + y \rightarrow s(x + y)$$

Then there are two different left reduction steps starting form $s(0) + s(s(0))$:

$$s(0) + s(s(0)) \ \rightarrow_{\mathcal{R},E} \ s(0 + s(s(0))) \qquad s(0) + s(s(0)) \ \rightarrow_{\mathcal{R},E} \ s(s(0) + s(0))$$

due to the fact that there are two different E-matching substitutions.

As a consequence it is not possible anymore to show that two different LSE derivations cannot generate the same substitution.

7 Conclusions

We developed a new method for proving the completeness of normalizing narrowing and obtained various new completeness results including results for conditional and equational narrowing. In particular, we showed that normalizing goals is in fact a way of restoring the completeness of narrowing strategies.

Acknowledgments: I am grateful to Claude Kirchner for fruitful discussion on the topic of the paper and on noetherian equational theories. I want to thank Alexander Bockmayr for fruitful discussion and comments on a previous version of this paper. I also want to thank Aart Middeldorp and the referees for their comments.

References

[BHS89] H.-J. Bückert, A. Herold and M. Schmidt-Schauß. On Equational Theories, Unification and Decidability. *Journal of Symbolic Computation*, 1989, volume 8, number 1 & 2, 1989, Special issue on unification, part two, pages 3 - 50.

[BKW92] A. Bockmayr, S. Krischer and A. Werner. An Optimal Narrowing Strategy for General Canonical Systems. In *CTRS 1992*, LNCS 656, Springer-Verlag, 1993.

[BKW93] A. Bockmayr, S. Krischer and A. Werner. *Narrowing Strategies for Arbitrary Canonical Systems*. Interner Bericht 22/93, Fakultät für Informatik, University of Karlsruhe, 1993. To appear in *Fundamenta Informaticae*.

[Boc90] A. Bockmayr. *Contributions to the Theory of Logic-Functional Programming*. PhD thesis, Fakultät für Informatik, Univ. Karlsruhe, 1990, (in German).

[Boc93] A. Bockmayr. Conditional Narrowing Modulo a Set of Equations. *Applicable Algebra in Engineering, Communication and Computing*, 1993, vol. 4, pages 147 - 168.

[BW94] A. Bockmayr and A. Werner. LSE Narrowing for Decreasing Conditional Term Rewrite Systems. *CTRS 1994*, Jerusalem, Israel, 1994, to appear in LNCS.

[DHK94] G. Dowek, T. Hardin, C. Kirchner. *Higher-order unification via explicit substitutions*. Technical Report, December 1994. To appear in Proceedings Logic in Computer Science 1995.

[DJ90] N. Dershowitz and J.P. Jouannaud. Rewrite Systems, in: *Handbook of Theoretical Computer Science*, volume B, pages 244 - 320, Elsevier, 1990.

[Han94a] M. Hanus. The Integration of Functions into Logic Programming: From Theory to Practice. *J. of Logic Programming*, 1994, vol. 19 & 20, pages 583 - 628.

[Han94b] M. Hanus. Combining Lazy Narrowing and Simplification. In *Proceedings PLILP'94*, 1994, Madrid, LNCS 844, Springer-Verlag, pages 370 - 384.

[Her86] A. Herold. *Narrowing Techniques Applied to Idempotent Unification*. SEKI Report SR-86-16, Univ. Kaiserslautern, 1986.

[HO80] G. Huet and D.C. Oppen. Equations and Rewrite Rules: A Survey. In R. Book (ed.), *Formal Languages: Perspectives and Open Problems*, Academic Press, 1980.

[Höl89] S. Hölldobler: *Foundations of Equational Logic Programming*. LNAI 353, Springer-Verlag, 1989.

[Hul80] J. M. Hullot. Canonical Forms and Unification, Proceedings of the *5th CADE*, 1980, LNCS 87, Springer-Verlag, page 318 - 334.

[JKK83] J.P. Jouannaud, C. Kirchner and H. Kirchner. Incremental Construction of Unification Algorithms in Equational Theories. In *Proc. 10th ICALP*, Barcelona, LNCS 154, Springer-Verlag, 1983, pages 361 - 373.

[Klp92] J. .W. Klop. Term Rewriting Systems. In S. Abramski, D. M. Gabbay and T. S. Maibaum, editors, *Handbook of Logic in Computer Science*, volume 2 - Background: Computational Structures, pages 1- 116. Oxford Uni. Press, 1992.

[LW91] R. Loogen and S. Winkler. Dynamic Detection of Determinism in Functional Logic Languages. In *Proc. 3th PLILP*, 1991, LNCS 528, Springer-Verlag, pages 335 - 346.

[MH94] A. Middeldorp and E. Hamoen. Completeness Results for Basic Narrowing. *Applicable Algebra in Engineering, Communication and Computing*, 1994, volume 5, pages 213 - 253.

[Rét87] P. Réty. Improving Basic Narrowing Techniques. In *Proc. 2nd RTA*, Bordeaux, LNCS 256, Springer-Verlag, 1987, pages 228 - 241.

[Rét88] P. Réty. *Méthodes d'unification par surréduction*. PhD thesis, Univ. Nancy, 1988.

[Wer95] A. Werner. *Normalizing Narrowing for Weakly Terminating and Confluent Systems*. Interner Bericht. Fak. f. Informatik, Univ. Karlsruhe, in preparation.

[Yam88] A. Yamamoto. Completeness of Extended Unification Based on Basic Narrowing. In *Proc. 7th Logic Programming Conference*, Jerusalem, pages 1-10, 1988.

On Termination of Constraint Logic Programs

Livio Colussi[1], Elena Marchiori[2], Massimo Marchiori[1]

[1] Dept. of Pure and Applied Mathematics, Via Belzoni 7, 35131 Padova, Italy
e-mail: {colussi,max}@euler.math.unipd.it
[2] CWI, P.O. Box 94079, 1090 GB Amsterdam, The Netherlands
e-mail: elena@cwi.nl

Abstract. This paper introduces a necessary and sufficient condition for termination of constraint logic programs. The method is based on assigning a dataflow graph to a program, whose nodes are the program points and whose arcs are abstractions of the rules of a transition system, describing the operational behaviour of constraint logic programs. Then termination is proven using a technique inspired by the seminal approach of Floyd for proving termination of flowchart programs.

1 Introduction

The aim of this paper is to introduce a sufficient and necessary condition for termination of constraint logic programs (clp's for short). Termination of clp's is a fairly recent topic, and the only contribution we are aware of is by Mesnard [Mes93], cited in the recent survey [DSD94] on termination of logic programs. However, the aim of that work is different, namely to provide sufficient conditions for the termination problem of clp's, based on approximation techniques. Here we aim at an exact description of terminating clp's, to provide a better understanding of the termination problem for clp's, and to provide a basis for the development of formal methods for reasoning about run-time properties of clp's.

Termination behaviour of clp's is more subtle than that of logic programs. For instance, the presence of some constraints can turn an execution into a (finite) failure, because the actual state does not satisfy a constraint. A similar behaviour can be observed in some built-in's of Prolog (see e.g. [AMP94]). Moreover, in most CLP systems, the state is divided into two components containing the so-called *active* and *passive* constraint, and only the consistency of the active constraint is checked. Then the fact that satisfiability of passive constraints is not checked, affects the termination behaviour of the program: a constraint in the passive component might lead to an inconsistency which is never detected, and which would otherwise have led to termination (with failure). These observations show that the presence of constraints plays a crucial role in the termination behaviour of a clp, and that methods for proving termination for logic programs cannot be applied to deal with clp's in full generality.

In this paper we give a necessary and sufficient condition for the termination problem of clp's. We consider termination w.r.t. an initial set of states (the precondition). Our approach is built on four main notions. First, the elementary computational steps of a clp are described by means of a *transition system*. Next, a *dataflow graph* is assigned to a program. Its nodes are the program points and its arcs are abstractions of the rules of the transition system. Further, a tuple of sets of states, called *invariant* is assigned to the dataflow, one set for each node of the dataflow graph. A set assigned to a node describes the final states of partial computations ending in that node. Finally, a function from states to a well-founded set W, called *W-function*, is associated with each node of the graph. These notions are combined in the definition of *termination triple*, which provides a characterization of terminating clp's (w.r.t. a precondition). Our approach is inspired by the technique introduced by Floyd [Flo67] to prove termination of flowchart programs. Intuitively, in a termination triple the invariants and the W-functions are chosen in such a way that every computation of the program is mapped into a decreasing chain of W. Then by the fact that W is well-founded it follows that every computation is finite.

The notion of termination triple provides a formal basis for reasoning about run-time properties of clp's. We introduce a methodology for finding termination triples, and we show how this method can be modified to yield a practical sufficient criterion for proving termination of normal clp's. To help the reader to focus more on the approach than on the technicalities, the presentation deals with *ideal* CLP systems, where the constraint inference mechanism does not distinguish between active and passive constraints. We discuss in the Conclusion how to extend the results to more general CLP systems.

We have organized the paper as follows. After a few preliminaries on notation and terminology, three sections present the main notions of our approach: Section 3 introduces our transition system, Section 4 the notion of dataflow graph of a program, and Section 5 introduces the notion of invariant for a program. Then in Section 6 we introduce the notion of termination triple, Section 7 contains a methodology for finding termination triples, Section 8 discusses the sufficient criterion. Finally, Section 9 discusses the results and related approaches to study termination of logic programs. For lack of space, we omitted the proofs. They can be found in the full version of the paper.

2 Preliminaries

Let *Var* be an (enumerable) set of variables, with elements denoted by x, y, z, u, v, w. We shall consider the set $VAR = Var \cup Var^0 \cup \ldots \cup Var^k \cup \ldots$, where $Var^k = \{x^k \mid x \in Var\}$ contains the so-called *indexed variables* (i-variables for short) of *index* k. These special variables will be used to describe the standardization apart process, which distinguishes copies of a clause variable which are produced at different calls of that clause. Thus x^k and x^j will represent the same clause variable at two different calls. This technique is known as 'structure-sharing', because x^k and x^j share the same structure, i.e. x. For an index k and a syntactic object E, E^k denotes the object obtained from E by replacing every variable x with the i-variable x^k. We denote by $Term(VAR)$ (resp. $Term(Var)$)

the set of terms built on VAR (resp. Var), with elements denoted by r, s, t.

A sequence $E_1, \ldots, E_k$ of syntactic objects is denoted by $\overline{E}$ or $\langle E_1, \ldots, E_k \rangle$, and $(s_1 = t_1 \wedge \ldots \wedge s_k = t_k)$ is abbreviated by $\overline{s} = \overline{t}$.

Constraint Logic Programs

The reader is referred to [JM94] for a detailed introduction to Constraint Logic Programming. Here we present only those concepts and notation that we shall need in the sequel.

A constraint c is a (first-order) formula on $Term(VAR)$ built from primitive constraints. We shall use the symbol $\mathcal{D}$ both for the domain and the set of its elements. We write $\mathcal{D} \models c$ to denote that c is valid in all the models of $\mathcal{D}$.

A *constraint logic program* $\mathcal{P}$, simply called program or clp, is a (finite) set of clauses $H \leftarrow A_1, \ldots, A_k$ (denoted by C, D), together with one goal-clause $\leftarrow B_1, \ldots, B_m$ (denoted by G), where H and the A_i's and B_i's are atoms built on $Term(Var)$ (primitive constraints are considered to be atoms as well) and H is not a constraint. Atoms which are not constraints are also denoted by $p(\overline{s})$, and $pred(p(\overline{s}))$ denotes p; for a clause C, $pred(C)$ denotes the predicate symbol of its head. A clause whose body either is empty or contains only constraints is called *unitary*.

3 Operational Semantics

To design our method for characterizing the termination behaviour of clp's, we start with a description of the operational behaviour of a clp by means of a transition system. In this transition system standardization apart plays a central role. The reason is that we want to use a suitable representation of program variables during the execution, which will be used in Section 7 where we study how to render *practical* our characterization.

As in the standard operational model states are consistent constraints, i.e.

$$States \stackrel{\text{def}}{=} \{c \in \mathcal{D} \mid c \text{ consistent}\},$$

denoted by c or α. We use the two following operators on states:

$$push, pop : States \rightarrow States,$$

where $push(\alpha)$ is obtained from α by increasing the index of all its i-variables by 1, and $pop(\alpha)$ is obtained from α by first replacing every i-variable of index 0 with a new fresh variable, and then by decreasing the index of all the other i-variables by 1. For instance, suppose that α is equal to $(x^1 = f(z^0) \wedge y^0 = g(x^2))$. Then $push(\alpha)$ is equal to $(x^2 = f(z^1) \wedge y^1 = g(x^3))$ and $pop(\alpha)$ to $(x^0 = f(u) \wedge v = g(x^1))$, where u and v are new fresh variables. These operators are extended in the obvious way to sets of states. *Push* and *pop* are used in the rules of our transition system to describe the standardization apart mechanism. The rules of this transition system, called TS, are given in Table 1. In a pair

$$\textbf{R} \ \ ((\langle p(\overline{s}) \rangle \cdot \overline{A}, \, \alpha) \longrightarrow (\overline{B} \cdot \langle pop \rangle \cdot \overline{A}, \, push(\alpha) \wedge \overline{s}^1 = \overline{t}^0 \,),$$
$$\text{if } C = p(\overline{t}) \leftarrow \overline{B} \text{ is in } \mathcal{P}$$
$$\text{and } push(\alpha) \wedge \overline{s}^1 = \overline{t}^0 \text{ consistent}$$

$$\textbf{S} \ \ (\langle pop \rangle \cdot \overline{A}, \, \alpha) \longrightarrow (\overline{A}, \, pop(\alpha))$$

$$\textbf{C} \ \ (\langle d \rangle \cdot \overline{A}, \, \alpha) \longrightarrow (\overline{A}, \, \alpha \wedge d^0 \,),$$
$$\text{if } d \text{ is a constraint}$$
$$\text{and } \alpha \wedge d^0 \text{ consistent}$$

Table 1. Transition rules for CLP.

$(\overline{A}, \alpha)$, α is a state, and $\overline{A}$ is a sequence of atoms and possibly of tokens of the form pop, whose use is explained below. We fix a suitable standardization apart mechanism: In the standard operational semantics of (C)LP, every time a clause is called it is renamed apart, generally using indexed variables. Here if a clause is called then $push$ is first applied to the state, and if it is released then pop is applied to the state. To mark the place at which this should happen the symbol pop is used. As mentioned above, this formalization will lead to an elegant method in Section 7. The rules of TS describe the standard operational behaviour of a clp (cf. e.g. [JM94]): Rule **R** describes a resolution step. Note that, the way the operators $push$ and pop are used guarantees that every time an atom is called, its variables can be indexed with index equal to 0. Then, in rule **R** the tuple of terms $push(\overline{s}^0)(= \overline{s}^1)$ is considered, because a $push$ is applied to the state. Rule **S** describes the situation where an atom has concluded with success its computation, i.e. when the control reaches a pop. In this case, the operator pop is applied to the state. Finally, rule **C** describes the execution of a constraint. Observe that we do not describe failure explicitly, by adding a corresponding *fail* state. Instead, a failure here occurs when no rule is applicable.

To refer unambiguously to clause variables, the following non-restrictive assumption is used.

Assumption 1 Different clauses of a program have disjoint sets of variables.

We call *computation*, denoted by τ, any sequence $\langle conf_1, \ldots, conf_k, \ldots \rangle$ of configurations s.t. for $k \geq 1$ we have that $conf_k \rightarrow conf_{k+1}$. We consider an operational semantics $\mathcal{T}(\mathcal{P}, \phi)$ for a program $\mathcal{P}$ w.r.t. a set ϕ of states, called *precondition*. This semantics describes all the computations starting in (G, α) (recall that G denotes the goal-clause of $\mathcal{P}$) with α in ϕ. It is defined as follows. We use $\cdot$ for the concatenation of sequences.

Definition 2. (partial trace semantics) $\mathcal{T}(\mathcal{P}, \phi)$ is the least set T s.t. $\langle (G, \alpha) \rangle$

is in T, for every $\alpha \in \phi$, and if $\tau = \tau' \cdot \langle(\overline{A}, \alpha)\rangle$ is in T and $(\overline{A}, \alpha) \rightarrow (\overline{B}, \beta)$, then $\tau \cdot \langle(\overline{B}, \beta)\rangle$ is in T. □

Observe that this is a very concrete semantics: the reason is that it is not meant for the study of program equivalence, but for the study of run-time properties of clp's, namely to characterize termination of clp's. Indeed, $\mathcal{T}(\mathcal{P}, \phi)$ will be used in Section 5 to define the notion of invariant for a program. This latter notion will play a central role in giving (in Section 6) a necessary and sufficient condition for the termination (w.r.t. a precondition) of clp's.

4 A Dataflow Graph for clp's

In this section we introduce the second notion used in our method, namely the dataflow graph of a program. Graphical abstractions of programs have been often used for static analysis of run-time properties. Here, we assign to a program a directed graph, whose nodes are the program points and whose arcs are abstractions of the transition rules of Table 1. In this choice, we have been inspired by the seminal work of Floyd [Flo67] for flowchart programs. To study termination, in general information on the form of the program variables bindings before and after the program atoms calls is needed. Methods for proving termination of logic programs based on graph abstraction, like for instance [BCF94, WS94], use inductive proof methods for proving such run-time properties, and use the graph only to detect possible sources of divergence by considering its cycles. Instead, in our approach, the graph is used both to derive run-time properties and for detecting possible sources of divergence.

We consider the leftmost selection rule, and view a program clause C : $H \leftarrow A_1, \ldots, A_k$ as a sequence consisting alternatingly of (labels l of) *program points* (pp's for short) and atoms,

$$H \leftarrow {}_{l_0} A_1 \, {}_{l_1} \cdots {}_{l_{k-1}} A_k \, {}_{l_k}.$$

The labels l_0 and l_k indicate the *entry point* and the *exit point* of C, denoted by $entry(C)$ and $exit(C)$, respectively. For $i \in [1, k]$, l_{i-1} and l_i indicate the *calling point* and *success point* of A_i, denoted by $call(A_i)$ and $success(A_i)$, respectively. Notice that $l_0 = entry(C) = call(A_1)$ and $l_k = exit(C) = success(A_k)$. In the sequel $atom(l)$ denotes the atom of the program whose calling point is equal to l. For notational convenience the following assumptions are used. Note that they do not imply any loss of generality.

Assumption 3 $l_0, \ldots, l_k$ are natural numbers ordered progressively; distinct clauses of a program are decorated with different pp's; the pp's form an initial segment, say $\{1, 2, \ldots, n\}$ of the natural numbers; and 1 denotes the leftmost pp of the goal-clause, called the *entry point of the program*. Finally, to refer unambiguously to program atom occurrences, all atoms occurring in a program are supposed to be distinct.

In the sequel, $\mathcal{P}$ denotes a program and $\{1, \ldots, n\}$ the set of its pp's. Program points are used to define the notion of dataflow graph.

Definition 4. (dataflow graph) The *dataflow graph* $dg(\mathcal{P})$ *of* $\mathcal{P}$ is a directed graph (*Nodes, Arcs*) s.t. *Nodes* $= \{1, \ldots, n\}$ and *Arcs* is the subset of *Nodes* × *Nodes* s.t. (i, j) is in *Arcs* iff it satisfies one of the following conditions:

- i is *call*(A), where A is not a constraint, j is *entry*(C) and *pred*(C) = *pred*(A);
- i is *exit*(C), j is *success*(A) and *pred*(A) = *pred*(C);
- i is *call*(A) for some constraint A and j is *success*(A).

An element (i, j) of *Arcs* is called *(directed) arc from i to j*. □

Arcs of $dg(\mathcal{P})$ are graphical abstractions of the transition rules of Table 1. Rule **R** is abstracted as an arc from the calling point of an atom to the entry point of a clause. Rule **S** is abstracted as an arc from the exit point of a clause to a success point of an atom. Finally, rule **C** is abstracted as an arc from the calling point of a constraint to its success point.

Example 1. The following program *Prod* is labelled with its pp's.

```
G:  ←  1 prod(u,v) 2
C1: prod([x|y],z) ←  3 z=x*w 4 prod(y,w) 5
C2: prod([ ],1) ←  6
```

The dataflow graph $dg(Prod)$ of *Prod* is pictured below.

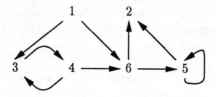

□

Remark. One can refine Definition 4 by using also semantic information, i.e. by pruning the arcs stemming from the first two conditions if $\mathcal{D} \models \neg(\overline{s} = \overline{t})$, i.e. if $p(\overline{s})$ and $p(\overline{t})$ do not 'unify', where $p(\overline{s})$ is A and $p(\overline{t})$ is (a variant of) the head of C. □

Our notion of dataflow graph differs from other graphical representations of (c)lp's, as for instance the *predicate dependency graph* or the *U-graph* (see e.g. [DSD94]), mainly because of the presence in $dg(\mathcal{P})$ of those arcs from exit points of clauses to success points of atoms, such as the arc from 5 to 2 in $dg(Prod)$. These arcs are crucial in our method, because we use the graph not only for detecting possible divergences but also for deriving information on the run-time behaviour of the program, information needed in the termination analysis. In contrast, methods for studying termination of logic programs, based on graph representation, use other static analysis methods for deriving this information.

A *path* is a finite non-empty directed path of $dg(\mathcal{P})$. Paths are denoted by π, and concatenation of paths by $\cdot$. Moreover, $path(i,j)$ denotes the set of all the paths from i to j, and $path(i)$ the set of all the paths from 1 to i.

5 Invariants for clp's

In this section we use the notion of dataflow graph to derive information on the run-time behaviour of programs which is relevant for the study of termination. To this end, we first relate paths of the dataflow graph and computations. Next, we use this relation to define the notion of assertion at a program point, which is the set containing the final states of all the partial traces ending in that program point.

We write *conf*, possibly subscripted, to denote a configuration $(\overline{A}, \alpha)$ used in the rules of TS. The relation *Rel* relating paths and computations is defined by induction on the number of elements of a computation as follows.

The base case is $\langle(\langle p(\overline{s})\rangle \cdot \overline{A}, \alpha)\rangle \; Rel \; \langle call(p(\overline{s}))\rangle$, and the induction case is as follows. Suppose that $\tau' \cdot \langle conf_1 \rangle \; Rel \; \pi$ and that $\tau = \tau' \cdot \langle conf_1, conf_2 \rangle$ (by definition this implies $conf_1 \rightarrow conf_2$). Then:

- $\tau \; Rel \; \pi \cdot \langle entry(C) \rangle$,
  if $conf_1 = (\langle p(\overline{s})\rangle \cdot \overline{A}, \alpha)$ and C is the selected clause;
- $\tau \; Rel \; \pi \cdot \langle success(A) \rangle$, if $conf_1 = (\langle pop \rangle \cdot \overline{A}, \alpha)$, where if $\pi = \langle l_1, \ldots, l_k \rangle$ then A is s.t.
  $call(A) = l_i$ for some $i \in [1, k]$ and for every B in $\mathcal{P}$

$$|I_{call(B)}| = |I_{success(B)}|$$

  with $I_{\star(B)} = \{j \mid i < j \leq k, \; l_j = \star(B)\}$, and $\star$ in $\{call, success\}$;
- $\tau \; Rel \; \pi \cdot \langle success(d) \rangle$, if $conf_1 = (\langle d \rangle \cdot \overline{A}, \alpha)$.

In the sequel we refer to a set of states also by calling it *assertion*, to make the reader acquainted with the intuition that an assertion of some specification language could represent a set of states. In particular, we define the notion of assertion at program point. For a partial trace $\tau = \tau' \cdot \langle(\overline{A}, \beta)\rangle$, we call β the *final state of* τ, denoted by $finalstate(\tau)$ and for a path π, we denote by $lastnode(\pi)$ its last element.

Definition 5. (assertion at pp) Let l be a pp of $dg(\mathcal{P})$. The *assertion at l* (w.r.t. ϕ), denoted by $\mathcal{I}_l(\mathcal{P}, \phi)$, is defined as follows:

$$\mathcal{I}_l(\mathcal{P}, \phi) = \{finalstate(\tau) \mid \tau \in \mathcal{T}(\mathcal{P}, \phi) \text{ and } \tau \; Rel \; \pi \\ \text{for some } \pi \text{ s.t. } l = lastnode(\pi)\}.$$

$\square$

For instance, $\mathcal{I}_1(\mathcal{P}, \phi) = \phi$. The notion of assertion at pp is needed to give a sufficient and necessary condition for termination. However, it is too strong to be practical, because it implies the exact knowledge of the semantics of a program. Indeed, for proving termination, it is often enough to have partial knowledge of the semantics, i.e. to replace assertions at pp with suitable supersets. These supersets form the so-called invariants for $\mathcal{P}$. To define this notion, we need to formalize how paths modify states. We use ϕ, ψ, possibly subscripted, to denote sets of states.

Definition 6. Let π be a path and let $\tau = \langle(\overline{A}, \alpha)\rangle \cdot \tau'$ be a computation s.t. τ Rel π. Then $finalstate(\tau)$ is called the *output of π w.r.t. α*, denoted by $output(\pi, \alpha)$. □

It can be shown that Definition 6 is well-formed, i.e. that if τ and τ' are s.t. both τ Rel π and τ' Rel π, then $\tau = \tau'$, hence $output(\pi, \alpha)$ is uniquely defined. Observe that in some cases $output(\pi, \alpha)$ is not defined, namely when there is no τ s.t τ Rel π.

Then the notion of invariant for $\mathcal{P}$ is defined as follows.

Definition 7. (invariant for $\mathcal{P}$) Let $\{1, \ldots, n\}$ be the set of nodes of $dg(\mathcal{P})$ and let ϕ be an assertion. We call the tuple $(\phi_1, \ldots, \phi_n)$ of assertions an *invariant for $\mathcal{P}$ (w.r.t. ϕ)* if: $\phi \subseteq \phi_1$; and for every $i, j \in [1, n]$, for every path $\pi \in path(i, j)$, and for every $\alpha \in \phi_i$ we have that if $output(\pi, \alpha)$ is defined, then it is in ϕ_j. □

6 Characterization of Termination

To give a characterization of terminating programs, the dataflow graph $dg(\mathcal{P})$ and an invariant $(\phi_1, \ldots, \phi_n)$ for $\mathcal{P}$ will be used. A function from states to a well-founded set W, called W-function, will be associated to certain nodes of $dg(\mathcal{P})$. The intuition is that for a terminating clp, each path of the graph can be mapped into a decreasing chain of W. For a path π from i to j, the W-function of i applied to a state α in ϕ_i is shown to be strictly greater than the W-function of j applied to $output(\pi, \alpha)$. To examine only a finite number of paths, we adapt a technique introduced by Floyd [Flo67] and formalized by Manna [Man70] to prove termination of flowchart programs: only those nodes of the graph which 'cut' some cycle are considered (see Definition 9), and only suitable paths connecting such nodes, called *smart*, are examined.

First, we define the notion of terminating w.r.t. a precondition clp.

Definition 8. (terminating clp's) Let ϕ be a set of states. A program is *terminating w.r.t. ϕ* if all the computations starting at (G, α), with $\alpha \in \phi$, are finite. □

Next, we define the notion of cutpoint set, originally introduced in [Flo67, Man70].

Definition 9. (cutpoint set) A set C of pp's of a program $\mathcal{P}$ is called a *cutpoint set for* $\mathcal{P}$ (and its members *cutpoints*) if every cycle of the dataflow graph contains at least one element of C. □

So, cutpoints are meant to be control loci to check for possible nontermination caused by loops (cycles in the dataflow graph). Now, as in Floyd [Flo67], one has to consider the paths connecting two cutpoints, whose internal nodes are not cutpoints. However, observe that a path could describe a possible divergence only if it is contained in a cycle of $dg(\mathcal{P})$. Moreover, only cycles of $dg(\mathcal{P})$ which contain at least one entry point of a non-unitary clause, could represent an infinite computation. Thus we introduce the notion of *smart path*.

Definition 10. (smart path) Let C be a cutpoint set for $\mathcal{P}$. Let $l, l' \in C$ and let π be a path in $path(l, l')$. Then π is *smart w.r.t.* C if the following conditions are satisfied:

1. there is a cycle in $dg(\mathcal{P})$ containing π and containing an entry point of a non-unitary clause of $\mathcal{P}$;
2. $\pi = \langle l \rangle \cdot \pi' \cdot \langle l' \rangle$ and no pp of π' is in C.

□

Now we have all the tools to define the notion of termination triple, which provides a necessary and sufficient condition for the termination of a clp. We call *W-function* a function from states to a well-founded set $(W, <)$. Moreover, for a tuple $\Phi = (\psi_1, \ldots, \psi_n)$ of assertions, and a set $C = \{i1, \ldots, ik\}$, with $1 \le i1 < \ldots < ik \le n$, we call $(\psi_{i1}, \ldots, \psi_{ik})$ the restriction to C of Φ.

Definition 11. (termination triple) Let ϕ be a set of states. Let C be a set of nodes of $dg(\mathcal{P})$; let $\Phi = \{\phi_l \mid l \in C\}$ be a set of assertions; and let $\mathbf{w} = \{w_l \mid l \in C\}$ be a set of W-functions. Then $(C, \Phi, \mathbf{w})$ is a *termination triple for* $\mathcal{P}$ *w.r.t.* ϕ if:

1. C is a cutpoint set for $\mathcal{P}$;
2. Φ is the restriction to C of an invariant for $\mathcal{P}$ w.r.t. ϕ;
3. for every $l, l' \in C$ and smart path (w.r.t. C) $\pi \in path(l, l')$, we have that if $\alpha \in \phi_l$ and $output(\pi, \alpha)$ is defined then $w_l(\alpha) > w_{l'}(output(\pi, \alpha))$.

□

Then we have the following necessary and sufficient condition for termination.

Theorem 12. (termination characterization) *Let ϕ be a set of states. Let C be any cutpoint set for the program $\mathcal{P}$. Then $\mathcal{P}$ terminates w.r.t. ϕ if and only if there is a termination triple $(C, \Phi, \mathbf{w})$ for $\mathcal{P}$ w.r.t. ϕ.*

In Sections 7 we shall introduce a method for finding termination triples. Moreover, in Section 8 we shall introduce a sufficient criterion based on this characterization.

7 Finding Termination Triples

We have seen how termination of a clp can be characterized by means of the notion of termination triple. This result is theoretically interesting. It provides a better understanding of the termination problem for clp's, and it can serve as a theoretical framework on which automatic techniques can be built. The attentive reader, however, will have observed that we have not used the special standardization apart mechanism incorporated in the rules of the transition system TS of Table 1. Indeed, as one would expect, the characterization we have given does not depend on the standardization apart mechanism.

The reason of the introduction of this mechanism is related with the issue of *finding* a termination triple. In this section we shall discuss a powerful methodology to prove that a triple $(C, \Phi, \mathbf{w})$ is a termination triple. This methodology relies on the specific form of the rules of TS, hence on indexed variables and on the operators *pop* and *push*.

First, we give an inductive description of the strongest postcondition of a path. Next, we introduce a sound and (relatively) complete method to prove that a tuple of assertions is an invariant for the program.

7.1 Outputs of Paths

We show here how the notion of output of a path can be given inductively, without using the relation *Rel*.

We have that $output(\langle 1 \rangle, \alpha) = \alpha$. Moreover, when the initial state α satisfies suitable conditions, then the $output(\pi, \alpha)$ can be inductively computed. To this end, the following set of states is needed:

$$free(x) = \{\alpha \mid \mathcal{D} \models \alpha \rightarrow \forall x.\alpha\};$$

it describes those states where x is a free variable. The intuition is that x is free in a state if it can be bound to any value without affecting that state. For instance, $y = z$ is in $free(x)$, because x does not occur in the formula. Also $y = z \wedge x = x$ is in $free(x)$, because $\mathcal{D} \models (y = z \wedge x = x) \rightarrow \forall x\,(y = z \wedge x = x)$. Further, we write $\phi \wedge c$ to denote the set $\{\alpha \wedge c \in States \mid \alpha \in \phi\}$. Moreover, it is convenient to make the following assumptions on non-unitary (goal-)clauses.

Assumption 13 The body of every non-unitary clause does not contain two atoms with equal predicate symbol; and at least one argument of its head is a variable.

This assumption is not restrictive. It can be shown that every program can be transformed into one satisfying Assumption 13. The transformation will in general modify the semantics of the original program (the set of pp's changes and new predicates could be introduced). However, it is easy to define a syntactic transformation that allows us to recover the semantics of the original program.

Because of the second assumption, we can fix a variable-argument of the head of a clause C, that we call *the characteristic variable of C*, denoted by x_C.

Also, a new fresh variable x_G is associated with the goal-clause G, called *the characteristic variable of* G. These variables play a crucial role in the following result, to be explained below.

Theorem 14. *Let α be a state and let $\pi = \pi' \cdot \langle l_k \rangle$ be a path, where $\pi' = \langle l_1, \ldots, l_{k-1} \rangle$. Suppose that $\beta = output(\pi', \alpha)$ is defined. Then:*

- *if $l_k = entry(C)$, $l_{k-1} = call(A)$ for some atom $A = p(\overline{s})$, and if $push(\beta) \wedge (\overline{s}^1 = \overline{t}^0)$ is consistent then:*

$$output(\pi, \alpha) = push(\beta) \wedge (\overline{s}^1 = \overline{t}^0),$$

  where $p(\overline{t})$ is the head of C;
- *if $l_k = success(A)$ with A not a constraint, $l_{k-1} = exit(D)$ for some clause D, and if $pop(\beta) \in \neg free(x_C^0)$ where C is the clause containing A, then*

$$output(\pi, \alpha) = pop(\beta);$$

- *if $l_k = success(A)$ with A a constraint, and if $\beta \wedge A^0$ is consistent then:*

$$output(\pi, \alpha) = \beta \wedge A^0.$$

The requirements on the characteristic variables are needed to rule out all those paths which are not semantic, i.e. which do not describe partial traces. Informally, whenever a state is propagated through a semantic path the variable x_C^0 is initially free (by assumption). Then, the index of x_C is increased and decreased by means of the applications of the *push* and *pop* operators. When C is called, then x_C^0 is bound (because by assumption it occurs in the head of C), hence x_C^0 is not free. From that moment on its index will be increased and decreased and it will become 0 *only* if the success point of an atom of the body of C is reached. If the success point of an atom of G is reached, then x_G^0 is not free. Moreover, for each clause C different from G, x_C^0 is free, because either C was never called, or x_C^0 has been replaced with a fresh variable by an application of *pop*.

Example 2. The following example illustrates the crucial role of the characteristic variables to discriminate those paths which are not *semantical paths*. Consider again the program *Prod*. Let $\pi = \langle 1, 3, 4, 6, 2 \rangle$ and let $\alpha = (x_G^0 = 0)$, where 0 is a constant. This path is not semantical, i.e. it does not describe a computation. Then, the output of this path w.r.t. α is not defined. Indeed, at program point 2 we obtain that x_G^0 is free, thus Theorem 14 is not applicable. The behaviour, with respect to freeness, of the characteristic variables during the propagation of α through π is described in Table 2.

Note instead that the path obtained from π by replacing 2 with 5 is a semantical path (i.e. x_{C1}^0 is not free at pp 5). $\square$

at pp	x_G^0	x_G^1	x_G^2	x_{C1}^0	x_{C1}^1	x_{C2}^0
1	not free	free	free	free	free	free
3	free	not free	free	not free	free	free
4	free	not free	free	not free	free	free
6	free	free	not free	free	not free	not free
2	free	not free	free	not free	free	free

Table 2. Characteristic variables through π

7.2 Proving Invariants for clp's

We introduce now a necessary and sufficient condition to prove that an n-tuple $(\phi_1, \ldots, \phi_n)$ of assertions is an invariant for $\mathcal{P}$.

Recall that we denote by $\{1, \ldots, n\}$ the set of pp's of a program $\mathcal{P}$. Moreover, $atom(l)$ denotes the atom of the program whose calling point is l. For a node j of $dg(\mathcal{P})$, let $input(j)$ denote the set of the nodes i s.t. (i, j) is an arc of $dg(\mathcal{P})$. Then we have the following theorem.

Theorem 15. (characterization of invariants for $\mathcal{P}$) *Let $(\phi_1, \ldots, \phi_n)$ be an n-tuple of assertions s.t. $\phi_1 \subseteq \neg free(x_G^0)$, and $\phi_1 \subseteq free(x_C^0)$ for every non-unitary clause C different from G. Then $(\phi_1, \ldots, \phi_n)$ is an invariant for $\mathcal{P}$ if and only if for $i \in [1, n]$ we have that:*

1. *if $i = entry(C)$ then $push(\phi_j) \wedge (\bar{s}^1 = \bar{t}^0) \subseteq \phi_i$, for every $j \in input(i)$, where $p(\bar{t})$ is the head of C and $p(\bar{s}) = atom(j)$;*
2. *if $i = success(A)$ and A is not a constraint then $pop(\phi_j) \cap \neg free(x_C^0) \subseteq \phi_i$, for every $j \in input(i)$,*
   where C is the clause containing A;
3. *if $i = success(A)$ and A is a constraint then $\phi_{i-1} \wedge A^0 \subseteq \phi_i$.*

Let us comment on the above theorem, using the transition system of Table 1: let $\overline{A}$ denote a generic sequence of atoms and/or tokens. Then 1 states that $\phi_{entry(C)}$ contains those states obtained by applying rule $\mathbf{R}$ to $(\langle atom(j) \rangle \cdot \overline{A}, \alpha)$, for every $\alpha \in \phi_j$ and every $j \in input(entry(C))$. Further, 2 states that when A is not a constraint, then $\phi_{success(A)}$ contains those states obtained by applying rule $\mathbf{S}$ to $(\langle pop \rangle \cdot \overline{A}, \alpha)$, for every $\alpha \in \phi_j$ and every $j \in input(success(A))$. Finally, 3 states that when A is a constraint, then $\phi_{success(A)}$ contains those states obtained by applying the transition rule $\mathbf{C}$ to $(\langle A \rangle \cdot \overline{A}, \alpha)$, for every $\alpha \in \phi_{call(A)}$.

This theorem is derived from a fixpoint semantics which has been introduced in a companion paper [CMM95]. The conditions 1-3 of Theorem 15 correspond to the three cases of the definition of an operator F on n-tuples of assertions whose least fixpoint μF yields a semantics equal to $(\mathcal{I}_1(\mathcal{P}, \phi), \ldots, \mathcal{I}_n(\mathcal{P}, \phi))$. For instance, 1 corresponds to the case where F maps a tuple $(\psi_1, \ldots, \psi_n)$ to a tuple $(\phi_1, \ldots, \phi_n)$ s.t. $\phi_i = \cup_{j \in input(i)}(push(\psi_j) \wedge (\bar{s}^1 = \bar{t}^0))$. The other cases of the definition of F are obtained analogously. Then the proof of Theorem 15 is an easy consequence of the equality between μF and $(\mathcal{I}_1(\mathcal{P}, \phi), \ldots, \mathcal{I}_n(\mathcal{P}, \phi))$.

7.3 A Methodology

Theorem 15 can be used as a basis for a sound and complete proof method for proving invariants of clp's. One has to define a specification language to express the properties of interest. Then, a formula of the language is interpreted as a set of states, conjunction is interpreted as set intersection, negation as set-complementation, and implication as set inclusion. The predicate relation *free* has to be in the specification language, and the operators *pop* and *push* should be defined in the expected way on formulas. Simpler methods can be obtained from Theorem 15, by loosing completeness. We shall introduce in the following section one of such methods.

To summarize, we obtain the following methodology to study termination of clp's. To find a termination triple for $\mathcal{P}$ w.r.t. ϕ:

- construct $dg(\mathcal{P})$;
- select a cutpoint set;
- use Theorem 15 to find an invariant for $\mathcal{P}$;
- find a suitable set of W-functions;
- use Theorem 14 to check condition 3. of the definition of termination triple.

We conclude this section with a simple example.

Example 3. Consider the program *Prod* of Example 1. Let *true* denote the set of all states and let $list(x)$ denote the set of states where x is a list. Take $\phi = (list(u^0) \wedge \neg free(x_G^0) \wedge free(z^0))$. We show that *Prod* terminates w.r.t. ϕ.

The dataflow graph $dg(Prod)$ for *Prod* was already given in Example 3.

$\mathcal{C} = \{3, 5\}$ is a cutpoint set for *Prod*.

Let $\phi_1 = \phi$, $\phi_2 = true$, $\phi_3 = \phi_4 = list(y^0)$, $\phi_5 = \phi_6 = true$. It is easy to check using Theorem 15 that $\Phi = (\phi_1, \ldots, \phi_6)$ is an invariant (w.r.t. ϕ) for *Prod*.

Consider the following W-functions, where the well-founded set W is here the set of natural numbers: $w_3 = w_5 = \|y^0\|$, where $\|t\|$ denotes the length of t if t is a list and 0 otherwise.

In order to show that $(\{3, 5\}, \{\phi_3, \phi_5\}, \{w_3, w_5\})$ is a termination triple, we have only to consider the smart path $\pi = \langle 3, 4, 3 \rangle$.

Let α in ϕ_3 and suppose that $w_3(\alpha) = k$. Then α is in $\phi_3 \wedge (\|y^0\| = k)$. Using Theorem 14 we have that $\beta = output(\pi, \alpha \wedge \|y^0\| = k)$ is defined, with $\beta = (list(y^1) \wedge \|y^1\| = k \wedge z^1 = x^1 * p^1 \wedge y^1 = [x^0|y^0] \wedge p^1 = z^0)$. Then $w_3(output(\pi, \alpha)) = (\|y^1\| - 1) = (k - 1)$; and from $k - 1 < k$ we obtain $w_3(output(\pi, \alpha)) < w_3(\alpha)$.

Thus $(\mathcal{C}, \{\phi_3, \phi_5\}, \{w_3, w_5\})$ satisfies the three conditions of Definition 11, and hence *Prod* is terminating w.r.t. ϕ. $\square$

8 A Sufficient Criterion

In this section we discuss a variation of the above methodology which will yield a sufficient criterion for termination which is more practical, yet less powerful, than the one given in the previous section. The idea is to extract a small subgraph of the dataflow graph, called *cyclic*, to be used in the termination analysis.

Definition 16. (cyclic dataflow graph) Consider the graph consisting of those arcs (l, l') of $dg(\mathcal{P})$ that belong to a cycle and s.t. l' is the entry-point of a non-unitary clause. This graph is called the *cyclic dataflow graph* of $\mathcal{P}$, denoted by $cdg(\mathcal{P})$. □

The cyclic dataflow of $\mathcal{P}$ extracts the minimal information on the program which is needed to prove termination.

For two W-functions w_1, w_2, we write $w_1 \preceq w_2$ if $w_1(\alpha \wedge c) \leq w_2(\alpha)$, for every state α and constraint c.

Definition 17. (termination pair)

Let ϕ be a set of states. Let N stands for the set of nodes of $cdg(\mathcal{P})$; let $\Phi = \{\phi_l \mid l \in N\}$ be a set of assertions; and let $\mathbf{w} = \{w_l \mid l \in N\}$ be a set of W-functions. Then $(\Phi, \mathbf{w})$ is a *termination pair for $\mathcal{P}$ w.r.t. ϕ* if:

1. Φ is the restriction to N of an invariant for $\mathcal{P}$ w.r.t. ϕ;
2. for every $l, l' \in N$, if l and l' belong to the same clause and $l < l'$, then $w_l \succeq w_{l'}$;
3. for every arc (l, l') of $cdg(\mathcal{P})$ and α in ϕ_l, if $push(\alpha) \wedge (\bar{s}^1 = \bar{t}^0)$ is consistent then

$$w_l(\alpha) > w_{l'}(push(\alpha) \wedge (\bar{s}^1 = \bar{t}^0)),$$

where $p(\bar{t})$ is the head of the clause containing l', and $p(\bar{s}) = atom(l)$. □

The definition of termination pair uses $cdg(\mathcal{P})$ to analyze possible divergences (Point 1). Point 3 states that when a pp is reached via a resolution step $\mathbf{R}$, then the value of the corresponding W-function decreases steadily. Point 2 deals with the other two transition rules, $\mathbf{C}$ and $\mathbf{S}$, which do not have to increase the value of the W-functions. The notion of termination pair provides a sufficient criterion for proving termination.

Theorem 18. *A program $\mathcal{P}$ terminates w.r.t. ϕ if there is a termination pair for $\mathcal{P}$ w.r.t. ϕ.*

8.1 Negation

In this subsection we show how all the previous results can be extended to provide sufficient criteria for termination of *normal* clp's, that is clp's where body clauses may contain negated atoms $\neg A$. We suppose that negated atoms are solved using the negation as finite failure procedure or one of its modifications which allow to deal also with non-ground literals (see e.g. [AB94]).

A dataflow graph is assigned to a normal clp $\mathcal{P}$, constructed by means of the following steps:

1. consider every negated atom $\neg A$ of the program $\mathcal{P}$ as an atom A and build the dataflow graph using Definition 4;
2. delete from the graph obtained in step 1. every arc (i, j), s.t. j is the success point of a negated atom;
3. add to the graph obtained in step 2. the arcs $(i, i + 1)$, for every i which is the calling point of a negated atom.

The three steps above describe the execution of a negated atom $\neg A$ as follows: the execution of A is started, and at the same time also the execution of the next literal is started. In this way, we approximate the real computation of the program, by possibly introducing extra computations, in the case that $\neg A$ would have failed. Note that this technique is also implicitly used in Wang and Shyamasundar [WS94].

Using this definition of dataflow graph, we can obtain a sound description of an invariant for $\mathcal{P}$: Theorem 15 can be restated as sufficient condition, where in case 1. a negative literal is treated as an atom (i.e. $\neg A$ is treated as A) and in case 3. it is treated as the constraint *true*. Thus, the notion of termination triple provides a sufficient criterion for termination. Also Theorem 18 can be extended to normal clp's:

Theorem 19. *A normal program $\mathcal{P}$ terminates w.r.t. ϕ if there is a termination pair for $\mathcal{P}$ w.r.t. ϕ.*

Remark. The above technique is based on the following program transformation. Consider a clause $H \leftarrow L_1, \ldots, L_{k-1}, L_k, L_{k+1}, \ldots, L_m$, where $L_k = \neg A$ is a negative literal. Split this clause as follows:

$$H \leftarrow L_1, \ldots, L_{k-1}, A, new.$$
$$H \leftarrow L_1, \ldots, L_{k-1}, L_{k+1}, \ldots, L_m.$$

where *new* is a new predicate symbol. This corresponds to the intuition that: the first clause starts the execution of A and then does not care about the computation (that is disregarded due to *new*); the second clause allows the execution continue, as if L_k had succeeded. Via repeated applications of this transformation, we can obtain from a normal clp a definite clp s.t. if this transformed program terminates then the original program terminates. □

We conclude this section with an example to illustrate the application of this method.

Example 4. Consider the normal program *Fastqueen* solving in an efficient way the N-queens problem.

```
←₁ fastqueens(number,solution) ₂
fastqueens(num,qns) ←₃ range(1,num,ns) ₄ queens(ns,[],qns) ₅
queens(unplqs,safeqs,qs) ←₆ select(q,unplqs,unplqs1) ₇
                    ¬ attack(q,safeqs) ₈ queens(unplqs1,[q|safeqs],qs) ₉
queens([],qs1,qs1) ←₁₀
range(m,n,[m|ns]) ←₁₁ m<n ₁₂ m1=m+1 ₁₃ range(m1,n,ns) ₁₄
```

```
range(u,u,[u])  ←₁₅
select(x,[x|xs],xs)  ←₁₆
select(v,[y|ys],[y|zs])  ←₁₇ select(v,ys,zs) ₁₈
attack(w,ws)  ←₁₉ att(w,1,ws) ₂₀
att(x1,n1,[y1|ys1])  ←₂₁ x1=y1+n1 ₂₂
att(x2,n2,[y2|ys2])  ←₂₃ x2+n2=y2 ₂₄
att(x3,n3,[y3|ys3])  ←₂₅ n4=n3+1 ₂₆ att(x3,n4,ys3) ₂₇
```

One obtains the following cyclic dataflow graph of *Fastqueens*:

$$8 \longrightarrow 6 \longrightarrow 17 \circlearrowright$$

$$13 \longrightarrow 11 \qquad\qquad 26 \longrightarrow 25$$

Consider the precondition

$\phi = ground(number^0) \wedge \neg free(x_G^0) \wedge free(unplqs^0) \wedge free(m^0) \wedge free(v^0) \wedge free(w^0) \wedge free(x3^0)$.

We show that *Fastqueens* is terminating w.r.t. ϕ. Consider the assertions:

$\phi_6 = \phi_8 = (list(unplqs^0) \wedge list(safeqs^0))$,
$\phi_{11} = \phi_{13} = list(ns^0)$,
$\phi_{17} = list(ys^0)$,
$\phi_{25} = \phi_{26} = list(ys3^0)$.

Consider the following W-functions (here $\| \ \|$ is the 'list-length' map seen in the previous Example 3):

$w_6 = w_8 = \|unplqs^0\|$,
$w_{11} = w_{13} = \|ns^0\|$,
$w_{17} = \|ys^0\|$,
$w_{25} = w_{26} = \|ys3^0\|$.

It is not difficult to check that this is a termination pair for *Fastqueens* w.r.t. ϕ. For instance, for condition 2 of Def. 17 note that whenever two pp's of the *cdg* are on the same clause the corresponding W-functions are equal.

Thus, for Theorem 19, *Fastqueens* terminates w.r.t. ϕ. □

9 Conclusion

In this paper we have provided a characterization of terminating clp's w.r.t. a precondition by means of the notion of termination triple. We have discussed how this characterization can be used in practice, by introducing a methodology for finding termination triples, and a sufficient criterion based on this methodology for proving termination of normal clp's.

A different graphical abstraction has been used to study termination of logic programs ([BCF94, WS94]), under the name of U-graph or specific graph. This notion is based on the so-called dependency graph of a program. In an U-graph, the program atoms are the nodes and there is a directed arc from a node n_1 to another node n_2 either if n_1 is the head of a clause and n_2 is one of its body atoms, or if n_1 is a body atom and n_2 is the head of a clause s.t. n_1 and n_2 unify. In this representation the first type of arc abstracts a clause, and the second one the flow of control. Then, the graph is used to detect possible divergences, and other proof methods ([BC89] and [DM88]) are used to obtain the information on the operational behaviour of the program which is needed to perform the termination analysis on the graph.

However, for our purpose, namely to give a characterization of terminating clp's, we found advantageous to have an uniform approach based uniquely on the dataflow graph of the program. For this reason, we have introduced a more *concrete* notion of dataflow graph, where also the backwards propagation of the state in a derivation is described.

We conclude by showing how the results can be extended to more general CLP systems.

All major implemented CLP systems are 'quick-check' and 'progressive' (cf. [JM94]). In these kind of systems, the state is divided into two components containing the *active* and the *passive* constraint, and only the consistency of the active constraint is checked. This improves the efficiency of the system. We sketch how our results can be easily extended to deal with 'quick-check' and 'progressive' systems.

$$States = \{(c_1, c_2) \mid c_1 \text{ and } c_2 \text{ are constraints s.t. } consistent(c_1)\},$$

where the test $consistent(c_1)$ checks for (an approximation of) the consistency of c_1.

Rules **R** and **C** are modified as below, where a state is denoted by (α_1, α_2):

$$\mathbf{R} \; (\langle p(\overline{s}) \rangle \cdot \overline{A}, \alpha) \longrightarrow (\overline{B} \cdot \langle pop \rangle \cdot \overline{A}, \; infer(\alpha_1', \alpha_2' \wedge \overline{s}^1 = \overline{t}^0)),$$

with $\alpha' = push(\alpha)$, if $C = p(\overline{t}) \leftarrow \overline{B}$ is in $\mathcal{P}$.

$$\mathbf{C} \; (\langle d \rangle \cdot \overline{A}, \alpha) \longrightarrow (\overline{A}, \; infer(\alpha_1, \alpha_2 \wedge d^0)),$$

if d is a constraint.

Finally, the definition of $\phi \wedge c$ has to be changed in:

$$\phi \wedge c = \{\alpha' \in States \mid \alpha' = infer(\alpha_1, \alpha_2 \wedge c) \text{ and } \alpha \in \phi\}.$$

The operator *infer* computes from the current state (c_1, c_2) a new active constraint c_1' and passive constraint c_2', with the requirement that $c_1 \wedge c_2$ and $c_1' \wedge c_2'$ are equivalent constraints. The intuition is that c_1 is used to obtain from c_2 more active constraints; then c_2 is simplified to c_2'.

Acknowledgements: We would like to thank Jan Rutten and the anonymous referees for their helpful comments. The research of the second author was partially supported by the Esprit Basic Research Action 6810 (Compulog 2).

References

[AB94]   K.R. Apt and R. Bol. Logic programming and negation: a survey. *JLP* 19,20: 9-72, 1994.

[AMP94]   K.R. Apt, E. Marchiori, and C. Palamidessi. A declarative approach for first-order built-in's of Prolog. *Applicable Algebra in Engineering, Communication and Computation*, 5(3/4), pp. 159-191, 1994.

[BC89]   A. Bossi and N. Cocco. Verifying correctness of logic programs. *TAPSOFT*, LNCS 352, pp. 96–110, 1989.

[BCF94]   A. Bossi, N. Cocco and M. Fabris. Norms on terms and their use in proving universal termination of a logic program. *TCS* 124: 297–328, 1994.

[CMM95]   L. Colussi, E. Marchiori and M. Marchiori. A dataflow semantics for constraint logic programs. In *Proceedings of PLILP'95*, to appear, 1995.

[DM88]   W. Drabent and J. Małuszyński. Inductive assertion method for logic programs. *TCS*, 59(1):133–155, 1988.

[DSD94]   D. De Schreye and S. Decorte. Termination of logic programs: the neverending story. *JLP* 19,20: 199-260, 1994.

[Flo67]   R.W. Floyd. Assigning meanings to programs. In J.T. Schwartz, editor, *Proceedings Symposium in Applied Mathematics*, volume 19 of *Math. Aspects in Computer Science*, pages 19–32. AMS, 1967.

[JM94]   J. Jaffar and M.J. Maher. Constraint Logic Programming: A Survey. *JLP* 19,20: 503-581, 1994.

[Man70]   Z. Manna. Termination of Programs Represented as Interpreted Graphs. Proc. Spring. J. Comp. Conf., pp.83-89, 1970.

[Mes93]   F. Mesnard. *Etude de la terminaison des programmes logiques avec constraintes aux moyens d'approximations.* PhD Thesis, Paris VI, 1993.

[WS94]   B. Wang and R.K. Shyamasundar. A methodology for proving termination of logic programs. *JLP* 21(1): 1–30, 1994.

Modelling Producer/Consumer Constraints

Helmut Simonis
COSYTEC SA
4, rue Jean Rostand
Parc Club Orsay Université
F-91893 Orsay Cedex
France

Trijntje Cornelissens
Beyers & Partners
Michielssendreef 42
B-2930 Brasschaat
Belgium

1. Abstract

In this paper we describe the modelling of producer/consumer constraints with the CHIP system. Producer/consumer constraints arise in scheduling problems with consumable resources like raw materials or money, in particular for batch based processing. The constraint assures that at each time point enough consumable resources are available. The modelling with CHIP uses the cumulative constraint to express conditions in a very declarative way, yet obtains very good propagation due to the reasoning power build into the cumulative constraint. We show that with producer/consumer constraints many resource scheduling problems can be easily expressed and give examples of its industrial use.

2. Introduction

Constraint logic programming (CLP) [FHK92][JM94] is increasingly used to solve hard scheduling and planning problems [BKC94] [BCP92] [BS92] [BDP94] [CDF94] [DS91] [Ev92] [FS90] [Wa94]. Special constraints like cumulative [AB93] and diffn [BC94] have been introduced to express constraints on renewable resources [Go92], like machines or personnel. These resources can be used over a time period up to a certain level of availability. In this paper we show how to model constraints on consumable resources with the same basic mechanisms. Consumable resources often are raw materials or amounts of money, which are available in limited amounts over certain time periods. A producer/consumer constraint on consumable resources expresses that at any time point more resources must have been produced than consumed. We use CHIP [DHS88] to express these constraints. CHIP is a constraint logic programming system originally developed at the ECRC in Munich [VH89][HSD92], and further developed by COSYTEC [KS95] [SB95]. We express producer/consumer constraints in the finite domain solver of CHIP, using the global cumulative constraint [AB93].

The paper is structured as follows:

In section 3, we introduce the producer/consumer constraint with several variations. Section 4 gives the declarative semantics of the constraint. Section 5 briefly introduces the cumulative constraint in CHIP. The next section describes the modelling of the producer/consumer constraint with the help of the cumulative. In section 7, we present different extensions of the constraint. Finally, we discuss the use of the constraint for the ATLAS scheduling system in section 8.

3. Producer/Consumer Constraints

Producer/consumer constraints arise in many different variants. We now discuss some typical examples.

3.1 Raw Materials

Consider a scheduling problem where each task requires certain amounts of different raw materials. The raw materials must be available at the beginning of each task in order to start the task. Some initial stock of the different raw materials is available, more becomes available with receivings of raw materials in given quantities at certain time points. The problem consists in scheduling the task in such a way that for each task all required raw materials are available at its start. In this case, the production of the resource is fixed (known), only the consumption can be varied by scheduling tasks at different time points. We call this type of constraint a *consumer constraint*.

3.2 Finished Products

The opposite problem occurs when scheduling with hard delivery dates of finished products. Each task produces a certain quantity of finished products at the end of the task. A certain initial stock of each finished product may be available. There are orders for defined quantities of finished products for fixed dates, which must be satisfied. The problem consists in scheduling the tasks in such a way that all orders can be satisfied. Since in this case the consumers are fixed and only the producers (tasks) are variable over time, we call this situation a *producer constraint*.

Note that this model is a generalisation of the usual production scheduling problem[Ba74][Go93][CC88][Fr82], where orders are matched one-to-one with production tasks. In this case, the producer constraint simply consists in scheduling all tasks before their due-date, which can be easily expressed by inequality constraints. This simplified model can be used in many situations where orders are few and known well in advance. It can not be used if many orders require the same finished product and there is no direct link between orders and production tasks.

3.3 Intermediate Products

This last type of constraint arises in multiple step scheduling problems, where some tasks create an intermediate product in certain quantities and other tasks use that intermediate product. Typical examples are batch based production in the chemical and food industry. We call this type of constraint the general *producer/ consumer constraint*.

Again this is a generalisation of a well known problem. In the job-shop scheduling problem [CC88][Pi88], each job consists of tasks which have to be scheduled in some order. This order often is caused by producer/consumer constraints between the tasks. The difference is that producers and consumers in job-shop scheduling problems are matched one-to-one, this is not the case for the general producer/consumer constraint, where the sequence of tasks is not predetermined.

4. Mathematical Formulation

A mathematical formulation of the producer/consumer constraint is quite simple. Given an initial quantity Q_0 at time 0, and given a set of producers P_i which produce amounts Q_{Pi} at times T_{Pi} and a set of consumers C_j which consume amounts Q_{Cj} at times T_{Cj}, the following inequalities must hold:
Let

$$a = \min\{T_{Ci}, T_{Pi}\} - 1$$

$$b = \max\{T_{Ci}, T_{Pi}\} + 1$$

$$\forall t \in [a, b] \quad Q_0 + \sum_{T_{Pi} \le t} Q_{Pi} - \sum_{T_{Cj} \le t} Q_{Cj} \ge 0 \tag{1}$$

Unfortunately, these constraints can not be easily expressed as sets of inequality constraints, except in the case that the T_{Pi} and T_{Cj} are fixed or that atleast a total (temporal) order is given for the P_i and C_j events. In that case, the constraint can be expressed as a set of recursive equalities and inequalities on the stock level S_t at time point t:

$$S_a = Q_0$$

$$\forall t \in [a, b-1] \quad S_{t+1} = S_t + \sum_{T_{Pi} = t} Q_{Pi} - \sum_{T_{Cj} = t} Q_{Cj} \tag{2}$$

$$\forall t \in [a, b] \quad S_t \ge 0$$

If the time points T_{Pi} or T_{Cj} are not fixed (resp. no total order given on the events), it is very difficult to express the constraints without adding many additional decision variables.

Fortunately, an alternative solution exists to this problem: using the cumulative constraint in CHIP.

5. Cumulative Constraint

Originally [AB93], the cumulative constraint was introduced in CHIP to tackle complex scheduling problems which could not be solved efficiently with current constraint logic programming systems. Also, experiments in solving complex decision making problems have shown the possibility of extending the use of the cumulative constraint in order to solve placement problems [BC94]. We now briefly describe the declarative semantics and the interpretation of the cumulative constraint

```
cumulative([S1,...,Sn], [D1,...,Dn], [R1,...,Rn], L)
```

where $[S_1,...,S_n]$, $[D_1,...,D_n]$ and $[R_1,...,R_n]$ are non-empty lists of domain variables that have the same length n, and where L is a natural number. For a domain variable V, we define respectively min(V) and max(V) as the smallest and the greatest value of the domain of the variable V.

Let:

$$a = \text{minimum}(\min(S_1),\ldots,\min(S_n))$$
$$b = \text{maximum}(\max(S_1)+\max(D_1),\ldots,\max(S_n)+\max(D_n))$$

The cumulative constraint holds if the following condition is true:

$$\forall t \in [a,b]: \sum_{j \text{ such that } S_j \leq t \leq S_j+D_j-1} R_j \leq L \tag{3}$$

Procedurally, the implementation of the cumulative constraint corresponds to a specialisation of the lookahead [VH89] declaration. From an interpretation point of view the cumulative constraint matches directly the single resource scheduling problem [Go93] [CC88], where $S_1,..S_n$ correspond to the start of the tasks, $D_1,..,D_n$ correspond to the duration of the tasks, and $R_1,..,R_n$ to the amount of resources used by each task. The natural number L is the total amount of available resource which must be shared at any instant by the different tasks. The cumulative constraint states that, at any instant t of the schedule, the sum of the amounts of resource for all tasks that are active at time t does not exceed the upper limit L.

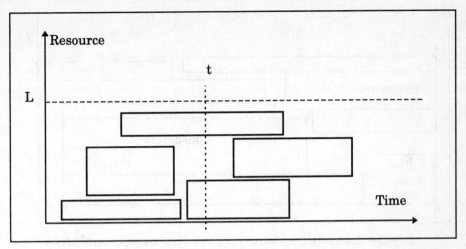

Figure 1: Cumulative Constraint

6. Modelling

We now face the question on how to express the producer/consumer constraint with the help of a cumulative constraint. We will describe the intuition of the modelling first, and then show its correctness formally.

The cumulative constraint models *tasks*, which have a start and an end date, a duration and a resource use, and a *resource availability* which constrains the amount of resource available at any given *time point*. The producer/consumer constraint models *events*, which occur at a *time point* with a given quantity and constrains the overall resource consumption over a *time period*.

In order to express the producer/consumer constraint with the cumulative constraint, we have to convert the events at a time point into tasks stretching over a time period and convert the constraints over resource use in a time period into constraints on individual time points. In a sense, the producer/consumer constraint is the dual of the cumulative constraint, in that time points and periods exchange their meaning.

The basic idea of the conversion is as follows:

A producer events makes some amount of resource available at a time point. We express this by a task which blocks a resource from the start until this time point.

A consumer event uses up some resource at its time point. This resource is no longer available and thus blocked until the end.

The consumer events can consume the initial stock and all production finished before them, the resource limit in the cumulative constraint is then the sum of all producer quantities plus the initial stock.

Graphically, we can express the situation with the following diagram:

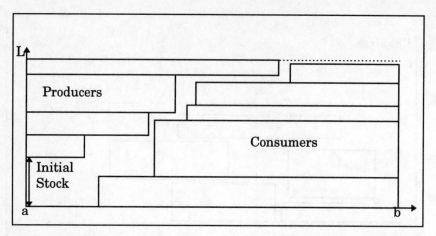

Figure 2: Producer/consumer constraint as cumulative

As long as the producer and consumer areas don't overlap, the constraint is satisfied.

Formally, we define *consumer tasks* and *producer tasks* to express the producer/consumer events.

The producer tasks for the P_i events are defined with a start date a, a duration T_{Pi}-a and a resource use Q_{Pi}.

The consumer tasks for the C_j events are defined with a start date T_{Cj}, a duration b-T_{Cj} and a resource use Q_{Cj}.

The overall availability level for the cumulative constraint is given by the equation:

$$L = Q_0 + \sum_{\text{All } P_i} Q_{Pi} \tag{4}$$

Using the declarative semantics defined for the cumulative constraint above, we can show the correctness of our modelling. For each time point t, the cumulative constraint expresses the inequality

$$\forall t \in [a,b]: \qquad \sum_{j \text{ such that } S_j \leq t \leq S_j + D_j - 1} R_j \quad \leq L \tag{5}$$

Using our descriptions for producer and consumer tasks, we obtain

$$\sum_{T_{Pi}>t} Q_{Pi} + \sum_{T_{Cj}\leq t} Q_{Cj} \leq \sum_{\text{All } Pi} Q_{Pi} + Q_0$$

$$\sum_{T_{Cj}\leq t} Q_{Cj} \leq \sum_{T_{Pi}\leq t} Q_{Pi} + Q_0 \tag{6}$$

$$Q_0 + \sum_{T_{Pi}\leq t} Q_{Pi} - \sum_{T_{Cj}\leq t} Q_{Cj} \geq 0$$

which is the definition of the producer/consumer constraint.

7. Extensions

In this section we discuss some extensions of the basic constraint which often occur in real-life situations. We show that the same modelling can be used after some simple transformations.

7.1 Margins

The basic constraint above states that at each time point the stock level of the consumable resource must be greater or equal to zero. In reality, this constraint will be strengthened to hold a minimum operational stock level l, which must be available at all times. The minimum stock is a safeguard against unexpected delays or requirements of the consumable resource. The actual amount for l will be carefully chosen as a compromise between the inventory cost of this stock and the possibility of running out of stock.

Handling this safety margin in our constraint modelling is trivial, we just reduce the initial stock by the value l.

7.2 Variable Resource Consumption

In the model above we have assumed fixed quantities for producer and consumer events. We can easily extend the modelling to cope with variable quantities by using an extension of the cumulative constraint which allows variable resource limits.

A possible alternative can be used in special cases of batch based production. In some batch production systems, the size of one batch can be adjusted between a minimum level Min and a maximum level Max. In order to produce an overall quantity Qty of a product, we can then find the minimum number N of batches required to fill the order given by:

$$N = \left\lceil \frac{Qty}{Max} \right\rceil \tag{7}$$

This number of batch tasks is then scheduled with a producer/consumer constraint, which controls the start and end of each batch. After this schedule has been obtained, a fine tuning of the batch sizes can be performed independently using the recursive equations 2. This fine tuning will minimise the batch sizes in such a way as to obtain the smallest possible inventory cost. This is done be reducing batch sizes at the beginning of the time period, while satisfying overall stock constraints.

This approach is worthwhile if the number of batches to be produced should be minimised, i.e. if the batch processing is a critical resource. If not, it may be better to split the production into more batches, so that the stock level can be further reduced.

7.3 Splitting Resource Use

Until now we have assumed that consumer events require the full quantity of the consumable resource at one time point, and that producer events make the total amount of resource available at one time point. This assumption works well for batch based production, where a given quantity of resource is either required at the beginning or becomes available at the end of a batch production step. This type of production is a *single step* producer/consumer.

This type of resource use is often coupled with other production steps, which continuously consume or produce resources. A typical example is a packaging line in food industry, which produces a constant flow of finished products and consumes a constant flow of raw materials. This type of production corresponds to a *continuous flow* producer/consumer constraint. As the flow rate is constant over time, we can treat this type of problem with the cumulative resource constraint, specifying that at each time point the quantities produced and consumed must be balanced.

A third type of constraint occurs if a process produces/consumes resources neither in a single step nor in a continuous flow, but rather in *multiple steps*. This often happens if (limited) buffers are available in front of a continuous line, or the finished product from a continuous line is stored in large containers. A typical example would be the packaging of many bottles in crates and palettes. Depending on the time scale, finished palettes may become available in discrete steps, not in a continuous flow.

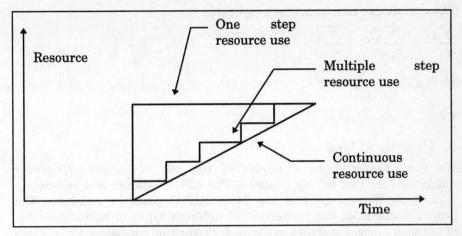

Figure 3: Different Resource Usage Pattern

In the modelling of the producer/consumer constraint, we can introduce multiple step consumption by splitting the producer/consumer tasks into sub tasks with smaller quantity and linked start/end times.

7.4 Limited Storage

The producer/consumer constraint expressed until now only assumes that a minimum limit exists on the stock available of the consumable resource. In practice, the overall storage space will often be limited as well. In this case, we also have to express a constraint on the maximum amount of stock available at each time point. This limit may be given for one resource (for example size of a storage tank) or may be given for the amount taken by several resources together (space in a warehouse). We can express this limit declaratively by the inequality:

$$\forall t \in [a,b] \quad Q_0 + \sum_{T_{Pi} \leq t} Q_{Pi} - \sum_{T_{Cj} \leq t} Q_{Cj} \leq S \tag{8}$$

To express this constraint with the cumulative formalism, we exchange the role of producer and consumer tasks. Consumer tasks now use storage space from the beginning and free storage space at their end, while producer tasks use up storage from their start to the end. The overall resource limit is given by

$$L = S + \sum_{\text{All } Cj} Q_{Cj} - Q_0 \tag{9}$$

The cumulative constraint then expresses

$$\sum_{T_{Pi \leq t}} Q_{Pi} + \sum_{T_{Cj} > t} Q_{Ci} \leq \sum_{All\ Cj} Q_{Cj} + S - Q_0$$

$$Q_0 + \sum_{T_{Pi \leq t}} Q_{Pi} + \sum_{T_{Cj} \leq t} Q_{Cj} \leq S \tag{10}$$

8. Practical Use

We now discuss some examples of the use of consumer/producer constraints for real-life applications. The ATLAS system is a scheduling application for one part of the MONSANTO plant in Antwerp. The program schedules the production of different types of herbicides. The production process is shown in figure 4. Production consists mainly of two steps, a batch formulation part and a continuous packaging (canning) operation.

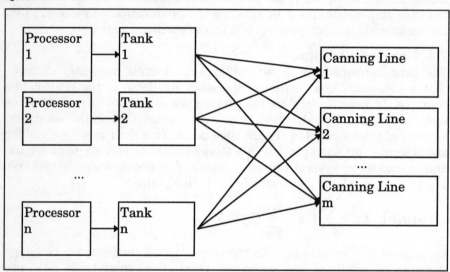

Figure 4: ATLAS production process

Besides many constraints associated with machine choice, set-up times and cumulative manpower constraints, producer/consumer constraints play a major role in the problem solver. The constraints occur in different places:

- Each batch processing step requires different raw materials from a set of available raw materials. Raw materials are stored and delivered at different (fixed) time points in the future. This is a typical consumer constraint where we schedule the use of the raw materials, but not their production.
- The chemicals produced in the batch process are then used to fill bottles and cans of different types and sizes. There is a limited number of storage tanks of fixed sizes which are used to store the

product between production and consumption. The materials for the canning operation must be available at the beginning of each shift. This producer/consumer constraint expresses both minimum and maximum values on the stock levels. Different packaging tasks may use the same intermediate product, which is produced in several batches. The consumption for one task is split in multiples of shift based demands.

- A fine tuning of the batch sizes is performed as a separate step after a schedule has been obtained and accepted. This fine tuning is used to reduce the storage requirements of the intermediate products.
- Besides the chemicals, the canning operations require other packaging materials like bottles, caps, labels, cartons, tape etc. Different canning tasks compete for some of the resources, which can be delivered with a fixed lead time only or by daily call-off from the manufacturer. Again, this is a consumer constraint which splits demands based on the shift pattern. Due to the number of different packaging materials and their storage requirements (empty bottles), only very limited stocks can be held inside the plant. Transfers from and to outside warehouses (also of limited size) must also be taken into account.
- The canning tasks do not correspond directly to orders, one task may serve different orders or several tasks may be needed to fill one order. In addition, some finished product stock may be available. A producer constraint expresses this type of problem.

Not all of these constraints are active in the actual system. Some stock levels (like raw materials) are not critical to the schedule, others (like finished products) are known to be unsatisfiable, as not all orders can be produced in the given time limits.

The actual system works with data sets of several dozen intermediate products and more than one thousand packaging materials, of which roughly one hundred are critical. A typical schedule may contain several hundreds of batches and canning tasks split into many sub-tasks to handle the stock level constraints with an eight hour resolution. In addition, (literally) several thousand other constraints are needed to express other parts of the scheduling problem.

The ATLAS system has been developed jointly by Beyers and Partners and COSYTEC. It is fully operational and in daily use since April 1994. Its overall size is around 30000 lines of CHIP and ORACLE forms/reports code, of which 4000 lines form the actual problem solver. A complete re-run of the problem solver takes some minutes to find a solution of high quality.

The producer/consumer model with the cumulative constraint made it possible to express and effectively solve this scheduling problem in CHIP. But the ATLAS system is not the only application using the producer/consumer modelisation. We just mention two others:

- A scheduling/planning system for crude oil transport in a pipeline network uses producer/consumer constraints for stock levels both for the different sources and for the different sinks.
- A transportation scheduling system for a food processing company uses producer constraints to ensure that raw material transports from many sources arrive in time to keep the different factories operating, while minimising the stock held at each site.

9. Summary

In this paper we have discussed the modelling of producer/consumer constraints for consumable resources with the cumulative constraint in CHIP. This modelling allows to express the constraint in a simple, yet very efficient manner.

Producer/consumer constraints arise in many scheduling and planning problems dealing with stock levels of raw materials and intermediate or finished products. The constraints state that at all time points the available stock level must be between minimum and maximum values. Producer/consumer constraints are a generalisation of sequence constraints arising in flow shop or job shop scheduling problems and occur in many scheduling problems with batch or continuous processing.

It is important to note that we could add this important class of constraints to CHIP without adding any new built-in constraint, just by re-using existing constraints in a novel way.

In addition to the formalism we have presented a typical example of the constraint use from the ATLAS system, a real-life application jointly developed in CHIP by Beyers and Partners and COSYTEC.

In conclusion, the producer/consumer constraint enables us to solve new, more complex scheduling problems with the CHIP system in a simple, yet efficient way.

10. References

[AB93] A. Aggoun, N. Beldiceanu
Extending CHIP in Order to Solve Complex Scheduling Problems
Journal of Mathematical and Computer Modelling, Vol. 17, No. 7, pages 57-73
Pergamon Press, 1993

[Ba74] K. R. Baker
Introduction to Sequencing and Scheduling.
John Wiley, 1974.

[BKC94] G. Baues, P. Kay, P. Charlier
Constraint Based Resource Allocation for Airline Crew Management
ATTIS 94, Paris, April 1994

461

[BS92] N. Beldiceanu, H. Simonis
Aircraft Maintenance Scheduling
COSYTEC TR, Nov 1992

[BC94] N. Beldiceanu, E. Contejean
Introducing Global Constraints in CHIP
Journal of Mathematical and Computer Modelling, Vol 20, No 12, pp 97-123, 1994

[BCP92] J. Bellone, A. Chamard, C. Pradelles
PLANE -An Evolutive Planning System for Aircraft Production.
First International Conference on the Practical Application of Prolog. 1-3 April 1992, London.

[BDP94] P. Bouzimault, Y. Delon, L. Peridy
Planning Exams Using Constraint Logic Programming
2nd Conf Practical Applications of Prolog, London, April 1994

[CC88] J. Carlier and P. Chretienne.
Problèmes d'ordonnancement.
Masson, Paris, 1988

[CDF94] A. Chamard, F. Deces, A. Fischler
A Workshop Scheduler System written in CHIP
2nd Conf Practical Applications of Prolog, London, April 1994

[DHS88] M. Dincbas, P. Van Hentenryck, H. Simonis, A. Aggoun, T. Graf and F. Berthier.
The Constraint Logic Programming Language CHIP.
In Proceedings of the International Conference on Fifth Generation Computer Systems (FGCS'88), pages 693-702, Tokyo, 1988.

[DS91] M. Dincbas, H. Simonis
APACHE - A Constraint Based, Automated Stand Allocation System
Proc. of Advanced Software Technology in Air Transport (ASTAIR'91)
Royal Aeronautical Society, London, UK, 23-24 October 1991, pages 267-282

[Ev92] O. Evans
Factory Scheduling Using Finite Domains
In Logic Programming in Action LNCS 636, 45-53, 1992

[FS90] M.S. Fox and K. Sycara.
Overview of CORTES: A Constraint Based Approach to Production Planning, Scheduling and Control.
In Proceedings of the Fourth International Conference on Expert Systems in Production and Operations Management, 1990.

[Fr82] S. French
Sequencing and Scheduling: an Introduction to the Mathematics of the Job-Shop
Horwood, Chichester, 1982

[FHK92] T. Fruewirth, A. Herold, V. Kuchenhoff, T. Le Provost, P. Lim, M. Wallace
Constraint Logic Programming - An Informal Introduction
In Logic Programming in Action LNCS 636, 3-35, 1992

[Go93] Gotha
Les Problemes d'Ordonnancement
Operations Research vol27, 1, 1993, pages 77-150

[JM94] J. Jaffar M. Maher
Constraint Logic Programming: A Survey
Journal of Logic Programming, 19/20: 503-581, May-July 1994

[KS95] P. Kay, H. Simonis
Building Industrial CHIP Applications from Reusable Software Components
3rd International Conference on Practical Applications of Prolog
Paris, April 1995

[Pi88] E. Pinson
Le Probleme de Job Shop
These de Doctorat de Univ Paris VI, 1988

[SB95] H. Simonis, N. Beldiceanu
The CHIP System
COSYTEC Technical Report, April 1995

[VH89] P. Van Hentenryck.
Constraint Satisfaction in Logic Programming.
MIT Press, Boston, Ma, 1989.

[HSD92] P. Van Hentenryck, H. Simonis, M. Dincbas
Constraint Satisfaction using Constraint Logic Programming
Journal of Artificial Intelligence, Vol.58, No.1-3, pp.113-161, USA, 1992

[Wa94] M. Wallace
Applying Constraints for Scheduling
In B. Mayoh, E. Tyugu, J. Penjaam (Eds) Constraint Programming, Springer Verlag, 1994

A Constraint-Based Approach to Diagnosing Software Problems in Computer Networks

Daniel Sabin, Mihaela Sabin, Robert D. Russell and Eugene C. Freuder

Department of Computer Science, University of New Hampshire, Durham, NH 03824
USA

Abstract. Distributed software problems can be particularly mystifying to diagnose, for both system users and system administrators. Model-based diagnosis methods that have been more commonly applied to physical systems can be brought to bear on such software systems. A prototype system has been developed for diagnosing problems in software that controls computer networks. Our approach divides this software into its natural hierarchy of layers, subdividing each layer into three separately modeled components: the interface to the layer above on the same machine, the protocol to the same layer on a remote machine, and the configuration. For each component knowledge is naturally represented in the form of constraints. User interaction modeling is accomplished through the introduction of constraints representing user assumptions, the finite-state machine specification of a protocol is translated to a standard CSP representation and configuration tasks are modeled as dynamic CSPs. Diagnosis is viewed as a partial constraint satisfaction problem (PCSP). A PCSP algorithm has been adapted for use as a diagnostic engine. This paper presents a case study illustrating the diagnosis of some problems involving the widely used FTP and DNS network software.

1 Introduction

One of the fundamental problems confronting users and managers of computer networks today is the diagnosis of problems arising within the network itself. The symptoms produced by such problems are often baffling since they are so unpredictable and so unrelated to the task for which the network is being used. Furthermore, the error messages from the system are usually so general and vague that little can be gleaned from them as to the exact cause of (and hence the fix to) the problem. Diagnosing under these circumstances is currently more art than science [14]. The situation has been summarized in a cartoon that pictures a visitor to a computing site staring at a swami sitting cross-legged in the corner, and receiving the explanation: "That's our network guru".

Techniques for model-based diagnosis have been used successfully in the diagnosis of physical systems [10]. We have applied and extended this approach to computer network software. We consider this software to be constructed in a *hierarchy of layers* fashion as described in the ISO OSI Reference Model [12].

We subdivide each layer into three separately modeled components: the interface to the layer above on the same machine (or to the user, in the case of the application layer), the protocol to the same layer on a remote machine, and the configuration. This decomposition is developed further in the paper.

Our approach considers diagnosis as a dynamic partial constraint satisfaction problem. Activity constraints are used to interface the model with the "real world" of the network, allowing the model to dynamically obtain data from the network and to use that data to change the problem as the search for a solution progresses. The partial solutions discovered by our system constitute the diagnosis.

The next section concentrates on individual components, presenting examples of problems from widely used *File Transfer Protocol* (FTP) and *Domain Name Service* (DNS) software. Sect. 3 presents the theoretical background for our approach. Sect. 4 gives some details on how problems are represented in our system, presents the actual dynamic partial constraint satisfaction algorithm and shows how one of the sample problems, previously presented in Sect. 2, is actually diagnosed by this algorithm.

This work concentrates on modeling the network *infrastructure* itself. We believe it gives us a solid foundation for understanding basic problems that occur at all levels in information networks, and that the techniques we have developed are applicable at higher levels as well.

2 FTP Case Study

The application protocol chosen for exemplification is FTP, described in RFC 959 [19]. It provides interactive file transfer and relies on Transmission Control Protocol (TCP) – a transport protocol in the TCP/IP hierarchy of protocols [4].

We decompose the problem domain into three components, each of which will be modeled separately, as shown in Fig. 1.

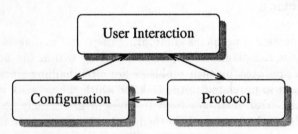

Fig. 1. Problem domain decomposition

1. The *User Interaction* component deals with commands given by the human user and the expectations that the user has about the system response to these commands.
2. The *Protocol* component is really the *network* software, and will later be further decomposed into layers corresponding to the actual implementation of the network software. For now it represents simply all *active software*.

3. The *Configuration* component represents all *passive* information about the network and the computing environment, such as machine names and addresses, routes, connectivity, etc. This information parameterizes the software in the protocol component.

The complete FTP service is structured in two distinct processes, plus the rules and formats, namely the protocol, for information exchange between them. These processes, a client (local) FTP program and a server (remote) FTP daemon, cooperate to accomplish the file transfer function. The client initiates the connection and forwards user commands to the remote server. The server, in response to the received commands, sends replies whose general format is a completion code (including any error code), followed by a textual description of the action taken. A user interface resides on the local machine through which the user requests the transfer of files to and from the remote machine. In our simple examples only two of the basic operations are used:

> **put** *local_file_name*   *remote_file_name*
> **get** *remote_file_name*   *local_file_name*

As a result, a local (remote) file is copied to (from) the remote (local) machine.

But in order to be able to communicate with the server, the client has to establish a connection with it first. Therefore, the client needs to know the server's IP address. Since people prefer names, while computers prefer numbers, programs that interface with users have to map names to numbers, and vice versa. Programs that utilize networking need to map between the names used by people to refer to host computers and the IP addresses (numbers) used to communicate over the network. The Domain Name Service (DNS) [18] consists of a method for constructing names of host computers in a hierarchical manner and a way to resolve these names in a distributed fashion. The Berkeley Internet Name Domain (BIND) is a set of procedures used to map DNS names to IP addresses and vice versa [1] [11]. It consists of a number of server daemons running at various locations in the Internet, each with the responsibility of resolving a subset of the names. On OSF/1 [5] a name is resolved as follows:

1. The file /etc/svc.conf is consulted to see what services are available and in what order they are to be used. Possibilities are *local* and *bind*. Each service in the list is attempted in turn until either the name is resolved or the list is exhausted, in which case the resolution fails.

2. The *local service* is provided by consulting the file /etc/hosts which contains a table of known names and IP addresses. Resolution consists of searching for the name in the table and it fails if the name is not there.

3. The *bind service* is provided by contacting a server daemon called **named**. If the configuration file /etc/resolv.conf is present, it is consulted to find an ordered list of the IP addresses of server daemons to contact. Each daemon in turn is contacted until one of them responds. Resolution fails if none of the servers responds, or if the first one that does respond is not able to resolve the name into an IP address. If the /etc/resolv.conf file is not present,

an attempt is made to contact a server daemon running on the local host. In this case, resolution fails if there is no such server, or if that server is not able to resolve the name into an IP address.

In the examples shown we have run the FTP program on two different machines whose operating systems are ULTRIX (a version of UNIX) and VMS. Their filesystems differ in the way files are represented and named.

According to our framework for network diagnosis we can group the FTP problems we encountered into three categories: user interaction, protocol and configuration problems. For each category we discuss some interesting examples for which we give the diagnosis solution produced by the diagnosis tool. The examples we will present are actual cases we have run and diagnosed. The format of each example explains the FTP command and its execution context, formulates the problem encountered and prints out the message produced by the diagnosis program.

To understand why the problems of the first two categories occurred, we mention briefly the VMS conventions in naming files, which are more restrictive than those for the UNIX filesystem. The name format requires three different fields for name, extension and version number. Only alphanumeric characters are allowed (plus the $ character) to specify the name field. The file extensions are predefined to indicate the type of the file. Other special characters are reserved for wildcards or delimiters in the file name syntax. Thus, names such as "@@" or "!!" are not accepted in the VMS filesystem. Choosing reserved characters to name files usually produces messages such as: "file specification syntax error", "invalid wildcard operation" or "not a plain file", which are self explanatory. However, there are cases in which the FTP server responses are rather cryptic or the transfer results are totally unexpected. We will explore these cases and explain both the FTP execution context and its effects.

2.1 Sample User Interaction Problems

The differences between the filesystems of the local and remote machine can cause surprising name mapping for the files transfered. Newly created file names on the remote machine are generated when the file specification is illegal. This is also a case of name mapping when the filesystems do not have the same naming conventions. An example is shown in Fig. 2.

There are cases in which the files get partially changed without violating naming rules. Even if the sequence of user commands shows no error, as presented in Fig. 3, examining the text files or running the executable files shows strange results. This may happen when the type of the transfer (ASCII or binary) does not match the type of the file transfered. For the ASCII type, conversion to a standard text file representation on the network is necessary to allow communication between different filesystems. The UNIX system considers the newline character as text line delimiter, while VMS uses a line length count. Thus, for the ASCII type of transfer, the sending and receiving sites perform the necessary transformations between the standard representation and their internal representation

```
FTP Command:       put @@ @@
FTP Error Message: ---
FTP Context:       - Local FTP running on UNIX, remote FTP running on VMS
                   - Local file "@@" exists, but is not a valid file name for VMS
Problem:           The transfer takes place, but the remote name is changed to "$A$A.;1"
Diagnosis:         *** Remote file name has the form "$?$?.;?"
```

Fig. 2. Invalid remote file name specification

of files. It is the user's responsibility to correlate the data representation used
and the transformation function performed during the transfer.

```
FTP Command:       put alpha alpha
FTP Error Message: ---
FTP Context:       - Local FTP running on UNIX, remote FTP running on VMS
                   - Local file "alpha" exists on UNIX, and is an ASCII file
                   - The transfer type is "binary"
Problem:           The content of the transfered file is not modified, since the conversion to the
                   standard representation does not apply when "binary" transfer is used. As a
                   result, <EOL> is not recognized on VMS and lines are incorrectly displayed
Diagnosis:         *** Change type to ASCII and redo the transfer
```

Fig. 3. Incorrect transfer type specification

2.2 Sample Protocol Problem

Sometimes illegal parameters in user transfer commands are discarded by the
FTP client and the FTP server receives incompletely specified requests. The
received error message has no useful meaning for the user, as shown in Fig. 4.

It is interesting to notice how the protocol knowledge helps isolate a problem
triggered at the user level. In this sense, a further exploration of the underlying
protocols could extend the problem domain we address.

2.3 Sample DNS Configuration Problem

We assume that all the basic configuration tasks, such as installing TCP/IP
in the kernel and configuring the network interfaces and routing, have been

FTP Command:	get !! !!
FTP Error Message:	RETR: command not understood
FTP Context:	- Local FTP running on VMS, remote FTP running on UNIX
	- File "!!" exists on the remote machine, but is not a valid VMS file name
Problem:	The lower level command RETR used for implementing the user GET
	command requires a nonempty argument. Due to an implementation error,
	the client sends to the server a RETR request with an empty argument.
	The server returns an error message which is not understood by the user.
Diagnosis:	*** FTP client implementation error --
	RETR request with no argument
	*** Invalid VMS file name "!!"

Fig. 4. Protocol implementation error

performed correctly and we look only at various configurations required by the name service.

All the problems in this category follow the same simple scenario: the user tries to connect to a remote host whose name is the parameter of the `ftp` command and the connection is refused. In all cases the remote system gives the same error message: `unknown host`. However, the underlying configurations can be vastly different. For each of these erroneous configurations our diagnostician program figures out what the problem is and provides more useful messages, as shown in the example in Fig. 5.

One type of configuration problem is caused by incompletely specifying the *host table* when only local resolution is used. If the `<remote-host>` name given by the `ftp` command is missing from the `etc/hosts` file, then this host is unknown. This diagnosis is shown in Fig. 5.

Configuration:	- Local resolution only indicated in `/etc/svc.conf`
	- *<remote-host>* name is not in `/etc/hosts`
Diagnosis:	*** Local resolution failed.
	No *<remote-host>* in `/etc/hosts`.

Fig. 5. Local resolution with incompletely specified host table

3 Background

Model-based diagnosis techniques compare observations of the behavior of a system being diagnosed to predictions based upon a model of the system in order to diagnose faults [10]. The fundamental presumption behind model-based diagnosis is that, assuming the model is correct, all the inconsistencies between observation and prediction arise from faults in the system. Given a model description and a set of observations, the diagnosis task is to find a set of faults that will explain the observations. Minimal diagnoses postulate sets of faulty components that are minimal in the sense that no proper subset provides an explanation.

3.1 Model-based Diagnosis as Partial Constraint Satisfaction

Constraint satisfaction is a powerful and extensively used artificial intelligence paradigm [7]. A *constraint satisfaction problem* (CSP) involves a set of problem variables, a set of values for each variable and set of constraints specifying which combinations of values are consistent. A solution to a CSP specifies a value for each variable such that all the constraints are satisfied.

If we assign costs to the values we can look for a solution with optimal cost. Model-based diagnosis can be viewed as a constraint optimization problem by associating system components with constraints that reflect their behavior, component inputs and outputs with problem variables, and introducing assumption variables associated with the system components, where a value of 0 for an assumption variable reflects normal behavior and a value of 1 abnormal behavior [6]. Observations force assignment of some of the problem variables. The task of finding a minimal diagnosis corresponds to finding an optimal solution of such a CSP.

We use a refinement of this approach based on the notion of a *partial constraint satisfaction problem* (PCSP) [8]. PCSPs were introduced for applications that settle for partial solutions that leave some of the constraints unsatisfied, e.g. because the problems are overconstrained or because complete solutions require too much time to compute.

We have found that PCSPs provide an elegant approach to viewing diagnosis in CSP terms. Regarding components as constraints, and faulty components as failed constraints, minimal diagnoses naturally correspond to PCSP solutions that leave minimal sets of constraints unsatisfied. These sets are minimal in that there is no solution which leaves only a proper subset unsatisfied. Bakker et al. [2] have taken the opposite approach, applying model-based diagnosis methods to partial constraint satisfaction.

Combinations of branch and bound and CSP techniques have been used in algorithms that search for a solution that leaves a minimal number of constraints unsatisfied [8]. We have adapted one of these algorithms to search for solutions with minimal sets of unsatisfied constraints. One of the advantages of viewing diagnosis as a PCSP is that it permits us to bring our experience with PCSP algorithms to bear on diagnosis.

3.2 Modeling Configuration as Dynamic Constraint Satisfaction

For synthesis tasks such as configuration and model composition, the constraint problem is of a more dynamic nature [15] [16] [17]. Any of the elements of the CSP might change during the search process. Mittal and Falkenhainer introduced the notion of a *dynamic constraint satisfaction problem* (DCSP) by adding a new type of constraint, called an *activity constraint*, on the variables considered in each solution. Activity constraints, expressed in terms of consistent assignment of values to some already instantiated set of variables, specify which variables and constraints should be added to or removed from the current CSP. The problem thus changes as search progresses.

The main advantage of this extension to the standard CSP is that inferences can now be made about variable activity, based on the conditions under which variables become active, avoiding irrelevant work during search.

The definitions of a dynamic constraint satisfaction problem and activity constraints, as stated in [15], are the following:

Given

- A set of variables V representing all variables that may potentially become active and appear in a solution.
- A non-empty *initial set of active variables* $V_I = \{v_1, \ldots, v_k\}$, which is a subset of V.
- A set of discrete, finite domains $D_1, \ldots, D_k$, with each domain D_i representing the set of possible values for variable $v_i \in V$.
- A set of *compatibility constraints* C^C on subsets of V limiting the values they may take on. These correspond to the standard set of CSP constraints. In addition, if any of the variables involved in the constraint are not active, the constraint is trivially satisfied.
- A set of *activity constraints* C^A on subsets of V specifying constraints between the activity and possible values of problem variables. There are four types of activity constraints, which can be divided into two groups:
  1. *require variable* and *require not*, which establish the activity (inactivity) of a variable based on an assignment of values to a set of already active variables. A require-variable constraint is logically equivalent to:
  $active(V_1) \wedge \ldots \wedge active(V_j) \wedge P(v_1, \ldots, v_j) \rightarrow active(V_k)$, where P is a predicate, v_i is the current value assigned to variable $V_i, \forall i, 1 \leq i \leq j$ and $V_k \notin \{V_1, \ldots, V_j\}$.
  2. *always require variable* and *always require not*, which establish the activity (inactivity) of a variable based on the activity of other variables, independent of their current value. An always require variable constraint is logically equivalent to:
  $active(V_1) \wedge \ldots \wedge active(V_j) \rightarrow active(V_k)$, where $V_k \notin \{V_1, \ldots, V_j\}$.

Find

- All solutions, where a solution is an assignment A which meets two criteria:

1. The variables and assignments in A satisfy $C^C \cup C^A$.
2. No subset of A is a solution.

4 Representation and Reasoning

We model each of the components of Fig. 1 – user interaction, protocol, configuration – as a separate PCSP knowledge base. Protocol diagnosis has been studied previously as a constraint satisfaction problem [3] [9] [20]. We apply a similar approach here to the FTP protocol. We demonstrate here that user interaction diagnosis can also be modeled as a constraint satisfaction problem, in particular by introducing constraints that reflect user assumptions. Finally, extending the representation used by [17], we are able to treat diagnosis of configuration tasks as a PCSP as well.

These three components are naturally modeled separately. They utilize different mechanisms to instantiate the general CSP paradigm, e.g. an intermediate finite state machine model for protocols. Applying the diagnostic engine successively to the three separate domains, until a diagnosis is found, may reduce the combinatorial complexity the engine faces. On the other hand, it is already clear that there are interesting interactions between these components, which may ultimately require a more sophisticated control architecture.

There was also a knowledge engineering, knowledge acquisition effort in developing the user interaction model. Considerable time was spent exploring different types of interaction that can occur, and discovering different types of problems that can arise.

4.1 User Interaction

The FTP commands specify the parameters for the data connection (data port, transfer mode, representation type, structure, etc) and the nature of the file system operation (store, retrieve, append, delete, etc).

Each time the user gives a command, the current state of the FTP client can be represented as a PCSP problem. The set of variables includes the transfer parameters: MODE, STRUCTURE, TYPE, the local and remote operating systems: CLIENT, SERVER, the file system operation, COMMAND, and the file pathname, PATH. In addition, there are some other variables which have no direct correspondent among the entities that characterize the state of the client. They represent instead, either the user's perception of the result of the operation, or, to some extent, the state of the user's mind at that moment. The variable OUTCOME represents the outcome of an FTP operation. Since the value of this variable cannot be determined at the time of the transfer, the user is responsible for supplying a value ("success", or, if something went wrong, his perception of "wrong", e.g. "ascii file incorrectly transferred"). Clearly, the motivation for introducing this variable in the PCSP is that it allows us to embody faulty behaviors in the model.

A "fault" at this level typically means a mismatch between the status of the real world and the user's mental representation of it. For example, data representations are handled in FTP by a user specifying a representation type, described in our model by the variable TYPE. When the user is specifying a value for the TYPE variable, he is in fact just making an assumption about the actual type of the file, represented by the value of the variable ACTUAL-TYPE. User's assumptions are modeled in a natural way with constraints. In this particular case, there is an equality constraint between variables TYPE and ACTUAL-TYPE.

This difference in semantics implies that all such PCSPs will have two sets of constraints:

1. constraints that will be part of all the PCSPs, representing the functional specification model of FTP (accounting for both correct and incorrect behavior);

2. constraints that change from problem to problem:

   (a) constraints modeling user's assumptions about the real world;

   (b) some FTP commands translate to unary constraints, forcing value assignments for the corresponding variables (e.g. the FTP command get restricts the domain of the variable COMMAND to a single value, namely *get*).

4.2 Protocol

Protocol specifications are typically represented in the form of finite automata, often referred to as *finite-state machines* (FSMs). Since simple FSMs have limited expressive power in representing such notions as timers, logical conditions, etc., a more powerful formalism is needed, and thus extended finite automata have been used for protocol testing and specification analysis or diagnosis [13] [21].

The idea of using model-based techniques to diagnose communication protocols based on extended finite automata is not new. To our knowledge, at least three protocol diagnosis systems have been proposed [3] [9] [20]. All these approaches attempt to diagnose protocols by analyzing conflicts between observations and the protocol model. This implies that observations must somehow be associated with the model.

The representation approach we are using is similar to the one used by Riese in [20]. The FTP protocol specification as an extended finite transducer is translated into a standard CSP form.

Where Riese is using a specialized algorithm for solving the diagnosis problem, he calls it HMDP, we are using a variant of a standard PCSP algorithm to produce the set of minimal diagnoses.

We make the same assumptions as Riese does, that the external observer resides outside of the node on which the system under diagnosis is implemented, and that the observer can time-stamp messages when they are observed.

In addition to the time stamp of the message, an observation also contains the type of the message (STOR, RETR, etc.), the corresponding arguments, if any, and the direction of the message, relative to the client (SEND or RECEIVE).

Each observation has a CSP variable associated with it. Considering the order given by the time stamps, let $OBS =< o_1, \ldots, o_n >$ be a sequence of observations and let v_i be the variable associated with observation o_i. The domain of values of such a variable is simply the set of all valid state transitions described by the extended finite transducer. Thus, to solve the CSP we have to assign one state transition of the protocol machine to each variable corresponding to an observation, subject to two kinds of constraints:

1. unary constraints, which check whether the value t_i assigned to some variable v_i has the same message type, direction and number and type of arguments as the associated observation o_i;
2. binary constraints, which relate a variable v_i to its neighbors v_{i-1} and v_{i+1} by checking whether the pairs of corresponding values t_i, t_{i-1} and t_i, t_{i+1} respectively, are part of a sequence of transitions allowed by the protocol machine. Due to transitivity, if all the binary constraints are satisfied, a solution to the problem will represent a complete transition sequence explaining OBS.

When the FTP implementation is faulty, conflicts between observations and the FTP model will result in partial satisfaction of the constraints, and the diagnosis algorithm applied to this PCSP will produce the set of minimal diagnosis in terms of errors at the level of the protocol commands (e.g. incorrect/missing arguments) and/or sets of faulty state transitions.

4.3 Configuration

We use the same approach as [15], but extend the definition of DCSP to that of *dynamic partial constraint satisfaction problem* (DPCSP), by relaxing two of the requirements in the previously presented DCSP definition.

First, we do not restrict the domains of values for variables to be predefined finite sets of values. In some cases domains are still finite sets of values, known from the beginning, but this is not always true. Due to the nature of our application, the values some variables may take are known only during the search, when these variables become active.

Second, since we are trying to solve a diagnosis problem which might have no complete solution, the (partial) solution we accept may violate some of the constraints, but we are still looking for an optimal solution, according to some criterion (e.g. minimal number of violated constraints).

Studying name service configuration and modeling it using the DCSP formalism, we found out that quite a simple language is sufficient for specifying the associated dynamic constraint satisfaction problem. Since a DCSP has four basic components, a program in this language will naturally have four sections:

1. a section defining the set of variables and corresponding domains of values,
2. a section specifying the set of activity constraints,
3. a section specifying the set of compatibility constraints, and
4. a section specifying the initial set of active variables.

Variable Specification Figure 6 presents the variable definition section for a simplified model of the name service.

// Variables

VAR	remote-host	ASK prompt-user("Remote host name:")
VAR	ping-path	DEF "/sbin/ping"
VAR	services-file	DEF "/etc/svc.conf"
VAR	resolve-file	DEF "/etc/resolv.conf"
VAR	hosts-file	DEF "/etc/hosts"
VAR	ping-response	ASK ping($remote-host)
VAR	resolution-type	ASK resolve-service($services-file, "hosts")
VAR	hosts	ASK resolve-host($hosts-file)
VAR	local-server	DEF "/etc/named.pid"
VAR	servers	ASK resolve-name-server($resolve-file)
VAR	domain	ASK resolve-domain($resolve-file), local-host())

Fig. 6. Variables definition section

In order to specify a CSP using the specification language, all variables have to be declared using a VAR statement. Each variable is completely specified by the value of two attributes: *name* and *domain* of possible values.

When the domains are known ahead of time, we simply need a way to directly express them as sets of values. But since the domains of values are not predefined finite sets of values for all variables, we also need a way of specifying a procedure by which a domain will be obtained when the variable becomes active during search. Accordingly, the language offers two built-in mechanisms for specifying the domain of values for a variable:

a) The user can supply a *default*, or predefined, domain as a set of values by using the DEF slot of the VAR statement.

b) In case the domain of a variable is not known at specification time, the user must supply, as the value of the ASK slot, the call to a function which, when executed, will return the set of values in the domain. Function execution will be triggered by the activation of the variable. The function may take as arguments either constants (e.g. string, number) or the current value of variables which, at the time of the call, are already active. The current value of a variable is selected by the expression *$variable*, where *variable* is the name of the variable.

Modeling the name service configuration, we have to provide several user-defined functions which inspect configuration files, invoke UNIX system calls or prompt the user in order to get the *asked* values for the current variable. The *prompt-user* function takes one parameter, the message to be displayed. All the functions that examine configuration files need at least one parameter, indicating the name of the file where the possible values might be found. Some of them require a second parameter, usually a string constant, to localize the line in the file where the information is stored.

Constraints Specification Activity and compatibility constraints are specified in the form of boolean expressions over variables and their possible values. The language provides the standard logical and relational operators, enhanced, for increased flexibility, with set-based operators (e.g. test for set membership, set inclusion, etc.). The operands can be constants, the current value of active variables, selected using the *$variable* expression, built–in and user–written functions, taking as arguments any of the above.

As an example, Fig. 7 presents the activity and compatibility constraints in the name service configuration model. The keywords START, ARV, RV stand for initial set of active variables (START), always require variable (ARV) and require variable (RV). When specifying a compatibility constraint, the user must also supply a formatted output statement which, in case the constraint fails, will be printed as the diagnostic message.

// *Initial Set of Active Variables*

START remote-host

// *Activity Constraints*

ARV remote-host ⇒ (ping-path ping-response)
RV $ping-response = "unknown" ⇒ (services-file resolution-type)
RV $resolution-type = "local" ⇒ (hosts-file hosts)
RV $resolution-type = "bind" ⇒ (resolve-file servers domain))
RV $servers = nil ⇒ local-server

// *Compatibility Constraints*

CON $remote-host IN $hosts
    "*** Local resolution failed. No $remote-host in $hosts-file."
CON $local-server != nil
    "*** Local resolution failed. No $remote-host in $hosts-file."
CON $servers = nil OR bind-resolve($remote-host $servers $domain)
    "*** BIND resolution failed."

Fig. 7. Activity and compatibility constraints definition section

4.4 Algorithm Description

Figure 8 provides a basic branch and bound algorithm for solving dynamic partial constraint satisfaction problems. It is a refinement of a partial constraint satisfaction algorithm presented in [8].

```
bound ← {{con|con is a compatibility constraint }}
algorithm BRANCH&BOUND (distance, search-path, variables, values)
   if (variables = ∅) then
      if (distance = ∅) then
         return true
      for each element D ∈ bound do
         if (distance ⊆ D) then
            bound ← bound \{D}
         □
      bound ← bound ∪{ distance }
      return false
   □
   if (values = ∅) then
      return false
   crrt-variable ← first variable in variables
   crrt-value ← first value in values
   new-distance ← distance
   subsumed ← false
   for each constraint C involving crrt-variable and variables in search-path
      until (subsumed = true) do
      if (C fails) then
         new-distance ← new-distance ∪ {C}
         if (∃ D ∈ bound such that D ⊆ new-distance) then
            subsumed ← true
      □
   if (subsumed = false) then
      required-variables ← RUN-ARV(crrt-var) ∪ RUN-RV(crrt-var, crrt-val)
      new-variables ← variables \{ crrt-variable }∪ required-variables
      if (BRANCH&BOUND(new-distance,
         search-path ∪⟨ crrt-variable, crrt-value ⟩,
         new-variables, domain of first variable in new-variables))
      then
         return true
   □
   return BRANCH&BOUND(distance, search-path, variables, values \{ crrt-value })
□
```

Fig. 8. Dynamic partial constraint satisfaction algorithm

Branch and bound operates in a similar fashion to backtracking in a context where we are seeking all solutions that violate minimal, under set inclusion, sets of constraints. The algorithm basically keeps track of the best solutions found so far and abandons a line of search when it becomes clear that the current partial solution cannot lead to a better solution. In fact, the notion of failure during search is the main difference between CSP and PCSP. A CSP search path fails as soon as a single inconsistency is encountered. A PCSP search path will fail only when enough inconsistencies accumulate to reach a cutoff bound.

The *bound* in our context is a set containing the sets of constraints left unsatisfied by the best solutions found so far. If at any time during the search the set of constraints violated by the current partial solution, which we call the *distance*, becomes a superset of any element in the *bound*, the current search path is abandoned.

Once the search path is complete, i.e. all variables have been assigned a value, if its *distance* is a subset of any element in the *bound*, then that element will be replaced by the *distance*. In other words, the partial solution we found is better than a previous solution in the sense that it violates only a subset of the constraints violated by the previous solution.

The search process stops when either a complete solution, one that satisfies all the constraints, is found, or when we exhausted all the values for all the variables. Finding a complete solution is equivalent, from the diagnostic point of view, to finding that the configuration under diagnosis is correct, i.e. it presents no "faults". In the second case, the *bound* represents exactly the set of minimal diagnoses, that is, the set of minimal sets of constraints, one for every "best" partial solution found.

For the sake of simplicity in presentation, the algorithm in Fig. 8 does not in any way use the partial solution it finds (*search-path*). In fact, each element in the *bound* is not only a set of constraints, but a pair: set of constraints and the corresponding partial solution.

When we presented the language, we said that the definition of each constraint includes an output statement, which represents the text of the diagnostic message, in case the constraint is violated. When the algorithm stops, each element in the *bound* represents a possible minimal diagnosis for the configuration being tested. Therefore, one diagnostic message will consists of all the strings included in the definitions of the constraints in one such element.

The algorithm can also produce, if requested by the user, an explanation for each diagnosis, by printing the values assigned to each variable in the corresponding search path.

4.5 Sample Trace

We show in Fig. 9 a trace of our algorithm solving the problem presented in Fig. 5. Initially, only variable *remote-host* is active. Since it has an ASK function of type PROMPT-USER, the user will be asked to provide the name of the remote host. Let's say the user typed in **xx.xx.xx**. Due to the ARV constraint, variables *ping-path* and *ping-response* become active (STEP 1). Using function PING, the value of *ping-response* is set to "unknown". One of the RV constraints is satisfied now and variables *services-file* and *resolution-type* are activated (STEP 2). Using function RESOLVE-SERVICE, the algorithm decides that the value of *resolution-type* is "local". A new RV constraint is satisfied. Accordingly, variables *hosts-file*

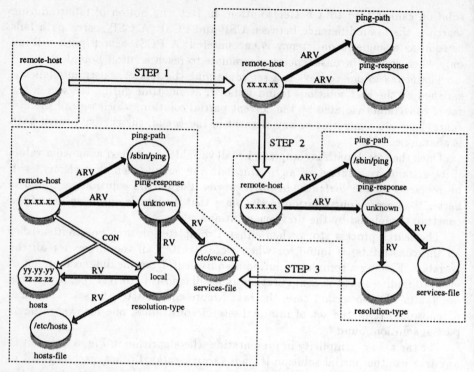

Fig. 9. Example trace for the problem presented in Fig. 2

and *hosts* become active (STEP 3). Variable *hosts* is initialized to the list of host names read from the etc/hosts file. Since all the variables involved in the compatibility constraint among *remote-host*, *hosts* and *resolution-type* have been instantiated, the constraint becomes active and the check fails. Because there are no other values to try, the current assignment represents the only solution of this DPCSP. So, the algorithm stops with the value of *bound* being a set with one element, the set containing only one constraint, the one that just failed. The diagnostic message is thus the string produced by the associated output statement:

```
*** Local resolution failed.
No XX.XX.XX in /etc/hosts.
```

which is the current diagnosis for this problem.

5 Conclusion

The prototype system we developed for diagnosing software problems in computer networks uses model-based diagnosis techniques. Given a model description of the software system, and a set of observations describing faulty behavior when the service is provided, the diagnosis task finds the set of errors that explain the observations and gives precise diagnosis messages. We use a PCSP approach to view the model-based diagnosis in CSP terms, where the interacting components that define the service are the constraints. Since we solve a diagnosis problem which might have no complete solution, we need to accept partial solutions which violate some of the constraints. Thus, minimal diagnoses correspond directly to PCSP solutions that leave minimal sets of constraints unsatisfied. The dynamic nature of a configuration task is described in terms of DPCSP: at any given point in the search process configuration components are added or removed dynamically from the current problem. This enables our system to obtain current information directly from the network by applying user-written functions supplied with the model. Data thus obtained is used to guide the search by determining which components to activate. We showed the effectiveness of our prototype system on several sample problems for which more meaningful diagnosis messages have been produced.

We consider two ways in which our system could be extended, to diagnose both widely used Internet high-level services, such as NFS, NIS, etc., and lower-level protocols in the protocol hierarchy. To achieve the second goal, the mechanism used in our system is powerful enough to allow *on-line diagnosis* of lower level protocols. In our initial exploration of configuration problems we chose BIND because it is high in the protocol hierarchy, at the application level, and there are already useful tools, such as "ping" and "nslookup", that can be coupled directly into our system to provide dynamic information. However, we need to extend the problem domain to involve the entire protocol stack to detect errors that might propagate up the stack. These errors may affect the system performance or, even if an error at one level is handled properly by the protocol at a higher level, it might signal future errors. For on-line diagnosis we need to be able to run our system in a *monitoring mode*, whereby normal situations are checked in order to detect faults before they propagate. For this, we need to develop appropriate data gathering tools that filter the huge amount of data exchanged by lower-level services.

Acknowledgments

This material is based on work supported by Digital Equipment Corporation, and by the National Science Foundation under Grant No. IRI-9207633.

References

1. Albitz, P. and Liu, C., *DNS and BIND*, O'Reilly & Associates, Inc., Sebastopol, CA, 1994.
2. Bakker, R.R., Dikker, F., Tempelman, F. and Wognum, P.M., Diagnosing and solving over-determined constraint satisfaction problems, *Proceedings of the 13th International Joint Conference on Artificial Intelligence*, 1, 276–281, 1993.
3. Bouloutas, A.T., Modeling Fault Management in Communication Networks, PhD Thesis, Columbia University, 1990.

4. Comer, D.E., *Internetworking with TCP/IP*, vol. **1**, Prentice Hall, Inc., Englewoods Cliffs, NJ, 1991.

5. DEC OSF/1, Configuring Your Network Software, *Digital Equipment Corporation*, 1993.

6. El Fattah, Y. and Dechter, R., Empirical Evaluation of Diagnosis as Optimization in Constraint Networks, *Working Papers of The Third International Workshop on Principles of Diagnosis (DX-92)*, (1992).

7. Freuder, E.C. and Mackworth, A.K., Special Volume, Constraint-Based Reasoning, *Artificial Intelligence*, **58**, 1992.

8. Freuder, E.C. and Wallace, R.J., Partial Constraint Satisfaction, *Artificial Intelligence*, **58**, 21–71, 1992.

9. Ghedamsi, A., von Bochmann, G. and Dssouli, R., Diagnosing multiple faults in finite state machines, Technical Report, Dept. d'IRO, Universite de Montreal, Canada, January 1993.

10. Hamscher, W., Console, L. and de Kleer, J., editors, *Readings in Model-based Diagnosis*, Morgan Kaufmann Publishers, Inc., San Mateo, CA, 1992.

11. Hunt, C., *TCP/IP Network Administration*, O'Reilly & Associates, Inc., Sebastopol, CA, 1994.

12. ISO, ISO Open Systems Interconnection - Basic Reference Model, Second Edition, *ISO/TC 97/SC 16(ISO CD 7498-1)*, 1992.

13. Lin, Y.J. and Wuu, G., A constraint approach for temporal intervals in the analysis of timed transitions, *Protocol Specification, Testing and Verification*, **XI**, 215–230, 1991.

14. Miller, M.A., *Troubleshooting TCP/IP*, M&T Books, 1993.

15. Mittal, S. and Falkenhainer, B., Dynamic Constraint Satisfaction Problems, *Proceedings of the Eighth National Conference on Artificial Intelligence (AAAI-90)*, 25-32, 1990.

16. Mittal, S., Reasoning about Resource Constraints in Configuration Tasks, *SSL Technical Report, XEROX Park*, 1990.

17. Mittal, S. and Frayman, F., Towards a Generic Model of Configuration Tasks, *Proceedings of the Eleventh International Joint Conference on Artificial Intelligence*, **2**, 1395–1401, 1989.

18. Mockapetris, P., Domain Names - Concepts and Facilities, *Request For Comments 1034*, 1987.

19. Postel, J., File Transfer Protocol, *Request For Comments 959*, ISI, October 1985.

20. Riese, M., Model-based Diagnosis of Communication Protocols, PhD Thesis, Swiss Federal Institute of Technology, Lausanne, 1993.

21. Wang, C.J. and Liu, M.T., A test suite generation method for extended finite state machines using axiomatic semantics approach, *Protocol Specification, Testing and Verification*, **XII**, 29–43, 1992.

Solving Crew Scheduling Problems
by Constraint Programming

Nabil Guerinik and Michel Van Caneghem *

Laboratoire d'Informatique de Marseille , URA CNRS 1787 **
Prologia ***

Abstract. Programming by linear constraints makes it possible to express complex problems of operations research. However, real industrial problems cannot be solved in a reasonable amount of time if one insists on coding everything only in constraint programming languages.
We have experienced this fact in the case of the Airline and bus Crew Scheduling problem. We propose a method based on constraint programming with a part of the implementation written in C. This allows us to solve more easily and also as efficiently as the best existing programs, difficult problems (300 flights and 500000 pairings). This program is currently used for a French airline company.

1   Introduction

The crew scheduling problem is one which has been studied continuously for the past 40 years. The problem involves assigning crews to flights. The goal is to minimize crew costs while satisfying the many constraints imposed by governmental and labor work rules.

Crew scheduling problems are now efficiently solved by operations research technics. However, the adaptation to different airline company rules is not very practical. We developed a methodology based on constraint programming in order to solve this kind of problems. Starting from a naive resolution of the problem with Prolog III language, we refine this program by adding operations research considerations. This makes it possible to develop efficient combinatorial algorithms. Next, we study in the same way specific problems related to the large size of the problems treated (preprocessing, selection and filtering).

In order to obtain reasonable performances, a small part of the algorithm had been rewritten in C (in particular the simplex). We show with benchmarks that our method gives results comparable to those of operations research. This is well worth a couple of extra pages in C!

This method has also been applied to the assignment of drivers for bus companies (Esprit project SuperbuS 8742).

---

* E-mail: nabil.guerinik@lim.univ-mrs.fr, michel.van.caneghem@lim.univ-mrs.fr

** Université de la Méditerranée, 163 avenue de Luminy, 13288 Marseille cedex 09 (France)

*** Prologia, case 919 Luminy, 13288 Marseille cedex 09 (France). E-mail: prologia@prologianet.univ-mrs.fr

2 Solving Crew Scheduling

We are going to illustrate the different algorithms used with an example which is simpler than the one concerning airplane crews. We will take the problem of driver assignment for a regional bus company. Following a schedule for passengers, the company allocates buses to satisfy this service.

The problem of crew scheduling is that of assigning drivers to these buses, knowing that safety regulations (periods of driving and rest) as well as trade union rules must be satisfied. This assignment must be done at minimal cost (number of drivers). The following is an example of this kind of schedule:

			16h	08h	↑	Paris			09h	16h	17h	17h
	18h	16h	↑	06h		Orléans			↓	18h	19h	↓
		↑	↑	14h		Troyes			11h		↓	19h
23h	16h	14h	↑			Chateauroux		10h	14h		21h	↓
21h			12h			Nevers	↓	12h	16h			22h

To deal with this problem, we need to have a few definitions. A *spell* represents a route connection between two cities (this is the basic unit). A bus driver performs what is called a *pairing* (or a duty), which is a valid succesion of spells. By validity, we mean the satisfaction of a set of contractual and trade union conditions. For example:

1. a driver must never travel uselessly, that is, all his trips must correspond to spells;
2. every duty lasts no more than one day between 6.00 and 23.00;
3. the duration of a duty (time spent between the departure of the first spell and the arrival of the last) does not exceed 12 hours;
4. a driver must not drive more than four hours without interruption.

We seek to minimize first the number of drivers needed to cover all of the spells, secondly the total service time.

2.1 The Natural Approach

The most natural solving method consists in partitioning the set of spells in valid subsets and in distinguishing among all the possible partitions the one with the smallest cardinality. Our program enumerates by consequent all the possible partitions.

```
solve(Part,Cost) :- minimize(Cost,solution(Part,Cost)).

solution(Part,Cost):-
    listOfSpells(Set), partition(Set,Part), partitionCost(Part,Cost).

partition(<>,<>).
partition(Set,<SubSet>.Part) :-
    subSet(SubSet,Set,Set1),
```

```
    validSubSet(SubSet),
    partition(Set1,Part)
    {Set # <>, SubSet # <>}.

subSet(<>,<>,<>).
subSet(<E>.SS,<E>.S,S1) :- subSet(SS,S,S1).
subSet(SS,<E>.S,<E>.S1) :- subSet(SS,S,S1).

validSubSet(S) :-
    spell(Id,Dt,At,Dp,Ap), feasableSubSet(At,Ap,S1), validDuty(S)
    {S = <Id>.S1}.

feasableSubSet(At,Dp,<>).
feasableSubSet(At,Dp,<Id>.S) :-
    spell(Id,Dt,At1,Dp,Ap), feasableSubSet(At1,Ap,S)
    {Dt >= At}.

validDuty(Duty) :-
    dutyStrech(Duty,DepTime,ArrTime)
    {6 =< DepTime, ArrTime =< 23, ArrTime - DepTime =< 12}.

dutyStrech(<Id>,Dt,At) :- spell(Id,Dt,At,_,_).
dutyStrech(<Id1>._.<Id2>,Dt,At) :-
    spell(Id1,Dt,_,_,_), spell(Id2,_,At,_,_).

partitionCost(<>,0).
partitionCost(<Duty>.Part,Cost + 100 + Ar - Dt) :-
    dutyStrech(Duty,Dt,Ar), partitionCost(Part,Cost).

listOfSpells(<a,d,h,g,i,l,f,k,b,c,e,n,m,j>).

spell(a, 6, 8,orl,par).      spell(b,16,18,par,orl).
spell(c,17,19,par,orl).      spell(d, 9,11,par,tro).
spell(e,17,19,par,tro).      spell(f,14,16,tro,par).
spell(g,12,14,nev,tro).      spell(h,10,12,cha,nev).
spell(i,14,16,cha,nev).      spell(j,21,23,nev,cha).
spell(k,16,18,cha,orl).      spell(l,14,16,cha,orl).
spell(m,20,22,tro,nev).      spell(n,19,21,orl,cha).
```

where:

- **minimize** finds the minimum cost by successive enumeration (each time a solution is found, everything starts again while imposing that the cost is strictly inferior to it);
- **validDuty** verify a few contractual rules (the rules 1,2 and 3);
- **partitionCost** calculate the cost of a pairing.

and here is the result:

```
?- solve(Part,Cost).
```

```
*** 746
*** 744
*** 743
*** 741
*** 739
*** 738
{Part = <<a,d,f,b>,<h,g>,<i,j>,<l>,<k>,<c,n>,<e,m>>, Cost = 738}
```

As soon as the number of elements is larger (which is the case for real-life problems) this method is no longer usable. This way of doing it also has the inconvienience of not imposing constraints before enumeration, these having as a goal the limitation of the search tree. It is therefore necessary to formulate the problem in another way.

2.2   Set Partitioning Modelling

One idea consists in generating all valid subsets of spells (valid pairings), then to choose a family of subsets forming a partition of the set of spells,which is of minimum cost. This is easily expressed with constraint programming although it is not always very efficient because of the combinatory aspect of the problem. To express this problem of partition we associate with each pairing j a variable x_j such that:

$$x_j = \begin{cases} 1 \text{ if the pairing } j \text{ is in the solution} \\ 0 \text{ if not} \end{cases}$$

then we construct a matrix $A = (a_{ij})_m^n$ where m is the number of spells and n the number of pairings generated which is defined by:

$$a_{ij} = \begin{cases} 1 \text{ if the spell } i \text{ is covered by the pairing } j \\ 0 \text{ if not} \end{cases}$$

A set of pairings forms a partition if and only if each spell is assured by a single pairing belonging to this set, which is expressed by the following constraints:

$$\forall\, 1 \leq i \leq m, \quad \sum_{j=1}^{n} a_{ij} x_j = 1$$

Let us denote by c_j the cost of the pairing j. Our problem can then by formulated by the following linear program:

$$\begin{cases} \min \sum_{j=1}^{n} c_j x_j \\ \sum_{j=1}^{n} a_{ij} x_j = 1 \,, \; \forall\, 1 \leq i \leq m \\ x_j \in \{0,1\} \,, \; \forall\, 1 \leq j \leq n \end{cases}$$

It involves a linear integer program. The integer constraint resolution algorithms are difficult and often inefficient. The method used consists in releasing in our system the constraint $x_j \in \{0,1\}$ by replacing it with the constraint $0 \le x_j \le 1$ followed by an enumeration procedure that is going to affect x_j either the value 0 or the value 1. The algorithm written in Prolog III appears as

```
solve(L,Cost) :-
    numberOfDuties(N),
    listOfSpells(S),
    positive(L),
    setPar(S,L),
    computeCost(L,1,Cost),
    minimize(Cost,enumerate(L))
    {L::N}.

positive(<>) .
positive(<X>.L) :- positive(L) {X >= 0}.

setPar(<>,L).
setPar(<S1>.S,L) :- setParBis(S1,1,L,Sum), setPar(S,L) {Sum = 1}.

setParBis(S,_,<>,0).
setParBis(S,I,<X>.L,Sum + X) :-
    cover(I,S), !, setParBis(S,I + 1,L,Sum).
setParBis(S,I,<X>.L,Sum) :- setParBis(S,I + 1,L,Sum).

cover(I,S) :- duty(I,_,L), member(S,L) .

computeCost(<>,_,0).
computeCost(<X>.L,I,Sum + Cost*X) :-
    duty(I,Cost,_), computeCost(L,I + 1,Sum).

enumerate(<>).
enumerate(<1>.L) :- enumerate(L).
enumerate(<0>.L) :- enumerate(L).

numberOfDuties(44).
```

where:

- positive(L) put the constraints $\forall j \; x_j \ge 0$ ($x_j \le 1$ follows from set partitioning equations);

- setPar(S,L) put set partitionning constraints ($\forall i \; \sum_{j=1}^{n} a_{ij}x_j = 1$);

- computeCost(L,Cost) represents $\sum_{j=1}^{n} c_j x_j$;

- enumerate(L,Cost) enumerates all the variables x_j.

Here is the result after 30 stages of optimization:

```
?- solve(L,Cost).
*** 1428

*** 1331
*** 1329
*** 1236
...
*** 741
*** 739
*** 738
{L = <0,0,0,1,0,0,0,0,0,0,0,0,1,0,0,0,0,0,0,0,0,0,0,0,0,0,0,0,0,1,0,1,
     0,0,1,0,0,1,0,0,0,0,1,0>, Cost = 738}
```

In this approach, the enumeration is done in the chronological order of the variables, which makes it impossible to process reasonable sizes of this problem within an acceptable amount of time. Recourse to a more intelligent enumeration will be necessary. This is described in the following section.

2.3 LP Based Resolution

If we look for an enumeration method which converges towards a good integer solution more quickly, it is necessary to find a procedure which brings us a variable order, in which the enumeration is done to get rapidly an integer solution close to the optimum.

Experience shows that the LP resolution of the set partitioning system is the most appropriate procedure to perform this role in the context of many $\{0, 1\}$-problems. We have seen for concrete examples which we have solved that this heuristic gives a near optimal solution having a very good quality (at a distance less than 10% from the optimal LP solution) in a reasonable execution time.

Let us look more closely at the mechanism of this routine of choice. This procedure gives us at each node of the enumerative tree the next variable on which the enumeration must be performed (this variable will first be given the value 1, then the value 0 if backtracking occurs). For this, we solve the linear program associated to the current set partitioning system, which is going to give us a fractional optimal solution having component values between 0 and 1. The procedure examines this solution and returns as next enumeration variable, the one with the value the closest to 1.

Everything we have described above is programmable in Prolog III which has a simplex algorithm implementation. The choice of pivot is made according to the method of M. Balinski and R. Gomory [1] which avoids cycling. Here, only the enumeration procedure which is coded in Prolog III has been changed as follows:

```
enumerate(<>,Cost).
enumerate(L,Cost) :-
```

```
        chooseVar(L,Cost,X,L1), oneZero(X), enumererate(L1,Cost).

    chooseVar(L,Cost,X,L3) :-
        min_value(Cost,Cost),
        chooseVarBis(L,<-1,0>,1,I),
        assert(chosenVar(I)),
        fail.
    chooseVar(L,Cost,X,L3) :-
        retract(chosenVar(I))
        {L = L1.<X>.L2, L1::I - 1, L3 = L1.L2}.

    chooseVarBis(<>,<Max,I>,_,I).
    chooseVarBis(<X>.L,Old,K,I) :-
        max_value(X,Max), chooseVarTer(Max,L,Old,K,I).

    chooseVarTer(1,_,_,I,I) :- !.
    chooseVarTer(Max,L,Old,K,I) :- !, chooseVarBis(L,New,K + 1,I)
        {Old = <OldMax,_>, New = <Max,K>, Max > OldMax}.
    chooseVarTer(Max,L,Old,K,I) :- chooseVarBis(L,Old,K + 1,I).

    oneZero(1).          oneZero(0).
```

where `min_value(X,Y)` is a predefined rule which computes the minimum value m of X satisfying the current constraint system, and adds the constraint $Y = m$.

Now we get to the optimum much more quickly

```
?- solve(L,Cost).
*** 1035
*** 1032
*** 937
*** 935
*** 843
*** 836
*** 751
*** 738
{L = <0,0,0,1,0,0,0,0,0,0,0,0,1,0,0,0,0,0,0,0,0,0,0,0,0,0,0,0,1,0,1,
     0,0,1,0,0,1,0,0,0,0,1,0>, Cost = 738}
```

One has to note that at each iteration, the cost of the LP optimal solution remains unchanged as long as the selected variable has the value 1 in that solution. Hence, the same solution can be used for the next variable selection. The Simplex is therefore only used when backtracking, or when the selected variable has a value strictly lower than 1 in the continuous solution. As a consequence, we start the enumeration by the variables which are set to 1 by the Simplex. In other words, we favour in the discrete optimisation the pairings which have been fully selected (by giving them the value 1) by the continuous optimisation. This is the main difference between our approach and the classical integer programming approach, which mostly consists in rounding fractional variables.

Furthermore, we have found in our experiments that if there are several variables which may be selected (*i.e.* they have the same value in the LP solution), it would be useful to choose the one with the smallest ratio $\frac{\text{cost}}{\text{number of covered flights}}$.

In order to get the exact optimal solution, we have to run this heuristic iteratively using at each step the last found integer solution as an upper bound. We can use the following property. Let (P) denote the set partitioning system and b the upper bound.

Proposition 1. *If* $(P) \cup \{x_j = 1\}$ *is unsolvable or admits an LP-solution greater then* b *then* x_j *is necessarily nil in all integer solutions inferior to* b.

The idea that comes to mind is to test this property on the set of system variables before starting the enumeration, which can be written:

```
fixAllVariable(<>,Cost,Bound).
fixAllVariable(<X>.L,Cost,Bound) :-
    not(lessCostly(X,Cost,Bound)), !, equal0(X),
    fixAllVariable(L,Cost,Bound) .
fixAllVariable(<X>.L,Cost,Bound) :- fixAllVariable(L,Cost,Bound) .

lessCostly(1,Cost,Bound) :- min_value(Cost,C) {C < Bound}.

equal0(0).
```

This idea remains very costly because it involves executing the simplex as many times as there are variables in the system. This leads us once to envisioning a new procedure.

2.4 The Use of the Dual Linear Program

In our problem, the linear program that we consider (using vectorial notations) is:

$$(I) \begin{cases} \min c^t x \\ Ax = \mathbf{1} \\ x \geq 0 \end{cases}$$

where $\mathbf{1}$ is the vector with m components all equal to 1.
Let us now turn to the following linear program:

$$(II) \begin{cases} \max y^t \mathbf{1} \\ y^t A \leq c^t \\ y \in I\!\!R^m \end{cases}$$

Note that by analogy to the fact that each variable x is associated with a pairing, each component of vector y (dual variables) corresponds to a spell. The linear program (II) is called the *dual* of (I). The fundamental theorem of the duality of linear programming says that if (I) is solvable then (II) is solvable and in addition $\min c^t x = \max y^t \mathbf{1}$. Let $\lambda = \min c^t x$. Consequently the system

$$\begin{cases} y^t \mathbf{1} = \lambda \\ y^t A \leq c^t \end{cases}$$

is solvable. Let us consider a solution y of this system. For each feasible solution x of (I), we have $y^t A x = y^t \mathbf{1} = \lambda$. The economic function of the linear program can then be expressed as follows

$$\begin{aligned} z &= c^t x \\ &= c^t x + \lambda - y^t A x \\ &= \lambda + (c^t - y^t A) x \\ &= \lambda + \sum_{j=1}^{n} (c_j - y^t A^j) x_j \end{aligned}$$

This last formulation of the economic function is of interest because the coefficient $cr_j = c_j - y^t A^j$ of each variable is non-negative. cr_j is called *reduced cost* of the variable x_j. This allows us to state the following property

Proposition 2. *Each variable x_j satisfying $\lambda + cr_j \geq b$ is nil in every integer solution of cost less than b.*

Proof. This property follows from the fact that $\lambda + cr_j$ is a lower bound of the continuous optimal solution (if it exists) of the linear program below:

$$\begin{cases} \min c^t x \\ A x = \mathbf{1} \\ x_j = 1, \, x \geq 0 \end{cases}$$

$\square$

It is clear that, in theory, the property 2 makes it possible to suppress less variables than property 1. Having noted this, we show experimentally that it enables us to suppress a significant quantity of variables, added to the fact that it requires a single execution of the simplex. Hence, it is this version of suppression by upper bound that we keep in the final implementation of our program. The rule fixAllVariables is then improved as follows:

```
fixAllVariables(L,TotalCost,Bound) :-
    dualConstraint(Dual,L,1),
    min_value(TotalCost,Z),
    sum(Dual,Z),
    getSolution(Dual),
    fixVariable(L,1,Dual,Z,Bound).

dualConstraint(_,<>,_).
dualConstraint(Dual,<X>.L,J):-
    duty(J,Cost,R),
```

```
        scalarProduct(Dual,R,P),
        dualConstraint(Dual,L,J + 1) {P <= Cost}.

    fixVariable(<>,_,_,_,_).
    fixVariable(<X>.L,J,Dual,Z,Bound) :-
        duty(J,Cost,R),
        scalarProduct(Dual,R,P), !,
        equal0(X),
        fixVariable(L,J + 1,Dual,Z,Bound)
        {Z + Cost - P >= Bound}.
    fixVariable(<X>.L,J,Dual,Z,Bound) :- fixVariable(L,J + 1,Dual,Z,Bound).
```

where:

- dualConstraint sets the constraints $\forall j$, $y^t A^j \leq c_j$ using for the computation of $p = y^t A^j$ the predicate scalarProduct;
- sum sets the constraint $y^t \mathbf{1} = Z$;
- getSolution(X) gives a particular solution of X satisfying the current constraint system;
- fixVariable performs the settings at 0 which proceed from the property 2.

3 The Pre-processing

The performances of our resolution system greatly depend on the size of the problem being treated. The idea of pre-processing is natural and is justified as soon as a much simpler algorithm makes it possible to reduce this size. The first idea comes from the observation that a same pairing can be generated more than once with eventually different costs. From the optimization point of view, only one of these pairings must be considered, the one with the lowest cost.

This can be simply programmed in Prolog III by going through the pairing list and comparing each pairing with all those not yet suppressed which follow it, which gives a processing in $O(n^2)$.

This becomes non-functional above a certain number of pairings and requires the use of an hash-code adapted for the comparison of pairings. The hash-code which seems to us the most useful rests on 3 keys corresponding respectively to the smallest index of the covered spell, to the largest index and to the average of the indices over the set of spells covered by the pairing. Obviously, this processing must be done just after the generation of pairings and before the setting of set partitioning constraints.

Other types of pre-processing are possible. We may be convinced that the particular structure of a set partitioning system allows for some reductions (certain of these are obvious, others less so) on the constraint system. This can be realized by a kind of pre-processing capable of fixing permanently some variables to 0 or 1 without altering the integer optimal solution of the initial constraint system. It may be noted that these variable affectations to values $\{0, 1\}$ mean that the distance between the optimal continuous value of the economic function and its optimal integer solution is diminished all while guaranteeing that the integer optimal solution of the original constraint system is not lost.

Prolog III is capable of automatically realizing part of this pre-processing due to fixed variables: once a variable can no longer take a single value, it takes this value. However, certain pre-processing types must be explicitly programmed for the simple reason that the constraint $x \in \{0, 1\}$ can not be placed in Prolog III. In what follows, we examine which of the pre-processing reductions are done directly by Prolog III and which must be coded.

3.1 Examples of Reductions Directly Realized by Prolog III

Setting of Variables to Value 1 When a spell becomes covered by a single pairing, the corresponding variable is automatically set to 1.
To the inquiry $\{x = 1, x + y + z = 1, t + y + z = 1, y >= 0, z >= 0, t >= 0\}$
Prolog III answers $\{x = 1, y = 0, z = 0, t = 1\}$.
Notice that when a variable is set to 1 in a row (spell), the other variables that cover this row are voided.

Processing of Dominated Rows Let two set partitioning constraints be C_i and C_j. Let I and J be the respective sets of variables present in C_i and C_j.
C_j is said to be dominated by C_i if $I \subset J$. In this case, we only need to substract the two equations in order to see that the variables belonging to $J \setminus I$ must be nil in all feasible solutions of the system. Next, one of the two constraints becomes redundant and has to be removed.
Prolog III correctly performs this kind of reduction. In fact, the answer to the inquiry $\{x + y + z + t = 1, y + t = 1, x >= 0, y >= 0, z >= 0, t >= 0\}$ is $\{x = 0, z = 0, y + t = 1\}$.

3.2 Examples of Simulated Reductions in Prolog III

The constraint $x_j \in \{0, 1\}$ can be simulated by the implication

$$\begin{cases} Ax = \mathbf{1} \\ x_j = 1 \qquad \text{non solvable} \implies x_j = 0 \\ x \in \{0, 1\} \end{cases}$$

As it is difficult to check the feasability of an integer constraint system, the preceding implication is relaxed as follows

$$\begin{cases} Ax = \mathbf{1} \\ x_j = 1 \qquad \text{non solvable} \implies x_j = 0 \\ x \geq 0 \end{cases}$$

which is equally valid but rapidly checked. As this stimulated pre-processing has to be performed for each variable of the system it is better to do it once before the enumeration starts. Two interesting reductions which follow this scheme can here be demonstrated

Establishment of Variable Equalities Let I and J be the sets of spells covered respectively by pairings i and j. i and j are called *orthogonals* if $I \cap J = \emptyset$. Let two set partitioning constraints which differ exactly by two variables be p and q. After subtracting the two equations we deduce $x_p = x_q$. If, moreover, p and q are non orthogonal then we can declare that $x_p = x_q = 0$.

The behaviour of Prolog III in this situation is such that if p and q are non orthogonal the equality $x_p = x_q$ is not detected, but that if p and q are non orthogonal then the fixing $x_p = 0$ (resp. $x_q = 0$) is realized after setting the constraint $x_p = 1$ (resp. $x_q = 1$) and the detection of a failure. As an illustration of this fact, the response of Prolog III to the inquiry $\{x+y+z = 1, x+y+t = 1\}$ is $\{z = -y - x + 1, t = -y - x + 1\}$. On the other hand, to the inquiry $\{x + y = 1, y + z = 1, x + z + t + u = 1, x = 1, y >= 0, z >= 0, t >= 0, u >= 0\}$ it answers that the constraint system is not feasible.

Processing of Strongly Dependant Pairings A pairing j is said to be *strongly dependant* if there exists a spell i not covered by j such that j is non-orthogonal to all pairings that cover the spell i. Let us show that j strongly dependant $\implies x_j = 0$. Let I be the set of pairings which cover spell i. We know that there exists $k \in I$ such that $x_k = 1$. The fact that j and k are non-orthogonal implies that x_j and x_k cannot be equal to 1 simultaneously. So, we necessarily have $x_j = 0$.

Let us now look at the reaction of Prolog III in this case:

```
> {y+z+t=1,x+y=1,x+z=1,x+t=1,x>=0,y>=0,z>=0,t>=0};
{y = 1/3, z = 1/3, t = 1/3, x = 2/3}
> {y+z+t=1,x+y=1,x+z=1,x+t=1,x=1,y>=0,z>=0,t>=0};
The constraint system of the inquiry is not feasible.
```

In this example, x represents a strongly dependant pairing.

Finally, the pre-processing is very simply coded in Prolog III like this:

```
preprocess(<>).
preprocess(<X>.L) :- not(equal1(X)), equal0(x), preprocess(L).
preprocess(<X>.L) :- preprocess(L).
```

3.3 Some Results of Pre-processing

Table 1 gives the size of the system after pre-processing (with and without strongly dependant pairing elimination) and the corresponding times. The size of the initial matrix appears in the left-hand column with the number of pairings then the number of spells.

Table 1.

Input	without strong_dept			with strong_dept		
	Nb_Rot	Nb_Spe	Time	Nb_Rot	Nb_Spe	Time
197x17	177	17	0.03	177	17	0.06
294x19	251	18	0.05	251	18	0.11
434x24	353	21	0.07	353	21	0.30
1220x23	910	22	0.25	725	22	1.87
1366x19	926	19	0.26	926	19	0.96
1783x20	1408	20	0.37	1244	20	1.83
2540x18	2034	18	0.56	2034	18	2.76
2879x40	2137	32	1.03	2137	32	2.86
3103x40	2303	38	0.65	2303	38	3.43
5172x36	3106	34	1.35	3106	34	5.88
7479x55	5957	47	5.92	5915	47	28.74
8820x39	6483	34	2.63	6483	34	54.72
10757x124	8446	110	4.16	8444	110	163.30
13635x100	10716	45	64.23		–	
16043x51	10904	50	5.35		–	
36699x71	16734	69	7.75		–	

4 Large-Size Problem Solving

In the real life problems which we have encountered (airline crew scheduling),
the system size is too large (400000 pairings) to consider direct processing. For
this reason we have chosen the following method:

A significant sub-problem of the initial problem is selected such that we can
quickly determine its optimal integer solution. The solution of this sub-problem
is used as an upper bound to filter the initial system by removing the pairings
which do not belong to any integer solution of cost less than or equal to this
bound.
The resulting reduced system is then small enough to be solved exactly.
The simplicity of this approach comes from the fact that all three steps rely on
the same basic algorithm, the simplex algorithm. On the other hand, the power
of this approach comes from the fact that for this kind of problem, several near
optimal solutions exist around the linear programming solution.

4.1 Selection

First of all, we establish the size of the sub-system we want to select, let us say
K pairings. The first step of the selection consists in solving the linear program
containing all the generated pairings. From this solution, we build our significant
sub-system by selecting all the pairings which are associated to a non-zero value
in the LP-solution. Then in order to have K pairings, we select among the
remaining pairings those with the smallest reduced costs. Unfortunately, there

is a limit to the size of a set partitioning matrix, after which it the execution time of the simplex becomes unreasonable. We must here then proceed by stages:

We start the process by a pre-selection which chooses K "good" pairings, for instance the K pairings which have the smallest costs. Let (S_0) be this set of pairings and $(\overline{S_0})$ the set of the remaining pairings. The selection then proceeds in an iterative manner. After each iteration, the sub-sets (S_i) and $(\overline{S_i})$ are updated by exchanging certain pairings. The selection ends when (S_i) containts the optimal LP solution of $(S_i) \cup (\overline{S_i})$ (i.e., when the reduced costs of $\overline{S_i}$ are positive). At each iteration, the linear program corresponding to (S_i) is solved by the simplex and the solution (non-zero variables) along with the dual variable values are recuperated. We then compute the reduced costs of the zero-value pairings of (S_i) and all pairings of $(\overline{S_i})$.

1. If all reduced costs of $(\overline{S_i})$ are non-negative (optimal solution), we then keep as significant sub-problem the set of pairings of (S_i) with non-zero values, to which we add some pairings from $(S_i) \cup (\overline{S_i})$ with the lowest reduced costs, and the selection process ends.
2. Otherwise the zero-value pairings of (S_i) with the largest reduced costs (necessarily non-negative) are exchanged with those of $(\overline{S_i})$ having the lowest negative reduced costs. A new set (S_{i+1}) is thus formed for the next iteration.

It is possible to have an unsatisfiable (in continuous) initial system S_0. We then need to add to S_0 an artificial pairing g covering all spells with a very high cost. This pairing is non-zero in the optimal solution of (S_i) if and only if (S_i) is not feasible. Let (S) denote the sub-system which corresponds to the last iteration, if $(S) \cup (\overline{S})$ is feasible, either $g \in (\overline{S})$ or $g \in (S)$ with a zero value. It is clear that in this case, we do not select g in the sub-problem.

4.2 Filtering

The system (S) is small enough (in the order of 20000 pairings) so that we can look for the optimal integer solution. This integer solution is of course one of the initial problem, but not necessarily optimal.

Filtering is used to remove from the initial system all pairings which cannot improve the cost of the solution previously found. Using the continuous solution of the initial system and the reduced costs, we look through the non-zero pairings of (S) and the pairings of $(\overline{S})$ in order to eliminate those whose reduced costs are greater than the difference between the integer solution and the continuous solution. This gives us a system which is sufficiently reduced to be solved exactly by the method described in Section 2.3. If the system is too large we can repeat the whole operation.

5 Coding in C Language

Despite all the efforts tried previously, we could not keep all the programs in Prolog III. Some parts had to be rewritten in C, either for reasons of performance or for reasons of memory.

1. In order to generate in an efficient way a large number of pairings according to company rules, we must divide the generation program into two parts. The first part stays in Prolog and deals with pairing segments of no more than one day. The second part (much more combinatoric) is rewritten in C to process pairings of 2, 3 and 4 days (we get up to a billion pairings).

2. The maximum problem size we are able to solve in Prolog III seems to be limited to a thousand or so pairings covering tens of spells. In order to solve industrial instances of crew scheduling problems, on the one hand, we have to divide the Prolog III program in several parts and, on the other hand, rewrite some of them in C language. In particular, we wrote a simplex having adapted calculations to set partitioning matrices. This is a dual simplex [3] (often used in integer programming) which limits degeneracy cases without including a specific treatment. We have adopted the *steepest-edge* criterion [4] for the choice of pivot. All these characteristics make our simplex implementation quite fast, without however reaching the same performance of commercial packages. In addition, this simplex directly provides us reduced cost values without having to solve the dual linear system.

3. Prolog III pre-processing makes as many system resolutions (in continuous) as there are variables, which makes it excessively costly. We have then restrained the pre-processing to the typical reductions types mentioned in section 3 by programming them in C.

4. Selection and filtering have been written directly in C using Unix sorting functions.

For the airplane company problem, the pairing generation procedure (with all the company rules) contains 600 lines of C and 800 lines of Prolog. The different resolution procedures contain, in all, 2500 lines of code C.

6 Performances

By coding our resolution program in C, we are able to solve real life problems containing as much as 300 spells and a half billion pairings, in a reasonable time on a standard work station (Sun SPARC Classic). We have performed many experiments by using real data from both *American Airlines* (mentioned in Padberg's paper [5]) and from the French airline company for whom the application has been realized. The same method has also been used for solving crew scheduling problems for buses, in the realm of the SuperbuS European project (ESPRIT 8742). We are satisfied by the results obtained, and a sub-set is presented below:

where:

input: size of the problem in number of spells then number of pairings;

D: density of the set partition matrix;

Z^*_{IP}: first integer obtained;

Z_{IP}: optimal integer solution;

Table 2. American Airlines

input		D (%)	time Z_{IP}^*	Z_{IP}^*/Z_{IP}	time Z_{IP}	Z_{IP}/Z_{LP}	time opt.	I	total time	time Pad.
17	197	22	0.05	1.047	0.06	1.030	0.00	4	0.06	0.06
19	294	24	0.10	1.048	0.13	1.021	0.00	4	0.14	0.17
31	467	19	0.09	1	0.09	1	0.00	1	0.09	0.10
18	1072	25	0.81	1.025	0.86	1.001	0.01	4	0.87	0.38
20	1217	30	0.51	1.108	0.62	1.018	0.03	4	0.65	0.62
20	1783	36	2.08	1.082	4.73	1.007	0.43	6	5.17	3.68
26	2662	28	2.05	1.097	2.10	1.007	0.04	4	2.14	1.43
40	3103	16	1.07	1	1.07	1	0.00	1	1.07	0.53
36	5172	22	0.78	1	0.78	1	0.00	1	0.78	0.74
50	6774	18	27.72	1.210	48.94	1.022	0.01	5	48.95	10.41
55	7479	13	31.73	1.002	36.03	1.002	5.28	3	41.31	35.40
39	8820	16	13.12	1.000	14.02	1.000	0.00	3	14.03	2.05
124	10757	6	121.69	1.091	232.11	1.004	0.04	4	232.15	62.49
100	13635	14	64.37	1	64.37	1	0.00	1	64.37	4.78
163	28016	6	273.17	1.013	274.25	1.007	0.00	2	274.26	11.19
71	36699	8	153.94	1.004	987.97	1.013	—	—	—	134.38

Z_{LP}: optimal continuous solution;
time Z_{IP}^*: time necessary for the computing of Z_{IP}^*;
time Z_{IP}: time necessary for the computing of Z_{IP};
time opt.: time necessary for proving the optimality of Z_{IP};
I: number of algorithm iterations. Let us recall that at each iteration, either a best solution is found or the optimality is proved;
total time: total time of the problem resolution (including the optimality proof);
time Pad.: resolution time of Hoffman and Padberg's algorithm [5] for the same data.

We have directly performed the integer resolution for *American Airlines* data, without selection and without filtering, because of their sizes.
It should be noted that we have sometimes had difficulty to prove the optimality of an integer solution (see the last example of table 2).
Hoffman and Padberg's algorithm uses as simplex the commercial package CPLEX which seems to be at the moment the fastest, and certainly faster than our simplex implementation.
It is likely that furnished with a high performance simplex, our algorithm can attain the same performance levels as Hoffman and Padberg.

where:
time selec: total selection time;
I_S: number of selection iterations;
Z_{IP}^*: optimal integer solution of the significant sub-problem;

Table 3. French Airline Company

input	D (%)	time selec	I_S	Z^s_{IP}/Z_{IP}	I_1	I_2	total time
108 108636	10	62	3	1	0	0	62
252 205928	4	859	13	1	4	1	969
257 157435	3	466	11	1.016	2	2	124
252 375939	4	1118	8	1.028	4	2	2431
182 152600	5	287	3	—	> 11	—	> 6000

I_1: number of integer resolution iterations of the significant sub-problem;
I_2: number of integer resolution iterations of the sub-problem after filtering.

In the last example of table 3, the best integer solution Z^s_{IP} found is such that $Z^s_{IP}/Z_{LP} = 1.403$. We failed to prove the optimality of Z^s_{IP} and to find a best solution in a reasonable amount of time.

7 Conclusion

We have showed that with a little effort, constraint programming can be used in order to efficiently solve a difficult industrial problem. As a positive result, This gives a program which is currently in service for the summer season 1995. However, this is not not very satisfactory.

In fact, in solving this crew scheduling problem we had to write several special programs (in Prolog and C), use a sophisticated simplex which we used for finding good bounds and for guiding the final enumeration. This allowed us to solve the problems of the airline company (Matrix A of size 500 rows and 500000 columns). But all the ingredients used can already be found in a language such as Prolog III or IV : The tools are the same. Only the methodology changes, for arriving at a solution one needs a great pragmatism.

In the future, we will systematically address this issue and investigate ways to reduce the gap separating a formal modelling by constraint programming and an efficient utilization of the existing tools.

Acknowledgments
We are grateful to Nathalie Vetillard, Engineer at Prologia, for her contribution to the computational experiments.

References

1. M.L. Balinski and R.E. Gomory, "A mutual primal-dual simplex method", *Recent Advances in Mathematical Programming*, McGraw-Hill, pp 17-26, (1963).
2. R.E. Bixby, "Progress in linear programming", *ORSA journal on computing*, vol. 6, No. 1, (1994), pp. 15-22.

3. V. Chvàtal, "Linear Programming", *W.H. Freeman and Company editors*, New York, 1983.

4. J.J. Forrest, D. Goldfarb, "Steepest-edge simplex algorithms for linear programming", *Mathematical Programming*, 57, p. 341-374, 1992.

5. K.L. Hoffman and M. Padberg, "Solving airline crew sheduling by Branch and Cut", *Management Science* vol. 39, No. 6, June 1993, 657-682.

6. Roseaux, "Exercices et problemes resolus de recherche operationnelle (T3 : programmation linéaire et extensions; problèmes classiques", *Masson*, Paris 1991.

A Visual
Constraint-Programming
Environment

Massimo Paltrinieri

Ecole Normale Supérieure
Département de Mathématiques et d'Informatique
45 rue d'Ulm
75005 Paris
France
palmas@dmi.ens.fr

Abstract

Design has not received much attention by the constraint-programming community, although in the development cycle of real-world applications it is probably the most expensive phase. Since constraint programming is declarative, design can go much further than for traditional imperative languages, as it can produce models that are executable. Because of the potentially huge number of constraints and variables of a real-world applications though, compactness of these models is a key issue. This paper abstracts the classical notion of constraint satisfaction problem to a new, more compact model. A design methodology based on such a model is then proposed. An interactive system that supports the methodology and integrates traditional constraint-programming languages to directly execute the resulting model is further presented. The system provides a visual environment that covers the full development cycle of constraint-based applications. Its benefits are finally illustrated on a real-world problem.

1 Introduction

The *design* process builds the model of a problem, consisting of abstractions and relationships. Equivalently, design can be referred to as *problem formulation* or *modeling*. The importance of design in the development of real-world constraint-based applications has been pointed out in [Pal94a].

Since real-world applications may include thousands of constraints and variables, compactness of the model obtained through design is a key issue, as it may determine whether the model is manageable in practice or not. Compactness has also relevant implications on the overall comprehension and on the possibility to compose and reuse models. For this reason, the formal model underlying constraint programming is abstracted with notions of the object-oriented paradigm, such as object, class, inheritance and with a new notion, *multi-class association*, for which *multi-class constraint* is a special case (this enhanced model is the topic of Section 3 and it is illustrated on a simple example in Section 4).

A design methodology based on such a model has been defined and a system that supports the methodology developed. For the enhanced model is just an abstraction of the classical one, the system can be integrated to traditional constraint-programming languages: the problem to be solved is first visually designed with the system; the resulting model, properly preprocessed, is then executed by the underlying language.

The integration of the design system to traditional constraint-programming languages has also been implemented. The result is an interactive environment (presented in Section 5) that supports the full development cycle of constraint-based applications. The environment has been employed to solve a number of problems taken from the constraint-programming literature. The resulting model has always turned out to be more compact than the original one (the solution to a real-life scheduling problem is presented in Section 6).

2 Related Work

Many real-life problems have been formulated as constraint satisfaction problems: temporal reasoning, belief maintenance, theorem proving, machine vision, microcomputer configuration, design of mechanical and electronic devices, financial analysis, several applications of planning and scheduling in manufacturing, aircraft routing, time tabling, genetic experiments, resource allocation, etc. (for a survey of some of these applications see [Nad90]).

Several constraint-programming languages are today available both at the academic and industrial level: Prolog III [Col90], CLP(R) [Jaf88] and Chip [Din88] are logic-programming languages replacing the pattern-matching mechanism of unification, as used in Prolog, by a more general operation called constraint satisfaction; Charme [Opl89] is the first industrial constraint-programming language and is based on a simplified Pascal-like syntax; Bertrand [Lel88] is a rule-based language that implements constraint-satisfaction through an augmented term rewriting mechanism; in TK!Solver [KoJ84] and Ideal [VaW82] constraints are stated as equations; CC [Sar93] implements concurrent constraint programming.

Our framework does not aim at providing a new constraint-programming language but rather a design methodology, with its support system, to visually define models that are automatically converted to programs for these languages.

Constraint-based systems integrating some object-oriented components are Equate [Wil91], Ilog-Solver [Pug92], Life [AKa93], Codm [SRR94], Yafcrs [Kök94] and Oz [HSW95].

Although we share some notions of the object-oriented paradigm, such as object, class, and inheritance, such notions are treated differently from these systems as we neither try to integrate objects and constraints at the same level, nor to extend object-oriented programming with constraints, but we rather take the model of constraint satisfaction problems and abstract it through these notions. Furthermore, these languages do not focus on design and provide programming environments that are just textual.

Constraint-based systems further integrating some object-oriented and graphical components are ThingLab [Bor79], Socle [Har86], Garnet [MGV92], Kaleidoscope [FBB92], Siri [Hor92] and Devi [ThS94].

ThingLab is a graphical-interface generator including a module addressing visual programming. For this reason, ThingLab is probably the closest system to ours. We extend that work in several ways, for instance by considering general combinatorial problems and by concentrating on the compactness of the resulting model. The main difference between our and the other mentioned systems is that graphics, in our system, is the means whereas in those systems it is the end: while our system uses graphics to solve constraint-based problems, those systems employ constraints to solve graphics-based problems. In other words, these systems are *constraints-for-graphics* systems, where textual definitions of constraints are stated in the definition of user-interfaces where relations among graphical objects have to be maintained, such as window *w1* must always be centered over window *w2*; on the other hand, we propose a *graphics-for-constraints* system, where a graphical environment allows to define constraint satisfaction problems on various application domains, such as those mentioned at the beginning of this section.

3 From CSP to OOCSP

Constraint-based systems differ in the programming paradigm they adopt, the syntax they follow, the resolution strategy they implement, the underlying domain, etc., but they are all made to solve, flexibly and efficiently, a large class of combinatorial problems, called *constraint satisfaction problems* (CSP), consisting of a set of *variables*, each associated with a *domain* of values, and of a set of *constraints* that limit the combination of values of the variables. Semantically, to each constraint is associated a relation given by a set of tuples having one value for each variable occurring in the constraint. A *solution* to a CSP is an assignment of values to the variables, such that for each constraint, the tuple determined by the solution is in the relation associated to the constraint. Each CSP can be graphically represented as a *constraint graph* where nodes represent variables and edges represent constraints.

Several notions, such as attribute, object, class, inheritance, association, etc., are added to the CSP model to obtain a new model, called OOCSP (*object-oriented constraint satisfaction problem*).

An *attribute* is a feature taking values from a domain. An *object* is a collection of attributes. Object attributes correspond to variables in CSP's. The set of attributes of an object defines the *structure* of the object. Objects sharing the same structure are grouped into *classes*. Classes are organized into a *hierarchy*. The structure of a lower class includes that of a higher class. Constraints can be defined both on object and class attributes. Constraints on object attributes have the same meaning as in CSP's, while constraints on class attributes induce constraints on object attributes. A solution to an OOCSP is an assignment of domain values to object attributes such that all the constraints are satisfied.

Associations can be defined over classes, objects, class attributes and object attributes and they are named accordingly. The naming convention is outlined in Table 1 and must be applied from top to bottom: if some class attribute occurs in the association, then it is a *class constraint*; otherwise, if there is some object attribute, then it is an *object constraint*; otherwise, if there is some class, then it is a *class relation*; otherwise, if there are just objects, it is an *object relation*.

Class constraints and class relations together are called *class associations*. Object constraints and object relations together are called *object associations*. Class constraints and object constraints together are called *constraints*. Class relations and object relations together are called *relations*. Class associations and object associations together are called *associations*. The syntactical difference between a constraint and a relation is that attributes occur in the former but not in the latter.

The association *adjacent_neq* in Section 4 is a class constraint because there is some class attribute, namely *region_1.color* and *region_2.color*. The *adjacent* association is a relation because there are no class attributes, object attributes or classes occurring in it, but just objects. The *disjunction*, *precedence*, and *k1-k5* associations in Section 6 are all class constraints as there is some class attribute occurring in each of them, namely *task_1.start*, *task_2.start*, *foundat.start*, etc.

A class association *induces* a set of object associations, obtained by replacing each class with its objects and the objects of its derived classes (this takes inheritance into account) in all the possible combinations. This rule is the main step in defining the semantics of OOCSP's, where constraints are defined on objects and classes organized in a hierarchy, in terms of CSP's, where constraints are defined on variables. Remark that this notion can be applied to *multi-class associations*, i.e., associations defined over different classes, and not just to associations on a given class. Examples of multi-class associations, more precisely *multi-class constraints*, are *disjunction* and *k1-k5* in Section 6, as they are defined over attributes of different classes, such as *task* and *resource* for *disjunction*, *formwork* and *foundat* for *k1*, etc.

Associations can span levels by relating, for instance, an object to a class. Coherently with the notion just presented, such a class association induces object associations each one relating the given object to an object of the given class and its derived ones. For instance, stating that the *formwork* task class uses the *carpentry* object resource, means that all the objects of the *formwork* class and of its derived classes use the *carpentry* resource.

Encapsulation is the ability to define an object's behavior *within* the object, where object behavior means "how an object acts and reacts, in terms of its state changes and message passing" [Boo94]. In our framework, associations, which are defined *over* (and not within) objects, completely define an object's behavior, as they refine the domains of its attributes (state changes) and they propagate the effects of such refinements to other objects (message passing).

if there is some...	...then the association is a
class attribute	class constraint
object attribute	object constraint
class	class relation
object	object relation

Table. 1. Naming convention for associations.

Recall that some traditional object-oriented design methodologies as well allow to define associations that violate the classical notion of encapsulation, for "some information inherently transcends a single class" [Rum91]. In this case, associations are usually modeled as class attributes pointing to the associated classes. This solution has a number of disadvantages, since modeling associations inside the associated classes inhibit reusability and modifiability. A new trend in modeling associations proposes that "the associated classes do not contain any information about the association, as this way of modeling avoids redundancy and removes any direct coupling between associated classes" [Tan95].

The expressive power of CSP and OOCSP is identical, as the CSP's class is the same as the OOCSP's class. In other words, each CSP can be represented as an OOCSP and vice-versa (the main objective of the OOCSP model is not to extend the class of CSP's to new problems, but to represent them more compactly). The proof is simple:

CSP -> OOCSP: a CSP is equivalent to an OOCSP where, for each variable, a class with an object with just one attribute with the variable's domain is defined and the constraints are those of the original CSP where variables are replaced by the corresponding object attributes.

OOCSP -> CSP: the CSP equivalent to a given OOCSP is obtained by

1. inducing object associations from class associations
2. replacing object relations in object constraints with their truth value
3. for each object attribute defining a variable with the same domain
4. replacing each object attribute in the object constraints with the corresponding variable.

Step 1 eliminates hierarchy, classes and class associations; step 2 object relations; step 3 objects; step 4 object constraints. Step 3 introduces variables and domains; step 4 constraints. The result is a set of constraints over a set of variables with an associated domain, i.e., a CSP.

Each OOCSP can be graphically represented as an *object constraint graph*, a structure on two levels: at the upper level, nodes represent classes while edges represent class associations; at the lower level, a graph can be associated to each class: nodes represent objects of the given class while edges represent object associations.

The object constraint graph is introduced as an enhancement of the constraint graph, since the size of the latter is untractable for real-world problems. The improvement is due to abstraction, since a graph of the lower level is seen as a node at the upper level and an edge between nodes of the upper level is a compact representation of possibly many edges between nodes of the lower level.

4 Example

A simple example of CSP is the Canadian-Flag Problem, the problem of coloring the four regions of the Canadian flag (see Fig. 1) using only red and white in such a way that each region has a different color from its neighbors and the maple leaf is red. In this problem, the variables are *left*, *center*, *right* and *leaf*, the four regions; the domains

are $D_{left} = D_{center} = D_{right} = \{red, white\}$, $D_{leaf} = \{red\}$; the constraints are *left !=
center, center != right, leaf != center* ("*!=*" means different from), establishing the
difference of values for pairs of adjacent regions.

The only solution is *left = red, center = white, right = red, leaf = red*, assigning the
value *red* to the left-hand region, *white* to the center region, *red* to the right-hand region
and *red* to the leaf region.

In our framework, the four regions of the Canadian flag are modeled as four objects,
left, *center*, *right* and *leaf*, of the same class *region*. Such a class has an attribute, *color*,
initialized to the set of values { *white, red* }. The attribute and its initialization are so
implicitly defined also for the four objects. The initialization of the *color* attribute of
the *leaf* object is overloaded to *red*, a subset of its class initialization.

There is just a class association, namely a class constraint being defined over the class
attribute *color* of the *region* class. The class constraint is called *adjacent_neq* (*neq*
stands for "not equal"), is depicted as a circular edge on *region*, and is defined by the
logical expression

adjacent_neq.   **if** *adjacent(region_1, region_2)*
                       then *region_1.color != region_2.color*

meaning that regions pairwise adjacent must be colored differently (*region_1* and
region_2 are two instances of the *region* class). The four objects are linked by the
adjacent object relation

adjacent.   *adjacent(left, center)*   *adjacent(center, right)*   *adjacent(center, leaf)*.

depicted as three edges joining the four object nodes.

The model obtained is directly executable to generate the assignment of colors to
regions solving the problem. The main modeling steps of the Canadian-Flag Problem
designed and solved through our system are shown in Fig. 2.

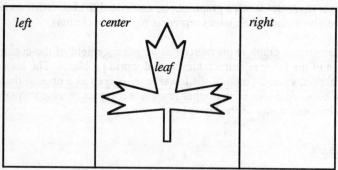

Fig. 1. The Canadian Flag.

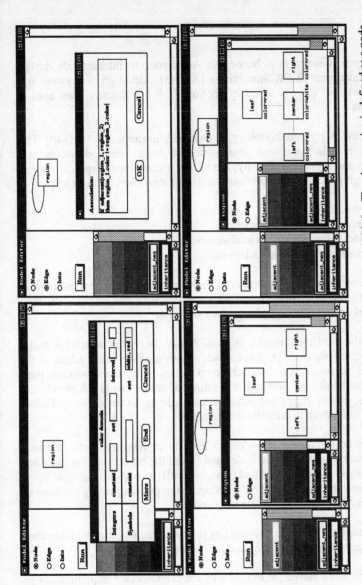

Fig. 2. The Canadian-Flag Problem. Top-left. The system is in mode **Node**. The class *region* is defined as a node of the object-constraint graph. The domain of the *color* attribute is being defined as a set of symbols initialized to *white* and *red*. **Top-right.** The system is now in mode **Edge**. The *adjacent_neq* association over the *region* class is formally stated through a simple logical expression meaning that if two regions are adjacent to each others, then they must be colored differently. **Bottom-left.** A new window called *region* is opened by clicking on the *region* class icon in mode **Into**. The *left*, *center*, *right* and *leaf* objects of class *region* are defined in this window, as well as the *adjacent* object association. **Bottom-right.** By clicking on the **Run** button, the model is executed and the solution, i.e., an assignment of values to object attributes such that all the constraints are satisfied, is displayed.

5 The System

A system called Gianna (Gianna Is A Name, No Acronyms) to interactively design OOCSP's has been developed in SICStus Prolog [And93]. Although the system still misses many functionalities (as discussed in Section 7), it has already been used to solve several problems.

The system supports the design methodology of OOCSP's presented in [Pal94b]. The methodology closely recalls traditional object-oriented design methodologies as it consists of a notation and a process. Briefly, the notation combines graphical entities into object constraint graphs, while the process consists of the following four steps:

- identify the abstractions
- identify the semantics of these abstractions
- identify the associations among these abstractions
- identify the semantics of these associations.

Concretely, abstractions are classes and objects; the semantics of classes and objects are the attributes and their domains; associations are relations and constraints; their semantics is the logical expression formalizing their meaning.

The system can be in three different modes: in mode *Node*, classes are defined as nodes of the object-constraint graph; in mode *Edge*, associations are defined as edges of the object-constraint graph; in mode *Into*, by clicking on a class node, a new window pops up and a new graph can be defined within the window: nodes of this graph are objects of the selected class, while edges are associations among these objects. Colors distinguish edges corresponding to different associations.

Attribute domains can be initialized at the object level or at the class level, in which case the same initialization is automatically defined for all the objects of that class and for all its derived classes. Attributes of classes, as well as logical expressions of associations, are defined through appropriate dialog boxes popping up by clicking on class and edge icons in *Node* and *Edge* mode respectively.

When the model is complete, it can be executed by pressing the *Run* button. Execution consists of two main phases: *preprocessing* and *propagation*.

Preprocessing. OOCSP's are converted to CSP's by the preprocessor implementing an optimized version of the algorithm presented in Section 3. Steps 1 and 2 are executed simultaneously, so relations are replaced by their truth value and expressions are simplified. For instance, if by preprocessing an implication the antecedent is evaluated to *true*, only the consequent is induced (when the condition cannot be evaluated statically, because it contains attributes, the whole implication is induced). For example, the result of preprocessing the *adiacent_neq* class constraint is given by the three object constraints

> *left.color != center.color*
> *center.color != right.color*
> *center.color != leaf.color*

as the three conditions

       adjacent (*left*, *center*)
       adjacent (*center*, *right*)
       adjacent (*center*, *leaf*)

are evaluated to *true*.

Propagation. In the current implementation of the system, the preprocessed problem is then treated by the ECL^{i}PS^e [WaV93] propagation engine, the ECRC successor of Chip [Din88]. The two systems, ECL^{i}PS^e and SICStus, are complementary: the result of preprocessing is a CSP in ECL^{i}PS^e syntax that is solved by instantiating all variables to singleton values; the solution is then handed back to SICStus to display variable (object attributes in this context) assignments under the corresponding object icons. Being the system architecture modular, it is possible to preprocess the model into programs for other constraint-programming languages besides ECL^{i}PS^e.

6 The Bridge Problem

The Bridge Problem [Van89] is a real-life project-planning problem consisting of determining the start time of the tasks necessary to build a five-segment bridge (see Fig. 3). The project (see Fig. 4) includes 46 tasks (*a1*, *p1*, etc.) that employ resources (excavator *ex*, concrete-mixer *cm*, etc.). The constraints of the problem include 77 disjunctive constraints (task *a1* and *a2* cannot overlap because they both employ the excavator, tasks *t2* and *t5* cannot overlap because they both employ the crane, etc.), 66 precedence constraints (execute task *t5* before task *v2*, execute task *m5* before task *t4*, etc.) and 25 specific constraints (the time between the completion of task *s1* and the completion of task *b1* is at most 4 days, the time between the completion of task *a4* and the completion of task *s4* is at most 3 days, etc.), for a total of 168 constraints.

The Bridge Problem has been modeled and solved with traditional constraint languages, such as Chip and Charme.

The Chip program [Van89] consists of 55 (Prolog-like) facts defining data and of 20 (Prolog-like) procedures defining the process. The size of the program is 90 lines, excluding declarations (35 lines). Data facts define tasks, durations, resources, components, relations and constraints. Process procedures basically iterate over data to set the appropriate constraints. No code concerns constraint propagation since it is taken into account by the language (it is in fact what differentiates Chip from Prolog).

The Charme formulation [Bul91], consists of 5 data (Pascal-like) declarations (arrays and structures) and of 10 (Pascal-like) procedures defining the program. The size of the program is 85 lines, excluding declarations (70 lines). As for the Chip formulation, the program accesses data and sets constraints. Again, no code concerns constraint propagation, as it is built into the language.

Our methodology is now employed to design the Bridge Problem.

Identify Classes and Objects. The basic class of the problem is *task*. Tasks can be of 14 different types (*excav*, *foundat*, etc.). Each concrete task is an object, instance of one of such classes. For example, *a1* is an instance of *excav*, *p1* is an instance of *foundat*, etc.

Identify the Semantics of These Classes and Objects. Each task is characterized by a *name*, *start time*, *duration*, *component* that it processes, and a *resource* that it employs. All these features are attributes of the generic class *task* and consequently of the 14 derived subclasses. The *start time* is the unknown to be determined, so it is a variable. The initial value is 0..200, meaning that the start time of each task is initially unknown, it will be automatically determined by the system, and it will be included between 0 and 200 days.

Identify the Associations Among These Classes and Objects. The 77 disjunctive constraints and the 66 precedence constraints can be expressed as two class constraints, referred to as *precedence* and *disjunction* respectively. The 25 specific constraints can also be expressed at the class level, with five class constraints referred to as *k1-k5*.

Identify the Semantics of These Associations. The semantics of these associations is specified through logical formulae on classes and objects:

disjunction. if $task\_1.resource = task\_2.resource$
then $[task\_1.start + task\_1.duration \le task\_2.start$ or
$task\_2.start + task\_2.duration \le task\_1.start]$
precedence. if $before(task\_1, task\_2)$
then $task\_1.start + task\_1.duration < task\_2.start$
k1. if $formwork.component = foundat.component$
then $foundat.start + foundat.duration - 4 \le formwork.start + formwork.duration$
k2. if $excav.component = formwork.component$
then $formwork.start - 3 \le excav.start + excav.duration$
k3. $house.start \le formwork.start - 6$
k4. $masonry.start + masonry.duration - 2 \le removal.start$
k5. $delivery.start = begin.start + 30.$

The design of the Bridge Problem is complete (see Fig. 5) and can automatically be interpreted and executed to determine the start time of the tasks. The model consists of 16 classes (*task*, *excav*, etc.), 53 objects (*a1*, *l*, etc.), 1 relation (*before*) and 8 class constraints (*disjunction*, *precedence*, *k1-k5*).

The *before* relation is not shown in Fig. 5: it relates 66 pairs of tasks to define the precedence constraint, but thanks to classes many pairs are factorized and only 29 edges are drawn (the text is entered just for the first pair, for instance "*before(a3, p1)*", then it is automatically generated by joining objects through edges of the same color).

The lack of constraints on objects means that the model is well conceived, because abstraction has been fully exploited to factor out common information. Compared to the Chip (90 lines) and the Charme (85 lines) programs, the textual part of our model consists of just 14 lines.

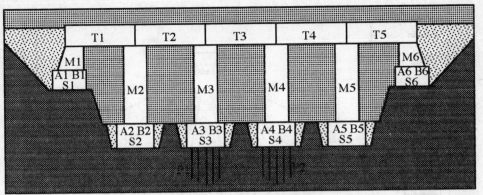

Fig. 3. The five-segment bridge.

N	Name	Description	Duration	Resource
1	pa	beginning of project	0	-
2	a1	excavation (abutment 1)	4	excavator
3	a2	excavation (pillar 1)	2	excavator
4	a3	excavation (pillar 2)	2	excavator
5	a4	excavation (pillar 3)	2	excavator
6	a5	excavation (pillar 4)	2	excavator
7	a6	excavation (pillar 5)	5	excavator
8	p1	foundation pile 2	20	pile-driver
9	p2	foundation pile 3	13	pile-driver
10	ue	erection of tmp. housing	10	-
11	s1	formwork (abutment 1)	8	carpentry
12	s2	formwork (pillar 1)	4	carpentry
13	s3	formwork (pillar 2)	4	carpentry
14	s4	formwork (pillar 3)	4	carpentry
15	s5	formwork (pillar 4)	4	carpentry
16	s6	formwork (abutment 2)	10	carpentry
17	b1	concrete found. (abutment 1)	1	concrete-mixer
18	b2	concrete found. (pillar 1)	1	concrete-mixer
19	b3	concrete found. (pillar 2)	1	concrete-mixer
20	b4	concrete found. (pillar 3)	1	concrete-mixer
21	b5	concrete found. (pillar 4)	1	concrete-mixer
22	b6	concrete found. (abutment 2)	1	concrete-mixer
23	c1	concrete setting (abutment 1)	1	-
24	c2	concrete setting (pillar 1)	1	-
25	c3	concrete setting (pillar 2)	1	-
26	c4	concrete setting (pillar 3)	1	-
27	c5	concrete setting (pillar 4)	1	-
28	c6	concrete setting (abutment 2)	1	-
29	m1	masonry work (abutment 1)	16	bricklaying
30	m2	masonry work (pillar 1)	8	bricklaying
31	m3	masonry work (pillar 2)	8	bricklaying
32	m4	masonry work (pillar 3)	8	bricklaying
33	m5	masonry work (pillar 4)	8	bricklaying
34	m6	masonry work (abutment 2)	20	bricklaying
35	l	delivery of bearers	2	crane
36	t1	positioning (bearer 1)	12	crane
37	t2	positioning (bearer 2)	12	crane
38	t3	positioning (bearer 3)	12	crane
39	t4	positioning (bearer 4)	12	crane
40	t5	positioning (bearer 5)	12	crane
41	ua	removal of tmp. housing	10	-
42	v1	filling 1	15	Caterpillar
43	v2	filling 2	10	Caterpillar
44	k1	costing point 1	0	-
45	k2	costing point 2	0	-
46	pe	end of project	0	-

Fig. 4. The 46 tasks are characterized by a name, a component they process, a duration and a resource they employ.

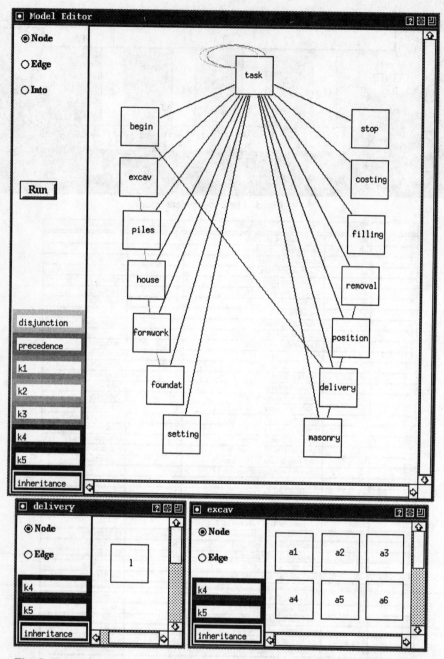

Fig. 5. The Bridge Problem formulated as an OOCSP: 14 classes of specific tasks are derived from the base class *task* on which two class constraints, *disjunction* and *precedence*, are defined; five more class constraints, *k1-k5*, are defined over other classes; the 46 tasks are represented as objects. Two out of the 14 class windows, *delivery* and *excav*, are also shown.

7 Discussion

This work integrates in one framework

- a *design methodology* supported by
- a *visual system* that produces
- *compact models* directly
- *executable* by traditional constraint programming languages.

We believe that this framework is original in providing an integrated environment for the whole development cycle of constraint-based applications.

This is achieved by adding abstraction levels to the classical CSP model through notions typical of the object-oriented paradigm, such as object, class and inheritance. Multi-class associations, i.e., associations over multiple classes, allow to factor out several associations into a single expression. The resulting model, OOCSP, represents CSP's more compactly.

Several problems presented in the literature have been reformulated as OOCSP always obtaining a significant gain in terms of model compactness. Besides comparing our formulation to that of traditional constraint languages, such as Chip and Charme (see Section 6), we also compared it to that of object-oriented constraint languages. For example, the formulation of the Bridge Problem in Ilog-Solver consists of 88 C++ lines (excluding data definition, 104 lines), whereas the textual part of our model consists of 14 lines. As another example, the Yafcrs formulation of the scheduling problem presented in [Kök94] consists of 145 Lisp lines (excluding data definition, 105 lines), whereas our formulation consists of 7 lines. Of course, besides the textual component, our model also includes a visual component, but we believe that visual information contributes to make the model more intuitive, composable and reusable.

Future developments will concentrate on the following issues.

Dynamic creation and removal of objects, classes and constraints. This functionality cannot be effectively included in the present implementation of the system, since preprocessing and propagation are done in two different languages. As soon as constraint propagation will be available in SICStus Prolog, the two phases will be performed in the same environment and dynamic creation and removal of model components will be implemented more easily.

The capability to combine models of different problems, or different views of the same problem. For instance, the formulation of the Bridge Problem in Section 6 represents resources as task attributes. If, on the other hand, a model of resources, possibly even more detailed, existed independently, then tasks in the new model could be associated to resources in the existing one. Composability has interesting implications also on reusability, since by using the existing resource model in combination with the new one, resources do not have to be redefined.

Effectiveness of the resulting model, through sound design rules, and efficiency of the propagation phase, through the specification of appropriate heuristics.

The construction of a library of models: to solve a problem, the user selects the appropriate model and customizes it by adding or deleting nodes and edges.

Acknowledgments

Many thanks to François Fages and to the whole Logic and Constraint Programming group at E.N.S. for fruitful discussions. Emmanuel Chailloux, Christian and Philippe Codognet encouraged new developments to the system. I am grateful to the following people for their help in positioning my system with respect to other systems: Alan Borning (ThingLab, ThingLabII), Bjorn Freeman-Benson (Kaleidoscope), Peter Chan (Charme and Chip), Tibor Kökény (Yafcrs), Michel Leconte (Ilog-Solver). Comments and criticism from anonymous reviewers were also very valuable.

References

[AKa93]   Hassan Aït-Kaci: An Introduction to LIFE - Programming with logic, Inheritance, Functions and Equations, in D. Miller (ed.), *Proc. of the Internat. Symp. on Logic Programming*, Vancouver, BC, pages 52-68, The MIT Press, Cambridge, MA, 1993.

[And93]   J. Andersson, S. Andersson, K. Boortz, M. Carlsson, H. Nilsson, J. Widen, T. Sjöland: Sicstus Prolog User's Manual, *Technical Report T93:01*, Swedish Institute of Computer Science, January 1993.

[Boo94]   G. Booch: *Object-Oriented Analysis and Design with Applications*, Second Edition, The Benjamin Cummings Publishing Company, Inc., California, 1994.

[Bor79]   A. Borning: Thinglab: A Constraint-Oriented Simulation Laboratory, *Ph.D. Thesis*, Stanford University, CA, 1979.

[Bul91]   Bull S.A.: *Manuel Charme First,* Bull Publication 95-F2-52GN-REV0, Cediag, 48 Route de Versailles, 78430 Louveciennes, France, 1991.

[Col90]   A. Colmerauer: An Introduction to Prolog III, *Communications of the ACM*, Vol. 33 (7), 1990.

[Din88]   M. Dincbas, P. Van Hentenryck, H. Simonis, A. Aggoun, T. Graf, F. Berthier: The Constraint Logic Programming Language CHIP, *Proc. of the Int. Conf. on Fifth Generation Computer Systems*, Tokyo, Japan, 1988.

[FBe90]   B. Freeman-Benson: Kaleidoscope: Mixing Objects, Constraints and Imperative Programming, *Proc. ECOOP/OOPSLA '90*, pages 77-88, Oct. 1990.

[FBB92a] B. Freeman-Benson, A. Borning: The Design and Implementation of Kaleidoscope'90, a Constraint Imperative Programming Language, *Proc. of the IEEE Computer Society International Conference on Computer Languages,* pages 174-180, April 1992.

[Har86]   D. R. Harris: A Hybrid Object and Constraint Representation Language, *AAAI-86*, pages 986-990, Philadelphia, Pennsylvania, 1986.

[Hor92]   B. Horn: Constraint Patterns as a Basis for Object Oriented Programming, *Proc. of the 1992 Conference on Object-Oriented Programming Systems, Languages and Applications*, pages 218-233, Vancouver, Canada, 1992, ACM Press.

[HSW95] M. Henz, G. Smolka, J. Würtz: Object-Oriented Concurrent Programming in Oz, in P. van Hentenryck and V. Saraswat (eds.), *Principles and Practice of Constraint Programming,* The MIT Press, pages 27-48, 1995, to appear.

[Jaf88] J. Jaffar, S. Michaylov, P.J. Stuckey: The CLP(R) Language System, *draft for Constraints & Languages W/S,* 1988.

[JaM94] J. Jaffar, M. Maher: Constraint Logic Programming: A Survey, Journal of Logic Programming, 19/20, pages 503-581, May-July 1994.

[KoJ84] M. Konopasek, S. Jayaraman: *The TK!Solver Book,* Osborne/McGraw-Hill, Berkeley, CA, 1984.

[Kök94] T. Kökény: Yet Another Object-Oriented Constraint Resolution System: An Open Architecture Approach, *XI Europen Conference on Artificial Intelligence,* Workshop: Constraint Processing, working notes, pages 115-120, Amsterdam, The Netherlands, 1994.

[Lel88] W. Leler: *Constraint Programming Languages,* Addison-Wesley Publishing Company, 1988.

[LFB93] G. Lopez, B. Freeman-Benson, A. Borning: Kaleidoscope: A Constraint Imperative Programming language, in *Constraint Programming,* B. Mayoh, E. Tõugu, J. Penjam (Eds.), NATO Advanced Science Institute Series, Series F: Computer and System Science, Springer-Verlag, 1993.

[LFB94] G. Lopez, B. Freeman-Benson, A. Borning: Implementing Constraint Imperative Programming Languages: The Kaleidoscope'93 Virtual Machine, in *Proc. of the 1994 ACM Conference on Object-Oriented Programming Systems, Languages and Applications,* Portland, Oregon, October 1994.

[MBF89] J. Maloney, A. Borning, B. Freeman-Benson: Constraint Technology for User Interface Construction in ThingLab II, in *Proc. of the 1989 ACM Conference on Object-Oriented Programming Systems, Languages and Applications,* pages 381-388, New Orleans, October 1989.

[MGV92] B. A. Myers, D. A. Giuse, B. Vander Zanden: Declarative Programming in a Prototype-Instance System: Object-Oriented Programming Without Writing Methods, *Proc. of the 1992 ACM Conference on Object-Oriented Programming Systems, Languages and Applications,* pages 184-200, Vancouver, Canada, 1992.

[Nad90] B. A. Nadel: Some Applications of the Constrain Satisfaction Problem, *Technical Report CSC-90-008,* Computer Science Department, Wayne State University, 1990.

[Opl89] A. Oplobedu: Charme: Un Langage Industriel de Programmation par Contraintes, *Actes 9eme Journée International sur les Systèmes Expert et Leur Applications,* Vol. 1, 55-70, Avignon, 1989.

[Pal94a] M. Paltrinieri: On the Design of Constraint Satisfaction Problems, *Principles and Practice of Constraint Programming,* A. Borning (ed.), Lecture Notes in Computer Science, N. 874, Springer-Verlag, 1994.

[Pal94b] M. Paltrinieri: Integrating Objects with Constraint-Programming Languages, *Object-Oriented Methodologies and Systems,* E. Bertino and S. Urban (eds.), Lecture Notes in Computer Science, N. 858, Springer-Verlag, 1994.

[Pug92] J.-F. Puget: Programmation Par Contraintes Orientée Objet, *12th International Conference on Artificial Intelligence, Expert Systems and Natural Language,* pages 129-138, Avignon, France, 1992.

[Rum91]   J. Rumbaugh, M. Blaha, W. Premerlani, F. Eddy, W. Lorensen: *Object-Oriented Modeling and Design*, Prentice-Hall Inc., Englewood Cliffs, N.J., 1991.

[Sar93]   V. A. Saraswat: *Concurrent Constraint Programming*, MIT Press, 1993.

[SRR94]   D. Srivastava, R. Ramakrishnan, P. Z. Revesz: Constraint Objects, *Second International Workshop on Principles and Practice of Constraint Programming*, Orcas Island, WA, May 1994.

[Tan95]   C. Tanzer: Remarks on Object-Oriented Modeling of Associations, *Journal of Object-Oriented Programming*, Vol. 7, No. 9, pages 43-46, February 1995.

[ThS94]   S. Thennarangam, G. Singh: Inferring 3-dimensional Constraints with DEVI, *Second International Workshop on Principles and Practice of Constraint Programming*, Orcas Island, WA, May 1994.

[Van89]   P. Van Hentenryck: *Constraint Satisfaction in Logic Programming*, The MIT Press, Cambridge, Massachusetts, 1989.

[VaW82]   C. J. Van Wyk: A High-Level Language for Specifying Pictures, *ACM Transactions on Graphics* 1(2), 163-182.

[WaV93]   M. Wallace, A. Veron: Two Problems - Two Solutions: One System ECLiPSe, *IEE Colloquium on Advaanced Software Technologies for Scheduling*, London, April 1993.

[Wil91]   M. Wilk: Equate: An Object-Oriented Constraint Solver, *OOPSLA '91*, pages 286-298, Phoenix, October 1991.

Polynomial Restrictions of SAT: What Can Be Done with an Efficient Implementation of the Davis and Putnam's Procedure?*

Antoine Rauzy

LaBRI - CNRS URA 1304 - Université Bordeaux I
51, cours de la Libération, F-33405 Talence (France)
email: rauzy@labri.u-bordeaux.fr

Abstract. Constraint Solving Problems are NP-Complete and thus computationaly intractable. Two approaches have been used to tackle this intractability: the improvement of general purpose solvers and the research of polynomial time restrictions. An interesting question follows: what is the behavior of the former solvers on the latter restrictions ?

In this paper, we examplify this problem by studying both theoretical and practical complexities of the Davis and Putnam's procedure on the two main polynomial restrictions of SAT, namely Horn-SAT and 2-SAT. We propose an efficient implementation and an improvement that make it quadratic in the worst case on these sub-classes. We show that this complexity is never reached in practice where linear times are observed, making the Davis and Putnam's as efficient as specialized algorithms.

1 Introduction

Let $\phi = C_1 \wedge C_2 \wedge \ldots \wedge C_m$ be a Boolean expression in conjunctive normal form, i.e. where each *clause* C_i is a disjunction of literals and each *literal* is either a variable p_i or its negation $\neg p_i$ $(1 \leq i \leq n)$.

The SAT(isfiability) problem consists in determining whether such an expression ϕ is true for some assignment of Boolean values to the variables $p_1, \ldots, p_n$. Cook [13] has shown that SAT is NP-complete and it is now the reference NP-complete problem [25]. A k-SAT instance is a SAT instance wherein all of the clauses have the same length k. For $k \geq 3$, k-SAT is NP-complete [13].

As the other Constraint Solving Problems and unless $P = NP$, SAT is thus computationally intractable. Two approaches have been used to tackle this intractability: the improvement of general purpose solvers and the research of restrictions for which there exists polynomial time algorithms. It must be pointed out that solving a restriction requires a *priori* two algorithms: the first one to recognize that a given instance belongs to the restriction, the second one to decide whether instances belonging to this restriction are satisfiable or not. Both must be polynomial to establish that the restriction is so.

---

* This work is supported by the french inter-PRC project "Classes Polynomiales"

SAT admits some (few) restrictions for which such algorithms are known. These restrictions are mainly Horn-SAT (satisfiability of sets of Horn clauses) and 2-SAT (satisfiability of sets of binary clauses) for which there exist linear time algorithms. These algorithms work on specialized data-structures (graphs or hypergraphs) and cannot be extended into general solvers for SAT. This raises an interesting question: what about the behavior of the general purpose solvers on these restrictions ?

In this paper, we aswer this question for what concerns the good old Davis and Putnam's procedure [17, 16], Horn-SAT and 2-SAT. This procedure is of a particular interest because, despite of its simplicity, it has never been shown inferior to any other complete algorithm. In particular, it outperforms the most efficient resolution based methods [6].

We first propose an efficient implementation and discuss how unit resolution and monotone literal propagation can be achieved in linear time. Then, we establish that this implementation is quadratic on Horn clauses and that an improvement we have proposed in [33] makes it quadratic on binary clauses. We give experimental results obtained on randomly generated sets of clauses. This provides evidence that the quadratic worst case complexity is never reached in practice where linear times are observed. We give elements to explain why. We examine also some related problems such as unique-satisfiability or truth of quantified boolean formulae.

The main interest of these results is that given any SAT instance, it is not necessary to test whether it belongs to one of the cited polynomial classes, in order to apply a specialized decision algorithm. The Davis and Putnam's procedure, that is a complete solver for SAT, ensures good practical results. This show a clear separation between hard instances, that are indeed hard for any algorithm, and easy instances that are symmetrically easy for well implemented general purpose solvers.

The remaining of this paper is organized as follows. We describe how the Davis and Putnam's procedure can be efficiently implemented at section 2. Then, sections 3 and 4 are respectively devoted to Horn instances and 2-SAT instances.

2 Implementation of the Davis and Putnam's Procedure

The paper by Davis and Putnam [17], that is cited by most of the authors, does not contain the procedure under its nowadays recursive presentation in terms of assignments of Boolean values to variables. Such a presentation has appeared for the first time in [16]. Nevertheless, even the latter paper does not give any detail about the underlying data structure (nor does the very often referenced [41]). However, this point is significant since linear time simplifications discussed below can only be achieved by choosing the appropriate data structure.

2.1 Data structure

We use a "sparse matrix" to store the clauses. Each row of the matrix encodes a clause (i.e. a list of literals). Each column encodes the list of occurrences of a variable. The design of an enumerative algorithm (i.e. one whose principle is to assign values to variables), on such a matrix requires a single basic instruction: the assignment of a value belonging to {*true, false, neutral*} to a variable. This operation is performed by visiting each occurrence of the variable and updating various counters that are used for multiple purposes, including the design of algorithms and heuristics.

- For each clause, counts of satisfied, falsified and neutral literals it contains in the current assignment are maintained, as well as a status belonging to {*unchanged, satisfied, shortened, falsified*}. A clause is *unchanged* when all its literals have the value *neutral*. It is *satisfied* when at least one of its literals is satisfied. It is *falsified* when all its literals are falsified. Finally, it is *shortened* otherwise, i.e. when it contains no satisfied literal and at least a falsified literal and a neutral literal. A clause is *active* if it is either unchanged or shortened. A clause is *unit* when it is active and it contains only one unassigned literal.
- Global counts of clauses of each of the fourth categories are maintained.
- The value of each variable is maintained, as well as counts of its positive and negative occurrences in the clauses of each category and counts of its positive and negative occurrences in unit clauses. Note that if a variable occurs both positively and negatively in unit clauses the current set of clauses is unsatisfiable.
- A list of unit literals and a list of monotone literals are maintained. A neutral literal is said to be *monotone*, if its opposite does not occur in active clauses. It is said to be an *unit-literal* if it is the only neutral literal of an unit clause. These lists are doubly chained ones, in order to allow constant time insertion and removal of items.

We denote by $E_{p_1 \leftarrow v_1, \ldots, p_k \leftarrow v_k}$ the matrix E in which values $v_1, \ldots, v_k$ belonging to {*true, false*} are assigned to variables $p_1, \ldots, p_k$. The other variables are assumed to have the value *neutral*. By extension, we denote E_q the matrix E in which the literal q has been satisfied. We denote by $1 - v$ the opposite value of v, i.e. $1 - v = false$ when $v = true$ and vice versa, and by $\neg q$ the opposite of a literal q. Note that the presented way of carrying out assignments is not the one described for instance in the Loveland's book [41]. In general, authors assume that the set of clauses is updated each time an assignment is performed. Of course, the set of clauses encoded by $E_{p_1 \leftarrow v_1, \ldots, p_k \leftarrow v_k}$ is obtained from the set of clauses encoded by E by deleting clauses that contain a satisfied literal and suppressing the occurrences of falsified literals from the other clauses. In our experience, our way of doing is not only simpler to program but also more efficient. In the following, we always say "set of clauses" but the underlying coding by means of a sparse matrix is implicitly assumed.

Lemma 1 Complexity of the basic operation. *The worst case complexity of the assignment of a value to a variable is in* $\mathcal{O}(L \times K)$, *where L denotes the maximum number of occurrences of a variable and K denotes the maximal size of a clause.*

In what follows, we keep the same meaning to L and K. We denote by V the number of variables, by C the number of clauses and by S the total number of literals occurring in the clauses. K and L are indeed majored by V and C.

2.2 Linear Time Unit and Monotone Propagation

A very interesting property of the proposed data structure is that it allows linear time unit and monotone propagations. We call *unit and monotone propagation* the process that consists in peeking repeatedly an unit or monotone literal and satisfying it until there is no more unit or monotone literals or a variable occurs both positively and negatively in unit clauses.

Lemma 2 Linear Time Unit and Monotone Propagation. *Unit and Monotone Propagation is in $\mathcal{O}(S)$.*

Since lists of unit and monotone literals are maintained, detection of such literals is done in constant time. Let us consider the maximum number of times a literal is visited. A clause may change at most two times of status during the propagation process (from *unchanged* to *shortened* then from *shortened* to *falsified* or to *satisfied*), thus its literals are visited at most two times in order to update counters of their owning variables. An additional visit may be necessary to detect the only unassigned literal of the clause (when this clause becomes unit). The list of occurrences of a variable is visited at most once, when a value is assigned to this variable. It follows that each literal is visited at most four times. □

This simple complexity analysis is not essentially new since Minoux in [44] have already remarked that unit resolution can be performed in linear time. We extend it here to monotone literals and to the updating of various counters. Moreover, the algorithm discussed here is far more natural and general than graph based algorithms proposed by Dowling and Gallier [18] (and corrected in [50]), Minoux [44] or Ghallab and Escalada-Imaz [27].

2.3 Algorithm

The Davis and Putnam's procedure, as it is implemented on a sparse matrix, can be described in an informal way as follows: let E the set of clauses to be tested.

- If the satisfiability of E is not immediately decidable (i.e. if neither E is empty nor it contains an empty clause or a variable occurring both positively and negatively in unit clauses), then there are two cases:
- E contains a monotone or a unit literal q. In this case, the value v that satisfies q is assigned to the corresponding variable, and the algorithm is called recursively. It is sound since in both cases, E is satisfiable if and only if E_q is satisfiable.
- E does not contain monotone or unit literal. In this case, a variable p and a value v are chosen and the algorithm is called recursively first on $E_{p \leftarrow v}$ and second on $E_{p \leftarrow 1-v}$, if $E_{p \leftarrow v}$ is not satisfiable.

Heuristics. In practice, a good heuristic for choosing the next literal to assign improves dramatically the performances of the algorithm. Of course, a compromise must be found between the cost of an heuristic and its efficiency. For this study, we used two simple heuristics.

The first one so-called `ffis` (for First Fail in Shortened Clauses) that consists in choosing the variable that has first the maximum number of occurrences in shortened clauses and second the maximum number of occurrences in unchanged clauses. The chosen value is the one satisfying the most frequent literal. `ffis` is not the best heuristic we know, however it is a very interesting tradeoff and seems — as far as we have tested them on a sufficiently large benchmark — as efficient as many other proposed ones [56, 34, 42, 20]. Its cost is in $\mathcal{O}(V)$ (a traversal of the table of variables).

The second heuristics so-called `bimo` (for Best In Matrix Order) is even simpler and consists in choosing the first unassigned variable in the matrix order. The chosen value is the one satisfying the most frequent literal. Its cost is in $\mathcal{O}(1)$ (it suffices to increment a pointer each time a variable is assigned).

On-Line Algorithms. Several authors have examined the case where new clauses are added on-line to the current set [4, 32, 54]. It is clear that the Davis and Putnam's procedure can be easily adapted without any additional cost to this case: it suffices to maintain the current execution stack, i.e. the current assignment plus a number of information to handle backtracking. In what follows, we will do not mention this point anymore, but it will be implicitly understood.

3 Horn Clauses

3.1 Worst Case Complexity

A *Horn clause* is a clause that contains at most one positive literal. Horn-clauses are used extensively in Artificial Intelligence (see e.g. [31]) A set of clauses E is said *Horn-renamable* if it exists a renaming transforming E into a set of Horn clauses (a *renaming* substitutes in the whole set and for some variables p, the occurrences of p for $\neg p$ and vice versa).

Several linear time algorithms have been proposed to test the satisfiability of Horn clauses [18, 44, 27]. These algorithms do not consider the recognition problem (i.e. they take sets of Horn clauses in input). Lewis showed in [39] that in order to decide whether a set of clauses is Horn-renamable or not it suffices to check the satisfiability of an associated set of binary clauses (as it will be discussed at the next section, it is possible the perform this test in linear time). The basic idea is to associate a binary clause $(\neg p \vee \neg q)$ with each pair (p, q) of literals occurring simultaneously in a clause. Each assignment satisfying the set of binary clauses defines a Horn-renaming: it suffices to rename the variables taking the value *false* in the assignment. Conversely, each Horn-renaming defines a satisfying assignment: the value *false* is assigned to renamed variables, the value *true* is assigned to the others. Roughly done this construction may generate a quadratic number of binary clauses. Many authors have proposed linear explicit or implicit constructions of the set of binary clauses [2, 43, 1, 40, 10, 30]. The following result is well known:

Theorem 3 Unit-Resolution. *The unit-resolution is complete for Horn clauses.*

It means that if a Horn-renamable set of clauses is unsatisfiable, the Davis and Putnam's procedure demonstrates it just by applying the unit-literal selection rule. Therefore, the following results holds:

Lemma 4 Unsatisfiable Horn-SAT. *The Davis and Putnam's procedure is in $\mathcal{O}(S)$ on unsatisfiable Horn-renamable instances.*

This result is already known and has been implicitly pointed out for instance in [24]. Unit literal propagation is sufficient to determine whether a Horn set is satisfiable or not. But this requires to know that the tested instance is Horn renamable. What we want to ensure is that our general decision procedure, here the Davis and Putnam's procedure, is polynomial on polynomial classes of SAT without testing before whether the tested instance belongs to a polynomial class or not. It thus remains to look at the complexity of the algorithm on Horn-renamable sets clauses that do not contain unit literal and that are thus satisfiable. Let E be such a set. We can assume without a loss of generality that E does not contain any monotone literal.

Let q be the literal chosen by the used heuristics. There are two cases:

- E_q is satisfiable. In this case, the algorithm does not backtrack on the satisfaction of q.
- E_q is unsatisfiable, and from the lemma 4, the Davis and Putnam's procedure detects this unsatisfiability in $\mathcal{O}(S)$. Thus it backtracks (with the same complexity), and then it falsifies q. The set $E_{\neg q}$ is a Horn-renamable set of clauses with at least one variable less than E.

Since the process "selection of variable / unit-literal propagation / detection of a falsified clause / backtrack" cannot be repeated more than V times, the following result holds:

Theorem 5 Horn-SAT. *The Davis and Putnam's procedure is in $\mathcal{O}(V \times S)$ on Horn-renamable instances.*

On the one hand, this shows that the worst case complexity of the Davis and Putnam's procedure is not as good as the worst complexity of specialized algorithms that first decide in $\mathcal{O}(S)$ whether a set of clauses is Horn-renamable then test in $\mathcal{O}(S)$ whether it is satisfiable. On the other hand, the obtained complexity is low and we will see that the practical complexity is actually linear. Note that the key point to obtain a linear worst case complexity stands in the proof of Horn-renamability and that this proof is in turn equivalent to a satisfiability test of a set of binary clauses.

3.2 Experimental Complexity

Fig. 1 shows the results obtained on randomly generated Horn-SAT instances. An instance consists of C non-tautological clauses of size 3 built independently over 1000 and 2000 variables, each variable having the same probability to be drawn. One of the literals of a clause is positive, the two others are negative (to be sure not to introduce biases, instances are randomly renamed). Presented curves have been obtained by interpolating points corresponding to the draw of 100 instances for the value 0.5, 0.6 and so on of ratio C/V. Fig. 1 shows that:
– Below the value 2.3 of the ratio C/V, curves of running times with both heuristics are quasi-identical.
– Beyond this value, running times grows linearly with the ratio C/V for bimo, and more than linearly with ffis.

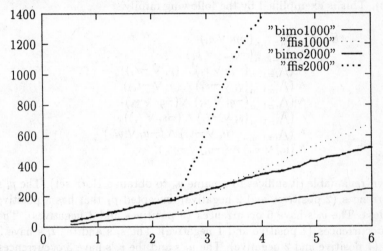

Fig. 1. Horn-SAT: Relation between sizes of instances and running times

This is explained as follows. For any value of the ratio C/V and for both heuristics, the procedure never backtracks. This is due to the choice of the most frequent literal (once the variable chosen). The number of assignments required to satisfy all of the clauses grows as C/V grows. Below the ratio 2.3, the satisfiability of instances is proved only by means of monotone literal propagation. No choice is performed, and thus the two curves are identical. Beyond this ratio, monotone literal propagation does not suffice. Some choices must be performed. The number of required choices increases as C/V increases. Conversely, the number of monotone literals decreases as C/V increases, even if it remains high for a long time. For instance, about 60% of assigned literals are monotone at $C/V = 6.5$. With bimo, each choice is performed in constant time and thus, even if a linear number of such choices must be done, the Davis and Putnam's procedure remains linear. With ffis, each choice is performed in linear time. The Davis and Putnam's procedure tends thus to be quadratic, since it must perform ρV choices, where ρ is a constant between 0 and 1 that depends on C/V.

These observations justify the way we draw instances: the easiness of a Horn-renamable instance depends on the number of monotone literals it contains, that depends on turn on the proportion of "positive" literals. Statistically, the more there are such literals, the less there are monotone ones. By compelling at least one literal per clause to be "positive", we ensure that there is a quite high proportion of such literals, namely about $1/3$. Note that drawing instances whose clauses are longer than 3 would decrease this proportion. On the other hand, introducing binary clauses makes the problem easier, as we will see at the next section.

How to reach the worst case complexity ? It is possible to build instances for which the worst case complexity is reached (even in terms of the number of assignments). This is exemplified by the following family.

$$
\begin{aligned}
E_n = \ & \bigwedge_{i=1..n}(\neg p_i \vee q_i) \\
& \wedge \bigwedge_{i=2..n}(\neg q_{i-1} \vee p_i) \\
& \wedge \left(\bigwedge_{i=1..n}(\neg p_i \vee r_i) \wedge (p_i \vee \neg r_i)\right) \\
& \wedge \left(\bigwedge_{i=1..n}(q_i \vee \neg s_i) \wedge (q_i \vee \neg t_i)\right) \\
& \wedge \left(\bigwedge_{i=1..n}(\neg q_i \vee u_i) \wedge (\neg q_i \vee v_i)\right) \\
& \wedge \left(\bigwedge_{i=1..n}(s_i \vee \neg t_i) \wedge (\neg s_i \vee t_i)\right) \\
& \wedge \left(\bigwedge_{i=1..n-1}(u_i \vee \neg v_i) \wedge (\neg u_i \vee v_i)\right) \\
& \wedge (u_n \vee v_n) \wedge (\neg u_n \vee \neg v_n)
\end{aligned}
$$

E_n is horn-renamable (it suffices to rename v_n to obtain a Horn set). The p_i's have 4 occurrences (2 positives and 2 negative), excepted p_1 that has a positive occurrence less. The q_i's have 6 occurrences (3 positives and 3 negatives). The r_i's have 2 occurrences (1 positive and 1 negative). The s_i's and the t_i's have 3 occurrences (1 positive and 2 negative). The u_i's and the v_i's have 3 occurrences (2 positive and 1 negative) Thus, E_n contains $24 \times V - 1$ literal occurrences and thus has a size linear in V. There is no unit and no monotone literal in E_n. ffis may choose to assign the value 1 to q_1, since q_1 is one of the most frequent variables and has as many positive and negative occurrences. The set $E_{n_{q_1 \leftarrow 1}}$ is shown unsatisfiable in at least $2n$ unit-literal assignments:

$$
q_1 \Rightarrow p_2 \Rightarrow q_2 \Rightarrow p_3 \Rightarrow \ldots \Rightarrow q_n \Rightarrow (u_n \wedge v_n)
$$

but the last two clauses constrain u_n and v_n to take different values. Thus, the algorithm backtracks and assigns the value 0 to q_1. It is easy to verify that

$$
E_{n_{q_1 \leftarrow 0}} \equiv (E_{n-1} \wedge \neg p_1 \wedge \neg r_1 \wedge \neg s_1 \wedge \neg t_1 \wedge (u_1 \Leftrightarrow v_1))
$$

The next chosen literal may be q_2, and so on. It follows that at least $n(n+1)/2$ assignments are necessary to find a model of E_n. The same result holds for **bimo** (with the appropriate variable ordering). Note that the above instances are compound of binary clauses.

3.3 Unique Horn Satisfiability

The unique satisfiability problem (unique-SAT) asks whether there exists a unique solution to a given SAT instance. Unique-SAT is known to be co-NP-complete [5]. In [48], D. Pretolani proposes linear time algorithm to solve unique-SAT on Horn clauses. This algorithm involves rather complex techniques. By going on after the first model was found (indeed in the case of satisfiable instances), the Davis and Putnam's procedure will check whether there exists a second model within the same complexity than for the first one: it will explore remaining alternatives, and on each unexplored right branch, either the corresponding set is unsatisfiable and it will be demonstrated it in $\mathcal{O}(S)$ in the worst case, or it is satisfiable and the procedure finds the second model in $\mathcal{O}(V \times S)$. Since the number of unexplored alternatives is majored by V, we have:

Theorem 6 unique-Horn-SAT. *The Davis and Putnam's procedure is in $\mathcal{O}(V \times S)$ on unique-Horn-SAT.*

In practice, determining whether a Horn-instance is unique satisfiable is not more costly than finding a solution: experiments reported above show that even for very large ratios C/V (50 for instance), there remain variables not valued in the found solution. Thus this solution is in fact a set of 2^k solutions, where k is the number of free variables.

4 Binary Clauses

Binary clauses play an important role in circuit design (see e.g. [37]). Satisfiability of quadratic clauses is the other well known polynomial time restriction of the SAT problem. As the matter of fact, there are a quadratic number of binary clauses (exactly $2n(n-1)$). Thus, simply by saturating a 2-SAT instance for the resolution principle, one obtains a polynomial decision algorithm. There exist linear time algorithms for solving 2-SAT [3, 22, 47]. Two different ways have been proposed to achieve linearity:

- By using the Tarjan's (linear) algorithm for exhibiting and sorting strongly connected components of a graph [52], as it is proposed by Apsvall, Plass and Tarjan in [3]. This implies a graph based formulation of the problem.
- By performing assignments of Boolean values to variables in "parallel" as suggested by Even, Itai and Shamir in [22].

However, as it is shown in [47], it appears that algorithms with a quadratic worst case complexity are more efficient in practice than those with a linear one. We will discuss this point latter.

4.1 A Frequent Error

Conversely to what many authors have written (including Petreschi and Simeone in [47]), the worst case complexity of the Davis and Putnam's procedure is not polynomial on binary clauses. To be convinced of that, it suffices to consider the following family of instances:

$$E_n = \left(\bigwedge_{i=1..n} (p_i \vee \neg q_i) \wedge (\neg p_i \vee q_i) \right) \wedge (r \vee s) \wedge (\neg r \vee s) \wedge (r \vee \neg s) \wedge (\neg r \vee \neg s)$$

The four last clauses form an unsatisfiable subset. It is easy to verify that the first ones, that encode the relations $p_i = q_i$ for $i = 1..n$, admit 2^n models. With a heuristics such as `bimo` presented at section 2, that chooses variables in the order $p_1, \ldots, p_n, r$, the Davis and Putnam's procedure goes through a complete binary tree on height n. Each leaf of this tree consists of the small search tree showing that the subset of the four last clauses is unsatisfiable.

This way of building sets of clauses – a big subset admitting a lot of solutions and a small unsatisfiable subset – often misleads enumerative methods. Note that it is always possible to mislead any reasonable heuristics (such as `ffis`), by duplicating some clauses, for these heuristics are based on counting arguments.

4.2   An improvement

Nevertheless, an improvement that we have introduced in [33] ensures the polynomiality of the algorithm on binary clauses (no complexity study was done in the cited paper). This improvement generalizes the notion of monotone literal to sets of literals. It uses the following property – so-called model separation:

Lemma 7 Model separation. *Let E be a set of clauses and σ a partial assignment of the variables of E. If E_σ does not contain any shortened (nor falsified) clause, then E is satisfiable if and only if E_σ is satisfiable.*

Proof it suffices to see that E_σ is a subset of E. Thus, if it is unsatisfiable, E is unsatisfiable too. Otherwise, σ extends any model of E_σ into a model of E. $\square$

This property is used in order to prune the search tree:

Assume the values $v_1, \ldots, v_k$ assigned to the variables $p_1, \ldots, p_k$ in this order. Assume too that the set $E_{p_1 \leftarrow v_1, \ldots p_k \leftarrow v_k}$ has been shown unsatisfiable (a complete subtree under the node labeled with p_k has been explored). Assume finally that $E_{p_1 \leftarrow v_1, \ldots p_k \leftarrow v_k}$ does not contain any clause shortened by the assignment of the variables $p_i, p_{i+1}, \ldots, p_k$ ($1 \leq i \leq k$).

Then, from the model separation lemma, the search tree can be pruned from the node labeled with p_{i-1} to the node labeled with p_k.

Let, for instance, E be the following set of clauses:

$$E = \begin{array}{l} (p_1 \vee \neg q_1) \wedge (\neg p_1 \vee q_1) \wedge (p_2 \vee \neg q_2) \wedge (\neg p_2 \vee q_2) \\ \wedge (r \vee s) \wedge (\neg r \vee s) \wedge (r \vee \neg s) \wedge (\neg r \vee \neg s) \end{array}$$

Assume that the procedure assigns first the value 1 to p_1 (and thus the value 1 to q_1 by unit literal propagation), then second the value 1 to p_2 (and thus the value 1 to q_2 by unit literal propagation). $E_{p_1 \leftarrow 1, q_1 \leftarrow 1, p_2 \leftarrow 1, q_2 \leftarrow 1}$ is unsatisfiable and contains no shortened clause. Thus, E is also unsatisfiable and it is not necessary to explore the assignments $p_1 \leftarrow 1, q_1 \leftarrow 1, p_2 \leftarrow 0, q_2 \leftarrow 0$ and $p_1 \leftarrow 0, q_1 \leftarrow 0$.

Note that the complexity of the detection of the model separation is linear w.r.t. the number of pruned branches, thanks to the counters described in the first section.

The improved Davis and Putnam's procedure, when applied to sets of binary clauses, is very similar to an algorithm proposed in [22] to solve instances of the timetable problem (which is reducible to 2-SAT). Model separation lemma also generalizes the notion of "autarch" proposed by Monien and Speckenmeyer in [46]. The key idea is that when a pair variable/value is chosen, either this assignment is demonstrate unsatisfiable by unit literal propagation, or it can be definitely kept.

4.3 Polynomiality of the improved Davis and Putnam's procedure

Let E be a set of binary clauses. We can assume without a loss of generality that E does not contain unit-clause, nor monotone literal.

Let $< p, v >$ be the pair variable/value chosen by the heuristic. The assignment of v to p creates eventually some unit-literals. These literals are chosen, thanks to the unit-literal selection rule. Their assignments may create new unit-literals that are themselves chosen and so on. At the end of this process, a set E_σ is obtained. There are two cases:

- At least one of the clauses of E is falsified by σ. Then, the algorithm backtracks and assigns the value $1 - v$ to p.
- None of the clauses of E_σ is falsified and E_σ does not contain any shortened clause, since a shortened binary clause is unit. In this case, the model separation lemma holds and E is satisfiable if and only if E_σ is satisfiable too. Thus, the partial assignment σ is definitive.

Since the process "selection of variable / unit-literal propagation / detection of a falsified clause / backtrack" cannot be repeated more than V times, the following result holds:

Theorem 8 2-SAT. *The improved Davis et Putnam's procedure is in $\mathcal{O}(V \times S)$ on binary clauses.*

4.4 Experimental Complexity

Before presenting experimental results of the Davis and Putnam's procedure on binary clauses, we must discuss recent works about threeshold phenomena and randomly generated k-SAT.

The interest in randomly generated k-SAT instances has been increased recently by an experimental result due to several authors independently [21, 45, 38, 15] that remarked that k-SAT instances obey a 0/1 law. Below a ratio C/V that depends on k, the probability to draw a satisfiable instance tends to 1 as

V tends to infinity. Beyond this ratio it tends (quickly) to 0. For $k = 2$ the threshold has been actually established equal to 1 by several authors [12, 28]. For $k = 3$ and $k = 4$ experimental values have been found (respectively 4.25 for $k = 3$ and 9.8 for $k = 4$). Researchers work hard to find (theoretical) lower and upper bounds for these values and Dubois in [20] gives a general equation $ln(2) - V.2^k - exp(kV/(2^k - 1)) = 0$, for which the upper zeros would be very close to the values of the thresholds of k-SAT instances (for $k=3$ and beyond). Threshold phenomena occur also in sets of clauses with different lengths [26].

In a practical point of view, one can observe that the hardest randomly generated k-SAT instances for Davis and Putnam's procedure (and for other algorithms, even incomplete ones such as Selman's GSAT [51]) are those around the threshold [11, 45, 20, 49] that is where about 50% of the drawn instances are satisfiable. Even for small numbers of variables (say 50) running times suddenly increase near the threshold and quickly decrease after. Satisfiable instances are significantly easier than unsatisfiable ones, but they are hard too, i.e. that running times quickly increase as V increases.

The Fig. 2 shows the results obtained on randomly generated 2-SAT instances (heuristics: bimo). An instance is compound of C different and non tautological clauses, all literals having the same probability. For 1000, 1500, 2000 and 2500 variables, 100 instances have been generated for the values 0.5, 0.55, 0.60, ..., 1.95 and 2 of the ratio C/V. This study enlighten the following phenomena:

– For a given the number of variables, the average running time reaches a maximum near the value 1 of the ratio C/V, i.e. near the threshold. The maximum is closer to 1 as V increases.

– At least for the ratio C/V around 1 (i.e. near the difficulty peek), running times grows linearly with V.

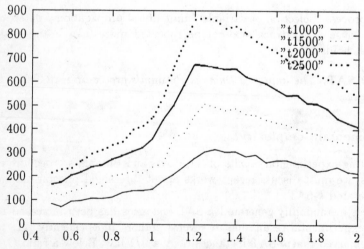

Fig. 2. 2-SAT: Relation between sizes and running times

This is explained as follows. Below the value 1 of the ratio C/V, instances are almost always satisfiable, and thus are Horn instances (since a 2-SAT instance is satisfiable if and only if it is Horn). The results obtained in the previous section apply here too, i.e. the procedure never bactracks. The difference stands in that here only one choice is necessary in average. The number of assignments increases as V increases, which explains that the running times (slowly) increases. Beyond the value 1 of the ratio C/V, instances tends to be unsatisfiable. For both heuristics (bimo and ffis), the procedure backtracks exactly once (in average). Thus unsatisfiablity is shown by means of two unit literal propagations. This has been already remarked by Petreshi and Simeone [47]. The "length" of each unit literal propagation depends on the ratio C/V: the more it is close to 1, the more propagations tend to be long. This explains why there is a difficulty peak.

How to reach the worst case complexity ? The example of the previous section that shows that the Davis and Putnam's procedure can actually reach its worst case quadratic complexity on Horn clauses is also a 2-SAT instance. Moreover, it is easy to verify that the model separation property never applies on this example.

Fig. 3, a Davis and Putnam's tree is pictured that sketches how the worst case complexity is reached on both Horn clauses and binary clauses. This tree clarifies the idea behind the Even, Itai and Shamir's algorithm. If the two unit literal propagations are performed in "parallel" (and fairly), one can stop immediatly after the first one is achieved. Thus, left branches of the pictured tree are "cut" at the same "length" than right branches. This trick ensures the linearity.

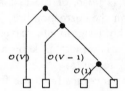

Fig. 3. 2-SAT: A worst case Davis and Putnam's tree

4.5 Related Problems

Unique Satisfiability A linear algorithm that determine whether set of binary clauses is uniquely satisfiable has been proposed in [29]. It is derived from the already cited algorithm proposed in [3]. The argumentation we have developed for Horn clauses applies here too. Thus, we have the following result:

Theorem 9 unique-2-SAT. *The improved Davis and Putnam's procedure is in $\mathcal{O}(S \times V)$ on unique-2-SAT.*

Note that, for the same reasons than for Horn instances, the Davis and Putnam's procedure is not more costly in practice to find the first solution than to determine whether it is unique (and thus there are good reasons to think that it is more efficient in practice than the algorithm of [29]).

Quantified Boolean Formulae Let $\psi = Q_1 x_1 Q_2 x_2 \ldots Q_n x_n \phi$, where each Q_i is either $\exists$ or $\forall$ and ϕ is a formula in conjunctive normal form built over the variables $x_1, \ldots, x_n$. The quantified Boolean formulae problem (QBF) consists in determining whether such a formula ψ is true. QBF is P-SPACE complete and limitations on the position and the number of quantifier alternations define the polynomial hierarchy (see [35] for a survey on complexity classes).

In [3], a linear algorithm for solving QBF for quadratic formulae is proposed. What we do here uses a similar trick (but translated from a graph based algorithm to a assignment based algorithm).

Let ψ a QBF instance in which all the clauses are at most quadratic. The quantifier alternation defines an order on variables: $x_1 < x_2 < \ldots < x_n$.

Consider the following adaptation of the Davis and Putnam's procedure:
– The terminal cases are those of the standard procedure (all the clauses are satisfied or a clause is falsified), plus the following one: if a universally quantified variable occurs into an unit-clause, then ψ is false (since the variable cannot take two values).
– The monotone literal selection rule is removed.
– The chosen variable, when there are no unit literal, is the least unassigned one. Let x_i be this variable, then examine successively $\phi_{x_i \leftarrow 0}$ and $\phi_{x_i \leftarrow 1}$ by propagating these assignments with the unit literal selection rule. Now, there are two cases : If x_i is existentially quantified, then either both assignments drive to failure cases and the formula ψ is false, or the last assignment is kept and the algorithm is called recursively on the corresponding formula. If x_i is universally quantified, then either one of the assignments drives to a failure case and the formula ψ is false, or the last assignment is kept and the algorithm is called recursively on the corresponding formula.

The soundness of the algorithm comes from the following lemma:

Lemma 10 Extended model separation. *Let $\psi = Q_1 x_1 Q_2 x_2 \ldots Q_n x_n \phi$ be quadratic QBF instance with no unit-clause, and such that the unit propagations of the assignments $x_1 \leftarrow 0$ and $x_1 \leftarrow 1$ don't drive to failure cases. Let ψ_0 and ψ_1 be the two obtained formulae (ϕ_0 and ϕ_1 being their respective sets of clauses).*

1. *ϕ_0 is satisfiable if and only if ϕ_1 is satisfiable.*
2. *For any variable y occurring in one of these formulae and that is not assigned in ϕ_0 and ϕ_1, $\phi_v \models y$ if and only if $\phi_{1-v} \models y$ ($v \in \{0, 1\}$).*

Proof. The first point comes from the model separation lemma. The second one is demonstrated as follows: Assume ϕ_0 and ϕ_1 satisfiable and $\phi_v \models y$. Since ϕ_v is a proper subset of ϕ, $\phi \models y$. Assume that there exists a model of ϕ_{1-v} that assigns the value 0 to y. Then by model separation lemma, this model can be extended into a model of ϕ. A contradiction. $\square$

The above lemma explains why it is not necessary to explore the two branches of the alternative when a choice point occurs: one suffices to make sure that either a universally quantified variable is implied and thus the whole formula is false, or that no universally quantified variable is implied and the formula is true.

Since the examination of least unassigned variable is in $\mathcal{O}(S)$, the following result holds:

Theorem 11 QBF restricted to quadratic clauses. *The extended improved Davis et Putnam's procedure is in $\mathcal{O}(V \times S)$ on the QBF problem restricted to sets of binary clauses.*

Note however that, on the contrary to what happens for 2-SAT and unique 2-SAT, this result requires to know that the given instance contains only quadratic clauses. Once again there are good reasons to think that the improved Davis and Putnam's procedure is more efficient in practice than the algorithm of [3].

5 Conclusion

What is done : In this paper, we provided worst case complexity bounds for the Davis and Putnam's procedure applied to Horn clauses and binary clauses. In both cases, this complexity is quadratic. In practice, the Davis and Putnam's procedure never reaches this complexity on randomly generated instances where linear times are observed.

We designed, on the same basis, algorithms to solve related problems such as the unique satisfiability or the truth of a quantified Boolean formula that have a good complexity on known polynomial restrictions of these problems.

What cannot be done : The variations studied here are designed without adding any functionality to the standard data structure used to implement the Davis and Putnam's procedure. They use two principles:
– A filtering principle : the unit literal propagation rule.
– An intelligent backtracking principle : the model separation property.

There exist polynomial classes that cannot be captured with these simple mechanisms. These classes are those defined by means of structural properties of the underlying graph of constraints. The Constraint Solving Problem community has extensively studied this kind of properties. It is well known, for instance, that if this graph is a tree, the problem is solvable in polynomial time. But this requires to assign values to variables in an order depending on the graph. Such an order cannot be induced by counting arguments (what do heuristics associated with the Davis and Putnam's procedure). In the case of SAT, several such classes have been exhibited [55, 1, 23, 36]. But, conversely to what happens for Horn-SAT and 2-SAT, it is doubtful that these classes have any practical interest, due to their very unnatural look. Nevertheless it could be interesting to randomly generate instances of these classes and see what happens.

What could be done : Other polynomial restrictions of SAT could be handled as we have done in this paper. It is the case of $r, r - SAT$ instances of Tovey [53] (improved by Dubois [19]) that are trivial to solve for they contain less clauses than variables. More interesting is the class of q-Horn clauses introduced in [7] that generalizes both Horn clauses and binary clauses. A linear algorithm has been proposed recently to recognize instances of this class in [9] (once recognized, solving them could be easily done in linear time). A complexity index of SAT instances based on this class has been proposed in [8]. In [49], we have proposed a variation on the Davis and Putnam's procedure that is polynomial on this class and once again linear in practice. However, our variation has a quite high complexity that can be surely improved.

More generally, it could be interesting to examine which simple filterings and/or pruning principles make enumerative algorithms (designed to solve constraint problems) polynomial on known polynomial restrictions. A first step in this direction has been done for CSPs in [14].

References

1. V. Arvind and S. Biswas. An $O(n^2)$ algorithm for the satisfiability problem of a subset of propositional sentences in CNF that includes horn sentences. *Information Processing Letters*, 24:67–69, 1987.

2. B. Aspvall. Recognizing Disguised NR(1) Instances of the Satisfiability Problem. *Journal of Algorithms*, 1:97–103, 1980.

3. B. Aspvall, M. Plass, and R. Tarjan. A Linear Time Algorithm for Testing the Truth of Certain Quantified Boolean Formulae. *Information Processing Letter*, 8(3):121–123, 1979.

4. G. Ausiello and G. Italiano. On-Line Algorithms for Polynomially Solvable Satisfiability Problems. *Journal of Logic Programming*, 10:69–90, 1990.

5. A. Blass and Y. Gurevitch. On the unique satisfiability problem. *Information and Control*, 55:80–88, 1982.

6. J.M. Boï and A. Rauzy. Two algorithms for constraints system solving in propositional calculus and their implementation in prologIII. In P. Jorrand and V. Sugrev, editors, *Proceedings Artificial Intelligence IV Methodology, Systems, Applications (AIMSA '90)*, pages 139–148. North-Holand, september 1990. Alba-Varna bulgarie.

7. E. Boros, Y. Crama, and P.L. Hammer. Polynomial-time inference of all implications for Horn and related formulae. *Annals of Mathematics and Artificial Intelligence*, 1:21–32, 1990.

8. E. Boros, Y. Crama, P.L. Hammer, and M. Saks. A complexity index for satisfiability problems. *SIAM Journ. Comp.*, 23:45–49, 1994.

9. E. Boros, P.L. Hammer, and X. Sun. Recognition of q-Horn formulae in linear time. *Discrete Applied Mathematics*, 55:1–13, 1994.

10. V. Chandru, C.R. Coulard, P.L. Hammer, M. Montanez, and X. Sun. On renamable Horn and generalized Horn functions. In *Annals of Mathematics and Artificial Intelligence*, volume 1. J.C. Baltzer AG, Scientific Publishing Company, Basel Switzerland, 1990.

11. P. Cheeseman, B. Kanefsky, and W.M. Taylor. Where the Really Hard Problems Are. In *Proceedings of the International Joint Conference of Artificial Intelligence*, *IJCAI'91*, 1991.

12. V. Chvátal and B. Reed. Miks gets some (the odds are on his side). In *Proceedings of the 33rd IEEE Symp. on Foundations of Computer Science*, pages 620–627, 1992.

13. S.A. Cook. The Complexity of Theorem Proving Procedures. In *Proceedings of the 3rd Ann. Symp. on Theory of Computing, ACM*, pages 151–158, 1971.

14. M.C. Cooper, D.A. Cohen, and P.G. Jeavons. Characterizing Tractable Constraints. *Artificial Intelligence*, 65:347–361, 1994.

15. J.M. Crawford and L.D. Auton. Experimental results on the crossover point in satisfiability problems. In *Proceedings of the Eleventh National Conference on Artificial Intelligence (Washington, D.C., AAAI'1993)*, pages 21–27, 1993.

16. M. Davis, G. Logemann, and D. Loveland. A Machine Program for Theorem Proving. *JACM*, 5:394–397, 1962.

17. M. Davis and H. Putnam. A Computing Procedure for Quantification Theory. *JACM*, 7:201–215, 1960.

18. W.F. Dowling and J.H. Gallier. Linear-time Algorithms for Testing the Satisfiablity of Propositional Horn Formulae. *J. Logic Programming*, 3:267–284, 1984.

19. O. Dubois. On the r,s-SAT satisfiability problem and a conjecture of Tovey. *Discrete Applied Mathematics*, 26:51–60, 1990.

20. O. Dubois, P. André, Y. Boufkhad, and J. Carlier. SAT versus UNSAT, 1994. Position paper, DIMACS chalenge on Satisfiability Testing, to appear.

21. O. Dubois and J. Carlier. Sur le problème de satisfiabilité. Communication at the Barbizon Workshop on SAT, october 1991.

22. S. Even, A. Itai, and A. Shamir. On the Complexity of Timetable and Multicommodity Flow Problems. *SIAM J. Comput.*, 5:691–703, 1976.

23. G. Gallo and M.G. Scutella. Polynomially Solvable Satisfiability Problems. *Information Processing Letters*, 29:221–227, 1988.

24. G. Gallo and G. Urbani. Algorithms for Testing the Satisfiablity of Propositional Formulae. *Journal of Logic Programming*, 7:45–61, 1989.

25. M.R. Garey and D.S. Johnson. *Computer and Intractability: A Guide to the Theory of NP-Completeness*. Freeman, San Fransisco, 1979.

26. I.P. Gent and T. Walsh. The SAT Phase Transition. In A.G. Cohn, editor, *Proceedings of 11th European Conference on Artificial Intelligence, ECAI'94*, pages 105–109. Wiley, 1994.

27. M. Ghallab and E. Escalada-Imaz. A linear control algorithm for a class of rule-based systems. *Journal of Logic Programming*, 11:117–132, 1991.

28. A. Goerdt. A treshold for unsatifiability. In I.M. Havel and V. Koubek, editors, *Proceedings of Mathematical Foundations of Computer Science, MFCS'92*, pages 264–272, August 1994.

29. P. Hansen and B. Jaumard. Uniquely solvable quadratic boolean equations. *Discrete Applied Mathematics*, 12:147–154, 1985.

30. J.-J. Hebrard. A linear algorithm for renaming a set of clauses as a Horn set. *Theoretical Computer Science*, 124:343–350, 1994.

31. L. Henschen and L. Wos. Unit refutations and Horn sets. *JACM*, 21(4):590–605, October 1974.

32. J.N. Hooker. Solving the Incremental Satisfiability Problem. *Journal of Logic Programming*, 15:177–186, 1993.

33. S. Jeannicot, L. Oxusoff, and A. Rauzy. Évaluation Sémantique en Calcul Propositionnel. *Revue d'Intelligence Artificielle*, 2:41–60, 1988.

34. R.J. Jeroslow and J. Wang. Solving Propositional Satisfiability Problems. *Annals of Mathematics and Artificial Intelligence*, 1:167–188, 1990.

35. D.S. Johnson. A Catalog of Complexity Classes. In J. Van Leeuwen, editor, *Handbook of Theoretical Computer Science*, volume A. Elsevier, 1990.

36. D.E. Knuth. Nested Satisfiability. *Acta Informatica*, 28, 1990.

37. T. Larrabee. Test Pattern Generation Using Boolean Satisfiability. *IEEE Transactions on Computer-Aided Design*, 11(1):4–15, January 1992.

38. T. Larrabee and Y. Tsuji. Evidence for a satisfiability threshold for random 3cnf formulas. In H. Hirsh and al., editors, *Proceedings of Spring Symposium on Artificial Intelligence and NP-Hard Problems (Stanford CA 1993)*, pages 112–118, 1993.

39. H.R. Lewis. Renaming a Set of Clauses as a Horn Set. *JACM*, 25(1):134–135, 1978.

40. G. Lindhorst and F. Shahroki. On renaming a set of clauses as a Horn set. *Information Processing Letters*, 30:289–293, 1989.

41. D. Loveland. *Automated Theorem Proving: A Logical Basis*. North Holland, 1978.

42. E.L. Lozinskii. A simple test improves checking satisfiability. *Journal of Logic Programming*, 15:99–111, 1993.

43. H. Mannila and K. Mehlorn. A fast algorithm for renaming a set of clauses as a Horn set. *Information Processing Letters*, 21:269–272, 1985.

44. M. Minoux. LTUR: A Simplified Linear-Time Unit Resolution Algorithm for Horn Formulae and its Computer Implementation. *Information Processing Letter*, 29:1–12, 1988.

45. D. Mitchell, B. Selman, and H. Levesque. Hard and Easy Distributions of SAT Problems. In *Proceedings Tenth National Conference on Artificial Intelligence (AAAI'92)*, 1992.

46. B. Monien and E. Speckenmeyer. Solving Satisfiability in Less than 2^n Steps. *Discrete Applied Math.*, 10:287–295, 1985.

47. R. Petreschi and B. Simeone. Experimental Comparison on 2-Satisfiability Algorithms. *RAIRO Recherche Opérationelle*, 25:241–264, 8 1991.

48. D. Pretolani. A linear time algorithm for unique Horn satisfiability. *Information Processing Letters*, 48:61–66, 1993.

49. A. Rauzy. On the Complexity of the Davis and Putnam's Procedure on Some Polynomial Sub-Classes of SAT. Technical Report 806-94, LaBRI, URA CNRS 1304, Université BordeauxI, 9 1994.

50. M.G. Scutella. A Note on Dowling and Gallier's Top-Down Algorithm for Propositional Horn Satisfiability. *Journal of Logic Programming*, 8:265–273, 1990.

51. B. Selman, H. Levesque, and D. Mitchell. A New Method for Solving Hard Satisfiability Problems. In *Proceedings of the 10th National Conference on Artificial Intelligence (AAAI'92)*, 1992.

52. R.E. Tarjan. Depth First Search and Linear Graph Algorithms. *SIAM J. Comput.*, 1:146–160, 1972.

53. C. A. Tovey. A Simplified NP-complete Satisfiability Problem. *Discrete Applied Mathematics*, 8:85–89, 1984.

54. A. van Gelder. Linear Time Unit Resolution for Propositional Formulas - in Prolog, Yet. submitted to the Journal of Logic Programming, 1994.

55. S. Yamasaki and S. Doshita. The satisfiability problem for a class consisting of horn sentences and some non-horn sentences in propositional logic. *Information and Computation*, 59:1–12, 1983.

56. R. Zabih and D. Mac Allester. A rearrangement search strategy for determining propositional satisfiability. In *Proceedings of the National Conference on Artificial Intelligence, AAAI'88*, pages 155–160, 1988.

Improved Branch and Bound in Constraint Logic Programming

Steven Prestwich and Shyam Mudambi

ECRC GmbH, Arabellastr. 17, D-81925 München, Germany

Abstract. Constraint logic programming has been applied to cost minimization problems such as job-shop scheduling with some success, using the (depth-first) branch and bound method. Recent work has shown that problem-specific heuristics can improve the performance of CLP systems on combinatorial optimisation problems. In this paper we take an orthogonal approach, by developing a generic parallel branch and bound strategy which improves existing CLP strategies in several ways: by avoiding the sometimes prohibitive overheads common to existing implementations; by speeding up convergence to optimal solutions; and by speeding up the proof of optimality for suboptimal solutions. The latter two improvements exploit parallelism in novel ways, which can be smoothly integrated with Or-parallelism. We evaluate these ideas on a set of job-shop scheduling problems, in some cases achieving order of magnitude speedups.

1 Introduction

CLP (Constraint Logic Programming) has been applied to cost minimization problems such as job-shop scheduling with some success [20], some implementations approaching the efficiency of hand-coded Operations Research algorithms [3]. The main advantage of the CLP approach is its ease of programming and its flexibility. For well-known problems Operations Research techniques are the best, but for new problems with complex constraints, the flexibility of CLP makes it the tool of choice.

The basic paradigm used in CLP is that of "constrain and generate". Since even after the constrain phase the remaining search space can be quite large, Or-parallel CLP systems attempt to explore the remaining search space in parallel. This combination of Or-parallelism and CLP was first suggested in [17]. The first real system to combine finite domain constraints with Or-parallelism was the Elipsys system [19] from ECRC. Or-parallelism has now been added to ECRC's ECL^{i}PS^e [8] CLP platform, on which the results in this paper have been obtained.

Both ElipSys and ECL^{i}PS^e have proven rather successful in practical applications [18, 4]. However, we have found that the current approaches to parallelising branch and bound in CLP are still not able to solve many of the larger optimisation problems in reasonable time spans (such as some 10×10 job-shop scheduling problems).

This paper describes a new application of parallelism which we call *cost-parallelism*. We combine cost-parallelism with Or-parallelism to find optimal solutions more quickly than pure Or-parallel branch and bound, and also find more accurate solutions within a given time frame. We also apply cost-parallelism in a different way to the task of finding suboptimal solutions for hard problems, improving the worst-case behaviour by reducing the sensitivity of the execution time to the choice of initial cost bounds. An implementation is described which combines these techniques and which also avoids certain overheads (restarting of the search and thrashing) from which some implementations suffer. The implementation is tested on several job-shop scheduling problems with good results.

In the next section we provide some necessary background and briefly review some related work. Section 3 describes a modified branch and bound strategy for CLP which avoids some of the overheads of the earlier approaches. Section 4 describes an enhancement to this strategy inspired by aspiration windows, a technique used in Game Theory to speed up the search for optimal solutions. Section 5 describes a different enhancement to speed up the search for suboptimal solutions of hard problems. Section 6 shows how to combine these techniques into a single strategy. Finally, Section 7 discusses the results and possible future work.

2 Parallel Branch and Bound

Combinatorial optimisation problems typically have many solutions. A cost C is assigned to each solution, and we are usually interested in finding any one of the optimal solutions, that is one with the lowest possible cost. For very hard problems this may be too expensive to find and we must be content with a suboptimal solution, that is one with a higher cost.

Most CLP systems provide functions for optimisation based on the branch and bound method. In a nutshell, branch and bound works by searching for a solution to the problem and then adding a further constraint that any new solution must be better than the current best. This strategy fits well with the standard backtracking search employed by most sequential logic programming systems. Two such branch and bound strategies were first implemented in CHIP [7] and are also available in ECL^{i}PS^e . Commercial versions of CHIP [1] and related constraint solving tools, such as CHARME and DECISIONPOWER [5], provide users with variants of these strategies.

We now describe these two strategies, as they provide a starting point for our work.

- MIN-MAX: Starting with known upper and lower cost bounds, first find any solution by standard backtracking search, using the initial upper and lower cost bounds C^{max} and C^{min} as a constraint $C^{min} \leq C \leq C^{max}$ to prune the space. Whenever a new solution is found with cost C_n the search is halted, and *restarted* using the tighter constraint $C^{min} \leq C \leq C_n - 1$ to further prune the search space. Eventually no further solutions can be found (or $C_n = C^{min}$) and the solution found in the previous search is optimal.

– MINIMIZE: This is an alternative version which does not restart the search, and thus avoids wasted effort in many cases because it does not need to re-traverse the initial empty part of the search tree. It maintains a global variable which records the lowest cost found so far. On finding a solution with cost C_n the global variable is updated. Whenever the domain of C changes, this variable is consulted and a new constraint $C \leq C_n$ added. However, MINIMIZE may suffer from another overhead, which occurs when a new solution has been found and MINIMIZE enforces backtracking to find a cheaper solution. If the last few labelings of domain variables did not affect the cost, MINIMIZE is forced to exhaust this subtree before it can use the new upper cost bound to prune the search. We shall refer to the behaviour as *thrashing*.

In both cases, the fruitless search of the tree after an optimal solution has been found can be called the *proof of optimality*, since it establishes the optimality of the last solution.

2.1 Or-parallelism

The usual way to exploit parallelism in branch and bound is to use Or-parallelism to speed up the cost bounded search. At certain nodes of the search tree (usually selected by a run-time scheduler) each branch is tried in parallel on different processors, [1] instead of in sequence by backtracking.

A limitation of Or-parallelism in general is that it is dependent on the particular program. A good way to improve CLP programs is to attempt to reduce the nondeterminism — the improvements described in [3] are due to the use of heuristics which prune the search space. This makes the algorithm more deterministic, and hence less amenable to OR-parallelisation.

Another limitation of Or-parallelism applies to MIN-MAX in particular: as soon as a solution is found within given cost bounds, all processes are halted and restarted. If the solutions tend to be at the left of the search tree then adding processors to explore the tree further to the right brings no benefit.

A number of researchers have worked on exploiting Or-Parallelism within branch and bound algorithms, both inside and outside the logic programming framework [10, 11, 15, 16]. In particular, Szeredi [16] investigated the use of Or-Parallel Prolog for such problems and had some encouraging preliminary performance figures using the Aurora system [12]. The MIN-MAX and MINIMIZE strategies can be seen as specialisations of the more general higher-order predicates (MINOF and MAXOF) which he suggests.

2.2 Suboptimal Solutions

Both the MINIMIZE and MIN-MAX strategies can be generalised to search for a solution which is optimal to within some tolerance E (where $0 < E \leq 1$ and

---

[1] The branches need not be explored by physically different processors, only by different processes. Multitasking could be used to simulate several processors, but in this paper we shall assume that each physical processor executes exactly one process.

$E = 1$ indicates complete accuracy). [2] A simple way to do this is, when a solution has been found with cost C_n, a new upper cost bound $C_n E - 1$ is subsequently used (rounded to the nearest integer) instead of $C_n - 1$. Thus the upper cost bound decreases more rapidly. When no solutions are found we know that the optimal solution is between C_n and this bound, and so the previous solution with cost C_n is optimal to within E.

This converges more quickly because it avoids finding many solutions which are only marginally better than the previous solutions. Moreover, the proof of optimality to within E may take much less time than the "real" proof of optimality. This is because we only have to show that there are no solutions with cost $C^{sub}E - 1$ instead of $C^{opt} - 1$ (where C^{opt} is the cost of an optimal solution and C^{sub} is the cost of the suboptimal solution found). Since $C^{sub}E \leq C^{opt}$ and the size of the search space typically varies exponentially as the upper cost bound, this is the main source of speedup in problems where the execution time is dominated by the proof of optimality.

However, in the worst case $C^{sub}E = C^{opt}$ so that the proof of optimality is the same as it would have been without approximating to E. In this case we have lost accuracy without significantly gaining speed. We improve this worst case behaviour below.

2.3 Aspiration Windows

An old but interesting idea in the field of Game Theory is the use of *aspiration windows*, often applied to alpha-beta search of game trees (see for example the survey paper [6]). The possible cost values are split into disjoint intervals, and these intervals are explored in parallel; that is, each processor searches for solutions with a unique range of cost values and uses these artificial cost bounds to prune the search.

Parallel aspiration windows have been used (for example) in chess-playing programs. An advantage is that there is no communication necessary between the parallel processors during the search. However, it has been shown that this method has a theoretical upper bound on its parallel speedup of about 5 or 6.

2.4 Cost-parallelism

In a previous paper [14] we described a modified version of MIN-MAX (here referred to as C-MIN-MAX) using what we call *cost-parallelism*. Cost-parallelism is related to aspiration windows insofar as searches are performed in parallel using different cost bounds, but we attempted to make C-MIN-MAX more adaptive in its choice of cost intervals.

The strategy works as follows. Based on Or-parallel MIN-MAX, where each search has upper cost bound $C_n - 1$, it adds N extra searches running on other processors, each starting off with a different upper bound but all with the same lower bound. As soon as a new solution with cost C_{n+1} is found by one of the

---

[2] In ECL^{i}PS^e E is specified in terms of an integer percentage.

searches, all the searches whose upper bounds are above C_{n+1} are terminated. Similarly, as soon as a search fails, this establishes a new lower bound and any searches with a lesser upper bound are terminated.

Hence both success and failure can be used to refine the upper and lower cost bounds, and the freed processors from the terminated searches can be used to start new searches with bounds which lie within the new, narrower interval. The choice of how many searches to start (the value of N), whether these should be sequential or Or-parallel, whether to limit how close two search bounds can be, and where to place the N searches within the interval lead to different variants of the same algorithm.

Although (like MIN-MAX) C-MIN-MAX suffers from the restarting overhead, it gives good speedup on the job-shop scheduling problems compared to MIN-MAX. In this paper we apply cost-parallelism to a new version of MINIMIZE and obtain better results than with C-MIN-MAX.

3 Branch and Bound With Low Overhead

As noted above, two common ways of implementing branch and bound are the MIN-MAX and MINIMIZE variants. These may suffer from the overheads of restarting and thrashing respectively. It is possible to avoid the thrashing problem in MINIMIZE by using a form of intelligent backtracking [9] but not all CLP systems have intelligent backtracking.

Here we describe a way of avoiding thrashing and restarting without using intelligent backtracking. It imposes an overhead of additional checks, but unlike thrashing and restarting this overhead is independent of the distribution of solutions. This strategy, which we call MIN, will form the basis of strategies described later.

3.1 The MIN Strategy

The MIN strategy differs from MINIMIZE only in the way it checks the global cost. It performs an exhaustive search of the space under the constraint $C^{min} \leq C \leq C_n$, where initially $n = 0$ and $C_0 = C^{max}$. The best-yet cost value C_n is maintained throughout the search as a global variable C_{best}. Whenever a new (cheaper) solution is found C_{best} is updated to the cost C_{n+1} of the new solution. The constraint $C \leq C_{best} - 1$ is checked after each labeling of a domain variable *even if the labeling did not affect C*. This is where MIN differs from MINIMIZE.

MIN avoids the restarting overhead of MIN-MAX because it does not restart the search after a new solution is found. Nor does it suffer from the thrashing overhead of MINIMIZE because as soon as C_{best} is reduced from C_n to C_{n+1}, the additional checks cause the search to move back up the tree until $C \leq C_{n+1} - 1$ holds. The large number of additional checks used by MIN do cause a significant overhead, but this pays off for at least some interesting problems (as we shall show). This illustrates a tenet of constraint programming: for hard problems it is worthwhile spending more time at each node pruning the remaining choices.

3.2 Or-parallelism

Or-parallelism can be applied to MIN exactly as in MIN-MAX and MINIMIZE: at some OR-nodes the alternatives are explored in parallel instead of by backtracking. The global variable C_{best} can be updated by any of the processors, and this value must be communicated to the other processors. Since improving the cost bound is a relatively infrequent event, this adds a negligible amount of communication overhead.

One of the advantages of using Or-parallelism with MIN is that it will almost always result in increased performance (ignoring questions of communication overhead) because it is much less speculative than the Or-parallel MIN-MAX strategy. In order to see why this is so, consider what happens when MIN-MAX is parallelised. As soon as one worker finds a solution which is better than the current best, all workers are halted and the search is restarted with a new upper bound on the cost function. Thus the Or-parallel version of MIN-MAX is akin to applying a series of one-solution parallel searches. Such a strategy will have no parallel speedup if solutions are quickly found by the default sequential search (in our case, near the left of the search tree). MIN, on the other hand, never aborts a search once a solution is found, but just updates a global value. In this sense MIN is akin to a parallel all-solution search, which is much more amenable to efficient parallelisation.

3.3 Empirical Results

Here and in future sections, we use a set of 21 job-shop scheduling problems: the Muth-Thompson 10×10 benchmark [13] (which we shall refer to as MT) with $C^{max} = 5000$, plus ten 10×10 and ten 8×8 problems, all randomly generated with $C^{max} = 1000$ and various values of C^{min}. The program used was a fairly straightforward ECL^{i}PS^e program which simply enumerates domain variables, exploiting built-in disjunctive constraints based on the Carlier-Pinson propositions [2]. All the results were obtained using the parallel ECL^{i}PS^e system on a Silicon Graphics Onyx Series multiprocessor equipped with 16 IP19 processors with 64 MB main memory. The IP19 processor is built upon a 150 MHz MIPS R4400 cpu with two 16KB primary caches for data and instructions and a 1 MB unified secondary cache. All the execution times shown for the job-shop problems include both the time to find the optimal solution *and* to prove optimality.

First, we note that on all these problems MINIMIZE is *very* inefficient, spending so much time thrashing that even the simplest problems did not terminate after several hours. This is probably a feature of our particular algorithm, because on some other programs we tried MINIMIZE outperforms MIN-MAX.

We therefore compare only MIN-MAX and MIN. In Figure 1 we compare the sequential and Or-parallel performance of the two strategies. This graph plots the execution times of the 21 problems on the two strategies sequentially and in Or-parallel (with 12 processors). Each point on the graph corresponds to one job-shop benchmark[3]. Points lying below the line labelled "equal" indicate that for

---

[3] Each benchmark was run three times and the mean time was used.

that benchmark MIN performed better than MIN-MAX and vice-versa for points lying above the line.

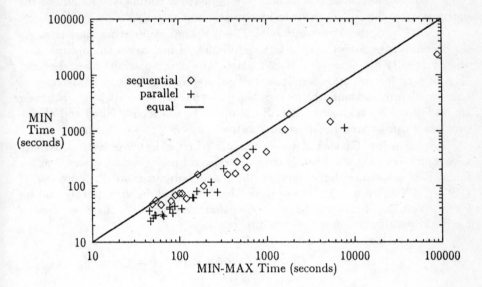

Fig. 1. Comparison of sequential and parallel (12 processor) execution of MIN-MAX and MIN on several job-shop scheduling problems on the SGI Onyx.

As one can see from Figure 1, MIN's performance is better than MIN-MAX on all the problems except one. In addition, as we expected, MIN takes much better advantage of Or-parallelism and outperforms MIN-MAX on all the parallel benchmarks.

4 Fast Optimal Solutions

As described above, Or-parallelism is often used to speed up the search for a solution, and can be implemented in MIN in the same way as in MIN-MAX and MINIMIZE. However, we can also apply parallelism in a different way by performing several searches in parallel with MIN, each with a different upper cost bound. If $C^{max} \gg C^{opt}$ this could lead to a cheap solution being found very quickly. We call the searches which look ahead for cheap solutions *optimistic searches*.

4.1 Optimistic Search

Here we describe a modified version of MIN we shall call O-MIN. We start with MIN, and introduce a number of optimistic searches. Each optimistic search works in the same way as MIN, but uses only one processor and has an artificial upper cost bound at some depth below C_n. As soon as C_n is updated by any of the searches (whether MIN or optimistic search) this is communicated to all the other searches, and their cost bounds are adjusted accordingly. The aim of the optimistic searches is to try for lucky cheap solutions early on.

Given P processors we start with $P - 1$ optimistic searches plus MIN. As C_n decreases, the lowest optimistic searches are pushed below the optimal cost and eventually die. The processors freed by the dying optimistic searches can then be used for Or-parallelism in MIN. We therefore begin with a high degree of cost-parallelism and smoothly reduce this in favour of Or-parallelism, until near the end of the branch and bound all optimistic searches have failed and all the processors can be used in Or-parallel to speed up the proof of optimality.

How far below C_n should the optimistic searches be? We could distribute their upper cost bounds linearly over the range of possible cost values, but we found that sometimes large gaps are best and sometimes small. Moreover, if $C^{min} \ll C^{opt}$ most or all of the optimistic searches will die very quickly and we lose the benefits of cost-parallelism earlier than necessary. We therefore chose a nonlinear distribution over the cost interval:

$$U_i = C_n - Di - e^{\alpha i + \beta} \quad \text{(for } i = 1 \ldots P - 1)$$

where D is a (user-defined or default) constant which controls how close optimistic search bounds can be to each other and to MIN — if they are too close there is no benefit from cost-parallelism. We choose α and β so that, at the start of the search when $n = 0$ and $C_0 = C^{max}$:

- as $i \to P$, $U_i \to C^{min}$ and
- as $i \to 0$, $U_i \to C^{max} - D$

Given these conditions we can derive

$$\alpha = \left(\frac{1}{P}\right) \ln \left(\frac{C^{max} - C^{min}}{D} - P\right) \qquad \beta = \ln(D)$$

As an example, say $D = 20$, $C^{max} = 1000$, $C^{min} = 200$ and $P = 4$. This gives optimistic search cost bounds $U_1 = C_n - 49$, $U_2 = C_n - 140$ and $U_3 = C_n - 334$. which decrease as C_n decreases. Initially $C_0 = C^{max}$ and so the search starts off with optimistic search bounds 951, 860 and 666. For larger values of P the interval is divided up more finely and the distribution tends to $C_n - D$, $C_n - 2D$, $C_n - 3D \ldots$

For all the empirical results in this paper, we set the value of D to 10. We are currently investigating the automation of the choice of D, based on factors such as the number of processors available, the range of the cost function and an estimate of how the size of the search tree grows with the upper cost bound.

4.2 Reducing Redundancy

The optimistic searches may explore much of the same part of the tree as each other or as MIN, giving some redundancy. This is partly a consequence of using only the upper cost bounds instead of dividing the problem into mutually disjoint aspiration windows — in our scheme the search tree corresponding to an upper bound contains the search tree for a lesser upper bound.

We can reduce this redundancy by forcing the optimistic searches to explore different parts of the tree from each other and from the MIN search. Of course the tree for any bound still contains that for a lower bound, but this is not important because only a fraction of the tree is explored by any optimistic search.

An optimistic search can be made to explore a different part of the tree by changing the enumeration order it uses for each domain variable. The standard enumeration order used by MIN is left-to-right, that is given a domain variable with d values $\{v_1, v_2, \ldots, v_d\}$ the values are tried in the order $\langle v_1, v_2, \ldots, v_d \rangle$ (ignoring Or-parallelism). An optimistic search can simply try these values in a permuted order. As well as changing the enumeration order for domain variable labeling, the same principle can be used with nondeterministic (sequential or Or-parallel) predicates: optimistic searches can use different clause orderings for such predicates.

The new enumeration orders can be chosen in many ways, but they should incur little extra overhead, be as different as possible from each other, and have a bias to the left of the tree to maintain a degree of user control over the search strategy. In particular, in the case of a domain of size 2 (or in the case of a nondeterministic predicate with 2 clauses) some optimistic searches should use the ordering $\langle v_1, v_2 \rangle$ and some use $\langle v_2, v_1 \rangle$.

Here we briefly describe the method we used. Say the domain is $\{1, 2, 3, 4, 5, 6, 7, 8\}$, then the optimistic searches use the orders

$$\text{optimistic search } \# 1: \langle 2, 4, 6, 8, 1, 3, 5, 7 \rangle$$
$$\text{optimistic search } \# 2: \langle 1, 3, 5, 7, 2, 4, 6, 8 \rangle$$
$$\text{optimistic search } \# 3: \langle 3, 6, 2, 5, 8, 1, 4, 7 \rangle$$
$$\text{optimistic search } \# 4: \langle 1, 4, 7, 2, 5, 8, 3, 6 \rangle$$
$$\text{optimistic search } \# 5: \langle 4, 8, 3, 7, 2, 6, 1, 5 \rangle$$
$$\text{optimistic search } \# 6: \langle 1, 5, 2, 6, 3, 7, 4, 8 \rangle$$
$$\vdots \qquad \qquad \vdots$$

That is any optimistic search $\#2n$ picks out elements using the ordering

$$1, \ 1 + (n + 1), \ 1 + 2(n + 1), \ 1 + 3(n + 1), \ \ldots$$
$$2, \ 2 + (n + 1), \ 2 + 2(n + 1), \ 2 + 3(n + 1), \ \ldots$$
$$\vdots$$

while any optimistic search $\#2n - 1$ picks out

$$\vdots$$
$$2, \ 2 + (n + 1), \ 2 + 2(n + 1), \ 2 + 3(n + 1), \ \ldots$$
$$1, \ 1 + (n + 1), \ 1 + 2(n + 1), \ 1 + 3(n + 1), \ \ldots$$

These orders satisfy the criteria listed above and seem to work quite well in practice.

4.3 Empirical Results

Figure 2 compares O-MIN with MIN, both with Or-parallelism (using 12 processors). As can be seen, in almost all the problems the use of optimistic search pays off. However, for a couple of the problems, where the optimal costs were close to the initial horizon, MIN does a little better.

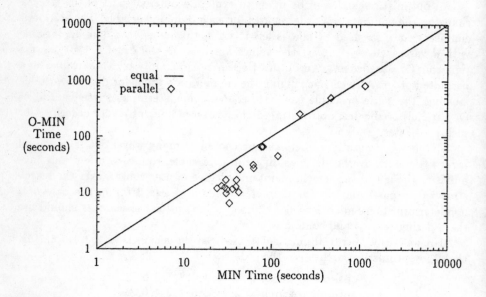

Fig. 2. Comparison of the parallel execution of MIN and O-MIN on several job-shop scheduling problems on the SGI Onyx with 12 processors.

Figure 3 compares the behaviours of MIN-MAX, MIN and O-MIN as the number of processors is varied for the MT problem (with a horizon of 5000): that is, to compare their speedup curves. Though the speedups are good for all three strategies, we see that MIN and O-MIN are almost an order of magnitude faster than the standard MIN-MAX approach.

The graph in figure 4 plots the value of the current best solution versus time for the MT problem, for all three strategies. The number of processors used was 12, hence the end points of each of the lines corresponds to the last row of the table in Figure 3. This graph illustrates one of the main advantages of using optimistic search: in less than 100 seconds, O-MIN has found a solution of cost less than 1000 (the optimal solution for this problem has a cost of 930), thus

Processors	MIN-MAX		MIN		O-MIN	
1	90131	(1.00)	22961	(1.00)	22976	(1.00)
4	13003	(6.93)	2941	(7.81)	3124	(7.35)
8	9761	(9.23)	2123	(10.82)	2140	(10.74)
12	7799	(11.56)	1139	(20.15)	777	(29.56)

Fig. 3. Execution times (in seconds) for the MT problem (speedup in brackets) on the SGI Onyx

O-MIN is well-suited to situations in which one has to find the best solution within a specified time bound.

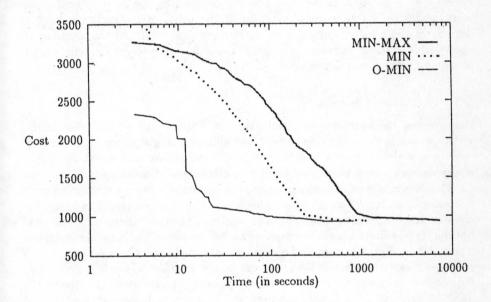

Fig. 4. Best cost versus time for the MT problem on the SGI Onyx with 12 processors

5 Fast Suboptimal Solutions

In the previous section we showed that the search for solutions can often be made faster by the use of optimistic searches, that is by searching for solutions with lower cost than is warranted by the solutions found so far. However, where the total execution time is dominated by the proof of optimality, optimistic searches have little effect. In this section we show that, for problems with hard proof of optimality, searching for suboptimal solutions with *higher* cost can lead to speedup. We call this *pessimistic search*.

We have not yet described how MIN can be used to find suboptimal solutions, but it works in the same way as MIN-MAX and MINIMIZE. When searching for suboptimal solutions, MIN prunes the search using a cost bound $C_n E - 1$ instead of $C_n - 1$. O-MIN can also be applied to finding suboptimal solutions in the same way, with the slight modification that instead of using optimistic search cost bounds of $U_i = C_n - Di - e^{\alpha i + \beta}$ it uses $U_i = C_n E - Di - e^{\alpha i + \beta}$.

5.1 Sensitivity to the Horizon

Consider the worst case for MIN, O-MIN, MIN-MAX and MINIMIZE, where the final best cost C_n is such that $C_n E = C^{opt}$. The proof of optimality then uses the cost bound $C^{opt} - 1$, which is the same cost bound used by the proof of optimality when searching for an *optimal* solution. If the proof of optimality is hard it dominates the total execution time, and so we have sacrificed the accuracy of the solution without any significant gain in speed — thus losing the whole point of searching for a suboptimal solution.

5.2 Pessimistic Search

Here we describe another cost-parallel variant of MIN which we shall call P-MIN. P-MIN works in the same way as MIN, but diverts a single processor to perform a cost-parallel search with cost bound $C_n - 1$: the pessimistic search. Note that either search (MIN or pessimistic) can update the global cost bound C_n.

The pessimistic search may seem counter-productive at first sight: why use a processor to search for solutions with *higher* cost than necessary? The advantage comes when the proof of optimality is expensive. The more expensive the proof of optimality, the more chance the pessimistic search has of finding a new solution. The point is that if it *does* find a solution, say with cost $C_n - k$, the proof of optimality can immediately lower *its* cost bound to $(C_n - k)E - 1$ and this may happen several times before the proof of optimality terminates. The harder the proof of optimality the lower its bound will become, and therefore the more it is speeded up by the pessimistic search.

Since the proof of optimality takes a time which is exponential in the cost bound, this speedup may be quite dramatic. In the extreme case where the proof of optimality is *very* expensive, the pessimistic search has time to reach an optimal solution with cost C^{opt} and the proof of optimality proceeds with the lowest possible cost bound $C^{opt} E - 1$ and hence the smallest possible search space. As a bonus, the harder the proof of optimality is the cheaper the final solution will be.

6 The Final Strategy

Optimistic searches are most useful when the proof of optimality is easy, and pessimistic search makes hard proofs of optimality easier. Therefore it may be worthwhile using optimistic searches for problems with hard proof of optimality, provided we also make the proof of optimality easier by using pessimistic search. In fact, combining the pessimistic search and optimistic searches in a single strategy should give a good general strategy for finding suboptimal solutions, as we usually do not know in advance whether the proof of optimality will be easy or hard.

A hybrid strategy, which we call OP-MIN, can be defined as a simple generalisation of O-MIN and P-MIN: starting from O-MIN, which is MIN plus optimistic searches, we divert a processor to a pessimistic search (if $E > 0$). If $E = 1$ then OP-MIN reduces to O-MIN. If only one processor is available then OP-MIN (like O-MIN) reduces to MIN. Given 2 processors, we could either have an optimistic or a pessimistic search. The current implementation chooses the pessimistic search, although the user can turn off pessimistic search altogether.

OP-MIN is our final strategy. It combines Or-parallelism with optimistic cost-parallelism, and in the case where suboptimal solutions are specified (by the user) it also uses pessimistic cost-parallelism. We believe that this is a good general strategy for finding both optimal and suboptimal solutions.

6.1 Empirical Results

On most of the job-shop problems pessimistic search is of little use; in fact OP-MIN is slightly slower than O-MIN because OP-MIN diverts a processor away from Or-parallelism and therefore finds solutions more slowly and takes longer to prove optimality.

However, the 7th 10×10 job-shop problem, has quite a hard proof of optimality and hence should benefit from the pessimistic search. To investigate the effect of pessimistic search on this example we measured the time taken to find a suboptimal solution ($E = 0.95$) as a function of the horizon C^{max}. The times are shown as a graph in Figure 5. Note that an optimal solution for this problem has a cost of 989.

As this shows, the time taken by both O-MIN and MIN-MAX is very dependent on the choice of the initial horizon (the same is true of MIN and MINIMIZE). This is because the total execution time depends largely on the last cost value in the sequence, which controls the size of the search space in the proof of optimality. On the other hand, the time taken by OP-MIN does not vary much at all with respect to the horizon.

These results show that for problems with hard proof of optimality, pessimistic search can reduce the sensitivity of the execution time to the choice of initial cost bounds, and hence improves the worst-case time.

7 Conclusion

Recent work has shown that encoding problem-specific heuristics can improve the performance of CLP systems on combinatorial optimisation problems. In this paper we took an orthogonal approach, by developing a generic parallel branch and bound strategy which improves existing CLP strategies in several ways:

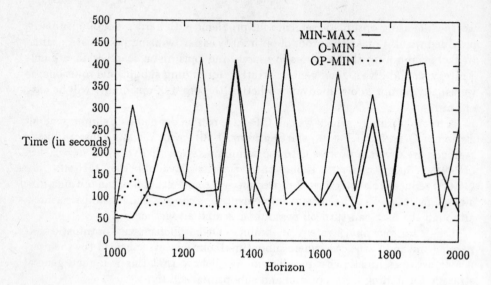

Fig. 5. Comparison of MIN-MAX, O-MIN and OP-MIN strategies on the 7th 10×10 problem (with $E = 0.95$) using the SGI Onyx with 8 processors.

- It avoids the overhead of "thrashing" incurred by the MINIMIZE strategy, and also avoids the overhead of restarting incurred by the more popular MIN-MAX strategy.
- When searching for an optimal solution it uses a novel form of parallelism to speed up convergence, and also to yield more accurate solutions within a given time frame.
- When searching for a suboptimal solution it uses another novel form of parallelism to reduce the sensitivity of the proof of optimality to the choice of initial cost bounds, and hence improves the worst-case behaviour for problems with hard proof of optimality.

We call these applications of parallelism *cost-parallelism* because they try different cost bounds in parallel. Cost-parallelism can be smoothly integrated with the more usual Or-parallelism.

The advantages of our cost-parallel strategies were demonstrated on a set of job-shop scheduling benchmarks, where they resulted in an order of magnitude performance improvement over the more conventional MIN-MAX strategy.

7.1 Future Work

The job-shop scheduling algorithm we used is quite a straightforward one, utilising a disjunctive constraint built-in (`disjunctive/3`) of ECL^{i}PS^e which implements some of the redundant constraints proposed by Carlier-Pinson [2]. However, it is clear from the discussion in [3] that the more sophisticated task intervals approach will also benefit from the use of cost-parallelism, as it is quite sensitive to the value of the initial horizon and a great deal of time is spent in creeping down to the optimal solution. In general we feel that generic methods such as cost-parallelism should combine well with problem-specific heuristics used in optimisation problems, enabling CLP to tackle problems which have previously been out of its scope.

We intend to further improve our strategy and test it on other optimisation problems. Not all the problems we tried so far are improved by our strategies: sometimes the extra checking overhead outweighs the other savings, and sometimes cost-parallelism has no other effect than to divert processors away from useful Or-parallelism. It is worth investigating other variants, for example a Cost-parallel MINIMIZE with intelligent backtracking to avoid thrashing. There are also variations on aspiration windows in the game theory literature which may be useful; for example the use of zero-width windows which search for solutions with a single cost. We have only experimented with a few fairly simple ideas, and there may be scope for further cross-fertilisation between CLP and game theory.

Acknowledgements

We would like to thank the Brandeis University Computer Science Department and Tim Hickey in particular for giving us access to their Silicon Graphics multiprocessor.

References

1. A. Aggoun and N. Beldiceanu. Extending CHIP in order to solve complex scheduling and placement problems. In *Proc. of JFPL'92*, 1992.
2. J. Carlier and E. Pinson. An algorithm for solving the job shop problem. *Management Science*, 35(2), 2 1989.
3. Yves Caseau and Francois Laburthe. Improved CLP scheduling with task intervals. In *Proc. of Eleventh International Conference on Logic Programming*, pages 369–383. The MIT Press, 1994.
4. D. Clark, C. Rawlings, J. Shirazi, Liang liang Li, Mike Reeve, Kees Schuermann, and Andre Veron. Solving large combinatorial problems in molecular biology using the ElipSys parallel constraint logic programming system. *Computer Journal*, 36(4), 1993.
5. Jean-Yves Cras. A review of industrial constraint solving tools. survey, AI Perspectives, 1994.
6. Claude G. Diderich and Marc Gengler. A survey of minimax trees and associated algorithms. Technical Report 94/50, Swiss Federal Institute of Technology, Lausanne, 1994.
7. M. Dincbas et al. The constraint logic programming language CHIP. In *Proceedings of the International Conference on Fifth Generation Computer Systems (FGCS'88)*, pages 693–702. ICOT, 1988.

8. European Computer-Industry Research Centre, Munich, Germany. *ECLiPSe 3.5.1 User Manual*, 1995.

9. Pascal Van Hentenryck. Personal communication, January 1995.

10. V. Kumar and V.N. Rao. Parallel depth first search - Part I. Implementation. *International Journal of Parallel Programming*, 16(6), 1987.

11. V. Kumar and V.N. Rao. Parallel depth first search - Part II. Analysis. *International Journal of Parallel Programming*, 16(6), 1987.

12. Ewing Lusk, Ralph Butler, Terence Disz, Robert Olson, Ross Overbeek, Rick Stevens, D.H.D Warren, Alan Calderwood, Peter Szerdi, Seif Haridi, Per Brand, Mats Carlsson, Andrzej Ciepielewski, and Bogumil Hausman. The Aurora Or-Parallel Prolog system. In *Proceedings of the International Conference on Fifth Generation Computer Systems (FGCS'88)*. ICOT, 1988.

13. J. F. Muth and G. L. Thompson. *Industrial Scheduling*. Prentice-Hall, Englewood Cliffs, New Jersey, 1963.

14. Steven Prestwich and Shyam Mudambi. Cost-parallel branch and bound in CLP. In *Proc. of ILPS 1994 post-conference workshop on Constraint Languages and Systems*, pages 141–149, 1994. Available as an ECRC technical report no. 94-38.

15. T. J. Reynold and P. Kefalas. Or-parallel prolog and search problems in AI applications. In *Logic Programming: Proceedings of the Seventh Internatinal Conference*, pages 340–354. MIT Press, 1990.

16. Peter Szeredi. Exploiting or-parallelism in optimisation problems. In *Proceedings of the JICSLP'92*, pages 703–716. MIT Press, 1992.

17. P. Van Hentenryck. Parallel constraint satisfaction in logic programming: Preliminary results of chip within PEPSys. In Giorgio Levi and Maurizio Martelli, editors, *Proceedings of the Sixth International Conference on Logic Programming*, pages 165–180, Lisbon, 1989. The MIT Press.

18. A. Veron, K. Schuerman, M. Reeve, and L. Li. APPLAUSE: Applications using the ElipSys parallel CLP system. In *Proceedings of the Tenth International Conference on Logic Programming*. MIT Press, June 1993.

19. A. Veron, K. Schuerman, M. Reeve, and L. Li. Why and how in the ElipSys Or-Parallel CLP system. In *PARLE'93: Parallel Architectures and Languages Europe*, pages 291–302. Springer-Verlag, 1993.

20. M. Wallace. Constraints in planning, scheduling and placement problems. In *Constraint Programming*. Springer-Verlag, 1994.

Reducing Domains for Search in CLP(FD) and Its Application to Job-Shop Scheduling *

Hans-Joachim Goltz

Research Institute for Computer Architecture
and Software Technology, GMD-FIRST
Rudower Chaussee 5, D-12489 Berlin, Germany
goltz@first.gmd.de

Abstract. This paper describes a generalization of the "labelling" search strategy and its application to scheduling problems. The assignment of a value to the selected variable is replaced by reduction of the domain of the variable. This strategy can be applied for solving problems modelled in CLP(FD).

We discuss the application of this domain-reducing strategy to the well-known problem of 10×10 job-shop scheduling. The computation results obtained using this strategy show its advantages. A good solution, coming to within 3% of the optimal solution, is generated in less than 1 second, using only a simple heuristics for variable selection and domain reduction. Compared with the standard strategy, the domain-reducing strategy exhibits more robustness with respect to the given planning horizon. Assuming that there is a choice of machines, a good solution can be generated with the same strategy, deviating from the optimal solution by less than 4%.

Our experience has shown that the domain-reducing strategy is suitable as a basic search strategy for solving job-shop problems by means of CLP, allowing good (near-to-optimum) solutions to be computed fast.

1 Introduction

Constraint logic programming (CLP) is a neat generalization of logic programming in which the basic operation of logic programming, the unification, is replaced by the more general concept of constraint solving over a computation domain. Large combinatorial problems can be solved using CLP. Constraint logic programming with linear constraints over finite integer domains, CLP(FD), has been established as a practical tool for solving discrete scheduling problems (see e.g. [8, 1, 5, 7]). A scheduling problem, together with the conditions to be satisfied, can be suitably modelled in terms of a set of constraints. To generate a solution, however, a search is necessary, and the choice of a good strategy is a problem. For instance, search behaviour depends largely on the order in which variables are instantiated.

---

* This research was funded by the *German Federal Minister for Education, Science, Research, and Technology* under grant 01 IW 206

In this paper, a general search strategy is proposed which can be applied to solving problems modelled in CLP(FD). The assignment of a value to the selected variable is replaced by reduction of the domain of this variable. The idea of domain reduction is not new. However, we suggest using a domain-reducing strategy as a basic search strategy for CLP(FD). Furthermore, we discuss the application of this domain-reducing strategy to the well-known problem of 10×10 job-shop scheduling ([11]).

The job-shop problem consists in scheduling a set of jobs on a set of machines, where the following conditions have to be satisfied: each machine can handle at most one job at any one time, and each job has a specified processing order over the machines. The objective is to schedule the jobs such that the maximum of their completion times is minimized.

Strategies for solving problems of job-shop scheduling are discussed in several papers (see e.g. [14, 8, 4, 7]). Several heuristics for variable selection are investigated in [4]. An interesting strategy for obtaining the optimal solution to a job-shop problem is presented in [7]. However, this method cannot be used if machine groups are considered (i.e. if there is a choice between resources).

The goal of our investigation was the development of a general search strategy for solving job-shop problems using CLP such that good (near-to-optimum) solutions can be computed fast. The computation results obtained with the suggested strategy show its advantages:

- A good solution, coming to within 3% of the optimal solution, is generated in less than 1 second, using only a simple heuristics for variable selection and domain reduction.
- A substantial improvement on the results presented in [4] was achieved, although the heuristics we used for variable selection were simpler than those considered in [4].
- Assuming that there is a choice of machines, a good solution can be generated with the same strategy (this solution deviating from the optimal solution by less than 4%).

Since the objective of this paper is the description of the basic idea behind the proposed search strategy, computation results only with respect to a well-known job-shop scheduling problem and to simple heuristics are discussed. Note that we have also obtained good computation results for other job-shop scheduling problems. Investigations of heuristics for domain reduction of the selected variable form a part of our current research work.

The paper is organized as follows: The following section is devoted to the well-known labelling strategy for search in CLP(FD). The proposed domain-reducing strategy is described in Section 3. In Section 4, the application of the domain reducing strategy to job-shop problems is discussed. Some computation results for solving the classical 10×10 job-shop problem with this strategy are given in Section 5. Some papers related to the discussed problems are mentioned in Section 6. The final section contains some conclusions. A description of the example considered in this paper is included in the Appendix.

2 Basic Strategy for Search in CLP(FD)

Generally speaking, a constraint solver over finite domains is not complete, since consistency is only proved locally. Thus, a search is necessary to find a solution. Often this search is called "labelling". The basic idea behind this search can be described as follows, variables always being variables on finite domains in the present context:

- select a variable from the set of problem variables considered
- choose a value from the domain of this variable and assign this value to the variable
- consistency techniques are used by the constraint solver in order to compute the consequences of this assignment
- backtracking has to be used if the constraint solver detects a contradiction
- repeat this until all problem variables have a value and the constraints are satisfied.

The basic algorithm of this search can be expressed by the following program:

```
labeling([]).
labeling(VarList) :-
        select_var(Var,VarList,NewVarList),
        choosing_value(Var),
        labeling(NewVarList).
```

The predicate select_var/3 may be defined in the following way: select from the list of domain variables the variable with the smallest domain (*first-fail principle*) and delete this variable from the list of variables. The predicate choosing_value/1 may be replaced by the built-in predicate indomain/1. This predicate instantiates a domain variable to elements of its domain and is contained in most CLP(FD) systems.

An important question to be answered when generating values for the variables is which variable to choose next for instantiation. It is well-known that the generated order for variable selection plays an important role in program behaviour, and that the choice of values to be assigned to a variable can also be of some importance (see e.g. [14]). The choice of the next variable to be instantiated and the choice of values to be assigned to the selected variable can be based on certain specific heuristics in which edge-finding methods can be integrated. Such heuristics for job-shop scheduling are investigated e.g. in [4].

3 Search by Reducing Domains

A generalization of the labelling method is proposed in this section. The assignment of a value to the selected variable is replaced by reduction of the domain of this variable. If backtracking has to be used, then the other part of the domain is considered for the corresponding variable.

```
reducing([]).
reducing(VarList) :-
      select_var(Var,VarList,NewVarList),
      reducing_domain(Var),
      reducing(NewVarList).
```

A solution is narrowed by this reduction procedure. However, this procedure does not normally generate a solution to the problem. Thus, after domain reduction, assignment of values to the variables has to be performed, which may also include a search. The main part of the search, however, is realized by the domain-reducing procedure.

The basic idea behind the algorithm is described in more detail below, but we do not consider the dependencies of all components. For instance, domain reduction of a variable may be dependent on the domains of the other variables. The conditions for reducing the domain of a variable are:

- The domain of a variable is only reduced if the number of elements belonging to the domain is greater than or equal to a given number `MinSize`, whereby we assume that this number is generated by the predicate `min_domain_size/1`.
- The domain is reduced in such a way that the number of elements belonging to the reduced domain is greater than or equal to a given number `Min` and is less than or equal to a given number `Max`. These numbers are generated by the predicate `limits/2`. Furthermore, we assume that the predicate `select_subdomain/4` selects a subdomain of a given domain such that the conditions with respect to `Min` and `Max` are satisfied.

If the constraint solver detects a contradiction during the domain reducing procedure, then backtracking has to be performed. In this case, the set difference between the old domain and the reduced domain is considered as the new domain for the corresponding variable. In the following description of the algorithm, the predicate `difference/3` stands for this generation of set difference.

```
reducing_domain(Var):-
      domain(Var, Domain, Size),
      min_domain_size(MinSize),
      limits(Min, Max),
      (   Size =< MinSize ->
              true
      ;
              select_subdomain(Domain, SubDom, Min, Max),
              restriction(Var, Domain, SubDom)
      ).

restriction(Var, Domain, SubDom):-
      NewVar :: SubDom,
      Var = NewVar.
```

```
restriction(Var, Domain, SubDom):-
    difference(Domain, SubDom, NewDomain),
    NewVar :: NewDomain,
    Var = NewVar,
    reducing_domain(Var).
```

Note that, for a given variable, the predicate domain/3 is assumed to generate the domain of this variable and the number of elements belonging to this domain. Furthermore, X :: Domain means that X is a domain variable with the domain Domain.

The choice of the numbers MinSize, Min, and Max depends on the problem under consideration. Specific heuristics can be used for determining these numbers. Furthermore, heuristics for the choice of a subdomain are necessary. If the numbers MinSize, Min, and Max are chosen as equal to 1, then the domain-reducing strategy corresponds to the labelling strategy.

The order of variable selection also plays an important role in the domain-reducing strategy, although this strategy shows considerable robustness in this context. Our experience has shown that in many cases either a solution can be found within only few backtracking steps, or a large number of backtracking steps are needed. We therefore use the following basic search method: the number of permitted backtracking steps is restricted, and different order of variable selection are tried out.

4 Job-Shop Scheduling with CLP(FD)

The class of typical job-shop problems is defined as follows:

- A set of jobs and a set of machines are given, each job consisting of a set of tasks.
- The only precedence relation is that each task must be performed after its predecessor in the job order.
- Each task has to be placed on a given machine within a limited time interval, a machine being able to execute only one task at any one time.
- Each machine is available during the entire given time interval.
- Each job is independent of all other jobs, and each machine is independent of all other machines.
- The objective is to schedule the jobs such that the maximum of their completion times is minimized.

Job-shop problems additionally satisfying the condition

- each task in a job needs a different machine

are often called $n \times m$ problems (i.e. n jobs, m machines, and consequently m tasks of each job). The importance of $n \times m$ problems is the result of the attention they have received in recent years. The well-known 10×10 problem was defined in the book *Industrial Scheduling* by Muth and Thompson [11] in 1963 and remained unsolved for over 20 years [6]. This problem has since been used as a benchmark for most OR algorithms.

Job-shop problems can be suitably described in CLP(FD) (see e.g. [14, 8, 5]). The main complexity in job-shop problems comes from capacity constraints. These constraints describe dependencies between tasks competing for the same resource. In the CHIP system, cumulative constraints can be used for describing such dependencies. Cumulative constraints were introduced in CHIP to solve complex scheduling problems efficiently [1].

The start time of a task is considered to be a problem variable. The objective is to assign values to these variables such that the constraints are satisfied and the maximum of the completion times of the jobs is minimized. Furthermore, we assume that a planning horizon is given. Often, the given planning horizon affects program behaviour.

Our application of the domain-reducing strategy to the problem of job-shop scheduling is described below. To investigate the program behaviour of the domain-reducing strategy, we choose relatively simple heuristics.

Note that, in job-shop problems, the domain of a variable can be regarded as an interval of natural numbers. Thus, the minimum and the maximum of a domain is considered instead of the domain itself, and a reduced domain can be determined by its new limits. Since we assume that the objective of scheduling is to minimize the completion time, the first part of the domain interval is considered first.

The numbers `MinSize`, `Min`, and `Max` are chosen in the following way, `Duration` being the average of the durations of the given tasks: `MinSize is Duration/3`, `Min is Duration/2`, `Max is Duration*1.3`. Our experience has shown that the choice of `Max` can significantly influence the success of the search. A number between `Duration` and `Duration*1.5` is a good candidate for `Max` to solve $n \times m$ problems.

The following definitions of predicates are modified versions of the definitions given in Section 3 and characterize the domain-reducing procedure for solving job-shop problems.

```
reducing_domain(Var):-
    min_max_of_domain(Var, MinDom, MaxDom),
    min_domain_size(MinSize),
    limits(Min, Max),
    (   MaxDom-MinDom =< MinSize ->
            true
    ;
            X is MaxDom-MinDom/2
            minimum(X,Max,Y),
            maximum(Y,Min,Diff),
            restriction(Var, MinDom, Diff)
    ).
```

```
restriction(Var, MinDom, Diff):-
    Var #<= MinDom + Diff.
restriction(Var, MinDom, Diff):-
    MinDom + Diff #< Var,
    reducing_domain(Var).
```

The possible start times of the tasks are restricted according to the order determined by `select_var/3`. Such a restricted domain can them be further reduced as a result of subsequent restrictions of start times. The simple heuristic chosen for the domain-reducing startegy has the following effect with respect to the placing of task on a machine: first, it is always attempted to restrict the possible start times such that the task in question is placed before as many tasks as possible that are assigned to this machine. This, in particular, enables a task B to be placed before a task A with an already restricted domain of start times and, hence, the earliest possible start time of task A may be increased. Of course, this procedure is not suitable in all cases. The search could be made even more efficient by choosing better heuristics for domain reduction. Evidently, the maximum permitted size of a reduced domain is also of great significance for the success of the described search strategy.

As mentioned above, the domain-reducing procedure does not normally generate a solution. In the worst-case of our tests, presented in the next section, we found six pairs of tasks after the search by domain reduction, with both tasks in each case occupying the same machine and the order between these tasks being undetermined. In most cases, there are at most three pairs of such tasks. Furthermore, in some cases, the choice of the order of such a task pair has no influence on the other tasks. Note that a job-shop problem can be regarded as solved if the order of the tasks that have to be placed on the same machine is determined. Thus, the main part of the search is realized by the domain-reducing procedure.

The order for variable selection is also important for the domain-reducing strategy. We use the following method for variable selection: after generation of the constraints that have to be satisfied, a priority of each task is computed, and the set of tasks is sorted according to these priorities. Thus, we use a static ordering for variable selection. The priority of a task depends on the following factors:

- the duration of the task
- the sum of the durations of the tasks that belong to the same job and have to be performed after the task under consideration
- the number of tasks that belong to the same job and have to be performed after the task under consideration
- the demand on the machine on which the task has to be placed, this depending on:
  - the sum of the durations of the tasks that have to be placed on this machine

- the difference between the latest due date and the sum of the earliest ready times and of the durations of the tasks (dates and durations relate to the tasks occupying this machine).

Furthermore, the priority of a task depends on a given set of weights for these factors. Thus, different order for variable selection can be defined by different sets of weights for the factors. The order for variable selection used in our implementation are always defined in this way.

5 Computation Results

Some computation results of the implemention of the proposed search strategy are given in this section. This implementation is realized in CHIP. Cumulative constraints are used for modelling capacity constraints. However, we get similar computation results if cumulative constraints are not used. The results given here relate to the well-known example of the 10×10 problem defined by *Muth* and *Thompson* in [11] (see also Appendix). All execution times given are for a Sun SPARC 20.

We define the number of search steps as the number of applications of the second clause of `restriction/3` (i.e. how many times the choice of the first part of the interval yields a contradiction). For the search, we use different orders for variable selection and restrict the number of search steps.

In the first table, the domain-reducing strategy is compared with other strategies. The other strategies are based on the strategy described in Section 2. The same order for variable selection are used for the strategies considered, i.e. we use the same definition of the predicate `select_var/3`. If some assignment of a value to a variable is unsuccessful, changing this value by 1 will often cause only minor changes to the search space. Thus, in [4], a value-selection heuristics is proposed that selects values in multiples of some chosen distance K, beginning with the first value in the domain. This strategy is denoted as "jump = K". Thus, the strategy "jump = 1" corresponds to the basic strategy with `indomain/1` mentioned in Section 2. Note that the strategy "jump = K" is logically incomplete if K is greater than 1.

We used 10 different orders for variable selection in the tests presented in Table 1. The order were not chosen systematically. The results may be improved if more specific heuristics for these orders are chosen. Note that, the advantages of the domain-reducing strategy have also been shown for other variable orders.

The figures in the first column show the given planning horizon. The other figures show the number of order for variable selection which make it possible to generate a solution within 100 search steps, the best solution for each case (within 100 search steps), and the best solutions within 200 search steps if the well-known branch-and-bound method is used. For the branch-and-bound method, the built-in predicate `min_max/2` of the CHIP system was applied. The sign "—" means that no solution was found for the corresponding case. The generation of the best solution requires in each case between 0.6 and 0.8 seconds.

horizon		strategies			
		jump = 1	jump = 12	jump = 17	domain reduction
	number of solutions	2	3	4	6
1,070	best solution	1,067	1,057	1,059	1,024
	best solution using b. & b.	1,058	1,047	1,057	958
	number of solutions	—	1	—	5
1,020	best solution	—	1,020	—	1,009
	best solution using b. & b.	—	999	—	958
	number of solutions	—	1	—	4
1,000	best solution	—	999	—	958
	best solution using b. & b.	—	996	—	958
	number of solutions	—	—	—	4
970	best solution	—	—	—	958
	best solution using b. & b.	—	—	—	958

Table 1. Comparison of several strategies

If the number of permitted search steps is restricted to 1,000, then only 3 further solutions can be found:

- with the strategy "jump = 1" and the given planning horizon 1,070 the solution 1,052 after 217 search steps
- with the domain-reducing strategy and the given planning horizon 1,070 the solution 1,067 after 453 search steps
- with the strategy "jump = 17" and the given planning horizon 1,020 the solution 1,015 after 268 search steps.

Some results with and without the branch-and-bound method are given in Table 2. If the branch-and-bound method was used, the search was restricted to 200 steps and the number of search steps in the table means that after this number of search steps the presented solution was achieved. The cpu-time includes the time for

- generating the constraints
- computing a priority for each task
- sorting the tasks according to these priorities
- generating the solution.

For instance, if the planning horizon 960 is given, the solution 958 is generated in 640 milliseconds. This time consists of 160 milliseconds for generating the constraints, 170 milliseconds for computing priorities and sorting, and 310 milliseconds for searching. Note that this solution coming to within 3% of the optimal solution 930.

The second column of the table contains the numbers of the chosen orders for variable selection, the orders being numbered beginning with 1. Note that the order with number 3 generates the following selection: first, the tasks that have to be placed on the first machine are considered, whereby we assume that the machines are ordered with respect to the demand on then (the sum of durations of the corresponding tasks); then, the tasks of the next machine are considered, etc.; the order of the tasks of a specific machine depends on these first two factors.

horizon	order	branch & bound	solution	search steps	cpu-time in sec.
2,000	4	no	1,105	0	0.8
2,000	4	yes	1,051	72	5.3
1,130	3	no	1,066	1	0.7
1,130	3	yes	958	9	5.4
1,070	3	no	1,024	1	0.7
1,070	3	yes	958	8	4.8
1,020	10	no	1,018	0	0.7
1,020	10	yes	967	63	7.7
1,020	3	yes	958	5	3.9
970	1	no	967	18	0.9
970	3	no	958	1	0.7
970	8	no	967	20	1.1
960	3	no	958	0	0.6

Table 2. Results with and without the branch and bound method

A comparison of the best results presented in [4] with our results is given in Table 3. In [4], the disjunction in the capacity constraints is represented by *disjunction as constraint*. For each task pair assigned to the same machine, a constraint of the following kind with an additional Boolean domain variable is generated (see also [5]):

```
disjunct(Start_A,Duration_A,Start_B,Duration_B) :-
        horizon(Max),
        Bool :: 0..1,
        Start_A + Duration_A #<= Start_B + Bool * Max,
        Start_B + Duration_B #<= Start_A + (1 - Bool) * Max.
```

The Boolean domain variable controls the choice between the two constraints. Each of both values activates one constraint and deactivates the other.

Except for the cpu-time, we get the same results if we do not use cumulative constraints. In this case, the disjunction in the capacity constraints is represented in the same way as in [4]. In Table 3, the first cpu-time for each horizon relates to the case of the use of cumulative constraints, and the second to the other case (disjunctions as constraints). Note that the generation of the 450 disjunctive constraints requires approximately twice as long as the generation of the 10 cumulative constraints.

	results of [4]		our results		
horizon	solution	search steps	solution	search steps	cpu-time in sec.
1,040	1,033	207	1,031	0	0.6 / 0.9
1,000	989	279	958	1	0.7 / 0.9
988	983	69,794	958	1	0.7 / 0.9
979	972	6,614	958	1	0.7 / 0.9

Table 3. Comparison of results

The domain reduction can also be applied to problems of job-shop scheduling if there are alternative machines available, i.e. machine groups are predetermined and there is a choice between the machines of the group. We modified the example of the 10 × 10 problem considered above in the following way: the 10 machines were grouped into the 4 machine groups { 1, 2 }, { 3, 4 }, { 5, 6, 7 }, and { 8, 9, 10 }. Table 4 contains some computation results for this new problem. We applied the same search strategy as in the tests presented above. However, only the order 1 of the tasks is used, and the definitions of the numbers MinSize, Min, and Max are modified.

horizon	branch & bound	solution	search steps	cpu-time in sec.
825	no	823	0	0.8
870	no	858	0	0.9
870	yes	823	104	7.8
930	no	860	0	0.9
930	yes	823	14	6.8
1000	yes	823	14	6.9
1100	yes	823	23	7.2

Table 4. Results of a modified problem

If the planning horizon 793 is given, the constraint solver detects a contradiction without performing any search. Thus, a lower bound for an optimal solution of this problem is 794, and the solution 823 deviates from the optimal solution by less than 3.7 %.

It proved possible to successfully apply the presented strategy to other job-shop problems as well. Thus, we considered, among others, nine different 10 × 10 problems automatically generated by *P. Breitinger and H.C.R Lock* in connection with their investigations presented in [4]. In a relatively short period of interactive work (less than 40 minutes for each problem and less than 10,000 search steps), estimations of the optimum were able to made for these problems with the following results: the optimum was determined for two problems, the difference between the upper and the lower bound being on average 5%, and for the worst case 9% (percentage with respect to the lower bound).

6   Related Work

The general scheme of constraint logic programming was first defined in [9]. Since 1987, a large number of publications relating to CLP have appeared, devoted to questions of semantics, new generalizations, implementation of concrete systems, applications, and other aspects. A survey on constraint logic programming is given in [10], and interesting papers on constraint logic programming are contained in [3]. In [14], the language CHIP (Constraint Handling In Prolog) is described and methods for solving discrete combinatorial problems are presented. The application of CLP to large combinatorial problems is discussed in [8]. The paper [5] is devoted to the use of CLP(FD) for solving realistic scheduling problems with large sets of tasks, the modelling of such problems also being described. Several methods for improving the search for problems of job-shop scheduling are investigated in [4], heuristics for variable selection, for example, being discussed there. An overview of variable selection heuristics can be found in [12]. In [7], an interesting technique for searching is presented. This technique can be successfully used for scheduling problems, but it cannot be directly applied if alternative resources are considered. An OR approach to job-shop problems is described e.g. in [2].

7   Conclusion

We have introduced a generalization of the labelling search strategy. The assignment of a value to the selected variable is replaced by reduction of the domain of this variable. The application of this domain-reducing strategy to the well-known problem of 10×10 job-shop scheduling has been discussed. The computation results demonstrate the advantages of this strategy, despite the fact that simple heuristics for domain reduction are used. For instance, a good solution, coming to within 3% of the optimal solution, was generated in less than 1 second, whereby only simple heuristics for variable selection and domain reduction were used.

In comparison with the standard strategy, the domain-reducing strategy shows more robustness with respect to the chosen order of variable selection and the given planning horizon. We expect that the presented results may be improved if more specific heuristics are integrated (see e.g. [4] or [7] for such heuristics). However, this was not the objective of the present paper. Investigations of heuristics for domain reduction of the selected variable form part of our current research work.

As we did not integrate specific heuristics of the 10×10 job-shop problem into the domain-reducing procedure, we were able to apply this strategy successfully to a modified problem. In the modified problem, we assumed that there is a choice of machines. A good solution, deviating from the optimal solution by less than 4%, was able to be generated with the same strategy in less than 1 second.

We propose using the domain reducing strategy as a basic search strategy for CLP(FD).

References

1. A. Aggoun and N. Beldiceanu. Extending CHIP in order to solve complex scheduling and placement problems. *Math. Comput. Modelling*, 17(7):57–73, 1993.
2. D. Applegate and W. Cook. A computational study of job-shop scheduling. *Operations Research Society of America*, 3(2), 1991.
3. F. Benhamou and A. Colmerauer, editors. *Constraint Logic Programming (Selected Research)*. MIT Press, Cambridge, London, 1993.
4. S. Breitinger and H.C.R. Lock. Improving search for job-shop-scheduling with CLP(FD). In M. Hermenegildo and J. Penjam, editors, *Programming Language Implementation and Logic Programming*, volume 844 of *Lecture Notes in Computer Science*, pages 277–291, Berlin, Heidelberg, 1994. Springer.
5. S. Breitinger and H.C.R. Lock. Modelling and scheduling in CLP(FD). In *[13]*, pages 95–110, 1994.
6. J. Carlier and E. Pinson. An algorithm for solving the job shop problem. *Management Science*, 35(2):164–176, 1989.
7. Y. Caseau and F. Laburthe. Improved CLP scheduling with task intervals. In P. Van Hentenryck, editor, *Proc. of the 11th International Conference on Logic Programming*, pages 369–383. MIT Press, 1994.
8. M. Dincbas, H. Simonis, and P. van Hentenryck. Solving large combinatorial problems in logic programming. *J. Logic Programming*, 8:75–93, 1990.
9. J. Jaffar and J.-L. Lassez. Constraint logic programming. In *Proc. 14th Principles of Programming Languages*, pages 111–119, Munich, 1987.
10. J. Jaffar and M. J. Maher. Constraint logic programming: A survey. *J. Logic Programming*, 19/20:503–581, 1994.
11. J.F. Muth and G.L. Thompson. *Industrial Scheduling*. Prentice-Hall, Englewood Cliffs, NJ, 1963.
12. N. Sadeh and M. Fox. Variable and value ordering heuristics for hard constraint satisfaction problems: an application to job-shop scheduling. Technical Report CMU-RI-TR-91-23, Carnegie Mellon University, Pittsburgh, Pennsylvania, 1991.
13. L. Sterling, editor. *Proc. Internat. Conf. on the Practical Application of Prolog*. London, 1994.
14. P. van Hentenryck. *Constraint Satisfaction in Logic Programming*. MIT Press, Cambridge (Mass.), London, 1989.

Appendix

We give below the data for the job-shop problem discussed in this paper. This problem is defined by Muth and Thompson in [11]. The first line of the table contains the job numbers, and the first column the task numbers. The pair n ; m means that the corresponding task has to be placed on machine "m" and the duration of this task is "n". For instance, the task 2 of job 3 has to be placed on the machine 1 and the duration of this task is equal to 85. The optimal solution of this problem is known to be 930 (see [6]), i.e. the jobs can be completed within 930 time units.

	1	2	3	4	5	6	7	8	9	10
1	29 ; 1	43 ; 1	91 ; 2	81 ; 2	14 ; 3	84 ; 3	46 ; 2	31 ; 3	76 ; 1	85 ; 2
2	78 ; 2	90 ; 3	85 ; 1	95 ; 3	6 ; 1	2 ; 2	37 ; 1	86 ; 1	69 ; 2	13 ; 1
3	9 ; 3	75 ; 5	39 ; 4	71 ; 1	22 ; 2	52 ; 6	61 ; 4	46 ; 2	76 ; 4	61 ; 3
4	36 ; 4	11 ; 10	74 ; 3	99 ; 5	61 ; 6	95 ; 4	13 ; 3	74 ; 6	51 ; 6	7 ; 7
5	49 ; 5	69 ; 4	90 ; 9	9 ; 7	26 ; 4	48 ; 9	32 ; 7	32 ; 5	85 ; 3	64 ; 9
6	11 ; 6	28 ; 2	10 ; 6	52 ; 9	69 ; 5	72 ; 10	21 ; 6	88 ; 7	11 ; 10	76 ; 10
7	62 ; 7	46 ; 7	12 ; 8	85 ; 8	21 ; 9	47 ; 1	32 ; 10	19 ; 9	40 ; 7	47 ; 6
8	56 ; 8	46 ; 6	89 ; 7	98 ; 4	49 ; 8	65 ; 7	89 ; 9	48 ; 10	89 ; 8	52 ; 4
9	44 ; 9	72 ; 8	45 ; 10	22 ; 10	72 ; 10	6 ; 5	30 ; 8	36 ; 8	26 ; 5	90 ; 5
10	21 ; 10	30 ; 9	33 ; 5	43 ; 6	53 ; 7	25 ; 8	55 ; 5	79 ; 4	74 ; 9	45 ; 8

What Is Symbolic Computation?

Bruno Buchberger

RISC (Research Institute for Symbolic Computation)

A4232 Hagenberg, Austria, Europe

In my editorial to the Journal of Symbolic Computation (see Vol. 1/1, pp. 1-6, 1995) I defined the scope of the journal by saying that "symbolic computation studies the algorithmic solution of problems dealing with symbolic objects". However, I was not really able to define precisely what we mean by "symbolic objects". Instead, I listed some of the typical domains and topics that are considered in the area of "symbolic computation".

After 10 years of editing the Journal of Symbolic Computation and 8 years of directing the Research Institute for Symbolic Computation, in this talk, I will make another attempt to define what symbolic computation is. Of course, most probably, there are so many views about what symbolic computation is as there are researchers working in this field. However, I will argue that a certain area can be defined rigorously by the mathematical domains studied and the methods permitted, which might encompass much of what most of the researchers in the area of symbolic computation are currently doing and excludes certain other areas.

Roughly, my definition will expand on the earlier definition by saying that "symbolic objects" are objects having infinite semantics. In more detail, I will start from a "definition" of "mathematics" and "algorithmic mathematics" and will finally define "symbolic computation" as a specific part of algorithmic mathematics, namely as the "area that tries to find algorithmic solutions of problems about non-algorithmic domains in algorithmic representation".

I will also briefly review some of the main achievements, in the past ten years, in the mathematical foundation, the software realization and also the application of symbolic computation.

Constraint Solving for Combinatorial Search Problems: A Tutorial

P. Van Hentenryck
Brown University, Box 1910
Providence, RI 02912, USA
Email: pvh@cs.brown.edu

Abstract

Combinatorial search problems are ubiquitous in numerous applications areas. This tutorial reviews some fundamental techniques from artificial intelligence, numerical analysis, and operations research to solve both discrete and continuous combinatorial problems. For discrete problems, we consider techniques such as branch and relax, branch and cut, and local search. For continuous problems, we consider techniques such as quasi-Newton methods, continuation methods, and interval methods. Our main goal is to give an informal understanding and intuition about these techniques and to review some constraint programming tools supporting them.

1   Introduction

Combinatorial search problems are ubiquitous in many areas of science and engineering. Most of these problems are computationally difficult (they are NP-hard) and require considerable expertise and development time. The purpose of this tutorial is to review some fundamental techniques from artificial intelligence, numerical analysis, and operations research to solve both discrete and continuous combinatorial problems. For discrete problems, we consider techniques such as branch and relax, branch and cut, and local search. For continuous problems, we consider techniques such as quasi-Newton methods, continuation methods, and interval methods. Our main goal is to give an informal understanding and intuition about these techniques and we often make simplification to ease understanding. We also try to connect some constraint programming tools with the techniques presented but make no effort to be comprehensive, the focus being on ideas and on showing which techniques have been considered at this point. We also try to give references to papers where additional information can be found.

The paper is organized as follows. We start by some preliminaries which review linear programming, a fundamental tool in combinatorial optimization, and some frameworks to state combinatorial search problems. We then move to discrete combinatorial search problems and review branch and relax, branch and cut, and local search. We conclude by continuous combinatorial search problems and review quasi-Newton, continuation and interval methods.

2 Preliminaries

The purpose of this section is to overview some frameworks that have been used to state combinatorial search problems. We first start by an overview of linear programming, which is a fundamental tool for combinatorial optimization. We then consider integer programming and constraint satisfaction problems for discrete problems, since the solution techniques are essentially different depending upon the angles chosen to represent the problem. Note that there are other frameworks that can be chosen to represent discrete combinatorial problems such as propositional logic but their solution techniques are essentially the same as those presented here. We finally consider polynomial systems for continuous problems.

2.1 Linear Programming

Linear programming [15] is a fundamental tool for combinatorial search problems, not only because it solves efficiently a large class of important problems, but also because it is the basic block of some fundamental techniques in this area, such as branch and relax and branch and cut. A linear program consists of minimizing a linear objective function subject to a set of linear constraints over real variables constrained to be nonnegative or, in symbols,

$$\text{minimize } \sum_{j=1}^{n} c_j x_j$$
$$\text{subject to}$$
$$\sum_{j=1}^{n} a_{ij} x_j = b_i \ (1 \le i \le m)$$
$$x_j \ge 0 \qquad (1 \le j \le n).$$

Note first that considering only equations, nonnegative variables, and minimization is not restrictive. An inequality $t \ge 0$ can be recast as an equation $t - s = 0$ by adding a new variable, an arbitrary variable can be expressed as the difference of two nonnegative variables, and maximization can be expressed by negating the objective function. In addition, decision problems (i.e., finding if a set of constraints is satisfiable) can be recast by adding a variable per constraint and minimizing their sum. The problem is satisfiable if and only if the optimum is zero. Note also that linear programs can be solved in polynomial time although the simplex algorithm, currently the most commonly used algorithm for solving them, is exponential in the worst-case. However, in practice, it is still difficult to outperform the simplex algorithm.

There are many fundamental geometrical results on this problem. Of particular interest is the fact that the set of constraints defines a polyhedron or a polytope (if the solution set is bounded which we will assume). Moreover, an optimal solution to the linear program is located on one of the vertices of the polytope. This of course immediately suggests a naive algorithm for linear programming: enumerate all the vertices and choose the one with the minimal value for the objective function. The simplex algorithm is a more informed way of exploring the vertices. It starts from a vertex and move to an adjacent vertex with a better value for the objective function until no such vertex exists. The convexity of the solution space guarantees that the optimal solution has been found, once no such adjacent vertex can be found.[1] To translate this geometrical intuition into a computer program, it is important to find out what a vertex looks like algebraically. This leads to the notion of solved form for a set of linear constraints. A set of linear constraint is in solved form iff it is of the form

$$x_1 = b_1 + \sum_{j=m+1}^{n} a_{1j}x_j \quad b_1 \geq 0$$
$$\dots$$
$$x_m = b_m + \sum_{j=m+1}^{n} a_{mj}x_j \; b_m \geq 0.$$

The variables $x_1, \dots, x_m$ are called basic variables, while the other variables are called non-basic variables. The solved form makes explicit a solution, usually called a basic feasible solution,

$$\{x_1 \leftarrow b_1; \dots; x_m \leftarrow b_m; x_{m+1} \leftarrow 0; \dots; x_n \leftarrow 0\}$$

which is the algebraic counterpart to the geometric notion of a vertex. Moving from one vertex to another consists of moving from one solved form to another by choosing a non-basic variable to enter the basis and a basic variable to leave the basis. The optimum is reached when the objection function, after elimination of the basic variables, contains only positive coefficients for the variables. The simplex algorithm has also some other attractive features for solving combinatorial search problems. For instance, it is relatively easy to add a new constraint and reoptimize. The main reason is duality theory. The dual problem (where constraints are variables and variables are constraints) is feasible but not optimal. Since the dual and the primal problems have the same optimum, it suffices to optimize the dual.

Link to Constraint Programming 1 (Linear Programming). Linear programming has been supported in constraint programming languages for about a decade now starting with languages like Prolog III [12],CHIP [20], and CLP($\Re$) [28]. The implementation techniques are however still far from the best techniques used in linear programming packages, although some effort are aiming at bridging this gap.

2.2 Integer Programming

The success of linear programming led many researchers to investigate some of its generalizations. Integer programming [22] is a natural extension of linear programming, where an additional constraint requires the variables to be integral, i.e.,

$$\text{minimize} \; \sum_{j=1}^{n} c_j x_j$$
subject to
$$\sum_{j=1}^{n} a_{ij}x_j = b_i \; (1 \leq i \leq m)$$
$$x_j \geq 0 \qquad\qquad (1 \leq j \leq n)$$
$$x_j \; \text{integer} \qquad (1 \leq j \leq n).$$

---

[1] The simplex algorithm can thus be viewed as a local search algorithm (see Section 3.3) but it has the property of converging towards the optimum.

Unfortunately, these additional constraints make the problem NP-complete, which excludes the application of simple techniques such as solving the corresponding linear program and rounding the solution.

Integer programming have been investigated extensively in the past and has produced some important techniques and insights to solve combinatorial search problems. There are commercial packages to solve integer programming problems but, in general, it is more effective to use special-purpose algorithms than to recast a problem into an integer programming problem and to use general-purpose codes.

There are however a number of interesting observations to be made at this point. Consider the linear program obtained by removing the integrality constraints (this program is called the linear relaxation). If the optimal solution to the linear relaxation is integral, then it is also the solution of the integer program. In general, the solution will be not be integral (except for some classes of problems where the coefficient matrix is totally unimodular). The linear relaxation still provides us with some information, since the optimum of the integer program must be greater or equal to the optimum of the linear relaxation.

2.3   Constraint Satisfaction Problems

We now turn to a completely different modelling paradigm, constraint satisfaction problems, that has been extensively investigated in the artificial intelligence community following the seminal work of Waltz [51], Montanari [35], and Mackworth [31].

A constraint satisfaction problem (CSP) consists of a set of variables x_i ($1 \leq i \leq n$), each of which has an associated finite domain D_i ($1 \leq i \leq n$) of values, and a set of constraints. A constraint c on variables $x_{i_1}, \ldots, x_{i_n}$ is a subset of the cartesian product $D_{i_1} \times \ldots \times D_{i_n}$ and we denote by $c(v_1, \ldots, v_n)$ the boolean value obtained when variables $x_{i_j}(1 \leq j \leq n)$ are replaced by values $v_j(1 \leq j \leq n)$. A solution to a CSP is an assignment of values to the variables such that all constraints are satisfied. Note that there are also various extensions to the CSP framework to take into account optimization and preferential constraints (e.g., [21]).

At first sight, one may wonder what this framework has to offer over integer programming. The framework has even less structure than integer programming, since the constraints can be arbitrary. The only real restriction is that the variables range over a finite set of values. There are at least two related reasons why this area has been worth investigating although, as in the case of integer programming, it is often more profitable to use special-purpose algorithms than recasting a problem into the CSP framework and using a general-purpose CSP algorithm. First, the added generality has led researchers to investigate pruning techniques very different from those developed for integer programming and these techniques appear to be effective for a variety of combinatorial search problems where the mathematical structure of the problem is difficult to extract. Second, the added generality allows CSP algorithms to manipulate disjunctive constraints which are not well handled in general by integer programming code. Consider for instance a disjunctive constraint

$$x_1 \geq x_2 + d_2 \ \lor \ x_2 \geq x_1 + d_1$$

occurring frequently in disjunctive scheduling. It is possible to recast this constraint into integer programming by adding a new Boolean variable b which indicates which disjunct should be selected to obtain three constraints

$$x_1 \geq x_2 + d_2 - bM$$
$$x_2 \geq x_1 + d_1 - (1-b)M$$
$$0 \leq b \leq 1$$

where M is a (sufficiently) large number. When $b = 0$, the first disjunct must hold while the second disjunct is automatically satisfied and vice-versa for $b = 1$. Unfortunately, the above constraints are not handled effectively by linear programming, i.e., the optimum of the linear relaxation is a poor approximation of the optimum of the integer program, since the assignment of 0.5 to b satisfies both constraints if M is large enough. Contrarily, the handling of disjunctions has been an active topic of research is the CSP community (e.g, [47, 49, 10, 17]). Note also that disjunctive linear programming [1] has also been an active research in operations research and that combinations of techniques developed in these two fields appear to be complementary to solve disjunctive linear programs [17].

2.4 Polynomial Systems

The last framework that we consider are polynomial systems of constraints over reals. The problem consists in finding whether a set of nonlinear constraints (built from rational numbers, the operators $+, -, \times$, and variables) is satisfiable over the reals. The problem is in NP-hard (in fact, it is in PSPACE). An important fact to mention in this context is that small problems (i.e., problems with less than 10 variables) can be extremely hard in this area, which is rarely the case in discrete combinatorial search problems.

3 Discrete Combinatorial Search Problems

In this section, we consider a number of techniques to solve discrete combinatorial search problems, i.e., problems where the variables are constrained to take a finite set of values. The techniques considered include branch and relax, branch and cut, and local search. Other techniques include dynamic programming [2], approximation algorithms (e.g, [13]), and decomposition techniques [18, 36] but they are not covered in this tutorial.

3.1 Branch and Relax

Branch and relax (often called branch and bound for optimization problems and branch and prune for decision problems) is a well-known technique to solve combinatorial search problems. It consists of iterating two steps

1. solving a relaxation of the constraints;
2. splitting the problem into subproblems.

A branch and relax procedure is in fact a tree search procedure where each node is a subproblem (the top-level node is the original problem) and a relaxation procedure is executed for each of the nodes. There are various ways of exploring the tree and depth-first search is often selected because of its good memory behaviour and its ability to produce early solutions.[2] A given branch and relax algorithm of course depends on the choice of the relaxation and branching procedures. We explore two traditional schemes in the following.

Linear Programming Relaxation This relaxation assumes that the original problem has been recast as an integer programming problem. The resulting problem is of course an optimization problem.

The relaxation procedure consists simply of using the linear relaxation. As mentioned previously, if the solution is integral, then the subproblem is solved optimally. If the solution is not integral, then the optimum of the linear relaxation is a lower bound on the value of the original problem. Hence, if this value is greater than the value of an already found solution, the subproblem can be pruned away: it cannot lead to an optimal solution.

The branching procedure in this context often consists of selecting a variable x which takes a fractional value f in the linear relaxation and of creating two new subproblems by adding the constraints $x \leq \lfloor f \rfloor$ and $x \geq \lceil f \rceil$ respectively. Adding these constraints can be done easily in a simplex with bounded variables and dual simplex can be used to reoptimize, which makes the whole procedure incremental.

Branch and relax algorithms using the linear relaxation are probably the most successful way to solve integer programming problems and they are available in a number of commercial packages. They have been successful in attacking large instances of a variety of problems such as set partitioning or set covering. However, small problems of the same nature cannot be solved in reasonable time. This is of course to be expected for NP-complete problems but it also indicates a weakness of this approach: it does not really exploit the structure of the problem at hand. We will study in Section 3.2 branch and cut algorithms which are refinements of branch and relax algorithms overcoming (at least partially) this problem.

---

[2] Note however that there has been a renewed interest in "intelligent" backtracking techniques in artificial intelligence in recent years. These techniques analyze the failures to determine a suitable node in the tree to backtrack. See [5] for more on this topic.

Link to Constraint Programming 2 (Linear Relaxation). 2LP [33] is an interesting constraint language which makes it easy to branch and relax algorithms based on the linear relaxation. It is also appropriate to implement branch and cut algorithms.

Local Consistency Relaxation This relaxation assumes that the problem can be modelled as a CSP, which is almost always the case for discrete combinatorial search problems. The resulting statement is a decision problem but it can be easily generalized to optimization problems when the domains are numerical values.

The relaxation procedure is to use constraints locally to reduce the domains of the variables. More precisely, the relaxation procedure uses each constraint to reduce the domains of its variables and terminates when no reduction takes place for any of the constraints. If any of the domains is empty, then the subproblem is unsolvable. The relaxation may seem inherently less precise than a linear relaxation. However, it is valuable for (at least) two reasons. First, sometimes weaker relaxations may lead to faster algorithms. Second, and most important, the local consistency relaxation may exploit the structure of the problem in a better way, especially in presence of disjunctive constraints. We will illustrate this on two examples later on in this section. There are of course many ways to use constraints locally to reduce the domains and this has been investigated intensively in the artificial intelligence community under the name *consistency techniques* [31] and in the operations research community for specific applications. We will discuss some of them in this paper but see for instance [32, 18] for an overview of the techniques developed in artificial intelligence.

The branching procedure in this context consists of creating several subproblems again. This can be done by instantiating a variable to its possible values or by splitting the domain of a variable in several parts. In practical applications, this procedure often uses the results of the relaxation step to make a more informed choice. For instance, a typical heuristics is to choose to instantiate the variable with the smallest domain.

Let us now consider two relaxation procedures: a general-purpose and a specific local consistency procedures. Section 4.3 will present a local consistency relaxation for continuous problems. One of the most successful general-purpose ways of using constraints is called arc-consistency and consists of reducing the domains by performing projection operations.

Definition 3 (Arc-Consistency). A constraint c over variables $x_1, \ldots, x_n$ is arc-consistent wrt x_i and $\langle D_1, \ldots, D_n \rangle$ iff $D_i = D_i \cap \{r_i \mid \exists r_1 \in D_1, \ldots, \exists r_{i-1} \in D_{i-1}, \exists r_{i+1} \in D_{i+1}, \ldots, \exists r_n \in D_n : c(r_1, \ldots, r_n)\}$. Constraint c is arc-consistent wrt $\langle D_1, \ldots, D_n \rangle$ if it is arc-consistent wrt x_i and $\langle D_1, \ldots, D_n \rangle$ $(1 \leq i \leq n)$. A system of constraints S is arc-consistent wrt $\langle D_1, \ldots, D_n \rangle$ if each constraint in S is arc-consistent wrt $\langle D_1, \ldots, D_n \rangle$.

A relaxation procedure based on arc-consistency reduces the domains of the variables (without removing any solution) until the system of constraints is arc-consistent. Arc-consistency can be enforced in time $O(ed^2)$ where d is the size of the largest domain and e is the number of constraints, even without taking into account the structure of the constraints.

Link to Constraint Programming 4 (Consistency Techniques). The integration of consistency techniques in constraint programming languages was pioneered by the CHIP system [46] and is now in use in numerous other constraint languages. These languages have been applied successfully to a large number of industrial applications.

Example 1 (Mobile Telephone Frequency Allocation). A nice application of this relaxation is the allocation of frequencies to mobile telephones. This application illustrates the interest of arc-consistency and the need to look for surrogate constraints which exploit specific properties of the solutions. It also indicates why using a general tool is not in general a good idea, since we cannot expect the tool to deduce these additional properties. We are given a number of stations (the variables of the problem) which must be assigned some frequencies (the domains of the problem) such that a number of constraints be satisfied. The constraints are of three forms

1. the distance between two stations x and y is fixed to some value d, i.e., $|x - y| = d$;
2. the distance between two stations x and y must be greater than some value d, i.e., $|x - y| > d$;
3. the distance between two stations x and y must be smaller than some value d, i.e., $|x - y| < d$. This constraint can be rewritten as $x - y < d$ & $y - x < d$.

The first two kinds of constraints are of course disjunctive because of the absolute values and enforcing arc-consistency will produce significant pruning of the domains but are not enough to solve most problems. To improve the relaxation, we can combine several constraints together.[3] Consider three constraints

$$|x - y| = d_1 \ \& \ |x - z| > d_2 \ \& \ |x - z| > d_3$$

and assume that $d_1 < d_2$ and $d_1 < d_3$. We can easily see that z cannot be between x and y and that these three constraints can be combined to produce significant pruning. The algorithm can thus apply arc-consistency on a constraint $c(x, y, z)$ defined as the above conjunction. Languages like cc(FD) have efficient way to enforce arc-consistency on such a constraint using constructive disjunction [49]. An algorithm based on this relaxation procedures is able to solve large instances of the problems involving several hundreds variables and several thousands constraints. $\square$

For certain applications however, problem-specific relaxations are preferable.

---

[3] This idea is due to Michel Van Caneghem.

Example 2 (Disjunctive Scheduling). A disjunctive scheduling problem is specified by a set of tasks t_i, each of which has a fixed duration, by a set of precedence constraints stating that a task can only start after completion of another task, by a set of disjunctive constraints stating that two tasks cannot be scheduled at the same time and by a deadline e indicating when the schedule must be completed. It is easy to model this problem as a CSP by associating a variable s_i with each task t_i to represent its starting date. The precedence constraints are of the form

$$s_i \geq s_j + d_j$$

where d_j is the duration of tasks t_j, and the disjunction constraints are of the form

$$s_i \geq s_j + d_j \vee s_j \geq s_i + d_i.$$

The domains of the variables are simply given as $\{0 \ldots e\}$. As should be clear, the linear programming relaxation (assuming the rewriting of disjunctive constraints presented previously) is not really helpful, since it would result in a shortest path relaxation which only takes into account the precedence constraints. The best algorithms known to solve this problem (e.g., [7]) uses a local consistency relaxation which manipulates disjunctions as a whole. Consider a set T of tasks $t_1, \ldots, t_n$ in disjunction. Let $d_1, \ldots, d_n$ be their durations and $D_1, \ldots, D_n$ their domains representing their possible starting dates. Denote by m_i (resp. M_i) the minimum (resp. maximum) of D_i. The key idea behind the local relaxation is to reduce the domains by considering a subset $S \subseteq T$ of tasks and finding out the tasks that cannot be scheduled first (resp. last) in S. The domain of these tasks can be updated, since these tasks must be scheduled after (resp. before) the completion (resp. starting) of some other tasks in S.[4] To detect if a task cannot be scheduled first, we simply determine if the following condition holds

$$m_i + \sum_{j \in S} d_j > max_{j \in S \setminus \{i\}} M_j. \quad \Box$$

Link to Constraint Programming 5 (Scheduling). Several constraint languages such as CHIP [20] and ILOG [42] supports this disjunctive relaxation directly. Other languages such as cc(FD) [49] and Laure [8] allow programmers to build them on top of the languages.

The above examples indicate clearly that the design of branch and prune algorithms is very much an art. Identifying properties of the solution and efficient relaxations to exploit them is problem-specific and requires insight into the nature of the problem.

---

[4] There are also some other rules to update the domains but we focus on the main idea here.

3.2 Branch and Cut

The techniques described in this section assume that the problem has been re-casted as an integer programming problem. It is based of course on the linear relaxation but its main idea is to add new linear constraints when the optimal solution of the relaxation is not integral. We first review cutting planes algorithms which generates constraints in a syntactic way and then moves to polyhedral cuts which exploits the nature of the problem to generate the constraints.

Cutting Planes Cutting planes algorithms originate from the work of Gomory (e.g., [24]) and are based on the following idea. The linear relaxation is solved. If the solution is integral, an optimal solution has been found. Otherwise, a new constraint is generated and the process is restarted. The new constraint should satisfy a number of conditions, two of which being

- it should cut off the current optimal solution to the linear relaxation;
- it should be valid, i.e., it should not remove any integer solution.

Let us first illustrate a simple cut proposed by Dantzig [14]. Consider the solved form of the linear relaxation at optimality.

$$x_1 = b_1 + \sum_{j=m+1}^{n} a_{1j} x_j \quad b_1 \geq 0$$
$$\dots$$
$$x_m = b_m + \sum_{j=m+1}^{n} a_{mj} x_j \quad b_m \geq 0.$$

Its optimal solution is thus

$$\{x_1 \leftarrow b_1; \dots; x_m \leftarrow b_m; x_{m+1} \leftarrow 0; \dots; x_n \leftarrow 0\}.$$

Assume that the solution is not integral. It follows that some x_k $(m+1 \leq k \leq n)$ is not zero in any integral solution, i.e., the constraint

$$\sum_{k=m+1}^{n} x_k > 0$$

must hold. Since the x_k are integer, this constraint can be rewritten as

$$\sum_{k=m+1}^{n} x_k \geq 1.$$

It is easy to see that the above constraint is valid and cut off the optimal solution. Unfortunately, this cut does not guarantee termination for a large class of problems, i.e., the above process would generate infinitely many cuts.

A valid cut that guarantees termination of the process (provided that the algorithm uses some guidelines on how to generate the cuts and that the linear relaxation uses a lexicographic pivoting rule) was proposed by Gomory [24]. Assume that b_i is not integral in the constraint

$$x_i = b_i + \sum_{j=m+1}^{n} a_{ij}x_j$$

of the solved form and rewrite the constraints as

$$x_i + \sum_{j=m+1}^{n} b_{ij}x_j = b_i$$

where $b_{ij} = -a_{ij}$. Since $x_k \geq 0$, we have that

$$\sum_{j=m+1}^{n} \lfloor b_{ij} \rfloor x_j \leq \sum_{j=m+1}^{n} b_{ij}x_j.$$

and thus

$$x_i + \sum_{j=m+1}^{n} \lfloor b_{ij} \rfloor x_j \leq b_i.$$

Moreover, since $x_i + \sum_{j=m+1}^{n} \lfloor b_{ij} \rfloor x_j$ is integral, we must have

$$x_i + \sum_{j=m+1}^{n} \lfloor b_{ij} \rfloor x_j \leq \lfloor b_i \rfloor.$$

which is Gomory cut.[5] It is also easy that the constraint cuts off the optimal solution of the linear relaxation.

Several algorithms based on these ideas have been developed (see for instance [44] for some computational experience) but these approaches are not very successful. Their main limitation is that the generated constraints are syntactic in nature and do not exploit the structure of the problem. This leads us directly to polyhedral cuts, an active and successful area in combinatorial optimization which can be traced back to the work of Dantzig, Fulkerson, and Johnson [16] and Gomory [25].

Polyhedra Cuts Consider an integer programming problem and the set S of all integer solutions to its constraints. Define *conv(S)* as the convex hull of all these solutions. If we had a constraint representation of this *conv(S)*, linear programming would solve the integer programming problem. It is of course impossible in general to find a constraint representation of *conv(S)* efficiently. However, this suggests the possibility of generating linear inequalities which are facets of *conv(S)*. These constraints are much stronger in general that the cutting planes described above which are not even guaranteed to intersect the convex hull. As

---

[5] This is not strictly true since Gomory cut is in fact a slight variation of this to reduce the size of the coefficients.

a consequence the linear relaxation is likely to produce much better results, i.e., the gap between the optimum of the linear relaxation and the integer programming solution is smaller [41]. Branch and cut algorithms are precisely based on this principle. The basic idea is to use the linear relaxation. If the problem is not solved, the algorithm tries to generate facets of *conv(S)*. If no facets can be found at this point, the algorithm branches as in traditional branch and bound algorithms. Once again, the identification of facets of *conv(S)* is problem-specific and very much an art. We give two examples in the following to illustrate this approach. The presentation of the first example is based on [39] and it illustrates how to find a constraint that is a facet. The second example is the travelling salesman problem for which branch and cut is a very effective approach.

Example 3 (Node Packing). Given a graph $G = (V, E)$ and an integer k, the problem consists in finding a node packing (i.e., a subset of V such that no two vertices are connected by an edge E) of maximal size. The integer program can be obtained by associating a Boolean variable x_i with each vertex in V

$$\text{maximize } \sum_{j=1}^{n} x_j$$
$$\text{subject to}$$
$$x_i + x_j \leq 1 \ (i, j) \in E$$
$$0 \leq x_i \leq 1 \ i \in V$$
$$x_i \text{ integer} \ i \in V$$

and we denote by S the set of node packings, i.e., all solution of the constraints. Let us illustrate how to find a valid cut which is a facet. Once again, the key idea is to look at properties of all solutions. In the case of the node packing problem, it is possible to obtain some facets of *conv(S)* by considering the maximal cliques of G. Recall that a clique is a subset C of vertices such that each two vertices in C are connected. Moreover, a clique C is maximal if any superset of C is not a clique. Given a clique C, the constraint

$$\sum_{j \in C} x_j \leq 1$$

defines a facet of *conv(S)*. To prove that the above constraint defines a facet, we need to show that the constraint contains n affinely independent points of S which, in this case, is similar to showing that the constraint contains n linearly independent points of S. Assume that $C = \{1, \ldots, k\}$ is a maximal clique. For each vertex i in $V \setminus C$, there exists a vertex c_i in C such that $(i, c_i) \notin E$. It is easy to see that the vectors constructed from the packings $\{1\}, \ldots, \{k\}, \{k+1, o_{k+1}\}, \ldots, \{n, o_n\}$ are linearly independent.

A branch and cut algorithm can then generate some or all the clique constraints. Note however that the clique constraints and the nonnegativity constraints do not generally define all the facets of *conv(S)*. Consider the set of constraints

$$x_1 + x_2 \leq 1$$
$$x_1 + x_3 \leq 1$$
$$x_1 + x_4 \leq 1$$
$$x_1 + x_5 \leq 1$$
$$x_2 + x_3 \leq 1$$
$$x_3 + x_4 \leq 1$$
$$x_4 + x_5 \leq 1$$
$$x_5 + x_6 \leq 1$$
$$x_1, x_2, x_3, x_4, x_5, x_6 \geq 0.$$

The clique constraints are given by

$$x_1 + x_2 + x_3 \leq 1$$
$$x_1 + x_3 + x_4 \leq 1$$
$$x_1 + x_4 + x_5 \leq 1$$
$$x_1 + x_5 + x_6 \leq 1$$
$$x_1 + x_2 + x_6 \leq 1.$$

However the assignment $\{x_1 \leftarrow 0; x_2 \leftarrow 0.5; \ldots; x_6 \leftarrow 0.5\}$ satisfies all constraints. To prune this fractional solution, it is necessary to consider another type of cuts based on cordless cycles. $\square$

Example 4 (Travelling Salesman Problem). We are given a complete graph with n vertices and, for each edge (i, j) of the graph, a positive number d_{ij} representing its cost. The problem is to find an Hamiltonian tour (i.e., a tour visiting each city exactly one) of minimal cost. The problem can be modelled as an integer programming problem by associating with each edge (i, j) a Boolean variable x_{ij}. A first approximation may be

minimize $\sum_{i=1}^{n} \sum_{i=1}^{n} d_{ij} x_{ij}$
subject to

$$\sum_{i=1}^{n} x_{ij} = 1 \qquad 1 \leq j \leq n$$
$$\sum_{j=1}^{n} x_{ij} = 1 \qquad 1 \leq i \leq n$$
$$0 \leq x_i \leq 1 \qquad i \in V$$
$$x_{ij} \text{ integer} \qquad i \in V$$

The first two sets of linear constraints guarantee respectively that each vertex i is entered exactly once and that each vertex j is left exactly once. The above approximation is in fact a matching problem that can be solved in polynomial time. It leaves out an important set of constraints (called the subtour constraints) that forbid subtours, i.e., a set of vertices which make up a tour which is not connected to other vertices. To express those constraints, consider a subset T of vertices. We must state that at least one vertex of T is connected to a vertex of $V \setminus T$ or, in symbols,

$$\sum_{i \in T} \sum_{j \in V \setminus T} x_{ij} \geq 1 \ \forall T \subset V$$

The main problem here is that there are exponentially many subtour constraints. An algorithm can thus solve the above approximation; if the result is not a tour, then violated subtour constraints can be added and the process repeated. When this process terminates however, the result does not in general correspond to a tour. We could resort to branch and bound at this point or we could generate other valid cuts. Another polyhedral cut for the TSP is a comb. A comb has a handle (a set of nodes) and an odd number (> 2) of teeth. A tooth is a set of nodes which has at least one node in common with the handle. The comb consists of all edges which have both ends in the handle or both ends in a tooth. It is possible to bound by above the number of edges in a comb that can belong to a tour and the resulting constraint is a polyhedral cut [9]. Branch and cut algorithms based on these techniques have been very successful, solving optimally problems with more than a thousand variables as shown recently by Padberg and Rinaldi on the one hand and Applegate, Bixby, Chvátal, and Cook on the other hand. □.

Link to Constraint Programming 6 (Polyhedral Cuts). The use of polyhedral cuts is studied by Barth and Bockmayr [4] in the context of pseudo Boolean constraints for constraint logic programming. Note also that the language 2LP can used to implement branch and cut algorithms.

3.3 Local Search

Local search is a fundamentally different technique than what we have seen so far. Contrary to the algorithms we have presented, local search is not a complete method, i.e., it does not guarantee to find a solution in decision problems (even if one exists) or it may not return the optimal solution in optimization problems. However, it works surprisingly well in practice for a variety of problems. It has a long tradition in operations research (e.g., [30]) and it is attracted much attention in artificial intelligence in recent years [34, 45]. Its basic idea is extremely simple and we present it in the context of optimization problems. It consists of starting with a solution and of modifying it locally to obtain better and better solutions. There are many issues in local search such as the definition of the local modification (usually called a neighborhood), the criteria to accept a move, and the termination criteria. We review some of those in the following. Our presentation often assumes the following model: "given a set S, find a subset T which satisfies a set of constraints C and minimizes an objective function f". For instance, in the travelling salesman, the set S is the set of edges, C states that the proposed solution must be a tour, and $f(T)$ computes the sum of all weight of the edges in S.

Local Improvement The simplest form of local search is local improvement. It can be described concisely by the following abstract code

```
T := some random solution to C;
while f(T) > f(transform(T)) do
    T := improve(T);
```

The key idea is to keep on modifying locally the current solution until no more improvement is possible. The main issue in local improvement algorithms is of course the choice of the transformation. Technically, this is achieved by choosing a *neighborhood* which defines a set of solutions closely related to the current solution.[6] The neighborhood should be large enough to produce good solutions and small enough for the runtime to be reasonable. A typical neighborhood, called *k-exchange*, consists of exchanging k elements of T by k elements from $S \setminus T$. We illustrate local search on two examples.

Example 5 (Graph Partitioning). Let $G = (V, E)$ be a complete graph with $2n$ vertices and associate a cost d_{ij} with each edge (i, j). The graph partitioning problem consists of finding a partition $V = A \cup B$ $(A \cap B = \emptyset)$ such that $\sum_{i \in A, j \in B} d_{ij}$ is minimized. Note that it is easy to find feasible solutions in this problem. Consider a feasible solution (A_1, B_1). The neighborhood can be defined as the set of all pairs (i, j) such that $i \in A_1$ and $j \in B_1$. Our transformation can simply select the pair (i, j) which produces the partition $(A_1 \setminus \{i\} \cup \{j\}, B_1 \setminus \{j\} \cup \{i\})$ minimizing the cost among all pair exchanges. □

Example 6 (TSP). In the TSP, the set T of the above model is the set of edges in the current tour. Note that it is not as trivial to generate a feasible solution and the neighborhood is also more complicated. A k-exchange neighborhood consists of exchanging k edges from T with k edges from $S \setminus T$ such that the result be a tour. For instance, if $k = 2$ and if $\langle i_1, \ldots, i_k, i_{k+1}, \ldots, i_l, i_{l+1}, \ldots, i_n \rangle$ is a tour, we could replace the edges (i_k, i_{k+1}) and (i_l, i_{l+1}) by the edges (i_k, i_l) and (i_{k+1}, i_{l+1}) to obtain the tour $\langle i_1, \ldots, i_k, i_l, i_{l-1}, \ldots, i_{k+1}, i_{l+1}, \ldots, i_n \rangle$. 3-exchange has been shown to produce excellent results for the TSP in reasonable time. 3-exchange produces much better results than 2-exchange. In addition, 4-exchange is only marginally better than 3-exchange but it requires much more computation. [30] □.

Note that there is no reason to limit ourselves to a unique initial starting solution. We could actually generate a large number (say 100) and select the best result from all these runs. This is a common technique in local search. An obvious limitation of the above local improvement schemes is that the neighborhood is fixed once for all to a given k and determining an appropriate k is very much an experimental endeavour. This limitation has been addressed in various ways in the past.

Dynamic Local Improvement An elegant solution was proposed by Kerninghan and Lin and consists of trying to identify k dynamically. Consider the graph-partitioning example again, let (A^*, B^*) be the optimum solution and (A, B) be the current partitioning. It is easy to see that we can find some sets

---

[6] Note that, in the simplex algorithm, the neighborhood is defined as the set of adjacent vertices.

$X \subseteq A$ and $Y \subseteq B$ such that

$$A^* = (A \setminus X) \cup Y$$
$$B^* = (B \setminus Y) \cup X$$

Therefore it is necessary to find $|X| = k$ elements in A to exchange in order to obtain an optimal solution. Of course, we do not know k but the key idea behind the scheme proposed here is to try to find it dynamically. This is achieved by exchanging $|A|$ elements of A sequentially and picking up the best partitioning obtained during this sequence of exchanges. The transformation procedure looks like this:

procedure transform(T)
$\quad T_0 := T$;
$\quad$**for** $i := 1$ **to** $|T|$ **do**
$\quad\quad$**choose** $x_i \in T \setminus \{x_1, \ldots, x_{i-1}\}$;
$\quad\quad$**choose** $y_i \in S \setminus (\{y_1, \ldots, y_{i-1}\} \cup \{T\})$;
$\quad\quad$**exchange** (x_i, y_i) in T_{i-1} to produce T_i at cost C_i;
$\quad$**return** T_k such that $C_k = min_{j=1}^{|T|} C_j$.

The above procedure has also the interesting side-effect of letting the transformation explore several solutions whose costs are worse than the current solution before producing eventually an improvement. As a consequence, it enables the algorithm to escape local minima. Escaping local minima has been a recurrent theme in local search.

Local Search Local search does not really require that the new selected solution be an improvement over previous ones. Many systems and algorithms, such as simulated annealling and GSAT allows transformations not producing improvements from time to time. The key issue then becomes the termination criteria and different algorithms adopt different criteria.

Link to Constraint Programming 7 (Local Search). They are a number of constraint tools based on local search. The most well-known is probably GSAT [45], which uses local search to solve propositional problems. GSAT [45] is probably the fastest method to solve a variety of propositional problems. The same techniques can be adapted to provide a general algorithm for CSP. However, in practice, it may be more efficient to exploit the specificities of the problem to choose the neighborhood and to update the solution efficiently.

4 Continuous Combinatorial Search Problems

In this section, we consider the solving of continuous combinatorial search problems expressed as polynomial systems. As stated previously, these problems are NP-hard and remains so even when floating-point approximations are considered acceptable. Moreover, these problems raise the issue of numerical accuracy. A well-known illustration of this problem [43] is given by the function

$$f(x, y) = 333.75y^6 + x^2(11x^2y^2 - y^6 - 121y^4 - 2) + 5.5y^8 + \frac{x}{2y}$$

when evaluated on $x = 77617$ and $y = 33096$. The evaluation produces, on some systems, the following results

Single Precision   1.172603...
Double Precision   1.1726039400531...
Extended Precision 1.172603940053178...

Although these results seem consistent with each other, they are completely wrong, since the correct answer is -0.8273960599468213 with an error of at most one unit in the last digit. This example shows that sometimes even verifying that an assignment of values is a solution may be difficult when floating-point numbers are used. The goal of this section is to review some numerical techniques to solve polynomial systems of equations. We do not review symbolic methods such as Groebner basis [6], cylindric decomposition [11], and resultant techniques [29]. Moreover, we focus here on the basic ideas and often restrict attention to simple cases to convey the underlying principles easily. The presentations here are based on [19, 37, 48].

4.1 Quasi-Newton Methods

Newton's method is a very effective way of solving an equation

$$f(x) = 0$$

when a reasonable guess of the solution(s) can be exhibited. Consider an approximation x_i of the solution. The key idea of Newton's method is to take the derivative at x_0, and to intersect it with the x-axis to obtain a new guess x_{i+1}

$$x_{i+1} = x_i - \frac{f(x_i)}{f'(x_i)}.$$

This method is very effective when the initial guess x_0 is closed to the root: it converges quadratically to the root. As a consequence, many numerical algorithms used to solve polynomial systems use Newton's method in one form or another. However, the method can also fail completely when the initial guess is poor. For instance, for the function $f(x) = \arctan x$, Newton's method produces the cycle $x_1 = -x_0; x_2 = x_0; x_3 = -x_0; \ldots$ for some $x_0 \in [1.39, 1.40]$. Quasi-Newton methods upgrades Newton's method by adding a more global component. The underlying principle is as follows. Suppose that the new guess x_{i+1} does not improve our current value x_i, i.e., $|f(x_{i+1})| > |f(x_i)|$. Since the derivative at x_i points in the direction of a local decrease of the absolute value of the function, the basic idea is to roll back from x_{i+1} to x_i in search of a point y such that $|f(y)| < |f(x_i)|$. A possible solution is to apply the following iteration step

$$x_{i+1} := x_i - f(x_i)/f'(x_i);$$
while $|f(x_{i+1})| > |f(x_i)|$ **do**
$$x_{i+1} := (x_i + x_{i+1})/2;$$

It should be mentioned however that quasi-Newton methods are not guaranteed to be complete and can miss solutions, especially on hard problems. This can be unfortunate in some situations where the system of constraints admits both physical and non-physical solutions. The method may possibly converge systematically towards a non-physical solution.

Link to Constraint Programming 8 (Newton's Method). Newton's method has been in a number of constraint-based graphics systems [23, 38].

4.2 Continuation Methods

We now turn to continuation (or homotopy) methods [37, 50] which are theoretically guaranteed to find all isolated solutions to polynomial systems. Continuation methods also exploit Newton's method but are extremely careful in choosing appropriate guesses. The basic idea behind continuation methods is as follows. Instead of solving the original problem directly, a continuation method solves another problem P_0 which has at least as many solutions as the original problem. Then this new problem is modified slightly to produce problem P_1 and the solutions of P_0 are used as guesses for P_1. The method thus generates a sequence of problems $P_0, P_1, \ldots, P_n$, the last one being the original problem, and the solutions for P_i are used as the guesses for P_{i+1}. Let us illustrate this on a quadratic equation

$$x^2 + ax + b = 0.$$

We know that such an equation has at most two solutions. To generate the sequence of problems, we use the continuation

$$c(x, t) = x^2 + atx + b$$

where t is a new variable. The sequence of problems to solve is simply

$$c(x, t) = 0$$

for various values of t. The initial problem P_0 is $c(x, 0) = 0$ which we can solve easily. The last problem P_n is simply $c(x, 1) = 0$ and the intermediary problems are given by choosing increasing values of t between 0 and 1. By choosing small increments, we can make sure that the solutions of problems P_i are appropriate guesses for the problem P_{i+1}. Consider the equation

$$x^2 + 3x - 4 = 0.$$

The two solutions of $c(x, 0) = 0$ are -2 and 2. We can use them as guesses for solving $c(x, 0.05) = 0$ to produce, say, 1.926 and -2.076 which can be used as guesses to solve $c(x, 0.1) = 0$ and so on until we obtain the two solutions of our initial problem.

To make this idea work in full generality, it is necessary to consider complex numbers to avoid the method to get stuck as shown by the equation

$$x^2 + 3x + 4 = 0.$$

Also, it is necessary to take care of an issue known as path crossing, which means that two solutions merge, making it impossible for the method to be complete. This happens for instance for the continuation

$$x^2 - 4tx + 1$$

when $t = 0.5$ in which case there is only one solution. This problem can be fixed by using randomization techniques.

The above ideas generalize easily to systems of equations. Consider two equations in two variables x, y

$$f_1(x, y) = 0$$
$$f_2(x, y) = 0$$

The continuation used to generate the problem for this example can be

$$(1 - t)(p_1^2 x^2 - q_1^2) + t f_1(x, y) = 0$$
$$(1 - t)(p_2^2 x^2 - q_2^2) + t f_2(x, y) = 0$$

where the p_i and q_i are random complex numbers. When t is zero, the system has four solutions that can be easily computed. Note that a system of two quadratic equations exhibit another issue that must be dealt with by continuation methods: solutions at infinity. Consider two equations

$$a_1 x^2 + b_1 y^2 + c_1 xy + d_1 x + e_1 y + f_1 = 0$$
$$a_2 x^2 + b_2 y^2 + c_2 xy + d_2 x + e_2 y + f_2 = 0$$

and assume that (v_x, v_y) is a solution to

$$a_1 x^2 + b_1 y^2 + c_1 xy = 0$$
$$a_2 x^2 + b_2 y^2 + c_2 xy = 0.$$

Hence, (rv_x, rv_y) is also a solution to this last system and r can be made arbitrary large. Plugging (rv_x, rv_y) in the original system and dividing by r^2 produces expressions

$$(a_1 v_x^2 + b_1 v_y^2 + c_1 v_x v_y) + \frac{1}{r}(d_1 v_x + e_1 v_y + f_1)$$
$$(a_2 v_x^2 + b_2 v_y^2 + c_2 v_x v_y) + \frac{1}{r}(d_2 v_x + e_2 v_y + f_2)$$

which go to zero when r is made very large. Detecting or finding solutions at infinity may be difficult but randomization techniques can be used to rewrite the system so that the problem disappears.

Continuation methods are excellent techniques when the constraint system is small (say, less than 10-20 variables). They cannot deal with large number of variables since they have to generate a number of initial solutions which depends on the degree of the systems.

4.3   Interval Methods

Interval methods are another technique which can be used to isolate all solutions to polynomial systems. Interval methods are branch and prune algorithms which associate an interval of floating point numbers with each variable of the problem. The relaxation step uses constraints to reduce the intervals of the variables. Intervals are also used to bound numerical errors in order to guarantee the completeness of the method.

We start with some definitions. An interval $[l, u]$ represents the set of real numbers

$$\{r \in \Re \mid l \leq r \leq u\}$$

and the set of intervals is denoted by $\mathcal{I}$ and is ordered by set inclusion.

Definition 9 (Enclosure and Hull). Let S be a subset of $\Re$. The enclosure of S, denoted by $\overline{S}$ or $box\{S\}$, is the smallest interval I such that $S \subseteq I$. We often write $\overline{r}$ instead of $\overline{\{r\}}$ for $r \in \Re$.

The main concept behind interval methods is the notion of interval extension.

Definition 10 (Interval Extension). $F : \mathcal{I}^n \to \mathcal{I}$ is an interval extension of $f : \Re^n \to \Re$ iff

$$\forall I_1 \ldots I_n \in \mathcal{I} : r_1 \in I_1, \ldots, r_n \in I_n \Rightarrow f(r_1, \ldots, r_n) \in F(I_1, \ldots, I_n).$$

An interval relation $C : \mathcal{I}^n \to Bool$ is an interval extension of a relation $c : \Re^n \to Bool$ iff

$$\forall I_1 \ldots I_n \in \mathcal{I} : [\, \exists r_1 \in I_1, \ldots, \exists r_n \in I_n \; c(r_1, \ldots, r_n) \,] \Rightarrow C(I_1, \ldots, I_n).$$

Example 7. The interval function $\oplus$ defined as

$$[a_1, b_1] \oplus [a_2, b_2] = [\lfloor a_1 + a_2 \rfloor, \lceil b_1 + b_2 \rceil]$$

is an interval extension of addition of real numbers. The interval relation $\doteq$ defined as

$$I_1 \doteq I_2 \; \Leftrightarrow \; (I_1 \cap I_2 \neq \emptyset)$$

is an interval extension of the equality relation on real numbers.

Newton's method can be generalized to work with intervals, producing the interval Newton method, a branch and prune algorithm which is one of the best tools to find roots of univariate polynomials. The relaxation step uses an interval version of the Newton iteration step. Given a function f, its derivative f', and interval extensions F and F' of f and f', the relaxation step uses the following property

"every zero of f in I lies also in $N(F, F', I)$"

where

$$N(F, F', I) = I \sqcap \overline{[center(I) - \frac{F(center(I))}{F'(I)}]}.$$

More precisely, the algorithm uses $N^*(F, F', I) = \bigcap_{i=0}^{\infty} I_i$ where

$$I_0 = I$$
$$I_{i+1} = N(F, F', I_i) \ (0 \leq i).$$

Newton Interval method can then be seen as the iteration of two steps:

1. a pruning step which applies $N^*(F, F', I)$ to the current interval I;
2. a splitting step which splits the current interval in two parts to define two new subproblems.

It is interesting to note that the pruning step is very similar to the basic step of Newton's method. The main difference is the fact that the derivative is evaluated over the intervals to avoid "overshooting" the roots.

The method can be generalized easily to systems of equations. See for instance [26] for a traditional algorithm which is guaranteed to isolate all zeros. Recently, much progress has been made in this area by applying consistency techniques to polynomial systems (e.g., [27, 48]). The Newton system enforces an approximation of arc-consistency, called box-consistency, that can be defined as follows:

Definition 11 (Box-Consistency). An interval constraint C is box-consistent wrt x_i and $\mathbf{I} = \langle I_1, \ldots, I_n \rangle$ iff

$$C(I_1, \ldots, I_{i-1}, [l, l^+], I_{i+1}, \ldots, I_n) \wedge C(I_1, \ldots, I_{i-1}, [u^-, u], I_{i+1}, \ldots, I_n).$$

where $l = left(I_i)$ and $u = right(I_i)$ and l^+, l^- denotes respectively the smallest floating point number greater than l and the largest floating point number smaller than l.

The resulting system has been shown to be competitive with continuation methods on their benchmarks and to outperform them a number of other benchmarks from numerical analysis. Interval techniques are also effective for (unconstrained and constrained) optimization problems. Viewing continuous problems as discrete problems seems thus to be a promising approach in this field.

Link to Constraint Programming 12 (Interval Methods). Interval methods have been introduced in constraint programming by BNR-Prolog [40] and they are now the basis of a number of systems. The above techniques are included in the constraint programming language Newton [3, 48] which is probably one of the fastest interval tools available for a wide range of applications.

5 Conclusion

This tutorial has reviewed a number of constraint-solving techniques for combinatorial search problems and has tried to link some of them to constraint programming research. It is worth mentioning that many available techniques are already in use in many constraint programming tools, although much progress remains to be achieved to develop tools that compare well with specific programs. It should be interesting to review how much constraint programming will achieve in the next few years.

Acknowledgments

I would like to thank Ugo Montanari for inviting me to give this tutorial and making me think about these issues. Special thanks also to Deepak Kapur, Philip Klein, and David McAllester for numerous discussions on this topic. This work was supported in part by the Office of Naval Research under grant ONR Grant N00014-94-1-1153, the National Science Foundation under grant numbers CCR-9357704, a NSF National Young Investigator Award with matching funds of Hewlett-Packard.

References

1. E. Balas. Disjunctive Programming. *Annals of Discrete Mathematics*, 5:3–51, 1979.
2. R.E. Bellman. *Dynamic Programming*. Princeton University Press, Princeton, NJ, 1957.
3. F. Benhamou, D. McAllester, and P. Van Hentenryck. CLP(Intervals) Revisited. In *Proceedings of the International Symposium on Logic Programming (ILPS-94)*, pages 124–138, Ithaca, NY, November 1994.
4. A. Bockmayr. 0-1 Constraints and 0-1 Optimization. In *Proc. 3rd Workshop on Constraint Logic Programming*, Marseilles, France, 1993.
5. Maurice Bruynooghe. In J.L. Lassez and G. Plotkin, editors, *Computational Logic, Essays in Honour of Alan Robinson*, pages 166–177. Cambridge, Massachusetts.
6. B. Buchberger. Groebner Bases: An Algorithmic Method in Polynomial Ideal Theory. In *Multidimensional Systems Theory*, pages 184–232. N.K. Bose Ed., D. Reidel Publishing Co., 1985.
7. J. Carlier and E. Pinson. Une Méthode Arborescente pour Optimiser la Durée d'un JOB-SHOP. Technical Report ISSN 0294-2755, I.M.A, Angers, 1986.
8. Y. Caseau, P.-Y. Guillo, and E. Levenez. A Deductive and Object-Oriented Approach to a Complex Scheduling Problem. In *Proc. of DOOD'93*, Phoenix, AZ, December 1989.
9. V. Chvátal. Edmonds Polytopes and Weakly Hamiltonian Graphs. *Mathematical Programming*, 5:29–40, 1973.
10. C. Codognet and P. Codognet. Guarded Constructive Disjunction: Angel or Demon? In *First International Conference on Principles and Practice of Constraint Programming (CP'95)*, Cassis, France, September 1995. Springer Verlag.

11. G.E. Collins. Quantifier Elimination for the Elementary Theory of Real Closed Fields by Cylindrical Algebraic Decomposition. In *Lecture Notes In Computer Science, Vol. 33*, pages 134–183. Springer Verlag, Berlin, 1975.

12. A. Colmerauer. An Introduction to Prolog III. *Commun. ACM*, 28(4):412–418, 1990.

13. T.H. Cormen, C.E. Leiserson, and R.L Rivest. *Introduction to Algorithms*. MIT Press, Cambridge, 1990.

14. G.B. Dantzig. A Note on Solving Linear Programs in Integers. *Naval Research*, 5(2):75–76, 1959.

15. G.B. Dantzig. *Linear Programming and Extensions*. Princeton University Press, Princeton, N.J., 1963.

16. G.B. Dantzig, D.R Fulkerson, and S.M. Johnson. Solution of a Large-Scale Travelling Salesman Problem. *Operations Research*, 2:393–410, 1955.

17. B. de Backer and H. Beringer. A clp language handling disjunctions of linear constraints. In *Proceedings of the Tenth International Conference on Logic Programming (ICLP-93)*, Budapest (Hungary), June 1993.

18. R. Dechter. Constraint Networks. In *Encyclopedia of Artificial Intelligence (Second Edition)*. Stuart C. Shapiro Editor, Wiley, 1992.

19. J.E. Dennis and R.B. Schnabel. *Numerical Methods for Unconstrained Optimization and Nonlinear Equations*. Prentice Hall, Englewood Cliffs, New Jersey, 1983.

20. M. Dincbas, P. Van Hentenryck, H. Simonis, A. Aggoun, T. Graf, and F. Berthier. The Constraint Logic Programming Language CHIP. In *Proceedings of the International Conference on Fifth Generation Computer Systems*, Tokyo, Japan, December 1988.

21. E. Freuder. Partial Constraint Satisfaction. *Artificial Intelligence*, 58, 1992.

22. R.S Garfinkel and G.L Nemhauser. *Integer Programming*. John Wiley & Sons, New York, 1972.

23. M. Gleicher. Practical Issues in Programming Constraints. In V. Saraswat and P. Van Hentenryck, editors, *Principles and Practice of Constraint Programming*. The MIT Press, Cambridge, Massachussetts, 1995.

24. R.E. Gomory. An Algorithm for Integer Solutions to Linear Programs. In R. Graves and P. Wolfe, editors, *Recent Advances in Mathematical Programming*, pages 269–302. McGraw-Hill, 1963.

25. R.E. Gomory. On the Relation between Integer and Non-Integer Solutions to Linear Programs. *Proceedings of the National Academy of Science*, 53:260–265, 1965.

26. E.R. Hansen and R.I. Greenberg. An Interval Newton Method. *Appl. Math. Comput.*, 12:89–98, 1983.

27. H. Hong and V. Stahl. Safe Starting Regions by Fixed Points and Tightening. *Computing*, 53(3-4):323–335, 1994.

28. J. Jaffar, S. Michaylov, P.J. Stuckey, and R. Yap. The CLP($\Re$) language and system. *ACM Trans. on Programming Languages and Systems*, 14(3):339–395, 1992.

29. D. Kapur, T. Saxena, and L. Yang. Algebraic and Geometric Reasoning using Dixon Resultants. In *Proceedings of Intl. Symp. on Symbolic and Algebraic Computation (ISSAC-94)*,, pages 99–107, Oxford, England, July 1994.

30. S. Lin. Computer Solutions of the Travelling Salesman Problem. *Bell System Tech. Journal*, 44:2245–2269, 1965.

31. A.K. Mackworth. Consistency in Networks of Relations. *Artificial Intelligence*, 8(1):99–118, 1977.

32. A.K. Mackworth. Constraint Satisfaction. In *Encyclopedia of Artificial Intelligence (Second Edition)*. Stuart C. Shapiro Editor, Wiley, 1992.

33. K. McAloon and C. Tretkoff. 2LP: Linear Programming and Logic Programming. In V. Saraswat and P. Van Hentenryck, editors, *Principles and Practice of Constraint Programming*. The MIT Press, Cambridge, Massachussetts, 1995.

34. S. Minton, M.D. Johnston, and A.B. Philips. Solving Large-Scale Constraint Satisfaction and Scheduling Problems using a Heuristic Repair Method. In *AAAI-90*, August 1990.

35. U. Montanari. Networks of Constraints : Fundamental Properties and Applications to Picture Processing. *Information Science*, 7(2):95–132, 1974.

36. U. Montanari and F. Rossi. An efficient algorithm for the solution of hierarchical networks of constraints. In *Workshop on Graph Grammars and Their Applications in Computer Science*, Warrenton, December 1986.

37. A.P. Morgan. *Solving Polynomial Systems Using Continuation for Scientific and Engineering Problems*. Prentice-Hall, Englewood Cliffs, NJ, 1987.

38. G. Nelson. Juno, a constraint-based graphics system. In *ACM SIGGRAPH'85*, pages 301–309, San Francisco, CA, July 1985.

39. G.L. Nemhauser and L.A. Wolsey. *Integer and Combinatorial Optimization*. John Wiley & Sons, New York, 1988.

40. W. Older and A. Vellino. Extending Prolog with Constraint Arithmetics on Real Intervals. In *Canadian Conference on Computer & Electrical Engineering*, Ottawa, 1990.

41. M. W. Padberg. Covering, Packing, and Knapsack Problems. *Annals of Discrete Mathematics*, 4:265–287, 1979.

42. J.F. Puget and P. Albert. PECOS: Programmation par Contraintes Orientee Objets. *Genie Logiciel and Systemes Experts*, 23, 1991.

43. S.M. Rump. Algorithm for Verified Inclusions-Theory and Practice. In *Reliability in Computing*, pages 109–126. Academic Press, San Diego, 1988.

44. H.M. Salkin and K. Mathur. *Foundations of Integer Programming*. North-Holland, 1989.

45. B. Selman, H. Levesque, and D. Mitchell. A NEw Method for Solving Hard Satisfiability Problems. In *AAAI-92*, pages 440–446, 1992.

46. P. Van Hentenryck. *Constraint Satisfaction in Logic Programming*. Logic Programming Series, The MIT Press, Cambridge, Mass., 1989.

47. P. Van Hentenryck and Y. Deville. The Cardinality Operator: A New Logical Connective and Its Application to Constraint Logic Programming. In *Eighth International Conference on Logic Programming (ICLP-91)*, Paris (France), June 1991.

48. P. Van Hentenryck, D. McAllister, and D. Kapur. Solving Polynomial Systems Using a Branch and Prune Approach. *SIAM Journal on Numerical Analysis*, 1995. (to appear).

49. P. Van Hentenryck, V. Saraswat, and Y. Deville. The Design, Implementation, and Evaluation of the Constraint Language cc(FD). In *Constraint Programming: Basics and Trends*. Springer Verlag, 1995.

50. J Verschelde, P. Verlinden, and R. Cools. Homotopies Exploiting Newton Polytopes For Solving Sparse Polynomial Systems. *SIAM Journal on Numerical Analysis*, 31(3):915–930, 1994.

51. D. Waltz. Generating Semantic Descriptions from Drawings of Scenes with Shadows. Technical Report AI271, MIT, MA, November 1972.

The Concurrent Constraint Programming Research Programmes

Vijay Saraswat

Abstract. Concurrent constraint programming (CCP) was introduced eight years ago as a simple combination of ideas from concurrent logic programming and constraint logic programming, developed in the style of process algebras.

It seems that three meta-themes have characterized the development of this subject. CCP has been explored as a foundational paradigm for concurrent computation, resulting in the development of mathematical models of computation characterized by monotonic accumulation of information. Several concrete results have been obtained, including general and fully abstract models for different combinations of control features, and connections between operational semantics and logical deduction. Second, CCP has been pursued as a clean conceptualization of concurrent logic programming — leading for example, to work on failure-free systems for distributed computation, such as Janus — and as an extension to constraint logic programming, as in the development of the language AKL, which emphasizes encapsulated non-determinism. Last, CCP has been used as the basis for instantiating an approach to software development (called model-based computing) based on explicit declarative modeling of the systems and processes at hand, and on the systematic, rigorous generation from these models of software for simulating, controlling, diagnosing and documenting these systems. This approach has proven to be particularly appropriate when the systems at hand are complex physical systems, such as those used for digital reprographics. Constraints arise very naturally in analyzing and modeling physical systems, and CCP languages therefore provide a powerful declarative cum procedural formalism for this approach. However, a flexible representation of time, and time-based control constructs, is crucial for modeling physical systems; and this focus has led to the development of discrete timed and hybrid CCP, obtained by integrating in ideas from synchronous programming. The talk will make an effort to cover the basic results in the theoretical, practical and implementational approaches in this field, and convey their underlying unity.

Automatic Generation of Invariants and Intermediate Assertions *

Nikolaj Bjørner, Anca Browne and Zohar Manna

Computer Science Department
Stanford University
Stanford, CA 94305

Abstract. Verifying temporal specifications of reactive and concurrent systems commonly relies on generating auxiliary assertions and strengthening given properties of the system. Two dual approaches find solutions to these problems: the *bottom-up* method performs an abstract forward propagation of the system, generating auxiliary properties; the *top-down* method performs an abstract backward propagation to strengthen given properties. *Exact* application of these methods is complete but is usually infeasible for large-scale verification. An *approximate analysis* can often supply enough information to complete the verification.
The paper overviews some of the exact and approximate analysis methods to generate and strengthen assertions for the verification of invariance properties. By formulating and analyzing a generic safety verification rule we extend these methods to the verification of general temporal safety properties.

Contents

1 Introduction

The deductive verification of reactive and concurrent systems commonly relies upon finding suitable auxiliary assertions and strengthened properties to complete the proof [MP95]. This paper describes a number of systematic methods for generating invariants and intermediate assertions that can help in the verification of temporal safety properties.

An invariant of a system S is a first-order formula (an *assertion*) that holds at every state of its computations. Deductive methods provide a verification rule

---

* This research was supported in part by the National Science Foundation under grant CCR-92-23226, the Advanced Research Projects Agency under NASA grant NAG2-892, the United States Air Force Office of Scientific Research under grant F49620-93-1-0139, and the Department of the Army under grant DAAH04-95-1-0317.

that establishes invariants from first-order premises. These premises require an auxiliary first-order assertion which strengthens the invariant being proved. We will examine two ways of finding the strengthening assertion: forward propagation is a symbolic forward execution of S that summarizes the set of reachable states as a first-order formula; backward propagation executes S backwards from the states satisfying the invariant and also generates a first-order formula. We will see that both methods, in principle, generate adequate candidates for the auxiliary assertion.

We formulate a verification rule applicable to arbitrary temporal safety properties, and show how forward and backward propagation can be generalized to this setting. General temporal safety properties can express properties such as first-in-first-out ordering, causality and bounded overtaking.

Exact forward or backward propagation of a system S may not terminate when the state space of S is infinite or unmanageably large. This motivates the study of approximate, but decidable, propagation methods over different domains. We overview techniques from linear algebra, linear programming and monadic second-order logic in a general framework. Early work on forward and backward propagation in program verification includes [GW75, KM76]. Linear algebra has long been applied to the automatic discovery of linear equalities between system variables [Lau73, Kar76]. Linear programming was proposed in [CH78] to express linear constraints among system variables in the form of convex polyhedra. It is also one of the most prominent examples of the abstract interpretation theory introduced in [CC77].[2] Monadic second-order logic applied in set-based program analysis [Hei92] provides unary constraints on the values of program variables. Table 1 categorizes the methods discussed in this paper.

Table 1. Approximation methods.

Domain	Constraint form	Solvers	Propagation
Linear equations	$A\bar{x} = b$	Linear algebra	Finite
Polyhedra	$A\bar{x} \leq b$	Linear programming	Approximate
Set-based	$x \in S, y \in T$	Tree automata	Implicit

Section 2 summarizes preliminary notions such as the computational model of reactive systems, linear-time temporal logic and fixedpoints. In Section 3 we present the verification rule for invariance and introduce bottom-up and top-down methods. The same is done for general safety properties in Section 4. Section 5 introduces approximation as a way to automatically perform the analysis presented in Sections 3 and 4. Finally, the surveyed methods are described in Sections 6, 7 and 8.

The methods described in this paper have proved useful as part of the verification system STeP, the _Stanford Temporal Prover_ [MAB+94]. STeP uses linear-time temporal logic in the specification of reactive and concurrent systems, and combines model checking with deductive techniques. The tools presented are auxiliary routines that can be invoked from STeP's deductive environment.

---

[2] Abstract interpretation is also being applied in connection with model checking [CGL92, DGG94].

2 Preliminaries

2.1 Transition Systems

Following [MP95], our computational model for reactive systems is that of a *transition system*, $S = \langle \mathcal{V}, \Theta, \mathcal{T} \rangle^3$, where $\mathcal{V}$ is a finite set of system variables, Θ is the initial condition, and $\mathcal{T}$ is a finite set of transitions. The vocabulary $\mathcal{V}$ contains data variables, control variables and auxiliary variables. The set of *states* (interpretations) over $\mathcal{V}$ is denoted by Σ. We assume a first-order assertion language $\mathcal{A}$ over $\mathcal{V}$. The initial condition Θ is an assertion in this language. A transition τ maps each state $s \in \Sigma$ into a (possibly empty) set of τ-successors, $\tau(s) \subseteq \Sigma$. It is defined by an assertion $\rho_\tau(\overline{x}, \overline{x}')$, called the *transition relation*, which relates the values $\overline{x}$ of the variables in state s and the values $\overline{x}'$ in a successor state $s' \in \tau(s)$. We require that $\mathcal{T}$ contain a transition τ_I, called the *idling transition*, such that $\tau(s) = \{s\}$ for every state s.

A computation of a system S is an infinite sequence of states $s_0, s_1, s_2, \ldots$, such that s_0 is an initial state satisfying Θ and for every $i \geq 0$ there is a transition $\tau \in \mathcal{T}$ satisfying $s_{i+1} \in \tau(s_i)$.

To facilitate the representation of systems, some of our examples are given in SPL (Simple Programming Language). SPL statements are translated into transitions in a straightforward manner. For example, the assignment statement

$$\ell_0 : x := y + 1;\ \ell_1 :$$

assigns $y + 1$ to x when control resides at location ℓ_0, and subsequently moves control to ℓ_1; it generates the transition τ with transition relation

$$\rho_\tau(\ell_0, \ell_1, x, y, \ell_0', \ell_1', x', y') : \quad \ell_0 \land x' = y + 1 \land y' = y \land \ell_1' \land \neg\ell_0' .$$

2.2 Preconditions and Postconditions

The weakest precondition $\mathrm{WP}(\tau, \varphi)(\overline{x})$ and strongest postcondition $\mathrm{SP}(\tau, \varphi)(\overline{x})$ of an assertion $\varphi(\overline{x})$, relative to a transition τ, are defined by

$$\mathrm{WP}(\tau, \varphi)(\overline{x}) \stackrel{\triangle}{=} \forall \overline{x}' \cdot \rho_\tau(\overline{x}, \overline{x}') \to \varphi(\overline{x}')$$
$$\mathrm{SP}(\tau, \varphi)(\overline{x}) \stackrel{\triangle}{=} \exists \overline{x}_0 \cdot \rho_\tau(\overline{x}_0, \overline{x}) \land \varphi(\overline{x}_0) .$$

WP characterizes the states that must reach a φ-state (i.e., a state satisfying φ) by taking τ. SP characterizes the states reachable from a φ-state by taking τ. For example, transitions associated with guarded assignments of the form **if** $c(\overline{x})$ **then** $\overline{x} := e(\overline{x})$ have transition relations of the form $\rho_\tau : c(\overline{x}) \land \overline{x}' = e(\overline{x})$. Their weakest precondition, $\mathrm{WP}(\tau, \varphi)(\overline{x}) : \forall \overline{x}'. c(\overline{x}) \land \overline{x}' = e(\overline{x}) \to \varphi(\overline{x}')$, can be simplified to $\mathrm{WP}(\tau, \varphi)(\overline{x}) : c(\overline{x}) \to \varphi(e(\overline{x}))$.

The two operators are monotone in φ since all occurrences of φ are positive, i.e., they are under the scope of an even number of negations. Thus,

$$(\varphi \to \psi) \to (\mathrm{WP}(\tau, \varphi) \to \mathrm{WP}(\tau, \psi)), \quad (\varphi \to \psi) \to (\mathrm{SP}(\tau, \varphi) \to \mathrm{SP}(\tau, \psi)).$$

---

[3] Fairness assumptions are ignored when establishing safety properties.

Let τ^{-1} be the inverse of τ, i.e., $\rho_{\tau^{-1}}(\overline{x}, \overline{y}) \triangleq \rho_\tau(\overline{y}, \overline{x})$. Then we observe

$$\text{WP}(\tau, \neg\varphi) \quad \leftrightarrow \neg\text{SP}(\tau^{-1}, \varphi) \qquad\qquad \text{SP}(\tau, \neg\varphi) \quad \leftrightarrow \neg\text{WP}(\tau^{-1}, \varphi)$$
$$\text{WP}(\tau, \varphi \wedge \psi) \leftrightarrow \text{WP}(\tau, \varphi) \wedge \text{WP}(\tau, \psi) \qquad \text{SP}(\tau, \varphi \vee \psi) \leftrightarrow \text{SP}(\tau, \varphi) \vee \text{SP}(\tau, \psi)$$
$$\text{WP}(\tau, \varphi \vee \psi) \leftarrow \text{WP}(\tau, \varphi) \vee \text{WP}(\tau, \psi) \qquad \text{SP}(\tau, \varphi \wedge \psi) \rightarrow \text{SP}(\tau, \varphi) \wedge \text{SP}(\tau, \psi).$$

We will also use the notation

$$\text{WP}(\mathcal{T}, \varphi) \triangleq \bigwedge_{\tau \in \mathcal{T}} \text{WP}(\tau, \varphi) \qquad\qquad \text{SP}(\mathcal{T}, \varphi) \triangleq \bigvee_{\tau \in \mathcal{T}} \text{SP}(\tau, \varphi) .$$

Notice that

$$\varphi \rightarrow \text{WP}(\mathcal{T}, \psi) \quad \text{iff} \quad \text{SP}(\mathcal{T}, \varphi) \rightarrow \psi .$$

2.3   Linear-Time Temporal Logic

We specify properties of reactive systems using linear-time temporal logic. A *temporal formula* is constructed from state formulas (called *assertions*), which are formulas from the first-order assertion language $\mathcal{A}$. To state formulas we apply boolean operators (such as $\vee$, $\neg$), quantifiers ($\forall$, $\exists$) and temporal operators. The temporal operators used in this paper are future operators $\square$ (*always in the future*), W (*waiting-for, unless*), $\bigcirc$ (*next*) and their past counterparts $\boxminus$ (*always in the past*), B (*back-to*) and $\ominus$ (*previously*).

A *model* for a temporal formula φ is an infinite sequence of states σ : $s_0, s_1, s_2, \ldots$, where each state s_j provides an interpretation for the variables occurring in φ. Given a model σ, we present an inductive definition of the notion of φ holding at position j, $j \geq 0$, in σ, denoted by $\langle \sigma, j \rangle \vDash \varphi$:

$$\langle \sigma, j \rangle \vDash \varphi \qquad \Longleftrightarrow s_j \vDash \varphi \qquad\qquad\qquad\qquad \text{if } \varphi \in \mathcal{A}$$

That is, φ is evaluated locally, using the interpretation in s_j

$$\langle \sigma, j \rangle \vDash \bigcirc \varphi \quad \Longleftrightarrow \langle \sigma, j + 1 \rangle \vDash \varphi$$
$$\langle \sigma, j \rangle \vDash \square \varphi \quad \Longleftrightarrow \forall j' : j' \geq j \cdot \langle \sigma, j' \rangle \vDash \varphi$$
$$\langle \sigma, j \rangle \vDash \varphi \, W \, \psi \Longleftrightarrow \forall j' : j' \geq j \cdot \langle \sigma, j' \rangle \vDash \varphi \ \text{ or}$$
$$\exists k : k \geq j \cdot \langle \sigma, k \rangle \vDash \psi \text{ and } \forall j' : j \leq j' < k \cdot \langle \sigma, j' \rangle \vDash \varphi$$
$$\langle \sigma, j \rangle \vDash \ominus \varphi \quad \Longleftrightarrow j > 0 \text{ and } \langle \sigma, j - 1 \rangle \vDash \varphi$$
$$\langle \sigma, j \rangle \vDash \boxminus \varphi \quad \Longleftrightarrow \forall j' : 0 \leq j' \leq j \cdot \langle \sigma, j' \rangle \vDash \varphi$$
$$\langle \sigma, j \rangle \vDash \varphi \, B \, \psi \Longleftrightarrow \forall j' : 0 \leq j' \leq j \cdot \langle \sigma, j' \rangle \vDash \varphi \ \text{ or}$$
$$\exists k : 0 \leq k \leq j \cdot \langle \sigma, k \rangle \vDash \psi \text{ and } \forall j' : j \geq j' > k \cdot \langle \sigma, j' \rangle \vDash \varphi$$

Other temporal connectives are defined as abbreviations, e.g., $\Diamond\varphi = \neg\,\square\neg\varphi$, $\diamondsuit \varphi = \neg\,\boxminus\neg\varphi$.

A temporal formula φ is $\mathcal{S}$-*valid*, denoted $\mathcal{S} \vDash \varphi$, if for each computation σ of $\mathcal{S}$, $\langle \sigma, 0 \rangle \vDash \varphi$. A state s is said to be an $\mathcal{S}$-*reachable* state if it can be reached by some computation of $\mathcal{S}$. A state formula φ is $\mathcal{S}$-*state valid* if $s \vDash \varphi$ for every $\mathcal{S}$-reachable state s of $\mathcal{S}$. See [MP95] for a more detailed discussion of linear-time temporal logic and reactive systems.

2.4 Fixedpoints

The least fixedpoint of a monotone operator $G : \mathcal{A} \mapsto \mathcal{A}$ is denoted by $\mu X.G(X)$ and the greatest fixedpoint of G is denoted by $\nu X.G(X)$. The denotation of an assertion φ in $\mathcal{A}$ is the subset of Σ, where φ holds, i.e., $[\![\varphi]\!] = \{s \in \Sigma \mid s \vDash \varphi\}$. If X is denoted by the set $S \subseteq \Sigma$, then $[\![G(X)]\!]_{[S/X]}$ is the denotation of $G(X)$. The denotations of the fixedpoint operators are defined as

$$[\![\mu X.G(X)]\!] \;\triangleq\; \bigcap \{S \subseteq \Sigma \mid [\![G(X)]\!]_{[S/X]} \subseteq S\}$$
$$[\![\nu X.G(X)]\!] \;\triangleq\; \bigcup \{S \subseteq \Sigma \mid S \subseteq [\![G(X)]\!]_{[S/X]}\} \;.$$

The monotonicity of G ensures that $[\![\mu X.G(X)]\!]$ is the unique least fixedpoint, i.e., the least set S such that $S = [\![G(X)]\!]_{[S/X]}$, and that $[\![\nu X.G(X)]\!]$ is the unique greatest fixedpoint.

When finding or approximating fixedpoints in the assertion language $\mathcal{A}$ itself we will examine sequences that may or may not converge to the fixedpoints in a finite number of steps: by applying G repeatedly to F (false) we generate the ascending sequence $\text{F}, G(\text{F}), G^{(2)}(\text{F}), \ldots$, which, when it converges in a finite number of iterations, produces an assertion in $\mathcal{A}$ equivalent to $\mu X.G(X)$. Similarly, by computing the descending sequence $\text{T}, G(\text{T}), G^{(2)}(\text{T}), \ldots$, starting from T (true), one may find an assertion in $\mathcal{A}$ equivalent to $\nu X.G(X)$.

3 Invariance

An assertion p is S-*invariant* (*invariant* for short) if $S \vDash \Box p$. To establish that a given assertion p is S-invariant, we use the verification rule INV (Figure 1). This sound and relatively complete proof rule reduces the verification of $\Box p$ to first-order premises. For a given transition system S and assertion p, to prove

For transition system $\langle \mathcal{V}, \Theta, \mathcal{T} \rangle$, and
assertions p and φ

$$
\begin{array}{ll}
I1 & \Theta \rightarrow \varphi \\
I2 & \varphi \rightarrow p \\
I3 & \{\varphi\}\, \mathcal{T}\, \{\varphi\} \\
\hline
& S \vDash \Box p
\end{array}
$$

Fig. 1. Rule INV (invariance)

that $\Box p$ is S-valid, we have to find a strengthened assertion φ such that the first-order premises are S-state valid.

In premise $I3$ we use the notation

$$\{\varphi\} \, T \, \{\psi\} = \bigwedge_{\tau \in T} \{\varphi\}\tau\{\psi\}$$

where each *verification condition* $\{\varphi\}\tau\{\psi\}$ can be expressed equivalently as

standard: $\qquad\qquad \forall \overline{x} \forall \overline{x}' \cdot [\varphi(\overline{x}) \,\wedge\, \rho_\tau(\overline{x}, \overline{x}') \rightarrow \psi(\overline{x}')]$
strongest postcondition: $\forall \overline{x}' \cdot [\mathrm{SP}(\tau, \varphi)(\overline{x}') \rightarrow \psi(\overline{x}')]$
weakest precondition: $\quad \forall \overline{x} \cdot [\varphi(\overline{x}) \rightarrow \mathrm{WP}(\tau, \psi)(\overline{x})]$.

When establishing the first-order premises $I1-I3$ of rule INV it is sound to assert any previously established invariant ψ as an axiom. This will be used throughout the paper.

The main difficulty in using rule INV is finding the strengthened assertion φ. We now show that the strongest and weakest candidates for φ can be given fixedpoint characterizations.

3.1 Forward propagation

Define the operator $\mathcal{F}$ by

$$\mathcal{F}(Y) \;\triangleq\; \Theta \vee \mathrm{SP}(T, Y)$$

A formula φ satisfies $I1$ and $I3$ iff $\mathcal{F}(\varphi) \rightarrow \varphi$. Since $\mathcal{F}$ is monotone, i.e., if $Y_1 \rightarrow Y_2$ then $\mathcal{F}(Y_1) \rightarrow \mathcal{F}(Y_2)$, the fixedpoint formula

$$\mu Y. \mathcal{F}(Y)$$

provides the strongest assertion $\varphi_{\mathcal{F}}$ satisfying $I1$ and $I3$. We have therefore

$$\text{(F1)} \quad \Theta \rightarrow \varphi_{\mathcal{F}} \qquad\qquad \text{(F2)} \quad \mathrm{SP}(T, \varphi_{\mathcal{F}}) \rightarrow \varphi_{\mathcal{F}} \; .$$

Notice that $\varphi_{\mathcal{F}}$ precisely characterizes the set of reachable states:

$$\text{a state } s \text{ is } S\text{-accessible} \quad \text{iff} \quad s \vDash \varphi_{\mathcal{F}} \; .$$

The implication from left to right holds for any formula satisfying $I1$ and $I3$; the converse holds because $\varphi_{\mathcal{F}}$ is the strongest such formula.

As $\mathcal{F}$ is monotone, if the sequence starting from F (false)

$$\underbrace{\text{F}}_{\varphi_0} \;\rightarrow\; \underbrace{\mathcal{F}(\varphi_0)}_{\varphi_1} \;\rightarrow\; \underbrace{\mathcal{F}(\varphi_1)}_{\varphi_2} \;\rightarrow\; \cdots$$

converges in finitely many steps, i.e., $\varphi_n \leftrightarrow \varphi_{n+1}$ is S-valid for some n, then its limit is $\varphi_{\mathcal{F}}$.

3.2 Backward propagation

Given p, define the monotone operator $\mathcal{B}$ by

$$\mathcal{B}(X) \ \triangleq \ p \wedge \text{WP}(\mathcal{T}, X) \ .$$

A formula satisfies satisfies $I2$ and $I3$ iff $\mathcal{B}(\varphi) \leftarrow \varphi$. The fixedpoint formula

$$\nu X.\mathcal{B}(X)$$

provides the weakest $\varphi_\mathcal{B}$ satisfying $I2$ and $I3$. We therefore have

(B1) $\quad \varphi_\mathcal{B} \rightarrow p \qquad\qquad$ (B2) $\quad \varphi_\mathcal{B} \rightarrow \text{WP}(\mathcal{T}, \varphi_\mathcal{B}) \ .$

$\varphi_\mathcal{B}$ precisely characterizes the states where p is invariant, that is, for a state s, $s \vDash \varphi_\mathcal{B}$ iff s is a p-*invariant state*, i.e., every computation of $\mathcal{S}$ starting in s satisfies $\square\, p$.

Since $\mathcal{B}$ is monotone, if the sequence starting from T (true)

$$\underbrace{\text{T}}_{\varphi_0} \ \leftarrow \ \underbrace{\mathcal{B}(\varphi_0)}_{\varphi_1} \ \leftarrow \ \underbrace{\mathcal{B}(\varphi_1)}_{\varphi_2} \ \leftarrow \ \cdots$$

converges in finitely many steps, then its limit is $\varphi_\mathcal{B}$.

3.3 The top-down/bottom-up duality

Abstract state space exploration from the set of initial states, also called *bottom-up analysis*, does not depend on the system property we want to establish. *Top-down analysis*, on the other hand, explores the state space starting with the states that satisfy an invariant candidate p.

Since $\varphi_\mathcal{F}$ captures exactly the reachable state space, whereas $\varphi_\mathcal{B}$ only collects enough information to establish p, one can make the following observation:

Property 1 *The following are equivalent: 1:* $\Theta \rightarrow \varphi_\mathcal{B}$, *2:* $\varphi_\mathcal{F} \rightarrow p$, *3:* $\varphi_\mathcal{F} \rightarrow \varphi_\mathcal{B}$.

Proof Assume $\Theta \rightarrow \varphi_\mathcal{B}$. By the fixedpoint characterization (B2) of $\varphi_\mathcal{B}$ and by the equivalence $(X \rightarrow \text{WP}(\mathcal{T}, Y)) \leftrightarrow (\text{SP}(\mathcal{T}, X) \rightarrow Y)$, we may infer $\Theta \vee \text{SP}(\mathcal{T}, \varphi_\mathcal{B}) \rightarrow \varphi_\mathcal{B}$. Since $\mathcal{F}(\varphi_\mathcal{B}) = \Theta \vee \text{SP}(\mathcal{T}, \varphi_\mathcal{B})$ and $\varphi_\mathcal{F}$ is the strongest assertion satisfying $\mathcal{F}(\varphi) \rightarrow \varphi$ we have $\varphi_\mathcal{F} \rightarrow \varphi_\mathcal{B}$. This establishes *1⇒3*. The argument establishing *2⇒3* is analogous, using (F2).

To establish *3⇒1*, assume $\varphi_\mathcal{F} \rightarrow \varphi_\mathcal{B}$. By the fixedpoint characterization of $\varphi_\mathcal{F}$ we have (F1) and *3⇒1* follows by transitivity of implication. The implication *3⇒2* is established in a similar way. ∎

The correspondence is best illustrated by the commuting diagram:

$$
\begin{array}{ccc}
\Theta & \xrightarrow{\ \ (\text{F1})\ \ } & \varphi_\mathcal{F} \\[4pt]
\downarrow & \swarrow & \downarrow \\[4pt]
\varphi_\mathcal{B} & \xrightarrow[\ (\text{B1})\ ]{} & p
\end{array}
$$

where the horizontal implications are given by the fixedpoint equations. If one of the downwards directed implications is present, all the others must also be.

The diagram suggests that if p is an invariant, then the $\varphi_{\mathcal{F}}$ states are a subset of the φ_B states as reflected in Figure 2.

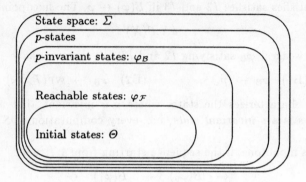

Fig. 2. State space.

As Figure 2 shows, the p-invariant states, given by φ_B, are a subset of the p-states, which are those states where p holds but is not necessarily preserved by the transitions.

Example (forward and backward propagation) We analyze program BAKERY (Figure 3) using both forward and backward propagation. The program guarantees mutual exclusion, that is, ℓ_3 and m_3 are never reached at the same time. Synchronization is provided by the integer variables y_1 and y_2, which can be thought of as numbers used in waiting-lines at bakeries.

$$\textbf{local } y_1, y_2 : \textbf{integer where } y_1 = y_2 = 0$$

$$P_1 :: \begin{bmatrix} \textbf{loop forever do} \\ \begin{bmatrix} \ell_0 : \textbf{noncritical} \\ \ell_1 : y_1 := y_2 + 1 \\ \ell_2 : \textbf{await } (y_2 = 0 \vee \\ \qquad\qquad y_1 \leq y_2) \\ \ell_3 : \textbf{critical} \\ \ell_4 : y_1 := 0 \end{bmatrix} \end{bmatrix} \;\Big\|\; P_2 :: \begin{bmatrix} \textbf{loop forever do} \\ \begin{bmatrix} m_0 : \textbf{noncritical} \\ m_1 : y_2 := y_1 + 1 \\ m_2 : \textbf{await } (y_1 = 0 \vee \\ \qquad\qquad y_2 < y_1) \\ m_3 : \textbf{critical} \\ m_4 : y_2 := 0 \end{bmatrix} \end{bmatrix}$$

Fig. 3. Program BAKERY (Bakery protocol for mutual exclusion)

Forward propagation   The method requires computing the sequence

$$\underbrace{\text{F}}_{\varphi_0} \;\rightarrow\; \underbrace{\mathcal{F}(\varphi_0)}_{\varphi_1} \;\rightarrow\; \underbrace{\mathcal{F}(\varphi_1)}_{\varphi_2} \;\rightarrow\; \cdots$$

until a limit is found.

Figure 4 represents the iterations of $\mathcal{F}$ as layers in a directed graph, growing bottom-up from the initial condition $\varphi_1 : \Theta$. The i-th iteration of $\mathcal{F}$, represented by φ_i, is the disjunction of the nodes that are reachable from the source on a path of at most depth $i - 1$.

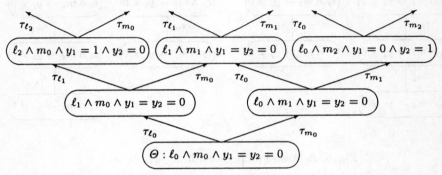

Fig. 4. Forward propagation

From the initial condition Θ we calculate

$$
\begin{aligned}
\text{SP}(\mathcal{T},\Theta) &= \bigvee_{\tau \in \mathcal{T}} \text{SP}(\tau,\Theta) \\
&= \text{SP}(\tau_{\ell_0},\Theta) \vee \text{SP}(\tau_{m_0},\Theta) \\
&= (\ell_1 \wedge m_0 \wedge y_1 = y_2 = 0) \;\vee\; (\ell_0 \wedge m_1 \wedge y_1 = y_2 = 0)
\end{aligned}
$$

which generates the two disjuncts just above Θ. One more iteration of $\mathcal{F}$ generates the three disjuncts at the third level. The sequence $\varphi_1, \varphi_2, \varphi_3, \ldots$ does not converge to a fixedpoint in a finite number of steps, since $\varphi_{5k} \wedge \ell_2 \wedge m_2$ is equivalent to

$$\ell_2 \wedge m_2 \wedge |y_1 - y_2| = 1 \wedge 1 \le y_1 \le k + 1 \wedge 1 \le y_2 \le k + 1 \,.$$

However, it is possible to express the strongest invariant (representing the reachable state space) of the protocol by the first-order formula:

$$
\begin{aligned}
\varphi_{\mathcal{F}} : \;\; & \ell_{0,1} \wedge (m_{0,1} \wedge y_1 = 0 \wedge y_2 = 0 \;\vee\; m_{2,3,4} \wedge y_1 = 0 \wedge y_2 \ge 1) \\
& \vee\; \ell_{2,3,4} \wedge m_{0,1} \wedge y_1 \ge 1 \wedge y_2 = 0 \\
& \vee\; \ell_2 \wedge (m_2 \wedge y_1 \ge 1 \wedge y_2 \ge 1 \wedge |y_1 - y_2| = 1 \;\vee\; m_{3,4} \wedge y_2 \ge 1 \wedge y_1 - y_2 = 1) \\
& \vee\; \ell_{3,4} \wedge m_2 \wedge y_1 \ge 1 \wedge y_2 - y_1 = 1 \,.
\end{aligned}
$$

Backward propagation   Backward propagation starts from an invariant candidate, in this case

$$\Box \neg(\ell_3 \wedge m_3),$$

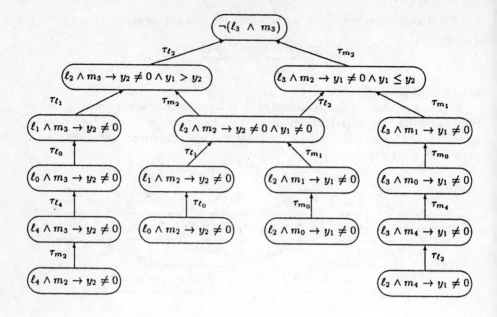

Fig. 5. Backward propagation from $\neg(\ell_3 \wedge m_3)$

which expresses mutual exclusion in the critical sections.

We compute the terms of the sequence

$$\underbrace{\mathrm{T}}_{\varphi_0} \leftarrow \underbrace{\mathcal{B}(\varphi_0)}_{\varphi_1} \leftarrow \underbrace{\mathcal{B}(\varphi_1)}_{\varphi_2} \leftarrow \cdots$$

until a limit is found. Applying $\mathcal{B}$ once generates $\varphi_1 : \neg(\ell_3 \wedge m_3)$. In the second iteration of $\mathcal{B}$ we calculate:

$$
\begin{aligned}
\mathrm{WP}(\mathcal{T}, \varphi_1) &= \bigwedge_{\tau \in \mathcal{T}} \mathrm{WP}(\tau, \varphi_1) \\
&= \mathrm{WP}(\tau_{\ell_2}, \varphi_1) \wedge \mathrm{WP}(\tau_{m_2}, \varphi_1) \\
&= (\ell_2 \wedge m_3 \rightarrow y_2 \neq 0 \wedge y_1 > y_2) \wedge (\ell_3 \wedge m_2 \rightarrow y_1 \neq 0 \wedge y_1 \leq y_2).
\end{aligned}
$$

Continuing mechanically in this fashion we obtain the formulas shown in Figure 5. The conjunction of the formulas is the greatest fixedpoint $\varphi_{\mathcal{B}}$ of $\mathcal{B}$. By calculating $\mathrm{WP}(\tau, \varphi)$, where τ labels an edge pointing to a node labeled by φ, one obtains the assertion labeling the source of the edge. The auxiliary invariants $\square(y_1 \geq 0)$ and $\square(y_2 \geq 0)$ were used to simplify the examined conjuncts. These invariants can be generated automatically by several of the methods described later in this paper. Finally, since $\Theta : \ell_0 \wedge m_0 \wedge y_1 = y_2 = 0$ implies $\varphi_{\mathcal{B}}$, we have indeed established mutual exclusion of the critical sections.

The example shows the power of backward propagation: a completely automatic search terminates with a strengthened invariant. The analysis described above is entirely automatic in STeP. Forward propagation, on the other hand, does not converge in finitely many steps because the protocol's set of states cannot be reached in finitely many iterations. ◢

4 General Safety

A *general safety* property p is one that can be expressed as

$$\Box\, q$$

where q is a past formula, i.e., it does not contain any future temporal operators.
Example (general safety formulas)   The state-causality formula

$$\Box\, \underbrace{[p\ \to\ \diamondsuit\, r]}_{\text{past}}$$

for assertions p and r, is a general safety formula. A model satisfies this formula if every p-position coincides with or is preceded by an r-position.

The nested waiting-for formula

$$\Box[p\ \to\ q_1\ W\ (q_2\ W\ r)]$$

for assertions p, q_1, q_2 and r is a general safety formula. A model satisfies this formula if every p-position initiates a q_1-interval, followed by a q_2-interval, that may be terminated by an r-position. Each q_i-interval, $i = 1, 2$, is a set of successive positions all of which satisfy q_i, and may be empty or extend to infinity. In the latter case, there need not be a following interval nor a terminating r-position. This is a general safety formula, since it is equivalent to the formula

$$\Box\, \underbrace{[(\neg q_2)\ \to\ q_1\ B\ ((\neg p)\ B\ r)]}_{\text{past}}\ .\quad ◢$$

An *assertion graph* $G = \langle N, N_0, E, \lambda \rangle$ is a labeled directed graph where

$$
\begin{aligned}
N &\quad -\ \text{set of nodes}\\
N_0 \subseteq N &\quad -\ \text{initial nodes}\\
E \subseteq N \times N &\ -\ \text{edges}\\
\lambda : N \mapsto \mathcal{A} &\ -\ \text{mapping from nodes to assertions.}
\end{aligned}
$$

G is an *assertion graph for p* if it describes exactly the models of p, i.e., for every model $\sigma : s_0, s_1, \ldots,\ \langle \sigma, 0 \rangle \vDash p$ iff there exists a path $n_0(\in N_0), n_1, \ldots$ in G such that $s_i \vDash \lambda(n_i)$ for every $i \geq 0$. An assertion graph for a given p can always be automatically generated ([MP95]). Conversely, any graph G is the assertion graph for some general safety property p. More precisely, we have,

Lemma 1. *Let* $G = \langle N, N_0, E, \lambda \rangle$ *be a labeled graph. There exists a temporal operator* C_G *of arity* $|N|$, *which is monotone in every argument, such that G is the assertion graph of* $C_G((\lambda(n))_{n \in N})$.

language $\mathcal{A}$ (assumed to be sufficiently expressive), it is possible to construct a formula $acc(\mathcal{S}, n)$ for each $n \in N$, such that:

$$s \vDash acc(\mathcal{S}, n) \quad \text{iff} \quad s \text{ is } (\mathcal{S}, n)\text{-accessible} .$$

The assertions $\{acc(\mathcal{S}, n)\}_{n \in N}$ trivially satisfy the premises of SAFE.

Finding useful strengthened assertions $\{\varphi_n\}_{n \in N}$ for rule SAFE is the main obstacle in its use; assertions $\{acc(\mathcal{S}, n)\}_{n \in N}$ are seldom very useful. Similar to the analysis of INV we now give fixedpoint characterizations of the strongest and weakest candidates for SAFE.

Notation: For an ordered set N we will use $(a_n)_{n \in N}$ or a_N for a tuple indexed by the elements in N.

4.1 Forward Propagation

To generate a unique least set of intermediate assertions for SAFE we need to work with deterministic assertion graphs. We say that an assertion graph G is *deterministic* if any model has at most one path in G, that is, for any n_1, n_2, if $n_1, n_2 \in N_0$ or for some $m \in N$, $(m, n_1), (m, n_2) \in E$ then $\lambda(n_1) \wedge \lambda(n_2)$ is unsatisfiable. We also define G to be *edge-complete* if any model whose first state satisfies $\bigvee_{n \in N_0}$ has at least one path in G, that is, for any $n \in N$, $\bigvee_{(n,m) \in E} \lambda(m)$ holds.

If G is not deterministic then there may be incomparable minimal (with respect to the order on $\mathcal{A}^{|N|}$ defined pointwise by the implication relation) tuples of assertions satisfying $S1-S3$.

Example (two minimal solutions for $S1-S3$) Consider a graph with two nodes, $N = N_0 = \{n_1, n_2\}$, labeled $\lambda(n_1) : x = 0$ and $\lambda(n_2) : y = 0$, such that any two nodes are connected. This graph is an assertion graph for the property $\square(x = 0 \vee y = 0)$ and is not deterministic because $n_1, n_2 \in N_0$ and $\lambda(n_1) \wedge \lambda(n_2) \leftrightarrow x = 0 \wedge y = 0$ is satisfiable. Consider the transition system with $\Theta : x = 0 \wedge y = 0$ and only one transition, τ_I, the idling transition, defined by the transition relation $\rho_\tau : x' = x \wedge y' = y$. In this system there are two minimal solutions to $S1-S3$, namely

$$\begin{cases} \varphi_{n_1} : x = 0 \wedge y = 0 \\ \varphi_{n_2} : \text{F} \end{cases} \qquad \begin{cases} \varphi_{n_1} : \text{F} \\ \varphi_{n_2} : x = 0 \wedge y = 0 \end{cases}$$

For deterministic assertion graphs G, we will show that we can define a forward propagation operator $\mathcal{F}_N : \mathcal{A}^{|N|} \mapsto \mathcal{A}^{|N|}$ such that if $S1-S3$ can be established and the propagation sequence associated with $\mathcal{F}$ converges after finitely many iterations, then its limit is the unique minimal solution to $S1-S3$. Note that a nondeterministic assertion graph can be transformed into a deterministic one by a standard automata-theoretic construction, so in the following we assume a deterministic G.

First observe that φ_N satisfies premises $S1-S3$ of rule SAFE iff it satisfies

For a node $n \in N$, we say that a state s is (S, n)-*accessible* if there exists a computation $s_0, s_1, \ldots, s_k, \ldots$, of S, where $s = s_k$, and a finite path $n_0, n_1, \ldots, n_k = n$ in G such that $n_0 \in N_0$ and $\forall i \in [0..k] \cdot s_i \vDash \lambda(n_i)$. An assertion φ is (S, n)-*valid* if it holds for every (S, n)-accessible state.

For transition system $S = \langle \mathcal{V}, \Theta, \mathcal{T} \rangle$,
general safety property p,
assertion graph $G = \langle N, N_0, E, \lambda \rangle$ for p, and
assertions $\{\varphi_n\}_{n \in N}$

$$
\begin{array}{lll}
S1 & \Theta \quad \rightarrow \bigvee_{n \in N_0} \varphi_n & \\
S2 & \varphi_n \rightarrow \lambda(n) & n \in N \\
S3 & \{\varphi_n\} \; \mathcal{T} \; \{\bigvee_{(n,m) \in E} \varphi_m\} & n \in N \\
\hline
& S \vDash p &
\end{array}
$$

Fig. 6. Rule SAFE (general safety)

The verification rule SAFE shown in Figure 6 reduces the verification of the general safety property p to first-order premises $S1-S3$. Suppose we have a transition system S, a general safety property p and an assertion graph G for p. To prove that p is S-valid, we have to find *intermediate assertions* $\{\varphi_n\}_{n \in N}$ such that premise $S1$ is S-state valid and for each $n \in N$, $S2$ and $S3$ are (S, n)-valid.

Lemma 2. *Rule* SAFE *is sound.*

Proof   Assuming the premises of $S1-S3$ of SAFE are satisfied, we must show that p is S-valid. Consider an arbitrary computation $\sigma : s_0, s_1, \ldots$ of S, i.e.,

$$
s_0 \vDash \Theta \quad \text{and} \quad \forall i \geq 0 \, \exists \tau \in \mathcal{T} \cdot (s_i, s_{i+1}) \vDash \rho_\tau(\overline{x}, \overline{x}') \; .
$$

We show that $\sigma \vDash p$. By premise $S3$ we have

$$
\forall i \geq 0 \, \forall n \in N \cdot [s_i \vDash \varphi_n \quad \rightarrow \quad \exists m \cdot (n, m) \in E \, \land \, s_{i+1} \vDash \varphi_m] \; .
$$

By premise $S1$, $\exists n \in N_0 \cdot s_0 \vDash \varphi_n$. Thus, by induction on i, it follows that $\forall i \geq 0 \, \exists n \in N \cdot s_i \vDash \varphi_n$. Hence, by $S2$, σ induces a path $n_0(\in N_0), n_1, \ldots$ on G such that $s_i \vDash \lambda(n_i)$ for every $i \geq 0$. Therefore σ is a model of p. ∎

Lemma 3. *Rule* SAFE *is complete.*

Proof (sketch)   Assuming p is S-valid we must establish that, given an assertion graph G for p, there are assertions $\{\varphi_n\}_{n \in N}$ satisfying premises $S1-S3$. By encoding finite sequences and elementary operations on these in the assertion

$(C1a)$ $\Theta \wedge \lambda(n) \rightarrow \varphi_n, \ n \in N_0$ $\qquad$ $(C1b)$ $\Theta \rightarrow \bigvee_{n \in N_0} \lambda(n)$

$(C2)$ $\varphi_n \rightarrow \lambda(n), \ n \in N$

$(C3a)$ $\mathrm{SP}(\mathcal{T}, \varphi_m) \wedge \lambda(n) \rightarrow \varphi_n, \ (m,n) \in E$ $\qquad$ $(C3b)$ $\{\varphi_n\}\mathcal{T}\{\bigvee_{(n,m) \in E} \lambda(m)\}$

This is because premise $S1$ holds iff conditions $(C1a)$ and $(C1b)$ hold, premise $S2$ coincides with condition $(C2)$ and premise $S3$ holds iff conditions $(C3a)$ and $(C3b)$ hold. Consider the monotone operator $\mathcal{F}_N : \mathcal{A}^{|N|} \mapsto \mathcal{A}^{|N|}$ defined pointwise, at each $n \in N$, by

$$\mathcal{F}_n(\varphi_N) \ \triangleq \ \left[(\Theta \wedge n \in N_0) \vee \bigvee_{(m,n) \in E} \mathrm{SP}(\mathcal{T}, \varphi_m) \right] \wedge \lambda(n) \ .$$

A tuple of formulas φ_N satisfies $(C1a)$ and $(C3a)$ iff φ_N satisfies $\mathcal{F}_n(\varphi_N) \rightarrow \varphi_n$ for any $n \in N$. If the sequence

$$(\mathrm{F})_{n \in N}, \quad \mathcal{F}_N((\mathrm{F})_{n \in N}), \quad \mathcal{F}_N^{(2)}((\mathrm{F})_{n \in N}), \quad \dots$$

reaches a limit $\varphi_{\mathcal{F},N}$ in finitely many steps, then $\varphi_{\mathcal{F},N}$ is the least fixedpoint of $\mathcal{F}_N$. $S1-S3$ have a solution iff $(C1b)$ holds and $\varphi_{\mathcal{F},N}$ furthermore satisfies $(C3b)$. $(C2)$ is always satisfied by $\varphi_{\mathcal{F},N}$. Notice that $\varphi_{\mathcal{F},N}$ precisely characterizes the $(\mathcal{S}, n)$-accessible states.

For a graphical interpretation of the propagation method associated with $\mathcal{F}_N$, we define the *extension* G^e of G, which is a deterministic, edge-complete supergraph of G. Suppose that n_f and $\{n^e\}_{n \in N}$ are new distinct symbols not in N. Let $G^e = \langle N^e, N_0^e, E^e, \lambda^e \rangle$, where

$N^e = N \cup \{n_f\} \cup \{n^e \mid n \in N\}$ $\qquad$ $\lambda^e(n) = \lambda(n)$ if $n \in N$

$N_0^e = N_0$ $\qquad$ $\lambda^e(n^e) = \neg(\bigvee_{(n,m) \in E} \lambda(m))$

$E^e = E \cup \{(n, n^e), (n^e, n_f) \mid n \in N\}$ $\qquad$ $\lambda^e(n_f) = \mathrm{T}$

The n^e nodes can be considered as escape nodes for those computations that after reaching n have nowhere to go in G. All the computations that fail to stay in G end looping in the node n_f. Using G^e, we can characterize the models of both p and $\neg p$. A model σ satisfies p iff its (unique) path in G^e stays in N and conversely, it satisfies $\neg p$ iff its first state does not satisfy $\bigvee_{n \in N_0} \lambda(n)$ or its path in G^e reaches a node in $N^e \setminus N$.

Example (G and G^e) For program BAKERY in Figure 3, the 1-bounded over-taking property for process P_1 is expressed by the general safety formula

$$p_{bound}: \quad \square[\ \ell_2 \ \rightarrow \ (\ell_2 \wedge \neg m_3) \ W \ ((\ell_2 \wedge m_3) \ W \ ((\ell_2 \wedge \neg m_3) \ W \ \ell_3))] \ .$$

That is, whenever process P_1 reaches ℓ_2, process P_2 can access its critical region at most once before P_1 reaches its critical region at ℓ_3.

An assertion graph G for p_{bound} and its extension G^e are shown in Figure 7. The nodes in $N^e \setminus N$ are drawn with two concentric ovals. Statechart conventions [Har84] are used for a more compact graphical representation. For example, the

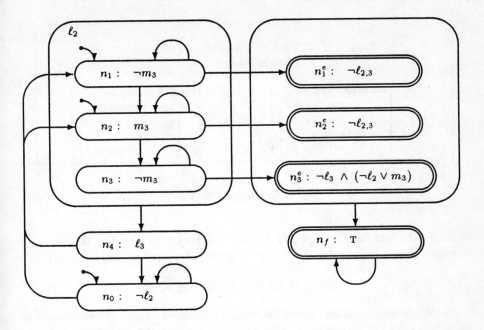

Fig. 7. Graph G and its extension G^e for property p_{bound}

edge departing the compound node containing n_1, n_2 and n_3 represents the edges $(n_1, n_4), (n_2, n_4), (n_3, n_4)$.

We extend the definition of the forward operator $\mathcal{F}_N$ to all the nodes of G^e, so for all $n \in N^e$,

$$\mathcal{F}_n(\varphi_{N^e}) \triangleq \left[(\Theta \wedge n \in N_0^e) \vee \bigvee_{(m,n) \in E^e} \mathrm{SP}(\mathcal{T}, \varphi_m) \right] \wedge \lambda^e(n) \ .$$

With this definition, condition $(C3b)$ can be replaced by the condition that $\varphi_{\mathcal{F},n}$ is unsatisfiable for any $n \in N^e \setminus N$. If the sequence $(\mathrm{F})_{n \in N^e}$, $\mathcal{F}_{N^e}((\mathrm{F})_{n \in N^e})$, $\mathcal{F}_{N^e}^{(2)}((\mathrm{F})_{n \in N^e})$, $\ldots$ converges in finitely many steps to $\varphi_{\mathcal{F},N^e}$, then

- $C_{G^e}(\varphi_{N^e})$ is $\mathcal{S}$-valid.
- p is $\mathcal{S}$-valid iff $(C1b)$ holds and for any $n \in N^e \setminus N$, $\varphi_{\mathcal{F},n}$ is unsatisfiable.

Thus the bottom-up approach to verifying p consists of the following steps: check that $(C1b)$ holds, generate the least fixedpoint, $\varphi_{\mathcal{F},N^e}$, of $\mathcal{F}_{N^e}$ and finally check that $\forall n \in N^e \setminus N$, $\varphi_{\mathcal{F},n}$ is unsatisfiable. Notice that, unlike the invariance case, forward propagation for general safety properties depends on the given property.
Example (generating intermediate assertions for rule SAFE) Consider program PROD-CONS (Figure 8), a simple version of a producer-consumer protocol. The statement **produce** x assigns some nonzero value to x and **consume** x sets x to 0. They do not change other variables. Statements **request** and **release**

$$
\boxed{
\begin{array}{l}
\qquad\text{local } e, f \;\; : \text{integer where } e = 1, f = 0 \\
\qquad\quad\; x, y, z : \text{integer where } x = y = z = 0 \\[2mm]
Prod ::
\begin{bmatrix}
\text{loop forever do} \\
\begin{bmatrix}
\ell_0: & \text{produce } x \\
\ell_1: & \text{request } e \\
\ell_2: & y := x \\
\ell_3: & \text{release } f
\end{bmatrix}
\end{bmatrix}
\; \| \; Cons ::
\begin{bmatrix}
\text{loop forever do} \\
\begin{bmatrix}
m_0: & \text{request } f \\
m_1: & z := y \\
m_2: & \text{release } e \\
m_3: & \text{consume } z
\end{bmatrix}
\end{bmatrix}
\end{array}
}
$$

Fig. 8. Program PROD-CONS

stand for the standard semaphores P and V. We want to establish the causality property that a given value u is not consumed unless it was first produced:

$$
p_{caus} : \quad \Box\,[z = u \;\rightarrow\; \diamondsuit\, x = u] \;.
$$

A deterministic graph G and its edge-complete extension G^e are shown in Figure 9. Forward propagation with program PROD-CONS and property p_{caus} generates disjuncts from φ_{n_1} as shown in Table 2. The first column is the disjunct number and the second is the iteration when it was obtained. The top row represents the result of the first iteration $\mathcal{F}_{n_1}((\mathrm{F})_{n \in N})$, the first two rows the result after the second iteration, and so on. As $\{n_1\}$ is a maximal strongly connected component that cannot be reached from other components, we can perform the forward propagation first on $\{n_1\}$. Each disjunct is obtained from the initial condition or is the result of applying strongest postcondition to a previously obtained disjunct. For instance, disjunct 5, obtained at the fifth iteration, generates disjuncts 6 and 7 in the table. The propagation is completed by the eleventh iteration. We can now propagate $\varphi_{\mathcal{F},n_1}$ to other components in the graph. We obtain $\varphi_{\mathcal{F},n_1^e} = \mathrm{F}$ and therefore $\varphi_{\mathcal{F},n_f} = \mathrm{F}$. We can also compute $\varphi_{\mathcal{F},n_2}$ and $\varphi_{\mathcal{F},n_3}$, but since $N^e \setminus N$ is not reachable from these nodes it is not important what the actual formulas are. (We could take $\varphi_{n_2} : x = u$ and $\varphi_{n_3} : \mathrm{T}$ together with the other formulas to satisfy conditions $S1 - S3$). As $\varphi_{n_e^1} : \mathrm{F}$, we have proved that program PROD-CONS satisfies property p_{caus}.

The bottom-up method for proving a safety property p can also be used for debugging. With a deterministic assertion graph G and its extension G^e for p we generate assertions φ_{N^e}, expressing the $(\mathcal{S}, n)$-accessible states, in stages. Stage $i + 1$ is obtained from stage i by applying $\mathcal{F}_{N^e}$. The propagation stops when we obtain a satisfiable $\varphi_{n,i}$ for $n \in N^e \setminus N$ and $i \geq 0$. By recording the history of previous iterations we can reconstruct the symbolic computation that ends outside G.

Example (counterexamples using forward propagation) Consider again program PROD-CONS (Figure 8). Suppose we want the protocol to have a lazy production property, namely that once the producer writes a value into x it

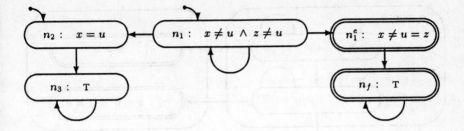

Fig. 9. Graphs G and G^e for the property p_{caus}

Table 2. The first few disjuncts of φ_{n_1} where $c: u \neq 0 \wedge u \neq x \wedge u \neq y$

#	it.	source	disjunct							
1	1	Θ	$\ell_0 \wedge m_0$	$\wedge$ $x = 0$	$\wedge$ $y = 0$	$\wedge$ $z = 0$	$\wedge$ $(e,f) = (1,0)$	$\wedge$ c
2	2	$n_1, 1$	$\ell_1 \wedge m_0$	$\wedge$ $x \neq 0$	$\wedge$ $y = 0$	$\wedge$ $z = 0$	$\wedge$ $(e,f) = (1,0)$	$\wedge$ c
3	3	$n_1, 2$	$\ell_2 \wedge m_0$	$\wedge$ $x \neq 0$	$\wedge$ $y = 0$	$\wedge$ $z = 0$	$\wedge$ $(e,f) = (0,0)$	$\wedge$ c
4	4	$n_1, 3$	$\ell_3 \wedge m_0$	$\wedge$ $x \neq 0$	$\wedge$ $y = x$	$\wedge$ $z = 0$	$\wedge$ $(e,f) = (0,0)$	$\wedge$ c
5	5	$n_1, 4$	$\ell_0 \wedge m_0$	$\wedge$ $x \neq 0$	$\wedge$ $y = x$	$\wedge$ $z = 0$	$\wedge$ $(e,f) = (0,1)$	$\wedge$ c
6	6	$n_1, 5$	$\ell_1 \wedge m_0$	$\wedge$ $x \neq 0$	$\wedge$ $y \neq 0$	$\wedge$ $z = 0$	$\wedge$ $(e,f) = (0,1)$	$\wedge$ c
7	6	$n_1, 5$	$\ell_0 \wedge m_1$	$\wedge$ $x \neq 0$	$\wedge$ $y = x$	$\wedge$ $z = 0$	$\wedge$ $(e,f) = (0,0)$	$\wedge$ c

...

will wait until that value is read by the consumer before assigning a new value to x. This property is expressed by the formula

$$p_{ord}: \quad \Box[x = u \;\rightarrow\; ((x = u \wedge z \neq u)\, W\, (x = u \wedge z = u))\, W\, x \neq u]$$

where u is an auxiliary integer variable used to record the value of x. Figure 10 shows the deterministic graph G of all models of p_{ord}, and its extension G^e.

Table 3 shows the disjuncts produced in the first six applications of the forward propagation operator $\mathcal{F}_N$ and maintains enough information to construct an abstract counterexample. We stopped when we obtained a satisfiable disjunct for a node in $N^e \setminus N$. A counterexample $s_1, s_2, \ldots, s_6, s_6, \ldots$ is generated by tracing back the origins of the first disjunct of $\varphi_{n_1^e}$:

$$s_1 \vDash \ell_0 \wedge m_0 \wedge 0 = x \neq u \wedge y = 0 \wedge z = 0 \wedge e = 1 \wedge f = 0 \quad \text{in node } n_0$$
$$s_2 \vDash \ell_1 \wedge m_0 \wedge 0 \neq x = u \wedge y = 0 \wedge z = 0 \wedge e = 1 \wedge f = 0 \quad \text{in node } n_1$$
$$s_3 \vDash \ell_2 \wedge m_0 \wedge 0 \neq x = u \wedge y = 0 \wedge z = 0 \wedge e = 0 \wedge f = 0 \quad \text{in node } n_1$$
$$s_4 \vDash \ell_3 \wedge m_0 \wedge 0 \neq x = u \wedge y = u \wedge z = 0 \wedge e = 0 \wedge f = 0 \quad \text{in node } n_1$$
$$s_5 \vDash \ell_0 \wedge m_0 \wedge 0 \neq x = u \wedge y = u \wedge z = 0 \wedge e = 0 \wedge f = 1 \quad \text{in node } n_1$$
$$s_6 \vDash \ell_1 \wedge m_0 \wedge 0 \neq x = u \wedge y = u \wedge z = 0 \wedge e = 0 \wedge f = 1 \quad \text{in node } n_1^e$$

The counterexample shows that it is possible that *Prod* produces a new value before *Cons* has a chance to read the previous one. A fix to this problem is to switch statements ℓ_0 and ℓ_1.

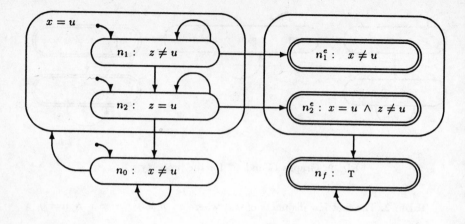

Fig. 10. Graphs G and G^e for the property p_{ord}

Table 3. Forward propagation for PROD-CONS and p_{ord} (6 iterations) where $c : z = 0$

	#	it.	source	disjunct										
φ_{n_0}	1	1	Θ	ℓ_0	$\wedge$	m_0	$\wedge$	$0 = x \neq u$	$\wedge$	$y = 0$	$\wedge$	$(e,f) = (1,0)$	$\wedge$	c
	2	2	$n_0, 1$	ℓ_1	$\wedge$	m_0	$\wedge$	$0 \neq x \neq u$	$\wedge$	$y = 0$	$\wedge$	$(e,f) = (1,0)$	$\wedge$	c
	3	3	$n_0, 2$	ℓ_2	$\wedge$	m_0	$\wedge$	$0 \neq x \neq u$	$\wedge$	$y = 0$	$\wedge$	$(e,f) = (0,0)$	$\wedge$	c
	4	4	$n_0, 3$	ℓ_3	$\wedge$	m_0	$\wedge$	$0 \neq x \neq u$	$\wedge$	$y = x$	$\wedge$	$(e,f) = (0,0)$	$\wedge$	c
	5	5	$n_0, 4$	ℓ_0	$\wedge$	m_0	$\wedge$	$0 \neq x \neq u$	$\wedge$	$y = x$	$\wedge$	$(e,f) = (0,1)$	$\wedge$	c
	6	6	$n_0, 5$	ℓ_1	$\wedge$	m_0	$\wedge$	$0 \neq x \neq u$	$\wedge$	$y \neq u$	$\wedge$	$(e,f) = (0,1)$	$\wedge$	c
	7	6	$n_0, 5$	ℓ_0	$\wedge$	m_1	$\wedge$	$0 \neq x \neq u$	$\wedge$	$y = x$	$\wedge$	$(e,f) = (0,0)$	$\wedge$	c
φ_{n_1}	1	2	$n_0, 1$	ℓ_1	$\wedge$	m_0	$\wedge$	$0 \neq x = u$	$\wedge$	$y = 0$	$\wedge$	$(e,f) = (1,0)$	$\wedge$	c
	2	3	$n_1, 1$	ℓ_2	$\wedge$	m_0	$\wedge$	$0 \neq x = u$	$\wedge$	$y = 0$	$\wedge$	$(e,f) = (0,0)$	$\wedge$	c
	3	4	$n_1, 2$	ℓ_3	$\wedge$	m_0	$\wedge$	$0 \neq x = u$	$\wedge$	$y = u$	$\wedge$	$(e,f) = (0,0)$	$\wedge$	c
	4	5	$n_1, 3$	ℓ_0	$\wedge$	m_0	$\wedge$	$0 \neq x = u$	$\wedge$	$y = u$	$\wedge$	$(e,f) = (0,1)$	$\wedge$	c
	5	6	$n_1, 4$	ℓ_0	$\wedge$	m_1	$\wedge$	$0 \neq x = u$	$\wedge$	$y = u$	$\wedge$	$(e,f) = (0,0)$	$\wedge$	c
	6	6	$n_1, 4$	ℓ_1	$\wedge$	m_0	$\wedge$	$0 \neq x = u$	$\wedge$	$y = u$	$\wedge$	$(e,f) = (0,1)$	$\wedge$	c
	7	6	$n_0, 5$	ℓ_1	$\wedge$	m_0	$\wedge$	$0 \neq x = u$	$\wedge$	$y \neq u$	$\wedge$	$(e,f) = (0,1)$	$\wedge$	c
φ_{n_2}	1	1	Θ	ℓ_0	$\wedge$	m_0	$\wedge$	$0 = x = u$	$\wedge$	$y = 0$	$\wedge$	$(e,f) = (1,0)$	$\wedge$	c
$\varphi_{n_1^e}$	1	6	$n_1, 4$	ℓ_1	$\wedge$	m_0	$\wedge$	$0 \neq x \neq u$	$\wedge$	$y = u$	$\wedge$	$(e,f) = (0,1)$	$\wedge$	c
$\varphi_{n_2^e}$														

4.2 Backward Propagation

The backward propagation operator $\mathcal{B}_N : \mathcal{A}^{|N|} \mapsto \mathcal{A}^{|N|}$, on an assertion graph G, is defined pointwise as

$$\mathcal{B}_n(\varphi_N) \stackrel{\triangle}{=} \lambda(n) \wedge \mathrm{WP}(\mathcal{T}, \bigvee_{(n,m) \in E} \varphi_m) .$$

A tuple of formulas φ_N satisfies $S2$ and $S3$ iff it satisfies $\mathcal{B}_n(\varphi_N) \leftarrow \varphi_n$ for any $n \in N$. If the sequence $(\mathrm{T})_{n \in N}, \mathcal{B}_N((\mathrm{T})_{n \in N}), \mathcal{B}_N^{(2)}((\mathrm{T})_{n \in N}), \ldots$ converges in finitely many steps to a tuple of formulas $\varphi_{\mathcal{B},N}$ then $\varphi_{\mathcal{B},N}$ is the maximal tuple satisfying $S2$ and $S3$. The formula $\varphi_{\mathcal{B},n}$ characterizes those states s with the property that for any sequence of states $\sigma : s_0 = s, s_1, \ldots$ originating in s such that $\forall i \geq 0 \cdot s_{i+1} \in \tau(s_i)$ there is a path $n_0 = n, n_1, \ldots$ in G starting in n such that for any $i \geq 0$, $s_i \vDash \lambda(n_i)$. Furthermore,

$$p \text{ is } S\text{-valid iff } \Theta \to \bigvee_{n \in N_0} \varphi_{\mathcal{B},n} .$$

Thus a top-down approach to verifying p consists of first generating the greatest fixedpoint, $\varphi_{\mathcal{B},N}$, of $\mathcal{B}_N$ and then checking that $\Theta \to \bigvee_{n \in N_0} \varphi_{\mathcal{B},n}$ holds.

Example (generating intermediate assertions for rule SAFE) Consider program BAKERY (Figure 3) and the 1-bounded overtaking property

$$p_{bound} : \quad \square [\ell_2 \to (\ell_2 \wedge \neg m_3) W ((\ell_2 \wedge m_3) W ((\ell_2 \wedge \neg m_3) W \ell_3))] .$$

An assertion graph G for p_{bound} and its extended graph G^e are shown in Figure 7. Forward propagation does not terminate, but the property can be proved using backward propagation. To compute the limit of the sequence $(T)_{n \in N}$, $\mathcal{B}_N((T)_{n \in N})$, $\mathcal{B}_N^{(2)}((T)_{n \in N}), \ldots$ we assume the invariant $\square(\ell_2 \to y_1 \geq 1)$. This invariant can be generated by the methods presented in Sections 7 and 8.

One iteration of $\mathcal{B}$ generates $\varphi_n = \lambda(n)$ for each $n \in N$. In the second iteration we get

$$\varphi_{n_3} = \lambda(n_3) \wedge \text{WP}(T, \lambda(n_3) \vee \lambda(n_4)) = (\neg m_3 \wedge \ell_2) \wedge \text{WP}(T, \ell_3 \vee (\neg m_3 \wedge \ell_2))$$
$$= (\neg m_3 \wedge \ell_2) \wedge \underbrace{(m_2 \to y_2 \geq y_1 \wedge y_1 \neq 0)}_{\text{WP}(\tau_{m_2}, \neg m_3 \wedge \ell_2)} = (\neg m_3 \wedge \ell_2) \wedge \underbrace{(m_2 \to y_2 \geq y_1)}_{\text{by } \square(\ell_2 \to y_1 \geq 1)}$$

The other φ's remain at their previous values. A third application of $\mathcal{B}$ shows that a fixedpoint was reached. Since Θ implies φ_{n_0} and $n_0 \in N_0$, premise $S1$ holds. Backward propagation has thus provided the necessary intermediate assertions to establish the 1-bounded overtaking property.

5 Approximate Analysis

As we have seen, there is no guarantee for success in forward and backward analysis. For infinite or even large finite-state systems, the propagation may not terminate or, even if the sequences converge in a finite number of iterations, we may not be able to prove it (we might not be able to prove for instance that $\mathcal{F}^{n+1}(\text{F}) \to \mathcal{F}^n(\text{F})$). A solution to the difficulties in generating invariants is to limit the search for valid properties and intermediate assertions to a domain $\mathcal{D}$ where we can find approximations to the least (greatest) fixedpoint of the forward (backward) operator. At a minimum, the domain $\mathcal{D}$ is required to support a partial order $\leq$ corresponding to implication in $\mathcal{A}$. The connection between $\mathcal{D}$ and the assertion language $\mathcal{A}$ is given by a monotone function

$$\gamma : \mathcal{D} \mapsto \mathcal{A} .$$

We say that $\mathcal{D}$ abstracts $\mathcal{A}$ and that γ is the *concretization function*.

Invariance

In the approximate analysis, the forward propagation operator $\mathcal{F}$ is relaxed to a weaker operator

$$\overline{\mathcal{F}} : \mathcal{D} \mapsto \mathcal{D} \qquad \text{such that} \qquad \mathcal{F} \circ \gamma \to \gamma \circ \overline{\mathcal{F}} .$$

This condition guarantees the properties

1. if $\overline{\mathcal{F}}(a) \leq a$ then $\mathcal{F}(\gamma(a)) \to \gamma(a)$,
2. p is $\mathcal{S}$-valid if $\overline{\mathcal{F}}(a) \leq a$ and $\gamma(a) \to p$.

These provide a general, domain-independent, justification of the the bottom-up approximate analysis method. The first property shows that an invariant can be obtained by first generating a solution $a \in \mathcal{D}$ of $\overline{\mathcal{F}}(a) \leq a$ and then computing its concretization $\gamma(a)$. The second property shows that p is $\mathcal{S}$-valid if such an invariant satisfies premise $I2$ of rule INV.

Similarly, $\mathcal{B}$ has to be approximated by a stronger monotone operator

$$\underline{\mathcal{B}} : \mathcal{D} \mapsto \mathcal{D} \qquad \text{such that} \qquad \mathcal{B} \circ \gamma \leftarrow \gamma \circ \underline{\mathcal{B}} .$$

The following properties are the basis for top-down approximate analysis:

1. if $\underline{\mathcal{B}}(a) \geq a$ then $\mathcal{B}(\gamma(a)) \leftarrow \gamma(a)$,
2. p is $\mathcal{S}$-valid if $\underline{\mathcal{B}}(a) \geq a$ and $\Theta \to \gamma(a)$.

The first property shows that a strengthening of p can be obtained by first generating a solution $a \in \mathcal{D}$ of $\underline{\mathcal{B}}(a) \geq a$ and then computing its concretization $\gamma(a)$. The second property shows that p is $\mathcal{S}$-valid if such an invariant satisfies premise $I1$ of rule INV.

In the domains described in Section 8, the least (greatest) fixedpoint of $\overline{\mathcal{F}}$ ($\underline{\mathcal{B}}$) can be directly computed by solving a system of constraints constructed from $\mathcal{S}$ and the property p. In other domains, solutions to $\mathcal{F}(\varphi) \to \varphi$ or $\mathcal{B}(\varphi) \leftarrow \varphi$ can be found by approximating the propagation methods. These domains must have a minimal element $\perp$ for forward propagation and a maximal element $\top$ for the backward propagation. The partial order $\leq$ should be decidable, so we can detect the convergence of the sequences. Furthermore, it should be possible to find a propagation sequence that converges in finitely many steps. The domain of linear systems of equations presented in Section 6 has this property because any monotone sequence of equations is guaranteed to converge in finitely many steps. In the polyhedra domain (Section 7) the propagation sequences do not necessarily converge after a finite number of iterations, but it is possible to achieve convergence by approximating the process further. Table 1 in Section 1 summarizes the properties of the approximate methods we review.

General Safety Properties

Let p be a safety property and $\mathcal{D}$ an abstraction of $\mathcal{A}$ with concretization function $\gamma : \mathcal{D} \mapsto \mathcal{A}$. It is possible to approximate the propagation methods for p in $\mathcal{D}$. Indeed, let G be an assertion graph for a safety property p. We will assume that G is deterministic whenever we consider forward propagation. The exact forward and backward operators are operators on $\mathcal{A}^{|N|}$. The domain $\mathcal{D}^{|N|}$ is an abstraction of $\mathcal{A}^{|N|}$ with the concretization function given on any component of a tuple in $\mathcal{D}^{|N|}$ by $\gamma : \mathcal{D} \mapsto \mathcal{A}$.

In the approximate bottom-up analysis, if condition $(C1b)$ holds, we are interested in generating assertions φ_N that satisfy conditions $(C2)$, $(C1a)$ and $(C3a)$ and then check if they also satisfy condition $(C3b)$. Property $(C2)$ cannot be guaranteed if the labelings $\lambda(n)$ are not in the image of γ. Therefore we first have to strengthen the graph G to a graph $\underline{G}$, which has the same structure as G but a stronger labeling function $\underline{\lambda} = \gamma(\lambda^{\mathcal{D}})$ where $\lambda^{\mathcal{D}} : N \mapsto \mathcal{D}$ is a a labeling of the nodes in the abstraction domain such that

$$\gamma(\lambda^{\mathcal{D}}(n)) \;\rightarrow\; \lambda(n) \ .$$

Thus $\underline{G}$ is an assertion graph dependent on the abstraction domain. Approximating G by $\underline{G}$ is sound: the only premise of rule SAFE that depends on the labeling λ is $(C2)$, and if φ_N satisfies $(C2)$ for $\underline{G}$ then it satisfies $(C2)$ for G as well. In the exact forward analysis of safety properties, we have used a complete deterministic extension of the assertion graph and replaced condition $(C3b)$ by the equivalent condition $\forall n \in N^e \setminus N.\neg\varphi_n$. In the abstraction domains we will make another conservative approximation and dispense with the requirement that the supergraph be deterministic. In this case, $(C3b)$ is only implied by $\forall n \in N^e \setminus N \cdot \neg\varphi_n$.

Let $\mathcal{F}_{N^e}$ be the forward propagation operator associated with $\underline{G}^e$ and let $\overline{\mathcal{F}}_{N^e}$ be an approximation of it in $\mathcal{D}^{|N|}$, that is, a monotone operator such that for each $n \in N^e$ and $a_{N^e} = (a_n)_{n \in N^e} \in \mathcal{D}^{|N^e|}$,

$$\mathcal{F}_n((\gamma(a_n))_{n \in N^e}) \;\rightarrow\; \gamma(\overline{\mathcal{F}}_n(a_{N^e})) \ .$$

The forward operator $\mathcal{F}_{N^e}$ has the following properties:

1. if $\forall n \in N^e \cdot \overline{\mathcal{F}}_n(a_{N^e}) \leq a_n$ then $\forall n \in N^e \cdot \mathcal{F}_n((\gamma(a_n))_{n \in N^e}) \rightarrow \gamma(a_n)$
2. p is $\mathcal{S}$-valid if there exists a tuple of assertions a_N such that
$$\Theta \;\rightarrow\; \bigvee_{n \in N_0} \lambda(n), \;\; \forall n \in N^e \cdot \overline{\mathcal{F}}_n(a_{N^e}) \leq a_n,$$
$$\forall n \in N^e \cdot a_n \leq \lambda^{\mathcal{D}}(n) \text{ and } \forall n \notin N \cdot \neg\gamma(a_n).$$

The first property implies that assertions satisfying conditions $(C1a)$ and $(C3a)$ can be obtained by first generating a tuple a_{N^e} that satisfies $\forall n \in N^e \cdot \overline{\mathcal{F}}_n(a_{N^e}) \leq a_n$ and then computing its concretization $\varphi_{N^e} = (\gamma(a_n))_{n \in N^e}$ in $\mathcal{A}^{|N^e|}$. Under these conditions, φ_N, the restriction of φ_{N^e} to the nodes in N, satisfies $(C1a)$ and $(C3a)$. Notice that if each a_n is bounded by $\lambda^{\mathcal{D}}(n)$ then the assertion tuple φ_N also satisfies condition $(C2)$. The second property shows that if in addition for any $n \notin N$, φ_n is unsatisfiable and condition $(C1b)$ holds, then p is $\mathcal{S}$-valid.

Let $\mathcal{B}$ be the backward operator for G and $\underline{\mathcal{B}}$ an approximation of it in $\mathcal{D}^{|N|}$, i.e., $\mathcal{B}$ is a monotone operator such that for each $n \in N$ and $a_N = (a_n)_{n \in N} \in \mathcal{D}^{|N|}$,

$$\mathcal{B}_n((\gamma(a_n))_{n \in N}) \;\leftarrow\; \gamma(\underline{\mathcal{B}}_n(a_N)) \ .$$

Similar to the invariance case, we have the properties

1. if $\forall n \in N \cdot \underline{\mathcal{B}}_n(a_N) \geq a_n$ then $\mathcal{B}_n((\gamma(a_n))_{n \in N}) \leftarrow \gamma(a_n)$,
2. p is $\mathcal{S}$-valid if $\forall n \in N \cdot \underline{\mathcal{B}}_n(a_N) \geq a_n$ and $\Theta \rightarrow \bigvee_{n \in N_0} \gamma(a_n)$.

The first property shows that assertions satisfying premises $S2$ and $S3$ of rule SAFE can be obtained by first generating a tuple a_N that satisfies $\underline{\mathcal{B}}_n(a_N) \geq a_n$ for all $n \in N$, and then computing its concretization $\varphi_N = (\gamma(a_n))_{n \in N}$ in $\mathcal{A}^{|N|}$. φ_N defines a strengthening of the safety property p, namely, $C_G(\gamma(a_n))_{n \in N}$. If φ_N also satisfies premise $S1$ of rule SAFE then, by the second property, p is $\mathcal{S}$-valid. These properties define the top-down approximate analysis method for the general safety case.

6 Systems of Linear Equations

We now present a method for discovering *linear relationships* between the variables of a system, that is, formulas expressible as conjuctions of linear equations:

$$(\overline{u}_1 \cdot \overline{x} + v_1 = 0) \wedge \ldots \wedge (\overline{u}_k \cdot \overline{x} + v_k = 0) \ .$$

The main ideas reviewed here can be found in [Kar76]. More recently the linear equation analysis was generalized to linear congruence equations in [Gra91]. Invariants of this flavor have also been studied extensively in the Petri net literature [Lau73, Rei85], where they are called S-invariants. In [MP95] these ideas are applied to fair transition systems with locations.

Linear invariants are generated in the abstraction domain Λ of linear systems of equations over the variables of the system $\overline{x} = x_1, \ldots, x_n$:

$$\Lambda \triangleq \{ \mathcal{E} \mid \mathcal{E}(\overline{x}) : U\overline{x} + \overline{v} = 0 \},$$

where U ranges over $m \times n$-matrices, and $\overline{v}$ is a column vector of length m. Two systems $\mathcal{E}_1(\overline{x})$ and $\mathcal{E}_2(\overline{x})$ are equal if they have the same set of solutions. Λ is partially ordered by $\sqsubseteq$, where

$\mathcal{E}_1 \sqsubseteq \mathcal{E}_2$ iff   the set of solutions of $\mathcal{E}_1$ is a subset of the set of solutions of $\mathcal{E}_2$.

Λ has the following minimal and maximal elements with respect to the order $\sqsubseteq$:

$\bot$:   the system with no solution, e.g., the system $0\overline{x} + 1 = 0$
$\top$:   the system that admits any solution, $0\overline{x} = 0$.

The concretization function $\gamma : \Lambda \mapsto \mathcal{A}$ is defined by

$$\gamma(\mathcal{E}) \triangleq \bigwedge_{i=1}^{m} (\sum_{j=1}^{n} u_{ij} x_j + v_i = 0) \ .$$

Dualization Consider the system of equations $\mathcal{E}(\overline{x}) : U\overline{x} + \overline{v} = 0$. Let $\overline{x}_0$ be a solution of $\mathcal{E}$ and $\{\overline{x}_1, \dots, \overline{x}_k\}$ a basis of solutions for $U\overline{x} = 0$. The homogeneous system of equations

$$\mathcal{E}^d(\overline{u}, v) : \begin{cases} \overline{x}_0 \cdot \overline{u} + v = 0 \\ \overline{x}_1 \cdot \overline{u} \quad = 0 \\ \dots \\ \overline{x}_k \cdot \overline{u} \quad = 0 \end{cases}$$

is called the *dual* of $\mathcal{E}$. Consider now a homogeneous system of equations $\mathcal{H}(\overline{u}, v) : X\overline{u} + \overline{y}v = 0$. Let $\{(\overline{u}_1, v_1), \dots, (\overline{u}_n, v_n)\}$ be a basis for the set of solutions of $\mathcal{H}$. The system of equations

$$\mathcal{H}^d(\overline{x}) : \begin{cases} \overline{u}_1 \cdot \overline{x} + v_1 = 0 \\ \dots \\ \overline{u}_n \cdot \overline{x} + v_n = 0 \end{cases}$$

is called the *dual* of $\mathcal{H}$.

Let $\mathcal{F}^\Lambda : \Lambda \mapsto \Lambda$ be the operator

$$\mathcal{F}^\Lambda(\mathcal{E}) \triangleq \mathcal{E}_\Theta \sqcup \bigsqcup_{\tau \in \mathcal{T}} \tau(\mathcal{E}), \text{ where :}$$

- $\sqcup : \Lambda \times \Lambda \mapsto \Lambda$ is defined by $(\mathcal{E}_1 \sqcup \mathcal{E}_2)^d(\overline{u}, v) \triangleq \left\{ \begin{matrix} \mathcal{E}_1^d(\overline{u}, v) \\ \mathcal{E}_2^d(\overline{u}, v) \end{matrix} \right\}$
- $\mathcal{E}_\Theta : U_\Theta \overline{x} + \overline{v}_\Theta = 0$, where $\Theta \to U_\Theta \overline{x} + \overline{v}_\Theta = 0$
- $\tau(\mathcal{E})$: Let A_τ and $\overline{b}_\tau$ be such that $\rho_\tau(\overline{x}, \overline{x}') \to \left[A_\tau \begin{pmatrix} \overline{x} \\ \overline{x}' \end{pmatrix} + \overline{b}_\tau = 0 \right]$. Suppose

$\mathcal{E} : U\overline{x} + \overline{v} = 0$. Let $\begin{pmatrix} \overline{x}_0 \\ \overline{x}'_0 \end{pmatrix}$ be a solution of $\left\{ \begin{matrix} A_\tau \begin{pmatrix} \overline{x} \\ \overline{x}' \end{pmatrix} + \overline{b}_\tau = 0 \\ U\overline{x} + \overline{v} = 0 \end{matrix} \right\}$, and

$\left\{ \begin{pmatrix} \overline{x}_1 \\ \overline{x}'_1 \end{pmatrix}, \dots, \begin{pmatrix} \overline{x}_k \\ \overline{x}'_k \end{pmatrix} \right\}$ be a basis of solutions of $\left\{ \begin{matrix} A_\tau \begin{pmatrix} \overline{x} \\ \overline{x}' \end{pmatrix} = 0 \\ U\overline{x} = 0 \end{matrix} \right\}$. Let $X =$

$(\overline{x}'_0 \ \overline{x}'_1 \ \dots \ \overline{x}'_k)^T$ and $y = (1 \ 0 \ \dots \ 0)^T$. Then, $\tau(\mathcal{E})$ is the system dual to $X\overline{u} + \overline{y}v = 0$.

This definition guarantees that for any system $\mathcal{E}$,

$$\mathcal{F}(\gamma(\mathcal{E})) \to \gamma(\mathcal{F}^\Lambda(\mathcal{E})) \ .$$

Thus $\mathcal{F}^\Lambda$ is a good approximation of the forward operator $\mathcal{F}$. When the transition system is *linear*, i.e., satisfies $\Theta \leftrightarrow \gamma(\mathcal{E}_\Theta)$ and $\rho_\tau(\overline{x}, \overline{x}') \leftrightarrow A_\tau \begin{pmatrix} \overline{x} \\ \overline{x}' \end{pmatrix} + \overline{b}_\tau = 0$ for every transition τ in $\mathcal{T}$, then $\mathcal{F}^\Lambda$ is the best possible approximation of $\mathcal{F}$ in Λ as summarized in the following proposition:

Proposition 4. (Linear completeness) *Let $\mathcal{S}$ be a linear transition system, and $\mathcal{E}_\infty$ be the least fixedpoint of $\mathcal{F}^\Lambda$. If $\mathcal{E}$ is a system of equations such that $\gamma(\mathcal{E})$ is $\mathcal{S}$-valid, then $\gamma(\mathcal{E}_\infty) \to \gamma(\mathcal{E})$.*

The least fixedpoint of $\mathcal{F}^A$ is computable. Indeed, in Λ, any strictly monotone sequence of systems of equations cannot have more than $n + 1$ distinct systems, where n is the number of variables. Therefore the sequence $\mathcal{E}_0 : \perp, \mathcal{E}_1 : \mathcal{F}^A(\mathcal{E}_0)$, $\mathcal{E}_2 : \mathcal{F}^A(\mathcal{E}_1)$, ... converges after at most $n + 1$ steps.

Example (generation of invariants) We illustrate the technique on the transition system STABLE (Figure 11) by showing how to derive the linear invariant $\Box(y + z - 2 = 0)$.

$$
\begin{aligned}
\mathcal{V} &: \{y, z\} \\
\Theta &: y = 0 \wedge z = 2 \\
\mathcal{T} &: \{\tau_I, \tau\} \text{ where } \rho_\tau : \quad y' = y - 1 \wedge z' = y + 2z - 1
\end{aligned}
$$

Fig. 11. Transition system STABLE

The invariant $\Box(y + z - 2 = 0)$ is found by computing the converging sequence $\perp \sqsubseteq \mathcal{E}_1 \sqsubseteq \mathcal{E}_2 \sqsubseteq \dots$ We use the notation $\overline{x} = (y\ z)^\mathrm{T}$ and similarly $\overline{x}' = (y'\ z')^\mathrm{T}$. First, notice that we have the following implications:

$$
\underbrace{y = 0 \wedge z = 2}_{\Theta} \quad \rightarrow \quad \underbrace{\begin{pmatrix} 1 & 0 \\ 0 & 1 \end{pmatrix}}_{U_\Theta} \begin{pmatrix} y \\ z \end{pmatrix} + \underbrace{\begin{pmatrix} 0 \\ -2 \end{pmatrix}}_{\overline{v}_\Theta} = \begin{pmatrix} 0 \\ 0 \end{pmatrix}
$$

$$
\underbrace{y' = y - 1 \wedge z' = y + 2z - 1}_{\rho_\tau} \quad \rightarrow \quad \underbrace{\begin{pmatrix} -1 & 0 & 1 & 0 \\ -1 & -2 & 0 & 1 \end{pmatrix}}_{A_\tau} \begin{pmatrix} y \\ z \\ y' \\ z' \end{pmatrix} + \underbrace{\begin{pmatrix} 1 \\ 1 \end{pmatrix}}_{\overline{b}_\tau} = \begin{pmatrix} 0 \\ 0 \end{pmatrix} \ .
$$

The system $\mathcal{E}_\Theta$ is the consequent of the first implication and $\mathcal{E}_\Theta^d$ (which is needed later) is determined by the system

$$
(a) \quad X = (0\ 2) \quad \text{and} \quad \overline{y} = (1),
$$

since a particular solution to $U_\Theta \overline{x} + v_\Theta = \overline{0}$ is $\overline{x} = (0\ 2)^\mathrm{T}$, and there are no nonzero solutions to the homogeneous system $U_\Theta \overline{x} = \overline{0}$.

The terms of the sequence $\mathcal{E}_0, \mathcal{E}_1, \dots$ are computed in stages:[4]

- $\mathcal{E}_0 = \perp$
- $\mathcal{E}_1 = \mathcal{E}_\Theta \sqcup \tau(\perp) = \mathcal{E}_\Theta$.
- $\mathcal{E}_2 = \mathcal{E}_\Theta \sqcup \tau(\mathcal{E}_1)$. We have to solve the system

$$
\begin{cases} A_\tau(\overline{x}, \overline{x}') + \overline{b}_\tau = 0 \\ U_\Theta(\overline{x}) + \overline{v}_\Theta = 0. \end{cases}
$$

---

[4] The idling transition τ_I can be ignored in the invariance case.

A solution of the system is $(\bar{x}_0 \ \bar{x}'_0)^T = (0 \ 2 \ -1 \ 3)^T$ and the homogeneous system of equations

$$\begin{cases} A_\tau(\bar{x}, \bar{x}') = 0 \\ U_\Theta(\bar{x}) \quad = 0 \end{cases}$$

has only the trivial $(0 \ 0 \ 0 \ 0)^T$ solution. $\tau(\mathcal{E}_1)^d$ is therefore determined by

$$(b) \quad X = (-1 \ 3) \quad \text{and} \quad \bar{y} = (1) \ .$$

Combining the systems defined by (a) and (b), which express $\mathcal{E}_\Theta^d$ and $\tau(\mathcal{E}_1)^d$, we get

$$\mathcal{E}_2^d : \quad \begin{pmatrix} 0 & 2 \\ -1 & 3 \end{pmatrix} \bar{u} + \begin{pmatrix} 1 \\ 1 \end{pmatrix} v = \begin{pmatrix} 0 \\ 0 \end{pmatrix} \ .$$

The set of solutions of $\mathcal{E}_2^d$ is a 1-dimensional vector space with basis given by $\{(\underbrace{1 \ 1}_{\bar{u}_1^T} \ \underbrace{-2}_{v_1})^T\}$ hence,

$$\mathcal{E}_2 : \quad \underbrace{(1 \ 1)}_{U_2} \bar{x} - \underbrace{2}_{v_2} = 0 \ .$$

$- \ \mathcal{E}_3 = \mathcal{E}_\Theta \sqcup \tau_1(\mathcal{E}_2) \sqcup \tau_2(\mathcal{E}_2)$. By performing calculations similar to the previous step, we arrive at a linear system identical to $\mathcal{E}_2$.

Hence, we have reached a fixedpoint, which is translated by the concretization function into the linear invariant $\Box(y + z - 2 = 0)$. ∎

7 Convex Polyhedra

The convex polyhedra abstraction was first studied as a tool in the analysis of programs in [CH78]. More recently, convex polyhedra have also been used in the analysis of linear hybrid systems [HRP94, HH95]. We first summarize the method (following [CH78]) and give an example of its use in the generation of invariants. Next we illustrate how the techniques can be extended to automatically generate polyhedral intermediate assertions for the verification of general safety properties.

A closed convex polyhedron P is a formula $\bigwedge_i L_i$ where each L_i is a weak inequality, i.e.,

$$L_i = \sum_j a_{ij} x_j \geq b_i \ .$$

P can be viewed as the set of solutions of its system of linear constraints

$$P = \{\bar{x} \mid A\bar{x} \geq \bar{b}\} \ .$$

We say that $P = \{\bar{x} \mid A\bar{x} \leq \bar{b}\}$ *satisfies a linear constraint* $\bar{c} \cdot \bar{x} \leq d$ if $P = \{\bar{x} \mid A\bar{x} \leq \bar{b}, \bar{c} \cdot \bar{x} \leq d\}$, that is, $\bar{c} \cdot \bar{x} \leq d$ is linearly dependent on the constraints in $A\bar{x} \leq \bar{b}$.

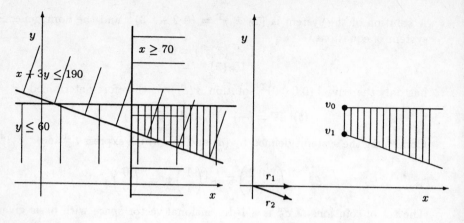

(a) Constraint representation   (b) Generator representation

Fig. 12. Representations of a polyhedron

Another representation of P is given by a system of generators: a finite set of *rays* R and a finite set of *vertices* V such that

$$P = \left\{ \sum_{v_i \in V} \lambda_i \cdot v_i + \sum_{r_j \in R} \mu_j \cdot r_j \;\middle|\; \lambda_i \geq 0,\ \mu_j \geq 0 \text{ and } \sum_i \lambda_i = 1 \right\}$$

where P is the convex closure of this system of generators. Both representations are used in the standard inclusion decision procedure.

Example (polyhedra representations) Consider the polyhedron shown in Figure 12. Its constraint representation is

$$\left\{ \begin{pmatrix} x \\ y \end{pmatrix} \;\middle|\; \begin{pmatrix} -1 & -3 \\ 1 & 0 \\ 0 & -1 \end{pmatrix} \begin{pmatrix} x \\ y \end{pmatrix} \geq \begin{pmatrix} -190 \\ 70 \\ -60 \end{pmatrix} \right\}.$$

The sets of rays and vertices R and V are

$$R = \left\{ \begin{pmatrix} 1 \\ 0 \end{pmatrix}, \begin{pmatrix} 3 \\ -1 \end{pmatrix} \right\}, \qquad V = \left\{ \begin{pmatrix} 70 \\ 60 \end{pmatrix}, \begin{pmatrix} 70 \\ 40 \end{pmatrix} \right\},$$

which determine the generator representation

$$\left\{ \lambda_1 \begin{pmatrix} 70 \\ 60 \end{pmatrix} + \lambda_2 \begin{pmatrix} 70 \\ 40 \end{pmatrix} + \mu_1 \begin{pmatrix} 1 \\ 0 \end{pmatrix} + \mu_2 \begin{pmatrix} 3 \\ -1 \end{pmatrix} \;\middle|\; \begin{array}{l} \lambda_1, \lambda_2, \mu_1, \mu_2 \geq 0 \text{ and} \\ \lambda_1 + \lambda_2 = 1 \end{array} \right\}.$$

7.1   Invariants

The closed convex polyhedra Φ are an abstraction of the assertion language $\mathcal{A}$ with the concretization function given by the inclusion $\gamma : \Phi \mapsto \mathcal{A}$. The partial order, minimal and maximal elements are the subset relation, the empty set, and the total set which are mapped by γ into the implication relation, F and T respectively.

An approximation of $\mathcal{F}$ in Φ is

$$\mathcal{F}^{\Phi}(\varphi) \;\stackrel{\triangle}{=}\; \alpha(\Theta) \vee^{\Phi} \mathrm{SP}^{\Phi}(\alpha(\mathcal{T}), \varphi), \text{ where :}$$

- $\vee^{\Phi}$ is the convex hull operator: $P_1 \vee^{\Phi} P_2$ is the smallest closed convex polyhedron that includes P_1 and P_2. The convex hull can be computed using the generator representations: if (R_1, V_1) and (R_2, V_2) are the generator representations for P_1 and P_2 then $(R_1 \cup R_2, V_1 \cup V_2)$ is a generator representation for $P_1 \vee^{\Phi} P_2$.
- $\mathrm{SP}^{\Phi}(\alpha(\mathcal{T}), \varphi) \stackrel{\triangle}{=} \bigvee_{\tau}^{\Phi} \mathrm{SP}(\alpha(\tau), \varphi)$, where $\mathrm{SP}(\alpha(\tau), \varphi)(V) \stackrel{\triangle}{=} \exists V^p \cdot (\alpha(\rho_\tau)(V^p, V) \wedge \varphi(V^p))$. Notice that $\exists x$ is an operator on Φ. Indeed, it can be shown that $\exists x.P = P \vee^{\Phi} (\bigwedge_{y \neq x}(y = 0))$.
- $\alpha(\varphi) \in \Phi$ is such that $\varphi \to \alpha(\varphi)$. For a given φ we can compute such an $\alpha(\varphi)$ by first rewriting $\varphi = c_1 \wedge \ldots \wedge c_k$ and then taking $\alpha(\varphi) \stackrel{\triangle}{=} \bigwedge \{c_i \mid c_i \text{ is linear}\}$.

The sequence

$$P_0 : \text{F}, \quad P_1 : \mathcal{F}^{\Phi}(P_0), \quad P_2 : \mathcal{F}^{\Phi}(P_1), \; \ldots$$

does not necessarily converge in finitely many steps (it actually might not even converge in Φ). However it is possible to achieve convergence using a *widening* operator [CH78]. This is an operator $\nabla : \Phi \times \Phi \mapsto \Phi$ such that

(W1) for any $P_1, P_2 \in \Phi$, $P_1 \vee^{\Phi} P_2 \to P_1 \nabla P_2$,
(W2) for any $P_0 \to P_1 \to \ldots$ in Φ, the sequence $P_0', P_1', \ldots$ defined by $P_0' = P_0$ and $P_{i+1}' = P_i' \nabla P_{i+1}$ converges in a finite number of steps.

Several widening operators appear in the literature. The simplest is defined by

$$P_1 \nabla P_2 \;\stackrel{\triangle}{=}\; \begin{cases} P_2 & \text{if } P_1 = \emptyset, \\ \text{the polyhedron defined by the} \\ \quad \text{constraints of } P_1 \text{ satisfied by } P_2 & \text{otherwise} \end{cases}$$

The widening operator can be used to obtain the sequence

$$P_0' : \text{F}, \quad P_1' : P_0' \nabla \mathcal{F}^{\Phi}(P_0'), \quad P_2' : P_1' \nabla \mathcal{F}^{\Phi}(P_1'), \; \ldots.$$

which, by (W2), converges after finitely many iterations. The above sequence conservatively approximates $P_0, P_1, \ldots$ and therefore its limit is a solution of $\mathcal{F}^{\Phi}(P) \to P$.

Most widening operators have the property that the constraints of $P_1 \nabla P_2$ are a subset of the constraints of P_1 (if $P_1 \neq \emptyset$). Thus the constraints of the limit polyhedron are a subset of the constraints of the polyhedron to which the first widening has been applied. For this reason, forward propagation with widening usually converges to a better solution if we start with a few iterations without widening. We will use this observation in our examples.

Example (generation of invariants) Consider program LOOP (Figure 13). Using polyhedra abstraction we can generate the invariant $0 \leq y \leq N$.

---

local y : integer where $y = 0$
$\quad\quad\quad N$: integer where $N \geq 0$

ℓ_0: **while** $y \leq N - 1$ **do** $y := y + 1$
ℓ_1:

Fig. 13. Program LOOP

To illustrate the method and the need for a widening operator, we present in Figure 14 a few terms of the infinitely increasing sequence

$$P_1 : \mathcal{F}^{\Phi}(\bot), \quad P_2 : P_1 \vee^{\Phi} \mathcal{F}^{\Phi}(P_1), \quad P_3 : P_2 \vee^{\Phi} \mathcal{F}^{\Phi}(P_2), \ldots$$

as well as a few terms of the sequence

$$P_1' : \mathcal{F}^{\Phi}(\bot), \quad P_2' : P_1' \vee^{\Phi} \mathcal{F}^{\Phi}(P_1'), \quad P_3' : P_2' \triangledown \mathcal{F}^{\Phi}(P_2'), \ldots$$

that converges in finitely many steps. A polyhedral forward propagation operator $\mathcal{F}^{\Phi}$ for LOOP can be defined as

$$\mathcal{F}^{\Phi} \overset{\triangle}{=} \alpha(\Theta) \vee^{\Phi} \mathrm{SP}^{\Phi}(\alpha(\mathcal{T}), \varphi))$$
$$\alpha(\Theta) \overset{\triangle}{=} y = 0 \wedge N \geq 0$$
$$\alpha(\tau_{\ell_0, \mathrm{T}}) \overset{\triangle}{=} y \leq N - 1 \wedge y' = y + 1$$
$$\alpha(\tau_{\ell_0, \mathrm{F}}) \overset{\triangle}{=} y \geq N$$

For simplicity we ignore the two label variables ℓ_0 and ℓ_1. (Taking them into account generates 4-dimensional polyhedra.)

Partitioning the state space into sets that have the same location we could generate a stronger invariant for the transition system LOOP:

$$\square \left[(\ell_0 \rightarrow 0 \leq y \leq N) \wedge (\ell_1 \rightarrow 0 \leq y = N) \right]$$

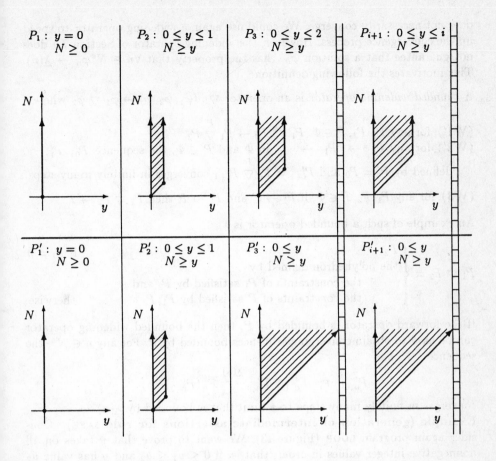

Fig. 14. The sequences $P_0, P_1, \ldots$ and $P'_0.P'_1, \ldots$

7.2 General Safety Properties

Let G be an assertion graph and $\underline{G}$ a strengthened graph labeled by $\underline{\lambda} : N \mapsto \Phi \subseteq \mathcal{A}$ such that

$$\underline{\lambda}(n) \to \lambda(n) \ .$$

Let $G^e \supset \underline{G}$ be an extension graph of $\underline{G}$ with labels in Φ.

An approximation of $\mathcal{F}_{N^e}$ in Φ is given by

$$\mathcal{F}_n^{\Phi}(P_N) \quad \triangleq \quad [\alpha(\Theta)_{n \in N_0} \vee^{\Phi} \bigvee_{(m,n) \in E}^{\Phi} \mathrm{SP}^{\Phi}(\mathcal{T}, P_m)] \wedge \underline{\lambda}(n)$$

where $\alpha(\Theta)_{n \in N_0}$ is defined to be $\alpha(\Theta)$ if $n \in N_0$ and $\bot$ otherwise. The other notations are the same as in Section 7.1. This operator has all the desired properties, except that the ascending sequence

$$\underbrace{(\emptyset)_{n \in N^e}}_{P_{N^e,0}}, \quad \underbrace{\mathcal{F}_{N^e}^{\Phi}(P_{N,0})}_{P_{N^e,1}}, \quad \underbrace{\mathcal{F}_{N^e}^{\Phi}(P_{N,1})}_{P_{N^e,2}}, \quad \ldots$$

does not necessarily converge. We could use again a widening operator to speed up the convergence process. However, the widening operator of Section 7.1 does not guarantee that a solution φ_{N^e} has the property that $\forall n \in N^e \varphi_n \to \underline{\lambda}(n)$. This motivates the following definition:

A *bounded widening operator* is an operator $\nabla : (\varphi_1, \varphi_2, \psi) \mapsto \varphi_1 \overset{\psi}{\nabla} \varphi_2$ where

(W1′) for any $P_1, P_2, P \in \Phi$. $P_1 \vee^\Phi P_2 \to P_1 \overset{P}{\nabla} P_2$

(W2′) for any $P_0 \to P_1 \to \ldots$ in Φ and $P \in \Phi$, the sequence $P'_0, P'_1, \ldots$
defined by $P'_0 = P_0$ and $P'_{i+1} = P'_i \overset{P}{\nabla} P_{i+1}$ converges in finitely many steps.

(W3) for any $P_1, P_2, P \in \Phi$, if $P_1 \to P$ and $P_2 \to P$ then $P_1 \overset{P}{\nabla} P_2 \to P$.

An example of such a bounded operator is

$$P_1 \overset{P}{\nabla} P_2 = \begin{cases} P_2 & \text{if } P_1 = \emptyset \\ \text{the polyhedron defined by} & \\ \quad \text{the constraints of } P_1 \text{ satisfied by } P_2 \text{ and} & \\ \quad \text{the constraints of } P \text{ satisfied by } P_1, P_2 & \text{otherwise} \end{cases}$$

If the forward operator is bounded by P, then the bounded widening operator can be used to obtain converging sequences bounded by P. For any $n \in N^e$, the sequence

$$P'_{n,0} : \text{F}, \quad P'_{n,1} : P'_{n,0} \overset{\underline{\lambda}(n)}{\nabla} \overline{\mathcal{F}}_n(P'_{N,0}), \quad \ldots$$

converges in finitely many steps to a limit that is bounded by $\underline{\lambda}(n)$.

Example (generation of intermediate assertions for rule SAFE) Consider again program LOOP (Figure 13). We want to prove that y takes on all nonnegative integer values in order, that is, if $0 \leq u_1 \leq u_2$ and y has value u_2 then previously y had value u_1. This property is expressed in temporal logic as

$$p_{caus} : \quad \Box(y = u_2 \to \diamondsuit y = u_1) \ .$$

The assertion $0 \leq u_1 \leq u_2$ will be used as a new axiom. An assertion graph G for p_{caus} and its extension G^e are presented in Figure 15.

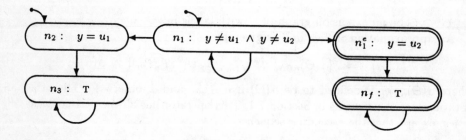

Fig. 15. Graphs $\underline{G}$ and $\underline{G}^e$ for the property p_{caus}

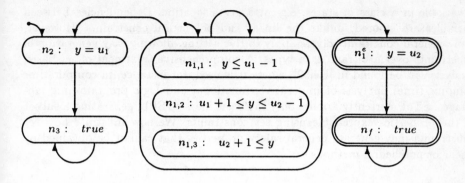

Fig. 16. Graphs $\underline{G}$ and $\underline{G}^e$ for the property p_{caus}

Table 4. Forward propagation for program LOOP and property p_{caus} where $c : N \geq y$

	Θ iteration	exact iteration	∇ iteration
$n_{1,1}$	$y = 0 \leq u_1 - 1 \wedge c$	$0 \leq y \leq 1 \leq u_1 - 1 \wedge c$	$0 \leq y \leq u_1 - 1 \wedge c$
$n_{1,2}$	F	F	F
$n_{1,3}$	F	F	F
n_2	$y = u_1 = 0 \wedge c$	$0 \leq y = u_1 \leq 1 \wedge c$	$0 \leq y = u_1 \wedge c$
n_3	F	$u_1 = 0 \leq y \leq 1 \wedge c$	$0 \leq u_1 \leq y \wedge c$
n_1^e	F	F	F
n^f	F	F	F

To conservatively approximate G we have to strengthen $\lambda(n_1)$ and $\lambda(n_2)$ and weaken $\lambda(n_1^e)$ in the polyhedra domain. In our example, all labels except for $\lambda(n_1)$ are closed convex polyhedra. The labeling of node n_1 is $y \neq u_1 \wedge y \neq u_2$. The negated equalities can be transformed into pairs of inequalities; furthermore, since the variables are integers they can be transformed into weak inequalities, e.g., $y \neq u_1 \ \leftrightarrow \ y \leq u_1 - 1 \ \wedge \ y \geq u_1 + 1$. Rewriting this expression into disjunctive normal form produces polyhedral disjuncts, so no further weakening is necessary. A node labeled by a disjunction can always be split into a cluster of nodes, one for each disjunct. Thus we get the graph in Figure 16. The assertion $0 \leq u_1 \leq u_2$ was used to simplify the labels of the generated nodes, and nodes with label F are not shown.

The forward propagation proceeds as shown in Table 4. The sequence converges after three iterations with empty polyhedra corresponding to the nodes n_1^e and n_f, which proves that p_{caus} is $\mathcal{S}$-valid. ⌐

8 Set-based Analysis

Set-based analysis approximates the state space by associating each system variable with an indexed collection of sets. Each set contains the possible values of a variable in a class of states, e.g. at a given location. Dependencies between variables are ignored, unlike the linear and polyhedral constraints. However, more general constraint solvers apply to this setting allowing easy generation of constraints over arbitrary data types. A comprehensive treatment of set-based analysis can be found in [Hei92], where it is used, for instance, in compile-time (binding-time) analysis of imperative, functional and logic programming languages. STeP currently applies only the basic ideas to SPL, generating a subset of the properties expressible using set constraints. We now illustrate how set constraints may generate general safety properties that cannot be obtained by linear or polyhedral methods.

8.1 Invariance

Given the system variables $\mathcal{V} = \{x_1, \ldots, x_n\}$, let $\mathbf{X}$ be a tuple of sets $(X_1, \ldots, X_n)$ corresponding to $\mathcal{V}$. We refer to a family of such tuples by $\{\mathbf{X}_i\}_{i \in I}$, where I is an index set.

$$
\boxed{
\begin{array}{c}
\textbf{local } x : \textbf{integer where } x = 0 \\[2mm]
P_1 :: \begin{bmatrix} \ell_0: & \textbf{await } x = 1 \\ \ell_1: & x := x + 1 \\ \ell_2: & \end{bmatrix} \quad \| \quad P_2 :: \begin{bmatrix} m_0: & x := 1 \\ m_1: & \textbf{await } x = 2 \\ m_2: & \end{bmatrix}
\end{array}
}
$$

Fig. 17. Program MONADIC

Example (indexed sets) For the trivial program MONADIC, shown in Figure 17, $\mathcal{V} = \{x\}$, and we take $I = \{\ell_0, \ell_1, \ell_2, m_0, m_1, m_2\}$, which gives the family $X_{\ell_0}, X_{\ell_1}, X_{\ell_2}, X_{m_0}, X_{m_1}, X_{m_2}$ of six singleton tuples.

A transition takes an indexed family and produces another according to the effect of the transition. Tuples that are not affected by the transition are set to be empty. Hence we can define

$$
\mathcal{F}^M(\{\mathbf{X}_i\}_{i \in I}) \triangleq \Theta_I \sqcup \bigsqcup_{\tau \in \mathcal{T}} \mathrm{SP}(\tau, \{\mathbf{X}_i\}_{i \in I})
$$

where $\sqcup$ is defined as

$$
\{(X_1, \ldots, X_n)_i\}_{i \in I} \sqcup \{(Y_1, \ldots, Y_n)_i\}_{i \in I} \triangleq \{(X_1 \cup Y_1, \ldots, X_n \cup Y_n)_i\}_{i \in I},
$$

and Θ_I is an indexed family, where tuples for the initial locations contain the initial values and all other tuples have empty sets.

Example For MONADIC, Θ_I is $\left\{ \{0\}_{\ell_0}, \emptyset_{\ell_1}, \emptyset_{\ell_2}, \{0\}_{m_0}, \emptyset_{m_1}, \emptyset_{m_2} \right\}$, and

$$
\begin{aligned}
\mathrm{SP}(\tau_{\ell_0}, \{X_i\}_{i \in I}) &: \left\{ \emptyset_{\ell_0}, (\{1\} \cap X_{\ell_0})_{\ell_1}, \emptyset_{\ell_2}, \emptyset_{m_0}, \emptyset_{m_1}, \emptyset_{m_2} \right\} \\
\mathrm{SP}(\tau_{\ell_1}, \{X_i\}_{i \in I}) &: \left\{ \emptyset_{\ell_0}, \emptyset_{\ell_1}, (X_{\ell_1}+1)_{\ell_2}, (X_{\ell_1}+1)_{m_0}, (X_{\ell_1}+1)_{m_1}, (X_{\ell_1}+1)_{m_2} \right\} \\
\mathrm{SP}(\tau_{m_0}, \{X_i\}_{i \in I}) &: \left\{ \{1\}_{\ell_0}, \{1\}_{\ell_1}, \{1\}_{\ell_2}, \emptyset_{m_0}, \{1\}_{m_1}, \emptyset_{m_2} \right\} \\
\mathrm{SP}(\tau_{m_1}, \{X_i\}_{i \in I}) &: \left\{ \emptyset_{\ell_0}, \emptyset_{\ell_1}, \emptyset_{\ell_2}, \emptyset_{m_0}, \emptyset_{m_1}, (\{2\} \cap X_{m_1})_{m_2} \right\}
\end{aligned}
$$

where $X_{\ell_1}+1$ is shorthand for $\{x+1 \mid x \in X_{\ell_1}\}$; thus $+ : \mathcal{Z} \times \mathcal{Z} \to \mathcal{Z}$ is lifted to its power-set version $+ : 2^{\mathcal{Z}} \times 2^{\mathcal{Z}} \to 2^{\mathcal{Z}}$. Combining the sets with $\sqcup$ we get

$$\mathcal{F}^{\mathcal{M}}(\{X_i\}_{i \in I}) = \left\{ \begin{array}{ll} (\{0,1\})_{\ell_0}, & (\{0\} \cup (X_{\ell_1}+1))_{m_0}, \\ (\{1\})_{\ell_1}, & (\{1\} \cup (X_{\ell_1}+1))_{m_1}, \\ (\{1\} \cup (X_{\ell_1}+1))_{\ell_2}, & ((\{2\} \cap X_{m_1}) \cup (X_{\ell_1}+1))_{m_2} \end{array} \right\} .$$

A crucial observation in set-based analysis is that the least fixedpoint of $\mathcal{F}^{\mathcal{M}}$ can be calculated directly by collecting its effect as constraints on the indexed tuples. The smallest solution to the constraints is the least fixedpoint.

Example (constraints)   For program MONADIC we generate the set constraints

$$X_{\ell_0} \supseteq \{0,1\}, \qquad X_{\ell_1} \supseteq \{1\}, \qquad X_{\ell_2} \supseteq \{1\} \cup (X_{\ell_1}+1),$$
$$X_{m_0} \supseteq \{0\} \cup (X_{\ell_1}+1), \ X_{m_1} \supseteq \{1\} \cup (X_{\ell_1}+1), \ X_{m_2} \supseteq (\{2\} \cap X_{m_1}) \cup (X_{\ell_1}+1) .$$

The least solution of these constraints is:

$$X_{\ell_0} = \{0,1\}, \quad X_{\ell_1} = \{1\}, \quad X_{\ell_2} = \{1,2\},$$
$$X_{m_0} = \{0,2\}, \quad X_{m_1} = \{1,2\}, \quad X_{m_2} = \{2\} .$$

Constraint-solving methods based on tree automata or set constraints [HJ91] are guaranteed to generate this least solution algorithmically.

Each indexed tuple is associated with a first-order constraint by mapping $\mathbf{X}_i$ to $\gamma(\mathbf{X}_i) = \varphi_i \to M_1(x_1) \wedge \ldots \wedge M_n(x_n)$, where the M_k are monadic predicates. $M_k(x)$ is true iff x is a member of each $X_{k,i}$ that satisfies the constraints.

Example (concretization)   The first-order constraints for MONADIC are

$$\gamma(X_{\ell_0}) \colon \ell_0 \to 0 \leq x \leq 1, \quad \gamma(X_{\ell_1}) \colon \ell_1 \to x = 1, \quad \gamma(X_{\ell_2}) \colon \ell_2 \to 1 \leq x \leq 2,$$
$$\gamma(X_{m_0}) \colon m_0 \to x=0 \vee x=2, \ \gamma(X_{m_1}) \colon m_1 \to 1 \leq x \leq 2, \ \gamma(X_{m_2}) \colon m_2 \to x = 2,$$

and the invariant extracted is $\square \bigwedge_{i \in I} \gamma(X_i)$.

8.2   General Safety

The ideas involved in generating general safety properties are similar to those presented for invariance. The following example illustrates the potential of having powerful constraint solvers at our disposal.

Example (parity)   Suppose we want to examine what happens between the point at which program BAKERY (Figure 3) sets y_1 to 1 and when both y_1 and y_2 are 0 again. A template of the events under examination is given in Figure 18.

With each node in G we associate a pair of sets, (Y_1, Y_2) corresponding to the variables y_1 and y_2, indexed by the node identifier, i.e., we have the tuples of sets $(Y_1, Y_2)_{n_1}, \ldots, (Y_1, Y_2)_{n_6}$. The propagation operator $\mathcal{F}_N^{\mathcal{M}}$ is defined for each node n following the general schema

$$\mathcal{F}_n^{\mathcal{M}}(\{(Y_1, Y_2)_n\}_{n \in N}) \triangleq \left[\Theta_{n \in N_0} \sqcup \bigsqcup_{\tau \in \mathcal{T}} \bigsqcup_{(m,n) \in E} \mathrm{SP}(\tau, (Y_1, Y_2)_m) \right] \sqcap \lambda(n)$$

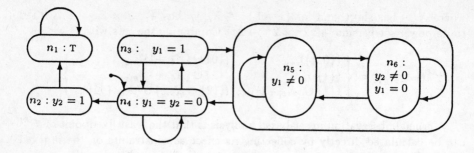

Fig. 18. Assertion graph G for BAKERY

where $\lambda(n)$ is a pair of sets constrained by the node labelings:

$$\lambda(n_1) = (\mathsf{T}, \mathsf{T}), \qquad \lambda(n_2) = (\mathsf{T}, \{1\}), \qquad \lambda(n_3) = (\{1\}, \mathsf{T}),$$
$$\lambda(n_4) = (\{0\}, \{0\}), \quad \lambda(n_5) = (\mathsf{T} \setminus \{0\}, \mathsf{T}), \quad \lambda(n_6) = (\{0\}, \mathsf{T} \setminus \{0\})$$

where T is the set of all possible values, and $\Theta_{n \in N_0} = (\{0\}, \{0\})$ for $n = n_4$ and $(\emptyset, \emptyset)$ otherwise. The operation $\sqcap$ is dual to $\sqcup$ and is characterized by $(X_1, Y_1) \sqcap (X_2, Y_2) = (X_1 \cap X_2, Y_1 \cap Y_2)$. In this case the operator SP takes a pair $(Y_1, Y_2)_n$ and produces a pair (Y_1', Y_2') corresponding to the effect of the transition. For instance,

$$\mathrm{SP}\big(\tau_{\ell_1}, (Y_1, Y_2)_{n_4}\big) = (Y_2 + 1, Y_2) \ .$$

We have also applied the auxiliary invariant $\square(y_2 \neq 0 \to m_2 \vee m_3 \vee m_4)$ to infer that transition τ_{m_1} is disabled at node n_6, hence $\mathrm{SP}(\tau_{m_1}, (Y_1, Y_2)_{n_6}) = (\emptyset, \emptyset)$.

From the fixedpoint equation $\mathcal{F}_N^{\mathcal{M}}(\{(Y_1, Y_2)_n\}_{n \in N}) = \{(Y_1, Y_2)_n\}_{n \in N}$ we extract, as in the invariance analysis, a set of constraints, whose minimal solution is the fixedpoint. For $n_3, \ldots, n_6$ the constraints are:

$$\{1\} \subseteq Y_{1,n_3} \quad \{0\} \subseteq Y_{1,n_4} \quad Y_{1,n_3} \cup (Y_{2,n_5} \cup Y_{2,n_6}) + 1 \subseteq Y_{1,n_5} \qquad \{0\} \subseteq Y_{1,n_6}$$
$$\{0\} \subseteq Y_{2,n_3} \quad \{0\} \subseteq Y_{2,n_4} \quad Y_{2,n_3} \cup (Y_{1,n_3} \cup Y_{1,n_5}) + 1 \subseteq Y_{2,n_5} \quad Y_{2,n_5} \setminus \{0\} \subseteq Y_{2,n_6}$$

whose minimal solution is

$$(Y_1, Y_2)_{n_3} = (\{1\}, \{0\}) \quad (Y_1, Y_2)_{n_5} = (\{n \in \mathcal{N} \mid odd(n)\}, \{n \in \mathcal{N} \mid even(n)\})$$
$$(Y_1, Y_2)_{n_4} = (\{0\}, \{0\}) \quad (Y_1, Y_2)_{n_6} = (\{0\}, \{n \in \mathcal{N} \mid even(n) \wedge n > 0\})$$

where $\mathcal{N}$ is the set of nonnegative integers. We have thus extracted the information that when y_1 is set to 1 (represented by n_3), y_2 remains even and y_1 either odd or 0 until both are simultaneously 0 again (represented by n_4). ◢

Acknowledgements We thank Henny Sipma and Tomás Uribe for their many helpful comments and suggestions.

References

[CC77]   P. Cousot and R. Cousot. Abstract interpretation: A unified lattice model for static analysis of programs by construction or approximation of fixpoints. In 4th *ACM Symp. Princ. of Prog. Lang.*, pages 238–252. ACM Press, 1977.

[CGL92]   E.M. Clarke, O. Grumberg, and D.E. Long. Model checking and abstraction. In 19th *ACM Symp. Princ. of Prog. Lang.*, pages 343–354, 1992.

[CH78]   P. Cousot and N. Halbwachs. Automatic discovery of linear restraints among the variables of a program. In 5th *ACM Symp. Princ. of Prog. Lang.*, pages 84–97, Jan. 1978.

[DGG94]   D.R. Dams, O. Grumberg, and R. Gerth. Abstract interpretation of reactive systems: Abstractions preserving ∀CTL*, ∃ECTL*, CTL*. In *IFIP Working Conference on Programming Concepts, Methods and Calculi (PROCOMET 94)*, pages 573–592, June 1994.

[Gra91]   P. Granger. Static analysis of linear congruence equalities among variables of a program. In *TAPSOFT 91, Vol.1: Colloq. on Trees in Algebra and Programming (CAAP '91)*, LNCS, pages 169–192. Springer-Verlag, April 1991.

[GW75]   S. M. German and B. Wegbreit. A Synthesizer of Inductive Assertions. *IEEE transactions on Software Engineering*, 1(1):68–75, March 1975.

[Har84]   D. Harel. Statecharts: A visual approach to complex systems. Technical Report CS84-05, Dept. of Applied Mathematics, Weizmann Institute of Science, 1984.

[Hei92]   N. Heintze. *Set Based Program Analysis*. PhD thesis, Carnegie Mellon University, 1992.

[HH95]   T.A. Henzinger and P.-H. Ho. Algorithmic analysis of nonlinear hybrid systems. In *Proc. 7th Intl. Conference on Computer Aided Verification*, LNCS, 1995.

[HJ91]   N. Heintze and J. Jaffar. A decision procedure for a class of Herbrand set constraints. Technical Report CMU-CS-91-110, Carnegie Mellon University, Feb. 1991. Abstract appears in *Proceedings of the 5th Annual IEEE Symposium on Logic in Computer Science*, 1990.

[HRP94]   N. Halbwachs, P. Raymond, and Y.-E. Proy. Verification of linear hybrid systems by means of convex approximations. In 1st *Intl. Static Analysis Symp.*, vol. 864 of *LNCS*, pages 223–237. Springer-Verlag, Sept. 1994.

[Kar76]   M. Karr. Affine relationships among variables of a program. *Acta Informatica*, 6:133–151, 1976.

[KM76]   S. Katz and Z. Manna. Logical analysis of programs. *Communications of the ACM*, 19(4):188–206, April 1976.

[Lau73]   K. Lautenbach. Exacte Bedingungen der Lebendigkeit für eine Klasse von Petri-Netzen. *St. Augustin, GMD Bonn*, 82, 1973.

[MAB⁺94] Z. Manna, A. Anuchitanukul, N. Bjørner, A. Browne, E. Chang, M. Colón, L. de Alfaro, H. Devarajan, H.B. Sipma, and T.E. Uribe. STeP: The Stanford temporal prover. Technical Report STAN-CS-TR-94-1518, Computer Science Department, Stanford University, July 1994.

[MP95]   Z. Manna and A. Pnueli. *Temporal Verification of Reactive Systems: Safety*. Springer-Verlag, New York, 1995.

[Rei85]   W. Reisig. *Petri Nets: An Introduction*, vol. 4 of *EATCS Monographs on Theoretical Computer Science*. Springer-Verlag, Berlin, 1985.

The OTI Constraint Solver:
A Constraint Library for Constructing
Interactive Graphical User Interfaces

Alan Borning[1] and Bjorn N. Freeman-Benson[2]

[1] Department of Computer Science and Engineering, University of Washington,
Box 352350, Seattle, Washington 98195-2350, USA; borning@cs.washington.edu
[2] Object Technology International Inc., R. Buckminster Fuller Laboratory,
201 - 506 Fort St., Victoria, B.C., Canada V8W 1E6; bnfb@oti.on.ca

Abstract. ENVY/Constraints is an IBM/Smalltalk library that provides a constraint satisfier and a collection of useful constraints, targeted at developing interactive graphical user interfaces. The solver supports multi-way constraints and constraint hierarchies. It uses a hybrid algorithm, combining local propagation with pluggable cycle solvers, allowing constraints to range over arbitrary objects, while at the same time satisfying constraints representing simultaneous equations over the reals.

1 Introduction

A variety of research projects have demonstrated the utility of constraints in building interactive graphical applications. Some applications of constraints in user interface software are maintaining consistency between application data and views of that data on the screen, maintaining consistency among multiple views, and determining the layout of windows and other graphical entities, in particular specifying geometric constraints on manipulable graphical objects. Early examples of such research projects include Sketchpad [10] and ThingLab [1]. More recent projects include Garnet [7], TRIP II [6], and many others. (See e.g. [8] for many additional references.)

In this project, we wanted to provide a commercial-quality constraint library, written in Smalltalk, to support writing interactive graphical applications. Our previous experience with such applications lead to the following choices for the constraint library:

1. The library must have good performance, so that we can, for example, move a constrained object on the screen with reasonable interactive feedback.
2. We wanted to support multi-way as well as one-way constraints, since multi-way constraints are more expressive, particularly for such uses as layout and geometric constraints.
3. We wanted to support constraint hierarchies [2], which allow soft or preferential constraints as well as required constraints. Such constraints are particularly useful in an interactive graphical environment to express the desire for stability in a figure—that some part shouldn't move unless some stronger

constraint forces it to. A variety of ways of selecting solutions to constraint hierarchies have been defined; we chose the locally-predicate-better comparator, since it is understandable and generally efficiently implementable.

4. We wanted to allow constrained variables to hold arbitrary kinds of Smalltalk objects, not just a few fixed data types. This allows application programmers to use constraints to accomplish such tasks as constraining colors, keeping a font consistent with a font string description, and the like.

5. We wanted more powerful constraint solvers than local propagation—in interactive user interfaces, simultaneous linear equations and inequalities arise naturally, for example.

Object Technology International, which has supported the work described here, is a software engineering company specializing in object-oriented systems. Its headquarters is in Ottawa, Canada; there are also some eight other R&D labs elsewhere in North America, in Europe, and in Australia. The company's primary business is joint development and technology licensing through alliances with major corporations. OTI develops and maintains a portfolio of software components, tools, and processes, which it uses in the development of object-oriented systems and products. OTI's interest in the constraint library is simple: it is a software tool that (we hope) will allow selected applications to be written more easily, that will be more maintainable, and to have additional capabilities that would be difficult to provide just by writing standard imperative code.

OTI has used the ENVY/Constraints library in a number of products, both internal and external. For example, we used the library to build a graphical editor application for a large database. The end user does not explicitly know that constraints are used, rather he or she just knows that the figures in the drawings all "behave correctly." Some of the figures move together (i.e., are constrained to move together), others are linked by stretchable lines (i.e., the lines are constrained to the figures), and still others are completely unconstrained.

Our own initial motivation for undertaking this project was a desire to move academic research into industrial use. However, as the project has progressed, it has become a research endeavor in its own right. The work has also fed back into academia; for example, the ENVY/Constraints solver is now used as the constraint engine underlying our current implementation of the Kaleidoscope'93 constraint imperative language [5].

There has been much industrial work in applying constraints to planning, scheduling, and optimization problems, which has already achieved excellent results. The techniques required for such applications are rather different, however, than those needed for interactive user interfaces. We need low latency response for interactivity. Also, we start with a solved set of constraints, perturb the state with a user input, and adjust the state to satisfy the constraints again. In contrast, the planning and scheduling applications don't always require an interactive response, and typically involve solving for the values of initially unbound variables (in the style of logic programming), in contrast to updating the current state and resatisfying the constraints (in the style of imperative programming).

2 The UltraViolet Algorithm

Unfortunately, some of the goals outlined in Section 1 conflict with each other. Efficient local propagation algorithms are available that meet the first four goals (efficiency, multi-way constraints, constraint hierarchies, constraints over arbitrary classes of objects)—but local propagation doesn't handle cycles or inequalities (Goal 5). However, one of the standard algorithms for handling e.g. collections of linear equality or inequality constraints wouldn't handle constraints over arbitrary classes of objects, and would be less efficient than local propagation.

We therefore designed a hybrid algorithm, named UltraViolet (in keeping with our shades-of-blue naming scheme for constraint satisfaction algorithms). UltraViolet uses local propagation when possible, and resorts to a cycle solver when necessary. It uses a modular architecture, which allows different cycle solvers to be plugged in and selected according to the kinds of constraints that are in the cycle.

The algorithm is incremental: as constraints and constrainable variables are added and deleted, the solution is updated. The constraints and variables are partitioned into connected subgraphs, since if there are no constraints that connect the two subgraphs, they can be solved independently. Within a connected subgraph, the constraints and variables are partitioned into cycles and acyclic local propagation regions, based on the topology of the constraint graph.

The local propagation regions are solved using the DeltaBlue algorithm [3, 9]. The local propagation algorithm communicates with the cycle solvers via variables that are shared by the cycle and the local propagation region—the information passed back and forth is a value for that variable and a walkabout strength (the strength of the weakest constraint that can be revoked to allow that variable to be set to any value).

The solver architecture selects the appropriate cycle solver based on the kinds of constraints that are in the cycle. In the current product we use only one cycle solver, although our architecture has been tested using several different solvers. This linear equation cycle solver handles constraints that can be represented as systems of simultaneous linear equations. These equations have strengths associated with them (corresponding to the strengths of their constraints), and may be redundant or inconsistent. (However, the variables will never be underconstrained—each variable has an implicit "stay" constraint at the weakest strength that attempts to keep it at its current value, so if the variable isn't given a value by some stronger constraint the weakest stay will cause it to remain at its current value.)

The design of the linear equation cycle solver is adapted from that of the linear equation solver used in CLP($\mathcal{R}$) [4]. The constraints in the cycle are first converted to linear normal form. (If no such form exists, the linear equation cycle solver reports failure to UltraViolet so that another cycle solver could be tried instead.) The variables in the cycle are classified as parametric variables, non-parametric variables, and known variables. The non-parametric variables are defined in terms of a linear expression containing parametric variables. Known variables are a special case of non-parametric variables, and have a known (constant) value. Initially all the variables are classified as parametric. The constraints are sorted by strength and processed strongest first. In constructing the normal form, non-parametric variables are replaced by their corresponding expressions. If, after simplification, the resulting equation is approximately $0 = 0$, the new constraint is redundant given the currently satisfied constraints, and can be ignored. If the result is $0 = c$ for some non-zero c, the constraint is inconsistent with the currently satisfied constraints. If the constraint was required, the solver reports that the required constraints can't be satisfied; otherwise the constraint can be ignored. Otherwise the constraint can be satisfied and adds new information. It is solved for one of its parametric variables, resulting in this variable being moved to either the non-parametric or known variables. Finally, after all the constraints have been processed, all of the variables will be in the set of known variables, and the sets of parametric and non-parametric variables will be empty.

The library includes a callback mechanism to notify imperative code when constrained variables have been changed by the solver. In typical applications, these callbacks are used to update the visual appearance of constrained objects after their defining constraints (position, color, shape, etc.) are satisfied. The callback mechanism is also used to signal the application program when required constraints cannot be satisfied or cycles cannot be solved.

3 Future Work

In the near future we plan to add support for inequality constraints (on real numbers) and for plan compilation. Linear inequality constraints occur frequently in interactive graphical applications—for example, a constraint that one window be somewhere to the left of another, or a constraint that a line lie within a rectangle. Our design supports both local propagation solutions for inequalities, which will be used when possible, and a simplex-based solver for cycles containing inequalities. Plan compilation is an important technique for achieving good performance in interactive applications involving repeated solutions of the same collection of constraints for different input values (e.g. when dragging part of a constrained figure with the mouse). Given the current set of constraints, Smalltalk code is produced that can be re-evaluated for each new input value, rather than re-invoking the constraint solver each time. Plan compilation can also be used to release constraint-based products without the ENVY/Constraints library—the effect of the constraints is captured in the compiled Smalltalk code.

Subsequently, we plan to design and implement other kinds of cycle solvers for different classes of constraints, and to add support for constraint visualization and debugging. Throughout the process, we will continue to work with industrial users of the constraint library, developing and using additional application frameworks, and feeding the results back to the design of the constraint satisfaction library.

Acknowledgements

Thanks to Gus Lopez for being an early user of the library, and to Richard Anderson for recent help on constraint satisfaction algorithm design. This project has been funded by Object Technology International. Preparation of this paper, as well as earlier research in this area on which this work draws, has been funded in part by the National Science Foundation under Grants IRI-9302249 and CCR-9402551.

References

1. Alan Borning. The programming language aspects of ThingLab, a constraint-oriented simulation laboratory. *ACM Transactions on Programming Languages and Systems*, 3(4):353–387, October 1981.

2. Alan Borning, Bjorn Freeman-Benson, and Molly Wilson. Constraint hierarchies. *Lisp and Symbolic Computation*, 5(3):223–270, September 1992.

3. Bjorn Freeman-Benson, John Maloney, and Alan Borning. An incremental constraint solver. *Communications of the ACM*, 33(1):54–63, January 1990.

4. Joxan Jaffar, Spiro Michaylov, Peter Stuckey, and Roland Yap. The CLP($\mathcal{R}$) language and system. *ACM Transactions on Programming Languages and Systems*, 14(3):339–395, July 1992.

5. Gus Lopez, Bjorn Freeman-Benson, and Alan Borning. Implementing constraint imperative programming languages: The kaleidoscope'93 virtual machine. In *Proceedings of the 1994 ACM Conference on Object-Oriented Programming Systems, Languages, and Applications*, pages 259–271, October 1994.

6. Satoshi Matsuoka, Shin Takahashi, Tomihisa Kamada, and Akinori Yonezawa. A general framework for bidirectional translation between abstract and pictorial data. *ACM Transactions on Information Systems*, 10(4):408–437, October 1992.

7. Brad A. Myers, Dario A. Giuse, Roger B. Dannenberg, Brad Vander Zanden, David S. Kosbie, Ed Pervin, Andrew Mickish, and Philippe Marchal. Garnet: Comprehensive support for graphical, highly-interactive user interfaces. *IEEE Computer*, 23(11):71–85, November 1990.

8. Michael Sannella. *Constraint Satisfaction and Debugging for Interactive User Interfaces*. PhD thesis, Department of Computer Science and Engineering, University of Washington, 1994. Forthcoming.

9. Michael Sannella, John Maloney, Bjorn Freeman-Benson, and Alan Borning. Multi-way versus one-way constraints in user interfaces: Experience with the DeltaBlue algorithm. *Software—Practice and Experience*, 23(5):529–566, May 1993.

10. Ivan Sutherland. *Sketchpad: A Man-Machine Graphical Communication System*. PhD thesis, Department of Electrical Engineering, MIT, January 1963.

Model-Based Computing:
Using Concurrent Constraint Programming for Modeling and Model Compilation

Markus P.J. Fromherz   Vijay A. Saraswat

Xerox PARC, 3333 Coyote Hill Road, Palo Alto, CA 94304
{fromherz,saraswat}@parc.xerox.com

Abstract. Writing software for simulating, controlling or diagnosing real-world physical devices is non-trivial, as it requires encoding the complex interactions of device components and processes. *Model-based computing* is an approach to developing such software that employs multi-use declarative machine descriptions to derive information from which machine software can be constructed automatically. Specifically, we have been using this approach to develop code for *scheduling reprographic machines.*

We discuss the modeling of hardware components for scheduling purposes using concurrent constraint programming. We show how standard symbolic manipulation techniques such as partial evaluation and abduction can be used to process these models into a form that is directly compilable into procedural (C++) code and usable within a conventional software architecture.

1   Introduction

In the industrial marketplace, the constant demand of ever greater functionality at ever lower prices results in products that are ever more complex. For many high-tech devices, this complexity has remained manageable only by using software for controlling systems composed of electro-mechanical and computational elements.

However, the construction of such software has become a gargantuan task. For instance, traditional product development methods for reprographic machines (photo-copiers, printers, fax machines etc.) involve dozens, if not hundreds of mechanical, electrical, software and systems engineers. The software is produced mostly by hand. Few, if any, automated tools are available to help in the design and analysis of machines, or in the production of software and documentation.

Such work practices are unable to deal with the increasing demand for faster time to market, and for greater flexibility in product lines. These demands can be addressed by faster, concurrent software development, and by "plug-and-play" machine modules, but this requires the development of software that is generic, reusable and customizable, rather than software that is custom-tailored for a particular configuration.

To address some of these problems, we are investigating the application of *model-based computing* techniques. The central idea is to develop compositional, declarative models of machines, at different levels of granularity, customized for different tasks. Together with such models, suitable software architectures with generic algorithms are developed for the tasks at hand (e.g., simulation, diagnosis, control-code generation, scheduling, etc.). Finally, linking the two are special-purpose, though configuration-independent, reasoners. Exploiting the declarative semantics of the modeling formalism (e.g., using partial evaluation and abduction techniques), these reasoners produce from the input models information in the right form for the given task architecture.

Using model-based computing in a particular application domain thus has two challenging parts to it: finding a suitable *generic software architecture* that can lead to efficient implementations, and developing a *domain theory* that is both powerful enough to describe relevant properties of the application domain and rigorous enough to permit the automatic synthesis and integration of the necessary software configuration information. This paper focuses on the second issue. After reviewing the scheduling problem for reprographic machines, we will provide details of our modeling language and describe the compilation of models to suitable run-time structures.

2 Scheduling Reprographic Machines

One application of model-based computing that we have studied extensively is the construction of real-time schedulers for modular, networked reprographic machines.

Fig. 1 shows a typical, simplified module, a *mark engine* that is able to produce sheets with one (simplex) or two images (duplex) on them. This sample module consists of several *components*: a marker, an inverter, merge and split components, and two transport components. A simplex sheet is printed once and moved to the output, bypassing the inverter. A duplex sheet is printed on one side, then inverted and moved back to be printed on the other side, before it is inverted again and moved to the output. Such a mark engine can typically handle many different sheet sizes, and can also be augmented to print color copies. Other types of machine modules are feeder modules (sheet sources) and finisher modules (for stapling, binding, etc.).

The scheduler. Conceptually, reprographic machines may be thought of as multi-pass assembly line machines, where parts (e.g., sheets, images) are moved along the assembly line (e.g., paper path, photo-receptor belt) and put together until a desired output is produced. At the heart of the control software for such a system is the *scheduler*. The scheduler receives a continuous stream of "jobs" from the electronic sub-system. A job describes what needs to be accomplished, and the scheduler must plan the sequence of actions that need to be taken by each module to produce the job. Typically, it is desired to *complete* the job as quickly as possible; sometimes it is also desired to *start* the job as quickly as possible. (In general, scheduling and execution happen in parallel, with a short lead time for the scheduler.)

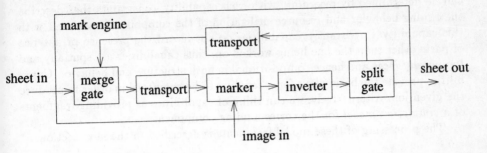

Fig. 1. Schematic view of a simple reprographic machine module

It should be clear that the transportation and printing of sheets is constrained in various ways by the physics of the machine. For example, sheets cannot overlap in the paper path (resource constraint), sheets and images have to be synchronized, images can be placed on the photo-receptor belt only at certain places, inversion takes longer than bypassing and therefore inverted sheets cannot immediately be followed by non-inverted sheets at the entrance of the inverter, etc. [3]. When sequencing module operations, the scheduler has to satisfy these constraints.

3   Modeling Reprographic Machines

The central idea of our approach to scheduling reprographic machines is to use *veridical, declarative* models of these machines. Veridical models directly capture the physics of components (at an appropriate level of abstraction), and the construction of systems from these components. Declarative models are represented as a conjunction of logical formulas that can directly be understood and interpreted in terms of the system at hand. Such models can be produced by people who are experts in the structure and behavior of the machine, rather than in programming languages or software engineering techniques. Such models enable a clear separation between generic application-oriented algorithms and machine-specific information, which in turn allows us to reuse models for more than one application.

Domain theory. Intuitively, each component is to be modeled as a transducer of timed streams; for example, a mark engine takes as input a stream of video images, sheets and control signals, and produces as output a stream of prints. This requires a representation of the basic "one-shot" (atomic) operations of each component, specifying which outputs can be produced from which inputs, given a control signal. We will call (the description of) these basic operations *capabilities.* For example, an inverter has capabilities to *bypass* or *invert* an input sheet.
 In order to produce the required job, several of these capabilities, from several components, need to be sequenced. The legality of sequences of capabilities

can be determined by recording, with each capability, constraints that describe the timing behavior and resource utilization of the component associated with this capability. Importantly, capabilities do not record the presence or absence of parts other than the one being worked on: thus capabilities are spatially and temporally *local*, and hence compositional in both structure and behavior. Capabilities provide the basic *plans* for scheduling to be composed in order to produce the given job. Alternatively, we can think of capabilities as providing fragments of a *simulation model* for the corresponding component.

The processing of these model fragments is described in the next section.

Modeling language. As basic representation language, we have designed a concrete concurrent constraint language cc(FT, Res) using feature-trees and a resource constraint system. An instance of the cc languages [6] was chosen for flexibility and expressiveness: concurrent processes define components that are running in parallel, channels (lists) correspond to component ports through which sheets and images are forwarded, and shared channels model connected ports. Furthermore, suitable constraint systems can easily be added, and various language techniques can be used for reasoning about behavior. The combinators used are ask, tell, parallel composition, hiding, together with definition via recursion. The language and its constraint systems will be explained in more detail in forthcoming papers.

The cc(FT, Res) language is our internal language of representation. For the modeler, we provide a domain-oriented modeling language that simplifies the specification of structural elements and has sections for attaching behavioral definitions. In this Component Description Language (CDL), behavior is defined using cc(FT, Res), and the resulting models are translated to cc(FT, Res) programs. The use of a separate modeling language enables us to add useful parameters to the models (e.g., for debugging, or for use in reasoning algorithms) by changing the compiler without affecting the original models.

More concretely, the following elements appear in component models for scheduling. The basic behavior of a component is to *move parts* (sheets or images) from entry to exit ports. Moving parts takes time, which is stated by *events and timing constraints*. Some component capabilities transform parts, which requires an explicit representation of *part features and constraints* on these features. For their operations, components need resources, declared by *resource allocations* together with their timing constraints. These elements — component structure, moving parts with changing features, and resource allocations with timings — together form the vocabulary from which component models are put together.

A more detailed description of the modeling elements is beyond the space of this paper. In order to get an intuition of CDL, consider a transporter component with one capability, "move". This capability forwards the sheet (not wider than 300 mm) unchanged, but with a delay given by the length and speed of the component. The following is a complete model of this component.

```
component transport(Length,Speed) is  % parameters Length, Speed
    entryPorts in;
    exitPorts  out;
    resources  inR: signal,      % resources that don't allow
               outR: signal;     % ... overlapping of allocations

    capability move(T_in) is       % capability with reference time T_in
        in.input(S, T_in),         % sheet S_in enters during T_in
        out.output(S, T_out),      % ... and exits as S_out during T_out
        inR.allocate(T_in, busy),  % space at entry and exit is
        outR.allocate(T_out, busy), % ... reserved during T_in and T_out
        S.width =< 300,            % feature constraint on the width
        T_in.start + Length/Speed = T_out.start, % timing constraints
        T_in.duration = T_out.duration           % ... on the intervals
    end move
end transport.
```

Component models can be put together (through parallel composition) to describe composite configurations. (Note, in particular, that parallel composition is powerful enough to describe configurations with loops.) Component models usually are instances of more generic descriptions obtained from design libraries. This means that designers often want to specialize the composite models with information further describing the intended use of the current configuration. As an example, in the configuration of Fig. 1, no sheet may be allowed to traverse the duplex loop more than once. In CDL these design restrictions can be elegantly stated using the underlying cc(FT, Res) language.

4   Model Compilation

Given the output job (goal), the scheduler performs two basic actions: *plan selection* (selection of capabilities for each component) and *sequencing* (determination of a legal timing for execution of the selected capabilities). We will concentrate on the former in this paper. Logically, it boils down to the following operation. Given input parts I and capability control commands C, machine model M would compute output parts O by executing the processes corresponding to the component capabilities selected by C. Logically, given M and O, it is desired to determine I and C such that:

$$M \vdash I, C \to O$$

and I, C is consistent.

One attractive aspect of the model-based computing approach is that it is possible to perform part of this work at design-time, through a process of *model compilation* (akin to knowledge compilation [4]): machine capabilities can be precompiled by partially evaluating the model.

Model compilation is done in two stages. First, CDL models are translated to cc(FT, Res) processes that exchange control commands, inputs, and outputs

on their communication channels. Recursive calls and additional parameters are
added automatically by the compiler. Each component capability is translated
into a clause for the corresponding process.

Second, the model can be evaluated at design-time to determine composite
capabilities for the entire machine. Conceptually, this is accomplished by performing fold/unfold transformations on the process corresponding to the composite configuration. In principle, a single clause representing a composite configuration is replaced by a collection of clauses, one for each *consistent, output-
complete*, and *input-complete* selection of component capabilities (clauses). A
selection is consistent if the constraints in the body of the clause are consistent.
A selection is output-complete if the output of each component (given the capability selected) is consumed by the downstream component (if any). A selection
is input-complete if the input to each component (given the capability selected)
is produced by the upstream component (if any). (Note that because the configuration may contain loops, the same component can be selected more than once,
for operation at different times; however, it is expected that design restrictions,
such as those described above, will ensure that the composite machine has a
finite number of capabilities.)

In practice, a more efficient data-driven approach is used to synthesize capabilities. A "seed" (e.g., a generic sheet) is placed at the output, and propagated
through the network via partial evaluation (for down-stream propagation) and
abduction (for up-stream propagation). (Note here that because of the monotone nature of execution in cc languages, partial evaluation can be implemented
merely by execution.) The cc(FT, Res)-to-CDL compiler facilitates this intended
usage of component models by introducing annotations to guide abduction, and
by adding constructs that automatically close all channels when a composite
capability has been synthesized.

These algorithms are currently implemented in Prolog, and provided as part
of a modeling tool for engineers. Other technology is needed if one wants to
embed this in a real-time controller for product machines.

5   Related Work

Model-based computing has its roots in *model-based reasoning*. There, relationships of structure, behavior and function of physical devices have been investigated with the intent of deriving knowledge about device behavior from "first
principles" [2, 1, 9]. What is emphasized in our framework is the use of a declarative, constraint-based modeling notation that is also powerful enough to function
as a programming language.

Constraint-based scheduling has long been used in "intelligent" scheduling
systems [5, 10]. The most general approach to constraint-based scheduling is
using a constraint programming language, as proposed for cc(FD) [7], CHIP [8]
and related languages. We follow a similar approach, building on a well-defined
semantics with flexibility in language extension and program manipulation. In

addition, we provide a domain-specific modeling language, and our technology interfaces well with software written in other languages.

6 Conclusions

The scheduler is one of the most complex pieces of code in the control software of reprographic machines. Using constraint-based representations, we have presented an approach to constructing part of this software from compositional models of the machine's components.

We believe that model-based computing — developing software that captures real-world objects in declarative executable descriptions — is an approach suitable for various application domains. Declarative models enable multi-use of the captured information, as well as flexibility and reusability of the resulting software. As more and more applications profit from explicit system models, modeling will become a core activity in software development.

Acknowledgments

The work reported here has been carried out in collaboration with a number of other researchers and engineers within Xerox Corporation, including the past and present members of the Machine Control project (Danny Bobrow, Vineet Gupta, Tim Lindholm and Pierre Berlandier) at PARC.

References

1. AAAI. *AAAI'90 Workshop on Model Based Reasoning*, July 1990.
2. B. Chandrasekaran and R. Milne, editors. Special Section on Reasoning about Structure, Behavior and Function. *Sigart Newsletter*, 93:4–55, 1985.
3. M. Fromherz and B. Carlson. Optimal Incremental and Anytime Scheduling. In P. Lim and J. Jourdan, editors, *Proc. Workshop on Constraint Languages/Systems and their Use in Problem Modelling at ILPS'94*, pages 45–59. ECRC, TR 94-38, Nov. 1993.
4. A. Goel, editor. Knowledge Compilation. *IEEE Expert*, 6(2):71–93, 1991.
5. P. Prosser and I. Buchanan. Intelligent Scheduling: Past, Present, and Future. *Intelligent Systems Engineering*, 3(2):67–78, 1994.
6. V. A. Saraswat. *Concurrent Constraint Programming*. Doctoral Dissertation Award and Logic Programming Series. MIT Press, Cambridge, MA, 1993.
7. P. Van Hentenryck. Scheduling and Packing in the Constraint Language CC(FD). [10], 137–167.
8. P. Van Hentenryck and T. Le Provost. Incremental Search in Constraint Logic Programming. *New Generation Computing*, (9):257–275, 1991.
9. D. S. Weld and J. de Kleer. *Readings in Qualitative Reasoning about Physical Systems*. Morgan Kaufmann, San Mateo, Calif., 1990.
10. M. Zweben, and M. S. Fox, editors. *Intelligent Scheduling*. Morgan Kaufmann, San Francisco, CA, 1994.

CLP in ECRC

Micha Meier and Alexander Herold

European Computer Industry Research Centre,
Arabellastr. 17, 81925 Munich, Germany
micha@ecrc.de, herold@ecrc.de

1   History

Constraint logic programming (CLP) has been one of main research topics of ECRC since its foundation in 1984. The CHIP system [3] was the first CLP system developed at ECRC and it was designed to tackle real world constrained search problems. It was based on the concept of active use of constraints and it included three computation domains: finite domain restricted terms, boolean terms and linear rational terms. For each of them CHIP used a specialised constraint solver tightly integrated with the Prolog engine.

In another research direction, the SEPIA system [5] has been developed with the goal of providing an efficient Prolog system with low-level support for developing new logic programming extensions especially in the control area.

The ElipSys system [8] was the first parallel CLP research system implemented at ECRC. It included only a finite domain constraint solver, but it was able to use OR-parallel execution on shared-memory multiprocessors to explore the huge search spaces in parallel. The interface to the constraint solver was done in a modular way, using *consecutively updatable fields* to attach data to logical variables.

The functionalities of all ECRC's logic-programming systems have been integrated in a common system, which became the main platform for the ECRC's work in the area of advanced information management. This is **ECL^{i}PS^e**, the ECRC Constraint Logic Parallel System.

2   ECL^{i}PS^e

The large and complex problems encountered in constraint programming make it necessary to experiment with new constraint types, new solvers, various control approaches and also combinations of different methods. The **ECL^{i}PS^e** system was designed to meet these requirements. Its main goal is to support prototyping, development and use of various system extensions that exploit different control schemes and to ensure that various extensions can smoothly work together in one system. While other CLP systems have used a more or less tightly integrated approach to constraint solver implementation, the **ECL^{i}PS^e** approach is modular and it is built on well-defined interfaces between basic building blocks, which are independent and programmed in **ECL^{i}PS^e** itself.

The constraint interface is based on two fundamental concepts:

- *Attributed variables* make it possible to associate additional data with logical variables and to add user-defined handlers to system primitives like e.g. the unification. The variable attributes are subject to module visibility rules. Different constraint solvers can thus be independently developed and included into the system.
- *Suspensions* correspond to suspended goals and they represent active agents waiting for particular events to occur. They can be used to implement various kinds of data-driven computations.

These data types make it possible to develop constraint solvers as well as various other extensions that go beyond the basic CLP scheme, without resorting to kernel modifications and low-level programming. The constraint extensions are implemented in the the **ECL^{i}PS^e** language as libraries. The interoperability of these libraries, a major problem for other constraint systems, is automatically guaranteed. **ECL^{i}PS^e** currently provides the following constraint libraries:

- **Suspend** is the library for basic coroutining, used by most other extensions. Previously, this functionality was provided by specialised kernel functions, WAM support and was coded in C. The current **ECL^{i}PS^e** code is much shorter, more general and still sufficiently efficient.
- The finite domains library **fd** provides data types, basic arithmetic and symbolic constraints and primitives to support writing of user-defined constraints over variables with finite atomic or ground domains.
- Linear rational arithmetic solver provides the CLP(Q) and CLP(R) functionality.
- **Propia**, the library for generalised propagation, makes it possible to run normal Prolog or finite domain predicates as constraints with specified amount of propagation.
- Constraint Handling Rules (**CHR**) is a system which provides a declarative high-level language to write constraint solvers.
- **Conjunto**, a constraint solver for finite sets built on top of the finite domain library.

The fact that all constraint solvers are written in **ECL^{i}PS^e** itself has several important consequences:

- All data can be directly accessed and manipulated, there are no hidden black boxes.
- The complete environment is directly available in all extensions, e.g. the compiler, garbage collector, debugger, graphics, etc.
- Modifications of the system kernel will not make the extensions incompatible. Moreover, improvements of the kernel (e.g. compilation technology or parallel execution) are immediately available.

3 Parallel CLP

The latest **ECL^{i}PS^e** release supports OR-parallel execution on shared-memory multiprocessors. This type of parallelism is very useful for large search problems typical for CLP, because the search space can be explored on several processors in parallel. The OR-parallel execution is transparent to the user, a sequential CLP program can be simply enhanced by **parallel** annotations for selected predicates and the system takes care of processor allocation and tasks scheduling.

4 Current and Future Work

4.1 Applications and Cooperative Projects

ECRC is concentrating mainly on the research and system development topics, but the **ECL^{i}PS^e** system is also being used in CLP applications. In the ESPRIT industrial projects CHIC [2] and APPLAUSE [1] a number of CLP applications from various areas like transportation, manufacturing, traffic control, planning or pollution control has been developed in cooperation with industrial and academic partners. ECRC's shareholders Bull, ICL and Siemens, as well as IC-PARC (Centre for Planning and Resource Control at the Imperial College in London) and a number of other licenced **ECL^{i}PS^e** users are also using **ECL^{i}PS^e** to develop CLP applications.

4.2 Distributed ECL^{i}PS^e

We are currently working on a distributed version of parallel **ECL^{i}PS^e**, which will run on a network of possibly heterogeneous computers [6]. Such a system will be able to exploit local networks, now available in most organisations, as a single large parallel computer. Alternatively, large and difficult problems can be tackled by connecting a number of parallel computers via the Internet.

4.3 Parallel CLP

With **ECL^{i}PS^e** we have obtained a platform that allows us to open up the area of parallel CLP. There is a number of research issues here, like e.g. parallel optimisation methods [7]. Complicated algorithms used for sequential solving can be simulated by very simple algorithms in the parallel setting and this area seems very promising. The high-level approach used to write extensions in **ECL^{i}PS^e** allows an easy programming and exploring of various parallel search strategies and mixed methods.

4.4 Integration of Different Solvers and Approaches

The **ECL^{i}PS^e** framework allows to combine different competitive or cooperative solvers in one system. We plan to use this framework to integrate and/or interface various approaches from mathematical programming and heuristic techniques into CLP and thus to give the user the possibility to combine different methods into new, powerful ones.

4.5 Program Development

The area of CLP methodology and program development is still in its infancy although it is vitally important for a practical use of CLP. We are currently working on several issues:

- Programming methodology for CLP(FD).
- Correctness and performance debugging of CLP programs [4].
- Tracing and optimising parallel CLP programs.

5 Conclusion

With ECL^{i}PS^e, a next generation CLP system has been developed. It is based on the strengths of its predecessors and it overcomes their limitations. It is not a proprietary black box designed for one particular purpose, but a system with an open architecture that allows cooperating solutions to be developed and used.

References

1. *The ESPRIT Project APPLAUSE*.
   URL http://www.ecrc.de/research/collaborations/applause/applause.html.
2. *The ESPRIT Project CHIC*.
   URL http://www.ecrc.de/research/collaborations/chic/.
3. M. Dincbas, P. Van Hentenryck, H. Simonis, A. Aggoun, T. Graf, and F. Berthier. The constraint logic programming language CHIP. In *International Conference on FGCS 1988*, Tokyo, November 1988.
4. Micha Meier. Debugging constraint programs. In *Proceedings of the First International Conference on Principles and Practice of Constraint Programming*, Cassis, September 1995.
   URL http://www.ecrc.de/eclipse/html/reports.html.
5. Micha Meier, Abderrahmane Aggoun, David Chan, Pierre Dufresne, Reinhard Enders, Dominique Henry de Villeneuve, Alexander Herold, Philip Kay, Bruno Perez, Emmanuel van Rossum, and Joachim Schimpf. SEPIA - an extendible Prolog system. In *Proceedings of the 11th World Computer Congress IFIP'89*, pages 1127–1132, San Francisco, August 1989.
6. Shyam Mudambi and Joachim Schimpf. Parallel CLP on heterogeneous networks. In *Proceedings of the ICLP'94*, 1994.
7. Steven Prestwich and Shyam Mudambi. Improved branch and bound in constraint logic programming. In *Proceedings of the First International Conference on Principles and Practice of Constraint Programming*, Cassis, September 1995.
8. André Véron, Kees Schuerman, Mike Reeve, and Liang-Liang Li. Why and how in the ElipSys OR-parallel CLP system. In *Proceedings of PARLE'93*, pages 291–304, Munich, June 1993.

Constraint Programming and Industrial Applications

Touraïvane*

*PrologIA***

Abstract. PrologIA has been designing and marketing AI languages and tools since 1984. The company occupies a active position in research into CLP and Natural Language processing. PrologIA has created expert systems for diagnosis aid, file rationalization etc ... and develops turn-key real-life applications. This paper presents two applications based on CLP technology : a decision support system in the field of middle term banking planning grounded on the Constraint Logic Programming technology and a crew scheduling application mixing Constraint Logic Programming and Set Partioning Modeling.

1 SD-Solver : CLP-based simulation tool

The CEFI[3] research center and La Hénin bank are building a Decision Support System (DSS) in the field of middle term banking planning. The first requirement for this banking DSS was to offer both forward and backward (i.e "multidirectional") simulations on the basis of a single dynamic model. Since the problem appeared to be quite general, it has been decided to develop a generic CLP-based simulation tool on the top of Prolog III. This tool, named SD-Solver [1], has been used to implement a banking application.

The decision process of the bank relies on a quarterly model. This model describes the dynamic behavior of the bank. Exploring the impact of alternative decisions ("what if" analysis) helps the decision maker to understand the dynamic behavior of the system he's supposed to control. However, his final objective is rather to make a decision which leads this system to a given position ("what for" analysis). Standard optimization packages are devoted to this task, they usually prove not flexible.

Within this context, the main objective has been to design a banking DSS using CLP technology on which a flexible multidirectional simulation system can be grounded in terms of constraints.

The system gives to the user a direct control on the solving process. A first reason for that comes from to fact that the definition of a well-posed problem will only be achieved after a "trial and error" process. At any moment the system

---

* E-mail : touraivane@prologianet.univ-mrs.fr

** Parc Technologique de Luminy - case 919, 13288 Marseille Cedex 09 France

[3] CEFI (Centre d'Économie et de Finances Internationales), Château La Farge, route des milles, 13290 Les Milles, France.

should be able to add constraints, to inspect the reached state and to remove constraints before performing a new trial.

A second reason is related to the backward simulation and the control on the search space. The user should be allowed to freely "navigate" on the search space, even to prune it "on the fly" in order to converge to an interesting solution. The third reason advocate for a real conversational mode. The main objective is to provide the decision maker with a tool at promoting a deep understanding of the system he manages.

Of course, SD-Solver inherits its main properties from Prolog III, but offers in many cases an easier way to implement applications grounded on array oriented numerical models. A first version of the banking DSS has been implemented using this environment. A shortened variant of the quarterly model has been written in a text file, and a specific graphical human interface has been implemented on top of SD-Solver.

The first results are demonstrative and the new compiler Prolog IV is expected to bring a better efficiency.

2   Crew Scheduling

The objective of this application [4] is to provide to a French airline company a flexible tool in order to help the experts to minimize crew costs while satisfying the many constraints imposed by governmental and labour laws. Flexibility is required to adapt the schedule to the evolution of these laws and and to the changes of commercial strategies. The structure of the company's network, the existence of multiple bases and services of middle sized cities make the crew scheduling problem difficult.

In order to solve this difficult problem, we have joined the advantages of CLP and set partioning modeling. Since set partioning involes linear integer programming, our approach uses linear relaxation followed by a specialized enumeration procedure.

The method used in this application consists in

1. selecting a significant sub-problem of the initial problem.
2. using then optimal integer solution of the sub-problem as an upper bound to filter the initial solution
3. solving the initial system (The system obtained by filtering is small enough to be solved exactly)

Each of three steps described above are performed using the same Simplex algorithm. On top of three steps, pre-processing is used to reduce the size of the problem.

In order to tackle large size problem, some parts of this tool – based on Prolog – is written in C, either for reasons of performance or for reasons of memory. It is the case for the kernel of the software : a specialized version of the simplex algorithm designed for set partitioning matrices.

This application is an example of the combination of constraint logic programming and constraint programming. It is characterized by the great simplicity of the methods it uses and by the small size of the code, while keeping a level of performance equivalent to its competitors. This tool will be in service in summer 1995.

Acknowledgments

SD-Solver was designed and implemented by Chistophe Bisière within the Esprit Project #5246 PRINCE.
Nabil Guerinik and Michel Van Caneghem are the authors of the Crew Scheduling application. Nathalie Vétillard contributes to the computational experiments.

References

1. Christophe Bisière. SD-Solver: "Towards a multidirectional CLP-based simulation tool", *Proceedings of IFAC'94*, Meeting on Computational Methods in Economics and Finance, Amsterdam, 1994.
2. Christophe Bisière. "SD-Solver: User Manual", CEFI, Les Milles, 1993
3. Nabil Guerinik, Guy Alain Narboni and Michel Van Caneghem. "Applications of set partitionning to Crew Scheduling", *Proceedings of APMOD'95*, Brunnel, U.K, 1995.
4. Nabil Guerinik and Michel Van Caneghem. "Solving Crew Scheduling Problems by Constraint Programming", *Proceedings of CP'95*, Marseilles, France, 1995

The CHIP System and Its Applications

Helmut Simonis
COSYTEC SA
4, rue Jean Rostand
F-91893 Orsay Cedex, France

1. Abstract

This tutorial presents the CHIP constraint logic programming system and some of its applications. We present the different constraint solving modules in the CHIP environment with special emphasis on the high-level global constraints in the finite domain solver.

2. System components

The CHIP system consists of a number of different components which together greatly simplify the development of applications. The tool extends the functionality of a *host language* with constraints and other sub systems. Two host languages are supported at the moment.

- The Prolog based version of CHIP uses intrinsic language features like *unification* and *backtracking search* to achieve a deep integration of the constraints with the host language. Constraints and search procedures can be easily defined and extended in the base language.
- The C/C++ version of the CHIP system takes the form of a constraint library which can be used inside application programs. Since search and variable binding are not part of the host language, the integration is not as seamless as the Prolog version.

Other modules of the CHIP environment include a graphical library based on Xwindows, interfaces to relational databases and foreign language interfaces. The different modules can be used together with an object modelling system to build large scale end-user systems [KS95].

3. History

CHIP [DVS88] was one of the first CLP systems together with PROLOG III and CLP(R). It was developed at the European Computer-Industry Research Centre (ECRC) in Munich during the period 1985-1990. Different constraint solvers were developed and integrated in a Prolog environment. At the same time the technology was tested on a number of example applications. The CHIP system is now being marketed and developed by COSYTEC. The early versions of CHIP were also the basis for a number of derivatives by ECRC shareholder companies. BULL developed CHARME, a constraint based system with a C like syntax, ICL produced DecisionPower based on the ECRC CHIP/SEPIA system and Siemens is using constraints in SNI-Prolog. ECRC has also continued research on constraints. The current CHIP version V4.1 differs from the earlier constraint system by the inclusion of powerful global constraints [AB93] [BC94] as high-level building blocks.

4. Constraint Solvers

The CHIP system contains a number of different constraint solver modules, which are useful for different types of problems.

The *complete rational solver* for linear arithmetic terms uses Gaussian elimination and an incremental Simplex method to solve equations and inequalities over a continuous domain. It is used mainly for financial and blending type of problems, where its flexibility offers some advantages over linear programming for small problem sizes.

The *Boolean solver* uses complete Boolean unification to solve constraints over Boolean algebra or in propositional calculus. Due to the exponential complexity of the problem solving process, its use is restricted to special application domains like hardware verification.

The *finite domain solver* is the core of the constraint solving system of CHIP. Originating in the CHIP system of ECRC, finite domain constraints have found many applications in very different areas. CHIP offers basic constraints like arithmetic and disequality, several symbolic constraints like element, handling of disjunction with conditional propagation, as well as user definable constraints with update demons and coroutining primitives.

4.1 Global Constraints

The simple constraint in the early finite domain systems were all based on syntactic, domain independent propagation methods. CHIP now contains some finite domain constraints based on semantic methods. These constraints use domain specific knowledge to derive better propagation results. Constraints of this type are called *global* constraints [AB93][BC94] and combine several important properties:

- They model a complex condition on sets of variables.
- The condition can be used in multiple contexts.
- The constraint reasoning detects inconsistency in many situations and reduces the search space significantly.
- They can be applied to large problem instances.

CHIP contains a number of these constraints:

- The *cumulative* constraint is used to express cumulative resource limits over a period.
- The *diffn* constraint expresses non-overlapping constraints on n-dimensional rectangles.

- The *cycle* constraint finds circuits in directed graphs.
- The *among* constraint expresses limits on occurrences of values in sequences of variables.
- The *precedence* constraint combines a set of precedence constraints and resource constraints on multiple resources in one model.

The constraints can be used and combined for many different problems and significantly extend the range of problems which can be handled with CLP. They provide high level building blocks to rapidly define and efficiently solve complex constraint problems.

5. Application examples

In this section we present some large scale, industrial systems developed with CHIP. These examples show that constraint logic programming based on Prolog can be used efficiently to develop end-user applications. The constraint solver is a crucial part of these applications. Other key aspects are graphical user interfaces and interfaces to data bases or other programs. Some background on how such applications can be developed with logic programming is given in [KS95].

ATLAS, [SC94] a tool for detailed production scheduling in a chemical factory, is based on a constraint model using numerous constraints on machines and consumable resources. The constraint solver is embedded in a user-friendly graphical environment and uses a relational database to exchange information with other information system tools. The program was co-developed by the Belgian company Beyers and Partners and COSYTEC.

FORWARD is a simulation and scheduling tool for oil refineries. In this application, CHIP is linked to a simulation tool written in FORTRAN which calculates flow rates and yields from a schedule obtained with the CHIP solver. The basic constraints express a non-linear optimisation problem over a continuous domain. The program was developed by the engineering company TECHNIP and COSYTEC and is currently used at three different refineries.

TACT combines planning, scheduling and assignment aspects for the operational transport fleet management in the food industry. The system uses several interacting solvers to create a schedule for drivers, lorries and other resources in a transportation problem. The system is used both to create working schedules and to handle 'what-if' decision support scenarios. The application was developed by COSYTEC.

Dassault Aviation has developed several applications with CHIP. *PLANE* is a medium-long term scheduling system for aircraft assembly line scheduling. *MADE* is controlling a complex work-cell in the factory, and *COCA* schedules micro-tasks in the production process.

The *LOCARIM* application is capable of designing a computer/phone network in large buildings. It is used by France Telecom to propose a cabling and estimate cabling costs for new buildings. The application was developed by Telesystemes together with COSYTEC.

EVA is used by EDF to plan and schedule the transport of nuclear waste between reactors and the reprocessing plant in La Hague. This problem is highly constrained by the limited availability of transport containers and the required level of availability for the reactors. The program was co-developed by EDF and the software house GIST.

TAP-AI [BKC94] is a planning system for crew assignment in an airline. It schedules and reassigns pilots and cabin crews to flights and aircraft respecting physical constraints, government regulations and union agreements. The program is intended for day-to-day management of operations with rapidly changing constraints.

SEVE is a portfolio management system for CDC, a major bank in Paris, developed in-house. It uses non-linear constraints over rationals and finite domain constraints to choose among different investment options. The system can be used for "what-if" and "goal-seeking" scenarios, based on different assumptions on the development of the economy.

6. References

[AB93] A. Aggoun, N. Beldiceanu
Extending CHIP in Order to Solve Complex Scheduling Problems. Journal of Mathematical and Computer Modelling, Vol. 17, No. 7, pages 57-73, 1993

[BKC94] G. Baues, P. Kay, P. Charlier
Constraint Based Resource Allocation for Airline Crew Management
ATTIS 94, Paris, April 1994

[BC94] N. Beldiceanu, E. Contejean
Introducing Global Constraints in CHIP. Journal of Mathematical and Computer Modelling, Vol 20, No 12, pp 97-123, 1994

[DHS88] M. Dincbas, P. Van Hentenryck, H. Simonis, A. Aggoun, T. Graf and F. Berthier. The Constraint Logic Programming Language CHIP.
In Proceedings of the International Conference on Fifth Generation Computer Systems (FGCS'88), pages 693-702, Tokyo, 1988.

[KS95] P. Kay, H. Simonis
Building Industrial CHIP Applications from Reusable Software Components
3rd Conference on Practical Applications of Prolog, Paris, April 1995

[SB95] H. Simonis, N. Beldiceanu
The CHIP System. COSYTEC Technical Report, April 1995

[SC94] H. Simonis, T. Cornelissens
Modelling Producer/Consumer Constraints
First International Conference on Principles and Practice of Constraint Programming, Cassis, France, September 1995

Applications of Constraint Programming

Jean-Francois Puget

ILOG SA, (rue de Verdun, BP 85, F-94253 Gentilly Cedex, FRANCE
email : puget@ilog.fr
http : //www.ilog.com

1 Introduction

Let us consider the following list of applications, taken from the recently held SOLVER and SCHEDULE user's meeting [11]: manpower planning at the Banque Bruxelles Lambert, a supermarket cashier assignment system, nursing rotas in an hospital, gate allocation for Singapore airport and Hong Kong airport, Heathrow airport ground movement planning, configuring control architecture at EDF, various production scheduling systems in USA, logistics and transportation optimization, time tabling for Singapore university, maintenance scheduling for US airlines and Long Island Lightning Company, geometric design at Chrysler and other cutomers. This gives an idea of the wide variety of problems where constraint programming has been succesfully employed. In order to get an idea of the complexity of such tasks, let's consider the Banque Bruxelles Lambert (BBL) application in more detail. (Our description of the problem is based on [6].) BBL has a department responsible for monitoring the computer and telecommunication system on a 24-hour basis. Organizing the time-tables of staff in this department, of course, entails serious scheduling problems. The staff assigned to this department is divided into units, called "rooms," of up to 30 people whose working hours are planned according specific rules. The general organization of a room includes three shifts: morning, afternoon, and night. In a given week, an employee must be assigned a working shift or must get a rest. During the week, an employee must keep the same type of shift from Monday through Friday. Any possible Saturday shift must be the same type as the previous weekdays, but any possible Sunday shift must be the same type as the following weekdays. Certain kinds of transitions between shifts are forbidden; for example, two consecutive weeks of night shifts (denoted night-night) for the same employee must not be scheduled. A minimum and maximum level of staffing for each shift is set for each day of the year. The annual count of the different types of shifts should be balanced for all employees at a given hierarchical level. This balance is particularly important for the night shifts because those shifts earn a substantial bonus. Holidays, training periods, and other absences of staff must be taken into account, of course. Besides those explicit constraints, certain factors are treated as preferences or objectives in a solution. In particular, staff is divided into teams, and those teams should work together as much as possible. Moreover, certain transitions between shifts are preferred by the staff, such transitions as rest-night, night-afternoon, afternoon-morning. The list of constraints and objectives is actually longer, but we can use this preliminary list as a working description of the problem.

Given all that information, we have to compute the time-tables for an entire year in a reasonably short time and in such a way that the time-tables can be recalculated, in whole or in part, as need be in the course of the year, even on a daily basis as changes in staff occur.

2 Solver overview

It must be now quite clear that the type of constraint needed for these applications are finite domain constraints. Indeed, SOLVER implements state of the art finite domain constraint solving algorithms, using a concise C++ syntax[8]. The constraint propagation algorithm we use is based on the AC-5 algorithm[3]. In order to give a flavor of SOLVERsyntax, the nqueen problem can be expressed as follows:

```
void main(){
    IlcInit();
    IlcInt i, nqueen = 1000;
    IlcIntVarArray Q(nqueen,0,nqueen-1),
                   Q1(nqueen), Q2(nqueen);
    for (i=0; i<nqueen; i++) {
        Q1[i] = Q[i]+i;
        Q2[i] = Q[i]-i;
    }
    IlcTell(IlcAllDiff(Q));
    IlcTell(IlcAllDiff(Q1));
    IlcTell(IlcAllDiff(Q2));
    IlcSolve(IlcGenerate(Q, IlcChooseMinSize));
    IlcEnd();
}
```

Effective Use

SOLVER relies on a general search algorithm to solve a wide variety of problems. For real problems however, the user may have to help th algorithm by incorporating knowledge about the problem to be solved.

First, there are many problems for which it is fairly easy to find one solution, but for which finding an optimal solution and verifying the optimality requires exponential running time in the worst case. For those problems, we can easily implement a search with the SOLVER algorithm that generates a preliminary solution very quickly and then gradually improves that result through further searches. Such an algorithm can be stopped at any time, and the best result found thus far can be returned.

Second, a SOLVER user can make the search itself more efficient by exploiting knowledge about the problem. For example, in a given problem, the order in which the variables are assigned values is very important.

A third possibility that SOLVER supports is the use of specialized algorithms as new constraints. One of the most successful operations research algorithms for updating time-bounds of activities submitted to unary resource constraints was proposed in [4][7]. We implemented this algorithm in the resource constraints of SCHEDULE, which is an add-on to SOLVER, used to develop finite capacity scheduling applications. SCHEDULE uses a natural object model for representing schedules in terms of activities that share and use resources. The model consists of a set of C++ classes, methods, and functions that implement the concepts of "resource" and "activity" in terms of SOLVER variables and constraints. More detailed description of SCHEDULEcan be found in [5],[2][1].

The following table give some benchmark results on well known job shop scheduling problems. The first one is the standard 10 by 10 jobshop stated in 1963, and that was not solved until 86. The best published runtime fo this problem is 135 seconds[4]. This table shows that we have a state of the art implementation.

Instance	CPU(one)	BT	CPU	TM
MT10	.2	13684	184.8	227
ABZ5	.2	19303	226.6	216
ABZ6	.2	6227	80.3	198
LA19	.3	18102	219.2	235
LA20	.2	40597	407.3	220
ORB1	.2	22725	323.7	243
ORB2	.2	31490	416.4	210
ORB3	.3	36729	488.4	262
ORB4	.2	13751	169.9	210
ORB5	.2	12648	168.5	232

The first column gives the time for the first solution, the next two gives the total number of backtracks and the total running time including the proof for optimality, the last columns gives the total memory used. Times are given on an RS6000 workstation.

When to Use Constraint Programming

Constraint programming, and especially SOLVER and SCHEDULE, have been quite successful recently. Other approaches could be used in principle. For instance, one could use an existing problem solver. That choice transforms the task into converting the model of the problem into the format acceptable as input for the existing package. A good example of such an approach is the widespread practice of defining problems as integer linear programming problems, regardless of the entities that actually appear in the problem model. The major advantage of this approach is that it exploits a powerful algorithm from operations research, the simplex algorithm. The major disadvantage is that if we find that the package at hand does not solve our problem satisfactorily, we will likely find it difficult to enhance performance by exploiting any problem-specific knowledge we may have since that knowledge may not readily convert to the acceptable format. See [10] and [9]for comparisons between constraint programming and integer linear programming.

The toolkit we presented here (SOLVER and SCHEDULE) have been successfully applied to a large number of industrial problems (more than 200, in fact). Does this mean that they represent the ultimate constrained optimization tools? The answer is no, of course. Much progress remains to be made: the basic technology could be refined; new algorithms from operations research could be integrated; more user friendly interfaces could be defines, including explanation and analysis support.

However, the major bottleneck we encounter is not tied to the problem-solving abilities of our tools. It is, rather, tied to the specification of the application to be developed. More precisely, the bottleneck deals with the representation of the problem to be solved: What has to be expressed as a decision variable? What are the constraints of the problem? What are the objectives to be achieved? In the same spirit, the objectives of an application may be fuzzy or even contradictory.

Here again, the facility with which SOLVER lets a developer try out alternative search strategies or impose new constraints as needed provides valuable assistance in application development.

References

1. Philippe Baptiste, Claude Le Pape and Wim Nuijten. *Incorporating Efficient Operations Research Algorithms in Constraint-Based Scheduling.* Proceedings of the First International Joint Workshop on Artificial Intelligence and Operations Research, Timberline Lodge, Oregon, 1995.
2. Philippe Baptiste and Claude Le Pape. *A Theoretical and Experimental Comparison of Constraint Propagation Techniques for Disjunctive Scheduling.* Proceedings of the Fourteenth International Joint Conference on Artificial Intelligence, Montréal, Québec, 1995.
3. Deville, Y. and Van Hentenryck, P., *An Efficient Arc Consistency Algorithm for a Class of CSP Problems,* Proceedings of IJCAI, pages 325-330,1991.
4. Jacques Carlier and Eric Pinson. *Adjustment of Heads and Tails for the Job-Shop Problem.* European Journal of Operational Research, 78:146-161, 1994.
5. Claude Le Pape. *Implementation of Resource Constraints in* ILOG SCHEDULE: *A Library for the Development of Constraint-Based Scheduling Systems.* Intelligent Systems Engineering, 3(2):55-66, 1994.
6. Jacques, P. *Solving a manpower planning problem using constraint programming,* Belgian Journal of Operations Research, Statistics and Computer Science, volume 33, issue 4.
7. W. P. M. Nuijten. *Time and Resource Constrained Scheduling: A Constraint Satisfaction Approach.* PhD Thesis, Eindhoven University of Technology, 1994.
8. Jean-François Puget. *A C++ Implementation of CLP.* Technical Report, ILOG S.A., 1994.
9. Jean-François Puget, Bruno De Backer *A comparison between Constraint programming and integer programming* INFORMS international conference, Singapore, 1995.
10. Barbara M. Smith (University of Leeds), Sally C. Brailsford, Peter M. Hubbard and H. Paul Williams (University of Southampton) The Progressive Party Problem: Integer Linear Programming and Constraint Programming Compared. In these proceedings.
11. Ilog, Proceedings of the first Solver/Schedule international users conference, 1995.

Author Index

Springer-Verlag
and the Environment

We at Springer-Verlag firmly believe that an international science publisher has a special obligation to the environment, and our corporate policies consistently reflect this conviction.

We also expect our business partners – paper mills, printers, packaging manufacturers, etc. – to commit themselves to using environmentally friendly materials and production processes.

The paper in this book is made from low- or no-chlorine pulp and is acid free, in conformance with international standards for paper permanency.

Lecture Notes in Computer Science

For information about Vols. 1–912

please contact your bookseller or Springer-Verlag